The

CHRISTIAN ALMANAC

The CHRISTIAN ALMANAC

A Dictionary of Days Celebrating History's Most Significant People and Events

GEORGE GRANT & GREGORY WILBUR

CUMBERLAND HOUSE
NASHVILLE, TENNESSEE

Published by Cumberland House Publishing, Inc., 431 Harding Industrial Drive, Nashville, TN 37211

Cover design: Karen Phillips
Text design: Mary Sanford

Library of Congress Cataloging-in-Publication Data
Grant, George, 1954-
    The Christian almanac : a dictionary of days celebrating history's most significant people and events / George Grant & Gregory Wilbur.
      p. cm.
    Includes index.
    ISBN 1-58182-061-5 (pbk. : alk paper)
      1. Church history--Chronology. 2. Devotional calendars. I. Wilbur, Gregory, 1968- II. Title.

BR149 .G64 2000
270'.02'02--dc21

                                                              00-043088

Printed in the United States of America
1 2 3 4 5 6 7—05 04 03 02 01 00

To Uz, Andy, and Keith:
Already Celebrating Endless Days

CONTENTS

ACKNOWLEDGEMENTS

*The work of an author is merely the agglomeration of everyone
and everything that has come before him.*

[HOLBROOK JACKSON (1874-1948)]

No book, of course, is merely the fruit of a single author's labor—it is rather the accumulation and collation of a thousand odd experiences, random collaborations, and peculiar inheritances. A book like this is even more dependent on such vagaries and intangibles than most. Who can say where we got most of these quotes, factoids, tidbits, rarities, and minutiae? Certainly, not us.

Oh sure, there were a number of favorite books, Web sites, reference guides, and anthologies we consulted during the actual writing of this book. But they were mostly for fact checking. In fact, writing this book was more like holding an intellectual garage sale than doing a research and writing project. Most of the items in this massive tome were scribbled in one notebook or another during our lifetimes of collecting historical and literary trivia. Thus, in a very real sense, all we did was clean out our closet, sort through our things, and try to make sense of long-neglected possessions. We vaguely remember accumulating all this stuff; we just can't quite remember why.

Like any good garage sale, we had lots of help getting things organized. Our students at Bannockburn College, Franklin Classical School, New Hope Academy, Knox House, Arx Axiom Academy, and the Gileskirk School kept us on our toes, telling us what was boring and what was interesting. They were also always willing to add to our collection with just one more strange fact or figure.

Likewise, our favorite authors were fit subjects for plunder—and always rich with treasure no matter how many times we returned to the coffers. Where would we be without G. K. Chesterton, Tim Powers, George MacDonald, J. R. R. Tolkien, John Buchan, Paul Johnson, Thomas Chalmers, Charles Spurgeon, Walter Scott, TR, C. S. Lewis, Samuel Johnson, John Ruskin, Thomas Carlyle, and of course, the inimitable Q: Arthur Quiller-Couch?

Music was provided by Puccini, Handel, Haydn, Richard Strauss, Jessye Norman, Mendelssohn, William Coulter, and Mike Card—with special thanks to Wes King.

Our dear friends at Cumberland House, Ron and Julia Pitkin, actually thought we could make something more of this than just another garage sale. For that we are grateful. And Mary Sanford, our patient editor, sorted through every scrap of detail to make sure it was good and right and true. To them we owe our deepest thanks and warmest praise.

Finally, our beloved families put up with all our ooing and ahing as we sorted through this mess of material—when they really just wanted us to put the stuff away, they nevertheless encouraged us in our fascinations. Our wives, Sophia and Karen, are our greatest gifts in life. For them we are eternally grateful.

Eastertide 2000
Kings Meadow

The
CHRISTIAN
ALMANAC

INTRODUCTION

Every day that passes should be lived in light of the past, in light of the future,
and in light of eternity.

[THOMAS CHALMERS (1780–1847)]

Every day is an anniversary. History is so rich and so resplendent that there is not a single date that does not offer great lessons in heroism or ignominy, brilliance or foolishness, inspiration or admonition. There is not a single date that does not point us toward the remarkable cultural and spiritual legacy of our Christian inheritance in Western civilization. And there is not even a wrinkle in time that does not bear the obvious impress of God's own good providence.

Alas, you could hardly tell that by looking at the average history textbook these days. If history is, as Stephen Mansfield has quipped, "More than dates and dead people," you would never know it based on most of the printed evidence.

There are very few things that modern historians can agree on. But when it comes to God there is sudden consensus. The long-held notion that history is His story is fiercely resisted in our day.

But history is full of the indecipherable mysteries of providence, and thus any attempt to reduce the process of its legends, epics, movements, heroes, and villains to a mere mechanical or material science is destined to be more than a little ridiculous—as the sad legacies of Marx, Toynbee, Wells, and Wilson have proven.

It is true that certain undeniably fixed milestones emerge—like the Battles of Hastings and Waterloo, the regicides of Louis XVI and Charles I, the triumphs of Bismarck and Richelieu, and the tragedies of the Hapsburgs and Hoenstauffens—and you can, from them, build up certain vague rules regarding the onward march of civilization. But for the most part, the events of history have the habit of coming up out of nothing, like the little particles of ice that float to the surface of the Seine at the beginning of a frost, or like the little oak trees that crop up everywhere like weeds in the broad fields of East Sussex. They arise silently and unpredictably.

And that surprises us. It is too easy for us to forget—or to try to ignore—the fact that the doings of man are on the knees of an inscrutable and sovereign God.

One of the most important and most neglected aspects of His story called history is the fact that the story is not yet complete—and will not be until providence has run its resolute course. We can only truly comprehend the events of the past when we recognize them as part and parcel of the ethical outworking of God's plan for the present—and even for the future.

The irony of this is so large that it may be too large to be seen. Thus, the writing and rewriting of history is often little more than the material preferences and prejudices of one age gazing into a distant mirror of another age.

Modern secular historians are especially prone to fall into this alluring trap. And so, they quixotically rail against the upstart evils of today by lambasting the tenured virtues of yesterday. They attempt to impose sanctions against some unacceptable form of behavior by instituting a kind of retroactive apartheid. It is the same odd impulse that induces certain politicians to attempt to cure the ills of Timbuktu by starting an agitation in Tulsa or to reform the administration of Montevideo by holding a referendum in Minneapolis.

Cultural paradoxes of that sort are clearly on the rise in our time despite the fact that they seem to be increasingly marked by an immobilizing hardening of the heart and a simultaneous softening of the head. Purveyors of politically correct consensus-terrorism have bemoaned in pious tones the cultural realignment that has followed on the heels of the establishment of the American City on a Hill, exposing us to a kind of insulated Hare Krishna disregard for reality and making us vulnerable to the fierce tyrannies that petty prejudices inevitably engender.

This day-by-day almanac is an attempt not only to recall many of the famous births, deaths, world events, and other notable anniversaries, but to provide us with tantalizing details of some of the most important lessons and most profound inspirations that history has to

offer us as well. In other words, it is an attempt to practice that old discipline called moral philosophy. It is hoped that the combination of facts we've gathered together here—some serious, some humorous, some just plain odd—will suggest practical ways to make such lessons and inspirations immediately applicable to our present circumstances in the hurly-burly of the modern world. Whether a reader is interested in simply browsing or in detailed study, our hope is that this will prove to be as informative and entertaining for you as it has been for us. Our intent was to create a book that every home and every classroom would find both delightful and useful.

In choosing the events that we did, we had to sort through several immediate difficulties. First, most dates prior to the middle of the eighteenth century are almost entirely unreliable, when they are available—and they are almost never available. Historians quibble over the few scraps of certainty that we have, making even them rather uncertain. You'll notice, as a consequence, that the vast majority of dates we've listed are from the last two centuries when date-keeping was more common.

Second, even when dates can be fairly reasonably verified, there is the problem of what calendar to use—the one in use when the event occurred or the one we use today. It makes a big difference—it is why, for instance, Russians celebrate their October Revolution in November.

There are about forty different calendar systems currently in use in the world. Some of these systems replicate astronomical cycles according to fixed rules, others are based on abstract, perpetually repeating cycles of no astronomical significance. Some carefully and redundantly enumerate every unit of passing time, others contain mystical ambiguities and metaphysical discontinuities. Some are codified in written laws while others are transmitted by oral tradition.

The common theme of each system is the desire to organize the calendar to satisfy the needs and preoccupations of society. Besides simply serving the obvious practical purposes, this process of organization provides a sense, however illusory, of understanding and managing time itself. Thus calendars have provided the basis for planning agricultural, hunting, and migration cycles, for divination and prognostication, and for maintaining cycles of religious and civil events. Whatever their scientific sophistication, or lack thereof, calendars are essentially social covenants, not scientific measurements.

Ultimately, that means that things get rather messy when we try to pinpoint exact dates. There are inevitable contradictions and variations—not just because people have remembered wrongly, but because they have remembered differently. It is why the 116-year-long conflict between England and France is called the Hundred Years' War. It is why Easter is celebrated according to one set of calculations in the West and an entirely different set in the East. It is why we can assert that the birth of Christ did not occur in the year 1 or 0, but in 3 or 4 b.c. And it is why there is no year 0 at all—thus making the exact timing of century and millennial changes a matter of some controversy.

What a mess, huh? Well, it gets worse. Even if all the calendar systems in the world could be regularized, there would still be difficulties in measuring the passing of time. There are three principal astronomical cycles that calendars attempt to measure. The first is the day, which is based on the rotation of the earth on its axis. Next is the month, which is based on the revolution of the moon around the earth. Finally, there is the year, which is based on the revolution of the earth around the sun. The complexity of creating a consistent calendar system arises because none of these cycles of revolution are regular. In other words, they do not comprise an integral number of days. From the vantage of Earth, astronomical cycles are neither constant nor perfectly commensurable with each other. The tropical year, for instance, is defined as the mean interval between vernal equinoxes—it therefore necessarily corresponds to the cycle of the seasons. As a result, a calendar year of an integral number of days cannot be perfectly synchronized to the tropical year. Approximate synchronization of calendar months with the lunar phases requires a complex sequence of months of 29 and 30 days. For convenience, it is common to speak of a lunar year of twelve synodic months, or 354.36707 days.

Three distinct types of calendars have resulted from this situation. There is the solar calendar—like the modern Gregorian or the ancient Julian calendar—which is designed to maintain synchrony with the tropical year. To do so, days are intercalated, forming leap years, to increase the average length of the calendar year. There is also the lunar calendar—like the modern Islamic calendar—which follows the lunar phase cycle without regard for the tropical year. Thus, the months of the Islamic calendar systematically shift with respect to the months of the Gregorian calendar. The third type of calendar is the lunisolar. It has a sequence of months based on the lunar phase cycle; but every few years a whole month is intercalated to bring the calendar back in phase with the tropical year. The Hebrew and Chinese calendars are examples of this type of system.

In most societies a calendar reform is an extraordinary event. Adoption of a calendar depends on the forcefulness with which it is introduced and on the willingness of society to accept it. For example, the acceptance of the Gregorian calendar as a worldwide standard spanned more than three centuries. Use of the Gregorian calendar in the United States stems from a British act of Parliament in 1751, which specified use of the Gregorian calendar in England and its colonies. However, its adoption in the United Kingdom and other countries was fraught with confusion, controversy, and even violence.

Thus, when a papal bull (edict) was issued to correct official date-keeping, confusion reigned. Crowds gathered in the streets all throughout Europe demanding that their days be given back to them. All because officials were trying to rectify difficulties with the current calendrical system.

Because the Julian calendar, promulgated by Julius Caesar, made the year too long by several minutes, the calendar had been displaced by three full days every four hundred years. In 1582 it was out of sequence with the equinoxes by a full ten days and with the original dates by fourteen days. Several church councils had discussed the issue—never arriving at a workable solution.

Gregory XIII was an energetic pope. Long active in church affairs and a patron of education, he was not one to let the matter continue indefinitely. He determined to correct the problem and on February 24, 1582, acting on the recommendations of a special council, issued a bull requiring all Catholic countries to follow October 4 with October 15 that year. To illiterate people, it seemed as if their days had actually been stolen from them.

The papal commission advised by scientist Christopher Clavius is generally credited with aiding the pope in making the reform. And he relied on a plan that had been propounded by Bishop Robert Grosseteste of England nearly three hundred years earlier. Ironically, the English, afraid of appearing to give too much deference to the pope by adopting the calendar he set forth, refused the Gregorian calendar and retained the Julian another two centuries, oblivious to the fact that it had been the proposal of their own native son Grosseteste. Britain and its colonies did not change over until 1752. By then the calendar was eleven days out of date.

The Gregorian calendar was intended primarily for the benefit of the church, which needed to plot the variable date of its most important feast, Easter. But the plan was the best yet devised—and it became an international standard. Although some nations, like China, Japan, and Russia, did not adopt the calendar until the twentieth century, all nations now use it for international business and for recording historical events.

Obviously, for the sake of internal consistency in this book, we simply had to settle on a single approach. We have used the Gregorian calendar whenever possible—even when events occurred prior to its adoption. That is bound to create some consternation here or there—but so be it. As Henry Cabot Lodge asserted, "Nearly all the historical work worth doing at the present moment in the English language is the work of shoveling off heaps of rubbish inherited from the immediate past."

That is precisely the kind of work that we have attempted to do in this book. Our aim has been to preserve the practical lessons and profound legacies of Christendom without the petty prejudice of modern fashions or the parsimonious preference of Enlightenment innovations. We wanted to avoid the trap of noticing everything that went unnoticed in the past while failing to notice all that the past deemed notable.

We believe that history is a series of lively adventure stories—and thus should be told without the cumbersome intrusion of arcane academic rhetoric or truckloads of extraneous footnotes. In fact, we believe that history is a romantic moral drama in a world gone impersonally scientific—and thus should be told with a measure of passion, unction, and verve. For us, the record of the ages is actually philosophy teaching by example—and because however social conditions may change, the great underlying qualities that make and save men and nations do not alter. It is the most important example of all. Because the past is ever present, giving shape and focus to all our lives, it is not what was, but whatever seems to have been, simply because the past, like the future, is part and parcel of the faith.

This book is our attempt, therefore, to revive a venerable old Christian tradition of charting the topography of that forgotten foreign land called the past. It is an effort to make the tales of yore a narrative worthy to be told at home round the hearth, to appeal to the heroic heart of all generations, and to reinvigorate the eternal infancy of mankind.

How to Use This Book

Some books are meant to be tasted, others to be swallowed, and some
few to be chewed and digested; that is, some books are to be read only
in parts; others to be read but not curiously; and some few to be read
wholly, and with diligence and attention.

[Francis Bacon (1561–1626)]

If Francis Bacon's sage counsel is to be trusted, then this book is rather schizophrenic—it is both a reference book and a guide; it is both a precise daily almanac and a vast amalgamation of trivia; it is meant both to be tasted around the edges and to be swallowed whole; it is both a book to browse and a book to study. So, before you begin, we thought it might be helpful to sort through the multiple personalities evident here, and point out ways to interact with them to best advantage.

For the Average Reader: If you are like most of us, you probably don't know a whole lot about history. It was not likely that history was your favorite class in school. But even if you are now a bit of a history buff there are undoubtedly large areas of unexplored territories of the past in which you would like to venture. For you, this book can serve as a kind of buffet table—dip in wherever you like. Look up special days or events. Note books you want to read later, music you need to pick up, videos you need to rent, or holidays you want to celebrate.

For the Homeschool or Classroom: The daily entries in this almanac may serve as regular academic exercises, hooks for curriculum items, springboards to further study, or just opportunities for fun breaks in long days of study. Read or retell the main story at the beginning of the day. Or start a class session with a "Today in History" feature. Use the quote of the day or particular books or pieces of music to set the theme for the day—or the week, for that matter.

For the Family: Celebrate the seasons, create new traditions, and make substantive memories by incorporating aspects of the almanac into your regular family schedule. The daily entries will point you to innumerable ways to integrate learning into your lifestyle. On Winston Churchill's birthday, why not have an English dinner? On the anniversary of the publication of Pilgrim's Progress, why not begin reading that classic aloud? During the Advent season leading up to Christmas, why not mark each day with the traditional festivities handed down to us by our great cultural legacy? Why not begin a yearly observance of the first performance of Handel's Messiah, or the publication of Tolkien's Lord of the Rings, or the completion of Milton's Paradise Lost, or the delivery of Henry's "Give Me Liberty or Give Me Death" speech?

FOR DAILY DEVOTIONS: While every day certainly has any number of inspirational stories associated with it, you'll also find selected Bible passages at the beginning of each date that combine to take you through the Book in a year. There is perhaps no single better discipline that a Christian can undertake than reading through the entire canon of the Scriptures. Why not begin today? After all, as the prince of the preachers, Charles Haddon Spurgeon, once said, "The devil is not afraid of a dust-covered Bible."

FOR READING SCHEDULES: A number of the great classics are mentioned in the daily entries—usually on the date of their publication. Instead of approaching the ominous task of a lifetime reading list, why not familiarize yourself with the great books chronologically? To be sure, you won't be able to read them all, but you will at least be able to begin sorting through your priorities. As Winston Churchill commented, "If you cannot read all your books, at any rate handle, or as it were, fondle them—peer into them, let them fall open where they will, read from the first sentence that arrests the eye, set them back on the shelves with your own hands, arrange them on your own plan so that you at least know where they are. Let them be your friends; let them be your acquaintances."

FOR A GUIDE TO THE ARTS: As in the case of books, there are far too many mentions of paintings, sculptures, works of architecture, musical compositions, films, and theatrical performances to actually enjoy on a day-to-day basis. But, the almanac may serve as a reminder or even a guide to areas within the world of the arts you may want to explore next. As poet Tristan Gylberd has argued, "We may rest assured that beauty, goodness, and truth are well able to fend for themselves. Mere affirmation affords stark contrast enough with the howling wasteland of modern bohemianism."

The main thing is to take joy in the journey—wherever your paths may lead you. After all, as the poet Percy Shelley has asserted, "The truest education is a redolent fountain—forever overflowing with the crystalline waters of wisdom and delight."

JANUARY

JANUARY

Basil of Caesarea (330–379) was born into a family of wealth and distinction. His grandmother Macri; his father, Battia; his mother, Emmelia; his sister, Macrina; and his two younger brothers, Gregory and Peter, were all numbered among the early saints of the church. One of his other brothers became chief counsel to the emperor and still another became an imperial governor. Three of his ancestors bore the Byzantine scepter and two others ascended to the bishopric. For nearly a millennium some member of this family held a high position in Constantinople. Basil was greater than all of them.

Renowned for his encyclopedic learning, he studied in all the great schools of his day and then practiced law with an eye toward a public career. But he yielded to a call to the ministry instead. It was not long before his reputation reached the farthest edges of the empire: He was a quick-witted adversary to the heretical Arians, he was a valiant defender of orthodoxy; he had a productive theological pen, and he was a man who combined a deep and sincere piety with a tough and realistic practicality.

Besides his many pastoral duties, Basil involved himself in the issues of the day. After being moved by the plight of the poor, he spent the rest of his life seeking practical ways to alleviate their suffering. He instituted the practice of almsgiving in Caesarea, utilizing the resources of the church to help transform poverty into productivity. Because health care was an important part of that process—and because the poor were generally denied access to anything but the crassest form of folk medicine—Basil opened the very first nonambulatory hospital.

When he lay dying on this day in the year 379, his last words were, "This day is a day of beginnings, not of endings. Lord, into Thy hand I commend my spirit; Thou hast redeemed me, O Lord God of Truth."

New Year's Day
National Day
  Cuba, Sudan, Haiti
Feast Day
  St. Felix of Bourges, St. Almachius, St. William of Dijon, St. Eugendus or Oyend, St. Peter of Atroa, St. Odilo, St. Fulgentius of Ruspe

NEW YEAR'S DAY

The celebration of the New Year did not occur on the first day of January at the introduction of the Gregorian calendar in 1582, which was accepted at that time only in France, the northern Italian city-states, Portugal, and in the Spanish nations of Castile and Aragon. The new calendar was not accepted until 1600 in Scotland and 1752 in England. From the earliest days of the Roman Imperial calendar the New Year was celebrated on March 25—which is why September, October, November, and December are derived from the Latin words septem (seven), octo (eight), novem (nine), and decem (ten). Throughout Christendom, January 1 has been celebrated as a day of renewal—of vows, vision, and vocation. It was on this day that guild members took their annual pledge, that husbands and wives renewed their marriage promises, and that young believers reasserted their resolution to walk in the grace of the Lord's great epiphany. In Edinburgh, beginning in the seventeenth century, revellers would gather at the Tron Church to watch the great clock tower mark the entrance into the new year—which was the inspiration behind the relatively recent Times Square ceremony in New York. But in Edinburgh, the purpose was not merely to have a grand excuse for a public party, but a way of celebrating the truth of Epiphany newness.

Each age has deemed the new-born year, the fittest time for festal cheer.

[SIR WALTER SCOTT (1771–1832)]

404 The last gladiatorial match was fought in the Roman Coliseum.

439 The Theodosian Code went into effect. Created by Emperor Theodosius II, it was the first Christian standard of justice for the Roman Empire.

1449 Lorenzo de Medici, later dubbed Lorenzo the Magnificent, was born in Florence.

1519 Ulrich Zwingli undertook his duties as the chief preacher at the Zurich Cathedral on his thirty-sixth birthday. He did so with the shocking announcement that he would abandon the Roman liturgy, undertaking a verse-by-verse study of the New Testament instead.

1545 Bishop Hugh Latimer presented Henry VIII with a Bible marked at the verse "Marriage is honorable in all, and the bed undefiled: but whoremongers and adulterers God will judge." The King was not amused, and Latimer was later burned at the stake.

1660 Samuel Pepys recorded the first entry in his famous diary: "This morning (we lying lately in the garret) I rose, put on my suit with great skirts, having not lately worn any other clothes but them."

1735 American patriot and master silversmith Paul Revere was born.

1766 The Old Pretender, James III, died in exile. To the end, the son of the last Stuart king never gave up hope that his loyal Jacobites would restore him to the British throne.

1785 London's oldest daily newspaper, the *Daily Universal Register*, renamed the *Times* in 1788, was first published.

1791 Austrian composer Franz Joseph Haydn arrived in London for an extended visit to compose and conduct. It was during this visit that Haydn heard Handel's *Messiah* and *Israel in Egypt*, which greatly influenced the writing of his own oratorio *The Creation*.

1801 Italian astronomer Giuseppe Piazzi became the first person to discover an asteroid. He named it Ceres.

1811 James Fenimore Cooper married Susan DeLancey in Upstate New York, where he ran his family's farm. She would later encourage him to try his hand at writing fiction after he expressed frustration at the poor selection available in local bookshops. His famed *Leatherstocking Tales* resulted.

1879 English novelist Edward Morgan Forster, known for such novels as *Howards End*, *A Room with a View*, and *Passage to India*, was born in London.

1892 The first immigrants arrived at Ellis Island. Eventually, more than twelve million immigrants would pass through the New York entry port during its sixty-two years of operation.

1898 The five boroughs of Manhattan, the Bronx, Brooklyn, Queens, and Staten Island were consolidated into New York City.

1959 Fidel Castro led Cuban revolutionaries to victory over Fulgencio Batista.

1993 Czechoslovakia split into two new nations, the Czech Republic and Slovakia.

13

JANUARY

HOLY NAME OF JESUS
FEAST DAY
St. Seraphim of Sarov, St. Basil, St. Gregory Nazianzen, St. Munchin, St. Adalhard or Adelard, St. Caspar of Bufalo, St. Macarius of Alexandria, St. Vincentian

A devoted son of the Scottish Reformation, Andrew Geddes (1518-1586) was a sterling example of compassion, integrity, and truth during the fierce religious conflicts that wracked his nation throughout the sixteenth century. Converted under the preaching of John Knox, he served as a deacon in that great Reformer's church and imbibed knowledge from the confessional truths he heard preached each Sabbath for nearly thirty years. He helped to craft the first liturgies, confessions, and catechisms utilized in the national Reform movement.

Taking his cue from the biblical injunction to faithfully demonstrate justice, mercy, and humility before God (Micah 6:8), he also utilized both the prominence of his office and the power of his influence as a force for effective social change: He helped to organize the famed "seasons of prayer" in cottages all across Scotland that so profoundly shaped the character of the times, he pioneered a ministry to rescue and care for abandoned and orphaned children, and he consulted with local magistrates in an effort to bring the standards of jurisprudence in line with scriptural principles of justice.

A newly published Latin translation of the widely read book *On the Help of the Poor*, by Jean Louis Vives, left a deep impression on Geddes—so much so that he used the book as a model for his various charitable activities. It was on this day, in 1569, that he first launched the Parish Relief Leal, a voluntary mercy ministry that was duplicated in local churches throughout Scotland in the years to come. Emphasizing what he called "covenantal compassion" and "community conciliation," Geddes left a lasting legacy for his beloved homeland and many of the Reform movements that would so indelibly mark its history—including those of Covenanters such as James Guthrie and James Renwick as well as Free Churchmen, including David Welch and Thomas Chalmers.

1863

The day after President Abraham Lincoln signed the Emancipation Proclamation the law took effect. It did not actually free any slaves within the jurisdiction of the Union. The document was essentially symbolic, designed to placate certain sectors within the Republic's abolitionist constituency, and to provide strategic wartime advantages. The fact is, the Northern Union never adopted an abolitionist stance during the lifetime of Lincoln. In his first inaugural speech, he admitted that in his view, the freeing of the slaves was not only inexpedient and impolitic but perhaps even unconstitutional as well. Reinforcing that position, several of the states that remained in the Northern Union were slave states—including Missouri, Maryland, West Virginia, East Tennessee, and Northern Kentucky. Nevertheless, when the administration finally did act on the issue with its proclamation in 1863, the decree laid the groundwork for freedom for the slaves—which would come with the ratification of the Thirteenth, Fourteenth, and Fifteenth Amendments to the Constitution.

> *Chivalry gives naught but itself and takes naught but from itself. Chivalry possesses not nor would it be possessed—for it is sufficient unto love.*
>
> [JAMES VILLARS (1891–1973)]

18 Ovid, the Roman poet best known for his *Metamorphoses*, died in exile at Tomi on the Black Sea. It was one year to the day since his friend Livy, the author of *The History of Rome*, had died in his beloved home near the Great Forum.

1492 The Reconquista was concluded when Christian forces under the command of Ferdinand of Aragon and Isabella of Castile overran the last Muslim fortress in Granada.

1635 The notorious Cardinal Richelieu, the real power behind the French throne for much of the tumultuous seventeenth century, established the Academie Francaise.

1839 French photographer Louis Daguerre took the first photograph of the moon.

1843 The opera *The Flying Dutchman*, by Richard Wagner, premiered in Dresden. This early opera included the development of Wagner's use of leitmotif, which are short, melodic phrases utilized to identify character, emotions, and ideas related to the plot and action of the work. The story tells of a Dutch captain who swears an oath in order to double the Cape of Good Hope. The devil overhears his oath and condemns the captain to sail the seas until the Day of Judgment unless he finds a woman to love him faithfully until death.

1896 *La Bohème*, Giacomo Puccini's opera masterpiece about the lives and loves of a poet, a painter, and a musician in the Latin Quarter of Paris, premiered at the Teatro Regio in Turin, Italy. It was based on the Henri Murger novel *La Vie de Bohème*.

1916 Robert Russa Moton was the only child of former slaves who were determined to provide him with a quality education. A graduate of Virginia's Hampton Institute—the alma mater of Booker T. Washington—on this day he became the second president of Alabama's celebrated Tuskegee Institute just months after Washington's death.

1920 Isaac Asimov was born in Petrovichi, Russia. After emigrating to America he established himself as a respected biochemist, and began writing science fiction stories. Eventually he became the third most prolific author in history, publishing more than four hundred titles—behind only Cotton Mather and Edward Stratemeyer.

1921 Religious services were broadcast on radio for the first time when KDKA in Pittsburgh aired the Sunday service of the city's prominent Calvary Episcopal Church.

1935 The notorious Lindbergh baby kidnapping trial began.

1945 The United States released its citizens of Japanese, Italian, and German descent from internment camps where they had been imprisoned throughout World War II.

1965 The New York Jets of the upstart American Football League signed Alabama quarterback Joe Namath for a reported $400,000. He would later lead them to victory in Super Bowl III.

JANUARY

3

India in the nineteenth century was hardly a place for a Victorian lady. It was a rough-and-tumble world of stark brutality and crass occultism. Anna Bowden (1852–1873) was a consummate English debutante. But she burst fearlessly onto that cultural landscape at a very tender age—forever changing it.

Sensing a calling to the foreign mission field, Anna left her family's comfortable social orbit at the age of eighteen to enroll in a missionary training school in London. Late in 1871, Robert Campbell-Green, an itinerant evangelist working in southern India, visited the school to deliver a short series of devotional talks on the many new missionary inroads there. Anna impulsively committed herself to the fledgling work. Just a month later, on this day in 1872, she set sail.

When she arrived at Conjeeveram, a seacoast town about forty miles south of Madras, she discovered that the mission compound had been abandoned. The remaining English residents in the region, a small community of fabric exporters, could say only that the mission had been vacant for quite some time and that the residents of the compound had suddenly disappeared without a trace. Anna remained undeterred. She refurbished the mission's decrepit facilities and reopened its tiny clinic and school. Despite warnings from British authorities to steer clear of "politically sensitive issues," Anna's concern for justice drew innumerable children and outcaste "untouchables" into her circle. After only a few months, her efforts began to reap a bountiful harvest.

But she soon ran into trouble. A mob of Hindu fanatics attacked the mission. They burned the buildings to the ground, raped a number of the young girls who had come to live there, and tortured and killed Anna. But death was not the end of Anna's impact. Her daring example sparked a revival within the missionary community in India and her journals—published shortly after her martyrdom—made a stunning impact throughout England and around the world by provoking new legal protections for the poorest of the poor in India.

1687 The Duke of Savoy issued an edict to a group of Protestants who had taken their name from the thirteenth-century mendicant Reformer Peter Waldo. These Waldensians could either leave their homes and cross over the Alps to Geneva, or renounce their faith and be given new homes in the malaria-infested Piedmont. Twenty-eight hundred decided to brave the winter march across the Alps. Many perished along the way, but more than two thousand reached Geneva.

Courage is not having the strength to go on; it is going on when you don't have the strength. Industry and determination can do anything that genius and advantage can do and many things that they cannot.

[Theodore Roosevelt (1858–1919)]

JANUARY

107 B.C. Roman orator and statesman Marcus Tullius Cicero was born in Arpinum.

1521 Martin Luther was excommunicated by Pope Leo X for his refusal to recant his commitment to reform the church. The Protestant Reformation was thus launched.

1745 David Brainerd committed himself to reach the Indian tribes of Colonial America with the gospel of Christ after a day of intense prayer and fasting. He would die just two years later at the age of twenty-nine. Nevertheless, his commitment—movingly recorded in his diary and published by his mentor, Jonathan Edwards—became a source of inspiration to an entire generation of missionaries.

1777 The troops of George Washington routed the British army under Lord Cornwallis at the Battle of Princeton. It was the first Revolutionary War victory for the Americans.

1795 The pioneering industrialist Josiah Wedgewood died at his palatial estate outside Manchester, England.

1803 Author, playwright, and wit Douglas William Jerrold was born in London. For years he was the heart and soul of the comic magazine *Punch,* which continues to bear the mark of his satirical humor to this day.

1868 The Meiji Restoration reestablished the authority of Japan's emperor and heralded the fall of the military rulers known as Shoguns.

1870 Construction began on the Brooklyn Bridge in New York City.

1882 Irish writer Oscar Wilde arrived in New York for his first visit to America. When asked if he had anything to declare, Wilde replied, "Nothing except my genius."

1892 John Ronald Reuel Tolkien, renowned philologist and author of *The Hobbit, The Lord of the Rings,* and other tales, was born in Bloemfontein, South Africa.

1898 Southern Presbyterian pastor, theologian, and educator Robert Lewis Dabney died in Austin, Texas, where he taught at the University of Texas. He had first gained prominence during the War Between the States as Stonewall Jackson's chaplain.

1909 Victor Borge, pianist, entertainer, and astute musical comedian, was born in Denmark. Borge, a Jew, fled his native country when the Nazis invaded in 1940.

1924 Working near Luxor, Egypt, in the Valley of the Kings, British archaeologist Howard Carter and his workmen uncovered the stone sarcophagus of King Tutankhamen containing the magnificent solid gold coffin and mummy of the boy pharaoh.

1938 The March of Dimes campaign to fight polio was organized—borrowing the old idea of nickel-and-dime subscriptions from the Scottish Presbyterian innovator Thomas Chalmers.

1959 President Eisenhower signed a proclamation admitting Alaska into the Union as the forty-ninth state.

JANUARY

NATIONAL DAY
Myanmar
FEAST DAY
St. Gregory of Langres, St. Roger of Ellant, St. Elizabeth Bayley Seton, St. Pharaïdis, St. Rigobert of Reims

When the brash socialist agitator Adolf Hitler first came to power as the chancellor of Germany in 1933, he was welcomed by most church members and leaders from around the nation. One prominent pastor and theologian leader even said that 1933 and Hitler's rise were a gift of mercy from God's hand. To be sure, Hitler used the rhetoric of a Christian restoration of law and order, morality, and traditional values.

Since the defeat of the nation in the First World War and the humiliation of the Versailles Treaty, the German Weimar Republic had allowed an extreme modernist culture to flourish, and many Christian leaders believed Hitler would bring a spiritual renewal to the German people. They hoped that at last a German national church might be established, and in May 1933 a constitution for a unified national church was produced by the new Nazi administration. But then in July two restrictions were placed by the government on the clergy—that they be politically subservient to the Nazis and that they accept the superiority of the Aryan race.

A small group of church leaders in Germany began to resist such ideas and oppose the restrictions. They believed that the church should have full freedom to serve God apart from political influence, and they began to organize formal opposition to the new national church. Prominent theologians like Karl Barth, Martin Niemöller, and Dietrich Bonhoeffer were among the leaders of this new opposition.

On this day in 1934, they met in Barmen and accepted Barth's *Declaration on the Correct Understanding of the Reformation Confessions in the German Evangelical Church.* By April the opposition had officially formed the Confessing Church as the underground Protestant church of Germany. At the first Synod of the Confessing Church, held openly at Barmen several months later, another declaration was written that ultimately became the confession of the church. The declaration stressed that unity, "can come only from the word of God in faith through the Holy Spirit." It added that in order to serve God properly, the church must be totally free from political influence. It resisted the Nazi contention that God was giving a new revelation through the history of the German nation. The Confessing Church maintained there was no revelation in addition to that of Jesus Christ and the Word of God.

Alas, each of the men who lead this confessing opposition to the Nazis paid dearly for their commitment—most died in prisons or suffered long and bitter confinements alongside the Jews and Gypsies in the concentration camps. Nevertheless, they kept alive the independent proclamation of the gospel during the difficult days of the Nazi terror.

I am of certain convinced that the greatest heroes are those who do their duty in the daily grind of domestic affairs whilst the world whirls as a maddening dreidle.

[FLORENCE NIGHTINGALE (1820–1910)]

1577 Hans Bret, a baker and lay preacher in the Spanish Netherlands, was tortured and burned at the stake for his Protestant faith in his hometown of Antwerp. His was the latest in a long series of martyrdoms during the great persecutions of 1531 to 1578, but his example will always be remembered because despite the horror of having his tongue clamped and cauterized, he boldly proclaimed the gospel until the flames consumed his body.

1785 Librarian, philologist, and children's author Jakob Grimm was born in Hanau, near Frankfurt am Main. Along with his brother Wilhelm, he collected and edited *Grimm's Fairy Tales*.

1809 Louis Braille, who developed a tactile system of reading and writing for the blind, was born in Coupvray, France. He himself was blind from the age of three.

1813 Sir Isaac Pittman, the British publisher and printer who invented shorthand, was born near London.

1821 The first native-born American saint recognized by the Roman Catholic Church, Elizabeth Ann Seton, died in Emmitsburg, Maryland.

1865 The New York Stock Exchange opened its first permanent headquarters near Wall Street in New York City.

1884 The socialist Fabian Society was founded in London.

1885 Dr. William W. Grant of Davenport, Iowa, performed what is believed to have been the first appendectomy on twenty-two-year-old Mary Gartside.

1896 Utah was admitted as the forty-fifth state following the prohibition of Mormon polygamy.

1936 The first pop-music chart was compiled, based on record sales. It was published in New York by *Billboard* magazine.

1958 Ralph Vaughan Williams, renowned English composer and hymn arranger, died in London.

1960 Albert Camus, the famed author of such books as *The Plague*, died in an automobile accident near Sens, France, at age forty-six.

1965 President Lyndon Johnson outlined the goals of a "Great Society" in his State of the Union address. The flurry of legislation that he pushed through in the days that followed created the modern welfare system.

1965 T. S. Eliot, best known for his antimodernist poem "The Waste Land," and his stinging essays on Christian civilization, died in London at the age of seventy-six.

4

JANUARY

FEAST DAY
St. Simeon Stylites, St. Gerlac,
St. Dorotheus the Younger,
St. Apollinaris, St. Convoyon,
St. Syncletica, St. John Nepomucene
Neumann

Edward the Confessor, son of Ethelred the Unready, was the only English king ever to be canonized a saint by the Church of Rome. Edward was the next to last Saxon king—but his successor, King Harold, did not enjoy the throne long. Just ten months after Edward's death his Norman cousins invaded England and claimed the crown.

Edward had himself spent much of his life in Normandy. The fierce Viking Danes had invaded England just as Edward was entering his teens. They had removed his father from the throne, so he fled with his mother and brother to Normandy, which was then ruled by Edward's uncle. There Edward came under the influence of the Norman monks and submitted himself to the rigors of a devout Christian life. The British church, rooted in ancient Celtic traditions, had always functioned quite independently of the bishops in Rome. So now Edward was exposed to an entirely new perspective of the faith—one that affected him profoundly. He vowed to make a pilgrimage to Rome; but his half brother died suddenly, and Edward was proclaimed king before he could fulfill his vow.

Edward never proved to be a particularly dynamic or visionary leader. He left most of the actual work of government to his lords, dukes, and earls. Nevertheless, it was evident that he fervently desired the good of his people. He was charitable, compassionate, gracious, and free from personal vanity. His piety became legendary. At the end of his life, Edward built a monastery dedicated to Saint Peter in a little village adjacent to London to satisfy the vow of pilgrimage he had made but was never able to fulfill. The church, which took more than fifteen years to build, was built in the grand style of churches attached to the royal palaces in Normandy. Today it is known as Westminster Abbey.

Edward died on this day in 1066, just one week after the church was dedicated, and he was buried there the next day—events that were later memorialized on the famed Bayeux Tapestry. On December 25, 1066, his cousin, William the Conqueror from Normandy, was crowned king of England in Westminster Abbey, and the church has continued to this day as the Coronation Church of the British monarchy.

1895

French Captain Alfred Dreyfus, convicted of treason, was publicly stripped of his rank. Though the Jewish officer was ultimately vindicated, his public humiliation heightened awareness of the discrimination most Jews suffered and proved to be an inspiration for the birth of the modern Zionist movement.

Of all the tyrannies, a tyranny sincerely expressed for the good of its victims may be the most oppressive. It may be better to live under robber barons than under omnipotent ideological busybodies.

[C. S. LEWIS (1898–1963)]

1477 Charles the Bold, king of France, was killed at the Battle of Nancey—one of the pivotal battles during the Hundred Years' War.

1589 Catherine de Medici, heir of one of the greatest royal families in Europe and power behind the throne of France, died at age sixty-nine.

1643 The first divorce was granted in the American colonies.

1782 Poet William Cowper, writing in his journal, assessed the propensities of John Dryden: "Never, I believe, were such talents and such drudgery united."

1821 Lord Byron wrote in his diary concerning Sir Walter Scott: "What a wonderful man! I long to get drunk with him." Apparently, Scott declined the offer.

1825 Alexandre Dumas, author of such books as *The Three Musketeers* and *The Count of Monte Cristo*, embarked on his career as a romantic at the age of twenty-three by fighting a duel in which his trousers fell down.

1855 King Camp Gillette, the American inventor of the safety razor, was born.

1896 German physicist Wilhelm Röntgen gave the first public demonstration of x-rays.

1909 When Marcel Proust dipped a rusk of toast in his tea, the flavor brought back a rush of childhood memories that became the basis for the famous madeleine episode in *Swan's Way*, from which the structure of his brilliant multivolume *Remembrance of Things Past* eventually evolved.

1919 The German Worker's Party was formed in Germany by Gottfried Feder. A disgruntled Adolf Hitler joined the left-wing party later that year, rose to a position of leadership, and changed the name to the National Socialist—or Nazi—Party.

1925 Nellie T. Ross succeeded her late husband as governor of Wyoming, becoming the first female governor in U.S. history.

1933 The thirtieth president of the United States, Calvin Coolidge, died in Northampton, Massachusetts, at age sixty, just four years after leaving the White House. He was the last president to substantially reduce the size and expense of the federal government.

1943 Educator and scientist George Washington Carver died in Tuskegee, Alabama, at age eighty-one. In addition to the innumerable technical breakthroughs he made throughout his career, he devoted his life to teaching young African Americans how to make themselves "indispensable to their communities."

1964 During his tour of the Holy Land, Pope Paul VI met with Patriarch Athenagoras I, the first meeting of the heads of the Roman Catholic and Eastern Orthodox Churches in more than five hundred years.

JANUARY

6

The legendary generosity and charity of Good King Wenceslaus of Bohemia (907–929), is no mere Yuletide fable. The young prince lived a life fraught with conflict and tragedy. Both his mother and grandmother—victims of court intrigue and anti-Christian conspiracy—were murdered when he was young. He himself was the object of several assassination attempts and revolts. Yet, despite such adversity, he was a model Christian regent. He reformed the penal system. He criminalized abuse of children and outcasts. And he exercised great compassion on the poor.

The little kingdom prospered under the young king's benevolent rule. At peace with their neighbors—Wenceslaus cultivated friendly relations with the Carolingian Empire by acknowledging Henry as the legitimate successor of Charlemagne in 926. The poor and the needy, the despised and the rejected, were the special beneficiaries of the newfound peace and prosperity.

Early on Epiphany morning in 929, as Wenceslaus made his way to church, he met his brother, Boleslaus. Apparently envious of the king's popularity and good fortune, Boleslaus struck him down. Wenceslaus murmured as he fell at the chapel door, "Brother, may God forgive you." The common people at once began to acclaim Wenceslaus a martyr. Amazingly, by his death he was able to achieve what he never could while he was living—the complete conversion of Bohemia and the codification of his deeds of mercy as a standard for Christian civic justice and mercy. His example became the pattern for living in light of the epiphany of Christ in the midst of this fallen world.

EPIPHANY
FEAST DAY
  St. John de Ribera, St. Erminold,
  St. Wiltrudis, St. Guarinus

EPIPHANY

The celebration of Epiphany is the culmination of what is traditionally called the Twelve Days of Christmas. The word literally means "revelation" or "sudden unveiling" or "manifestation." It commemorates the day when wise men from the East were conducted by a miraculous star to the Nativity in Bethlehem. The magi were thus the first to comprehend that Jesus was not merely the prophetic fulfillment of Jewish aspirations. Instead, He was the Light of the World and the joy of every man's desiring. They beheld the very glory of God that day—for in the City of David, the Savior was born. As a result, Epiphany is the celebration of unveiling of good news.

The happy appearance of Christ in the world has made for a new dispensation of civic virtue. Because the Lord abides forever, He has established His Throne for judgment, and He will judge the world in righteousness. He will surely execute judgment for the peoples with equity. The Lord also will be a Stronghold for the oppressed, a Stronghold in times of trouble. As a consequence, a royal regent must needs be a bastion of both justice and mercy.

[WENCESLAUS OF BOHEMIA (907–929)]

871 Alfred the Great, the young king of Wessex, defeated the Danes at the Battle of Ashdown. It was the first step toward the unification of all the scattered English realms.

1367 Richard II, the last of the eight Plantagenet kings of England, was born. His memory has been grossly distorted—though gloriously preserved—by the eponymous play by William Shakespeare.

1412 Joan of Arc, known as the Maid of Orleans, was born in the little village of Domremy. She was a French national heroine during the calamitous Hundred Years' War. Emerging from obscurity, she helped to liberate the city of Orleans from the English so that the Dauphin might ascend to the throne. Eventually, she was captured and burned at the stake as a witch.

1540 England's King Henry VIII married his fourth wife, Anne of Cleves. The marriage lasted about six months.

1649 Cardinal Mazarin spirited Queen Anne of Austria and the boy-king of France, Louis XIV, out of Paris to escape angry near-revolutionary crowds. High taxes and the growing authority of the Crown were responsible for the discontent of the Parisians.

1759 George Washington married the wealthy widow Martha Dandridge Custis.

1832 The French engraver and illustrator Gustave Doré was born in France. His illustrations of the Bible and books such as *The Rhyme of the Ancient Mariner* were stunning for their close technical detail and historical accuracy.

1838 The first public demonstration of the electric telegraph was given by its inventor, Samuel Morse, in Morristown, New Jersey.

1850 Unable to reach his own church because of a snowstorm, fifteen-year-old Charles Haddon Spurgeon ducked into a tiny chapel. There were only a few other parishioners who had braved the storm—even the preacher had failed to come. But a faithful deacon read a brief salvation message, and the boy was converted. It was a propitious moment, for he would become one of the greatest preachers in all of history, proclaiming the gospel to millions of souls throughout the course of his ministry. Indeed, more than a century after his death all of his more than 150 books remain in print, and his name is practically synonymous with substantive orthodox and evangelical ministry.

1854 The character Sherlock Holmes was "born" in the North Riding of Yorkshire.

1878 The renowned American poet Carl Sandburg was born in Galesburg, Illinois. He was best known not for his poetry, but for his magisterial biography of Abraham Lincoln, for which he won the Pulitzer Prize.

1919 Theodore Roosevelt died at his home on Long Island, Sagamore Hill. He was not yet sixty-one years old, but he was able to accomplish in those few years what most men could hardly expect to squeeze into a half dozen lifetimes. He had served as a New York State legislator, the under-secretary of the U.S. Navy, police commissioner for the city of New York, U.S. Civil Service Commissioner, the governor of the state of New York, the vice president under William McKinley, a colonel in the U.S. Army, and two terms as president of the United States. In addition, he had run a cattle ranch in the Dakota Territories, served as a reporter and editor for several journals, newspapers, and magazines, and conducted scientific expeditions on four continents. During his career he was hailed by supporters and rivals alike as the greatest man of the age—perhaps one of the greatest of all ages. His passing was mourned around the world.

JANUARY

According to his own account, Christopher Columbus first went to sea when he was about ten—probably to supplement his family's meager income. He began to venture out on short sailing excursions to Portofino to load dry fish, to Savona with bolts of his father's cloth, or to Corsica to sell Genoese dry goods in the festival markets.

Like so many of Genoa's progeny, he was immediately smitten by the romance and grandeur of the sea. Over the next seven or eight years he sailed whenever he could. Apparently he was a quick study and never wanted for opportunities to sail. By the time he was eighteen he knew the western Mediterranean like the pocket of a familiar cloak—and he abandoned the weaver's loom altogether for a life at sea.

On this day in 1474, he signed on with a crew delivering cargo to far-away Chios. Strategically located just off the coast of Asia Minor in the eastern Aegean, the small island was Genoa's gateway to the Orient. Its markets and bazaars overflowed with spices, silks, pearls, and precious stones. The varicolored costumes, alluring perfumes, abstruse customs, strange tongues, and exotic sagacity of its merchants, hawkers, traders, peasants, shysters, tradesmen, charlatans, shamans, and seamen concocted an intoxicating cultural brew—a stunning introduction to the esoteric wiles of the East. But the smells were what arrested first-time visitors to Chios. Genoese slang dubbed the island "mirovolos"—the land of a thousand aromas—and for good reason. Its ambiance is in fact a fabulous harmony of many flavors—sage, thyme, oregano, and pepper each liberally garnish the pungent air. But dominating them all is the sweet fragrance of mastic. Obtained from the bark of a peculiar strain of a Lentisk tree that grows abundantly along the southern shores of the island—like nowhere else in the world—the resin's unique scent is all-pervasive and unmistakable. It was treasured around the Mediterranean for its use in making colognes, drinks, candies, and a popular aphrodisiac.

Columbus was utterly bewitched—and would remain so for the rest of his life. The esoteric whimsy of the Orient captivated him. He had begun the long journey that would lead him inevitably and inexorably to the shores of America.

CHRISTMAS DAY, ORTHODOX
FEAST DAY
St. Valentine, St. Raymund of Peñafort, St. Aldric, St. Lucian of Antioch, St. Tillo, St. Canute Lavard, St. Reinhold

---

ST. DISTAFF'S
DAY

This was the day in England that women returned to their spinning after the holiday season of Christmas and Epiphany. The staff was used to wind wool or flax to aid in the spinning process. Men would playfully set the women's flax or wool on fire this day, and the spinners retaliated by drenching the men with pails of water. English poet Robert Herrick mentions these activities of Distaff Day in a poem:

Partly work and partly play; Ye must on St. Distaff's Day.
From the plow soone free the teame; Then come home and fother them.
If the Maides a-spinning goe; Burn the flax and fire the tow.
Bring the pailes of water then; Let the maides bewash the men.
Give St. Distaff all the right; Then bid Christmas sport good night;
And next morrow, every one, to his owne vocation.

> *The most extraordinary thing in the world is an ordinary man and an ordinary woman and their ordinary children.*
>
> [G. K. CHESTERTON (1874-1936)]

367 Athanasius, bishop of Alexandria, established for the first time an authoritative list of the canon of the Old and New Testaments in his annual Lententide letter.

1610 The astronomer Galileo Galilei sighted four of Jupiter's moons.

1789 In the first national election under the new Constitution, George Washington was elected president of the United States.

1800 The man who would one day become the thirteenth president of the United States, Millard Fillmore, was born in Summerhill, New York.

1867 Mark Twain was sent by his editor on the "first organized pleasure party ever assembled for a transatlantic voyage." It was a "Grand Tour" for the rich and famous of America, who, weary of war and reconstruction at home, set out to see the sights in Europe and beyond. During the trip that would ultimately make his reputation as an author of incomparable wit, Twain wrote, "Passengers growl less this trip than any I ever saw, but they growl some on all trips, no matter how favorable everything is." The quip, written in his notebook on this day, would eventually find its way into his breakthrough book, *Innocents Abroad.*

1894 One of the earliest motion picture experiments took place at the Thomas Edison studio in West Orange, New Jersey, as comedian Fred Ott was filmed sneezing.

1899 French composer Francis Poulenc, known for his tight harmonies and vocal music, was born in France.

1867 The prominent literary editor Max Perkins met with the promising Thomas Wolfe for the first time to discuss the young author's manuscript *Look Homeward Angel.* Perkins later recalled that Wolfe's "wild hair and bright countenance" reminded him of the romantic poet Percy Shelley.

1924 At the age of twenty-six, George Gershwin completed his composition *Rhapsody in Blue,* a successful fusion of art music and jazz.

1927 Transatlantic telephone service was inaugurated between New York and London.

1953 President Harry Truman announced in his State of the Union address that the United States had developed a hydrogen bomb.

1967 Contralto Marian Anderson debuted at the Metropolitan Opera in New York City as the first African American to sing at America's most prestigious opera venue.

1999 For only the second time in history, an impeached American president went on trial before the Senate. Eventually acquitted on a procedural technicality, President Bill Clinton faced charges of perjury and obstruction of justice.

JANUARY

One of the most remarkable men Africa ever produced—standing shoulder to shoulder with such giants as Athanasius, Origen, and Tertullian—was Augustine of Hippo. He would eventually prove to be a pillar of Western thought—perhaps Christendom's single most important cultural influence from the time of the Roman Empire until the Reformation more than a thousand years later.

He was born in 354 at Tagaste—in present-day Algeria—of a pagan father and a Christian mother. Monica, his mother, was a vital and invigorating influence on him from his earliest remembrance. She was unusually gifted—and determined to see her son advance. She secured for him the best possible classical education—and then, because he proved to be an able scholar, prodded him on toward advanced studies. As a result, he studied rhetoric at the great University of Carthage to become a lawyer, but later gave up his plan for a career in teaching. His study of rhetorical philosophy—with an emphasis on Platonism and Manichaeanism—resulted in a complete renunciation of Christianity.

Augustine also began to live a self-confessedly debauched life—including keeping a mistress for fifteen years by whom he had a son. Those early years of unbridled sensuality revealed him to be a man of innate passion—a character trait that would continue to dominate the rest his life. Even after he committed himself to a chaste and virtuous Christian life, his natural vitality, vibrancy, and verve were evident.

In pursuit of opportunities to improve his academic standing, he took teaching posts—opportunities Monica secured for him first in Rome and later in Milan. It was in this latter city that he fell under the sway of the eloquent bishop and rhetorician Ambrose. After a long and tortured battle of the soul, Augustine was converted to orthodox Christianity under Ambrose's ministry and was baptized—much to the relief of Monica.

After some two years of intensive discipling and catechizing, he returned to Africa and established a scholastic community in Hippo. There he founded the Classicum Academae—a kind of prototype for the modern university devoted to study, writing, and the work of cultural transformation. The school was famed for its emphasis on logic, rhetoric, art, music, politics, theology, and philosophy. But it was equally recognized for the brilliance of its founder. On this day in 391 the steadfastness, holiness, and giftedness of Augustine was recognized and he was ordained—though very much against his own objections. In 394 he was asked to serve as coadjutor in the diocese. And in 396 he was elevated to the bishopric of the city.

During his career he wrote more than a thousand works, including nearly three hundred hefty books. Several of them have claimed a central place in the canon of the Western literary masterpieces. His autobiography, *Confessions,* practically invented the genre and remains a devotional and inspirational classic. But he is probably best known for his analysis of the great culture war between truth and error. *The City of God* is a book that both summarizes his other works and crowns them with the full achievement of maturity. It was a fitting monument to this, the greatest of all Western philosophers.

The longing for home is woven into the fabric of our lives and is profoundly affected by our inescapable connection to places, persons, and principles: the incremental parts of community.

[JONATHAN JELLISTON (1891–1977)]

1642 Astronomer Galileo Galilei died in Arcetri, Italy.

1815 Andrew Jackson led American troops to a stunning victory over the British in the Battle of New Orleans. The best of the 8,000-man-strong British army, the same soldiers who had defeated Napoleon, were bested by a group of backwoods Tennessee riflemen, Kentucky hunters, pirates, and Creoles. The British suffered 1,971 casualties. The Americans had seven killed and six wounded. The astounding American victory gained a new respect for America in Europe and made a hero out of the American commander Andrew Jackson, paving the way for his becoming president of the United States.

1821 Mr. Huddy, the ninety-seven-year-old postmaster of Lismore, Scotland, on a wager delivered the mail from Lismore to Fermoy in a Dunvargon oyster-tub—drawn by a pig, a badger, two cats, a goose, and a hedgehog, with a pig-driver's whip in one hand, a cow's horn in the other, and a red nightcap on his head.

1824 English novelist Wilkie Collins, best known for *The Woman in White* and his origination of the genre of detective fiction with his novel *The Moonstone,* was born in London.

1894 Fire caused serious damage at the World's Colombian Exposition in Chicago.

1918 President Woodrow Wilson outlined his "Fourteen Points" for peace after World War I.

1918 Mississippi became the first state to ratify a proposed amendment to the U.S. Constitution prohibiting the sale, manufacture, and transportation of liquor.

1935 Rock-and-roll legend Elvis Presley was born in Tupelo, Mississippi.

1964 President Lyndon Johnson declared a "War on Poverty."

1973 Secret peace talks between the United States and North Vietnam began near Paris.

1982 The virtual telecommunications monopoly held by the American Telephone and Telegraph Company—known as AT&T—was broken up by the Justice Department when the company agreed to government demands that it divest itself of the twenty-two local Bell System phone providers.

1987 For the first time, the Dow-Jones industrial average closed above 2000, ending the day at 2002.25.

JANUARY

Birmingham, Alabama, was a wild and untamed mining town in the heart of the reconstructed South when James Alexander Bryan came to pastor the Third Presbyterian Church there on this day in 1888. When he died in 1941, Birmingham had become a vibrant industrial center. In the years between, Brother Bryan—as he was affectionately called—won the hearts of generation after generation of its citizens. He was an unlikely hero for the bustling town, though. For one thing, he was noticeably inept as a pulpiteer. His sermons were often halting, rambling, and inarticulate. Though entirely committed to the authority of the Scriptures and the centrality of preaching, he simply was not a skilled orator.

He was also a poor administrator. Though perpetually busy, he was easily distracted and rarely kept up with his workload. He didn't even maintain a particularly winsome appearance. He was more often than not disheveled, shabbily dressed, and hastily groomed. In a day when manliness and imposing presence were especially esteemed, he was shy, soft-spoken, and had a slight stutter.

Nevertheless, he was practically a cultural icon in the city. Near the end of his life, he was honored by local dignitaries in a citywide celebration. The president of the City Commission said: "No man in Birmingham is better known or better loved than Brother Bryan. There is one man in this city about whom we are all agreed, and he is Brother Bryan." The editor of the city newspaper agreed: "Brother Bryan is the only man, whom we have ever known, whose motives have never been questioned. He is the one man for whom we are all unanimous." The city erected a statue of the humble pastor at one of its busiest intersections near downtown. It portrayed him in a posture of prayer and proclaimed him "the patron saint of Birmingham."

How had this seemingly inept pastor won over an entire city so completely? How had this painfully ordinary man accomplished a feat so extraordinary as this? Very simply, Brother Bryan was a common man who proved to be an uncommon example of the Christian mandate of loving his neighbor. He made it a habit to make a circuit every morning just before dawn to all the factories, shops, fire and police stations, schools, and offices downtown to pray with as many common workingmen and -women as he could. He would simply announce himself, drop to his knees wherever he was, and begin to intercede for each of them. The words most often on his lips were, "Let us pray."

He also distinguished himself with his selfless service to the poor, the needy, the brokenhearted, and the sick. His indefatigable efforts to encourage the distressed led him to establish several city outreaches to the homeless, to orphans and widows, and to the victims of war and pestilence overseas. More than any rich philanthropist, he demonstrated the power and effect of merciful service on the fabric of a community. Though he violated all the rules of success, he seemed to incarnate the essence of the Christian faith. He was, as many called him, "religion in shoes."

The smiling little cottage, where at eve
He meets his rosy children at the door,
Prattling their welcomes, and his honest wife,
With good brown cake and bacon slice, intent
To cheer his hunger after labor hard:
Such is the heart, the soul, the very essence,
Of parish life: the hearth, the home, domesticity.

[THOMAS CHALMERS (1780–1847)]

1324 Marco Polo died in Venice at the age of seventy. Twenty-five years earlier, while a prisoner of the Genoese, he dictated to a fellow inmate the memoirs of his days with Kublai Khan, *The Travels of Marco Polo.*

1788 Connecticut became the fifth state to ratify the new federal Constitution.

1793 Frenchman Jean Pierre Blanchard, using a hot-air balloon, flew between Philadelphia and Woodbury, New Jersey.

1799 The British prime minister, William Pitt the Younger, introduced income tax to raise funds for the Napoleonic Wars.

1863 The dome of the Church of La Madonna del Sasso in Locarno, Switzerland, collapsed through the roof and entombed fifty-three women who were worshipping there.

1866 Fisk University in Nashville, Tennessee, started classes for former slaves as The Fisk School. The students met in former Union army barracks.

1873 Napoleon III, the nephew of Bonaparte and his successor in the revived French Empire, died in exile.

1902 New York State introduced a bill to outlaw flirting in public.

1904 Choreographer Georgi Balanchivadze—anglicized to George Balanchine—was born. Best known for his work on *Apollo, Orpheus, Firebird, Swan Lake,* and *The Nutcracker,* he also founded the School of American Ballet and the New York City Ballet.

1913 Richard Milhous Nixon, the thirty-seventh president of the United States, was born in Yorba Linda, California.

1924 Virginia Woolf leased a house at 52 Tavestock Square in Bloomsbury, where she would ultimately lead a renowned colony of artists, writers, and musicians.

1928 The Seeing Eye, the first school to train dogs to guide the blind, was opened in Nashville, Tennessee.

1972 In Hong Kong harbor, the *Queen Elizabeth,* the world's largest passenger liner for more than thirty years, was gutted by fire.

1972 Reclusive billionaire Howard Hughes, speaking by telephone from the Bahamas to reporters in Hollywood, said a purported biography of him by Clifford Irving was a fake.

1980 Saudi Arabia beheaded sixty-three people for their involvement in the November 1979 raid on the Grand Mosque in Mecca.

JANUARY

10

By an ironic sort of providence, Thomas Mifflin (1744–1800) served as George Washington's first aide-de-camp at the beginning of the Revolutionary War, and, when the war was over, he was the man, as president of the United States, who accepted Washington's resignation of his commission. In the years between, Mifflin greatly served the cause of freedom while serving as the first Quartermaster General of the Continental army. He obtained desperately needed supplies for the new army. Although experienced in business and successful in obtaining supplies for the war, Mifflin preferred the front lines, and he distinguished himself in military action on Long Island and near Philadelphia.

Born on this day in 1744, he was reared in a strict Quaker home. As a young man, much to his dismay, he was excluded from Quaker meetings because of his military activities. Nevertheless, he maintained throughout his life a pattern of devotion to his family and their traditions. Somehow, though, that did not protect him from public controversy. Mifflin lost favor with Washington, for instance, and was part of the Conway Cabal—a rather notorious plan to replace Washington with General Horatio Gates. And Mifflin narrowly missed court-martial action over his handling of funds by resigning his commission in 1778.

In spite of all these problems—and of repeated charges that he was a drunkard—Mifflin continued to be elected to positions of responsibility—as president and governor of Pennsylvania, delegate to the Constitutional Convention, as well as the highest office in the land—where he served from November 3, 1783, to November 29, 1784. In addition, he was heralded by friends and supporters as a pious and gracious man who cared for nothing more than the sacred honor of his God and his nation.

Most of Mifflin's significant contributions occurred in his earlier years; in the First and Second Continental Congresses he was firm in his stand for independence and for fighting for it, and he helped obtain both men and supplies for Washington's army in the early critical period. In 1784, as president, he signed the treaty with Great Britain that ended the war. Although a delegate to the Constitutional Convention, he did not make a significant contribution beyond signing the document.

Although he was accused of negligence, as governor of Pennsylvania he supported improvements of roads and reformed the state penal and judicial systems. He had gradually become sympathetic to Jefferson's principles regarding states' rights; even so, he directed the Pennsylvania militia to support the federal tax collectors in the Whiskey Rebellion. In spite of charges of corruption, the affable Mifflin remained a popular figure. A magnetic personality and an effective speaker, he managed to hold a variety of elective offices for almost thirty years and make an indelible mark on the critical Revolutionary period.

FEAST DAY

St. Marcian of Constantinople; St. William of Bourges; St. Agatho, pope; St. Dermot or Diarmaid; St. Peter Orseolo; St. John the Good

No abounding of material prosperity shall avail us if our spiritual senses atrophy. The foes of our own household will surely prevail against us unless there be in our people an inner life which finds its outer expression in a morality like unto that preached by the seers and prophets of God when the grandeur that was Greece and the glory that was Rome still lay in the future.

[Theodore Roosevelt (1858–1919)]

1645 William Laud, the archbishop of Canterbury and arch-persecutor of the Puritans during the reign of Bloody Mary, was beheaded on Tower Hill after being found "guilty of endeavoring to subvert the laws, to overthrow the Protestant religion, and to act as an enemy of Parliament."

1713 Composer and violin virtuoso Arcangelo Corelli died in Rome, Italy. He was the first composer of instrumental music to gain an international reputation, and his style of playing became the basis of violin technique for the next two centuries.

1738 Revolutionary War hero and leader of the Green Mountain Boys, Ethan Allen was born in Litchfield, Connecticut. He formed the Green Mountain Boys as a militia group to fight for the establishment of the Republic of Vermont. When the Revolutionary War began, the militia fought against the British and were instrumental in the capture of Fort Ticonderoga on May 10, 1775. Allen called for the surrender of the British troops "in the name of the Great Jehovah and the Continental Congress."

1812 The fog and smoke were so thick around London that shops and offices lit lamps in the middle of the day as if it were night. The streets were not lighted and great care had to be taken to avoid accidents in the darkness.

1840 Sir Rowland Hill implemented his system of prepaid postage by means of a stamp. Until this time in Britain, letters were charged according to the number of enclosures and the distance traveled. The Penny Post replaced this system by charging the flat rate of a penny for any letter under a certain weight.

1847 The United States Marines captured Los Angeles from Mexico.

1863 The Tube, London's underground railway system, was opened to passengers with trains running from Paddington to Farrington Street at fifteen-minute intervals.

1870 John D. Rockefeller incorporated Standard Oil. Eventually the company became a huge monopoly, making Rockefeller the richest man on earth.

1920 The League of Nations convened as the Treaty of Versailles went into effect.

1928 The Soviet Union ordered the exile of Leon Trotsky.

1946 The first General Assembly of the United Nations convened in London.

1957 Harold Macmillan became prime minister of Britain, succeeding Anthony Eden.

1967 Massachusetts Republican Edward W. Brooke, the first black elected to the U.S. Senate by popular vote, took his seat.

1984 For the first time in more than a century, the United States established full diplomatic relations with the Vatican.

10

31

JANUARY

11

FEAST DAY
St. Salvius or Sauve of Amiens,
St. Theodosius the Cenobiarch

The great Victorian preacher Charles Spurgeon read it more than a hundred times. E. M. Bounds kept a copy by his bedside and read from it every night before retiring. Stonewall Jackson kept a copy in his knapsack throughout his Southern campaigns. Its enduring value was confirmed by C. S. Lewis, who said it was "a literary and spiritual masterpiece." Translated into more languages than any other book save the Bible, it is *Pilgrim's Progress,* a fanciful allegory of the Christian life written primarily from a prison cell midway through the seventeenth century by John Bunyan.

The son of a poor brazier, born in 1628, Bunyan was a witness to some of the momentous events in English history: the civil war, the regicide of King Charles, the Cromwell protectorate, the Great Fire, the restoration of the monarchy, and the great Puritan purge. Those days left an indelible mark of change upon the souls of both men and nations. Bunyan was no exception. After a dramatic adult conversion, he immersed himself in the life and work of a very small nonconformist congregation.

For nearly a decade, Bunyan served as an unordained itinerant preacher and frequently took part in highly visible theological controversies. Thus, he was an easy target for the very restrictive laws concerning religion in his day. He was arrested for preaching without a license. The judges threatened Bunyan, but he was unshakable. Finally, they told him he would not be released until he was willing to foreswear his illegal preaching. And so he was sent to the county gaol, where he spent twelve long years.

Because of his wife's strong exhortations to use his time of incarceration wisely, Bunyan began writing the allegorical *Pilgrim's Progress* as a sort of spiritual autobiography. Almost immediately, *Pilgrim's Progress* struck a nerve. Bunyan was able to throw a searchlight of understanding on the soul of Everyman. As literary critic Roger Sharrock said: "A seventeenth-century Calvinist sat down to write a tract and produced a folk-epic of the universal religious imagination instead."

Today, in the center of Bedford, England, there stands a statue of Bunyan carrying a tinker's burden upon his back and a Bible in his hand. It marks the place where that great Puritan spent the long years of his imprisonment for the offense of preaching without the permission of the state. Near the foot of the statue is a little bronze plaque. On it are engraved the words of the prosecutor—the Lord Judge Magistrate of Bedford—spoken at Bunyan's sentencing on this day in 1673. The judge said: "At last we are done with this tinker and his cause. Never more will he plague us: for his name, locked away as surely as he, shall be forgotten, as surely as he. Done we are, and all eternity with him." Of course, it is not Bunyan who is forgotten. Instead, it is the Lord Judge Magistrate of Bedford who remains unnamed and unremembered.

Strong Son of God, Immortal Love,
Whom we, that have not seen thy face,
By faith, and faith alone, embrace.

[ALFRED, LORD TENNYSON (1809–1892)]

1757 The first secretary of the U.S. Treasury, Alexander Hamilton, was born in the West Indies.

1776 The first copies of Thomas Paine's little booklet *Common Sense* were sold in bookshops in Boston, New York, and Philadelphia. It was said that it made possible the final break from Britain. Though the American war had already been under way for nearly two years, it would be another six months before independence was declared.

1805 The federal territory of Michigan was created.

1815 Sir John A. Macdonald, the first prime minister of Canada, was born in Glasgow, Scotland.

1817 Timothy Dwight, grandson of Jonathan Edwards and president of Yale College, died. When he came to Yale twenty-two years earlier, the institution had suffered through a long season of decline and skepticism. The revival he provoked there became a major impetus for the Second Great Awakening.

1842 William James, psychologist, philosopher, and brother of Henry, was born in New York City.

1913 The first sedan-type automobile, a Hudson, went on display at the 13th Automobile Show in New York.

1922 Leonard Thompson, a fourteen-year-old Canadian boy, received the first injection of insulin to help regulate his diabetic condition. Canadian physiologists Charles Herbert Best and Frederick Grant Banting had isolated the hormone the year before.

1928 British novelist Thomas Hardy died at his home near Dorchester. His heart was buried in the grave of his wife in Dorset, and his ashes were deposited next to those of Charles Dickens in Westminster Abbey's Poet's Corner.

1935 Aviator Amelia Earhart began the trip from Honolulu to Oakland, California, that made her the first woman to fly solo across the Pacific Ocean.

1936 Noir detective fiction pioneers Dashiell Hammett and Raymond Chandler were introduced to one another at a dinner for *Black Mask* contributors in Los Angeles.

1942 Japan declared war against the Netherlands, the same day that Japanese forces invaded the Dutch East Indies.

1943 The United States and Britain signed treaties relinquishing extraterritorial rights in China.

1964 U.S. Surgeon General Luther Terry issued the first government report saying smoking may be hazardous to one's health.

He was just twenty-eight years old when he joined an extraordinary group of Southern historians, poets, political scientists, novelists, and journalists on this day in 1930, publishing a prophetic collection of essays warning against the looming loss of the original vision of American life—a vision of both liberty and virtue. The symposium, entitled "I'll Take My Stand"—poignantly voiced the complex intellectual, emotional, and spiritual consternation of men standing on the precipice of catastrophic cultural change. Andrew Nelson Lytle (1902–1995) was still a graduate student at Vanderbilt University, but already he was recognized by the literary luminaries that made up the group as a brilliant writer and a wise exponent of their philosophy of chivalry and agrarian virtue.

The Agrarians—as the group came to be called—were alarmed by what they perceived to be a steady erosion of public virtue in modern American life. They feared that—as was the case in the eighteenth century—our liberties were facing a fearsome challenge from the almost omnipresent and omnipotent forces of monolithic government. Lytle, like the other Agrarians, was the product of the post-Reconstruction era in the South. It was a difficult time in a difficult place. The virtues of Southern gentility, though sorely tested since the War Between the States and its horrendous aftermath, were still very much in evidence. Despite the region's captivity to the economic and cultural domination of the North, the old precepts survived. Indeed, in some quarters they actually thrived.

He was born in 1902, into a family with deep roots in both the soil and the society of the Old South. He was reared on a rich diet of family closeness, hard work in the fields, community cohesiveness, deep piety, and a legacy of storytelling that would ever afterward shape his vision of the good life.

But of course, Lytle knew full well that he, his Agrarian cohorts, and all the other advocates of that residual Southern civilization, were essentially standing against the rising tide of industrial modernity. Though "I'll Take My Stand" caused a stir when it was first released, very few critics gave it much chance of actually affecting the course of events. It was assumed that "the wheels of progress could not be redirected." For some fifty years it looked as if the critics might be right. The Agrarian commitment to the old standards of chivalry seemed to be a hopelessly lost cause. But recent turns of events have vindicated their emphasis on less government, lower taxes, family values, minimal regulation, and localism. Their innate distrust of professional experts in politics, media, and academia have suddenly been translated into populist megatrends.

Lytle actually lived to see the genesis of the cultural about-face. His long career as a gentleman farmer, novelist, essayist, university professor, and writing mentor earned him a tenured place among Southern belles-lettres. His log cabin on Monteagle became a gathering place for a kind of cultural expatriate movement. His chivalrous demeanor and his venerable mien became for generations of young Southern writers the very embodiment of the social and spiritual ideal. At his death in 1995, he was lauded as a prophet—not of a way of life now long gone, but of a hope merely deferred.

Real valor consists not in being insensible to danger, but in being prompt to confront and disarm it.

[SIR WALTER SCOTT (1771–1832)]

576 B.C. On this day Roman slaves forgot their condition and became their own masters for a day during the celebration of the Compitalia.

1519 Holy Roman Emperor Maximilian I died, opening the door for the Hapsburg descendants of Ferdinand and Isabella to once again dominate the Catholic world.

1588 On this day in the year in which the Spanish Armada invaded England, John Winthrop was born into an English Puritan home. Years later, in 1629, a group of Puritans had formed the Massachusetts Bay Company to begin settlement in America. John Winthrop was elected governor of the company, and within a short period of time he had enlisted seven hundred colonists for the new settlement. He organized the Great Migration of Puritans, which sailed for America in 1630. In a sermon Winthrop preached during the voyage to America, the Massachusetts governor used imagery from Jesus' Sermon on the Mount when he said New England was to be "as a City upon a Hill, the eyes of all people are upon us." From Winthrop and the Puritans, America inherited the idea that in some way this land was to be an example and beacon of light to the rest of the world.

1729 Edmund Burke, the British statesman, philosopher, and father of modern Conservatism, was born. His strong defense of liberty—including the right of American colonists to throw off the shackles of Parliament—was epitomized in his famous call to action: "The only thing necessary for the triumph of evil is for good men to do nothing."

1737 John Hancock, American patriot, confederation president, and signer of the Declaration of Independence, was born in Boston.

1773 The first museum in America was established in Charleston, South Carolina.

1822 Jean Joseph Étienne Lenoir, the French inventor who created the first safe, inexpensive, and functional internal combustion engine, was born in France.

1865 Almost forty years before the Wright brothers successfully flew their powered aircraft, the Aeronautical Society of Great Britain was organized.

1876 John Chaney—known by his pen name, Jack London—was born. The author of *The Sea Wolf*, *The Call of the Wild*, and *White Fang*, he celebrated the spirit of adventure and courage on the vanishing American frontier.

1915 Congress rejected a proposal to give women the right to vote.

1969 The underdog New York Jets defeated the Baltimore Colts 16-7 in Super Bowl III, played at the Orange Bowl in Miami.

1976 English mystery writer Dame Agatha Christie died in Wallingford, Oxfordshire. She wrote numerous books and plays, many featuring detectives Hercule Poirot or Miss Jane Marple, which have sold more than 100 million copies.

JANUARY

13

Dympna Caelrhynn was born near the end of the eighth century, the eldest daughter of a heathen Celtic prince, Eadburh. When she was still just a child, her beloved Christian mother was claimed by a plague. Apparently stricken mad with grief, Eadburh conceived a perverted passion for his daughter. In order to escape his incestuous intentions, she fled abroad with her chaplain, Gerebernus, first to the newly Christianized port city of Antwerp, and then to the small village of Gheel about twenty-five miles away. There she began to rebuild a life for herself.

With the help of Gerebernus, she devoted herself to the care of the needy and the forlorn. She rescued dozens of orphaned children from a life of begging in the streets. She gave shelter to the lame, the mentally impaired, and the infirm. She fearlessly lobbied for justice for the poor. And she fought to expose the dark secrets of abortionists whose flourishing contraband was wreaking havoc among the peasantry.

There in the Flemish lowlands, Christian medievalism was progressively making its mark. As a result, many of the most insidious practices from antiquity were passing from the scene—including the age-old pagan procedures of infanticide, abandonment, and exposure. Even so, when there were serious problems with a pregnancy or when handicapped children were born, many families reverted to the pagan practices.

Dympna boldly challenged this, arguing that if human life is sacred, then all human life must be protected—regardless of how unlovely or inconvenient it might be. She sought to demonstrate that there was no such thing as an unwanted child. She made her home a haven for the otherwise unwanted. In the span of just three years, her household grew to include more than forty handicapped children and another twenty mentally impaired adolescents and adults.

Before long, she had gained a remarkable reputation for selflessness, graciousness, and charity. Eadburh, upon hearing of his daughter's whereabouts, followed her to Gheel. There was an awful confrontation. When she refused to return home with him, he flew into a rage and brutally slew her on this day in 795.

Amazingly, Dympna's vision did not die with her that day. Stricken with sorrow, the citizens of Gheel decided to continue her mission of mercy. That work continues to the present day. It includes a hospital for the mentally ill, a foundling center, an adoption agency, and the world's largest and most efficient boarding-out program for the afflicted and disturbed, run as a private association by the Christian families of Gheel.

FEAST DAY
St. Hilary of Poitiers, St. Agrecius, St. Berno

1910

The first broadcast of opera from the stage of the New York City Metropolitan Opera consisted of arias from *Cavelleria Rusticana* and *I Pagliacci* sung by Mme. Emmy Destinn and Enrico Caruso.

Courage is not simply one of the virtues, but the form of every virtue at the testing point, which means, at the point of highest reality. A chastity or honesty or mercy which yields to danger will be chaste or honest or merciful only on conditions. Pilate was merciful until it became risky.

[C. S. LEWIS (1898–1963)]

1695 Jonathan Swift was ordained an Anglican priest in Ireland and appointed prebend of Kilroot.

1733 James Edward Oglethorpe and 116 colonists arrived at Charleston, South Carolina, to settle the British territory of Georgia. Oglethorpe was a philanthropist and member of the House of Commons.

1752 With the implementation of the Change of Style Act, the new year in England officially started on the first of January instead of March 25.

1794 President George Washington approved a measure adding two stars and two stripes to the American flag, following the admissions of Vermont and Kentucky to the union.

1834 Horatio Alger was born in Revere, Massachussetts. In 1867 he would publish *Ragged Dick*, and over the next thirty years repeat that rags-to-riches story scores of times, prompting George Jurgens to remark, "Horatio Alger wrote the same novel 135 times and never lost his audience."

1864 Composer Stephen Foster died in New York.

1893 Britain's Independent Labor Party first convened.

1898 When Emile Zola sent his famous defense of Captain Alfred Dreyfus in the form of an open letter to the president of the French Republic, his friend Georges Clemenceau printed it in the Paris newspaper *L'Aurore* under the title "J'accuse."

1915 The government *Gazette* of Nigeria printed a black-bordered notice, "It is with the deepest regret that His Excellency the Governor-General has to announce the death at Itu, on this day, of Miss Mary Mitchell Slessor. For thirty-nine years, with brief and infrequent visits to England, Miss Slessor has laboured among the Eastern Provinces in the south of Nigeria. By her enthusiasm, self-sacrifice, and greatness of character she has earned the devotion of thousands of the natives among whom she worked, and the love and esteem of all Europeans, irrespective of class or creed, with whom she came in contact. She has died, as she herself wished, on the scene of her labours, but her memory will live long in the hearts of her friends, Native and Europeans, in Nigeria." Thus passed one of Africa's greatest missionaries.

1919 The concept of submarine warfare was introduced by the German General Staff.

1928 The War Office of Great Britain abolished the use of the lance as a battle weapon.

1941 Irish novelist James Joyce died in Zurich, Switzerland.

1966 Robert C. Weaver became the first black cabinet member as he was appointed Secretary of Housing and Urban Development by President Lyndon Johnson.

13

JANUARY

Like Samuel Adams and Patrick Henry, Samuel Chase (1741–1811) was a firebrand political activist. His daring speeches against British tyranny stirred fellow Marylanders as well as members of the Continental Congress to support the cause of independence.

Of powerful build and persuasive manner, Chase won a position of leadership in the Maryland colonial legislature while in his twenties. He vigorously opposed the Stamp Act and helped establish the patriotic committee of correspondence in Maryland. At the Continental Congress he was one of the first to speak out for independence.

Early in 1776 he went to Canada as a congressional commissioner—with Benjamin Franklin and John and Charles Carroll—to try to persuade the French-Canadians to join in fighting the British, but the mission was unsuccessful. Chase returned to Philadelphia in time to learn of Richard Lee's resolution on independence, introduced on June 7, but at that time the Maryland delegates were not authorized to vote for independence. Chase left Philadelphia and made a special trip through Maryland to win the people's support, and before the end of June the Maryland Convention voted for independence—and its delegates in Philadelphia were authorized to sign the Declaration of Independence.

After the war Chase was against the idea of a national government and refused to attend the Constitutional Convention, but by 1790 he was identified with the Federalist Party, and President Washington appointed him to the Supreme Court on this day two years later. As an associate justice, Chase became known for his positive, often impressive opinions, some of which provided an enduring base for the new judicial system. But he was on occasion too much the loyal Federalist: He strongly supported the sedition laws, passed during the Adams administration, which prohibited political opposition to the government, and which Jefferson and his fellow Democrat-Republicans saw as an abridgment of the First Amendment.

In 1804, after Chase had uttered some exceedingly intemperate remarks, the House of Representatives initiated impeachment action, but the Senate did not find him guilty. He remained in office, although he was in later years overshadowed by the new chief justice, John Marshall. But he had already made a substantial contribution to the judicial system—and gained the dubious distinction of being the only Founding Father to undergo impeachment proceedings.

FEAST DAY
The Martyrs of Mount Sinai,
St. Barbasymas or Barbascemin,
St. Antony Pucci, St. Datius,
St. Macrina the Elder, St. Sava,
St. Felix of Nola, St. Kentigern or
Mungo

1894

His career as a seaman over, Joseph Conrad returned to London and took up the manuscript of a tale he had been writing aboard ship and in port for five years. *Almayer's Folly,* his first novel, would be published the following year.

All stations are so oriented that they serve others.

[MARTIN LUTHER (1483–1546)]

1529 The Castilian Reformer Juan de Valdes published his *Dialogue on Christian Doctrine.* The work presented many Protestant ideas, especially the idea of justification by faith alone, in Spanish. Valdes emphasized that faith and religious feeling were more important than church hierarchy or tradition. The Spanish Inquisition did not look favorably on Valdes's work, and he had to flee Castile for Naples. He Italianized his name to Valdesso and continued to write of the need for a spiritual reformation of the church. Valdes was a great Spanish prose writer and could have become a leading humanist in his day, but he was more interested in Bible study and the Christian life. Personal piety to him was more important than intellectual and philosophical pursuits. He translated into Spanish and wrote commentaries on the books of Matthew, Romans, 1 Corinthians, and Psalms. Though he was reluctant to break with the Catholic Church, Valdes strongly believed in justification by faith alone. His writings spread this Reformation emphasis in the Italian and Spanish worlds.

1639 Connecticut earned the title of the "Constitution State" for the passing of the first constitution in the American colonies. The "Fundamental Orders" were adopted in Hartford by representatives from Wethersfield, Windsor, and Hartford.

1733 Yeneseisk, Siberia, recorded a temperature of 120 degrees below zero Fahrenheit. The air was so frigid that birds dropped frozen to the ground and smoke was unable to rise.

1742 English astronomer Edmond Halley, who observed the comet that now bears his name, died at age eighty-five.

1784 The Continental Congress ratified the Treaty of Paris, which established the United States officially as an independent and sovereign nation.

1858 French emperor Napoleon III narrowly escaped an attempt on his life.

1886 Hugh Lofting, creator of the *Dr. Dolittle* series, was born in Maidenhead, Berkshire.

1900 Puccini's opera *Tosca* received a mixed reception at its Rome world premiere.

1925 In Tokyo, novelist and playwright Yukio Mishima was born into a samurai family.

1943 President Franklin Roosevelt and British Prime Minister Winston Churchill opened a wartime conference in Casablanca.

1952 NBC's *Today* show premiered.

1953 Croatian war hero Josip Broz Tito was elected president of Yugoslavia by the country's Parliament. He would rule the nation with an iron fist for the next twenty-five years.

1963 George C. Wallace was sworn in for his first term as governor of Alabama with a pledge of "segregation forever."

14

JANUARY

Thomas of Villanueva (1488–1535) grew up in the region of Don Quixote's La Mancha in a devout Christian home where virtuous living and gracious charity were constantly modeled for him by his parents. Thus it was no surprise when he committed himself to a life of Christian service after graduating from the new university at Alcala.

On this day in 1518, at the age of thirty, he was ordained and began a brilliant career as an anointed and effective preacher. His ministry was most distinguished not by his very evident pulpit skills, however, but rather by his care and concern for the poor and needy. He was especially involved in providing relief for abused children and orphans—securing new homes for them as well as meeting their immediate material needs.

He was involved in other merciful activities as well—once, when he discovered an abortion cabal operating illicitly in a nearby city, he flew into a frenzy of righteous indignation. He used his influence to provoke a criminal investigation. He lobbied for stronger laws for the protection of children. And he worked with authorities to ensure local enforcement of the new laws.

At the time, the Iberian peninsula contained no fewer than eleven separate kingdoms—besides Portugal—including Aragon, Castile, Leon, Catalonia, Valencia, Andalusia, Granada, Galicia, Asturias, Navarre, and Murcia. Relying on neither legalism nor lawlessness, recidivism nor revolution, he raised the standard of biblical justice in these diverse lands—ultimately laying the groundwork for a unified Spanish legal code once the various kingdoms were united under the Hapsburg descendants of Ferdinand and Isabella. In a very real sense, then, he was the father of modern Spain—and that great nation was birthed out of a concern for the needy and helpless.

FEAST DAY
St. Macarius the Elder, St. Isidore of Alexandria, St. Bonitus or Bonet, St. Ida, St. John Calybites

1697

Though the Puritan clergy of Massachusetts had unanimously opposed the Salem witch trials, the episode was seen by them all as a terrible example of misdirected zeal. Thus, in December 1696, the General Court passed a resolution calling for a general fast day to be held on this day, "That so all of God's people may offer up fervent supplications unto him, that all iniquity may be put away, which hath stirred God's holy jealousy against this land; that he would show us what we know not, and help us, wherein we have done amiss, to do so no more." Judge Samuel Sewell and the jury of the trials all confessed their error and implored God's forgiveness and further direction.

O world, thou choosest not the better part!
It is not wisdom to be only wise,
And on the inward vision close the eyes,
But it is wisdom to believe the heart.
Columbus found a world, and had no chart,
Save one that faith deciphered in the skies;
To trust the soul's invincible surmise
Was all his science and his only art.

[GEORGE SANTAYANA (1863–1952)]

1559 Elizabeth I was crowned queen of England after the death of her half sister, Bloody Mary. Protestantism, which had been fiercely persecuted under Mary, was immediately restored under the sponsorship of the Crown.

1752 Tobias Smollett anonymously published his controversial booklet *Habbakkuk Jibling*, which charged the novelist Henry Fielding with plagiarism.

1762 The DeLancey Mansion was purchased by innkeeper Samuel Francis. This tavern is the oldest building in modern New York City.

1829 Honoré de Balzac signed a contract with publisher Urbain Canel for the novel *Les Chouans*, the first work to appear under his own name. He was so anxious to perfect the text that Canel had difficulty getting him to surrender the manuscript.

1844 The University of Notre Dame received its charter from the state of Indiana.

1870 The Democratic Party was represented as a donkey for the first time in a cartoon by Thomas Nast, the same cartoonist who created the modern image of Uncle Sam and Santa Claus. The cartoon was published in *Harper's Weekly*.

1891 Russian poet Osip Mandelstam, memorialized by his widow Nadezhda's "Hope Against Hope," was born in Warsaw.

1892 The rules of basketball were published for the first time, in Springfield, Massachusetts, where the game originated.

1919 Pianist and statesman Ignace Jan Paderewski became the first premier of the newly created Republic of Poland.

1922 The Irish Free State was established after more than three hundred years of bitter struggle against Great Britain.

1928 Civil rights leader Martin Luther King Jr. was born in Atlanta, Georgia.

1943 Work was completed on the massive five-sided maze, the Pentagon, which was to serve as the headquarters for the U.S. Department of Defense.

1967 The first Super Bowl was played when Vince Lombardi's Green Bay Packers of the National Football League defeated Lamar Hunt's Kansas City Chiefs of the American Football League, 35-10.

1973 President Nixon announced the suspension of all U.S. offensive action in North Vietnam, citing progress in peace negotiations.

1992 The Yugoslav Federation, founded in 1918, effectively collapsed as the European Community recognized the republics of Croatia and Slovenia.

JANUARY

Described as the "Morning Star of the Reformation," John Wycliffe (1329–1384) was an unlikely hero. He was a quiet academic at the esteemed Oxford. His patron was John of Gaunt, son of the great Black Prince, regent for Richard II, and by all accounts the most powerful man in all of Europe. Wycliffe taught the law, theology, and philosophy of the old classical order. He was hardly a revolutionary.

Nevertheless, he became thoroughly convinced that ordinary people needed to have access to the Scriptures in their own language. At the time, the only people who could read the Bible were the very few educated men in the universities who were fluent in Greek, Latin, or Hebrew. Even most pastors had never seen a copy of the entire canon.

Thus, the venerable Oxford don set out on this day in 1560 to make a translation of the Bible that every Englishman might be able to read. Wycliffe unleashed a revolution in vernacular translation that would alter all of Christendom within just a few generations.

But not only did Wycliffe revive interest in the Scriptures during a particularly dismal and degenerate era with his translation of the New Testament into English, he also unleashed a grassroots movement of lay preachers and relief workers that brought hope to the poor for the first time since the unlanding of the peasants more than two generations before. Those common Lollards, as they were most often called, carried Wycliffe's determined message of grace and mercy to the entire kingdom, laying the foundations for the Reformation in England more than a century and a half later.

Persecuted in life and vilified in death, Wycliffe nevertheless committed himself to the task of reform, whatever the cost.

FEAST DAY
St. Henry of Cocket; St. Marcellus, pope, St. Berard and Others; St. Fursey; St. Priscilla; St. Honoratus of Arles

1786

The Virginia legislature passed the Ordinance of Religious Freedom, which disestablished the Anglican Church as the state church and guaranteed that no person would be molested for his or her religious beliefs. The law gave Virginia complete religious freedom and was the model for the guarantees of religious freedom written into the U.S. Constitution's Bill of Rights. Thomas Jefferson had worked for seven years to get the Virginia legislature to pass such a law. He often allied himself with Baptists and Presbyterians, who had endured much hardship from the lack of religious freedom in colonial Virginia. Jefferson was very proud of his role in this piece of legislation. Indeed, the three accomplishments he wanted carved on his tombstone were "Author of the Declaration of Independence, Founder of the University of Virginia, and Author of the Statute of Virginia for Religious Freedom."

After the suffering of decades of violence and oppression, the human soul longs for higher things, warmer and purer than those offered by today's mass living habit, introduced as by a calling card by the revolting invasion of commercial advertising, by TV stupor and by intolerable music.

[ALEKSANDR SOLZHENITSYN (1918–)]

1547 Ivan the Terrible was crowned as the first of the Russian czars.

1599 The English poet's poet, Edmund Spenser, best known for his work *The Faerie Queene*, died and was buried in Poet's Corner in Westminster Abbey, London.

1872 The first Orient Express railway train arrived at the station in Stamboul, thus connecting Turkey with the rest of Europe.

1883 The U.S. Civil Service Commission was established.

1919 *The Kid*, an early film starring Charlie Chaplin and Jackie Coogan, was released for distribution.

1920 Prohibition began in the United States as the Eighteenth Amendment to the U.S. Constitution took effect. It was later repealed by the Twenty-first Amendment.

1938 Benny Goodman refused to play at Carnegie Hall when he learned that the black members of his band would not be allowed to perform. The management of the hall reversed their decision.

1942 Actress Carole Lombard, her mother, and about twenty other people were killed when their plane crashed near Las Vegas, Nevada, while returning from a war-bond promotion tour.

1944 General Dwight D. Eisenhower took command of the Allied Invasion Force in London.

1964 The musical *Hello, Dolly!* opened on Broadway, beginning a run of 2,844 performances.

1967 Alan S. Boyd was sworn in as the first secretary of transportation.

1991 The White House announced the start of Operation Desert Storm to drive occupying Iraqi forces out of Kuwait.

16

JANUARY

The first extended period of peace came to the young American nation with the administration of James Monroe (1758–1831). The serene years that followed came to be known as the Era of Good Feeling.

The European nations, exhausted by the Napoleonic Wars, let the new nation develop in peace, and Monroe—and the United States—made the most of it: The country persuaded Britain to agree to disarm forever along the Canadian border and purchased Florida from Spain. At home the problem of slavery was temporarily ameliorated by the Missouri Compromise, which admitted Missouri as a slave state but prohibited slavery north of the Mason-Dixon Line.

Perhaps the greatest achievement of the strapping young nation in these years was the assertion of its growing authority by proclaiming the Monroe Doctrine—the warning to European nations against further conquest or colonization in the Western Hemisphere. Drafted by John Quincy Adams, son of the former president and able secretary of state in the Monroe administration, the final document was revised by Monroe himself on this day in 1823 and then presented to Congress in an address later in the year. The Monroe Doctrine has served as the basis for American foreign policy ever since.

Before reaching the presidency, Monroe served in a variety of posts: He began as an eighteen-year-old lieutenant in the Revolution; forty years later he held the cabinet position of secretary of state and war. His long career was punctuated with controversy: As Washington's minister to France, he earned Federalist disapproval and, finally, removal by his sympathy for the French cause; as Jefferson's minister to England, he concluded a treaty on naval problems that failed to uphold American rights and was, therefore, rejected by Jefferson. However, as Jefferson's minister extraordinary in France he won a share of the credit for the purchase of Louisiana by signing the treaty that concluded the greatest of real estate transactions.

Monroe's administration brought to an end almost a quarter century of rule by the close friends that the Federalists called the Virginia Dynasty—Jefferson, Madison, and Monroe. Like his friends, Monroe almost exhausted his fortune in a lifetime of public service; with them he helped block the Federalists' drift toward class rule and furthered the establishment of the government according to Jeffersonian principles of democracy.

FEAST DAY
St. Sabinus of Piacenza; St. Julian Sabas; St. Antony the Abbot; St. Geulf or Genou; St. Sulpicius II or Sulpice of Bourges; Saints Speusippus, Eleusippus, and Meleusippus

FEAST DAY OF ST. ANTHONY

This festival, celebrated with baking and feasting throughout the Slavic lands of Central Europe as well as the old Christian communities of the Middle East, commemorates the life and work of the Egyptian hermit and missionary who died in 365.

> *An atheist is a man who has no invisible means of support.*
>
> [JOHN BUCHAN (1875–1940)]

1536 François Rabelais, the great French poet, was absolved of apostasy by Pope Paul II and allowed to resume the practice of medicine in Montpellier.

1604 The Hampton Court Conference of King James I appointed fifty-four scholars to produce a new translation of the Bible. The scholars included Anglicans, Puritans, linguists, theologians, clergy and laymen. They were divided into six groups. Each translator was assigned a portion of Scripture, but he had to present his work to the others in his group for approval. Each book was then sent to the other five groups for review and criticism. With this procedure, each book went through the entire group for review. By 1611 the translation was complete. Though never officially authorized, the 1611 translation was called the "Authorized Version," but is best known as the King James Version. Ultimately, it became a major influence in forming the Christianity and molding the language of English-speaking people around the world for three centuries.

1706 Printer, philosopher, and statesman Benjamin Franklin was born in Boston.

1746 Bonnie Prince Charlie and his Highlanders defeated the British at the Battle of Falkirk. This was their last victory in the 1745 uprising of the Jacobites before their eventual defeat three months later at Culloden.

1860 Anton Chekhov was born in Tagnrog, Russia. In 1904, the year he died, his last play, *The Cherry Orchard*, would open at the Moscow Art Theater on his forty-fourth birthday.

1871 On the 165th anniversary of the birth of Benjamin Franklin, a statue of the inventor, statesman, and philosopher was unveiled in the city of New York as a gift from the printers of the city. Horace Greeley spoke on the occasion in honor of Franklin.

1893 Hawaii's monarchy was overthrown as a group of businessmen and sugar planters forced Queen Liliuokalani to abdicate.

1893 The nineteenth president, Rutherford B. Hayes, died in Fremont, Ohio, at age seventy.

1899 Alphonse Capone, the notorious Chicago gangster who was finally convicted for tax evasion, was born in Brooklyn, New York.

1917 The United States purchased the West Indies from Denmark for $25 million.

1945 Swedish diplomat Raoul Wallenberg, credited with saving tens of thousands of Jews, disappeared in Hungary while in Soviet custody.

1955 The United States Navy launched the *Nautilus*, the first atomic submarine.

1961 In his farewell address, President Eisenhower warned against the rise of "the military-industrial complex."

1991 U.S., British, and Saudi forces began air raids on Iraq, thus starting the "Gulf War" and the liberation of Kuwait.

JANUARY

The remarkable explosion of wealth, knowledge, and technology that occurred during the Renaissance and the Enlightenment completely reshaped human society. No institution was left untouched. Local communities were shaken from their sleepy timidity and thrust into the hustle bustle of mercantilism and urbanization. The church was rocked by the convulsions of the Reformation, the Counter-Reformation, Anabaptism, Deism, and neo-paganism. Kingdoms, fiefs, baronies, and principalities began to take the torturous path toward becoming modern nation-states. Such revolutionary changes are not without cost. Ultimately, the cost to Western civilization was devastating. Immorality and corruption ran rampant. Disparity between rich and poor became endemic. Ruthless and petty wars multiplied beyond number. Even the old horrors of abortion, infanticide, abandonment, and exposure began to recur in the urban and industrialized centers.

Vincent De Paul was born on this day in 1581 for just such a time as this—to tackle these kinds of problems. Raised the son of a peasant farmer in Gascony, he surrendered to the ministry at the age of twenty. Spurred on by a passionate concern for the poor and neglected, he quickly developed a thriving outreach to the decayed gentry, deprived peasantry, galley slaves, unwanted children, and convicts of France. Over the ensuing years, he mobilized hundreds of Christians for charitable work and established innumerable institutions—hospitals, shelters, foundling centers, orphanages, and almshouses throughout all of Europe.

Despite its many advances in art, music, medicine, science, and technology, the Renaissance and Enlightenment were essentially nostalgic revivals of ancient pagan ideals and values. The dominating ideas of the times were classical humanism, pregnable naturalism, and antinomian individualism—or in other words: godlessness, materialism, and hedonism. Taking their cues primarily from ancient Greece and Rome, the leaders of the epoch were not so much interested in the Christian notion of progress as they were in the heathen ideal of innocence. Reacting to the artificialities and contrivances of the medieval period, they dispatched the Christian consensus it had wrought with enervating aplomb.

Vincent made it clear to his fellow laborers that merciful service in such a time was not an option for the believer—it was mandatory. By the time he died in 1660, the charitable relief movement he had sparked was alive and well—alert to the threat against the innocents that inevitably comes when men turn their hearts away from Christian truth and toward the delusions of this world. To this day all around the globe, members of the Society of Vincent De Paul continue the momentum that he began by modeling a life of obedience to the truth.

FEAST DAY
St. Prisca, St. Peter's Chair, Rome,
St. Desle or Deicolus, St. Volusian

> *When I was a boy of 14, my father was so ignorant I could hardly stand to have the old man around. But when I got to be 21, I was astonished at how much the old man had learned in seven years.*
>
> [MARK TWAIN (1835–1910)]

1689 Satirist and philosopher Charles de Montesquieu was born into a wealthy nobleman's family at their country home near Bordeaux.

1778 Captain James Cook discovered and named the Sandwich Islands after the First Lord of the Admiralty, Lord Sandwich.

1779 Peter Roget, the physician who compiled the *Thesaurus of English Words and Phrases,* was born in London, and educated at the University of Edinburgh. He amassed the Thesaurus in 1852, and it went through twenty-eight editions in his lifetime.

1788 The first English settlers arrived in Australia's Botany Bay to establish a penal colony.

1862 The tenth president of the United States, John Tyler, died in Richmond, Virginia, at age seventy-one. At the time, he was serving as a member of the Confederate Congress.

1863 Konstantin Stanislavsky, actor, producer, and teacher of "method" acting, was born in Russia.

1882 Pooh Day: A. A. Milne, author of *Winnie the Pooh, The House at Pooh Corner, When We Were Very Young,* and *Now We Are Six,* was born in St. John's Wood, London. Of his chosen profession he quipped, "Almost anyone can be an author; the difficult business is to actually collect money from this state of being."

1896 The first college basketball game with five players on each side was played between the University of Iowa and the University of Chicago.

1912 English explorer Robert F. Scott and his expedition reached the South Pole, only to discover that Roald Amundsen had beaten them to it. Scott and his party perished during the return trip.

1919 The First World War Peace Congress opened in Versailles, France.

1943 Due to the industrial restrictions imposed by the Second World War, a ban was placed on the sale of presliced bread in an effort to limit the demand on metal replacement parts by bakeries.

1967 Albert DeSalvo, who claimed to be the "Boston Strangler," was convicted in Cambridge, Massachusetts, of armed robbery, assault, and sex offenses. Sentenced to life, DeSalvo was killed by a fellow inmate in 1973.

1975 The situation comedy *The Jeffersons,* a spinoff of *All in the Family,* premiered on CBS-TV.

1991 Financially strapped Eastern Airlines shut down after sixty-two years in business.

18

JANUARY

It was only after years of tenacity and long suffering that Konstantin von Tischendorf was able to discover one of the oldest complete copies of the New Testament and thus transform biblical scholarship for the modern era. Born in Saxony on January 18, 1815, he became a Bible scholar who decided to search for old Bible manuscripts so he could produce an edition of the Bible that was as close to the original manuscripts as possible.

In 1843 he visited Italy looking for Bible manuscripts, and in 1844 he traveled throughout Egypt, Sinai, Palestine, and the Middle East. In May of 1844 he was staying in the monastery of St. Catherine on Mount Sinai, which had been founded by the Emperor Justinian in the sixth century. He noticed in the hall of the monastery a large basket filled with old and tattered parchments. The librarian said they were to be burned as rubbish and two other similar basketfuls had already been burned. Tischendorf looked through the basket and found 129 leaves of a manuscript of the Old Testament in Greek. His enthusiasm was visibly stirred, for this manuscript was the oldest Bible he had ever seen, probably dating from the fourth century.

The monks became very suspicious and began carefully guarding the fragments. Tischendorf was not able to see the manuscripts again until he revisited the monastery in 1859. On this day—the last day of his visit—the steward pulled down an old manuscript of the Greek New Testament from a shelf filled with old coffee cups. It was like the pages once seen in the trash bin. Tischendorf persuaded the monastery to give the manuscript to the czar of Russia, the sponsor of Tischendorf's travels and a former benefactor of the monastery.

The ancient book became known as *Codex Sinaiticus*. It includes a large section of the Old Testament and the earliest complete manuscript of the New Testament. When the Communists took over Russia in 1917, they had no interest in the manuscript. It was purchased by the British Museum on Christmas Day, 1933.

FEAST DAY

St. Canute IV of Denmark, Saints Abachum and Audifax, St. Fillan or Foelan, St. Albert of Cashel, St. Charles of Sezze, St. Germanicus, Saints Marius and Martha, St. Messalina, St. Henry of Uppsala, St. Nathalan, St. Wulfstan

---

1568

Miles Coverdale, who had printed a complete Bible in 1535, died at the age of eighty-one. His was the first complete Bible printed in English. Once an assistant to William Tyndale, he was not actually a particularly capable Greek or Hebrew scholar, but he had a good literary style. Working from Tyndale's notes, he was able to hammer out a masterpiece that formed the basis for every other translation over the course of the next three hundred years.

I long to accomplish a great and noble task, but it is my chief duty to accomplish humble tasks as though they were great and noble. The world is moved along not by the mighty shoves of its heroes, but by the aggregate of the tiny pushes of each honest worker.

[HELEN KELLER (1880–1968)]

1714 Richard Steele published *The Crisis*, a defense of the Hanoverian succession, for which he would be denounced and expelled from Parliament.

1729 Dramatist William Congreve, famed for his play *Love for Love*, died in London at the age of fifty-eight.

1736 James Watt, the Scottish inventor of the condensing steam engine and for whom the unit of power the watt was named, was born in Scotland.

1807 Robert Edward Lee, scion of one of America's most revered patriot families—and the only man who was offered the command of both the Union and Confederate armies prior to the uncivil War Between the States—was born in Stratford, Virginia.

1809 Edgar Allan Poe, the originator of the modern detective story and well known for stories and poems such as *Fall of the House of Usher, The Raven, Masque of the Red Death*, and *Murder at the Rue Morgue*, was born in Boston, Massachusetts, where his parents were working as itinerant actors. He would be orphaned three years later.

1813 Sir Henry Bessemer, inventor of the process that bears his name of converting pig iron to steel, was born in England.

1825 The process of food storage in tin cans was patented by Ezra Daggett and Thomas Kensett of New York.

1839 French painter Paul Cézanne was born in Aix-en-Provence. He was influenced by and exhibited with the early impressionists but later broke with them and pursued his own techniques.

1853 Verdi's opera *Il Trovatore* premiered in Rome.

1861 Georgia seceded from the Union.

1944 The federal government relinquished control of the nation's railroads following settlement of a wage dispute.

1955 A presidential news conference was filmed for television for the first time, with the permission of President Dwight Eisenhower.

1966 Indira Gandhi was elected prime minister of India.

1977 In one of his last acts of office, President Gerald Ford pardoned Iva Toguri D'Aquino, an American citizen who had made radio propaganda broadcasts for Japan during the Second World War.

1981 The United States and Iran signed an agreement paving the way for the release of fifty-two Americans held hostage for more than fourteen months.

JANUARY

A Philadelphia merchant of great wealth who became the "financier of the Revolution," Robert Morris (1734–1806) frequently risked his fortune on behalf of the Continental army—and in the end, did indeed lose everything. With Roger Sherman, Morris shares the distinction of having signed all three of the principal founding documents—the Declaration of Independence, the Articles of Confederation, and the Constitution.

A conservative among the patriots, Morris did little besides sign a protest against the Stamp Act before he was elected to Congress in 1775, and he did not originally support the idea of independence, believing that the time was not ripe. He did, however, sign the Declaration—after he had abstained from the initial vote. And, in 1778, he signed the Articles of Confederation.

In 1776, as chairman of the executive committee of Congress, Morris was left in charge of the government when Congress fled Philadelphia, then threatened by the British. Later that year Washington requested funds for an offensive, and Morris, pledging his personal credit, obtained the money that enabled Washington to defeat the Hessians at Trenton in December. For the remainder of the war, Morris was, either officially or unofficially, the chief civilian in charge of finance and supply.

In May 1781, Congress appointed him to the new position of Superintendent of Finance, and that summer he worked closely with Washington in planning the support for the major offensive against Cornwallis at Yorktown. Again Morris backed the purchase of ammunition and supplies with his personal pledge.

After the war Morris continued as principal finance officer for Congress, caught between the obligations of the Confederation and the States' continued refusal to support it. He all but exhausted his own credit and repeatedly planned to resign, but he stayed on. He established the first national bank, but Pennsylvania challenged its charter. By 1784, when he finally resigned, the United States had practically no credit abroad—and he himself was nearly bankrupt. As a result, he urged the establishment of a stronger national government. At the Annapolis convention he supported the idea of the convention in Philadelphia. Host to Washington during the Constitutional Convention, Morris nominated Washington to preside and signed the completed document in September.

Morris declined Washington's offer of the position of Secretary of the Treasury in the new government and was elected one of Pennsylvania's first senators. After he returned to private life his debts finally caught up to him. From this day in 1798 until 1801 he was incarcerated in Philadelphia's debtor's prison. He came out a broken and forgotten man.

FEAST DAY
St. Sebastian; St. Fabian, pope; St. Euthymius the Great; St. Fechin

When idle, be not solitary; when solitary, be not idle.

[SAMUEL JOHNSON (1709–1784)]

1265 Simon de Montfort, the earl of Leicester, called the first English Parliament during the reign of Henry III. Although councils of landholders had been previously held, this meeting in the halls of Westminster included commoners in the form of two knights for each county and two citizens for each borough.

1327 King Edward II of England was deposed by his eldest son, who became King Edward III five days later.

1669 Susanna Wesley was born this day, the twenty-fifth child of Puritan minister Samuel Annesley. At age nineteen she married the Anglican minister Samuel Wesley. Seventeenth-century Puritans were encouraged to have large families as seed and fruit for the Lord's kingdom, so she was delighted in her own eighteen children. Two of those children gained renown as the founders of Methodism, John and Charles Wesley.

1835 The Extraordinary Exhibition of the Industrious Fleas, the first Flea Circus, was reopened after a cold spell forced the exhibit to close to enable the exhibitor "to fill up the vacancies that grim death had made." Performances were given from 11 A.M. to 3 P.M. and from 5 P.M. to 9 P.M., and admission was fifty cents.

1841 The island of Hong Kong was ceded to Great Britain. It returned to Chinese control in July 1997.

1887 Congress approved an agreement to lease Pearl Harbor in Hawaii as a naval base.

1896 Comedian George Burns was born Nathan Birnbaum in New York City.

1900 John Ruskin died of influenza at his Brantwood home at Coniston, in the Lake District. The great artist, critic, author, and aesthete was eighty-one.

1920 Movie director Federico Fellini was born in Rimini, Italy.

1936 Britain's King George V died; he was succeeded by Edward VIII, who would later abdicate the throne to marry an American divorcée.

1937 Franklin D. Roosevelt became the first president sworn into office in January at the beginning of his second term. The original date for the start of the presidential term was March 4.

1942 Nazi officials held the notorious Wannsee Conference, during which they arrived at their "Final Solution" that called for exterminating Jews.

1961 Robert Frost recited "The Gift Outright" at the inauguration of John F. Kennedy.

1981 Iran released fifty-two Americans it had held hostage for 444 days, minutes after the presidency had passed from Jimmy Carter to Ronald Reagan.

1986 The United States observed the first federal holiday in honor of slain civil rights leader Martin Luther King Jr.

JANUARY

FEAST DAY
St. Agnes, St. Fructuosus of Tarragona, St. Patroclus of Troyes, St. Alban or Bartholomew Roe, St. Epiphanius of Pavia, St. Meinrad

It is a cruel irony of history that Cotton Mather (1663–1728) is generally pictured unsympathetically as the archetype of a narrow and severe intolerance, who proved his mettle by prosecuting the Salem witch debacle of 1692. In fact, he never attended the trials—he lived in the distant town of Boston—and actually denounced them once he saw the tenor they had taken. And as for his Puritanism, it was of the most enlightened sort. Mather was a man of vast learning, prodigious talent, and expansive interests. He owned the largest personal library in the New World—consisting of some four thousand volumes ranging across the whole spectrum of classical learning. He was also the most prolific writer of his day, producing more than 450 books on religion, science, history, medicine, philosophy, biography, and poetry. His greatest work, *Magnalia Christi Americana*, dripping with allusions to classical and modern sources, was published on this day in 1702.

He was the pastor of the most prominent church in New England—Boston's North Church. He was active in politics and civic affairs, serving as an advisor to governors, princes, and kings. He taught at Harvard and was instrumental in the establishment of Yale. He was the first native-born American to become a member of the scientific elite in the Royal Society. And he was a pioneer in the universal distribution and inoculation of the smallpox vaccine.

His father, Increase Mather, was the president of Harvard, a gifted writer, a noted pastor, and an influential force in the establishment and maintenance of the second Massachusetts charter. In his day he was thought to be the most powerful man in New England—in fact, he was elected to represent the colonies before the throne of Charles II in London. But according to many historians, his obvious talents and influence actually pale in comparison to his son's.

Likewise, both of Cotton Mather's grandfathers were powerful and respected men. His paternal grandfather, Richard Mather, helped draw up the Cambridge Platform, which provided a constitutional base for the Congregational churches of New England. And with John Eliot and Thomas Weld, he prepared the *Bay Psalm Book*, which was the first text published in America. It achieved worldwide renown and remains a classic of ecclesiastical literature to this day. His maternal grandfather was John Cotton, who wrote the important Puritan catechism for children, *Milk for Babes*, as well as drawing up the Charter Template with John Winthrop as a practical guide for the governance of the new Massachusetts Colony. The city of Boston was so named to honor him—his former parish work in England was at St. Botolph's Boston.

According to historian George Harper, together these men laid the foundations for a lasting "spiritual dynasty" in America. Even so, according to his lifelong admirer, Benjamin Franklin, "Cotton Mather clearly out-shone them all. Though he was spun from a bright constellation, his light was brighter still." And according to George Washington, "He was undoubtedly the Spiritual Father of America's Founding Fathers."

A man is wise as long as he searches for wisdom; he becomes a fool the moment he thinks he has found it.

[TRISTAN GYLBERD (1954–)]

1525   The first baptisms of the Anabaptists were performed by the Swiss separatists Conrad Grebel and Felix Manz. The men were originally friends of Ulrich Zwingli in Zurich but broke with him when the pace of reforms did not meet their expectations.

1789   The first American novel, William Hill Brown's epistolary romance, *The Power of Sympathy or the Triumph of Nature*, was published anonymously in Boston.

1793   King Louis XVI of France was executed by guillotine during the French Revolution after he had been sentenced to death for treason the day before. His final words echoed through the square in front of the Palace of the Tuileries, "I die innocent of the crimes imputed to me," and "I pardon the authors of my death, and I pray heaven that the blood you are about to shed may never be visited upon France."

1824   Thomas Jonathan "Stonewall" Jackson, Confederate military hero, was born in Clarksburg, Virginia (now West Virginia).

1861   Jefferson Davis of Mississippi and four other Southerners reluctantly resigned from the U.S. Senate.

1924   Russian revolutionary and mastermind of the Communist dictatorship, Vladimir Ilyich Lenin, died at age fifty-four. Aided by the Germans who wanted Russia out of the First World War, Lenin took advantage of the overthrow of the Russian czar to impose the Soviet government on both the Russians and fifteen other independent states—thus creating the U.S.S.R.

1929   The British Broadcasting Company—better known as the BBC—broadcast its first programming from London to the world.

1941   Operatic tenor Placido Domingo was born in Madrid, Spain. He is regarded as one of the premier tenors of his generation and has sung all over the world.

1950   George Orwell, author of *1984* and *Animal Farm*, died in London.

1950   Former State Department official Alger Hiss, accused of being part of a Communist spy ring, was found guilty in New York of lying to a grand jury. Hiss, who had been instrumental in negotiating the Yalta Accords at the end of the Second World War as well as the establishment of the United Nations, was sentenced to five years in prison; he served less than four.

1977   President Jimmy Carter pardoned almost all Vietnam War draft evaders.

1997   Speaker Newt Gingrich was reprimanded and fined as the House voted for the first time in history to discipline its leader for ethical misconduct.

1998   President Bill Clinton angrily denied reports that he'd had an affair with former White House intern Monica Lewinsky and had tried to get her to lie about it. He later admitted that he was in fact lying himself and was consequently impeached by Congress.

JANUARY

Like so many of the best political minds in his day, Cyrus Griffin (1736–1796) was trained in London's Inner Temple to be a lawyer—and thus was counted among his nation's legal elite. And like so many other Virginians, he was an anti-Federalist, though he eventually accepted the new Constitution with the promise of the Bill of Rights as a hedge against the establishment of an American monarchy—which still had a good deal of popular currency in the years immediately following American independence. The Articles of Confederation afforded such freedoms that he had become convinced that even with the incumbent loss of liberty, some new form of government would be required.

A protégé of George Washington, having worked with him on several speculative land deals in the West, he was a reluctant supporter of the constitutional ratifying process. His hesitation was that the new system might cause the federal government to grow ever larger, ever more powerful, and ever more intrusive in the lives of ordinary Americans. He believed that government was "a necessary evil; thus, the smaller it is, the less powerful it can be, the better all men are apt to be." Nevertheless, he was reassured by Washington that the restrictions imposed by the Bill of Rights and other constitutional provisions would never allow the national bureaucracy to grow "beyond the bounds of the absolutely essential maintenance of order."

It was just prior to his term in the office of the presidency—the last before the new national compact went into effect—that ratification was formalized and finalized. As a result, he served in a kind of caretaker's role as the nation's chief executive from this day in 1788 until George Washington's inauguration on April 30, 1789.

Griffin was thus notable in the annals of American freedom in that he was the only chief executive officer in the nation to oversee the peaceful transition from one governmental system to another.

1973

In perhaps its most divisive and controversial decision since Dred Scott, the Supreme Court overturned the infanticide and homicide laws in abortion cases in all fifty states by legalizing abortion procedures from the moment of conception until just before the moment of birth. Delivered on January 22, 1973, the Roe v. Wade decision sent shock waves throughout the nation—the effects of which are still felt. In a remarkably argued majority opinion, Associate Justice Blackmun introduced several creative constitutional innovations—including a heretofore unrecognized "right to privacy." Like the Dred Scott decision before it, this case actually only exacerbated the debate the court set out to resolve.

Those who are quick to promise are generally slow to perform. They promise mountains and perform molehills. He who gives you fair words and nothing more feeds you with an empty spoon. People don't think much of a man's piety when his promises are like pie-crust: made to be broken.

[CHARLES H. SPURGEON (1834–1892)]

1561 English essayist and philosopher Francis Bacon, Baron Verulam, was born in Yorkhouse, London. Alexander Pope considered him "the wisest, brightest, meanest of mankind" for taking bribes during his term as a judge. He is best known as the founder of the philosophical school of inductive logic.

1775 André Marie Ampère, the scientist most connected with understanding electrical current and their units of amps (named for him), was born in France.

1788 English Romantic poet Lord George Gordon Byron, Baron Byron of Rochdale, was born in London. He is best known for *Childe Harold's Pilgrimage, Manfred, Don Juan*, and his friendship and influence over fellow Romantic poet Percy Bysshe Shelley.

1875 Early film director D. W. Griffith, who advanced film through such early classic epics as *Birth of a Nation*, was born in La Grange, Kentucky. Known as the Father of the Motion Picture, Griffith pioneered several film techniques such as utilizing dramatic situations instead of episodes, the close-up, the fade-out, the flashback, and cross-cutting of simultaneous action.

1901 After reigning longer than any other English monarch (sixty-three years), Queen Victoria died. Her forty grandchildren married into almost every royal family in Europe.

1917 President Wilson pleaded for an end to war in Europe, calling for "peace without victory." By April, however, America also was at war.

1922 Pope Benedict XV died; he was succeeded by Pius XI.

1938 *Our Town*, the Pulitzer Prize–winning play by Thornton Wilder, premiered at the McCarter Theater in Princeton, New Jersey.

1944 During World War II, Allied forces began landing at Anzio, Italy.

1953 The Arthur Miller drama *The Crucible* opened on Broadway.

1968 The comedy show *Rowan & Martin's Laugh-In* premiered on NBC-TV.

1970 The first regularly scheduled commercial flight of the Boeing 747 began in New York and ended in London some six and a half hours later.

1973 Former President Lyndon Johnson died at age sixty-four.

1996 Norma McCorvey, the woman named as "Jane Roe" in the Roe v. Wade decision, asked the Supreme Court to reverse their ruling in light of the fact that the case was based on fraudulent evidence. The court declined.

22

JANUARY

John Calvin (1509–1564) established Geneva as the epicenter of the Reformation with his profound theological insight and his rich devotional piety. His careful and systematic codification of the biblical foundations for Reform was like a magnet for the best and brightest throughout Christendom. The city quickly became an island of intellectual integrity and economic prosperity.

A Frenchman who only came to Geneva reluctantly after he was exiled from Paris during a persecution of Protestants there, Calvin nevertheless gave himself heart and soul to his adopted city. It was there that he would write his greatest work, *The Institutes of Christian Religion*. A massive systematic theology, the work would set the pace for generations of scholars after him and provide the lodestone for Reform movements all over the world—from Knox's Scotland and Whitefield's England, to Mather's America and Kuyper's Holland. His weekly preaching was comprehensively biblical and practically pastoral. As a result, Geneva became a center for Christian scholarship.

In addition though, the city became renowned for its charitable compassion. It was a kind of safe haven for all of Europe's poor and persecuted, dispossessed and distressed. There they found that Calvin had not only instructed the people in such things as the providence of God, but he also had taught them the importance of mercy in balancing the Christian life. On this day in 1555, he reorganized the diaconate of the city for the task of caring for the flood of poor refugees pouring into the city from the persecution in provinces all over Western Europe. Ever since, Geneva has been known as a haven for peace and reconciliation—a reputation it maintains to this day.

FEAST DAY
St. Bernard of Vienne, Saints Clement and Agathangelus, St. Asclas, St. John the Almsgiver, St. Emerentiana, St. Maimbod, St. Ildephonsus, St. Lufthidis

1845

The United States Congress fixed the presidential election day as the first Tuesday after the first Monday in November. The only injunction before then from 1792 was that elections were to occur "within 34 days preceding the first Wednesday in December."

When you are a Bear of Very Little Brain, and you Think of Things, you find sometimes that a Thing which seemed very Thingish inside you is quite different when it gets out into the open and has other people looking at it.

[A. A. MILNE (1882–1956)]

1732 France extended its colonial position in the New World as Louisiana became a royal province.

1752 Muzio Clementi, composer, pianist, and piano manufacturer, was born in Italy.

1789 Georgetown University was established in present-day Washington, D.C.

1832 French painter Edouard Manet—recognized as one of the fathers of modern art because of his break with the salon techniques and his scandalous subject matter—was born in Paris.

1849 English-born Elizabeth Blackwell became the first woman in America to receive a Doctor of Medicine degree, from the Medical Institution of Geneva, New York.

1899 Pope Leo XIII sent a formal letter to James Cardinal Gibbons, archbishop of Baltimore and senior hierarch of the Catholic Church in America. This was not an encyclical, which would have been addressed to the entire church, but a pastoral warning against what has been called the "phantom heresy." And that heresy was Americanism. The letter, titled "Testem Benevolentiae," condemned secularist tendencies, flagrant materialism, a denigration of religious vows, and any attempt to adapt the church's traditional teaching to conform to the needs of the modern world.

1920 The Dutch government refused demands from the victorious Allies to hand over the exiled kaiser of Germany.

1932 New York Governor Franklin D. Roosevelt announced his candidacy for the Democratic presidential nomination.

1936 George Orwell wrote a review confessing, "I worshiped Kipling at 13, loathed him at 17, enjoyed him at 20, despised him at 25, and now again rather admire him."

1948 American composer David Diamond's Symphony no. 4 was premiered by the Boston Symphony Orchestra under the direction of Leonard Bernstein.

1950 The Israeli Knesset approved a resolution proclaiming Jerusalem the capital of Israel.

1968 North Korea seized the U.S. Navy ship *Pueblo*, charging that it had intruded into the Communist nation's territorial waters on a spying mission. The crew was released eleven months later.

1971 The lowest recorded temperature in the United States—80 degrees below zero—occurred at Prospect Creek, Alaska.

1972 President Nixon announced that an accord had been reached to end the Vietnam War.

23

JANUARY

The Elizabethan Age produced a number of the greatest stylists of the English language, including William Shakespeare, Sir Walter Raleigh, Sir Francis Drake, and of course, John Donne. When the venerable poet was born in London on this day in 1573, Queen Elizabeth was in the middle of her long and glorious reign, and Donne was able to partake of all the benefits the age afforded. Indeed, as a young man John Donne was quite attracted to the extravagance of English Renaissance life. During England's war with Spain in the 1590s, Donne sailed as a gentleman adventurer. He took a government position as secretary to the Keeper of the Great Seal—a position he ultimately lost when he secretly married his employer's daughter. In 1609 he applied for the secretaryship of the new colony of Virginia, but he failed to get the job.

It was Donne's marriage that brought about in him a dramatic transformation. The deepening love of his faithful wife provoked him to grow in the love of God. Eventually, his piety entirely replaced his earlier flamboyance—and it was evident to everyone who knew him. King James encouraged Donne to enter the ministry, and though he felt very unworthy, Donne consented. With a great sense of his own sinfulness and God's forgiveness, Donne was eager to preach God's forgiveness to others. In 1621 he was appointed dean of St. Paul's in London and became one of the most prominent and eloquent preachers of his day.

Donne was a man of immense scholarship and learning, yet he preached that "all knowledge that begins not with His glory is but a giddy, but a vertiginous circle, but an elaborate and exquisite ignorance."

The death of his wife in 1617 brought about another profound change in Donne. She was thirty-three and died of exhaustion one week after giving birth to her twelfth child. Her death brought home to Donne the fleeting nature of earthly happiness, and he saw his whole life as God's wooing of him. He gained strong convictions about the providence and goodness of God and the coming resurrection in the face of certain death.

In his many poems and sermons Donne often challenged his people to ready themselves for death: "All our life is but a going out to the place of execution, to death. Now was there ever any man sent to sleep in the cart?" His famous lines "No man is an Island, entire in itself" and "For whom does the bell toll? It tolls for thee," have become almost commonplaces in the English language. When the death bell tolled for Donne in 1631, his trust in God enabled him to tell a friend, "I am full of inexpressible joy and shall die in peace."

FEAST DAY
St. Francis of Sales, St. Babylas of Antioch, St. Felician of Foligno, St. Macedonius the Barley-eater

For right is right,
Since God is God,
And right the day must prevail;
To doubt is but disloyalty,
To falter is but travail.

For right is right,
Let it be known
And right the day must win;
To dither is but apostasy,
To hesitate is thus sin.

[MARTIN HEVER (1766–1839)]

1527 Felix Manz was executed by drowning in Zurich. Manz was a Hebrew scholar and an illegitimate son of a canon of Grossminster Church in Zurich, had become an Anabaptist and was undermining the authority of the City Council. He was exiled from the city, but he returned secretly, was arrested, and condemned—not for heresy but for sedition.

1732 Pierre-Augustin-Caron de Beaumarchais was born in Paris. He would become a watchmaker, pamphleteer, and secret agent, as well as a successful dramatist. His best-known works include *The Marriage of Figaro* and *The Barber of Seville.*

1848 James Wilson Marshall found a gold nugget at Sutter's Mill on a branch of the Sacramento River near Colomo, California. This discovery sparked the "forty-niners'" gold rush to California, which included more than 200,000 fortune hunters.

1862 Edith Wharton, author of such books as *The House of Mirth,* was born to a distinguished New York family.

1908 The first Boy Scout troop was organized in England by Robert Baden-Powell.

1913 Franz Kafka, the surrealist author, stopped work on his classic work *Amerika,* never to complete it.

1922 Christian K. Nelson of Onawa, Iowa, patented the Eskimo Pie.

1924 The Russian city of St. Petersburg was renamed Leningrad in honor of the late revolutionary leader. After the fall of Communism it was renamed St. Petersburg.

1943 President Roosevelt and British Prime Minister Churchill concluded a wartime conference in Casablanca, Morocco.

1965 Sir Winston Churchill died at the age of ninety and was buried at Bladon near Blenheim Palace. In addition to his public career, Churchill also was the author of several important historical works including *The Second World War* (6 vol., 1948–53), and *A History of the English-Speaking Peoples* (4 vol., 1956–58). In 1953 he received the Nobel Prize for literature as well as knighthood.

1972 The Supreme Court struck down laws that denied welfare benefits to people who had resided in a state for less than a year.

1978 A nuclear-powered Soviet satellite plunged through Earth's atmosphere and disintegrated, scattering radioactive debris over parts of northern Canada.

1986 The *Voyager Two* space probe swept past Uranus, coming within 50,679 miles of the seventh planet of the solar system.

1993 Civil rights pioneer and retired Supreme Court Justice Thurgood Marshall died in Bethesda, Maryland, at age eighty-four.

JANUARY

Callistus of Rome was a Christian slave who was imprisoned and sentenced to hard labor in the Sardinian quarries late in the second century after becoming involved in a scandalous financial scheme. After his release he was emancipated and put in charge of the church's shelter and cemetery on the Appian Way, which still bears his name. He faithfully occupied himself with his duties—caring for the poor, comforting the bereaved, and giving refuge to the dispossessed.

But it was his compassion for abandoned children that proved to be especially noteworthy—it was Callistus who helped to organize the famed "Life Watches" that placed hundreds of exposed children into Christian homes. It seemed that unwanted newborn children were simply taken outside the city to infanticide walls where they were left to die from exposure or from the assaults of foraging beasts. The Christians of Rome would take these children into their own homes and raise them as their own. This selfless sacrifice was a hallmark of the early church's work of mercy.

Callistus believed that eventually service would afford Christians the authority to speak into the lives of many Roman citizens who were searching. In any case, it earned him authority—because of the prominence of his sacrificial work, Callistus was chosen to serve as bishop of Rome. He died on or about this day in 222.

FEAST DAY

Saints Juventinus and Maximinimus, the Conversion of St. Paul, St. Apollo, St. Artemas, St. Publius, St. Dwynwen, St. Poppo, Saint Praejectus or Prix

BURNS NIGHT

The birthday of Scottish poet Robert Burns (1759–1796) has become an occasion for Scotsmen, their descendants, and their romantic wannabes to gather together wherever they may be to the lilt of bagpipers and the strains of Burns's poetry. Celebrants traditionally enter the rooms with the shout "Hail Great Chieftan o' the Puddin-Race." While the drinking of Scotch—and the requisite carousing that often attends it—often marks such festivities, the traditional celebration is a dinner. The bill of fare generally includes roast lamb, haggis—a traditional grain sausage—boiled potatoes, and shortbread for dessert.

A man with a definite belief always appears bizarre, because he does not change with the world; he has climbed into a fixed star and the earth whizzes below him like a zoetrope. Millions of mild black-coated men call themselves sane and sensible merely because they always catch the fashionable insanity, because they are hurried into madness after madness by the maelstrom of the world. The man with a definite belief is sure to be the truer friend.

JANUARY

[G. K. CHESTERTON (1874–1936)]

1533 England's King Henry VIII secretly married his second wife, Anne Boleyn. She later gave birth to Elizabeth I.

1579 The Dutch provinces of the Low Countries signed the Union of Utrecht to break away from Spain and form the new country of the Netherlands. Sporadic fighting occurred with Spain until the signing of the Peace of Westphalia in 1648, which ended the Thirty Years' War and granted formal independence to the United Provinces of the Netherlands.

1759 Robert Burns, the highly revered Scottish National Poet, was born in Alloway, Ayrshire, Scotland. His best-known works include "Auld Lang Syne," "Comin' Thro' the Rye," "A Red, Red Rose," "To a Mouse," and his collection *Poems, Chiefly in the Scottish Dialect.* In 1859, at a centenary dinner in Boston, Ralph Waldo Emerson would affirm, "The 'Confession of Augsburg,' the Declaration of Independence, the 'French Rights of Man,' and the 'Marseillaise,' are not more weighty than the songs of Robert Burns."

1787 Shays's Rebellion suffered a setback when debt-ridden farmers led by Captain Daniel Shays failed to capture an arsenal at Springfield, Massachusetts.

1874 Author William Somerset Maugham was born in Paris at the British Embassy. He would later observe, "To write simply is as difficult as to be good."

1890 The United Mine Workers of America was founded.

1909 Adapted by Hugo von Hofmannsthal from the Greek tragedy by Sophocles, Richard Strauss's opera *Elektra* premiered at the Hofoper in Dresden. The opera's modern composition and use of dissonance, while disturbing and shocking to early twentieth-century audiences, aptly portrayed the psychological undertones of the libretto.

1915 The inventor of the telephone, Alexander Graham Bell, inaugurated U.S. transcontinental telephone service.

1946 The United Mine Workers rejoined the American Federation of Labor—best known as the AFL.

1947 Chicago gangster Al Capone, who at one time practically ran that city, died in Miami Beach, Florida, at age forty-eight.

1959 American Airlines opened the jet age in the United States with the first scheduled transcontinental flight of a Boeing 707.

1961 President John F. Kennedy held the first presidential news conference carried live on radio and television—it was beamed coast to coast via a series of broadcast tower relays.

1971 Charles Manson and three members of his bizarre personality cult were convicted in Los Angeles of murder and conspiracy in the 1969 slayings of seven people, including actress Sharon Tate.

1981 The fifty-two Americans from the American Embassy in Tehran who had been held hostage by Iranian Shi'ite revolutionaries finally arrived home in the United States after 444 days of captivity. They were met with an exuberant welcome by a grateful and relieved nation adorned with yellow ribbons.

JANUARY

Variously called the "Guru of the Fundamentalists," "Missionary to the Intellectuals," and "Godfather of Evangelicalism," Francis A. Schaeffer was undoubtedly one of the most influential thinkers, theologians, authors, and apologists of the past generation. His books, tapes, and films gave new credibility to Evangelicals interested in the arts, culture, politics, and society.

After serving for a short time in Presbyterian congregations in the United States, he moved to Switzerland in 1948 to begin a unique missionary outreach—to whoever God would send to his door. Over the years literally thousands of students, skeptics, and searchers found their way to the door of the small mountain chalet that he shared with his wife and four children. Calling his work *L'Abri*—the French word for "shelter"—he set up a study center on this day and simply attempted to provide "honest answers to honest questions."

Asserting the lordship of Christ over the totality of life, he wrote a series of intellectually stimulating books documenting the drift of Western art, music, ideas, and law from their Christian moorings. Though he had a wide following among academically minded Evangelicals beginning in the mid-sixties, it was not until the release of his book and film series *How Should We Then Live?* that he gained national and international notoriety. He followed that with another book and film series, *Whatever Happened to the Human Race?* which brought new prominence to the struggle against abortion, infanticide, and euthanasia. But it was his book *A Christian Manifesto* that catalyzed the burgeoning Evangelical consensus in the culture.

Despite a difficult and protracted battle against cancer over the last five years of his life, he gave the lion's share of his time, energies, and efforts to promoting the authority of Christ over every aspect of life and society. In both word and deed, Schaeffer confirmed the gospel's message of light and life.

NATIONAL DAY
Australia, India
FEAST DAY
St. Timothy, St. Margaret of Hungary, St. Alberic, St. Paula, St. Conan of Man, St. Titus, St. Eystein, St. Thordgith or Theorigitha of Barking

1788 — Captain Arthur Phillip, leading a fleet of ships carrying convicts from England, landed in Sydney Cove. This day is observed as the National Day of Australia. Phillip eventually became the governor of New South Wales. It was not until 1865 on this day that England was no longer allowed to send convicts to Australia.

We must all measure ourselves by our friendships—apart from the Scriptures, there is no surer measure to be had in this poor fallen world.

[FRANCIS A. SCHAEFFER (1912–1984)]

166   Saint Polycarp was martyred in the city of Smyrna. Polycarp refused to blaspheme Christ and was burned at the stake.

1500   Vicente Yanez Pinzon discovered Brazil when he reached the northeastern coast during a voyage. Formerly, the Spanish explorer had commanded the *Niña* during Christopher Columbus's first expedition to the New World.

1564   When the Protestants during the Reformation of the sixteenth century pointed out errors and problems in the Catholic Church, many Catholics agreed that there was need for reform and change in their church. Pope Paul III appointed a commission of Reform-minded theologians and hierarchs to prepare for a council to deal with the church's sundry controversies. The commission's list of the issues and controversies included a clergy that was too worldly, rampant bribery in the church, immoral monastic orders, abuses in indulgences, and prostitutes in Rome. The Council of Trent began meeting in 1545 to deal with these problems and to respond to the Reformation. Three sessions were held, the last one ending in 1563. Though the Council of Trent did bring about some moral reforms in the church, its final decrees upheld the medieval doctrines of the church to which many Protestants had objected—doctrines such as the Mass, the seven sacraments, justification by faith and works, purgatory, the celibacy of the priesthood, and indulgences. The Council also asserted that the church alone could interpret the Scriptures; therefore, the Bible should not be translated into the language of the people. The Latin Vulgate continued to be the Bible used by the Roman Catholic Church until after Vatican II in the 1960s. On this day in 1564, Pope Pius IV accepted and confirmed the decrees of the Council of Trent. The council had improved church organization, elevated the papacy to a stronger position, and blocked any reconciliation with the Protestants. The council had a defining influence upon Roman Catholic faith and practice until well into the twentieth century.

1784   In a letter to his daughter, Benjamin Franklin expressed unhappiness over the choice of the eagle as the symbol of America, and expressed his own preference: the turkey.

1789   Wolfgang Mozart's opera *Cosi Fan Tutti* was first presented as a command performance before Emperor Joseph II of Austria at the Burgtheater in Vienna.

1802   Congress passed an act calling for a library to be established within the U.S. Capitol. This new institution would evolve over time into the Library of Congress.

1837   Michigan became the twenty-sixth state.

1841   Britain formally occupied Hong Kong, which the Chinese had ceded to Queen Victoria's growing world empire.

1870   Virginia rejoined the Union.

1911   The Richard Strauss opera *Der Rosenkavalier* premiered in Dresden, Germany.

1942   The first American expeditionary force to go to Europe during the Second World War went ashore in Northern Ireland.

1950   India officially proclaimed itself a republic as Rajendra Prasad took the oath of office as president.

1962   The United States launched *Ranger Three* to land scientific instruments on the moon—but the probe missed its target by some twenty-two thousand miles.

JANUARY

27

The beautiful and beguiling Elizabeth of Bratislava (1207–1231) was the daughter of King Andrew II of Hungary. Her marriage at the age of fourteen to Ludwig of Thuringia, though arranged for political reasons, was a happy one, and the couple had three children. Their enlightened rule was prosperous and benevolent, making their kingdom a beacon light to all of Central Europe.

In 1227, Ludwig died suddenly shortly after joining a band of crusaders bound for the Holy Land. Grief stricken for some months, the young Elizabeth finally vowed to give the rest of her life in service to the needy. She helped to establish one of the first foundling hospitals in Europe, as well as several orphanages and almshouses.

Justice and mercy were the hallmarks of her worldview, but they were defined by the parameters of humility and faith. Though her life was short, her legacy was enduring both in heaven and on earth. Her sons, who ruled following her regency, carried on her work, establishing a legacy of hospitality, graciousness, and kindness that helped to define Hungarian culture down through the years—many say, even down to the present day.

FEAST DAY
St. Julian of Le Mans; St. Marius or May; St. Angela Merici; St. Vitalian, pope

1756

Johannes Chrysostomus Wolfgangus Theophilus Mozart was born in Salzburg, Austria. He created a vast number of works in an astonishingly short amount of time, including the operas *The Marriage of Figaro, The Magic Flute, Don Giovanni,* many symphonies, chamber works, and his final work, *Requiem.* Two of his melodies are still regularly sung in many churches as the tunes to "O Could I Speak That Matchless Worth" and "Jesus, I My Cross Have Taken." Mozart was a musical genius who constantly had music playing in his head. From the time he was four until his death, Mozart worked nonstop. At the age of six he wrote his first minuets; just before his ninth birthday he composed his first symphony. By eleven he had written his first oratorio and had completed his first opera at twelve. By the time of his death he had produced more than six hundred compositions. Music was his one joy and passion. A century after his death, famed music critic Joseph Machlis would assert, "Something of the miraculous hovers about the music of Mozart. One sees how it is put together, whither it is bound, and how it gets there; but its beauty of sound and perfection of style, its poignancy and grace defy analysis and beggar description. For one moment in the history of music all opposites were reconciled, all tensions resolved. That luminous moment was Mozart." Even so, when Mozart died at the age of thirty-six he was buried in a pauper's grave.

Poets and friends are born to what they are.

[ALEXANDER STEPHENS (1812–1883)]

407   Saint John Chrysostom died. Known as John of Constantinople during his life, he was later named Chrysostom, which means "golden tongued," in reference to his great powers of oratory.

1302   Dante Alighieri was expelled from his hometown, Florence, when a political faction he opposed seized power. For the next two decades, until the end of his life, he would remain in exile.

1832   Mathematician Charles Lutwidge Dodgson, better known as the English children's author Lewis Carroll, writer of such works as *Alice's Adventures in Wonderland* and *Through the Looking Glass,* was born in Daresbury, Chesire, the eldest of eleven children.

1851   Naturalist and painter of North American birds, John James Audubon, died in New York City.

1880   Thomas Edison received a patent for his electric incandescent lamp.

1885   Jerome Kern, one of the primary composers in early American musical theater with such works as "Ol' Man River," "The Way You Look Tonight," and "Smoke Gets in Your Eyes," was born in New York City.

1926   Scottish inventor John Logie Baird gave the fist public demonstration of television, which utilized the technology of a mechanical scanning system suggested in 1884 by Paul Nipkov.

1944   The Soviet Union announced the end of the deadly German siege of Leningrad, which had lasted for more than two years.

1945   The Soviet Red Army liberated the Nazi concentration camp of Auschwitz near the Polish town of Oshwiecim where between two and three million people were killed during World War II. The Soviet soldiers discovered about eight thousand survivors in the three main camps comprising Auschwitz. These people had either been too sick or too hungry to be part of the forced death march the Nazis organized before the camp's liberation.

1951   An era of atomic testing in the Nevada desert began as an air force plane dropped a one-kiloton bomb on Frenchman Flats.

1967   Three United States astronauts, Gus Grissom, Edward White, and Roger Chaffee, died in a launch pad fire in Florida during a preflight simulation. Faulty electrical wiring in the *Apollo 1* command module was the probable cause.

1967   More than sixty nations signed a treaty banning the orbiting of nuclear weapons.

1973   The Vietnam peace accords were signed in Paris.

1977   The Vatican reaffirmed the Roman Catholic Church's ban on female priests.

1981   President Reagan greeted the fifty-two former American hostages released by Iran at the White House, telling them simply, "Welcome home."

27

JANUARY

He was supposedly the most powerful man on the face of the earth. He had armies at his command. Whole hosts of fierce warriors would hasten to his merest demand. Yet, Henry IV, emperor of the Holy Roman Empire, found himself kneeling in the snow outside the walls of the Canossa Castle, shivering in the cold for three days begging for mercy. It was one of the coldest winters on record. From November through April the Rhine River was frozen solid. Despite this, Henry did not even think about any alternative other than this—much to the surprise of all who knew him. After all, he had never been known to bend his knee to anyone before.

Henry was only six years old when his father died and he was thrust into a position of almost unimaginable power and privilege. He had been spoiled as a boy, and as a young man he lived a licentious life. When he came of age and began to rule in his own right, he was despotic and had little regard for justice or his subjects' welfare. He bribed priests to get their support and paid his soldiers from church funds. His mistresses were given jewels taken from the sacred vessels of the church. Virtually all of his subjects were horrified by such perverse defiance of basic Christian morality, but Henry was adamantly recalcitrant. Aware of such brazenness, the bishop of Rome urged his repentance, but Henry shrugged off his exhortations.

Henry, however, had met his match in this bishop. Pope Gregory VII, best known as Hildebrand, moved decisively to define and enforce the authority of the church and insisted that the see of St. Peter had preeminence over such spiritual concerns—even to the point of deposing wicked kings and emperors. He asserted that Jesus, the King of Glory, had given Peter and his successors, the bishops of Rome, very tangible responsibilities in the affairs of the world. When Emperor Henry IV continued in his belligerence, Pope Gregory VII simply excommunicated him from the church and deposed him from his throne, absolving his subjects from all allegiance to the deposed ruler.

Henry suddenly realized this was no idle threat. Talk of rebellion began to rumble throughout Henry's domains. Once-loyal nobles began to question the security and stability of Henry's reign. Sobered by this change in circumstances, Henry decided to placate the prelate. A few days before Christmas in 1076, Henry journeyed across the Alps with his wife and six-year-old son, Conrad, to seek the pope. Once in Italy he climbed the steep hill to Canossa, a fortress where Gregory was staying. He arrived at the castle on January 21, 1077, but the pope wanted to thoroughly humble him and would not receive him. Henry begged; he offered assurances of his repentance. It must have been quite a sight to behold.

Finally, on January 28 the pope granted Henry's forgiveness and restored him to the church and to his throne. Henry's humiliation at Canossa was a triumph of the church over the moral corruptions of the state of the day, preserving the balance of power that was the heart and soul of medieval civilization.

FEAST DAY
St. Thomas Aquinas, St. Amadeus of Lausanne, St. Peter Nolasco, St. Peter Thomas, St. Paulinus of Aquileia

Bad company corrupts good character.

[PAUL OF TARSUS (C. 10–65)]

814 Saint Charlemagne's Day is celebrated in France to commemorate the death of Charlemagne in 814.

1547 England's King Henry VIII died; he was succeeded by his sickly but pious nine-year-old son, Edward VI.

1596 Off the coast of Porto Bello—in present-day Panama—Sir Francis Drake died of dysentery on his ship and was buried at sea. Drake, a favorite of Queen Elizabeth I, was the first Englishman to circumnavigate the globe.

1754 Based on his reading of a 1722 fairy tale, *The Travels and Adventures of Three Princes of Sarendip,* English writer Horace Walpole coined the term "serendipity" in a letter to describe the princes' curious ability of making accidental discoveries. Sarendip was an early name for Ceylon, later Sri Lanka.

1853 Cuban revolutionary Jose Marti was born in Havana.

1871 France surrendered in the Franco-Prussian War, finally ending the long reign of Napoleon III.

1889 Arthur Rubinstein, the American pianist who played solo with the Berlin Symphony at the age of twelve, was born on this day.

1909 A decade after the end of the Spanish-American War, the United States ended direct control over Cuba.

1912 American abstract expressionist artist Jackson Pollock—known for his technique of dripping paint from cans onto vast canvases in an effort to capture action and the expression of the subconscious (psychic automatism)—was born in Cody, Wyoming. He died in a car accident in 1956.

1915 The Coast Guard was created by an act of Congress.

1916 Louis D. Brandeis was appointed by President Wilson to the Supreme Court, becoming its first Jewish member.

1980 Six American diplomats, who had evaded capture when their fellow workers were taken hostage in Tehran, flew out of Iran with the help of Canadian diplomats.

1982 Italian antiterrorism forces rescued U.S. Brigadier General James L. Dozier, forty-two days after he had been kidnapped by Communist terrorists from the Red Brigades.

1986 The world looked on in horror when the space shuttle *Challenger* exploded seventy-three seconds after liftoff from Cape Canaveral, killing all seven crew members aboard.

28

JANUARY

Thomas Jefferson called him, "The wisest man of his generation." Although he signed neither the Declaration of Independence nor the Constitution, George Mason (1725–1792) was the source of some of the most revolutionary ideas in both of those documents. The drafters of both drew ideas from documents that were largely his—the Virginia Declaration of Rights and the Virginia Constitution.

A Southern aristocrat with a five-thousand-acre plantation, which he managed himself, Mason was a neighbor and friend of Washington. As a member of the House of Burgesses in 1769, Mason prepared resolutions against the importing of British goods, which Washington presented and the legislature adopted. On this day in 1774 Mason wrote the Fairfax Resolves, advocating that all the colonies meet in congress and that Virginia cease all relations with Britain. He was also primarily responsible for Virginia's relinquishing its claim to the lands beyond the Ohio River, the Northwest Territory, and he influenced Jefferson in his drafting of the Northwest Ordinance, with its prohibition of slavery and its provision for the formation of new states.

This Virginia planter played an unusual role at the Constitutional Convention, for he hated slavery, which he called "diabolical in itself and disgraceful to mankind," and he urged delegates at the convention to give the new government the power to prevent the expansion of slavery. When the Constitution was completed, he refused to sign, partly because he felt the Constitution failed to deal strongly enough with the institution of slavery, permitting the importing of slaves until 1808, and partly because it gave the Senate and president too much power and provided no protective bill of rights. He continued his opposition at the Virginia Ratification Convention, joining Patrick Henry, Benjamin Harrison, Richard Henry Lee, and others who feared too powerful a central government. But Mason lived to see his most cherished ideas of the rights of the individual incorporated into the Constitution as the Bill of Rights Amendments in December 1791.

A rationalist who had little faith in the workings of governmental bodies, Mason fought passionately for the freedom of the individual—citizen or slave; and he was largely responsible for ensuring that protection of the rights of the individual would be such an essential part of the American system.

FEAST DAY
St. Sainian of Troyes, St. Sulpicius "Severus," St. Gildas the Wise

1936 The first members of baseball's Hall of Fame, including Ty Cobb and Babe Ruth, were named in Cooperstown, New York.

Books and friends should be few but good.

[PATRICK HENRY (1736–1799)]

1571 Robert Campbell Sproul, son of one of the early Scottish Reformers and himself a leader among the Covenanters, was born in Edinburgh.

1685 In the wake of the Reformation, religious wars raged across Europe. In France a civil war involving both religious and political issues was carried on between the Huguenots, as the French Protestants were called, and the Roman Catholics. The fighting came to an end in 1589 when the Protestant Henry IV ascended the French throne. In that year he issued an edict, known in history as the Edict of Nantes, which gave the Huguenots civil liberty as well as liberty of conscience, allowing them to worship publicly. There was much opposition to the Edict, but it remained law for almost a century. When Louis XIV became king in 1665, he began issuing a series of more than two hundred orders and laws that took away the protection given to the Huguenots by the Edict of Nantes. In 1685 Louis XIV totally revoked the edict, declaring, "The best of the larger part of our subjects, who formerly held the so-called Reformed religion, have embraced the Catholic religion, and therefore the Edict of Nantes has become unnecessary." Though some Protestants did convert to Catholicism under governmental pressure, about a half million more fled to Geneva, Germany, England, and America in the face of fierce persecution. The leaders of the new colony of South Carolina circulated pamphlets encouraging the Huguenots to come to their American colony. Many of the Huguenots were skilled craftsmen, and their exodus severely hampered France's economy for several generations afterward.

1817 John Callcott Horsley, the designer and artist of the first commercial Christmas cards, was born in England.

1820 Britain's King George III died insane at Windsor Castle, ending a reign that saw both the American and French Revolutions.

1843 The twenty-fifth president of the United States, William McKinley, was born in Niles, Ohio.

1845 *The Raven* was published in the *New York Evening Mirror* under a pseudonym. Edgar Allan Poe signed his poem "Quarles."

1850 Henry Clay introduced in the Senate a compromise bill on slavery, which included the admission of California into the Union as a free state.

1861 Kansas became the thirty-fourth state of the Union.

1879 William Claude Dukinfield, better known as the wisecracking comedian and film actor W. C. Fields, was born in America.

1900 The American League, consisting of eight baseball teams, was organized in Philadelphia.

1958 Actors Paul Newman and Joanne Woodward were married.

1963 The first members of football's Hall of Fame were named in Canton, Ohio.

1963 Poet Robert Frost died in Boston.

1979 President Carter formally welcomed Chinese Vice Premier Deng Xiaoping to the White House, following the establishment of formal diplomatic relations.

29

JANUARY

At two o'clock in the afternoon on this day in 1649, Charles I, king of England, stepped upon a scaffold outside the banqueting hall at Whitehall Palace in London. A few moments later he was beheaded by executioner Richard Brandon and England was without a king. His death brought to an end the Civil War between the king and his Parliament. It was just four years after the king's royalist forces lost at Naseby to the army led by the Parliamentarians' Oliver Cromwell.

Charles had offended a large majority of his subjects by refusing to accept accountability to Parliament, flirting with Catholicism, and continually raising tax rates. He went so far as to dissolve Parliament on several occasions for several years at a time. The struggle between the Parliament and the Crown erupted in a war in which Charles was opposed by well-trained Roundhead and Cavalier forces. After several contentious battles, Charles surrendered to a Scottish army in 1646. He was convicted of treason in 1648 and executed in 1649.

Cromwell was afterward named Lord Protector of the English Commonwealth—though he repeatedly refused to accept Parliament's offer of the Crown. The monarchy was restored in 1660 when Parliament invited Charles II to assume his father's throne. The whole incident was fraught with difficulty. Even so staunch a supporter of the cause of constitutional freedom in England as the Anglican bishop of Liverpool, J. C. Ryle (1816–1900), could not approve of the regicide. He noted in his book *Light from Old Times,* "It is a vulgar error to suppose, as many do, that the whole Parliamentary party are accountable for that wicked and impolitic act. The immense majority of the Presbyterians protested loudly against it." It was, in fact, the army that took the lead. Ryle was particularly anxious to make it clear that the Puritans "were entirely guiltless of any participation in the trial and death of the King." Nevertheless Ryle admitted that as much as the civil war was to be regretted, "we must in fairness remember that we probably owe to it the free and excellent Constitution which we possess in this country."

FEAST DAY
St. Martina, St. Bathildis, St. Adelelmus or Aleaume, St. Aldegundis, St. Barsimaeus, St. Hyacintha Mariscotti

1577

A sudden and glorious conversion transformed Camillus de Lellis (1555–1589) from a gruff soldier of fortune into a meek and compassionate servant of Christ. Because he himself had suffered from a chronic affliction, shortly after his decision to trust the Lord he offered himself to serve in the church's indigents' hospital of San Giacomo in Rome, of which he quickly became bursar. This experience opened his eyes to the shocking brutalities of Renaissance life. He began to train and supervise teams of Christian workers not only to care for the sick but also to deal with some of the entrenched problems of the poor, the homeless, and the abandoned that led to disease and contagion. Before the end of the sixteenth century, he had established several new hospitals and hospices in Naples to handle the second- and third-order consequences of both the legalism and the lawlessness that had become so much a part of the Renaissance worldview. As a result, he became a champion of justice for thousands.

A Christian should follow his occupation with contentment. Is your business here clogged with any difficulties and inconveniences? Contentment under those difficulties is no little part of your homage to that King who hath placed you where you are by His call.

[COTTON MATHER (1663–1728)]

1649 Famed English poet John Milton wrote *The Tenure of Kings and Magistrates*, in which he defended regicide and the execution of King Charles. Probably as a reward, he was appointed Latin secretary to England's Council of State, and became official apologist of the new Commonwealth under Oliver Cromwell.

1798 A brawl broke out in the House of Representatives in Philadelphia, as Matthew Lyon of Vermont spat in the face of Roger Griswold of Connecticut—it was to be only the first of many indignities over the course of two centuries of governance.

1835 An attempt was made on the life of President Andrew Jackson in the rotunda of the Capitol.

1882 The thirty-second president of the United States, Franklin Delano Roosevelt, was born in Hyde Park, New York.

1933 Adolf Hitler was named chancellor of Germany by President Hindenburg after the Nazi Party made a surprisingly strong showing in parliamentary elections.

1933 The first episode of the *Lone Ranger* radio program was broadcast on station WXYZ in Detroit.

1939 Adolf Hitler called for the extermination of European Jews.

1946 The Franklin Roosevelt dime was first issued on the former president's birthday.

1948 The political and spiritual leader of the Indian independence movement, Mahatma Karamchand Gandhi, was shot and killed by a Hindu fanatic in New Delhi.

1962 Two members of the "Flying Wallendas" high-wire circus family were killed when their seven-person pyramid collapsed during a performance in Detroit.

1964 The United States launched *Ranger Six*, an unmanned spacecraft carrying television cameras that was to crash-land on the moon.

1968 The Tet Offensive began as Communist forces launched surprise attacks against South Vietnamese provincial capitals.

1979 The civilian government of Iran announced it had decided to allow Ayatollah Ruhollah Khomeini, who'd been living in exile in France, to repatriate. His return ultimately sparked a violent revolution that toppled the government and brought to power a radical Islamic regime.

30

JANUARY

Education was the privilege of the very few and the very rich until Jean Baptist De La Salle (1621–1688) began his great work midway through the seventeenth century. After giving up a life of ease, he dedicated himself to teaching the children of the very poor. He opened day schools, Sunday schools, vocational training schools, teachers colleges, and continuing education centers—actually pioneering many modern techniques and concepts while maintaining the discipling and mentoring standards of a covenantal, Christian, and classical curriculum—in more than fourteen cities throughout Europe.

He fought hard against the insipid humanistic tendencies within the scholastic community and deplored the corresponding decline in Christian morality. He believed that if youngsters could be educated in accordance with gospel principles, the barbarities of the emerging Enlightenment modernism would disappear; but if they were not given the opportunity to advance, such wickedness would eventually prevail—because, as he often quipped, evil desires nothing better than hopelessness and ignorance.

It was on this day in 1671 that he established the Harilaman Academy, a preparatory school for underprivileged students, providing the means for poor but gifted young men to advance into the greatest universities of Europe.

FEAST DAY

Saints Cyrus and John of Alexandria, St. Francis Xavier Bianchi, St. Adamnan of Coldingham, St. Aidan or Maedoc of Ferns, St. Eusebius of St. Gall, St. Marcella of Rome, St. John Bosco, St. Ulphia

1955

John Raleigh Mott died after a lifetime devoted to promoting missions, evangelism, and ecumenism. In 1886 Dwight Moody led a student conference at Northfield, Massachusetts. J. R. Mott was among one hundred volunteers for foreign missions who attended the conference. Afterward he helped to revitalize the YMCA movement in America and around the world. He helped to organize the Student Volunteer Movement for Foreign Missions (SVM), he founded the World's Student Christian Federation (WSCF), and served as the president of the World Alliance of YMCAs. In 1946 he was awarded the Nobel Peace Prize.

Exertion, self-denial, endurance, these make the hero,
but to the spoiled child they connote the evil of nature
and the malice of man.

[RICHARD WEAVER (1910–1963)]

1606 Guy Fawkes of York, convicted for his part in the "Gunpowder Plot" against the English Parliament and King James the First, was executed.

1788 Bonnie Prince Charlie died as an exile in Rome after a lifetime of attempting to regain the British throne of his Stuart forebears.

1797 Art song composer and symphonist Franz Peter Schubert was born in Vienna, Austria. He died at the age of thirty-two in 1828. He was known as the Father of German Lieder for his more than six hundred art songs. Although he wrote with classical forms, his evocative harmonies place him in the Romantic period.

1815 With the installation of Thomas Jefferson's 6,457-volume personal library, the Library of Congress was reestablished after its destruction during the War of 1812.

1865 General Robert E. Lee was named general-in-chief of all the Confederate armies in what was already seen to be a hopelessly lost cause.

1901 Anton Chekhov's *Three Sisters* opened to a mixed reception at the Moscow Art Theater in a production directed by Konstantin Stanislavsky. Olga Knipper, Chekhov's wife, played the part of Masha.

1905 Arthur G. MacDonald was the first person to exceed 100 miles per hour in an automobile, at Ormond Beach, Florida. He traveled 1 mile in 34.40 seconds for a speed of 104.65 miles per hour. He was driving a Napier.

1905 Novelist John O'Hara was born in Pottsville, Pennsylvania.

1915 Thomas Merton, author of *The Seven Storey Mountain*—a bestseller describing his journey from his cosmopolitan Columbia University days to his decision to become a Trappist monk—was born in France.

1917 Germany served notice that it was beginning a policy of unrestricted submarine warfare.

1923 Controversial modernist writer Norman Mailer was born in Long Branch, New Jersey. In 1973 he would charge $50 per couple to attend his fiftieth-birthday celebration at New York's Four Seasons restaurant. He sent out 5,000 invitations, but only 500 showed up.

1935 Ezra Pound met the Italian fascist dictator, Benito Mussolini, and read aloud several lines from a draft of *Cantos*, which he gave the dictator as a present. Apparently, Il Duce found the reading most entertaining.

1945 Private Eddie Slovik became the only U.S. soldier since the Civil War to be executed for desertion as he was shot by an American firing squad in France.

1948 J. D. Salinger's groundbreaking short story "A Perfect Day for Banana Fish" appeared in the *New Yorker* magazine.

1949 The first daytime television soap opera, *These Are My Children*, was broadcast from the NBC station in Chicago.

1956 When asked in a *Newsweek* magazine interview about writing free verse, Robert Frost snapped, "I'd just as soon play tennis with the net down."

1958 The United States entered the Space Age with its first successful launch of a satellite into orbit, *Explorer One.*

1971 Astronauts Alan B. Shepard Jr., Edgar D. Mitchell, and Stuart A. Roosa blasted off aboard *Apollo 14* on a mission to the moon.

February

FEBRUARY

The greatest scholar of his day, Desiderius Erasmus, was the forerunner of the Reformation. Born in Rotterdam in 1466, he taught Classical Greek at the great universities of Paris and Cambridge. Concerned about the moral corruption of the church in his day, he used his pen to prime the spiritual and ecclesiastical cannons that would ultimately fire shattering salvos in the hands of Martin Luther.

First, he wrote the scathing satire *In Praise of Folly.* The book made a mockery of both the pious pretensions and the ribald depravity of the established order. It represented a clarion call for fundamental reform. Next, he undertook a new translation of the Greek New Testament. For centuries Jerome's Latin translation, the Vulgate, had been the church's only reliable text of the Bible. Unfortunately, the Vulgate was not without errors. From Greek texts, Erasmus reconstructed the original as best he could. In a parallel column he provided a new Latin translation. At great risk he also annotated the text with notes pointing out the church's flagrant departures and errors. He attacked its refusal to let priests marry—though they were allowed to live with mistresses. He also challenged such pet doctrines as prayers to the saints, indulgences, and relic worship.

The work of translation took the careful scholar several years. Finally, on February 1, 1516, Erasmus dedicated it to Pope Leo X. In a soothing letter, he tried to assure the pope that he meant no harm. "We do not intend to tear up the old and commonly accepted edition, but amend it where it is corrupt, and make it clear where it is obscure." He then cited a number of revered church fathers in support of his corrections. In essence, he was recalling the church to its patristic roots—a challenge that would later be picked up by other Reformers, from Luther and Calvin to Zwingli and Knox. Though it was clearly not his intention to fuel the discontent of the Protestants, eventually, the work of Erasmus made their reforms possible.

FEAST DAY
St. John of the Grating, St. Henry Morse, St. Pionius, St. Bride or Brigid of Kildare, St. Seiriol, St. Sigebert III of Austria

1949   This day was established by presidential proclamation as National Freedom Day in the United States for the purpose of celebrating the 1865 signing of the Thirteenth Amendment to the Constitution. This day is to be observed in perpetuity.

The world desires to know what a man can do, not what he knows.

[Booker T. Washington (1856–1915)]

107   Saint Ignatius, bishop of Antioch, Syria, was martyred by being thrown to the wild beasts at the amphitheater in Rome. Ignatius Theophoros (Greek for "God Bearer") is best known for his seven letters written to the early church. It is probable that he was discipled by the apostle John.

1788   The state of Georgia issued the first steamboat patent in the United States to Briggs and Longstreet.

1790   The United States Supreme Court opened its first session in the Royal Exchange Building on Broad Street in New York. Chief Justice John Jay of New York presided. The court was recessed until the following day because only three of the six justices were present.

1861   Texas voted to secede from the United States, the only state in the Federal Union with an explicitly stated and undisputed right to do so.

1892   At a grand ball for the socially elite, Mrs. William Astor invited four hundred guests to her mansion, thus beginning the use of "400" to indicate social hierarchy.

1893   Inventor Thomas A. Edison completed work on the world's first motion picture studio, his "Black Maria," in West Orange, New Jersey.

1906   The first federal penitentiary was completed in Leavenworth, Kansas.

1920   The Royal Canadian Mounted Police came into existence.

1945   Berlin, Germany, was raided by one thousand American bombers.

1946   Norwegian statesman Trygve Lie was chosen to be the first secretary-general of the United Nations.

1949   The RCA Record Company released the first single record which played at 45 revolutions per minute.

1959   Texas Instruments obtained a patent on their Integrated Circuit.

1960   After they were refused service, four black college students began a sit-in at the all-white Woolworth's lunch counter in Greensboro, North Carolina. This peaceful protest sparked many other such protests throughout the United States.

1968   During the Vietnam War, Saigon's police chief, Nguyen Ngoc Loan, executed a Viet Cong spy with a pistol shot to the head in a scene captured in a now-infamous news photograph.

1979   Ayatollah Ruhollah Khomeini received a tumultuous welcome in Tehran as he ended nearly fifteen years of exile.

1989   East Germany's Communist premier, Hans Modrow, appealed for negotiations with West Germany to forge a "united fatherland."

1992   After a meeting in Washington, President George Bush and Russian President Boris Yeltsin officially declared the end of the Cold War.

FEBRUARY

Writing in her journal when she was just eight years old, Fanny Crosby composed a verse, "Oh what a happy child I am, although I cannot see! I am resolved that in this world, contented I will be! How many blessings I enjoy that other people don't! So weep or sigh because I'm blind I cannot— no, I won't!" And indeed, she never did though her life was filled with adversity. She had not been born blind. A minor eye infection was mistreated by a quack doctor and became permanent blindness when scars formed on her eyes. Shortly afterward, her father died. In order to support the young girl, Fanny's mother hired out as a maid. She was essentially raised by her grandmother and a kindly neighbor.

Early on, the child was encouraged to take solace in the Bible. She memorized large portions of Scripture, even entire chapters, every day. She began to write verse as a means of expressing her love for Christ and His Word.

On this day in 1864, her pastor arranged for her to meet William B. Bradbury, a prominent organist and music publisher who had gained popular acclaim as the composer of the beloved children's tune "Jesus Loves Me." Bradbury was searching for quality Christian verse to set to his music. He was immediately impressed by young Fanny, and they began to collaborate. Later, Bradbury would introduce her to William H. Doane with whom she would also write.

Before her death in 1915, she and her collaborators would write some of the most popular and memorable hymns in the history of the American church, including "A Wonderful Savior Is Jesus My Lord," "Praise Him! Praise Him!," "Jesus Our Blessed Redeemer," "To God Be the Glory, Great Things He Hath Done," "All the Way My Savior Leads Me," and "Blessed Assurance." She never did weep or sigh over her blindness—today many see far more clearly as a result.

CANDLEMAS *(Wives Feast Day)*
FEAST DAY
The Purification, St. Joan de Lestonnac, St. Adalbald of Ostrevant, The Martyrs of Ebsdorf

CANDLEMAS DAY

This day a festival is held in honor of the presentation of the infant Jesus in the temple in Jerusalem in accordance with Mosaic Law (Leviticus 12:6–7). When Jesus was presented, Simeon took Him in his arms and called Him "a light to lighten the gentiles" (Luke 2:32). Traditionally, churches would host a procession of communicants holding candles in commemoration of Christ as the Light of the World. According to an old bit of folklore: "If Candlemas Day be fair and bright, Winter will have another flight; But if it be dark with clouds and rain, Winter is gone, and will not come again."

GROUNDHOG DAY

According to folklore, if a groundhog sees its own shadow upon venturing outside its den on this day, there will be six more weeks of winter. If it does not see its shadow, winter will soon give way to spring.

If you have a job without aggravations, you don't have a job.

[MALCOLM FORBES (1919–1990)]

1536 The Argentine city of Buenos Aires was founded by Pedro de Mendoza of Spain.

1594 Renaissance Church composer Giovanno Pierluigi da Palestrina died in Rome. His compositions are acknowledged as the climax of sixteenth-century technique and music with austere and clear harmonies. Writing almost all of his music in service to the church and for the purpose of worship, he was known as the "Prince of Music," and his works were recognized as the "absolute perfection" of the church style.

1653 New Amsterdam, now New York City, was incorporated.

1848 The Treaty of Guadalupe Hidalgo was signed. This ended the Mexican War and extended the boundaries of the United States to the Pacific Ocean. The United States acquired this territory, which included Texas, California, New Mexico, Arizona, and parts of Wyoming and Colorado for $15 million.

1863 Journalist Samuel Clemens used the moniker Mark Twain for the first time when he sent a report to the *Virginia City Enterprise* from Carson City, Nevada.

1865 Fritz Kreisler, naturalized American violin virtuoso and composer of *Caprice Viennois, Tambourin Chinois, Liebesfreud*, and *La Gitana*, was born in Austria.

1876 The National League of baseball was formed with the charter members Chicago, Boston, New York, Philadelphia, Hartford, St. Louis, Cincinnati, and Louisville.

1882 James Joyce, renowned poet and author of *Ulysses* (1922), *Portrait of the Artist as a Young Man* (1916), and *Finnegan's Wake* (1939), was born in Dublin, Ireland. He is best known for his experimental use of language and stream of consciousness style.

1888 *Cleopatra's Needle*, a stone obelisk from Egypt, arrived in London and was floated up the Thames River to its resting place opposite the houses of Parliament. It was met by cheering crowds and fired salutes despite its inordinate cost to taxpayers.

1901 Jascha Heifetz, who was one of the greatest violinists of modern times, was born in Russia. He made his first public appearance at the age of six.

1905 Social critic and author Ayn Rand was born as Alissa Rosenbaum in St. Petersburg, Russia. She emigrated to the United States in 1926 and began work as a screenwriter in Hollywood. Her major works, *The Fountainhead* (1943) and *Atlas Shrugged* (1957), presented her philosophy of objectivism, which is a repudiation of the Judeo-Christian work ethic with individualism and selfishness as virtues.

1913 Grand Central Terminal was opened in New York City.

1942 Because of safety concerns following the Japanese attack on Pearl Harbor, the *Los Angeles Times* urged additional security measures be established against Japanese Americans, stating that a Japanese American "almost inevitably grows up to be a Japanese, not an American." This mindset was the precursor to the internment of American citizens of Japanese descent during the Second World War. More than 100,000 Japanese Americans were placed in prison camps throughout the war.

1971 Idi Amin assumed power in Uganda, following a coup that ousted President Milton Obote. Afterward he began a slaughter of more than 300,000 people.

FEAST DAY
St. Laurence of Spoleto, St. Anskar, St. Ia the Virgin, St. Laurence of Canterbury, St. Blaise, St. Werburga, St. Margaret "of England"

Opposed to secession prior to the hostilities and a strong proponent for peace all throughout them, Alexander Stephens was an unlikely prospect for the vice-presidency of the Confederacy during the tempestuous War Between the States. The Georgia congressman had strong personal and political ties to the old Whig Party in the North and thus was intimate with many of the men he was later forced by regrettable circumstances to oppose. Like so many of the leading Southerners, he opposed slavery and cherished his connections to the old union and to the gentlemen he had served with in Washington.

Thus, when his duty bade him home to join his fellow countrymen in what turned out to be a futile quest for independence, he left Capitol Hill burdened with great sadness and foreboding—though he remained honorably chivalrous in all his personal dealings.

It was this chivalrous character that first endeared him to one of his oldest and dearest friends, Abraham Lincoln. The contrasts between the two men were obvious enough. Stephens was a conservative from the old Democratic and Republican school; Lincoln was a liberal from the new progressive and nationalist school. Stephens was an urbane scholar of some renown; Lincoln was a self-educated backwoods lawyer. Stephens was devout throughout his life; Lincoln was a belligerent skeptic. Stephens had been successful all his life in business, marriage, family, community, and politics; Lincoln suffered a long string of failures, sorrows, and humiliations in business, marriage, family, community, and politics. Lincoln's lanky and rugged frame stood out in any crowd; Stephens was extraordinarily diminutive and frail.

The men first met when they served together in the House of Representatives. The two men seemed to be polar opposites. Yet they immediately found an appreciation for one another's company. Their friendship would endure to the end of their lives, even when war pitted them against one another.

Indeed, from the end of 1863 to the beginning of 1865 the two communicated with each other several times in an attempt to get serious peace talks under way. On this day in 1865, they held a shipboard peace conference off the Virginia coast. Both men were encouraged by the initial talks. But all hopes of a negotiated peace were dashed in April when first, Lee surrendered at Appomattox, and then five days later, Lincoln was assassinated at Ford's Theater in Washington.

In later years Stephens served his state as a congressman, governor, publisher, professor, and civil rights advocate. He forever rued the tragic loss of his friend—both for his own sake and for that of the nation. Indeed, he believed that the bonds of friendship they had shared might well have served to bring healing between the sundered regions and the divided land.

The fear of the Lord is the beginning of wisdom: and the knowledge of the holy is understanding.

[KING SOLOMON (C. 1000 B.C.)]

590 Following the death of Pope Pelagius II, all eyes turned to one man, the beloved and energetic Gregory of Rome. But Gregory resisted, saying, "Let not the ruler forsake the inner care of divine ministration for occupation of outer works." He had seen enough of politics and had recently retired from public life. His ardent wish was to return to one of the monasteries he had founded. The senate, clergy, and Roman populace were deaf to his protestations. By unanimous vote they elevated him to the papacy on this day. Acceding to their wishes, he became one of the papacy's greatest administrators, reforming the ministries, services, music, liturgy, and dogmatic theology of the church.

1690 The first paper money in America was issued by the colony of Massachusetts. The currency was used to pay soldiers fighting a war against Quebec.

1809 The great Romantic composer Felix Mendelssohn was born in Hamburg, Germany. In 1816, his family added Bartholdy to their name when they converted from Judaism to Christianity. Mendelssohn had reached a fully developed compositional style by the age of sixteen, and is best known for his incidental music to *A Midsummer Night's Dream*; the *Scottish, Italian,* and *Reformation Symphonies*; *Fingal's Cave* and *Hebrides* overtures; and the oratorios *St. Paulus* and *Elijah.*

1809 Congress created the federal territory of Illinois.

1876 With an initial investment of $800, the Spalding brothers started a sporting goods company. They manufactured the first official baseball, tennis ball, basketball, golf ball, and football.

1882 P. T. Barnum enlarged the animal attractions at his renowned circus through the purchase of the world-famous elephant Jumbo.

1894 Norman Rockwell, the American artist best known for his realistic and charming cover art for the *Saturday Evening Post*, was born in New York City. He sold his first of 317 covers to the magazine in 1916. A detailed craftsman, Rockwell's style is highly realistic in its often humorous portrayals of families and small-town life. In 1977 he was awarded the Presidential Medal of Freedom. He died in Stockbridge, Massachusetts, on November 8, 1978.

1913 The Sixteenth Amendment to the Constitution, providing for a federal income tax, was ratified—the first of three new amendments in a single year that would radically alter the character of American government and freedom.

1916 Canada's original Parliament Buildings, in Ottawa, burned down.

1917 The United States broke off diplomatic relations with Germany, which had announced a policy of unrestricted submarine warfare.

1924 Woodrow Wilson, former president of the United States, died in Washington at age sixty-eight, less than three years after leaving office.

1930 Former president William Howard Taft resigned as chief justice of the United States for health reasons.

1942 After being struck by a torpedo, the U.S. transport ship *Dorchester* sank. Four army chaplains went down with the ship after they gave their life belts to four other men.

1959 A plane crash near Clear Lake, Iowa, claimed the lives of rock-and-roll stars Buddy Holly, Ritchie Valens, and J. P. "The Big Bopper" Richardson. The tragedy was immortalized as "the day the music died," in Don McLean's hit song "American Pie."

FEBRUARY

4

Early in the morning on this day in 1555, John Rogers was burned at the stake in the center of London. He was the first martyr during the violent reign of Bloody Mary—and thus, his was the opening chapter of that torturous period immortalized in the remarkable chronicle *Foxes Book of Martyrs.*

Rogers's scholarly youth certainly did not suggest his cruel fate. Born in 1500, he was educated at Cambridge, becoming a master at the university. Afterward, he became an orthodox Catholic priest. It was at that time that he befriended the reformer William Tyndale, who was working on his translation of the Bible into English. Their friendship ultimately led Rogers to convert to Protestantism. In short order, Tyndale suffered martyrdom and Rogers returned to England to pastor a small Reformed congregation.

Determined to see Tyndale's work into print, Rogers obtained a license to print a full English language Bible. Utilizing the text Tyndale completed—the entire New Testament and half the Old—as well as Miles Coverdale's emendations, Rogers set the work into type and added his own interpolary notes. The work constituted not only the first English language Bible but also the first English language commentary on the Bible. Fully cognizant of Tyndale's fate, Rogers cautiously printed the work under the pseudonym Thomas Matthews. To this day it is known as the Matthews Bible. Later it became the basis of the Bishop's Bible and, through it, of the Authorized Version.

Eventually, the official acceptance of Protestantism in England under Henry VIII and Edward VI brought Rogers new prominence. But when sickly Edward VI died, his bitter half sister Mary ascended the throne. A staunchly fanatical Roman Catholic, she was determined to stamp out Protestantism altogether. Three days after Mary entered London, Rogers preached a message urging his congregation to remain faithful to the doctrines they had been taught. For this sermon he was questioned and placed under house arrest. A few weeks later he was transferred to the notorious Newgate Prison where he was tried, convicted, and sentenced to death.

Rogers begged to be allowed to speak a few words to his wife before his execution. This was denied him—though he did meet her and his eleven children in the street as he was marched to the site of his execution, singing psalms all the while. At the stake he was offered a pardon if he would only recant and return to Catholicism. He refused, the fire was lit, and so began Mary's reign of terror.

NATIONAL DAY
Sri Lanka
FEAST DAY
St. Theophilus the Penitent, St. Nicholas Studites, St. Andrew Corsini, bishop, St. Joan of Valois, St. Isidore of Pelusium, St. John de Britto, St. Modan, St. Phileas, St. Joseph of Leonessa, St. Rembert

DISMAL DAY

Also called the Egyptian's Woe, this day was associated with the plagues of Egypt during the early Christian era and thus was believed to be a day of woe and mourning. The word *day* in the phrase is actually an etymological tautology since the word *dismal* was originally the English form of the Latin *dies mali* or "evil days." *Dismal* was at first used as a noun; only later did it become an adjective. Observed somberly, this occasion was intended to be a reminder of the consequences of rejecting the gracious beckoning of God.

A prudent question is one-half of wisdom.

[FRANCIS BACON (1561–1626)]

1783 Britain declared a formal cessation of hostilities with its former colonies, the United States of America.

1818 At an evening at Leigh Hunt's home, the famed poets Keats, Shelley, and Hunt vied with one another in composing sonnets on the subject of the Nile. Hunt's was deemed by them all as the best.

1861 Following the election of Abraham Lincoln as president of the United States, delegates from six of the seceding Southern states met in Montgomery, Alabama, to form the Confederate States of America. Jefferson Davis was elected president of the Confederacy, which was initially comprised of Georgia, Florida, Louisiana, Mississippi, and South Carolina.

1901 Charles Lindbergh, "Lucky Lindy," was born in the United States. Lindbergh flew the *Spirit of St. Louis* as the first pilot to fly solo from New York to Paris.

1905 Dietrich Bonhoeffer, the German theologian and Lutheran pastor who was hanged by the Nazis, was born in Germany.

1921 Activist and author Betty Friedan was born in Peoria, Illinois. She helped to formulate the doctrines and dogmas of feminist orthodoxy in her 1963 blockbuster *The Feminine Mystique.* In that manifesto, she warned that depression, addiction, frigidity, menstrual problems, and even suicide stalk women who spend too much time in their home harboring Victorian ideals. Perhaps feeling that she wasn't quite making herself clear on the issue, she went on to argue that none but the mentally retarded could find housework fulfilling, and that women who accept the role of housewife are in as much danger as the millions who walked to their own deaths in Nazi gas chambers. Not too subtle, but apparently she got her point across.

1938 Walt Disney Productions released its full-length animated film *Snow White.*

1945 Winston Churchill, Joseph Stalin, and Franklin D. Roosevelt gathered for the Yalta Conference to discuss the dividing of Europe at the close of the Second World War.

1974 Newspaper heiress Patricia Hearst was kidnapped in Berkeley, California, by the Symbionese Liberation Army.

1980 Abolhassan Bani-Sadr was installed as president of Iran by the virtual spiritual dictator of the Islamic Revolution, Ayatollah Ruhollah Khomeini.

1997 Despite his acquittal in the criminal trial, a civil jury in Santa Monica, California, found O. J. Simpson liable for the deaths of his ex-wife, Nicole Brown Simpson, and her friend Ronald Goldman.

FEBRUARY

Calvin Coolidge delivered his famous "Have Faith in Massachusetts" speech on January 7, 1914, to the state senate of Massachusetts. It was then published nationwide in the venerable *Harper's Weekly* the next month, on this day. The speech was the crowning plea of scholarly conservatism in a day of reaction and radicalism. Its laconic style and quiet confidence thrust the taciturn Calvin Coolidge upon the national stage and established a new platform for traditional civic restraint. In many ways it heralded the advent of a fresh new Conservative movement. The speech was like the man—a simple Vermont performance: immovable but majestic granite.

In the speech, Coolidge articulated the essential tenets of modern Conservatism including the need for essential Christian covenantalism and a reliance on moral absolutes: "This Commonwealth is one. We are all members of one body. The welfare of the weakest and the welfare of the most powerful are inseparably bound together. Industry cannot flourish if labor languish. Transportation cannot prosper if manufactures decline. The general welfare cannot be provided for in any one act, but it is well to remember that the benefit of one is the benefit of all, and the neglect of one is the neglect of all. The suspension of one man's dividends is the suspension of another man's pay envelope."

He concluded, "Men do not make laws. They do but discover them. Laws must be justified by something more than the will of the majority. They must rest on the eternal foundation of righteousness. That state is most fortunate in its form of government which has the aptest instruments for the discovery of laws. The latest, most modern, and nearest perfect system that statesmanship has devised is representative government. Its weakness is the weakness of us imperfect human beings who administer it. Its strength is that even such administration secures to the people more blessings than any other system ever produced. No nation has discarded it and retained liberty. Representative government must be preserved."

Thus was launched one of the most unlikely ascendancies in American political history—as well as one of the most dynamic and consistent Conservative movements in all of history. It would not only put Coolidge in the White House, it would offer a distinctive-view government that altogether altered the political landscape of Washington and defined the terms of Conservative political discourse for the rest of the century.

FEAST DAY
St. Agatha, Saints Indractus and Dominica, St. Adelaide of Bellich, St. Bertulph or Bertoul of Renty, St. Avitus of Vienne, St. Vodalus or Voel

Nothing is more common than for men to make partial and absurd distinctions between vices of equal enormity, and to observe some of the divine commands with great scrupulousness, while they violate others, equally important, without any concern, or the least apparent consciousness of guilt. Alas, it is only wisdom which perceives this tragedy.

[SAMUEL JOHNSON (1709–1784)]

FEBRUARY

1631 Roger Williams, the founder of Rhode Island, arrived in Boston from his former home in England.

1778 South Carolina became the first colony to ratify the Articles of Confederation.

1783 Sweden recognized the independence of the United States.

1850 Du Bois D. Parmelee of New Paltz, New York, received a patent (No. 7074) for the first adding machine to utilize depressible keys. This impractical and unused machine was called a calculator.

1881 Phoenix, Arizona, was incorporated.

1881 Scottish essayist and historian Thomas Carlyle died in London, never having quite recovered from the death of his wife, Jane. He was a leading figure of the Victorian era and is best known for his three-volume historical work, *The French Revolution*. Carlyle also served as rector of Edinburgh University.

1887 Giuseppe Verdi, at the age of seventy-four, produced his operatic masterpiece *Otello* at La Scala in Milan. The story is taken directly from Shakespeare with minimal alterations.

1901 Edwin Prescott received a patent for the loop-the-loop centrifugal roller coaster.

1917 Congress passed an immigration act severely curtailing the influx of Asians.

1917 Mexico's democratic constitution was adopted.

1934 Henry "Hank" Aaron, Baseball Hall of Famer, member of the Milwaukee and Atlanta Braves, and home-run champion—beating Babe Ruth's astonishing career record of 714—was born in Mobile, Alabama.

1937 President Franklin Roosevelt attempted to pack the Supreme Court with sympathetic judges who would allow his radical expansion of federal power, proposing to simply increase the number of Supreme Court justices.

1940 At the Victor studio in Manhattan, Glenn Miller and his band recorded "Tuxedo Junction" for RCA's Bluebird label.

1958 Gamel Abdel Nasser was formally nominated to become the first president of the new United Arab Republic.

1962 French President Charles de Gaulle called for Algeria's independence after a long and tortuous struggle.

1989 Soviet leader Mikhail S. Gorbachev told the Communist Party it had to give up its unchallenged right to rule in favor of earning that right, instead of taking it for granted.

1994 White separatist Byron De La Beckwith was convicted in Jackson, Mississippi, of murdering civil rights leader Medgar Evers in 1963, and was immediately sentenced to life in prison.

FEBRUARY

6

For nearly a quarter century, John Calvin had led the Swiss city of Geneva with tireless devotion. In the process he not only brought the city to a place of great prominence and prosperity, he also had planted the seeds of our modern democratic freedoms, our representative governing institutions, and our free and open economic markets. In addition, he expounded a winsome and practical perspective of the Reformation doctrines of grace.

On this day in 1564, the man who had done most to stamp his intellect on the Reformation, on Western civilization, and on the modern world, preached his last sermon. Unable to walk, he was carried to church in a chair. Just a month later, he succumbed to illness and died.

When he first came to Geneva in July 1536, he intended to spend just one night. He had just recently published the first edition of his magisterial work of systematic theology, *The Institutes of the Christian Religion.* In Paris, he had received a fine classical education—in preparation for a career in either the church or in law. As a result, he had a highly developed and disciplined mind.

William Farel, the leader of the Protestant movement in the city of Geneva and one of the most prominent evangelists and preachers anywhere in Europe, saw in Calvin the gifts and callings necessary to take Reformation to the next necessary stage of development. He attempted to persuade Calvin to stay. But the young man resisted his pleas. The city was not ready, he argued, for authentic and consistent reform. It seemed to him that sin ran rampant through its streets, day and night. Farel would not take no for an answer—he fulminated with warnings as if from the Lord. In the end, Calvin finally relented. Thus began an odd partnership between the fiery Farel and the scholarly Calvin.

Alas, it quickly became apparent that Calvin was right about the condition of the city. Within a year the two Reformers were expelled from the city. When given the news, Calvin calmly replied, "If we had sought to please men, we should have been badly rewarded, but we serve a higher Master, who will not withhold from us our reward." He settled into a much quieter life as the pastor at nearby Strassburg.

But the citizens of Geneva eventually had a change of heart. Calvin and Farel were invited back. At first, Calvin again resisted, knowing that years of fierce opposition lay before him if he accepted. But he was once again compelled by conscience—and by Farel's tenacity—to return. And thus began the remarkable transformation of the city into a beacon light of freedom, virtue, and faithfulness that shaped the world in ways that millions—who may never have heard the name of Calvin—enjoy to this day.

NATIONAL DAY
New Zealand
FEAST DAY
St. Paul Miki and his Companions, St. Vedast or Vaast, St. Hidegund, St. Amand, Saints Mel and Melchu, St. Guarinus of Palestrina

| WAITANGI DAY | A national holiday in New Zealand marking the 1840 Treaty of Waitangi, which forged peace between the European settlers and the indigenous Maori tribes. |

A wise old owl sat on an oak,

The more he saw the less he spoke;

The less he spoke the more he heard;

Why aren't we like that wise old bird?

[EDWARD RICHARDS (1842–1911)]

1756 America's third vice president, Aaron Burr, was born in Newark, New Jersey.

1778 The United States won official recognition from France with the signing of treaties in Paris.

1788 Massachusetts became the sixth state to ratify the U.S. Constitution.

1894 George Herman "Babe" Ruth was born in Baltimore, Maryland. Ruth was one of the first inductees into the Baseball Hall of Fame as well as the holder of the records for most appearances in the World Series and the first to score 60 home runs in a single season. The "Sultan of Swat" played for the New York Yankees. Traded to New York by the Boston Red Sox in 1920, he almost singlehandedly made the Yankees the preeminent sports franchise—indeed, the Bronx landmark, Yankee Stadium, is still known as the "House that Ruth Built." He retired in 1935 after twenty-one years of playing baseball professionally and died thirteen years later of cancer. Although he was a bit rough around the edges, Ruth was the most celebrated athlete of his time.

1899 A peace treaty between the United States and Spain was ratified by Congress, thus ending the Spanish-American War.

1911 President Ronald Reagan was born in Tampico, Illinois.

1933 The Twentieth Amendment to the Constitution was declared in effect; the so-called "lame duck" amendment moved the start of presidential, vice-presidential, and congressional terms from March to January.

1952 Britain's King George VI died. He was succeeded by his young daughter, Elizabeth II.

1959 The United States successfully test-fired for the first time a Titan intercontinental ballistic missile from Cape Canaveral.

1978 Muriel Humphrey took the oath of office as a United States senator from Minnesota, filling the seat of her late husband, former Vice President Hubert Humphrey.

1989 Pulitzer Prize–winning historian Barbara W. Tuchman died in Greenwich, Connecticut, at age seventy-seven. Her works on the First World War and its causes revitalized the field of moral philosophy, which had been spurned by historians throughout most of the twentieth century.

1993 Tennis Hall of Famer and human rights advocate Arthur Ashe died of AIDS in New York at age forty-nine. His infection with the disease was the result of a tainted blood transfusion during coronary surgery.

FEBRUARY

When the first section of the Erie Canal opened in 1825, it was a marvel of engineering and human labor. Cut through the rolling hills and wide fertile valleys of Upstate New York, it would become the superhighway of antebellum America. From Albany to Buffalo, it opened up the American frontier and made westward expansion inevitable. It turned New York Harbor into the nation's number one port. It shaped social and economic development. With branches that eventually crisscrossed the entire state, cities and industries developed along the canal and flourished—including Rochester, Syracuse, and Binghamton.

Until the American colonies declared independence in 1776, European settlement of the New World was largely confined to the eastern seaboard. The Appalachian Mountains were a formidable obstacle to westward movement. Only the Mohawk River Valley in New York offered both a land and a water passage through the mountains.

By 1817, plans for a man-made waterway fed by the Mohawk River and bypassing its waterfalls and rapids had been made. This plan was to traverse the entire state of New York, connecting the Hudson River in the east with the Great Lakes in the west. When it was opened, vast parcels of land became accessible for the first time. Shipping costs dropped dramatically. Immigrants to America, in search of new lands and new opportunities in the West, crowded canal boats. The westward movement of the nation was begun.

This great feat of American tenacity and ingenuity was immortalized in an old boatman's folksong. The "Erie Canal Song," also known as "Low Bridge," was first published on this day in 1913. It was composed to protest the coming of the mechanized barge, which would replace the mule that had been used previously. Its refrain was familiar to generations of Americans afterward. "Low bridge, everybody down/Low bridge for we're coming to a town/And you'll always know your neighbor/ And you'll always know your pal/If you've ever navigated on/The Erie Canal." The song not only captured a slice of nostalgia, it also epitomized the American covenantal spirit.

FEAST DAY
St. Luke the Younger, St. Theodore of Heraclea, St. Adaucus, St. Moses, St. Richard, "King of the English," St. Silvin

1812

Charles John Huffham Dickens was born in Portsmouth, Hampshire, England. Dickens is regarded as the greatest novelist of the Victorian period for his concern over social issues in such works as *The Pickwick Papers* (1837), *Oliver Twist* (1838), *A Christmas Carol* (1843), *David Copperfield* (1850), *A Tale of Two Cities* (1859), and *Great Expectations* (1861). He journeyed to America in the 1840s for a five-month vacation and was lionized by the people. He died on June 9, 1870, in Kent.

Wisdom is found only in truth.

[JOHANN GOETHE (1749–1832)]

1478 Sir Thomas More, the first layman to become Lord Chancellor of England, was born on this day. Refusing to recognize Henry VIII as head of the church, More was executed for high treason in 1535. It is said that as he placed his head on the block, he drew his beard aside and said, "This hath not offended the King."

1867 Author Laura Ingalls Wilder, who wrote the semi-autobiographical *Little House on the Prairie* series between 1932 and 1943, was born in Lake Pepin, Wisconsin. She died on February 10, 1957, in Mansfield, Missouri.

1904 A fire began in Baltimore that raged for almost thirty hours and destroyed more than 1,500 buildings.

1936 Franklin Roosevelt authorized a flag and seal for the office of the vice president.

1943 The government announced that shoe rationing would go into effect in two days, limiting consumers to buying three pairs per person for the remainder of the year.

1944 Bing Crosby and the John Scott Trotter Orchestra recorded "Swinging on a Star" for Decca Records in Los Angeles.

1945 Lutheran theologian Deitrich Bonhoeffer was transferred to the Nazi's terrible Buchenwald concentration camp where many thousands of prisoners died, some while undergoing cruel medical experiments. Three months later Bonhoeffer was added to the list of the dead. He was hanged days before Allied Army forces freed the camp. Safe in exile in America during the first part of Hitler's terrible reign, he had abruptly returned to Germany. "I have come to the conclusion that I have made a mistake in coming to America. I shall have no right to participate in the reconstruction of the Christian life in Germany after the war if I did not share in the trials of this time with my people. Christians in Germany face the terrible alternative of willing the defeat of their nation in order that civilization may survive, or willing the victory of their nation and thereby destroying civilization. I know which of these alternatives I must choose. But I cannot make that choice in security." In Germany Bonhoeffer worked with the underground resistance. He helped guide Jews to safety. Believing that Hitler was like a madman "driving a car into a group of innocent bystanders," he even joined a plot to kill the Führer. After he was arrested for his aid to the Jews, his role in the plot was discovered. There was little hope that he would survive the Nazi wrath. Nonetheless, Bonhoeffer was personally at peace. Suffering, he said, had become a better key for understanding the world than happiness ever had been. In the end, he had fulfilled the aspirations of his own theology, aptly expressed in his book *The Cost of Discipleship*: "The one thing that matters is practical obedience. That will resolve man's difficulties and make him free to become the child of God."

1948 General Dwight D. Eisenhower resigned as army chief of staff and was succeeded by General Omar Bradley.

1949 Joe DiMaggio commanded the first six-figure contract in the major leagues when he signed with the Yankees for $100,000.

1964 The Beatles began their first American tour as they arrived at New York's John F. Kennedy International Airport, where they were greeted by thousands of screaming fans.

1984 Space shuttle astronauts Bruce McCandless II and Robert L. Stewart went on the first untethered space walk.

1986 Haitian President-for-Life Jean-Claude Duvalier fled his country, ending twenty-eight years of his family's rule. Five years later on this same day, the Reverend Jean-Bertrand Aristide was sworn in as the island nation's first democratically elected president.

Athanasius (300–373) was one of the giants of the church's Patristic Age. As a young deacon from Alexandria, he attended the First Ecumenical Council at Nicaea where he took a leading role in shaping the Nicene Creed. His bold defense of the doctrine of the Trinity against the Arian heresy demanded his attentions throughout his life and resulted in repeated exiles from his beloved home. He was also involved in various conflicts in the arenas of politics, the arts, liturgical renewal, monastic development, New Testament canonisity, and judicial reform. He wrote several important works including biographies, commentaries, systematic theologies, and devotional treatises. His short classic, *On the Incarnation,* is still a staple of any solid theological education.

Late in the evening on this day in 356, nearly five thousand Byzantine troops surrounded the church of St. Theonas in the Egyptian city of Alexandria. Inside, Athanasius was leading an all-night prayer vigil. When the troops burst through the doors, he was reading Psalm 103, "Bless the Lord, O my soul: and all that is within me, bless his holy name."

Amazingly, the members of his congregation, in all the confusion of the moment, managed to spirit him away. And so for the third time since the Council of Nicaea, Athanasius was exiled from his beloved city. George of Kallistos, an Arian, had been sent with imperial authority to assume the bishopric. He unleashed a spate of persecution. Sixteen bishops were banished from Alexandria. Using terror and murder, George tried to force an Arian creed on the people. A price was placed on the head of Athanasius. Agents searched everywhere for him. But the Alexandrians loyally hid their beloved teacher. Eventually George was ousted. Athanasius returned—only to be forced into exile twice more.

Despite a life filled with furious activity and controversy, it was for his personal piety and humble faith that he earned for himself the sobriquet "Athanasius conta mundum," or "Athanasius against the world." Long seasons of prayer and fasting punctuated his life with an air of humility and faithfulness that his opponents simply were unable to match.

1587 For her alleged part in a conspiracy to usurp her cousin Queen Elizabeth I, Mary, Queen of Scots, was beheaded in Fotheringhay Castle in Northamptonshire county. Her remains were moved to Westminster Abbey in 1612 and placed next to Elizabeth's by order of her son, King James I of England—also known as James VI of Scotland.

They say you may praise a fool till you make him useful: I don't know much about that, but I do know that if I get a bad knife I generally cut my finger, and a blunt axe is far more trouble than profit. A handsaw is a good thing, but not to shave with.

[CHARLES H. SPURGEON (1834–1892)]

1693 A charter was granted for the College of William and Mary in Williamsburg, Virginia.

1819 English writer, critic, and artist John Ruskin was born in London. Ruskin championed the Gothic Revival movement in architecture and the decorative arts. He greatly influenced public taste in art in Victorian England through such works as *Modern Painters, The Seven Lamps of Architecture,* and *The Elements of Drawing.* In 1869, Ruskin was elected as the first Slade Professor of Fine Art at Oxford where his public lectures drew great crowds. He died on January 20, 1900, in Lancanshire.

1828 Jules Verne, the French author of such tales as *A Journey to the Center of the Earth* (1864), *Twenty Thousand Leagues Under the Sea* (1869–70), and *Around the World in Eighty Days* (1873) and the pioneer of modern science fiction, was born in Nantes, France. He died in 1905, in Amiens. His writings included a foreshadowing of future technological advances such as the submarine, the aqualung, television, and space travel.

1837 The Senate had to select the vice president of the United States, choosing Richard Mentor Johnson, after none of the candidates received a majority of electoral votes.

1874 The Russian folk-opera *Boris Godounov,* by Modeste Moussorgsky, was first performed in its entirety at the Imperial Opera House in St. Petersburg, Russia. This story of an ambitious councilor to the czar who has visions of power was adapted from a historical play by Alexander Pushkin. This opera is most often performed in the reorchestrated and edited version by Rimsky-Korsakov.

1904 The Russo-Japanese War began. The war raged on destructively, threatening to engulf the entire Pacific Rim until President Theodore Roosevelt brought the two sides together and forged a lasting peace settlement. For his role in the negotiations, Roosevelt was awarded the Nobel Peace Prize in 1906.

1910 The Boy Scouts of America was incorporated in the District of Columbia and was granted a federal charter by an act of Congress six years later, on June 15, 1916.

1915 D. W. Griffith's silent movie epic about the difficult days following the War Between the States, *The Birth of a Nation,* premiered in Los Angeles. Engendering tremendous controversy for its favorable portrayal of the South, it nevertheless was heralded as one of the most remarkable artistic advances in the history of the film industry.

1922 President Warren Harding had the first radio installed in the White House.

1925 John Towner Williams, the American composer and conductor of film scores and former conductor of the Boston Pops Orchestra, was born in New York. His film music for *Jaws,* the Star Wars movies, *E.T.,* and the Indiana Jones movies helped to resurrect and redeem artistic film scoring with its use of large orchestras, derived ideas from art music, and the use of Wagnerian leitmotifs that identify certain characters and thoughts. Williams studied music at UCLA and the Julliard School.

1968 Three college students were killed in a confrontation with highway patrolmen in Orangeburg, South Carolina, during a civil rights protest at a whites-only bowling alley.

1973 Senate leaders named seven members of a select committee to investigate the Watergate scandal, including the chairman, Democrat Sam J. Ervin Jr. of North Carolina.

FEBRUARY

9

Addai of Edessa was one of the apostle Thomas's earliest disciples. Sometime at the end of the first century—traditionally believed to be around the year 94—he was sent out by the fledgling churches of the Indus Valley as a missionary to what is now Urfa in Iraq. There he pioneered innumerable evangelistic enterprises and planted the first Christian congregations outside the Roman world.

He was known for his powerful preaching, his gentle pastoral spirit, and his effective organization. He became an influential force among the ruling families of the region and helped them reshape the system of justice to match biblical ethics.

When Tatar warlords swept through the territory shortly after the turn of the century, he was forced into hiding—though he continued to boldly proclaim the gospel of grace. Eventually though, he was betrayed into the hands of the new pagan rulers. Recalcitrant to the end, he was martyred for his faith on this day in the year 108.

FEAST DAY
St. Apollonia, St. Sabinus of Canossa, St. Teilo, St. Alto, St. Ansbert, St. Nicephorus of Antioch

1825

The House of Representatives elected John Quincy Adams president after none of the candidates received a majority of electoral votes—this despite the fact that Andrew Jackson out-polled him in popular vote. The son of former President John Adams, he had served as a lawyer, senator, diplomat, and secretary of state. He was a stubborn man whose motto was "Watch and Pray," and won his nickname, "Old Eloquence," for championing principle and attacking the institution of slavery. Having rejected the doctrines of Unitarianism, then popular among the New England elite, he devotedly read two to five chapters of the Bible every day—in the original Hebrew and Greek. But not content merely to read, he acted on what he read. So often did he put principle before party, he became highly unpopular with his followers. Nevertheless, John Quincy Adams did not let it alter his course. "The Sermon on the Mount commends me to lay up for myself treasures, not on earth, but in Heaven. My hopes of a future life are all founded upon the Gospel of Christ." After his single term as president, he returned to Congress.

The greatest advances in human civilization have come when we recovered what we had lost: when we learned the lessons of history.

[WINSTON CHURCHILL (1874–1965)]

1567 The second husband of Mary, Queen of Scots, Lord Darnley, died when his house near Edinburgh was blown up by gunpowder while he was sick in bed. The Earl of Bothwell, who became Mary's third husband three months later, and Mary were thought to be involved in the murder.

1590 The British established workhouses for the poor and punished vagabonds through an act passed by Parliament.

1773 William Henry Harrison was born in Charles City County, Virginia. He was the first United States president to die in office just a month after his inauguration in 1841—he caught pneumonia after making a three-hour inaugural speech on a cold and blustery Washington day. After his death, his vice president, John Tyler, assumed the office of president.

1849 Most of Italy was united for the first time since the fall of Imperial Rome when the revolutionary Mazzini replaced the fractured kingdoms of the peninsula with a republic.

1861 The Provisional Congress of the Confederate States of America elected Jefferson Davis president and Alexander H. Stephens vice president.

1870 President Ulysses Grant signed a bill establishing the Federal Meteorological Service, later known as the U.S. Weather Bureau.

1885 Alban Berg, one of the three main composers utilizing the twelve-tone method of composition in such works as the operas *Wozzeck* and *Lulu*, was born in Austria. The twelve-tone, or serial, method of composition as developed by Arnold Schoenberg stripped Western music of tonality, hierarchy of pitch, and other ideals. Berg considered his music to be the musical equivalent of the expressionistic painters.

1941 In a radio broadcast specifically directed toward U.S. President Franklin Roosevelt, Winston Churchill said, "We shall not fail or falter; we shall not weaken or tire. Neither the sudden shock of battle nor the long-drawn trials of vigilance and exertion will wear us down. Give us the tools and we will finish the job."

1942 The U.S. Joint Chiefs of Staff held its first formal meeting to coordinate military strategy during World War Two.

1942 Daylight-Saving War Time went into effect in the United States, with clocks turned one hour forward. After the war the temporary policy was discontinued until 1970, when President Richard Nixon permanently reinstated it.

1943 The bloody World War II Battle of Guadalcanal in the Southwest Pacific ended with an American victory over Japanese forces.

1950 In a speech in Wheeling, West Virginia, Joseph McCarthy, a Republican senator from Wisconsin, charged that the State Department was riddled with Communists. He called for a full governmental investigation into "un-American activities."

1964 The Beatles made their first live American television appearance on *The Ed Sullivan Show*.

1971 The *Apollo 14* spacecraft returned to Earth after man's third landing on the moon.

1984 Former KGB Director Yuri V. Andropov died at age sixty-nine, less than fifteen months after succeeding Leonid Brezhnev as the Soviet dictator. He was succeeded by Konstantin Chernenko, whose tenure in office was even shorter—leading to the accession of Mikhail Gorbachev, the last man to preside over the Soviet Union.

FEBRUARY

10

Alban of Verlamium is widely venerated as the first Christian martyr on the Island of Britain. During the last few decades of the second century he offered refuge to those fleeing the persecution of the church. He succored the sick, cared for the poor, and saved abandoned children from certain death.

He had been converted during a trading expedition to the imperial province of Gaul—now France—and brought the message of the gospel to his home village on the Thames River just downstream from the Roman citadel city of Londinium.

Venerable Bede, the historian, some four centuries later recorded his brutal martyrdom on Holmhurst Hill on this day in 288 after he tried to intercede on behalf of a pitiful family of refugees. An enraged centurion senselessly hacked at him with his sword and staff until he perished.

In the days following his death, however, his sacrificial concern for the needy became a model for the early English church and he became a patron of British Christianity ever after.

FEAST DAY
St. William of Maleval,
St. Scholastica, St. Trumwin,
St. Austreberta, St. Soteris

1899

The Authorized Version of the Bible, long venerated by the English-speaking world, was revised for the first time. Three million copies of the New Testament sold within a year, and the text was printed in full in two Chicago newspapers within two days of reaching the United States. When the original King James Version was first published in 1611, it was based on earlier English translations, all of which traced back to Tyndale's translation, whose New Testament was in turn made directly from the Greek text of Erasmus. In truth, the Authorized Version was not really a translation at all, since the compilers simply selected the text from existing English versions with only a few changes. After the 1611 edition was published, several Greek texts came to light, all older than Erasmus' manuscript. These discoveries underscored the need for revisions in the accepted text to make it as accurate as possible. The revised translation was not a modern language version, however. It merely solved a handful of textual problems, regularized spelling, and clarified a few grammatical issues. As a concession to the traditionalists, the revisers retained the cadence, structure, and vocabulary of the King's English—in fact, they sometimes even opted for idioms predating Shakespeare. The new Authorized Version that resulted is the King James Version that we have today.

A nation which does not remember what it was yesterday, does not know what it is today, nor what it is trying to do. We are trying to do a futile thing if we do not know where we came from or what we have been about. Ours is a rich legacy. Rich but lost.

FEBRUARY

1354 In Oxford, England, a conflict occurred between students of the University of Oxford and the townspeople. This was one in a number of skirmishes between the two sides; however, on this day, the townspeople sought reinforcements from the surrounding country folk and managed to overpower and wound or kill several students. The citizens had several rights and privileges revoked, and an annual penance was decreed. To this day, every anniversary of the massacre must be marked by the mayor and sixty-two citizens who attend St. Mary's Church, and an offering of one penny per man is required.

1680 New England settlers returned to a more normal life after the disappearance of the Great Comet, which had terrorized them; however, Sir Isaac Newton had utilized the comet's appearance to discover the parabolic form of the comet's trajectory of orbit.

1763 France ceded its Canadian provinces to England under the Treaty of Paris, which ended the French and Indian War.

1840 Britain's Queen Victoria married Prince Albert of Saxe-Coburg-Gotha.

1846 Members of the Church of Jesus Christ of Latter-day Saints, the Mormons, began an exodus to the West from Illinois under the leadership of their newly appointed leader, Brigham Young.

1846 Thomas McLean published Edward Lear's *A Book of Nonsense*, which contained seventy-two limericks in two volumes.

1861 After a wild night on the town, romantic poet and artist Dante Gabriel Rossetti returned home to find his wife, Elizabeth, dead from an overdose of laudanum.

1926 Famed lyric soprano Leontyne Price was born in Laurel, Mississippi. The daughter of a maid, Leontyne sang around the house as she helped her mother. Her extraordinary voice was recognized by her mother's employer, who paid for voice lessons for the young girl. When Leontyne made her debut at the Metropolitan Opera House in New York City in the opera *Il Trovatore* by Giuseppe Verdi, she received a forty-two-minute standing ovation from the enthusiastic crowd.

1933 The first singing telegram was sold by the Postal Telegram Company in New York.

1942 The former French liner *Normandie* capsized in New York Harbor a day after it caught fire while being refitted for the U.S. Navy.

1942 RCA presented Glenn Miller and his orchestra with a "gold record" for their recording of "Chattanooga Choo Choo," which had sold more than one million copies.

1949 Arthur Miller's play *Death of a Salesman* opened at Broadway's Morosco Theater.

1950 Mark Spitz, the American swimmer who was the first person to win more than five gold medals at one Olympiad, was born in California. At the 1972 Olympics, Spitz won seven gold medals and set a new world record time for each win. In all, Spitz won eleven medals at the 1968 and 1972 Olympics, five gold medals at the 1967 Pan Am Games, set twenty-six world records, and won numerous championships, awards, and honors.

1962 The Soviet Union exchanged captured American U-2 pilot Francis Gary Powers for Rudolph Ivanovich Abel, a Soviet spy held by the United States.

1967 The Twenty-fifth Amendment to the Constitution, dealing with presidential disability and succession, went into effect.

1989 Ron Brown was elected chairman of the Democratic National Committee, becoming the first African American to lead a major U.S. political party.

FEBRUARY

On this day in 1625, Nicholas Ferrar (1579–1637) retired from a promising parliamentary career in London and moved to a Christian community in Huntingdonshire. The community was marked by extreme Puritan piety: they fasted regularly—both publicly and privately; twice a day they all attended the liturgical offices in their tiny church; at every hour during the day some members joined in a little office of prayer so that the whole Psalter was recited daily; and at night, at least two members of the household maintained a "nightwatch of prayer" and the Psalter was again recited.

The members of the community were marked by their charity and merciful service as well—so that their spiritual disciplines were not merely turned inward. Ferrar focused their practical concern on abandoned boys that roamed the byways. Ultimately, the community developed one of the most effective alternatives to the barbarous orphanage system of the day through simple Christian service and unfaltering spiritual devotion.

FEAST DAY

Saints Saturninus and Dativus; St. Benedict of Aniane; St. Gregory II, pope; St. Caedmon; St. Pascal, pope; St. Lazarus of Milan; St. Lucius of Adrianople; St. Severinus of Agaunum

1929

On this day Benito Mussolini negotiated the Lateran Treaty with the pope, recognizing the sovereign status of the church's 109-acre Vatican enclave for the first time in nearly a century—constituting it as the smallest nation in the world. For more than a thousand years the church had been the biggest landlord in Italy. And when Pope Pius IX was crowned in 1846, the church still controlled the Papal States, seventeen thousand square miles of Italian territory, as well as the city of Rome. But on February 9, 1849, most of Italy was united for the first time since the fall of Imperial Rome when the revolutionary Mazzini replaced the old fractured kingdoms of the peninsula—including virtually all of the territory within the Papal States—with a republic. After various shifts of control, the new Italian state completed the takeover of papal lands in 1870 and denied the Vatican's status as a separate nation. The Vatican, which had always dealt directly with foreign powers, continued to receive foreign ambassadors anyway. An uneasy coexistence existed between church and state until Mussolini relented and granted the pope absolute authority over his little enclave within the city of Rome.

If we take the generally accepted definition of bravery as a quality which knows not fear, I have never seen a brave man. All men are frightened. The more intelligent they are, the more they are frightened. The courageous man is the man who forces himself, in spite of his fear, to carry on.

[GENERAL GEORGE PATTON (1885–1945)]

FEBRUARY

1732 President George Washington was born on his parents' plantation near Fredericksburg, Virginia. The date of his birth is February 11 in accordance with the Old Style (Julian) calendar, which was in effect at the time—the modern use of the Gregorian calendar necessitates adjusting his birth date to February 22.

1778 Voltaire received more than three hundred visitors following his return to Paris after twenty-eight years of exile for impudent behavior and his satiric writings.

1812 Massachusetts Governor Elbridge Gerry signed a redistricting law favoring his party—giving rise to the term "gerrymandering."

1847 Thomas Alva Edison, the first man to record sound in 1877 as well as the inventor of the ticker tape machine, the light bulb, and other devices, was born in Milan, Ohio. Edison's genius lay in his ability to make practical applications of scientific principles despite only three months of formal schooling and a progressive loss of hearing. He was one of the most productive inventors of his time.

1858 A French girl, Bernadette Soubirous, claimed for the first time to have seen a vision of the Virgin Mary near Lourdes. A number of miraculous healings at the site were reported shortly thereafter, and Lourdes became a major attraction for holy pilgrimages.

1861 President-elect Lincoln departed Springfield, Illinois, for Washington.

1937 A sit-down strike against General Motors ended, with the company agreeing to recognize the United Automobile Workers Union.

1940 John Buchan, 1st Baron Tweedsmuir, died in Montreal, where he was serving as governor-general of Canada. He had an amazing career as a journalist, statesman, spy, adventurer, churchman, historian, and educator. His writing career alone was astonishingly varied—including the creation of the genre of spy thrillers (*The Thirty-nine Steps, Greenmantle, Mr. Standfast*) as well as writing critically acclaimed historical fiction (*Witchwood, John Burnet of Barns*), adventure stories (*John MacNab, Prester John*), biographies (*George V, Augustus, Montrose, Walter Scott*), history (*The History of the Great War, The Scots Fusiliers*) and poetry (*The Bairns of the Soul*).

1945 President Roosevelt, British Prime Minister Winston Churchill, and Soviet leader Joseph Stalin signed the Yalta Agreement during World War Two, effectively partitioning Europe between east and west, thus enabling the opportunistic Stalin to draw down what Churchill would later call "The Iron Curtain."

1975 Margaret Thatcher became the leader of the British Conservative Party as the first woman in that position. She would proceed to lead her party to an extraordinary electoral success in 1979, becoming the first woman to serve the Crown as prime minister—a post she would hold for a near-record eleven straight years.

1979 The radical Shi'ite followers of Ayatollah Ruhollah Khomeini's Islamic Revolution seized power in Iran.

1990 South African black activist Nelson Mandela was freed after serving twenty-seven years in prison for his role in several antiapartheid terrorist attacks and assassinations.

1993 President Clinton announced his choice of Miami prosecutor Janet Reno to be the nation's first female attorney general.

FEBRUARY

Cotton Mather was born on this day in 1663. He was the scion of a rich heritage that helped to shape American civilization in remarkable ways. His grandfather Richard Mather brought the family to the American colonies in 1635 after a distinguished career as a Puritan minister in England. There he became a vital member of the leadership of Boston—both through his articulate pulpit manner and through production of the *Bay Psalm Book*—the first book produced in America.

Richard's son, Increase Mather, was likewise an influential pastor, educator, and author. He earned America's first Doctor of Divinity degree. He also served as president of Harvard and as a diplomat for the Massachusetts Bay Colony, helping to renegotiate the colonial charter at the court of King Charles II following the restoration of the monarchy.

But the greatest of all the Mathers was Increase's son, Cotton. Like his father and grandfather, he was an influential pastor, statesman, and author. Indeed, he ultimately proved to be the most prolific author in American history—more than 450 of his works were printed in his lifetime, including books on an astonishing variety of subjects from theology and philosophy to natural science and history.

He left his mark in virtually every arena of human endeavor. So profound was his influence, in fact, that George Washington later called him the "Father of the Founding Fathers."

FEAST DAY
St. Julian the Hospitaller, St. Ethelwald of Lindisfarne, St. Anthony Kauleas, St. Marina or Pelagia, St. Meletius, St. Ludan

1554 — Lady Jane Grey, queen of England for thirteen days, was killed at the Tower of London along with her husband, Lord Guildford Dudley, by order of her stepsister, Bloody Mary. She was maneuvered into the role of queen at the age of sixteen when Edward VI died in July 1553.

> *The fear of God makes a hero; the fear of man makes a coward.*
>
> [ALVIN YORK (1887–1964)]

1653 Composer Arcangelo Corelli was born in Fusignano, Italy. Corelli was the composer of numerous violin concertos that were the height of Italian Baroque ensemble compositions.

1709 The Scottish seaman Alexander Selkirk was taken off Juan Fernandez Island after living there alone for more than four years. His adventures inspired Daniel Defoe to write *Robinson Crusoe.*

1733 English adventurers led by James Oglethorpe founded the new crown colony of Georgia—named for the king—and laid out the town of Savannah.

1809 Charles Darwin, the English naturalist, was born in Shrewsbury, on the Welsh border. Works such as *The Origin of Species* were an attempt to extricate biblical ideas from the realms of science. The theories of evolution are a product of his writings.

1809 Abraham Lincoln, who would one day become the sixteenth president of the United States and lead the nation through the War Between the States, was born in present-day Larue County, Kentucky.

1870 Women in the Utah Territory gained the right to vote—the first in the nation.

1892 President Lincoln's birthday was declared a national holiday.

1907 More than three hundred people died when the steamer *Larchmont* collided with a schooner off New England's Block Island.

1908 Six automobiles left Times Square, New York City, for a race around the world. The cars—three French, one Italian, one German, and one American—traveled a route that led them through Seattle, Yokohama, and Paris. The American car won the race in 170 days.

1909 A new civil rights organization, the National Association for the Advancement of Colored People (NAACP), was founded by a group of African-American intellectuals who desired to make a break from Booker T. Washington's strategy of peaceful coexistence and cooperation.

1915 The cornerstone for the Lincoln Memorial was laid in Washington, D.C.

1915 The American hymn writer Fanny Crosby died. She left behind thousands of hymns—the equivalent of fifteen hymnbooks full—many of them classic favorites of the Christian Church.

1924 The first performance of George Gershwin's "Rhapsody in Blue" occurred at the Aeolian Hall in New York City, by Paul Whiteman and his orchestra, with Gershwin at the piano. The name of the concert was "An Experiment in Modern Music." This fusion of jazz idioms in an art music context enabled Gershwin to "make a lady out of jazz."

1940 The radio play *The Adventures of Superman* debuted on the Mutual network with Bud Collyer reading the part of the Man of Steel.

1973 The first American prisoners of war from the Vietnam conflict were released. The 116 POW's were flown from Hanoi to the Philippines.

2000 Charles Schulz, the beloved creator of the "Peanuts" comic strip, died of cancer one day before the final installment of Charlie Brown, Snoopy, Linus, and Lucy ran in Sunday newspapers across the country.

FEBRUARY

13

On this day in 1859, Jonathan Blanchard left his position as president of Knox College in Galesburg, Illinois, to lead the struggling Illinois Institute, founded out in the countryside due west of Chicago by the Wesleyan Methodists in 1854. This able and pious administrator was an heir to the old Scotch-Irish stock of American immigrants who brought their strong faith and diligent work ethic to bear on the Western frontier.

It was Blanchard's desire that the little college commit itself to a combination of intellectual growth by reaffirming the old tradition of classical education and the evangelical zeal evidenced in the great prairie revivals of the mid-nineteenth century.

Shortly after he arrived in the area, a local community leader who shared that vision gave a small parcel of pastureland to the Institute. Warren L. Wheaton was convinced that if the old ideals of the American founding vision were to be transplanted in the West, such institutions would be needed. In gratitude, Blanchard later had the school renamed Wheaton College.

Touched almost at once by the calamity of the War Between the States, the college said farewell to some sixty-seven matriculators, most of whom never returned. Nevertheless, the school managed to survive and even prosper. Its reputation grew as it provided students with a liberal arts education undergirded with classical studies and a distinctively Christian emphasis.

The village around Wheaton had been a picket fence and white steeple kind of community from its earliest days. Eventually, under Blanchard's gentle leadership, the whole area became a quiet enclave of conservative Christian publishing houses, educational suppliers, and evangelistic ministries in the midst of the vibrant metropolitan milieu of Chicago nearby. Indeed, by the turn of the century it had practically become the buckle of the Midwest's Bible Belt—so much so that in many circles the very name "Wheaton" had become synonymous with evangelical Christianity.

FEAST DAY
St. Catherine dei Ricci, St. Stephen of Rieti, St. Ermenilda or Ermengild, St. Martinian the Hermit, St. Polyeuctes of Melitene, St. Licinus or Lesin, St. Modomnoc

1974

Nobel Prize–winning novelist, essayist, and historian Aleksandr Solzhenitsyn was expelled from the Soviet Union. A prominent founding member of the Samzat movement—an underground resistance to Communist rule organized by artists and writers—Solzhenitsyn was the author of several books exposing Soviet tyranny that proved to be very embarrassing to the Kremlin and the Politboro. His books *A Day in the Life of Ivan Denisovich, The Gulag Archipelago, Cancer Ward, Full Circle, The Oaken Calf,* and *August 1914* are undeniable classics. After his exile, he became a media darling in the West. In 1978, he created a firestorm of controversy when in a commencement address at Harvard, he indicted Liberals in the West with the same politically correct tendencies to impose tyranny in the name of freedom as his former Soviet masters in the gulag.

The nomad spirit of modernity has dashed the integrity of community—but not the deep need for it.

[HAROLD BEEKSER (1922–1997)]

1542 The fifth wife of England's King Henry VIII, Catherine Howard, was executed for presumed adultery.

1689 The Dutch noble William III of Orange and his wife, Mary Stuart, came to the throne of England in a bloodless revolution. William's father-in-law, James II, then reigning from his palace at Whitehall, had been deposed just the day before for exerting his royal prerogative to promote Roman Catholicism. Thus, on this day Parliament granted the throne to William with certain religious and civil conditions: "Whereas the late King James II did endeavor to subvert and extirpate the Protestant religion, and the laws and liberties of this kingdom," they wrote, "we do resolve that William and Mary, Prince and Princess of Orange, be declared King and Queen of England, Scotland, Ireland, France, and the Dominions."

1741 Three days ahead of Benjamin Franklin's *Saturday Evening General Magazine*, Andrew Bradford of Philadelphia published the first American periodical, *The American Magazine*. Edited by John Webbe, only three issues appeared, each containing the sundry proceedings of the colonial assemblies and brief reprints from the *London Magazine*.

1804 Educator, philosopher, and theologian Immanuel Kant died in Konigsberg, Prussia, his lifelong home. His book *Critique of Pure Reason*, published in 1781, was a response to David Hume's empiricism—and it subsequently launched its own school of metaphysical enlightenment.

1903 The incredibly prolific novelist Georges Simenon, creator of the *Inspector Maigret* mysteries, was born in Liege.

1914 To protect the copyrighted musical compositions of its members, composer Victor Herbert founded the American Society of Composers, Authors, and Publishers, known as ASCAP, in New York City.

1920 Because segregation barred African-American athletes from participating in major league baseball, the National Negro Baseball League was organized.

1920 The League of Nations recognized the perpetual neutrality of Switzerland.

1935 A jury in Flemington, New Jersey, found Bruno Richard Hauptmann guilty of first-degree murder in the kidnapping and death of the infant son of Charles and Anne Lindbergh. Hauptmann was later executed.

1945 Allied planes began bombing the beautiful German city of Dresden.

1960 France tested its first atomic weapon.

13

FEBRUARY

14

Cyril, who with his brother Methodius was the pioneer missionary to the Slavs and architect of the Cyrillic alphabet, died while still serving in the realm of Moravia. He left behind him one of the greatest legacies any man has been graced to give the world. His influence—along with that of his brother—essentially reshaped the entire structure of Eastern European culture. So lasting was their impact that the two are called "the Apostles of the Slavs."

Around 860, Rastislav, a prince of the Moravian tribes, asked the Byzantine hierarchy to send missionaries to proclaim the gospel among subjects. Patriarch Photius delegated the noble-born brothers Cyril and Methodius to the task. Natives of Thessalonica, they were no strangers to Eastern Europe and had already carried out diplomatic missions for Byzantium to the Abassid Caliph and later to the Alambahd Khazars.

Both men were learned and pious. Cyril was a professor of philosophy at the university in Constantinople. Methodius was a renowned linguist—it was said that he was fluent in more than a dozen languages. Of Slavic origin themselves, the brothers were already familiar with the structure of the language and began developing a special alphabet to capture its sounds shortly after they arrived on the field. Their Glagolitic script was the basis for modern Cyrillic, which became the alphabet of learning and commerce throughout Central and Eastern Europe. Utilizing this script the brothers were able to translate the Scriptures, church liturgies, and other writings into the Slavic tongue.

The two brothers faced innumerable obstacles throughout their lives, but their faith and forbearance enabled them to make a lasting impact that is felt even to this day across the wide expanse of a continent—from the Russian Steppe and the Caspian Ridge to Dalmatian Strand and the Balkan Upland.

St. Valentine's Day
Feast Day
St. John the Baptist of the Conception, St. Antoninus of Sorrento, St. Maro, St. Abraham of Carrhae, St. Adolf of Osnabrück, St. Auxentius, Saints Cyril and Methodius, St. Conran

St. Valentine's Day

Valentine was a third-century pastor who was imprisoned for his faith. He wrote small pastoral notes to members of his congregation on leaves he was able to pluck from a maple tree just outside his cell. These little "Valentine's cards" expressed his love for the flock, and his desire that they demonstrate like love toward one another. Gradually the tradition grew up for Christians to exchange notes of love and encouragement to one another on this, his birthday.

You have, to be sure, known pain and fear,

And the anguish of failure and frustration are near;

Yet your eyes read companionship not distance,

Your home beckons forth, with no hint of resistance;

Indeed, your cloak, though threadbare, is half mine,

You are my friend, and I, most assuredly, am thine.

[TRISTAN GYLBERD (1954–)]

FEBRUARY

1400 Richard II, the deposed king of England, was murdered at Pontefract Castle, Yorkshire—presumably by thugs hired by his cousin and successor, Henry IV.

1778 The American ship *Ranger* carried the recently adopted banner of the Stars and Stripes to a foreign port for the first time as it arrived in France.

1797 Against overwhelming odds, Admirals Jervis and Nelson of the British navy defeated the revived Spanish Armada at the Battle of Cape St. Vincent, off the coast of Portugal.

1848 Famed pioneering photographer Matthew Brady captured President James K. Polk on film in New York, making the chief executive the first president to be photographed.

1859 Oregon was admitted to the Union as the thirty-third state.

1894 Actor and comedian Benjamin Kubelsky, best known as Jack Benny, was born in Waukegan, Illinois. Benny played a endearing tightwad who was the willing recipient of others' jokes. In addition, he maintained a lifelong passion for playing the violin.

1895 British wit Oscar Wilde's final play, *The Importance of Being Earnest*, opened at the St. James's Theatre in London.

1899 Congress approved, and President William McKinley signed, legislation authorizing states to use voting machines for federal elections.

1903 The Department of Commerce and Labor was established.

1912 Arizona became the forty-eighth state of the Union.

1919 The United Parcel Service—best known for its ubiquitous brown trucks and UPS moniker—was founded.

1920 The League of Women Voters was founded in Chicago; its first president was Maude Wood Park.

1924 Thomas Watson created the International Business Machine Corporation—the company best known as either IBM or Big Blue.

1929 The "St. Valentine's Day Massacre" took place in a Chicago garage as seven rivals of Al Capone's gang were gunned down.

1962 First lady Jacqueline Kennedy conducted a televised tour of the White House.

1989 Iran's Ayatollah Khomeini called on all faithful Muslims around the world to assassinate Salman Rushdie, the British author of *The Satanic Verses*, a novel condemned by Khomeini and his Shi'ite revolutionaries as blasphemous.

FEBRUARY

FEAST DAY
St. Tanco or Tatto, St. Agape of Terni, St. Walfrid or Galfrid, St. Sigfrid of Växjö

Niagara Falls was established as the ideal honeymoon destination by the French at the beginning of the nineteenth century. Napoleon's brother, Jerome Bonaparte, traveled by stagecoach from New Orleans to spend his honeymoon at the remarkable natural wonder on this day in 1802. He returned home with glowing reports. Since then, it gradually gained a reputation as the undisputed honeymoon capital of the world. And for good reason.

The Niagara River is actually a mere thirty-five miles in length, stretching between Lake Erie and Lake Ontario. But along that short distance are some of the most stunning sights on the face of the earth. The imposing Horseshoe Falls on the Canadian side of the river drop 177 feet, and the stupendous Vertical Falls on the American side of the river drop 184 feet. Together with the thunderous crash of the waters, the rising mist from the pool below, and the wide panorama across the gorge, the Falls create a surreal spectacle of titanic proportions. Winter brings an added dimension of beauty and outdoor activity to Niagara. Thousands of gulls and terns flock around the Falls and rapids. The clinging spray of the Falls blankets the nearby trees, rocks, and lampposts, forming luminescent frozen shapes. When Charles Dickens visited the Niagara Falls in 1841, he wrote, "Niagara was at once stamped upon my heart, an Image of Beauty; to remain there, changeless and indelible, until its pulses cease to beat, forever."

In May 1535, Jacques Cartier left France to explore the New World. Although he never saw Niagara Falls, the Indians he met along the St. Lawrence River told him about it. Samuel de Champlain explored the region in 1608. He, too, heard stories of the mighty cataract, but never visited it. Etienne Brule, the first European to see Lakes Ontario, Erie, Huron, and Superior, apparently was also the first to behold the Falls, in 1615. Later that same year, the Recollet missionary explorers arrived in Ontario. They were followed a decade later by the Jesuits. It was a Jesuit father, Gabriel Lalemant, who first recorded the Iroquois name for the river—*Onguiaahra,* meaning "Strait." In December 1678, Recollet priest Louis Hennepin visited Niagara Falls. A few years later, he published the first engraving of the Falls in his book *Nouvelle Decouverte.*

Although Napoleon's greatest contribution to America was undoubtedly the Louisiana Purchase, the discovery of this marvel as a place to nurture young love must rate a close second.

Work is much more fun than fun.

[NOEL COWARD (1899–1973)]

1386 Pressured by the onslaughts of the Teutonic Knights—an order of Crusaders who had returned to Europe to conquer the last remaining pagan territories—Jagiello, king of the Lithuanians, converted to Christianity. The Teutonic Knights had already conquered Estonia, Livonia, Prussia, and East Pomerania. Though the Lithuanian kingdom had been able to resist all their assaults—indeed, Jagiello's kingdom was vast, stretching from the Baltic in the north to the Black Sea in the south and eastward almost to Moscow—he was wise enough to realize that absorption into Christendom was now only a matter of time. He decided that he would rather choose that time than let the Teutons choose it for him. Jagiello's conversion marked the end of established paganism in Europe.

1564 Galileo Galilei, the renowned astronomer and physicist, was born in Pisa, Italy. Besides his famous investigations into planetary movements, he was a great innovator in structural engineering and mechanical physics. He demonstrated his theorem of equal velocity by dropping objects from the leaning tower in Pisa.

1764 The city of St. Louis was established on the banks of the Mississippi River by French traders intent on opening a gateway to the West.

1799 Samuel Johnson satirically recommended that Jean Jacques Rousseau be hired out to work on plantations. This comment exacerbated a famous argument between the writers Rousseau, Voltaire, and Hume, which resulted in the fiercest ideological salvos in Enlightenment thought.

1820 American suffragist and Christian temperance crusader Susan B. Anthony was born in Adams, Massachusetts.

1888 Horatio Nicholls, also known as Lawrence Wright, was born in England. Nicholls was a songwriter and publisher who was known as the "Father of Tin Pan Alley," the area in New York City—West Twenty-eighth Street between Broadway and Sixth Avenue—which sparked great creativity in the area of popular song with such composers as George M. Cohan, George Gershwin, Cole Porter, Jerome Kern, and Scott Joplin. It was called "Tin Pan Alley" because the sound of tinny pianos in various offices and workrooms could be heard from the street.

1898 The battleship USS *Maine* was sunk in the harbor at Havana, Cuba, by an explosion of unknown origin. The deaths of 260 crew members heightened tensions with Spain, despite the fact that no clear evidence of foul play was discovered. This event sparked the Spanish-American War and inspired its battle cry, "Remember the Maine."

1903 The first teddy bear was introduced in America, named in honor of President Theodore Roosevelt.

1908 In a wry war of words, George Bernard Shaw nicknamed his literary and philosophical rivals G. K. Chesterton and Hilaire Belloc "the Chesterbelloc . . . a very amusing pantomime elephant."

1925 Yale University received the original Gutenberg Bible, printed in fifteenth-century Germany, which was bought in New York for $106,000.

1933 President-elect Franklin Roosevelt narrowly escaped an assassination attempt in Miami that claimed the life of Chicago Mayor Anton J. Cermak.

1965 The Canadian Maple Leaf Flag of red and white was unfurled for the first time in Ottawa on Parliament Hill.

1970 Great Britain adopted a currency system based on decimals, thus replacing the 1,200-year-old method of pounds, shillings, and pence—which was based on twelve pennies to the shilling.

FEBRUARY

16

Over the course of the past three centuries, the Gulf Coast of Mississippi has served under a variety of flags: the French Fleur de Lis, the Golden Spanish Imperium, the Great Mississippi Magnolia, the Stars and Bars of the Confederate States of America, the Star-Spangled Banner of the United States, and briefly during the War of 1812, the British Union Jack. But perhaps most intriguing was its tenure under the Bonnie Blue of the Republic of West Florida.

Early in 1802, Napoleon concluded that it would be in his best interest to sell his American colonies to the United States. Negotiations took about two weeks, and the territories—extending from New Orleans to the Canadian border—were sold for $15 million in 1803. The transaction is known in history as the Louisiana Purchase.

Specifically exempt from the sale was the land east of the Mississippi. Over the course of the next several months, the settlers there formed an independent nation extending from the Mississippi in the west to Pensacola Bay in the east and stretching as far north as present-day Montgomery, Alabama. The founders of this Gulf Coast state called their nation the Republic of West Florida and established their capital at Baton Rouge. Thomas Jefferson's near relative Fulwar Skipwith was elected president shortly afterward—and it was Skipwith who encouraged the adoption of the Bonnie Blue Flag, the old Celtic symbol of covenantal freedom, as the nation's official banner.

Independence brought both liberty and prosperity to the region—but it was to be short-lived. On this day in 1810, the sovereignty of West Florida was brought to an untimely and ignominious end when President James Madison ordered a detachment of American cavalrymen under the command of General William Claiborne to conquer the territory for the United States. Legislators were marched out of the Capitol Building at bayonet-point and forced to pledge allegiance to the federal United States and its governmental emissaries. The Bonnie Blue flag was torn down and replaced by the Stars and Stripes. The conquest was made in the name of American Manifest Destiny—but it remained a point of contention in the region and contributed to its quick acceptance of secession in the earliest days of the War Between the States.

FEAST DAY
St. Juliana of Cumae; St. Onesimus the Slave; St. Gilbert of Sempringham; Saints Elias, Jeremy, and their Companions

1948 | The first nightly newscast began airing on NBC-TV. Known as *The Camel Newsreel Theatre*, the broadcast consisted of Fox Movietone Newsreels.

If you get into the habit of putting in hard and conscientious work, doing a little duty well, no matter how insignificant; if you get into the habit of doing well whatever falls to your hands, whether in the light or in the dark—you will find that you are going to lay a foundation for success.

[BOOKER T. WASHINGTON (1856–1915)]

1497 Philip Melanchthon, the comrade of Martin Luther and a German Protestant Reformer, was born in the house of his grandparents in the electoral Saxon residential town of Bretten. He was well learned and held the position of professor of Greek at the University of Wittenberg—his name is the Greek rendering of the German Schwarzerdt, which means "black earth." It was at Wittenberg that he first met Martin Luther, and in 1521 he wrote *Loci Communes*, a systematic presentation of the principles of the Reformation for people outside the movement. In addition, Melanchthon wrote the *Augsburg Confession* (1530). He represented Luther at various conferences and also established a friendship with John Calvin.

1519 Gaspard de Coligny was born in France. He was a French soldier and Protestant leader who was one of the first victims of the St. Bartholomew's Day Massacre of the Huguenots.

1804 Lieutenant Stephen Decatur led a successful raid into Tripoli Harbor to burn the U.S. Navy frigate *Philadelphia*, which had fallen into the hands of pirates. The daring attack established the reputation of American fighting men as among the most fearless in the world.

1838 Historian Henry Brooks Adams was born in Boston. The great-grandson and grandson of presidents, the son of a prominent diplomat, he was the Brahmin of one of America's most prominent families. In his most famous work, *The Education of Henry Adams*, published in 1910, he wrote, "I want to look like an American Voltaire or Gibbon, but am slowly settling down to be a third-rate Boswell hunting for a Dr. Johnson." His *Chartres and Mont St. Michel* would become the most articulate repudiation of modernism of the Victorian Age.

1862 During the War Between the States, some fourteen thousand Confederate soldiers surrendered at Fort Donelson, Tennessee. Union General Ulysses S. Grant's tenacious strategy there marked the beginning of his rise to prominence in the Union army and earned him the nickname "Unconditional Surrender Grant."

1876 Author, educator, and historian George Macaulay Trevelyan, best known for his *English Social History* and *History of England*, was born at Stratford-upon-Avon, the purported home of William Shakespeare.

1918 Taking advantage of the disarray that enveloped Europe in the aftermath of the First World War and the Communist Revolution in Russia, Lithuania proclaimed its independence.

1923 The burial chamber of King Tutankhamen's recently unearthed tomb was unsealed in Egypt.

1937 Dr. Wallace H. Carothers, a research chemist for Du Pont who invented nylon, received a patent for the synthetic fiber.

1945 American troops landed on the island of Corregidor in the Philippines during World War II.

1968 Haleyville, Alabama, instituted the nation's first 911 emergency telephone system.

FEBRUARY

17

The little kingdom of Portugal differed from almost every other realm at the end of the fourteenth century in that it was already a single and united whole. From Algarve in the south to Minho in the north there were no conflicting dialects, no semi-independent provinces, and no feudal lords with vassals and rear-vassals of their own. All fiefs were held directly from the king, all castles were Crown property, and there were no robber barons carving out autonomous manorial estates. The four great indigenous crusading orders—Saint John, Santiago, Aviz, and Christo—were still garrisoned in their fortresses, but all their attentions had been focused on the Saracens of North Africa since the defeat of the Moors a century earlier.

Into these happy circumstances came the Infante Dom Henrique on this day in 1394—the fourth son of King Joao. Future generations would call him Henry the Navigator because of his efforts to forge nautical advancement. At Cape St. Vincent, he built a marine laboratory that transformed the enterprise of discovery from happenstance into science. There, he gathered the greatest pilots, navigators, cartographers, shipbuilders, geographers, astronomers, mathematicians, and mariners in the world. He accumulated a vast library of sailing charts and portolanos. He investigated the ancient tales of St. Brendan, of the norsemen, of the Antipodes, of Prester John, and of Marco Polo with the objectivity of an academician. He sponsored the discovery and colonization of innumerable farflung isles—including Madeira, Porto Santo, the Verdes, and the Azores. And he advanced the design of oceangoing vessels by building the caravel.

As progressive as Henry may appear—a medieval anomaly of purposefulness, logic, and moderation—it is clear enough that he was very much a man of his day. The great and overriding motivation behind his enterprise was the simple desire to carry the crusading sword over to Africa in Christendom's holy war against Islam. He ultimately led three crusades—in 1415 against Mauritania, in 1436 against Tangier, and in 1458 against Fez.

North Africa had once been a jewel of Christian civilization. It produced some of the finest minds of the early church—Augustine, Tertullian, Anthony, Clement, Cyprian, Origen, and Athanasius. But during the seventh and eighth centuries it was put to the scimitar and vanquished. Almost every trace of Christianity was swept away. Henry wanted more than anything to remove that shame. In the process, he launched the world's greatest adventurers, discoverers, and mariners.

FEAST DAY
Saints Theodulus and Julian, St. Evermod, St. Loman, St. Fintan of Cloneenagh, St. Finan of Lindisfarne

As pride sometimes is hid under humility, idleness is often covered by turbulence and hurry.

[SAMUEL JOHNSON (1709–1784)]

1776 The first volume of Edward Gibbon's *History of the Decline and Fall of the Roman Empire* was published in London.

1801 The House of Representatives broke an electoral tie between Thomas Jefferson and Aaron Burr, making Jefferson the new president and Burr his vice president.

1817 The Gas Light Company of Baltimore was the first gas company to utilize gas streetlights "to provide for more effectual lighting of the streets, squares, lanes and alleys of the city of Baltimore."

1865 Columbia, South Carolina, was practically burned to the ground as the Confederates evacuated and Union forces moved in.

1879 The Waldenses received a guarantee of civil and religious rights for the first time. The religious sect began in 1176 when the rich merchant Peter Waldo first heard the words of Christ to the rich young ruler, "If thou wilt be perfect, go and sell that thou hast, and give to the poor, and thou shalt have treasure in heaven; and come and follow me." Immediately, Waldo sold all he had and began a life of itinerant preaching. He and his small band of followers were often persecuted, and most were sent into exile. With the coming of the Reformation, many of the remaining Waldenses joined the Protestants. Allowed refuge in Switzerland, they nevertheless pined for their homeland and in 1691, they made a "glorious return." But it was not until the Italian revolutions of the mid-nineteenth century that the remnant, now dwelling in alpine valleys of northern Italy, guaranteed their rights.

1897 The forerunner of the National PTA, the National Congress of Mothers, was founded in Washington.

1901 Marian Anderson, the renowned contralto who was the first African American to sing at the Metropolitan Opera House, was born in Philadelphia. Anderson was the first black singer to be named a permanent member of the Metropolitan Opera Company (1955) as well as the first to perform in the White House. Conductor Arturo Toscanini described her as "the voice that comes once in 100 years." She died in 1993.

1904 Giacomo Puccini's opera *Madame Butterfly* was poorly received at its world premiere at La Scala in Milan. It was, however, quickly received as a masterpiece by critics elsewhere. The story of a Japanese bride and her brazen and insolent American husband, Pinkerton, originated as a story by John Luther Long and then became a successful New York play in 1900 before being immortalized by Puccini's composition.

1913 The infamous Armory Exhibition introduced modern art to Americans. There was public outcry over the contemporary works of the French and Spanish painters Picasso, Matisse, Braque, and Duchamp exhibited in the Sixty-ninth Regiment Armory in New York. Despite the flaunting of objective aesthetics and the deliberate attempt to shock patrons, modern art established a firm hold in the United States, and New York City soon surpassed Paris as the center of the art world.

1933 *Newsweek* was published by the *Washington Post* to rival the popular *Time*.

1947 *The Voice of America* began broadcasting into the Soviet Union.

FEBRUARY

Next to the Bible, the best-loved and most-read book during the first three hundred years of American colonial and national life was John Bunyan's *Pilgrim's Progress*. Its plot was familiar to every schoolchild. Its characters became cultural icons. Its imagery was seamlessly woven into the art, music, literature, and ideas of the people.

The opening lines of the saga were etched into the memories of untold thousands and became a kind of yardstick against which to measure literary and devotional excellence: "As I walked through the wilderness of this world, I lighted on a certain place where was a den, and I laid me down in that place to sleep, and as I slept I dreamed a dream. I dreamed, and behold I saw a man clothed in rags, standing in a certain place, with his face from his own house, a book in his hand, and a great burden on his back. I looked and saw him open the book, and read therein; and as he read he wept and trembled, and not being able to longer contain, he brake out with a lamentable cry, saying: What shall I do?"

First published on this day in 1678, the vivid allegory detailed the trials and tribulations of a young man named Christian as he made his way through the treacherous world. He was a pilgrim—journeying toward his ultimate home, the Celestial City. Along the way he passed through such tempestuous places as Vanity Fair, the Slough of Despond, Strait Gate, the Hill of Difficulty, Delectable Mountains, By-Path Meadow, Lucre Hill, Doubting Castle, and Mount Caution. Those inhospitable locales were populated by a variety of carefully drawn villains such as Obstinate, Pliable, Mr. Worldly-Wiseman, Mistrust, Timorous, Wanton, Talkative, Envy, Mr. Money-Love, Faint-Heart, and Little-Faith. Despite the fact that he was helped from time to time by a whole host of heroic characters such as Evangelist, Faithful, Good Will, Hopeful, Knowledge, Experience, Watchful, and Sincere, the hapless pilgrim had to struggle through one difficulty or distraction after another. Again and again he was forced to decide between compromise or faithfulness, between accommodation with the world or holy perseverance, between the wide way to destruction or the narrow road to glory. After overcoming a number of chilling risks and hazards, the story was ultimately resolved—like virtually all great classic works of literature—with a happy ending.

NATIONAL DAY
Gambia, Nepal
FEAST DAY
St. Coleman of Lindisfarne, St. Flavian of Jerusalem, St. Simeon of Jerusalem, St. Theotonius, St. Helladius of Toledo

Though written in a coarse, speech-patterned prose—a far cry from the polite literary convention of the seventeenth century—the book was almost immediately acclaimed as a masterpiece of imagination and inspiration. Even those Christians who chafed a bit at Bunyan's gallant Puritan theology, his stalwart Calvinistic doctrine, and his intrepid nonconformist practice readily identified with his beautifully realized vision of life in this poor fallen world. What appeared on the surface to be little more than an episodic series of adventures or a blithe narrative of folk-tale ups and downs was, in fact, a penetrating portrayal of the universal human experience.

Pilgrim's Progress struck a nerve. As literary critic Roger Sharrock said, "A seventeenth-century Calvinist sat down to write a tract and produced a folk-epic of the universal religious imagination instead."

A wise man will make more opportunities than he finds.

[Francis Bacon (1561–1626)]

1478 George, the Duke of Clarence, was murdered in the Tower of London for opposing his brother Edward IV, king of England.

1516 Mary I, known as Bloody Mary for her persecution of Protestants during her reign from 1553 until her death in 1558, was born in Greenwich Palace. She was the first child of Henry VIII and the wife of his youth, Catherine of Aragon—the daughter of the famed Ferdinand of Aragon and Isabella of Castile.

1546 Martin Luther, the German Protestant Reformer, died on this day.

1564 The artist Michelangelo, whose greatest works included the sculptures of the *Pieta, David,* and *Moses,* as well as the paintings covering the ceiling of the Sistine Chapel, died in Rome.

1745 Count Alessandro Volta, the scientist who invented the electric battery and utilized his name for the unit of electromotive force, the volt, was born in Italy.

1861 Jefferson Davis was sworn in as president of the Confederate States of America in Montgomery, Alabama.

1868 The first complete performance of Johannes Brahms's *Ein Deutsches Requiem* (German Requiem) took place in Leipzig. The text was taken from Martin Luther's translation of the Bible. This was the first of more than one hundred performances throughout Europe over the next ten years.

1885 Mark Twain's masterpiece, *The Adventures of Huckleberry Finn,* was published for the first time.

1930 Elm Farm Ollie, a Guernsey cow, flew in an airplane with a group of reporters. During the flight, she was milked, and the milk was parachuted over St. Louis sealed in paper containers.

1930 The planet Pluto was discovered by Clyde William Tombaugh at the Lowell Observatory in Flagstaff, Arizona. Dr. Percival Lowell had mathematically predicted the location of the planet, but did not live to see the confirmation of his predictions.

1953 Lucille Ball and Desi Arnaz received a then-astronomical $8 million contract to continue the *I Love Lucy* television show through 1955.

1986 Despite having lost a leg to cancer, Jeff Keith, a twenty-two-year-old student from Boston College, completed a run across the United States.

18

FEBRUARY

At the Council of Toulouse, held in 1229, the hierarchy of the church had determined that the laity was to be denied direct access to the Scriptures. The assumption was that the masses of people in the church were too ignorant to be trusted with the holy Writ. A century and a half later John Wycliffe openly challenged that notion—and nearly paid with his life.

After earning his doctorate in 1372, Wycliffe was widely regarded as the greatest living philosopher in all of Europe. He was also an eloquent preacher. In passionate sermons, preached not in Latin, but in the English his fellows could understand, he blasted the worldliness of the clergy and the corruptions of the church.

Among the corruptions he challenged were the sale of indulgences, the worship of saints, the veneration of relics, the idleness of monks and priests, the inaccessibility of the Bible, and the empty ritual of many church services. Church authorities lashed back. They summoned Wycliffe on this day in 1377 to a trial at St. Paul's Cathedral. He came with the powerful Prince John of Gaunt—regent of the realm and son of the famed Black Prince. The meeting broke up inconclusively with a violent quarrel between the bishops and the prince.

Apparently though, the confrontation made Wycliffe more determined than ever to bring the Word of God to the common people. He not only began to work on a translation of the Bible in common English, he also trained and sent forth preachers to proclaim its doctrines clearly—these were the men the prelates called Lollards, or "mutterers."

Alas, many of his followers were persecuted and killed. In Bohemia, Jan Hus became a giant of faith from hearing Wycliffe's words. In England, too, his testimony could not be stamped out. Lollards preached for more than a century. Years after his death the church ordered Wycliffe's bones dug up, burned, and scattered. It was too late to undo the good he had done. It is no wonder, then, that he came to be called "The Morning Star of the Reformation."

FEAST DAY
St. Boniface of Lausanne, St. Barbatus, St. Conrad of Piacenza, St. Mesrop

1803   Congress voted to accept Ohio's borders and constitution. Interestingly, Congress did not get around to formally ratifying Ohio statehood until 1953 after the territory had provided the nation with several prominent presidents, congressmen, and federal judges.

I would have everybody able to read, and write, and cipher; indeed I don't think a man can know too much; but mark you, the knowing of these things is not education; and there are millions of your reading and writing people who are as ignorant as neighbor Norton's calf.

[CHARLES H. SPURGEON (1834–1892)]

FEBRUARY

1473 The astronomer Copernicus was born in Torun, Poland. His astronomical observations led him to conclude that the earth revolved around the sun—a rather novel notion at the end of the Medieval Epoch.

1674 The Treaty of Westminster provided for the ceding of American Dutch colonies to British rule.

1807 Former Vice President Aaron Burr was arrested in Alabama. He was subsequently tried for treason. Though he was eventually acquitted, his reputation never recovered, and his public career was ruined.

1846 The Texas state government was formally installed in Austin. It was the second time that an independent nation joined the U.S. as a state—the first was Vermont in 1791.

1878 Thomas Edison received a patent for his phonograph.

1881 Kansas became the first state to prohibit all alcoholic beverages.

1913 The first prize was inserted into a box of Cracker Jacks. It was a spindle jack and ball.

1932 In Oxford, Mississippi, William Faulkner completed work on his classic novel *Light in August.*

1942 President Roosevelt signed an executive order giving the military the authority to relocate and intern Japanese Americans. Later, German Americans were also forced to spend the war years in the prisonlike camps.

1942 About 150 Japanese warplanes attacked the Australian city of Darwin.

1945 Nearly thirty thousand U.S. Marines landed on Iwo Jima, where they began a bloody monthlong battle to seize control of the Pacific island from Japanese forces.

1951 Andre Gide died in Paris at the age of eighty-one. He had arranged to have a telegram sent to the Sorbonne a few days after his death—with his signature attached. It read, "Hell doesn't exist. Better notify Claudel." Paul Claudel was a poet who had attempted to share the gospel with Gide over the previous decade. Sadly, it was too late for Gide to change either the veracity of the note, or its irony.

1959 An agreement was signed by Britain, Turkey, and Greece granting the bitterly disputed Mediterranean island of Cyprus its independence.

1960 The comic strip *Family Circus* by Bil Keane appeared for the first time.

1997 Deng Xiaoping, the last of China's major Communist revolutionaries, died.

19

FEBRUARY

20

FEAST DAY
St. Eleutherius of Tournai, St. Eucharius of Orléans, St. Tyranno, St. Zenobius, St. Wulfric

In 1947 a Palestinian Bedouin was tending his flocks in the desolate hills adjacent to the Dead Sea. As he was whiling the hours away, he poked his head into a small cave and accidentally stumbled across a few ancient-looking pots. They were filled with some old scrolls covered in archaic writing.

Thinking that the leaves might be of some value, he took them to Khalil Iskander, an antiques dealer in Jerusalem. He thought they might be a curiosity that a collector or perhaps even a museum might buy. Iskander supposed they were probably Syrian and thus they had some value, but not too terribly much. Nevertheless, before he sold them he decided to consult with a friend who was a manuscript expert. The friend was slightly more interested and spoke to Orthodox Archbishop Athanasius Yeshua Samuel about the find. Also interested, the archbishop asked to see the scrolls. Almost at once he recognized that the scrolls contained portions of the Old Testament. Unable to suppress his excitement, he immediately made arrangements to purchase them from Iskander. Even so, he was not entirely sure what he had purchased.

The archbishop began showing the parchments to a number of experts. His own archivist believed them to be very old, but was uncertain about their ultimate value. Most of the other experts who viewed them, however, believed that they were basically worthless. Months passed in which his efforts to learn the value of the scrolls were thwarted. In desperation, he contacted the American University of Beirut. There he met John Trever, a careful biblical scholar who was trained in photographing old scrolls. Trever was intrigued.

On this day in 1948, Trever saw the scrolls for the first time and was certain that the find was quite significant. After photographing the leaves of the scrolls, he sent the images out to the best paleographers in the world. In short order, it became evident that the scrolls were older than any other portion of Scripture yet discovered—dating from sometime around 100 B.C. Significant, indeed.

Soon the whole world was electrified with the announcement of the Dead Sea Scrolls. Not only did they confirm the accuracy of the Old Testament, but they also shed light on the years just before Christ's coming. They turned out to be the greatest archaeological discovery of the twentieth century.

Forewarned, forearmed; to be prepared is half the victory. Wisdom comes of such a recognition.

[MIGUEL DE CERVANTES (1547–1616)]

1790 Holy Roman Emperor Joseph II died, leaving a leadership vacuum that would eventually result in a series of calamitous Enlightenment revolutions that would bring to an end the *ancien régime* of Christendom.

1790 Karl Czerny, the pianist, composer, and piano teacher, was born in Austria. Czerny was a pupil of Ludwig van Beethoven and the teacher of pianist and composer Franz Liszt. His teaching etudes are still used by piano instructors.

1792 President George Washington signed an act creating the United States Postal Service.

1809 The Supreme Court ruled that the power of the federal government is greater than that of any individual state—a notion construed by many as a direct contradiction of the Tenth Amendment and the ultimate cause of the bitter War Between the States.

1816 Gioacchino Rossini's opera masterpiece, *The Barber of Seville*, was first performed at the Argentina Teatro in Rome. Rossini's version is the most famous of the five opera settings of the Pierre Beaumarchais plays; however, the first performance was met with bitter resentment as the public was overly fond of a now-forgotten version by Paisiello from twenty-five years before.

1839 Dueling was prohibited in the District of Columbia by an act of Congress.

1852 Emily Dickinson's mock Valentine, "Sic Transit," appeared in the *Springfield Republican*.

1872 Cyrus Baldwin received a patent for a vertical-geared hydraulic electric elevator that was installed in a New York hotel.

1872 In New York City, the Metropolitan Museum of Art was opened to the public.

1872 A machine for manufacturing square-bottomed paper bags was patented by Luther Crowell.

1895 Abolitionist and statesman Frederick Douglass died in Washington, D.C., leaving a void in African-American leadership—a void that would only be filled by the emergence of Booker T. Washington during the succeeding decade.

1902 Renowned nature photographer Ansel Adams was born in San Francisco. In opposition to the art world of the 1930s, Adams photographed outstanding landscapes of primarily the American Southwest. In addition, he wrote technical manuals for photography and helped to found the first museum and college photography departments.

1933 The House of Representatives completed congressional action on an amendment to repeal Prohibition.

1944 The syndicated comic strip *Batman and Robin* made its debut in newspapers around the country.

1950 Dylan Thomas arrived in New York for his first series of American poetry readings.

1962 Colonel John Glenn orbited the earth three times, becoming the first American astronaut and the first man to orbit the earth more than once. He traveled in the Mercury space capsule *Friendship 7*.

20

FEBRUARY

21

FEAST DAY
St. Robert Southwell, St. Peter
Damian, St. George of Amastris,
St. Germanus of Granfel

James Monroe was the last of the Southern aristocrats of the Virginia dynasty to serve as president. The man who succeeded him was the last of the Northern aristocrats of the Massachusetts dynasty—the Adams family of Braintree. For John Quincy Adams (1767–1848), though not born to the purple, was born to the red, white, and blue.

He literally grew up with the country—as a boy he watched the Battle of Bunker Hill from a hill near home; at fourteen he served as secretary to the minister to Russia; at sixteen he was secretary at the treaty ending the Revolution; and he later held more offices than any earlier president.

The only son of a president to reach that office during the first two centuries of American history, Adams followed a career that closely resembled his father's—both attended Harvard, studied law, and were successful ministers and peace commissioners in Europe; both were elected president for only one term; both became involved in party conflicts and spent their least-successful years in the White House.

Studious and crotchety, Adams was more successful as a diplomat and statesman than as a politician. As Monroe's secretary of state he negotiated with the Spanish for Florida and was largely responsible for the document that became known as the Monroe Doctrine.

In the unusual election of 1824, four Democrat-Republicans contended for the presidency. Andrew Jackson received almost fifty thousand votes more than Adams, but less than the required majority. The decision thus rested with the House of Representatives, and when Henry Clay threw his support to Adams, the House elected Adams. Jackson felt cheated. The strong feeling that developed between Jackson and Adams ruined Adams's administration and finally drove the two men into separate parties—Adams to the National Republicans and Jackson to the Democrats.

Adams was more successful in Congress, where he served his last seventeen years. There he distinguished himself by his dedicated fight to remove the "gag rule," which prevented Congress from considering any antislavery petitions. He won the freedom of slave mutineers aboard the ship *Amistad,* persuaded Congress to accept the gift of James Smithson to set up a national museum, the Smithsonian Institution, and helped to establish a fund for a national observatory. After fourteen years of struggle he finally won. But his service did not end until he collapsed on the floor of Congress on this day in 1848, sixty-six years after he first served his country at his father's side.

The next best thing to being wise oneself is to live in a circle of those who are.

[C. S. LEWIS (1898–1963)]

1594 After three years of imprisonment and torture, Robert Southwell, the English religious poet and Jesuit martyr, was hanged, drawn, and quartered at Tyburn. He was arrested in 1592 while celebrating Mass and was tried for treason under the anti-Catholic laws of 1585. His poetry is infused with simplicity and directness and is related to the later Metaphysical poetry by its use of paradox and striking images.

1791 The Presidential Succession Act was approved by Congress and provided for the succession to the office of president and vice president in case of removal, death, resignation, or disability.

1801 Cardinal John Henry Newman was born in London, England. During his days as a student at Oxford University, he helped to organize and became the leader of the Oxford Movement, and attempted to reform the Church of England. He left the Anglican church and joined the Roman Catholic Church on October 9, 1845, after resigning his position as vicar of St. Mary's, Oxford. An influential man of letters, he wrote a number of hymns and books including the eloquent *Apologia pro Vita Sua* (1864) and *The Idea of the University* (1880). He died in Birmingham, Warwick, England, on August 11, 1890.

1866 Lucy B. Hobbs became the first woman to graduate from a dental school, the Ohio College of Dental Surgery in Cincinnati.

1878 The first telephone directory, which included the names of fifty subscribers, was issued by the New Haven Connecticut Telephone Company.

1885 The soaring monolith of the Washington Monument was dedicated on the Washington Mall between the Capitol and the White House.

1893 Andrés Segovia, the pioneer of classical guitar techniques who was famous for his renditions of art music transcriptions as well as the revival of interest in his instrument, was born in Spain.

1905 Wystan Hugh Auden, the English poet and man of letters, was born in York, Yorkshire, England. His first book of poetry was published in 1924, the year before he entered Christ Church, Oxford. After graduating in 1928, Auden spent a year in Berlin and the next five years as a school master in England and Scotland. His early poems and dramas were experimental and leftist in conception. In the late 1930s and early 1940s Auden's longer poems, *For the Time Being (A Christmas Oratorio)*, *The Sea and the Mirror*, and *The Age of Anxiety* (winner of the Pulitzer Prize in 1948), reflected his move toward Christianity. His final years consisted of literary criticism, working as an editor, and translating poetry. He died in Vienna, Austria, on September 29, 1973.

1916 The decisive Battle of Verdun during the First World War began in France.

1925 The venerable literary magazine *The New Yorker* made its debut.

1931 Alka-Seltzer was introduced as a new "cure-all remedy" and "digestive aid."

1947 Inventor Edwin H. Land publicly demonstrated his Polaroid Land camera, which could produce a black-and-white photograph in sixty seconds.

1953 The double helix structure of the DNA molecule was discovered by Francis Crick and James Watson.

1965 Former Black Muslim leader Malcolm X was shot to death in New York by assassins identified as Black Muslims. He was thirty-nine years old.

FEBRUARY

Though a number of prominent generals had occupied the White House—from George Washington to Andrew Jackson—tobacco-chewing General Zachary Taylor (1784–1850) was the first regular army man to become president. It was solely on the strength of his popularity as a military hero that the Whigs chose him in 1848; never had a candidate known less about government, law, or politics. "Old Rough and Ready" had practically no formal education, had spent his entire life moving from one army post to another, and had never voted in an election in his life.

Commissioned a first lieutenant in the infantry in 1808, he served in almost every war and skirmish for the next forty years. As a young captain in the War of 1812 he showed himself a cool and courageous leader; he won further recognition in the wars with the Black Hawks and Seminoles in later years.

But it was his dramatic success in leading the American forces against the Mexican army in 1846–47 that caught the imagination of the American people and made him a national hero. In battle after battle he defeated the Mexicans—at Palo Alto, Reseca de la Palma, and Monterrey—and then on February 22, 1847, he won his greatest victory at Buena Vista when his troops routed a large army led by General Santa Anna.

In the White House, Taylor saw his job as the civilian counterpart of a military commander; untutored in politics, he tried to remain nonpartisan, to leave legislative matters to Congress and simply execute the laws himself. But running the government proved more complex: Before long he became embroiled in the issue that haunted the country—slavery.

Although unskilled in politics, he was a forthright and determined leader: When Southern congressmen threatened trouble over the admission of California as a free state, Taylor, who owned slaves himself, warned that he would lead the army against them and hang any who resisted as traitors. Thus the hero of the Mexican War, who died unexpectedly on this day in 1850, proved that, for all his lack of skill, he yet was able to take a stand on the issue the country dreaded facing. No successor until Lincoln was to show such courage.

1732 According to the New Style (Gregorian) calendar, George Washington, who became the first president under the current U.S. Constitution, was born at his parents' plantation in the Virginia Colony near Bridge's Creek. Throughout his life, though, he celebrated his birthday on February 11, in accordance with the Old Style Calendar.

If your ship doesn't come in, swim out to it.

[ANDY TANT (1980–1996)]

1630 Quadequina, brother of Massosoit, brought popped corn in a deerskin bag to the colonists at the first Thanksgiving dinner.

1819 Spain ceded Florida to the United States.

1819 Poet, essayist, and diplomat James Russell Lowell was born in Cambridge, Massachusetts.

1857 Lord Robert Baden-Powell, a former soldier who was the founder of the Boy Scouts in 1908, was born in Britain. The foundation of the Boy Scouts was the chivalric code as synthesized by St. Benedict.

1876 Johns Hopkins University was founded in Baltimore, Maryland.

1879 Frank Winfield Woolworth opened the first five-cent store in Utica, New York. Disappointing sales of as little as $2.50 a day led Woolworth to move his store to Lancaster, Pennsylvania, in June of that year, where the idea proved successful. Eventually, he was able to build a commercial empire that proved to be the first international retail conglomerate.

1882 Engraver, writer, and typographer Eric Gill was born in Brighton, England. A passionate convert to Christianity and a protégé of G. K. Chesterton and Hilaire Belloc, Gill's designs—including Perpetua, Bunyan, and Gill Sans Serif—are now used all over the world.

1889 President Grover Cleveland signed a bill to admit the new states of the Dakotas, Montana, and Washington into the Federal Union.

1892 *Lady Windermere's Fan,* by Oscar Wilde, was first performed at London's St. James's Theater.

1892 Edna St. Vincent Millay was born in Rockland, Maine

1924 President Calvin Coolidge, known as "Silent Cal," delivered the first presidential radio broadcast from the White House.

1954 Billy Graham began a three-month long evangelistic crusade in London—filling an 11,000-seat arena every night of the crusade. Though he had received negative publicity in the press, wherever Graham went he was mobbed by crowds. Extra meetings had to be scheduled. Londoners sang hymns in the subways. More than two million people attended the meetings. Thousands came to Christ. Winston Churchill met Billy and, in private, received the gospel. That London crusade did much to establish Mr. Graham's international ministry, which continued to expand over the next four decades.

1973 The United States and Communist China agreed to establish liaison offices.

1980 In a stunning upset, the United States Olympic hockey team defeated the Soviets at Lake Placid, New York, 4-3. The U.S. team went on to win the gold medal.

1987 Pop artist Andy Warhol died at a New York City hospital at age fifty-eight.

22

FEBRUARY

The historical origins of Mardi Gras are much debated, but many of its traditions seem to have their roots in early Celtic Christian rituals in ancient Gaul, Ireland, and Scotland—which, in turn, seem to have even earlier Greek and Egyptian antecedents. Mardi Gras, or Fat Tuesday, was a celebration of life's excesses before the austere self-sacrifices of the Christian season of Lent. It received its name from the tradition of slaughtering and feasting upon a fattened calf on the last day of the Winter Carnival that followed the Twelfth Night, or Epiphany.

Lent began on Ash Wednesday, forty days before Easter, and included a much more proscribed lifestyle for faithful Christian families—traditionally a season of severe fasting and asceticism. The day prior to Ash Wednesday was thus the final hurrah, and excesses frowned upon at any other time of the year were actually embraced and exulted.

The ancient Mardi Gras tradition was first brought to the New World by the French, and it became a vital component of the culture settlers established along the Gulf Coast. Though it is most often associated with the city of New Orleans, all throughout the region, festive carousers celebrate during the two weeks before the beginning of Lent with parades, balls, masquerades, street dances, concerts, amusements, jocularity, and merry banquets.

In 1682, French explorer Robert Cavalier, Sieur de la Salle, claimed the region from where the Mississippi drained into the ocean all the way to Pensacola Bay in the name of King Louis XIV of France. Spanish explorers had already discovered the region, but abandoned it when they failed to discover gold. La Salle attempted to return to the region two years later, but ended up in Texas instead. He spent the next two years searching for his discovery—a search that ended when his men finally murdered him.

War prevented France from continuing its colonization efforts until 1697. King Louis XIV then commissioned a Canadian, Pierre le Moyne, Sieur D'Iberville, to secure a colony and French interests in the region. Iberville's flotilla finally landed on this day, twelve miles off the Mississippi Gulf Coast, and he established his headquarters on the site of present-day Ocean Springs, Mississippi. The following spring, he built a fort near present-day Phoenix, Louisiana—the first permanent French colony on the Gulf Coast.

But ongoing wars and other concerns kept the attentions of King Louis away from the New World. When he died in 1715, he was succeeded in name by his five-year-old great-grandson, and in practice by Philippe, Duke of Orleans, who served as regent for the young king. One of the regent's friends was John Law, who devised a get-rich-quick strategy of promoting Louisiana's riches. The scheme virtually bankrupted France, but not before the dramatic expansion of the colony and the founding of New Orleans, Biloxi, Mobile, and Pensacola in the spring of 1718.

Progress in the new towns was slow, but Mardi Gras festivities are believed to have begun in their earliest days. It provided them with a sense of cultural cohesion and identity. Indeed, it seemed that early on the Mardi Gras of the colonies took on a character and a flavor it never had back in France.

We have been slobbered upon by those who have chewed the mad root's poison, a poison that penetrates to the spirit and rots the soul.

[ANDREW NELSON LYTLE (1902–1995)]

303   After more than eighteen years of laissez-faire rule, the Roman emperor Diocletian instituted a number of reforms aimed at reviving the sprawling political entity he was responsible to oversee. He reorganized the provinces and made the army more mobile while increasing its size. To battle inflation, he issued a new coinage, established a uniform system of taxation, and implemented wage-price controls. In addition, he launched a massive crackdown on the burgeoning church—believing that the loyalty of Christians could not be counted on. All this was put into effect on this day in 303. In the persecution that followed, church leaders were dragged off and tortured to death. Christian books and Scriptures were burned. The rack, the scourge, slow fires, crucifixion, and every other barbarity was employed against the faithful. In the end however, the blood of the martyrs proved to be the seed of the faith—the church only proved its mettle and as a consequence, grew by leaps and bounds.

1633   Samuel Pepys was born in London, England. In 1660, he began keeping his famous diary that gave an honest picture of life in the upper-class during Restoration England. He chronicled the coronation of Charles II, the plague, and the Great Fire of London. He amassed a great library in his later years, which he left to Magdalene College, Cambridge, at his death on May 26, 1703, in London.

1685   Composer George Frideric Handel was born in Halle, Germany. Handel was best known for his *Water Music, Music for the Royal Fireworks,* and his numerous oratorios including *Israel in Egypt* and *Messiah.*

1820   Famed Romantic lyric poet John Keats died in Rome at the age of twenty-five of tuberculosis. He had gone to Rome with his friend Joseph Severn to escape the winter. His most famous poems include *Lamia, The Eve of St. Agnes, Ode on a Grecian Urn, Ode to a Nightingale, To Autumn,* and *Hyperion.*

1836   The siege of the Alamo began in San Antonio during the struggle for control of Texas. Though Mexican forces under the dictator Santa Anna ultimately slaughtered the entire force of Texan defenders, the massacre served to rally Texans elsewhere, and they eventually won their independence.

1847   U.S. troops under General Zachary Taylor defeated Mexican general Santa Anna at the Battle of Buena Vista in Mexico. The confrontation served as the first battlefield experience for many of the men, who would later square off against one another in the War Between the States.

1848   Former President John Quincy Adams died of a stroke at age eighty while still serving in the House of Representatives.

1861   President-elect Abraham Lincoln arrived secretly in Washington to take office, an assassination plot having been foiled in Baltimore.

1896   Leo Hirshfield introduced the chewy chocolate candy the Tootsie Roll.

1945   Joe Rosenthal, an Associated Press photographer, captured the drama of the moment when six members of the U.S. Marines raised the American flag over the Pacific Island of Iwo Jima. The scene was later immortalized in a bronze monument in Washington, D.C.

1954   In Pittsburgh, the first mass inoculation of children against polio with Jonas Salk's revolutionary vaccine began just as a massive epidemic of the dread disease was sweeping across the nation.

FEBRUARY

A tall Virginia gentleman, John Tyler (1790–1862) was the first vice president to complete the unexpired term of a president, but it is almost certain that the Whigs would never have chosen him as their vice-presidential candidate had they known he was to serve all but a month of Harrison's term. By the time he acceded to the highest office in the land "Honest John" had clearly demonstrated that he was not a party man: During his years in Washington as a nominally Democratic congressman and senator he had followed such an independent course—fighting the Missouri Compromise, fighting high tariffs, fighting Jackson—that it finally led him, by 1833, out of the Democratic Party altogether; yet his views on states' rights and on strict construction of the Constitution would never permit him to be at home with the Whigs.

Nevertheless, the Whigs had nominated him, and after Harrison's death they had to live with him—as their chief executive. It is not surprising that Tyler's years in the White House were tempestuous ones. When his stand on states' rights led him to veto a bill for a Bank of the United States, every member of Harrison's original cabinet except Daniel Webster promptly resigned, and Webster, as secretary of state, was at the time deeply involved in settling the northeastern boundary dispute with Great Britain. Tyler further alienated the Whigs by repudiating the spoils system and refusing to replace some well-qualified Democratic ministers abroad. Throughout his term he was unable to work in harmony with the Whig majority in Congress, who were led by Henry Clay, the actual political leader of the party. They did agree with Tyler, however, on the annexation of Texas, which was accomplished in the final days of Tyler's term. But in the election of 1844 only an irregular Democratic convention nominated Tyler, and he withdrew before election.

At a time when political parties were emerging as powers on the national political scene, John Tyler left the White House, a president without a party. But even though he had no party, he said he still had "plenty of principle and a clear conscience, things many party men are never able to enjoy."

At the end of his life he worked to forge a compromise with fire-eaters from both the North and the South who he feared might wreck the nation over the issues of nullification and secession. He chaired a peace conference attended by twenty-one states on this day in 1861, but was unable to negotiate a settlement and war broke out a short time later. He subsequently served in the Confederate Congress until his death a year later.

FEAST DAY
St. Praetextatus; Saints Montanus, Lucius, and their Companions

Indifference in questions of importance is no amiable quality.

[SAMUEL JOHNSON (1709–1784)]

FEBRUARY

1582 Because the Julian calendar—promulgated by Julius Caesar—made the year too long by several minutes, the calendar was displaced by three full days every 400 years. By the middle of the sixteenth century it was out of sequence with the equinoxes by a full ten days and with the original dates by fourteen days. The energetic and Reform-minded Pope Gregory XIII was not one to let the problem continue indefinitely. He determined to correct the calendar and on February 24, 1582, acting on the recommendations of a special council, issued a bull requiring all Catholic countries to follow October 4 with October 15 that year. To illiterate people, it seemed as if eleven days had actually been stolen from them and panic ensued. The new Gregorian calendar was only reluctantly adopted by countries around the world during the next three centuries, but eventually, it became the standard measurement for the passing of time.

1766 Samuel Wesley, organist and composer and the younger son of Charles Wesley, the hymn writer, was born in England.

1786 Wilhelm Grimm, younger brother of Jakob Grimm, with whom he wrote fairy tales, was born in Hanau, Germany. Some of their most famous tales were "Rapunzel," "Hansel and Gretel," "Cinderella," "Snow White," and "Rumplestiltskin."

1803 The United States Supreme Court ruled that it was the final authority with regard to issues of constitutional interpretation in Marbury vs. Madison.

1821 Mexico declared its independence from Spain.

1863 Arizona was organized as a federal territory.

1868 The House of Representatives impeached President Andrew Johnson following his attempted dismissal of Secretary of War Edwin M. Stanton—an ignominy shared by only one other administration in history. Johnson was later acquitted by the Senate.

1903 The United States signed an agreement acquiring a naval station at Guantanamo Bay in Cuba—a controversial foothold on the island that remains to this day.

1942 *The Voice of America* went on the air for the first time.

1945 American soldiers liberated the Philippine capital of Manila from Japanese control during World War II.

1955 Cole Porter's musical *Silk Stockings* opened at the Imperial Theater on Broadway.

1981 Buckingham Palace announced the engagement of Britain's Prince Charles to Lady Diana Spencer.

1988 In a ruling that was roundly denounced by civil libertarians and conservative family advocates alike, the Supreme Court overturned a $200,000 award that the Reverend Jerry Falwell had won against *Hustler* magazine and publisher Larry Flynt for a lewd and libelous parody.

FEBRUARY

NATIONAL DAY
Kuwait
FEAST DAY
St. Ethelbert of Kent, St. Walburga,
St. Gerland, St. Louis Versiglia, St.
Caesarius of Nazianzen, St.
Calixto Caravario

Unique among the Founding Fathers, John Marshall (1755–1835) was a young officer in the Continental army who played only a minor role in the Revolution. He did not contribute to, or sign, either the Declaration of Independence or the Constitution. But, as chief justice of the Supreme Court, he did perhaps more than any other man to institutionalize the new national government by establishing the authority of the Court as co-equal with the Legislative and Executive branches, and by clarifying the fundamental relationship between the States and the national government. Contributions of such magnitude place John Marshall among the first rank of the nation's founders.

Although Marshall was only a junior officer in the Revolution—he fought at Brandywine, Germantown, and Monmouth, and endured Valley Forge—his experience in the war led him to see the need for a strong national government, for he believed that a stronger, better-organized government might have more effectively managed the limited resources available to the colonies to wage war. In addition, his military service provided the kind of experience that permitted him to think in national terms.

Raised in the near wilderness of the frontier, Marshall was thrust into the world of the Continental army as a teenager. Later he acknowledged that he became an American before he had had a chance to become a Virginian. In the 1790s Marshall was well established as a leader of the Federalists in Virginia. He declined President Washington's offer of the position of Attorney General; he publicly defended the Jay Treaty; and on this day in 1797 he was appointed by President Adams as a commissioner to France—for what became known as the XYZ Affair.

When Marshall was appointed Chief Justice, the Supreme Court stood far below the Executive and Legislative branches in power and prestige. By sheer force of intellect he produced decisions that won wide approval from constitutional lawyers, associates on the Court, and eventually American citizens generally. He was so successful, so inevitably right in many of his views, that he made the Court the recognized interpreter of the Constitution. From 1801 to 1835 he delivered the opinion in more than five hundred cases, over twenty-five of which were fundamental constitutional questions. Marshall's influence on our system was so great that the Constitution as we know it is, in large measure, Marshall's interpretation of it. A century and a half later, Marshall is still considered foremost of constitutional lawyers. According to a contemporary, Judge Jeremiah Mason, without Marshall's monumental efforts the government of the new nation "would have fallen to pieces."

There are, indeed, many truths which time necessarily and certainly teaches, and which might, by those who have learned them from experience, be communicated to their successors at a cheaper rate: but dictates, though liberally enough bestowed, are generally without effect, the teacher gains few proselytes by instruction which his own behavior contradicts; and young men miss the benefit of counsel, because they are not very ready to believe that those who fall below them in practice, can much excel them in theory. Thus the progress of knowledge is retarded, the world is kept long in the same state, and every new race is to gain the prudence of their predecessors by committing and redressing the same miscarriages.

FEBRUARY

[SAMUEL JOHNSON (1709–1784)]

1570   Pope Pius V excommunicated England's Queen Elizabeth I for embracing the Protestantism of her father.

1723   Famed architect Sir Christopher Wren, who helped to rebuild London after the Great Fire as well as design many other buildings in London, Oxford, and throughout England, died at the age of ninety. He was buried over the interior of the north door in his renowned St. Paul's Cathedral, London. His son provided the inscription, which reads, "Si monumentum requiris, circumspice"—"If you would seek his monument, look around."

1792   George Washington met with the United States government department heads at his home, Mount Vernon, in what was the first cabinet meeting.

1836   Inventor Samuel Colt patented his revolver.

1841   French impressionist painter Pierre Auguste Renoir—famous for *A Girl with a Watering Can, The Umbrellas, Luncheon at the Boating Party, Dance at the Moulin de la Galette, La Loge,* and numerous other distinctive paintings—was born in Limoges, France.

1873   The world-renowned operatic tenor Enrico Caruso was born in Naples, Italy. Regarded for his excellent interpretations of roles by Verdi and Puccini as well as others, the range, beauty, and power of his voice made him one of the greatest tenors of all time. He sang more than fifty roles

in the United States, Latin America, and Europe.

1899   Paul Julius Reuter, founder of the British news agency that bears his name, died in Nice, France.

1901   United States Steel Corporation was incorporated by J. P. Morgan.

1919   Oregon became the first state to tax gasoline.

1924   In honor of the birth of renowned operatic tenor Enrico Caruso in 1873, his hometown of Naples, Italy, started the tradition of lighting the world's largest candle. It is dedicated to his memory and is eighteen feet high and seven feet in circumference. It is expected to last through 1,800 years of birthday celebrations.

1948   With the military aid of the Soviet Union, Communists seized power in Czechoslovakia.

1950   *Your Show of Shows* made its television debut on NBC.

1986   President Ferdinand E. Marcos fled the Philippines after twenty years of dictatorial rule in the wake of a tainted election. Corazon Aquino assumed the presidency in the wake of new democratic elections.

1990   Nicaraguans went to the polls in an election that resulted in an upset victory for opponents of the ruling Communist Sandinistas. International pressure, particularly from Britain and America, ensured a peaceful transition to democratic rule.

FEBRUARY

In 1821, Dr. John Rippon, pastor of the New Park Street Chapel in Southwark, London, began a ministry to the homeless poor. A complex of almshouses was erected on a property adjacent to the church and the monumental task of rehabilitation was begun. Rippon wrote, "Christian compassion is driven by a holy and zealous compulsion when sight be caught of deprived distress. Talk not of mild and gentle acts, of soft provisions and hesitant walk. Christian compassion knows only boldness and sacrifice. Lest we strike the Judas bargain and go the way of the goats, let us invite the strangers in. Let us shelter the aliens beneath a covering of charity and Christlikeness."

When Charles Haddon Spurgeon succeeded Rippon in the pastorate of New Park Street Chapel in 1854, the work with the poor continued unabated. When the church moved to larger facilities in 1861, it was apparent to Spurgeon that the almshouses, too, would need to be moved into larger and more up-to-date facilities. Therefore, he launched the construction of a new building for them. According to press reports at the time, "No greater effort has ever been expended on behalf of the city's destitute."

The new structure consisted of seventeen small homes, which, in the manner of the times, were joined together in an unbroken row. There, in home-style fashion, the poor were not only sheltered, but also provided with food, clothing, and other necessities. In succeeding years, a school, an orphanage, and a hospital were added, each an expression of that holy and zealous compulsion: Christian compassion.

Both Rippon and Spurgeon looked upon their work of sheltering the homeless as part and parcel with the rest of their ministry. It was inseparable from their other labors: preaching, writing, praying, and evangelizing. It was inseparable, in fact, from their faith in Christ.

On this day in 1870, a renowned doubter accosted Spurgeon on a London thoroughfare and challenged the authenticity of his faith. Spurgeon answered the man by pointing out the failure of the secularists in mounting practical and consistent programs to help the needy thousands of the city. In contrast, he pointed to the multitudinous works of compassion that had sprung from faith in Christ: Whitefield's mission, Mueller's orphanage, Jamison's hospice, Chalmers's poor school, Bernardo's shelter, Welch's job corps, and Martin's hospital. He then closed the conversation by paraphrasing the victorious cry of Elijah, boisterously asserting, "The God who answereth by orphanages, let Him be God!"

FEAST DAY
St. Alexander of Alexandria, St. Porphyry of Gaza, St. Nestor of Magydus, St. Victor the Hermit

1870

New York City's first attempt at a subway line opened. The single car was propelled like a sailboat by means of a rotary blower to create wind. The fare was 23 cents.

Every great nation owes to the men whose lives have formed part of its greatness not merely the material effect of what they did, not merely the laws they placed upon the statute books or the victories they won over armed foes, but also the immense but indefinable moral influence produced by their deeds and words themselves upon the national character.

[THEODORE ROOSEVELT (1858–1919)]

398 Against his own wishes, John Chrysostom was pressed into service as the bishop of Constantinople.

1802 Victor-Marie Hugo, poet, dramatist, and author of *The Hunchback of Notre Dame* (1831) and *Les Misérables* (1862), was born in Besançon, France. By the time of his death on May 22, 1885, in Paris, he was a national hero and was buried in the Panthéon.

1815 Napoleon Bonaparte escaped from the Island of Elba to begin his second conquest of France. His bid to recover his former glory ended at the Battle of Waterloo.

1846 Wild West personality William F. "Buffalo Bill" Cody was born in Scott County, Iowa. He left home at the age of eleven and worked herding cattle, driving a wagon train, trapping fur, mining for gold, riding for the Pony Express, and scouting for the army. His Wild West show was a display of skill and daring that captured the imaginations of Americans. In 1887, Cody and his show were invited to be the main American attraction at Queen Victoria's Golden Jubilee celebration. Visited by nobility, royalty, and commoners, Cody was credited with improving relations between the English and the United States.

1848 The Second French Republic was proclaimed following the failure of the revived Bourbon monarchy.

1919 Congress established the Grand Canyon as a national park.

1929 President Calvin Coolidge signed a measure establishing Grand Teton National Park.

1932 Country music performer Johnny Cash—known as the Man in Black—was born.

1940 The United States Air Defense Command was created. Just over a year later, the airspace of the nation was penetrated in a massive surprise attack by Japanese warplanes on Pearl Harbor.

1951 In the wake of nearly a decade and a half of Franklin Roosevelt's rule, the Twenty-second Amendment to the Constitution was ratified. It limited a president to two terms of office.

1952 Prime Minister Winston Churchill announced that Britain had developed its own atomic bomb.

1986 Robert Penn Warren, one of the original Southern Agrarians, became the first poet laureate of the United States.

26

FEBRUARY

Henry Meldith (1544–1572) was a young Huguenot pastor in central Navarre renowned for both his boldness in preaching and his humility of bearing. During the early days of the Reformation—when passions were high and tempers were short—he taught his congregation discretion and long-suffering through an exercise of the basic biblical disciplines of prayer and fasting. In a society riven by political and theological strife, they were able to build bridges of reconciliation.

Meldith himself became a legate to Henry of Navarre, who eventually assumed the throne of France. He carried a message of humility, faithfulness, and quiet obedience to the great Conference of Poissy on this day in 1561 and again to the Conference of New Rochelle in 1571. Several accounts of those meetings note the powerful influence his prayerful attitude and life of discipline had upon the other attendees.

That he was accidentally killed in the riotous St. Bartholomew's Day Massacre in Paris the following year probably sealed the fate of the Huguenot community more than any other single event. The still-wavering king lamented his death as "the loss of France's humblest Christian."

FEAST DAY
St. Alnoth, St. Herefrith of Louth,
St. Leander of Seville

1807

American poet Henry Wadsworth Longfellow was born in Portland, Massachusetts (now in Maine). He was the first American poet to earn a living solely from the writing of verse. He traveled to Germany in 1835 and was greatly influenced by German Romanticism. While presiding over the modern-language program at Harvard for eighteen years, Longfellow wrote *The Wreck of the Hesperus* and *Evangeline,* which became a popular favorite. Later works included *Hiawatha, Paul Revere's Ride,* and *Christus: A Mystery*—a trilogy relating the history of Christianity from its beginnings. Longfellow died on March 24, 1882, in Cambridge, Massachusetts.

1902

American author John Steinbeck, best known for his social criticism in such works as *The Grapes of Wrath* (1939), *The Red Pony* (1937), *Cannery Row* (1945), *The Pearl* (1947), and *East of Eden* (1952), was born in Salinas, California. In 1962, he received the Nobel Prize for literature. He died on December 20, 1968, in New York City.

My son, ill-gotten gains do not profit, but righteousness delivers from death. The Lord will not allow the righteous to hunger, but He will thrust aside the craving of the wicked. Poor is he who works with a negligent hand, but the hand of the diligent makes rich. The soul of the sluggard craves and gets nothing, but the soul of the diligent is made fat. Wealth obtained by fraud dwindles, but the one who gathers by labor increases it. A man can do nothing better than find satisfaction in his work.

[KING SOLOMON (C. 1000 B.C.)]

FEBRUARY

304 Barlaam of Antioch was a cobbler for the Imperial forces who devoted all his free time to the care of orphans and widows in his church. Because he himself had been saved from the infanticide wall outside the city, he was especially concerned for exposed children. Even though he was not a pastor or church leader, his good deeds were so widely known that the enemies of the faith sought to have his witness silenced. During a period of calamitous persecutions, they succeeded in having him martyred on this day.

304 George of Diospolis, patron of both England and Lebanon, was a Christian soldier who gained fame after several daring rescues of children in distress. He was known as the "Dragonslayer" not so much because of exploits with rare and dangerous reptiles, but because of his willingness to snatch innocent life out of the jaws of death. Eventually, he, too, fell victim to Diocletion's wrath in the persecution of 304, and was beheaded in Nicomedia. Later, innumerable legends made much of his exploits—associating him romantically with damsels and dragons—but it was his willingness to risk all for the sake of the sanctity of life that earned him his place in history.

380 Although it was the emperor Constantine who legitimized Christianity after his conversion, it was one of his successors, Theodosius, who made Christianity the official faith of the empire on this day. The Theodosian Codes and Edicts were the first attempt to substantially codify the Christian faith in the wider culture.

1801 Congress established jurisdiction of the District of Columbia. With donations from the states of Maryland and Virginia, the land along the banks of the Potomac River was the site of the nation's new capital city.

1848 Following the Communist revolutions that shook all the monarchies of Europe, Louis-Philippe, the last of the Bourbon kings of France, abdicated the throne and a republic was proclaimed.

1879 Constantine Fahlberg of Johns Hopkins University discovered the artificial sweetener saccharin.

1910 Comic writer Peter de Vries was born in Chicago. He stated the obvious, saying, "I love being a writer; it's the paperwork I can't stand."

1922 The Supreme Court unanimously upheld the Nineteenth Amendment to the Constitution, which guaranteed the right of women to vote.

1933 Germany's Parliament Building, the Reichstag, caught fire. The National Socialist Party—best known as the Nazis—blamed the Communists and used the fire as a pretext for suspending civil liberties, thus tightening their control over the nation.

1973 Members of the American Indian Movement occupied the hamlet of Wounded Knee in South Dakota, the site of the 1890 massacre of Sioux men, women, and children. The occupation lasted until May.

1997 Divorce-on-demand became legal in Ireland for the first time since the introduction of Christianity by St. Patrick.

27

FEBRUARY

On this day in 1901, English author, journalist, and wit G. K. Chesterton wrote a rather obscure short story that would ultimately define his work as a popular philosopher. It was about a man who traveled around the world in an effort to find his true home—only to end up precisely where he began. Thomas Smythe had been born, brought up, married, and became the father of a family in a little white farmhouse by a river. The river enclosed it on three sides like a castle—on the fourth side there were stables and beyond that a kitchen garden and beyond that an orchard and beyond that a low wall and beyond that a road and beyond that a wood and beyond that slopes meeting the sky—but Smythe had known nothing beyond what he could see from his house. Its walls were the world to him and its roof the sky. Indeed, in his latter years he hardly ever went outside his door. And as he grew lazy, he grew restless; angry with himself and everyone. He found himself in some strange way weary of every moment and hungry for the next.

His heart had grown stale and bitter toward the wife and children whom he saw every day. His home had become drab and wearisome to him. Yet there was a fragment of a memory that yet remained of happier days when the thatch of his home burned with gold as though angels inhabited the place. Even so, he remembered it as one who remembers a dream. One calamitous day, his mind snapped under the weight of the contradiction—the contradiction between his fond remembrances of the past and his drab circumstances in the present. He presently announced that he was setting out to find his home—that fine white farmhouse by the river. Though his beloved wife and children tried to make him see that he was already there, he could not be persuaded. His delusion was complete.

Thomas Smythe then set out on an epic journey. He crossed hill and vale, mountain and plain, stream and ocean, meadow and desert. Like a transmigrating soul, he lived a series of existences but never diverged from the line that girdled the world. At long last though, he crested a hill and suddenly felt as if he had crossed the border into elfland. With his head a belfry of new passions, assailed with confounding memories, he came at last to the end of the world. He had arrived at the little white farmhouse by the river—he had arrived at home. His heart leapt for joy as he saw his wife run to meet him in the lane. The prodigal had returned.

The story struck a chord with Chesterton's readers for a thousand different reasons—it was a powerfully told parable of the universal human experience, it was a poignant prose poem of Everyman's heart longing, and it was a stern rebuke to the vagabond spirit that drags all the Cains, the Esaus, and the Lots eastward away from Eden. But they probably loved it most of all because it was their own story—the testimony of their own, as yet incomplete, pilgrimage home.

FEAST DAY
St. Oswald of Worcester;
St. Lupicinus; St. Hilarius, pope;
St. Proterius; St. Romanus

For our titanic purposes of faith and revolution, what we need is not the old acceptance of the world as a compromise, but some way in which we can heartily hate and heartily love it. We do not want joy and anger to neutralize each other and produce a surly contentment; we want a fiercer delight and fiercer discontent. We have to feel the universe at once as an ogre's castle, to be stormed, and yet as our own cottage, to which we can return at evening.

[G. K. CHESTERTON (1874–1936)]

FEBRUARY

399   Fabiola Fabii was a wealthy member of a prominent patrician family who, after a scandalous life, was converted in middle age and then devoted the rest of her days to good deeds. Together with Pammachius of Bethlehem, she channeled her vast resources into the establishment of a large hospice for sick and needy travelers in Porto. It was the first institution of its kind and was widely heralded for its unbending Christian convictions. She died in the plague on this day.

1533   Michel de Montaigne was born at the Chateau de Montaigne in Perigord, France.

1759   The pope gave permission for the first time for the Bible to be translated and made available in the vernacular languages of all peoples in Catholic states.

1827   The Baltimore and Ohio Railroad Company was incorporated as the first United States railroad chartered to carry passengers and freight.

1849   The ship *California* arrived at San Francisco, carrying the first of the prospectors during the California Gold Rush.

1861   The federal territory of Colorado was organized.

1910   A. E. Houseman published his most famous work, *A Shropshire Lad*. He later commented on his sparce output, "In barrenness I hold a high place among English poets, excelling even Gray."

1916   Henry James died in London at seventy-two. His last words were, "So here it is at last, the distinguished thing." T. S. Eliot commented acidly on the occasion, "James had a mind so fine that no idea could violate it."

1928   Smokey the Bear, mascot of the United States Forest Service, was born.

1944   Corrie ten Boom, her sister Betsy, and her father were betrayed into the hands of the Nazis for attempting to aid and abet the escape of Jews from the Holocaust. The story immortalized by the book and film *The Hiding Place* had now begun. It would end in death in the concentration camps for everyone except Corrie, who became a "tramp" for the Lord, spreading the gospel of forgiveness from sins to many nations.

1993   A gun battle erupted at a compound near Waco, Texas, when Bureau of Alcohol, Tobacco and Firearms agents tried to serve warrants on a religious community known as the Branch Davidians. Four agents and six Davidians were killed as a fifty-one-day standoff began. Eventually, the entire community was burned to the ground and one hundred men, women, and children inside were killed.

FEBRUARY

John, Lord of Joinville spent six years of his life on Holy Crusade—beginning on this day in 1248—at the side of his liege King Louis IX of France. Joinville wrote his famous *Crusade Chronicle* detailing all that he and Louis—who was later canonized as St. Louis—had experienced.

Written nearly fifty years after the events, the *Chronicle* is a loving, longing, and lingering look at both an age of chivalry and a man of faith. Part biography, part memoir, and part wartime journal, his is an anecdotal account that epitomizes the Medieval Epoch and the Crusader spirit. He tells stories as he remembers them—telling how people looked, describing their manners and customs, and relating their fears and fancies. Though he offers a narrative of battles, strategies, and troop movements, he stops to tell of a tumbler's tricks, to describe a fossil that struck his fancy, to report at length his long-ago conversations, to moralize, to illustrate, to elaborate, and to reminisce.

The crusade he describes was an ill-fated attempt to recover territories overrun by the Moslem hoard following the disasters of the Albigensian, Baltic, and Children's Crusades. But even though it did not succeed militarily, it was an inspiration to generations of Christians afterward. Louis was gallant, saintly, and a veteran soldier. He was an ideal feudal lord, and he led his loyal army in an ideal quest. As a result, Joinville was able to capture most of the very best about medievalism in a very short span without resort to hagiography. Not even in Malory or Chaucer do we get so close to the heart of the Old World order of Christendom.

Interestingly, Joinville's vivid account is often paired in modern English editions with the *Crusade Chronicle* of Villehardouin—but the two could hardly be more different. Villehardouin wrote almost a century before Joinville and described the insidious Fourth Crusade—a conflict marred by the very worst corruption, prejudice, greed, avarice, and betrayal. He served as a dispassionate observer—much like the modern historian—while Joinville was an unabashed partisan. He betrayed a jaded, wanton, and skeptical disillusionment while Joinville was ever the Christian romantic and idealist. He anticipated the emergence a New World disorder with the naiveté of the worldly-wise, whereas Joinville yearned to preserve the Old World order with all the stout-heartedness of the devout.

Probably somewhere between the two the truth about the Crusades may be found. Nevertheless, there is little doubt that Joinville's *Chronicle* makes for the more edifying reading.

LEAP YEAR DAY

LEAP YEAR

The leap year system was adopted by Julius Caesar to keep the calendar from getting out of whack and was adjusted in 1582 by Pope Gregory XII. An extra day is added every four years, except for years ending in 00—unless the year is divisible by 400. Thus 2000 was a leap year, and so was 1600, but 1700, 1800, and 1900 were not.

One horse-laugh is worth ten-thousand syllogisms.

[H. L. MENCKEN (1880–1956)]

FEBRUARY

46 B.C. The addition of February 29 to the calendar was made with the adoption of the Julian calendar.

468 The forty-sixth pope, St. Hilarius (or Hilary), died on this day. He was recognized as a wise administrator who corrected abuses and solved disputes. The Roman synod he sponsored in 465 is the oldest synod from which the acts are extant. His feast day is celebrated on February 28.

992 The Archbishop of York, St. Oswald, died on this day. Of Danish parentage, the Anglo-Saxon bishop was credited with making many monastic reforms as well as establishing many Benedictine monasteries throughout Gloucestershire, Worcestershire, and other areas. His feast day is celebrated on February 28 except in leap years.

1288 In Scotland, the Parliament established this day as one when a woman could propose marriage to a man. If he refused, he was required to pay a hefty fine. This is the origin of Sadie Hawkins Day.

1504 Christopher Columbus, stranded in Jamaica during his fourth voyage to the West, used a correctly predicted lunar eclipse to frighten hostile natives into providing food for his crew.

1528 Patrick Hamilton, the Scottish Reformer and martyr, was burned at the stake for heresy. His death may have done more for the cause of the Scottish Reformation than his extended life could have done.

1792 Gioacchino Antonio Rossini, composer of such works as *The Barber of Seville* and *William Tell*, was born in Pesaro, Italy.

1796 President George Washington signed Jay's Treaty, which settled some of the final outstanding differences between the United States and Great Britain.

1836 *The Huguenots*, an opera by Giacomo Meyerbeer, premiered at the Grand Opéra in Paris. The action takes place in Touraine and Paris in the year 1572 during the St. Bartholomew's Day Massacre in which the Catholics plotted the demise of the Protestant Huguenots.

1904 President Theodore Roosevelt appointed a seven-member commission to facilitate completion of the Panama Canal.

1940 *Gone with the Wind* won eight Oscars at the Academy Awards presentation in Los Angeles, including Best Picture. Hattie McDaniel, who played the role of Mammy, was the first African American to win an Oscar.

1956 President Eisenhower announced that he would seek a second term of office.

1968 The discovery of the first pulsar, a star that emits regular radio waves, was announced by Dr. Jocelyn Bell Burnell at Cambridge, England.

1968 President Lyndon Johnson's National Advisory Commission on Civil Disorders warned that racism was causing America to move "toward two societies, one black, one white—separate and unequal."

1971 The first major-league baseball player to receive $200,000 a year was Hank Aaron, who signed a contract with the Atlanta Braves.

MARCH

MARCH

When Hudson Taylor arrived at the port of Shanghai on this day in 1854, he did not speak the language, he did not know where to go, he did not know a soul, and he did not have a place to stay. Evening was just descending when he disembarked from his ship and began walking alone through the bewildering alien streets. Nevertheless, he wrote in his diary that he was exultant: "My feelings on stepping ashore I cannot attempt to describe. My heart felt as though it had not room and must burst its bonds, while tears of gratitude and thankfulness fell from my eyes."

Though he was ultimately able to find his way to a friendly mission compound in the teeming city that night, just about nothing else seemed to go his way. The days and weeks that followed were dreary and lonely. A civil war erupted just days after he arrived, and people were slaughtered before his eyes. He struggled with the language and the seemingly impenetrable cultural barriers between himself and the Chinese people he had come to serve.

Eventually though, Taylor was able to overcome every one of these difficulties and many more. He learned the language and made up his mind to adopt native dress. He went to work planting an indigenous church and English board, and he founded the China Inland Mission to expand his work throughout the entire land. He never told anyone about his financial needs, trusting that the Lord would provide whatever was needed. At his death the China Inland Mission had 205 missionaries. Though Chinese Christianity grew slowly at first, and has always suffered severe persecution, the fruit of Taylor's labors is evident. Today the Chinese church is thought by some analysts to be the fastest growing in the world. Who could have ever imagined such an outcome on that day so long ago when Taylor stepped out in faith and into Shanghai?

FEAST OF
ST. DAVID,
PATRON OF
WALES

During a battle against the Saxons, Saint David suggested to King Cadwallader that the Britons wear leeks in their hats to distinguish them from their enemies. They won the battle, and Welshman celebrate the day by fixing leeks to their hats.

There is only one form of political strategy in which I have any confidence, and that is to try to do the right thing—and sometimes be able to succeed.

[CALVIN COOLIDGE (1872–1933)]

1469 William Caxton began work on the first book printed in English. He translated *Receuil of the Histories of Troy* from the original French. He set up his own printing office to publish the work.

1642 The first city to become incorporated in North America was Georgeana, Maine.

1781 The Continental Congress adopted the Articles of Confederation. The bill authorizing the new constitutional framework was signed by then President Thomas McKean but did not take effect until the next administration under President John Hanson.

1790 Congress authorized the first U.S. Census.

1810 Frédéric Chopin, the renowned Polish composer and pianist, was born in Zelazowa Wola near Warsaw. Chopin studied piano from the age of four and gave his first recital at the age of eight. Almost all of his compositions are for piano. A composer in the Romantic style, his lyrical melodies are supported by adventurous harmony and subtle rhythm. His music reflects the elements of Polish folk music and was wildly popular in his war-torn homeland.

1845 President Tyler signed a congressional resolution to annex the Republic of Texas. It was only the second time that a sovereign nation had joined the American Federal Union—the first was when the Republic of Vermont became the fourteenth state in 1791.

1867 Nebraska became the thirty-seventh state.

1872 Congress authorized creation of Yellowstone National Park.

1875 The United States Congress passed a Civil Rights Act; however, it was invalidated by the Supreme Court in 1883.

1904 Glenn Miller, American band leader, composer, and leader of the U.S. Army Band during World War II, was born in Clarinda, Iowa. He dropped out of college to concentrate on music. In 1943, Miller and his band joined the military and gave more than eight hundred performances. His biggest hits included "Moonlight Serenade" and "In the Mood."

1932 The infant son of Charles and Anne Lindbergh was kidnapped from the family home near Hopewell, New Jersey. Remains identified as those of the baby were found the following May.

1937 Connecticut issued the first permanent license plates for automobiles.

1954 Five United States congressmen were wounded when Puerto Rican nationalists started shooting from the spectators' gallery in the House of Representatives.

1961 President John Kennedy established the Peace Corps.

1974 Seven people, including former Nixon White House aides H. R. Haldeman and John D. Ehrlichman, former Attorney General John Mitchell and former Assistant Attorney General Robert Mardian, were indicted on charges of conspiring to obstruct justice in connection with the Watergate break-in. All four of these defendants were ultimately convicted the following January, although Mardian's conviction was later reversed.

MARCH

MARCH

As a young woman, Bathild of Chelles (631–680) was carried away from her English home by pirates and indentured to the court of Clovis II, ruler of the Frankish kingdom. Her great beauty and piety attracted the attentions of the king, and he made her his wife on this day in 649.

Some years later, upon the king's death, Bathild became regent for their eldest son, Chlotar III. Utilizing the powers of her position, she stridently opposed the profligate slave trade and the practices of infanticide, exposure, abandonment, and abortion. She encouraged evangelism among the barbaric Celts, she supported local ministries to the needy, and she helped to bring reform to the old Roman legal code.

Her patronage of the arts and commitment to the sciences was also notable, as was her devotion to the disciplines of the Christian life. Her life of balance served as an inspiration to the emerging French nation—which emphasized her vision of justice, mercy, and humility before God long before they embraced liberty, equality, fraternity. Indeed, many historians rank her alongside her great-great-grandchild, Charlemagne, as one of the founders of the French culture.

1938

Martin Niemöller was tried in a Nazi court for the crime of preaching a "rebellious" sermon. He was convicted and sentenced to seven months in prison. Hitler had him arrested again almost as soon as he was released. This time his resistance placed him in concentration camps at Sachsenhausen and Dachau until the end of World War II. He was an ex-submarine captain, who after he entered the ministry had become one of the leaders of the Confessing Church, which offered fierce resistance to Hitler's repressive regime. Altogether he spent eight years in prison. Nonetheless, he apologized with deep regret in October 1945, after the war, for failing to speak out earlier and more strongly against Nazism. Often he would say, "First they came for the socialists and I did not speak out because I was not a socialist. Then they came for the trade unionists and I did not speak out because I was not a trade unionist. Then they came for the Jews and I did not speak out because I was not a Jew. Then they came for me and there was no one left to speak for me."

> *Hooey pleases boobs a great deal more than sense.*
>
> [H. L. MENCKEN (1880–1956)]

1492 King Ferdinand V banished nearly 800,000 Jews from the Iberian kingdom of Aragon—which along with Queen Isabella's Castile was one of the two primary lands that would one day comprise the nation of Spain.

1545 Sir Thomas Bodley was born in England. He was a bibliophile who founded the library at Oxford that bears his name. The Bodleian Library serves as a depository of British publications, housing approximately twenty 20 million volumes, requiring some six kilometers of new shelves per year.

1793 The first president of the Republic of Texas, Sam Houston, was born near Lexington, Virginia. He had a checkered political career serving as a congressman and governor in Tennessee. He moved to the Texas Territory following a personal and political scandal. He led the Texans to victory over the Mexican dictator, Santa Anna, and became one of the founders of an independent republic there. After Texas was annexed to the U.S. he served as a governor and senator from that state.

1799 The Congress standardized the system of weights and measures for the United States.

1836 The Republic of Texas was founded by a group of fifty-nine former American and Mexican citizens.

1863 In order to facilitate the advancement of rail travel, the U.S. Congress authorized a standard track width of 4' 8½" for the Union Pacific Railroad. This gauge became the standard around the world.

1877 Republican Rutherford B. Hayes was declared the winner of the 1876 presidential election over Democrat Samuel J. Tilden, even though Tilden had won the popular vote. The controversial ruling came after the Republican-held Congress cut a deal with Southern state electors, promising to end Reconstruction in exchange for Hayes votes.

1899 President William McKinley signed a measure creating the rank of admiral of the navy for Admiral George Dewey in recognition of his great exploits in the Spanish-American War.

1899 Mount Rainier National Park in Washington State was established.

1917 Nineteen years after their island was acquired by American expeditionary forces during the Spanish-American War, Puerto Ricans were granted U.S. citizenship.

1923 *Time* magazine made its debut as a news weekly.

1933 The movie *King Kong*, starring Fay Wray, premiered in New York.

1939 The Massachusetts legislature, realizing that the state had never ratified the Bill of Rights, voted to accept the amendments to the Constitution 147 years after they had actually gone into effect.

1949 The U.S. Air Force B-50 Superfortress *Lucky Lady II* completed the first nonstop flight around the world, flying some 23,452 miles.

1969 The *Concorde*, the French-built supersonic passenger aircraft, made its maiden flight.

NATIONAL DAY
Morocco
FEAST DAY
St. Ailred of Rievaulx, St.
Cunegund, empress, St. Marinus of
Caesarea, St. Non, St. Winwaloe,
St. Anselm of Nonantola, St.
Artelais, St. Chef, St. Emeterius

MARCH

3

By the middle of the fifth century, the forces of disintegration had almost destroyed the western half of the Roman Empire. Various Germanic barbarian warlords—from the Vandal, Visigoth, Frankish, and Herulian tribes—had replaced the old Imperial power with their own. For several decades they had placed puppet emperors on the throne and had taken control of the once-great military.

The eastern half of the venerable empire was struggling with troubles of its own. A usurper drove the emperor, the young Zeno, from his throne. Needing a strong base of support, this usurper placed a large number of Monophysite heretics in key positions.

Monophysitism had actually begun as a response to another heresy known as Nestorianism. A bishop, Nestorius, had refused to call Mary the "Mother of God," for, said he, the child in her womb was thoroughly human. In contradistinction to this, the Monophysites taught that Christ's human nature was dissolved in His divine nature as a drop of honey dissolves in the ocean. Each faction was attempting to preserve a part of the truth about Christ's incarnation—but each had gone to one extreme or another. Eventually the church restored a sense of biblical balance at the Council of Chalcedon in 451, declaring that Christ was both truly God and truly man—thus denouncing the Monophysite and Nestorian polar opposites.

Instead of resolving the issue though, the council's ruling only incited further fighting. The Monophysites refused to accept defeat. The Imperial usurper ordered the acts of Chalcedon burned and nearly five hundred bishops complied. In Alexandria, the controversy was particularly fierce. Rivals tortured and killed one another. A Monophysite monk known as Timothy the Cat had the patriarch of Alexandria butchered three days before Easter and triumphantly seized his place, consigning his corpse to flames.

Thus, when Simplicius became bishop of Rome on this day in 468, he inherited a roiling mess. He immediately used his influence to help Emperor Zeno regain his throne and oust the Monophysite bishops. But when Zeno—out of fear of the powerful Monophysite faction—determined to arrange a compromise, Simplicius threatened to topple him once again. Compromise was not possible, he argued. Unless Christ is fully God, He cannot redeem us. Unless He is fully man, He cannot stand in our place.

Eventually the unflinching defense of Simplicius for the principles laid down at the Council of Chalcedon saved the church from a fatal compromise during one of the most volatile epochs in history. With Athanasius, he stood contra mundum, and as a result, preserved orthodoxy.

The most dangerous form of sentimental debauch is to give expression to good wishes on behalf of virtue while you do nothing about it. Justice is not merely words. It is to be translated into living acts.

[THEODORE ROOSEVELT (1858–1919)]

1634 The first public ale tavern in the Puritan city of Boston opened on this day. It was cause for celebration and prayers of thanksgiving by all the most prominent and pious citizens.

1791 The United States Congress established the U.S. Mint by resolution.

1817 The state of Mississippi and the territory of Alabama were established when the Mississippi Territory was divided.

1837 The number of Supreme Court justices was increased from seven to nine by an act of Congress.

1842 The first performance of Felix Mendelssohn's "Scottish" Symphony no. 3 was held in Leipzig, Germany.

1845 Florida became the twenty-seventh state.

1847 The inventor of the telephone, Alexander Graham Bell, was born in Edinburgh, Scotland.

1849 Congress created the Minnesota Territory.

1855 The secretary of war received an appropriation of $30,000 from Congress for the purpose of importing and testing camels from the Orient for military purposes.

1875 The first performance of Georges Bizet's opera *Carmen* was held at the Opéra Comique in Paris. This colorful and melodramatic opera was an early failure before gaining respect and position in the opera repertoire.

1885 The American Telephone and Telegraph (AT&T) was incorporated.

1885 The U.S. Post Office began offering special delivery for first-class mail.

1915 The National Advisory Committee for Aeronautics—the precursor to NASA—was created.

1931 The United States formally adopted "The Star-Spangled Banner" as its national anthem.

1931 The first jazz album to sell a million copies, *Minnie the Moocher*, was recorded by Cab Calloway on this day.

1940 Artie Shaw and his orchestra recorded "Frenesi" for RCA Victor.

1991 In a case that sparked a national outcry, motorist Rodney King was severely beaten by Los Angeles police officers in a scene captured on amateur video.

FEAST DAY
St. Peter of Cava, St. Casimir of Poland, St. Adrian and his Companions

MARCH

It seemed only natural that Washington's vice president, John Adams (1735–1826), should succeed Washington, for in his own contentious but courageous way, he had contributed much to the new nation. Unlike Washington, Adams was not a great leader: He had neither a commanding nor a magnetic personality; he was a lawyer and an intellectual who made his greatest contributions before he became president. Nevertheless, he was second only to Washington in the hearts and minds of most Americans.

A man of bristling integrity, he could devote himself to a cause with a fierce intensity: He condemned the Stamp Act of 1765, was one of the first to support the idea of independence, and, at the Continental Congress when the colonies wavered before the mighty decision, he vigorously fought for acceptance of the Declaration of Independence. He further distinguished himself by representing the infant country with dignity—and success—in the leading courts of Europe.

By 1789 Adams was a respected but not a popular figure. In finishing second to Washington he barely received enough votes to secure the vice presidency—and for eight years he was continually in the shadow of the commanding figure of Washington. Unfortunately, his own term was little better. After his inauguration on this day in 1797, he struggled through one controversy after another.

His conflict with Alexander Hamilton and his cabinet members created factional strife in both the Federalist Party and the government. Through the bitter disputes Adams remained essentially a Federalist, maintaining the strong central government established by Washington and Hamilton. When the Federalists passed the oppressive Alien and Sedition Laws in 1789, they assumed such sweeping powers over all critics of government that they challenged the essential freedoms of the individual; the party, already too closely allied with the propertied colonial aristocracy, carried the idea of a strong central government too far.

Both Adams and the party lost favor: In the 1800 election Adams was defeated by Jefferson and the new Republican Party. Interestingly, Jefferson and Adams—once fierce rivals—became close friends in their elder years. They even died on the same day, within hours of one another—on July 4, 1826.

INAUGURATION DAY	Every American president from George Washington to Franklin Roosevelt was inaugurated on this day. The passage of the Twentieth Amendment in 1933 changed the date to January 20.

*So to be patriots as not to forget
we are gentlemen.*

[EDMUND BURKE (1729–1797)]

1461   The Duke of York was proclaimed King Edward IV, after Henry VI was deposed.

1583   Bernard Gilpin was known during the English Reformation as "The Apostle of the North." Exposed to the teaching of Erasmus at Oxford, he only gradually moved toward Protestant views. But his love of the common man eventually put him at odds with the corrupt Catholic hierarchy. As a young rector, he would ride in winter through districts that were without pastors and preach, distributing alms to the poor and caring for the ill. In this way he exerted a great Reforming influence on Northumberland and Yorkshire. The people adored him. But clerics resented him. They denounced him as a heretic, and he was brought up on charges in 1558. Providentially, Queen Mary died before he could come to trial. After the ascendancy of the Protestants, Gilpin rejected all offers of high position, choosing instead to serve his own community with great humility. He died on this day, after being crushed by an ox at market while making his rounds, gathering food for distribution to the poor.

1678   The Italian composer and violinist Antonio Vivaldi, best known for *The Four Seasons* and *Gloria*, was born in Venice. He entered the priesthood in 1703 and was known as the "red priest" because of the color of his hair.

1789   The Constitution of the United States went into effect as the first Federal Congress met in New York. The lawmakers were forced to immediately adjourn for the lack of a quorum.

1791   The Republic of Vermont joined the U.S. in a treaty that made the territory along Lake Champlain between New Hampshire and New York the fourteenth state.

1829   An unruly crowd of backwoodsmen mobbed the White House during the inaugural reception for President Jackson.

1837   The Illinois state legislature granted a city charter to Chicago.

1861   Abraham Lincoln was inaugurated president, sparking the secession of several border and Southern states.

1891   The United States Congress passed the International Copyright Act, which sought to halt the practice of American publishers pirating the content and intellectual property of books from Britain, Belgium, France, and Switzerland.

1902   The American Automobile Association was founded in Chicago.

1925   President Calvin Coolidge's inauguration was broadcast live on twenty-one radio stations coast to coast—a first.

1933   In his inaugural address of 1933, Franklin D. Roosevelt uttered the words, "This nation asks for action, and action now. We must act, and act quickly. The only thing we have to fear is fear itself."

1933   The start of Roosevelt's first administration brought with it the first woman to serve in the cabinet, Labor Secretary Frances Perkins.

143

MARCH

From the time he was a small boy, George Müller's father had intended that he would one day become a clergyman. But Müller resisted that notion violently. As a young man, he squandered one opportunity after another in drunkenness, thieving, fornication, cheating, and lying. On several different occasions, he was arrested and jailed. Yet his father never doubted.

When he went away to study at the university, a friend introduced him to a prayer meeting. There, he came under heavy conviction and was powerfully converted. He suddenly had an insatiable hunger for Scripture. Though he found it difficult to throw off his old habits all at once, he made a valiant effort, and he was eventually able to effectually renounce the evils that had such a grip on him for so long. For the sake of Christ, he burned a novel he was writing. He even renounced the stipend his father supplied him, believing it wrong to accept it since his father opposed the various schemes for mission work he now proposed to do.

Eventually Müller became a pastor, focusing his ministry on the care of the poorest of the poor. He taught his parishioners principles of biblical stewardship—each was to give as God laid on his or her heart. He placed an offering box at the back of the church where they could give in sight of God alone. He made it a habit to make the church's needs known only to God. When he married, he and his wife sold all they had and gave the proceeds to the poor.

His concern for the poor led him to build a network of orphanages. And again, he determined that the work would proceed entirely on faith. He prayed for every penny, never announcing his needs. At every turn, God gave him great success.

On this day in 1834, Müller and his friend Henry Craik announced their intention to form a new missionary society. It was to be called "The Scripture Knowledge Institution, for Home and Abroad." The grand name and bold vision of the new organization belied the fact that the two men had no money whatsoever and no visible means of raising the necessary support for the scheme. Indeed, true to form, they had determined ahead of time that they would not seek out donations, would not accept donations from non-Christians, and would not incur any indebtedness.

Nevertheless, the little venture that the men intended to aid inner-city Sunday schools, circulate the Scriptures to the poor, and provide support for missionaries abroad was soon thriving. Within just a few short years it had obtained a world wide influence and was counted among the most successful Christian organizations anywhere.

Müller always believed that his great faith against all odds was rooted in the great faith of his father—who believed that he would one day serve Christ despite all evidence to the contrary.

Beware of those with whom you rake and round,
Alert to dangers and snares,
And you will find that security and surety abound.
Listless discernment cares,
But little, so spent are lives upon the merest sound.
Thus the wise soul prepares,
And establishes an apprehension of solid ground.

[STEPHEN STEWART (1816–1888)]

1133 Henry II, the first monarch of the house of Anjou, or Plantagenet, was born in Le Mans, France. He solidified his claim to the English throne through the defeat of his cousin Stephen of Blois. He added to his territory by his marriage to Eleanor of Aquitaine and his conquests in the northern counties of England, North Wales, and Ireland. Because of a dispute with Thomas à Becket over ecclesiastical authority, Henry had the archbishop murdered. At his death, he was succeeded by his son, Richard the Lionheart.

1512 Flemish geographer, mapmaker, and pioneer of modern cartography Gerhardus Mercator was born in Rupelmonde, Flanders. Because of his knowledge of geography and his invention and use of map-drawing instruments and survey equipment, he was regarded as the premier geographer of the Renaissance. In addition to maps, Mercator also produced a terrestrial globe in 1541 and was the first to use the term "atlas" for a group of maps. He fled to Germany in 1552 to escape persecution for his Protestant beliefs.

1770 The Boston Massacre occurred when British soldiers who were being taunted by a crowd of colonists opened fire. One of the five people killed was Crispus Attucks, a black man. Two British soldiers were later convicted of manslaughter.

1933 In German parliamentary elections, the National Socialists—an upstart left-wing political party popularly known as the Nazis—won a surprising 44 percent of the vote, enabling it to join with the Nationalists to gain a slender majority in the Reichstag.

1946 At Westminster College in Fulton, Missouri, Winston Churchill made his historic "Iron Curtain" speech. "From Stettin in the Baltic to Trieste in the Adriatic, an Iron Curtain has descended across the Continent," he asserted, "allowing police governments to rule Eastern Europe."

1953 Soviet dictator Joseph Stalin, the creator of the Iron Curtain, died. He was seventy-three years old. During his twenty-nine years in power he ordered the slaughter of millions of his own people—outstripping even Hitler in his genocidal efficiency.

1963 A private plane crash near Camden, Tennessee, claimed the lives of country music performers Patsy Cline, "Cowboy" Copas, and "Hawkshaw" Hawkins.

1970 The Nuclear Non-Proliferation Treaty went into effect after forty-three nations ratified it.

NATIONAL DAY
Ghana
FEAST DAY
*Saints Baldred and Billfrith, St.
Chrodegang, St. Colette, St. Conon,
St. Cyneburga, St. Fridolin, St.
Tibba*

MARCH

6

Often called the "Prince of the Preachers," Charles Haddon Spurgeon (1834–1892) was heralded as the greatest orator to grace the Christian pulpit since the apostle Paul—both during his lifetime and in the years ever since. His sermons delivered at London's Metropolitan Tabernacle were undoubtedly used in accord with God's good providence as dynamic forces for righteousness in Victorian England and around the world.

But his many years of ministry were marked not only by his masterful pulpiteering, but by his many social and cultural labors as well. In 1861, he erected an almshouse for the elderly. In 1864, he established a school for the needy children of London. In 1866, he founded the Stockwell Orphanages. And on this day in 1866, to these many enterprises he added still another, a private hospital. He wanted to revive the venerable Christian tradition of I John 3:18, "My little children, let us not love in word, neither in tongue; but in deed and in truth."

Though he was a best-selling author, the pastor of the single largest church in the world, a sought-after evangelist, a friend and counselor to innumerable lords, members of the Royal family, and a succession of prime ministers and cabinet officers, he believed that his work in mercy ministry was the most important that he had ever undertaken.

In all he was responsible for some sixty different institutions—schools, seminaries, colportage societies, missionary agencies, and mercy ministries. His commitment to fulfilling the Great Commission led him to a fully integrated and dynamically engaged worldview—and ultimately established him as a paragon of balanced and effective evangelical leadership.

1643

Pope Urban VIII forbade the reading of *Augustinus.* The book had been written by Cornelius Jansen who had been a Catholic professor of theology at Louvain. Before his death two years before, he had participated in a running feud with the Jesuits over the issue of scriptural authority and salvation by grace. In Jansen's view, the Jesuits had allowed works and human reason to replace a genuine Christian faith. "Heresy," sniffed the church. "Calvinism in a new cloak," argued the Jesuits. But *Augustinus,* based on the teachings of the church father Augustine, was winsomely convincing. Nearly a fifth of the French clergy admitted that they had accepted Jansenist teachings. As a result, the pope issued his controversial ban.

Man was made for work. The Fall unmade him. Now, in Christ made anew, man can once again work. But he must be ever mindful of the salvific connection: the call to work must not, cannot, go out unaccompanied by the call to salvation.

[LANGDON LOWE (1843–1919)]

MARCH

1475 Michelangelo Buonarroti—Renaissance painter of the Sistine Chapel ceiling and sculptor of the *Pieta, Moses,* and *David*—was born in the Medici city-state of Florence just as the Renaissance was beginning to flower there.

1713 Clement XI issued a new papal bull, Unigenitus, condemning the Jansenist teachings. Among the propositions condemned in this edict were the claims that the Scriptures may be read by all men, that the Lord's Day should be sanctified by reading the Bible, and that fear of unjust excommunication shouldn't prevent us from doing our duty.

1716 The skies of Europe, from the west coast of Holland to the interior of Russia, were lit by an especially brilliant display of the aurora borealis—the northern lights.

1806 Elizabeth Barrett Browning, the English poet, and wife of Robert Browning, was born near Durham, England. Her most famous work, *Sonnets from the Portuguese,* recounts her courtship with Browning.

1834 The city of York in Upper Canada was incorporated as Toronto.

1836 The Alamo, a former mission in San Antonio, Texas, fell after a thirteen-day siege to Mexican dictator General Antonio López de Santa Anna. The whole garrison was slaughtered. Davy Crockett, Colonel James Bowie, and their Texan comrades were outnumbered 15 to 1.

1853 Verdi's opera *La Traviata* premiered in Venice.

1857 The Supreme Court handed down the *Dred Scott* decision, which said that since black Americans are not full citizens, an escaped slave could not sue his master for his freedom.

1933 A nationwide bank holiday declared by President Roosevelt went into effect.

1935 Retired Supreme Court Justice Oliver Wendell Holmes Jr. died in Washington.

1944 Dame Kiri Te Kanawa, renowned operatic soprano, was born in New Zealand. She became an opera star overnight after an enthusiastic debut in 1971 at the Royal Opera House, Covent Garden, London, in the role of the Countess in *The Marriage of Figaro.* She is known for her lyric soprano roles in the operas of Strauss, Mozart, Verdi, and Puccini, but she also has a wide repertoire of French, German, and British art songs.

1944 U.S. heavy bombers staged the first American raid on Berlin during the Second World War.

1950 Silly Putty was invented.

1957 The former British African colonies of the Gold Coast and Togoland united to become the independent state of Ghana.

147

MARCH

John Chrysostom (347–407) was one of the greatest preachers of the Patristic Age. In fact, his name actually means "golden tongue." His many extant sermons on family life, personal holiness, and Christian social responsibility remain models of wise erudition and faithful exposition. In addition, he was an influential liturgical reformer. His work continues to define the parameters of orthodox worship to this day.

When he became the bishop of Constantinople on this day in 397, pious men and women throughout Byzantium rejoiced. A champion of charity to the poor, mercy to the lost, and tenderheartedness to the outcast, he was plainspoken about the ills and excesses of his day. As a result, he was extremely popular among the people. Unfortunately, his forthrightness also quickly earned him the enmity of many rich and powerful officials in the Byzantine court, including the empress.

Though political intrigue surrounded him from the moment he arrived in the capital city, he faithfully carried out his pastoral responsibilities, making a dynamic impact on the city in a very short time. A great revival of interest in the gospel and its incumbent responsibilities swept through even the most cosmopolitan circles.

Eventually though, his clear expositions could be tolerated no longer. He was exiled and put through innumerable humiliations. Throughout his ordeals, however, he remained steadfast, and even after his ignominious death, his impact upon the whole fabric of Byzantine culture was profoundly felt.

1897

Johannes Brahms attended his last concert—a performance of his Fourth Symphony in Vienna. Brahms sat in the artists' box and both the orchestra and audience honored him, realizing that they were probably seeing him for the last time. The audience broke into wild applause at the end of each movement and were only quieted when the maestro stepped to the edge of the balcony. At the end of the performance, Brahms, shrunken in stature with lank white hair, stood in the balcony with tears running down his face. When he died on April 3, 1897, all of musical Vienna accompanied the funeral procession.

The heart of a fool is in his mouth, but the mouth of a wise man is in his heart.

[BENJAMIN FRANKLIN (1706–1790)]

MARCH

1804 Wales had recently experienced a sweeping revival. One thing, however, was lacking. There were not enough Bibles for everyone. Reverend Thomas Charles, a notable figure in the revival, visited the Religious Tract Society in London in 1802 and pleaded with them for Scriptures. Alas, the society had to turn him away for lack of resources. As the members discussed the request, the Reverend Joseph Hughes said, "A society might be formed for the purpose—and if for Wales, why not for the Kingdom; why not for the whole world?" Fifteen months later the spark of his suggestion became reality. Thus, the British and Foreign Bible Society was formed. It was to be the first of many similar organizations founded throughout the world.

1821 Franz Schubert's art song the "Erlkönig" received its first public performance, sung by Johann Vogel. It received such a warm reception that Schubert's friends decided to publish it, along with some of his other songs, at their own expense. After many years of composition, Schubert's Opus I was published. The composition of the "Erlkönig" was accomplished in a single sitting. Schubert would often write six to eight songs in a single day.

1849 Horticulturist Luther Burbank was born in Lancaster, Massachusetts.

1850 In a three-hour speech to the U.S. Senate, Daniel Webster endorsed the flawed Compromise of 1850, which had been drafted by his old rival, Henry Clay, as perhaps the last hope of preserving the Union.

1875 French composer Maurice Ravel was born in Ciboure, France. His most important compositions were *Pavane pour une Infante Defunte* (Pavane for a Dead Infant), *Mother Goose Suite, Bolero*, and *Daphnis et Chloe* (a ballet commissioned by Diaghilev). He was best known for his rich, sensual orchestrations diffused with light, making full use of the exquisite palette of orchestral color.

1876 Alexander Graham Bell received a patent for his talking device called the telephone—three days before the device actually worked.

1897 Dr. John Kellogg first served his corn flakes to patients at a mental hospital in Battle Creek, Michigan, years before they were sold in stores.

1911 The United States sent twenty thousand troops to the Mexican border as a precaution in the wake of the Mexican Revolution.

1926 The first successful trans-atlantic radio-telephone conversation took place, between New York and London.

1933 The game of Monopoly was invented, although it was not mass-marketed by Parker Brothers until 1935.

1936 Adolf Hitler ordered his troops to march into the Rhineland, thereby breaking the Treaty of Versailles and the Locarno Pact.

1945 U.S. forces crossed the Rhine River at Remagen, Germany, during the last days of the Second World War. They used the damaged but still usable Ludendorff Bridge.

1965 A march by civil rights demonstrators was broken up in Selma, Alabama, by state troopers and a sheriff's posse. When the demonstration and its aftermath was broadcast to the entire nation by television network news, public opinion began to shift.

MARCH

When Hugh Goldie (1806–1881) joined a mission station in Old Calabar on the West Coast of Africa early in the nineteenth century, he was horrified by many of the things he found there. The living conditions of the people were utterly deplorable. Their nutrition was abominable. Their hygiene was disgraceful. Their social and commercial arrangements were in utter disarray.

But it was their cavalier attitude to the sanctity of human life that most disturbed him. Although they had recently abandoned the centuries-old practice of human sacrifice, they still freely practiced abortion, abandonment, and infanticide. Even though Goldie was met with stiff opposition by the tribal chiefs—and even by many of his fellow missionaries who felt that his pro-life convictions would compromise their evangelistic efforts—he stood firmly on what he believed was the essential integrity of the whole counsel of God.

He faithfully taught the people. He worked hard to ensure that every man, woman, and child had access to adequate health care so that there would be no excuse for the taking of innocent lives. And he established a pattern of care and concern for the least desirable people in the community—rather than focusing his attentions on the most prestigious—thus modeling a consistent ethic of the sanctity of all human life.

Finally, as a result of his lifelong crusade for life, tribal decrees on this day in 1851 banned the terrible customs. He eventually went on to his eternal reward having "run the race, fought the fight, and held the course" (see 2 Timothy 4:7).

1984

In the months following Pope John Paul's visit to his homeland, the Communist regime in Poland tried to crack down on expressions of faith. The government ordered all crosses to be removed from public buildings—including schools. Only one school in the entire nation voluntarily complied. As a result, the state police began to enforce the decree in a series of raids. On this day, riot police were sent to the Staszic Agricultural College when two-thirds of the students staged a sit-in to protest the removal of their seven crosses. Within days thousands of Polish students from around the country joined them, waving crucifixes in the air. The government tried to force parents of the Agricultural College seniors to sign forms acknowledging that the school was secular in nature as a condition of graduation. Most of the parents refused. Eventually the government was forced to retreat—and its concession was the first step toward the democratization of the nation.

Those who have not discovered that worldview is the most important thing about a man, as about the men composing a culture, should consider the train of circumstances which have with perfect logic proceeded from this. The denial of universals carries with it the denial of everything transcending experience.

[RICHARD WEAVER (1910–1963)]

MARCH

1702 England's Queen Anne ascended the throne upon the death of King William III. Though she would bear eighteen children, none would survive her. Thus, she was the last of the British monarchs connected to the old Stuart line.

1714 Composer Carl Philipp Emanuel Bach, son of J. S. Bach, was born in Weimar (in modern-day Germany). His innovations, technique, and compositions for the keyboard paved the way for the compositions of Haydn, Beethoven, and Schubert.

1841 Supreme Court Justice Oliver Wendell Holmes Jr., the "Great Dissenter," was born in Boston.

1854 Commodore Matthew C. Perry landed in Japan. Within a month, he concluded a treaty with the Japanese emperor. The treaty ended Japan's long-standing isolationism and opened two ports for trade with the United States.

1859 Kenneth Grahame, the creator of Mole, Rat, Badger and Toad in the children's classic *The Wind in the Willows,* was born in Edinburgh, Scotland. Portions of *The Wind in the Willows* were written in the form of letters to his young son.

1874 The thirteenth president of the United States, Millard Fillmore, died in Buffalo, New York.

1911 New York City police utilized latent fingerprint evidence in the prosecution of a burglary for the first time. The presence of the defendant at the scene of the crime was established and accepted, and Caesar "Charley Crispi" Cella was convicted.

1917 The Russian Revolution began with rioting and strikes in St. Petersburg. It is often called the "February Revolution" because of the Old Style calendar used by Russians at the time.

1930 The twenty-seventh president of the United States, William Howard Taft, died in Washington.

1935 Thomas Wolfe's second novel, *Of Time and the River,* was published by Scribner's to great acclaim.

1965 The United States landed about 3,500 marines in South Vietnam—the first significant American military mobilization in the war that had already been raging since the end of the Second World War in the former French colonies of Indo-China.

1977 The United States Army announced that it had conducted 239 germ warfare tests in open-air situations.

151

MARCH

The first Crusade to liberate the once-Christian lands of the Near East was a great success. An army of about fifty thousand Europeans, supported by Byzantium, drove south through Syria and Palestine, finally retaking Jerusalem in 1099. During the next few years, the Crusaders carved up their conquests into several small kingdoms—realms that they dubbed as Outremer. They built castles, churches, and markets. They constructed fortified walls, dug fresh wells, and cultivated the fields. They restored the holy places. They opened the trade routes. And they rebuilt the roadways.

Many of the men committed their lives to making the region a flourishing Christian culture once again. The feudal order that they instituted there brought dramatic changes to the lives and the fortunes of the citizenry. Under their ambitious building program, cities like Acre, Edessa, and even Jerusalem itself, blossomed into architectural marvels. Out of the rubble of war they brought forth peace and prosperity.

But restoring the lands to their former glory was no easy task. Provisions had to be shipped across long distances. Communications with the West were difficult at best. Petty jealousies between competing clans, commanders, chiefs, and would-be-czars weakened their solidarity, stalled their progress, and diverted their attentions. But, regardless of all that, in the end there simply were not enough of them to hold their tiny strip of territory against the persistent onslaught of Muslim assassins and warlords.

On this day in 1144, the Saracens reorganized their armies and swept through Syria. Edessa fell. A renewed Crusade led by the kings of France and Germany failed to recover it. All of Europe was stunned. And the worst was yet to come. In 1150, Saladin united the Islamic world under his leadership and began to chip away at the remaining Christian holdings. In 1187, he defeated the Crusaders at the decisive Battle of Hattin. He then captured Jerusalem and overran virtually all the Latin territories except Acre.

Another series of Crusades was launched by such notables as King Richard I of England, Emperor Frederick II of Germany, and King Louis IX of France. Under their leadership the Western armies valiantly won back a few swatches of the lost lands between Joppa and Acre. But the flagging campaigns were generally ineffectual. Jerusalem was lost again in 1244. Acre fell in 1291. And the Christian Near East has been held in the grips of Islam ever since.

Commend me to sterling honesty, though clad in rags.

[SIR WALTER SCOTT (1771–1832)]

1454 Amerigo Vespucci was born in Florence. During an expedition in 1499–1500, he explored the northern coast of South America. He claimed to have reached the North American mainland even earlier. Regardless, the newly discovered continents were named America in his honor.

1796 The future emperor of France, Napoleon Bonaparte, married Josephine de Beauharnais. The couple divorced in 1809.

1862 The *Monitor* and the *Virginia*—formerly the *Merrimac*—engaged in the first recorded submarine battle. The ironclads fought for five hours off the coast of Virginia.

1910 American composer Samuel Barber, best known for his *Adagio for Strings*, was born in West Chester, Pennsylvania. "When I'm writing music for words, then I immerse myself in those words, and I let the music flow out of them. When I write an abstract piano sonata or a concerto, I write what I feel. I'm not a self-conscious composer . . . it is said that I have no style at all but that does not matter. I just go on doing, as they say, my thing. I believe this takes a certain courage."

1916 Mexican raiders led by Pancho Villa attacked Columbus, New Mexico, killing more than a dozen people.

1933 Congress, called into special session by President Roosevelt, began its "hundred days" of enacting New Deal legislation in an effort to end the Great Depression.

1945 Tokyo and other parts of Japan were devastated by bombing attacks from U.S. B-29 bombers. The incendiary bombs killed at least 120,000 in Tokyo alone.

1956 British authorities exiled Makarios III, archbishop of Cyprus, charging that the cleric was actively supporting terrorism. Makarios had earlier pledged to achieve self-determination for his people. The politics of the situation were more than a little complex, however. Eighty percent of the islanders were Christians. They wanted to unite with Greece. Islamic Turkey, which controlled the island from 1571 to 1878, threatened to invade rather than let the people federate with Greece. Britain, which had held the island as a Crown colony since 1925, was caught in the middle of an ancient struggle. In exile, Makarios became an effective spokesman for the dissidents. By 1959 he was allowed to return from exile, and the island eventually won its independence. Rather than let Greece annex the island, Turkey invaded in 1974 and forcibly partitioned it into Greek and Turkish sectors. The island remains divided to this day.

1964 Ford Motor Company produced the first Ford Mustang. It was sold a few weeks later and became an instant classic.

1974 A Japanese guerrilla operating in the Philippines finally surrendered twenty-nine years after the end of the Second World War. He had never gotten word of the Japanese surrender and was still faithfully carrying out his orders.

1981 Filming for the science fiction film noir classic *Blade Runner*, under the direction of Ridley Scott, began in California. Despite the disappointing initial reaction, the film, based on Philip K. Dick's novel *Do Androids Dream of Electric Sheep?* has since been highly praised for its masterful use of ambiance, special effects, cinematography, and probing insights into the question of what it means to be human and have a soul.

Feast Day
St. Kessog; St. John Ogilvie; St. Attalas; St. Hymelin; St. Macarius of Jerusalem; St. Simplicius, pope; St. Anastasia Patricia

MARCH

On this day in 1528, Martin Luther, father of the Reformation and a great man of letters, edited and published a curious little book entitled *Liber Vagatorum* (The Book of Vagabonds and Beggars). Arguing that there was a direct relationship between religious reform and the elimination of homelessness, he offered the book as a practical manual for poverty relief, "the next and most important item on the agenda of revival." It marked a major turning point in Western thought.

The book urged the abolition of begging and vagrancy by the establishment of a social welfare system coordinated by the civil magistrates. Until that time, virtually no one would have or could have imagined that the magistrates could match the efficiency of the church in caring for the poor.

The church's system was comprehensive, being divided into two spheres: parish relief and monastic hospitality. From the earliest days, local churches gave charity central prominence in their ministries. Much of the structure even of parish life was determined by the exigencies of relief. The combined effect of the teaching of virtually all the early church fathers, however much they may have differed in other matters, was to make almsgiving an indispensable aspect of church life. Charity became a symbol of faithfulness. It was looked for as a sign of spiritual vitality.

Luther's plan called for the establishment of a "common chest." He recommended that "there shall be ordered for the burghers and kept in place for all times, two casks or council chests in which bread, cheese, eggs, meat, and other foods and provisions shall be placed; and there shall also be a box or two wherein money may be put for the upkeep of the common chest." In addition to voluntary contributions from various sources there was to be a "tax requirement" committing each inheritor, merchant, craftsman, and peasant to contribute to the chest each year. Servants and young laborers who did not own property but had "burgher and parish rights" would have their portion deducted by their employers. All this was to be above and beyond the tithe and would finance all relief as well as cover the costs of public education and pay the salaries of the clergy. The fund was to be expended by ten supervisors or overseers, independent of the church but "chosen in an open burgher's meeting in the parish hall."

A social welfare revolution occurred almost overnight. Like the Reformation itself, it swept across the Continent, leaving it forever altered. Luther's plan shifted responsibility for the poor from the church to the state. This jurisdictional turnaround was based upon his conviction that the church was "an institution of grace," while the state was an "institution of works." He wanted a wall of separation between the two. He wanted to limit the church to "spiritual authority" and the state to "cultural authority," having suffered long under the corrupted Medieval Church bureaucracy. Every change in the social welfare system in the West since 1600 has simply been a development of this Lutheran presupposition: Relief is the state's responsibility, not the church's. Alas, thus was born modern statism that lent us socialism, fascism, and welfarism.

Life is not so short but that there is always time enough for courtesy and chivalry.

[RALPH WALDO EMERSON (1803–1882)]

MARCH

1302   The greatest poet of the Medieval era, Dante Alighieri, settled into a home in Venice after having been banished from Florence upon penalty of burning. Dante had been one of seven noblemen who oversaw the government of his birthplace. When an accidental collision in the streets during the May Festival of 1300 led to a brawl and then civil war, Dante and his party were overthrown. He spent the rest of his life in exile—mostly in Venice. It would be there that he would write his masterpiece *The Divine Comedy*. Banishment drew out Dante's genius. An epic of love and faith, Dante envisioned *The Divine Comedy* in three parts, Inferno, Purgatorio, and Paradisio. It yearns with utopian nostalgia for a Pan-Christian empire and radiates a Boethian sense of divine reality. T. S. Eliot said that "Dante and Shakespeare divide the modern world between them. There is no third." W. B. Yeats called him "the chief imagination of Christendom."

1775   Daniel Boone was sent by the Transylvania Company to forge and cut the Wilderness Road through Kentucky.

1785   Thomas Jefferson was appointed minister to France, succeeding Benjamin Franklin.

1849   Former Congressman Abraham Lincoln applied for a patent for an inflatable airbag to help lift grounded boats from sandbars and shoals.

1864   Ulysses S. Grant became commander of the Union armies in the Civil War.

1876   Alexander Graham Bell sent the first telephone message, "Come here, Watson, I want you," to his assistant located on another floor of Bell's home at 5 Exeter Place, Boston, Massachusetts.

1892   The United States government issued paper money in the denominations of $5, $10, $20, $100, $500, and $1,000 for the first time.

1915   Sergei Rachmaninoff's choral work *Vespers* was premiered in Moscow. This work is a musical setting for an all-night vigil celebrated in Russian monasteries and on the eves of holy days in Russian Orthodox churches.

1965   Neil Simon's play *The Odd Couple*, starring Walter Matthau as Oscar Madison and Art Carney as Felix Unger, opened on Broadway.

1969   James Earl Ray pleaded guilty in Memphis, Tennessee, to the assassination of Martin Luther King Jr. Ray later repudiated that plea, maintaining his innocence until his death thirty years later.

1985   Konstantin U. Chernenko, Soviet leader for just thirteen months, died at age seventy-three.

10

MARCH

The long boot of Italy, where the Renaissance would be born at the end of the fifteenth century, consisted of five principal parts: the kingdom of Naples, the republic of Florence, the dukedom of Milan, the Papal States, and Venice. A hodgepodge of minor city-states—like the Ligurian republic of Genoa—completed the scene. Each of the realms was obstinate, noisy, and vain about its storied ancestry, but only Venice actually remained a great power—run by an austere, ironfisted, and farsighted oligarchy, with overseas possessions along the Adriatic and throughout the Aegean. Italy for the most part remained only a shell of its former self.

But the decline and ultimately the fall of Byzantium brought a flood of learned exiles to the West—with their uninterrupted access to the ancient and patristic classics—suddenly enriching nascent intellectual endeavors with a volatile mixture of ideas, philosophies, and theologies. In the same way that Greek knowledge had vivified the Arab world during the Great Captivity, so it now catalyzed the Latins.

Thus, a large group of Italian geniuses, heirs of that classical legacy, stretched the limits in the fields of geography, philosophy, politics, science, the arts, and music. Christopher Columbus was born on this day in 1451. Botticelli was born six years earlier. Two years before that saw the birth of Lorenzo de Medici and Domenico Ghirlandaio. A year later came the birth of Leonardo da Vinci. Two years later Giuliano de Medici was born. And three years later still, Amerigo Vespucci, Pinturicchio, and Politian were all born. When Columbus was undertaking his first seafaring experiences in the Ligurian and Tyrrhenian Seas, Pico della Mirandola and Machiavelli were born—in 1463 and 1469 respectively. In the years in which he was thinking up the idea of going west to reach the East, Ariosto in 1474, Michelangelo in 1475, and Titian in 1477 were born. Piero della Francesca died in the same year that the navigator discovered San Salvador. In 1500, when Columbus was seeking the Western Passage in order to circumnavigate the globe, Benvenuto Cellini was born. A year before Columbus's death, Raphael was born. Mantegna and Columbus died in the same year.

If these names were erased from existence, the Renaissance—and all that ultimately produced the modern world of Western civilization—would vanish into thin air, and all of history would be radically and irretrievably altered.

Zealous, yet modest; innocent, though free;
Patient of toil, serene amidst alarms; Inflexible
in faith, invincible in arms.

[JAMES BEATTIE (1735–1803)]

1302 In Italy at Cittadella, the marriage union of Romeo Montevecchio and Juliet Cappelletto was solemnized.

1810 Emperor Napoleon of France was married by proxy to Archduchess Marie Louise of Austria.

1829 The young composer Felix Mendelssohn provoked a revival of interest in the music of J. S. Bach after he conducted the masterful *St. Matthew Passion*. It was only then that scholars began to analyze and appreciate the artistic majesty of Bach—who was relatively unknown. For more than fifty years no Bach piece was published separately on its own merits. Mendelssohn had long been in awe of Bach, however. His performance of the *St. Matthew Passion* came almost exactly a century from the date of its first, long-forgotten performance. "Never," wrote one participant, "have I known any performance so consecrated by one united sympathy." More than one thousand people were unable to get tickets. Two further concerts had to be scheduled at once. So great was the sensation that composer Hector Berlioz marveled, "There is but one god—and Bach and Mendelssohn are His prophets." Today many consider Bach the greatest composer who ever lived.

1861 The Confederate Convention in Montgomery, Alabama, adopted a constitution. The form of government the Southern states adopted for their Confederacy was a deliberate imitation of the original American Constitution—since they believed that they were the philosophical heirs of the Founders and that the Northern states had departed from that decentralized vision. The confederation also drew from the old Articles of Confederation in protecting the autonomy and rights of the individual states. Though its cause was lost, the essence of its flexible form has served as a model for a number of conservative democratic experiments in the years since.

1941 President Roosevelt signed into law the Lend-Lease Bill, providing war supplies to countries fighting the Axis.

1942 As Japanese forces continued to advance in the Pacific during the Second World War, General Douglas MacArthur left the Philippines for Australia, vowing, "I shall return." He kept that promise nearly three years later.

1953 A B-47 bomber accidentally dropped a nuclear bomb on South Carolina; however, the bomb did not detonate due to six safety catches.

1954 The U.S. Army charged that Wisconsin Senator Joseph R. McCarthy and his subcommittee's chief counsel, Roy Cohn, had exerted pressure to obtain favored treatment for Private G. David Schine, a former consultant to the subcommittee.

1959 The Lorraine Hansberry drama *A Raisin in the Sun* opened at New York's Ethel Barrymore Theater.

1965 Reverend James J. Reeb, a white minister from Boston, died after being beaten by whites during civil rights disturbances in Selma, Alabama.

1991 The Metropolitan Museum of Art in New York City acquired $1 billion worth of art through the bequeath of Walter H. Annenberg.

MARCH

12

Charleston, South Carolina, was still reeling from the effects of the calamitous War Between the States and the even more calamitous Radical Reconstruction when Langdon Lowe began his work with the poor in 1881. Hundreds of former sharecroppers and plantation slaves had made their way into the city, hoping to find jobs as dockhands, or perhaps even serving in the merchant marine. But jobs were few and far between. The city was deeply depressed. The corruption and decay of the *inter alia* government had left the city treasury thoroughly depleted, so that the streets, the docks, the harbor, the sewers, and the financial district had fallen into near ruin. That, of course, inhibited business growth and reinvestment. For a time, it looked as if Charleston, once "the emerald of the South," would go the way of Carthage and Troy and slowly die. But Lowe had other ideas.

The former Confederate colonel had been converted to faith in Christ during the great revival among the Southern armies in 1863. Over the next eighteen years, the dashing Southern gentleman devoted his energies to church, family, business, and politics, rising to a place of moderate prominence in the community. But a chance encounter one evening along the Charleston strand with a destitute family of nine forced him to reevaluate his life completely. Not only did that disturbing encounter revitalize his Christian devotion, but it also lit a fire of compassion in his heart that would ultimately spark Charleston's revival.

Lowe began by organizing work crews to repair the streets and docks. In exchange for a day's food and shelter, plus a few coppers, unemployed and homeless workers would gather rubbish, clear away debris, cut down overgrowth, and do light repairs. Lowe solicited financial and material assistance from the various benefiting businesses. Before long, not only were many of the city's poor working again, but a full-scale revitalization had begun. Suddenly Charleston was on the road to becoming a hive of industry, activity, and prosperity again.

Just three years after beginning his ambitious private-initiative program of biblical charity, Langdon Lowe died. But the legacy he left Charleston and all Christendom lived on. His diary, first published in 1896, is not only a classic glimpse into the spiritual vitality of this Southern Presbyterian layman, but it also is a detailed description of how churches, businesses, families, and community coalitions can coordinate their efforts and pool their resources for the benefit of the needy. "The Lord God on High has ordained and prescribed obedience in all matters," Lowe wrote just a month before his death. "Huddled against the cold of the ocean, shivering urchins and penniless Confederate widows are but prods to the fullest expression of that obedience, drawing from the unified strengths of mercantilists, churchmen, craftsmen, and seamen. Akin to the primordial Gospel society in Jerusalem following Pentecost, our work corps allows the attention of each concern to be focused on provisions of mercy, grace, and peace. For the welfare of our own, we turn, not to Rome or Babylon, or Washington, we turn to hearths of our own making."

Amor vincit omnia. (Love conquers all.)

[GEOFFREY CHAUCER (1343–1400)]

604 Pope Gregory the Great, who collected and codified the melodies of the church into what came to be known as Gregorian chant, died.

1663 Reformer, educator, and philanthropist August H. Francke was born. He was a renowned professor of Hebrew at the University of Leipzig in Germany. But he launched a number of other ministries as well. The orphanage he built served as a model to George Müller's more famous work in Bristol. The Bible school he founded awakened university students to a deeper spirituality—including a number, such as Count Zinzindorf, who would later go on to accomplish great feats of faith themselves.

1664 New Jersey became a British colony as King Charles II granted land in the New World to his brother James, the Duke of York.

1894 Coca-Cola was first sold in bottles.

1912 Juliette Gordon Low founded the Girl Guides, which later became the Girl Scouts of America.

1925 Republican Chinese revolutionary leader Sun Yat-sen died.

1930 Indian political and spiritual leader Mohandas K. Gandhi began a two-hundred-mile march to protest a British tax on salt.

1933 President Franklin Roosevelt delivered the first of his radio "fireside chats," telling Americans what was being done to deal with the nation's economic crisis.

1934 Wilhelm Furtwängler conducted the premiere of Paul Hindemith's symphony *Mathis der Maler* in Berlin. Attempts to stage the opera version of the work met with disapproval from the Nazis. Because of Hindemith's marriage to a half-Jewish woman, his refusal to stop association with Jews, and the subject matter of the opera, which dealt with a peasant uprising against the aristocracy, Hindemith was forced to flee the country. Furtwängler incurred the wrath of Hitler and was removed from his musical posts and denied permission to leave the country. Hindemith went on to lead a successful career in composition and teaching abroad.

MARCH

1938 The Anschluss—Hitler's plan to unite the entire German-speaking world under his Third Reich—began as German troops entered Austria.

1939 Pope Pius XII was formally crowned in ceremonies at the Vatican.

1940 Finland and the Soviet Union concluded an armistice during the Second World War. Fighting between the two countries flared again the following year.

1947 President Harry Truman established what became known as the "Truman Doctrine" to help Greece and Turkey resist Communism.

1956 The Dow-Jones industrial average closed above 500 for the first time.

1969 Former Beatle Paul McCartney married photographer Linda Eastman in London.

12

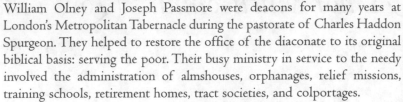

MARCH

13

William Olney and Joseph Passmore were deacons for many years at London's Metropolitan Tabernacle during the pastorate of Charles Haddon Spurgeon. They helped to restore the office of the diaconate to its original biblical basis: serving the poor. Their busy ministry in service to the needy involved the administration of almshouses, orphanages, relief missions, training schools, retirement homes, tract societies, and colportages.

In a lecture to young Bible college students in 1862, Olney stated, "Deacons are called of God to a magnificent field of service, white unto harvest. . . . Ours is the holy duty of stopping by the way, when all others have passed by, to ministrate Christ's healing. Thus, we take the Good Samaritan as our model, lest the pilgrim perish."

To that same audience, Passmore said, "It is ironic indeed that our type of diaconal faithfulness comes not from the life of a disciple of our blessed Lord. Nay, not even is our type from the ancient fathers of faith, the Jews. Instead, our type is from the life of a Samaritan. Mongrel, as touching doctrine, this Good Samaritan is all of pedigree as touching righteousness. Oh, that the church of our day had such men. Oh, that the church of our day bred such men, men of unswerving devotion to the care of the poor and broken-hearted. Oh, that the church of our day was filled with such men, men driven by the Good Samaritan faith . . . offering both word and deed, the fullness of the Gospel."

According to their pastor, Spurgeon, the two men were able to "demonstrate that the words of the Gospel could be translated into actual, tangible deeds. As a result, they were to be counted among the greatest evangelists of our day."

1904

Argentina and Chile successfully negotiated a peaceful settlement of the border war in the Tierra del Fuego region, high in the Andes. Brokered by President Theodore Roosevelt and King Edward VII of England, the peace averted certain conflict that would have plunged all of South America into war. To commemorate the event Monsignor Marcolino del Carmel Benavente, the bishop of San Juan, suggested the erection of a statue—as a way to remind the people in both countries of Christ's words, "And I, if I be lifted up from the earth, will draw all men unto me." Tourists traveling the Pan American Highway can see the result: a 26-foot-tall bronze Christ holding out His right hand in blessing over the disputant nations. His left hand clings to a cross. Under His feet is the Western Hemisphere. Located thirteen thousand feet up in Uspallata Pass, Mount Aconcagua forms its backdrop, lofting thirteen thousand feet higher. This is the highest readily accessible point on the boundary between the two nations. Sculptor Mateo Alonso modeled the work. Señora Angela de Oliveira Cézar de Costa raised the financing. Old cannons were melted down to make the casting. The statue was dedicated on this day as the *Christ of the Andes*. A plaque at its base asserts, "He is our peace who hath made us one." Such monuments are rare in this tumultuous globe, where plowshares are more often beaten into swords than swords into plowshares.

Fear can keep a man out of danger, but courage can support him in it.

[THOMAS FULLER (1608–1661)]

MARCH

4 B.C. Historian Josephus recorded an eclipse of the moon in Rome.

1395 John Barbour—author of the first major work of Scottish literature, the national epic *The Bruce*, whose central event is the Battle of Bannockburn of 1314—died in Aberdeen, Scotland.

1758 Edmund Halley, an English scientist, predicted in 1682 that the comet named for him would reach its nearest point to the sun (perihelion) on this day in 1758. He was correct.

1781 Uranus, the seventh planet from the sun, was discovered by Sir William Herschel, a German-born astronomer living and working in England at the Royal Naval Observatory in Greenwich. He named the planet Georgium Sidus in honor of England's King George III.

1833 The "Italian Symphony" (Symphony no. 4) by Felix Mendelssohn was premiered.

1852 The cartoon character of Uncle Sam—based on Samuel Wilson, who served in the War of 1812—was published in the *New York Lantern*.

1868 The impeachment trial of President Andrew Johnson began in the Senate.

1884 Standard Time was adopted throughout the United States, dividing the continental states into the Eastern, Central, Mountain, and Pacific zones.

1901 The twenty-third president of the United States, Benjamin Harrison, died in Indianapolis.

1906 American suffragist Susan B. Anthony died in Rochester, New York.

1925 A law went into effect in Tennessee prohibiting the teaching of evolution. This was the pretext for the American Civil Liberties Union's infamous Scopes Monkey Trial case in Dayton, Tennessee. Clarence Darrow was the ACLU's lawyer. Former Secretary of State William Jennings Bryan was the state prosecutor. The ACLU lost the case.

1933 Banks began to reopen after a government "holiday" declared by President Franklin Roosevelt in an effort to quell public panic.

1947 The Lerner and Loewe musical *Brigadoon* opened on Broadway.

1964 In a notorious case, thirty-eight residents of a Queens, New York, neighborhood failed to respond to the cries of Kitty Genovese, twenty-eight, as she was being stabbed to death.

1969 The *Apollo 9* astronauts splashed down, ending a mission that included the successful testing of the Lunar Module.

1988 Yielding to student protests, the board of trustees of Gallaudet University in Washington D.C., a liberal arts college for the hearing-impaired, chose I. King Jordan to become the school's first deaf president.

13

MARCH

14

Girolamo Savonarola (1452–1498) was an early Italian Reformer and the composer of the beautiful hymn "Glorious, All Glorious He." During the moral and social tumult of the Medici reign in Florence he captured the attentions of the populace, attacking every sort of laxity with special eloquence. For several years he stood practically alone as a stalwart defender of all that was good and just.

When the Medicis were finally deposed in 1494, the city turned to the fiery preacher for leadership and guidance. He instituted dizzying reforms and quickly distanced the city from the corruptions of both the empire of Charles VII and the papal see of Alexander VI. The city prospered, and a new era of liberty was celebrated among all classes.

Eventually, the political intrigues of his opponents succeeded in turning the tide of public opinion against him and he was dubiously convicted of heresy, treason, and schism. Nevertheless, his commitments to freedom and justice served as essential inspirations of the Reformation just a few years later and formed the basis for the Western conception of liberty under law.

1937

Pope Pius XI issued an encyclical that was smuggled into Germany and read on Palm Sunday from every Catholic pulpit. Amazingly, not a single copy fell into Nazi hands first. *"Mit brennender sorge,"* Pius began. "With burning concern and mounting consternation," he wrote, "we have been observing for some time now the cross carried by the church in Germany and the increasingly difficult situation of those men and women who have kept the faith." The encyclical especially urged Christians to resist the idolatrous cults of state and race. "Race, nation, state all have an essential and honorable place within the secular order. To abstract them, however, from the earthly scale of values and make them the supreme norm of all values, including religious ones, and divinize them with an idolatrous cult, is to be guilty of perverting and falsifying the order of things created and commanded by God."

The world has no room for cowards. We must all be ready somehow to toil, to suffer, to die. And yours is not the less noble because no drum beats before you when you go out into your daily battlefields, and no crowds shout about your coming when you return from your daily victory or defeat.

[ROBERT LOUIS STEVENSON (1850–1894)]

MARCH

1361 Icelandic monk Eysteinn Ásgrímsson died at the Helgisetre Monastery in Norway. He was the author of *Lilja* (The Lily) which is a survey of Christian history from Creation to the Last Judgment and is considered to be the finest example of pre-Reformation Icelandic poetry.

1629 Massachusetts Bay colony was established by a royal charter.

1743 The first recorded town meeting in America was held, at Faneuil Hall in Boston.

1794 Eli Whitney of Mulberry Grove, Georgia, received a patent on "a machine for ginning cotton" that mechanically separated seed from cotton. Whitney had applied for a patent on June 20, 1793, but his model was stolen and manufactured dishonestly before he actually received his patent. The invention was so valuable that Whitney had no legal recourse.

1836 Isabella Mary Beeton, author of *Household Management*, was born on this day. Although there had been other works on the same subject—including the first guides composed during the Middle Ages—her book was the standard household management guide due to its organization and efficiency. She learned her household skills from her mother, who had eighteen children. Beeton died at the age of twenty-nine.

1879 Mathematical Physicist Albert Einstein, who revolutionized the world of science by his Theory of Relativity and other findings, was born in Ulm, Germany.

1883 German political philosopher Karl Marx died in London.

1900 Congress ratified the Gold Standard Act.

1903 President Teddy Roosevelt created the first nature refuge when he established the bird sanctuary on Pelican Island, Sebastian, Florida.

1916 Pulitzer- and Academy Award–winning playwright Horton Foote was born in Wharton, Texas. His many plays and screenplays—such as *1918, The Trip to Bountiful, Tender Mercies, To Kill a Mockingbird* (from the Harper Lee book), and *The Death of the Old Man*—chronicle a very personal and poignant perspective on small-town life.

1923 President Harding became the first chief executive to file an income tax report.

1939 The republic of Czechoslovakia was dissolved, opening the way for Nazi occupation.

1943 George Szell conducted the premiere performance of Aaron Copland's *Fanfare for the Common Man* in New York.

1951 During the Korean War, United Nations forces liberated Seoul from the Communist occupation.

1964 A jury in Dallas, Texas, found Jack Ruby guilty of murdering Lee Harvey Oswald, the accused assassin of President Kennedy, the previous November.

1967 The body of President John Kennedy was moved from a temporary grave to a permanent memorial site at Arlington National Cemetery.

FEAST DAY
St. Longinus; St. Louise de Marillac; St. Zacharias, pope; St. Lucretia; St. Matrona; St. Clement Mary Hofbauer

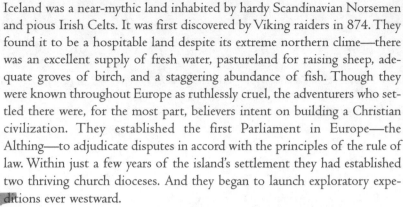

MARCH

Iceland was a near-mythic land inhabited by hardy Scandinavian Norsemen and pious Irish Celts. It was first discovered by Viking raiders in 874. They found it to be a hospitable land despite its extreme northern clime—there was an excellent supply of fresh water, pastureland for raising sheep, adequate groves of birch, and a staggering abundance of fish. Though they were known throughout Europe as ruthlessly cruel, the adventurers who settled there were, for the most part, believers intent on building a Christian civilization. They established the first Parliament in Europe—the Althing—to adjudicate disputes in accord with the principles of the rule of law. Within just a few years of the island's settlement they had established two thriving church dioceses. And they began to launch exploratory expeditions ever westward.

In 982, Eric the Red negotiated the treacherous conditions of the Danish Channel and stumbled onto a vast new land. He was so used to the barren rocks, ice, and wastes of lava on Iceland that he dubbed his discovery Greenland because of its lichen-covered hillsides. He established a small but lively settlement along the southwest coast, and on this day in 1120, a diocese was authorized by papal decree. But the Norse explorers did not stop there. They plunged westward and reached the stark coast of Labrador—which they named Helluland. Pushing farther south, they came to the wooded coast of Nova Scotia (Markland) and then mainland Canada (Vinland).

The explorers established no permanent settlements in any of these new territories, but they did record their visits there—and they even drafted crude maps and charts that ultimately made their way into the hands of cartographers throughout Christendom. The Petrus Vesconte map of 1321, the Andrea Bianco map of 1436, the Basel map of 1443, the Catalan Este map of 1450, and the Giovanni Leardo map of 1452 all indicated at least some familiarity with the Norse adventures from the North Atlantic. None thought the data was terribly significant though. Only Iceland secured an accurate placement. The reason was understandable enough: The northwestern lands were thought to be frozen wastes and barely habitable. It was commonly assumed that the Norsemen had simply stumbled upon Utima Thule—the northern limit of the Eurasian continental land mass. Thus, their epic accomplishments were not counted as discoveries at all—only chance encounters.

Even so, hearing such stories, seeing such waters, and visiting such places stirred the imagination and longing of men like Christopher Columbus. In fact it was while he was sailing in *Ultima Thule* that he began to wonder if perhaps it was possible to reach the Asian shore by sailing west. If it could be done in the frozen north, why not in the more hospitable south?

THE IDES OF MARCH	The Roman lunar calendar divided each month into Kalends, Nones, and Ides—rooted in the phases of the moon. The Ides of each month marked the half-moon phase.

*I*n valor there is hope.

[Tacitus (c. 55–120)]

44
B.C. Roman general and statesman Gaius Julius Caesar died at the hands of a group of nobles in the Senate House.

459 While profaning the divine at a wedding banquet, Attilla the Hun developed a nosebleed and bled to death. He was known as the Scourge of God because of his ravaging of the Roman Empire.

1493 Christopher Columbus returned to Spain, concluding his first voyage to the Western Hemisphere.

1517 When Giovanni de Medici became bishop of Rome, taking the name Pope Leo X, he was determined to rebuild the dilapidated palace and basilica of St. Peter. The problem was that the Vatican was bankrupt. And so on this day he declared that anyone who contributed to the cathedral would be granted indulgence from sins. Some months later, Leo sent a Dominican monk named Tetzel to preach the indulgence in Germany. Tetzel was rather exorbitant in his promises, implying that the indulgence might even cover any future sins that the buyer was then harboring. Wary of all such schemes, Frederick the Wise refused to allow the indulgence to be preached in his territory of Saxony. So Tetzel came as near the border of Saxony as he could so that people from the city of Wittenberg could cross over and buy the prized papers. Afterward several concerned city leaders solicited the opinion of a middle-aged monk named Martin Luther. Enraged by Leo's scheme, Tetzel's brazenness, and the people's gullibility, Luther refused to confirm the value of the indulgences. Instead, as had many before him, he posted theses for debate on the door of Wittenberg Castle Church where a large crowd was expected. From those ninety-five theses the Reformation was born.

1767 The seventh president of the United States, Andrew Jackson, was born in Waxhaw, South Carolina.

MARCH

1820 Maine became the twenty-third state, having split from Massachusetts.

1823 Michigan began taxing property for the sake of supporting a university—the first state to do so.

1869 When organizers George Ellard and Harry Wright announced that they would start to pay players, the Cincinnati Red Stockings became the first pro baseball team.

1875 The Roman Catholic archbishop of New York, John McCloskey, was named the first American cardinal by Pope Pius IX.

1913 President Woodrow Wilson held the first open presidential news conference.

1949 In Great Britain, the rationing of clothes was officially ended, almost four years after the conclusion of World War II.

1956 The Lerner and Loewe musical *My Fair Lady* opened on Broadway at the Mark Hellinger Theater in New York.

1972 Francis Ford Coppola's film masterpiece, *The Godfather*, opened in theaters.

1975 Greek shipping magnate Aristotle Onassis died near Paris at age sixty-nine.

1998 The news program *60 Minutes* aired an interview with former White House employee Kathleen Willey, who said President Clinton had made unwelcome sexual advances toward her in the Oval Office in 1993, a charge denied by the president.

FEAST DAY
*St. Finan Lobur, St. Abraham
Kidunaia, St. Julian of Antioch,
St. Eusebia of Hamage, St.
Heribert of Cologne, St. Gregory
Makar*

MARCH

Wherever committed Christians have gone, throughout Europe, into the darkest depths of Africa, to the outer reaches of China, along the edges of the American frontier, and beyond to the Australian outback, the faith of the good Samaritan—authentic concern for the needy—has always been in evidence. In fact, most of the church's greatest heroes are those who willingly gave the best of their lives to serve the less fortunate.

Nathaniel Samuelson, a Puritan divine of some renown, was a great spokesman for Christ who devoted his life and ministry to the poor. He established a network of clinics, hospitals, and rescue missions that in later years served as the primary inspiration for William Booth in founding the Salvation Army.

His preaching was noted for its emphasis on mercy ministry. In a sermon that he preached at his little parish church in Yorkshire, England, he said, "Sodom was crushed in divine judgment. And why, asks me? Was it due to abomination heaped upon abomination such as those perpetuated against the guests of Lot? Nay, saith Scripture. Was it due to wickedness in commerce, graft in governance, and sloth in manufacture? Nay, saith Scripture. In Ezekiel 16:49, thus saith Scripture: Behold this, the sin-guilt of thine sister Sodom: she and her daughters wrought arrogance, fatness, and ill-concern, but neglected the help of the poor and need-stricken. Thus, they were caught, committing blasphemy before me. Therefore, I removed them in judgment as all see. Be ye warned by Sodom's example. She was crushed in divine judgment simply and solely due to her selfish neglect of the deprived and depressed."

1517

The fifth Lateran Council ended. It had been called together two years earlier to deal with the dangers of new technologies—particularly, the printing press. Though the Bible was Johann Gutenberg's first project, within sixty years of his invention of movable type, printed pornography had begun to be produced. Thus, the council decreed that books should no longer be printed without ecclesiastical examination and consent. Every book published was to feature a license to print. Hence, each bishop automatically became censor for his diocese. Of course, their decree was largely unenforceable. Months later Luther posted his ninety-five theses and made masterful use of the new technology to spread his theories across the breadth of Europe. Other reformers, such as William Tyndale, resorted to secret printing and pious smuggling. As for pornography, we know how it has fared.

The strength and glory of a land does not depend upon its wealth, its defenses, its great houses, its powerful armaments; but on the number of its gracious, serious, kind, and wise citizens.

MARCH

1621 Samoset, the Indian chief from the Island of Monhegan, visited the new colony of Plymouth—the first chief to do so.

1751 James Madison, fourth president of the United States, was born in Port Conway, Virginia.

1792 Sweden's King Gustav III was shot and mortally wounded during a masquerade party.

1802 West Point Military Academy was established by an act of Congress in West Point, New York.

1830 Only thirty-one shares were traded on this day at the New York Stock Exchange—its slowest day ever.

1836 The Republic of Texas approved a constitution.

1849 Nathaniel Hawthorne's bitter caricature of the Puritans, *The Scarlet Letter*, was published.

1894 The opera *Thais*, composed by Jules Massenet, premiered in Paris.

1915 The Federal Trade Commission was organized.

1926 Professor Robert Hutchins Goddard launched the first successful liquid-fuel rocket in Auburn, Massachusetts. The rocket traveled 184 feet in 2.5 seconds, reaching speeds of 60 mph along its trajectory.

1935 Adolf Hitler formally abandoned the Treaty of Versailles.

1945 During the Second World War, Iwo Jima was declared secured by the Allies.

1968 During the Vietnam War, the My Lai Massacre was carried out by U.S. troops under the command of Lieutenant William L. Calley Jr.

1969 The musical *1776*, about the writing of the Declaration of Independence, opened on Broadway.

1978 Italian politician Aldo Moro was kidnapped by left-wing urban guerrillas, who later murdered him.

1991 Americans Kristi Yamaguchi, Tonya Harding and Nancy Kerrigan swept the World Figure Skating Championships in Munich, Germany.

1995 The state of Mississippi ratified the Thirteenth Amendment, 130 years after it was originally adopted at the end of the War Between the States.

16

NATIONAL DAY
Ireland
FEAST DAY
*St. Patrick, St. Withburga, St.
Gertrude of Nivelles, St. Joseph of
Arimathea, St. Paul of Cyprus, the
Martyrs of the Serapaeum*

MARCH

The great Scottish pastor, social reformer, educator, author, and scientist Thomas Chalmers (1780–1847) was born on this day in 1780 at Anstruther on the Fife coast. During the course of his long and storied career he served as the pastor of three congregations, taught in three colleges, published more than thirty-five best-selling books, and helped to establish in excess of one hundred charitable relief and missions organizations. He practically reinvented the Scottish parish system as well as the national social welfare structure. He counted such luminaries as the Duke of Wellington, Sir Walter Scott, King William IV, Thomas Carlyle, William Wilberforce, and Robert Peel as his friends. Indeed, he was among the most influential and highly regarded men of his day.

In 1809, having already made his mark as a brilliant professor of mathematics at St. Andrews and serving a small rural parish, he underwent a spiritual transformation following an extended illness. Afterward, he completely abandoned himself to his little covenantal community. He married and had his first children there. He established a classical school at the heart of the parish. He set about a reform of the ministry to the poor, the widows, and the orphans. He established a pioneer missionary society and a Bible society and he began his prodigious and prolific publishing career.

Chalmers went to Glasgow at the invitation of the magistrates and town council in 1815. He served first in the Tron Church until 1819, and then he was transferred to the newly created parish of St. John's, a poorer parish with a very high proportion of factory workers, where he had the freedom to develop ministry to the poor and needy.

Chalmers was concerned that his ministry should first and foremost be to the parish—where some eleven or twelve thousand people lived and worked. He commenced a program of visitation from house to house that took two years to complete. He organized the eldership to cooperate in this task and developed Sabbath evening schools. He undertook care of the poor, education of the entire community, and reform of the local political economy. In addition, he became a popular author, at times even besting his friend Walter Scott in sales.

In later years, he prepared others for a similar impact in ministry at the University of Edinburgh—always modeling mercy himself. In 1843, he led the Evangelicals in the establishment of the Free Church and in 1846 laid the cornerstone for its New College.

Thomas Carlyle said of him, "What a wonderful old man Chalmers is. Or rather, he has all the buoyancy of youth. When so many of us are wringing our hands in hopeless despair over the vileness and wretchedness of the large towns, there goes the old man, shovel in hand, down into the dirtiest puddles, cleans them out, and fills the sewers with living waters. It is a beautiful sight." By the end of his life, Chalmers had changed his land like no other since Knox.

| ST. PATRICK'S DAY | Celebrated by Irish and would-be Irish all across the globe, this day is marked by parades, wearing green clothing, adorning homes with shamrocks and leprechauns, and parties. |

Faith is always at a disadvantage; it is a perpetually defeated thing which survives all conquerors.

[G. K. CHESTERTON (1874–1936)]

461 According to tradition, Saint Patrick, the patron saint of Ireland, died on this day. As a result, this is his feast day.

1776 British forces evacuated Boston during the Revolutionary War.

1846 Kate Greenaway, English artist and children's book illustrator, was born in London. Her little "Toy-books," *The Birthday Book, Mother Goose, Little Ann,* and others, created a revolution in book illustration and were praised by art critics around the world.

1870 The Massachusetts legislature authorized the incorporation of Wellesley Female Seminary. It later became Wellesley College.

1905 Distant cousins Eleanor Roosevelt and Franklin D. Roosevelt were married in New York.

1906 President Theodore Roosevelt first used the term "muckrake" to describe tabloid journalism in a speech to the Gridiron Club in Washington.

1910 The Camp Fire Girls organization was formed. It was formally presented to the public exactly two years later.

1941 The National Gallery of Art opened in Washington, D.C.

1942 General Douglas MacArthur arrived in Australia to become supreme commander of Allied forces in the Southwest Pacific theater during the Second World War.

1950 Scientists at the University of California at Berkeley announced that they had created a new radioactive element, which they named "californium."

1966 An American midget submarine located a missing hydrogen bomb that had fallen from an American bomber into the Mediterranean off the coast of Spain.

1969 Golda Meir, a high school teacher from Milwaukee, became Israel's fourth prime minister.

1993 Helen Hayes, the "First Lady of the American Theater," died in Nyack, New York, at age ninety-two.

MARCH

FEAST DAY
St. Cyril of Jerusalem, St. Alexander of Jerusalem, St. Christian, St. Edward the Martyr, St. Finan of Aberdeen, St. Anselm of Lucca, St. Frigidian, St. Salvator of Horta

John C. Calhoun was the only American politician to serve as vice president under two different presidents. He also served as secretary of war and secretary of state under two more presidents. He was born in the South Carolina upcountry on this day in 1782. The son of a small-holding farmer, Calhoun was educated at a classical log college in Georgia. His advanced studies were pursued at Yale under the tutelage of the strong antiunionist Timothy Dwight—the renowned grandson of Jonathan Edwards.

Upon his return to his beloved South, his soaring ambitions enabled his career to advance with astonishing speed. He served in the state legislature and in Congress. Appointed secretary of war in the cabinet of James Monroe in 1817, Calhoun was a War Hawk who supported what was then called the American System—calling for the use of federal power to enforce mercantilist policies and the imposition of high protective tariffs.

Calhoun sought to succeed Monroe as president in 1824. Lacking support, however, he withdrew to run for the vice-presidency with endorsement from both Jacksonians and the followers of eventual winner, John Quincy Adams. At the time of his election as vice president in 1824, Calhoun was not yet identified with the states' rights position he would later make famous. His views on federal power, however, were undergoing a dramatic transformation—and before long he was converted to both the orthodox Calvinism and the traditional constitutionalism that dominated his native region. No longer persuaded that the interests of the South could be served by an active federal government fostering industry, he abandoned the ideas of political pragmatism for those of principle. As a result Calhoun began repudiating the mercantilist system and broke with the Adams administration. He secretly authored the South Carolina Exposition and Protest, which asserted that a state had the power of nullification over any federal law it deemed unconstitutional.

Supporting Andrew Jackson's presidential candidacy in 1828, Calhoun was reelected to the vice-presidency. His efforts to dominate the Jackson administration were frustrated by Jackson's refusal to endorse a strong states' rights position. In addition, Calhoun was outraged by Jackson's high-handed rule. After the president opposed South Carolina's efforts to nullify the Tariff of 1832, Calhoun resigned from the administration.

Calhoun remained an influential statesman until his death. Serving briefly as secretary of state in 1844–45 under John Tyler, he engineered the annexation of Texas. He spent the remainder of his career serving in the Senate defending Southern rights, advocating strict construction of the Constitution, and predicting disunion and civil war if those principles were not respected. Near the end of his life he delineated his principles in writing. Published just before his death in 1850 as *A Disquisition on Government,* the work attempted to forge reasonable legal and political protections for minorities from majority rule. It became the manifesto of the South and remains an undoubted classic.

You must not begin to fret the successes of cheap people.

[WILLA CATHER (1873–1947)]

MARCH

978 Edward, king of England, was stabbed in the back and murdered at the encouragement of his stepmother. His body was then buried in unhallowed ground.

1543 Hernando de Soto made the first known record of the flooding of the Mississippi River while on an exploration trip. The river overflowed its banks on this day and did not crest until April 20. The river receded by the end of May.

1766 Britain repealed the Stamp Act after protests, boycotts, and appeals from the American colonies.

1837 The twenty-second and twenty-fourth president of the United States, Grover Cleveland, was born in Caldwell, New Jersey.

1902 Italian tenor Enrico Caruso received $500 from the Gramaphone Company for making a phonograph recording. Caruso, who was one of the first artists to recognize the potential of the phonograph as a medium for musicians, recorded ten operatic arias in a hotel room in Milan, Italy, that had been converted into a temporary studio.

1909 Einar Dessau of Denmark used a shortwave transmitter to converse with a government radio post about six miles away in what's believed to have been the first broadcast by a "ham" operator.

1931 Schick Razor Blade Company marketed the first electric razor.

1937 More than four hundred people, mostly children, were killed in a gas explosion at a school in New London, Texas.

1944 Twenty-five hundred women rushed into a Chicago department store in a panic to obtain one of 1,500 alarm clocks advertised for sale. Alarm clocks had been scarce during the Second World War.

1959 President Dwight Eisenhower signed the Hawaii statehood bill.

1965 The first space walk took place as Soviet cosmonaut Aleksei Leonov left his *Voskhod Two* capsule, secured by a tether.

1974 Most of the Arab oil-producing nations ended their embargo against the United States, thus bringing to a close the nation's worst energy crisis marked by high prices and long gas lines.

1979 Iranian authorities detained American feminist Kate Millett, a day before deporting her and a companion for what were termed "perverse provocations." Millett had been protesting the radical Shi'ite regime's treatment of women.

18

MARCH

The Charity Organization Society was England's leading private charity agency in the late nineteenth century. It operated on the biblical principle of aid to foster self-help. According to Charles Loch Mowat, the historian of the society, it embodied an idea of charity that claimed to reconcile the divisions in society, to remove poverty, and to produce a happy, self-reliant community. It believed that the most serious aspect of poverty was the degradation of the character of the poor man or woman. Indiscriminate charity only made things worse; it demoralized. True charity demanded friendship, though, the sort of help that would restore a man's self-respect and his ability to support himself and his family. True charity demanded "gainful employ."

The society aimed to implement to the fullest extent possible the bootstrap ethic so predominant in Scripture. Again, according to Mowat, it sought: "First, to place in gainful employ those able to work; Second, to occupy, with industry within the Society, all those incapable of placement; And, third, to acquire the means with which to supply the other incapacitated needy with the necessities of life."

Charles Haddon Spurgeon, the premier Victorian pulpit master, was a public advocate and avid supporter of the society. He heralded it as "a charity to which the curse of idleness is subjected to the rule of the under-magistrate of earthly society: work."

This was the appropriate aim of biblical charity, he said, "to rid the impoverished of the curse of idleness" and to "rebuild self-reliance and productivity." More than anything else, he argued, "the poor need jobs." So, the society sought to explore the markets, equip the applicants, and expand the opportunities so that full employment could be secured for all but the totally infirm.

The results were remarkable—a revolution not unlike that of Thomas Chalmers in Scotland a generation earlier took place in the industrialized centers all throughout Britain. Poverty was transformed into productivity, and the poor themselves became engines of prosperity.

SAN JUAN CAPISTRANO DAY	This is the day that the swallows traditionally return to the San Juan Capistrano Mission in California.

In one sense, Babylon is the acceptance of matter as the only meaning, the source of the mystery. That man could accept the shell for the total meaning, that his vanity could lead him into thinking he can control matter and hence life, is the ultimate folly.

[ANDREW NELSON LYTLE (1902–1995)]

721 B.C. The Greek astronomer Claudius Ptolemaeus (Ptolemy) recorded the first known eclipse of the moon.

1813 British missionary to Africa Dr. David Livingstone was born on this day. While working in Kuruman, Livingstone met Mary Moffat, daughter of a fellow missionary. The two married in 1845 and lived at Mabosta. It was there that Livingstone lost the full use of his right arm after a lion attacked and mauled his shoulder. Not to be daunted, Livingstone undertook a journey of 4,300 miles, declaring the gospel as he went through the heart of the continent. The transcription of his diaries into a book entitled *Missionary Travels* became an instant bestseller in Britain.

1821 The English scholar, explorer, and orientalist Sir Richard Francis Burton was born in Torquay, Devonshire, England. Because of his travels all over the world, Burton learned twenty-five languages and an additional fifteen dialects, which enabled him to translate and publish almost thirty volumes of foreign literature including the skillful and original English version of *The Thousand and One Arabian Nights* and the beguiling *Kama Sutra*. As the first Englishman to visit Mecca (disguised as an Afghani Muslim) as well as many other locales, Burton wrote an astonishing forty-three volumes of travel literature. At his death in 1890, his widow, Isabel, burned hundreds of his unpublished manuscripts, thinking them to be obscene.

1872 The Russian ballet master Sergei Pavlovich Diaghilev was born in Gruzine, Novgorod Province. He was gifted with the ability to stimulate creative gifts as well as providing the catalyst to bring together some of the best artists of his era. Diaghilev brought together scenic design by Henri Matisse, Georges Braque, Jean Cocteau, and Pablo Picasso with new compositions by Igor Stravinsky, Maurice Ravel, Manuel de Falla, Darius Milhaud, and Erik Satie. He revived a serious interest in ballet in the twentieth century.

1931 Nevada legalized gambling.

1942 Men between the ages of forty-five and sixty-four were required to register for nonmilitary duty, as ordered by President Franklin D. Roosevelt.

1945 Nearly eight hundred troops were killed as kamikaze planes attacked the American aircraft carrier *Franklin* off the coast of Japan. The ship, however, was saved.

1945 Adolf Hitler issued his so-called "Nero Decree," ordering the destruction of German facilities that could fall into Allied hands.

1953 The Academy Awards ceremony was televised for the first time. *The Greatest Show on Earth* was named best picture of 1952.

1976 Buckingham Palace announced the separation of Princess Margaret and her husband, the Earl of Snowdon, after sixteen years of marriage.

1987 Televangelist Jim Bakker resigned as chairman of his PTL ministry organization amid a sex and money scandal involving Jessica Hahn, a former church secretary from Oklahoma.

1998 Completing baseball's transformation from family ownership to corporate control, Rupert Murdoch's Fox Group won approval to buy the Los Angeles Dodgers for a record $350 million.

FEAST DAY
St. Cuthbert, St. Wolfram, St. Herbert of Derwentwater, St. Martin of Braga, St. Photina and her Companions, the Martyrs of Mar Saba

MARCH

20

By the time Hilaire Belloc visited Rome in 1901—after a long journey on foot from France, across the Alps, and through Lombardy—it was universally recognized as one of the grandest cities in the world. Tens of thousands of pilgrims and tourists came to admire, and be awed by, its treasures of architecture, art, and history every year. It was a well-worn cliché that all roads led to Rome. Certainly that was true for Belloc (1870–1953), a close friend and confidant of G. K. Chesterton and himself a renowned poet, journalist, novelist, and apologist for the Catholic faith.

Belloc was born outside Paris in 1870. Two years later, his father, a French citizen, died. His mother removed the youngster and his sister to her native England where they would be raised. He was trained in the finest schools in the land and quickly gained renown as a fine poet, an incisive historian, and an essayist of great promise. An ardent Catholic and proud of his dual citizenship and heritage, he maintained close ties to his father's family in France and upheld his responsibilities to serve in the French armed services. It was following one of his tours of duty there that he impetuously decided to walk all the way to Rome as a kind of modern-day pilgrimage. He wanted to find the roots of his faith—and to discover the sites and sights of Christendom's genesis.

That he did and more. The story of his remarkable journey was recorded in his classic book *The Path to Rome.* But the insights he gained and the perspective that he solidified also pervaded his more than one hundred books that followed in his long and accomplished career as a historian, apologist, controversialist, politician, economic theorist, novelist, poet, journalist, and pundit.

It was there, amid the unearthed splendors of the pagan Antiquity and the rebuilt glories of the pagan Renaissance that he found the genius of Western civilization, its ultimate continuity, and its conflict with the Reformation—themes that would shape his social criticism and define his curmudgeonly prophecies against the advancing horrors of modernity. In essence, it was his trip to Rome that made him so interesting and so infuriating.

SPRING EQUINOX

This day marks the beginning of spring in the Northern Hemisphere, when the sun moves north across the celestial equator marking the vernal equinox.

When I am dead, I hope it may be said, though his sins were scarlet, his books are read.

[HILAIRE BELLOC (1870–1953)]

43 B.C. Ovid, the outstanding Roman poet, was born in Sulmo near Rome. His greatest known work is the fifteen-book *Metamorphoses.*

1413 England's King Henry IV died. He was succeeded by his gallant son, Henry V.

1455 When Guido di Pietro became a monk at Fiesole, he changed his name to Giovanni and became known as Giovanni da Fiesole. Italians called him Beato, "Blessed One." But fourteen years after his death, on this day, he was given the name by which he is best known today: Fra Angelico, "angelic father." He gained early renown as a masterful painter—first illuminating manuscripts and later creating altarpieces. Wherever he resided—Cortona, Fiesole, and San Marco—he left frescoes and paintings. When the decayed monastery at San Marco in Florence was restored by the Dominicans, he and his pupils painted fifty frescoes in its rooms as aids to contemplation. As his fame as an artist spread, he was called to Rome to decorate the Vatican. Most of the frescoes he created in the Eternal City have perished with their buildings. Among those that remain are scenes from the lives of St. Lawrence and St. Stephen. Thanks to Fra Angelico the Vatican possesses portraits of many of his contemporaries, including Thomas Aquinas and Albertus Magnus. The pope wanted to make Angelico archbishop of Florence, but the unworldly priest declined the offer. In 1449 he was elected abbot of Fiesole and served three years, after which he returned to Rome to paint. He and Fra Filippo Lippi are considered the two greatest artists of the Medieval Epoch.

1727 Sir Isaac Newton died after serving as president of the Royal Society since 1703. His many contributions to science and mathematics include the invention of calculus, the formulation of the three laws of motion, which bear his name, and the understanding of light and optics. A graduate of Trinity College, Cambridge, he resisted the efforts of King James II to make the institution Catholic.

1815 Having returned from exile on the island of Elba, Napoleon Bonaparte entered Paris, beginning his "Hundred Days" rule.

1816 The Supreme Court affirmed its right to review state court decisions.

1828 Norwegian dramatist and poet Henrik Ibsen was born in Skien, Norway. Ibsen created a new order of moral analysis set in a realistic middle-class background with sparse action and penetrating dialogue. His most famous works were *Peer Gynt, A Doll's House, Ghosts,* and *Hedda Gabler.*

1857 *Uncle Tom's Cabin* by Harriet Beecher Stowe was published. In one week the initial printing of five thousand copies sold out. More than one million copies had sold in a period of sixteen months. Though she had never visited the South or witnessed slavery firsthand, she constructed a compelling narrative that Abraham Lincoln said ultimately caused the War Between the States.

1896 American marines landed in Nicaragua to protect U.S. citizens in the wake of a violent revolution.

1954 "High-fidelity" recordings were first introduced by Decca, Columbia, and MGM.

1963 The first exhibition of "Pop Art" took place in New York City.

1991 By a unanimous ruling of the Supreme Court, it was decided that employers were not allowed to exclude women from jobs in which exposure to toxic chemicals could cause damage to a developing fetus.

MARCH

21

Composer Johann Sebastian Bach was born in Eisenarch, Thuringia (now Germany), on March 21, 1685. Thus began a life filled with incredible labor and beauty. Bach was a master craftsman and artisan, and he regarded himself as such. Rarely did he talk about his own work and never in a way that exalted art for its own sake or relied on rapturous inspiration for a guide. When asked about his work, he simply replied, "I worked hard." His insatiable desire for learning was manifested throughout his life by copying the music of other composers to understand their technique or in creating musical puzzles to unravel compositionally.

And he wrote and wrote. When his music was catalogued and published it took forty-six years to compile and filled sixty volumes. He did all of this while fulfilling the role of organist, conductor, and musical director of church services, and teaching a class of boys. Bach never received widespread fame or fortune, and yet he continued to be faithful in the vocation in which God had called him. His life was one of struggles: the death of his first wife, the death of children, the lack of money or favor, the strenuous work, conflict with church officials, eventual blindness, and obscurity. From his pen flowed some of the best-crafted and most beautiful music known in music history. Works such as *The Saint Matthew Passion, Mass in B-minor, The Brandenburg Concertos,* more than three hundred cantatas, multiple sonatas for solo instruments, and many works for keyboard were written and crafted through times of personal hardship.

Bach understood the role of the artist as one of artisan in service to the glory of God. His eventual renown, influence, and fame were left to the hand of God, who exalted Bach's faithfulness almost eighty years after his death. Service to God does not necessarily mean worldly success or fortune; God's economy is based on willingness, sacrifice, submission, and faithfulness. As Bach always noted at the end of each of his compositions, *Soli Deo Gloria,* "To God alone belongs all glory."

1747

The bitter old slave-trader John Newton and his crew were caught in a violent storm on the Atlantic Ocean. Their ship was in a sad state of disrepair, and its sails and rigging were worn. Wakened by a crushing wave smashing against the vessel, Newton barely escaped as water filled his cabin. He hurried above where he found that timbers had been ripped away. Men pumped water desperately. Clothes and bedding were stuffed into holes and boards nailed over them. Exhausted after battling for more than an hour, Newton was lashed to the wheel to try to steer the ship. The storm raged on and on. In this desperate moment Newton cried out to the God he had been taught to worship as a child. Eventually, the ship was delivered from distress—and so was Newton. He became an abolitionist and a minister. Reflecting on his hard life, he wrote one of the world's most loved hymns, which begins: "Amazing grace, how sweet the sound that saved a wretch like me."

We trust, not because a God exists, but because this God exists.

[C. S. Lewis (1898–1963)]

543 Saint Benedict, the founder of the Bendictine Order, died. While abbot of Monte Casino, he developed the foundation of the order on the principles of obedience, charity, and voluntary poverty.

1292 John of Peckham was raised to the archbishopric of Canterbury in England by the pope in Rome. Born in the Surrey region, his early education came in the priory of Lewes. He later studied in Paris, where he defended the innovative theology of St. Thomas Aquinas. At the university he lectured on theology, was provincial minister of the Franciscans, and acted as an instructor to the papal curia. Even after he was appointed to become archbishop, he insisted on following the strictest Franciscan rules, such as walking rather than riding a horse. Humble and sincere, he prayed and fasted assiduously. But Peckham was a scientist as well as a churchman. Inspired by the newly translated Arabic writings of Alhazen, he began to study the nature of light and optics. With more than average skill, he applied mathematics to the problem. The elementary textbooks he wrote were successful in achieving his goal of popularizing science as a legitimate Christian vocation.

1556 The archbishop of Canterbury, Thomas Cranmer, was burned at the stake in Oxford for heresy. Protestants respected the courage and learning of this pious martyr.

1617 Mrs. John Rolfe, formerly Indian princess Pocahantas, died in London. She saved the life of Captain John Smith, who had been imprisoned by her father, Chief Powhattan. In 1612, she married the colonist Mr. Rolfe, who took her to England.

1678 *The London Gazette* offered a reward to anyone who might be able to reveal the author of the scandalous *An Account of the Growth of Popery*, published anonymously the year before.

1790 Thomas Jefferson reported to President Washington in New York as the new secretary of state.

1806 Mexican statesman Benito Juarez, who was Mexico's first president of Indian ancestry, was born in Oaxaca.

1843 Robert Southey, historian and poet laureate for thirty years, died at Greta Hall, Keswick, in England.

1891 The feuding between the Hatfields and McCoys of West Virginia ended when a son from one family announced his engagement to a daughter from the rival clan.

1963 The Alcatraz federal prison island in San Francisco Bay was emptied of its last inmates at the order of Attorney General Robert F. Kennedy.

1965 Martin Luther King Jr. led three thousand civil rights demonstrators on a march from Selma to Montgomery, Alabama. They were under the protection of federal troops since local police had assaulted the group two weeks earlier.

1979 The Egyptian Parliament unanimously approved a peace treaty with Israel.

EASTER *(earliest possible date)*
FEAST DAY
   St. Deogratius, St. Basil of Ancyra,
   St. Paul of Narbonne, St. Nicholas
   Owen, St. Benvenuto of Osimo

MARCH

22

The original Poor Laws, enacted on this day in 1589, sought to "reinforce righteousness," to strengthen "the family bond," and to "set the poor to work" and turn the country into "a hive of industry." Although far from ideal, the laws accomplished just that, and became the model for three centuries of unprecedented liberty and prosperity.

The Poor Laws determined that if welfare was to be a compromise, it was to be a carefully conditioned compromise. Workhouses and labor yards were established so that those willing to work could "pull themselves up by their own bootstraps" while maintaining family integrity. Cottage apprenticeships were initiated so that the youth would "be accustomed and brought up in labor, work, thrift, and purposefulness." Disincentives were deliberately incorporated so that unfaithfulness, irresponsibility, sloth, and graft could be kept to a minimum. From all but the disabled, industry was required.

This legacy of conditioning government welfare on faith, family, and work was carried across the sea by the early American settlers. Knowing that the Poor Laws were based on the fundamental scriptural balance between discipline and responsibility, the colonists maintained the old consensus. As a result, the poor could expect justice and compassion even along the rough-hewn edges of the new frontier. But it was a justice and compassion that demanded responsibility, effort, and diligence of the beneficiaries. It was a justice and compassion rooted in the biblical family and work ethic. It was a justice and compassion that were administered, not by an army of benevolent bureaucrats, but by a gracious citizenry. It was a justice and compassion that offered opportunities, not entitlements.

American statesman Alexander Hamilton wrote, "Americans hold their greatest liberty in this, our poor arise from their plight of their own accord, in cooperation with, but not dependent upon, Christian generosities." Likewise, philanthropist Thomas MacKay wrote, "American welfare consists in a re-creation and development of the arts of independence and industry." And Benjamin Franklin was fond of paraphrasing the old Talmudic proverb, asserting that American charity "is the noblest charity, preventing a man from accepting charity, and the best alms, enabling men to dispense with alms." So America came to be known the world over as the home of the free and the brave, the land of opportunity. The old consensus remained an unchallenged bastion in the determination of domestic social policy. But that old consensus died in 1964 when President Lyndon Johnson launched his famous "war on poverty."

1730

The first gambling legislation in the colonies was passed at Boston, Massachusetts, stating, "It is likewise ordered that all persons whatsoever that have cards, dice or tables in their houses, shall make away with them before the next court under pain of punishment."

Man is what he believes.

1312 The Poor Knights of Christ and of the Temple of Solomon—who were more commonly known as the Knights Templars—were abolished and banned by Philip the Fair of France. They had come into existence as an order of fighting monks dedicated to protecting the Christians who visited the Holy Land. Bernard of Clairvaux, teacher of Christian love, wrote their rule. Sworn to poverty, they nevertheless became rich with lands in the years following the Crusades. Like the Teutonic Knights and Knights Hospitallers, they had quickly grown beyond their original purpose. After the loss of Jerusalem, the Templars returned to Europe. Their castles became repositories of the wealth of Europe, bank vaults, protected by sword and spear, the only place a rich man could be sure his gold was safe. Rivals eyed them with envy. Nations feared their international military might. Like so many other monarchs, Philip the Fair desired to get his hands on Templar wealth. He tried to get the pope to take action. When the pope would not, believing none was called for, Philip arrested every Templar in a single day. He tortured them into confessing all sorts of wrongs against themselves and their order. With this "proof," Pope Clement V was prodded into action. He called a council at Vienne, which voted overwhelmingly to abolish the Templars. Nevertheless, Clement V refused to condemn the knights; he merely dissolved them as a managerial step. Even so, the order's assets were transferred to either the Knights Hospitallers or the French treasury. The knights, many of those who recanted the confessions forced from them under torture, were burned as heretics, fifty-four of them in one day. Their master was sentenced to life imprisonment. Relieved, he repudiated the lies he'd been forced to tell. At once he, too, was seized and burned.

1599 Flemish artist and portrait painter Sir Anthony Van Dyck was born in Antwerp. His talent was recognized early, and he was admitted to the Antwerp guild of painters in 1618 at the age of eighteen. He spent the following two years as part of the Peter Paul Rubens workshop. Travels to Italy and England helped to solidify his style and reputation as one of the best portrait painters—especially of royalty and aristocracy. His paintings are characterized by his use of color, the luminous effect of fabrics and metals in the works, and expressive hands.

MARCH

1638 Civil and religious dissident Anne Hutchinson was expelled from the Massachusetts Bay Colony.

1673 The first regular mail service was established between New York and Boston.

1687 French composer Jean Baptiste Lully died in Paris from injuries sustained while conducting a rehearsal of his *Te Deum*. Overcome with the excitement of the music, Lully accidentally struck himself on the toe with his cane. A doctor recommended amputation of the inflamed toe, but Lully procrastinated until the infection had spread too far to be cured.

1882 Congress outlawed polygamy as a means of dealing with the innumerable utopian or millennial cults that had sprung up in the second half of the nineteenth century—chief among them were the Mormons of Joseph Smith and Brigham Young.

1919 The first international airline service was established between Paris and Brussels with a regular weekly flight.

1946 The British mandate in Transjordan came to an end.

1976 Filming began on the first of George Lucas's *Star Wars* films.

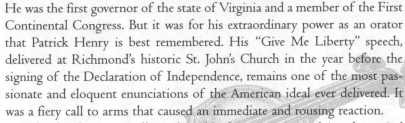

NATIONAL DAY
Pakistan
FEAST DAY
St. Gwinear, St. Turibius, St.
Benedict the Hermit, St. Victorian,
St. Ethelwald the Hermit, St.
Joseph Oriol

MARCH

23

He was the first governor of the state of Virginia and a member of the First Continental Congress. But it was for his extraordinary power as an orator that Patrick Henry is best remembered. His "Give Me Liberty" speech, delivered at Richmond's historic St. John's Church in the year before the signing of the Declaration of Independence, remains one of the most passionate and eloquent enunciations of the American ideal ever delivered. It was a fiery call to arms that caused an immediate and rousing reaction.

What has been generally neglected by historians in studying the period is the fact that Henry was in the throes of an aching grief at the time he issued that famous clarion call. Less than thirty days prior to the assembly on this day in 1775, Henry's beloved wife, Sarah, had died after a short illness. Henry's grief was so deep that he confided to his family physician that he was "a distraught old man."

His bereavement was smothering. Indeed, many of his fellow delegates to the Virginia Convention, including President Peyton Randolph, questioned whether he was fit to attend the deliberations of government. No doubt they were all stunned by the power and suasion of his words, which appear in the box below. Despite his personal anguish—or perhaps because of it—Patrick Henry stirred himself to sound for the theme of that which is right and good and true.

An appeal to arms and to the God of Hosts is all that is left us! They tell us, sir, that we are weak, unable to cope with so formidable an adversary. But when shall we be stronger? Will it be the next week, or the next year? Will it be when we are totally disarmed, and when a British guard shall be stationed in every house? Shall we gather strength by irresolution and inaction? Shall we acquire the means of effectual resistance by lying supinely on our backs and hugging the delusive phantom of hope, until our enemies shall have bound us hand and foot? Sir, we are not weak, if we make a proper use of the means which the God of nature hath placed in our power. Three millions of people, armed in the holy cause of liberty, and in such a country as that which we possess, are invincible by any force which our enemy can send against us. Besides, sir, we shall not fight our battles alone. There is a just God who presides over the destinies of nations, and who will raise friends to fight our battles for us. The battle, sir, is not to the strong alone; it is to the vigilant, the active, the brave. Besides, sir, we have no election. If we were base enough to desire it, it is now too late to retire from the contest. There is no retreat but in submission and slavery! Our chains are forged! Their clanking may be heard on the plains of Boston! The war is inevitable—and let it come! I repeat it, sir, let it come! It is in vain, sir, to extenuate the matter. Gentlemen may cry, peace, peace!—but there is no peace. The war is actually begun! The next gale that sweeps from the north will bring to our ears the clash of resounding arms! Our brethren are already in the field! Why stand we here idle? What is it that gentlemen wish? What would they have? Is life so dear, or peace so sweet, as to be purchased at the price of chains and slavery? Forbid it, Almighty God! I know not what course others may take, but as for me: Give me liberty, or give me death!

—*Patrick Henry, March 23, 1775*

The most exalted virtue has ever been found to attract envy.

[PATRICK HENRY (1736–1799)]

MARCH

1743 At the London premiere of Handel's oratorio *Messiah*, the entire audience at the Covent Garden theater rose to their feet with King George II at the beginning of the "Hallelujah Chorus." Thus began the tradition of always standing during the singing of this glorious refrain.

1792 Joseph Haydn's Symphony no. 94 in G Major (the "Surprise" symphony) was performed publicly for the first time, in London.

1806 Explorers Lewis and Clark, having reached the Pacific Coast, began their journey home.

1857 Cookbook author Fannie Merritt Farmer was born in Boston, Massachusetts. *The Fannie Farmer Cookbook* (originally *The Boston Cooking-School Cook Book*) was an American household standard, and has lived through thirteen editions. Farmer was ahead of her time in sharing important nutritional information to her readers. She stressed buying the freshest eggs, fish, and poultry, and was careful to include wonderful bread recipes in her book, as she detested the poor bread available from bakers of her day. In the preface to the cookbook's first edition, Fannie Farmer wrote, "But for life the universe were nothing; and all that has life requires nourishment."

1891 The first jazz concert was held at Carnegie Hall in New York City.

1899 Robert Koldewey, an archaeologist sponsored by the German Oriental Society, made a startling discovery of a basket full of three hundred cuneiform tablets at the site of the ancient city of Babylon. Earlier he had found a bas-relief that spanned nearly 960 feet. He had uncovered the enormous city walls, so wide that four span of horses could drive abreast. He found bricks stamped with Nebuchadnezzar's name. But it turned out that the tablets were the most astonishing discoveries of all—here, on cuneiform, was verification of a long-disputed biblical text, listing the supplies given King Jehoiachin of Judah.

1901 Australian soprano Helen Porter Mitchell, known to audiences as Dame Nellie Melba, explained her method for preparing toast, which involved baking paper-thin slices of bread until they were crisp and dry.

1911 Rocket pioneer Wernher von Braun was born in Wirsitz (now Wyrzysk, Poland). He was instrumental in the development of the V2 liquid-fuel rockets that Germany used against Britain in 1944 during World War II. After the war, von Braun was moved to the United States, where he led American efforts in space exploration. He led the Redstone missile program and was the director of development operations at NASA in Huntsville, Alabama. He was directly responsible for the *Saturn V* launch vehicle that enabled the *Apollo* spacecraft to travel to the moon.

1919 Benito Mussolini founded his fascist political movement in Milan, Italy.

1929 The first telephone was installed in the White House.

1933 The German Reichstag adopted the Enabling Act, which effectively granted Adolf Hitler dictatorial legislative powers.

1956 Pakistan became an independent republic within the British Commonwealth.

23

FEAST DAY

St. Dunchad, St. Hildelith, St. Macartan, St. Aldemar, St. Simon of Trent, St. William of Norwich, St. Catherine of Vadstena, St. Irenaeus of Sirmeum

MARCH

Originally populated by various indigenous peoples of the Algonquin, Iroquois, and Abenaki nations, the land now known as Vermont was first seen by European eyes on this day in 1609, when the French explorer Samuel de Champlain sailed the still partly frozen lake that now bears his name. The French must have paid their visits during the warmer months, for when they gazed upon the mountains that form the spine of the state, they named them Les Verts Monts—or the Green Mountains. The quaint capital of the state, Montpelier, also got its name from the French—it means the "naked mount" or the "mountain without trees." As happens with language, Les Verts Monts was somehow transliterated into Vermont. And as generally happens with explorers, Champlain claimed all he saw in the name of France.

In 1763, England was granted the area via the Treaty of Paris, which ended the Seven Years' War—a global imperial conflict known in the Americas as the French and Indian War and celebrated in our folklore by the tales of Washington Irving and James Fenimore Cooper. The land was at various times claimed by the colonial governors of both New Hampshire and New York; however, the fiercely independent residents maintained their autonomy. By 1775, they had joined the spreading rebellion against British rule—but rather than join forces with the other thirteen Atlantic coast colonies, Vermonters, naturally, chose to go it alone.

Ethan Allen and his Green Mountain Boys did not fight for American independence; rather, they fought for Vermont's freedom. The great victory at Fort Ticonderoga was won not by American forces but by the militias of a sovereign Vermont under the authority of President Thomas Crittenden and the national legislature convened in Windsor. Even after the other thirteen colonies had confederated into a single American nation, the little state of Vermont remained an independent republic. It was not until 1791, some fifteen years after declaring autonomy, that it joined the United States as that fledgling nation's fourteenth member state.

Even after Vermont joined the Union, its rugged citizens maintained their distance and independence—they reserved the right to secede at any time by a simple majority vote of the state legislature. It is the only state to continue to have that statutory prerogative to this day.

1820 — The American hymn writer Fanny Crosby was born in Putnam County, New York. Although she lost her sight in infancy, she wrote more than six thousand hymns, including "Blessed Assurance," "All the Way My Savior Leads Me," and "I Am Thine, O Lord."

Many of our people, without knowing it, are Christian heathen, and demand as much missionary effort as the heathen of foreign lands.

[BOOKER T. WASHINGTON (1856–1915)]

MARCH

304 Late in the third century, Afra of Augsburg (277–304) developed a ministry to the abandoned children of prisoners, thieves, smugglers, pirates, runaway slaves, and brigands. Herself a former prostitute, she cared for the despised and the rejected with a special fervor, taking them into her home, creating an adoption network, and sacrificing all she had, that out of her lack they might be satisfied. Her faith and piety were renowned. Her struggle for justice was unparalleled. And her ministry of mercy was an inspiration to thousands. Ultimately, her well-integrated and balanced approach to the work of the gospel in the world came under the scrutiny of the authorities. Considered a grave danger to state security because of her influence, she was martyred during the great persecution of Diocletian.

1580 The first recorded use of bombs was upon the town of Watchendonck in Guelderland, Germany. Galen, bishop of Munster, is usually credited with the invention.

1721 J. S. Bach completed the *Brandenburg Concertos*—a set of six concertos composed while Bach was the Court Kapellmeister of Prince Leopold of Anhalt-Köthen.

1765 American colonists were required to provide housing for British troops according to the Quartering Act, which Great Britain enacted on this day.

1882 German scientist Robert Koch announced in Berlin that he had discovered the bacillus responsible for tuberculosis.

1883 Long-distance telephone service was inaugurated between Chicago and New York.

1934 President Franklin Roosevelt signed a bill granting future independence to the Philippines. The United States had ruled the country since the Spanish-American War at the end of the previous century.

1944 Seventy-six Allied airmen tunneled out of the German prison camp Stalag Luft III in what came to be known as the Great Escape. Only three of the men made it back home.

1955 Tennessee Williams's play *Cat on a Hot Tin Roof* premiered on Broadway.

1958 Rock-and-roll pioneer Elvis Presley was inducted into the army in Memphis, Tennessee.

1976 The president of Argentina, Isabel Peron, was deposed by her country's military.

1980 Archbishop Oscar Arnulfo Romero was assassinated while serving Communion in war-torn El Salvador—he had been nominated for the Nobel Peace Prize just the year before for his efforts to halt the violence in his homeland.

1989 The nation's worst oil spill occurred as the supertanker *Exxon Valdez* ran aground on a reef in Alaska's Prince William Sound and began leaking eleven million gallons of crude.

24

NATIONAL DAY
   Greece
FEAST DAY
   *St. Barontius, St. Alfwold, St.
   Dismus, St. Lucy Filippini, St.
   Hermenland, St. Margaret
   Clitherow*

MARCH

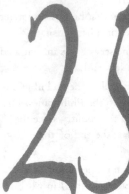

Born on this day in 1734 in Edinburgh, Scotland, during the tumultuous days of the final Jacobite Rising and the Tartan Suppression, Arthur St. Clair (1734–1818) was the only president of the United States born and bred on foreign soil. Though most of his family and friends abandoned their devastated homeland in the years following the Battle of Culloden—after which nearly a third of the land was depopulated through emigration to America—he stayed behind to learn the ways of the hated Hanoverian English in the Royal Navy. His plan was to learn of the enemy's military might in order to fight another day.

During the global conflict of the Seven Years' War—generally known as the French and Indian War—he was stationed in the American theater. Afterward, he decided to settle in Pennsylvania, where many of his kin had established themselves. His civic-mindedness quickly became apparent: He helped to organize both the New Jersey and the Pennsylvania militias, led the Continental army's Canadian expedition, and was elected to Congress. His long years of training in the enemy camp were finally paying off.

He was elected president in 1787, and he served from February 2 of that year until January 21 of the next. Following his term of duty in the highest office in the land, he became the first governor of the Northwest Territory and the founder of Cincinnati.

Though he briefly supported the idea of creating a constitutional monarchy under the Stuart's Bonnie Prince Charlie, he was a strident anti-Federalist—believing that the proposed federal Constitution would eventually allow for the intrusion of government into virtually every sphere and aspect of life. He even predicted that under the vastly expanded centralized power of the state the taxing powers of bureaucrats and other unelected officials would eventually confiscate as much as a quarter of the income of the citizens—a notion that seemed laughable at the time but that has proven to be ominously modest in light of our current governmental leviathan.

St. Clair lived to see the hated English tyrants who destroyed his homeland defeated. But he despaired that his adopted home might actually create similar tyrannies and impose them upon themselves.

1894

Jacob S. Coxey began leading an "army" of unemployed people from Massillon, Ohio, to Washington, D.C., to demand help from the federal government. It marked the beginning of the radical populist and labor movement, which would dominate American politics for the next five decades.

God's in His heaven—all's right with the world.

[Robert Browning (1812–1889)]

1409 The Council of Constance ended a period of papal schism during which three rival popes ruled at once. The council deposed all the claimants, including the one who called the hierarchy together in the first place.

1643 The colony of Maryland was established by Englishmen sent by Lord Baltimore.

1811 Percy Shelley was expelled from Oxford for refusing to admit that he had written *The Necessity of Atheism.*

1823 William Blake signed an agreement to illustrate and engrave *The Inventions to the Book of Job.*

1867 Italian conductor Arturo Toscanini was born in Parma, Italy. Toscanini studied cello, but took advantage of his first opportunity to conduct. While he was on tour with an Italian opera company in South America, the Brazilian conductor resigned, and Toscanini was called upon to take over direction with almost no notice. He was brilliant, and it is reported that he went on to conduct performances of eleven more operas, apparently from memory. He served as principal conductor at La Scala, and was appointed principal conductor at the Metropolitan Opera in 1908. He conducted the opening concert of the Palestine Symphony Orchestra in 1936, and in 1938 conducted at a festival in Switzerland with the orchestra made up of Jewish musicians who had fled from Germany. His perfectionism and adherence to the composer's intentions were evident in the recordings and broadcasts he conducted with the NBC Symphony Orchestra.

1881 Hungarian composer and ethnomusicologist Béla Bartók—who awakened serious interest in Hungarian folk music by collecting about six thousand folk melodies—was born in Nagyszentmiklós, Hungary (now Sînnicolau, Romania). He emigrated to the United States in 1940 and conducted research at Columbia University. His works were not accepted, and he struggled for the rest of his life financially. His best-known works were *Music for Strings, Percussion, and Celesta* (1937) and *Concerto for Orchestra* (1943), and a series of six string quartets that have since been recognized as the best additions to the repertoire since Beethoven.

March

1882 In New York City, passersby were amazed, when strolling by a department store window, at the first public demonstration of pancake-making. Coincidentally, waffles are traditionally consumed on this day in Sweden in observance of Waffle Day.

1896 The first modern Olympic Games were held in Athens, Greece, from March 25 to April 3.

1913 The home of vaudeville, the Palace Theatre, opened in New York City.

1918 French composer Claude Debussy died in Paris.

1925 Flannery O'Connor, heir of the great Southern literary tradition and author of *Wise Blood, A Good Man Is Hard to Find,* and *The Violent Bear It Away,* was born in Savannah, Georgia.

1957 The Treaty of Rome established the European Economic Community.

1965 The Reverend Martin Luther King Jr. led twenty-five thousand marchers to the state capitol in Montgomery, Alabama, to protest the denial of voting rights to African Americans.

1992 Soviet cosmonaut Sergei Krikalev who had spent ten months aboard the orbiting *Mir* space station, finally returned to Earth-during the time he was in space, Communism had fallen and the Soviet Union had ceased to exist.

FEAST DAY
St. William of Norwich, St. Liudger, St. Felix of Trier, St. Castalus of Rome, St. Braulio, St. Basil of Rome

MARCH

The steadfast political correctness of Northampton today belies—and perhaps even betrays—its historical roots. The town actually began as a Puritan settlement purchased from the Nonotuck Indians in 1654. For the price of something like a hundred fathom of wampum, ten coats, and a few trinkets, the Puritans acquired the area of rich farmland. Throughout the first century of its existence, Northampton remained a strict New England Christian community.

It was within the bounds of that staid and upright cultural context that the ministry of Jonathan Edwards took place. He was not a particularly enthralling master of pulpit theatrics or hermeneutical technique. Instead, he won his reputation as a thinker. He was highly regarded as a precise dogmatician. He was widely admired as a careful systemizer. And he was deeply appreciated as a cogent preceptor. His books were among the greatest achievements of the human intellect. He was to prove himself, according to many accounts, superior to Locke, Newton, Descartes, and a couple of Pascals combined.

But as a preacher, he apparently left a little something to be desired. In fact, he read his densely theological and tautly philosophical sermons from painstakingly researched longhand manuscripts—often in a flat, monotonous voice. Only rarely did he deign to make eye contact with his congregation. Though not unpleasant in demeanor, he hardly cut a dashing or charismatic figure.

Nevertheless, it was here that he read what was perhaps the most famous sermon ever delivered in the history of America. Titled "Sinners in the Hands of an Angry God," the sermon was an exposition of the imminence of judgment and the horrors of perdition. It was about what we today derisively call hellfire and damnation.

Though he actually preached the sermon at a neighboring town first, the rhetorical masterpiece was preached in Northampton on this day in 1742. It was astonishingly gripping and terrifyingly vivid. It caused an immediate sensation. Even before the sermon was finished, people were moaning, groaning, and crying out. In fact, there was so much distress and weeping that Edwards had to quiet and calm the people several times so he could conclude. The fervor of the Great Awakening that had thus far bypassed the region now swept through it with a white-hot intensity. Suddenly the people were bowed down with an awful conviction of their sin and danger.

The sermon not only won for Edwards even greater renown than he already enjoyed, but it also provoked a further awakening among its distant readers. Since then it has been reprinted hundreds of times—perhaps thousands. To this day it is not only a standard text for the study of great preaching, it also has passed into the realm of classic literature—and thus is the most anthologized sermon in the English language.

Perhaps more important for Northampton, it made the sleepy New England settlement one of the most prominent towns in all of the colonies—because it was from Northampton that the fires of renewal and revival had first come.

A lie can only seize the mind of that man who has forgotten the *I*ncarnation.

[ANDREW NELSON LYTLE (1902–1995)]

MARCH

752 When Stephen II died after the shortest pontificate in history—four days—a Roman deacon became Stephen III. His papacy is highly significant. Up to his day, popes had exercised little temporal power. But with Italy practically abandoned by the emperors, popes increasingly tended to step into the breach. In this way they came to possess lands. Stephen became the first papal monarch when Ravenna was placed under his control by the king of the Franks, Pepin the Short.

1699 On this day, John Evelyn wrote in his diary, "After an extraordinary storm, there came up the Thames a whale which was fifty-six feet long. Such, and a larger of the Serpent kind, was killed there forty years ago. That year died Cromwell."

1788 Massachusetts, the North American center for the slave trade, abolished the practice, forcing traders to move their ports of entry to Rhode Island and Deleware.

1804 The Louisiana Purchase was divided into the Territory of Orleans and the District of Louisiana.

1827 Ludwig van Beethoven died in Vienna. On his deathbed, he was heard to utter the words "I shall hear in heaven."

1873 American poet Robert Frost was born in San Francisco, California. Frost's use of colloquial language, simple rhythms, and New England settings in such poems as "Stopping by Woods on a Snowy Evening," "The Road Not Taken," and "Mending Wall" garnered for him Pulitzer Prizes in 1923, 1930, 1936, and 1942.

1892 Poet Walt Whitman died in Camden, New Jersey.

1912 American playwright Tennessee Williams was born in Columbus, Mississippi. His characters, walking on the edge of ruin and self-destruction, thinly robed themselves in the cloaks of fading Southern gentility and social custom. Early success came with *The Glass Menagerie* (1945), and he won the Pulitzer Prize for *A Streetcar Named Desire* (1947) and *Cat on a Hot Tin Roof* (1955).

1964 The musical play *Funny Girl* opened on Broadway.

1971 East Pakistan proclaimed its independence, taking the name Bangladesh.

1979 The Camp David peace treaty brokered by American President Jimmy Carter was signed by Israeli Prime Minister Menachem Begin and Egyptian President Anwar Sadat at the White House.

1982 Groundbreaking ceremonies took place in Washington, D.C., for the Vietnam Veterans Memorial.

Louise De Marillac (1626–1691) married a high official of the French court and enjoyed a life of privilege and pleasure. Happily married and carefree, she gave little thought to the plight of those less fortunate than herself.

Her husband's shockingly violent death left her a widow at the age of thirty-three. That tragedy effected in her a deep desire to serve Christ, and she committed herself to His kingdom. Shortly thereafter, she became a companion and coworker of Vincent De Paul in Paris, caring for the sick and helpless. With him, she launched a sheltering ministry for women in crisis.

At the time of her death, her ministry had more than forty houses throughout France and twenty-six more in Paris, where abused and exploited women could learn to rebuild their lives. She maintained throughout her life that this service was simply the outward expression of an inward commitment to yield every aspect of her life to the ministry of the church and its sovereign King, her Savior.

FEAST DAY
St. Rupert, St. Athilda, St. John of Egypt

MARCH

27

1416

St. Francis of Paola was born in southern Italy. At the age of twelve he spent a year with the Franciscans. Afterward he made a pilgrimage to Rome. Upon his return he sought parental permission to seclude himself as a hermit near Paola. Unsatisfied with that location, he moved into a cave beside the sea. His isolated habitation was soon discovered by a group of hunters who noised abroad a report of his sanctity. At nineteen, he accepted followers, the nucleus of the order he would found: the Minims. The name was derived from the Latin for "least." Christ taught that whoever would be greatest must become the least. The name was also intended to show that the order held to stricter poverty than even the Franciscan Friars Minor. The Minim rule was only the fifth that had been approved by the church. Among the order's special purposes was assistance to the poor and needy. Francis himself boldly defended the oppressed before the tyrants of the age. Minims also sponsored retreats and missions. A Minim accompanied Columbus on his second voyage to America. One of the most famous Minims was Marin Mersenne, who more than any other man facilitated communication between scientists in the seventeenth century. His monastic cell was not only a meeting place of the learned but the center of voluminous correspondence. Leo X canonized him in 1519. Because Minims pastored seamen, Francis was eventually declared patron saint of sailors.

To be happy at home is the end of all labor.

[SAMUEL JOHNSON (1709–1784)]

1512 Spanish explorer Juan Ponce de Leon sighted Florida in his search for the fabled Fountain of Youth.

1625 Charles I ascended the English throne upon the death of James I. He would later be executed by Parliament after a long civil war.

1794 President Washington and Congress authorized creation of the U.S. Navy.

1836 The first Mormon temple was dedicated in Kirtland, Ohio.

1892 American composer Ferde Grofé was born in New York City. His family included many talented musicians, including his father who sang light opera, his mother who played cello, his grandfather who was premier cellist in the Los Angeles Symphony, and his uncle who was concertmaster in the same symphony. His grandfather and uncle taught him to play brass instruments, violin, viola, and coached him in chamber music. He was most known for his orchestration of George Gershwin's *Rhapsody in Blue* and his own compositions' attempt to capture scenic beauty as evident in the titles—*The Grand Canyon Suite*, *The Hudson River Suite*, *Niagara Falls Suite*, *Symphony in Steel*, and *World's Fair Suite*. He died on April 3, 1971, in Santa Monica, California.

1913 First Lady Helen Herron Taft and Viscountess Chinda, wife of the Japanese ambassador, planted the first cherry trees around the Potomac Tidal Basin in Washington, D.C.

1917 The Seattle Metropolitans became the first American team to win the Stanley Cup as they defeated the Montreal Canadiens.

1927 Renowned cellist and conductor Mstislav Rostropovich was born in Baku, Azerbaijan Soviet Socialist Republic (now Azerbaijan). He studied and taught at the Moscow Conservatory. He risked the retribution of Soviet Officials to help Soviet dissident and author Aleksandr Solzhenitsyn. Rostropovich forfeited his citizenship and emigrated to the United States in 1974 where he became the conductor of the National Symphony Orchestra in Washington, D.C. He is regarded as the best cellist of his generation.

1945 Nearing the end of the Second World War, General Dwight Eisenhower told reporters in Paris that German defenses on the Western Front had been broken.

1952 The film musical *Singin' in the Rain*—starring Gene Kelly, Debbie Reynolds, Donald O'Connor, and Jean Hagen—premiered at Radio City Music Hall in New York City.

1958 Nikita Khrushchev became Soviet premier in addition to first secretary of the Communist Party.

1964 Alaska was rocked by a powerful earthquake that killed 114 people.

1968 Soviet cosmonaut Yuri Gagarin, the first man to orbit the earth, died in a plane crash.

1989 Boris N. Yeltsin and other antiestablishment candidates claimed victory in parliamentary elections for the new Congress of People's Deputies in the Soviet Union.

1994 Ukraine held its first parliamentary elections since the collapse of the Soviet Union.

MARCH

Just as it is generally assumed that politics and religion do not make for particularly pleasant dinner table conversation, it is generally assumed that they do not make for particularly pleasant poetry either. John Milton sundered both assumptions in his masterful work *Paradise Lost*. In it he created a work that was explicitly political and inescapably religious. Indeed, it was a prime example of the most unbending ideological and theological dogmatism of the zealously partisan seventeenth century. And yet, it was also magnificent poetry. Its beauty and grace were undeniable. Its majestic cadence, its lofty vision, and its soaring images earned Milton a place in English letters second only to Shakespeare. Its ornate symmetry, its fertile allusions, and its rich profundity have secured for him a tenured place even in the curriculums of those who despise his ideas.

A bloody civil war was waged in what once was Merry England from 1642 to 1648. That calamitous time was followed by the regicide of King Charles I in 1649, ten years of Puritan parliamentary rule under Oliver Cromwell from 1649 to 1659, and finally by the restoration of the Stuart monarchy in 1660. These events were not merely the background to John Milton's life: They were his life. He was an active, passionate, and crucial player in those revolutionary events. And his poetry is indelibly marked by his activism and devotion.

Milton was raised in a reasonably well-to-do household. His family had lived in London for several generations, which remained Milton's home for most of his life. His father was a scrivener—a combined banker, notary, investment broker, and accountant—who was wealthy enough to afford private tutors for his son, then schooling at the most elite schools in England. Some critics have argued that as a result of this extended period of intensive study, Milton was one of the most learned men England has ever produced. Indeed, he wrote poetry in Latin, Greek, Hebrew, and Italian, and read almost all the literature surviving from the Greek and Roman periods in addition to the best of all the major literary traditions of Christendom. Just before the religious and political quarrels in England came to a head, he had the opportunity to travel abroad for fifteen months, meeting and talking with learned men all over Europe. He even met Galileo and looked through his telescope, a fact Milton mentions more than once in *Paradise Lost*.

When he returned, he committed his vast learning and considerable rhetorical skills to the Puritan cause. As an aide to Cromwell, Milton championed one controversy after another with great vigor—and in the process, he made himself not only well known but also well hated. The restoration of the Stuart monarchy in 1660 obviously meant the end of Milton's government job. Indeed, for a time he was actually in danger of his life and had to be hidden by friends—one of his earlier pamphlets had argued strongly in defense of the king's beheading. Milton retired from public life and devoted himself to the composition of *Paradise Lost*. Though his work was interrupted by the Great Plague in 1665 and the Great Fire in 1666, the epic was finally completed on this day in 1667.

Fate chooses your relations, you choose your friends.

[CHRISTOPHER WREN (1632–1723)]

MARCH

1380   The Venetians were the first Europeans to use gunpowder in a battle against the Genoese, though gunpowder had been invented by the early Chinese, and utilized by the Arabs as early as 690 in a battle near Mecca.

1592   Pioneering educator John Comenius was born in Prague. Like most of the other followers of John Hus, he was forced into exile during the Thirty Years' War. He and most of the members of his small covenant community settled in Leszno, Poland. There Comenius wrote several textbooks on education. These were so original in their conception of classical and covenantal discipleship that they won him the name "Father of Modern Education."

1797   Nathaniel Briggs of New Hampshire received a patent for his invention of the washing machine.

1834   The Senate voted to censure President Jackson for the removal of federal deposits from the Bank of the United States.

1854   During the Crimean conflict, allies Britain and France declared war on czarist Russia.

1866   The first ambulance for use by a hospital went into service.

1868   Maxim Gorky (a pen name meaning "most bitter" in Russian) was born in Nizhni Novgorod (renamed Gorky in his honor by Stalin in 1932). His considerable literary income was devoted almost exclusively to revolutionary socialism.

1896   The opera Andrea Chenier, by Umberto Giordano, premiered in Milan, Italy.

1898   The Supreme Court ruled that a child born in the United States to Chinese immigrants was a U.S. citizen.

1930   The names of the ancient Byzantine Christian cities of Constantinople and Angora were changed by the Islamic Turkish government to Istanbul and Ankara.

1939   The Spanish Civil War ended when Madrid fell to the traditionalist coalition forces under the command of Francisco Franco.

1941   Novelist and critic Virginia Woolf drowned in the River Ouse, near the south coastal village of Lewes, in England. She had left a note to her husband beforehand, so the death was ruled a suicide.

1943   Composer Sergei Rachmaninoff died in Beverly Hills, California.

1969   The thirty-fourth president of the United States, Dwight Eisenhower, died in Washington at age seventy-eight.

28

FEAST DAY
Saints Gwynllyw and Gwladys;
St. Cyril of Heliopolis; St.
Berthold; St. Mark of Arethusa; St.
Rupert of Salzberg; Saints Jonas,
Barachisius, and Others; Saints
Armogastes, Masculas, Achinimus,
and Saturus

MARCH

29

Joseph Damien de Veuster (1840–1889) grew up in the lowlands of Belgium. After posting a promising academic record, he disappointed his family's expectations of a brilliant professional career in business, law, or politics by submitting to a call to the mission field. Assigned to the newly reopened islands of Hawaii, he served as a pastor in the burgeoning village of Honolulu for nearly a decade.

His concern for the sanctity of all human life led him not only to fight against the few remaining abortionists among the natives, but also to eventually request a transfer to the wretched leprosium on Molakai. There, Damien helped the people to build homes, schools, roads, civic halls, and treatment clinics. He protected the integrity of each resident from persecution and rejection—both from within and without the colony.

Encouraging the essential Christian values of faith, family, and work, he helped restore dignity, hope, and purpose to the despised and rejected. His sacrificial character was soon lauded around the globe. Even the renowned literary skeptic, Robert Louis Stevenson, was struck by Damien's saintly service to the unwanted—actually risking his fortune and his reputation by publishing a defense of the great man.

Eventually contracting leprosy himself, Damien died at the age of forty-nine. On his tombstone were engraved the words, "Died a Martyr of Charity."

1630

"Anno Domini 1630, March 29, Easter Monday. Riding at the Cowes, near the Isle of Wight, in the *Arbella,* a ship of three hundred and fifty tons." So begins one of the most famous journals ever written, a journal that remains a treasure mine of information for historians of New England. John Winthrop, the writer of the journal, was a well-educated, upper-class Englishman. Although a moderately successful lawyer, he left it all to join the Massachusetts Bay Company. Motivating his decision was a personal inclination toward Puritanism and distress over the religious condition of Europe. Eventually, the Puritans settled in the New World. There Winthrop was for nine years a governor and for ten years deputy governor. John Winthrop maintained his sporadic journal entries until 1649.

People are judged by both the company they keep and the company they keep away from.

[BONNIE PRINCE CHARLIE (1720–1788)]

1461 Edward IV defeated the forces of Henry VI and his Lancastrians at the Battle of Towton in Yorkshire, thus securing his claim to the English throne.

1483 Italian Renaissance painter Raphael was born Raffaello Santi or Raffaello Sanzio in Urbino. One of his most famous works was *The School of Athens*, which depicts the philosophers Aristotle and Plato discussing the nature of the world. Old Style calendars place his birth and death on April 6.

1638 Swedish colonists settled in present-day Delaware.

1751 The founder of the London Foundling Hospital, Captain Thomas Coram, died. The hospital opened in 1741 and complied with an act of Parliament requiring that a basket be hung outside the hospital for foundling infants. The ringing of a bell notified hospital officials when an infant had been left. The hospital received 3,296 infants in its first year of operation.

1790 The tenth president of the United States, John Tyler, was born in Charles City County, Virginia.

1847 Due to a unique series of natural events, the Niagara River stopped flowing, and the falls were silenced for thirty hours. A fierce wind from Lake Erie caused an ice jam to block the river near Buffalo, New York.

1847 Victorious forces led by General Winfield Scott occupied the city of Vera Cruz after Mexican defenders capitulated.

1867 The British Parliament passed the North America Act to create the Dominion of Canada.

1902 English composer Sir William Turner Walton was born in Oldham. He was trained as a chorister in Christ Church Cathedral, Oxford. Despite early leanings toward fashionable and modern compositions, Walton moved to the point of writing contemporary music with a neo-Romantic bent. He is best known for the oratorio *Belshazzar's Feast*, the opera *Troilus and Cressida*, and the suites of music derived from his film scores for Shakespearean films.

1943 In the United States rationing began for meat, butter, and cheese—a precaution necessary to maintain supplies for the Second World War.

1951 Julius and Ethel Rosenberg were convicted of conspiracy to commit espionage. They were executed in June 1953.

1951 Based on Margaret Langdon's novel *Anna and the King of Siam*, the Rodgers and Hammerstein musical *The King and I* opened on Broadway for 1,246 performances.

1962 Jack Paar hosted NBC's *Tonight Show* for the final time. He would be succeeded by Johnny Carson.

1971 Army Lieutenant William L. Calley Jr. was convicted of murdering at least twenty-two Vietnamese civilians in the My Lai Massacre. Calley ended up spending just three years under house arrest.

1973 United States troops left South Vietnam, ending direct military involvement in the Vietnam War.

1998 The Lady Vols of Tennessee won a third straight NCAA basketball championship, defeating Louisiana Tech 93-75.

MARCH

30

Impassioned and dramatic painter Vincent van Gogh was born in Groot Zundert on this day in 1853. Throughout his life he desperately wanted to serve the church. He was brought up in a Dutch Reformed manse where his father served as the pastor of a small country parish, and he yearned to follow in those footsteps. He taught and preached at a Methodist chapel, but he failed his courses in the rudimentary seminary. Van Gogh then attempted to serve as a missionary to coal miners in Belgium; however, the mission society stopped his support. Deeply hurt by feelings of continued rejection, he abandoned the institutional church altogether.

Van Gogh was tormented by mental illness and emotional instability, and it was obvious that he was not suited to be a pastor. However, he was suited to be an artist. Van Gogh painted as a means of relief from his madness; his art was not a product of it. The colors and brush strokes of his works belie an intensity and passion that reveal the turbulence of his mind while engaging in the forms and structure of balanced art. As Gene Edward Veith says, "Tragically, his church did not understand his gifts and refused to tolerate his admittedly quirky personality. If the church had affirmed him as an artist and had the patience to offer him the love, the healing, and the discipleship he so desperately needed, his story might have had a happier ending." Van Gogh died two days after he shot himself in a deranged relapse of his delusional madness. Van Gogh's desire to serve the church was correct; he just needed to be taught that all of life glorifies God—especially when it is used to fulfill the vocation that God has given.

1533

Thomas Cranmer was consecrated Archbishop of Canterbury by King Henry VIII. Believing himself subject to the king, Cranmer promptly granted Henry an annulment of his marriage. Already leaning toward Protestantism, Cranmer became the chief architect of the English Reformation. He urged the king to place Bibles in England's churches and it was done. He wrote the first *Book of Common Prayer*. On his deathbed the king clung to Cranmer's hand. Under Edward VI, Henry's young son and successor, Cranmer advanced Protestantism even more, helping draft doctrines that became the basis for the Church of England's Thirty-Nine Articles. Cranmer supported Lady Jane Gray to succeed Edward. It was not to be. Bloody Mary took the throne instead and charged him with treason and heresy. In the face of death he recanted his Protestant opinions. When he learned he was to die anyway, he publicly renounced his recantation. "As for the pope, I refuse him, as Christ's enemy and Antichrist, with all his false doctrine." When the fire was lit, he held the hand that had signed the recantation into the flame, burning it off before the fire touched his body, saying, "This unworthy right hand." As death approached he repeated several times, "Lord Jesus, receive my spirit."

Our greatest wealth is not measured in terms of riches but relationships. Likewise, our greatest debts are incurred because of wastrel companions.

MARCH

1820 Anna Sewell, the author of *Black Beauty*, was born in Norfolk, England. Her concern for the humane treatment of horses led to her writing the novel during the last seven or eight years of her life.

1822 Florida became a United States territory after its purchase from Spain.

1842 Dr. Crawford W. Long of Jefferson, Georgia, first used ether as an anesthetic during a minor operation.

1858 Hyman L. Lipman received a patent for a pencil with an attached eraser. The pencil was unique because of the eraser, which was a "secured . . . piece of prepared rubber, glued in at one end."

1867 The United States purchased Alaska from Russia for $7.2 million, or a little more than 2 cents an acre. William Seward, the U.S. secretary of state, had pushed for the deal, and the purchase was ridiculed as "Seward's Folly."

1870 The Fifteenth Amendment to the Constitution, giving African-American men the right to vote, was declared in effect despite irregularities in its ratification.

1870 Texas was readmitted to the Union.

1909 The Queensboro Bridge, linking the New York boroughs of Manhattan and Queens, opened.

1942 In an effort to save precious fabric, American manufacturers of men's suits were ordered to omit cuffs, pleats, and patch pockets for the duration of the war.

1945 The Soviet Union invaded Austria near the end of the Second World War.

1964 John Glenn withdrew from the Ohio race for the U.S. Senate because of injuries suffered in a fall.

1970 The musical *Applause* opened on Broadway.

1981 President Reagan was shot and seriously wounded outside a Washington, D.C., hotel by John W. Hinckley Jr. Also wounded were White House Press Secretary James Brady, a Secret Service agent, and a District of Columbia police officer.

30

Bernard of Clairveaux (1090–1153) was one of the most brilliant Christian apologists, theologians, and Reformers of the High Medieval period as well as the inspirational composer of innumerable hymns, including the beloved "O Sacred Head, Now Wounded." A determined holy life, a commitment to charitable compassion, and an unusual eloquence earned Bernard a reputation in his day as a wise and astute counselor to kings, emperors, and popes.

Even so, his willingness to embrace unpopular truths often made his high profile a very precarious position. His ardor for biblical justice, combined with his passion for peace, made him a key player in most of the great events of his day: monastic establishments, agrarian reforms, peasant revolts, ecclesiastical reconciliations, Teutonic crusades, and attempts to liberate Jerusalem and the old Christian realms of the East.

On this day in 1146, Bernard of Clairvaux received permission from Pope Eugenius III to preach a crusade. Many Europeans, after the conquest of the Christian stronghold of Edessa by fierce Moslem warriors, were nervous that Islam was erupting to retake the Holy Land. Holy sites would be vandalized. Innocent Christians would be persecuted, tortured, and killed. And the heart of the Christian world would fall into the hands of infidels.

With this in mind, Bernard said a terrible judgment faced those who did not take up the cross of the crusade. In a field outside Vézelay he read the pope's encyclical and then preached a stirring sermon. "This is a plan not made by man, but coming from heaven and proceeding from the heart of divine love." To violent men, terrified of facing Christ's judgment, indulgence from their crimes was a promise worth a great deal. Thousands flocked to join the expedition. Alas, the Second Crusade failed miserably. It did not even retake Edessa.

Though Bernard's reputation suffered as a result of the failure, his conscience did not. He later recorded, "I must not seek the applause of men, now or ever. My sole responsibility is to walk in the light of the grace Christ affords me day by day, regardless of how unpopular that course may be."

Never be ashamed to own you have been in the wrong; 'tis but saying you are wiser today than yesterday.

[JONATHAN SWIFT (1667–1745)]

MARCH

1492 King Ferdinand of Aragon and Queen Isabella of Castile, Spain, issued a joint edict expelling Jews from Spanish soil, except for those willing to convert to Christianity.

1596 French philosopher René Descartes was born in La Haye near Tours. Known as the "father of modern philosophy," he focused his theory of knowledge by locating the point of certainty in the awareness of self as conveyed in the maxim *Cogito ego sum*—I think, therefore I am.

1621 English poet Andrew Marvell, best known for his metaphysical poems ("To His Coy Mistress"), political satire, and odes in praise of Oliver Cromwell, was born in Yorkshire. He is recognized as one of the greatest of the secular metaphysical poets.

1630 John Donne, English metaphysical poet and Dean of St. Paul's, died in London. He had written, "Any man's death diminishes me, because I am involved in Mankind; and therefore never send to know for whom the bell tolls; it tolls for thee." He is best known for his religious poetry as well as love poetry. His work is striking for its use of images.

1732 Franz Joseph Haydn was born in Rohrau, Austria. Haydn is best known for his many symphonies and his oratorios *The Seasons* and *The Creation.*

1855 English writer Charlotte Brontë, author of *Jane Eyre* (1847), died in Haworth, Yorkshire.

1889 Despite protests by one hundred leading writers, composers, and artists, the Eiffel Tower was officially opened in Paris. Famed engineer Alexandre Gustave Eiffel unfurled the French tricolor from atop the distinctive tower, officially marking its completion. The protesters were concerned that the architecture of the tower was not in keeping with French taste.

1917 The United States took possession of the Virgin Islands from Denmark.

1918 Sponsored by the National Daylight Saving Association, the first daylight-saving time was implemented on Easter Sunday, when U.S. clocks were set one hour ahead.

1923 The first U.S. dance marathon, held in New York City, ended with Alma Cummings setting a world record of twenty-seven hours on her feet.

1925 An act of Congress authorized sculptor Gutzon Borgium to carve the likenesses of Presidents Washington, Jefferson, Lincoln, and Theodore Roosevelt on the granite face of Mount Rushmore in the Black Hills of South Dakota.

1933 Congress authorized the Great Depression measure of the Civilian Conservation Corps in an effort to get the unemployed back to work.

1943 Rodgers and Hammerstein's musical *Oklahoma!* opened on Broadway.

1945 *The Glass Menagerie* by Tennessee Williams was premiered on Broadway.

1949 Newfoundland entered the Dominion confederation as Canada's tenth province.

1968 President Lyndon Johnson stunned the country by announcing that he would not run for another term of office.

1976 The New Jersey Supreme Court ruled that coma patient Karen Anne Quinlan could be disconnected from her respirator. Quinlan did not die as expected—she remained comatose for an additional nine years.

APRIL

ALL FOOLS' DAY
FEAST DAY
St. Agilbert, St. Gilbert of
Caithness, St. Tewdric, St. Walaric,
St. Catharine of Palma, St. Melito,
St. Valery, St. Hugh of
Bonnevaux, St. Hugh of Grenoble

APRIL

Benignus of Dijon was a missionary from Lyons who was martyred in Epagny in the late second century—contemporary accounts place his death on this day in 197 or 198. He was renowned for his generosity and charity especially to the sick and suffering. He was not a pastor or evangelist, rather he was a tradesman—belonging to a leatherworking guild—who offered his services to fledgling churches and opened his home to the needy.

Apparently a mob of superstitious citizens in that pre-Christian Gallic region slew him because he nursed, supported, and protected a number of deformed and crippled children that had been saved from death after failed abortions or exposures. Believing that the children were accursed, the townsmen were enraged by his acts of mercy.

Afterward, Benignus became an inspiration to many dedicated Christian workers, who though they were not gifted for preaching or teaching roles, were nevertheless called to missionary activity. Thus, he became the patron of "tent-makers."

1872

Frederick Denison Maurice died of exhaustion. He had written books and pamphlets, edited newspapers, preached, attended the sick, and taught in both traditional and workingmen's schools all his life, despite physical weakness, rising early each day and not slacking pace until after evening dinner. He was a founder and the chief voice of the Christian Socialists. He edited their newspaper, *The Athenæum.* But his view of socialism was not so much an economic theory tied to the ideas of the Fabians or the Marxists as it was an outworking of the doctrine of the Incarnation—Christians must become "socialists," he contended; that is, they must become socially active. Likewise, socialists must become Christians. In an effort to put his ideas into practice, he created institutions for workers, such as the Workingman's College. Education, he believed, could do much to rectify society. A trained lawyer, he helped secure passage of a bill through Parliament which gave legal status to cooperatives. This was a big boost to workers who sought to unite.

APRIL FOOLS' DAY

Since at least the seventeenth century this day has been celebrated with practical jokes and spurious news. Mark Twain commented in his *Pudd'nhead Wilson's Calendar,* "This is the day upon which we are reminded of what we are on the other three hundred and sixty-four."

*A wise man will not leave the right to the mercy of chance,
nor wish it to prevail through the power of the majority.
There is but little virtue in the action of masses of men.*

[HENRY DAVID THOREAU (1817–1862)]

1578   William Harvey, the physician who discovered the process of the circulation of the blood, was born in England.

1789   The United States House of Representatives convened for its first full meeting in New York City. Frederick Muhlenberg of Pennsylvania was elected the first House Speaker.

1826   Samuel Morey received a patent for the internal combustion engine.

1853   Cincinnati, Ohio, became the first American city to pay its firefighters a regular salary.

1873   Russian composer and pianist Sergei Rachmaninoff was born in Oneg, near Novgorod. Although his compositions have since gained a place in the orchestral repertoire, it was as a pianist—perhaps one of the greatest of all time—that he was primarily known. His poetic vision, the delicate shadings of aural color, and his creative vision are unsurpassed. In 1917 Rachmaninov left his estates and homeland for good because of the Russian Revolution, and he sought to earn a living in the West by conducting and performing. His best-known compositions are the second and third Piano Concertos, Symphony no. 2, *Vespers,* and *Rhapsody on a Theme of Paganini.*

1918   The Royal Air Force was established in Britain at the behest of Parliamentary back-bencher Winston Churchill.

1933   The governing Nazi Party began sponsoring and encouraging a general boycott of Jewish-owned businesses.

1939   The United States recognized the government of Generalissimo Franco in Spain following the end of the Spanish civil war.

1945   American forces invaded the Japanese island of Okinawa during the Second World War.

1946   Tidal waves struck the Hawaiian islands, resulting in more than 170 deaths.

1947   Greece's King George II died.

1954   *The Tender Land,* an opera by American composer Aaron Copland, premiered at the City Center with the New York City Opera Company. The story is set on a lower-middle-class farm in the Midwest and continued Copland's use of open harmonies and expansive melodies that capture the spirit of the open spaces of the West. Of particular note is the ensemble "The Promise of Living" which plays a prominent role in the opera as well as in the orchestral suite from the opera.

1960   The first weather satellite, *TIROS-One,* was launched from Cape Canaveral.

1963   The daytime drama *General Hospital* premiered on ABC-TV.

1970   President Nixon signed a measure banning cigarette advertising on radio and television, to take effect after January 1, 1971.

1976   Stephen Wozniak and Steve Jobs launched their little company, Apple Computer, when they sought to market a circuit board that they had built and designed in Jobs's garage in Los Altos, California. Their first sales call for their revolutionary design resulted in an immediate order for fifty units.

APRIL

The only Founding Father who in 1776 was not in favor of independence, William Johnson (1727–1819), grew into a strong supporter of the new nation. He helped draft the Constitution, signed it, and stoutly defended it at the Connecticut Ratification Convention.

Although he attended the Stamp Act Congress in 1765 and served as a special agent for Connecticut in England, Johnson during these years was firmly convinced that the colonies and Great Britain would settle their differences. His stay in London, where he associated with Dr. Samuel Johnson, the great critic and lexicographer, and other notables, undoubtedly strengthened his ties with England, although in London he worked closely with Benjamin Franklin, then agent for Pennsylvania and other colonies, in representing colonial interests. And he supported the American policy of nonimportation of British goods as a protest against the Townshend Acts. After returning, Johnson was elected to serve in the First Continental Congress, but since he was against the idea of independence, he declined the position. Still devoted to the idea of a peaceful settlement, in 1775 he visited the British commander General Thomas Gage in Boston—sent by the Connecticut legislature. His mission was unsuccessful, and he was for a time held by patriots there. He resigned from the Connecticut legislature, and from 1777 to 1779 his refusal to support independence cost him his law practice—which the state permitted him to resume after he swore allegiance to Connecticut.

Despite his tardy adoption of the cause of independence, Johnson was an influential member of the Congress of Confederation. At the Constitutional Convention, Johnson, a soft-spoken but effective speaker, helped defend and explain the "Connecticut Compromise," the proposal for representing the States in the Senate and the people in the House of Representatives that was finally adopted—to settle the dispute between the large and small states.

The scholarly Johnson, who was one of the colonies' leading classicists and who was then serving as president of Columbia College, was chairman of the committee on style that produced the final version of the Constitution—though Gouverneur Morris wrote most of it. He eloquently defended the Constitution at the Connecticut Ratification Convention, and, after ratification, his state selected him to serve as one of the men to sit in the newly formed Senate on this day in 1791.

Nine-tenths of wisdom is being wise in time.

[THEODORE ROOSEVELT (1858–1919)]

742 Charlemagne, king of the Franks, was born.

1513 Castilian explorer and adventurer Juan Ponce de Leon landed in Florida. Though he did not find the fabled Fountain of Youth, he marveled at the beauty of the land, calling it a "demi-paradise."

1725 Giovanni Jacopo Casanova was born in Venice. The infamous gigolo would later scandalize polite society with an account of his sundry amorous adventures in his *Memoirs.*

1792 Congress passed the Coinage Act, which authorized establishment of the U.S. Mint.

1805 Children's fairy-tale author Hans Christian Andersen was born the son of a cobbler, near Copenhagen at Odense, Denmark. Although he wrote plays and other fiction, he was most famous for his fairy tales, including "The Ugly Duckling" (1843), "The Emperor's New Clothes" (1837), "The Snow Queen" (1844), "The Red Shoes" (1845), and "The Little Mermaid" (1837).

1836 Charles Dickens and Catherine Hogarth were married at St. Luke's Church, Chelsea. Although she bore him ten children, the marriage was unhappy. They finally separated in 1858.

1840 The master of the French literary world, Emile Zola, was born in Paris.

1842 The Philharmonic Society of New York was founded by Urieli Hill.

1860 The first Italian Parliament met at Turin.

1865 Confederate President Davis and most of his cabinet fled the Confederate capital of Richmond, Virginia.

1872 Artist, inventor, and philanthropist Samuel F. B. Morse died in New York. Best known as the developer of the electric telegraph, Morse was a committed Christian who dedicated all his work to the "honor and glory of Christ Jesus."

APRIL

1902 The first cinema in the United States opened in Los Angeles. Admission to the Electric Theatre was ten cents for a one-hour show.

1914 The Assemblies of God were organized at a conference at the Grand Opera House in Hot Springs, Arkansas. Called together by Eudorus N. Bell, publisher of *Word and Witness,* the meeting was intended only to provide the framework for annual conferences where Pentecostal teachings might be conducted. But the proceedings evolved into the foundation of a new denomination.

1917 Declaring that "the world must be made safe for democracy," President Woodrow Wilson asked Congress to declare war against Germany.

1921 Albert Einstein arrived in New York to lecture on his new theory of relativity.

1974 French president Georges Pompidou died in Paris.

1982 Several thousand troops from Argentina seized the disputed Falkland Islands, located in the South Atlantic, from Britain. Margaret Thatcher immediately mobilized the Royal Navy and Britain seized the islands back less than two months later.

Feast Day

*Saints Agape, Chionia, and Irene;
St. Pancras of Taormina; St.
Richard of Chichester; St. Nicetas;
St. Burgundofara; St. Sixtus I,
pope*

APRIL

3

He was the most dominant figure of the eighteenth-century literary world. The renown of Samuel Johnson was due in part to his moral essays, poetry, and prayers, in part to his remarkable *Dictionary of the English Language,* and in part to his amazing novel *Rasselas.* But in spite of all his carefully composed contributions to the prose of his native land, he may have never attained the stature that places him in the same rank as Shakespeare and Milton were it not for his famous trip to Scotland with his friend and biographer, James Boswell.

Born in Litchfield in 1709, the son of a failed bookseller, Johnson struggled throughout his early life against the ravages of poverty. Though he demonstrated a precocious mind and a prodigious literary talent, he was unable to complete his education at Oxford, and instead began his lifelong labors as a hack freelance writer in London for a series of newspapers, magazines, journals, and book publishers. As a result, he became phenomenally prolific and adept at virtually every genre—from criticism, translation, poetry, and biography to sermons, parliamentary reports, political polemics, and dramatic stage plays. Though his work was recognized as brilliant, he was never quite able to climb out of the miry privation that seemed to bog him down throughout his life.

At last, when he was nearly fifty, he received a commission to produce a dictionary. Over the course of the next seven years, he single-handedly took on the great task of comprehensively documenting English usage—which when completed, set the standard for etymology forever afterward. The work was indeed, stunning. Each word was not only carefully and succinctly defined, but illustrated from classic or poetic literature.

The dictionary earned Dr. Johnson a royal allowance that enabled him to pay off the bill collectors and to live with a modicum of ease. It was during this season of his life that he first met James Boswell, a Scottish ne'er-do-well and spendthrift who had already spent half a lifetime squandering his father's considerable estate on the pleasures of the flesh. Johnson was a pious, thoughtful, bookish, and venerable elder statesman. Boswell was an impetuous, ingratiating, bombastic, and irreverent young turk. But amazingly, the two men struck up a fast friendship. By that time, Johnson was nearly incapacitated with gout, corpulence, and arthritis. By all accounts he was built for a stationary life—overweight and slovenly, asthmatic and awkward. First impressions of him always surprised people. He was big-boned, six feet tall, stout, and stooped. Over a crop of wiry, frizzy hair he wore varying, ill-fitting wigs in unfetching shades of gray. His short-sightedness led to his reading so close to lamps and candles that the wigs frequently bore scorch marks.

Despite the fact that he was eloquent of speech and elegant of mind, he was hardly a fit candidate to become a dominating literary figure. But Boswell would see to that. Over the next several years, the unlikely pair carried on a conversation that, when documented in Boswell's biographies and journals, would enchant the world. And thus, an unlikely star in the already brilliant English literary constellation was born.

It is natural to mean well, when only abstracted ideas of virtue are proposed to the mind, and no particular passion turns us aside from rectitude; and so willing is every man to flatter himself, that the difference between approving laws, and obeying them is frequently forgotten.

[SAMUEL JOHNSON (1709–1784)]

1327 In his book *Defensor pacis*, Marsilius of Padua denounced the corruptions of the Roman prelacy and called for a radical reformation of the church. In short order both Marsilius and his copyist, John of Jandun, had been forced to flee for asylum from Paris to Bavaria. On this day, the pope issued a bull denouncing the pair as "sons of perdition and fruits of malediction." Nevertheless, copies of the book survived their condemnation and it was printed in 1517, the same year Luther posted his Ninety-five Theses. In fact, Luther was accused of resurrecting Marsilius's ideas.

1367 King Henry IV of England was born on the same day that John of Gaunt, his father, and Edward, the Black Prince, his uncle, were victorious at the Battle of Najara.

1593 Metaphysical poet George Herbert, known for his mastery of metrical form and allegory as well as his themes of Christian devotion, was born in Montgomery Castle, Wales. Herbert studied at Trinity College, Cambridge, and eventually became rector at Bemerton in 1630. From his deathbed in 1633, he sent his poems to a friend, asking him to decide whether they ought to be published. His collection of poems, *The Temple*, included such poems as "The Church Militant," "The Church Porch," "The Pulley," and the remarkable poems "The Collar" and "The Call." Other poems, such as "The Altar" and "Easter Wings," are pattern poems, which are written in the shape of the subject. Herbert said of his poetry that they were "a picture of the many spiritual conflicts that have passed between God and my soul, before I could subject mine to the will of Jesus, my Master, in whose service I have

now found perfect freedom." Herbert died at the age of forty of tuberculosis in 1633.

1783 The "First American Man of Letters," Washington Irving, was born in New York City. The last of eleven children, Irving worked as a lawyer until he was able to make a living at writing. His first great success, both in the United States and England, was *The Sketch Book* (1819–20), a collection of stories and essays that included his most famous short stories, "The Legend of Sleepy Hollow" and "Rip Van Winkle." These stories mix fact and fiction with satire and whimsy. He traveled in Spain for several years, but finally settled at "Sunnyside," his home on the Hudson River in Tarrytown, New York where he died in 1859.

1860 Two riders simultaneously left St. Joseph, Missouri, and Sacramento, California, for the first exchange of mail via the Pony Express. The service was discontinued on October 24, 1861.

1882 Outlaw Jesse James was shot to death in St. Joseph, Missouri, by Robert Ford.

1897 Composer Johannes Brahms died in Vienna from cancer and was buried near the graves of Beethoven, Schubert, and Mozart. One of his last works was a Chorale Prelude for organ based on the tune "O World I Must Now Leave Thee."

1968 Less than twenty-four hours before he was assassinated in Memphis, Tennessee, civil rights leader Martin Luther King Jr. delivered his famous "Mountaintop" speech to a rally of striking sanitation workers.

NATIONAL DAY
Hungary
FEAST DAY
St. Ambrose, St. Isidore, St. Plato,
St. Tigernach, St. Benedict the
Black, Saints Agathopus and
Theodulus

APRIL

In 1840 the Whig Party took the gamble of nominating the oldest man ever to run for president, sixty-eight-year-old William H. Harrison (1773–1841), and they won the election but lost the gamble, for Harrison lived only one month after his inauguration. On March 4, 1841, he made a three-hour inaugural speech in a drenching rain and caught pneumonia. One month later, on this day, he died in the White House.

He served the shortest term of any president, but his election ended the Jacksonian reign and brought the growing Whigs to power, even though John Tyler, the vice president who succeeded Harrison, was an ex-Democrat with rather watery Whig convictions.

The election of 1840 marked the beginning of elaborate national campaigns—by then the Whigs had become established as a second party, a development that helped to institutionalize the party system as the country's method of selecting candidates. Smarting from their defeat in 1836, when they were new and poorly organized, the Whigs met almost a year before the election for their first national convention. They then proceeded to build an elaborate campaign around everything but the issues: Harrison's military exploits against the Indians—especially the Battle of Tippecanoe; and his service as a simple man of the West—the Ohio and Indiana Territories where he served as a civil and military leader.

Campaign posters pictured Harrison as "The Hero of Tippecanoe" or "The Farmer of North Bend," hand to the plow in front of a log cabin. The catchy slogan "Tippecanoe and Tyler, too" rang out at the largest political rallies and mass meetings ever held in America. And it is one of the ironies of politics that the log cabin developed into a potent campaign symbol for Harrison, a man who was born in a white-pillared mansion into one of the aristocratic families of Tidewater Virginia. His father, Benjamin Harrison, was one of the Founding Fathers of the nation, a member of the Continental Congress, and a signer of the Declaration of Independence.

And so it was that the man to hold the presidency for the shortest time may have made the biggest impact—if only from the standpoint of having invented the modern presidential campaign.

Truth is that golden chain
It links together the terrestrial,
With that greater plane,
Which is but glorious celestial.

Truth sets the seal of heaven
On all the things of this sphere,
And infuses with the leaven
That maketh life so dear.

[Simon Fraser (1776–1862)]

APRIL

397 St. Ambrose, bishop of Milan, died. Known as the "Father of Hymnody," he encouraged the singing of hymns, wrote several, and codified the Ambrosian chant for the early church. Legend says that when Ambrose baptized St. Augustine, they spontaneously composed the *Te Deum*, singing alternating stanzas as they came out of the water.

1581 At Deptford, Francis Drake hosted Queen Elizabeth I for dinner on board his ship *The Pelican* in which he had recently circumnavigated the globe. After dinner, the Queen bestowed the rank of knighthood upon Drake. *The Pelican* was subsequently broken up, and pieces of it were fashioned into a chair, which now stands in the Bodleian Library in Oxford.

1648 Grinling Gibbons, the woodcarver and sculptor employed by Christopher Wren to execute his works for St. Paul's Cathedral in London, was born in Holland.

1739 The first performance of Handel's *Israel in Egypt* was held in London at the King's Theatre in Haymarket. Second only to *Messiah* in popularity, this oratorio tells the story of the Exodus from Egypt with vivid portrayals of the plagues and jubilant praise for the salvation of the Lord for He hath triumphed gloriously.

1774 Oliver Goldsmith, a literary protégé of Samuel Johnson, died at the age of forty-five.

1818 Congress decided that the flag of the United States would consist of thirteen red-and-white stripes and twenty stars, with a new star to be added for every new state of the Union.

1850 The city of El Pueblo de Nuestra Senora la Reina de Los Angeles de Porcioncola was incorporated in California.

1897 Campbell's Soup was first introduced.

1902 British financier, adventurer, and entrepreneur Cecil Rhodes left ten million dollars in his will to provide scholarships for Americans at Oxford University.

1914 *The Perils of Pauline,* a very early movie thriller, opened in New York City to rave reviews.

1939 Glenn Miller recorded his signature tune, "Moonlight Serenade," on this day.

1945 American forces liberated the Nazi death camp Ohrdruf in Germany. The true nature of the Holocaust was revealed to the outside world for the first time.

1949 Twelve nations, including the United States, signed the North Atlantic Treaty.

1968 Civil rights leader Martin Luther King Jr. was assassinated in Memphis, Tennessee. He was just thirty-nine years old.

1974 Hank Aaron of the Atlanta Braves tied Babe Ruth's home-run record by hitting his 714th round-tripper in Cincinnati.

APRIL

The centerpiece of the Tuskegee University campus in southern Alabama is the Booker T. Washington monument. Upon a grand classical pedestal stands a remarkable bronze statue sculpted by Charles Keck in 1922. Washington himself is portrayed—stately, dignified, and venerable—standing with his eyes set upon the horizon while one hand is extended toward the future. With the other hand he is resolutely pulling back a thick veil—presumably the smothering cloak of Strabo—from the brow of a young man seated at his side. The man is obviously poor—he is only half-clothed, in stark contrast to the dapper presence of Washington—and is sitting upon the symbols of his labor, an anvil and a plow. But he too is gazing off into the distance while he grasps a massive academic textbook upon his knee. The inscription beneath this arresting image asserts, "He lifted the veil of ignorance from his people and pointed the way to progress through education and industry."

The monument is a perfect tribute to the man. While his life—the long and difficult journey from the obscurity of slavery to the heights of national influence and renown—is a remarkable testimony of individual achievement and personal sacrifice, the greatest legacy of Booker T. Washington was not what he accomplished himself, but what he helped thousands of others accomplish—both black and white.

He was born on this day in 1856, on a small tobacco plantation in the backcountry of Franklin County, Virginia. His nine years in slavery were spent in abject poverty. And even after emancipation, his family faced a grim hardscrabble existence.

When he was sixteen, he gained admittance to the Hampton Institute—one of the first schools established for former slaves. Though he worked full-time as a janitor to pay his tuition, he graduated with honors in a mere three years. Upon graduation, he returned to his family and taught in the local grammar school. Before long though, his mentor at Hampton beckoned him to return to that institution, where he became an instructor and assistant to the president. Shortly afterward, the state of Alabama contacted the school about the possibility of establishing a similar college there. Washington was recommended for the job. Thus, on July 4, 1881, at the age of twenty-five, Washington founded Tuskegee.

The obstacles facing him were enormous. There was no money, no faculty, no campus, no land, and no student body. Indeed, there was nothing except the resolution of the state to launch the school and the determination of Booker T. Washington to raise up a whole new generation of leaders from the rubble of the South and the legacy of slavery. Nevertheless, before his death in 1915, Tuskegee had grown to encompass a 2,000-acre campus of 107 buildings with more than 1,500 students and nearly 200 faculty members. As a result of his efforts, Washington became a celebrity and the first great leader for civil rights for all Americans.

My worth to God in public is what I am in private.

[OSWALD CHAMBERS (1874–1917)]

636 Isidore, Bishop of Seville, published a twenty-volume encyclopedia of scientific knowledge. The *De Rerum Natura*—literally, *On the Nature of Things*—was the first Christian attempt to improve on the work of the Roman Pliny.

1614 Matoaka, an Algonquin Princess—the word for Princess in the Algonquin language was *Pocahontas*—known as Rebecca since her baptism, married the English colonist Avis McJohn Rolfe. The wedding took place in Jamestown, Virginia. The bride's two brothers and an uncle stood for her. The marriage initiated a period of friendly relations between Indians and colonists. The story behind the marriage is rather complicated by legend and lore, but this much we know.

1621 The *Mayflower* sailed from Plymouth, Massachusetts, on a return trip to England.

1649 Elihu Yale, the English philanthropist for whom Yale University is named, was born.

1792 George Washington cast the first presidential veto, rejecting a congressional measure for apportioning representatives among the states.

1869 The last known surviving solider in the American War for Independence, Daniel Bakeman, died at the age of 109.

1874 *Die Fledermaus* (The Bat), the light comic opera by Johann Strauss the younger, premiered in Vienna and in a few years was famous throughout the world. The story of jokes, mistaken identities, and class mobility was set to glorious waltzes by the master of the form.

1895 Playwright Oscar Wilde lost his criminal libel case against the Marquess of Queensberry, who had accused the writer of homosexual practices.

1908 Herbert von Karajan, renown conductor of the Berlin Philharmonic Orchestra, was born in Austria. At a concert at the Mozarteum on January 22, 1929, with works by Tchaikovsky, Mozart, and Strauss, Herbert von Karajan conducted so well that the director of Ulm Stadttheater invited him to Ulm for a trial performance. His early start in music prepared him for a career as one of the greatest interpreters of orchestral music.

1916 Silent-film star Charlie Chaplin signed a contract making him the highest paid actor at $675,000 for one year's work.

1964 Army general Douglas MacArthur died in Washington at age eighty-four.

1974 The World Trade Center opened in New York City. The structure has 110 floors.

1975 Nationalist Chinese leader and founder of the Taiwanese resistance, Chiang Kai-shek, died at age eighty-seven.

1976 Reclusive billionaire Howard Hughes died in Houston at age seventy-two.

1997 Allen Ginsberg, the counterculture guru who shattered conventions as poet laureate of the Beat Generation, died in New York City at age seventy.

APRIL

APRIL

6

Despite having run on a platform of determined neutrality, President Woodrow Wilson found his administration being drawn inexorably toward war. On March 5, 1917, he delivered his second inaugural address as the nations of the world engaged in a great global war. "The tragical events of the thirty months of vital turmoil through which we have just passed have made us citizens of the world. There can be no turning back. All nations are equally interested in the peace of the world and in the political stability of free peoples, and equally responsible for their maintenance."

Less than a month later, the president, citing Germany's policy of unlimited submarine warfare against its enemies as well as neutral countries, including the United States, asked Congress for a declaration of war against the Imperial German government.

Though many were reluctant to abandon America's traditional neutrality, the president's words were persuasive. "I have called the Congress into extraordinary session because there are serious, very serious, choices of policy to be made, and made immediately, which it was neither right nor constitutionally permissible that I should assume the responsibility of making," he began. After detailing the Kaiser's many violations of international law, he asserted, "We have no quarrel with the German people. We have no feeling toward them but one of sympathy and friendship. It was not upon their impulse that their government acted in entering this war. It was not with their previous knowledge or approval. It was a war determined upon as wars used to be determined upon in the old, unhappy days when peoples were nowhere consulted by their rulers and wars were provoked and waged in the interest of dynasties or little groups of ambitious men who were accustomed to use their fellow men as pawns and tools."

Thus, he concluded, "the world must be made safe for democracy. Its peace must be planted upon the tested foundations of political liberty. We have no selfish ends to serve. We desire no conquest, no dominion. We seek no indemnities for ourselves, no material compensation for the sacrifices we shall freely make. We are but one of the champions of the rights of mankind. We shall be satisfied when those rights have been made as secure as the faith as the freedom of nations can make them. It is a fearful thing to lead this great peaceful people into war, into the most terrible and disastrous of all wars, civilization itself seeming to be in the balance. But the right is more precious than peace, and we shall fight for the things which we have always carried nearest our hearts—for democracy, for the right of those who submit to authority to have a voice in their own governments, for the rights and liberties of small nations, for a universal dominion of right by such a concert of free peoples as shall bring peace and safety to all nations and make the world itself at last free. God helping her, she can do no other."

And so did the United States enter the First World War.

Time after time mankind is driven against the rocks of the horrid reality of a fallen creation. And time after time mankind must learn the hard lessons of history—the lessons that for some dangerous and awful reason we can't seem to keep in our collective memory.

[HILAIRE BELLOC (1870–1953)]

884   Methodius, who with his brother Cyril was the pioneer missionary to the Slavs and architect of the Cyrillic alphabet, died while still serving in the Eastern European realm of Moravia.

1199   Richard Cœur de Lion, king of England, was slain by an arrow from a crossbow near Limoges in France at the siege of the castle of Chaluz.

1327   Poet and lyricist Francesco Petrarca—known as Petrarch—saw a beautiful married woman in the Church of Santa Clara in Avignon. He would later write more than 360 poems to her throughout his life, addressing her always as "Laura," never revealing her true identity.

1520   Italian Renaissance painter Raphael died in Rome on his thirty-seventh birthday. Originally from the town of Urbino, Raphael moved to Florence in 1504. His study of the works of Leonardo da Vinci, Michelangelo, and Fra Bartolommeo resulted in the development of his painting style and technique. From this point on, he created works that were more animated and informal, with elements of light and shade, a better understanding of anatomy, and dramatic action. One of his most famous works is the depiction of the great philosophers in *The School of Athens* (1509-1511).

1830   The Mormon Church—officially, the Church of Jesus Christ of Latter-day Saints—was organized by Joseph Smith in Fayette, New York, after he was supposedly led to buried tablets describing a lost American civilization by angel messengers.

1862   The bloody Battle of Shiloh began in Tennessee during the War Between the States. The two-day-long clash of arms pitted Union generals Ulysses Grant and D. C. Buell against Confederate generals A. S. Johnston and P. T. Beauregard and cost nearly ten thousand lives on each side. Except possibly Gettysburg, it has been the subject of more controversy than any other American battle.

1874   Illusionist and escape artist Harry Houdini (Ehrich Weiss) was born in Hungary.

APRIL

1909   Explorers Robert E. Peary and Matthew A. Henson became the first men to reach the North Pole. The claim, disputed by skeptics, was upheld in 1989 by the Navigation Foundation.

1930   Bakery executive James Dewar invented the Hostess Twinkie.

1947   The first Tony awards for excellence in Broadway theater were held at the Waldorf-Astoria in New York City.

1957   New York City ceased operating trolley cars on this day.

1971   Russian-born composer Igor Fyodorovich Stravinsky died in New York. Known mostly for his early experimental music (i.e., *The Rites of Spring*), Stravinsky also broke free from the weight of late Romanticism and developed the neoclassical style. He believed firmly that the heart of every musician should be the study of the cantatas by J. S. Bach. A consummate craftsman and diligent worker, he railed against the lack of restraints and discipline encouraged by modern artists. He once said, "For a beginner, in whatever field, there is only one possibility, namely to submit himself to an external discipline, with the double aim of learning the language of his profession, and, in the process, of forming his own personality."

FEAST DAY
St. Celsus, St. Goran, St. Finan Cam, St. George the Younger, St. Hegesippus, St. Aphraates, St. Henry Walpole, St. Herman Joseph, St. John Baptist de la Salle

APRIL

All too rare is the literary work that completely chronicles an epoch—a work that opens a window on the entirety of a culture: from its art, music, and ideas to its fancies, fables, and foibles. *The Canterbury Tales* is just such a rarity. But this remarkable work not only described an age, it also defined it. Written by Geoffrey Chaucer in the late fourteenth century—though not published until this day in 1499, almost a hundred years after his death—the book is a true masterpiece in every sense of the word.

Besides his fascinating insights into the roots and origins of our language, in this work Chaucer gives us a glimpse into the odd nuances of daily life during the halcyon days of the High Middle Ages. He offers us a remarkably enlightened approach to the questions of medieval love, marriage, and family. He affords us a firsthand look at the contemporary sciences, especially astronomy, medicine, psychology, physics, and alchemy. He gives a chronicler's account of the raging social, political, and theological issues of the time. He parodies the social oddities, exults in the cultural profundities, and scrutinizes the civic moralities of his time. He has a genius for capturing the quirks and nuances of ordinary life, the twists and turns of ordinary conversation, and the motivations and inclinations of ordinary people. He expands barnyard fables into cosmic comedies, he transforms old wives' tales into morality plays, and he develops the tidbits of everyday gossip into observations of the universal human condition. He observed what everyone recognized and recognized what everyone observed. And that is precisely what made him so great.

Thus he painted a vivid portrait of an entire nation—an entire civilization—high and low, male and female, old and young, lay and clerical, learned and ignorant, rogue and righteous, land and sea, town and country, cosmopolitan and provincial—in some of the most beautiful descriptions ever penned. On any given page you'll find poetry, mythology, history, science, theology, practical ethics, biography, linguistics, art, geography, music, and philosophy—all rendered in a rollicking good storyline brimming over with mystery, adventure, romance, and good humor. And he did this in a language that was hardly usable until he used it; he did this for a nation that was hardly recognizable until he recognized it.

The book is not a classic because some stuffy old professors in musty ivory towers decreed it so; it is a classic because it is classically good and vitally important. Almost two centuries before Shakespeare was born, Chaucer crafted an immortal work that should take a priority place in any Christian's must-read list. As G. K. Chesterton asserted, "The Poet is the Maker; he is the creator of a cosmos; and Chaucer is the creator of the whole world of his creatures. He made the pilgrimage; he made the pilgrims. He made all the tales told by the pilgrims. Out of him is all the golden pageantry and chivalry of the Knight's Tale; all the rank and rowdy farce of the Miller's. And he told all his tales in a sustained melodious verse, seldom so continuously prolonged in literature; in a style that sings from start to finish."

Tradition wears a snowy beard,
Romance is always young.

[JOHN GREENLEAF WHITTIER (1807–1892)]

1250 Louis IX of France—later dubbed Saint Louis—was captured by Egyptian Muslims during his ill-fated Crusade.

1770 Poet William Wordsworth, one of the prime forces behind the English Romantic movement, was born in Cockernouth, Cumberland, England. In 1798 he published a collection of poems with his friend Samuel Taylor Coleridge called *Lyrical Ballads,* which contained Wordsworth's poem "Tintern Abbey." The success of this volume helped to replace neoclassical verse, and in 1843, Wordsworth became poet laureate of England.

1798 The area of land that is comprised of the current states of Alabama and Mississippi was organized as the Mississippi Territory.

1824 The first complete performance of Ludwig van Beethoven's *Missa Solemnis* was held in St. Petersburg. Beethoven considered this work to be his most accomplished composition. During the writing of this monumental work, he wrote in his notebooks: "God above all things! For it is an eternal providence which directs omnisciently the good and evil fortunes of human men . . . Tranquilly will I submit myself to all vicissitudes and place my safe confidence in Thine unalterable goodness. O God! Be my rock, my life, forever my trust." Unfortunately, the *Missa Solemnis* is less an act of humility by a devout believer and more a display of defiant pride by one who feels divinity within the creative process of the human spirit.

1927 An audience in New York saw an image of Commerce Secretary Herbert Hoover in the first successful long-distance demonstration of television.

APRIL

1939 Italy invaded Albania, which offered only token resistance. Less than a week later, Benito Mussolini annexed the conquered territory.

1940 The first African American depicted on a U.S. postage stamp was the educator Booker T. Washington, whose likeness appeared on the 10 cent stamp issued this day.

1947 Auto pioneer Henry Ford died in Dearborn, Michigan, at age eighty-three.

1949 The Rodgers and Hammerstein musical *South Pacific* opened on Broadway.

1957 The last of New York's electric trolleys completed its final run from Queens to Manhattan.

1969 The Supreme Court unanimously struck down laws prohibiting private possession of obscene material.

1994 Civil war erupted in Rwanda, a day after a mysterious plane crash claimed the lives of the presidents of Rwanda and Burundi. In the months that followed, hundreds of thousands of minority Tutsis, plus Hutu intellectuals, were slaughtered.

APRIL

Born in 1676 in the obscure village of Duns, Berwickshire, Thomas Boston died on this day in 1732 in the equally obscure parish of Ettrick in the Scottish Borders. But his fifty-six years of life, forty-five of them spent in conscious Christian discipleship, lend credibility to the spiritual principle that it is not where a Christian serves, but what quality of service he renders, that really counts.

Graduating with a degree in the classical arts from Edinburgh University, Boston was able to afford only one session of theological training. He then underwent a rigorous self-guided study program, completing all his studies extramurally. With arduous discipline, sustained by only a meager library, his autodidactic studies earned him a widespread reputation. Indeed, as a Hebrew scholar he was, according to the renowned linguist George Morrison, "welcomed as an equal by the finest Hebrew scholars in the world." As a theologian, Jonathan Edwards wrote that he was "a truly great divine."

But it was as a loving, faithful, rigorously self-disciplined Christian pastor, and one deeply committed to the grace of God, that Boston was best remembered. Leaving his first charge at Simprin, where he served 1699–1707, he settled in Ettrick for a twenty-five-year ministry that saw the numbers of communicants rise from a mere sixty in 1710 to nearly eight hundred in 1731.

Constantly burdened for his congregation, Boston taught them in season and out of season, in pulpit and in home. Burdened for the truth of the gospel, he overcame all natural timidity to engage in confronting heretical doctrine and dealing with the critical cultural issues of the day. Though he was a quiet man, by all accounts he became a roaring lion in the pulpit. According to James Heatherton, "There was a grip in it that no preacher wins who is a stranger to his own heart."

He was thus counted as one of the most powerful and effective ministers of his day—and this despite the fact that he labored for Christ in an obscure, out-of-the-way place all his life, never desiring for anything more. According to Thomas Chalmers, "He so understood the covenant that he found his greatest reward amongst those who knew him best; so he never desired to leave them."

1869

The American Museum of Natural History opened in New York City. It is the largest natural history museum in the world and is comprised of twenty-three interconnected buildings that cover several city blocks. The entire facility, which includes a library of 450,000 volumes, consists of 1,265,381 square feet including exhibitions of anthropology, archaeology, geology, mineralogy, paleontology, and biology.

The age of chivalry is gone, alas; that of sophisters, economists, and calculators has succeeded.

[EDMUND BURKE (1729–1797)]

626 Maedoc of Ferns was an early Irish believer who traveled and studied widely throughout the British Isles in his youth. He established a Christian community in Wexford where he gave shelter to numbers of infant children who survived primitive abortion surgeries at the hands of pagan Druids. Throughout his life he fought against their deadly rites. He died on this day, but the community has survived to the present day, and it continues to provide institutional care for the helpless and the unwanted.

1341 Petrarch was crowned poet laureat on the steps of the capitol in Rome.

1492 Lorenzo de Medici, the great patron of Renaissance art and despot of the city of Florence, died.

1513 Ponce de Leon named his new discovery Florida, near the present site of St. Augustine. It is likely that the Castilian explorer chose that name in recognition of the fact that he made the discovery near the time of the Easter feast (Pasqua Florida).

1541 Francis Xavier, a disciple of Ignatius Loyola, left Portugal to serve as a missionary to Asion. Over the course of the next ten years, he traveled nine thousand miles, an incredible feat in those days of primitive transportation. He brought the gospel to more than fifty kingdoms, and baptized over one million converts. The church he planted in Japan endured three centuries of persecution without Bible or priests—just parents passing the Word on to children. He died at forty-six, worn out from his labors. He is remembered as the Apostle of the Indies.

1614 One of the greatest painters of Spanish art, El Greco, died in Toledo and was buried in Santo Domingo el Antiguo. He was born Domenikos Theotokopoulos in Candia, Crete (part of the Republic of Venice). His early art was most likely in the Byzantine style. He studied in Venice and Rome, but it was his move to Spain that caused him to develop in a style called Mannerism, which was the progeny of the High Renaissance art.

1819 Because of illness and pain, Sir Walter Scott was forced to give up writing his new novel *The Bride of Lammermoor.* But rather than cease work altogether, he lay upon a couch and dictated the story to a secretary.

1871 Robert Louis Stevenson beckoned his father to join him for a walk through the streets of Edinburgh. He wanted to tell him that he had decided to give up his career in engineering to devote himself full-time to writing.

1898 Maurice Bowra was born in Kiukiang, China. Among his brilliant classical Greek translations would be Pindar's *Pythian Odes.*

1935 The Works Progress Administration (WPA) was approved by Congress.

1946 The League of Nations assembled in Geneva for the last time.

1973 Artist Pablo Picasso died at his home near Mougins, France. He was ninety-one years old and worked right up until his final brief illness.

1974 Hank Aaron of the Atlanta Braves hit his 715th career home run in a game against the Los Angeles Dodgers, breaking Babe Ruth's career record.

1975 Frank Robinson, major-league baseball's first African-American manager, got off to a winning start as his team, the Cleveland Indians, defeated the New York Yankees, 5-3.

1994 Former Secretary of Defense Robert S. McNamara, in an interview with AP Network News and *Newsweek* magazine to promote his memoirs, called America's Vietnam War policy "terribly wrong."

APRIL

APRIL

Born in Northern Ireland to a wealthy Presbyterian family, Amy Carmichael (1867–1951) became one of the best-known missionaries of the first half of the twentieth century. Her ministry took her first to Japan, then to Ceylon, and finally to the Dohnavur province of India.

Although the brutal Hindu traditions of sarti and immolation—burning widows alive on the funeral pyres of their deceased husbands—had been legally banned, to her horror she discovered that ritual abortion and female infanticide were still quite common. In addition, many of the young girls that she had come to work with were still being systematically sold off as slaves to the nearby pagan temples to be raised as cult prostitutes.

She immediately established a ministry to protect and shelter the girls. Although she had to suffer the persecution of various Hindu sects and the bureaucratic resistance of the British colonial government, Carmichael built an effective and dynamic ministry renowned for its courage and compassion. Sadly, many of her fellow missionaries in India—having partially accepted the presuppositions of Planned Parenthood's Malthusian thought—believed that her effort to build an orphanage and school was actually a "worldly activity" that distracted her from the "saving of souls." To such accusations she simply replied, "Souls are more or less firmly attached to bodies."

Since her death in 1951, her Dohnavur Fellowship has continued to carry on ministries of evangelism, education, and medical aid among the poor and helpless. It remains one of the most dynamic Christian works on the Indian subcontinent.

1553 François Rabelais, author of *Gargantua* and *Pantagruel,* died in Paris. In his last will and testament he caustically wrote, "I have nothing. I owe much. I leave the rest to the poor."

1865 General Robert E. Lee surrendered the Army of Northern Virginia to General Ulysses S. Grant at Appomattox Courthouse, thus ending the American Civil War. Great respect was shown on all sides, as Union soldiers tipped their hats in salute to their opposing brethren in arms.

Every tradition grows ever more venerable—the more remote its origin, the more confused that origin is. The reverence due to it increases from generation to generation. The tradition finally becomes holy and inspires awe. Is this ill or fine? If the accumulated wisdom and the tested habits of the ages accounts for naught, then surely it is ill. But if such things afford security and sanity, then it is an augur of great good. Sense and sensibility should sway us toward the confident latter and not the impetuous former.

[JAMES GLEASON ARCHER (1844–1909)]

APRIL

1626 Francis Bacon, philosopher and man of letters, died in London. Between 1608 and 1620, he prepared at least twelve drafts of his most celebrated work, the *Novum Organum*, a presentation of his scientific method. His *Essays* mark him as a master of English prose. "Some books are to be tasted," he wrote, "others to be swallowed, and some few to be chewed and digested."

1682 After traveling down the Mississippi River, French explorer Robert LaSalle reached the Gulf of Mexico and claimed this area of the lower Mississippi for France.

1816 America's first African-American bishop, Richard Allen, was consecrated when a new denomination, the African Methodist Episcopal Church, was established.

1821 Charles Baudelaire was born in Paris. His translations of Edgar Allan Poe's work would eventually make Poe better known in France than in his native America.

1859 After serving a two-year apprenticeship, Samuel Clemens—who would later gain fame as Mark Twain—was licensed as a pilot of Mississippi steamboats in the District of St. Louis.

1915 Critic Alexander Woolcott took the management of the Schubert Theaters to court after they banned him from their productions for "rancor, malice, and venom."

1939 After she was denied the use of Constitution Hall by the Daughters of the American Revolution, African-American singer Marian Anderson performed a concert on the steps of the Lincoln Memorial in Washington, D.C. First Lady Eleanor Roosevelt helped to arrange the substitute venue for the concert.

1940 Germany invaded Denmark and Norway.

1942 American and Philippine defenders on Bataan capitulated to Japanese forces. The surrender was followed by the notorious "Bataan Death March," which claimed nearly ten thousand lives.

1959 NASA announced the selection of America's first seven astronauts: Scott Carpenter, Gordon Cooper, John Glenn, Gus Grissom, Wally Schirra, Alan Shepard, and Donald Slayton.

1963 By an act of Congress, Winston Churchill became the first person to be made an honorary citizen of the United States.

1965 The newly built Houston Astrodome was hailed as the "Eighth Wonder of the World." The occasion featured its first baseball game, an exhibition game between the Astros—previously called the Colt 45s, the team was renamed for the occasion—and the New York Yankees. The Astros won, 2-1. The stadium was retired from pro sports after the 1999 season.

1992 Former Panamanian ruler Manuel Noriega was convicted in Miami of eight drug and racketeering charges.

FEAST DAY

St. Hedda of Peterborough, Saints Beocca and Hethor, St. Bademus, St. Macarius of Ghent, St. Paternus of Abdinghhof, St. Michael de Sanctis, St. Fulbert of Chartres, the Martyrs under the Danes

Nestorius was consecrated bishop of Constantinople on this day in 428. Although there was little indication of it at the time, it was eventually to prove to be a momentous occasion. A firm opponent of the Arian heresy, he nevertheless, fell into a contrary error.

The Arians taught that Christ was a created being. To refute this and other points, Nestorius argued that at the Incarnation, the divine nature joined with the human merely as a man might enter a tent or put on his clothing. Instead of depicting Christ as one person with two natures, Nestorius saw Him as a conjunction of two natures so distinct as to be different persons who had merged.

Thus, Nestorius refused to call Mary the *Theotokos* or "Mother of God." Her baby was very human, he said. The human acts and sufferings of Jesus were of His human nature and not of His divine nature. To say Mary was Mother of God was to say God had once been a few hours old. "God is not now nor has He ever been a baby," he argued. He never actually denied that Christ was divine. On the contrary, he asserted, it was to protect His divinity that he argued as he did—lest it be lost in worship of the human child.

Cyril, the patriarch of Alexandria, condemned Nestorius's position on the Incarnation as heresy by issuing twelve anathemas against him. Nestorius responded in kind. The two men proved to be fierce antagonists. There was no chance of reconciliation. Emperor Theodosius II called a council at Chalcedon in 433 to settle the question. Working quickly, Cyril deposed Nestorius before his Syrian supporters could reach the council site. Rome backed Cyril's move and Nestorius was stripped of his position and exiled.

But the followers of Nestorius did not easily yield. In regions controlled by Persia they formed their own church. It was a strong body that evangelized eastward as far as China. Nestorian churches appeared in Arabia, India, Tibet, Malabar, Turkostan, and Cyprus. Many exist to this day, especially in Iraq.

Meanwhile, the Orthodox Church created a formula to describe Christ's person at the Council of Chalcedon. The assembled bishops declared Christ was two natures in one person. "We all with one voice confess our Lord Jesus Christ one and the same Son, at once complete in manhood, truly God and truly man, consisting of a reasonable soul and body; of one substance with the Father as regards his Godhead, of one substance with us as regards his manhood, like us in all things, apart from sin."

Weak things must boast of being new, like so many new German philosophies. But strong things can boast of being old. Strong things can boast of being moribund.

[G. K. CHESTERTON (1874–1936)]

787 The church of St. Corneille at Conpiègne installed an organ at the request of Frankish king Pepin—in what is modern-day France. This is the first recorded mention of this musical instrument.

1841 The first issue of the *New York Tribune* was published by Horace Greeley, who edited the paper for more than thirty years.

1847 Joseph Pulitzer was born in Mako, Hungary, the son of a wealthy grain merchant of Magyar-Jewish origin and a German mother who was a devout Roman Catholic. He gained influence and wealth in the newspaper industry and eventually he established the award bearing his name that grants prizes for literature, drama, music, and journalism for American citizens.

1866 The American Society for the Prevention of Cruelty to Animals (ASPCA) was incorporated.

1869 By act of Congress the number of Supreme Court Justices was raised from seven to nine.

1912 The White Star liner *Titanic* sailed on this day on her maiden voyage from Southampton to New York. Fourteen years before *Titanic's* first and only voyage, a novel called *Futility*, written by Morgan Robertson, was published. It concerned an unsinkable and glamorous Atlantic liner, the largest in the world. Like *Titanic*, the fictional vessel was a triple-screw design and could make 24–25 knots; at 800 feet it was a little shorter than *Titanic*, but at 70,000 tons its displacement was 4,000 tons greater. Also like *Titanic*, its passenger list was the crème de la crème and there were not enough lifeboats. On a cold April night, the fictional "unsinkable" vessel struck an iceberg and glided to the bottom of the Atlantic. The name of the liner in the story? *Titan*.

1925 F. Scott Fitzgerald's novel of the Jazz Age, *The Great Gatsby*, was published in New York by Scribner's.

1932 German war hero Paul von Hindenburg was reelected president of the republic—but the socialist candidate, Adolf Hitler, came in second.

APRIL

1947 Brooklyn Dodgers president Branch Rickey announced he had purchased the contract of Jackie Robinson from the Montreal Royals. It would mark the beginning of racial integration in Major League Baseball.

1953 The three-dimensional horror movie *House of Wax*, produced by Warner Brothers and starring Vincent Price, premiered in New York.

1956 While performing a concert at the Municipal Hall in Birmingham, Alabama, Nat King Cole was attacked on stage and beaten by a group of racial segregationists.

1959 Japan's Crown Prince Akihito married a commoner, Michiko Shoda.

1963 The nuclear-powered submarine USS *Thresher* failed to surface off Cape Cod, Massachusetts, in a disaster that claimed 129 lives.

1972 The United States and the Soviet Union joined some seventy nations in signing an agreement banning biological warfare.

1974 Golda Meir, the former Milwaukee schoolteacher, announced her resignation as prime minister of Israel.

10

APRIL

The American interstate system—on which new construction began on this day in 1958—is a marvel of social order and engineering prowess. Nowhere else on this planet is it possible to travel so far on good roads without going through an international border crossing, risking life and limb at the hands of brigands and banditos, or getting shaken down by the secret police. The ancient world was united more by Roman roads than by Roman armies. Similarly, the nationwide highway grid has made the transcontinental empire we call the United States a single navigable geographical entity.

The whole system is very nearly as orderly as arithmetic—all east-west routes are even-numbered beginning in the South; all north-south routes are odd-numbered beginning in the West; all triple-digit routes beginning with even numbers are loops around metropolitan areas; those beginning with odd numbers are spurs into city centers. It follows therefore that Interstate 10 underlies the nation, linking Atlantic and Pacific with a line running from Jacksonville to Los Angeles; Interstate 90 links the oceans with a line running from Providence to Seattle; Interstate 95 connects Miami and Boston, while Interstate 5 runs between Vancouver and San Diego. And every road ultimately leads to every other road.

Of course, the great disadvantage of this marvel of uniformity is that the interstate system has imposed a smothering standard of sameness on the wild diversity of the North American continent. As travelers drive along the interstate—any interstate—they could literally be anywhere—the roadways that crisscross the land have no distinctive identity. The highways are as blindly and blandly generic as a cafeteria soy-burger. As a result, critics have imagined it as the "geography of nowhere." Scattered all along the system at predictable intervals are a series of copycat tourist traps pockmarked with tacky metal sheds emblazoned with garish neon, selling cheap trinkets and bad food—all comprising a human environment not actually intended for humans, but rather for automobiles. Nevertheless, it has become a defining feature of modern American life.

1970

The troubled *Apollo 13* space capsule blasted off from Cape Canaveral carrying astronauts James Lovell, Fred Haise, and Jack Swigert. An explosion during the flight resulted in the aborting of the planned lunar landing and a race against time to return the astronauts safely to Earth despite numerous obstacles.

There are two ways: the way of life and the way of death, and the difference between these two ways is great.

[DIDACHE (C. 100)]

1506 St. Peter's basilica in Rome was first constructed by Constantine the Great at the beginning of the fourth century. It sat on the site where tradition says Peter was buried when executed in A.D. 67. As early as A.D. 90 an oratory had memorialized the spot. By the beginning of the sixteenth century, the walls of the old church were veined with cracks. At first, Pope Nicholas V simply planned to remodel the building, making structural enhancements where necessary. It would be a long, drawn-out process, taking decades. However, one of his successors, Julius II, determined to replace the basilica completely. He laid the cornerstone on this day. He hired the greatest Renaissance artists and architects to do the work—Bramante, Raphael, Sangello, Verone, Sangallo, Peruzzi, and Michelangelo all worked on the project at one time or another. The great cathedral was not finished until 1626, 120 years after Julius laid the first stone. Interestingly, it was to pay for the construction costs that Leo X authorized, the indulgence of which led to Luther's Ninety-five Theses and ultimately, the Reformation.

1689 William III and Mary II were crowned as joint sovereigns of Britain. Mary was the daughter of the deposed king, James II, who fled into exile in France. William was the Dutch elector of Orange.

1722 Christopher Smart was born in Shipbourne, Kent. In and out of asylums for almost seven years, the poet was finally released in 1763 and he published his masterpiece, *A Song to David,* shortly thereafter.

1814 Napoleon Bonaparte abdicated as emperor of France and was banished to the island of Elba.

1898 President William McKinley asked Congress to issue a Declaration of War against Spain. Exactly one year later he signed a treaty ending the Spanish-American War. It was a magnificent victory for the U.S. and greatly raised the young nation's international stature.

1914 George Bernard Shaw's play *Pygmalion* opened at His Majesty's Theater in London with Herbert Beerbohm Tree as Higgins and Mrs. Patrick Campbell as Eliza.

APRIL

1921 Iowa became the first state to impose a cigarette tax.

1931 Dorothy Parker stepped down as the drama critic for the *New Yorker,* ending her self-described "reign of terror."

1934 The strongest wind gusts on Earth were recorded at the top of Mt. Washington in New Hampshire at 231 miles per hour.

1945 At the close of the Second World War, American soldiers liberated the notorious Nazi concentration camp Buchenwald in Germany.

1951 President Harry Truman created a firestorm of controversy when he relieved General Douglas MacArthur of his commands in the Far East.

1968 President Johnson signed into law the Civil Rights Act of 1968, a week after the assassination of Dr. Martin Luther King Jr.

1979 The brutal dictator Idi Amin was deposed as president of Uganda as rebels and exiles backed by Tanzanian forces seized control.

11

Telemachus of Laddia was a monk from Syria who, while on a pilgrimage to Rome, launched a crusade to put an end to gladiatorial contests. He met with senators, nobles, and local church leaders in an effort to sway them to join his cause.

One day during the winter of 399, after many months of fruitless lobbying, he rushed into the great arena of the Colosseum to separate the bloody combatants. The infuriated spectators mobbed him and he died in the crush. Even so, his sacrifice was not for naught. Horrified by the story of this courageous defender of life, a number of prominent Romans took up his cause.

Less than five years later—an amazingly short amount of time given the cumbersome nature of the Roman judicial system—the emperor Honorius abolished all such contests throughout the empire. Telemachus became a model for genuine social and cultural reform. His life and death afforded Christians ample demonstration that the deleterious effects of sin in the world could in fact be ameliorated by righteous action. Thus, he became the patron of Christian political action.

Interestingly, Telemachus was cited by reformers like John Knox and George Buchanan as they attempted to bring substantial change to their world—more than a millennium later.

1861

The American War Between the States began when Union forces attempted to resupply Fort Sumter, a harbor garrison just offshore from Charleston, South Carolina. During a monthlong standoff, Confederate forces had kept the Union garrison supplied with food and water. But when President Abraham Lincoln ordered his soldiers to receive armaments from supply ships, the commander of the South Carolina forces, P. T. Beauregard, demanded immediate capitulation. When the Union forces refused, Beauregard opened fire. The fort quickly surrendered, but the war had begun.

He has shown you, O man, what is good and what the Lord requires of you: to do justice, to love mercy, and to walk humbly with your God.

[MICAH OF MORESETH (C. 700 B.C.)]

65 The Roman philosopher Seneca was, on this day, forced by the emperor Nero to commit suicide. Despite the fact that he was Nero's tutor and minister, Seneca fell out of favor when he warned the emperor against his life of gross excess.

1709 Richard Steele published the first issue of London's premier magazine of news, reviews, and commentary, *The Tattler*.

1775 Samuel Johnson, dining at a favorite London tavern with a number of companions made the offhand comment, "Patriotism is the last refuge of a scoundrel." The comment was immortalized when the ever-present James Boswell quickly jotted it down and then included it prominently in his biography of Johnson some years later.

1816 Charles Gavan Duffy, Irish nationalist, Australian politician—as well as a renowned journalist, poet, editor, and historian—was born at County Monaghan. His Shilling series, *The Library of Ireland*, popularized Irish belles-lettres. He was best known for his *Conversations with Carlyle* as well as his autobiography, *My Life in Two Hemispheres*.

1934 *Tender Is the Night* by F. Scott Fitzgerald was first published. It was a novel about rich expatriates—and thus was unenthusiastically received during the difficult days of the Great Depression.

1945 President Franklin Delano Roosevelt died of a cerebral hemorrhage while on vacation in Warm Springs, Georgia, at age sixty-three. He was succeeded by Vice President Harry S. Truman.

1955 In the midst of a raging polio epidemic, researcher Jonas Salk successfully tested a vaccine against the disease. On this day it was declared safe and effective and mass public vaccinations began immediately.

1961 Soviet cosmonaut Yuri Gagarin became the first man to fly in space, orbiting the earth once before making a safe landing. The journey lasted 108 minutes.

1972 Watchman Nee, the mystical Chinese Christian leader and author of such books as *The Normal Christian Life* and *Sit, Walk, Stand*, completed twenty years in prison, five years more than his maximum sentence. Ten days later he wrote in good spirits to his sister, possibly from a country prison. Within weeks he was dead. He had been accused by Communist authorities of exercising "a dark, mysterious control" over the more than 450 churches he had helped to plant all over China. His works remain influential, particularly in Pentecostal and Arminian Holiness circles.

1981 The space shuttle *Columbia* blasted off from Cape Canaveral on its first test flight.

1983 Chicagoans went to the polls to elect Harold Washington the city's first black mayor.

1985 Senator Jake Garn of Utah became the first senator to fly in space as the shuttle *Discovery* lifted off.

1989 Radical activist Abbie Hoffman was found dead at his home in New Hope, Pennsylvania, at age fifty-two.

1992 Euro Disneyland opened in the French countryside outside Paris.

APRIL

12

FEAST DAY
St. Guinoch; St. Martin I, pope; Saints Carpus, Papylus, and Agathonice; St. Hermenegild; St. Martius

APRIL

13

Thomas Jefferson was born this day in 1743 in Albemarle County, Virginia. Though he served as America's first secretary of state, its second vice president, and its third president, and though he was also at various times a member of the Continental Congress, an ambassador to France, governor of the state of Virginia, the founder of the Library of Congress, and the founder of the University of Virginia, the accomplishment he was most proud of was his authorship of the Declaration of Independence. It was in that document, he believed, that his credo of the rule of law was best enunciated.

It was his conviction that if left to the mere discretion of human authorities, even the best-intended statutes, edicts, and ordinances inevitably devolve into some form of tyranny. There must, therefore, be some absolute against which no encroachment of prejudice or preference may interfere. There must be a foundation that the winds of change and the waters of circumstance cannot erode. There must be a basis for law that can be depended upon at all times, in all places, and in every situation.

Apart from this uniquely Christian innovation in the affairs of men and nations, Jefferson believed that there could be no freedom. There never had been before, and there never would be again. Thus, in the opening refrain of the Declaration, he affirmed the necessity of that kind of absolute standard upon which the rule of law can then be established, "We hold these truths to be self-evident, that all men are created equal; that they are endowed by their Creator with certain inalienable rights; that among these are life, liberty, and the pursuit of happiness. That, to secure these rights, governments are instituted among men, deriving their just powers from the consent of the governed."

Appealing to the "Supreme Judge of the World" for guidance, and relying on His "Divine Providence" for wisdom, Jefferson called on his fellow Founders to commit themselves and their posterity to the absolute standard of "the laws of nature and of nature's God." A just government exists, he argued, solely and completely to "provide guards" for the "future security" of that standard. Take away those guards, he argued, and the rule of law is no longer possible.

That is precisely why he felt compelled to so boldly declare autonomy from the British realm. The activist government of the Crown had become increasingly intrusive, burdensome, and fickle and thus the possibility of rule of law had been thrown into very real jeopardy. Jefferson was therefore merely protesting the fashion and fancy of political, bureaucratic, and systemic innovation that had alienated the inalienable.

His credo contended that no one in America could be absolutely secure under the king, because absoluteness had been thrown out of the constitutional vocabulary. The liberties of all the citizens were at risk because suddenly arbitrariness, relativism, and randomness had entered into the legal equation. Thus, Jefferson induced his fellow Founders to act boldly to "form a more perfect union." And as a result, he had a hand in launching a sublime experiment in liberty never before surpassed, never again matched.

Nothing costs so little, goes so far, and accomplishes so much as a single act of merciful service.

[AUGUSTE RENIOR (1841–1919)]

1385 The pilgrimage that inspired Chaucer's *Canterbury Tales* began at the Tabard Inn.

1742 The first public performance of Handel's *Messiah* was held in Dublin, Ireland. Handel had been invited to Dublin by the Duke of Devonshire, the Lord Lieutenant of Dublin, and the governors of three charitable organizations to conduct one of his works for the purpose of charity. Handel decided to compose a new work, and in twenty-five days of intense labor, he completed the score to *Messiah*. The concert was greatly anticipated and even better received, and the three charities were able to split about $1,800 in revenue.

1845 Victor Hugo was made a peer of France—thus, he became Viscomte Hugo.

1870 The Metropolitan Museum of Art was founded in New York. The chairman of the committee was Theodore Roosevelt, father of the future president.

1909 Eudora Welty was born in Jackson, Mississippi. She would later remark, "Whatever our theme in writing, it is old and tired. Whatever our place, it has been visited by the stranger; it will never be new again. It is only the vision that can be new; but that is enough."

1912 Theodore Dresser sailed home from Europe on the *Kroonland*, too miserly to pay for passage on the *Titanic*. For once, his friends and family were grateful for his penny-pinching habits.

1943 President Roosevelt dedicated the Jefferson Memorial in Washington, D.C.

1958 Van Cliburn from Kilgore, Texas, won the Tchaikovsky International Piano Competition in the Soviet Union at the age of twenty-three—the first American to do so.

1970 *Apollo 13*, four-fifths of the way to the moon, was crippled when a tank containing liquid oxygen burst. The astronauts managed to return safely.

1986 Pope John Paul II visited a Rome synagogue in the first recorded papal visit of its kind.

1992 The Great Chicago Flood took place as the city's century-old tunnel system and adjacent basements filled with water from the Chicago River.

1997 Tiger Woods became the youngest person to win the Masters Tournament and the first player of at least partly African heritage to claim a major golf title.

13

APRIL

George Frideric Handel's life (1685–1759) was a continuing struggle between great success and precipitous failure. In 1715 he was the most famous composer alive, but fifteen years later he was disgraced and in debt due to the dissipation of his fame and popularity. In his fifties he was faced with the realization that his influence and popularity were dead in the field of opera—an arena that had garnered him previous success and for which he was uniquely productive. The greatest blow was his blindness, which left him unable to compose; however, Handel continued his musical career as an incomparable organist and conductor of his own great oratorios. In all, he completed forty-six operas, thirty-two oratorios, more than a hundred large choral works, other dramatic works, and many solo instrumental and orchestral compositions. The only explanation for his prodigious output despite his struggles was Handel's ability to divorce the ebbs and flow of his personal life from his productive life as an artist. In fact it was during the times of grief and stress that he was able to write some of his most lighthearted music.

Though his father opposed his pursuit of a musical career, he was a prodigy who caught the eye of powerful patrons. He studied throughout the German and Italian centers of music and served as the organist at the Cathedral of Moritzburg and Kapellmeister to the Elector of Hanover. Handel later established his reputation in London with the production of his opera *Rinaldo*. The opera sold out fifteen performances. Although he was instructed to return to Germany "in a reasonable period," Handel spent the next forty-seven years in England where he became a citizen in 1727.

In 1714, Queen Anne died and was succeeded by the Elector of Hanover, George I, Handel's former employer. Handel was a favorite with the court. In 1719, Handel was appointed the artistic director of the newly formed Royal Academy of Music in London. After he found success with his oratorios *Esther, Deborah, Saul,* and *Israel in Egypt,* his greatest work, *Messiah,* was premiered in 1742 in Dublin. The acclaim over *Messiah* was astonishing. The following years were an outpouring of genius as Handel wrote at the top of his creative powers such works as *Samson* (1741), *Semele* (1744), *Belshazzar and Hercules* (1745), *Judas Maccabaeus* (1746), *Joshua* (1747), *Solomon* (1748), *Theodora* (1749), *Choice of Hercules* (1750), and *Jephtha* (1751).

During the composing of *Jephtha* in 1751, Handel began to go blind. He underwent several operations from various surgeons, including the surgeon who attempted to restore Bach's sight, but all to no avail. Refusing to admit defeat, Handel continued to perform organ concerts and to conduct performances of his oratorios. It was during a performance of *Messiah* on April 6, 1759, that Handel felt somewhat lightheaded and later fainted during the ovation. He was carried home and put to bed. He told his friends that he wanted "to die on Good Friday in the hope of rejoining the good God, my sweet Lord and Savior, on the day of His resurrection." He died Easter weekend on this day, 1759, and was buried in the Poet's Corner of Westminster Abbey according to his wishes. Over his grave stands a statue depicting Handel standing in front of his work table littered with quills and the score of Messiah opened to the passage "I know that my Redeemer liveth."

Do unto the others as if you were the others.

[Leonardo da Vinci (1452–1519)]

1682 Archpriest Avvakum—the leader of a traditionalist movement within the Russian Orthodox Church known as the Old Believers—was martyred. While awaiting execution, he spent several years in prison where he wrote hundreds of pages of doctrine. He also produced an autobiography. Written in a zestful, contemporary Russian, it is considered a milestone of the language much as Pascal's *Provincial Letters* are for French and Chaucer's *Canterbury Tales* for the English. Its concise immediacy was unsurpassed until Tolstoy. Friendly jailers winked as Avvakum's well-wishers smuggled out his tracts and the text of the autobiography. Finally, at Czar Theodore's order, he and his fellow prisoners were locked in a log cabin and burned alive. Thus perished in flame a remarkable spiritual hero and literary genius whose remembrance endures to this day.

1828 The first edition of Noah Webster's *American Dictionary of the English Language* was published in the United States.

1865 President Abraham Lincoln was shot by actor John Wilkes Booth during a performance of *Our American Cousin* at Ford's Theatre in Washington, D.C. He died the following day. At the same time an accomplice of Booth's stabbed Secretary of State William Seward in his home but was fought off by Seward's son. An additional conspirator succumbed to fear and failed to strike down Vice President Andrew Johnson.

1902 J. C. Penney opened his first store, in Kemmerer, Wyoming. His life credo was, "You can't outgive God." He proved it by building a multimillion-dollar commercial empire while always giving away 90 percent of his personal income to Christian evangelistic and charitable work.

1912 The RMS *Titanic* struck an iceberg and sank on the following day as the ship's band played "Nearer, My God to Thee." More than 1,500 passengers and crew perished.

1931 King Alfonso XIII of Spain went into exile, and the Spanish Republic was proclaimed, precipitating the bitter Spanish Civil War.

1935 The Midwest came to be known as the Dust Bowl because of the layers of blown sand caused by vicious sandstorms.

1939 The motion picture *Wuthering Heights,* starring Merle Oberon and Laurence Olivier, premiered in New York.

1939 John Steinbeck's depression era novel filled with biblical imagery, *The Grapes of Wrath,* was published by Viking Press.

1956 At a price of $75,000, Ampex Corporation introduced the first commercial magnetic tape recorder for sound and picture. The unit was about four feet by three feet with five 6-foot racks of additional circuitry.

1981 The first test flight of America's first operational space shuttle, the *Columbia,* ended successfully with a landing at Edwards Air Force Base in California.

1989 Testimony concluded in the Iran-Contra trial of former National Security Council staff member Oliver L. North.

April

Although the campaign for president in 1888 was quite heated, the Republican candidate remained remarkably calm throughout the long ordeal. The grandson of a former president, Benjamin Harrison knew only too well the ebb and flow of politics and popular opinion, and simply refused to allow the process to disrupt his emotional equilibrium.

On election night his chief interest seemed to be in the polling results of his own state of Indiana. When the numbers there were safely announced in the Republican column, just after ten, he went to bed. The following morning a friend, having called to congratulate him late the night before, asked why he had retired so early. The president-elect explained, "I knew that my staying up would not alter the result if I were defeated, while if I was elected I had a hard day in front of me. So a good night's rest seemed the best course in either event."

Later he added, by way of explanation, "A fellow who fails to take into account the divine is bound to miss a good deal of sleep unnecessarily—it can help but little. Our charge is simply to render our services aright and leave the results to providence."

Harrison could sleep peacefully because he knew that God ordains civil government—it is a sacred institution and an honorable and holy vocational field—and thus those who serve in that arena are ministers under the hand of Providence. He knew that he was merely in the service of God's good purposes in the world—and so to worry or fret was not only utterly futile, it was utterly faithless.

1989 Students in Beijing launched a series of pro-democracy protests upon the death of former Communist Party leader Hu Yaobang. The protests culminated in the Tiananmen Square massacre.

Swallow Day According to ancient calendars and almanacs, the first swallows are expected to return to England for the spring and summer seasons. According to the eighteenth-century verse, "The Swallow, for a moment seen, Skim'd this morn the village green; Again at eve, when thrushes sing, I saw her glide on rapid wing. O'er yonder pond's smooth surface, when I welcom'd her back again."

Lay hold of something that will help you, and then use it to help somebody else.

[BOOKER T. WASHINGTON (1856–1915)]

1415 Greek scholar and translator of Homer and Plato, Manuel Chrysolaras, died in Konstanz. He helped to reintroduce Greek literature to the West and was instrumental in trying to arrange a council to consider the union of the Latin and Greek churches.

1452 Leonardo da Vinci, self-proclaimed "painter, architect, philosopher, poet, composer, sculptor, athlete, mathematician, inventor, and anatomist," was born in Vinci.

1729 J. S. Bach conducted the premiere performance of the *St. Matthew Passion* at the St. Thomas Church in Leipzig, Germany. The two contrasting sections are derived from the twenty-sixth and twenty-seventh chapters of Matthew with supplemental text by Christian Friedrich Henrici, a postal clerk. The sufferings of Christ are portrayed through music of humility, sorrow, and adoration. Some records indicate that the premiere occurred on April 11, 1727.

1817 The first American school for the deaf opened in Hartford, Connecticut.

1859 Oxford University won the annual Oxford-Cambridge boat race on the Thames River when the Cambridge boat was swamped by a passing steamer.

1850 The city of San Francisco was incorporated.

1861 The former superintendent of West Point, Robert E. Lee, was offered the command of the Union army by President Abraham Lincoln. He declined.

1865 President Lincoln died several hours after he was shot at Ford's Theater in Washington by John Wilkes Booth. Andrew Johnson became the nation's seventeenth president. It was four years

to the day since Lincoln had declared a state of insurrection and called for a full excursionary force to invade the South.

1874 The New York legislature passed a law mandating education as compulsory.

APRIL

1879 Ivory Soap was created by Harley Procter.

1888 English poet Matthew Arnold, most famous for his poem "Dover Beach," died in Liverpool. At the end of his life, he returned to religion as the center of his thoughts and wrote several essays dealing with literature and the church. This was a departure from his earlier thinking that poetry would replace religion and that people would "turn to poetry to interpret life for us, to console us, to sustain us."

1912 In the early morning hours, the British luxury liner *Titanic* sank in the North Atlantic off Newfoundland, less than three hours after striking an iceberg. About 1,500 people died.

1923 Diabetics had access to insulin for the first time.

1945 British and Canadian troops liberated the Nazi concentration camp Bergen-Belsen at the end of the Second World War.

1947 Jackie Robinson, baseball's first African-American major-league player, made his official debut with the Brooklyn Dodgers on opening day. The Dodgers defeated the Boston Braves, 5-3.

1951 The Franklin National Bank in Franklin Square, New York, issued the first bank credit card.

1959 Cuban leader Fidel Castro arrived in Washington to begin a goodwill tour of the United States. The goodwill did not last very long.

APRIL

16

The Rising of '45 under Bonnie Prince Charlie (1720–1788) very nearly succeeded in gaining Scotland independence from Britain. After a series of minor field victories, the prince ordered his troops toward London in the south. Along the borders of Northumbria at the field of Prestonpans, the young prince engineered a stunning victory over the vastly better equipped English. The trained British troops were simply unprepared to face the unfettered fury and untempered loyalty of the Highlanders. Then, in one stunning maneuver after another, he outwitted the English commanders and was able to eventually control more than three-quarters of the land. He came within fifty miles of London. The Hanoverian king, George II, was in a panic, making haste to leave for his German homeland.

It was treachery that eventually turned Bonnie Prince Charlie back, spoiling his fairy-tale aspirations. Betrayed by several of his nobles, he was forced to retreat back toward Scotland. The English armies, taking advantage of this turn of events, pursued with all haste. Over the next several months, the Highlanders were harried by both their enemies and the weather.

Though they were able to prevail in several of the skirmishes and battles that followed—including the decisive Battle of Falkirk—it was clear that the Hanoverians had taken the upper hand. The prince and his men were on the defensive. The final pitched battle between the two forces took place on the Culloden Moor just outside Inverness, on this day in 1746. The calamitous slaughter took less than half an hour. The well-equipped Hanoverian troops swept over the field and exacted the horrible price of vengeance.

The prince escaped with his life, but little else. Over the next five months Bonnie Prince Charlie wandered as a fugitive in the Highlands while the Hanoverians ravaged Scotland, raping and pillaging their way across the whole land. The Scots tongue, Gaelic, was banned, as were all the distinctive aspects of Scots culture—from bagpipes and kilts to tartans and clan badges. Alas, the prince could do little to ameliorate the sufferings of his people.

Eventually, he was able to steal away into exile, where he spent the rest of his life. He never gave up on the Stuart cause though. He maintained his claims. And his descendants to this very day claim the royal prerogative.

See the same man in vigor, in the gout;
Alone, in company, in place, or out;
Early at business, and at hazard late;
Mad at a fox chase, wise at debate;
Grogged at a borough, civil at a ball;
Friendly at Hackney, faithless at Whitehall.

[ALEXANDER POPE (1688–1744)]

APRIL

1789 President-elect Washington left his home at Mount Vernon, Virginia, for his first inauguration in New York.

1844 Literary stylist Anatole France was born in Paris.

1862 A full year after the War Between the States had begun, a bill ending slavery in the District of Columbia became law. Utilizing the appeals process, owners of the world's largest slave market—just two blocks from President Lincoln's bedroom in the White House—would remain open for business for another eighteen months.

1889 Sir Charles Spencer Chaplin—best known as Charlie Chaplin—was born in East Street, Walworth, London. The legendary comic actor, director, and producer left the vaudeville stage of his impoverished, precocious boyhood for Hollywood in 1914, where he created his beloved "Little Tramp" character. Chaplin went on to make more than eighty short and feature films, and is recognized as a pioneer of cinematography.

1912 Harriet Quimby became the first woman to fly across the English Channel.

1917 Vladimir Ilyich Lenin returned to Russia after years of exile. With gold from German and American financiers—who wanted the Russians out of the First World War—he was able to finance the Communist revolution and establish the Soviet totalitarian state.

1926 The Book of the Month Club began in the United States.

1945 In his first speech to Congress, President Harry Truman pledged to carry out the war and peace policies of his late predecessor, Franklin Roosevelt.

1945 American troops reached Nuremberg, Germany, at the end of the Second World War.

1947 Financier and presidential confidant Bernard M. Baruch said in a speech at the South Carolina statehouse, "Let us not be deceived, we are today in the midst of a Cold War." Thus, he coined a phrase that would define the era.

1947 America's worst harbor explosion occurred in Texas City, Texas, when the French ship *Grandcamp* blew up; another ship, the *Highflyer*, exploded the following day after fire from the first blast crossed an oil spill and engulfed the bow. The blasts and resulting fires killed 576 people.

1962 Famed war correspondent Walter Cronkite succeeded Douglas Edwards as anchorman of *The CBS Evening News.* He became America's most trusted source of news, closing each broadcast with the words, "And that's the way it is."

1994 Ralph Ellison, author of *Invisible Man*, died in New York at age eighty.

APRIL

17

John of Amathus was born on the eastern Mediterranean island of Cyprus toward the end of the sixth century. The greater part of his life was spent engaged in public service and civil affairs. He married young and faithfully raised his children in the nurture and admonition of the Lord.

Despite the fact that he was entirely untrained in theology, his unflagging piety and wisdom encouraged the people of the ancient North African Alexandria to call him to be their patriarch and pastor at the age of fifty on this day in 641. He threw himself into his new responsibilities with characteristic zeal. He injected new life into that old church by establishing innumerable ministries to the needy. He endowed several healthcare institutions—including the very first maternity hospital. He founded several homes for the aged and infirm. He opened hospices and lodges for travelers. He tore down the remnants of the old infanticide walls outside the city with his own hands and called on his parishioners to join him in defending the sanctity of human life in the future.

He also fought corruption in the political administration of the city. The people, weighed down with oppressive tax rates of more than 20 percent of their incomes, had allowed the once-thriving economy to sour. By pressing for tax reform, John hoped that prosperity would return, bringing benefits to everyone, but particularly to the poorest of the poor. He succeeded to such a degree that not only was Alexandria restored as the primary commercial center of North Africa and one of the three richest cities in Byzantium, but also dispossession and destitution were all but eliminated altogether. So prolific were his good deeds that he eventually became known as John the Almsgiver.

1842

Charles Henry Parkhurst was born. The pastor of the prominent Madison Square Presbyterian Church in New York City, he gained renown as the man who dared to expose the corruption of Tammany Hall, the powerful political machine that ran the city. He proved his charges by hiring a private detective to accompany him as he went undercover penetrating the brothels, gambling halls, and bootleg bars in places like Hell's Kitchen and the Bowery. Later he combined his efforts with the young Theodore Roosevelt, the city's police commissioner. Together they brought about the first significant reforms in city politics and the administration of justice.

A bold Christian is the highest style of a man.

[THOMAS YOUNG (1722–1799)]

1421 Seventy-two villages and more than 100,000 people were swept away in a immense flood in Holland.

1492 A contract was signed by Christopher Columbus and a representative of Aragon's King Ferdinand and Castile's Queen Isabella, giving Columbus a commission to seek a westward ocean passage to Asia.

1521 German theologian and Reformer, Martin Luther appeared at the first hearing of the Diet of Worms. An official of Trier pointed to a table of books and asked Luther if he was willing to recant. Luther saw that some of the books were his writings on Scripture, and he asked for a recess in order to respond appropriately.

1524 Genoese explorer Giovanni da Verrazano reached present-day New York Harbor.

1790 On his deathbed, 84-year-old Benjamin Franklin was asked by his daughter to shift positions. He replied, "A dying man can do nothing easy." They were his last words.

1861 Following the outbreak of hostilities between Federal troops and South Carolina, the Virginia State Convention reluctantly voted to secede from the Union. It was the consensus of opinion that President Lincoln had violated the charter of the Constitution by authorizing an invasion on one of the constituent states.

1912 Al Jolson recorded "Ragging the Baby to Sleep" for the Victor Talking Machine Company—it was the first unofficial gold record.

1961 Cuban forces routed an invasion at the Bay of Pigs that had been sponsored by the United States government in an effort to overthrow the Communist government of Fidel Castro. The CIA had trained 1,500 Cuban exiles for the assault.

1964 Ford Motor Company unveiled its revolutionary new Mustang model. It would almost immediately capture the affections of car buyers and pass into classic status.

1964 Jerrie Mock of Columbus, Ohio, became the first woman to complete a solo airplane flight around the world.

APRIL

1969 A jury in Los Angeles convicted Sirhan Sirhan of assassinating Senator Robert F. Kennedy.

1969 Czechoslovak Communist Party chairman Alexander Dubcek was deposed by forces backed by the Soviet government in Moscow. A moderate, he had ushered in the "Prague Spring," a time of extraordinary freedom.

1970 The astronauts of *Apollo 13* splashed down safely in the Pacific, four days after a ruptured oxygen tank crippled their spacecraft.

1975 Phnom Penh fell to Communist insurgents, ending Cambodia's five-year war.

1991 The Dow-Jones industrial average closed above 3000 for the first time.

1993 A federal jury in Los Angeles convicted two former police officers of violating the civil rights of beaten motorist Rodney King; two other officers were acquitted.

1998 A Thai military team collected evidence from the body of Pol Pot, the former chief of Cambodia's Khmer Rouge guerrillas, to lay to rest doubts that one of the century's worst tyrants was truly dead.

17

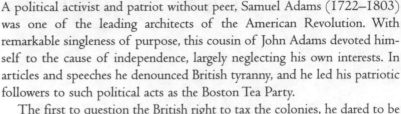
A political activist and patriot without peer, Samuel Adams (1722–1803) was one of the leading architects of the American Revolution. With remarkable singleness of purpose, this cousin of John Adams devoted himself to the cause of independence, largely neglecting his own interests. In articles and speeches he denounced British tyranny, and he led his patriotic followers to such political acts as the Boston Tea Party.

The first to question the British right to tax the colonies, he dared to be identified as a rebel leader—and he was the one, along with John Hancock, that British troops were after when they came to Lexington on April 19, 1775. In 1765 Adams openly encouraged citizens to defy the Stamp Act, and he was the prime mover behind the meeting of all the colonies at the Stamp Act Congress in New York. Adams worked against the British as a member of the Massachusetts legislature, in the powerful position of clerk, and less openly as founder of the Massachusetts committee of correspondence and a leader of the secret society, the Sons of Liberty. This patriotic—and radical—group resorted to violence and demonstrations on several occasions, storming the governor's home and hanging the British tax collector in effigy.

On March 5, 1770, a group of colonists threatened British soldiers in Boston, precipitating an incident in which three colonists were killed. Adams and Joseph Warren called it the Boston "Massacre," and news of the "massacre" helped promote anti-British feeling. Adams helped create another incident in December 1773, when the Sons of Liberty, encouraged by Adams, boarded British ships and dumped hundreds of chests of tea overboard—to protest the tax on tea. Adams had a genius for the daring act that would strike political flint.

Adams attended the First Continental Congress in 1774, and, on this day in 1775, he was with Hancock in Lexington, about to go to the Second Congress, when Paul Revere arrived with news that British troops were after them—and they rode off early the next day before the troops arrived and those first shots were fired. Although he remained active in politics to the end of his life—even serving as the governor of his state—signing the Declaration of Independence was the apex of his career. In his search for freedom and independence Adams was ever impatient, but thanks to his abiding Christian faith, he had the will and the ability to shape events that helped make independence in America a reality in his own time.

Let your hand feel for the afflictions and distresses of everyone, and let your hand give in proportion to your purse; remembering always the estimation of the widow's mite, that it is not everyone that asketh that deserveth charity; all however are worthy of the inquiry, or the deserving may suffer. Thus is the mettle of true character.

[GEORGE WASHINGTON (1732–1799)]

1521 Brought to the city of Worms to recant by Emperor Charles V, Martin Luther uttered the immortal words that launched the Reformation: "Since your majesty and your lordships desire a simple reply, I will answer without horns and without teeth. Unless I am convicted by scripture and plain reason—I do not accept the authority of popes and councils for they have contradicted each other—my conscience is captive to the Word of God. I cannot and I will not recant anything, for to go against conscience is neither right nor safe. Here I stand, I cannot do otherwise. God help me. Amen." With a victory gesture he then slipped out of the room.

1775 Silversmith Paul Revere rode from Boston to Lexington through the Massachusetts countryside to warn the colonists of the approaching British army. This event is often regarded as the start of the American Revolution. During his midnight ride, Revere did not shout, "The British are coming!" but rather "The regulars are coming!" Regulars was the name for British troops.

1882 Conductor Leopold Stokowski was born in London—although he claimed that it was in 1887. At a time in which it was assumed the only qualified conductors came from Eastern Europe, Stokowski affected a Germanic accent for his entire life. Often controversial in his conducting methods, he nevertheless made important contributions to art music in America and was a recognizable figure as evidenced in a Bugs Bunny cartoon parody of the demanding, unorthodox, yet respected musician.

APRIL

1906 Four square miles of buildings were destroyed in San Francisco and almost seven hundred people died when the San Andreas Fault in California settled and caused earthquakes throughout the region at 5:13 A.M.

1934 The first Laundromat—called a washateria—opened in Fort Worth, Texas.

1942 An air squadron from the USS *Hornet*, led by Lieutenant Colonel James H. Doolittle, raided Tokyo and other Japanese cities.

1945 Famed American war correspondent Ernie Pyle, age forty-four, was killed by Japanese gunfire on the Pacific island of Ie Shima, off Okinawa.

1946 The League of Nations went out of business.

1949 The Irish republic was proclaimed.

1955 Physicist Albert Einstein died in Princeton, New Jersey.

1977 Alex Haley, who chronicled the history of his family through slavery in *Roots*, was awarded the Pulitzer Prize.

1978 The U.S. Senate voted 68-32 to turn the Panama Canal over to Panamanian control on December 31, 1999.

1994 Former President Richard Nixon suffered a stroke at his home in Park Ridge, New Jersey, and was taken to New York Hospital–Cornell Medical Center. He died four days later.

APRIL

First settled on this day in 1796, Cleveland remained a sleepy little village at the mouth of the Cuyahoga River on the shores of Lake Erie for nearly two decades. But the nearby exploits of naval commander Oliver Perry during the War of 1812 highlighted its strategic position. The completion of the Ohio and Erie Canal in 1832 and the arrival of the railroad in 1851 cemented its importance—accessible to both the coal and oil fields of Pennsylvania and the iron ore mines of Minnesota. Following the War Between the States, it became a center of political and economic power—giving the nation five presidents during the next fifty years, including Rutherford B. Hayes, James Garfield, William McKinley, William H. Taft, and Warren G. Harding, as well as several of the greatest industrial monopolists, including Marcus A. Hannah and John D. Rockefeller.

The city boasted many notable firsts—the nation's first African-American newspaper, the *Aliened-American*, was published here in 1853; the Arcade, built in 1890 and located in the heart of downtown, was the first indoor shopping mall in the nation; the Negro Welfare Association, the forerunner of the Urban League, was established here in 1917; NACA, the forerunner of NASA, was established here in 1940; the first black mayor of a major American city was elected here in 1967.

By the end of the twentieth century, Cleveland had very nearly died. Once the fifth largest city in the nation, today it does not even rank in the top twenty. Though once a hub for transportation, a model of industrialization, and a progressive leader in social and cultural reform, by the second half of the twentieth century, it had begun a precipitous decline. In some ways it became emblematic of what became known as America's Rust Belt. Its once-busy factories had become decrepit, its vibrant communities had become depressed, its wonderful location had become spoiled by polluted air and water, and its massive modern infrastructure had become obsolete. It became an embarrassing blight. The proud metropolis was derisively referred to by critics as the Mistake on the Lake. Population declined by nearly half.

Nevertheless, its rich heritage—it has been estimated that there are some eighty different ethnic groups in the city speaking more than sixty different languages, representing nearly every race, tongue, and tribe on the planet—and progressive leadership have brought tremendous renewal to the city. By the time of its bicentennial, the city was once again demonstrating its strategic significance.

One friend in a lifetime is much; two are many; three are hardly possible.

[HENRY ADAMS (1838–1918)]

526 John the bishop of Rome served the liturgy in Constantinople's gloriously decorated cathedral, the Santa Sophia—the Hagia Sophia of Justinian had not yet been built. Afterward, with oriental splendor he crowned Justin the new emperor. It would be the last time Eastern and Western churches demonstrated such remarkable harmony.

1012 The archbishop of Canterbury, Saint Alphege, died today at the hands of marauding Danes. Previously his cathedral had been burned and he was captured and imprisoned; nevertheless, he attended to the needs of his captors who had contracted the plague. When a ransom for his release was not paid, the Danes drove a stake through his heart.

1526 The citizens of Strasburg, Nuremburg, Ulm, and nine other cities with the support of a few electors and princes, protested a decree of the Diet and petitioned the emperor to revoke what the assembly of the German states had decreed. These Reformers of religion were thus first given the name of Protestants.

1775 American colonists and British troops had their first exchange of fire in the towns of Lexington and Concord in the "first shot heard 'round the world." The British general Thomas Gage sent a force to capture military weapons at Concord.

1824 English Romantic poet Lord George Gordon Byron died of malaria at Missolonghi in Greece. He was in Greece to assist the country in its fight against the Turks.

1897 The first Boston Marathon was run from Ashland, Massachusetts, to Boston. Winner John J. McDermott ran the course in two hours, fifty-five minutes and ten seconds.

1898 Congress passed a resolution recognizing Cuban independence and demanding that Spain relinquish its authority over Cuba.

1933 President Franklin Roosevelt took the United States off the gold standard and issued a call for gold and silver certificates to be handed in to the government.

1938 RCA-NBC began an experiment of transmitting five hours of regular television programming a week.

APRIL

1943 Jews numbering in the tens of thousands began a valiant but ultimately futile battle against Nazi forces in the occupied Warsaw ghetto in Poland.

1945 The Rodgers and Hammerstein musical *Carousel* opened on Broadway.

1951 General Douglas MacArthur, relieved of his command by President Harry Truman, bid farewell to Congress, quoting a line from a ballad: "Old soldiers never die; they just fade away."

1993 Horrified, Americans watched live television footage as federal agents stormed the Branch Davidian religious community with tanks and tear gas. The fifty-one-day siege near Waco, Texas, ended as fire engulfed the structure. Dozens of men, women, and children perished in the blaze.

1995 A truck bomb devastated the Alfred P. Murrah Federal Building in Oklahoma City, killing 168 people. Timothy McVeigh and Terry Nichols were later convicted of charges related to the bombing.

1998 Mexican poet-philosopher Octavio Paz died at age eighty-four.

19

The first installment of Plutarch's famous *Lives* was published on this day in the year 118. He came to his vocation rather late in life—during the reigns of Trajan and Hadrian. This period at the beginning of the second century was a momentous time in the history of Western civilization for any number of reasons.

Greece, of course, had lost by this time the last vestiges of her independence. Her population had fallen precipitously since the days of her glory—the riches of Rome and the Asian provinces had not only attracted her most able administrators but also her most capable laborers. Thus, materially, culturally, and politically Plutarch's homeland was in decline. Though he could do little to arrest this trend, he felt obliged to put it into perspective—and that he did quite ingeniously in the *Lives.*

At the same time, the Roman Empire was in its most stable and vibrant stage. The economy was prosperous. The military was invincible. And the culture was vibrant. Education, the arts, and the sciences were all flourishing. Despite the decrepit paganism of the day, there was a degree of personal freedom unprecedented in all of history.

But the most significant feature of the age was the sudden emergence of Christianity as a major societal force. Although Plutarch does not deal with Christianity directly, it is clear that he was attempting to revive interest in the very best of ancient paganism. In the face of the moral challenge that Christian evangelism posed to the *ancien régime* he wanted to reignite the moral vitality of classicism. Thus, we see in the *Lives* the last great gasping apologetic for Greco-Roman civilization on the threshold of an ascendant Christendom.

When later writers, thinkers, and social activists would appeal to the classical Age for reforms in their own time, they would picture its ideals as seen through Plutarch's rose-colored glasses. This is why the American founders could remain so enamored with the ancients—despite their unhesitating commitment to Christian truth, their comprehension of the pagan essence of Greece and Rome was myopically obscured by Plutarch.

1227

Pope Gregory IX appointed a board of Inquisitors to sit against heresy in Florence. Shortly afterward, he issued formal rules to insure that the Inquisition would aim at the discipline and restoration of erring Catholics only. Jews, Muslims, and other non-Christians were not to be touched. The Inquisition would inquire into the spread of heresy, summon suspected heretics before tribunals, and punish infidelity so as to convert and save the souls. As his Inquisitor in France, Gregory appointed the brutal Robert le Bougre, former heretic. Shortly thereafter he had 180 individuals burned at the stake in one day and performed many other atrocities until recalled and imprisoned.

If all the world were just, there would be no need of valor.

[Plutarch (c. 49–120)]

1233 Pope Gregory IX issued a papal bull placing the operation of the Inquisition into the hands of the Dominicans due to the fact that the institution had already demonstrated terrible excesses. The methods employed by his order were hardly gentle. They included torture and execution, usually by burning. Although instructions for interrogation limiting the use of torture were issued, the tendency was to exceed them. Many faithful Dominicans never participated in the Inquisition. Others were mild in their measures. Some resigned rather than continue the brutal work. Nonetheless the good name of the Dominicans was forever stained by their participation in this cruel activity. Before long the order became popularly known as *Domini canes,* Latin for "God's dogs."

1721 Colonial statesman and one of the drafters of all four American founding documents, Roger Sherman, was born.

1779 The Scottish Jacobite Society was incorporated in Charleston, South Carolina, with the express intention of making Bonnie Prince Charlie, the Stuart Pretender, the king of America.

1789 It was while serving as a surgeon on the British warship *Arundel* that James Ramsay got his first glimpse of the conditions of chattel slavery. It would haunt him for the rest of his life, and would in fact completely redirect his ambitions and abilities. In time, he would submit to a call to the ministry and a mission to free England from the curse of inhuman servitude. A small book of memoirs advocating abolition—which he composed while serving in a quiet village pastorate—placed him at the center of a storm of controversy. Working with some of the greatest Christian thinkers and activists of the day— Granville Sharp, Charles Middleton, Thomas Clarkson, Ignatius Latrobe, and the young

William Wilberforce—he applied the principles of the Christian pro-life legacy to the question of slavery. By the time he died in 1789 on this day, the erosion of morality that Renaissance and Enlightenment thinking had begun in England had been checked to some degree—and the end of chattel slavery was within sight.

APRIL

1812 The fourth vice president of the United States, George Clinton, died in Washington at age seventy-three, becoming the first vice president to die while in office.

1841 Edgar Allan Poe's *Murder in the Rue Morgue*—the very first detective story—was published.

1853 Harriet Tubman began her work on the Underground Railroad in an effort to give escaping slaves a safe passage to the North.

1859 The first volume of Charles Dickens's *A Tale of Two Cities* was published. Its opening lines alone made the book a certain classic, "It was the best of times, it was the worst of times. . . ."

1889 Adolf Hitler was born in Braunau, Austria.

1902 Scientists Marie and Pierre Curie isolated the radioactive element radium.

1914 Charlie Chaplin, starring as the Little Tramp, directed his first short film "Twenty Minutes of Love," with the Keystone Film Co. He became the legendary director of such films as *The Kid, City Lights,* and *The Gold Rush.*

1949 Scientists at the Mayo Clinic announced that they had succeeded in synthesizing a hormone found to be useful in treating rheumatoid arthritis; the substance was named "cortisone."

1971 The Supreme Court upheld the use of busing to achieve racial desegregation in schools.

FEAST DAY
*St. Anselm, St. Beuno, St.
Maelrubba, St. Ethilwald, St.
Anastasius of Antioch, St. Conrad
of Prazham, St. Simeon Barsabas
and Others*

APRIL

He did not sign the Declaration, the Articles, or the Constitution. He did not serve in the Continental army with distinction. He was not renowned for his legal mind or his political skills. He was instead a man who spent his entire career in foreign diplomacy. Nevertheless, Elias Boudinot (1741–1802) is ranked among the greatest of America's Founding Fathers.

Born on this day in 1740 in the city of Philadelphia, he was active in civic affairs from his late teens until his death at the age of eighty-one. He earned the respect of his fellow patriots during the dangerous days following the traitorous actions of Benedict Arnold. His deft handling of relations with Canada also earned him great praise. After being elected to the Congress from his home state of New Jersey, he served as the new nation's Secretary for Foreign Affairs—managing the influx of aid from France, Spain, and Holland.

Then in 1783 he was elected to the presidency. He served in that office from November 4, 1782, until November 2, 1783. Like so many of the other early presidents, he was a classically trained scholar, of the Reformed faith, and an anti-Federalist in political matters. He was the father and grandfather of frontiersmen—and one of his adopted grandchildren and namesakes eventually became a leader of the Cherokee nation in its bid for independence from the sprawling expansion of the United States.

1109

Archbishop of Canterbury Anselm died. He had won a name for Reform because of his efforts to end such injustices as the slave trade, royal interference in the affairs of the church, and the infanticide of unwanted children. But perhaps his most notable legacy was what has become known as the ontological proof for the existence of God. Can the existence of God be proven? Anselm thought so. His argument was straightforward: When we discuss the existence of God, we define Him as a perfect being, greater than anything else that can be conceived. If God does not exist, then the name "God" refers to an imaginary being. This makes the definition of "God" contradictory, for to be real, to be living, to have power is greater than to be imaginary. It is clear I cannot even discuss the word God as defined if He does not exist, because I have to conceive of Him as really existing for Him to be greater than anything else, for a God who does not exist is not greater than anything else. In short, no philosopher can legitimately argue that God does not exist if he defines God as a perfect being greater than any which can be imagined; for to be perfect God must have real existence. Those who acknowledge He exists do not have a problem with self-contradiction when they affirm His existence. Since we can indeed raise the question of God's existence and argue the point, then God must exist.

Any coward can fight a battle when he's sure of winning; but give me the man who has the pluck to fight when he's sure of losing. That's my way, sir; and there are many victories worse than a defeat.

[GEORGE ELIOT (1819–1880)]

1142 Theologian, philosopher, and musician Peter Abelard died in Burgandy.

1649 The Maryland Toleration Act, which provided for freedom of worship for all Christians, was passed by the Maryland assembly.

1789 John Adams was sworn in as the first vice president of the United States.

1816 English writer Charlotte Brontë, author of *Jane Eyre* (1847), was born in Thornton, Yorkshire, England.

1836 With the war cry of "Remember the Alamo," Sam Houston achieved the independence of Texas by defeating the Mexicans at the Battle of San Jacinto. The entire battle took eighteen minutes with six hundred Mexicans losing their lives and only nine Texans.

1910 Author Samuel Langhorne Clemens, better known as Mark Twain, died in Redding, Connecticut—he was born at the appearance of Halley's comet and died at its next appearance.

1918 The World War I German fighter pilot ace, the Red Baron (Baron von Richthofen), was shot down and killed. He had brought down a record eighty enemy aircraft.

1929 The Soviet Union placed a comprehensive ban on all charitable activities by churches—assuming that there was to be no challenge to the state's claim on the heartstrings of the Soviet peoples.

APRIL

1940 The quiz show that asked the "$64 question," *Take It or Leave It*, premiered on CBS Radio.

1943 A fire station in New York installed the first sliding pole.

1945 In the cartoon short "Hare Trigger" released by Warner Brothers, the character of Yosemite Sam was introduced as a foil for Bugs Bunny.

1955 The Jerome Lawrence–Robert Lee play *Inherit the Wind*, very loosely based on the Scopes trial of 1925, opened at the National Theatre in New York.

1960 Brazil inaugurated its new capital, Brasilia, transferring the seat of national government from Rio de Janeiro.

1975 South Vietnamese president Nguyen Van Thieu resigned after ten years in office. Later that year, he fled to the United States when the Communists took Saigon.

1977 The Broadway musical *Annie* opened in New York.

1989 Tens of thousands of people crowded into Beijing's Tiananmen Square, cheering students who waved banners demanding greater political freedoms.

21

FEAST DAY
*St. Theodore of Sykeon; St.
Opportuna; St. Agipatus I, pope;
St. Leonides of Alexandria; Saints
Epipodius and Alexander*

APRIL

22

The Council of Constance was convened on this day in 1414. For thirty-three years Christendom had suffered schism. Popes in Rome and popes in Avignon claimed to be the legitimate successors of Peter. As a result, confusion reigned and corruption was unchecked. There seemed to be no hope of resolving the conflicts that created the schism in the first place. An earlier council held at Pisa to end the schism only worsened the problem. It actually created a third pope.

The Constance conclave got off to an equally rocky start. Jan Hus, the theology professor from Prague who had stirred the fires of revival by calling for substantive reform in the church, voluntarily appeared before the bishops. His purpose was to persuade them to legitimize his burgeoning Bohemian Reform movement. Although he arrived under promise of "safe conduct," he was seized and imprisoned by the bishop of Constance.

Told he must recant, he resolutely refused. After a mock trial he was summarily declared a heretic. That same day, they had him burned at the stake. Since his teachings were based on the work of John Wycliffe, the council also condemned Wycliffe, ordering his bones dug up and burnt. Both the English and Bohemian representatives left in protest.

Still, the council dragged on. After four more years of contentious deliberations, the convened bishops finally dealt with the issue that had brought them together in the first place. Because they were unable to sort through the conflicting claims of the three rival popes, they did the only thing they could—they removed all three and appointed a fourth. Amazingly, all sides agreed to this compromise, and the council adjourned with the schism at last healed.

1724

German philosopher Immanuel Kant was born in Königsberg, Prussia (now Kaliningrad, Russia). He studied and lectured in science and mathematics, but eventually broadened his concentration to cover the branches of philosophy. His unorthodox religious teachings, which were based on rationalism instead of revelation, included a personal epistemology for human knowledge. In his seminal work, *Critique of Pure Reason* (1781), Kant expressed his thoughts with the concept that people cannot understand the nature of the aspect of the universe, but they can be rationally certain of the things that they themselves experience. His thought had a profound impact on Marxism.

We cannot expect a more cordial welcome than disturbers of complacency have received in any other age.

[RICHARD WEAVER (1910-1963)]

APRIL

1348 The Order of the Garter, the highest order of English knighthood, had its origins at a royal ball in which the countess of Salisbury was dancing quite enthusiastically with King Edward III. One of her garters loosened and fell to the floor, but the gallant king swooped it up from the ground and fastened it to his own leg. This act became associated with the grandest ideals of chivalry.

1509 Henry VIII ascended the throne of England following the death of his father, Henry VII, at his palace in Greenwich. Soon afterward, he married his older brother Arthur's widow. Catherine of Aragon was the daughter of Ferdinand of Aragon and Isabella of Castile. Twenty-four years later, he would sue for divorce—and as a result break from the Catholic Church.

1861 The Virginia forces named Robert E. Lee as their commander.

1870 Vladimir Ilyich Ulyanov—best known as Nikolai Lenin—was born at Simbirsk (later called Ulyanovsk in his honor). With the help of the German and American financiers, Lenin took advantage of the Russian Revolution in February of 1917 to establish a Soviet totalitarian state based on the Communist ideas of Karl Marx.

1889 The Oklahoma Land Rush began at noon as thousands of homesteaders staked claims.

1896 The first shot of the Spanish-American War was fired off the coast of Key West, Florida, when the USS *Nashville* captured a Spanish merchant ship.

1926 The United States Congress authorized the use of the motto "In God We Trust" to be incorporated onto U.S. coins. This suggestion had been made by the Reverend M. R. Watkinson.

1930 The United States, Britain, and Japan signed the London Naval Treaty, which regulated submarine warfare and limited shipbuilding.

1952 An atomic test in the desert of Nevada became the first nuclear explosion shown on live television.

1964 President Lyndon Johnson opened the New York World's Fair.

1970 Thousands of Americans concerned about the environment observed the first "Earth Day."

1992 The Holocaust Memorial Museum in Washington, D.C., was dedicated.

1994 Richard M. Nixon, the thirty-seventh president of the United States, died at a New York hospital four days after suffering a stroke. He was eighty-one.

1998 A young woman charged, along with her high school sweetheart, with murdering their newborn at a Delaware motel pleaded guilty to manslaughter. Amy Grossberg was later sentenced to two and a half years in prison. Brian Peterson received a lesser sentence of two years because he'd cooperated with authorities.

22

NATIONAL DAY
England
FEAST DAY
St. George; St. Gerard of Toul; St. Ibar; St. Adalbert of Prague; Saints Felix, Fortunatus, and Achilleus

APRIL

Written under the authority of the new national federation, the Northwest Ordinance was a document guiding the formation and implementation of government for the once-disputed American territories northwest of the Ohio River. After successfully convincing the individual states to give up their competing claims in the region, the federal government initiated a pattern for annexation that would be followed throughout the nation's rapid conquest of much of the rest of the North American continent.

In addition, the document sheds light on the original intentions of the Founders concerning the role and function of government in society. For instance, Article I, begins with a declaration of religious freedom, "No person, demeaning himself in a peaceable and orderly manner, shall ever be molested on account of his mode of worship or religious sentiments in the said territory."

But that religious freedom was clearly understood as a freedom to exercise faith—as opposed to the modern notion of federally mandated freedom from religion. Article III makes that abundantly clear: "Religion, morality, and knowledge being necessary to good government and the happiness of mankind, schools and the means of education shall forever be encouraged."

The founders also made it evident that the American government was to deal honorably with the Native American residents of the frontier: "The utmost good faith shall always be observed toward the Indians; their lands and property shall never be taken from them without their consent; and in their property, rights, and liberty they shall never be invaded or disturbed unless in just and lawful wars authorized by Congress; but laws founded in justice and humanity shall from time to time be made for preventing wrongs being done to them, and for preserving peace and friendship with them."

Finally, Article VI made the founders views on slavery crystal clear: "There shall be neither slavery nor involuntary servitude in the said territory, otherwise than in punishment of crimes whereof the party shall have been duly convicted; Provided, always, that any person escaping into the same, from whom labor or service is lawfully claimed in any one of the original states, such fugitive may be lawfully reclaimed, and conveyed to the person claiming his or her labor or services as aforesaid." The ordinance was ratified on July 13, 1787.

ST. GEORGE'S DAY

The Patron Saint of England, Lybia, and Lebanon, George was a soldier who rose through the ranks of the Roman army. He confronted the emperor Dioclesian concerning his harshness and bloody commands. For his candor and courage, George was immediately imprisoned and was soon after beheaded. The legend of George is centered around his slaying of the dragon that had demanded the children of the town of Sylene in Libya. George wounded the dragon and led him back into the town where he proclaimed that he would kill the dragon if the people of the city would covert to Christianity and be baptized. Led by the king, fifteen thousand citizens were baptized.

He has not learned the lesson of life who does not every day surmount a fear.

[Ralph Waldo Emerson (1803–1882)]

997 Czech saint, bishop, missionary, and martyr Adalbert of Prague, who founded the first Benedictine houses in Bohemia and Poland, died on this day. Born a Vojtech, Adalbert was related to the princely Slavnik family. Prague's first bishop was German. On his death, the talented and devout Adalbert was elevated to bishop. With great energy and austerity, he set out to reform the clergy and eliminate pagan practices. Many pagans still clung to their old ways as nationalist traditions, however. Among these was the powerful Duke Boleslav of Bohemia, who fiercely opposed Adalbert's reforms. Ultimately, the bishop was driven into exile. He entered a Benedictine abbey in Rome. Four years later, he was invited to return to Prague. But resistance again mounted, and he gave up the lost cause. Under the protection of Emperor Otto III, he traveled into Germany, intending to extend his work among the Poles and Magyars. Poland's King Boleslav I invited him to bring the gospel to the Prussians of the northern coast. A pagan priest, jealous for his own prerogatives, murdered him on this day. Bohemia, which had rejected the martyr while he lived, now clamored for his relics, which were reputed to possess miraculous powers. Poland agreed, but stipulated that Bohemia must accept the reforms Adalbert had tried so fruitlessly to introduce while he was bishop to them. The Bohemians agreed and Adalbert's body was returned.

1344 The Feast Day of St. George was honored by the creation of the noble order of St. George, or the Blue Garter. Although the original implementation of the Order of the Blue Garter consisted of a grand joust, it was still common up until the ninth century for gentlemen to wear blue on this day.

1616 Spanish writer and poet Miguel de Cervantes, author of *Don Quixote*, died in Madrid. As the most important figure in Spanish literature, Cervantes led an adventurous life that included fighting as a Spanish infantry man in Naples, fighting in the decisive naval battle against the Turks, and being sold into slavery in Algiers by the Turks until he was ransomed five years later. His personal life was filled with financial woes and illicit relationships.

APRIL

1616 The apparently illiterate real estate speculator Guillame Shakspar—often dubiously identified as the playwright William Shakepeare—died in his home at Stratford-upon-Avon.

1635 The colonies in Maryland and Virginia engaged in a naval skirmish off the coast of Virginia concerning a boundary dispute.

1789 President-elect George Washington and his wife, Martha, moved into the executive mansion in New York called the Franklin House.

1791 The fifteenth president of the United States, James Buchanan, was born in Franklin County, Pennsylvania.

1899 Russian-American author Vladimir Nabokov was born in St. Petersburg.

1954 Hank Aaron of the Milwaukee Braves hit the first of his record 755 major-league home runs, in a game against the St. Louis Cardinals. The Braves won, 7-5.

1985 The Coca-Cola Company announced that it was changing the secret-flavor formula for Coke. Negative public reaction forced the company to resume selling the original version.

1998 James Earl Ray, the ex-convict who confessed to assassinating Dr. Martin Luther King Jr. in 1968 and then insisted he was framed, died at a Nashville hospital.

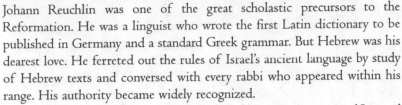

APRIL

Johann Reuchlin was one of the great scholastic precursors to the Reformation. He was a linguist who wrote the first Latin dictionary to be published in Germany and a standard Greek grammar. But Hebrew was his dearest love. He ferreted out the rules of Israel's ancient language by study of Hebrew texts and conversed with every rabbi who appeared within his range. His authority became widely recognized.

Alas, his reputation was nearly the cause of his ruin. A converted Jew and a Dominican Inquisitor obtained from Emperor Maximilian an order to burn all Hebrew works except the Old Testament, charging they were full of errors and blasphemies. Before the edict could be carried out, the emperor had second thoughts and consulted the greatest Hebraist of the age: Reuchlin.

Reuchlin urged preservation of the Jewish books as aids to study, and as examples of errors against which champions of faith joust. To destroy the books would give ammunition to church enemies. The emperor revoked his order.

The Dominicans were furious. Selecting passages from Reuchlin's writings, they tried to prove him a heretic. The Inquisition summoned him and ordered his writings burnt. Sympathetic scholars appealed to Leo X. The pope referred the matter to the Bishop of Spires, whose tribunal heard the issue. On this day in 1514, the tribunal declared Reuchlin not guilty.

But the Dominicans were not so easily deterred. They instigated the faculties at Cologne, Erfurt, Louvain, Mainz, and Paris to condemn Reuchlin's writings. Thus armed, they approached Leo X once again. Leo demurred. He appointed yet another commission. It backed Reuchlin. Still Leo hesitated. At last he decided to suspend all judgment. This in itself was a victory for Reuchlin. The cause of the embattled scholar became the cause of the innovators. Reuchlin's nephew, Melancthon, rejoiced as did the renowned Greek scholar Erasmus.

In 1517 Luther posted his Ninety-five Theses. "Thanks be to God," said the weary Reuchlin when he heard the news. "At last they have found a man who will give them so much to do that they will be compelled to let my old age end in peace." Thanks to Reuchlin, the Hebrew texts were preserved. His studies formed the basis for most of the better translations of the Old Testament—including Luther's. And his influence assured Melancthon a position among the learned and a vital place in the Reformation.

No coward soul is mine,

No trembler in the world's storm-troubled sphere:

I see Heaven's glories shine,

And faith shines equal, arming me from fear.

[EMILY BRONTË (1818–1848)]

APRIL

1558 The first two new candidates for the ministry since the beginning of the Reformation in Scotland were ordained by John Knox at Gileskirk in Edinburgh. Both Robert Campbell Sproul and James Grant were members of prominent Highland families and carried the message of the Reformation deep into the northern Gaelic lands near Inverness.

1704 *The News-Letter* was published in Boston by the brothers John and Duncan Campbell, thus instituting the first continuous newspaper on the American continent.

1792 The national anthem of France, "La Marseillaise," was composed by Captain Claude Joseph Rouget de Lisle.

1800 President John Adams gave approval for the appropriation of $5,000 for the purchase of "such books as may be necessary for the use of Congress." This was the beginning of the Library of Congress—though it would not get its present foundation until Thomas Jefferson donated his library following the War of 1812.

1833 Jacob Ebert and George Dulty patented the first soda fountain.

1898 Spain declared war on the United States after rejecting America's ultimatum to withdraw from Cuba.

1905 Poet and novelist Robert Penn Warren was born in Guthrie, Kentucky. Warren won three Pulitzer Prizes, including one for the novel *All the King's Men*. He became the first poet laureate of the United States in 1986. His work reflected an interest in Southern history and maintained the moral choices that confront those who face corruption.

1915 The Ottoman Turkish Empire began the brutal mass deportation of Armenians during World War I.

1916 Some 1,600 Irish nationalists launched the Easter Rising by seizing several key sites in Dublin, including the General Post Office. The rising was put down by British forces several days later.

1947 American frontier novelist Willa Cather, best known for her novels *O Pioneers!* (1913), *My Antonia* (1918), *Death Comes for the Archbishop* (1927), and *Song of the Lark* (1915), died in New York City. Her novel *Song of the Lark* is a beautiful portrayal of the development of an artistic mind as displayed in the life of a musician.

1953 British statesman Winston Churchill was knighted by Queen Elizabeth II.

1968 Leftist students at Columbia University in New York began a weeklong occupation of several campus buildings.

1985 The first verse works of American poet Tristan Gylberd were published by a small press in Texas under the title *Vorthos*.

1986 Wallis, the duchess of Windsor, for whom King Edward VIII gave up the British throne, died in Paris at age eighty-nine.

24

247

APRIL

In the spring of 1630 eleven small cargo vessels set sail across three thousand perilous miles of ocean. On board were some seven hundred men, women, and children who were risking their very lives to establish a godly, Puritan community on the shores of Massachusetts. John Winthrop, the leader of the group, composed a lay sermon, "A Model of Charity," during the journey—which he probably read to the assembled ship's company on this day.

The sermon expressed his intention to unite his people behind a single purpose, the creation of a due form of government, ecclesiastical as well as civil, so that their community would be a model for the Christian world to emulate. Theirs was to be a peculiar experiment, he said, a "City upon a Hill."

Their experiment was first and foremost to be a model society rooted in gracious kindness. If they were to succeed, he believed that all the world would look to them as apt adherents of the biblical ideal. The reasons were, he said, threefold: "First, to hold conformity with the rest of His works, being delighted to show forth the glory of His wisdom in the variety and difference of the Creatures and the glory of His power, in ordering all these differences for the preservation and good of the whole, and the glory of His greatness that as it is the glory of princes to have many officers, so this great King will have many stewards counting Himself more honored in dispensing His gifts to man by man, then if He did it by His own immediate hand."

Second, he said, "That He might have the more occasion to manifest the work of His Spirit: first, upon the wicked in moderating and restraining them: so that the rich and mighty should not eat up the poor, nor the poor, and despised rise up against their superiors, and shake off their yoke; secondly, in the regenerate in exercising His graces in them."

Third, he asserted, "That every man might have need of other, and from hence they might be all knit more nearly together in the bond of brotherly affection; from hence it appears plainly that no man is made more honorable than another or more wealthy . . . but for the glory of his Creator and the common good of the creature, man."

This was, he said, the "duty of mercy," which was to be the hallmark of the new American colonies. He concluded with a profound charge: "Beloved, there is now set before us life, and good, death and evil in that we are commanded this day to love the Lord our God, and to love one another to walk in His ways and to keep His Commandments and His ordinance, and His laws, and the articles of our covenant with Him that we may live and be multiplied, and that the Lord our God may bless us in the land whether we go to possess it. But if our hearts shall turn away so that we will not obey, but shall be seduced and worship other gods, our pleasures, and profits, and serve them; it is propounded unto us this day, we shall surely perish out of the good land whether we pass over this vast sea to possess it. Therefore let us choose life that we, and our seed may live; by obeying His voice, and cleaving to Him, for He is our life, and our prosperity."

If a thing is worth doing, it is worth doing badly.

[G. K. Chesterton (1874–1936)]

1507 Geographer Martin Waldseemuller used the name America for the first time to identify the New World, mistakenly giving credit of discovery to Amerigo Vespucci.

1599 Oliver Cromwell was born in Huntingdon, Oxfordshire. He would rise to a place of leadership among Parliamentarians opposed to the oppressive measures of Charles II. Eventually, he took command of their forces in a civil war that deposed and then executed the king. Parliament afterward named him Lord Protector of the Commonwealth, and he ruled England in that capacity until his death.

1800 English poet and hymn writer William Cowper died on this day. Racked with spiritual doubts, he fought bouts of depression throughout his life. Nevertheless, he wrote such enduring hymns as "God Moves in a Mysterious Way" (1774) and "There Is a Fountain Filled With Blood" (1771). He was greatly helped by clergyman Morley Unwin, and collaborated with John Newton.

1844 The British War Office issued further injunctions against duelling, declaring that "it is suitable to the character of honourable men to apologise and offer redress for wrong or insult committed, and equally so for the party aggrieved to accept, frankly and cordially, explanation and apologies for the same."

1859 Ground was broken by British and French engineers for the Suez Canal.

1915 During World War I, Allied soldiers invaded the Gallipoli peninsula in an unsuccessful attempt to take the Ottoman Turkish Empire out of the war.

1918 American jazz singer Ella Fitzgerald, known as "The first lady of song," was born in Newport News, Virginia, but she was raised in Yonkers where she had moved with her mother and stepfather as an infant.

1923 The legalization of an infanticide procedure called "abortion" first occurred in the United States when Governor John Love signed a Colorado bill into law.

1926 Giacomo Puccini's operatic masterpiece *Turandot* was first performed at La Scala in Milan. The last duet and finale were completed after Pucinni's death by Franco Alfano. The Oriental subject matter, the majesty and splendor of the music (including extensive use of the chorus), and the story all combine to form one of the greatest works of opera.

1945 Delegates from some fifty countries met in San Francisco to organize the United Nations.

1945 American and Soviet forces linked up on the Elbe River, a meeting that dramatized the collapse of Nazi Germany's defenses in the Second World War.

1959 The St. Lawrence Seaway opened to shipping.

1990 Violeta Barrios de Chamorro was inaugurated as president of Nicaragua, ending eleven years of Communist Sandinista rule.

APRIL

The first recorded history of the exploits of King Arthur was written by Geoffrey of Monmouth sometime around 1136 and circulated beginning this day in 1139. A Welsh chronicler during the waning days of Celtic independence, he wrote the richly inventive *Historia Regum Britanniae* in an effort to preserve the final remnants of the old culture in the face of French and Norman dominance. He collected the folk tales and legends from the earliest days of English regency on the island—a beguilingly beautiful Celtic knot of fact, fiction, and fantasy.

The stories he thus recorded, being patriotic, nostalgic, and romantic, quickly became an attractive subject for the jongleurs, troubadours, and minstrels of the High Middle Ages. They were thus repeated, adapted, retold, recast, and transmogrified by innumerable poets and jesters throughout England, Scotland, Wales, Normandy, Aquitaine, France, Burgundy, Lombardy, and the German and Italian domains of the Holy Roman Empire.

The story lines varied greatly—as did the focus. In the realms of Gaul, Lancelot and his quixotic quest for the Holy Grail became the central element of the story cycle. Among the British lands it was the betrayal of Arthur by Guinevere that dominated the saga. For the Teutonic peoples it was the sinister connivings of Mordred and Morgaine that possessed the attentions of the tale-bearers. But for each of them the Eden-like theme of an idyllic kingdom spoiled, not by external defeat but by dissension from within, claimed a tenured place in popular folk literature and music.

There is very little historical data from the time of King Arthur. About all we know is that there actually was such a king who had a kingdom called Camelot sometime after the Roman legions abandoned the British Isles in the fifth century. Other than that, virtually everything about the legendary king and his times is shrouded in mystery.

Monmouth added little or nothing to our scanty knowledge. His work made no pretense of being an accurate historical record. It was quite forthrightly portrayed as the noble stuff of fairy tales. It was designed to be a morality play not a biography. It was purposefully romantic. And that may well be the key to comprehending its genius.

1866

A group of women from Columbus, Mississippi, placed flowers on the graves of both Confederate and Union soldiers at Friendship Cemetery. This practice led to the official Decoration Day, which was first celebrated on May 30, 1868, as the day "for the purpose of strewing with flowers or otherwise decorating the graves of comrades who died in defense of their country during the late rebellion and with the hope that it will be kept up from year to year."

Genius is seldom recognized for what it is: a great capacity for hard work.

[HENRY FORD (1863–1947)]

322 St. Basil was martyred by torture and beheading after he sheltered a Christian maiden named Glaphiga from the wanton clutches of Roman emperor Lucinius.

387 "And we were baptized and all anxiety for our past life vanished away." With these joyous words Augustine recorded his entrance into the church on Easter day 387. Born in North Africa in 354 of a Christian mother and pagan father, Augustine became at twelve years of age a student at Carthage, and at sixteen a teacher of grammar. His mother was determined to see him become a Christian and baptized. He was equally determined to have his pleasures. He took a mistress and she bore him a son, Adeodatus. At twenty-nine his restless spirit drove him to Italy. In Rome he taught rhetoric for a year, but was cheated of his fees. He then moved to Milan, where he came under the influence of Ambrose, bishop of the city. In spite of himself he began to drift toward faith. At last, in a moment of crisis, he came to grace. Immediately he thrust aside those sins of the flesh that had held him bondage. At his mother's death, he returned to Africa where he founded a monastery, became bishop of Hippo and a subtle theologian, who more than any other stamped his imprint upon the Western church.

860 The first book written exclusively on the Eucharist was published by Paschasius Radbertus. The book, *On the Body and Blood of the Lord*, though it did not use the term, essentially taught the doctrine of transubstantiation—the belief that the substance of the bread and wine really become Christ's body and blood by faith. Later confirmed as the teaching of the Catholic Church at the Lateran Council in 1215, the doctrine of transubstantiation was refined further by the Council of Trent (1545–1563). It became one of the main issues that would separate Protestants and Catholics.

1607 An expedition of English colonists, including Captain John Smith, went ashore at Cape Henry, Virginia, to establish the first permanent English settlement in America.

1783 American ornithologist and painter John James Audubon was born in Les Cayes in Santo Domingo (now Haiti). He illustrated all known species of North American birds in his ten-volume series *Birds of America*.

APRIL

1826 The Rensselaer School, the first engineering college in the United States, was opened in Troy, New York.

1865 John Wilkes Booth, the assassin of President Lincoln, was surrounded by federal troops near Bowling Green, Virginia, and killed.

1919 The Allied nations sought the first of many payments from Germany as reparation for the cost of the First World War. These excessive payments, along with other oppressive measures, helped to spark the fire of nationalism in Germany, which greatly contributed to the outbreak of the Second World War.

1937 Planes from Nazi Germany raided the Basque town of Guernica during the Spanish Civil War.

1961 Roger Maris of the New York Yankees hit the first of a record 61 home runs in a single season. The homer was off Detroit's Paul Foytack at Tiger Stadium.

1964 The African nations of Tanganyika and Zanzibar merged to form Tanzania.

1968 The United States exploded beneath the Nevada desert a one-megaton nuclear device called "Boxcar."

1986 The world's worst nuclear accident occurred at the Chernobyl plant in the Soviet Union. An explosion and fire killed at least thirty-one people and sent radioactivity into the atmosphere.

26

APRIL

William Billings (1746–1800) was one of the first true American composers. Born in Boston to a family of small tradesmen, he was apparently a self-taught composer, yet Billings became a pioneer in both musical composition and music publishing around the time of the American Revolution. Billings had a profound impact on American music, overcoming severe physical handicaps from birth—a blind eye, a withered arm, and legs of differing lengths.

Billings entered the tannery business, but he wound up marking up the hides and walls of his shop with jottings of musical composition. He also worked as a singing school master which was one of the only ways a New Englander could make a living in music. His job was to teach a course to musical amateurs in the basics of singing and reading music. These classes were held from time to time in churches in Boston as well as throughout the region. On this day in 1770, his first tunebook, *The New-England Psalm-Singer*, appeared in print and was followed by a succession of other music publications. *The Continental Harmony* (1794) contained some of the last tunes by Billings. Although published as an act of charity for the impoverished musician, the tunebook reveals a composer still at the height of his powers.

Billings's music marks a departure from the relatively sophisticated European style of the time. It is enthusiastic, vigorous, and bursting with melodic activity in all voice parts. It is also remarkably different from the more genteel and regular rhythm of conventional nineteenth-century hymnals that displaced the *New England Psalmnody*. Consequently, his music fell out of favor in the nineteenth century. However, much of the style of Billings's music, as well as some of his own works, have been preserved in the South among the shape-note singers from the Sacred Harp tradition. *The Sacred Harp* is a tunebook first published in 1844 that contains old New England music, American folk hymns, and early camp meeting songs. *The Sacred Harp* continues to be revised and republished and utilized by an entire musical tradition.

Billings is probably best remembered as the composer of the defiant Revolutionary War battle hymn that begins with the line "Let tyrants shake their iron rod." This song was a morale booster equivalent to the song "Over There" in the First World War. His music was pervasive in the northeastern colonies, and was often sung by soldiers during the Revolutionary War in their camps. Billings is also sometimes referred to as the "Father of the American Church Choir" because of his involvement with church music as a director and composer. Choral and vocal music were the most pervasive forms of music available in the colonies. Instrumental music was rare, and most churches could not afford an organ even in a large city like Boston. Billings's music is easily accessible and may even appear to be rough around the edges. However, there is a vitality and energy in his compositions that capture not only the meaning of the text, but also the atmosphere of a small band of colonists struggling to plant a nation of liberty.

We know that all men were created to busy themselves with labor for the common good.

[JOHN CALVIN (1509–1564)]

1509 Pope Julius II excommunicated everyone in the entire Italian state of Venice—from the Doge right down to the common gondolier.

1521 Portuguese explorer Ferdinand Magellan was killed by natives in the Philippines.

1667 John Milton sold the rights for *Paradise Lost* to Samuel Simmons. Although the author was well known, the sale roused little notice and the book went for a pittance—£5 upfront and an additional £5 after the 1,300 copies of the first edition were sold. *Paradise Lost* was not to be published until August 20. But in time it would be ranked by many next to Shakespeare and the King James Bible as the most magnificent example of English prose ever penned.

1749 G. F. Handel's *Music for the Royal Fireworks* was first performed in Green Park, London, as part of the public thanksgiving celebrations for the peace of Aix-la-Chapelle. A rehearsal six days earlier was attended by twelve thousand people.

1805 A force led by American marines captured the city of Derna on the shores of Tripoli. The conflict, between the Barbary pirates and the United States, gave the marines their special identity—and the lyrics to their famous fight song.

1822 The eighteenth president of the United States, Ulysses S. Grant, was born in Point Pleasant, Ohio, the son of Scottish immigrants.

1861 West Virginia seceded from Virginia after Virginia seceded from the Union. Despite specific constitutional prohibitions, the Lincoln administration welcomed the territory and offered it statehood status.

1865 On the Mississippi River near Memphis, Tennessee, the boiler on the steamer *Sultana* exploded, killing 1,547 people. Most of those killed were Union soldiers on their way home after the Civil War.

APRIL

1889 Sergei Prokofiev was born in the Ukranian village of Sontsovka. Escaping the political unrest in his country, he toured the West, where his music was likened to aural cubism and found to be "alarmingly ultra-modern and an anarchy of noise and steel." His later period, a neo-Romantic return to a mature and masterful writing style, was condemned by the Soviets, who sought for all art to serve as propaganda.

1932 American poet Hart Crane drowned after jumping from a steamer while en route to New York; he was thirty-two.

1937 The nation's first Social Security checks were distributed.

1954 *White Christmas*, starring Bing Crosby, Danny Kaye, and Rosemary Clooney, with music by Irving Berlin, premiered at Radio City Music Hall.

1967 Expo 67, the Canadian World's Fair, was officially opened in Montreal by Canadian Prime Minister Lester B. Pearson.

27

FEAST DAY
St. Louis de Montfort, St. Vitalis, St. Peter Mary Chanel, St. Cyril of Turov, St. Valeria, St. Pollio, Saints Theodora and Didymus, St. Pamphilus of Sulmona, St. Cronan Roscrea

APRIL

Very little is known about the life and career of Guillame Shakspar—later dubiously presumed to be the playwright William Shakespeare. Apparently, he was born into a tradesman's family in Stratford-upon-Avon on this day in 1564. When he was eighteen, he married Anne Hathaway, ten years older than he. The young couple had a baby girl named Susanna six months later on May 26, 1583. In 1585 the birth of fraternal twins, Hamnet and Judith, completed the new family. But shortly afterward, Shakspar left Stratford and moved to London, leaving his family behind.

No one knows quite what Shakspar did for a living before he arrived in London. We do know that he established himself in the London theater by 1592. He had become an actor with London's most prestigious theatrical troupe, the Lord Chamberlain's Men, headquartered in the first professional theater building built since the fall of the Roman Empire. It was called, simply, the Theater.

There is no evidence that Shakspar was ever actually literate—there are no extant manuscripts of his writing, and the only evidence we have of his hand are two barely legible signatures. He had no formal education, owned no books, never traveled abroad as far as we know, and never claimed authorship of the works attributed to him. His parents were illiterate, his wife was illiterate, and his children were illiterate—hardly what you might expect from the single greatest author of English prose.

Shakspar died in Stratford on April 23, 1616. During his lifetime, the only written documents that can be directly tied to him are a few real estate transactions, a will—which mentions no literary properties, and a citation from the city of Stratford for having a dung hill that exceeded the limits of health and propriety. He left no male heirs to continue his name. His only son, Hamnet, had died at age eleven. Susanna and Judith both married, but Susanna's only child, Elizabeth, was Shakspar's last direct descendant. She died childless in 1670.

In 1623, seven years after his death, two of Shakspar's former colleagues in the theater published thirty-six plays and attributed them to him. This is what scholars refer to as the "First Folio." Though the plays evidence vast education, intimate familiarity with life in the court, and wide experience in the great cities of Europe, the Stratfordian authorship seems to have been accepted early on. In a prefatory poem, Ben Jonson even praised his old carousing friend as "the wonder of our stage."

Through the centuries, doubts about the Stratfordian authorship of the Shakespearean canon have produced innumerable theories about who the actual author was—some have suggested the Earl of Oxford, or Francis Bacon, or even Queen Elizabeth. While it is likely that Shakspar was incapable of producing such masterpieces as *Hamlet, King Lear, Henry V, Othello, Romeo and Juliet, Macbeth, A Midsummer Night's Dream, Much Ado About Nothing, Richard III,* and *The Taming of the Shrew,* it is just as likely that no one will ever be able to find convincing proof that any of the other possible authors wrote them either. It will likely remain one of history's great enigmas.

> *The wise does at once
> what the fool does at last.*
>
> [BALTASAR GRACIAN (1601–1658)]

1220 Bishop Poore laid the first five stones of the famed Salisbury Cathedral, one each for himself, Archbishop Stephen Langton, Pope Honorius III, Earl William, and Countess Ela of Salisbury. By 1237 the choir and east transepts were built, and by 1258 the nave and main transepts. The plans and their implementation experienced few alterations. Consequently, Salisbury has more unity of design than almost any other cathedral in the world. The great landscape artists, John Constable and Joseph Turner, portrayed it many times, as did other less eminent artists. Because of its distinctive cross-tipped spire, straining to a point 404 feet into the air, people who otherwise know little of architecture know the Salisbury Cathedral. It may be even more recognizable than that other great English architectural monument, St. Paul's Cathedral in London.

1758 The fifth president of the United States, James Monroe, was born in Westmoreland County, Virginia.

1788 Maryland became the seventh state to ratify the U.S. Constitution.

1789 There was a mutiny on the HMS *Bounty* as the crew of the British ship set Captain William Bligh and eighteen sailors adrift in a launch in the South Pacific.

1927 The song "Ol' Man River" from the musical *Show Boat* by Jerome Kern hit number one on the pop singles chart.

1942 Because of short supplies during World War II, the rationing of coffee began in the United States.

1945 Italian dictator Benito Mussolini and his mistress, Clara Petacci, were executed by Italian partisans as they attempted to flee the country.

1947 A six-man Scandinavian expedition sailed from Peru aboard a balsa wood raft named the Kon-Tiki on a 101-day journey to Polynesia.

1958 Vice President Nixon and his wife, Pat, began a goodwill tour of Latin America that was marred by hostile mobs in Lima, Peru, and Caracas, Venezuela.

1967 World heavyweight boxing champion Muhammad Ali—formerly known as Cassius Clay—refused to be inducted into the army, the same day General William C. Westmoreland told Congress the U.S. "would prevail in Vietnam."

1969 The French hero of the Second World War, President Charles de Gaulle, resigned his office, marking the end of an era.

1974 A federal jury in New York acquitted former Attorney General John Mitchell and former Commerce Secretary Maurice H. Stans of charges in connection with a secret contribution to President Nixon's reelection campaign from financier Robert Vesco.

1998 The Senate opened a new round of hearings on alleged abuse and mismanagement at the Internal Revenue Service.

APRIL

Franz Joseph Haydn's oratorio *The Creation* was first performed on this day in 1798. Composed late in his life, *The Creation* was an ambitious portrayal of the beginning of the world through the texts of Genesis and John Milton. Influenced by the works of Handel, which he had heard in London, Haydn "prayed to God with earnestness that He would enable me to praise Him worthily." The power, energy, and action of God's work of creation is abundantly displayed in this work in a manner that expands the understanding of God's creative nature.

Haydn was born in March 1732, to a working-class family in the small southeastern Austrian village of Rohrau. Though he remained quite poor throughout his youth, he worked hard and perfected his prodigious musical gifts, devoting himself unceasingly to practice. Eventually, Haydn's industry began to pay off, and his work began to attract attention.

By 1861, Haydn was a well-known and respected composer and conductor. He secured the post of Second Kapellmeister at Prince Esterházy's palace in Eisenstadt—a post he held for three decades. His fame spread throughout Austria and from Austria to the rest of Europe. Commissions came to him from many countries, and the great personages of Austria came to pay him homage, including the empress Maria Theresa. Despite his increasing notoriety, he never lost touch with his humble roots and was proud that he had made something of himself "out of nothing." Late in life he said, " I have associated with kings and many great ones, and have received from their lips much flattery. But I have never wished to live on a level of intimacy with them, for I had rather hold to the people of my own station."

The great friendship of Haydn's life was with Mozart. They met for the first time in 1781 when Haydn was forty-nine years old and Mozart was twenty-five. They not only respected each other's genius, they also cared for and influenced one another. Mozart respectfully called the elder composer Papa Haydn. Haydn would visit Mozart on his visits to Vienna. One day in 1785, Mozart and colleagues performed a set of quartets that Mozart had written in honor of Haydn. Haydn approached Mozart's father after the performance and said, "I tell you before God and as an honest man—your son is the greatest composer I know, either personally or by name."

After his patron died in 1790, Haydn moved to London—and immediately took the city by storm. It was then that he became familiar with the oratorios of Handel. It was during a performance of *Messiah* in 1791 at Westminster Abbey that Haydn burst into tears and exclaimed, "He is the master of us all." It was with this new understanding of the power and majesty of the oratorio form that Haydn undertook the writing of *The Creation* in 1796, when he was sixty-six years old.

He died on May 30, 1809, and was mourned not only by his countrymen but also the French. Napoleon ordered a special guard of honor to be placed at his house and an honor guard of officers to convey Haydn's body to the churchyard of Hundsthurm where it was buried. On June 15, Mozart's *Requiem*, his final composition, was sung in honor of Haydn at the Scots Church.

Wisdom is oft times nearer when we stoop than when we soar.

[WILLIAM WORDSWORTH (1770–1850)]

1861 Maryland's House of Delegates voted to secede from the Union but were prohibited from doing so by federal troops sent to detain all representatives until they agreed to reverse their vote.

1879 Thomas Beecham, the influential English conductor and founder of the London Philharmonic Orchestra (1932) and the Royal Philharmonic Orchestra (1946), was born on this day.

1882 John Nelson Darby died in Bournemouth, England. The theological innovator who systemized eschatological dispensationalism and founded the Plymouth Brethren movement spent his life attempting to awaken the church to an expectation that Christ would soon return. His system became the basis of such institutions as Dallas Theological Seminary and the Moody Bible Institute, the teachings of men like Hal Lindsey and Tim LaHaye, as well as the widely circulated *Scofield Reference Bible.*

1899 Composer, bandleader, and pianist Edward Kennedy "Duke" Ellington was born in Washington, D.C. Ellington was recognized in his lifetime as one of the greatest jazz composers and performers. Nicknamed "Duke" by a boyhood friend who admired his regal air, the name stuck and became indelibly associated with the finest creations in big band and vocal jazz. He was described by the English conductor and composer Constant Lambert as "no mere bandleader or arranger, but a composer of uncommon merit, probably the first composer of character to come out of America."

1912 Gideon Sandback of Hoboken, New Jersey, received a patent for the zipper—a device he claimed would revolutionize the fastening of clothing.

1916 The Easter Rising in Dublin collapsed as Irish nationalists surrendered to British authorities.

1945 American soldiers liberated the Dachau concentration camp—where tens of thousands of Jews, Gypsies, and Christians had perished. That same day, Adolf Hitler married Eva Braun and designated Admiral Karl Doenitz his successor.

APRIL

1974 President Nixon announced that he was releasing edited transcripts of some secretly made White House tape recordings related to Watergate.

1983 Harold Washington was sworn in as the first black mayor of Chicago.

1989 In a sign that student demonstrators in Beijing had gained influence, China's government conducted informal talks with leaders of the democracy protests, and then televised the discussions.

1992 Deadly rioting erupted in Los Angeles after a jury in Simi Valley, California, acquitted four Los Angeles police officers of almost all state charges in the videotaped beating of Rodney King.

1994 Israel and the PLO signed an agreement in Paris granting Palestinians broad authority to set taxes, control trade, and regulate banks under self-rule in the Gaza Strip and Jericho.

1998 Israelis began marking the fiftieth anniversary of the founding of their country—even though, according to the Western calendar, the anniversary fell on May 14.

NATIONAL DAY
The Netherlands
FEAST DAY
St. Erkenwald; St. Pius V, pope; St. Forannan; St. Wolfhard; St. Maximus of Ephesus; St. Eutropus of Saintes; Saints Marianus, James, and Others

APRIL

30

It was to General George Washington (1732–1799), hero of the American War of Independence, that fell the unprecedented task of organizing a national administration that was somehow to govern the thirteen separate states and yet preserve the freedoms for which the independent men of these states had so recently fought. It was his extraordinary task to make the radical idea of a government of free men, by free men, actually work, with nothing but the noble words of the freshly written Constitution to guide him.

When he took the oath of office on this day in 1789, there were no existing buildings or departments, no procedures, precedents, or traditions. There were no advisors, no staff, and no support infrastructure. There was no White House, no Capitol, and perhaps most ominously, no capital. There was simply the Constitution and the man—and the mighty task.

Like other colonial landholders, Washington was a new kind of man in history—part cultivated gentleman, part rugged pioneer, a man in whom the ideas of Western civilization were combined with the great physical strength and fierce spirit of independence of the frontiersman. Among such men, Washington was outstanding. His performance as a surveyor and a soldier on the western frontier earned him, at twenty-three, the command of Virginia's troops, and he served in the House of Burgesses for years before the Continental Congress chose him to lead the Continental army. As its commander he held the struggling patriots together during the long war years; with victory, he quietly retired from the field.

The presidential electors from the nearly sovereign states, cautious in selecting the man to hold power over all the states, had little to fear from one who had so willingly relinquished control of a victorious army. Already one of the country's leading citizens, Washington carried out his duties as president with simple dignity. Although he tried to remain free of parties, he was closer to the Federalist Hamilton, his secretary of the Treasury, than to the Democrat Jefferson, his secretary of State.

He firmly declined a third term, and spent his last years peacefully at his beautiful plantation Mount Vernon, where his tomb now stands. Of all memorials, the most dramatic is the graceful shaft of the monument in the District of Columbia that symbolizes the aspirations of America as they were so nobly embodied in the undoubted "Father of Our Country."

I wish to preach not the doctrine of ignoble ease but the doctrine of the strenuous life; the life of toil and effort; of labor and strife; to preach that highest form of success which comes not to the man who desires mere easy peace but to the man who does not shrink from danger, hardship, or from the bitter toil, and who out of these wins the splendid ultimate triumph.

[THEODORE ROOSEVELT (1858–1919)]

APRIL

1087 Julian Katarva died at his home on the Adriatic in Dalamatia. He was a nobleman who through a tragic error was responsible for the deaths of several members of his family. He never fully recovered from that awful accident and devoted the rest of his life to the care of the sick, the troubled, and the suffering. He endowed several hospitals all over Central Europe during the eleventh century. He also went on a personal crusade against those who took life lightly: abortionists, mercenaries, highwaymen, and occultists. Several times he risked his own life by rescuing children or women in distress. Eventually, he became known as Julian the Hospitaller.

1367 Peaceful, timid Pope Clement V could not endure turbulent Rome and wandered through Italy and France until 1309. In that year he bought the small town of Avignon in the papal territory of Venaissin. He established papal court there and surrounded himself with Frenchmen. So commenced the Avignon exile, the "Babylonian captivity" of the papacy. His successors, John XXII, Benedict XII, Clement VI, and Innocent VI, all of whom were French, toyed with the idea of returning to Rome. But it was their successor, Urban V, who was to sail from Marseille on this day to return the papacy to Rome.

1803 The size of the United States doubled when Thomas Jefferson and Napoleon Bonaparte struck a deal for the young American republic to purchase the Louisiana Territory from the French empire for $15 million.

1812 Louisiana became the eighteenth state of the Union.

1900 Hawaii was organized as a U.S. territory.

1900 Engineer John Luther "Casey" Jones of the Illinois Central Railroad was killed in a wreck near Vaughan, Mississippi, after staying at the controls in an effort to save the passengers.

1938 In the cartoon "Porky's Hare Hunt," wisecracking Bugs Bunny made his debut.

1939 The New York World's Fair officially opened.

1945 As Russian troops approached his bunker under the chancellory building in Berlin, Adolf Hitler committed suicide along with his wife of one day, Eva Braun.

1970 President Nixon announced the U.S. was sending troops into Cambodia, an action that sparked widespread protest.

1973 President Nixon announced the resignations of top aides H. R. Haldeman and John Ehrlichman, along with Attorney General Richard G. Kleindienst and White House counsel John Dean.

1975 The South Vietnamese capital of Saigon fell to Communist forces, who renamed it Ho Chi Minh City.

30

MAY

MAY DAY
FEAST DAY
St. Asaph, St. Corentin, St. Joseph,
St. Brioc, St. Amator, St. Marcoul,
Saints Philip and James, St.
Peregrine Laziosi, St. Sigismund of
Burgundy, St. Theodard of
Narbonne

MAY

By all accounts, it was the fairest fair of them all. The gates opened a year late but the extravaganza that celebrated the quadricentennial of the discovery of America was anything but behind the times. Called the World's Columbian Exposition and held in Chicago's resplendent Jackson Park in 1893, the mammoth gala was a magnet that drew more than twenty million merchants, peddlers, tourists, gawkers, sightseers, and thrill-seekers from around the world.

Even though America had long since proved her military and technological prowess to Europe, critics still regarded the young nation as a cultural backwater populated with presumptuous philistines. So, even though Columbus and his discovery were the ostensible reasons for the fair, the planners of the exposition viewed it as an opportunity to showcase America's newfound cultural savoir-faire.

Led by the renowned Chicago architect Daniel Burnham, an elite cadre of builders, artists, engineers, and craftsmen hammered out an ambitious design for each of the main exhibit buildings. The plan revolved around an imposing courtyard of Babylonian proportions in which all the buildings would be of strict classical design, all white, ordered by uniform cornice heights, and apportioned architectural embellishments.

From the day the fair opened—on this day in 1893—until its close some five months later, visitors wandered awestruck through the ethereal white city, whose atmosphere was so unlike that of real-life cities that it was often described as a kind of New Jerusalem. It didn't seem to matter that the façades of the buildings were made of an insubstantial mixture of plaster, cement, and jute, or that their interiors were more like warehouses than the palaces they were sometimes called. Instead, their harmonious architecture, lighted fountains, and beautiful gardens—along with the total absence of carriages, horse dung, and coal soot—infused visitors with a sorely needed dose of optimism at a time of severe economic constriction and increasing impersonalization.

The exposition also featured an on-site amusement area—the first of its kind. Located on a narrow, mile-long strip of parkland known before the fair as the Midway Plaisance, the amusements were designed to ensure the economic success of the fair. Along the midway—for a price—visitors could ogle the lions and tigers and bears of Hagenbeck's Animal Show, explore a Bedouin desert encampment, watch the volcanic force of Vesuvius erupt in a fabulous diorama, quaff beer in old Vienna, or visit an African ostrich farm. The two most popular attractions on the midway were at opposite ends of the technological scale. A reenacted street in old Cairo transported fairgoers to the markets, bazaars, and fleshly delights of that mysterious Eastern city. Just a few yards away was a giant wheel designed by George Ferris.

The grounds covered more than six hundred acres and included separate buildings sponsored by thirty-eight states, nineteen countries, and forty-two trades and disciplines. By the time the fair closed, there was little doubt in anyone's mind that the next century would be an American century. And so it was.

The wicked flee when no one pursues, but the righteous are bold as a lion.

[KING SOLOMON (C. 1000 B.C.)]

1672 English essayist, poet, and dramatist Joseph Addison was born in Milston, Wiltshire, England. He became one of the greatest stylists of the English language. His Latin poetry is considered among the best ever produced by an Englishman. But his real fame comes from the magazines he and Richard Steele produced together: the *Tatler,* the *Spectator,* and the *Guardian*—all of which survive in one form or another to the present day. Though he won great critical acclaim throughout his career, perhaps his highest praise came from John Wesley, who quipped, "God raised up Mr. Addison and his associates to lash the prevailing vices and ridiculous and profane customs of this country, and to show the excellence of Christ and Christian institutions."

1700 John Dryden, the first English poet laureate officially appointed to the post, died in London. Dryden so dominated the literary scene of his day through his poetry, plays, and literary criticism that this period came to be known as the Age of Dryden. Dryden wrote several stageworks with music by Henry Purcell and devoted the end of his life to translating works of Juvenal, Persius, and Virgil along with verse adaptations of the writings of Ovid, Geoffrey Chaucer, and Giovanni Boccaccio.

1704 *The Boston Newsletter* published America's first newspaper advertisement.

1786 Wolfgang Mozart's opera *The Marriage of Figaro* was first performed at the Burgtheater in Vienna. The story for the opera was adapted from a play by Pierre Beaumarchais and is a sequel to *The Barber of Seville.* There are characters that appear in both plays and in the operas by Rossini and Mozart.

1851 Queen Victoria of England opened the Great Exhibition in London.

1852 *The Carpet Bag,* a Boston weekly newspaper, published the writing debut of Samuel L. Clemens, forever known as Mark Twain.

1883 William F. Cody (Buffalo Bill) presented his first Wild West Show.

1884 Moses Walker became the first African-American player for baseball's Major League. Shortly thereafter, segregation was reasserted for another half century.

1884 Construction began on the first skyscraper, a ten-story structure in Chicago built by the Home Insurance Company of New York.

1898 Commodore George Dewey gave the command, "You may fire when you are ready, Gridley," as an American naval force destroyed a Spanish fleet in Manila Bay during the Spanish-American War.

1931 New York's 102-story Empire State Building was dedicated.

1931 Gospel singer Kate Smith began her long-running radio program on CBS.

1935 After four years and 354 days of construction, Boulder Dam was completed.

1941 General Mills introduced the world to Cheerios.

1941 The film masterpiece of Orson Welles, *Citizen Kane,* premiered at New York City's RKO Palace Theater.

MAY

It was William Blake who first gave the name Jerusalem to all that was tender and lovely in the human soul. He wrote of it as a beautiful woman who maintains her virtue despite the indignities imposed by the ages. Blake's poetic instinct grasped the truth that this city, perhaps more than any other, has always paradoxically and paradigmatically nourished both sincere holiness and sincere betrayal.

FEAST DAY
St. Gennys, St. Athanasius, St. Wiborada, St. Waldebert, Saints Exuperius and Zoe, St. Ultan of Fosses

In Jerusalem the present is but a gossamer haze above ages past. History is inescapable. It hangs in the air like the wail of the faithful before the Western Wall. It intrudes on every conversation like the wheedling cries of the Arab merchants at the Jaffa Gate. It pierces every waking moment like the glinting gold of the Haram es Sherif against the Judean sky. And yet the gossamer is thick and dull.

That was what most impressed Mark Twain when he visited the city on this day in 1867 as a part of the "first organized pleasure party ever assembled for a transatlantic voyage." It was a Grand Tour for the rich and famous of America, who, weary of war and reconstruction at home, set out to see the sights in Europe and beyond.

MAY

Twain was not yet able to assume the pose of a laureate ex-officio—he had only published a few newspaper articles, editorials, humor pieces, and a single book of frontier-style short stories. All of his great work—and the fame and fortune that would accompany it—still lay ahead of him. Nevertheless, his quick wit, ready criticism, and unerring eye lent the trip remarkable clarity and vision.

Everywhere he looked in Jerusalem, he saw the evidence of paradox. As yet, Zionism had not brought waves of Jewish immigrants to the city from Europe. And there were hardly any Palestinian Muslims in the city either. Instead, the largest part of the meager population was comprised of Christians. Some were the native remnant of the old Byzantine culture. Others were pilgrims who found their souls' rest in the city of their Lord's passion. Thus, as it had been for a great part of its existence through the ages, Jerusalem was a Christian city, dominated by Christian concerns.

The Ottoman Turks who ruled over the region at the time had allowed the little town to fall into a shameful state of disrepair. As a result, the Christians, along with the tiny community of Hasidic Jews who lived there, were the caretakers of its glorious spiritual, historical, and cultural heritage. Yet, apart from a few crumbling relics there was hardly any visible evidence of that heritage to be found. Twain had to wonder what there was in the city that was actually worth fighting over.

Despite the presence of the Church of the Holy Sepulchre, the Al Aqusa Mosque, the meandering Via Dolorosa, and the walls of Sulieman the Magnificent, Jerusalem seemed to be utterly devoid of interesting sites to visit. There were no great museums as there had been in all the other cities of the Grand Tour. There were no marvels of architectural wonder. There were no great paintings to admire, no remarkable statues to appreciate, and no public spaces to amble about. Nevertheless, his visit to the city clearly affected Twain. The themes of history and spirituality he encountered there would continue to dominate his writing—even haunt it—long after he left to return home.

Weasel words from mollycoddles will never do when the day demands prophetic clarity from greathearts. Manly men must emerge for this hour of trial.

[THEODORE ROOSEVELT (1858–1919)]

1519 Artist Leonardo da Vinci died at Cloux, France.

1602 The polymath Athanasius Kircher was born. At one time or another, the Jesuit scientist turned his hand to acoustics, archaeology, arithmetic, astronomy, chemistry, geography, geology, geometry, magnetism, medicine, music theory, optics, philology, philosophy, physics, and theology. In forty-four books and thousands of letters, he disseminated throughout all Europe his amazingly advanced speculations.

1670 King Charles II of England granted a charter to the Hudson's Bay Company. Prince Rupert, the king's Bohemian-born cousin, led seventeen other noblemen in the monopoly over trade in the vast region around the Hudson Bay in Canada. The area came to be known as Rupert's Land, and it retained its fur trading interests until the 1990s.

1863 Confederate General Thomas "Stonewall" Jackson was accidentally wounded by his own men at the Battle of Chancellorsville. He died eight days later to the great distress of Robert E. Lee who lamented, "I have lost my right arm." Many historians believe that this strategic loss was actually the turning point in the war, which the South seemed to be winning at the time.

1885 In Holyoke, Massachusetts, Clark W. Bryan published the first issue of *Good Housekeeping* magazine.

1890 The Oklahoma Territory was organized.

1919 The first airplane passenger service began in the United States when Robert Hewitt flew two women from New York City to Atlantic City.

MAY

1932 Jack Benny's first radio show made its debut on the NBC Blue Network.

1936 *Peter and the Wolf*, a symphonic tale for children by Sergei Prokofiev, had its world premiere in Moscow.

1939 After his 2,130-game streak spanning nineteen years, baseball great Lou Gehrig took himself out of the Yankee's lineup due to health problems. Shortly thereafter, he retired altogether.

1945 The Soviet Union announced the fall of Berlin, and the Allies announced the surrender of Nazi troops in Italy and parts of Austria.

1957 Senator Joseph R. McCarthy, the controversial Republican senator from Wisconsin, died at Bethesda Naval Hospital in Maryland.

1960 Convicted sex offender and best-selling author Carl Chessman was executed at San Quentin Prison in California.

1965 *The Early Bird* satellite transmitted television pictures across the Atlantic.

1972 After serving forty-eight years as head of the FBI, J. Edgar Hoover died in Washington.

MAY

3

Lachlan Macquarie was born on the tiny island of Ulva, just off the coast of Mull, in the Inner Hebrides. When he was just fourteen, he joined the British army on this day in 1776 and served in Nova Scotia as well as New York and Jamaica. As a lieutenant he served in India from 1787 to 1801 and later in Egypt where he was involved in defeating the army of Napoleon. On this day in 1810, Macquarie was appointed by the Prince Regent to be governor of New South Wales. Much of Australia was still being used as a penal colony, so the assignment was a difficult one. Indeed, the previous governor had been Captain William Bligh, who not only suffered the mutiny of his crew on the ship HMS *Bounty*, but also of the penal colony during the famous Rum Rebellion of 1808.

Macquarie followed a policy of encouraging the former convicts to settle in Australia—despite fierce opposition from the "free settlers" who wanted to retain privileges only for themselves. He also issued a call to fellow Hebrideans and Highlanders from Scotland to come make a new life in the vast open lands down below. Ultimately, a fourth of the population of Australia was made up of his fellow countrymen. Quite obviously, Australia would have been a very different place had he not succeeded. His strict administrative hand and warm faith in the doctrines of grace helped to transform Australia into a thriving country. It was his overarching vision of a Christian civilization near the heart of the Asian Pacific that transformed Sydney from a dreary shanty town to a magnificent Georgian city.

As a result of his efforts, Macquarie is often regarded as the "Father of Australia." Due to ill health, he left his adopted home in 1822 to receive medical treatment in Britain—but he never returned. Two years later he died and was entombed in a mausoleum on the island of Mull.

SCOTTISH DISMAL DAY

For Scottish Highlanders, it was especially important to refrain from impious acts as it was believed that this was the day on which Lucifer and his minions among the fallen angels were expelled from Paradise for their rebellion against God's sovereign rule.

326

Helena, the mother of Constantine the Great, went on a pilgrimage to Palestine in search of relics. It was on this day that after great lengths she isolated what she believed was Golgotha and the remains of the true Holy Cross of Christ. The Church of the Holy Sepulchre was built on the site. Rebuilt by the Crusaders in the eleventh century, it remains one of the chief pilgrimage sites in Jerusalem.

Beyond the poet's sweet dream lives
The eternal epic of the man.

[JOHN GREENLEAF WHITTIER (1807–1892)]

1469 Niccolò Machiavelli was born on this day in Florence, to the underprivileged side of a wealthy and prominent Florentine family. His writings and his primary work, *The Prince*, gave the writer, statesman, and largely self-educated political theorist a reputation of cynicism and immorality. He was the first philosopher to promote a study of politics based on the study of man, based on the principle that human nature does not change.

1494 Christopher Columbus sighted the island of Jamaica during his second journey.

1654 At Rowley, Massachusetts, the first toll bridge in America was erected across the Newbury River. Tolls applied not to people, but to their animals.

1721 Nearly a millennium after Eric the Red discovered it, Norwegian Hans Egede sailed with his wife for the inhospitable regions of Greenland, where he established a mission station and founded the colonial town of Godthab in an effort to reach the Eskimos with the gospel. Known as Nuuk today, it is the capital of the nation—and the missionary Egede is recognized as its founding father.

1802 Washington, D.C., became an official city with its incorporation on this day.

1810 English poet Lord Byron swam across the Dardanelles, which is the body of water connecting the Aegean Sea with the Sea of Marmara. Though partially lame, the robust Byron swam over four miles aided by currents.

1851 The four-year-old city of San Francisco was almost entirely destroyed by fire for the seventh time.

1916 Irish nationalist Patrick Henry Pearse was executed by the British for his role in the Easter Rising—thus becoming a martyr of the independence movement.

1921 West Virginia imposed the first state sales tax.

1944 The Paramount Pictures musical *Going My Way*, starring Bing Crosby, debuted.

1948 The Supreme Court ruled that covenants prohibiting the sale of real estate to African Americans or members of other racial groups were legally unenforceable.

1971 Antiwar protesters began four days of demonstrations in Washington, D.C., aimed at shutting down the nation's capital.

1971 National Public Radio made its debut on American airwaves.

1978 "Sun Day" was celebrated on a Wednesday as thousands of people extolling the virtues of solar energy held events across the country.

1979 Conservative Party leader Margaret Thatcher was chosen to become Britain's first female prime minister as the Tories decisively ousted the incumbent Labor government in parliamentary elections.

1986 In NASA's first post-*Challenger* launch, an unmanned Delta rocket lost power in its main engine shortly after liftoff, forcing safety officers to destroy it by remote control.

Martin Van Buren (1782–1862) was America's first political boss. Elegant in dress, amiable and courteous in manner, "Little Van" early on demonstrated such political skill that he rapidly rose to prominence in New York State politics: He became one of the leaders of the "Albany Regency," a political machine that developed a spoils system on a large scale and gained control of state politics in the 1820s. A masterful organizer, he welded diverse regional interests into the first effective national political party—the new Democrat Party, which, in 1828, supported Andrew Jackson for the presidency.

Coming to the presidency after the fiery general, Van Buren inherited thorny financial problems. Shortly after he took office, there were bread riots and banks failed—the country was caught up in the Panic of 1837. On this day, two months to the day after his inaugural, banks in New York suspended converting paper money into silver and gold. Banks elsewhere around the country followed suit, touching off a nationwide panic that gave way to an economic depression that lasted until 1843.

The skilled politician who had earned such names as "The Little Magician" and "The American Talleyrand" was unable to avert the financial upheaval, but he courageously attempted to improve matters. He established what later became the Treasury Department, independent of any bank. But his administration was generally held responsible for the panic. He never regained his earlier popularity and was defeated by William Harrison in 1840.

No more was the charming little gentleman in a snuff-colored coat seen gliding the streets of Washington in an elegantly fitted coach attended by liveried footmen. Although he remained a national figure for many years, and was an unsuccessful presidential candidate for the Free Soil Party in 1848, he spent most of his time in retirement at Lindenwald, his estate at Kinderhook, the quiet little village on the Hudson where he was born.

FEAST DAY

St. Pelagia of Tarsus, St. Florian of Lorch, St. Robert Lawrence, St. Augustine Webster, St. Gothard, St. John Houghton, St. Venerius of Milan, St. Cyriacus

MAY

4

1904 — President Theodore Roosevelt authorized the start of construction on the Panama Canal. The fifty-mile canal crossed the Isthmus of Panama and enabled ships to travel from the Pacific and Atlantic Oceans without rounding South America. The construction—which continued for just over a decade—involved many innovative engineering and medical advances, employed tens of thousands of workers, and cost an estimated $350 million.

1968 — McDonald's, the hamburger restaurant chain franchised by entrepreneur Ray Kroc, debuted its signature sandwich, the "Big Mac."

Mercy offers whatever is necessary to heal the hurts of others.

[DOLLY MADISON (1768–1849)]

1626 Peter Minuit, a Dutch colonist, arrived on the island of Manhattan along with four boats of settlers and 300 head of cattle. Minuit purchased the 20,000 acres of the island of Manhattan from the Indians for 60 quilders' (around $25) worth of cloth, beads, and brass buttons. He later served as the settlement's governor.

1655 Bartolommeo Cristofori, the harpsichord maker who invented the piano, was born in Italy. The piano was derived from the harpsichord and the clavichord. Its main distinctive was the introduction of a hammer-and-lever action that enabled the player to control the intensity of sound with a stronger or weaker touch. The earliest known model was called a *gravicembalo col pian e forte*—Italian for "harpsichord with soft and loud."

1776 The Rhode Island Colony declared itself free from British rule two months before the other twelve colonies represented by the Continental Congress adopted the Declaration of Independence.

1873 Father Damien, a Flemish missionary, joined the lepers of Molokai Island in the Hawaiian archipelago where he would spend the rest of his life. He transformed the miserable conditions of the little colony—before he himself contracted the disease and succumbed. His quiet heroism won worldwide renown. It brought new donations for the island and a staff of nurses and other helpers. By his own sacrificial life and death he assaulted the gates of hell.

1886 At Haymarket Square in Chicago, a labor demonstration for an eight-hour workday turned into a riot when a bomb exploded.

1916 Responding to a demand from President Wilson, Germany agreed to limit its submarine warfare, thereby briefly averting a diplomatic break with Washington.

1927 The Academy of Motion Picture Arts and Sciences, renowned as the organization that sponsors the Academy Awards, or Oscars, was formed.

MAY

1932 Chicago crime boss Alphonse Capone was incarcerated in an Atlanta penitentiary. The FBI was unable to pin any of his robberies, murders, or extortions on him. So, the U.S. Justice Department's "Public Enemy Number One" was convicted and jailed for the minor offense of tax evasion.

1942 The Battle of the Coral Sea, the first naval clash fought entirely with carrier aircraft, began during World War II.

1961 A group of civil rights "Freedom Riders" left Washington for New Orleans to challenge racial segregation on interstate buses and in bus terminals.

1970 At Kent State University, panicking members of the Ohio National Guard opened fire on students protesting the Vietnam War. Four students were killed, and nine were wounded.

1980 Marshal Josip Broz Tito, longtime Communist dictator of Yugoslavia, died three days before his eighty-eighth birthday. Less than a decade later, the amalgam nation broke apart into the vicious warring factions of Serbs, Croats, Slovenes, Macedonians, Bosnians, Muslims, and Kosovars.

When William Ellery Channing was installed in 1803 as pastor of the Federal Street Church in Boston, Puritan Calvinism was still the reigning theological system of New England. But many young ministers just out of seminary, like Channing, had begun to question whether that system was actually driven more by fear than by faith. As a consequence, they began to openly explore the various Unitarian theories then in vogue in Europe. They helped to revive the old Arian heresy—the idea that Jesus, though a great teacher, was but a mere man. Likewise, they toyed with the old Socinian heresy—the idea that although Jesus was just the Son of God, His teachings showed the way for all men to attain a similar status of sonship.

FEAST DAY
St. Hydroc, St. Hilary of Arles, St. Hilary of Galeata, St. Angelo, St. Jutta, St. Avertinus, St. Mauruntius

MAY

Sensing the revival of such heresy in their midst, the older orthodox ministers demanded either discipline or expulsion of these neo-Arians and Socinians. Channing met the Calvinists head-on. At the ordination of his friend and protégé Jared Sparks, held on this day in 1819, he delivered the speech that separated the Unitarians from the Calvinists.

Like the opponents of the arch-heretic Arius, Channing's opponents could find little to disparage in his personal character. He was courteous, gentle, refined. Although he became the focus of a great religious controversy, his writings were always calm and dispassionate. On the great moral issues of the day, his views also seemed unimpeachable to the average New Englander—he abhorred slavery, for instance, but he equally abhorred any violent and unconstitutional means to overthrow it; he preached against war; he supported Horace Mann's government-educational efforts and championed American literature. His ideals would be trumpeted by liberals for many generations. For example, he blamed society for alcoholism, rather than the alcoholic, and taught that man's depravity could be overcome through education.

But while his character was never in question, the heterodox nature of his theology could not be denied. The first half of his speech in 1819 defended the use of human reason in interpreting Scripture—altogether ignoring the role of the Holy Spirit in illumination. In the second half of the speech, he outlined the practical fruit of this theology of the unaided human mind. First, he rejected the doctrine of the Trinity: "We object to the doctrine of the Trinity, that it subverts the unity of God." Then he denied, in turn, the doctrines of the Incarnation, the authority of Scripture, and justification by faith.

Channing expressed these views forthrightly, even exultantly, in his speech. Christ was not both God and man, nor a member of the Godhead. The vicarious atonement of Christ for sin was absurd. Election by grace was a preposterous notion. In short, virtually every doctrine that seems fundamental to Christian religion, Channing renounced that day. He was brazenly declaring himself to be an arch-heretic—but all in the name of religion, morality, toleration, and truth. Amazingly, his winsome manner overcame every objection to his fulsome theology, and thus began the great apostasy of the New England Church and the birth of Universalist Unitarianism—the basis of the Religious Left, which remains a powerful cultural and political influence in America to this day.

It is to be steadily inculcated, that virtue is the highest proof of understanding, and the only solid basis of greatness.

[Samuel Johnson (1709–1784)]

1813 The founder of existentialist philosophy, Søren Aaby Kierkegaard was born on this day in Copenhagen, Denmark. Kierkegaard grew up in a strict Lutheran home with a father who stressed the importance of the logic of formal argument. The religious philosopher and critic of rationalism is known for his critique of systematic rational philosophy, especially that of Hegel.

1818 The Radical atheist and revolutionary author of Communist social and economic theories, Karl Heinrich Marx, was born in Trier, Rhine province, Prussia (in present-day Germany). With Friedrich Engels he published *Manifest der Kommunistischen Partei* (commonly known as *The Communist Manifesto*) in 1848, launching the socialist movement and the violent revolutions that shook all of Europe that year. His book *Das Kapital* and other writings by Marx and Engels formed the basis of Marxism, which inspired the totalitarian Communist movement of the early twentieth century.

1821 Napoleon Bonaparte died of cancer on the rat-infested South Atlantic island of St. Helena. He had been imprisoned there by British authorities ever since his defeat at Waterloo in 1815.

1891 Peter Ilich Tchaikovsky helped to celebrate the opening of Carnegie Hall—then known simply as the Music Hall—in New York City by conducting the "1812 Overture." As he toured the East Coast during this trip, Tchaikovsky was amazed at the warm reception given to him by the American people.

1893 Panic hit the New York Stock Exchange. By the end of the year, the entire country was in the throes of a severe depression.

1925 Public school teacher John T. Scopes was arrested in Dayton, Tennessee, after he agreed to test a statute in a manipulated test case for the American Civil Liberties Union (ACLU). His offense was in purposefully excluding all other possible origins theories and teaching Darwinian evolution as an exclusive and indisputable fact in his biology class.

MAY

1945 In the only fatal attack of its kind during the Second World War, a Japanese balloon bomb exploded on Gearhart Mountain in Oregon, killing the pregnant wife of a minister and five children.

1955 A decade after the end of the Second World War, West Germany became a sovereign state.

1955 New York City's 42nd Street Theater premiered *Damn Yankees*—a modern retelling of the story of Faustus.

1961 Launching from Cape Canaveral, Florida, Alan Shepard became the first American space traveler. He successfully completed a fifteen-minute suborbital flight in the *Freedom 7* capsule.

1962 The soundtrack album for Leonard Bernstein's *West Side Story* hit the #1 position on the *Billboard* chart, and remained there for fifty-four weeks.

The father of modern urban design, Patrick Geddes, was born in Ballater in Aberdeenshire, Scotland, and grew up in Perth. After his secondary studies, he gained practical business experience working at the National Bank of Scotland, but three years later he went to study botany at Edinburgh University. He left after only a week, going instead to the University of London. It was while he was there that he was influenced by the radical thinker Thomas Huxley. Later, during a visit to France to recuperate from illness, he developed his lifelong love of that country, its food, its aesthetic beauty, and its culture.

MAY

6

On this day in 1880 he returned to work at Edinburgh University. His wide field of varied interests—biology, botany, town planning, social thinking, politics, and literature—led him to pioneer a number of innovative urban-renewal projects, including the creation of the first student hall of residence at the university. He advocated improvements to the environment on the basis that humans prospered where there were fresh air, gardens, good housing, and pleasing aesthetics—things modern city dwellers would take for granted a generation later but that were revolutionary in his day.

His outspoken radicalism caused him to be bypassed for the Chair of Botany at the university. Nevertheless, both his talents and his message were so obviously meritorious that he was able to obtain a tenured position at University College, Dundee, where he taught intermittently for the rest of his life.

Shortly after his career move to University College, he obtained a building at the top of the Royal Mile near Edinburgh Castle that he converted into a sociological observatory—its famous camera obscura is still part of Outlook Tower there. He reconstructed Ramsay Gardens into the much-admired masterpiece it is today and introduced good civic planning in Dublin. In frequent trips to India he created plans for fifty Indian cities during the period of 1915 to 1929. He also traveled to America and Continental Europe and influenced architecture, park planning, and zoning ideas there. He was a fierce opponent of modern architecture, which he described as "inhuman mechanical ugliness," and fought for a more "Christian vision of beauty, goodness, and truth" until his death in 1932.

1937

The German dirigible *Hindenburg* exploded at Lakehurst, New Jersey, as it was landing after a transatlantic flight. The largest rigid airship ever built, the *Hindenburg* was 804 feet long, had a maximum speed of 84 miles per hour, and cruised at 78 miles per hour. The ship began commercial air service across the Atlantic by carrying 1,002 passengers on ten scheduled trips between Germany and the U.S. in 1936. The hydrogen explosion and fire killed 35 of the 97 people on board and a navy crewman on the ground. The disaster of this day ended the use of such airships in commercial transportation.

Chivalry is knowing what to do in a given situation and then having the courage to act without regard to the outcome.

[REX PAGE (1952–)]

878 The Christian king of Wessex, Alfred the Great, defeated the pagan Viking warlord Guthrum at the Battle of Ethandun. The battle not only ensured that Christianity would survive in England, it also made the unification of that land possible for the first time since the departure of Roman legions in the fifth century.

1758 Radical Jacobin leader and a primary figure in the French Revolution, the "Sea Green Incorruptible" Maximilien Robespierre was born in Arras, France. By the end of 1793, Robespierre had risen to dominate the Committee of Public Safety, the Revolutionary government's main arm during the Reign of Terror. In 1794, however, he was deposed and executed in the Thermidorian Reaction.

1813 J. F. Hummel of Philadelphia, Pennsylvania, was granted a patent for rubber.

1833 John Deere manufactured his first steel plow.

1851 Dr. John Forrie of New Orleans, Louisiana, was awarded a patent for a mechanical refrigeration machine.

1856 Sigmund Schlomo Freud was born in Frielberg, now in the Czech Republic. When he was four years old, Freud's family moved to Vienna, then a greenhouse of radical thought in politics, philosophy, and the arts and sciences. As a young man, Freud focused on studying neurology. Financial constraints, however, led him from research to clinical work. He became known as the "Father of Psychoanalysis," a dubious science associated with modern psychology.

1889 The Paris Exposition formally opened, featuring the just-completed Eiffel Tower.

1910 Britain's King Edward VII died, just nine years after his ascension to the throne. His funeral proved to be the last great gathering of royalty from around the world.

1915 American actor, writer, producer, and director Orson Welles was born on this day in Kenosha, Wisconsin. His masterpiece *Citizen Kane* is considered one of the most influential films of all time, creating new standards in the techniques of narrative, photography, lighting, and music.

1940 American author John Steinbeck was awarded the Pulitzer Prize for his classic novel of the Oklahoma Dust Bowl, *The Grapes of Wrath*.

MAY

1941 Dictator Joseph Stalin assumed the Soviet premiership, replacing his rival, Vyacheslav M. Molotov. Thus, he gained complete control over the apparatus of the Communist totalitarian state.

1942 During the Second World War, some fifteen thousand Americans and Filipinos on Corregidor surrendered to the Japanese.

1954 Roger Bannister, a British medical student, became the first man to run the mile in less than four minutes at a track meet in Oxford, England.

1994 Britain's Queen Elizabeth II and French President François Mitterrand formally opened the controversial railway Channel Tunnel—or Chunnel—between their countries after five years of construction. The first trip from Folkestone, England, to Calais, France, took a little over half an hour.

1994 Former Arkansas state worker Paula Jones filed suit against President Bill Clinton, alleging he had made untoward sexual advances against her three years earlier. It was the third sex scandal to swirl around the president—though it was by no means the last.

On this day in 1253, the year before Marco Polo was born, a courageous monk from Flanders left Constantinople on a trip to the Far East, visiting the court of the Great Khan Mangu in the very heart of Mongolia. But William of Ruisbroek traveled across the Asian continent for the sake of evangelism, not fame, fortune, or adventure.

Louis IX, the saintly king of France, heard that the Mongol warlord Sartak, son of Batu, was a Christian. He determined to make contact and encourage these distant brothers in the faith. William, a Franciscan friar, was the man chosen for the job. Accompanied by a fellow friar, Bartholomew of Cremona, and a small diplomatic contingent, he left for Sartak's camp just to the north of the Crimea. He hoped to establish a mission there.

The rumors about Sartak proved to be false—he was by no means a Christian. But apparently his father had been greatly influenced by Nestorians. So, to complete their mission, the travelers determined to visit the Batu camp along the northern Volga. Batu in turn sent them on to Mongolia with two Nestorian priests and a guide. The little party crossed the Russian Steppes and the broad expanse of Mongolia in the depths of winter and arrived at the Tartary capital of Karakoram in January of 1254.

Other Europeans, captives of war, were already present in the city. Nestorian Christians had long since penetrated the region with the gospel. Their ministry had little effect though, perhaps because their heterodox theology and loose morals actually mitigated against the doctrines of grace.

There in Karakoram, William met the Khan, discussed theology in his presence, and was allowed to preach. Once he grew vehement and upset the Khan. Nevertheless, William ministered there for eight months and baptized sixty Christians. In August, William left Tatary, bearing a letter from Mangu demanding submission of all Western kings and the pope. God had appointed him master of the world, claimed the Khan, and not even mighty seas and high mountains would prevent him from conquering the West. William of Ruisbroek arrived at Acre in May 1255, bearing this grandiose proclamation. He forwarded it to King Louis with a careful and accurate report. It included the best descriptions of Asia that had reached Europe to that point. In its pages were suggestions for further mission work. Though this never did materialize, William's eleven-thousand-mile missionary journey opened the world of Asia to the West for the first time.

MAY

Courage is a character trait most oft attributable to men. In fact, it is the universal virtue of all those who choose to do the right thing over the expedient thing. It is the common currency of all those who do what they are supposed to do in a time of conflict, crisis, and confusion.

[FLORENCE NIGHTINGALE (1820–1910)]

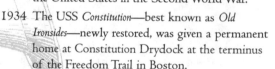

1274 One of the greatest minds of the Medieval period was Bonaventure of Bagnorea. A brilliant Franciscan theologian and apologist, he was also a devoted philanthropist. Over the long span of his life, he worked in hospitals, orphanages, foundling homes, hospices, monasteries, poor schools, and mendicant clinics. Always a peacemaker, he was a friend to both Thomas Aquinas and the patriarch of Constantinople—in fact, he was at least partially responsible for the great council at Lyons on this day in 1274 when the Eastern and Western churches were briefly reconciled.

1789 The first inaugural ball was held in New York in honor of President and Mrs. George Washington.

1824 After twelve years of labor, Ludwig van Beethoven's Ninth Symphony, with its soaring choral finale, *Ode to Joy*, was first performed in Vienna, to thunderous ovations which the deaf composer saw but could not hear.

1833 German composer Johannes Brahms was born in Hamburg. Though writing in a Romantic idiom, Brahms was a devout craftsman who balanced the emotional and intellectual aspects of composition as few composers have. He once said, "It is not hard to compose . . . but it is hard to let the superfluous notes fall under the table." His best-known works are his Protestant *German Requiem*, four symphonies, and various songs and concertos.

1840 Composer Peter Ilich Tchaikovsky was born in Votkinsk, Russia. Thoroughly Russian in his style and sensibilities, he incorporated elements of Western music to convey his love for his homeland.

1915 Twelve thousand people—including 120 Americans—died when a German torpedo sank the British ocean liner *Lusitania* off the Irish coast. Though passengers had been warned by German authorities that the ship was loaded with war materials and was therefore to be considered a hostile vessel, the American government expressed outrage. It sank in less than twenty minutes. This event ultimately led to the involvement of the United States in the Second World War.

MAY

1934 The USS *Constitution*—best known as *Old Ironsides*—newly restored, was given a permanent home at Constitution Drydock at the terminus of the Freedom Trail in Boston.

1939 Germany and Italy announced a military and political alliance known as the Rome-Berlin Axis.

1941 Glenn Miller recorded "Chattanooga Choo Choo" for RCA Victor.

1945 The interim German government formally offered an unconditional surrender to General Eisenhower, the Allied commander, at 2:41 A.M. in Rheims, France. The capitulation was to take effect the following day, ending the European conflict of the Second World War.

1954 The fifty-five-day Battle of Dien Bien Phu in Vietnam ended with Vietnamese insurgents overrunning French forces.

1963 The United States launched the *Telstar 2* communications satellite.

1975 President Gerald Ford formally declared an end to the "Vietnam Era." In Ho Chi Minh City, formerly Saigon, the Vietcong staged a rally to celebrate their takeover.

After a lengthy exchange of letters, the curators and burgomasters of Leiden officially appointed Jacobus Arminius professor of theology at their university on this day in 1603. When first proposed for the position, Arminius doubted he would take the job. He had formed loving ties with his congregation in Amsterdam. Furthermore, he had found theological researches a hindrance to his growth in personal sanctity. His working relationship with Amsterdam's authorities was good, and he seldom found it necessary to oppose them for the sake of conscience. Most important, he had a lifelong contract with Amsterdam that he could not simply abrogate.

At the time, Arminius was also Amsterdam's favorite minister. He had served there fifteen years. Yet the possibility of appointment to Leiden raised the question of his orthodoxy. John Calvin and Theodore Beza had taught that Romans 7 referred to the regenerate. Arminius held that it was the description of the unregenerate. His chief opponent in Leiden, Franciscus Gomarus, confessed that he had never read Arminius's work. After Arminius explained his views, Gomarus agreed that they were a defensible if not a preferred interpretation. Arminius showed his position to be the view of a score of eminent theologians from church history. Amsterdam was persuaded to release Arminius. The city promised to provide his widow a pension should he die and gave him a substantial gift.

Arminius had not cleared his last hurdle of controversy, however. At Leiden he became embroiled in a host of theological arguments against his will. He was compelled by the lecture schedule to speak on predestination, a topic on which his views were already suspect to strict Calvinists. His lecture consisted almost entirely of Scripture with minimal comment. Arminius's careful pastiche of scriptural quotes was clearly constructed to undermine the orthodox position, and a number of eminent Calvinists challenged him.

The crux of the issue was that Arminius put human will at the center of soteriology—in other words, man had to choose God, God could not simply and sovereignly choose man. The orthodox were outraged. Arminius tried hard to keep peace, even deliberately withholding some of his views. He was careful to avoid saying anything that smacked of Pelagianism. Nevertheless, he could hardly help but create a firestorm of controversy.

After his death, Arminius's views were condemned at the Synod of Dort. Ever since, Protestant groups have generally been divided into two broad theological camps—those who follow his free-will teaching (Arminians), and those who follow the traditional sovereign grace teaching (Calvinists).

He has done the work of a true man,
Crown him, honor him, love him.
Weep over him, tears of woman,
Stoop manliest brows over him.
No duty could overtask him,
No need his will outrun;
Or ever our lips could ask him,
His hand the work had done.

[JOHN GREENLEAF WHITTIER (1807–1892)]

MAY

1541 At a point somewhere near the present city of Memphis, Tennessee, explorer Hernando de Soto first sighted the broad expanse of the Mississippi River.

1846 The first major battle of the Mexican War was fought at Palo Alto, Texas, resulting in victory for General Zachary Taylor's forces.

1854 Dr. Hugh Hodge was one of the most prominent researchers in the field of embryology in the nineteenth century. He often exhorted his medical students at the University of Pennsylvania to protect innocent human life. His research had convinced him beyond any shadow of a doubt that life began at conception and that the destruction of that life before or after birth was unmitigated murder. On this day, he began to lobby the American Medical Association—in cooperation with the young Dr. Horatio Storer—to call a halt to the slaughter of children in the surreptitious abortion clinics of the land. Although it took many years, Dr. Hodge never wavered. His faith in Christ bolstered him through every trial, and ultimately he was successful. The AMA strongly denounced the brutal practice in September 1871.

1884 The thirty-third president of the United States, Harry S. Truman, was born near Lamar, Missouri.

1886 The first Coca-Cola was sold by Dr. John Styth Pemberton at Jacob's Pharmacy in Atlanta, Georgia.

1944 The first "eye bank" was established, in New York City.

1945 VE Day—Victory in Europe—was celebrated in Great Britain when Prime Minister Winston Churchill stood at the side of King George VI and announced the previous day's unconditional surrender by the German forces to the Allies, marking the end of the European phase of the Second World War.

1945 President Harry Truman announced the victory in Europe during a radio address on his sixty-first birthday.

1958 Vice President Nixon was shoved, stoned, booed and spat upon by anti-American protesters in Lima, Peru.

1962 The musical comedy *A Funny Thing Happened on the Way to the Forum* opened on Broadway.

1973 Militant American Indians who had held the South Dakota hamlet of Wounded Knee for ten weeks surrendered.

1987 An angry and defiant Gary Hart, dogged by questions about his personal life, including his relationship with Miami model Donna Rice, withdrew from the race for the Democratic presidential nomination.

277

It was the primary textbook of the Greek and Roman world for generations of students throughout Christendom. It was the historical source for many of Shakespeare's finest plays. It forever set the pattern for the biographical arts. It was the inspiration for many of the ideas of the American political pioneers—evidenced by liberal quotations in the articles, speeches, and sermons of Samuel Adams, Peyton Randolph, Patrick Henry, Samuel Davies, Alexander Hamilton, James Madison, Henry Lee, John Jay, George Mason, Gouverneur Morris, and Thomas Jefferson. Indeed, after the Bible it was the most frequently referenced source during the Founding era. For these and a myriad of other reasons, Plutarch's *The Lives of Noble Grecians and Romans* is one of the most vital and consequential of all the ancient classics.

First published in America on this day in 1699, it was written sometime during the tumultuous days of the second century. Organized as a series of parallel biographies—alternating between famous Greeks and Romans—a character from the Golden Age like Pericles, Alcibiades, Lycurgus, Alexander, or Solon was compared with one from the Splendorous Age like Cicero, Brutus, Cato, Anthony, or Caesar. Plutarch's aim was primarily didactic, and so *The Lives* abounds with lessons about honor, valor, wisdom, temperance, and duty. It was a paean to moral paganism. It was the original "Book of Virtues."

Interestingly, the various profiles are notorious for their mixture of fact and fiction, history and myth, verity and gossip. Plutarch was a lover of tradition, and his prime concern was to both memorialize past glories and reassert them as living ideals. Thus, whether an event actually occurred was of little consequence to him—what mattered was how the lessons from those events had passed into the cultural consciousness. "When a story is so celebrated and is vouched for by so many authorities," he commented in his profile of Croesus, "I cannot agree that it should be rejected because of the so called rules of chronology." And again, in his biography of Theseus, he wrote, "May I therefore succeed in purifying fable, making her submit to reason and take on the semblance of history. But where she obstinately disdains to make herself credible and refuses to admit any element of probability I shall pray for kindly readers and such as receive with indulgence the tales of antiquity."

Thus did Plutarch become the father of that modern branch of the theological arts we oddly call "Political Science." And thus did he forge the cardinal model for all succeeding disciplines of the "Divinities" such as sociology, psychology, history, and the social sciences. Indeed, the tenured place of "Moral Philosophy" in Western thought owes more to Plutarch than to almost any other single artisan—at least in form if not in substance.

FEAST DAY
St. Beatus of Lungern, St. Gerontius of Cervia, St. Beatus of Vendôme, St. Pachomius

MAY

*There is no outward sign of true chivalry
that does not rest on a deep moral foundation.*

[JOHANN GOETHE (1749–1832)]

1502 Christopher Columbus left Cadiz, Spain, on his fourth and final trip to the Western Hemisphere, during which he would accurately calculate the land mass of the South American continent based on the amount of fresh water pouring into the sea from several coastal rivers.

1671 Rogue and enemy of the throne Colonel Thomas Blood attempted to steal the crown, orb, and scepter of the king from the Tower of London. He nearly succeeded but was brought before King Charles II to explain his actions. However, he so intimidated the king that he was granted an estate in Ireland—the king was hopeful that he would just go away. His accomplices each received £200.

1754 The first American newspaper cartoon was published in Benjamin Franklin's *Pennsylvania Gazette*. It showed a snake cut into sections, each part representing an American colony. The caption read, "Join or die."

1860 Sir James Matthew Barrie, Scottish author of *Peter Pan* (1904), was born in Kirriemuir, Angus, Scotland.

1902 William Howard Taft—who would later become president of the United States and still later the chief justice of the Supreme Court—secured a deal with the Vatican to purchase 400,000 acres of prime land in the Philippines from the Spanish Franciscan friars who had served as the chaplains of the former colonial rulers. It was a tricky deal to negotiate and marked a landmark in church-state relations.

1913 The Seventeenth Amendment to the United States Constitution was ratified, providing for the election of senators by popular vote rather than their appointment by state legislatures.

1926 Americans Richard Byrd and Floyd Bennett became the first men to fly over the North Pole.

1936 Italy annexed Ethiopia—young Emperor Hailie Selassie was forced into exile.

1961 In a speech to the National Association of Broadcasters, Federal Communications Commission Chairman Newton N. Minow condemned television programming as a "vast wasteland."

1974 The House Judiciary Committee opened hearings on whether to recommend the impeachment of President Nixon.

1994 South Africa's newly elected Parliament chose former political prisoner and convicted terrorist Nelson Mandela to be the country's first black president. Mandela promised a South Africa for "all its people, black and white."

MAY

9

MAY

He was America's first celebrity. Though just twenty-five years old when he began touring the sparsely settled colonies in 1738, George Whitefield (1714–1770) was an immediate sensation. And he remained so for the rest of his life. Over the next thirty years, amid some seven visits from his native England, he would leave his mark on the lives of virtually every English-speaking soul living on this side of the Atlantic—from the cosmopolitan businessmen of Philadelphia and the seasoned traders of Boston to the yeomen farmers of Virginia and the frontier adventurers of Canada.

Perhaps it is surprising to us that an evangelist would be the most outstanding man of that day—a day graced by the likes of so many great men: Peyton Randolph, Samuel Adams, Patrick Henry, John Hancock, Alexander Hamilton, John Jay, George Mason, Gouverneur Morris, Charles Pinckney, Edmund Randolph, James Madison, and George Washington. But it was no surprise to the people he affected.

Whitefield literally took America by storm. "When he arrived in the colonies," says historian Mark Noll, "he was simply an event." Wherever he went, vast crowds gathered to hear him. Commerce would cease. Shops would close. Farmers would leave their plows midfurrow. And affairs of the greatest import would be postponed. One of his sermons in the Boston Common actually drew more listeners than the city's entire population. Another in Philadelphia, held on this day in 1744, spilled over onto more than a dozen city blocks. Still another in Savannah recorded the largest single crowd ever to gather anywhere in the colonies—despite the scant local population.

Some said he blazed across the public firmament like a "heavenly comet." Some said he was a "magnificent fascination of the like heretofore unknown." Others said he "startled the world awake like a bolt from the blue." There can be little doubt that he lived up to his reputation as the "marvel of the age." As historian Harry Stout has written: "He was a preacher capable of commanding mass audiences—and offerings—across two continents, without any institutional support, through the sheer power of his personality. Whitefield wrote best-selling journals and drew audiences totaling in the millions. White and black, male and female, friends and enemies—all flocked in unprecedented numbers to hear the Grand Itinerant. Whenever he visited, people could do anything, it seemed, but stay away."

By all accounts, he was the "Father of Modern Evangelism." He sparked a deeply affecting revival of portentous proportions—the Great Awakening. He helped to pioneer one of the most enduring church reform movements in history—Methodism. And he laid the foundations for perhaps the greatest experiment in liberty the world has yet known—the American Republic. In many respects, he was the spiritual father of the Founding Fathers.

A coward dies a thousand deaths, the valiant dies but once.

[WILLIAM SHAKESPEARE (C. 1564–1616)]

1774 Louis XVI ascended the throne of France. He and his pious wife, Marie Antoinette, would eventually be the victims of regicide during the French Revolution.

1775 Ethan Allen led a successful assault on Fort Ticonderoga. Allen called for the surrender of the British troops "in the name of the Great Jehovah and the Continental Congress." Though Allen is named among the greatest of the Revolutionary War heroes as the leader of the Green Mountain Boys, he and his men did not fight for American independence. Rather, they were from the Republic of Vermont—which did not join the other American colonies in establishing a federal government, preferring to remain independent until 1791.

1818 American patriot Paul Revere died in Boston.

1863 Thomas Jonathan "Stonewall" Jackson died. Virginia bred and West Point trained, Thomas Jackson turned out to be the South's most versatile—and unbeatable—military commander. Nicknamed "Stonewall," his quirky habits, sincere piety, and brilliant battlefield maneuvers made him a legend on both sides of the battlefield. At the Battle of Chancellorsville, Jackson was accidentally struck by the fire of his own men and mortally wounded. It was one of the most severe blows to the cause of the South.

1865 Union forces captured Confederate President Jefferson Davis in Irwinville, Georgia.

1869 In Promontory Point, Utah, Governor Stanford of California completed the first transcontinental railway in America by driving a gold spike into the last railroad tie.

1886 German neo-Orthodox theologian Karl Barth was born in Basle.

1899 Actor, dancer, and singer Frederick Austerlitz— otherwise known as Fred Astaire—was born in Omaha, Nebraska. Having studied dance since he was four, Astaire partnered with his sister Adele for such early Broadway hits as Gershwin's *Lady, Be Good!* Astaire is best known for his musical comedy films with partner Ginger Rogers, including *The Gay Divorcee* (1934), *Top Hat* (1935), and *Swing Time* (1936).

1908 Based on a suggestion of Miss Anna Jarvis, Philadelphia, Pennsylvania, adopted the first Mother's Day. National recognition for the day, which occurs on the second Sunday of May, was granted on May 12, 1914.

1910 Igor Stravinsky completed the score for *L'Oiseau de feu* (The Firebird), which was presented at the Paris Opéra. The ballet was commissioned by the renowned choreographer Serge Diaghilev, who had wanted to produce a work based on the old Russian legend. The instantaneous success of the ballet catapulted Stravinsky to fame.

MAY

1930 The first planetarium in the United States opened in Chicago. The domed building that housed the model of the heavens was a $1 million gift from Max Adler.

1934 Incredible dust storms swept away an estimated three hundred million tons of topsoil in Arkansas, Colorado, Oklahoma, and Texas.

1940 First Lord of the Admiralty, Winston Churchill, became prime minister of Great Britain after Neville Chamberlain resigned the post. Regarding this day Churchill said, "I felt as if I was walking with destiny, and that all my past life had been but a preparation for this hour and this trial."

1941 Adolf Hitler's deputy, Rudolf Hess, parachuted into Scotland on what he claimed was a peace mission. Hess ended up serving a life sentence at Spandau Prison until 1987, when he apparently committed suicide.

FEAST DAY

St. Comgall, St. Credan, St. Maieul, St. Tudy, St. Ansfrid, St. Walter of l'Esterp, St. Richard Reynolds, St. Francis di Girolamo, St. Ignatius of Laconi, St. Asaph, St. Gengulf, Mamertus

Margaret of Scotland was the royal daughter of one king, wife to another, and mother to yet another. Granddaughter of Edmund Ironside, her father briefly bore his crown as king of the English in the tumultuous days preceding the Norman invasion of William the Conqueror in 1066. When it became evident that the Norman conquest had succeeded, she and her brother escaped to the friendlier atmosphere of Scotland.

Not only did Malcolm of Canmore, king of the Scots, give the family refuge, he also courted the beautiful young Margaret. Though both royal households opposed the union—the Saxons because they felt it compromised any possible bid to recover their perogatives in England and the Scots because they saw no political advantage in the marriage—the two quickly fell in love and were married.

They had a wonderful romance and a happy marriage, rearing six sons and two daughters. A strong-willed queen, she was noted for her solicitude for orphans and the poor and for her rabid intolerance of slavery, abandonment, or abortion. She was also noted for her piety. It was Margaret who first introduced Catholic traditions to the Church of Scotland. The Celtic church there—the fruit of the work of Ionian missionaries sent out by Saint Patrick, Saint Columba, and Saint Finian—had developed an entirely separate tradition much more akin to Protestantism. Through her efforts, it was gradually absorbed into Western Christendom.

Her son David became one of the best Scottish kings and, like his mother, came to be revered as a saint for his merciful concerns and his selfless generosity toward the needy. Her daughter married Henry I of England and brought a similar saintly influence to the British royal line. Thus, by the time she died on this day in 1093, Margaret had not only left her gracious mark on her subjects, she had also left it on the whole of the fabric of British history.

1153 | Scotland's King David I died at the Edinburgh Castle. It was sixty years to the day after his saintly mother died there.

Have courage for the great sorrows of life and patience for the small ones. And when you have laboriously accomplished your daily task, go to sleep in peace. God is awake.

[VICTOR HUGO (1802–1885)]

MAY

1647 Peter Stuyvesant arrived in New Amsterdam to become governor.

1751 Pennsylvania Hospital opened as the first hospital in the United States.

1792 United States Army Captain Robert Gray discovered and named the Columbia River.

1812 The British prime minister, Spencer Perceval, was shot and killed in the lobby of the House of Commons by John Bellingham, a broker who had gone bankrupt.

1816 The American Bible Society was founded in New York. Elias Boudinot, the former president of the United States during the Confederation period, was the first chairman. The organization's purpose, "to encourage the wider circulation of the Holy Scriptures throughout the world," has resulted in translations of the Scriptures into more than a thousand languages all around the world.

1858 Minnesota became the thirty-second state of the Union.

1888 Israel Isidore Baline—otherwise known as Irving Berlin—was born in Mogilyov, Belarus. Starting in 1907 he published more than eight hundred songs, including "Oh, How I Hate to Get Up in the Morning," "Puttin' on the Ritz," "God Bless America," and "There's No Business Like Show Business." In his score for the movie *Holiday Inn,* he introduced the ballad "White Christmas."

1894 Choreographer and dancer Martha Graham was born in Allegheny, Pennsylvania. She trained a generation of American dancers in a self-devel-oped style that emphasized austere and angular movement and body lines, the relation between breathing to feeling and movement, and contraction and release.

1904 Salvador Dali, the most popular painter in the surrealist movement, was born in Figueras, Spain. Influenced deeply by French surrealists and by Sigmund Freud's writings, Dali was in the habit of putting himself into hallucinatory stupors. The images of melting clocks in *The Persistence of Memory* are his most memorable legacy.

1910 Glacier National Park in Montana was established.

1946 The first packages from the relief agency CARE—Cooperative for American Remittances to Europe—arrived at Le Havre, France.

1949 Israel was admitted to the United Nations as the world body's fifty-ninth member.

1949 The Kingdom of Siam changed its name to Thailand.

1973 Charges against Daniel Ellsberg for his role in the *Pentagon Papers* case were dismissed by Judge William M. Byrne, who cited government misconduct.

1989 To protect the lives of United States citizens, President George Bush deployed nearly 2,000 combat troops to Panama.

1998 A French mint produced the first coins of Europe's single currency, the Euro.

"If I had a vein that did not beat with the love of my country, I myself would open it." Such were the sentiments of Charles Cotesworth Pinckney (1746–1825), a Southern patriot who, though educated in England, was one of the principal Southern leaders of the new nation.

Pinckney was twice the unsuccessful Federalist candidate for president—in 1804 against Jefferson and 1808 against Madison—but he is remembered primarily as a courageous army officer, a signer of the Constitution, and as the commissioner to France who, in 1798, refused a veiled request for bribes with, "Millions for defense but not one cent for tribute."

After studying law under the famed William Blackstone at Oxford, Pinckney attended the Royal Military Academy in France, gaining training that helped him, after he returned to America, to win a commission as a captain in the Continental army in 1775. He fought in several battles and was captured when the British took Charleston on this day in 1780. By the end of the war he was a brigadier general.

Even before the war Pinckney was active in the patriotic movement. In 1775 he was a member of a group responsible for the local defense, and in February 1776 he was chairman of a committee that drafted a plan for the temporary government of South Carolina. At the Constitutional Convention, Pinckney stoutly defended Southern interests and states' rights; he revealed little faith in elections by the people, but he accepted the decisions of the convention, signed the Constitution, and supported it at the South Carolina ratification convention.

One of the most successful lawyers in South Carolina, Pinckney was offered a seat on the Supreme Court by Washington, but he declined—as he did later offers from Washington of the positions of secretary of war and secretary of state. However, in 1796 he accepted the position of minister to France, but, after he arrived in Paris, the French Directory chose not to accept him, and he went to Holland. In 1797 President Adams appointed Pinckney, John Marshall, and Elbridge Gerry commissioners to France in an attempt to settle differences, but the three were insulted by the French officials known as X, Y, and Z, and Pinckney made his famous reply and returned home something of a hero. He was soon appointed major general in the newly formed army, hastily organized by Washington because of the rupture with France, but by 1800 tensions were reduced.

Although he was twice unsuccessful in seeking the presidency, Pinckney was honored by his fellow officers of the Revolution and served from 1805 until his death as president of their association, the Society of the Cincinnati.

FEAST DAY

St. Dominic of the Causeway, St. John Stone, St. Ethelhard, St. Fremund, Saints Nereus and Achilleus, St. Pancras of Rome, St. Epiphanius of Salmis, St. Germanus of Constantinople, St. Modoaldus, St. Rictrudis

MAY

Where courage is not, no other virtue can survive except by accident.

[SAMUEL JOHNSON (1709–1784)]

1621 Edward Winslow and Susanna White became the first couple to marry in Plymouth Colony.

1819 Born on this day in Florence and named for her birthplace, Florence Nightingale pioneered the profession of nursing by her care of wounded soldiers during the Crimean War.

1828 English poet and painter Dante Gabriel Rossetti, founder of the Pre-Raphaelite Brotherhood, was born in London. The organization Rosetti began was known for the nonacademic manner in which they treated religious and moral subjects.

1850 Unites States historian and statesman Henry Cabot Lodge was born on this day in Boston, Massachusetts. In 1876 he was the recipient of Harvard University's first Ph.D. in political science. He served in the U.S. House of Representatives for six years, then was elected to the U.S. Senate, serving as chairman of the Foreign Relations Committee. When President Woodrow Wilson pushed for membership in an international peacekeeping organization, Lodge fought to protect the nation's sovereignty.

1870 Manitoba entered Confederation as a Canadian province.

1888 Yale track team's Charles Sherrill became the first runner to start a footrace in the now-familiar fast-break crouching position.

1932 The body of the kidnapped son of Charles and Anne Lindbergh was found in a wooded area of Hopewell, New Jersey.

1937 The first worldwide radio broadcast covered the coronation of England's King George VI, who was crowned at Westminster Abbey following the abdication of his brother, Edward Windsor.

1942 A German U-boat sank an American cargo ship at the mouth of the Mississippi River.

1943 Axis forces in North Africa surrendered during the Second World War.

1949 The Soviet Union announced an end to the Berlin Blockade.

1965 West Germany and Israel exchanged letters establishing diplomatic relations.

MAY

1970 The Senate voted unanimously to confirm Harry A. Blackmun as a Supreme Court justice. Just three years later, he would deliver the most notorious decision since the case of *Dred Scot* when he overturned the homicide and infanticide laws in all fifty states by legalizing abortion through all nine months of pregnancy.

1978 Bowing to pressure from feminist groups, the Commerce Department said hurricanes would no longer be given only female names.

1982 In Fatima, Portugal, security guards overpowered a Spanish priest armed with a bayonet who was trying to reach Pope John Paul II.

1994 The Senate joined the House in passing a bill providing extraordinary new privileges, exemptions, and protections for abortion clinics not afforded any other kind of medical facility.

2000 Franklin Classical School presented the premiere of Ruth: The Song of th;e Covenant composed by Gregory Wilbur in Nashville, Tennessee.

12

Three Portuguese shepherd children on their way to Cova da Iria, a natural depression near their hamlet, met a lady "brighter than the sun." According to the three, Lucia dos Santos, and Francesco and Jacinta Marto, on this day in 1917, the lady spoke to them and instructed them to return each month on the thirteenth. She said that she had an important message for all nations and for all men and women. In October, she would, by the power of God, work a great miracle that would substantiate her veracity.

The children reported this unusual event. It was met with a good deal of incredulity and remains controversial to this day. They were interrogated by the local clergy, but stuck to their story. In August they were kidnapped and held by a civil prefect for two days during the usual time of the apparition. Interest mounted when it became known the lady would work a miracle in October. In June, fifty people appeared on the site in the Parish of Fatima. By September this number had swelled to thirty thousand. The children alone saw and spoke with the lady, and she offered them a number of prophecies. The others saw only movement in trees and clouds.

By October, a crowd of fifty thousand amassed on the site. On this dreary, rainy, miserable day, the lady appeared to the children and told them that she was Our Lady of the Rosary. Eyewitnesses later reported that at midday the sun suddenly appeared in the cloud-covered sky. It rotated fantastically, shooting off colored rays, its rim a rainbow. It was not too bright to gaze upon. The sun began to roam among the clouds, half disappearing behind cloud puffs. From time to time it would stop and spin fantastically as at first. Finally it became stationary and pulsated. Without warning it hurtled toward the crowd, growing brighter and hotter. People screamed and cried for pardon from their sins. The children called to the crowd to pray.

As quickly as the phenomenon had begun, apparently, it reversed itself. The sun returned to the clouds. It took on its usual unbearable noonday brilliance. A great wind arose but the trees did not bend. The soggy ground where the people had stood was now baked mud. Roman Catholic authorities authenticated the miracle. A shrine was built to the Lady of Fatima. Though a large number of the prophecies the children gave remain unfulfilled—and several actually have been proven incorrect—the site remains a major Catholic pilgrimage destination to this day.

Courage is almost a contradiction in terms. It means a strong desire to live taking the form of a readiness to die.

[G. K. CHESTERTON (1874–1936)]

1607 Just over a hundred colonists disembarked from the *Sarah Constant, Godspeed,* and *Discovery* ships at Jamestown, Virginia, the first permanent British settlement in North America. It would get off to a rocky start when most refused to work. According to the captains of the company, John Smith and Christopher Newport, "Only twelve are laborers, ten or twelve are mechanics, while forty-eight are gentlemen, and there are no women."

1648 The first printing of the *Larger and Shorter Catechisms* of the Westminster Assembly were made available for distribution and sale in England and Scotland. The books were the fruit of five years of labor and remain one of the clearest expressions of Reformed Protestantism ever formulated. The question-and-answer format has been used to train tens of thousands of young children in the faith ever since.

1842 Sir Arthur Sullivan—the musical half of the Gilbert and Sullivan operetta duo—was born in England. Sullivan received strict academic training in the composition of music, and was regarded by the *London Times* in 1866 as a musician "who, if we are to expect anything lasting from the rising generation of national composers, Sullivan is the one from whom we may reasonably and on the fairest grounds expect it." Because of his fast lifestyle, Sullivan turned to the easy money he received from writing popular works such as *HMS Pinafore* (1878), *The Pirates of Penzance* (1879), and *The Mikado* (1885).

1846 The United States declared that a state of war already existed against Mexico.

1918 The first U.S. airmail stamps, featuring a picture of an airplane, were introduced. On some of the stamps, the airplane was printed upside down, making them collector's items.

1940 In a speech to the House of Commons, Winston Churchill declared, "I have nothing to offer but blood, toil, tears and sweat." That sentiment would become the hallmark of the solitary British resistance to Hitler's Nazi regime.

MAY

1954 President Dwight Eisenhower signed into law the St. Lawrence Seaway Development Act.

1954 The musical play *The Pajama Game* opened on Broadway.

1981 Pope John Paul II was shot and seriously wounded in St. Peter's Square by an Islamic assassin, Mehmet Ali Agca. He later claimed that he had been hired by a Moscow-backed Communist spy ring in Eastern Europe.

1985 A confrontation between Philadelphia authorities and the radical group "MOVE" ended as police dropped an explosive onto the group's headquarters; eleven people died in the resulting fire.

1989 In unusually strong language, President Bush called on the people of Panama and the country's defense forces to overthrow their military leader, General Manuel Antonio Noriega.

1998 President Bill Clinton ordered harsh sanctions against an unapologetic India, which had gone ahead with a second round of nuclear tests despite global criticism.

John Henry Newman was created a cardinal by Pope Leo XIII on this day in 1880. The move was extraordinary. Although he was an ordained priest, he held no churchly function of any sort and was only a recent convert to Catholicism. The honor was given because of Newman's piety, zeal, erudition, and other virtues.

As a young Anglican vicar, he had spurred a great revival at the University of Oxford after a series of chapel sermons on repentance and the simultaneous publication of a series of *Tracts for the Times*. Through these he hoped to define more clearly the Church of England's doctrine and position so that the church would not be subject to the whims of fashion and fancy. The sermons and tracts had a tremendous influence, and the revival became known around the world as the Oxford Movement.

A few years after the Oxford Movement began and Newman became a celebrity throughout England, one of his tracts created a storm of controversy. In it, Newman argued that the Church of England had only disassociated itself from the excesses of the Roman Catholic Church, not its fundamentals. This stirred a cry of outrage from the more conservative and evangelical branches of the Anglican communion. The furor became so great that Newman was forced to resign his posts at the university.

He retreated with a group of friends to rethink his place in the church. After much deliberation and prayer, he decided he must join the Catholic Church. On a visit to Rome, he was ordained. His secession from the Anglicans threw England into an even greater uproar than before, so influential had been his sermons and writings.

He remained both influential and controversial for the rest of his life. He was the author of several influential books including the masterpiece *Apologia Pro Vita Sua* (Apology for My Life) and *The Idea of the University*. He was also a gifted poet, writing such classic hymns as "Lead, Kindly Light"—he actually threw away the famous "Dream of Gerontius," thinking it of little worth, but thankfully a friend rescued it.

The Oxford Movement, in which he was so influential, persisted with great strength even after he had become a Catholic. Oxford itself elected him an honorary fellow, restoring his association with them.

MAY

14

1948

The independent state of Israel was proclaimed in Tel Aviv as British rule in Palestine came to an end. Immediately, all of its Arab neighbors declared war and vowed to destroy the nation altogether. Arab troops greatly outnumbered the entire Jewish population, but of the eighty-five thousand Jews in Palestine, thirty thousand took up arms to defend their fledgling nation. When overt hostilities ceased, the Arabs managed to retain possession only of the old quarter of Jerusalem and the West Bank territories, and Israel had a nation again—after 1,878 years of exile.

No other success in life—not being president, or being wealthy, or going to college, or anything else—comes up to the success of the man and woman who can feel that they have done their duty and that their children and grandchildren rise up to call them blessed.

[THEODORE ROOSEVELT (1858–1919)]

MAY

14

1643 Louis XIV became king of France at age four upon the death of his father, Louis XIII. Eventually the "Sun King" became one of the most powerful monarchs in all of history.

1686 Physicist and inventor Daniel Gabriel Fahrenheit was born in Gdansk, Poland. He invented alcohol and mercury thermometers, and developed the Fahrenheit temperature scale. Among his discoveries are the facts that water can remain liquid below its freezing point, and the boiling point of liquids depends upon atmospheric pressure.

1796 English physician Edward Jenner administered the first vaccination against smallpox to an eight-year-old boy.

1804 Captain Meriwether Lewis and William Clark left St. Louis, Missouri, on an expedition to chart and explore the recently acquired Louisiana Purchase. They reached the Pacific Coast at the mouth of the Columbia River on November 8, 1805, and returned to St. Louis on September 23, 1806.

1848 The Associated Press news service was established.

1852 Mrs. Gail Borden developed a process for making condensed milk for which she applied for a patent. At first there was some uncertainty as to the value of the product, but condensed milk was eventually successfully marketed and became the foundation of success for the Borden Company.

1856 The first commercially imported camels arrived in the United States, making their landing in Texas.

1897 John Philip Sousa's march, "The Stars and Stripes Forever," received its first performance.

1904 Opening ceremonies for the first Olympic games to be hosted by the United States were held in St. Louis, Missouri.

1942 Commissioned and conducted by Andre Kostelanetz, Aaron Copland's *Lincoln Portrait* made its debut, played by the Cincinnati Symphony Orchestra.

1942 The Women's Army Corps was established.

1955 Representatives from eight Communist bloc countries, led by the Soviet Union, signed the Warsaw Pact in Poland.

1973 The United States launched *Skylab 1,* its first manned space station.

1980 President Carter inaugurated the Department of Health and Human Services.

1994 The West Bank town of Jericho saw its first full day of Palestinian self-rule following the withdrawal of Israeli troops, an event celebrated by Palestinians.

1998 The absurdist television sitcom *Seinfeld* aired its final episode after nine years on NBC.

On this day in 1856, *The Wonderful Wizard of Oz* author Lyman Frank Baum was born in Chittenango, New York. In all, Baum wrote fourteen *Oz* books, delighting children around the world. But many scholars believe that the books were actually never intended for children, and that Baum drew the symbolism of the saga from William Jennings Bryan's campaign for the national government to back its paper money with silver as well as gold. Bryan's opponent in the 1896 and 1900 presidential elections was William McKinley, who supported the gold standard. Bryan argued that the gold standard depressed the economy, thereby crucifying America on a "cross of gold."

MAY

According to some scholars, the economic hard times are represented in the *Oz* books by the bleakness of the Kansas countryside in which Dorothy finds herself at the beginning of the saga. Dorothy represents Everywoman, and the cyclone that carries her to the land of Oz is apparently a Bryan silverite victory at the polls. The land gets its name from the silverites who wanted sixteen ounces of silver—abbreviated of course, as oz—to be the monetary equivalent of one ounce of gold. Dorothy's own house lands on the Wicked Witch of the East—who represents the eastern Wall Street and banking elite—killing the witch and freeing the Munchkins—who represent the ordinary folks—from their bondage. The good Witch of the North—representing the more enlightened Northern electorate—tells Dorothy that the Wizard of Oz might be able to help her get home. To reach him, she has to travel the yellow brick road—the pathway made of gold ingots—which might be done only with silver slippers (alas, the Hollywood version changed them to ruby for better visual contrast). She then meets Bryan's supporters along the way. There is the Scarecrow—who represents a farmer who thinks he has no brains. There is the Tin Woodsman—who represents the industrial laborer who thinks he has no compassion. And there is Bryan himself, represented by the Cowardly Lion—he might be the king of the jungle if he would only recognize his destiny and boldly, bravely claim it.

This ragtag electoral coalition goes to the national capital, the Emerald City, whose greenish hue is an optical illusion, just as the greenback dollar was illusory money. The wizard proves to be a complete charlatan. As he confesses to himself, "How can I help being a humbug when all these people make me do things that everybody knows can't be done? It was easy to make the Scarecrow and the Lion and the Woodsman happy, because they imagined I could do anything." To get Dorothy back to Kansas, he suggests a hot-air balloon, but the old windbag carries him away, leaving Dorothy behind. In the end, Dorothy learns that she has always had the means to return home. The message of the story was that ordinary people can take care of themselves if they realize their full potential, work together, and do not put themselves into the thrall of self-professed experts wielding the powers of government.

This populist message was uncongenial to Yip Harburg, the socialist and New Dealer who had the most to do with scripting the movie version. Thus, the subtle respinning of the story turned its meaning on its head. In the book, Dorothy sought the security of home in the national capital, but found there nothing but trickery and discovered in the process that she and her fellow citizens already had what it took to live the good life.

Do not bemoan the turn of fortune that makes of a simple matter a heroic act.

[Andrew Nelson Lytle (1902–1995)]

1556 John Knox appeared at the Church of the Blackfriars in Edinburgh to face charges of heresy. The Catholic bishops had hoped to humble him. Instead he turned the tables and scored a stunning triumph. Humiliated, Regent Mary of Guise, the mother of Mary, Queen of Scots, dismissed the summons, and Knox went on to preach to large crowds in Edinburgh. He also wrote her a letter of thanks asking for toleration of all Protestants. She treated it with contempt. Though he was briefly forced into exile one more time, Knox had clearly gained the upper hand. Eventually he brought the Reformation to Scotland and transformed the land.

1567 Composer Claudio Monteverdi was baptized on this day in Cremona, Italy. Monteverdi served as the transitional composer between the music of the Renaissance and the florid music of the Baroque era. He wrote five books of madrigals between 1587 and 1606, and his opera *Orfeo* (produced in 1607) was one of the earliest examples of that new genre. His music is still an active part of the modern repertoire.

1602 Captain Bartholomew Gosnold became the first Englishman to land on the New England coast when he anchored at what is now New Bedford, Massachusetts.

1857 The Royal Opera House in London opened at Covent Garden.

1862 The first enclosed baseball field in America, Union Grounds, opened in Brooklyn, New York.

1886 Poet Emily Dickinson died in Amherst, Massachusetts.

1911 The Supreme Court ordered the dissolution of John D. Rockefeller's Standard Oil Company, ruling it was in violation of the Sherman Antitrust Act.

1930 Ellen Church, the first airline stewardess, went on duty aboard a United Airlines flight between San Francisco and Cheyenne, Wyoming.

1942 Second World War gasoline rationing went into effect in seventeen states, limiting sales to three gallons a week for nonessential vehicles.

1948 Hours after declaring its independence, the new state of Israel was attacked by Jordanian, Egyptian, Syrian, Iraqi, and Lebanese army regulars as well as Palestinian insurgents.

1963 Astronaut L. Gordon Cooper blasted off aboard *Faith* 7 on the final mission of NASA's Project Mercury space program.

1972 George C. Wallace was shot by Arthur Bremer and left paralyzed while campaigning in Laurel, Maryland, for the Democratic presidential nomination.

1988 The Soviet Union began the process of withdrawing its troops from Afghanistan, more than eight years after Soviet forces had entered the country.

MAY

15

Widely known as the "Penman of the Revolution," John Dickinson (1732–1808) wrote many of the most influential documents of the period—from the Declaration of Rights in 1765 and the Articles of Confederation in 1776 to the Fabius Letter in 1787, which helped win over the first states to ratify the Constitution—Delaware and Pennsylvania.

Having studied law in England, Dickinson was devoted to the English common law system, and his writings before 1776 aimed to correct the misuse of power and preserve the union of the colonies and Britain. His most famous works included the eloquent "Letters from a Farmer in Pennsylvania," which condemned the Townshend Acts and were widely read throughout the colonies. He also penned "Petition to the King" which was a statement of grievances and an appeal for justice, with a pledge of loyalty adopted by Congress. But perhaps his greatest manifesto was "Declaration on the Causes and Necessity of Taking Up Arms"—adopted by Congress as its own official statement on the matter, which defended the colonies' use of arms for "the preservation of our liberties," and stated that the colonists were simply fighting to regain the liberty that was theirs as Englishmen.

In the Continental Congress, Dickinson opposed the idea of declaring independence at first, but, once it was done, he supported the cause and prepared a draft of the Articles of Confederation. Although over forty, Dickinson enlisted in the militia and saw action in New Jersey and Pennsylvania. He returned to Congress on this day in 1779, in time to sign the Articles of Confederation.

Because Delaware and Pennsylvania were under a single legal proprietor in those early days of independence, a citizen could hold office in either one, and Dickinson served as president of first Delaware and then Pennsylvania. He played the important role of conciliator at the Constitutional Convention. He saw the need for a stable national government, and so he joined Roger Sherman of Connecticut in supporting the idea of two legislative bodies—one with proportional, one with equal representation. This became known as the Great Compromise, which ultimately broke the deadlock between the large and small states.

After the Constitution was sent to the states, Dickinson published a series of letters that explained and defended the Constitution and helped win the first ratifications. The penman had done his work well: Jefferson called him "one of the great worthies of the Revolution."

FEAST DAY
St. Brendan the Navigator, St. Carantoc, St. Peregrine of Auxerre, St. Simon Stock, St. Domnolus of Le Mans, St. Honoratus of Amiens, St. Germerius, St. John Nepomucen, St. Possidius, St. Ubaldus of Gubbio

MAY

16

The family is the primary building block of our culture. Nay, it is itself our culture.

[HENRY CABOT LODGE (1850–1942)]

587 Irish monk Saint Bredan, known for setting out in the Atlantic with two other monks in a skin boat and possibly traveling as far as North America, died on this day.

1393 King Wenceslaus IV was a wicked and cruel man—hardly fit to bear the name of his forebearer. On this day he became enraged after the church balked over some lands he was trying to illegally confiscate. Wenceslaus ordered John of Nepomuk, the vicar-general of the diocese, and several other churchmen tortured. In his fury he personally assisted in the cruelties, applying a burning torch to John's side. His anger sated, Wenceslaus decided to free the victims but stipulated that they must say nothing of what he'd done to them. John, however, was too far gone to be released. Seeing that John was dying, Wenceslaus determined to get rid of the evidence of his brutal handiwork and trussed John up with a gag so he could not cry out. His heels were tied to his head and he was carried secretly through town and dumped in the river Moldau. But John's body washed ashore the next day. The people immediately recognized the corpse. They buried John in the cathedral of St. Vitus. From that day on, the Bohemians considered him both martyr and saint, honoring him much as Ireland honors Patrick, and paving the way for the reforms of Jan Hus in the next generation.

1763 James Boswell first met Dr. Samuel Johnson on this day. Boswell became a companion to Johnson and wrote the masterful biography of the literary giant, *Life of Samuel Johnson* (1791). Reportedly, their first conversation went as follows: "Boswell: I do indeed come from Scotland, but I cannot help it. Johnson: That, Sir, I find, is what a very great many of your countrymen cannot help."

1770 The Hapsburg princess, Marie Antoinette, age fourteen, married the Burbon Dauphin, the future King Louis XVI of France, who was just fifteen.

1866 Congress authorized minting of the five-cent piece.

MAY

1868 The Senate failed by one vote to convict President Andrew Johnson as it took its first ballot on one of eleven articles of impeachment against him.

1920 Joan of Arc was canonized in Rome.

1929 The first Academy Awards were presented during a banquet at the Hollywood Roosevelt Hotel. *Wings* won Best Picture, Emil Jannings won Best Actor, and Janet Gaynor took home the prize for Best Actress.

1946 The musical *Annie Get Your Gun* opened on Broadway.

1948 The body of CBS News correspondent George Polk was found in Solonica Harbor in Greece, several days after he'd left his hotel for an interview with the leader of a Communist militia.

1977 Five people were killed when a New York Airways helicopter, idling atop the Pan Am Building in midtown Manhattan, toppled over, sending a huge rotor blade flying.

1988 The Supreme Court ruled that police can search discarded garbage without a search warrant.

1991 Queen Elizabeth II became the first British monarch to address the United States Congress.

16

Robert Murray McCheyne was born in Edinburgh on this day in 1813, the youngest child in a family of five. His father was a prosperous lawyer and a man of social importance. Their spacious home, with its gardens, commanded a glorious view across to the shores of Fife. Here in Edinburgh McCheyne spent his childhood and youth. After passing successfully through the high school, he entered the arts faculty of the university in autumn 1827. There he turned his attention to elocution and poetry and the pleasures of society. But he was the subject of his elder brother's fervent prayers, and the early death of this brother in 1831 was a stroke used to awaken Robert from the sleep of nature. He began to be serious and to sit under the evangelical ministry of Thomas Chalmers.

MAY

In the winter of 1831, he entered the Divinity Hall of the university. Under the leadership of men like Chalmers and David Welsh there was a new stir of spiritual life in the college at this time; indeed, it proved to be a new stir in the life of the Church of Scotland. McCheyne was a diligent student, and after the completion of his studies he was licensed by the presbytery of Annan in 1835 and became an assistant to John Bonar in Larbert and Dunipace. His piety and eloquent preaching commended him the next year to his own parish, and so he was ordained minister of St. Peter's, Dundee, in 1836.

It was a new church built in a sadly neglected district containing some four thousand souls. McCheyne poured himself into the work—sleeping only three hours a night and never taking leisure at all. He visited, prayed, and preached as few had ever seen before in all of Scotland—and as a result won the hearts of even the most confirmed doubters in the district. Though he had so quickly achieved a measure of success, he was deeply concerned to deepen his ministry by continual study. Few ministers had ever maintained such an undecaying passion for the advantages of study. Though always conscious that souls were perishing every day, he never fell into the error of thinking that his main pastoral work consisted of outward activity.

By the end of 1838 the course of his ministry was sadly interrupted by serious illness—the effect of unremitting labor. It soon increased, and his doctors insisted on a total cessation of work. Accordingly, McCheyne with deep regret returned to his parents' home in Edinburgh to rest until he could resume his ministry. This separation from his people occasioned some of the richest pastoral letters since the time of the apostle Paul.

Though his condition had hardly improved, he returned to his flock a year later, and revival broke out almost immediately. Aware that his time was short, he threw himself into a hectic schedule. To the very end, he was relentless in his pursuit of holiness and the proclamation of the doctrines of grace. At last, in the spring of 1843—the year of the great Disruption—he succumbed to his lingering illness. His death was the cause of grievous mourning all throughout the nation. It was said that the brief ministry of Robert Murray McCheyne—just seven and a half years—had stamped an indelible impress on Scotland, and though he died in his twenty-ninth year, more was wrought by him that will last for eternity than most accomplish in a lifetime.

Caesars and Satraps attempt to succor our wounds and wants with opulent circuses and eloquent promises. All such dolations are mere pretense, however, in comparison to the genuine Christian care afforded at even the coarsest family hearth.

[METHODIUS (C. 815–885)]

1792 The New York Stock Exchange was first organized on this day by brokers meeting under a tree located on what is now Wall Street.

1814 Norway's constitution was signed, providing for a limited monarchy.

1918 Swedish soprano Birgit Nilsson was born in West Karup. With her renowned, rich voice, she was known as a master of Wagnerian opera, though her roles included those created by Verdi, Puccini, Strauss, Beethoven, and von Weber. In 1969 she was awarded the title of Kammersangerin (court singer) by the Austrian government.

1921 French Horn player Dennis Brain (1921–1957) was born into an English musical family and achieved international success as the incomparable master of his instrument despite the fact that he died at the age of thirty-six.

1938 Congress passed the Vinson Naval Act, providing for a two-ocean navy.

1939 Britain's King George VI and Queen Elizabeth arrived in Quebec on the first visit to Canada by reigning British sovereigns.

1940 Nazi troops occupied Brussels, Belgium, during the Second World War.

1946 President Harry Truman seized control of the nation's railroads, delaying a threatened strike by engineers and trainmen.

1947 The Conservative Baptist Association was formed in Atlantic City, New Jersey, after doctrinal disputes prompted a split within the liberal-leaning American Baptist Association. It was the second time theological liberalism had sundered the denomination—in 1921 the Conservative Baptist Fellowship had been created.

1948 The Soviet Union recognized the new state of Israel.

1954 The Supreme Court issued its landmark *Brown vs. Board of Education of Topeka* ruling, which held that racially segregated public schools were inherently unequal.

1973 The Senate opened its hearings on the Watergate scandal.

1989 More than one million people swarmed into central Beijing to express support for Chinese students calling for democracy. It was apparent that troops in the capital that had witnessed the protests were uninclined to use force against them, so the Communist government began to mobilize forces from the distant provinces for what would prove to be a tragically violent crackdown less than a month later.

MAY

17

It was at the end of his life, when his reputation was well established, his contribution to the life of Scotland, England, and Ireland fully recognized, and his fame spread around the world that the greatest test came to Thomas Chalmers (1780–1847). During the course of his long and storied career the great Scottish Reformer had served as the pastor of three congregations, taught in three colleges, published more than thirty-five best-selling books, and helped to establish more than a hundred charitable relief and missions organizations. He practically reinvented the Scottish parish system as well as the national social welfare structure. He counted such luminaries as the Duke of Wellington, Sir Walter Scott, King William IV, Thomas Carlyle, William Wilberforce, and Robert Peel as his friends and confidants. Indeed, he was among the most influential and highly regarded men of his day. Even so, he did not hesitate to involve himself in—and ultimately lead—a movement that was to set him in apparent disregard of the authority of the highest civil court in the land.

MAY

With the disappearance of Catholic authority in Scotland, Reformers worked hard to replace it with a faithful national church. Their struggle for spiritual independence had been a long and costly one under the leadership of John Knox and Andrew Melville among others. At long last, in 1690, their Reformed Church was legally recognized by the Crown as the established Church of Scotland. The danger of such an establishment was that the state might attempt to manipulate the internal affairs of the church.

That danger was realized when Parliament imposed conformity with the standards of English patronage upon the Scottish church. In reality, patronage was hardly different from the medieval practice of lay investiture—it gave landowners the right to appoint to a parish a minister who might or might not be biblically qualified for the post or acceptable to the elders of the congregation. The patronage conflict came to a head in 1838 when several ministers were forced on congregations opposed to their settlement. Many, including Chalmers, believed that the integrity of the gospel was at stake.

At about the same time, it was decided by Parliament that the church did not have the power to organize new parishes or to give the ministers there the status of clergy of the church. It had no authority to receive again clergy who had left it. And perhaps worst of all, a creeping liberal formalism was slowly smothering the evangelical zeal of the whole land—in large part due to the assumption of pastoral duties by men altogether unfit for such a solemn vocation.

After a ten-year struggle to regain the soul of the church, the evangelical wing, led by Chalmers, laid a protest on the table of the assembly, and some four hundred ministers left the established Church of Scotland on this day in 1843, to form the Free Church. When the new church was constituted that grave morning, Thomas Chalmers was, of course, called to be its moderator. He was the man whose reputation in the Christian world was the highest; he was also the man whose influence had been greatest in directing the events that led to what would eventually be called the "Disruption."

If we look externally there is a difference betwixt the washing of dishes and preaching of the Word of God; but as touching to please God, in relation to His call, none at all.

[WILLIAM TYNDALE (1494–1536)]

MAY

1281 After one hundred years of Christian occupation, Muslim forces besieged the Crusader city of Acre for thirty-three days, ending with the storming of the city and the massacre or enslavement of sixty thousand Christians.

1642 The French-Canadian city of Montreal was founded.

1652 Rhode Island banned slave ownership, the first colony to do so—but its maritime industry remained at the center of the slave trade for another two centuries.

1675 French missionary and explorer Jacques Marquette died near present-day Ludington, Michigan.

1703 Charles Perrault had a long and scholarly life. When he became a father late in life, he put aside his studies and devoted time to the raising of his son, including the writing of fables for his amusement. These stories of "Tom Thumb," "Bluebeard," and "Cinderella" were later collected and published in Paris in 1697 with the title *Tales of Mother Goose*. Perrault died on this day in 1703.

1804 The French Senate proclaimed Napoleon Bonaparte emperor.

1863 Ulysses S. Grant's Union troops surrounded the city of Vicksburg, Mississippi, beginning the siege that eventually put the strategic city into Union hands.

1896 The Supreme Court endorsed the concept of "separate but equal" racial segregation with its *Plessy vs. Ferguson* decision, a ruling that was overturned fifty-eight years later in the case of *Brown vs. Board of Education*.

1897 A public reading of Bram Stoker's new novel, *Dracula, or the Un-Dead*, was staged in London.

1920 Pope John Paul II, the first Polish pope was born Karol Wojtyla in Wadowice, Poland. He would be the first non-Italian pope since 1523, and his travels, firm religious conservatism, and energetic approach ultimately made him an influential and popular world figure.

1926 Evangelist Aimee Semple McPherson vanished while visiting a beach in Venice, California; she reappeared a month later, claiming to have been kidnapped.

1933 The Tennessee Valley Authority was created to bring electrical power to the mid-south.

1951 The United Nations moved from its temporary headquarters in Lake Success, New York, to its permanent home in Manhattan.

1980 The Mount St. Helens volcano erupted, leaving fifty-seven people dead.

MAY

Sir William Walton was born in Oldham, Lancashire, England, in 1902. As the son of two voice teachers, Walton showed an early acumen to music to the point of being able to sing airs of Handel before he could speak. His father gave him early lessons in music, and he was so advanced in his musical understanding and abilities that he became a regular member of his father's choir at the church in Oldham at the age of five. By the age of ten, Walton had won a scholarship to Christ Church and become a chorister at the cathedral in Oxford. It was during his early years at Oxford that he first heard a symphony orchestra stirring within him a desire to compose.

At the age of sixteen, Walton became the youngest student to ever earn his baccalaureate in music from Oxford. Despite his young age, he petitioned and was accepted as an undergraduate at Christ Church in 1918. Walton spent hours in the music library at Oxford and familiarized himself with the masters of contemporary music: Stravinsky, Bartók, Prokovfiev, Strauss, Holst, Schoenberg, and Satie. The deans of English music, Hubert Parry and Ralph Vaughan Williams, both knew and appreciated Walton's early compositions. Walton's monomaniacal focus on all things musical caused him to neglect his other subjects and lead to his expulsion from Oxford in 1920 though he was made an Honorary Fellow of Christ Church years later.

Walton's concert overture for orchestra, *Portsmouth Point*, was first performed in 1926 and solidified his reputation as an important young composer. In 1929, fellow composer Paul Hindemith premiered Walton's *Concerto for Viola and Orchestra* in London as soloist. This work marked Walton's ascension as a serious composer "capable of noble sentiments, eloquent musical expressiveness, and a most serious and sober attitude toward his mission as a composer." In other words, Walton moved from being modern to a true sense of being contemporary. Nowhere is this fact more evident than in his great biblical oratorio *Belshazzar's Feast*.

Interest in Walton and his music surged to the point that the London Symphony Orchestra premiered his first symphony even before he had had a chance to finish the last movement. It received its second premiere in 1935 when it was complete. He was drafted during the Second World War and wrote music for films from the Ministry of Information and War Office as well as for the coronations of both George VI and Elizabeth II. Walton also wrote some of the most effective and skillful music for cinema with his scores to Laurence Olivier's Shakespeare trilogy, *Henry V, Hamlet,* and *Richard III.*

Walton was essentially a self-taught composer and conductor who pursued his vocation with a dedication and passion. Few English composers received as many honors as he: honorary degrees from Oxford and Cambridge, the coveted Gold Medal from the Royal Philharmonic; he was knighted on this day in 1951 and given the Queen's Order of Merit in 1967. He died in 1983 just a day after discussing a new composition project with a friend.

You can choose your friends, but you can have only one mother.

[HILAIRE BELLOC (1870–1953)]

804 The English medieval scholar Alcuin of York died. He was an educator who made beauty, goodness, and truth the hallmarks of Charlemagne's Frankish Empire. From 782 to 790 he transplanted Celtic learning to the Continent. He founded the Carolingian palace library, for which he developed a script of small characters called Carolingian Minuscule, which allowed more letters than ever before to be written on a single expensive page of parchment. Of great beauty, this script was later employed by the earliest printers. His great hunger for learning revived the Augustinian tradition of Christian classical education and helped to lay the foundations of Europe's civilization of Christendom.

1588 The Spanish Armada set sail for England; it was roundly defeated by the English fleet the following August.

1643 Delegates from four New England colonies met in Boston to form a confederation.

1795 James Boswell, friend and biographer of Samuel Johnson, died in London.

1862 The United States Congress passed the Homestead Bill, granting 160-acre plots of land to settlers meeting certain residency requirements.

1906 The Federated Boys Clubs, forerunner of the Boys Clubs of America, were organized.

1921 Congress passed the Emergency Quota Act, which established national quotas for immigrants.

1928 The first annual Frog Jumping Jubilee was held in Calaveras County, California, in commemoration of Mark Twain's story "The Celebrated Jumping Frog of Calavares County." Of the fifty-one frogs entered, the "Pride of San Joaquin" won the contest with a jump of three feet four inches.

MAY

1935 T. E. Lawrence, also known as "Lawrence of Arabia," died in England from injuries he sustained in a motorcycle crash.

1943 In an address to the American Congress, British Prime Minister Winston Churchill pledged his country's full support in the war against Japan.

1958 The United States and Canada formally established the North American Air Defense Command.

1964 The State Department disclosed that forty hidden microphones had been found in the American embassy in Moscow.

1967 The Soviet Union ratified a treaty with the United States and Britain banning nuclear weapons from outer space.

1992 The Twenty-seventh Amendment to the Constitution, which prohibits Congress from giving itself midterm pay raises, went into effect after first being proposed and ratified in 1789.

19

The first Ecumenical Council was convened in the Byzantine city of Nicea on this day in 325 by the recently converted Roman emperor, Constantine. It was a momentous occasion—the first time the church had convened a universal synodical meeting since the time of Peter, James, John, Barnabas, and Paul at Jerusalem to discuss the initial outreach of the largely Jewish church to the Gentiles.

MAY

Three hundred and twelve bishops gathered. In the center of the room, on a throne, lay the four Gospels. The emperor himself, dressed in a purple gown and wearing a silver diadem, opened the council, saying, "I rejoice to see you here, yet I should be more pleased to see unity and affection among you." The next few days would be devoted to achieve that purpose, if at all possible, by finding an agreeable way to describe precisely who Jesus was.

The problem was that a prominent Eastern bishop, Arius, had been preaching that Christ was actually a creation of God—the first of all His creatures, of course, but a creation nonetheless. He was not of the substance or nature of God. "There was a time when the Son was not," he and his followers insisted. They even made up Unitarian songs, slogans, and jingles with catchy tunes to propagandize their ideas among the masses.

Bishop Alexander of Alexandria was horrified. Jesus, the Word, had coexisted eternally with God the Father, he argued. If Christ were not God, then man could not be saved, for only the infinite and holy God could forgive sin. He deposed Arius. Arius did not go quietly. He gathered followers and continued to teach his pernicious doctrine. The factions rioted. The unity of the empire was shaken. Constantine was alarmed. And that was why he called the council in the first place.

As the council progressed, the bishop of Nicomedia defended Arius's views, attempting to prove logically that Jesus, the Son of God, was a created being. Opposition bishops snatched his speech from his hand and flung it in shreds to the floor. They had suffered for Christ, some of them greatly, in the persecutions of Diocletian. They weren't about to stand by and hear their Lord blasphemed. Otherwise, to what purpose had they borne their gouged eyes, scourged backs, hamstrung legs and scorched hands?

The issues of Nicea boiled down to this: If Christ is not God, how can He overcome the infinite gap between God and man? If a created being could do it, there were angels aplenty with the power. Indeed, why could not any good man himself bridge the gap? On the other hand, Jesus had to be truly man, otherwise how could He represent mankind?

The orthodox bishops ultimately prevailed. Arius was condemned. At that point the council decided to write a creed that clarified the Bible's teaching on the nature of Christ's person and incarnation. The Nicene Creed became a document of fundamental importance to the church and gave clarity to the issues of orthodoxy and heterodoxy.

Be slow in choosing a friend, slower in changing.

[BENJAMIN FRANKLIN (1706–1790)]

1506 Christopher Columbus died in poverty in Castile, having just completed his book of biblical commentary, *The Prophecies*.

1536 English King Henry VIII married his third wife, Jane Seymour, the day after his second wife, Anne Boleyn, was beheaded in the Tower of London. Henry had sentenced Anne to death for treason and adultery after she gave birth to a stillborn son.

1777 The Cherokee Indians relinquished all their territory in South Carolina by signing the Treaty of DeWitts Corner.

1799 French author Honoré de Balzac was born in Tours, France.

1861 North Carolina voted to secede from the Union.

1861 The capital of the Confederacy was moved from Montgomery, Alabama, to Richmond, Virginia.

1873 A patent for riveted-pocket denim pants was granted to Jacob Davis and Levi Strauss.

1902 The United States ended its occupation of Cuba that had begun following the Spanish-American War.

1927 Charles Augustus Lindbergh left Roosevelt Field, New York, at 7:52 A.M. in the *Spirit of St. Louis* and landed at Paris 33 hours, 32 minutes later, completing the first transatlantic solo flight and winning $25,000 in prize money.

1932 Amelia Earhart Putnam became the first woman to fly solo over the Atlantic. She left Harbor Grace, Newfoundland, at 5:50 P.M., and arrived at Londonderry, Ireland, 14 hours, 56 minutes later.

1939 Regular transatlantic air service began as a Pan American Airways plane, the *Yankee Clipper*, took off from Port Washington, New York, bound for Europe.

1961 A white mob attacked a busload of civil rights "Freedom Riders" in Montgomery, Alabama, prompting the federal government to send in U.S. marshals to restore order.

1969 American and South Vietnamese forces captured Apbia Mountain, referred to as "Hamburger Hill" by the Americans, following one of the bloodiest battles of the Vietnam War.

1970 Some 100,000 people demonstrated in New York's Wall Street district in support of American policy in Vietnam and Cambodia.

1989 Communist officials in Beijing ordered CBS and CNN to end their live on-scene reports of China's pro-democracy protests.

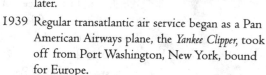

For generations, most Americans believed that no Europeans came to the New World until the time of Columbus—who, as every schoolchild knows, sailed the ocean blue in 1492. But this is far from certain. We now know that Vikings and Celts made their way to the shores of the Americas long before Columbus—and there is a good possibility that various Gaels, Chinese, Phoenician, Jewish, and African expeditions may have also accomplished the feat. Some of the evidence for this is quite startling.

In Wyoming County of West Virginia, there is an inscription carved into a mountain using an ancient language called Ogam. The inscription reads, "At the time of sunrise a ray grazes the notch on the left side on Christmas Day, a Feast-day of the Church, the first season of the Christian year, the season of the blessed Advent of the Savior, Lord Christ—Salvatoris Domini Christi. Behold, He is born of Mary, a woman."

Indeed, researchers have found that every December 25, the day of the Winter Solstice, a shaft of light penetrates a notch in the rock face and a picture of a sunburst next to this inscription is illuminated, just as it describes. Astoundingly, Dr. Robert Meyer, professor of Celtic studies at Catholic University, has determined that the inscription dates from early in the sixth century and was probably placed there by Irish monks. That Irish monks might have been in the hills of West Virginia only five centuries after the resurrection of Jesus, probably evangelizing Indians, is certainly a challenge to the standard textbook history of the coming of Europeans to the New World.

A stone found at Bat Creek in Tennessee contains a Hebrew inscription with the words "A comet for the Jews." This was a standard phrase indicating the Bar-Kochbar revolt of the second century, which was associated with a prophecy regarding a comet. Scholars date the stone between the third and seventh centuries and again wonder if Irish monks might have ventured as far as east Tennessee.

Similarly, on this day in 1818 a coin was found near the Elk River where the town of Fayetteville, Tennessee, now stands. The coin was engraved with the words "Antonius Augustus Pius, Princeps Pontifex Tertio Consule" on one side, and "Aurelius Caesar" on the other. Scholars believe the coin was issued sometime in the middle of the second century from Roman-occupied Wales. It is possible that some later explorers dropped the coin at Elk River—but it is more likely that the world of antiquity has far more mysteries yet to be unraveled than we may be prepared to admit.

FEAST DAY
St. Godric, St. Collen, St. Andrew Bobola, St. Theophilus of Corte

We must diligently strive to make our young men decent, God-fearing, law-abiding, honor-loving, justice-doing, and also fearless and strong, able to hold their own in the hurly-burly of the world's work, able to strive mightily that the forces of right may be in the end triumphant. And we must be ever vigilant in so telling them.

[THEODORE ROOSEVELT (1858–1919)]

1382 Stow's *Chronicles* recorded an earthquake in England: "There was a great earthquake in England, at nine of the clock, fearing the hearts of many; but in Kent it was most vehement, where it sunk some churches and threw them down to the earth."

1471 Albrecht Dürer, the most famous artist of Reformation Germany, was born in Nürnberg. Renowned as a painter, engraver (possibly the inventor of etching), and author of theoretical writings, he had a profound impact on other artists. His interest in understanding geometry and mathematical proportions and his ability to observe nature contributed to the quality of his work.

1632 Otto Blumhardt was one of the earliest Lutheran missionaries to Africa. Setting out alone in the first decade of the seventeenth century at a time when most of that great continent still remained unexplored and uncharted, he took the message of Christ and His glorious grace to several primitive jungle tribes—learning their languages, caring for their sick, and training their young. When he encountered gruesome child-killing rites in several of the tribes he was not startled in the least—witnessing abortion and exposure during his childhood in the slums of Hildesheim had prepared him for the depths of depravity in fallen man. That is not to say that he accepted it, of course. On the contrary, for the rest of his life, he devoted himself to the fight for human life. By the time of his death on this day in 1632, he was known by the natives of the region as the "Father of the Jungle" because so many of them literally owed their lives—their very existence—to his faithfulness.

1738 On this Pentecost Sunday, Charles Wesley was converted. Charles woke up, hoping that this would be the day. He would later pen such classic hymns as "And Can It Be?"; "Arise, My Soul, Arise"; and "Hark! The Herald Angels Sing." A year after his conversion, he commemorated the event by writing what is possibly his best-known hymn, "O for a Thousand Tongues to Sing."

1832 The first Democratic National Convention got under way in Baltimore. Delegates overwhelmingly approved the nomination of Andrew Jackson and his controversial choice for vice president, Martin van Buren.

1840 New Zealand was declared a British colony.

1881 Clara Barton organized the American Red Cross in Washington, D.C., and served as its first president.

1892 Ruggiero Leoncavallo's two-act operatic masterpiece, *Pagliacci*, was first performed at the Teatro dal Vèrme in Milan. This play within a play is most famous for its aria *Vesti la Giubba* (On with the Play), which ends with the line "Laugh for the pain that now is breaking your heart" and the clown characters which have become synonymous with the image of operatic tenors (especially Enrico Caruso).

1927 Charles A. Lindbergh landed his *Spirit of St. Louis* near Paris, completing the first solo airplane flight across the Atlantic Ocean.

1956 The United States exploded the first airborne hydrogen bomb over Bikini Atoll in the Pacific.

1989 Thousands of native Chinese marched in Hong Kong, Paris, Tokyo, and scores of other cities in a worldwide show of support for the pro-democracy demonstrators in Beijing.

The only man ever to serve two nonconsecutive terms as president, Grover Cleveland (1837–1908) performed the greatest comeback in American politics—he succeeded his successor.

With a limited formal education, Cleveland managed to study law and establish himself as a scrupulously honest officeholder in Buffalo and western New York State. By 1882 his reputation as a dedicated and effective administrator won him the governorship of New York, a post in which he gained further renown by fighting the New York City Democratic machine in cooperation with a young Republican assemblyman, Theodore Roosevelt. "We love him for the enemies he has made," said the delegate nominating Cleveland for the presidency at the 1884 Democratic convention, for "Grover the Crusader" had not hesitated to stamp out corruption, even in his own party.

To many of both parties he was the incarnation of clean, honest government. After the corruption, oppression, injustice, and outright tyranny of the Reconstruction era, it was time for a change: "Grover the Good" was elected in 1884, the first Democratic president in twenty-four years. In office Cleveland was a doer—and as a result, he made plenty of enemies as doers are wont to do in Washington. He made civil service reform a reality by courageously placing a number of political jobs under the protection of civil service, and he stood firmly against a high protective tariff, moves that contributed to his defeat in 1888.

While out of office Cleveland assumed the role of party spokesman and became an active critic of the new administration of Benjamin Harrison. In 1892 he soundly defeated the man who had replaced him in the White House. But he returned to power in grim times. With a depression cutting deep into the nation's economy, strong measures were called for—and in forcing the repeal of silver legislation and halting a Pullman labor strike, Cleveland demonstrated a firm hand. Nevertheless, rioting broke out on this day in Chicago and several other cities, as panic spread across the nation. Cleveland, however, did not yield to the pressures of the tyranny of the moment and slowly was able to steer the nation's affairs toward stability.

Throughout a difficult term he remained an honest, independent leader, a man who left office with the hard-won respect of members of both parties.

MAY

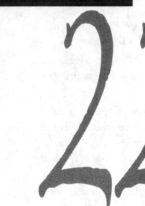

One man with courage makes a majority.

[Andrew Jackson (1767–1845)]

1455 The War of the Roses began with the first Battle of St. Albans in which Henry VI was taken prisoner by the Yorkists. It was called the War of the Roses because the red rose was the emblem of the Lancastrians and the white rose that of the Yorkists.

1761 The first life insurance policy in the United States was issued, in Philadelphia.

1813 German composer Richard Wagner was born in Leipzig to a nonmusical family. His incredible egotism and vanity propelled him to the forefront of innovations with regard to opera, music, composition, drama, and the grand presentation of the combination of all these elements.

1819 The first steam-propelled vessel to attempt a transatlantic crossing, the *Savannah*, departed from Savannah, Georgia. It arrived in Liverpool, England, on June 20.

1836 Felix Mendelssohn's oratorio *St. Paul* (Paulus) was first performed in Dusseldorf at the Lower Rhine Festival to great enthusiasm.

1859 Sir Arthur Conan Doyle, creator of detective Sherlock Holmes, was born in Edinburgh, Scotland. Holmes's character, who first appeared in *A Study in Scarlet* (1887), is partly derived from one of Doyle's professors at the University of Edinburgh, who was noted for his deductive logic. When, in 1893, Doyle tired of writing about Sherlock Holmes, he killed him off—only to have an angry public force him to bring Holmes back to life.

1868 The "Great Train Robbery" took place near Marshfield, Indiana, as seven members of the Reno gang made off with $96,000 in loot.

1877 The German Academy announced on this day that the second part of the Old Testament translation by Martin Luther in his own handwriting had recently been discovered in the Ducal Archives at Zerbst (Anhalt). The text from Joshua to Esther was comprised of 216 quarto pages and dated from 1523.

1907 Laurence Olivier, Baron Olivier of Brighton, was born in Dorking, Surrey, England. The actor, director, and producer was known for his brilliant portrayals of Shakespearean roles on stage and for his American films *Wuthering Heights* (1939), *Rebecca* (1939), and *Pride and Prejudice* (1940). In 1947 he was knighted for his service to the theater and was made a life peer in 1970.

1939 Adolf Hitler and Benito Mussolini signed a "Pact of Steel," committing Germany and Italy to a military alliance.

1950 The exquisite and hauntingly beautiful *Four Last Songs (Vier letzte Lieder)* for soprano and orchestra by Richard Strauss were premiered in London more than a year after the composer's death.

1969 The lunar module of *Apollo 10* flew to within nine miles of the moon's surface in a dress rehearsal for the first lunar landing.

1972 President Richard Nixon became the first United States president to visit the Soviet Union when he arrived in Moscow on this day.

1972 The island nation of Ceylon became the republic of Sri Lanka.

1989 More than one hundred top Chinese military leaders vowed to refrain from entering Beijing to suppress pro-democracy demonstrations.

1990 Pro-Western North Yemen and pro-Soviet South Yemen merged to form a single nation, the Republic of Yemen.

1992 After a reign of nearly thirty years, Johnny Carson hosted NBC's *Tonight Show* for the last time. In a controversial move, the network bypassed David Letterman to take his place, choosing Jay Leno instead.

MAY

22

FEAST DAY
Saints Montanus and Lucius, St. William of Rochester, St. Aldhelm, St. Euphrosyne of Polotsk, St. Ivo of Chartres, St. Leontius of Rostov, St. Desiderius of Vienne, St. John the Baptist dei Rossi

MAY

23

In 1540 when Hernando de Soto began exploring North America, searching for "gold-bearing mountains," his reputation preceded him. Though many of the earliest Spanish explorers were pious men intent on the conversion of the tribes they encountered in the Americas, de Soto was apparently not among their number. Already his troops had brutalized the men, women, and children they had encountered—torturing those who resisted their authority and stealing whatever valuables they found. "Intent upon capturing Indian slaves," they "brought along iron neck collars attached to chains and by cruelties inflicted upon the natives spread hatred and terror as the expedition advanced." The commander's own secretary, Rangel, "whose priestly soul deplored de Soto's lack of effort to convert the heathen," was grieved as well by the utter farce the venture became: "I have often wondered at the venturesomeness, stubbornness, and persistency of firmness, to use a better word, for the way these baffled conquerors kept on from one toil to another, from one danger to many others; here losing a companion, there three, again still more; going from bad to worse without learning from experience. Wonderful God that they should have been so blinded and dazed by a greed so uncertain, and by vain discourse which Hernando de Soto was able to utter to these deluded soldiers. He thought that his experience in the south—in Peru—was sufficient to show him what to do in the north, and he was deceived, as history will tell."

De Soto made his way inland to a Cherokee encampment near present-day Chattanooga, Tennessee, where he camped for a while and then trekked across the northern portions of Alabama and Mississippi, reentering Tennessee near another encampment called Quizquiz. There he had the unfortunate experience of battling the fierce Chickasaw, who almost defeated him. De Soto died on this day in 1542, still searching for gold. His men buried him in the great Mississippi he had discovered. As Rangel movingly recorded, "So, onward to his grave in the great river which he was to discover, marched the conquistador, Hernando de Soto, until on the banks of the father of waters, finding all things against him, he sickened and died."

1785

Benjamin Franklin, annoyed at having to carry two pairs of glasses, had both sets of lenses split and joined together to create the first pair of bifocals. He wrote from France to George Whatley, "I have only to move my eyes up and down as I want to see distinctly far or near." Due to the exorbitant price of having bifocals created, however, they did not become immediately popular.

The only thing we have to fear is fear itself.

[Franklin Delano Roosevelt (1882–1945)]

1430 Joan of Arc was captured by the Burgundians, who sold her to the English.

1498 The humble friar Savonarola, who had overturned the cruel tyranny of Medici Florence and ushered in a short season of reformation, was arrested, tortured repeatedly, and then executed. He was resolute to the end. After he had been hanged and burned, scoffers shouted, "If you can work miracles, work one now!" Immediately, his hand flew up, two fingers extended, as if blessing the crowd. The crowd panicked and fled the square, crushing several children to death.

1533 The marriage of England's King Henry VIII to Catherine of Aragon was declared null and void.

1618 The Thirty Years' War, which wasted Central Europe from 1618 to 1648, erupted when the famous Defenestration of Prague occurred. "Defenestration" is from the Latin *de* meaning "out of" and *fenestra*, meaning "window." Apparently in a dispute between Protestant and Catholic negotiators, two of the emperor's regents were hurled out of a window. Though the men were not killed, offense had been taken and war erupted.

1701 The notorious Scottish pirate Captain William Kidd was hanged on the bank of the Thames River in London. The British privateer had sailed for his country against the French in the West Indies, and was for a time a ship's captain in New York City, eventually turning to piracy as a more lucrative career. His name has become synonymous with the romantic, swashbuckling pirate of Western literature.

1788 South Carolina became the eighth state to ratify the United States Constitution.

MAY

1873 Canada's Northwest Mounted Police force was established. Their motto was, "We always get our man."

1895 By combining the collections of the Astor and Lenox libraries, the New York Public library was established.

1911 The New York Public Library, with its characteristic stone lions, was dedicated.

1915 Italy declared war on Austria-Hungary in the First World War.

1934 Bank robbers Bonnie Parker and Clyde Barrow were shot to death in a police ambush as they were driving a stolen Ford Deluxe along a road in Bienville Parish, Louisiana.

1937 Industrialist John D. Rockefeller died in Ormond Beach, Florida.

1945 Nazi official Heinrich Himmler committed suicide while imprisoned in Luneburg, Germany.

1960 Israel announced it had captured former Nazi official Adolf Eichmann in Argentina.

1997 The United States Post Office issued a postage stamp featuring cartoon legend Bugs Bunny.

307

The third president of the fledgling United States under the previous constitution was a patriot, rebel leader, and merchant who signed his name into immortality in giant strokes on the Declaration of Independence on July 4, 1776. The boldness of his signature has made the memory and example of John Hancock (1737–1793) live in American minds as a perfect expression of the strength and freedom—and defiance—of the individual in the face of British tyranny.

As president of the Continental Congress during two widely spaced terms—the first from May 24, 1775, to October 30, 1777, and the second from November 23, 1885, to June 5, 1786—Hancock was the presiding officer when the members approved the Declaration of Independence. Because of his position, it was his official duty to sign the document first—but not necessarily as dramatically as he did.

Hancock figured prominently in another historic event—the Battle at Lexington: British troops who fought there April 10, 1775, had known Hancock and Samuel Adams were in Lexington and had come there to capture these rebel leaders. And the two would have been captured, if they had not been warned by Paul Revere. As early as 1768, Hancock defied the British by refusing to pay customs charges on the cargo of one of his ships.

One of Boston's wealthiest merchants, he was recognized by the citizens, as well as by the British, as a rebel leader—and was elected president of the first Massachusetts Provincial Congress. After he was chosen president of the Continental Congress in 1775, Hancock became known beyond the borders of Massachusetts and, having served as colonel of the Massachusetts Governor's Guards, he hoped to be named commander of the American forces—until John Adams nominated George Washington. In 1778 Hancock was commissioned major general and took part in an unsuccessful campaign in Rhode Island.

But it was as a political leader that his real distinction was earned—as the first governor of Massachusetts, as president of Congress, and as president of the Massachusetts constitutional ratification convention. He helped win ratification in Massachusetts, gaining enough popular recognition to make him a contender for the newly created presidency of the United States, but again he saw Washington gain the prize. Like his rival, George Washington, Hancock was a wealthy man who risked much for the cause of independence. He was the wealthiest New Englander supporting the patriotic cause and, although he lacked the brilliance of John Adams or the capacity to inspire of Samuel Adams, he became one of the foremost leaders of the new nation—perhaps in part because he was willing to commit so much at such risk to the cause of freedom.

FEAST DAY
St. David of Scotland, St. Vincent of Lerins, Saints Donatian and Rogation, St. Nicetas of Pereaslav

MAY

Tell a man he is brave, and you help him to become so.

[THOMAS CARLYLE (1795–1881)]

1485 Posing as King Edward VI of England, Albert Simnel was crowned in Dublin. King Henry VI, who had had the real Edward put to death, pardoned Simnel and made him his royal falconer.

1543 The founder of modern astronomy, Nicolaus Copernicus, died just after the printing of his book describing the revolution of the celestial orbs. He had delayed the publishing of this book for some time for fear of official reaction. He was the first to determine that we live in a heliocentric solar system, with planets, including Earth, orbiting the sun.

1738 John Wesley was converted at a meeting in Aldersgate, London. A passage from Luther's *Preface to the Epistle to Romans* was read aloud. Wesley later recounted, "While he was describing the change which God works in the heart through faith in Christ, I felt my heart strangely warmed. I felt I did trust in Christ, Christ alone for salvation; and an assurance was given me that He had taken away my sins, even mine, and saved me from the law of sin and death." Wesley went on to be mightily used of the Lord to reform England. His Methodists became a national force. John rode thousands of miles—often as many as twenty thousand a year—preaching as only a man filled with the Holy Spirit can preach, proclaiming the gospel to all who would listen. He acted, he said, "as though he were out of breath in pursuit of souls." It is widely agreed that his preaching helped spare England the kind of revolution that occurred in France.

1819 Queen Victoria was born in London.

1830 The first passenger railroad in the United States began service between Baltimore and Elliott's Mills, Maryland.

1844 Samuel F. B. Morse sent his first telegraph message from Washington, D.C., to Baltimore, Maryland. His message simply said, "What hath God wrought!"

1869 John Wesley Powell launched the first exploration of the Grand Canyon.

1883 The Brooklyn Bridge, designed by John A. Roebling, opened on this day, connecting New York City to Brooklyn over the East River. At a total length of 5,989 feet, it was the largest suspension bridge in the world.

MAY

1915 Several years before the establishment of the FBI, Thomas Edison announced his invention of the telescribe, designed to record telephone conversations.

1935 The Cincinnati Reds defeated the Philadelphia Phillies during the first major-league baseball game played at night. From Washington, D.C., President Franklin D. Roosevelt pressed a button that illuminated the 363 lights at Crosley Field in Cincinnati.

1941 The German battleship *Bismarck* sank the British dreadnought HMS *Hood* in the North Atlantic.

1958 United Press International was formed through a merger of the United Press and the International News Service.

1962 Astronaut Scott Carpenter became the second American to orbit the earth as he flew aboard the Mercury capsule *Aurora 7*.

24

MAY

On this day in 1787 a constitutional convention convened in Philadelphia with representatives from seven states. Though the meeting was not authorized by Congress, they were among the most eminent men in the young American republic—and several were actually members of Congress. Their purpose was to draft amendments to the Articles of Confederation. Under other circumstances, the meeting might have been considered a coup d'état.

Eventually the conferees determined that in order to achieve their ends they would have to create an entirely new document. After several compromise plans had been proposed by the larger and the smaller states, on September 17, 1787, twelve state delegations had contributed to an acceptable draft of the new document.

Requiring the ratification of only nine states to take effect, the document met stiff opposition. Anti-Federalists charged that the document afforded too much power to the central government and predicted that if the document were actually ratified, a gargantuan bureaucracy, high taxes, and invasive intrusions into personal freedoms would result. It was only after supporters of the document amended the document ten times—in a series of postscripts known as the Bill of Rights—that the new constitution was made official on June 21, 1788. But it would be May 29, 1790, before all of the thirteen original states would actually ratify.

The soaring rhetoric of the opening words offered a glimpse of the document's essential genius: "We the people of the United States, in order to form a more perfect union, establish justice, insure domestic tranquillity, provide for the common defense, promote the general welfare, and secure the blessings of liberty to ourselves and our posterity, do ordain and establish this Constitution for the United States of America."

Though it was a document greatly influenced by such Christian ideas as checks and balances, separation of powers, and magistratal interpositionalism, its closing words offered the only explicit nod to Christianity: "Done in convention by the unanimous consent of the states present the seventeenth day of September in the year of Our Lord one thousand seven hundred and eighty-seven and of the Independence of the United States of America the twelfth. In witness whereof we have hereunto subscribed our names."

In the years since, despite the fact that the fears of the anti-Federalists have been realized to some extent, the much-emulated, often-copied Constitution has proven to be one of the most remarkable engines of freedom that the world has ever known.

SCOTLAND FLITTING DAY

On this day most property leases expired in Scotland. Tenants were forced to decide whether they would sit—stay in the house for another year—or "flit" to a new abode. As Scots generally liked to move about, many households were transported on this day.

*Courage is what it takes to stand up and speak;
courage is also what it takes to sit down and listen.*

[WINSTON CHURCHILL (1874–1965)]

735 Celtic historian and theologian the Venerable Bede, author of *The Ecclesiastical History of the English People (Historia Ecclesiastica Gentis Anglorum)*, died on this day. He was the first British author to utilize the modern dating system of anno Domini.

1570 John Eudes was born in Normandy at a time when anticlerical and anti-Christian sentiment there was at a fever pitch. Because his parents remained pious, he tasted the bitter draught of discrimination early in life. Not surprisingly, as an adult he dedicated himself to the care of the persecuted—refugees, the feeble-minded, Jews, the sick, Huguenots, and mendicants. He even organized teams of Christian women to care for women reclaimed from prostitution. His fearless and selfless care of the dying distinguished him during two virulent epidemics that swept through France in 1634 and 1639. But it was for his piety before the Lord and his devotion to the church that he was best known. He was unswerving in his commitment to utilize every moment he had breath to serve his sovereign Lord.

1787 When enough delegates to reach a quorum arrived in Philadelphia, George Washington opened and presided over the Constitutional Convention.

1803 Essayist and poet Ralph Waldo Emerson was born in Boston, Massachusetts.

1810 Argentina launched a war for independence against Spain.

1844 The first telegraphed news dispatch, sent from Washington, D.C., to Baltimore, appeared in the *Baltimore Patriot*.

1895 Playwright Oscar Wilde was convicted of a morals charge in London. He was sentenced to prison.

1935 Jesse Owens, the African-American athlete, set six world records in track and field in less than one hour at Ann Arbor, Michigan.

1935 Babe Ruth hit the 714th and final home run of his career, for the Boston Braves in a game against the Pittsburgh Pirates.

1946 Transjordan—now known simply as Jordan—gained independence from Britain and became a kingdom as it proclaimed its new monarch, King Abdullah Ibn Ul-Hussein. Two of his brothers also became kings in Iraq and Hejaz—now a part of Saudi Arabia.

1961 President Kennedy asked the nation to work toward putting a man on the moon by the end of the decade.

1963 The Organization of African Unity was founded in Addis Ababa, Ethiopia.

1968 In St. Louis, Missouri, the famed Gateway Arch was dedicated as part of the Jefferson National Expansion Memorial.

1977 Director George Lucas's film phenomenon *Star Wars* opened in theaters around the world. Two of the movie's sequels were also released on this day: *The Empire Strikes Back* in 1980, and *The Return of the Jedi* in 1983.

1992 Jay Leno made his debut as full-time host of NBC's *Tonight Show*, succeeding Johnny Carson.

MAY

25

Few men who have reached the presidency have been less prepared for that high office than was Andrew Johnson (1808–1875). It is reported that he never spent a single day in a schoolroom. Bound as apprentice to a tailor when only a boy of ten, Johnson spent his youth working long hours in the shop. Only after he had established himself as a tailor in the mountain town of Greenville, Tennessee, and married did he—with the help of his wife—make progress with his education.

But determined as he was, he never achieved the polish of the formally educated. Unfortunately, he also lacked the complex human qualities of his immediate predecessor, Abraham Lincoln. But this rough-hewn politician who was plagued with political handicaps of background and personality left his mark on history, for through all his faults and failings shone the kind of integrity and courage that command universal respect.

Never in sympathy with the Southern aristocracy, Johnson alone of the twenty-two Southern senators refused to leave his senate seat in 1861 when his state seceded from the Union. Firm in his resolve, he served the Union as military governor of Tennessee until he was elected vice president in 1864. And after Lincoln's death, the presidency provided him further occasions for courageous action.

Fighting the radical Republicans who wanted to grind the war-torn South under the Northern boot, Johnson fearlessly brought the wrath of the Republican Congress on his own head and narrowly missed impeachment—only one of two presidents ever to be involved in impeachment proceedings. But he survived that ordeal and was acquitted on this day in 1868.

Six years after leaving office, he had the pleasure of being elected once again to the Senate, where he had the opportunity to fight against the crushing tyranny of Reconstruction policies put into effect after his tenure in the White House. To the end, he remained a man of principle—which inevitably made him an outcast in Washington.

FEAST DAY

St. Priscus, St. Augustine of Canterbury, St. Philip Neri, St. Lambert of Venice, St. Quadratus of Athens, St. Mariana of Quito

MAY

1865 — The American War Between the States officially ended when Confederate General Edmund Kirby Smith surrendered to Union General E. R. S. Canby in New Orleans. More than 600,000 people died during the war and $5 billion worth of property was destroyed.

1868 — The impeachment trial of President Andrew Johnson ended when the Senate found it was one vote short of the two-thirds majority required for conviction.

It is impossible for any culture to be sound and healthy without a proper respect and proper regard for the soil.

[Andrew Nelson Lytle (1902–1995)]

1521 Martin Luther and all of his writings were placed under a ban by the Edict of Worms because of his views regarding the reform of the Catholic Church.

1564 Philip Neri began a series of lectures on spiritual disciplines at the church of Giovanni dei Fiorentini. Often the talks and Bible readings were accompanied by musical pieces composed by his follower Palestrina. Thus was born the form of Catholic service known as the oratorio. The Congregation of the Oratory was approved by Pope Gregory XIII in 1575 for prayer and preaching. About fifty such congregations exist today. Next to Loyola, Neri became the greatest of the Roman Catholic Counter-Reformation figures.

1568 Queen Elizabeth sponsored an Eisteddfod competition for Welsh bards and minstrels at Cayroes, in Flintshire. Simon ap Williams ao Sion won the grand prize of a silver harp.

1702 Samuel Pepys, known for his revealing diary that documented Restoration England and the events such as the Great Fire of London, died in London. He was a graduate of Magdalene College, Cambridge, and he left his papers to their library.

1805 Napoleon Bonaparte was crowned king of Italy.

1886 Asa Yoelson—otherwise known as Al Jolson—was born in Srednike, Russia. He was brought to the United States at the age of seven, and as a teenager performed with his brother in vaudeville. He quickly gained popularity in New York, and in the show *Sinbad* (1918), he took Gershwin's heretofore unsuccessful song "Swanee" as his trademark. Some of his biggest hits included the songs "Toot, Toot, Tootsie," "California, Here I Come," and "April Showers." In 1927 he starred in the first "talkie" film, *The Jazz Singer.*

1896 The *Wall Street Journal* first published the Dow-Jones industrial average.

1899 At the age of twenty-seven, Mary Reed left her family home in Ohio for a life of missionary endeavors on the subcontinent of Asia. Just three years later, after an exhausting tour of ministry among poor low-caste Hindus, she was diagnosed as having leprosy. Clinging to the promises of Scripture concerning the good providence of God, she resolved to redouble her efforts on behalf of the "untouchables." For several years she directed a concerted campaign against immolation and sarti from a quarantined sickbed. Later, after it became apparent that her disease had gone into complete remission, she launched a dramatic crusade against abortion and abandonment that involved the development of an "underground railroad," a network of sheltering homes, and mobile medical teams providing prenatal and gynecological care to the needy. When she died on this day in 1899, she left behind a legacy of care that gradually became codified into law throughout the vast Maharashtra province west of Bombay in southern India.

MAY

1940 The evacuation of Allied troops from Dunkirk, France, during the Second World War began.

1960 United Nations Ambassador Henry Cabot Lodge accused the Soviets of hiding a microphone inside a wood carving of the Great Seal of the United States that had been presented to the U.S. embassy in Moscow.

1978 The first legal casino in the eastern United States opened in Atlantic City, New Jersey.

1994 President Bill Clinton renewed trade privileges for China and announced that his administration would no longer link China's trade status with its human rights record.

26

George Alfred Henty's life (1832–1902) was filled with exciting adventure. Completing Westminster School, he attended Cambridge University. Along with a rigorous course of study, Henty participated in boxing, wrestling, and rowing. The strenuous study and healthy, competitive participation in sports prepared Henty to be with the British army in Crimea as a war correspondent, witnessing Garbaldi fight in Italy, being present in Paris during the Franco-Prussian war, in Spain with the Carlists, at the opening of the Suez Canal, touring India with the Prince of Wales—who later became King Edward VII—and a trip to the California gold fields.

He lived during the reign of Queen Victoria (1837–1901) and began his storytelling career with his own children. After dinner, he would spend an hour or two in telling them a story that would continue the next day. Some stories took weeks! A friend was present one day and after seeing the spellbound reaction of his children suggested that he write down his stories so others could enjoy them. He did just that.

On this day in 1877 his first volume was published. Over the next twenty-four years Henty wrote approximately 144 books plus innumerable stories for magazines and was dubbed the "Prince of Story-Tellers" and the "Boy's Own Historian." Henty would quickly pace back and forth in his study, dictating stories to a secretary as fast as the secretary could record them.

Each of Henty's stories revolved around a fictional boy hero during fascinating periods of history. His heroes were diligent, courageous, intelligent, and dedicated to their country and cause in the face, at times, of great peril. His histories, particularly battle accounts, were recognized by historian scholars for their accuracy. In fact, the only criticism Henty faced by the liberals of his day was that his heroes were "too Christian." There was nothing dry in Henty's stories and thus he removed the drudgery and laborious task often associated with the study of history.

His fiercely accurate narratives range across the whole spectrum of human achievement, highlighting the greatest characters and the most decisive moments in history. Other writers have succeeded admirably in capturing a single culture or area, but Henty was equally adept at telling the story of the Crimean War or the Peloponnesian War, of the Franco-Prussian conflict or the Norman conquest, of the adventures of the conquistadors or the trials of the pharaohs. Henty's heroes fought wars, sailed the seas, discovered land, conquered evil empires, prospected for gold, and a host of other exciting adventures. They met famous personages such as Josephus, Titus, Hannibal, Robert the Bruce, Sir William Wallace, Sir Francis Drake, Moses, Robert E. Lee, Frederick the Great, the Duke of Wellington, Huguenot leader Coligny, Cortez, King Alfred, and Napoleon—among many others. Henty's heroes lived through tumultuous historic eras, meeting the leaders of that time. Apparently, Henty's virtuosity knew no bounds.

FEAST DAY
St. Julius the Veteran, St. Eutropius of Orange, St. Restituta of Sora, St. Melangel

MAY

Brethren, standfast.

[PAUL OF TARSUS (C. 10–65)]

1096 Archbishop Ruthard of Mainz, in an attempt to protect the Jews of his city from persecution and massacre at the hands of Godfrey of Bouillon's crusaders, hid 1,300 men, women, and children in the Mainz cathedral.

1564 The French Reformer who helped to transform the city of Geneva into one of the most free and prosperous places the world had ever seen, John Calvin, died.

1818 Women's rights campaigner Amelia Jenks Bloomer, who popularized the garment that bears her name—bloomers—was born in Homer, New York.

1871 French painter Georges Rouault was born in Paris. He was associated with both the fauves and the expressionists. He was apprenticed to a stained-glass artisan, and his original works are characterized by thick reds, blues, and greens separated by heavy black outlining reminiscent of stained glass. Often considered the greatest modern religious painter, Rouault's subject matter included the passion of Christ, sorrowful kings, clowns, corrupt judges, and prostitutes, which he used to convey the gospel.

1919 Charles Strite of Minnesota was awarded a patent for the first pop-up toaster.

1933 Walt Disney's Academy Award–winning animated short *The Three Little Pigs* debuted in Hollywood.

1935 The Supreme Court struck down the National Industrial Recovery Act, a key component of Franklin Roosevelt's New Deal.

1936 The Cunard ocean liner *Queen Mary* left England on its maiden voyage.

1937 The Golden Gate Bridge in San Francisco was opened to pedestrian traffic. The majority of engineers of the day said that such a bridge could not be built. However, bridge designer Joseph B. Strauss submitted preliminary plans and estimated that the cost would be $27 million, far less than other engineers' $100 million projection. Strauss was chosen as chief engineer, and he received a War Department permit for a 4,200-foot main span with a vertical midspan clearance of 220 feet. The world-renowned bridge is one of the most visited sites on Earth.

1941 Amid rising world tensions, President Franklin Roosevelt proclaimed an "unlimited national emergency."

1941 The German battleship *Bismarck* was sunk off the coast of France, with a loss of 2,300 lives.

1964 Independent India's first prime minister, Jawaharlal Nehru, died.

1985 In Beijing, representatives of Britain and China exchanged instruments of ratification on the pact that would return the thriving capitalist city of Hong Kong to the control of the Communist Chinese in 1997.

1994 Nobel Prize–winning author Aleksandr Solzhenitsyn returned to Russia to the emotional cheers of thousands after spending two decades in exile.

MAY

27

Dante Alighieri's world was fraught with dissention, confusion, and disarray. Caught between two worldviews—the glorious worldview of fading Christendom and the deleterious worldview of emerging Renaissance—Dante (1265–1321) was in a very real sense a man out of time.

The remarkable explosion of wealth, knowledge, and technology that occurred during the late Medieval period leading up to the Renaissance completely reshaped human society. No institution was left untouched. Families were transformed from mere digits within the larger baronial or communal clan into nuclear societies in and of themselves. Local communities were shaken from their sleepy timidity and thrust into the hustle bustle of mercantilism and urbanization. The church was rocked by the convulsions of ecclesiastical scandal. Kingdoms, fiefs, baronies, and principalities began to take the torturous path toward becoming modern nation-states.

FEAST DAY

St. Bernard of Aosta, St. Ignatius of Rostov, St. Senator of Milan, St. William of Gellone, St. Germanus of Paris, St. Justus of Urgel

MAY

Such revolutionary changes were not without cost. Ultimately, the cost to Christian civilization—both East and West—was devastating. Immorality and corruption ran rampant. Disparity between rich and poor became endemic. Ruthless and petty wars multiplied beyond number.

Despite its many advances in art, music, medicine, science, and technology, the days leading up to the Renaissance were essentially marked by nostalgic revivals of ancient pagan ideals and values. The dominating ideas of the times were classical humanism and antinomian individualism. Taking their cues primarily from ancient Greece and Rome, the most prominent leaders of the epoch were not so much interested in the Christian notion of progress as in the heathen ideal of innocence. Thus, they dispatched the Christian consensus it had wrought with enervating aplomb. They threw the baby out with the bathwater. Nothing was sacred any longer. Everything—every thought, word, and deed, every tradition, institution, and relationship—was redefined.

No society can long stand without some ruling set of principles, some overriding values, or some ethical standard. Thus, when the men and women of high medievalism gradually began to throw off Christian mores, they necessarily went casting about for a suitable alternative. And so, Greek and Roman thought was exhumed from the ancient sarcophagus of paganism. Aristotle, Plato, and Pythagoras were dusted off, dressed up, and rehabilitated as the newly tenured voices of wisdom. Cicero, Seneca, and Herodotus were raised from the philosophical crypt and made to march to the tune of a new era.

Every forum, every arena, and every aspect of life began to reflect this newfound fascination with the pre-Christian past. Art, architecture, music, drama, literature, and every other form of popular culture began to portray the themes of classical humanism, pregnable naturalism, and antinomian individualism. A complete reversion took place. Virtually all the great Christian advances that the Medieval era brought were lost in just a few short decades.

It was in that sort of atmosphere that Dante began writing his masterpiece, *Inferno*, the first volume of *The Divine Comedy*, on this day in 1302.

Hearth and home are the cornerstones of help and hope and happiness.

[MARK TWAIN (1835–1910)]

1431 Charged with sorcery and heresy, Joan of Arc spoke at her trial, saying, "If I said that God did not send me, I should condemn myself, truly God did send me. . . . All this I have done, I did for fear of the fire and my retraction was against the truth. . . . I prefer to do penance once, by dying rather than suffer long punishment in prison."

1453 The last Christian service was held in the great domed cathedral Hagia Sophia in Constantinople as the Turks burst into the city and within days converted the church into a mosque.

1533 England's Archbishop Thomas Cranmer declared the marriage of King Henry VIII to Anne Boleyn valid.

1779 Irish poet and musician Thomas Moore was born in Dublin. Moore's *Irish Melodies,* a compilation of works written over twenty-seven years, contained the familiar poems "The Last Rose of Summer" and "Oft in the Stilly Night." Moore was a great friend of Lord Byron, and at the time was as well known and read. His poem "Lalla Rookh" (1817) garnered for him the highest price paid by an English publisher for a poem.

1830 By signing the Removal Act, President Andrew Jackson mandated that all Indians be resettled west of the Mississippi River. The result was the Trail of Tears—the horrific dispossession of the largely Christian Cherokee tribe.

1863 The first African-American regiment from the North left Boston to fight in the War Between the States. The South already had several free African-American regiments fighting on the field.

1892 The Sierra Club was organized in San Francisco.

1929 The first all-color talking picture, *On with the Show,* premiered in New York.

1937 President Franklin Roosevelt pushed a button in Washington signaling that vehicular traffic could cross the just-opened Golden Gate Bridge in California.

1937 Neville Chamberlain became prime minister of Britain.

1938 The first Rainy Season Bible School was founded in the Lisu region of China by Isobel and John Kuhn. Just before the Second World War both the schools and the missionaries were used of God to usher in a great wave of revival in that vast land.

1940 During the Second World War, the tiny Belgian army surrendered to invading German forces.

1972 The Duke of Windsor, who had abdicated the English throne to marry Wallis Warfield Simpson, died in Paris at age seventy-seven.

MAY

28

On this day in 1787, Edmund Randolph (1753–1813) introduced the Virginia Plan to the Constitutional Convention then meeting in the city of Philadelphia—the first time the idea of a new national form of government was formally presented to the delegates at Philadelphia. Although his friend James Madison contributed much to the plan, it was the handsome thirty-three-year-old governor of Virginia, spokesman for his state, who began the convention's serious deliberations by outlining the fifteen resolves that called for national executive, judiciary, and legislative branches. It was a dramatic moment: The delegates, officially gathered "for the sole and express purpose of revising the Articles of Confederation," were confronted with a radical proposal to create a completely different governmental system. That they heard Randolph out—for more than three hours—and even considered the plan he offered, testifies to Randolph's success.

Though he was perhaps more responsible than any other man for the existence of the new Constitution, he was not pleased with some of the additions and revisions to the Virginia Plan that delegates introduced later, and he several times shifted his position, for and against. In September he refused to sign the final document. However, at the Virginia Ratification Convention, he shocked anti-Federalists like Patrick Henry by reversing himself and supporting the Constitution. Randolph explained his new position: By this time eight states had already ratified the Constitution, only one more was needed, and other states had already urged that the Bill of Rights amendments should be enacted soon after ratification, satisfying his objection to the original Constitution. In a telling speech, Patrick Henry slyly suggested that perhaps there were other reasons—not going so far as mentioning a promised post in the new government, but the hint was enough: The two men came close to fighting a duel.

After Washington was elected president, he named Randolph the first attorney general, but Randolph denied that this was in any way related to his supporting the Constitution. As attorney general he established the office and the beginnings of the Justice Department, and after Jefferson resigned as secretary of state, Randolph assumed that position also. In 1795 he was accused of seeking bribes from the French ambassador, and though he proved himself innocent, he resigned and never held another public office.

FEAST DAY

St. Cyril of Caesarea; St. Bernard of Montjoux; St. Theodosia of Constantinople; St. Maximinus of Trier; Saints Sisinnius, Martyrius, and Alexander; Saints William, Stephen, Raymund, and their Companions

MAY

1874

English author, essayist, novelist, poet, and journalist Gilbert Keith Chesterton was born in London. His witty style and mastery of the paradox made him an apt defender of the faith by engaging a reader and then turning their world upside down or rather right side up. Although most known for his short stories of detection by Father Brown, Chesterton's most influential writings continue to be works such as *Orthodoxy, What's Wrong with the World,* and *The Everlasting Man.*

A person must be able to earn his living before he can be of much benefit to himself and the community in which he lives.

[BOOKER T. WASHINGTON (1856–1915)]

1736 Patrick Henry, the American orator and statesman who helped to fire the colonists toward revolution, was born in Studley, Virginia. Henry was a self-educated man who was admitted to the Virginia bar in 1760 and later elected to the Virginia House of Burgesses. It was there that he introduced seven resolutions against the Stamp Act, saying, "Caesar had his Brutus; Charles the First his Cromwel; and George the Third—may profit by their example." Henry became a member of the revolutionary convention of Virginia when the House of Burgesses was dissolved in 1774. It was there, when urging for the adoption of a resolution for a state of defense, that he uttered his most famous words, "I know not what course others may take, but as for me, give me liberty or give me death!" Henry went on to serve in both Continental Congresses and opposed the U.S. Constitution until the passage of the Bill of Rights, which helped to define the rights of states and individuals. He died on June 6, 1799.

1765 On his twenty-ninth birthday, Patrick Henry denounced the Stamp Act before Virginia's House of Burgesses, saying, "If this be treason, make the most of it!"

1790 Rhode Island became the last of the original colonies to ratify the United States Constitution.

1848 Wisconsin became the thirtieth state of the Union.

1897 The world was introduced to Jell-O on this day.

1900 The Otis Elevator Co. manufactured the first escalator in New York City. It was exhibited at the Paris Exhibition of 1900, and installed in a building in Philadelphia the following year. In 1889, the Otis Elevator Co. had built the first successful electric elevator for the Demarest Building on the corner of Fifth Avenue and Thirty-third Street in New York City.

1913 Igor Stravinsky's ballet *The Rite of Spring*, which recounts stories of pagan Russia, was premiered in Paris to a divided reception. The ballet, with choreography by Nijinsky, was met with shouts, whistles, hisses, booing, and stomping. Several people were injured by slaps and canes. The shifting rhythms and unresolved chords in the music are considered to have begun the modernist movement in music. Reportedly, Stravinsky left in the middle of the performance. Afterward, he was widely known as "the composer of *The Rite of Spring*," while in reality he soon moved away from such experimental music.

MAY

1917 The thirty-fifth president of the United States, John F. Kennedy, was born in Brookline, Massachusetts.

1932 First World War veterans began arriving in Washington to demand cash bonuses they weren't scheduled to receive for another thirteen years.

1942 The movie *Yankee Doodle Dandy*, starring James Cagney, premiered at a war bonds benefit in New York.

1942 Bing Crosby, the Ken Darby Singers, and the John Scott Trotter Orchestra recorded Irving Berlin's "White Christmas" in Los Angeles for Decca Records. It became the best-selling single of all time.

1953 Mount Everest was conquered by Edmund Hillary of New Zealand and Sherpa guide Tenzing Norgay of Nepal.

1973 Tom Bradley was elected the first African-American mayor of Los Angeles, defeating incumbent Sam Yorty.

29

No tale has more completely captured the imagination of every generation since the Medieval epoch as the story of King Arthur, his Knights of the Round Table, and their search for the Holy Grail. Even the most dearly beloved of literary classics—like the stories of Robin Hood, Moby Dick, Scrooge, Huck Finn, and Aslan—pale in popular comparison to the glories of Sir Thomas Malory's landmark book, originally entitled *Le Morte d'Arthur.* The vividly drawn characters from its pages—such as Lancelot, Mordred, Merlin, Guinevere, and Arthur himself—have been so assimilated into the common currency of popular culture that they are familiar even to the youngest of schoolchildren. That is quite a feat for a fable written by an obscure knight-errant during the shameful years of his imprisonment more than half a millennium ago.

MAY

But even without its amazing popularity, *Le Morte d'Arthur*—composed sometime before 1469 and published on this day fifteen years later in 1483—would still classify as a remarkable feat of ingenuity, creativity, and intellect. Malory was hardly a man of letters. Instead he was a hapless medieval soldier who identified himself as "a servant of Jesu, both day and night." Thus, it is not at all surprising to find that he did not actually invent the great Arthurian legends. He merely collated them from extant documentary histories, ballads, and minstrel songs and then provided them with a coherent narrative structure. Prior to his work, most of the ancient stories of Camelot's chivalry had been passed from one troubadour to another—mostly in stiff, formal, and inaccessible languages—through a disconnected series of Romantic cycles. Malory took those odd stories and forged them into an epic work of heroic fiction.

Most commentators and critics agree that Malory's literary accomplishment was significant for three reasons: First, he unraveled the incoherent lore of medievalism and cast it in a popularly accessible plotline; second, he practically invented a whole new fictional form in the process; and finally, he did it all in the just-emerging prose vernacular of English rather than in literary Latin or classical French. Like his countrymen and near-contemporaries, John Wycliffe and Geoffrey Chaucer, he was an amazing innovator: one of the greatest of the founders of the English literary tradition.

Despite these profound achievements, the chief triumph of Malory was simply that he could spin a yarn like almost no one before or after. Malory translated the heritage of the people into the language of the people—and he did it without ever patronizing the people. He did it by raising standards rather than lowering them. But most important, he did it by touching hearts and sparking imaginations with a rip-roaring plot and characters that readers still care about half a millennium later.

The novelistically connected stories Malory tells probe the lives, exploits, and loves of Arthur and Merlin, of Lancelot and Guinevere, of Excalibur and the Grail—but even more they explore the escapades, travails, and adventures of the human heart in this poor fallen world. Rooted in a thoroughgoing Christian worldview, they expose evil, exalt good, and illumine truth. And though the stories are by no means simplistic or devoid of symbolic mystery and intrigue, the moral of the story is never in doubt.

320

Faith is the force of life.

[LEO TOLSTOY (1828–1910)]

542   As legend has it, King Arthur died from wounds he received in battle from his nephew Mordred. King Arthur, ruler of the Britons, creator of the Knights of the Round Table, and son of valiant king Uther Pendragon, was buried on the Isle of Avalon (Glastonberry).

1431   Joan of Arc, French patriot and martyr, was burned at the stake in Rouen by the English.

1453   The cruel and patient Mehmed II, sultan of the Ottomans, besieged the great Christian city of Constantinople. He erected a fortress across the strait from the city, brought up ships and his dreaded janissaries, who were captured Christians who had been trained into an effective fighting force. Mehmed also cast a cannon that could hurl five-hundred-pound stones a mile. With this and other guns he lashed Constantinople, which had been ruled by nearly one hundred Christian emperors since Constantine had dedicated the city in 311. When the defenses finally failed, enraged Muslims murdered indiscriminately. Churches were looted and the sacramental chalices that had memorialized Christ's shed blood slaked Muslim throats. Christians were ravished on the altars. The land where Paul and Barnabas preached salvation through Christ's death and resurrection now belonged entirely to Islam. To Byzantium's few survivors, it was the last day of the world.

1539   Spanish explorer Hernando de Soto landed in Florida.

1778   François Marie Arouet, who wrote under the name Voltaire, died in Paris at the age of eighty-four. Most famous for his novel *Candide*, he also worked with revolutionary forces and served in French politics. He fought against what he believed was tyranny, which included Judeo-Christian beliefs. After his death, the English poet William Cowper (1731–1800) wrote the following epitaph: "The Frenchman first in literary fame; (Mention him if you please—Voltaire?—the same); With spirit, genius, eloquence supplied; Liv'd long, wrote much, laugh'd heartily and died; The Scriptures was his jest-book whence he drew; Bon-mots to gall the Christian and the Jew."

1783   The Pennsylvania *Evening Post* made its debut as the United States' first daily newspaper.

1883   Twelve people were trampled to death when a rumor that the recently opened Brooklyn Bridge was in imminent danger of collapsing triggered a stampede.

1896   The first automobile accident occurred in New York City when Henry Wells of Springfield, Massachusetts, in a Duryea Motorwagon, collided with Evelyn Thomas, a bicycle rider. She was taken to the Manhattan Hospital with a fractured leg, while Wells spent the night in jail, awaiting the report as to the extent of her injuries.

1899   Legendary MGM production executive Irving G. Thalberg was born in Brooklyn, New York.

1922   In Washington, D.C., the Lincoln Memorial was dedicated on this day by Chief Justice William Howard Taft.

1989   Student demonstrators at Tiananmen Square in Beijing erected a thirty-three-foot statue they called the "Goddess of Democracy."

MAY

30

Jan Hus began preaching the doctrines of the Reformation almost a century before Martin Luther when he brought the writings of John Wycliffe to his native Bohemia. Hus's friend Jerome of Prague was likewise convinced of the Wycliffian truths and began to seriously think through their implications.

MAY

At Hus's suggestion Jerome sailed to England and studied at Oxford, Wycliffe's old seat of learning. For the next several years, Jerome moved about a good deal, disseminating Reform doctrines in Paris, Jerusalem, Heidelberg, Vienna, Moscow, Budapest, and Cologne. He became a traveling ambassador for the fledgling Reform movement. He became very active in public affairs throughout Christendom. In his native Bohemia he sided with nationalistic students and denounced a bull proclaiming an indulgence for a crusade against Naples.

When Hus was arrested by the Council of Constance, Jerome secretly followed, hoping to defend his friend. He discovered he could do nothing and was, in fact, in great danger himself, and so he went to neighboring Idelberg and asked for safe conduct. Unwilling to stand idly by while grave injustices were being perpetrated, he had placards posted throughout Constance saying he was willing to appear before the bishops, that his character had been maligned, and that he would retract any error which could be proven against him. All he asked was a pledge of security.

When no pledge was forthcoming, Jerome headed home. On the way he was seized and sent in irons to the Council. A long chain was attached to the irons, and by this he was dragged into the cloister to be insulted and then locked in a tower. His legs were fastened in stocks. For many days he was kept in this miserable condition. After Hus was burned at the stake, Jerome was threatened with torments if he would not recant. In a moment of weakness, he yielded.

Still he was not released. On the contrary, a second recantation was demanded. He said he would recant only in public. By then he had been a prisoner almost a year. At the public "recantation," he took back his earlier recalcitrance and demanded a hearing to plead his cause. The Council refused this plea. Indignantly he protested, "To my enemies you have allowed the fullest scope of accusation; to me you deny the least opportunity of defense."

Jerome insisted he protested only against the bad behavior of the clergy. Unlike Hus he did not reject the doctrine of transubstantiation. Nonetheless, he was condemned to die in the flames as Hus had. For two days the council kept him in suspense, hoping to frighten him into a capitulation. The cardinal of Florence personally reasoned with him. Jerome remained steadfast. When a cap was made for him painted with red devils, he said, "Our Lord Jesus Christ, when He suffered death for me, a most miserable sinner, did wear a crown of thorns upon His head; and I for His sake will wear this adorning of derision and blasphemy." He sang hymns on his way to execution. Because of his vigor and health he was a long time dying in the flames. On this day in 1416, he and his paper crown were burned.

*The great cleavage throughout the world lies
between what is with, and what is against
the faith.*

[Hilaire Belloc (1870-1953)]

1578 Forbidden to bury their dead in regular burial grounds, the Christians of Rome interred them in underground vaults used by the poor. These catacombs were built outside the city and subject to severe building codes because of fear that they might collapse. So many martyrs found their final rest in these sites that Christians began to hold special memorial services in them. Except during the worst persecutions, Christians were allowed control of their own catacombs. Widespread use of catacombs for Christian burial seems to have dated from the third century. An entrance into the ancient catacombs was accidentally discovered north of Rome, on the Via Salaria. The import of the find, however, was not recognized until 1593 when Antonio Bosio, who committed himself to the lifelong study of archaeology, explored the catacombs and found a number of narrow passageways had been dug from one to another. Some passages were blocked. Twenty-seven years after his first descent, he completed a book on the catacombs, *Roma Sotterranea*, the first landmark work of modern archaeology.

1809 Composer Franz Joseph Haydn died in Vienna, Austria. Papa Haydn was a friend of Mozart, a teacher of Beethoven, and the father of the symphony. He is best known for his many symphonies and his oratorios *The Seasons* and *The Creation*.

1819 American poet and journalist Walt Whitman was born in West Hill, New York.

1889 A dam in Johnstown, Pennsylvania, gave way after heavy rains, killing 2,295 people.

MAY

1902 The Treaty of Vereeniging ended the Boer War. The war, also called the South African War, was fought between Great Britian and the two Boer Republics. Having fought for more than two and a half years, the Boers gave up rights to their independence on this day.

1910 The Union of South Africa was founded.

1913 The Seventeenth Amendment to the Constitution, providing for the popular election of U.S. senators, was ratified.

1916 During the First World War, British and German fleets fought the Battle of Jutland off the coast of Denmark.

1955 The United States Supreme Court banned racial segregation in public schools.

1961 South Africa became an independent republic.

1962 Second World War Gestapo official Adolf Eichmann was hanged in Israel for his role in the Nazi Holocaust.

1977 The Trans-Alaska oil pipeline, three years in the making, was completed.

31

JUNE

JUNE

NATIONAL DAY
Tunisia
FEAST DAY
St. Gwen of Brittany, St. Justin, St. Nicomedes, St. Ronan, St. Whyte, St. Wistan, St. Symeon of Syracuse, St. Caprasius of Lérins, St. Pamphilus of Caesarea, St. Inigo, St. Produlus the Soldier, St. Proculus the Bishop, St. Theobald of Alba

Most Americans were saddened—though the Republican establishment was relieved—when Teddy Roosevelt announced that he would not seek a third term. His successor was the country's largest president, a jovial, warm-hearted mountain of a man with a brilliant legal mind—an excellent administrator but a poor politician.

William H. Taft (1857–1930) served with distinction as the first governor of the Philippines and as Roosevelt's secretary of war, positions in which his amiable nature served to advantage. But it was Taft's great misfortune to succeed such a dazzling political figure as Roosevelt in the presidency and attempt to carry out his many new policies. Probably no successor could have pleased Roosevelt, but the fall from grace of the devoted friend Roosevelt had practically placed in the White House is one of the most tragic affairs in the history of the presidency. Near the end of Taft's administration, when it was clear that he had not completely supported Roosevelt's Square Deal and had made concessions to the conservatives, Roosevelt fiercely attacked him in speeches and articles.

In the 1912 election Roosevelt won every primary and was poised to sweep back into office when the Republican establishment stripped the credentials of hundreds of delegates and denied the great man the opportunity. They renominated the compliant Taft instead. Roosevelt helped to organize the Progressive Party and nearly won the day anyway.

With less than a month to go in the campaign, however, a nearly successful assassination attempt took Roosevelt out of the race and the Democratic opponent, Woodrow Wilson, was able to barely eke out a win. Taft and the bosses of the Republican Party were humiliated.

In spite of that, Taft continued to serve his country. After teaching law at Yale he was appointed by President Harding to the post that he had long sought, one that probably meant more to him than the presidency: On this day in 1921 he became chief justice of the Supreme Court, the only man ever to hold both offices.

1593

English playwright Christopher Marlowe, author of *Doctor Faustus,* was murdered at a tavern in Deptford near London. Allegedly a fight broke out over the bar bill; however, one theory holds that Marlowe was acting as a secret agent for the throne and was killed in the line of duty.

*Chivalry is the ideal code of ethical behavior—
ultimately based on scripture—that defines the
limits of proper action toward other people.*

1792 Kentucky became the fifteenth state of the Union.

1796 Tennessee became the sixteenth state of the Union.

1813 Aboard his frigate *Chesapeake*, Captain James Lawrence is reported to have uttered his dying words, "Don't give up the ship." Thus, the U.S. Navy gained its motto.

1841 Born to a poor but pious Scottish family, David Livingstone (1813–1873) committed his life early on to the work of the priesthood of believers. Driven by the dictates of the Great Commission, he went to Africa on this day in 1841 as a missionary-explorer. Going where no white man had ever gone before, Livingstone penetrated the deepest reaches of the continent proclaiming the good news of Christ. He understood only too well though, that the purpose of missions extended far beyond merely extending the offer of heaven to the hapless and hopeless. In his widely influential book, *Missionary Travels and Researches in Southern Africa,* he wrote, "The indirect benefits, which to the casual observer lie beneath the surface and are inappreciable, in reference to the wide diffusion of Christianity at some future time, are worth all the money and labor that have been extended to produce them." Among those "indirect benefits" in Livingstone's work were the dramatic curtailment of both the native abortion and slave trades. A legend in his own time and a paradigm of missionary efficacy ever since, Livingstone demonstrated the power of the authentic church in the face of the horrors of heathenism.

1865 In New Haven, Connecticut, the first public telephone booth in the United States began operation.

1868 James Buchanan, the fifteenth president of the United States, died near Lancaster, Pennsylvania.

1921 A racial massacre occurred in Tulsa, Oklahoma, when white citizens and law enforcement officers instigated attacks surrounding the African-American neighborhood of Greenwood. For almost eighty years, this was reported as a "race riot," though in reality at least thirty-six people were killed, hundreds were injured, and more than a thousand black-owned businesses and homes were destroyed in two days of violence. Nothing has yet been done to secure justice in this matter.

1943 A civilian flight from Lisbon to London was shot down by the Germans during the Second World War, killing all aboard, including actor Leslie Howard.

1958 Hero of the Second World War, Charles de Gaulle, became premier of France.

1967 The Beatles released their remarkably progressive album, *Sergeant Pepper's Lonely Hearts Club Band.*

1968 Author-lecturer Helen Keller, who earned a college degree despite being blind and deaf almost all of her life, died in Westport, Connecticut.

1979 Control of the African nation of Rhodesia passed into black-majority hands and was renamed Zimbabwe.

1980 Cable News Network (CNN) made its debut.

JUNE

JUNE

NATIONAL DAY
Italy
FEAST DAY
*St. Erasmus; St. Oda; St. Attalus;
Saints Marcellinus and Peter; St.
Eugenius I, pope; St. Nicholas the
Pilgrim; St. Stephen of Sweden; St.
Pothinus and his Companions*

Theodore Roosevelt believed that there were absolutes. To his mind virtue must always be accountable to that set of unchanging principles—ones that are not affected by the movement of the clock or the advance of the calendar. And he believed that those absolute principles could only be reliably found in the Book of books—the Bible.

Thus, he made Bible reading and Bible study a vital part of his daily life—and he encouraged others to likewise partake of its great wisdom. "A thorough knowledge of the Bible," he argued, "is worth more than a college education." The reason for this was not simply that the Bible outlined a good and acceptable system of personal morals and social etiquette. He believed that the Bible was far more than that—it was, in fact, the very warp and woof of the fabric of Western civilization. It was therefore an essential element of the maintenance of order, civility, and prosperity. Indeed, without it, the great American experiment in liberty would be thrown into very real jeopardy: "Every thinking man, when he thinks, realizes that the teachings of the Bible are so interwoven and entwined with our whole civic and social life that it would be literally impossible for us to figure ourselves what that life would be if these standards were removed. We would lose almost all the standards by which we now judge both public and private morals; all the standards which we, with more or less resolution, strive to raise ourselves."

He quoted the Bible often—evincing his intimate familiarity with it. One biographical archivist examined just his published works and found that he had so integrated Scripture into his thought processes that there were actually more than 4,200 biblical images, references, inferences, and complete quotations contained therein. And his unpublished letters, articles, and speeches contained hundreds—perhaps even thousands—more.

On this day in 1902, during the height of an extremely tense diplomatic showdown with Britain and Germany over their forcible recovery of debt service in Venezuela, several key military advisors were summoned to the White House. When they entered Roosevelt's office they found him furiously poring over a well-worn Bible and an exhaustive concordance. After a long and uncomfortable silence during which the president failed to acknowledge their presence, one of the generals cleared his throat and addressed the great man: "You asked for us, sir?" Without looking up from the volumes before him the president responded, "Well, don't just stand there, men. I need help. I can't remember why I hold to the Monroe Doctrine. I know that it's got to be in here somewhere." Still not quite comprehending what it was he wanted them to do, the men moved toward his desk whereupon the president handed each of them a Bible of their own to peruse. "Get to work, men," he told them. "I can't act without warrant. I can't pronounce policy without precedence or precept."

The Christian and the hero are inseparable—chiefly because of the effects of chivalry upon the character.

[SAMUEL JOHNSON (1709–1784)]

1840 Thomas Hardy, English novelist and poet, was born in Upper Bockhampton, Dorset. Many of Hardy's novels and poems were set in imagined "Wessex," a county in southwest England based upon the author's home. Hardy combined strong regionalism with a stoic pessimism concerning the tragedy of human life. His best-known works are *The Return of the Native* (1878), *The Mayor of Casterbridge* (1886), *Tess of the D'Urbervilles* (1891), and *Jude the Obscure* (1895).

1857 English composer Sir Edward Elgar was born in Broadheath. In appearance and manner, Elgar was the very model of an Edwardian gentleman. His post-Romantic compositional style, with homage to Wagner, Strauss, and Brahms, was tempered with individuality and luminous orchestrations. His most familiar works include *Enigma Variations* (1899), *The Dream of Gerontius* (1900—with text by Cardinal Newman), and *Pomp and Circumstance* (1901).

1861 Russian Orthodox missionary Nikolai Ivan Kasatkin first arrived in Japan. At the time, Christianity was a prohibited religion. He was very cautious—his first three years in the country he worked quietly with only a few disciples as he mastered the language. Not until 1868 did he baptize his first converts—but his plan was nothing less than to evangelize all of Japan. His plan was to make the church indigenous from the start, as free as possible of Russian influence. The church would be organized not around priests, but around lay workers. The Japanese church would have its own synod, to meet every two years. In this way, Nikolai hoped, the church would survive—no matter what happened between Russia and Japan. By 1873 the Japanese had legalized Christianity. By the time of

Nikolai's death, the Japanese church had thirty-three thousand converts.

1865 Confederate troops surrendered the port at Galveston, Texas, to Union troops as the final naval action of the American War Between the States

1883 Two thousand people witnessed the first baseball game played at night, at League Park, Ft. Wayne, Indiana, between a club of boys known as the M.E. College, and the Quincey Professionals. Quincey won by a score of 19-11.

1886 President Grover Cleveland married Frances Folsom in a White House ceremony.

JUNE

1897 Responding to rumors that he had died, Mark Twain told the *New York Journal* that "the report of my death has been greatly exaggerated."

1924 Congress granted American citizenship to all Native American Indians.

1941 Baseball's "Iron Horse," Lou Gehrig, died in New York of a degenerative disease. Amyotrophic lateral sclerosis quickly became popularly known as Lou Gehrig's disease.

1946 At the end of the Second World War the Italian monarchy was abolished in favor of a republic.

1953 Queen Elizabeth II of Britain was crowned in Westminster Abbey, sixteen months after the death of her father, King George VI.

1966 The American space probe *Surveyor 1* landed on the moon and began transmitting detailed photographs of the lunar surface.

1979 Pope John Paul II arrived in his native Poland on the first visit by a pope to a Communist country.

The students in America's earliest schools, academies, and colleges were educated according to the great traditions of the Christian classical heritage—beginning at the Latin School of Plymouth, established on this day in 1623. They were the beneficiaries of a rich legacy of art, music, and ideas that not only had trained the extraordinary minds of our Founding Fathers but also had provoked the remarkable flowering of culture throughout Western civilization. It was a pattern of academic discipleship that had hardly changed at all since the dawning days of the Reformation and Renaissance—a pattern, though, that has almost entirely vanished today.

Indeed, those first Americans were educated in a way that we can only dream of today despite all our nifty gadgets, gimmicks, and bright ideas. They were steeped in the ethos of Augustine, Dante, Plutarch, and Vasari. They were conversant in the ideas of Seneca, Ptolemy, Virgil, and Aristophanes. The notions of Athanasius, Chrysostom, Anselm, Bonaventure, Aquinas, Machiavelli, Abelard, and Wycliffe informed their thinking and shaped their worldviews.

The now carelessly discarded traditional medieval trivium—emphasizing the basic classical scholastic categories of grammar, logic, and rhetoric—equipped them with the tools for a lifetime of learning: a working knowledge of the timetables of history, a background understanding of the great literary classics, a structural competency in Greek and Latin-based grammars, a familiarity with the sweep of art, music, and ideas, a grasp of research and writing skills, a worldview comprehension for math and science basics, a principle approach to current events, and an emphasis on a Christian life paradigm.

The methodologies of this kind of classical learning adhered to the time-honored principles of creative learning: an emphasis on structural memorization, an exposure to the best of Christendom's cultural ethos, a wide array of focused reading, an opportunity for disciplined presentations, an experience with basic academic skills, and a catechizing for orthopraxy as well as orthodoxy.

The object of this kind of classical education was not merely the accumulation of knowledge. Instead it was to equip a whole new generation of leaders with the necessary tools to exercise discernment, discretion, and discipline in their lives and over their callings. Despite their meager resources, rough-hewn facilities, and down-to-earth frontier ethic, they maintained continuity with all that had given birth to the wisdom of the West. It was the modern abandonment of these classical standards a generation later that provoked G. K. Chesterton to remark, "The great intellectual tradition that comes down to us from the past was never interrupted or lost through such trifles as the sack of Rome, the triumph of Attila, or all the barbarian invasions of the Dark Ages. It was lost after . . . the coming of the marvels of technology, the establishment of universal education, and all the enlightenment of the modern world. And thus was lost—or impatiently snapped—the long thin delicate thread that had descended from distant antiquity; the thread of that unusual human hobby: the habit of thinking."

FEAST DAY
Genesius of Clermont, St. Kevin, St. Charles Lwanga, St. Isaac of Cordova, St. Morand, St. Cecilius, St. Clothilde, St. Joseph Mkasa, St. Lucillian and his Companions, Saints Liphardus and Urbicius, Saints Pergentinus and Laurentinus

JUNE

3

Courage is grace under pressure.

[ERNEST HEMINGWAY (1899–1961)]

1097 The Crusaders recaptured the ancient Christian city of Antioch from the Muslims.

1162 The close friend and former chancellor of King Henry II, Thomas Becket, was consecrated as the new archbishop of Canterbury. As chancellor, Becket had lived a life of great wealth. He had fought brilliantly beside the king and been a vigorous champion of his monarch's interests. Whatever his faults, his noble character could not betray any trust that he undertook, and he became immediately a devout, austere, studious, pure, and energetic archbishop. Conflict between the two old friends soon emerged over the boundaries of church-state jurisdictions. In utter frustration after several years of fitful wrangling, Henry wished aloud to be rid of the recalcitrant archbishop. Four knights, thinking they were doing the king's will, cut Becket down in front of Canterbury's altar. Becket, who could have escaped, refused to do so. He died bravely. "I am ready to die for my Lord, that in my blood the church may obtain liberty and peace. But in the name of almighty God I forbid you to hurt my people whether clerk or lay." Because of Becket, Canterbury became the most visited shrine in Christendom. It was to his shrine the pilgrims were headed in Geoffrey Chaucer's famed *Canterbury Tales.*

1621 The Dutch West India Company was organized by the States General of the Netherlands with the mission of colonizing the New World and parts of Africa. Competition with Spain and Portugal eventually forced the resignation of all rights by the company but not before the establishment of New Netherlands (later New York), Suriname, and Curaçao.

1808 Jefferson Davis, the first and only president of the Confederate States, was born in Christian County (now Todd), Kentucky. He served in the military, worked as a farmer in Mississippi, and served as a United States representative and two-term senator from Mississippi. While serving as the secretary of war for President Franklin Pierce, he encouraged the president to sign the Kansas-Nebraska Act, which further exacerbated the issue of slavery. Although he was a strong proponent of states' rights, he opposed secession from the Union. His actions as president of the Confederate States included the appointment of Robert E. Lee as commander for the Army of Virginia, raising the troops, and the unsuccessful attempts to secure recognition and help from foreign governments. He was captured after the war and imprisoned but was eventually released.

JUNE

1875 Opera composer Georges Bizet died at the age of thirty-six thinking that his magnum opus, *Carmen*, was a failure.

1888 The poem "Casey at the Bat," by Ernest Lawrence Thayer, was first published in the San Francisco *Daily Examiner.*

1924 Austrian novelist Franz Kafka died at the age of forty without having published any of his major works, which adroitly express modern man's angst and alienation. On his deathbed, he requested that all his manuscripts be destroyed, but his instructions were ignored by his literary executor.

1937 The Duke of Windsor, who had abdicated the British throne, married Wallis Warfield Simpson in Monts, France.

1963 Pope John XXIII died at the age of eighty-one. He was succeeded by Pope Paul VI.

1965 Astronaut Edward White became the first American to "walk" in space, during the flight of *Gemini 4.*

4

FEAST DAY
St. Edfrith, St. Ninnoc, St. Petroc,
St. Metrophanes, St. Francis
Caracciolo, St. Optatus of Milevis,
St. Quirinus of Siscia, St.
Vincentia Gerosa

Plutarch wrote his famous *Lives of Noble Greeks and Romans* rather late in life—during the reigns of Trajan and Hadrian. This period at the beginning of the second century was a momentous time in the history of Western civilization for any number of reasons: Greece, of course, had lost by this time the last vestiges of its independence. The population had fallen precipitously since the days of Greece's glory—the riches of Rome and the Asian provinces had attracted not only Greece's most able administrators but also its most capable laborers. Thus, materially, culturally, and politically Plutarch's homeland was in decline. Though he could do little to arrest this trend, he felt obliged to put it into perspective—and that he did quite ingeniously in *Lives*.

At the same time, the Roman Empire was in its most stable and vibrant stage. The economy was prosperous. The military was invincible. And the culture was vibrant. Education, the arts, and the sciences were all flourishing. Despite the decrepit paganism of the day, there was a degree of personal freedom unprecedented in all of history.

But the most significant feature of the age was the sudden emergence of Christianity as a major societal force. Although Plutarch does not deal with Christianity directly, it is clear that he was attempting to revive interest in the very best of ancient paganism. In the face of the moral challenge that Christian evangelism posed to the ancien régime, he wanted to reignite the moral vitality of classicism. Thus, we see in his *Lives* the last great gasping apologetic for Greco-Roman civilization on the threshold of an ascendant Christendom.

When later writers, thinkers, and social activists would appeal to the classical age for reforms in their own time, they would picture its ideals as seen through Plutarch's rose-colored glasses. This is why the American founders could remain so enamored with the ancients. Plutarch was actually a part of the first required curriculum at Harvard College published on this day in 1637. Despite an unhesitating commitment to Christian truth, the founders' comprehension of the pagan essence of Greece and Rome was myopically obscured by Plutarch.

1989

The Communist Chinese government, utilizing troops from distant provinces, crushed the burgeoning pro-democracy protests centered around Beijing's Tiananmen Square, killing hundreds—and according to some reports thousands—of demonstrators. The Red Army regulars then moved quickly to arrest any surviving leaders of the outlawed China Democracy Party as well as the cell-based underground Christian Church, which had been instrumental in feuling the pro-democracy movement. Those leaders were then sentenced to long jail terms for "counterrevolutionary" crimes. Many of them later succumbed to brutal maltreatment in prison.

Courage consists not in hazarding without fear, but being resolutely minded in a just cause.

1133   Lothar II became emperor of the Holy Roman Empire.

1260   Kublai became Khan of the Mongols.

1639   The first American constitution was ratified by the colony of New Haven. The entire community assembled in a newly erected barn where the eminent Puritan pastor John Davenport preached and prayed earnestly—and then proposed fundamental articles for the governance of the colony. His four articles were simple: First, they were to affirm that Scripture contains the perfect rule for government by men in commonwealth, church, and family; second, they were to affirm that they were therefore to be guided by Scripture in all matters; third, they would covenant to create a church as soon as possible; and fourth, they would only then establish a civil order to implement the articles and ensure prosperity for themselves and their descendants. The organization they created was theocratic. Twelve members were chosen to rule the "colony" and seven of them also to serve as the seven pillars of the church. They also elected a magistrate and imposed wage and price controls. This was the first truly autonomous government by colonists in the New World. The inhabitants of New Haven swore allegiance only to their own civil government and not to king or parliament. After twenty-three peaceful years, they were compelled, in 1662, to unite with Connecticut. John Davenport fought this merger fiercely, saying that Christ's interests would be miserably lost by the unification. Men of Davenport's caliber played leading roles in the young American colonies, giving them a strongly Christian tone at their birth.

1647   The English parliamentary army seized King Charles I as a hostage during the English Civil War.

1812   The Louisiana Territory was renamed the Missouri Territory.

1845   *Leonora*, by William Henry Fry, was performed at the Chestnut Theater in Philadelphia, Pennsylvania. This was the first American opera.

1896   In a brick shed in Detroit, Michigan, Henry Ford completed his first automobile.

1917   Awarded on this day were the first Pulitzer Prizes. The awards were established in a provision of the will of Joseph Pulitzer, the publisher of such exploitive tabloids as the *New York World*. The twenty-one awards are for outstanding achievement in drama, letters, music, and journalism.

1929   The first technicolor movie was shown by inventor George Eastman.

1939   During what became known as the "Voyage of the Damned," the SS *St. Louis*, carrying more than nine hundred Jewish refugees from Germany, was turned away from the Florida coast. The ship, which was also denied permission to dock in Cuba, eventually returned to Europe. Many of the refugees later died in Nazi concentration camps.

1942   The Battle of Midway began. It was the first major American victory over Japan in the Second World War.

1944   The American Fifth Army began liberating Rome during the Second World War.

1954   French Premier Joseph Laniel and Vietnamese Premier Buu Loc initialed treaties in Paris according "complete independence" to Vietnam.

1961   Beneath the waters of the North Atlantic, twenty-two Soviet sailors gave their lives to avert an explosion aboard the *K-19*, the first Soviet submarine armed with nuclear weapons. The sub had lost its coolant system during a training exercise.

JUNE

Fresh on the heels of America's remarkable victories during the Second World War, Secretary of State George C. Marshall delivered the commencement address at Harvard University on this day in 1947. In his address he formulated what would later be called the Marshall Plan. In concert with the Truman Doctrine—a commitment to support democracy abroad—the plan was to undertake economic reconstruction of all of Europe, east and west alike, following the devastation of the late great war. Eventually the plan became official policy as the European Recovery Program, and had an immediate galvanizing effect in Europe. The economic and political recovery of modern Europe can well be said to have begun the day after this speech.

In the speech he warned of the dangers of retreating into America's prewar tradition of isolation: "I need not tell you gentlemen that the world situation is very serious. That must be apparent to all intelligent people. I think one difficulty is that the problem is one of such enormous complexity that the very mass of facts presented to the public by press and radio make it exceedingly difficult for the man in the street to reach a clear appraisement of the situation. Furthermore, the people of this country are distant from the troubled areas of the earth and it is hard for them to comprehend the plight and consequent reactions of the long-suffering peoples, and the effect of those reactions on their governments in connection with our efforts to promote peace in the world."

The reason, he said, was simple enough: "The feverish preparation for war and the more feverish maintenance of the war effort engulfed all aspects of national economies. Machinery has fallen into disrepair or is entirely obsolete. Under the arbitrary and destructive Nazi rule, virtually every possible enterprise was geared into the German war machine. Long-standing commercial ties, private institutions, banks, insurance companies, and shipping companies disappeared, through loss of capital, absorption through nationalization, or by simple destruction. In many countries, confidence in the local currency has been severely shaken. The breakdown of the business structure of Europe during the war was complete. Recovery has been seriously retarded by the fact that two years after the close of hostilities a peace settlement with Germany and Austria has not been agreed upon. But even given a more prompt solution of these difficult problems, the rehabilitation of the economic structure of Europe quite evidently will require a much longer time and greater effort than had been foreseen."

The crisis was everywhere evident, he argued. "The town and city industries are not producing adequate goods to exchange with the food-producing farmer. Raw materials and fuel are in short supply. Machinery is lacking or worn out." The result was that "governments are forced to use their foreign money and credits to procure these necessities abroad. This process exhausts funds which are urgently needed for reconstruction. Thus a very serious situation is rapidly developing which bodes no good for the world." If the world was to stabilize and not plunge into war again, America would have to rebuild it. And so it did.

JUNE

NATIONAL DAY
Denmark
FEAST DAY
St. Boniface, St. Dorotheus of Tyre,
St. Tudno, St. Sanctius

Courage: the footstool of the virtues, upon which they stand.

[ROBERT LOUIS STEVENSON (1850–1894)]

1723 Adam Smith was born on this day in Kirkcaldy, Scotland. He wrote the first serious book of political economic theory, *An Enquiry into the Nature and Causes of the Wealth of Nations.*

1783 The French brothers Montgolfier successfully completed the first ascent by a hot-air balloon that lasted ten minutes.

1794 Congress passed the Neutrality Act, which prohibited Americans from enlisting in the service of a foreign power.

1826 Composer Carl Maria von Weber, the "Hero of German Romantic Opera," died in London. Weber is considered to be the first true Romantic, and it was he who unleashed the storm of Romanticism through his opera *Der Freischütz.* His works had an overwhelming impact on Mendelssohn, Liszt, Berlioz, and especially Wagner.

1851 Harriet Beecher Stowe's *Uncle Tom's Cabin* was published as a serial story in a Washington, D.C., antislavery newspaper.

1883 John Maynard Keynes was born in Cambridge, England. His theories of economics, which included state control of the economy, influenced countries and economies all over the world.

1917 About ten million American men began registering for the draft in the First World War.

1933 Franklin Roosevelt fulfilled a half century of Populist, Communist, and Democratic Party aspirations when he took the currency of the United States off the gold standard.

1967 War erupted in the Mideast when Israel stymied Egyptian military plans to encroach on its territory. Syria, Jordan, and Iraq entered the conflict. Against all odds, Israel won the war in an astonishingly short period of time—just six days.

JUNE

1968 Senator Robert F. Kennedy was shot and mortally wounded just after claiming victory in California's Democratic presidential primary. Gunman Sirhan Bishara Sirhan, a Palestinian immigrant, was immediately arrested.

1977 The Apple II, the world's first computer designed for personal use, went on the market.

1989 In one of the most remembered images of China's crushed pro-democracy movement, a lone man stood defiantly in front of a line of tanks in Beijing until friends pulled him out of the way.

1998 Volkswagen bought Rolls-Royce Motor Cars. It immediately sold the passenger car division to another German automaker, the Bavarian Motor Works (BMW).

The most famous orator of the Revolution, Patrick Henry (1736–1799), delivered dramatic speeches that kindled the spark of liberty in colonial Virginians and were, according to Thomas Jefferson, "far above all in maintaining the spirit of the Revolution." In 1765, before the House of Burgesses, Henry spoke out boldly against the Stamp Act, firing the colony's opposition and, on this day in 1775, just weeks before Lexington and Concord, he closed a stirring appeal to arm the militia with the immortal phrase, "Give me liberty, or give me death!"

A failure as a farmer and storekeeper, Henry studied law and quickly won a reputation as a lawyer. In 1763, in the *Parson's Cause* case, he gained fame throughout Virginia by winning a point of law against the king's nullification of a Virginia law. In the House of Burgesses in 1765, he responded to news of the Stamp Act by offering five daring resolutions that declared the colonists' rights, including the exclusive right to tax themselves, and he sought support with a fiery speech that evoked cries of treason. But Henry's powerful words helped stiffen resistance to the Stamp Act throughout the colonies and added to his reputation.

In Virginia, he had more real power than the governor. At the First Continental Congress, Henry strongly supported the Continental Association, a union of colonies for the purpose of boycotting British imports. It was at Virginia's revolutionary convention at Richmond that Henry, after proposing immediate arming of the militia, delivered the most famous speech of the Revolution, concluding, "Gentlemen may cry peace, peace—but there is no peace. The war is actually begun. Is life so dear, or peace so sweet, as to be purchased at the price of chains and slavery? Forbid it, Almighty God! I know not what course others may take, but as for me, give me liberty, or give me death!" The convention promptly approved his proposal, crying out, "To arms! To arms!"

In the Continental Congress in 1775, Henry favored the idea of a Continental army. No soldier himself, Henry resigned a commission after a short time. As a member of the Virginia patriotic convention, he helped draft the state's constitution and Bill of Rights. He became Virginia's first governor on July 5, 1776, and held the position for the legal limit of three years.

Although a leader of the Revolution, Henry was first and foremost a Virginian—when the Constitution came to Virginia for ratification, he fought it, believing it placed too much power in the federal government, depriving the states and the people of essential rights. And his fight against the Constitution and for the Bill of Rights brought that issue to public notice throughout the colonies—contributing to the early adoption of the Bill of Rights amendments.

JUNE

NATIONAL DAY
Sweden
FEAST DAY
St. Jarlath, St. Gudwal, St. Ceratius, St. Norbert, Saints Primus and Felician, St. Claude of Besançon, St. Eustorgius II of Milan, St. Philip the Deacon

SIBELIUS DAY	Annually on this day in Helsinki, the Finnish people hold a festival honoring Johan Julius Jean Sibelius, Finland's most famous composer.

On the battlefield, when surrounded and cheered by pomp, excitement, and admiration of devoted comrades, and inspired by strains of martial music and the hope of future reward, it is comparatively easy to be a hero, to do heroic deeds. But to uphold honor in ordinary circumstances, to be a hero in common life, that is a genuine achievement meriting our highest admiration.

[BOOKER T. WASHINGTON (1856–1915)]

1799 Russia's first great poet, Aleksandr Pushkin, was born in Moscow.

1832 Jeremy Benton, author of utilitarian ethics and founder of the *Westminster Review*, died in London.

1844 Twelve men met in the London flat of English businessman George Williams and created the Young Men's Christian Association (the YMCA). Its original intent was merely to extend their witness by hiring halls and seeking to reach men through lectures, exercise, and innocent amusement. In short order a number of prominent men threw their weight behind the work. Lord Shaftesbury was the YMCA's president for a time. Thomas Binney and other evangelical leaders gave their support. The organization caught on like wildfire. Long before Williams's death in 1905, it had achieved a membership of 150,000 in Britain and half a million in America with thousands of branches worldwide. For his service to the well-being of the nation, Queen Victoria knighted him.

1868 American poet Henry Wadsworth Longfellow arrived in England for the purpose of receiving an honorary bachelor of law degree from Cambridge University.

1875 Thomas Mann, author of such books as *Budenbrooks* and *The Magic Mountain*, was born in Lubeck, Germany.

1925 Walter Percy Chrysler left his job at General Motors to establish his own car company.

1934 Author Christopher Morley convened the first meeting of the Baker Street Irregulars, a literary club, at 144 East Forty-fifth Street in New York. Eight other authors attended the meeting.

1934 The Securities and Exchange Commission was established.

JUNE

1944 Allied forces launched Operation Overlord, also known as the D-Day invasion of Europe and the decisive turning point of World War II. The allies crossed the English Channel under the cloak of fog and stormed Omaha and Normandy Beaches in France at great cost of human life. The invasion was the largest in human history and involved four thousand ships, which eventually landed over four million Allied troops. Plans for the invasion had been under way since January. In a speech before the invasion, General Dwight D. Eisenhower told his troops, "The eyes of the world are upon you. The hopes and prayers of liberty-loving people everywhere march with you."

1966 Civil rights activist James Meredith was shot and wounded as he walked along a Mississippi highway to encourage African-American voter registration.

1968 Senator Robert F. Kennedy died at Good Samaritan Hospital in Los Angeles, a day after he was shot by Sirhan Bishara Sirhan.

His resolution "that these United Colonies are, and of right ought to be, free and independent States," approved by the Continental Congress June 7, 1776, was the first official act of the United Colonies that set them irrevocably on the road to independence. It was not surprising that it came from the pen of Richard Henry Lee (1732–1794). As early as 1768 he proposed the idea of committees of correspondence among the colonies, and in 1774 he proposed that the colonies meet in what became the Continental Congress. From the first, his eye was on independence.

A wealthy Virginia planter whose ancestors had been granted extensive lands by King Charles II, Lee disdained the traditional aristocratic role and the aristocratic view. In the House of Burgesses he flatly denounced the practice of slavery. He saw independent America as "an asylum where the unhappy may find solace, and the persecuted repose."

In 1764, when news of the proposed Stamp Act reached Virginia, Lee was a member of the committee of the House of Burgesses that drew up an address to the king, an official protest against such a tax. After the tax was established, Lee organized the citizens of his county into the Westmoreland Association, a group pledged to buy no British goods until the Stamp Act was repealed. At the First Continental Congress, Lee persuaded representatives from all the colonies to adopt this nonimportation idea, leading to the formation of the Continental Association, which was one of the first steps toward union of the colonies. Lee also proposed to the First Continental Congress that a militia be organized and armed the year before the first shots were fired at Lexington; but this and other proposals of his were considered too radical—at the time.

Three days after Lee introduced his resolution in June of 1776, he was appointed by Congress to the committee responsible for drafting a declaration of independence, but he was called home when his wife fell ill, and his place was taken by his young protégé, Thomas Jefferson. Thus Lee missed the chance to draft the document—though his influence greatly shaped it and he was able to return in time to sign it.

He was elected president—serving from November 30, 1784, to November 22, 1785, when he was succeeded by the second administration of John Hancock. Elected to the Constitutional Convention, Lee refused to attend, but as a member of the Congress of the Confederation, he contributed to another great document, the Northwest Ordinance, which provided for the formation of new states from the Northwest Territory. When the completed Constitution was sent to the states for ratification, Lee opposed it as antidemocratic and anti-Christian. However, as one of Virginia's first senators, he helped assure passage of the amendments that, he felt, corrected many of the document's gravest faults—the Bill of Rights. He was the great-uncle of Robert E. Lee and the scion of a great family tradition.

JUNE

FEAST DAY
St. Meriasek, St. Robert of Newminster, St. Anthony Gianelli, St. Gottschalk, St. Vulflagius, St. Willibald, St. Colman of Dromore, St. Paul I of Constantinople

We make men without chests and expect of them virtue and enterprise. We laugh at honor and are shocked to find traitors in our midst. We castrate and bid the geldings be fruitful.

[C. S. Lewis (1898–1963)]

1502 Pope Gregory XIII was born Ugo Buoncompagni in Bolgna, Italy. He introduced the New Style calendar that is named for him. A prominent theologian at the Council of Trent, he used his office of pontiff (1572–1585) to spread anti-Protestant propaganda as well as to build colleges for the education of Catholics. He even aided Philip II, the king of Spain, in his wars on the Protestant Netherlands and England.

1769 Daniel Boone first saw the woodlands of present-day Kentucky.

1848 French post-impressionist painter Paul Gauguin was born in Paris. He exhibited with the impressionists on five different occasions. He eventually turned from impressionism and adapted a style derived from Japanese prints, the art of indigenous peoples, and stained glass. Due to indebtedness, he abandoned his family to live in Tahiti and the Marquesas Islands and devoted himself to painting natives. He sought to escape "everything that is artificial and conventional" about European society. His masterpiece, *Where Do We Come From? What Are We? Where Are We Going?* (1897), was painted before a failed suicide attempt. Gauguin's use of color, two-dimensional forms, and his choice of subject matter provided the impetus for the fauvist style and greatly influenced Edvard Munch and the expressionists, thus having a great impact on modern art.

1864 Abraham Lincoln was narrowly renominated for a second term as president at his party's convention in Baltimore.

1891 Charles Haddon Spurgeon, "Prince of Preachers," preached his last sermon at the Tabernacle in London. He had labored in that building thirty years—usually preaching to an overflow crowd of six thousand every Sunday and Thursday. He chose as the topic of his final talk what it means to have Christ as our captain. With power he amplified on the story of David at Ziklag. He and his men returned to find their city burned and their wives and children taken. His men wanted to stone him. But when they returned victorious from recapturing their wives and children, David stood up for the exhausted men who had guarded the baggage: "We are all one in Christ Jesus. Surely this ought to comfort those of you who, by reason of feebleness, are made to feel as if you were inferior members of the body." Spurgeon showed that David attributed recovery of their families to the Lord and drew this conclusion: "If it is all of free grace, then, my poor struggling brother, who can hardly feel assured that you are saved, yet if you are a believer, you may claim every blessing of the Lord's gracious covenant." Christ, the Son of David, is "the most magnanimous of captains."

JUNE

1945 English composer Benjamin Britten premiered his opera *Peter Grimes* at Sadler's Wells Theater in London. The story is set in a Suffolk fishing village around 1830 in which the townspeople suspect Peter Grimes, a fisherman, of murdering his apprentices. Despite a trial in which Grimes is acquitted, he is driven to insanity by the hostility and suspicions of the gossiping people.

1948 Communist insurgents backed by the Soviet Union completed their takeover of Czechoslovakia with the resignation of President Eduard Benes.

1965 The Sony Corporation displayed the first black-and-white home video tape recorder.

1967 Author-critic Dorothy Parker, famed for her caustic wit, died in New York.

Geoffrey Chaucer was born into an Anglo-Norman family of well-to-do vintners in about 1342. He was educated at St. Paul's Almonry in London and early on was sent to be a page in the household of the countess of Ulster, who later became the duchess of Clarence, wife of Lionel, the third son of King Edward III. His star rose as a young and talented courtier, and he drew the attentions of the famed duke of Lancaster, John of Gaunt. For the rest of his life he was a trusted confidant of the royal family, serving as a knight during the Hundred Years' War in France, as a Royal justice of the peace in Kent, as His Majesty's comptroller of customs in London, and as an ambassador to Lombardy among the northern Italian city-states.

It was then that Chaucer first came to Florence on this day in 1364. And it was there that his literary visions were awakened. It was there that his native interests in poetry were heightened and focused. He socialized with Petrarch, came to admire Dante, and was delighted by Boccaccio. He hobnobbed with the greatest poets and thinkers of the slowly emerging Renaissance. There in the world of the Medicis, in the palaces of the Florentine intelligencia, he discovered a thrilling world of art, music, and ideas that would forever change his worldview and his sense of calling.

Though he gleefully immersed himself in that world of the European literati, he was nevertheless disturbed by the lack of a cohesive English poetic tradition. Indeed, the English had no sense of a distinctive tradition of any kind. The Norman Conquest had essentially smothered the once-proud Anglo-Saxon culture, annexing it to the Gallic milieu of the continent. But Chaucer was a patriot. He loved his homeland. All the sights and sounds, the people and peculiarities, the habits and humors of England stirred in him a poetic passion that no other place on earth possibly could.

JUNE

FEAST DAY
St. Medard, St. William of York,
St. Cloud of Metz, St.
Maximinius of Aix

Moved by a love of hearth and homeland, Chaucer committed himself to literary pursuits as a self-conscious exercise in civil and social correction. Since French was still the official language of England, his decision to work in the colloquial of the common people of the streets and fields was very propitious. Like his contemporary John Wycliffe he believed that the future of his beloved realm and its emerging culture of liberty were inextricably tied to its indigenous tongue. While Wycliffe worked at translating the Bible, Chaucer undertook the arduous task of translating several of the important medieval works he had encountered in Florence expounding the doctrines of chivalry and amour courtois from Latin, Burgundian, Castilian, Italian, and of course, French. Thus was born—or at the very least, thus was confirmed and established—the English language.

During his lifetime Chaucer witnessed the end of the Plantagenet dynasty, the beginning of the conflict between the Houses of Lancaster and York, the decline of the Crusades, the rise of the Reconquesta, the earliest European naval explorations, and the horrors of the Black Death. Taken together, the man of the times and the times of the man made for a fascinating work of art.

The Canterbury Tales was composed at the end of Chaucer's life. In fact it was never completed due to his premature death in 1400. It thus represents the full fruit of his greatest and most mature labors. But *The Canterbury Tales* also represents the full fruit of his times. And they were remarkable times indeed.

Better to die ten thousand deaths, than wound my honor.

[JOSEPH ADDISON (1672–1719)]

632 The prophet Muhammad died having only recently mobilized his pseudo-religious army and consolidated his violent conquest of the central Hejaz.

1778 The United States Secret Service was established and Aaron Burr named its first director.

1786 In New York City, commercially made ice cream was sold for the first time on this day.

1809 Robert Schumann was born in Zwickau, Germany. Most of the successes in his life came with a great cost and struggle. Even at the age of seventeen he recognized, "I possess imagination, but I am not a profound thinker." Although he wrote four symphonies that continue to be part of the repertoire, Schumann truly excelled in his composition of short pieces for piano and his many art songs.

1845 Andrew Jackson, seventh president of the United States, died in Nashville, Tennessee.

1867 American architect and pioneer of the modern style Frank Lloyd Wright was born in Richland Center, Wisconsin. Greatly influenced by Louis Sullivan, Wright opened an architecture firm in Chicago in 1893. His central philosophy of design came to be known as "organic architecture," which meant that the building should be a developed concept from its natural surroundings. He was greatly interested in the choice of building materials for their natural textures and colors and a sense of spaciousness with rooms flowing into one another. He pioneered the use of air conditioning, indirect lighting, and precast concrete blocks. He designed the first building (Larkin Building in Buffalo, New York—1904) to use air conditioning, double-glass windows, glass doors, and metal furniture. His most famous works include the Imperial Hotel in Tokyo (built on a floating foundation to withstand earthquakes), the Robie House, Fallingwater at Bear Run, Pennsylvania (remarkable for its use of cantilevers), and the Guggenheim Museum in New York City.

JUNE

1869 Mr. Ives W. McGaffey received a patent for the vacuum cleaner, the machine he invented.

1915 Secretary of State William Jennings Bryan resigned from the Wilson administration in a disagreement over U.S. handling of the sinking of the *Lusitania.*

1978 Exiled Russian author Aleksandr Solzhenitsyn shocked Harvard graduates during a commencement address by censuring the West as stridently as he did the East: "The fight for our planet, physical and spiritual, a fight of cosmic proportions, is not a vague matter of the future; it has already started. The forces of evil have begun their decisive offensive. You can feel their pressure, yet your screens and publications are full of prescribed smiles and raised glasses. What is the joy about?"

JUNE

During the Senate hearing following the tragic sinking of the *Titanic* the doctrine of "women and children first" was very much the topic of discussion. Surviving second officer Charles Lightoller indicated that despite the fact that there were actually no maritime laws that mandated such chivalry in times of danger, he, and perhaps many others like him, believed that the doctrine was a universally recognized and uniformly practiced principle of conduct. It was why the overall death toll in the *Titanic* disaster was nine men for every woman—for the most part the men gave their places in the few available lifeboats to women.

That was the motivating virtue behind Nellie Taft's efforts to establish a memorial to chivalry in Washington, D.C., shortly after the *Titanic* disaster. The First Lady mounted a national campaign to raise funds for a monument to be built in Washington, D.C. Mrs. Taft explained, "I am happy to do this in gratitude to the chivalry of American manhood."

Using the one-dollar donations of American housewives, nearly $90,000 was raised and a commission was given to a prominent team of artists, architects, and landscape designers.

The monument, dedicated at a very prominent location near the White House on this day in 1913, bears the inscription: "To the brave men who gave their lives that women and children might be saved." Atop a grand pedestal a beautiful bronze statue of a man, arms outstretched, eyes toward the horizon, was placed.

Sixty years later, the entire monument was removed and placed in a storage facility where it languished, all but forgotten, for several years. Finally, in 1979 it was given a new home overlooking the Potomac River, where it stands to this day as a reminder of the old virtue of chivalry and sacrifice.

1895

After Thérèse of Liseaux died of tuberculosis, her sister nuns found a little document in the New Testament that she had always carried at her heart. It was an act of oblation, a complete dedication of herself to Christ for life. In her autobiography Thérèse admitted that she longed for martyrdom, for heroic acts, to be a great preacher. Instead the Lord demanded of her love, a love that showed itself in every action and word of every day. She lived out that love in extraordinary ways for the rest of her life. After her death the usual fifty-year wait was waived and she was canonized in only twenty-eight years.

It is a greater honor to be right than to be president—or popular, for statesmanship consists rather in removing causes than in punishing or evading results—thus, it is the rarest of qualities.

[JAMES A. GARFIELD (1831–1881)]

68   The brutal and paranoid Roman emperor Nero committed suicide.

597 Saint Columba, as he was known to the Irish, died this day. Columba spread the gospel from Ireland to the northern British Isles, where he was known as Columkille or Colum Cille to the Scots. A Highland song about the Saint says, "Day of Colum Cille the beloved; day the harp should be put to use; day to put the sheep to pasture."

1374 Geoffrey Chaucer was appointed comptroller of the Customs and Subsidy of Wools by his patron, John of Gaunt.

1534 Jacques Cartier, a French navigator, sailed into the mouth of the St. Lawrence River.

1732 James Oglethorpe received a royal charter for the Georgia Colony.

1870 English novelist Charles Dickens died in London. He specifically requested in his will that only his name and dates be put on his tomb, and that no monument would be erected in his memory. He said, "I rest my claim to the remembrance of my countrymen on my published works." Nevertheless, the author was given an honored place in the Poet's Corner of Westminster Abbey. Two days after his death, Queen Victoria wrote in her diary, "He is a very great loss. He had a large loving mind and the strongest sympathy with the poorer classes."

1880 Fyodor Dostoevsky interrupted his work on *The Brothers Karamazov* to address the Moscow Society of Lovers of Russian Literature at a centenary celebration of Aleksandr Pushkin's birth, averring, "He is a phenomenon never seen and never heard of before."

1881 Leo Tolstoy set out on a pilgrimage to the Optina-Pustyn monastery accompanied by two bodyguards.

1893 Playwright Samuel Nathaniel Behrman, best known for *No Time for Comedy*, was born in Worcester, England.

1903 Marguerite Yourcenar, the first woman admitted to the Academie Francaise in its 345-year history, was born in Brussels.

JUNE

1940 Norway surrendered to the Nazis during the Second World War.

1940 In her diary, novelist and Bloomsbury leader Virginia Woolf reflected, "I will continue—but how can I? The pressure of this battle wipes out London pretty quick. It strikes me that one curious feeling is, that the writing 'I' has vanished. No audience. No echo." Less than a year later, she committed suicide.

1978 Leaders of the Church of Jesus Christ of Latter-day Saints struck down a 148-year-old policy of excluding black men from the Mormon priesthood.

1993 Japanese Crown Prince Naruhito wed commoner Masako Owada in an elaborate Shinto religious ceremony.

9

By any modern measure, the obstinate resolve of the antebellum South to maintain the principles of regionalism, localism, agrarianism, and state sovereignty was impossibly exotic and prosaic. In fact, those notions were generally assumed as normative by the men and women living in the first half of the nineteenth century—even as they had been throughout the entire history of Christendom.

Instead, it was the whole idea of nationality—and even the mood of nationalistic sentiment that gave rise to that idea—that was the innovation in the affairs of men. Indeed, it was an idea that until just a short time ago was utterly remote from the experience of Western civilization. Even the vocabulary of nationalism was of a very recent vintage—it was not until well into the nineteenth century that the institutional terms taken so for granted today—like "state," "polity," "federal," "government," or even "nation"—came into common usage. As short a time ago as the founding of the American republic, political discourse preferred to speak of "the commonwealth," "the people," "the confederation," "the common land," "the public," "the community," or "the cooperative welfare" to avoid the centralizing and unitary implications of "nationhood." The *New English Dictionary* underscored that distinction when it was published on this day in 1908—it stated that the old meaning of *nationality* envisaged "little more than an ethnic unit" but that a wholly new meaning had begun to emerge that stressed the notion of "political unity and independence."

At virtually no time in the past did men identify themselves in terms of a particular nation-state. Instead, they saw themselves as members of a family or a community—or, even more likely, of a faith. Jurisdictions and boundaries were set according to these relational and covenantal loyalties rather than by governmental edicts. Thus patriotism was interpersonal rather than institutional.

Most Americans—whether from the North or the South, the East or the West—generally did not see themselves first and foremost as citizens of the United States. Their sense of purpose was rooted in who they were rather than where they were from or what they did. As difficult as it may be for us to comprehend, this is the most significant clue to understanding their motivations, their ideals, their aspirations, and ultimately, their actions. They saw themselves fundamentally as co-heirs of a united vision of liberty rather than subjects of a particular magistraical jurisdiction.

Though the systemic and ideological notions of Enlightenment nationalism had gained more and more favor with the Western world's political elites since the time of the French Revolution, it was still remote enough from the day-to-day existence of Americans to be practically unnoticed. That is why today any map of the world from those days can be so mind-bogglingly indecipherable—it portrays a forgotten philosophy as well as a forgotten geography. There did not yet exist such nation-states as Germany, Italy, Poland, or Belgium. And the United States were plural sovereignties confederated together—not a singular federal union. The wrenching War Between the States was thus not merely a struggle over slavery, tariffs, and nullification. At root it also was a struggle between an Old World order and a New World order.

JUNE

FEAST DAY
St. Ithamar, St. Bogumilus, St. Landericus of Paris, St. Getulius and his Companions

Mercy has converted more souls than zeal, or eloquence, or learning or all of them together.

[SØREN KIERKEGAARD (1813–1855)]

1194 Much of the town of Chartres, France, was destroyed by fire.

1248 Bergen, Norway, was devastated by fire as well.

1376 Good King Wenceslaus was elected king of Bomeia.

1652 John Hull established the first United States mint in Boston.

1682 The first recorded tornado in the American colonies occurred at New Haven, Connecticut, about 2:30 P.M.

1695 Author, educator, and Reformer François Fenelon was consecrated archbishop of Cambrai, one of the richest and most important sees in France.

1793 Washington, D.C., became the nation's capital when all federal government offices were moved from Philadelphia.

1801 The North African state of Tripoli declared war on the United States in a dispute over safe passage of merchant vessels through the Mediterranean.

1829 The first boat race was held between Oxford and Cambridge, from Hambledon Lock to Henley Bridge on the Thames River. The race, which lasted fourteen minutes and thirty seconds, was won by Oxford.

1859 The richest mine in the United States, the Comstock Lode, was discovered by Peter O'Riley and Patrick McLaughlin in the Utah Territory.

1865 *Tristan und Isolde,* the opera by Richard Wagner, was first performed at the Hoftheater in Munich. Wagner's use of shifting and unresolving tonalities serves to heighten the tension in this old legend about star-crossed lovers.

JUNE

1922 Singer-actress Judy Garland was born in Grand Rapids, Minnesota.

1935 Alcoholics Anonymous was founded in Akron, Ohio, by William G. Wilson and Dr. Robert Smith.

1940 Benito Mussolini declared war on Great Britain and France.

1944 In an apparent reprisal for the D-Day invasion, German soldiers in the French town of Oradour-sur-Glane shot all the men of the town and forced all the women and children into the church, which was subsequently burned down. The town has remained unoccupied as a memorial to those who died in this atrocity.

1964 The Senate voted to limit further debate on a proposed civil rights bill, shutting off a filibuster.

Like so many of the Founding Fathers, Nathaniel Gorham (1738–1796) was a self-made man. Arising from poverty, he became a successful Boston merchant who then risked all he had for the cause of freedom. He believed that "the gospel of liberty in Christ compels us, by God's good providence, to pursue justice on earth as it is in heaven. Though we may never fully attain such a goal in this poor fallen world, it must ever be our aspiration. Woe be unto us should we ever settle, in our comforts, for less."

He was first elected to the Massachusetts General Court in 1771. His honesty and integrity won him acclaim, and he was thus among the first delegates chosen to serve in the Continental Congress. He remained in public service throughout the war and into the constitutional period, though his greatest contribution was his call for a stronger central government. But even though he was an avid Federalist, he did not believe that the union could be—or even should be—maintained peaceably for more than a hundred years. He was convinced that eventually, to avoid civil or cultural war, smaller regional interests should pursue an independent course. His support of a new constitution was rooted more in pragmatism than ideology.

When John Hancock was unable to complete his second term as president, Gorham was elected to succeed him—serving from June 6, 1786, to February 1, 1787. It was during this time that the Congress actually entertained the idea of asking Prince Henry, the brother of Frederick II of Prussia, and Bonnie Prince Charlie, the leader of the ill-fated Scottish Jacobite Rising and heir of the Stuart royal line, to consider the possibility of establishing a constitutional monarch in America. It was a plan that had much to recommend it, but eventually the advocates of republicanism held the day.

During the final years of his life, Gorham was concerned with several speculative land deals that nearly cost him his entire fortune. Nevertheless, he was honored at his death on this day in 1796 as one of the nation's greatest Christian statesmen.

JUNE

FEAST DAY
St. Barnabas, Saints Felix and Fortunatus, St. Parisio

ST. BARNABUS DAY

Before the change in calendars, the summer solstice fell on this day, which was known as the beginning of midsummer, or nightless days. An old saying connecting St. Barnabus with the solstice says, "Barnaby Bright, Barnaby Bright: the longest day and the shortest night."

The unbought grace of life, the cheap defense of nations, the nurse of manly sentiment, and the heroic enterprise is lost to us in all but the hearts of romantic visionaries and poets. Lament for the lost cause of chivalry.

[EDMUND BURKE (1729–1797)]

1509 England's King Henry VIII married his elder brother's widow, Catherine of Aragon. She was the elegant daughter of King Ferdinand of Aragon and Isabella of Castile.

1572 Ben Jonson, the playwright responsible for the only contemporary information about William Shakespeare, was born in Westminster. Today he is better known for his dubious Shakespearean lore and his poetry ("Drink to me only with thine eyes") than he is for his theatrical works.

1776 President John Hancock and several members of the Continental Congress asked Virginia representative Richard Henry Lee to create a new committee to draft a declaration of secession from the dominions of the English king and Parliament. On June 29, Lee's committee—composed of Thomas Jefferson, John Adams, Benjamin Franklin, Roger Sherman, and Robert Livingston—presented their draft for debate and a vote. On July 4, an amended version of that draft was accepted. The war that had been raging for more than a year had finally driven the reluctant revolutionaries to sever all ties with their motherland and draft a Declaration of Independence from Britain.

1776 English landscape painter John Constable was born in East Bergholt, Suffolk. He broke from the traditions of the Dutch and English painters by rejecting the use of brown underpainting. He achieved more luminous and natural effects through his use of color, which he employed to capture the effects of reflection in water and the light on clouds. His method of painting outdoors and his interest in the effects of light provided an inspiration to the later school of impressionism.

1864 German composer and conductor Richard Strauss, best known for his tone poems *Death and Transfiguration, Also Sprach Zarathustra, Don Quixote,* and for his operas *Salome, Der Rosenkavalier,* and *Elektra,* was born in Munich. He wrote as a post-Romantic with sweeping melodies, lush and evocative orchestrations, and shifting harmonic centers.

1910 French naval officer, marine explorer, and inventor Jacques Cousteau was born in Saint-Andre-de-Cubzac, France. During his naval career, Cousteau served as president of the French Oceanographic Campaigns and commander of his beloved ship *Calypso.* Cousteau founded the French Office of Underseas Research at Marseille, renamed the Center of Advanced Marine Studies in 1968. His many inventions included the Aqua-Lung diving gear and a process for using television underwater. His numerous books and films brought new understanding of the world's oceans and oceanographic life to millions.

JUNE

1919 Sir Barton, a horse, won the first Triple Crown of horse racing by winning the Belmont Stakes after winning the Kentucky Derby on May 1 and the Preakness on May 14.

1947 The government announced the end of household and institutional sugar rationing, to take effect the next day. It was the last of the Second World War consumer restrictions to go.

1963 After a standoff with the National Guard, Alabama governor George Wallace stepped aside from the steps of the gym at the University of Alabama to allow two black students to enroll in classes.

Charles Haddon Spurgeon is commonly heralded as the greatest preacher to grace the Christian pulpit since the apostle Paul. His metropolitan Tabernacle was undoubtedly a dynamic force for righteousness in Victorian England. But his many years of ministry were marked not only by his masterful pulpiteering, but by his many labors on behalf of the poor and needy as well.

On this day in 1861, he erected an almshouse for the elderly. In 1864, he established a school for the needy children of London. In 1866, he founded the Stockwell Orphanages. And, in 1867, to these many enterprises was added still another, a private hospital.

Explaining this furious activity on behalf of the poor, Spurgeon said, "God's intent in endowing any person with more substance than he needs is that he may have the pleasurable office, or rather the delightful privilege, of relieving want and woe. Alas, how many there are who consider that store which God has put into their hands on purpose for the poor and needy, to be only so much provision for their excessive luxury, a luxury which pampers them but yields them neither benefit nor pleasure. Others dream that wealth is given them that they may keep it under lock and key, cankering and corroding, breeding covetousness and care. Who dares roll a stone over the well's mouth when thirst is raging all around? Who dares keep the bread from the women and children who are ready to gnaw their own arms for hunger? Above all, who dares allow the sufferer to writhe in agony uncared for, and the sick to pine into their graves unnursed? This is no small sin: it is a crime to be answered for, to the Judge, when He shall come to judge the quick and the dead."

JUNE

NATIONAL DAY
  The Philippines
FEAST DAY
  St. Basilides, St. Eskil, St. Leo II, St. Odulf, St. Onuphrius, St. Ternan, St. Peter of Mount Athos, St. Antonia, St. John of Sahagun, St. Paula Frassinetti

1716

Francis Di Girolamo was consecrated to the work of the gospel as a very young man. The victim of a very cruel and harsh childhood himself, he pledged his life to the alleviation of the pains and woes of the poor and destitute. In search of sinners, he entered the prisons, brothels, galleys, back lanes, and tenements of urban Naples. He rescued hundreds of children from deplorable conditions and crusaded against a contraband abortifacient trade that was enjoying a new resurgence—once he burst into a laboratory where parricides were being concocted and, like Jesus in the Temple, literally decimated the room, overturning the equipment and scattering the drugs single-handedly. Over the years, he opened a thrift shop for the poor, several almshouses, a network of small hospices, and a foundling hospital. At his funeral on this day in 1716, the poor came from miles around—representing more than a dozen provinces. They thronged the church in grief, praying that God would raise up another champion of the despised and rejected.

At a time when liberty is under attack, decency is under assault, the family is under siege, and life itself is threatened, the good will arise in truth; they will arise in truth with the very essence and substance of their lives; they will arise in truth though they face opposition by fierce subverters; they will arise in truth never shying from the Standard of truth, never shirking from the Author of truth.

[HENRY LAURENS (1724–1792)]

JUNE

1667 A fifteen-year-old French boy was cured of a fever when Jean-Baptiste Denys, personal physician to Louis XIV, performed the first blood transfusion on a human being using lamb's blood.

1748 In addition to great lightning storms and hail of unusual size over much of Europe, a solar eclipse also occurred on this day.

1776 Virginia's state legislature became the first American government jurisdiction to adopt a comprehensive Bill of Rights in order to secure the liberty of all its citizens. The bill served as a model for the first ten amendments to the new federal Constitution approved nearly a decade and a half later.

1838 The Iowa Territory was organized.

1898 Philippine nationalists declared independence from Spain. Before the end of the year, the island nation would come under a protectorate of the United States—during the short-lived Spanish-American War.

1939 The National Baseball Museum and Hall of Fame was dedicated in the little town where baseball was created, Cooperstown, New York. The first group of inductees had been elected on January 29, 1936—Ty Cobb, Babe Ruth, Honus Wagner, Christy Mathewson, and Walter Johnson.

1963 Civil rights leader and NAACP field secretary Medgar Evers was murdered in front of his home in Jackson, Mississippi. He helped to register black voters and organized boycotts of firms that openly practiced racial discrimination. Byron De La Beckwith, a member of the Ku Klux Klan, was able to evade conviction for more than thirty years despite having repeatedly claimed responsibility for the crime. Finally he was found guilty of the murder in February 1994.

1967 The Supreme Court struck down all state laws prohibiting or restricting interracial marriages.

1979 Cyclist Bryan Allen flew the man-powered *Gossamer Albatross* across the English Channel.

1987 President Reagan, during a visit to the divided German city of Berlin, publicly challenged Soviet leader Mikhail S. Gorbachev to "tear down this wall." Two years later, the people of the city did so despite the Communist leader's reticence.

1994 In a crime that would captivate the nation and the world, Nicole Brown Simpson and Ronald Goldman were slashed to death outside her Los Angeles home. Former football star O. J. Simpson was later acquitted of the killings in a highly publicized criminal trial.

"I would rather be right than president," Henry Clay once said. He got his wish. He was often right but never president, though he ran for the office four times. Franklin Pierce (1804–1869), on the other hand, was a genial New Hampshire lawyer who said that the presidency would be "utterly repugnant" to him. Pierce became president in spite of himself—without ever making a single campaign speech.

Like his predecessor, James K. Polk, Pierce had not even been considered a candidate before the Democratic convention, but he was reluctantly pushed into the role of compromise candidate when the convention reached a stalemate at the forty-eighth ballot on this day in 1852. Although he had served honorably in his state legislature and in the House and Senate, Pierce gradually developed a marked distaste for politics—in 1842 he resigned from the Senate to return to private practice, and later he refused several opportunities to return to office. Handsome, friendly Pierce remained in committed retirement from all political involvement for a decade until he was caught up in the swirl of events that suddenly put him in the White House. The nation saw his ambivalence to party pandering refreshing. He won over a divided field after his friend Nathaniel Hawthorne wrote a flattering campaign biography.

In 1852 slavery was still a dominating issue. Pierce took office with the belief that he should support the Compromise of 1850 and, like Fillmore, he alienated the North by enforcing the law then on the books: the Fugitive Slave Act. The Kansas-Nebraska Act, which created new territories in 1854, simply provided a new arena for the great struggle. In these new territories nothing was settled as abolitionists and pro-slavery groups resorted to force and bloodshed: "Bleeding Kansas" became an open wound.

On other fronts Pierce fared little better. Part of his expansionist policy was a plan to purchase Cuba, but he was forced to denounce three of his ministers—one of them was his successor, James Buchanan—when they declared in the Ostend Manifesto that America should take Cuba, if Spain refused to sell it. However, Pierce was able to purchase land from Mexico which gave us our present southwest border, completing our expansion in the West. Pierce was probably grateful when his party neglected to nominate him for another term. At last he could have his privacy.

1967 President Johnson nominated Solicitor General Thurgood Marshall to become the first African-American justice on the Supreme Court. He first won fame as the lawyer who won the groundbreaking *Brown vs. Board of Education* case in 1954.

Happy homes are the responsibility of husbands and fathers—but inevitably it is wives and mothers who make it so.

1374 John of Gaunt granted Geoffrey Chaucer a pension—which allowed the civil servant to focus his attentions on his writing. Even so, he was only able to finish about half of his masterpiece, *The Canterbury Tales.*

1865 William Butler Yeats, considered one of the greatest twentieth-century poets of the English language, was born in Dublin, Ireland. He received the Nobel Prize for literature in 1923.

1888 Congress created the Department of Labor.

1893 Dorothy Leigh Sayers was born in Oxford, England. She is popularly known for her mystery stories featuring the witty, charming and dapper Lord Peter Wimsey in such novels as *Whose Body* (1923), *Strong Poison* (1930), *Murder Must Advertise* (1933), and *Busman's Honeymoon* (1937). Along with G. K. Chesterton and others, Sayers founded the Detection Club, which produced a parody of the detective story entitled *The Floating Admiral,* with each member of the club writing one chapter. For the last twenty years of her life, Sayers concentrated on writing Christian apologetics, theological dramas, and radio plays (*The Man Born to Be King,* 1943), and scholarly translations of *The Song of Roland* and *Dante's Divine Comedy.*

1898 The Yukon territory of Canada was organized.

1900 China's Boxer Rebellion—which targeted xenophobic paranoia against foreigners and Chinese Christians—erupted into terrifying street violence.

1911 Igor Stravinsky's ballet *Petrushka* was premiered in Paris. Nijinsky danced the lead role of the puppet to Stravinsky's music, which was increasingly experimental and dissonant.

JUNE

1927 Charles Lindbergh received a ticker-tape parade in New York City in which over 750,000 pounds of paper were showered upon the famous aviator. He had just returned from his successful solo flight over the Atlantic.

1942 President Franklin Roosevelt created the Office of War Information, and appointed radio news commentator Elmer Davis to be its head.

1944 During the Second World War, Germany first used the technologically advanced flying bomb against Britain. The V-I bomb *(Vergeltungswaffe 1)* was known in Britain as the "doodlebug."

1971 The *New York Times* began publishing the Pentagon Papers, a secret study of America's involvement in Vietnam.

1983 The *Pioneer Ten,* an unmanned United States space probe, crossed the orbit of Neptune becoming the first spacecraft to leave the solar system. The probe had been launched eleven years earlier.

It was on this day in 1912 that the United States Senate held hearings investigating the tragic sinking of the magnificent White Star liner *Titanic*, two months earlier. The doctrine of "women and children first" was described by second officer Charles Lightoller as "the law of human nature . . . and of Christian chivalry."

However, mention chivalry today and most of us are apt to think of knights in shining armor, damsels in distress, crusaders embarking on a great challenge, or pilgrims intent on a great quest. It is a rather romantic notion that brings Arthur and his Round Table, Ivanhoe and his lost honor, Guenevere and her threatened virtue, and Rapunsel and her dire straits. It evokes images of the long ago and the far away. It is, for us, rather passé. It is a positively medieval concept—a long-forgotten relic of the sentimental past.

But chivalry is a code of honorable conduct that need not necessarily be tied to any particular time or place or cultural context—variously described as a combination of mannerliness, courtesy, loving-kindness, manly valor, and noblesse oblige. As wise men and women throughout all time have known, it is a standard of virtuous behavior that has inspired great men and women through the ages—causing them to long for a kinder, gentler yet bolder, stronger society that abides by the conditions of genuine civilization.

Alas, like the virtue it memorializes—chivalry is little known and little noticed these days. Even in *Titanic* lore, it is overshadowed by the hulk of the political correctness and historical revisionism of Hollywood's film interpretations. Nevertheless, it stands overlooking the Potomac River, bearing quiet testimony to the long-held ideals of Christian civilization.

JUNE

FEAST DAY
St. Dogmael, Saints Valerius and Rugnius, St. Methodius I of Constantinople

FLAG DAY

Congress formally adopted the stars and stripes of the American flag as the National Standard on this day. With the exception of the adding of a star for each new state and the geometric arrangement of those stars, the flag as we know it is the same as the original one Betsy Ross sewed for George Washington—based on the design of his ancient family crest. Thus, this day is celebrated as Flag Day by the displaying and honoring of the flag.

True social security affords the broadest distribution of property through legitimate work as is humanly possible.

[ABRAHAM KUYPER (1837–1920)]

1594 Composer Orlando di Lasso, one of the greatest composers of sacred music in his era, died in Munich. His most famous motets are his settings of the *Penitential Psalms*, but his total oeuvre consists of some two thousand works. He was quite cosmopolitan for his day and traveled extensively.

1666 As of this date, Lutherans in the New Netherlands were allowed the privilege of worshipping in their own homes.

1775 The United States Army was founded.

1819 From 1796 to 1820, Henry Bicknell served with the London Missionary Society on the Pacific island of Tahiti. There his earnest labors— preaching the gospel and teaching the precepts of faithful living—bore abundant fruit. For years his efforts to legally protect the lives of innocents were met with frustration, however, due to the reign of King Pompare. The Tahitian king was renowned for his bloodthirsty indulgence in human sacrifice. During the thirty years of his rule, he commanded the ritual deaths of more than two thousand of his subjects. Regardless of the occasion—whether it was preparation for war, the consecration of a funeral, or the launching of a canoe—the pagan king insisted on offering a human sacrifice. Bicknell's unflagging efforts to rescue the innocent just before the lethal ceremonies and his uncompromising witness before the throne ultimately won the king over. Pompare converted and was baptized on this day in 1819. Before the diligent and dedicated missionary died the following year, he helped the once-murderous king frame Christian laws prohibiting abortion, infanticide, abandonment, and euthanasia.

1841 The first Canadian Parliament opened in Kingston.

1846 A group of U.S. settlers in Sonoma proclaimed the Republic of California.

1936 Journalist, humorist, and novelist G. K. Chesterton died in Beaconsfield, Buckinghamshire. A master of thoughtful epigrams and insightful paradoxes, he became— besides William Shakespeare and Samuel Johnson—the most quoted author in the English language.

1940 German troops entered Paris during the Second World War.

1940 In German-occupied Poland, the Nazi regime opened its notorious concentration camp at Auschwitz.

1951 The first UNIVAC (Universal Automatic Computer) was installed in the United States Census Office.

1954 President Dwight Eisenhower signed an order adding the words "under God" to the Pledge of Allegiance.

1989 Former President Ronald Reagan received an honorary knighthood from Britain's Queen Elizabeth II.

1998 The Chicago Bulls clinched their sixth NBA championship—an unprecedented double "threepeat" separated by a two-year interval.

JUNE

14

An expansionist mood dominated the country in the mid-1840s, and the man who caught the spirit of the times and came from nowhere to lead the country through the period of its greatest expansion was the Tennessean James K. Polk (1795–1849). In spite of this distinction, Polk has been one of the most neglected of our presidents. Emerging from comparative oblivion to become president, he has somehow managed to return there—in spite of a successful administration, one called by several leading historians "the one bright spot in the dull void between Jackson and Lincoln."

When the delegates to the Democratic convention met in Baltimore in 1844, Polk was not even considered for the presidency; before the convention was over he had become the first dark-horse candidate. And, in the election, when the Whigs made "Who is Polk?" their battle cry, he answered them by soundly defeating their very well-known, well-connected, and well-funded candidate Henry Clay, who was running in his third presidential race.

As president the little-known Polk was a strong, though not radical, expansionist. During his administration the nation acquired the vast lands in the Southwest and far West that extended the borders of the country almost to the present continental limits. He proved to be a forceful president in his direction of the Mexican War and in settling the Oregon boundary dispute with Great Britain; yet he did not yield to the extremists who wanted all of Mexico, nor to those who cried "Fifty-four forty or fight!" and claimed the Oregon Territory clear to the Alaskan border.

But the man who successfully led the country through its period of expansion strangely faded away when his work was done. Still popular at the end of his term but exhausted from overwork, Polk declined to be a candidate and returned to his home in Nashville, where he died on this day, only three months after leaving the White House at the age of fifty-three.

JUNE

FEAST DAY
St. Trillo, St. Vitus and his Companions, St. Bardo, St. Aleydia, St. Germaine Cousin of Pibrac, St. Hesychius of Durostorum, St. Landelinus, St. Edburga of Winchester, St. Tatian Dulas, St. Orsiesus

FLOOD DAY

This is the day on which ancient Egyptians expected the beginning of the annual flooding of the Nile River, whose waters fertilized the land. If the waters were late to begin rising by as little as one day, young girls were sacrificed by being drowned to appease the gods.

Two may walk together under the same roof for many years, yet never really meet; and two others at first speech are old friends.

[ROBERT HOWIE (1568–1646)]

1215 The Magna Carta, drafted by Archbishop Stephen Langton, was forced upon King John at the field of Runnymead. England's barons had been on the verge of revolt against the high-handed king who had never been able to match the popularity of his dashing older brother Richard Coeur de Lion. Though the charter was not the genesis of Western liberty as is often claimed—that honor should go to Robert the Bruce's Arbroath Declaration of 1420—the Magna Carta did guarantee several key provisions of common law for the nobles, including trial by jury and a prohibition against new taxes without permission of mediating magistrates-both of which afforded them the rudimentary beginnings of a representational Parliament. John, loath to yield even a fraction of his power, appealed to the pope, promising to become his vassal. The pope promptly voided the Magna Carta.

1509 The brilliant English Catholic academic John Fisher, who founded both St. John's College and Christ College at Cambridge University, published his famed sermon series, *Seven Penitential Psalms* for the king's mother, Lady Margaret Beaufort. The sermons, consisting of his comments on Psalms 6, 32, 38, 51, 102, 130, 143, went through several editions in his lifetime. They were recited during the Lenten season leading up to the Easter celebration.

1752 Benjamin Franklin made a demonstration showing the relationship between lightning and electricity at Philadelphia, Pennsylvania. A letter he wrote describing his experiments was read before the Royal Society in December of that year. Based upon his experiments, Franklin declared that electricity is "an element diffused among, and attracted by, other matter, particularly water and metals," and as such might be able to be harnessed.

1775 George Washington was named commander in chief of the Continental Army on this day.

1811 Harriet Beecher Stowe, author of the incendiary best-selling book *Uncle Tom's Cabin*, was born in Litchfield, Connecticut, the sixth child of Lyman Beecher, an ardent Calvinist and Puritan.

1836 Arkansas became the twenty-fifth state.

1843 Composer Edvard Grieg was born in Bergen, Norway, where he is considered a national hero as the embodiment of the land and its people. His most recognizable work is *Peer Gynt*, incidental music for the play by fellow countryman Henrik Ibsen.

JUNE

1844 Charles Goodyear received a patent for the process of vulcanizing rubber. After endless experimentation, he was finally able to prevent rubber from sticking and melting in hot temperatures.

1845 The United States and England, with the signing of the Oregon Treaty, agreed on the 49th parallel as the boundary between the United States and Canada.

1864 Union Secretary of War Edwin M. Stanton signed an order confiscating the home of General Robert E. Lee—the decree authorized it as the Arlington National Cemetery.

1978 King Hussein of Jordan married twenty-six-year-old American Lisa Halaby, who became Queen Noor.

For the first time, on this day in 1757 a Catholic prelate declared that all nations and peoples could have the Bible translated into their own vernacular tongues. The surprise concession of Pope Benedict XIV sent shock waves all across the Catholic world.

The patristic and medieval church had willingly translated the Scriptures into local languages. John Chrysostom had made a vernacular translation of the Bible for the Byzantines. The Venerable Bede had rendered the Gospels into Saxon. Alfred the Great translated the psalms. Charlemagne, after failing to force Latin on his people, sponsored a French vernacular translation. Cyril and Methodius had made an early Slavic version. And of course, the efforts of John Wycliffe and Jan Hus were widely disseminated.

But during the late Middle Ages, authority had been ascribed to Jerome's Vulgate version. Latin had become the official language of the church. It was held that control of Scripture was tantamount to control of authority. Churchmen and rulers alike seemed fearful of the liberating effects of the Bible in society at large, and so both sought to keep it out of the hands of the common people. The official line of the church was that it feared abuse and profanation of the Word of God in the hands of laymen, since it was too deep even for the greatest scholars to fully understand.

In England, Lollard preachers were forbidden to disseminate Wycliffe's English translation. Church councils actually forbade translation into the vernacular. By the middle of the fifteenth century, translation could be made only with the approval of a bishop—but the early rumblings of reform made even this policy too permissive.

In 1478 Pope Sixtus IV advocated censorship, saying that women foolishly "arrogate to themselves the knowledge of Scripture." Book burnings that included Bibles were common after 1521. The Synod of Sens in 1528 forbade all vernacular translations. Sometimes the translators and publishers themselves were burned. Possession of a Bible became criminal and often resulted in the execution of the accused.

In 1546 the Council of Trent allowed Bibles to be produced in the local languages as long as they had Catholic annotations and were attended by explanatory lectures. In 1713 a papal bull titled "Unigenitus" condemned the proposition that the Bible was for everyone. Thus, Benedict's decree was more than a little revolutionary.

JUNE

FEAST DAY
St. Cyricus, St. Ismael, St. Aurelian, St. John Francis Regis, Saints Cyr and Julietta, St. Benno of Meissen, St. Lutgarde, Saints Ferreolus and Ferrutio, St. Tychon of Amathus

Leaders are those who make the most of every moment, of every opportunity, and of every available resource.

[THEODORE ROOSEVELT (1858–1919)]

1456 Twenty-five years after being burned at the stake, Joan of Arc was exonerated of the charge of heresy by King Charles VII of France.

1502 The Sainte Chapelle was completed for the Duke of Savoy to house the much-disputed, but often venerated Shroud of Turin—a cloth in which Christ was reputedly wrapped following His crucifixion. Though scientists have been divided ever since, the general consensus is that the shroud is a brilliant forgery, painted in tempera—a carbon dating test that places its earliest possible date at 1000, though it was most likely created sometime between 1260 and 1390, the very time period in which it first drew the attention of the Savoy regents.

1567 Mary, Queen of Scots, was imprisoned in Lochleven Castle in Scotland.

1775 The U.S. Army Corps of Engineers, the primary engineering component of the United States Army, was organized when the Continental Congress authorized the use of engineers to prepare the fortifications for the Battle of Bunker Hill. Although the original duties of the Corps were military (coastal fortification, mapmaking, topographical survey), Congress passed the General Survey Act in 1824, which provided for the use of the corps for road, canal, and railroad surveys, lighthouse construction, and other improvements to rivers and harbors. In addition, the Corps planned and built the United States Capitol, the Lincoln Memorial, the Library of Congress, and the Washington Monument.

1846 The longest papacy in history began. Giovanni Maria Mastai Ferretti became Pope Pius IX on that day. But his thirty-two years as pontiff were very troubled times for the Roman Church. When he took office, the papacy ruled vast lands, most of which were lost during his reign. He was most notable though, for his promulgation of two very controversial dogmas: Immaculate Conception, which teaches that Mary was purified from original sin before her birth; and Papal Infallibility, which teaches that the pope cannot err when speaking ex cathedra on matters of faith and morals.

1858 In his acceptance speech for nomination to the United States Senate, Abraham Lincoln declared, "I believe this government cannot endure permanently, half slave and half free.... A house divided against itself cannot stand."

1897 President William McKinley signed a treaty of annexation with Hawaii.

1903 Ford Motor Company was incorporated.

1933 As part of the New Deal, the United States Congress voted to establish the Federal Bank Deposit Insurance Corporation and the National Recovery Administration in the Banking Act of 1933, and the National Industrial Recovery Act, respectively.

1955 Pope Pius XII excommunicated Argentine president Juan Domingo Peron.

1961 Soviet ballet dancer Rudolf Nureyev defected to the West while his troupe was in Paris.

1963 The world's first female space traveler, Valentina Tereshkova, was launched into orbit by the Soviet Union aboard *Vostok 6.*

JUNE

16

357

On this day in 1825, to commemorate the fiftieth anniversary of the great Battle of Bunker Hill in Boston—as well as to dedicate the site of a new monument—the venerable Senator from New Hampshire, Daniel Webster, delivered one of the most eloquent orations in American political history. Long studied both for its rhetorical brilliance and its civic perspective, the speech outlines the basic principles and precepts of the nation's extraordinary experiment in liberty.

He began by asserting, "We are among the sepulchers of our fathers. We are on ground distinguished by their valor, their constancy, and the shedding of their blood. We are here, not to fix an uncertain date in our annals, nor to draw it into notice an obscure and unknown spot. If our humble purpose had never been conceived, if we ourselves had never been born, June 17, 1775, would have been a day on which all subsequent history would have poured its light, and the eminence where we stand a point of attraction to the eyes of successive generations. But we are Americans. We live in what may be called the early age of this great continent; and we know that our posterity, through all time, are here to enjoy and suffer the allotments of humanity. We see before us a probable train of great events; we know that our own fortunes have been happily cast; and it is natural, therefore, that we should be moved by the contemplation of occurrences which have guided our destiny before many of us were born, and settled the condition in which we should pass that portion of our existence which God allows to men on earth."

He continued, saying, "These are excitements to duty; but they are not suggestions of doubt. Our history and our condition, all that is gone before us, and all that surrounds us, authorize the belief, that popular governments, though subject to occasional variations, in form perhaps not always for the better, may yet, in their general character, be as durable and permanent as other systems. We know, indeed, that in our country any other is impossible. The principle of free governments adheres to the American soil. It is bedded in it, immovable as its mountains. And let the sacred obligations which have developed on this generation, and on us, sink deep in our hearts."

Finally, he concluded, "In a day of peace, let us advance the arts of peace and the works of peace. Let us develop the resources of our land, call forth its powers, build up its institutions, promote all its great interests, and see whether we also, in our day and generation, may not perform something worthy to be remembered. Let us cultivate a true spirit of union and harmony. In pursuing the great objects, which our condition points out to us, let us act under a settled conviction, and an habitual feeling, that these twenty-four States, are one country. Let our conceptions be enlarged to the circle of our duties. Let us extend our ideas over the whole of the vast field in which we are called to act. Let our object be, Our Country, Our Whole Country, And Nothing But Our Country. And, by the blessing of God, may that country itself become a vast and splendid monument, not of oppression and terror, but of Wisdom, of Peace, and of Liberty, upon which the world may gaze with admiration for ever."

As Theodore Roosevelt later recounted, "It was perhaps the greatest oration since Cicero excoriated Cataline."

JUNE

NATIONAL DAY
Iceland
FEAST DAY
St. Moling, St. Adulf, St. Nectan, St. Botulf, St. Alban, St. Avitus, St. Bessarion, St. Hypatius, St. Rainerius of Pisa, St. Emily de Vialai, St. Hervé, Saints Nicander and Marcian, Saints Teresa and Sanchia of Portugal

A man can do nothing better than to find satisfaction in his work.

[KING SOLOMON (C. 1000 B.C.)]

1579 Sir Francis Drake sailed into San Francisco Bay and named the region New Albion.

1722 A little band of religious fugitives from Moravia (in modern Czechoslovakia) asked Count Ludwig von Zinzindorf if they might settle on his land. He consented, and thus the village of Herrnhut was founded. Ultimately, Herrnhut became the gathering place for innumerable religious exiles, including persecuted Lutheran, Schwenkfelder, Separatist, Reformed, and Brethren believers. In short order, a twenty-four-hour around-the-clock prayer vigil was established that lasted one hundred years. The fervent prayers resulted in the sending out of missionaries to many lands, the first Protestant missions outside Europe and North America. Thus Herrnhut reached out and touched other lands—even John and Charles Wesley were influenced by these Moravians.

1775 The Battle of Bunker Hill was fought on this day. It was the first battle of the American War for Independence—though King George III called it the Presbyterian Parsons' War. Although the British won a slight victory, the Americans were greatly encouraged by their ability to match the British and their great firepower. It was during this battle that Colonial Colonel William Prescott declared, "Men, you are all marksmen: don't one of you fire until you see the whites of their eyes."

1856 In Philadelphia, the Republican Party opened its first convention.

1882 Composer Igor Fyodorovich Stravinsky was born near St. Petersburg, Russia. When he became an American citizen he mistakenly adjusted his birth date from June 5 Old Style to June 18.

1885 The Statue of Liberty arrived in New York City aboard the French ship *Isere*.

1928 Amelia Earhart embarked on a transatlantic flight from Newfoundland to Wales—the first by a woman.

1942 Attempting sabotage, eight Germans were caught as they landed on the coasts of Long Island and Florida.

JUNE

1963 The Supreme Court declared that the recitation of the Lord's Prayer or reading of biblical verses in government schools was unconstitutional—beginning the process toward making American public institutions officially atheistic.

1969 The perverse Broadway musical review *Oh! Calcutta!* opened in New York.

1972 Washington, D.C., police arrested five men for a break-in at the Democratic Party National Committee's headquarters in the posh Watergate office and apartment complex. This incident led to the investigation of the "Watergate Affair," which eventually led to the resignation of President Nixon in 1974.

1994 After leading police on a slow-speed chase on Southern California freeways, football hero O. J. Simpson was arrested and charged with murder in the slayings of his ex-wife, Nicole, and her friend Ronald Goldman. Simpson was later acquitted in his sensational criminal trial.

359

FEAST DAY

*Saints Mark and Marcellian, St.
Amandus of Bordeaux, St.
Eliisabeth of Schönau, St. Gregory
Barbarigo*

One of the largest landholders in America, Charles Carroll (1737–1832) was a leader of the Catholic community in Maryland and the only Catholic to sign the Declaration of Independence. Like Washington and Hancock, he risked a great fortune by defying the mother country.

After years of study in Europe, Carroll returned to a country indignant over new British taxation, especially the Stamp Act. Although as a Catholic he was unable to hold office, he became a leader of the opposition—partly through newspaper articles he wrote under a pen name. He was a member of the colony's committee of observation, a group directing activities of patriots; the provincial committee of correspondence; and Maryland's unofficial legislature. He actively supported the policy of nonimportation of British goods.

In 1776 Congress appointed Carroll, his cousin John, Samuel Chase, and Benjamin Franklin as commissioners to Canada—to try to bring Canada into the struggle on the side of the colonies. However, American troops had already invaded Canada, turning the French-Canadians against the American cause. The mission failed. Carroll returned from Canada on this day in 1776, in time to take a firm stand for independence in the Maryland legislature. After helping to win the legislature's approval, he was selected as a delegate to the Continental Congress, where he signed the Declaration of Independence.

For the next twenty-five years, Carroll played a prominent part in both state and national affairs. In Congress, during the war he served with the Board of War and other important committees. A champion of freedom of religion, Carroll contributed to the Maryland constitution, and though he declined to attend the Constitutional Convention, he supported the new national Constitution. As one of Maryland's senators in the first Congress under that new form of government, he was instrumental in bringing Rhode Island, which had not yet ratified the Constitution, into the Union, and he assisted in drafting the amendments to the Constitution known as the Bill of Rights, finally assuring the freedom of worship and other freedoms for which he had risked so much.

When Carroll died in 1832 he was reputed to be the wealthiest man in America—and the last surviving signer of the Declaration of Independence.

Where you are liberal of your loves and counsels, be sure you be not loose; for those you make friends and give your heart to, when they once perceive the least rub in your fortunes, fall away like water from ye, never found again but where they mean to sink ye.

[WILLIAM SHAKESPEARE (c. 1564–1616)]

286 Roman emperor Fabian condemned twin brothers Marcus and Marcellianus to die. Despite the fact that the brothers were from a prominent family, they were stabbed to death with lances for the crime of remaining firm in their Christian faith.

373 Ephrem the Syrian, one of the great saints of the Patristic period, died. Originally from Nisibis in Mesopotamia, when the Persians forced Emperor Jovianus to relinquish Nisibis, Ephrem and many other Christians migrated to Edessa. Ephrem was already a famed teacher. In Edessa he founded a school of exegesis, which was neither as literal as that of Antioch nor as typological as that of Alexandria. He was the school's most famous representative. A true ascetic, during his years at Edessa, Ephrem lived in a cave, eating only barley bread and vegetables. Nonetheless he took an active part in the affairs of the city where his dirty, patched robe must have made him a comical sight. During his long and honored ministry, Ephrem wrote many hymns. He so emphasized their place in formal worship that the practice spread from Edessa to the whole Christian world. He saw hymns as a means of Christian education. Hence many of his songs take faith as their theme. Others were written to counter the heresies of Marcion, Manicheism, and Bardesanes. These were widely sung and "lent luster to the Christian assemblies," according to one early church historian. To this day Syrian Christians call him the "Harp of the Holy Ghost." He produced commentaries on virtually the whole Bible. His last public act was to distribute grain to Edessa's starving poor during a famine. No one else was trusted for the task.

1682 The city of Pennsylvania was officially established by patriot William Penn.

1778 American forces entered Philadelphia as the British withdrew during the Revolutionary War.

1812 The United States, desiring to expand its territories into the Canadian provinces, declared war against Britain.

1815 Napoleon Bonaparte was defeated as British and Prussian troops foiled the emperor's careful strategy on the battlefield of Waterloo in the Lower Netherlands (later gaining independence as Belgium).

JUNE

1873 Suffragist Susan B. Anthony was fined $100 for attempting to vote in the 1872 presidential election. The fine was never paid.

1940 British Prime Minister Winston Churchill encouraged his beleagered countrymen to conduct themselves with valor in the intensifying Second World War: "Let us therefore brace ourselves to our duty, and so bear ourselves that if the British Commonwealth and Empire last for a thousand years, men will say, 'This was their finest hour.'"

1948 Columbia Records publicly unveiled its new long-playing phonograph record in New York.

1953 Warner Brothers introduced yet another foil for the irrepressible Bugs Bunny in the form of the Tasmanian Devil who debuted in "Devil May Hare."

1979 President Carter and Soviet President Leonid I. Brezhnev signed the SALT II strategic arms limitation treaty in Vienna.

18

On this day in 1795, Louis XVII, the last little Bourbon king of France, died in the notorious Temple prison during the chaotic days of the French Revolution. Amazingly though, that fact was not confirmed with any certainty until more than two centuries later when a series of complicated DNA tests confirmed the identity of the child's remains.

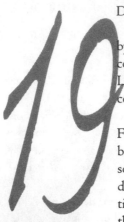

After his parents, King Louis XVI and Marie Antoinette, were beheaded by the mad tyrant Robespierre in 1793, the dauphin was locked away in the cold, damp Temple, which was originally a fortified monastery in Paris. Less than two years later he died a slow and painful death—apparently of complications from tuberculosis—at the age of ten.

The fate of the heir to the Bourbon throne had long been one of France's most enduring mysteries. Some historians believed that the dead boy was indeed Louis XVII. But others believed that the royal heir had somehow escaped and another child died in his place to save official face during the unstable days that followed the Revolution. One guard at the time said that he had seen a large number of bathtubs being carried out of the prison. When the porters carrying one stumbled, he claimed that he had heard a child's cry from within. Ever since, romantic royalists have hung on to every shred of hope that some member of the royal family escaped the calamity of the times. As a result, myths, legends, rumors, and speculations have continually circulated. Nearly eight hundred books have been written on the subject.

But science came to the aid of history. Genetic and pathology researchers from two European universities compared DNA from the scant remains of the dead boy—a long-preserved heart—to DNA from hair cut from Marie Antoinette when she was a child in Austria. Philippe Delorme, the French historian who organized the tests, said they laid the riddle to rest at last.

The child's remains took a circuitous route over almost two hundred years before ending up in a crystal vase in the royal crypt outside Paris. The heart was stolen by the doctor who performed the autopsy on the dead child in 1795. He pickled it in alcohol for eight to ten years. One of his students subsequently stole it, but on his deathbed, the student asked his wife to return it to the doctor. After the restoration of the French monarchy in 1814, the heart was offered to various members of the royal family, but they were reluctant to accept a relic of such dubious provenance. It finally found its way to the Spanish branch of the Bourbon family. They returned it to Paris in 1975 and it was placed in the royal crypt.

Now that the rumors are laid to rest, another sordid chapter of the French Revolution has been written—and as is par for the course, it has been written with a sad and morbid ending.

JUNE

FEAST DAY

Saints Gervase and Protase, St. Juliana Falconieri, St. Romuald, St. Boniface of Querfurt, St. Deodatus of Nevers, St. Odo of Cambrai

When the pale of chivalry is broken, rudeness and insult soon enter the breach.

[SAMUEL JOHNSON (1709–1784)]

1586 English colonists sailed from Roanoke Island, North Carolina, after failing to establish England's first permanent settlement in America.

1623 French scientist and philosopher Blaise Pascal was born. He was a mathematical prodigy who published his first treatise at the age of sixteen. His tutors, trying to direct his focus toward the classics, removed all of his mathematics texts. However, they admitted defeat when they discovered him working out Euclid's theorems of geometry on the floor with a piece of charcoal, from memory. Pascal voluntarily gave up mathematics for religion when he was just twenty-five.

1910 The first widely promoted Father's Day celebration was held in Spokane, Washington. Louise Dodd suggested the idea to her pastor. Eventually the mayor of the city and the governor of the state endorsed her concept and issued proclamations in support. Even the famed politician William Jennings Bryan weighed in with words of support. The third Sunday in June was established as the date of the celebration. Mrs. Dodd wanted to find a way to honor her own father. When his wife died in childbirth, he was left with six children. Somehow he overcame the difficulties of rearing them and operating his farm. The idea was slow to catch on. But by 1916 President Woodrow Wilson had endorsed the idea, and in 1924 Calvin Coolidge recommended national observance of the day "to impress upon fathers the full measure of their obligation" and strengthen intimate ties between fathers and children.

1917 During the First World War, King George V ordered the British royal family to dispense with all their German titles and surnames—the Hanover family had first come to England when the Stuart monarchy was deposed and the throne was offered to George I, the German imperial elector. Thus, the Saxe-Colburg-Gotha family took the new name of Windsor.

1934 The Federal Communications Commission was created.

JUNE

1953 Convicted of passing atom bomb secrets to the Soviet Union, Julius and Ethel Rosenberg were executed at Sing Sing prison in Ossining, New York. They were the first people to be executed for espionage in the United States.

1961 The Supreme Court struck down a provision in Maryland's constitution requiring state officeholders to profess a belief in God.

1964 The Civil Rights Act of 1964 was approved after surviving an eighty-three-day Senate filibuster.

1977 Pope Paul VI proclaimed a nineteenth-century Philadelphia bishop, John Neumann, the first American male saint.

1987 The Supreme Court struck down a Louisiana law requiring any public school teaching the theory of evolution to teach creationism science as well.

19

Though you might never know it by reading some of our modern history textbooks, the capture and imprisonment of Henry Laurens on this day in 1779 proved to be one of the most important events of the entire Revolutionary War period. He was a wealthy merchant from South Carolina who had served as a member of the first provincial convention in Charleston in 1775. The next year he was elected vice president of the sovereign state under its new constitution and was chosen to serve as a representative in the Continental Congress in Philadelphia. He was so highly regarded by his fellow delegates there that when John Hancock resigned his position as president, they unanimously elected Laurens to succeed him in 1777.

His tenure as the fourth president of the newly independent United States was terribly tumultuous. But Laurens served admirably. Furiously outspoken, unflaggingly ambitious, and decisively brilliant, his obvious leadership abilities won him the admiration of the American patriots—and the enmity of the court at Westminster. At the end of his distinguished term he was appointed to supervene John Adams as the legate to the Dutch government at the Hague. And it was to that assignment that he was traveling when he was captured.

Laurens was transported to London where he was imprisoned in the infamous Tower. Although he had been a lifelong churchman, he was not particularly known for his piety. But cut off from the noisy forgetfulness of public life, he resolved his faith into what he called a "God-fearing, Bible-reading, hymn-singing passion for permanent things." The experience of prison often changes the outlook of men. Every sham pretense, every false motive, every empty ideal, every corrupt ambition, and every shallow desire is exposed for what it is. Prison either drives men to greater sagacity and keenness or to deeper vapidity and tedium. It either breaks men or makes men. It made Laurens.

Though he was no less irascible in his resistance to English rule, no less belligerent in his revolutionary insurgency, and no less antithetical in his sedition against tyranny, he was far more pensive, far more judicious, and far more principled. Giving glory to God through works of excellence became far more important to him than mere political pragmatism or popular acclaim.

After he was released in a prisoner exchange—for Lord Cornwallis following the Battle of Yorktown—he applied his newfound perspective of service to his country to the great benefit of all. Although he had always been a man of great ability and accomplishment, Laurens redoubled his commitment to do all things excellently and to the glory of God. Of course, among his peers, that kind of commitment would not have been terribly unusual—George Washington, Patrick Henry, Samuel Adams, and Gouverneur Morris were all sticklers for covenantal excellence. For them maintaining a standard of excellence in all that they might undertake in life was an outworking of Christian virtue. But it was also a significant part of the legacy of leadership.

JUNE

FEAST DAY

Edward the Martyr; St. Alban; St. Govan; St. John of Matera; St. Silverius, pope; St. Bain; St. Adalbert of Magdeburg

To see what is right and not to do it is cowardice. It is never a question of who is right but what is right.

[JOHN BUCHAN (1875–1940)]

1599   The irregular synod of Diamper was called by Alexis de Menzez, archbishop of Goa, to correct lapses and errors of the Indian Christians. His methods were somewhat arbitrary and high handed, revealing a colonial mindset. He even unilaterally changed the articles after they had been adopted. Six hundred and sixty Indian lay-Christians and one hundred thirty of their Christian leaders gathered at the synod and accepted the Menzez articles. According to observers they did not understand what they were signing. Later, India's Christians repudiated the Diamper agreement and had to be wooed back by the Roman Church.

1756   In India, a group of British soldiers was imprisoned in a suffocating cell that gained notoriety as the "Black Hole of Calcutta." Most died.

1782   Congress approved the Great Seal of the United States.

1837   At the age of eighteen, Victoria became the queen of England when her uncle, William IV, died. She was awakened before dawn by the archbishop of Canterbury and Lord Chamberlain. Rather than keep them waiting, she threw a shawl over her nightgown-clad shoulders, and stood before them in her slippers, perfectly collected and dignified, but with tears in her eyes.

1863   Granted a waiver from explicit constitutional regulations prohibiting any part of one state from seceding and becoming a separate state, West Virginia was admitted to the Union as the thirty-fifth state.

1893   A jury in New Bedford, Massachusetts, found Lizzie Borden innocent of the ax murders of her father and stepmother.

JUNE

1898   During the Spanish-American War, the cruiser USS *Charleston* captured the Spanish-ruled island of Guam.

1943   Race-related rioting erupted in Detroit; federal troops were sent in two days later to quell the violence that resulted in more than thirty deaths.

1947   Las Vegas casino pioneer Benjamin "Bugsy" Siegel was shot dead at the Beverly Hills, California, mansion of his girlfriend, Virginia Hill, apparently at the order of mob associates.

1948   The variety series *Toast of the Town*, hosted by Ed Sullivan, debuted on CBS television from a theater on Upper Broadway.

1963   The United States and Soviet Union signed an agreement to set up a hotline communications link between the two superpowers.

1967   Boxing champion Muhammad Ali was convicted in Houston of violating Selective Service laws by refusing to be drafted. Despite the fact that the conviction was ultimately overturned by the Supreme Court, he was stripped of his titles.

20

JUNE

When the famed St. Paul's Cathedral burned down in the great London fire of 1666, King Charles II appointed Christopher Wren chief architect of the rebuilding project. Although he had no formal training as an architect, Wren was a genius who contributed to many sciences and built several public works. Wren's simple and elegant proposals were fiercely contested by a royal oversight committee that countered with a graceless alternative design.

Wren, a patient, practical man, agreed to the committee's plan—with the stipulation that he be allowed to make such modifications as would prove necessary during the actual construction. He modified continuously with the result that the finished work was almost identical to his own original design—a fortunate turn of events in any case: The completed building is one of European ecclesiastical architecture's greatest achievements. Of course, Wren's wry machinations hardly endeared him to the committee—despite his obvious brilliance, they determined to remove him from consideration for any future royal commissions.

As a result of all this controversy, only a handful of official onlookers were present to observe as the first stone was lowered deep into the earth overlooking the Thames River and set in place by Thomas Strong, a master mason. There was no special service. There was no fanfare. There was no dedicatory speech. There was no citywide ceremony. It was almost as if a warehouse or even a theater were being constructed, not the city's cathedral.

Nevertheless, Wren's project was imminently successful. Few cathedrals are built in a lifetime but Wren was able to complete the project in just 35 years. Interestingly, when he first began to lay out on the floor of the reconstructed cathedral the shape of his proposed dome, he called a workman to bring him a bit of stone. The workman grabbed the first piece that came to hand. Inscribed on it in Latin was the word *Resurgam*—May I Rise Again. St. Paul's did indeed rise—and it rose swiftly.

To Wren, a staunch Protestant, the preaching of the gospel was the primary function of a church. As a result, he designed the interior so that the pulpit would be the center of attention. He forbade his workmen to curse on the project, reminding them, on pain of dismissal, that they were engaged in a holy work. After his death Christopher Wren was entombed within the Cathedral. On his commemoration stone is written: *Si monumentum requiris, circumspice*—If you would see his monument, look around.

FEAST DAY
St. Aloysius Gonzaga, St. Leufred, St. Mewan, St. Engelmund, St. John Rigby, St. Eusebius of Samosata, St. Leutfridus

SUMMER SOLSTICE As the first day of summer in the Northern Hemisphere, the earliest known poem written in English was about this day: "Summer is ycomen in, loud sing cuckoo; groweth seed, and bloweth mead, and springeth the weed new."

> *The courage we desire and prize is not the courage to die decently but to live manfully.*
>
> [THOMAS CARLYLE (1795–1881)]

1611 The discoverer of the Hudson River, the Hudson Straits, and Hudson's Bay, Henry Hudson, and his son were last seen in a small boat set adrift from his ship *Discovery* by mutineering seamen.

1684 The charter of the Massachusetts Bay Colony was revoked on the grounds that the colonial administration had engaged in active discrimination against the Church of England.

1788 The United States Constitution went into effect as New Hampshire became the ninth state to ratify it.

1834 Cyrus Hall McCormick received a patent for his reaping machine.

1868 *Die Meistersinger von Nuremberg*, the opera by Richard Wagner, was first performed at the Hoftheater in Munich. The story is based on the practices and traditions of the German Mastersingers of the fourteenth, fifteenth, and sixteenth centuries. Working together in societies similar to guilds comprised of various grades of membership from apprentice to master, the merits of a particular member were judged according to an elaborate set of rules and a series of tests. The plot of the opera is centered around the historic figure of Hans Sachs (1494–1576) of Nuremberg and a song contest.

1889 Dwight L. Moody (1837–1899) was America's foremost evangelist throughout the difficult days that immediately followed the cataclysm of the War Between the States and disruption of Reconstruction. Literally thousands came to know Christ because the former shoe salesman faithfully proclaimed the gospel wherever and whenever he had opportunity—pioneering the methods of both modern crusade evangelism

and Sunday school outreach. But in addition to preaching to the masses, he cared for the masses. He was responsible for the establishment of some one hundred and fifty schools, street missions, soup kitchens, colportage societies, and other charitable organizations—including Chicago's first street boys clinic on this day in 1889. He believed it was essential that Christians proclaim the gospel in both word and deed. As a result, his impact on the nation is still felt through many of those institutions that continue their vital work—nearly a century after his death.

JUNE

1905 Jean-Paul Sartre, the radical French novelist, playwright, philosopher, atheist, and existentialist, was born in Paris. He declined the Nobel Prize for literature in 1964.

1932 Heavyweight Max Schmeling lost a title fight by decision to Jack Sharkey, prompting Schmeling's manager, Joe Jacobs, to exclaim, "We was robbed!"

1963 Cardinal Giovanni Battista Montini was chosen to succeed the late Pope John XXIII. The new pope took the name Paul VI.

1964 Civil rights workers Michael H. Schwerner, Andrew Goodman, and James E. Chaney disappeared in Philadelphia, Mississippi. Their bodies were found buried in an earthen dam six weeks later.

1973 The Supreme Court ruled that states may ban materials found to be obscene according to local standards.

The contentious Third Ecumenical Council was held in the ancient city of Ephesus in Asia Minor on this day in 431. It had been called to resolve a doctrinal controversy that had split the entire church into two warring camps.

The teachings of Nestorius, the prominent archbishop of Constantinople, had been challenged by Cyril, the equally prominent archbishop of Alexandria. The emperor Theodosius, who called the council, believed that the strength of his empire depended upon true worship of God without the intermingling of any manner of falsehood. Thus, he was determined not to allow the controversy to remain unresolved.

The conflict actually originated in the school of Antioch, when Diodorus and Theodore, bishop of Mopsuestia, argued that the human and divine natures of Christ could not have been united from the moment of conception in the womb of Mary. The orthodox position had always been that Mary was the Theotokos—literally, the God Bearer or Mother of God. The church had thus always taught that though the Virgin Mary was not the progenator of the eternal and indivisible Trinity, she was nevertheless the mother of the incarnate second person of the Trinity, the God-Man, Jesus. Thus Theotokos was an important honorific title intended to emphasize the union of the two natures of Christ. Nestorius though, taking his cues from his mentors in Antioch, refused to accept the title Theotokos, arguing that it rationally belittled the character and nature of Christ's humanity.

The Council at Ephesus opened before Nestorius and his followers were able to arrive to explain their position more fully. Thus, they were never actually able to answer the charges against them. Nevertheless, the heresy seemed clear-cut. As a result, Cyril, with the agreement of Theodosius and Celestine, the archbishop of Rome, issued a series of anathemas. In effect, he served as both accuser and judge—but it was more than evident to most of the other two hundred theologians, pastors, and bishops that Nestorianism undermined an essential aspect of the very nature of Christ, the Incarnation, and the Trinity.

JUNE

431

St. Paulinus, known as the inventor of bells, died in Nola, Italy. It was said that at the time of his death, a slight tremor was felt in the earth, which caused his bells at the St. Felix Church to ring.

Courage is resistance to fear, mastery of fear—not absence of fear. Except a creature be part coward, it is not a compliment to say it is brave.

1679 At the battle of Bothwell Bridge, the Duke of Monmouth crushed the stalwart resistance of the Scottish Covenanters.

1815 Napoleon Bonaparte abdicated the French imperial throne for a second time following his defeat at Waterloo.

1870 Congress created the Department of Justice.

1906 Film director Billy Wilder, born Samuel Wilder, was born in Sucha, Austria, now a Polish city. In his early days, Wilder served as a reporter and part-time scriptwriter in Vienna and Berlin. In 1933, his Jewish heritage forced his emigration to the U.S. where, in 1944, he gained professional respect as director of *Double Indemnity*. In 1945, Wilder was back in Germany as director of the U.S. Army's Psychological Warfare Division. Wilder wrote and directed several films noted for their humorous tackling of taboo subjects such as alcoholism and POW camps. He brilliantly explored the futile emptiness of modern life with *Sunset Boulevard* in 1950, then created some of the great film comedies with *Sabrina* in 1954, *The Seven Year Itch* in 1955, *Love in the Afternoon* in 1957, and *Some Like It Hot* in 1959.

1910 The *Deutchland*, a Zeppelin airship, began regular passenger service between Friedrichshafen and Dusseldorf, a distance of three hundred miles. Such airships were named for their German creator, Count Zeppelin.

1912 Theodore Roosevelt accepted the presidential nomination of the Progressive Party after a power struggle at the 1912 Republican Convention disqualified all the Roosevelt delegates, thus denying him the nomination—this, despite the fact that Roosevelt had won every primary. William H. Taft, Roosevelt's named successor, had failed to live up to the leadership demands and policies of the former president. Incensed by the inability of Taft to lead effectively, Roosevelt once again sought the office of president. He condemned Taft for being too beholden to big business. Running on a platform consisting of the Ten Commandments, he sought to promote the prohibition of child labor, women's suffrage, national social insurance, and limits on government incursion in labor disputes. The Progressive ticket got more votes than the Republicans, but the split enabled Woodrow Wilson, a Democrat, to eke out a victory.

JUNE

1938 Heavyweight boxing champion Joe Louis knocked out Max Schmeling in the first round of their rematch at Yankee Stadium.

1940 At the advent of the Second World War, Adolf Hitler gained a stunning victory as France was forced to sign an armistice eight days after German forces overran Paris.

1941 Germany invaded the territory of its ally, the Soviet Union, during the Second World War.

1944 President Franklin Roosevelt signed the GI Bill of Rights.

1945 The battle for Okinawa officially ended. Nearly 12,520 Americans and 110,000 Japanese were killed in the eighty-one-day campaign.

1970 President Nixon signed a measure that lowered the voting age to eighteen.

22

Thomas Malthus was a nineteenth-century cleric and sometime professor of political economy whose theories of population growth and economic stability quickly became the basis for national and international social policy throughout the West. According to his scheme, population grows exponentially over time, while production only grows arithmetically. He believed a crisis was therefore inevitable—a kind of population time bomb was ticking that he believed threatened the very existence of the human race. Poverty, deprivation, and hunger were the evidences of this looming population crisis. He believed that the only responsible social policy would be one that addressed the unnatural problem of population growth—by whatever means necessary. Every social problem was subordinate to this central cause. In fact, Malthus argued, to deal with sickness, crime, privation, and need in any other way simply aggravates the problems further—thus he actually condemned charity, philanthropy, international relief and development, missionary outreaches, and economic investment around the world as counterproductive.

In his magnum opus, *An Essay on the Principle of Population*, first published on this day in 1798, Malthus wrote, "All children born, beyond what would be required to keep up the population to a desired level, must necessarily perish, unless room be made for them by the deaths of grown persons. . . . Therefore . . . we should facilitate, instead of foolishly and vainly endeavoring to impede, the operations of nature in producing this mortality; and if we dread the too frequent visitation of the horrid form of famine, we should sedulously encourage the other forms of destruction, which we compel nature to use. Instead of recommending cleanliness to the poor, we should encourage contrary habits. In our towns we should make the streets narrower, crowd more people into the houses, and court the return of the plague. In the country, we should build our villages near stagnant pools, and particularly encourage settlements in all marshy and unwholesome situations. But above all, we should reprobate specific remedies for ravaging diseases; and restrain those benevolent, but much mistaken men, who have thought they were doing a service to mankind by projecting schemes for the total extirpation of particular disorders."

Malthus's disciples—the Malthusians and the neo-Malthusians—believed that if Western civilization were to survive, the physically unfit, the materially poor, the spiritually diseased, the racially inferior, and the mentally incompetent had to somehow be suppressed and isolated—or perhaps even eliminated. And while Malthus was forthright in recommending plague, pestilence, and putrefaction, his disciples felt that the subtler and more "scientific" approaches of education, contraception, sterilization, and abortion were more practical and acceptable ways to ease the pressures of the supposed overpopulation.

NATIONAL DAY
 Luxembourg
FEAST DAY
 St. Cyneburg, St. Etheldreda, St. Agrippina, St. Lietbertus, St. Joseph Cafasso, St. Thomas Garnet

MIDSUMMER NIGHT'S EVE

Observances of Midsummer Night's Eve during the Middle Ages included the building of huge bonfires around and through which people danced and jumped. Another ritual involved rolling a flaming straw-filled wheel down a hill. Those who could roll themselves down the hill and keep up with the wheel were said to have good luck for the coming year. Shakespeare, in his play *King Henry IV*, used the description, "As full of spirit as the month of May, and gorgeous as the sun at midsummer." And again, in *Twelfth Night*, he wrote, "This is very midsummer madness."

Courage and resolution are the spirit and soul of virtue.

[THOMAS FULLER (1608–1661)]

303 Saint Alban was martyred in Rome. His countenance and faith were such that his executioner was converted on the way to the site of the beheading. The executioner begged to die with him, so another executioner had to be found.

1626 At the Cambridge fish market in England, a fish cleaner discovered a copy of John Frith's *Book of Religious Treatises* inside a large cod.

1836 Congress approved the Deposit Act, which contained a provision for turning over surplus federal revenue to the states—a provision steadfastly ignored ever since.

1863 J. E. Renan published his infamous biography of Christ, *Vie de Jésus*. In it he claimed that Jesus was a magnetic teacher with a vivid personality and "merely an incomparable man." None of the supernatural elements in His scriptural biographies were true. The book immediately created a storm of controversy. Atheists said it did not go far enough in stripping veneration from the person of Christ. Believers deplored its blasphemous denial of Christ's divinity.

1868 Christopher Latham Sholes received a patent for an invention he called the Type-Writer.

1931 Aviators Wiley Post and Harold Gatty took off from New York on the first round-the-world flight in a single-engine plane.

1938 The Civil Aeronautics Authority was established.

1947 The Senate joined the House in overriding President Harry Truman's veto of the Taft-Hartley Act.

JUNE

1955 Walt Disney's *Lady and the Tramp*, the first animated feature filmed in CinemaScope, opened in theaters.

1956 Gamal Abdel Nasser was elected president of Egypt.

1972 President Richard Nixon and White House chief of staff H. R. Haldeman discussed a plan to use the CIA to obstruct the FBI's Watergate investigation. Revelation of a tape recording of this conversation sparked Nixon's resignation in 1974.

1989 The Supreme Court refused to shut down the dial-a-porn industry, ruling Congress had gone too far in passing a law banning all sexually oriented phone message services.

23

In an effort to relieve the besieged Stirling Castle, England's King Edward II, the effeminate son of the cruel Longshanks, sent troops northward into Scotland—a land that had been in constant rebellion against his sovereignty for more than a decade. First there were William Wallace and his ragged corps of Highland warriors. Now there was the loyal army of the presumptive king of an independent Scottish nation, Robert the Bruce.

Though the great castle overlooking the wide plain of Bannockburn had thus far been able to resist Bruce's assault, Edward knew it would not be able to hold out much longer. The taking of this fortress was an achievement of which Edward was prouder than of anything else he had done in his invasion of Scotland—in the royal annals, he made it of far greater moment than even his victory over Wallace at Falkirk.

The time and the place of the inevitable battle were thus fixed by necessity on this day in 1314: The English were bound to relieve Stirling Castle; the Scots must prevent them. If the invaders were not met and fought at Bannockburn, they might outflank the Scots and reach the castle. And if the Scots did meet and fight them there, it was not likely there would be any other favorable field for a pitched battle anywhere in the whole of the land. The battle, therefore, would of necessity be under the walls of the castle. The Scots were outnumbered by at least three to one. They would have to rely on strategy—and Bruce had a brilliant strategy.

At daybreak they met the fierce charge of the English armies. A detachment of English archers quickly wheeled around the Scottish flank and took up a position where they could rake the compact clumps of Scots spearmen. But the lines held just long enough for a host of decoys to appear along the horizon of a neighboring hill. The women and children were mistaken for a fresh army of the Scots—just exactly what Bruce had hoped. The confused English lines began to scatter. Scottish pikemen were then able to confine the English to a small land mass between the Bannock Burn—Gaelic for "river"—and the Firth of Forth. With little room to maneuver effectively, the massive English were forced into flight by a final charge of fewer than two thousand Scots swarming down from Gillies Hill. On that hill today stands the William Wallace Memorial.

The end was rout, confused and hopeless. Through all the history of its great wars before and since, never did England suffer a humiliation deep enough to even approach comparison with this. Besides the vast inferiority of the victorious army, Bannockburn was exceptional among battles by the utter helplessness of the defeated. There seemed to have been no rallying point. It was as if the Scripture had been fulfilled: "The wicked flee when no man pursueth." At last, Scotland was free.

JUNE

FEAST DAY
St. John the Baptist, St. Bartholomew of Farne, St. Simplicius of Autun, St. Ralph of Bourges

MIDSUMMER DAY

Activities on this day in rural English villages included the lavish decorating of the village well. This area became the focal point for music recitals and morris dancing throughout the day. As the traditional carol asserted, "When bloody Herod reignéd king, within Judea's land, much woes his cruel will did bring, by bloody fierce command. Amongst the rest with grief oppressed, was good Saint John there slain, who on this day, 'midst sport and play, a martyred death did gain."

> *O Caledonia, stern and wild,*
> *Meet nurse for a poetic child,*
> *Land of brown heath and shaggy wood*
> *Land of the mountain and the flood.*
>
> [SIR WALTER SCOTT (1771–1832)]

64 The first state-sponsored terror against Christians in the Roman Empire came at the order of one of the most debased of all emperors, Nero. So despised was Nero that when Rome caught fire, popular opinion attributed the catastrophe to him. A rumor spread that Nero had appeared on a stage during the catastrophe and sung a song. Nero tried to counter this downturn in his public approval ratings by throwing open his own resources to the homeless. He sponsored a number of religious activities designed to show himself innocent. Nothing worked. And so he determined to find scapegoats. He fastened onto the Christians as most suitable to his diabolical purpose. And thus began the first wave of Imperial persecutions.

1497 The first recorded sighting of North America by a European in more than two centuries took place as explorer John Cabot spotted land, probably in present-day Canada.

1509 Henry VIII was crowned king of England.

1786 In commemoration of the victory at Bannockburn, Scottish poet Robert Burns penned one of his most famous verses: "Scots! wha hae wi' Wallace bled, Scots! wham Bruce has aften led, welcome to your gory bed, or to victory! Now's the day, and now's the hour; see the front o' battle lour: See approach proud Edward's power; chains and slavery! Wha will be a traitor knave? Wha can fill a coward's grave? Wha sae base as be a slave? Let him turn and flee! Wha for Scotland's King and law; freedom's sword will strongly draw, freeman stand, or freeman fa'? Let him on wi' me! By oppression's woes and pains! By your sons in servile chains! We will drain our dearest veins, But they shall be free! Lay the proud usurpers low! Tyrants fall in every foe! Liberty's in every blow! Let us do or die! So may God ever defend the cause of truth and liberty, as He did that day! Amen."

JUNE

1793 The first republican constitution in France was adopted.

1842 Author, journalist, and humorist Ambrose Bierce was born in Meigs County, Ohio. His most famous work was a collection of cynical definitions in *The Devil's Dictionary.*

1908 The twenty-second and twenty-fourth president of the United States, Grover Cleveland, died in Princeton, New Jersey, at age seventy-one.

1948 The Republican National Convention, meeting in Philadelphia, nominated New York Governor Thomas E. Dewey for president. Though highly favored to win, he was narrowly defeated by Harry Truman in the general election.

1948 Communist forces cut off all land and water routes between West Germany and West Berlin, prompting the Western allies to organize the massive Berlin Airlift.

1968 Resurrection City, a shantytown constructed as part of the Poor People's March on Washington, D.C., was closed down by authorities.

On this day in 1939, Margaret Sanger, the founder of Planned Parenthood, announced the organization's new "Negro Project" in response to requests from Southern state public health officials—men not generally known at that time for their racial equanimity. "The mass of Negroes," her project proposal asserted, "particularly in the South, still breed carelessly and disastrously, with the result that the increase among Negroes, even more than among Whites, is from that portion of the population least intelligent and fit." The proposal went on to say that "Public Health statistics merely hint at the primitive state of civilization in which most Negroes in the South live."

In order to remedy this "dysgenic horror story," her project aimed to hire three or four "Colored Ministers, preferably with social-service backgrounds, and with engaging personalities" to travel to various black enclaves and propagandize for birth control.

"The most successful educational approach to the Negro," Margaret wrote sometime later, "is through a religious appeal. We do not want word to go out that we want to exterminate the Negro population and the Minister is the man who can straighten out that idea if it ever occurs to any of their more rebellious members."

Of course, those black ministers were to be carefully controlled—mere figureheads. "There is a great danger that we will fail," one of the project directors wrote, "because the Negroes think it a plan for extermination. Hence, let's appear to let the colored run it." Another project director lamented, "I wonder if Southern Darkies can ever be entrusted with . . . a clinic. Our experience causes us to doubt their ability to work except under White supervision." The entire operation then was a ruse—a manipulative attempt to get African Americans to cooperate in their own elimination.

The program's genocidal intentions were carefully camouflaged beneath several layers of condescending social service rhetoric and organizational expertise. Like the citizens of Hamelin, lured into captivity by the sweet serenades of the Pied Piper, all too many African Americans all across the country happily fell into step behind Margaret and the Eugenic racists she had placed on her Negro Advisory Council.

Soon taxpayer-supported clinics throughout the South were distributing contraceptives to African Americans, and Sanger's science fiction dream of discouraging "the defective and diseased elements of humanity" from their "reckless and irresponsible swarming and spawning" appeared at last to be on the road to fulfillment. Planned Parenthood had its first real success in social engineering.

JUNE

FEAST DAY
St. Adalbert, St. Febronia, St. Maximus of Turin, St. Eurosia, St. Gohard, St. Gallicanus, St. Prosper of Reggio, St. Prosper of Aquitaine, St. Moloc, St. Thea, and St. Willaim of Vercelli

A man should stop his ears against paralyzing terror, and run the race that is set before him with a single mind.

[ROBERT LOUIS STEVENSON (1850–1894)]

1115 In an isolated valley in Champagne, France, the energetic and ambitious Cistercian monk Bernard founded the famed monastery of Clairvaux. It became the most magnificent in all of Europe—but also its most morally pure. There he sought a return to the strict rule of St. Benedict. As a result of this spiritual integrity, Clairvaux grew so rapidly that it soon became necessary for it to found sister monasteries. In all, Bernard directly founded seventy monasteries. These in turn founded some 183 others.

1630 Governor John Winthrop first introduced the people of Massachusetts to the table fork, complete with leather carrying case. He had brought the flatware from England.

1788 The state of Virginia ratified the Constitution.

1876 Lieutenant Colonel George Armstrong Custer and his force of some two hundred men lost their lives at the Battle of Little Big Horn in Montana. The Sioux and Cheyenne Indians, led by Sitting Bull, decimated Custer's troops in a period of twenty minutes. This incident has come to be known as Custer's Last Stand.

1886 When the regular conductor failed to appear at the Rio de Janeiro Opera House, nineteen-year-old cellist Arturo Toscanini was called upon to conduct *Aida*. He was so successful that he decided to pursue a career as a conductor.

1908 Stanford White, the architect of Madison Square Garden as well as several buildings for New York University and the Washington Square Arch, was shot and killed by Harry Thaw, a prominent Pittsburgh millionaire, on the roof of the Garden. The resulting trial was one of the most sensational in all of society.

1910 The premiere of Igor Stravinsky's ballet *The Firebird* at the Paris Opéra catapulted the young composer into the Parisian limelight, and established his reputation as one of the greatest musical geniuses of his generation.

1948 The Republican national convention in Philadelphia chose California Governor Earl Warren to be Thomas E. Dewey's running mate.

1950 North Korean troops executed a carefully planned attack and crossed the 38th parallel, starting the Korean War. In an emergency session, the United Nations Security Council, in the absence of the Soviet Union delegate, resolved that all members should join in halting the invasion. Two days later, President Truman ordered U.S. troops' involvement in the UN "police action," despite the fact that he had not asked the U.S. Congress for a formal declaration of war.

JUNE

1951 The CBS Network first broadcast television programming in color as it transmitted a one-hour special from New York to four other cities.

1962 The United States Supreme Court declared that the use of an unofficial, nondenominational prayer read in New York State government schools was unconstitutional.

1967 The Beatles performed their new song "All You Need Is Love" during a live international telecast.

1973 Former White House Counsel John W. Dean began testifying before the Senate Watergate Committee.

1988 American-born Mildred Gillars, better known during the Second World War as Axis Sally for her Nazi propaganda broadcasts, died in Columbus, Ohio, at age eighty-seven. Gillars had served twelve years in prison for treason.

FEAST DAY
Saints Salvius and Superius, Saints John and Paul, St. Anthelmus, bishop, St. Maxentius, St. Vigilius of Trent

In the days that followed its tragic sinking in the North Atlantic, the *Titanic* came to symbolize different things to different groups. Many perceived the ship to be a modern incarnation of the Tower of Babel. The sinking represented God's unwillingness to allow man to build any edifice of invincibility or to seek salvation through technology. The frequent boasts of *Titanic's* indestructibility by builders and promoters of the leviathan were viewed as a direct challenge to the Creator.

According to Charles Linden, pastor of the prominent Yarborough Presbyterian Church in New York, that calamitous night when the White Star liner went down to the ocean floor "was both the darkest and brightest night in modern maritime history." In a sermon on this day in 1912 that was reprinted around the country, he asserted, "Where the sin of human presumption abounds, the grace of God abounds all the more."

Consequently, he argued that many Christians could take great solace in the profoundly moving examples of courage and bold manhood represented by the men who faithfully honored the command "women and children first," men who gave up their lives when they gave up their seats on the few available lifeboats. With only a few exceptions, he said, *Titanic's* men willingly gave up their places for others, thus exemplifying the verse "Greater love hath no man than he lay down his life for another."

The most poignant examples Linden cited came from the many incidents in which families were split up. Husbands literally looked into the eyes of their wives and children, whispered tender last words, and lowered their families into lifeboats with the full realization that they would never see them again. Thus, he argued, "One of *Titanic's* greatest ironies was that she became a symbol of duty and faith."

The suffragettes of 1912 had another opinion. To them the *Titanic* was a symbol of patriarchal oppression. They reacted negatively to Linden's sermon. The philosophy that man should be protector and defender of womankind was a fundamental impediment to their cause. They resented the fact that the suffragette movement was criticized by newspapers that ran articles asking questions like "Boats or votes?" Consequently, feminists argued that the policy "women and children first" was little more than a patriarchal sentiment that hid an agenda of suppression. Leading suffragettes actually argued that *Titanic* women were wrong to have accepted seats on the boats from men.

The more things change, the more they stay the same.

By faith we know His existence, in glory we shall know His nature.

[Blaise Pascal (1623–1662)]

1284 The Pied Piper of Hamelin, Germany, had his revenge today when he lured 130 children to their deaths in the town's river. He had previously rid the town of rats and mice, also drowning them in the river, but the town fathers refused to pay him his fee of 1,000 guilders.

1614 The Virginia Company held a lottery for the purpose of obtaining funds. The Great Prize was 4,500 crowns.

1721 Dr. Zabdiel Boylston vaccinated his six-year-old son and two servants against smallpox. These were the first vaccinations given for this disease in the United States.

1788 Wolfgang Mozart wrote Symphony no. 39 in E-flat, in its entirety—in a single day.

1819 William Clarkson received a patent for the first bicycle in the United States.

1828 After serving as a successful missionary nun to French colonial Africa, Mother Javouhey was asked by the French government to travel to its dark dominions in South America in an effort to bring it some measure of civilization. On this day, she sailed with one hundred people to the outcast French Guiana—an inhospitable colony that also included Devil's Island. Her work quickly brought a measure of prosperity to the region. When asked how she managed to subdue the tough characters she dealt with, she often replied, "I just acted like a mother among her children." She was an indefatigable traveler on behalf of the various mission works she started. Altogether she traveled 75,000-plus miles by land and sea. Her many successes led the English

to plead for her help in Sierra Leone—where governments failed, the gospel always prevailed.

1844 John Tyler married Julia Gardiner on this day, becoming the first president to marry while in office.

1870 The first section of Atlantic City's Boardwalk was opened to the public.

1900 A commission led by Dr. Walter Reed began the fight against the deadly disease yellow fever.

JUNE

1917 The first troops of the American Expeditionary Force arrived in France during the First World War. One million Americans arrived at St. Nazaire in France as the advance guard for the subsequent troops committed to the cause.

1945 The charter of the United Nations was signed by fifty countries in San Francisco.

1948 The Berlin Airlift began in earnest after the Soviet Union cut off land and water routes to the isolated western sector of Berlin.

1959 President Dwight Eisenhower joined Britain's Queen Elizabeth II in ceremonies officially opening the St. Lawrence Seaway.

1963 President John Kennedy visited West Berlin, where he made his famous declaration: *"Ich bin ein Berliner."*

1979 Heavyweight boxing champion Muhammad Ali confirmed to reporters that he'd sent a letter to the World Boxing Association resigning his title, saying his third announced retirement was indeed final.

The science fiction tales of H. G. Wells were far more than imaginative stories or speculative fables. To him they were instruments of scientific prophecy. His utopian vision of the future was spawned by the peculiar and innovative worldview he shared with all too many progressive thinkers at the dawn of the twentieth century. It was a system of thought rooted in the superiority—even the supremacy—of science over every other discipline or concern. A fantastic world could be expected in the days just ahead, Wells believed, because the sovereign prerogative of science would, no doubt, make short work of curing every cultural ill, correcting every irrational thought, and subverting every cantankerous disturbance. There was no obstacle too great, no objection too considerable, and no resistance too substantial to restrain the onward and upward march of the scientific evolution of human society.

That kind of unswerving confidence in the good providence of industry and technology gave its adherents a conceited algebraic certainty about their forecasts and predictions. In one of his most forthright books, published on this day in 1916, Wells boldly asserted his sanguine futurism: "For some of us moderns, who have been touched with the spirit of science, prophesying is almost a habit of mind. Science is very largely analysis aimed at forecasting. The test of any scientific law is our verification of its anticipations. The scientific training develops the idea that whatever is going to happen is really here now—if only one could see it. And when one is taken by surprise, the tendency is not to say with the untrained man, 'Now, who'd ha' thought it?' but 'Now, what was it we overlooked?' Everything that has ever existed or that will ever exist is here—for anyone who has eyes to see. But some of it demands eyes of superhuman penetration."

For Wells, and all those who shared his Flash Gordon optimism, science was a kind of new secular predestination. It not only affirmed what could be, it also confirmed what would be. And more, it discerned what should be. Scientific experts were thus not only the caretakers of the future, they were the guardians of Truth. They were a kind of superhuman elite—not at all unlike Plato's philosopher-kings—who ruled the untrained with a firm but beneficent hand in order to realize the high ideals of progress. That meant that science had to necessarily be intermingled with ideology. It had to become an instrument of social transformation. It had to be harnessed with the idealism of the farsighted elite. It had to be wielded by the cognoscenti as a tool for the preordained task of human and cultural engineering. It had to be politicized.

Thus, in the early days of the twentieth century, science and millenarian politics were woven together into a crazy quilt of idealism, fanaticism, and ambition. It enabled a few powerful men and movements to believe the unbelievable, conceive the inconceivable, and imagine the unimaginable. Until that starry-eyed orthodoxy crumbled under the weight of two world wars and a myriad of other twentieth-century horrors, the future that never happened was sustained by it as the future that almost was.

FEAST DAY
St. Cyril of Alexandria; St. Zoilus; St. Samson of Constantinople; St. George Mtasmindeli; the Martyrs of Arras; St. John of Chinon; St. Ladislas, king of Hungary

If I find in myself a desire which no experience in this world can satisfy, the most profitable explanation is that I was made for another world.

[C. S. Lewis (1898–1963)]

1736 George Whitefield preached his first sermon. A member of the Holy Club, to which John and Charles Wesley also belonged, he took as his topic the need for Christians to help one another. At first his speech was awkward, for his mother, his brothers and sisters, and many who had known him as a youngster were in the audience. But as he proceeded, he later recalled, the Spirit filled him. Those who came to listen were so moved by the authority of his words that parishioners complained to the bishop that some had gone "mad." Whitefield himself wrote, "Glory! Glory! Glory! be ascribed to an Almighty Triune God." He went on to preach thousands more powerful sermons. He became a force in the Great Awakening, which brought fresh life to America's churches. His last sermon was preached in 1770. He was then desperately ill but, mounting a barrel, urged his listeners to examine themselves whether they were in the faith. To be saved, they must be born again, he urged. The following morning he died.

1777 After being hidden for a year beneath the floor of a church in Allentown, the Liberty Bell was returned to Philadelphia.

1829 English scientist James Smithson died and left an endowment to the United States to found the Smithsonian Institution.

1844 Cult leader Joseph Smith and his brother, Hyrum, were killed by an anti-Mormon mob in Carthage, Illinois.

1846 The Smithsonian Institution was established by act of Congress.

1847 The cities of New York and Boston were linked for the first time by telegraph wires.

1880 Helen Adams Keller, who was deaf and blind from the age of nineteen months, was born in Tuscumbia, Alabama. At the age of seven she started formal education with Anne Mansfield Sullivan, who taught her Braille and sign language. She also learned to speak, and entered Radcliff College in 1900. After graduating with honors, she wrote and lectured around the world on behalf of the blind as well as socialist and pacifist causes. She wrote *The Story of My Life*, her autobiography, in 1902.

1893 Four years of deep depression followed a crash on the New York Stock Exchange.

1942 The FBI announced the capture of eight Nazi saboteurs who had been put ashore from a submarine on New York's Long Island.

1950 President Harry Truman ordered the air force and navy into the Korean conflict following a call from the UN Security Council for member nations to help South Korea repel an invasion from the North.

1969 Patrons at the Stonewall Inn, an illicit homosexual bar in New York's Greenwich Village, rioted against local police in an incident considered the birth of the homosexual rights movement.

JUNE

27

The Great War—as the First World War was called by contemporaries—ended on November 11, 1918, and President Wilson brought to the Paris Peace Conference an outline for peace composed of fourteen points, which he had presented in an address to Congress eleven months earlier. The speech had met with great enthusiasm on both sides of the Atlantic, and when the Treaty of Versailles was signed on this day in 1919, Wilson's cornerstone proposal, the establishment of a League of Nations, was included. The president embarked on a cross-country speaking tour to take his case for Senate ratification of the League of Nations Covenant directly to the people.

The fourteen points he espoused were aimed at remaking the old world order into an entirely new one. And what were the essential policies of his program? First, he demanded "open covenants of peace, openly arrived at, after which there shall be no private international understandings of any kind but diplomacy shall proceed always frankly and in the public view."

Second, there was to be "absolute freedom of navigation upon the seas, outside territorial waters, alike in peace and in war." Third, there was to be "the removal of all economic barriers and the establishment of an equality of trade conditions among all the nations." Fourth, there were to be "adequate guarantees given and taken that national armaments will be reduced to the lowest point consistent with domestic safety." Fifth, "a free, open-minded, and absolutely impartial adjustment of all colonial claims" would be made. Sixth, "the evacuation of all Russian territory and such a settlement of all questions affecting Russia as will secure the best and freest cooperation of the other nations of the world." Seventh, Belgium was to be "evacuated and restored, without any attempt to limit her sovereignty." Eighth, all French territory was to be "freed and the invaded portions restored," including the territory of Alsace-Lorraine, which had been in German hands since 1871. Ninth, a "readjustment of the frontiers of Italy" was to be effected "along clearly recognizable lines of nationality." Tenth, the peoples of Austria-Hungary were to be accorded "the freest opportunity of autonomous development." Eleventh, "Rumania, Serbia, and Montenegro should be evacuated and occupied territories restored." Twelfth, "the Turkish portions of the present Ottoman Empire should be assured a secure sovereignty," but the other nationalities under Turkish rule were to be freed. Thirteenth, "an independent Polish state should be erected." And fourteenth, "a general association of nations" was to be formed.

On September 26, in the midst of the tour, Wilson suffered a stroke, from which he never recovered. The Senate rejected the utopian fourteen-point covenant in March 1920, and the United States never joined the League of Nations. Nevertheless, many of its aims were put into effect—and the awful wars that followed in the twentieth century testified to their supreme lack of wisdom and foresight.

JUNE

FEAST DAY
St. Austell; Saints Potamiaena and Basilides; St. Irenaeus; St. Heimrad; St. John Southworth; Saints Sergius and Germanus of Valaam; St. Paul, pope

One does not discover new lands without consenting to lose sight of the shore.

[ANDRÉ GIDE (1869–1951)]

1491 England's King Henry VIII was born at the royal palace in Greenwich.

1687 William Phipps became the first native-born American to be honored with British Knighthood.

1778 Mary Ludwig Hays—best known as Molly Pitcher—carried water to American soldiers at the Revolutionary War battle at Monmouth, New Jersey.

1810 Sir John Throckmorton went to great lengths to win a £1,000 wager. He had bet that he could sit down to dinner in a well-made wool suit on the same day that the sheep had been shorn to produce the wool. On June 28, at five o'clock in the morning, two sheep were shorn, and the wool was washed, carded, stubbed, roved, spun and woven. The resulting cloth was subsequently scoured, fulled, tented, raised, sheared, dyed, and dressed. A tailor used the finished cloth to make a garment that Sir John wore to dinner at a quarter to six that evening, a thousand pounds richer.

1836 The fourth president of the United States, James Madison, died in Montpelier, Virginia.

1838 Britain's Queen Victoria was crowned in Westminster Abbey.

1890 Samuel Zwemer sailed from his homeland in the United States on a Dutch liner called the *Obdam*. He stopped briefly in Europe to contact the only evangelical missionary group then working among Muslims and then by train and boat headed for Beirut. In London he bought a copy of *Arabia Deserta*. Years later he sold it to Lawrence of Arabia. Zwemer's exploits have none of the popular renown of T. E. Lawrence's, but were, nonetheless, of great boldness. He lived, breathed, and thought of one thing alone: cracking open the Muslim world for Christ. He set up presses, especially under British protection in Cairo. These poured out a continual stream of books to educate Westerners about the need of Islam and Arabic language books to share Christ with the Arabs. He authored or coauthored at least forty-eight books in English: titles such as *Arabia, The Cradle of Islam; Childhood in the Moslem World;* and *The Moslem Doctrine of God*. He noted that in Islam the tender fatherhood of God was unknown. Printed Christian prayers from his presses were prized by some Islamic people who found them to have more meat than their own. Zwemer penetrated Islam, but the great work he began remained unfulfilled at his death.

JUNE

1914 A Serbian student, Gavrilo Princp, assassinated Archduke Francis Ferdinand of Sarajevo, heir to the throne of Austria, and his wife, Sofia. The crisis that followed sparked the cataclysm of the First World War.

1928 New York Governor Alfred E. Smith was nominated for president at the Democratic national convention in Houston—he was the first Catholic to run on a major party ticket.

1938 Because of a large egg surplus, Pennsylvania farmers sought methods to dispose of their excess. Slot machines that dispensed hard-boiled eggs were installed in cafés and taverns throughout the state. The cost was a nickel per egg.

1939 Pan American Airways began regular transatlantic air service as the *Dixie Clipper* left Port Washington, New York, for Portugal.

381

The great Flemish master Peter Paul Rubens was born in 1577 near the village of Siegen in the heart of Westphalia. As befitted tradition in the Lower Netherlands, he was named in honor of the two saints commemorated on this feast day.

When he was just a toddler, his father began reading the various theological tomes circulating among the literate and urbane. In short order, he was thoroughly convinced by the doctrines of grace and consequently converted to Calvinism. When persecution against Reformed believers broke out in his adopted city of Antwerp he was forced to flee with his young wife and child.

Over the next eight years, young Peter Paul was carefully catechized, nurtured on the strong biblical preaching of the Dutch exile community, and discipled by his diligent father. Alas, in 1587, his father died. Having nowhere else to turn, his wife and children returned to Antwerp where they had extended family. There, they were required to rejoin the Catholic Church.

Later biographers would comment that the artist eventually drew from the deep wells of both traditions—the Reformed and the Catholic—in his later work: It was vivid, literal, down to earth, and filled with wonder at ordinary things as might be expected of a Reformed artist; but it was also transcendent, transfigurational, and sacramental as might be expected of a Catholic artist—the combination of the two made his work particularly rich and multifaceted.

By the time he was twenty-two years old, he had reached the rank of master painter in the Antwerp Guild of Saint Luke. He drew on the great legacy of the early Flemish and Dutch masters. But never entirely content with his range and virtuosity, Rubens decided to travel to Italy to study the Renaissance masters as well. There he was influenced by the works of Titian, Paolo Veronese, Tintoretto, Michelangelo, and Raphael.

His associations with the leading artists, intellectuals, and politicians of the day secured his position and created demand not only for his works but also for his skill as an emissary and diplomat. At various times throughout his career, he was sent as an ambassador and was in the employ of the Iberian Hapsburg kings Phillip III and Phillip IV (where he served as mentor to Diego Velázquez), and he led a diplomatic mission to England (where he was knighted by the Stuart king Charles I).

He spent the majority of his final years in Antwerp, where he was recognized as the greatest painter of the post-Reformation era. His animated, bold, and vibrant style bridges the intellectual and the emotional as well as the classical and the Romantic—his compositions were stunning achievements drawing on the strengths of each of Christendom's rich inheritances.

JUNE

FEAST DAY
St. Peter, St. Paul, St. Elwin, Saints Judith and Salome, St. Cassius of Narni

FEAST DAY OF ST. PETER AND ST. PAUL | Throughout Christendom, this day has been cause for a celebration of the proclamation of the gospel—not just the two men whose lives are synonymous with it. Children born on this day have invariably been named for both saints—as was the case with Rubens.

A churchless society is most assuredly a society on the downgrade.

[THEODORE ROOSEVELT (1858–1919)]

67 According to tradition, the apostle Paul was beheaded with a sword near Rome on this day. The year is, of course, open to dispute—indeed, it has been variously placed anywhere between 62 and 67.

1613 During a performance of Shakespeare's *King Henry VIII*, the Globe Theater outside of London burned to the ground.

1767 The British Parliament approved the Townshend Revenue Acts, which imposed import duties on such things as glass, lead, paint, paper, and tea shipped to America. The colonists bitterly protested the acts—arguing that the very idea of taxation by Parliament, without any sort of representation, was a violation of their colonial charters and of English common law. The acts were subsequently repealed three years later, in 1770.

1776 The Virginia state constitution was adopted, and Patrick Henry elected the state's first governor.

1851 In a letter to Nathaniel Hawthorne, Herman Melville lamented, "Though I wrote the literary gospel of this century, I shall die in the gutter."

1861 The poet Elizabeth Barrett Browning, fifty-five, died at her home, the Casa Guidi, in Florence, Italy.

1900 Antoine de Saint-Exupery, the author of such works as *Night Flight* and *The Little Prince*, was born in Lyon, France.

1941 Polish statesman, pianist, and composer Ignace Jan Paderewski died in New York at age eighty.

1946 British authorities arrested more than 2,700 Jews in Palestine in an attempt to stamp out alleged terrorism.

1949 The government of South Africa enacted a ban against racially mixed marriages.

1954 The Atomic Energy Commission voted against reinstating Dr. J. Robert Oppenheimer's access to classified information. Though he had been a pioneer in the field, his political statements were deemed to be suspect by anti-Communist groups who were then ferreting out a myriad of spies at every level of the American system.

1966 The United States bombed fuel-storage facilities near the North Vietnamese cities of Hanoi and Haiphong.

1967 Jerusalem was reunified as Israel removed barricades separating the Old City from the Israeli sector in the days following the Six Days' War.

1970 The United States ended a two-month military offensive into Cambodia.

1972 The Supreme Court ruled that the death penalty, as it was then being meted out, could constitute "cruel and unusual punishment" and thus, be prohibited by the Constitution. The ruling prompted states to revise their capital punishment laws and methods.

1988 The Supreme Court, in a 7 to 1 decision, upheld the power of independent counsels to prosecute illegal acts by high-ranking government officials.

JUNE

29

383

When European settlers first began to ask the Cherokee about their history, one of the stories they told was of a white-skinned people who preceded them. The Cherokee called these people the "Welsh tribe" and knew that they claimed descent from white forebears who had "crossed the Great Water." A legend like this among the Cherokee would probably have gone unnoticed except that in Wales there are indeed tales of a local prince named Madoc ap Owen Gwynedd who sailed west and discovered land sometime after the year 1190. There is sufficient evidence for some to conclude that Madoc's company actually landed at Mobile Bay and made their way into what is today Tennessee, thus accounting for several mysterious stone forts just outside of Chattanooga and Manchester. According to this reconstructed account, the band continued through the Ohio Valley to present-day Kentucky—near Louisville—where they eventually intermarried with the Mandan Sioux and moved up the Missouri River into the Black Hills of the Dakotas.

If Cherokee legends and Welsh tales were the only support of this fantastic story, it probably would not have had the strength to survive the centuries. However, in his *Principal Navigations*, published on this day in 1589, Richard Hakluyt offered the story of Madoc in support of English territorial claims to the New World. Hakluyt insisted that because of Madoc, "it is manifest that that country was by Britons discovered, long before Columbus led any Spaniards thither" and offered also a few lines of the famous Madoc ballad, "Madoc I am the son of Owen Gwynedd; with stature large, and comely grace adorned: No lands at home nor store of wealth did please; my mind was whole to search the Ocean seas."

Additional support for the legend is found in the writings of American artist George Catlin. While drawing pictures of the Mandan Sioux in northern Missouri, Catlin discovered Indians with uncommonly pale complexions and blue or gray eyes. He believed they might indeed be descendants of the legendary Welsh colony of Madoc and argued the case in his famous *North American Indians*, written in 1841.

None of this proves the Madoc legend, of course. Nor are we entirely certain, for that matter, that Irish monks ever traversed the American inlands before the Spanish and English explorers began coming in the fifteenth and sixteenth centuries. What we know for certain is that many throughout American history have believed these legends—and not just the Cherokee. Even prominent statesmen like Tennessee's John Sevier believed in the Welsh tribe and more than one American's heart has been stirred by the vision of heroic monks whose religious zeal brought them to the New World a millennium before Columbus. Perhaps the true value of these legends, though, is what they say about the faith of later generations and how very much they wanted to believe in the exploits of early Christians who braved all to claim both native hearts and virgin lands for God.

JUNE

FEAST DAY
St. Theobald of Provins, the Martyrs of Rome, St. Emma, St. Bertrand of Le Mans, St. Erentrude, St. Martial of Limoges

It is an equally awful truth that four and four makes eight, whether you reckon the thing out in eight onions or eight angels, eight bricks or eight bishops, eight minor poets or eight pigs. Similarly, if it be true that God made all things, that grave fact can be asserted by pointing at a star or by waving an umbrella.

[G. K. CHESTERTON (1874–1936)]

1832 During a particularly furious storm in Birmingham, England, a shower of white frogs fell in the suburb of Mosely. They were found scattered among several gardens.

1857 Charles Dickens gave his first public reading of his works at St. Martin's Hall in London. He read from *A Christmas Carol*.

1864 Yosemite Valley Park, by vote of Congress, was established as the first state park in the United States.

1870 Ada H. Kepley of Effingham, Illinois, became America's first female law school graduate.

1906 The Pure Food and Drug Act and the Meat Inspection Act became law.

1907 Several square miles in the Tungaska region of Siberia were totally devastated by a gigantic meteor. The meteorite weighed one million tons, but broke up in the earth's atmosphere before impact at more than 90,000 miles per hour. The effects were felt over 1,500 square miles.

1921 President Warren Harding appointed former President William Howard Taft chief justice of the United States Supreme Court.

1934 Adolf Hitler began his "blood purge" of political and military leaders in Germany.

1936 The blockbuster novel about the War Between the States and its aftermath, *Gone with the Wind* by Margaret Mitchell, was published in New York. It was the only book she ever wrote.

1938 Action Comics debuted the new character of Superman.

1952 *The Guiding Light*, a popular daytime radio program, made its TV soap opera debut on CBS.

1958 The development of the transistor was announced by researchers of Bell Laboratories.

1963 Pope Paul VI was crowned the 262nd primate of the Roman Catholic Church.

JUNE

1971 The Twenty-sixth Amendment to the Constitution, lowering the minimum voting age to eighteen, was ratified as Ohio became the thirty-eighth state to approve it.

1971 When the Soviet spacecraft *Soyuz 11* returned to Earth, all three cosmonauts aboard, Viktor Patsayev, Georgi Dobrovolski, and Vladislav N. Volkov, were found dead. Although they successfully lived on the *Salyut 1* space station for three weeks, a faulty valve allowed their air supply to escape. They were the first men to have died in space.

1986 In a 5 to 4 decision, the Supreme Court ruled that states could outlaw homosexual acts between consenting adults.

30

JULY

NATIONAL DAY
Canada
FEAST DAY
St. Gall of Clermont, Saints Aaron and Julius, St. Eparchius of Cybard, St. Oliver Plunket, St. Carilephus or Calais, St. Thierry or Theodoric of Mont d'Or, St. Servanus or Serv, St. Simeon Salus, St. Shenute

JULY

Today he is hardly considered a major figure in the annals of American letters. In his own day, however, novelist and poet Stephen Crane was recognized as a literary prodigy. Indeed, he was among the brightest orbs in the starry American literary constellation. He was frequently compared with Tolstoy, Zola, and Kipling. Mark Twain praised him as "an undeniable master of the literary crafts." Buchan, Tolkien, and Lewis each acknowledged his "stunning evocative abilities." Chesterton ranked him "before Meredith, Alcott, and the Brontë sisters" and "perhaps only behind Scott, Austen, Stevenson, and Dickens" among the great Victorian novelists. Conrad dubbed him "non-comparable as an artist." And Howells inscribed his name "among the brightest of the sons of genius." He helped to launch the naturalist movement through his use of detached narration, great attention to detail, and characters from lower social classes.

Early on, Crane evidenced extraordinary gifts. He began to compose stories, satires, and verses at the age of fourteen. When his mother, an impoverished widow, secured a college scholarship for him, he turned his hand to political essays, elegies, criticism, and social commentary.

Alas, even the greatest gifts, the best advantages, and the finest opportunities can be easily squandered. He plunged into a life of wastrel bohemianism and concupiscence. He ventured into the rough and tumble literary world at the turn of the century. He frequented the theaters, dressed fashionably, and drank profligately. He boldly rejected the faith of his childhood and embraced a life of defiant worldliness.

He continued to write prodigiously as well—often in dissipated all-night binges. He managed to create an arresting style from a unique conflation of his reading and his own invention, that offered readers an eerie sense of eye witness authenticity—though it was entirely speculative and romantic.

As Crane became more and more adept at manufacturing his fantasies—fantasies of stark realism—his excesses became even more pronounced. Though his piddling advances and royalties were quickly squandered, he actually intensified his dissolute lifestyle. Going without food or sleep for days on end, he wrote ceaselessly with a tortured passion unequaled in American journalism letters. Then he would indulge in drinking sprees, carousings, and fierce street brawls.

His greatest work, *The Red Badge of Courage*, was published in the autumn of 1895. It quickly went through two editions before the end of the year. On this day the next summer, his publishers confirmed that the novel had become an international bestseller. Remarkably, it has never been out of print since. Though Crane achieved almost overnight celebrity, unremunerative contracts with the publishers and a general lack of good business sense kept Crane insolvent throughout his life while his debauched lifestyle seriously eroded his health. As quickly as his star had risen, it suddenly fell. Within four years of his first publishing triumph, he was dead at the age of twenty-eight.

God has not called me to be successful; He has called me to be faithful.

[MOTHER TERESA (1910–1997)]

1847 The post office of New York issued the first stamps in the United States. The Benjamin Franklin stamp was available for five cents, and the George Washington for ten cents.

1860 Six months after the publication of the *Origin of Species*, evolution was the topic of a meeting of the British Association. Seven hundred people attended, anticipating a lively discussion, including several imminent churchmen, among them the popular Bishop Sam Wilberforce. Though he had been coached by the great anatomist Sir Richard Owen, Wilberforce was not well grounded in the sciences. He merely castigated Darwin's theory with good humor. At one point he turned to the famed agnostic Thomas Huxley, and asked, "Was it through your grandfather or grandmother that you claim descent from a monkey?" Huxley slapped his knee and whispered a very unagnostic comment, "The Lord hath delivered him into mine hands." Wilberforce sat down to applause. Huxley then rose with defiance. Utilizing unproven but impressive-sounding research and scientific jargon, he exposed what he claimed was Wilberforce's ignorance and error. He would not be ashamed of a monkey in his ancestry, he said. Rather, he would be ashamed to be "connected with a man who used great gifts to obscure the truth." Thus was the tone set for an ideological struggle that would consume the better part of two centuries.

1862 The United States Congress enacted the International Revenue law, which sought to raise money for the war effort by levying a tax on practically everything other than the grave.

1863 The Battle of Gettysburg, the decisive battle of the American Civil War, began in Pennsylvania. The Confederate army under General Lee was defeated by General Meade and his Union troops. More than thirty-seven thousand men were killed or wounded in the three days of fighting.

1867 Canada became a self-governing dominion of Great Britain as the British North America Act took effect.

1898 Theodore Roosevelt and his Rough Riders volunteer cavalry regiment secured a U.S. victory in the Battle of Santiago by storming San Juan Hill in Cuba. To avoid capture, Spanish Admiral Pascual Cervera retreated from Santiago Harbor on July 3. The Spanish ships were attacked by the U.S. fleet, burned and sunk. Two weeks later, Spain surrendered.

JULY

1916 In the First World War, the Battle of the Somme began. More than twenty-one thousand men were killed on the first day. The British and French launched an attack along a twenty-one-mile front just north of the Somme River, but were slaughtered by the securely entrenched Germans. The British introduction of the tank in September did little to help their efforts; by the battle's end on November 13, the Allied forces had only gained five miles of French soil.

1941 The first television commercial—advertising Bulova clocks—was aired on New York's WNBT.

1980 "O Canada" was proclaimed the national anthem of Canada.

JULY

He was the last of the presidents to go from a log cabin to the White House. Left fatherless when only an infant, James A. Garfield (1831–1881) was forced to work from his earliest years on the family farm in Ohio. Besides helping his widowed mother, he also succeeded in earning enough—as a canal boat driver, carpenter, and teacher—to put himself through college.

His love of learning led him into a teaching career, serving as a professor of Latin and Greek and later a college president. The initiative that catapulted Garfield into the scholarly ranks ultimately carried him into public life as well. He became known as a powerful antislavery speaker and grew active in local politics.

When Abraham Lincoln was assassinated in 1865, James A. Garfield happened to be visiting in New York. Known as one of the president's most trusted political and military advisors, he was implored by city officials to address the agitated throngs that had gathered in the streets. He climbed aloft a scaffold and won the crowd's attentions. He simply said, "My fellow citizens, the president is dead, but the republic lives—and God Omnipotent reigns."

Garfield, who would himself one day attain the highest office in the land only to be struck down by an assassin's bullet, had been a fire-breathing Yankee enthusiast during the War Between the States. But the uncivil horrors of the battlefields in Virginia and the inhuman manipulations of the politicians in Washington had tempered his passions considerably. He no longer believed that men and governments, ideologies and policies, or parties and factions were ends unto themselves. He had embraced instead a perspective of politics rooted in a far deeper and more profound reality, of which he reminded the crowd from the pinnacle of that scaffold in New York: "Fellow citizens, clouds and darkness are round about Him. His pavilion is dark waters and thick clouds of the skies. Justice and judgment are the establishment of His throne. Mercy and truth shall go before His face. Fellow citizens, God reigns, e'en o'er the government in Washington—despite all appearances."

He served for eighteen years in Congress, emerging in 1880 as the leader of his party. Nevertheless, when the Republicans met in Chicago in 1880, Garfield was not considered a presidential contender. The struggle was between Grant, who was willing to try a third term, and Senator James Blaine from Maine. But as happened before, the convention was so divided that neither could win. It was not until the thirty-sixth ballot that the dark-horse candidate Garfield was nominated.

The surprise gift of the highest office in the land was not one that Garfield could enjoy for very long. In the White House he showed signs of being a strong executive, independent of party as was Hayes. But he was in office less than four months when he was fatally shot by an assassin as he was about to catch a train in the Washington depot on this day in 1831. Like that earlier log-cabin president, Garfield left the White House a martyr, having spent less time in office than any president except William Harrison.

Understanding is the reward of faith. Therefore seek not to understand that you may believe, but believe that you may understand.

[St. Augustine (354–430)]

1566 French astrologer, physician, and alchemist Nostradamus died in Salon.

1776 The Continental Congress passed a resolution saying that "these United Colonies are, and of right, ought to be, Free and Independent States."

1778 In Ermonville, near Paris, Jean Jacques Rousseau, author of *The Social Contract*, died of apoplexy.

1877 German novelist Herman Hesse, who would receive the Nobel Prize for literature in 1946, was born in a small town in the Black Forest.

1908 Thurgood Marshall was born in Bethesda, Maryland. He would become the first black U.S. Supreme Court justice, founder of the NAACP's Legal Defense and Educational Fund. He first won fame as a lawyer whose victory in *Brown vs. Board of Education* (1954) outlawed segregation in American public life.

1915 A German teacher at Cornell University, Eric Muenter—who also went by the alias Frank Holt—planted a bomb that exploded in the reception room of the United States Senate. The following day, he shot and wounded J. P. Morgan, who was involved with war contracts with the British government. Meunter was imprisoned and later committed suicide.

1921 More than two and a half years after the First World War Armistice was signed, a joint resolution of the United States Congress declared that the state of war with Germany was over.

1932 John and Betty Stam, missionary martyrs in China during the days of the Communist Revolution, left the comfort and safety of their home in America for the wild and dangerous world of Shanghai under the authority of the China Inland Mission. While there on the field in 1934, a daughter was born to them. Only a few days later they were captured and summarily executed for their faith. Though only able to minister for a very short time, their ultimate sacrifice helped to establish the house church movement—which thrives in China to this day.

1937 Aviator Amelia Earhart and navigator Fred Noonan disappeared over the Central Pacific Ocean while attempting to make the first round-the-world flight at the equator.

1947 An object crashed near Roswell, New Mexico; the Army Air Force later insisted it was a weather balloon, but contradictory eyewitness accounts gave rise to speculation it might have been an alien spacecraft.

1961 Ernest Hemingway took his own life at his home in Idaho. Hemingway's spare prose largely shaped the style of twentieth-century Western fiction. In 1953, he was awarded the Pulitzer Prize in fiction for his novel *The Old Man and the Sea*, and, just the next year, he received the Nobel Prize for literature. Hemingway used his widely varied life experiences to form the basis for many of his most successful works. His experience as a First World War ambulance driver influenced his novel *A Farewell to Arms* (1929); his love of Spain and of bullfighting is readily apparent in *Death in the Afternoon* (1932); and an account of a big-game safari he took is seen in *The Green Hills of Africa* (1935). As a journalist during the Second World War, Hemingway crossed the English Channel with U.S. troops on D-Day, and participated in the liberation of Paris, his former home. He moved to Cuba after the war, but was forced out in 1960 by Castro's revolution. Settling in Ketchum, Idaho, the author unsuccessfully fought depression and anxiety.

JULY

FEAST DAY

St. Thomas the Apostle; St.
Anatolius of Constantinople;
Saints Irenaeus and Mustiola; St.
Leo II, pope; St. Anatolius of
Laodicea; St. Rumold or Rombaut;
St. Bernardino Realino; St.
Helidorus of Altino

JULY

As one of America's greatest composers, Duke Ellington pioneered the Big Band sound, and brought artistic credibility to African-American jazz. Born in 1899 to a middle-class family in the nation's capital, Ellington took his first piano lessons at age seven and immediately exhibited a gift for music. He began playing professionally as a teenager for local parties and dances in a popular style derived from ragtime.

Determined to pursue a musical career, despite the reservations of his parents, on this day in 1922 Ellington moved to New York City, which had emerged as the nation's jazz capital. He played with theater orchestras during the week and with jazz bands on the weekends—including the renowned Elmer Snowden Ensemble. In 1924, he began to write and play for musical theater. Later that year, Ellington took over the Snowden band, and that six-man group became the nucleus of the Ellington orchestra. He steered them toward a bluesy and improvisational jazz, which ultimately became their signature sound.

By the thirties he had developed a lush approach to orchestration that introduced new complexity to the simplistic conventions of swing-era jazz. Essentially, he took what had begun as a vernacular dance music and created larger and more artistically challenging musical forms, exemplified in his three-movement composition "Black, Brown, and Beige." Alas, due to the fame of Ellington as a bandleader and composer, Ellington as an instrumentalist was often overlooked. Yet particularly during his later career his astonishing range and creativity on the piano were all too evident. In fact, his mastery of the instrument was the foundation of his orchestral virtuosity. As a young player in New York—at such venues as Harlem's famed Cotton Club—he came under the sway of the Harlem "stride" piano style, exemplified in the playing of James P. Johnson and Willie "the Lion" Smith. The stride style essentially divides the keyboard into three ranges. The pianist's left hand covers the two lower ranges, alternating single bass notes at the bottom with chord clusters struck higher up. The style takes its name from the characteristic bouncing "oom-pah, oom-pah" produced by the pianist's "striding" left hand. The pianist's left hand thus establishes a propulsive beat and outlines the tune's harmonic structure; the right hand plays melody, adds ornamentation, and improvises solo lines. Ellington evolved from this rather florid piano style, in part, by simplifying it and by adding harmonic complexities and dissonance that at times foreshadowed the emergence of "free-jazz" and "bop" music. Building on this innovative base, by 1928 his orchestra had emerged as the nation's foremost jazz ensemble—and it would remain so for nearly four decades.

Over the years, Ellington made dozens of recordings that became the heart and soul of the Big Band movement. They often featured the growling, plunger-muted solos of Miley and Nanton—producing such classics as "East St. Louis Toodle-Oo," "Black and Tan Fantasy," "Black Beauty," "Creole Rhapsody," and the soundtrack for the popular Amos 'n' Andy films. By the time of his death in 1974, he had established an enduring body of work that remains a national treasure.

There is a spiritual cancer at work in the world. The piracy of man's fallen nature invariably mitigates against freedom and justice. Therefore voluntary associations must needs balance us—without force of state but nonetheless with force of community—and hold us to accounts.

[JAMES STUART (1849–1901)]

1608 The city of Quebec was founded by Samuel de Champlain.

1775 General George Washington took command of the Continental army at Cambridge, Massachusetts.

1778 The last fluent and native speaker of the Cornish language, Dolly Pentreath, died in the village of Mousehole in Cornwall, England, at the age of 102. Her epitaph reads, *"Coth Doll Pentreath eans ha dean, Marow ha kledyz ed Paul pleu."* Translated, this reads, "Old Doll Pentreath, one hundred aged and two, deceased, and buried in Paul Parish too."

1835 In Paterson, New Jersey, children went on strike seeking a more equitable eleven-hour workday and six-day workweek.

1840 Søren Kierkegaard was examined for his theological degree at the University of Copenhagen. His thesis, "On the Concept of Irony with Constant Reference to Socrates," presaged his agonizing work as an existential Christian mystic and philosopher. Shortly afterward, he became an eccentric who wandered the streets of his city by day, frantically writing by night. He died at the age of forty-three having established himself as one of the most original thinkers of the nineteenth century—but also, one of its most tortured souls.

1863 During the War Between the States, Robert E. Lee's Confederate Army of Northern Virginia was defeated after a charge of fifteen thousand Confederate soldiers failed to break the Union lines held under George Meade at Gettysburg. The three-day battle, culminated by the filed Pickett's Charge, resulted in the Confederacy losing one-third of their troops, and the Union seeing 23,049 casualties out of their total 88,289 fighting men.

1878 Today is the birthday of songwriter and playwright George M. Cohan, composer of "You're a Grand Old Flag," "Yankee Doodle Dandy," "Give My Regards to Broadway," and "Mary's a Grand Old Name."

JULY

1890 Idaho became the forty-third state of the Union.

1898 During the Spanish-American War, a fleet of Spanish ships in Cuba's Santiago Harbor attempted to run a blockade of U.S. naval forces; practically all of the Spanish ships were destroyed in the four-hour battle that followed.

1954 Almost nine years after the end of the Second World War, food rationing ended in Britain.

1962 Algeria became an independent nation after 132 years of French rule.

1988 The *Vincennes*, a U.S. missle cruiser, mistakenly downed an Iranian commercial jet over the Persian Gulf. All 290 people on board were killed.

JULY

On June 9, 1776, the Continental Congress accepted a resolution made two days earlier by Virginia delegate Richard Henry Lee to appoint a committee to draft a declaration of secession from the dominions of the English king and Parliament. On June 29, the committee—composed of Thomas Jefferson, John Adams, Benjamin Franklin, Roger Sherman, and Robert Livingston—presented their draft for debate and a vote. Finally, on July 4, an amended version of that draft was accepted. The war that had been raging for more than a year had finally driven the reluctant revolutionaries to sever all ties with their motherland.

The original draft of that Declaration of Independence had been penned by the youngest member of the committee, Thomas Jefferson (1743–1826), but it hardly bore the mark of immaturity: "We hold these truths to be self-evident: that all men are created equal, that they are endowed by their Creator with certain unalienable rights, that among these are life, liberty, and the pursuit of happiness."

That day would not be the last time Jefferson's words would launch a revolution. A quarter century later, his election to the presidency marked a profound but peaceful change in the administration of the young nation. Indeed, it was called by many the "Bloodless Revolution of 1800." The revolutionist who boldly wrote religious and ethical beliefs into the Declaration of Independence brought to the office a philosophy of government firmly rooted in those same beliefs, a philosophy that concerned itself, above all, with the rights and liberties of the individual. It was Jefferson's democratic views, with his enduring faith in the individual, that, more than anything else, turned the country away from the class rule of the Federalists.

Few men have been better equipped to become president. A graduate of William and Mary College and an able lawyer, Jefferson helped shape the destiny of the struggling nation from the beginning. He served in the Virginia House of Burgesses, in the Continental Congress—writing the final draft of the Declaration, as a minister in the French court, as governor of Virginia, as secretary of state under Washington, and vice president under Adams. But as president, Jefferson proved that philosophic ability and experience in office were no replacements for political leadership. He was a remarkable inventor, scientist, writer, artist, planter, architect, musician, and educator—but he was a poor politician and administrator. He was able, however, to bring a profound sense of democracy to the nation's highest office, an accomplishment that ranks with the celebrated purchase of the Louisiana Territory as an outstanding achievement of his administration. A complex man, Jefferson was one of the most accomplished of our presidents—he was talented as few men are in any age—the living example of his own belief in the capacity of men to learn and to grow under freedom.

There are no tricks in plain and simple faith.

1623 William Byrd, one of the greatest composers of Anglican choral music as well as Latin Masses and motets, died in Essex, England.

1754 During the French and Indian War, British forces under the command of Col. George Washington were defeated by the French near Fort Duquesne. As a result, the Ohio Valley was placed under French rule.

1826 Stephen Collins Foster, composer of such American classics as "Camptown Races," "Oh, Susannah," "My Old Kentucky Home," and "Beautiful Dreamer," was born on this day.

1826 The semicentennial celebration of the signing of the Declaration of Independence was touched with sorrow by the deaths of Thomas Jefferson, the third president and principal author of the Declaration, and John Adams, the second president and the Declaration's chief advocate. The two old friends died within hours of one another.

1831 The fifth president of the United States, James Monroe, died in New York City—the third of the founding fathers and presidents to die on the nation's greatest holiday.

1832 Schoolchildren in Boston sang the song "America" for the first time at the Park Street Church in Boston. The song was written by Dr. Samuel Francis Smith on a scrap of paper in just half an hour.

1845 Henry David Thoreau began his two-year experiment in simpler living at Walden Pond, near Concord, Massachusetts.

1848 The cornerstone of the Washington Monument was laid by President James Polk.

1872 The thirtieth president of the United States, Calvin Coolidge, was born in Plymouth, Vermont. He was named for the great Reformer, John Calvin.

1881 At the age of twenty-five, Booker T. Washington founded the Tuskegee Institute. There was no money, no faculty, no campus, no land, and no student body. Indeed, there was nothing except the resolution of the state to launch the school and the determination of Washington to raise up a whole new generation of leaders from the rubble of the South and the legacy of slavery. Nevertheless, before his death in 1915, Tuskegee had grown to encompass a 2,000-acre campus of 107 buildings with more than 1,500 students and nearly 200 faculty members.

1895 "America the Beautiful," by Katherine Lee Bates, was first published on this day.

1917 During a ceremony in Paris honoring the French hero of the American Revolution, U.S. Lieutenant Colonel Charles E. Stanton declared solidarity with the French in the great struggle of the First World War, saying, "Lafayette, we are here!"

JULY

1918 American troops joined the British for the first time in military action against the Germans during the First World War.

1939 Baseball's "Iron Horse," Lou Gehrig, said farewell to his fans at New York's Yankee Stadium, declaring that he was "the luckiest man in the world."

1959 America's forty-nine-star flag, honoring Alaskan statehood, was officially unfurled. One year later an additional star was added honoring Hawaiian statehood.

1976 Israeli commandos raided the Entebbe airport in Uganda, rescuing almost all of the passengers and crew of an Air France jetliner seized by pro-Palestinian hijackers.

JULY

Presented with a Bank Renewal Bill by Congress on this day in 1832, President Andrew Jackson declined to sign based upon his concerns about a new and narrow concentration of wealth and power in America—thus denying the central bank its monopolistic charter. Such a monopoly, he believed, only exacerbated the tendency to tyranny toward which all nations eventually drift. Eventually, the principle of his argument became one of the cornerstones of American conservatism—so despite the fact that its economics no longer enliven the national debate, its politics do.

At the time, he wrote, "Having considered it with that solemn regard to the principles of the Constitution which the day was calculated to inspire, and come to the conclusion that it ought not to become a law, I herewith return it to the Senate, in which it originated, with my objections." It wasn't so much that Jackson opposed having a national bank at all, rather if there was to be such an institution he argued, it must yield to the rule of law in the Constitution. "A bank of the United States is in many respects convenient for the Government and useful to the people. Entertaining this opinion, and deeply impressed with the belief that some of the powers and privileges possessed by the existing bank are unauthorized by the Constitution, subversive of the rights of the States, and dangerous to the liberties of the people, I felt it my duty at an early period of my Administration to call the attention of Congress to the practicability of organizing an institution combining all its advantages and obviating these objections. I sincerely regret that in the act before me I can perceive none of those modifications of the bank charter which are necessary, in my opinion, to make it compatible with justice, with sound policy, or with the Constitution of our country."

The matter was simple; as far as Jackson was concerned, "This is a matter of liberty." And so, once again, Old Hickory proved himself to be a champion of the people and their freedom: "Experience should teach us wisdom. Most of the difficulties our Government now encounters and most of the dangers which impend over our Union have sprung from an abandonment of the legitimate objects of Government by our national legislation. Many of our rich men have not been content with equal protection and equal benefits, but have besought us to make them richer by act of Congress. By attempting to gratify their desires we have in the results of our legislation arrayed section against section, interest against interest, and man against man, in a fearful commotion which threatens to shake the foundations of our Union. It is time to pause in our career to review our principles, and if possible revive that devoted patriotism and spirit of compromise which distinguished the saga of the Revolution and the fathers of our Union. If we can not at once, in justice to interests vested under improvident legislation, make our Government what it ought to be, we can at least take a stand against all new grants of monopolies and exclusive privileges, against any prostitution of our Government to the advancement of the few at the expense of the many, and in favor of compromise and gradual reform in our code of laws and system of political economy."

Faith begins to make one abandon the old way of judging. Averages and movements and the rest grow uncertain. The very nature of social force seems changed to us. And this is hard when a man has loved common views.

[HILAIRE BELLOC (1870–1953)]

1801 American naval hero David G. Farragut was born in Knoxville, Tennessee.

1811 Venezuela became the first South American country to declare independence from Spain.

1832 During his long and productive ministry, Samuel Francis Smith composed nearly two hundred hymns. But it is for one he wrote while still in seminary that he is best known. Musician Lowell Mason had asked him to translate some German verses for a song book he was preparing. Among the tunes he handed Smith was a German patriotic hymn, "God Bless Our Native Land." When Smith read it, he immediately felt that the United States also needed a stirring national poem. Writing on scraps of paper that February 1832, he finished within thirty minutes a poem he titled "America"—though it is best known today by the title "My Country 'Tis of Thee." It was first sung several months later at an Independence Day celebration by a children's choir in Boston. The lyrics were then published in local newspapers on this day. It gained immediate popularity. The tune was actually the official or semiofficial melody of about twenty other national anthems—as early as the seventeenth century it had been found in Swiss music and had a long history of usage in Germany, Sweden, England, and Russia. Nine years after Smith adopted it, Beethoven wrote piano variations on the melody.

1853 Cecil John Rhodes was born this day. This South African statesman founded and gave his name to the country of Rhodesia and to scholarships at Oxford for students outside of Britain.

1865 William Booth founded the Salvation Army in London.

1940 During the Second World War, Britain and the Nazi puppet Vichy government in France broke diplomatic relations.

1946 The bikini made its debut during an outdoor fashion show at the Molitor Pool in Paris. Model Micheline Bernardini wore the skimpy two-piece swimsuit, which was the creation of designer Louis Reard.

1947 Larry Doby signed a contract with the Cleveland Indians, becoming the first African-American player in the American League.

JULY

1948 Britain's National Health Service Act went into effect, providing government-financed medical and dental care.

1954 Elvis Presley's first commercial recording session took place at Sun Records in Memphis, Tennessee; the song he recorded was "That's All Right (Mama)."

1975 Arthur Ashe became the first African-American man to win a Wimbledon singles title as he defeated Jimmy Connors.

1984 The Supreme Court weakened the seventy-year-old "exclusionary rule," deciding that evidence seized with defective court warrants could be used against defendants in criminal trials.

JULY

On this day in 1054, the Christian Church suffered a permanent schism when the four eastern patriarchates of Constantinople, Alexandria, Jerusalem, and Antioch, broke off fellowship with the one in the west, Rome.

The division came during the prelacies of Michael Cerularius, patriarch of Constantinople, and Leo IX, pope in Rome. The year before, Cerularius had circulated a treatise criticizing a number of the practices of the Roman church in unusually strong terms. Catholics did not allow their clergy to marry, for instance. This was contrary to both Scripture and tradition, according to Cerularius. In addition, Catholics used unleavened bread in their Eucharist, again in contradistinction to the long-held standards of church dogma.

But the most serious concern was that the Latin church had added the word *filoque* to the Nicene Creed, asserting that the Holy Spirit proceeded from both Father and Son. This, it seemed to the hierarchs of the East, was a heinous flirtation with heresy. Cerularius excommunicated all bishops of Constantinople who used the Western ritual and closed down their churches.

Both the criticisms and the actions incensed Leo. He demanded that Cerularius cease and desist—and then as if to add insult to injury, he demanded that each of the other patriarchs submit to the pope. Any church that refused to recognize the pontiff as supreme was an assembly of heretics, he said—a synagogue of Satan. The Eastern patriarchs weren't about to accept this characterization. The five patriarchates had always been held to be equal.

In an effort to enforce his decrees, Leo sent a delegation to Constantinople. The legates were led by a brilliant, though unyielding man, Cardinal Humbert. But Humbert was so rude to Cerularius that the patriarch refused to speak with him. Aggravated by this treatment, the legates issued a series of anathemas. To make matters worse, before they could get any further direction from Rome, Leo died.

Thus, taking matters into his own hands, Humbert and his delegation marched into St. Sophia on July 6, 1054, and placed a bull on the altar, that excommunicated Cerularius. After this act, Humbert made a grand exit, shaking the dust off his feet and calling on God to judge.

In turn, Cerularius convoked a council and once more blasted Western practices. Humbert was anathematized. The Orthodox condemned all who had drawn up the bull. There was no chance of reconciliation between the factions. The unity of fellowship, forbearance, and love that Christ said should mark His followers was irrevocably broken.

Better faithful than famous. Honor before prominence.

[THEODORE ROOSEVELT (1858–1919)]

1415 The council condemned Jan Hus as a heretic because of his Bohemian reforms. That same day they had him burned at the stake. The following year, Jerome of Prague suffered the same fate from the bishops. He had protested against indulgences. Angry, the nobility of Bohemia revolted from the church and remained Hussite for two hundred years, until Catholicism was forcibly restored by the Hapsburgs.

1483 England's King Richard III was crowned.

1535 Sir Thomas More, an English genius of letters, was executed at the Tower of London. Days earlier he had been sentenced to be hung and disemboweled, but King Henry VIII had changed the sentence to beheading. At one time or another he had served as the undersecretary of the Treasury, speaker of Parliament, high steward of both Oxford and Cambridge, and Lord Chancellor. A loyal Catholic, More wrote against the Reformers, especially William Tyndale. He opposed Tyndale's attempts to put the Bible into the English language. As Lord Chancellor he applied force against "heretics." His loyalty to the church was bound to bring him afoul of Henry when the king proclaimed himself head of the English church.

1755 Much of Wedgwood's original pottery was designed by English sculptor John Flaxman, who was born on this day in York, England. As a boy in London, Flaxman spent much time in his father's plaster-casting studio, and was thoroughly instructed in classical literature, whose characters and stories influenced his work for the rest of his life. Sometime after 1775, Flaxman went to work for the potter Josiah Wedgwood and learned how to translate designs based on antique models into beautiful silhouettes.

1777 During the American Revolution, British forces captured Fort Ticonderoga.

1862 "Taps" was played for the first time during the beginning week of July. General Daniel Butterfield wrote the music on the back of a torn envelope while resting after fighting in Virginia.

1885 Louis Pasteur, the French bacteriologist, inoculated a human being for the first time. The subject was a boy who had been bitten by a mad dog—he tested an antirabies vaccine on him. Not only did the boy survive, but he also went on to become the superintendent of the Pasteur Institute in Paris.

1917 During the First World War, Arab forces led by T. E. Lawrence captured the port of Aqaba from the Turks. It was this incident that gained the British officer the moniker Lawrence of Arabia.

JULY

1923 More than six years after the Russian Revolution and five years after launching a bitter civil war, the Communist cabal of Trotsky, Lenin, and Stalin established the Union of Soviet Socialist Republics.

1957 Althea Gibson became the first black tennis player to win a Wimbledon singles title, defeating fellow American Darlene Hard.

1967 The territorial war of independence in the Horn of Africa known as the Biafran War erupted. The war, which lasted two and a half years, claimed some 600,000 lives and began a course of conflict, revolution, famine, pestilence, and plague that has tormented the region ever since.

6

JULY

On this day in the year 476, the fierce barbarian military commander of the Germanic Heruli tribe, Odoacer, marched the Roman legions under his command into the city of Rome. There was little resistance in the city, and those few troops that remained loyal to the emperor, Romulus Augustulus, fled at the sight of the Heruli. The emperor himself had already sought exile in Ravenna. Odoacer simply marched to the Imperial palace and claimed it as his own.

Thus, the presumed fall of the Roman Empire was hardly a fall at all. Indeed, though historians make much of this date—supposing it to mark the ignominious end of the Roman Imperial era—in reality, no one then supposed that the empire ceased to exist.

For centuries before, even though it was governed by two competing emperors—one in the East at Constantinople and one in the West at Rome or Ravenna—the empire continued to be regarded as a single whole. So, when Romulus Augustulus was forced into exile, Odoacer and the other barbarian leaders did not hesitate to recognize the formal and universal overlordship of the Eastern emperor in the great Byzantine city of Constantinople, Zeno.

Though the Ostrogoths, Vandals, Franks, Visigoths, Lombards, and Burgundians all set up new kingdoms in the Western provinces, they never questioned the abiding significance of the confederated empire. Kingship merely denoted leadership of a clan or a community: Such leaders continued to look to the emperor to grant them titles to both land and authority. They used the emperor's image on their coins. They adopted Roman law throughout the provinces, and they paid fealty to their acknowledged lord in goods, services, and arms.

Thus the empire never really ended in an actual fall—it slowly and naturally faded away. Though its actual influence waxed and waned from time to time, deep respect remained for the unity it officially enshrined well into the Medieval era. In fact, some traditionalists—particularly in such places as the Central European domains of Austria and Hungary—maintained some kind of continuity with the old Roman imperium up until the dissolution of the venerable Hapsburg Empire at the conclusion of the First World War.

Thus, when Charlemagne, the king of the Franks, was crowned emperor by Pope Leo III in the church of Saint Peter's at Rome on Christmas Day in the year 800—restoring at long last the Western imperial throne—there was less a sense of resurrecting a long-lost legacy than of revitalizing a long-cherished ideal.

Nothing is ended with honor which does not conclude better than it began.

[SAMUEL JOHNSON (1709–1784)]

1438 The decrees of Basel were adopted by the Roman Catholic Church. The result of the conciliar movement, which began in 1414 at the Council of Constance and continued in 1431 at the Council of Pavia, was to restrict the authority of the popes and impose a degree of accountability to the cardinals and bishops of the church. European attempts to create parliaments to limit absolutism among their kings were thus paralleled in the church. By accepting these limitations, the Catholic world was able to heal—at least for a time—the deep schisms that had sundered the church. In addition to declaring that the pope was under conciliar authority, the pragmatic sanctions demanded a reduction in the use of excommunication and interdiction, revised the celebration of the liturgy, called for further councils to be held at regular intervals, and reduced papal income and power. Although superseded by the Concordat of Bologna in 1516, the decrees continued to be accepted by the French church for centuries afterward and fostered the anticlericalism of the French Revolution. The view still held wide currency until 1870, when the first Vatican Council declared that the pope was infallible when speaking ex cathedra on matters of faith and morals. A small number of Catholics refused to accept this change. They withdrew from the Roman Catholic Church and became known as Old Catholics. They have been in full communion with the Church of England since 1932.

1754 King's College in New York City opened. After independence from Britain the school was renamed Columbia College.

1846 The American annexation of California was proclaimed at Monterey after the surrender of the Mexican garrison there.

1860 Composer and conductor Gustav Mahler was born in Austria. Mahler was the last of the great post-Romantic composers who stretched tonality and Romanticism to the breaking point with great excesses.

1865 Four people were hanged in Washington, D.C., for conspiring with John Wilkes Booth to assassinate President Lincoln.

1887 The first surrealist painter, Marc Chagall, was born in Vitsyebsk, Russia (now Belarus). He lived most of his life in France where he was influenced by cubism, which he combined with Russian expressionism. Many of his themes and symbols were derived from Russian-Jewish folklore and traditions. Poetic inspiration formed much of his unique imagery and choice of color.

JULY

1898 The United States annexed the Pacific islands of Hawaii.

1899 Film director George Cukor was born in New York City.

1930 Construction began on the Boulder Dam—which was later renamed Hoover Dam.

1949 The police drama *Dragnet*, starring Jack Webb and Barton Yarborough, premiered on NBC radio.

1958 President Dwight Eisenhower signed the Alaska statehood bill.

1969 Canada's House of Commons gave final approval to a measure making the French language equal to English throughout the nation.

1981 President Ronald Reagan announced that he was nominating Arizona Judge Sandra Day O'Connor to become the first female justice of the U.S. Supreme Court.

JULY

"Curse the day," the fleet messengers announced. "Constantinople has fallen to the Turks. Byzantium is no more." The shattering news was announced in Genoa at wharfside early in the afternoon on this day in 1453. The great city had gone down fighting, with Emperor Constantine bravely positioned at the head of his troops. But the fierce Muslim tide was too much. All Christian resistance was quickly thwarted. The conquest was complete by midmorning. The massacre that followed was utterly horrifying—Byzantine citizens were cut down like grass in a meadow, holy relics were tossed into the sea, diplomatic consuls from the West were tortured and executed, women were raped, children were enslaved, and the once magnificent city was reduced to ruin. Pera, the nearby Ligurian trading outpost—and the heart of Genoa's booming foreign mercantile enterprise—had suffered a similar fate, but several ships were able to make good their escape.

It was one of those ships that now brought the shocking news to their home city. The commander had gone to the doge's palace to give him a first-hand report. Meanwhile, sailors related the sketchy sordid details to the stunned crowd gathered along the pier facing the harbor. Christopher Columbus would never forget that moment—though he was but a toddler. It was etched in his mind forever. Who could forget? Not since the days of the plague had so much emotion been unleashed in Genoa's dreary, earnest, and businesslike streets.

The storied Byzantine civilization had long been a symbol of the beneficence of Christian community life. Throughout the Middle East, across North Africa, and deep into the heart of Europe, the stability and steadfastness of the Eastern Empire had spawned a remarkable flowering of culture for more than a millennium. The legal system it had pioneered under Justinian was just and efficient. The form of government it had developed under Constantine was limited and decentralized. The trade it had spawned under Alexius was free and prosperous. It was a model society. Its families had been stable and secure. Perversity and corruption had been suppressed while personal liberty and civil rights were enhanced. Its advancement in the sciences had been unprecedented. Art, music, and ideas had flourished as in no other time in human history. And its literary output had been bedazzling.

The fall of the city was an unimaginable catastrophe. The bulwark of Constantinople was no longer. The site of the Holy Sepulchre had been desecrated by the infidels. And the brightest light that Christian erudition had ever known was unceremoniously snuffed out. Many, both there in Genoa and throughout all the rest of Christendom, would be possessed by that awful realization for the rest of their lives—as would the young and impressionable Columbus, who eventually set out across the sea in an effort to set the world aright.

Do your duty in all things. You cannot do more. You should never wish to do less.

[ROBERT E. LEE (1807–1870)]

1621 Poet and author of fables Jean de la Fontaine was born in France. Known for his epigramatic morals, he authored such well-known phrases as: "The stronger man's argument is always the best," "This fellow did not see farther than his own nose," "Help yourself, and heaven will help you," and "A hungry stomach has no ears."

1654 Jacob Barsimon became the first known Jew to settle in North America when he made his home in New York.

1663 King Charles II of England granted a charter to Rhode Island.

1776 Colonel John Nixon gave the first public reading of the Declaration of Independence, to a crowd at Independence Square in Philadelphia.

1796 The Passport Division of the U.S. State Department issued the first passport to Francis Barre, being "a citizen having occasion to pass into foreign countries about his lawful affairs."

1822 English Romantic poet Percy Bysshe Shelley drowned when his boat sank during a storm in the Bay of Spezia.

1835 The Liberty Bell, one of the symbols of American freedom, received its famous crack on this day as it tolled for the death of Chief Justice John C. Marshall. Originally hung in 1753 in Independence Hall in Philadelphia, the Liberty Bell bore the inscription, "Proclaim Liberty throughout all the Land unto all the inhabitants thereof." During the British occupation of Philadelphia from 1777 to 1778, it was removed and hidden for fear of its destruction.

1839 American entrepreneur and industrialist John D. Rockefeller was born in Richford, New York.

1853 An expedition led by Commodore Matthew Perry arrived in Yedo Bay, Japan, on a mission to seek diplomatic and trade relations with the Japanese.

1882 Composer, pianist, and folk-song enthusiast Percy Grainger was born in Australia. Grainger traveled throughout the British Isles with a cylindrical recording machine that he used to record authentic renditions of traditional songs and melodies. He wove these melodies throughout his music for piano, voice, wind ensemble, and orchestra.

JULY

1889 The *Wall Street Journal* was first published.

1907 Florenz Ziegfeld staged his first Follies, on the roof of the New York Theater.

1932 The United States stock market hit its lowest point during the Great Depression, having lost nearly two-thirds of its value.

1947 Demolition work began on New York's West Side to make way for the new permanent headquarters of the United Nations.

1950 General Douglas MacArthur was named commander in chief of United Nations forces in Korea.

JULY

In a speech delivered on this day at the Democratic National Convention in Chicago in 1896, William Jennings Bryan made his mark in the annals of American history. It was quite probably the most effective oration ever given in American party politics. Bryan, then only thirty-six, had come to Chicago as a leader of the Nebraska delegation, but with the avowed intention of vaulting from this relatively obscure role into the presidential nomination. And that he did.

The great issue before the convention was whether the party should take its place behind President Grover Cleveland and the conservative Democrats in a continued defense of the gold standard or yield to the fervent demand of populists in the West for free coinage of silver as the remedy for depressed prices, unemployment, and the blight of depression. Bryan was perhaps the most articulate advocate of the silver strategy—essentially calling for government to inflate the money supply.

Bryan made the issue of monetary policy a matter of utmost principle: "This is not a contest between persons. The humblest citizen in all the land, when clad in the armor of a righteous cause, is stronger than all the hosts of error. I come to speak to you in defense of a cause as holy as the cause of liberty—the cause of humanity." Indeed, he said, "the individual is but an atom; he is born, he acts, he dies; but principles are eternal; and this has been a contest over a principle."

He believed the cause he espoused was of vital import to the future of the nation—the great divide of modernity: "Never before in the history of this country has there been witnessed such a contest as that through which we have just passed. Never before in the history of American politics has a great issue been fought out as this issue has been, by the voters of a great party."

Indeed, for him, the religious connotations of the conflict were altogether inescapable. He thundered with the fierce logic of his policy and then ended with a rhetorical flourish that sent the galleries into a frenzy of cheering, shouting, and stomping, "You shall not press down upon the brow of labor this crown of thorns, you shall not crucify mankind upon a cross of gold."

A shoo-in for the nomination, he went on to lead one of the most spirited campaigns in American history marked by brilliant oratory and carefully hewn rhetoric. Though he was ultimately defeated by William McKinley in the general election, he had established himself as a political force to be contended with. Indeed, he would dominate Democratic Party politics for the next two decades.

1497

The Portuguese admiral Vasco da Gama set sail from Lisbon on a voyage to the East Indies. This difficult and long voyage (over two years and two months in duration) discovered the Cape of Good Hope as a passage to the East. This discovery diverted the flow of Eastern commerce away from the Italian states to parts of Northern Europe and shifted the commercial center of the region away from Venice.

If honor calls, where'er she points the way
The sons of honor follow, and obey.

[WINSTON CHURCHILL (1874–1965)]

1540 England's King Henry VIII had his six-month-old marriage to his fourth wife, Anne of Cleves, annulled.

1741 Jonathan Edwards traveled a few miles from his home into western Connecticut and read to a small congregation assembled there the most famous sermon ever delivered in the history of America. Titled "Sinners in the Hands of An Angry God," its subject was the imminence of judgment and the horrors of perdition. It was about what we today derisively call hellfire and damnation. Later described by literary and historical critics as a rhetorical masterpiece, the sermon was astonishingly gripping and terrifyingly vivid; it caused an immediate sensation in the town of Enfield where it was preached. Even before the sermon was finished, people were moaning, groaning, and crying out such things as "What shall I do to be saved?" In fact, there was such a breathing of distress and weeping that Edwards had to quiet and calm the people several times so he could conclude. The fervor of the Great Awakening that had thus far by-passed Enfield, now swept through the little town with a white-hot intensity. In short order, the sermon was printed and widely distributed throughout the Americas. It not only won for Edwards great renown, but it also provoked a further awakening among its distant readers. Since then it has been reprinted hundreds of times—perhaps thousands. To this day it is not only a standard text for the study of great preaching, it also has passed into the realm of classic literature—and thus is the most anthologized sermon in the English language.

1776 The Declaration of Independence was read aloud to General George Washington's troops in New York.

1816 Argentina declared independence from Spain.

1850 The twelfth president of the United States, Zachary Taylor, died after serving only sixteen months in office.

1872 John F. Blondel of Thomaston, Maine, received patent No. 128,783 for a donut cutter, which pushed dough out of a center tube, creating a hole in the middle.

1879 Italian composer Ottorino Respighi was born in Bologna. While playing viola for the St. Petersburg opera, Respighi took composition and orchestration lessons from Rimsky-Korsakov. His compositional abilities quickly moved him to the forefront of Italian music, with such works as *Fountains of Rome, Pines of Rome,* and *Ancient Airs and Dances.*

1915 American composer and symphonist David Diamond was born in Rochester, New York. In response to the experimentation of twentieth-century music, Diamond said, "It is my strong feeling that a romantically inspired contemporary music tempered by reinvigorated classical technical formulas is the way out of the present period of creative chaos in music." His music soars with a balance of exuberance and energy, as well as structure and form that are unmistakably American in sound.

1947 The engagement of Britain's Princess Elizabeth to Lieutenant Philip Mountbatten was announced.

1951 President Harry Truman asked Congress to formally end the state of war between the United States and Germany.

1986 The Attorney General's Commission on Pornography released the final draft of its report, which linked hard-core porn to criminal activity.

JULY

9

During his astonishingly varied fifty-year career in public life, Thomas McKean (1734–1817) held almost every possible position—from deputy county attorney to president of the United States under the Confederation. Besides signing the Declaration of Independence, he contributed significantly to the development and establishment of constitutional government in both his home state of Delaware and the nation. At the Stamp Act Congress he proposed the voting procedure that Congress adopted: that each colony, regardless of size or population, have one vote—the practice adopted by the Continental Congress and the Congress of the Confederation, and the principle of state equality manifest in the composition of the Senate. Also, as county judge in 1765, he defied the British by ordering his court to work only with documents that did not bear the hated stamps.

In June 1776 at the Continental Congress, McKean joined with Caesar Rodney to register Delaware's approval of the Declaration of Independence, over the negative vote of the third Delaware delegate, George Read—permitting it to be "the unanimous declaration of the thirteen United States." And at a special Delaware convention, he drafted the constitution for that state.

McKean also helped draft—and signed—the Articles of Confederation. It was during his tenure of service as president—from July 10, 1781, to November 4, 1782—that news arrived from General Washington in October 1781 that the British had surrendered following the Battle of Yorktown. As chief justice of the Supreme Court of Pennsylvania, he contributed to the establishment of the legal system in that state, and in 1787 he strongly supported the Constitution at the Pennsylvania Ratification Convention, declaring it "the best the world has yet seen."

At sixty-five, after forty-plus years of public service, McKean resigned from his post as chief justice. A candidate on the Democratic-Republican ticket in 1799, McKean was elected governor of Pennsylvania. As governor, he followed such a strict policy of appointing only fellow Republicans to office that he became the father of the spoils system in America. He served three tempestuous terms as governor, completing one of the longest continuous careers of public service of any of the Founding Fathers.

JULY

138

Roman emperor Hadrian died after a reign of twenty-one years. He is most famous for the construction of Hadrian's wall, which was built between the Tyne and the Solway in Britain for the purpose of fortifying the Roman frontier from the Northern tribes. Hadrian had visited Britain in 122 and personally begun the process of reorganizing the border. The wall was eight to ten feet thick and had seventeen forts and about eighty castles along its seventy-three-mile length.

True conscious honor is to feel no sin:

He's armed without that's innocent within.

[ALEXANDER POPE (1688–1744)]

1220 London Bridge, as well as parts of the city on each end of it, was consumed by a horrible fire that caused the collapse of the bridge and the deaths of three thousand people who perished in the flames.

1509 Theologian and pastor John Calvin was born in Noyon, France. He published the first edition of *Institutes of the Christian Religion* in 1536, which propelled him to the forefront of the Protestant movement as a thinker and spokesman. Calvin made his first trip to Geneva that same year while on the way to Strasbourg. He stayed and helped to establish the church until asked to leave two years later. In 1541 he was asked to return to Geneva to continue his work with the reformation of the church and city, and he remained there the rest of his life. Calvin improved the life of Geneva's citizens through health care, industry, and education, and he added to the life of the church through his many commentaries, hymns, and catechism.

1737 The first Protestant missionary to South Africa arrived at the request of the Dutch church. He was a Moravian, a man who had suffered great brutality in the prisons of his homeland for the crime of sharing his faith. Georg Schmidt was determined to reach the Hottentots for Christ. Though mocked by the Dutch and ignored by the Hottentots, he persevered and succeeded in planting an indigenous church among them— though he himself was eventually expelled from the country by the Boers.

1790 John Philpot, an Irish judge, declared in a speech, "The condition upon which God hath given liberty to men is eternal vigilance."

1820 French impressionist painter Camille Pissarro was born in Saint Thomas, Virgin Islands. After

he moved to Paris in 1855, he studied with Camille Corot but quickly became part of the impressionist movement. He was interested in the representation of light whether in rural landscapes or street scenes. He influenced many painters including Paul Gauguin, Paul Cézanne, Lucien Pissarro (his son), and Mary Cassatt.

1850 Vice President Millard Fillmore assumed the presidency following the death of President Zachary Taylor.

1875 Ernest Creux and Paul Berthoud, seminary friends, founded a mission to the Gwamba people at Valdezia in the Spelonken area of South Africa. The Boers warned them that the language could not be learned. Creux and Berthoud not only learned it, they also translated the Scripture into it. Before their deaths, the church had grown to many hundreds. Berthold lost his wife and five children to disease. Creux lost three children. He was also imprisoned by the Dutch when they fought the Gwamba. The Boers suspected he might favor the natives. In spite of such difficulties, their work succeeded to a remarkable degree.

JULY

1890 Wyoming became the forty-fourth state.

1913 The highest temperature ever recorded in the United States occurred this day when the temperature in Death Valley, California, registered 134 degrees Fahrenheit.

1919 President Woodrow Wilson personally delivered the Treaty of Versailles to the Senate, and urged its ratification.

1940 The 114-day Battle of Britain began as Nazi forces began an aerial bombardment of England.

JULY

Frederick Douglass was one of the greatest men of the nineteenth century. The abolitionist, reformer, author, and orator was born in Talbot County, Maryland, in 1818. The son of a slave, he was raised by his grandparents, and was actually spared direct contact with the institution of slavery throughout much of his childhood. When he was eight years old, he was sent to live with the Baltimore in-laws of his master. For Douglass, the move opened a new world and instilled a lifelong conviction that education was the path to self-betterment. His new mistress took the initiative in his education, reading to him from the Bible. Before long he was reading himself. Shortly afterward, he bought a copy of *The Columbian Orator*, which reflected the conviction that oratory offered the best means to instill civic virtue and respect for liberty. It is likely that this book helped to shape his later eloquence. At about the same time, Douglass was caught up in the evangelical fervor of the South's vibrant antebellum Christianity.

His relatively happy life was shattered when he was hired out to a cruel taskmaster on a hardscrabble farm overlooking the Chesapeake. He immediately made up his mind to escape, but his first attempt failed. Shortly afterward, he met and fell in love with a free black woman named Anna Murray, and the two conspired to take flight. Douglass made his way to freedom in 1838 via the Underground Railroad.

As soon as Anna was able to join him, the two were married and started a family. Douglass found work on the New England wharves. In 1839 he heard a speech by William Lloyd Garrison, who rekindled his resolve to become an orator. In 1841 he was invited to speak at a rally that included a number of prominent abolitionists. At the close of the meeting, the Massachusetts Anti-Slavery Society offered to employ him as a speaker. It was in that role that Douglass entered the stage of history.

Douglass's career as an abolitionist made him a celebrity—but it also made him a target: He was just as apt to speak out against Northern segregation as against slavery. Even so, the publication of his autobiographical *Narrative* gained him recognition as the nation's preeminent spokesman for civil rights.

When the War Between the States began, Douglass struggled to broaden its aims. At the outset, Abraham Lincoln insisted that the war was simply intended to preserve the Union, and that slavery would not be affected. He was further outraged by the calculated ruse of the Emancipation Proclamation. And the days of Reconstruction only confirmed the fact that the war did little to confront racial animus in the North or the South.

During his later years, Douglass also held several low-level but symbolically important government posts, including United States marshal for the District of Columbia (1877–1881), recorder of deeds for the District of Columbia (1881–1886), chargé d'affaires for Santo Domingo, capital of the Dominican Republic, and minister to Haiti (1889–1891). Though he never achieved his primary goals, he served as a model for every significant African-American leader who followed him.

Associate yourself with men of good quality if you esteem your own reputation; for 'tis better to be alone than in bad company.

[GEORGE WASHINGTON (1732–1799)]

1274 Robert the Bruce, the Scottish king who defeated the English army of Edward II on the fields of Bannockburn, was born in Scotland.

1533 Pope Clement VII excommunicated England's King Henry VIII following his ignominious divorce from Catherine of Aragon.

1767 John Quincy Adams, the sixth president of the United States, was born in Braintree, Massachusetts, to Abigail and John Adams, the second president.

1798 The United States Marine Corps was established on this day. The marines are a separate military service within the Department of the Navy and under the control of the secretary of the navy. They are trained to fulfill integrated land, sea, and air operations.

1804 Alexander Hamilton was shot and killed by his enemy Aaron Burr when the two met to settle their differences in a duel in Weehawken, New Jersey.

1864 General Jubal Early marched into Silver Spring with his Confederate forces and prepared to attack Washington, D.C., the next day. President Lincoln came under fire at one point while watching a skirmish at Fort Stevens with his wife. Reinforcing Union forces arrived shortly afterward and Early ceased his attack. It was later discovered that many of the reinforcements were actually fresh recruits without any battle experience whatsoever—had Early pressed on, the capital, the president, and the war might well have been history.

1871 Novelist Marcel Proust was born in Auteuil, outside Paris, during the turbulent summer of the Paris Commune. He would later blame his chronic bad health on his mother's nervousness caused by street violence during her pregnancy.

1915 Saul Bellow, Nobel Prize–winning novelist, was born in Lachine, Quebec, to parents recently emigrated from strife-torn Russia.

1934 President Franklin Roosevelt became the first chief executive to travel through the Panama Canal—which had been constructed at the behest of his cousin Theodore Roosevelt.

JULY

1955 The U.S. Air Force Academy was dedicated at Lowry Air Base in Colorado.

1962 AT&T successfully accomplished the first satellite transmission, made via the *Telstar* satellite.

1977 The Medal of Freedom was awarded posthumously to civil rights champion Dr. Martin Luther King Jr.

1979 The abandoned American space station *Skylab* made a spectacular return to Earth, burning up in the atmosphere and showering debris over the Indian Ocean and Australia.

FEAST DAY
St. John the Iberian, St. Jason, Saints Hermagoras and Fortunatus, St. John Gualbert, St. John Jones, St. Veronica, St. Felix

JULY

Unlike his friend George Whitefield, Jonathan Edwards was not a particularly enthralling master of pulpit theatrics or hermaneutical technique. Instead, he won his reputation as a thinker. He was highly regarded as a "precise dogmatician." He was widely admired as a "careful systemizer." And he was deeply appreciated as a "cogent preceptor."

As a philosopher, his greatness was unmatched. Thomas Chalmers said that he was "undoubtedly the greatest of all the theologians." Benjamin Franklin said that he "had a rational mind unmatched for generations untold." Daniel Webster said that his books were among the "greatest achievements of the human intellect." James Hollister said he was "the most gifted man of the eighteenth century, perhaps the most profound thinker in the world." Robert Hall said that "he was the greatest of the sons of men." Moses Tyler said he was "the most original and acute thinker yet produced in America." And Georges Lyon said he was "superior to Locke, Newton, Descartes, and a couple of Pascals combined."

But as a preacher, he apparently left a little something to be desired. In fact, he read his densely theological and tautly philosophical sermons from painstakingly researched longhand manuscripts—often in a flat, monotonous voice. Only rarely did he deign to make eye contact with his congregation. Though not unpleasant in demeanor, he hardly cut a dashing or charismatic figure.

A member of his church described these deficiencies sympathetically: "His appearance in the pulpit was with a good grace, and his delivery easy, natural, but very solemn. He had not a strong voice but appeared with such gravity, and spake with such distinctness and precision—his words so full of ideas and set in such a plain and striking light—that few speakers have been so able to demand the attention of an audience as he. His words often discovered a great degree of inward fervor, without much noise or external emotion, and fell with great weight on the minds of his hearers. He made but little motion of his head or hands in the pulpit, but spake as to discover the motion of his own heart, which tended in the most natural and effectual manner to move and affect others."

But another said, "I can little explain how the assembly remains awake during his discourses—which are over-long, boorish, and often incomprehensible to the simple man. Though there is evidence of some great passion in thought, yet to the eye and ear, little or none."

Nevertheless, his sermons were generally rushed into print and widely distributed throughout the Americas and all the rest of the English-speaking world. Indeed, his most famous sermon, "Sinners in the Hands of an Angry God"—printed for the first time on this day in 1749—has become a standard text for the study of great preaching as the most anthologized sermon in the English language.

Resolved: Never to do anything which I should be
afraid to do if it were the last hour of my life.

[JONATHAN EDWARDS (1703–1758)]

101 B.C. Roman general and dictator Caius Julius—later given the honorific title of Caesar—was born into the revered patrician family of Julii.

1543 England's King Henry VIII married his sixth and last wife, Catherine Parr.

1690 Protestant forces led by William of Orange defeated the Roman Catholic army of James II at the Battle of the Boyne in Ireland, ensuring that the royal House of Stuart would not regain their old dominions in Great Britain.

1730 Josiah Wedgwood was born into a family of potters in Burslem, Staffordshire. Wedgwood founded the famous pottery works in the English Midlands village of Etruria near Stoke-on-Trent where he made several innovations in ceramics.

1739 After a season of profound spiritual searching and self-examination, David Brainerd was converted. Though he lived only twenty-nine years, those years inspired many to follow Christ. Some, like William Carey and Henry Martyn, followed his footsteps onto the mission field. He was commissioned by the Scotland Society for the Propagation of Christian Knowledge as a missionary to the Indians. He labored for about three years among several races until ill health forced him to leave. Engaged to marry one of Jonathan Edwards's daughters, he was nursed in the preacher's home and died there October 9, 1747. Edwards preached Brainerd's funeral service and edited his journal with comments of his own under the title "The Life of David Brainerd."

1812 American forces led by General William Hull entered Canada—an incident that helped to provoke the War of 1812 against Britain. Hull's invasion was repulsed, and he was forced to retreat shortly thereafter to Detroit. The dream of the American war hawks was thus frustrated at the very outset of the conflict.

1817 American philosopher, naturalist, and transcendental anarchist Henry David Thoreau was born in Concord, Massachusetts. For two years he lived in a small hut on the edge of a pond near Concord, which provided the reflections in *Walden; or, Life in the Woods* (1854). In his essay "Resistance to Civil Government," he discussed the concept of passive resistance, which was adopted as a method of protest by Gandhi in India and by civil rights activists fighting segregation in the South.

1854 George Eastman, who invented the Kodak camera, was born on this day in Waterville, New York. He made photography affordable and available through mass-produced cameras and film. He also pioneered flexible film, which made motion pictures possible.

1862 The Union Congress authorized the Medal of Honor during the War Between the States.

1888 Toyohiko Kagawa was born into wealth, the son of a concubine. Both of his parents died while he was very young. As a teenager he became a Christian under the influence of Presbyterian missionaries and was baptized. He took theological training at Kobe and at Princeton University. Returning to his homeland, he committed himself to caring for the poor. For the rest of his life he devoted himself to community development and evangelism among the neediest of his people. His books—including the best-selling autobiographical novels *Across the Death Line* and *Before the Dawn*—brought new attention to the impoverished laborers in Japan's emerging capitalist economy. He won begrudging respect even among those who despised his faith. Amazingly, at his death Emperor Hirohito awarded him Japan's highest honor, the Order of the Sacred Treasure.

JULY

12

FEAST DAY

Saints Bridget and Maura, St. Henry the Emperor, St. Silas or Silvanus, St. Francis Solano, St. Eugenius of Carthage

JULY

On this day in 1896 George Washington Carver, a recent graduate of Iowa State College of Agriculture and Mechanical Arts—now Iowa State University—accepted an invitation from Booker T. Washington to head the agricultural department at Tuskegee Normal and Industrial Institute for Negroes—now Tuskegee University. During a tenure that lasted nearly fifty years, Carver elevated the scientific study of farming, improved the health and agricultural output of Southern farmers, and developed hundreds of uses for their crops.

As word of Carver's work at Tuskegee spread across the world, he received many invitations to work or teach at better-equipped, higher-paying institutions but decided to remain at Tuskegee, where he could be of greatest service to his fellow African Americans in the South. Carver epitomized Booker T. Washington's philosophy of black solidarity and self-reliance. Born a slave, Carver worked hard among his own people, lived modestly, and avoided confronting racial issues preferring to directly undermine segregation, prejudice, and discrimination by means of the excellence of his work and the indispensability of his service.

When he arrived in Tuskegee, Carver faced a whole host of challenges. The facilities were abysmal. Funds for the agricultural department—which consisted of little more than a dilapidated barn, a cow, and a few chickens—were altogether nonexistent. Nevertheless, he simply rolled up his sleeves and went to work. A resourceful individual, he assembled a small group of students to collect materials that could be used to construct laboratory equipment—pots, pans, tubes, wire, and anything else they thought might be useful—and made the tools and devices necessary to conduct agriculture-related experiments.

Carver also had to overcome concerns among the students—many of the students at Tuskegee associated agriculture with sharecropping and poverty. They were generally much more interested in learning the various industrial trades that would allow them to work in the factories and mills of urban America. But Carver knew better—the soil was the surest path toward self-sustaining community. Quietly and resolutely he dignified farming by infusing the discipline with science: botany, chemistry, and soil study. Over the course of just a few years, Carver's department began attracting the best and brightest students.

Over the years, Carver patented only three of his five hundred agriculture-based inventions, reasoning, "God gave them to me, how can I sell them to someone else?" He lived frugally, accepting only a small portion of his salary, and donated his life savings to a fund in his name that would encourage research in agricultural sciences. In 1916 Carver was appointed to The Royal Society of Arts in London, England, and in 1923 he was awarded the prestigious Spingarn Medal for his contributions to agriculture. His ingenuity and resourcefulness can be seen today in the hundreds of scientific and artistic items on display at the Carver Memorial Museum on the campus of Tuskegee University.

When I get a little money, I buy books. If there is anything left, I buy food and clothes.

[DESIDERIUS ERASMUS (1467–1536)]

1536 The brilliant Renaissance academic Desiderius Erasmus died in Basel, Switzerland. Though he became a central figure in the Reformation, his reforming zeal was always tempered by his commitment to the unity of the Catholic Church.

1787 In America's pre-Constitution government, Congress passed the Northwest Ordinance of 1787, defining the method by which the Union would create and admit the western states.

1793 French revolutionary writer Jean Paul Marat was stabbed to death in his bath by Charlotte Corday.

1798 William Wordsworth, while on a walking tour through the Wye valley, visited the ruins of Tintern Abbey. He composed one of this most famous poems after being inspired by the site.

1832 Henry Schoolcraft led the expedition that discovered the source of the Mississippi River on this day at Lake Itasca, Minnesota.

1852 Famed historian Thomas Babington Macaulay was elected to Parliament as a representative of the city of Edinburgh.

1863 Deadly rioting erupted in New York City. Entire neighborhoods were destroyed in protest of President Abraham Lincoln's determination to continue to prosecute the War Between the States and impose a military draft on the young men of the Union states.

1878 The Treaty of Berlin amended the terms of the Treaty of San Stefano, which had ended the Russo-Turkish War of 1877–1878.

1951 Austrian composer and music pioneer Arnold Schoenberg died. Obsessed with numerology (he had been born on September 13) to the extent of misspelling the name of his opera *Moses und Aron* so that it would not have thirteen letters, he ironically died on the thirteenth. Schoenberg is best known for his twelve-tone theory of composition, which simply meant that all twelve tones of the chromatic scale must be utilized before they could be repeated. The result was to destroy the hierarchy of pitches present in the relation between notes in tonal music. This was an outworking of his atheist philosophy that there is no order, relationship, or connection between elements of life. This left Schoenberg open to superstitions such as numerology.

JULY

1960 John F. Kennedy won the Democratic presidential nomination at his party's convention in Los Angeles.

1967 Race-related rioting broke out in Newark, New Jersey. By the time the violence ended, twenty-seven people had been killed.

1977 A blackout that would last twenty-five hours hit the New York City area.

1978 Lee Iacocca was fired as president of Ford Motor Company by chairman Henry Ford II. Iacocca went on to revive the flagging fortunes of Chrysler Corporation.

1985 Live Aid, an international rock concert in London, Philadelphia, Moscow, and Sydney, took place to raise money for relief efforts aimed at millions of the victims of famine in Africa.

NATIONAL DAY
France (Bastille Day), Iraq
FEAST DAY
St. Marcellinus or Marchelm, St.
Camillus de Lellis, St. Ulric of
Zell, St. Deusdedit of Canterbury

On this day in 1852, one of the worst naval disasters in modern history occurred in the shark-infested waters of the South Atlantic. The British troopship *Birkenhead* struck a rock shelf just off the coast of South Africa. The decrepit wood-hulled vessel carried the famed regiment of the 78th Highlanders—Scottish warriors who had distinguished themselves in every imperial scrap from the Napoleonic Wars to the Crimean Conflict. Also aboard were their wives and children—and of course, the ship's crew.

It was almost immediately evident that the foundering ship was going to sink. Unfortunately, there were very few lifeboats aboard. Nevertheless, calm prevailed. Orders were given to remove the women and children first by placing them into the few precious lifeboat seats—there was just enough room for them. Within twenty minutes the boat sank.

Not one woman or child was lost; not one man was saved. To make matters worse, the Highlanders and the crew of the *Birkenhead* had to endure grisly deaths—the sharks began circling even as the ship began to list. Their wives and children were forced to watch helplessly from the safety of the lifeboats.

Amazingly, in the last few moments before the boat dipped beneath the waves these brave and self-sacrificing men lined up in perfect military formation. Their piper band played the national air as the ship went down. Like the men of the *Titanic* a half century later, the Scottish stalwarts aboard the *Birkenhead* willingly exercised the age-old Christian virtue of Chivalry—that in times of crisis men must give their lives that women and children may live.

The *Birkenhead* incident inspired poet Rudyard Kipling, one of the twentieth century's most accomplished defenders of bold manhood, to pen his famous memorial verse, "So they stood an' was still to the Birken'ead drill; Soldier and sailor too." And thus, the phrase "Birken'ead Drill" came to be synonymous with courage, valor, and self-sacrificing chivalry.

JULY

BASTILLE DAY

This day is celebrated as the anniversary of the French Revolution and as the French national holiday. This despite the fact that the Bastille was hardly a prison at all when it was "liberated" by the Republican mobs that ultimately brought anarchy to the streets and the tyranny of guillotine justice to the Parliament.

It was the pipes of the Highlanders,
And now they played Auld Lang Syne
It came to our men like the voice of God,
And they shouted along the line.

[ROBERT LOWELL (1816–1891)]

1642 The first native American, Benjamin Thompson, best known for "New England Crisis," was born in Quincy, Massachusetts.

1798 Congress passed the Sedition Act, making it a federal crime to publish false, scandalous, or malicious writing about the United States government.

1813 Adoniram and Anne Judson, the first American foreign missionaries, laid eyes on the teeming city of Rangoon for the very first time. It would be five years before the Judsons baptized their first convert. But before the two of them died more than seven thousand Burmese would come to Christ—and today the Burmese church has grown to over two million Christians.

1823 King Kamehameha II of Hawaii and his wife died of measles while on a visit to Great Britain.

1841 The British humor magazine *Punch* was founded.

1853 Commodore Matthew Perry relayed to Japanese officials a letter from former President Millard Fillmore, requesting trade relations.

1860 Novelist Owen Wister, best known for his agrarian adventure story *The Virginian*, was born in Philadelphia.

1881 Outlaw William H. Bonney Jr., alias "Billy the Kid," was shot and killed by Sheriff Pat Garrett in Fort Sumner, New Mexico.

1903 Novelist Irving Stone, best known for *Lust for Life*, was born in San Francisco.

1904 Novelist Isaac Bashevis Singer was born in Radzymin, Poland. His many works of literary fiction ultimately earned him the Nobel Prize for literature in 1978.

1916 Tristan Tzara delivered the first Manifesto of Dada—an absurdist and modernist movement of artists and architects—in Zurich, Switzerland.

1933 All German political parties except the National Socialist—or Nazi—Party, were outlawed.

1958 The Iraqi military seized control of Baghdad and declared a republic in a coup d'état that brought the death of King Feisal II and the Crown Prince Abdul Illah, who were the last of the Hashemites to rule that beleaguered nation. The Hashemite dynasty in Hejaz met a similar fate—though the one in Jordan remains to this day.

1959 The first American nuclear warship, the USS *Long Beach,* was launched.

1965 The American space probe *Mariner 4* flew by Mars, sending back photographs of the planet.

1965 American Ambassador Adlai E. Stevenson—the scion of one of the nation's most prominent political families—died in London at the age of 65.

1976 Jimmy Carter won the Democratic presidential nomination at the party's convention in New York.

1978 Soviet dissident Natan Sharansky was convicted of treasonous espionage and anti-Soviet agitation, and sentenced to thirteen years at hard labor. Sharansky was released in 1986 and emigrated to Israel where he formed one of the most powerful political parties in that nation—mobilizing the vast Jewish Russian population.

JULY

14

415

JULY

Mark Twain once defined a literary classic as "a book which people praise but don't read." Fortunately, Joseph Malaby Dent, founder of J. M. Dent & Sons, never took that quip to heart. Over the course of his career he probably did more than any other single individual to inculcate a popular appreciation for the classics—his Everyman's Library editions provided excellent translations in durable bindings at extraordinarily cheap prices. Walk into almost any used-book shop in the English-speaking world today and there is apt to be a whole section filled with the little volumes that throughout the first half of the twentieth century became synonymous with the literary life.

Born in the old English village of Darlington, he was the tenth child of George Dent, a housepainter. As a youngster, he received elementary instruction at a local grammar school that emphasized little more than basic reading and writing skills. But by the time he was thirteen, he had already entered the workforce as an apprentice to a printer. Shortly thereafter, he turned to bookbinding. A voracious reader, he became especially enamoured with the classics—the ragged old volumes he was most likely called upon to rebind.

In 1867, he moved to London, where he set up his own bookbinding shop. He quickly gained a reputation for fine craftsmanship; indeed, his customers frequently rued the fact that his fine leather bindings put to shame the unattractive Victorian typography of the sheets they bound.

Encouraged by his rather elite clientele, Dent founded his publishing business in 1888. His first production, Charles Lamb's *Essays of Elia*, was edited by Augustine Birrell and illustrated by Herbert Railton, followed in 1889 by Goldsmith's *Poems and Plays.* Works by Jane Austen, the Brontë sisters, Geoffrey Chaucer, Daniel Defoe, Maria Edgeworth, Henry Fielding, Samuel Johnson, Lord Tennyson, and W. B. Yeats followed between 1889 and 1894. All of these early editions were expensively produced in limited quantities on handmade paper. Nevertheless, they enjoyed remarkable following among the literary cognoscenti.

In 1893, the bookseller Frederick Evans suggested that Dent publish a series of pocket volumes of William Shakespeare's plays. Though there did not seem to be much demand for cheap editions of the classics—in fact, sales of the great books had suffered a serious and steady decline throughout the latter half of the Victorian Age—Dent decided to follow the inclinations of his own heart and mind. He established the Temple Shakespeare series in 1894. The series was an almost immediate success. Then in 1904, Dent began to flesh out his ambitious vision for the Everyman's Library. It was to be a series of one thousand classics—practically the whole canon of Western civilization's great books—sold at an affordable price. Production began in 1906 and more than 150 titles were issued by the end of that first year.

Thus it was Dent and his passion for the classics that ensured great literature would be available to the general public in durable editions and at affordable prices.

When I was about ten or eleven years old I formed the habit of reading which has never since been broken. I developed peculiar literary affections and habits which inevitably generated an insatiable appetite for the classic masterworks then passing into popular disfavor. My career was thus established not upon any market sensibility, but upon my own predilection to preserve the good, the true, and the beautiful.

[JOSEPH MALABY DENT (1849–1926)]

1606 Dutch painter Rembrandt Harmenszoon van Rijn was born in Leiden to a family of modest means. Rembrandt coupled brilliant technique with a profound understanding of human emotion and nature. Much of his prodigious output portrayed biblical and theological themes despite the fact that orthodox ideas and scriptural vignettes were not considered serious subjects for art at the time in Holland. His works are characterized by chiaroscuro, or the contrast between light and dark.

1796 Thomas Bulfinch, best known for his multivolume compilation of myths, legends, fables, and tales, *Bulfinch's Mythology*, was born in Newton, Massachusetts.

1820 Edwin Jones became the first person known to have climbed Pikes Peak.

1870 Georgia became the last of the Confederate states to be readmitted to the Union.

1878 French literary master Gustave Flaubert wrote to his young charge, Guy de Maupassant, "You must—do you hear me young man?—you must work more than you are presently working. Do not waste your prodigious gifts. Talent will only take you so far. Work will be the difference between mediocre success and true literary merit."

1908 Jean Cocteau published his first poem at the age of eighteen in the chic Parisian journal *Je Sais Tout*.

1916 Boeing Company, originally known as Pacific Aero Products, was founded in Seattle.

1918 The Second Battle of the Marne began during the First World War.

1919 Irish novelist Dame Jean Iris Murdoch was born in Dublin. She had a penetrating ability to embody philosophy and thought in characters and narrative.

1964 Senator Barry M. Goldwater of Arizona was nominated for president by the Republican national convention in

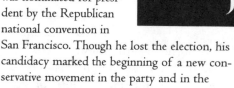

JULY

San Francisco. Though he lost the election, his candidacy marked the beginning of a new conservative movement in the party and in the nation.

1971 President Richard Nixon announced that he would visit the People's Republic of China to seek a "normalization of relations."

1979 President Jimmy Carter delivered his "malaise" speech in which he lamented what he called a "crisis of confidence" in America.

1992 Arkansas Governor Bill Clinton accepted the Democratic presidential nomination at the party's convention in New York despite a host of nagging scandals regarding his personal behavior, relationships, and finances.

FEAST DAY
St. Mary Magdalen Postel, St. Fulrad, St. Athenogenes, St. Helier, St. Eustathius of Antioch, St. Reineldis

JULY

On this day in 1930, an extraordinary group of Southern historians, poets, political scientists, novelists, and journalists published a prophetic collection of essays warning against the looming loss of the original vision of American life—a vision of both liberty and virtue. Including contributions from such literary luminaries as Robert Penn Warren, Donald Davidson, Allen Tate, Andrew Nelson Lytle, Stark Young, and John Crowe Ransom, the symposium, titled "I'll Take My Stand," poignantly voiced the complex intellectual, emotional, and spiritual consternation of men standing on the precipice of catastrophic cultural change.

The men were alarmed by what they perceived to be a steady erosion of the rule of law in modern American life. They feared that—as was the case in the eighteenth century—our liberties were facing a fearsome challenge from the almost omnipresent and omnipotent forces of monolithic government. They said, "When we remember the high expectations held universally by the founders of the American union for a more perfect order of society, and then consider the state of life in this country today, it is bound to appear to reasonable people that somehow the experiment has very nearly proved abortive, and that in some way a great commonwealth has gone wrong."

They were determined to warn against the creeping dehumanization of an ideological secularism that they believed was already beginning to dominate American life: "There is evidently a kind of thinking that rejoices in setting up a social objective which has no relation to the individual. Men are prepared to sacrifice their private dignity and happiness to an abstract social ideal, and without asking whether the social ideal produces the welfare of any individual man whatsoever."

Short-term pessimists but long-term optimists, they believed that eventually a grassroots movement would restore the principles of the rule of law and that the American dream could be preserved for future generations. Though they were not economists or sociologists or activists, their vision was a comprehensive blueprint for a genuinely principle-based conservative renewal.

Though the book received a great deal of attention and sold well—attaining near cult status in some places around the country—critics blasted the authors for their recondite naiveté. For some fifty years it looked as if the critics might be right. The course of twentieth century appeared to be a stern rebuke to the basic principles of the symposium. Like the English Distributists and the Continental Christian Democrats, with whom they shared so many basic presuppositions, the contributors seemed tragically out of step with the times.

But the recent resurgence of moderatism in politics, conservatism in economics, and communitarianism in social ethics have vindicated the Agrarians' emphasis on less government, lower taxes, family values, minimal regulation, and localism. Their innate distrust of professional politicians, propagandizing media, and commercial tomfoolery have suddenly been translated by a spontaneous grassroots advent into populist megatrends. The fulfillment of their improbable prophetic caveat is even now unfolding.

If a man does not make new acquaintances as he advances through life, he will soon find himself left alone.

[SAMUEL JOHNSON (1709–1784)]

622 The Islamic calendar started on this day—when Muhammad fled from Mecca to Medina. The day has been known as *Hejira*—Arabic for "flight"—ever since.

1723 Sir Joshua Reynolds, English portrait painter and first president of the Royal Academy of Arts, was born in Plympton, Devonshire, the son of a cleric. Interested in all of the arts, Reynolds founded the Literary Club, which consisted of Samuel Johnson (essayist and critic), Edmund Burke (statesman), David Garrick (actor), Oliver Goldsmith (writer), James Boswell (writer), and Richard Brinsley Sheridan (dramatist). Reynolds created more than two thousand portraits.

1769 The first permanent Spanish settlement in San Diego was founded by Father Junipero Serra.

1790 The District of Columbia was established as the seat of the United States government.

1862 David G. Farragut became the first rear admiral in the United States Navy.

1918 Czar Nicholas II, his empress, and their five children—the entire Russian royal family—were executed by the Bolsheviks at a remote Siberian compound, thus ending any hope of a Romanov restoration. Nevertheless, a civil war continued to rage in the beleaguered country for another five years before the Communists gained complete control.

1945 The first atomic bomb was exploded at 5:30 A.M. in a test in the New Mexico desert near Alamogordo.

1951 The controversial novel *The Catcher in the Rye* by J. D. Salinger was published.

1953 Author and poet Hilaire Belloc died in Guildford, Surrey, England. Born in France, he was educated at Oxford and became a British citizen, eventually serving in Parliament from 1906 to 1910. A good friend of G. K. Chesterton, they edited a weekly journal for many years that espoused their conservative social views. He was amazingly prolific, writing more than a hundred volumes in his life—in every genre and on every subject imaginable, including fiction, poetry, social criticism, history, philosophy, economics, politics, biography, science, military strategy, travel, art, geography, and theology. His best works include *The Path to Rome* (1902), *The Bad Child's Book of Beasts* (1896), *Hills and the Sea* (1906), *The Four Men* (1908), and *The History of England* (1925). His text *The Servile State* (1912) was a profoundly influential analysis of biblical economics that provided a devastating free-market critique of both mercantilist socialism and monopolist capitalism.

JULY

1957 Marine Major John Glenn set a transcontinental speed record when he flew a jet from California to New York in 3 hours, 23 minutes, and 8 seconds.

1964 In accepting the Republican presidential nomination in San Francisco, Barry M. Goldwater said, "Extremism in the defense of liberty is no vice" and "moderation in the pursuit of justice is no virtue."

1969 *Apollo 11* blasted off from Cape Kennedy on the first manned mission to the surface of the moon.

16

JULY

The great biographer James Boswell once asserted that Plutarch was "the prince of the ancient biographers." Indeed, our conception of the heroic men of ancient Greece and Rome owes more to Plutarch than to any other writer or historian—perhaps more than all the others put together. Thanks to his carefully researched labors, we have access to intimate details about the careers, struggles, enmities, and passions of Caesar, Alexander, Demosthenes, Antony, Solon, Cato, Pericles, Cicero, and Lycurgus. Without them, the era would be a virtual blank.

Interestingly, though Plutarch wrote prolifically on the lives of others, he left very little urge to indicate the course of his own. He threw the search-light of understanding upon the achievements of others, but his own remain shrouded in conjecture.

This much we do know—he was born just after the time of Christ on this day in 46, in the small Greek province of Boeotia—the broad and fertile plateau northwest of Athens. He came from an ancient and renowned Theban family, and thus was given access to the finest educational opportunities. He excelled in his wide-ranging travels and studies in Athens, Corinth, Alexandria, and Ephesus. He later became a respected member of the Imperial diplomatic corps and made his mark as a wise and effective adjudicator. In Rome, his reputation as a scholar earned him a number of influential contacts, friends, and opportunities. He served every emperor from the accession of Vespasian until his death in 126 during the reign of Hadrian. He was even granted an honorary consular rank.

Despite all these cosmopolitan experiences, he never lost his deep affection for his hometown of Chaeronea. Though a loyal supporter of the Empire, he remained a Greek patriot throughout his life. He was both a firm believer in and a committed practitioner of the ideals of the ancient city-state. Thus, he held a succession of magistracies in Chaeronea and nearby Delphi. His attachments at home were evidently reinforced by the sublime happiness of his marriage and family. It appears that his tender devotion to his wife, Timoxena, and their five children defined his mission and focused his philosophical vision.

It is this fact—the commitment of Plutarch to hearth and home—more than any other, that illumines the work of Plutarch. His beloved homeland was a shell of its former self. Many Greeks had all but forgotten the glories that once attended their land. The heritage of his community—and thus, of his own progeny—was very nearly lost. The splendor of the Roman Empire seemed to overshadow all that had come before. But Plutarch believed that the achievements of Rome were merely the extensions of those of Greece. All of his historical and literary work was aimed at showing the foundational role that Grecian greatness played in the Roman ascendancy. In fact, it was his thesis that there was direct continuity between the culture of Caesar, Brutus, and Antony and that of Pericles, Alcibiades, and Alexander. The entire parallel structure of the *Lives* was aimed at demonstrating this. And thus was created the notion of Greco-Roman culture.

I prefer to strive in bravery with the bravest, rather than in wealth with the wealthiest, or in greed with the greediest.

[PLUTARCH (C. 46–120)]

977 Vladimir began his rule over the Kievan Rus as a cruel tyrant and tireless playboy. He was, however, wise enough to recognize that a common faith could give his country unity. According to legend, it was on this day that he sent messengers to investigate the four great faiths of the civilized world: Islam, Judaism, Roman Catholicism, and Eastern Orthodoxy. The epicure in Vladimir thought Judaism and Islam, with their dietary restrictions, undesirable. He found Roman Catholicism "too simple." But his messengers sold him with their report of the ritual they witnessed in Byzantium. Speaking of the worship they saw in the great church of Constantinople, Hagia Sophia, they said, "We did not know whether we were in heaven or on earth. It would be impossible to find on earth any splendor greater than this. . . . Never shall we be able to forget so great a beauty." Vladimir embraced Orthodoxy and wed Anna, the sister of a Byzantine emperor. Thus began the spread of Christianity all through the land that would one day become Imperial Russia.

1453 Hostilities between France and England ceased as the Hundred Years' War concluded with the defeat of the English at the Battle of Castillon. English king Henry VI's holdings in France were reduced to just the region of Calais.

1492 Wearing a suit of armor, Joan of Arc crowned Charles VII of France at the Cathedral of Rheims as the culmination of her struggle to drive the English from France and restore the Crown.

1580 The Spanish navy defeated the French in a naval battle off the coast of modern Florida, bringing to an end French influence in that part of the New World.

1674 Isaac Watts, the English pastor and hymn writer of "Joy to the World," was born in Southampton. He wrote over 750 hymns, including the versification of all the psalms. Watts's great hymns of the church, such as "When I Survey the Wondrous Cross," "O God, Our Help in Ages Past," "Jesus Shall Reign Where're the Sun," and "How Sweet the Name of Jesus Sounds" have increasingly fallen out of use in the modern church, despite the glorious truth they declare.

1717 George Frideric Handel's *Water Music* was first performed on a barge on the River Thames at London.

JULY

1821 Spain ceded Florida to the United States.

1899 Tough-guy actor James Cagney was born in New York City.

1917 The royal family in Britain first publicly used the name Windsor.

1955 Animator Walt Disney's entertainment theme park, Disneyland, debuted in Anaheim, California.

1975 An American *Apollo* spaceship docked with a Soviet *Soyuz* spacecraft in orbit in the first superpower link-up of its kind.

1979 Nicaraguan President Anastasio Somoza resigned and fled into exile in Miami.

1997 Woolworth Corporation announced that it was closing its four hundred remaining five-and-dime stores across the country, ending 117 years in business.

JULY

When the Royal Society was chartered by Charles II on this day in 1662, it was the first scientific society in history. Interestingly, devout Christians, with their interest in God's creation, were most responsible for bringing it into existence. In fact, its membership was overwhelmingly Puritan in makeup.

The society originally grew out of the meetings of the so-called "invisibles" who gathered at the home of Katherine Boyles. Earlier she had supported the Parliamentarians and Puritans in the revolt against Charles I. Of deep intelligence, she welcomed the group into her house so that she might share the new scientific findings.

The other stalwarts of the society were likewise quite conservative in their theological inclinations. Theodore Haak, a professor at the largely Puritan Gresham College, initiated those early meetings of the "invisibles." Chief architect and secretary of the Royal Society after the Restoration was John Wilkins, whose religious inclinations later led him to become a bishop and to prepare arguments in defense of Scripture. John Willis also helped inaugurate the society. Considered one of the greatest physicians of his generation, he was so strong in his attachment to the Church of England that he was cold-shouldered at the royal court which inclined to Romanism. Among his many charities, he funded a clergyman to conduct worship services at hours when average workingmen could attend.

Likewise, Robert Boyle was a devout believer. He not only engaged in a series of apologetics projects, he also endowed a lecture series to defend Christianity, assisted persecuted Welsh clergymen, and subsidized Scripture translation. An innovative chemist, he developed Boyle's Law of Gases and wrote a book that debunked the pseudo-sciences of alchemy. He is often called the "Father of Modern Chemistry." Perhaps the most accomplished man of his day, Christopher Wren was also a founder of the society. Best known for rebuilding St. Paul's Cathedral, he was an anatomist who prepared the drawings for Willis's *Cerebri Anatome,* a geometer (Newton classed him among the best), a physicist pioneering a number of vital impact studies, a meteorologist, and a surveyor. He attempted some of the first blood transfusions and made microscopic studies of insects.

Since each of these founders was a sincere Christian, it is not surprising that the motto adopted by the new organization was "Nothing by mere authority." The history of the Royal Society affords further evidence that modern science, rather than being contrary to Christianity, is in fact its natural fruit.

1927

On this day, Ty Cobb, the "Georgia Peach," got his four-thousandth hit. Considered by many to have been baseball's greatest player, Cobb's statistics are astonishing: 12 batting titles (his first when he was 20), 4,189 hits, and a lifetime batting average of .366, with three .400 seasons and, in 1911, a .420 season. In his twenty-four years of playing, he stole 892 bases, with his 96 steals in 1915 standing as a record for nearly a half century.

The world does not consider labor a blessing, therefore, it flees and hates it but the pious who fear the Lord, labor with a ready and cheerful heart; for they know God's command and will, they acknowledge His calling.

[MARTIN LUTHER (1483–1546)]

63   Roman emperor Nero blamed Christians for the calamitous fire that destroyed most of the city of Rome. The accusation brought about the first great wave of persecutions.

954   Princess Olga of Kiev, the grandmother of the man credited with Christianizing Russia, became regent for her son Svyatoslav upon the assassination of her husband, Igor I. Believed to be of Viking ancestry, Olga ruled for the next twenty years, implementing fiscal and other reforms throughout the principality. Possibly already a convert to Christianity, she visited Constantinople and in 957 was baptized there.

1792   The Scot-born American naval hero John Paul Jones died in Paris at age forty-five.

1811   English novelist William Makepeace Thackeray was born in Calcutta, India. Among the pseudonyms he would use were A. M. Titmarsh, P. H. Yellowplush, G. S. Fitzboodle, and Theophile Wagstaff.

1817   English novelist Jane Austen, best known for her novels *Pride and Prejudice, Sense and Sensibility,* and *Emma,* died in Winchester, Hampshire, England.

1833   The Oxford Movement, a stirring toward reformation by the high church adherents of the Church of England, was officially launched during a chapel service led by Hugh Keble and attended by the notable scholars John Henry Newman, Richard Hurrell Froude, Edward Pusey, and Charles Marriott. Though some members of the movement later left Anglicanism for the Roman Catholic Church, the overall effect of the movement was to restore a higher level of spirituality among the English clergy. It also forced a re-examination of the doctrinal and authoritative bases of the church and brought genuine revival.

1872   Britain introduced the concept of voting by secret ballot.

1932   The United States and Canada signed a treaty to develop the St. Lawrence Seaway.

1936   The Spanish Civil War began as General Francisco Franco led an uprising of army troops based in Spanish North Africa.

JULY

1944   Hideki Tojo was removed as Japanese premier and war minister because of setbacks suffered by his country in the Second World War.

1947   President Harry Truman signed the Presidential Succession Act, which placed the Speaker of the House and the Senate president pro tempore next in the line of succession after the vice president.

1969   A car driven by Senator Edward M. Kennedy—a Democrat representing the state of Massachusetts and scion of one of America's elite political families—plunged off a bridge on Chappaquiddick Island near Martha's Vineyard. His passenger, twenty-eight-year-old Mary Jo Kopechne, died.

18

FEAST DAY

Saints Justa and Rufina; St. Ambrose Autpert; St. Macrina the Younger; St. Arsenius the Great; St. James of Nisibia; St. Symmachus, pope; St. John Plesington

JULY

On this day in 1871, Augustus St. Clair was given an extremely dangerous undercover investigative assignment for the *New York Times*—he was to infiltrate and ultimately expose the city's prosperous and profligate "medical malpractice" industry—the common euphemism for the abortion trade. For several weeks, he and a "lady friend" visited a number of the most heavily trafficked clinics in New York, posing as a couple facing a crisis pregnancy. They were shocked with what they saw.

It wasn't that the clinics were sordid back-alley affairs. They weren't. It wasn't that they were operated by shady or seedy quacks. They weren't. It wasn't that they were dark, dangerous, and disreputable. They weren't. On the contrary, it was that the rich splendor of the entrepreneurial abortuaries—fine tapestry carpets, expensive mahogany furniture, elegant decorations, and spacious parlors—contrasted so sharply with the desperation, helplessness, and poverty of their clientele. It was that the smug complacency of the proprietors—men and women who made quite an opulent living out of the sordid trade—contrasted so sharply with the dispiritedness of their patients. It was that their frank and forthright commerce—advertised openly in all the magazines, newspapers, and digests of the day—contrasted so sharply with the secretive shame of their customers. It was that the dens of iniquity were simultaneously dens of inequity.

As a result of his discoveries St. Clair wrote a hard-hitting three-column article which the *Times* published in late August. Entitled "The Evil of the Age," the article opened with a solemn warning: "The enormous amount of medical malpractice that exists and flourishes, almost unchecked, in the city of New York, is a theme for most serious consideration. Thousands of human beings are thus murdered before they have seen the light of this world, and thousands upon thousands more of adults are irremediably robbed in constitution, health, and happiness."

Skillfully, St. Clair portrayed virtually every dimension of the slick and professional abortion industry: from its bottom-line economics to its medical methodologies; from its marketing savvy to its litigal invulnerability. Told with passion and insight, the story hit the city like a bombshell. Almost single-handedly, the young reporter put abortion on the public agenda for the first time in decades.

Being on the public agenda is not enough in itself to bring about widespread social change, however. Something more is needed—an incident to galvanize the concern of the public. In the good providence of God, just such an incident occurred in New York just days after St. Clair's article appeared in the *Times*. The body of a beautiful young woman was discovered inside an abandoned trunk in a railway station baggage room. A police autopsy determined that the cause of death was a botched abortion.

A national campaign was launched that eventually made abortion illegal in every state, condemned by the American Medical Association, and vilified by the national press. And it all began with St. Clair's story in the *New York Times*—of all places.

The Christian faith has not been tried and found wanting. It has been found difficult, and left untried.

[G. K. CHESTERTON (1874–1936)]

1374 The Medieval poet Petrarch died in Tuscany one day shy of his seventieth birthday.

1553 Fifteen-year-old Lady Jane Grey, the greatest and best hope of the Protestant party, was deposed as queen of England after claiming the crown for nine days. Bloody Mary—the Catholic daughter of King Henry VIII and Catherine of Aragon—was proclaimed queen. Lady Jane was summarily executed along with a number of her supporters, and a terrible wave of persecution broke out all across the land—documented in the classic work *Foxe's Book of Martyrs*.

1663 Samuel Pepys entered in his diary, "Read over my vows and increased them by a vow against all strong drink until November next."

1797 While out for a walk in his garden, Mr. Wright of Norwich, England, was suddenly covered by a swarm of bees. He stood completely still for a period of two hours while the bees were removed from his head and put into a hive. Amazingly, he survived the incident without a single sting.

1834 French painter Edgar Degas was born in Paris to a wealthy family. He exhibited with the impressionists, although he preferred to work in the studio and was not interested in the portrayal of light. He was primarily interested in the theater, and his most famous works are of ballet dancers on stage. He experimented with the placement of the focal point in his works and often direct-ed the gaze of the viewer through the action in the painting.

1848 A pioneer women's rights convention convened in Seneca Falls, New York.

1870 The Franco-Prussian War began. France eventually lost the war and Napoleon III was deposed.

1898 Following the public uproar surrounding his trial for libel, Emile Zola fled France on the advice of his lawyers.

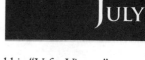

JULY

1941 British Prime Minister Winston Churchill launched his "V for Victory" campaign in Europe.

1979 The Nicaraguan capital of Managua fell to Sandinista guerrillas, two days after President Anastasio Somoza had fled the country.

1985 Christa McAuliffe of New Hampshire was chosen to be the first schoolteacher to ride aboard a space shuttle. McAuliffe and six other crew members died when the *Challenger* exploded shortly after liftoff.

1993 President Bill Clinton announced his controversial "Don't ask, don't tell" compromise allowing homosexuals to serve in the military but only if they veiled all their sundry homosexual activities from public scrutiny.

19

NATIONAL DAY
Colombia
FEAST DAY
*St. Margaret of Antioch, St. Elias
of Jerusalem, St. Ansegisus, St.
Aurelius of Carthage, St. Flavian
of Antioch, St. Wulmar, St. Gregory
Lopez, St. Wilgefortis or Liberata,
St. Joseph Barsabas the Just*

JULY

The religious wars that followed the Reformation saw a number of outbreaks of persecutions—by both Catholics and Protestants. Courageous men and women met their fates with steadfast faith and unwavering assurance that their cause—whichever it might have been—would one day be vindicated. Many a martyr was sacrificed during these difficult years.

Once called a "diamond of England," Edmund Campion was one of them. He was a Catholic academic who fled into exile following the ascension of Queen Elizabeth. He had long been an approving persecutor of the Protestants during the horrific persecutions unleashed by Bloody Mary. But at her death, the tables suddenly turned and he was forced out of his homeland.

On the Continent, he took vows as a Jesuit. Posted at first to Prague, he later was recalled to Rome. There he was ordered to infiltrate England and minister to English Catholics. Though he knew this to be a death warrant, he enthusiastically obeyed his orders. In preparation for his inevitable capture and death he wrote his *Challenge to the Privy Council*, more generally known as *Campion's Brag*. In this he insisted that his reasons for returning to his homeland were not political: "My charge is of free cost to preach the gospel, to minister the sacraments, to instruct the simple, to reform sinners, to confute errors; in brief, to cry alarm spiritual against foul vice and proud ignorance, wherewith many of my dear countrymen are abused."

For more than a year he eluded his captors, escaping from home to home. He met secretly with the Catholic elite, saying the Mass in their homes and distributing the elements of the sacraments. But, in the end he was betrayed on this day in 1581. Though he was hidden away in a secret cubbyhole in the wall, he was discovered and arrested.

Campion was racked and tortured. He was offered bribes and threats. But because he refused to recant, he was eventually hanged and drawn and quartered at Tyburn. At his sentencing he said, "In condemning us you condemn all your own ancestors—all the ancient priests, bishops, and kings— all that was once the glory of England."

Campion's execution was widely heralded by Protestants as due justice—since he had been responsible for so many of the awful tortures and killings described in *Foxe's Book of Martyrs*. But many of the ablest Puritan spokesmen decried the death as just one more sad chapter in the ongoing saga of Catholic-Protestant enmity.

1842	Nathaniel Hawthorne and his bride, Sophia Peabody, moved into the Old Manse in Concord, Massachusetts, to find a garden already plowed, weeded, and tilled for them by Henry David Thoreau.

There is little extraordinary about the achievements of a genius, a prodigy, or a savant. Inevitably, a great leader is someone who overcomes tremendous obstacles and still succeeds. That is the essence of courage. It is the ability to maintain, in the face of grave perils, a kind of incognizance of the consequences of doing right. It is the ability to maintain great strength without any impulsive compulsion to use it—that strength is to be held in reserve until and unless it becomes necessary to use it for the cause of right.

[TRISTAN GYLBERD (1954–)]

1304 Francesco Petrarca—best known as Petrarch—was born in Arezzo, Tuscany. Along with Chaucer and Dante, he established the literary form that would flower into Renaissance rhyme, poesy, and verse.

1389 Richard II named Geoffrey Chaucer chief clerk of the king's works at Westminster.

1698 Isaac Watts, the great hymn writer, preached his first sermon at Mark Lane in London. He had been born in Southampton, England on July 17, 1674. He fell under conviction in 1688 and learned to trust Christ in a personal way a year later. His father was twice imprisoned for refusing to bend to the Church of England's beliefs. Some of that pluck carried over to Isaac, who refused to take an all-expenses-paid education rather than conform himself to the Church of England. After completing his education, his gifts were so readily apparent that the little church at Mark Lane soon named him its assistant pastor. He published his *Hymns and Spiritual Songs*—including such classics as "Joy to the World" and "When I Survey the Wondrous Cross." And in 1719, he published a collection of Christianized psalms. These helped to transform hymnody and introduce an entirely new form of music for worship.

1810 Colombia—including the territory now contained in Panama—declared independence from Spain.

1861 The Congress of the Confederate States began holding sessions in Richmond, Virginia.

1871 British Columbia entered the Confederation as a Canadian province.

1872 Mr. Mahlon Loomis was awarded a patent for the first wireless telegraph.

1881 Sioux Indian leader Sitting Bull, a fugitive since the Battle of the Little Big Horn, surrendered to federal troops.

1942 The first detachment of the Women's Army Corps—later known as the WAC—began basic training at Fort Des Moines, Iowa.

1944 An attempt by a group of German officials to assassinate Adolf Hitler failed as a bomb explosion at Hitler's Rastenburg headquarters only wounded the Nazi leader. The blast was shielded by a heavy table.

1944 President Franklin Roosevelt was nominated for an unprecedented fourth term of office at the Democratic convention in Chicago.

1951 Jordan's Hashemite king Abdullah Ibn Ul-Hussein was assassinated in Jerusalem in the presence of his young grandson, the future King Hussein.

1969 *Apollo 11* astronauts Neil Armstrong and Edwin "Buzz" Aldrin became the first men to walk on the moon as they stepped out of their lunar module.

1976 The *Viking I* became the first spacecraft to land on Mars.

JULY

20

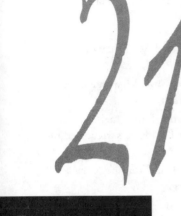

NATIONAL DAY
Belgium
FEAST DAY
St. Laurence of Brindisi, St. Victor
of Marseilles, St. Arbrogastes, St.
Praxedes

JULY

When Thurgood Marshall died in 1993, he was only the second justice to lie in state in the Supreme Court's chambers—Chief Justice Earl Warren, who had written the opinion in Marshall's most celebrated case, *Brown vs. Board of Education*, was the other. This honor capped the outpouring of praise for the Court's first African-American justice, a man who would likely have had an honored place in American history even if he had never sat on the bench of the highest court in the land.

His accomplishments were indeed, remarkable. He had served as the chief counsel for the National Association for the Advancement of Colored People—the NAACP—and was the founder of its Legal Defense and Educational Fund. He then began thirty years of public service—first as a federal appeals court judge, then as America's first African-American solicitor general. He was undeniably one of America's most influential and well-known lawyers, having helped millions of African Americans exercise their long-denied constitutional rights in a series of landmark civil rights cases.

Both of Marshall's parents—William, who worked as a dining steward at an all-white private club, and Norma, a grade school teacher in the segregated schools—instilled in their son a strong sense of pride and self-confidence. As a child, Marshall later recalled, he was a "hell-raiser," whose high school teacher punished him by sending him to the school's basement to read and copy passages from the United States Constitution. It was valuable training for the future lawyer, who claimed that by the time he graduated he could recite nearly the entire document by heart. From Baltimore's Douglass High School, Marshall entered Lincoln University in Oxford, Pennsylvania, where he won respect as a debater and graduated with honors in 1930.

Denied admission to the University of Maryland's all-white law school—an institution whose segregation he later challenged and defeated in *Murray v. Maryland* in 1936—Marshall entered the law school at Howard University. There, he met Charles H. Houston, the school's vice dean, who became the NAACP's first chief counsel and the first African American to win a case before the U.S. Supreme Court. Shortly after graduating magna cum laude in 1933, Marshall went to work for Houston at the NAACP, replacing him as chief counsel in 1938.

Marshall brought thirty-two cases before the Supreme Court; he won twenty-nine of them. He had an even more impressive record as a judge for the U.S. Court of Appeals, a position to which President John Kennedy appointed him in 1961. Of the 112 opinions he wrote for that court, not one was overturned on appeal. His tenure on the Supreme Court, though marked by the strenuous ideological wrangling of the day, was equally stellar. Nevertheless, he remained unshakable in his humility. When asked by a reporter at the end of his life how he wished to be remembered, Marshall was characteristically plainspoken, saying, "He did the best he could with what he had."

Faith declares what the senses do not see, but not the contrary of what they see. It is above them, not contrary to them.

[BLAISE PASCAL (1623–1662)]

1591 The premier American feminist, Anne Hutchinson, was born in Alford, England. Having come under the sway of John Cotton's preaching, she and her husband, William, followed Cotton in migrating to the new colony of Puritans and Pilgrims in Massachusetts. Within a short time however, she ran afoul of authorities by teaching heterodox ideas to a large number of women who gathered in her home each evening. Eventually she was banished from Boston and joined William Rogers at Rhode Island. Alas, her heretical ideas were too much even for him, and she was sent out into the wilderness where she was killed by Indians.

1759 Saint Seraphim of Sarov was born at Kursk, Russia. He entered the monastery of Sarov when he was nineteen years of age, and for the next forty-five years he led the life of a contemplative, first in the monastery and then in an isolated hut—eventually becoming one of the most renowned holy men in all of Eastern Orthodoxy.

1773 Pope Clement XIV dissolved the Society of Jesus—popularly known as the Jesuits. It had already been banned in France and Spain. It was a stunning decision, given the prominence the order had enjoyed in years past. It had been founded during the Reformation era in 1534. Ignatius of Loyola became its first superior when Pope Paul III approved it in 1540. Famed missionary Francis Xavier was one of the original seven men in the order. Indeed, the Jesuits had been a driving force in the Counter-Reformation. Their energy and organizational acumen had carried Catholicism beyond its pre-Reformation bounds and regained much of the territory lost to Protestants. By emphasizing missions and education, the Jesuits from the first exerted influence beyond their numbers—though in time it became the largest Roman

Catholic order. Jesuits became known as the schoolmasters of Europe and were prominent as confessors to kings and emperors. But the order suffered from a hefty dose of hubris and ran afoul of the church hierarchy. The Society eventually was restored in 1814, but it has never regained the prominence it once had.

1796 Robert Burns, who wrote songs and poems in Scottish dialect, died at Dumfries, Scotland. Only thirty-eight years old, he was survived by a pregnant wife and five small children. He was buried in a mausoleum at Dumfries.

1816 Paul Julius Reuter, founder of the British news agency bearing his name, was born in Hesse, Germany.

1831 Belgium asserted its independence from the Netherlands when Leopold I was proclaimed king of the Belgians.

JULY

1861 Stonewall Jackson picked up his nickname during the Battle at Bull Run Creek near Manassas, Virginia. Jackson, along with other Confederate forces, made a strong defensive stand that enabled the South to hold off the Union advance.

1899 Modern minimalist author Ernest Hemingway was born in Oak Park, Illinois.

1925 The American Civil Liberty Union's manipulated test case on evolution and creation—the so-called Scopes Monkey Trial—ended in Dayton, Tennessee. William Jennings Bryan won a conviction against teacher John T. Scopes, who had violated the state law against teaching Darwin's Theory of Evolution as scientific fact rather than as speculative theory.

1954 France surrendered North Vietnam to the Communist revolutionaries.

21

JULY

On this day in 1680 a company of English dragoons surprised and surrounded a Scottish preacher and a small band of armed men. Deciding to fight to the death, their leader, Richard Cameron, prayed, "Lord, spare the green and take the ripe." The skirmish took place at Ayrsmoss and sprang out of the complicated web of religious and political relations that strained English and Scottish relations at the time.

England had unilaterally imposed Episcopalian worship on most of Scotland. Cameron was a member of the historic but now-outlawed Covenanter movement—men and women who continued to worship in accordance with their Presbyterian convictions. Because of his natural gift of oratory, Covenanter leaders felt Cameron was called to preach the gospel. And so, though not yet ordained, he became an outdoor preacher. He embraced the most steadfast position of the Scottish Reformers and proclaimed the doctrines of grace with great fervor.

No doubt his patriotic Scots fervor for freedom from the despised English helped to shape his fierce recalcitrance; nonetheless, there was little doubt about the authenticity of his message. Thousands hung on his sermons, weeping when his eloquent appeals for repentance and submission to Christ touched their hearts. After receiving ordination in the Netherlands—it was closed to him and all the other Covenanters in Scotland—Cameron returned to Scotland to plant churches.

In his absence, Charles II had offered a broad indulgence for the Scots—if only the Covenanters would recant. Cameron attacked it savagely. With a number of other leaders he drew up the revolutionary Sanquhar Declaration, which disowned Charles II's authority and went so far as to boldly declare war on him. He prophesied the overthrow of the Stuart line for, among other things, "usurping the royal prerogatives of King Jesus." As a result, he was aptly nicknamed the "Lion of the Covenant."

A reward of £5,000 was immediately placed on his head. A small band of guards had to accompany him wherever he went to preach. But their swords proved insufficient on the day of disaster. The dragoons charged and hacked the Scots to death—though they offered fierce resistance. Cameron was slain and his body was desecrated—his head and hands were cut off to be displayed on an Edinburgh gate.

Even so, Cameron's prophecy was fulfilled in short order. Charles II was succeeded by his brother James II, who was driven into exile. The English Parliament then ended the Stuart royal line by summoning William III of Orange to the throne in a bloodless revolution.

1937 The Senate rejected President Franklin Roosevelt's proposal to add more justices to the Supreme Court—a power play to ensure the passage of his radical New Deal legislation.

I can only say that I am nothing but a poor sinner, trusting in Christ alone for salvation.

[ROBERT E. LEE (1807–1870)]

1515 Teresa of Avila was born in the heart of the fiercely Catholic Castile. While still a young teen, she committed herself to a convent and began a life of notable holiness, service, and study. With the ecstatic mystic St. John of the Cross, she foundered the discalced—or shoeless—Carmelite Order. The author of such books as the *Way of Perfection* and *Meditations on the Canticle*, she eventually was declared the first ever woman doctor of the church—taking her place beside such heroes of the faith as Saint Augustine and Saint Jerome.

1587 An English colony—fated to vanish under mysterious circumstances—was established on Roanoke Island off North Carolina by Sir Walter Raleigh.

1750 With the death of Johann Sebastian Bach in Leipzig, Germany, the period of music known as Baroque effectively came to a close.

1796 Cleveland, Ohio, was founded by General Moses Cleveland.

1812 English troops defeated the French at the Battle of Salamanca in Spain—it was the first major victory by any force against the Napoleonic army.

1821 Austrian botanist Gregor Johann Mendel was born. He developed the theory of heredity known as Mendelism.

1884 Still gripped by a recalcitrant paganism in the nineteenth century, Japan was inhospitable to the gospel and its proponents. Even so, a handful of pioneer missionaries persevered and bore fruit in the midst of terribly difficult circumstances. The life and ministry of Jai Ishii was just such fruit. Born into a powerful and influential samurai family, he was converted to the faith on this day while still a teenager at a Presbyterian mission school. Inspired by a visit of George Mueller two years later, Ishii committed his life to caring for the myriads of abandoned and neglected children that roamed Japan's medieval provinces. His courage and valor in standing against the tide of the culture became so widely heralded that guilds of abortionists regularly contracted with assassins to take his life. More often than not, however, Ishii was able to vanquish his foes—not with power or by might but with the gospel. Eventually, the orphanage, school, and hospital founded by him grew to the point that they housed nearly three hundred children at a time, provided primary health care for the entire feudal region, and asserted the principal outlet of higher culture in all of

JULY

Okayama. His ministry became a paradigm of Christian compassion and faithfulness in the midst of an emerging Japanese prowess as well as the model the government used—and still uses—in providing legal protection to the unwanted and the rejected.

1899 Poet Hart Crane was born in Garrettsville, Ohio.

1934 A man identified as bank robber John Dillinger was shot to death by federal agents outside Chicago's Biograph Theater.

1943 American forces led by General George S. Patton captured Palermo, Sicily, during World War II.

1975 The House of Representatives joined the Senate in voting to restore the American citizenship of Confederate General Robert E. Lee.

22

NATIONAL DAY
  Ethiopia, United Arab Republic
FEAST DAY
  St. Anne or Susanna, St. John Cassian, St. Romula and her Companions, St. Apollinaris of Ravenna, The Three Wise Men, St. Bridget of Sweden, St. Liborius

General Ulysses S. Grant (1822–1885) was one of the nation's greatest military heroes but one of its most unsuccessful presidents. Decisive and masterful on the battlefield, a dynamic leader and a horseman of great prowess, he proved to be ingenuous in the political arena—but being a great general and a great politician does not necessarily translate into presidential success.

Raised on a farm, he developed a love of horses early on and seemed always at his best on horseback. As leader of the victorious forces of the North, Grant was considered one of the saviors of the Union—even though he was held suspect by the abolitionists since he was a slaveholder all through the war and allowed emancipation only after he was forced to release his slaves by the passage of the Sixteenth Amendment in 1865. Indeed, he once asserted that "if the war had been about slavery," he "would have fought for the South." Ironically, his greatest on-the-field adversary, Robert E. Lee, had averred quite the opposite.

Nevertheless, after Andrew Johnson's unhappy term, Republicans turned readily to Grant, although he knew nothing about politics. Innocent and sincere, Grant committed errors of judgment from the beginning: He appointed two unknowns from his hometown in Illinois to cabinet positions. Later he allowed himself to be entertained by two stock manipulators—Jay Gould and Jim Fisk—who tried to corner the gold market, a mistake that left him open to charges of incompetence and corruption.

As the years passed, the evidences of corruption in his administration were such that Grant lost much of the popularity that first brought him into office. However, he managed to be reelected to another term, one tarnished by even more corruption, more scandal.

In spite of the scandals, Grant scored a few victories. Passage of the Amnesty Bill in 1872 restored civil rights to many Southerners, relieving some of the harsh conditions of Reconstruction. And, against considerable opposition, Grant took courageous steps to fight the growing threat of inflation. But the battle-torn country was still in distress; the general who had brought the great uncivil war to a successful close was not the man to bind up the nation's wounds.

His last years were sadly encumbered with woeful money problems. From the fall of 1884 until his death on this day in 1885, he raced against terminal cancer to finish his memoirs so that his widow would not live out her days as a pauper. As he had always been able to do before, he came through just in the nick of time.

1880   Mystery writer Raymond Chandler—best known for his noir gumshoe adventures *Farewell My Lovely* and *The Big Sleep*—was born in Chicago. Though he was educated in England, France, and Germany, he settled in Southern California, which formed the background for all of his novels.

Knowing is not enough; we must apply. Understanding is not enough; we must do. Knowing and understanding in action make for honor. And honor is the heart of wisdom.

[JOHANN GOETHE (1749–1832)]

1825 Kidnapped by Muslim slave-traders from his Yoruba homeland in north-central Africa, Samuel Adjai Crowther was rescued by missionaries and baptized into the church on this day. Six months after acquiring a rudimentary alphabet card he had taught himself to read the New Testament. His extraordinary intellectual gifts and spiritual initiative became further evident five years later when he was admitted into the Fourah Bay College at the top of his class—within a few months even becoming a tutor there. He was part of the first Niger expedition in which the British partook—partly for the sake of geographical knowledge, but also to end the slave trade in that region. In 1864, Crowther was consecrated in Canterbury Cathedral as the missionary bishop of the Niger Territory. That same year Oxford awarded him a doctor of divinity degree. Throughout his life he was an ardent and successful opponent of slavery, human sacrifice, infanticide, and other traditional African customs. After his death in 1891, a fellow missionary testified that through Bishop Crowther's labor "the horrible slave trade received a great check; the practice of human sacrifice is at an end within the Niger country, and the neighboring chiefs find themselves unable to procure slaves to be immolated by their priests. Instead of the indolence which accompanies the easy gains of the slave-dealer, commerce, with its attendant activity, has had to flee far up the rivers."

1829 William Austin Burt of Mount Vernon, Michigan, received a patent for his typographer—a forerunner of the typewriter.

1846 Protesting slavery and American involvement in the Mexican War, Henry David Thoreau refused to pay his one-dollar poll tax and was put in jail by his friend, a Concord, Massachusetts, constable. The experience prompted him to write his classic tract, *Civil Disobedience.*

1886 New York saloonkeeper Steve Brodie claimed to have made a daredevil plunge from the Brooklyn Bridge into the East River.

1904 Charles E. Menches filled a waffle pastry cone with two scoops of ice cream, thus inventing the ice cream cone. He prepared the concoction for the Louisiana Purchase Exposition in St. Louis, Missouri.

JULY

1914 Austria-Hungary issued a series of ultimatums to Serbia following the killing of Archduke Francis Ferdinand by a Serb assassin. Within days the dispute escalated to the point of arms—and thus began the First World War.

1948 American pioneer filmmaker D. W. Griffith died in Los Angeles at age seventy-three.

1952 Egyptian military officers led by Gamal Abdel Nasser overthrew the monarchy and sent King Farouk I into exile.

1967 Racial unrest in the city of Detroit erupted into rioting. The violence ultimately claimed forty-three lives.

23

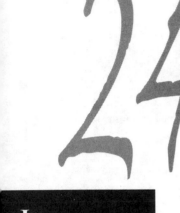

JULY

Determined to reclaim his family's inheritance, Bonnie Prince Charlie (1720–1788) landed on the shores of Scotland on this day in 1745. His seven elderly companions—loyal courtesans to the expatriate royal cause—hardly constituted a fighting force. He had virtually no hope of attracting allies for his cause, he had no contacts in the land, he carried no money, and had no foreign support. He had no military experience, no weapons, and no clear plan. Nevertheless, he was committed to the legacy of his family, the justness of his claim, and the nobility of his charge.

His grandfather James II, defeated by parliamentary troops at the Battle of the Boyne, sealed the Great Revolution of 1688 and deposed the Stuart monarchy of Great Britain. Living in exile in France, the family pressed its claim against the Hanoverian usurpers again and again over the next seventy years—but all to no avail. The British repeatedly repulsed the royal family and its loyal subjects so that the hope of a Stuart restoration increasingly became little more than a romantic lost cause.

Resigned to his restless exile, the prince's father, James III, was a morose and defeated man. As a result Bonnie Prince Charlie grew up in a hopeless environment of despair. But somehow he was never infected with that sense of futility and finality. He held on to the dream that one day his family might again reign supreme in London and Edinburgh—as was their due. His princely qualities—and deep devotion to his family's rich legacy of nobility—were evident to all.

In 1745, at the age of twenty-five, he determined that he must attempt to recover his father's inheritance. At first, the landlords, nobles, and lairds he met scoffed at the idea that the long-deposed Stuarts might be able to mount a legitimate claim for the throne. The Hanoverians and Parliamentarians controlled the greatest military force on the face of the earth. They commanded the world's largest treasury. And the citizens were enjoying an unprecedented season of peace and prosperity.

But the young prince would not be deterred. And his utter sincerity, his courageous bearing, his inspiring devotion, and his articulate oratory made believers out of nearly everyone he came in contact with. Traversing from cotter village to clan castle and from loch settlement to noble palace, he began to attract the attentions and command the loyalties of the stalwart Highlanders. He walked from the outer Hebrides in the far west to the heart of the country at Glenaladale. There, with his wild and untamed partisans around him—tartans blazing, bagpipes wailing, and chieftans shouting—he raised the standard of the Stuarts.

He very nearly succeeded, too. It was only treachery that eventually turned the prince back, spoiling his fairy-tale aspirations. Betrayed by several of his nobles, he was forced to retreat toward Scotland and ultimate defeat at the Battle of Culloden. Nevertheless, the bravery, loyalty, and noble bearing of Bonnie Prince Charlie continued to endure in the hearts of his countrymen—so much so, his great lost cause remains one of the most romantic affections in Scotland, even to this day.

Step out in faith.

[Johann Sebastian Bach (1685–1750)]

478 Saint Lupus, the bishop of the city of Troyes, died in France. Lupus protected Troyes from destruction at the hand of Attila the Hun. As Attilla approached the city, Lupus went out to meet him and asked who he was. Attila responded, "I am the scourge of God." St. Lupus replied, "Let us respect whatever comes from God. But if you are the scourge with which heaven chastises us, remember you are to do nothing but what that Almighty hand, which governs and moves you, permits." Attila spared the city.

1783 Latin American revolutionary Simon Bolivar was born in Caracas, Venezuela.

1802 French novelist Alexandre Dumas, known best for *The Three Musketeers* and *The Count of Monte Cristo*, was born in Paris.

1824 The Harrisburg *Pennsylvanian* suggested that candidate Andrew Jackson held the lead in the upcoming presidential election, in the first public opinion poll published in the United States.

1847 Mormon leader Brigham Young and his followers arrived in the valley of the Great Salt Lake in present-day Utah.

1862 The eighth president of the United States, Martin Van Buren, died in Kinderhook, New York.

1866 Tennessee became the first state to be readmitted to the Union after the War Between the States.

1870 Horatio Robinson Storer was a third-generation Boston physician and a specialist in obstetrics and gynecology. He became concerned about the booming abortion trade prior to the War Between the States and immediately sought ways to utilize his family influence to halt the slaughter. He wrote to his friends and contacts in the profession all over the country inquiring about the abortion laws in each of their states. He then began to bombard medical societies and professional journals with information, resolutions, and litigation. He confronted, cajoled, and preached. He lobbied, argued, and prayed. He became the lightning rod for the national debate over abortion. He wrote two widely circulated and popularly lauded books: *Why Not? A Book for Every Woman* and *Is It I? A Book for Every Man*— which detailed the "criminality and physical evils" of child-killing procedures. Clearly, he was the greatest and most influential pro-life advocate of his generation. The American Medical Association ultimately appointed him on this day as the chairman of a select committee to oppose child-killing procedures altogether. And thus was born America's first national right to life organization—as an ancillary of the AMA.

JULY

1874 Oswald Chambers, Scottish Bible teacher, missionary, and author, was born in Aberdeen. His best-selling book, *My Utmost for His Highest*, was published shortly after his death in 1917—he had been serving British troops in Egypt during the First World War. The book remains the most popular daily devotional guide in print more than three quarters of a century later.

1954 The obscure but often quoted American poet, critic, and educator Tristan Gylberd was born in Houston, Texas.

1959 During a visit to the Soviet Union, Vice President Richard M. Nixon engaged in a "Kitchen Debate" with Communist leader Nikita Khrushchev at an American exhibition in Moscow.

FEAST DAY
St. Christopher; Saints Thea, Valentina, and Paul; St. James the Greater; St. Magnericus

Prentice Herman Polk was fascinated with photography from as early as he could remember. He began studying through a correspondence course, which he paid for with ten dollars he was mistakenly given as change for a candy bar at a local store. Before he was in his teens he had begun taking photographs of the everyday lives of former slaves and sharecroppers—the kinds of subjects that would occupy his work for the rest of his long and storied career.

In 1916, he had the opportunity to attend the famed Tuskegee Institute. Although the school was technically chartered by the Alabama state legislature to repay black voters for their support, its early history is almost synonymous with the name of its founder and first administrator, African-American leader Booker T. Washington. Tuskegee's roots were in the post-Reconstruction era in the South, when higher educational opportunities for African Americans were still severely limited.

Washington's most significant contribution was his strong belief in industrial education and training as the key to success for African Americans. Students were required to learn a trade and perform manual labor at the school, including making and laying the bricks for the buildings that became the first campus. Tuskegee's charter had mandated that tuition would be free for students who committed to teaching in Alabama public schools. The students' labor helped with financial costs, and Washington solicited much of the remaining funding from northern white philanthropists.

Tuskegee was incorporated as a private institution in 1892. Because social conventions would have prohibited white instructors from serving under a black principal, Tuskegee became the first black institution of higher learning with a black faculty. In 1896 the school hired a young teacher who would become famous—George Washington Carver, whose groundbreaking agricultural research received international recognition. Washington also became nationally accepted as a black leader during the 1890s, because many whites appreciated his accomodationist approach to race relations, and Tuskegee gained wide recognition and substantial funding.

When Polk completed his course of study on this day in 1920, he was appointed to the faculty of the photography department—which he and several other pioneers built from scratch. He then served as department head from 1933 to 1938. From 1933 to 1982 he was the official school photographer, taking pictures of members of the Tuskegee community as well as visitors such as Henry Ford and Eleanor Roosevelt.

Perhaps his greatest contribution to history, though, was the fact that he also chronicled the experiences of George Washington Carver—his experiments, discoveries, innovations, and triumphs. By the time Polk retired in 1982, he had documented virtually the entire history of the Tuskegee Institute community in the twentieth century—a history that helped to shape the very destiny of the civil rights movement and African-American opportunity.

Only the sheerest relativism insists that passing time renders unattainable one ideal while forcing upon us another.

[RICHARD WEAVER (1910–1963)]

1593 In an effort to consolidate the vacillating support for his claim to the French throne, Henry IV of Navarre converted from Protestantism to Roman Catholicism.

1788 Wolfgang Mozart, the Austrian composer, wrote Symphony no. 40 in G Minor in its entirety.

1866 Following his successful prosecution of the War Between the States and negotiation of the Confederate surrender at Appomattox, Ulysses S. Grant was named general of the army, the first officer to hold that rank—a rank somewhat analogous to chairman of the Joint Chiefs of Staff today.

1868 Congress passed an act creating the Wyoming Territory.

1897 Adventure writer Jack London, bitten by gold fever, headed for the Klondike aboard the steamer *Umatilla*.

1909 French aviator Louis Bleriot flew across the English Channel in a monoplane, traveling from Calais to Dover in thirty-seven minutes.

1914 The day before leaving Barcelona for the United States, eleven-year-old Anais Nin made the first entry in her diary: "I am sad to think we are leaving a country that has been like a mother and a lucky charm for me." Except for a short interval in 1917, she would continue the diary for the rest of her life and it would serve as the source for many of her most famous stories and articles.

1944 Bing Crosby and the Andrews Sisters recorded Cole Porter's "Don't Fence Me In" in Los Angeles for Decca Records.

JULY

1946 The United States detonated an atomic bomb at Bikini Atoll in the Pacific in the first underwater test of the device.

1952 Puerto Rico became a self-governing commonwealth of the United States.

1969 A week after the Chappaquiddick accident that claimed the life of Mary Jo Kopechne, Edward M. Kennedy—the Democratic senator representing the state of Massachusetts—pleaded guilty to a charge of leaving the scene of an accident.

1978 Louise Joy Brown, the first "test tube baby," was born in Oldham, England. She had been conceived through the technique of in vitro fertilization.

1984 Soviet cosmonaut Svetlana Savitskaya became the first woman to walk in space as she carried out more than three hours of experiments outside the orbiting space station *Salyut 7*.

NATIONAL DAY
Liberia
FEAST DAY
*St. Anne, St. Simeon the
Armenian, St. Joachim, St.
Bartholomea Capitanio*

No man in all of history fought as hard or as long to abolish slavery as William Wilberforce did throughout his life. A member of the British Parliament, he introduced antislavery measures year after year for forty years until he retired in 1825. On this day in 1833, as he lay dying, word was brought to him that the bill to outlaw slavery everywhere in the British Empire had finally been passed. The dream for which he had struggled for decades was now within sight of fulfillment.

Wilberforce had not always been such a vigorous opponent of slavery. As a youth he was a witty, somewhat dissipated man about town who had misspent his time at Cambridge and squandered his considerable talents on silly amusements. He was a member of the high society elite and he reveled in it.

A friend of William Pitt—who later became prime minister—and himself a member of Parliament, Wilberforce seemed assured of a bright political future. But then in 1784, after winning his election in Yorkshire, he accompanied his sister to the Riviera for her health. As an afterthought, Isaac Milner, a tutor at Queen's College Cambridge and acquaintance from college days, was asked along.

Milner had become a deeply pious evangelical Christian. He began to share his testimony with the vacationers—particularly urging Wilberforce to commit his life to Christ. Wilberforce had always thought himself a Christian. But it became evident to him that a total commitment to Christ was demanded by the nature of the gospel itself. He struggled in anguish for several months. Part of that time he read Philip Doddridge's *The Rise and Progress of Religion in the Soul.* Here was a faith far deeper than anything he had known. Gradually he yielded.

After he returned home he had to wonder if it was proper for him to hold a seat in government. He confided his dilemma to Pitt. The ever-ambitious Pitt, wanting Wilberforce as an ally, urged him to remain. Still unsettled in his conscience, Wilberforce spoke to John Newton. Best remembered as the author of the hymn "Amazing Grace," Newton had been converted while a blasphemous sailor and slaver. He counseled Wilberforce to remain in politics as the champion of good causes.

Several of his new evangelical friends suggested that he take up the slavery issue. Even Pitt requested it. After many doubts, Wilberforce decided it was what God wanted. He also felt he must tackle causes that would raise the standard of life and morals in England. The friends who gathered around him became known as the Clapham Sect because most lived in the village of Clapham.

Rarely in history have so many owed so much to so few. These dozen or so Clapham men and women fought not only against slavery but against every other sort of modern vice. Many were wealthy—and they employed their worldly goods on behalf of godly causes. Everything from education for the poor masses, support of Bible societies, and private relief organizations to protection of day laborers, creation of Sunday schools, and establishment of orphanages received their attention.

But it was the abolition of slavery that remains their greatest achievement—Wilberforce died content just days after his triumph.

The motives to a life of faith are infinite.

[SAMUEL JOHNSON (1709–1784)]

1775 Benjamin Franklin was named the first postmaster general when the Second Continental Congress established the United States Postal System.

1788 After a bitter debate, New York became the eleventh state to ratify the U.S. Constitution.

1874 Russian conductor, composer, and double bass player Serge Koussevitsky was born in Vishny-Volotchok. He went to Paris after the Russian Revolution and eventually became the conductor of the Boston Symphony Orchestra, a position he held from 1924 to 1949. He was instrumental in promoting the works of contemporary American composers as well as commissioning such works as *Symphony of Psalms* (1930) by Igor Stravinsky.

1875 Swiss psychoanalyst Carl Jung was born in Kesswil, Switzerland, the son of a Protestant minister. Jung pioneered several aspects of psychology, such as word association, the idea of "complexes," the concept of the personality types introvert and extrovert, and the collective unconscious of all humans as displayed in universal desires, symbols, mythologies, religions, and primordial images. Jung attempted to create a state of wholeness of self through understanding how the personal unconscious integrated with the collective unconscious. He also wrote extensively on the relationship of psychotherapy and religious belief.

1882 Richard Wagner's last opera, *Parsifal*, was premiered at the Festspielhaus in Bayreuth. The story is set in the Middle Ages and deals directly with the Holy Grail legend. Wagner develops his compositional ideas of the leitmotif to their greatest evolution with specific musical ideas representing the Last Supper, the Grail, faith, Parsifal and other characters, and Good Friday.

1908 U.S. Attorney General Charles J. Bonaparte—a distant relative of the family of Napoleon—issued an order creating an investigative agency that was a forerunner of the Federal Bureau of Investigation.

1945 Winston Churchill resigned as Britain's prime minister after his Conservatives were soundly defeated by the Labor Party despite having led the nation to victory over the Nazi menace in the Second World War. Clement Attlee, the Socialist candidate, became the new prime minister.

1947 President Harry Truman signed the National Security Act, creating the Department of Defense, the National Security Council, the Central Intelligence Agency and the Joint Chiefs of Staff.

1948 President Truman signed a pair of executive orders prohibiting discrimination in the U.S. armed forces and federal employment.

1952 Argentina's first lady, Eva Peron, died in Buenos Aires at age thirty-three.

1968 Pope Paul VI issued his encyclical *Humanae Vitae—Of Human Life*—banning birth control and all other child-killing procedures from abortion to infanticide.

1989 Mark Wellman, a twenty-nine-year-old paraplegic, reached the summit of El Capitan in Yosemite National Park after hauling himself up the granite cliff six inches at a time over nine days.

JULY

26

439

FEAST DAY
The Seven Sleepers of Ephesus; St. Theobald of Marly; The Martyrs of Salsette; Saints Aurelia, Natalia, and their Companions; St. Pantaleon

Charles I, king of England and Scotland, like so many of his Stuart forebears, ruled in accordance with the doctrine of the divine right of kings. As a result, he was constantly in conflict with the rather independent-minded nobles in Parliament. Eventually, the irreconcilable differences between the two would lead to a bitter civil war—a conflict the king was destined to lose at the cost of his life. In fact, his fate was sealed long before that calamitous clash of arms—when he elevated a tyrannical bishop to become archbishop of Canterbury, the highest position in the Church of England.

William Laud was a stickler for minute forms and details in worship. Like Charles, he yearned to see the church return to the forms and standards of Catholicism—in every way that the rupture with Rome would permit. Indeed, it was largely supposed that Charles I wished to eventually reconcile with the papacy and restore Catholicism in full. Laud's various liturgical mandates seemed to be nothing less than a prelude to this.

Not surprisingly, then, Laud persecuted Puritans fiercely. The Puritans were those who desired to see the English church purified—and thus, they wanted worship to reflect a strictly biblical liturgy. Laud treated the Puritans as enemies of the Crown, enemies of the church, and enemies of God.

When Laud introduced his new mandatory standards for worship—in a new edition of the *Book of Common Prayer*—hundreds of churches responded with righteous indignation and spontaneous outrage. Indeed, most congregations caused such a stir that their bishops wisely did not even try to implement Laud's orders.

In Edinburgh, however, at a service in the great Gileskirk on High Street just a block from John Knox's manse, the clergy determined to follow the archbishop's order. There were a number of the king's dignitaries present for the service on this day in 1637. Unfortunately for the dean who began to perform the revised ritual, a large number of common folk were also in attendance.

The people were immediately outraged by the formal cant of the service and began murmuring—yet the service continued on. At long last a young woman, Jenny Geddes, could stand the affront no longer. A child of the Reformation, she suddenly stood and stoutly grasped the stool she had been straddling. With a gush of holy gall, she shouted, "Wilt thou say Mass at my lugs, thou popish-puling fool? No! No!" And at his head she flung her stool. Suddenly a flurry of other stools were hurled toward the pulpit with the resounding shouts, "Well, done, Jenny," "Bravo, Jenny," "That's the proper tool, Jenny. When the Deil will out, and shows his snout, just meet him with a stool."

The crowd had to be cleared by force, refusing to listen to their magistrates. Laud's experiment in restoring the high church services ultimately failed. Laud himself was imprisoned in 1640 and brought to trial a few years later on charges of high treason. The Puritan William Prynne, whom he had mutilated, was set as judge over him and returned a guilty verdict with relish—but it was said that it was not with nearly as much relish as the stool hurled by Jenny Geddes.

Mercy is two hearts tugging at one load.

[SARAH ORNE JEWETT (1835–1882)]

1373 Birgitta of Sweden, the founder of the nunnery at Vadstena, died on this day just after her return from a trip to Palestine. The convent, based on the Augustine rule, later became the literary center of Sweden. King Mangus, by the way, frightened by her warnings, funded this convent.

1586 Sir Walter Raleigh returned to England from Virginia, bringing the first tobacco known in England with him.

1694 The Bank of England received a royal charter as a commercial institution.

1789 Congress established the Department of Foreign Affairs, the forerunner of the Department of State.

1861 Union General George B. McClellan was put in command of the Army of the Potomac.

1866 Cyrus W. Field finally succeeded, after two failures, in laying the first underwater telegraph cable between North America and Europe.

1870 French-born author and poet Hilaire Belloc was born in La Celle-Saint-Cloud. He was educated at the University of Oxford and eventually became a British citizen. A friend of G. K. Chesterton, throughout his long and prolific career he published thousands of articles and poems as well as more than a hundred books on every conceivable subject.

1931 Thousands of acres of crops in Iowa, Nebraska, and South Dakota were destroyed by a giant swarm of grasshoppers.

1940 Bugs Bunny made his official debut in the Warner Brothers animated cartoon "A Wild Hare."

1946 On her deathbed, Gertrude Stein uttered her last words to Alice Toklas: "What is the answer?" Toklas did not know what to say and remained silent. With her last gasp, Stein insisted, "In that case, what is the question?"

1953 The signing of the armistice at Panmunjon, Korea, ended the Korean War. The war had lasted three years, thirty-two days, while the armistice negotiations between North Korea and the United States representing South Korea lasted two years, seventeen days.

1967 In the wake of urban rioting, President Lyndon Johnson appointed the Kerner Commission to assess the causes of the violence. The same day, black militant H. Rap Brown said in Washington that violence was "as American as cherry pie."

1995 The Korean War Veterans Memorial was dedicated in Washington, D.C., by an American veterans delegation and South Korean President Kim Young Sam.

JULY

27

Sir Thomas Malory always seemed to give his readers more of a glimpse of his own age than of the age he was purportedly writing about. His tales were ostensibly about the daring-do exploits of King Arthur and his knights—but his times invariably showed through. And for good reason— he lived during the days when the Hundred Years' War had finally ended and the Wars of the Roses had suddenly erupted. Like his mentor, Geoffrey Chaucer, he was caught in the midst of this horrendous power struggle between the two great houses of the English royal line. And like Chaucer he served the Lancastrian line against the Yorkists. It was a time of anarchy, confusion, and widespread destruction.

Malory looked back longingly on the fading glory of chivalric feudalism. Beginning on this day in 1466, when he was imprisoned during one of the lawless scuffles that marked the Wars of the Roses, he determined to recall that time and those values in some permanent form. *Le Morte d'Arthur* was the result.

Not surprisingly, the ancient code of chivalry plays a prominent role in every aspect of the book—from character development to plotlines to conflict resolution. The code—formalized in the eleventh century by Bernard of Clairveaux—consists of a list of twelve distinctive qualities that all true Christian knights shared.

- *integritas*—trustworthy to all in his covenantal community
- *fidelitas*—steadfastly loyal to all his friends and relations
- *succurrere*—helpful to any and all who might be in need
- *benevolus*—gracious and mannerly to everyone he met along the way
- *urbanus*—courteous upon every occasion
- *benignus*—selflessly kind
- *referre*—obey all those that God had place in authority over him
- *hilaris*—joyous and cheerful in the face of even the worst adversities
- *frugalis*—marked by an evident thrifty stewardship
- *fortitudo*—brave despite all the dangers that might cross his path
- *abulere*—scrupulously clean in all his personal habits and hygiene
- *sanctus*—piously reverent

Interestingly, the twentieth-century British war hero Robert Stephenson Baden-Powell utilized Bernard's code as the basis for the virtues to be inculcated in his Boy Scouts. But centuries before Lord Baden-Powell tapped the principles and elements of chivalry for his fledgling movement, Thomas Malory was building his tales of Arthurian romance around them.

There is perhaps no better guide to understanding the purpose and intent of Malory—and the times that he baptized upon the Arthurian legends—than this remarkable ethical code.

The nameless pioneers and settlers, the obscure mothers and fathers, the quiet craftsmen and tradesmen; it is only among these that the real story of America is told; it is only among them that the brilliance of liberty may be comprehended.

[THEODORE ROOSEVELT (1858–1919)]

1540 King Henry VIII's chief minister, Thomas Cromwell, was executed. That same day Henry married his fifth wife, Catherine Howard.

1794 Maximilien Robespierre, a leading figure of the French Revolution, was sent to the guillotine—a fate which confirmed the notion that in the end men reap what they sow.

1804 Ludwig Andreas Feuerbach was born. His father was a well-known jurist who exerted tremendous influence in the field of German law. He was also a petty, moralizing tyrant at home who betrayed Feuerbach's mother for another man's wife. It is perhaps not surprising that the ranks of atheists are most often joined by men who hate their fathers. Feuerbach, who had much reason to dislike his father, attacked Christianity mercilessly. Like his follower Karl Marx, he adopted materialist presuppositions and therefore considered his critique of the faith scientific. As a member of the faculty of Theology at the University of Berlin, he wrote such books as *Thoughts on Death and Immortality* and *Essence of Christianity*. The books mockingly asserted that religion was little more than a fantasy—an attempt at wish-fulfillment. After the failed Communist revolutions of 1848 Feuerbach's work faded into virtual oblivion—though not before greatly influencing Richard Wagner, Frederick Nietzsche, and Nikolai Lenin. Indeed, he was, as C. S. Lewis asserted, "the father of the madness of the twentieth century."

1821 Peru declared its independence from Spain.

1844 Gerard Manley Hopkins, English poet and Jesuit priest, was born in Stratford, Essex. He attended Balliol College, Oxford, and converted to Catholicism in 1866. Hopkins attempted to capture the inscape of natural objects or their uniqueness. He utilized internal rhyme, alliteration, compound metaphor, and sprung rhythm, which imitates the stresses of natural speech. His most famous poems include "The Wreck of the Deutschland," "Pied Beauty," "The Windhover," "Henry Purcell," and "Duns Scotus' Oxford."

1866 Beatrix Potter, creator of Peter Rabbit, Jeremy Fisher, Jemima Puddle-Duck, Mrs. Tiggywiggle, and Benjamin Bunny, was born in South Kensington, Middlesex, England. She designed her small books with small hands in mind.

JULY

1868 The Fourteenth Amendment to the U.S. Constitution, guaranteeing due process of law and granting citizenship to anyone born or naturalized in the United States, was declared in effect.

1896 The city of Miami, Florida, was incorporated.

1914 Austria-Hungary declared war on Serbia one month after the assassination of Archduke Ferdinand in Sarajevo, thus beginning the First World War.

1945 An Army Air Corps B-25 bomber crashed into the Empire State Building, entering at the seventy-ninth floor and killing fourteen people. Damage to the building cost $1 million to repair, but the building's structural integrity was not affected.

1976 The trans-Alaska pipeline opened, carrying oil from Prudhoe Bay to Valdez.

JULY

His life was a monument to the vitality of heritage. His writing captured the essence of the heroism, romanticism, and dynamism of the past. His character was a testimony to the vibrant virtues of days gone by. His habits recalled the rites and rituals of a hoary yore. Even his home was a saga in stone, a ballad of yesteryear in pitch and gable and crenelation, and a reliquary of legend, fable, and custom. Everything about Sir Walter Scott (1771–1832) bespoke tradition.

He was born in 1771 to a respectable, middle-class Edinburgh family, but much of his childhood was spent at his grandfather's farm in the beautiful Border country. It was there that he was first acquainted with the rituals, songs, ballads, folklore, and legends of Scotland that captivated him for the rest of his life. He demonstrated early genius and followed in his father's footsteps, becoming a barrister after completing his university training at the extraordinary age of seventeen. But a practice of the law was not able to fully occupy his precocious mind, and so he began composing verse and collecting the great ballads of his beloved Border lands. He wrote a great narrative poem, *The Lay of the Last Minstrel,* which proved to be a tremendous commercial and critical success and convinced him that literature should be the main business of his life.

Happily married and with a growing family to support, he determined to pursue the literary life away from the constant and pressing demands of the city. He bought a large farm along the Tweed Valley in the Border countryside. He called it Abbotsford, and for the rest of his life he made the estate a living demonstration of his highest ideals. Over the years he transformed the humble farmhouse into a magnificent castle estate chock-a-block with remnants, relics, and reminders of the rich history of the region. It was there in his museum-like environs that he created a series of historical novels that made Scott the most popular author in the world. Beginning with *Waverly* in 1814 and continuing through an astonishing thirty-two volumes over the next eighteen years—and including such classics as *Ivanhoe, Rob Roy, Tales of a Grandfather, Old Mortality, The Antiquary,* and *Red Gauntlet*—Scott reinvented an entire genre of literature.

He added immeasurably to the Scottish sense of identity. Indeed, he almost single-handedly revived interest in kilts, tartans, Gaelic, bagpipes, Highland dancing, haggis, Celtic music, and all the other distinctive elements of Scottish culture. Tales of the Covenanters, Wallace and Bruce, the Jacobites, Bonnie Price Charlie, and Rob Roy were all brought into the light of day by his intrepid commitment to regaling the past.

All of his books were stamped with his overarching conviction about the importance of tradition. On the cusp of the magnificent flowering of industrial advance, it seemed to Scott that men were sadly afflicted with a kind of malignant contemporaneity. He was alarmed that their morbid preoccupation with self—and thus their ambivalence and ignorance of the past—had trapped them in a recalcitrant present.

As a result, all of Scott's work essentially argued stridently that stable societies must be eternally vigilant in the task of handing on their great legacy—to remember and then to inculcate that remembrance in the hearts and minds of their children.

Mercy is the golden chain by which society is bound together.

[WILLIAM BLAKE (1757–1827)]

1588 The English soundly defeated the Spanish Armada in the Battle of Gravelines.

1805 Statesman and writer Alexis de Tocqueville was born in Paris. After a two-year visit to the United States, he would write *Democracy in America* in 1835.

1869 Novelist Booth Tarkington was born in Philadelphia. He would later win the Pulitzer Prize twice, for his novels *The Magnificent Ambersons* and *Alice Adams*.

1890 Vincent van Gogh died two days after shooting himself. He had just completed the ominous painting *Crows in the Wheatfields*. His paintings often depicted the emotional turmoil in his soul through the use of strong color and thickly laid paint—sometimes straight from the tube.

1914 Transcontinental telephone service began with the first phone conversation between New York and San Francisco.

1948 Britain's King George VI opened the Olympic Games in London—though the city was still recovering from the Second World War.

1957 Jack Paar made his debut as host of NBC's *Tonight Show*.

1958 President Eisenhower signed the National Aeronautics and Space Act, which created NASA and launched the American space program.

1968 Pope Paul VI reaffirmed the Roman Catholic Church's stance against abortion, infanticide, and artificial methods of birth control.

JULY

1974 Eleven women, with the connivance of four bishops, determined to smash the barriers of sexism in the Episcopal Church. Fifteen hundred people crowded the sanctuary of the Episcopal Church of the Advocate in Philadelphia to witness this confrontation with church rules and authority. A banner shouted Paul's words: "In Christ there is neither male nor female." Bishop Corrigan asked if there was any known impediment to ordination of the eleven. "Yes!" shouted several. Five priests stepped forward to take the microphones. What was about to be done was illegal and divisive they said. Their objections were dismissed and the ordination ceremony proceeded. The eleven women became priests and offered the cup and bread. But soon afterward the procedure was annulled by higher authorities. Too many rules had been broken. Three of the bishops were retired and not permitted to ordain without express approval. The other bishop was out of jurisdiction. Furthermore, none of the women had been approved by their local bishops as required by Episcopal law. The confrontation would prove to be just the first salvo in a long struggle for the soul of the church.

1975 President Gerald Ford became the first American president to visit the site of the Nazi concentration camp Auschwitz in Poland as he paid tribute to the victims.

29

JULY

Although most civil rights leaders focused on voting, education, and other fruits of governmental intervention, A. Philip Randolph (1889–1979) spent his long career as a labor leader working to bring more and better jobs to African Americans. After a long, successful battle to win representation for the nation's Pullman porters, Randolph—who was the founder and president the of Brotherhood of Sleeping Car Porters—was instrumental in the formation of the Fair Employment Practices Committee (FEPC), which protected African Americans against job discrimination in the army and defense industries.

The son of a minister, Randolph grew up in Jacksonville, Florida, and graduated from the Cookman Institute in 1907. A lack of economic opportunity for African Americans led Randolph, the class valedictorian, into a series of menial jobs until this day in 1911, when he moved to New York City. Working as an elevator operator and living in Harlem, Randolph took classes at the City College of New York and New York University, acted in amateur theatricals, and eventually took a job with a Harlem employment agency.

In 1914 Randolph met Chandler Owen, whose progressive politics and interest in civil rights matched his own. In 1917 the two founded *The Messenger*. Though the magazine was never profitable, it was influential, offering a more activist voice than that of W. E. B. Du Bois's *The Crisis* or the even more conventional *New York Age. The Messenger*, with its advocacy of labor unions, was especially popular among Pullman porters—all of whom were African American—who served railroad passengers in luxurious sleeping cars. Founded just after the Civil War, the Pullman company had by the 1920s become the nation's single largest employer of African Americans. Many of the Pullman porters were college graduates who enjoyed great respect within their communities, but at work they were subjected to grossly discriminatory practices.

Randolph served as president of the National Negro Congress before resigning in protest over its increasing domination by radical Socialists and Communists. During the Second World War and the years immediately following, he went to work with the National Association for the Advancement of Colored People (NAACP) to pressure Franklin Roosevelt and Harry Truman to desegregate the military and defense industries. Later, he met with President Dwight Eisenhower to push for faster school integration in the wake of *Brown v. Board of Education*.

Randolph's brainchild, the March on Washington, bore fruit in 1963 with the help of Bayard Rustin and the Reverend Martin Luther King Jr. who, along with Randolph, mobilized the largest demonstration of the Civil Rights Movement. Speaking just before King, the seventy-four-year-old Randolph exhorted the crowd of 250,000 to take part in a "revolution for jobs and freedom." The next year, President Lyndon Johnson signed the Civil Rights Act of 1964 and awarded Randolph the Presidential Medal of Freedom.

Upon his death in 1979, it was said of him, "No individual did more to help the poor, the dispossessed, and the working class than A. Philip Randolph."

Call it faith, call it vitality, call it the will to live, call it the religion of tomorrow morning, call it the immortality of man, call it whatever you wish; it is the thing that explains why man survives all things and why there is no such thing as a pessimist.

[G. K. CHESTERTON (1874–1936)]

1511 Artist, architect, and biographer Giorgio Vasari was born in Arezzo. His book *Lives of the Artists* provided a firsthand account of the artists of the Italian Renaissance—many of whom he knew personally. Filled with anecdotes and personal reflections, Vasari helped to shape an understanding of the artists and their works in one of the most influential periods of artistic endeavor.

1619 An old church in Jamestown, Virginia, was the site of the first Legislative Assembly on American soil. The participants agreed that the general assembly, known as the House of Burgesses, should meet on a annual basis summoned by the governor, and that the twenty-two members should be elected by "every free man."

1729 The city of Baltimore was founded.

1771 English poet Thomas Gray died and was buried next to his mother at Stoke Poges, the graveyard which inspired his "Elegy Written in a Country Churchyard."

1792 The French national anthem *La Marseillaise,* by Claude Joseph Rouget de Lisle, was first sung in Paris.

1817 Emily Brontë, English novelist and poet, and author of *Wuthering Heights* (1847), was born in Thornton, Yorkshire, England.

1844 The New York Yacht Club was founded.

1862 Automobile manufacturer Henry Ford was born on his family's farm in Dearborn, Michigan. He pioneered the assembly line method of automobile production.

1909 The first airplane purchased by the United States government was a 25 h.p. bi-plane from the Wright brothers of Ohio. It was delivered on this day. The cost of the aircraft: $31,250.

1922 On this Sunday morning, the great journalist, critic, novelist, and apologetic G. K. Chesterton took a walk with Father O'Connor. His more than 300-pound heft was to be baptized into the church that he had defended all his life. Looking for his prayer book, he accidentally pulled out a three-penny thriller instead. He was an amazingly gifted writer who had an uncanny knack of seeing what was crucial in any author's work and the clarity to smell the real worth or the real flaw of any argument. But paradox was his real forte. Paradox, he said, "is truth standing on her head to attract attention." As used by Chesterton paradox was either a statement that at first glance seems false but actually is true, or a "commonsense" view exposed as false. Of course, the greatest paradox was Chesterton himself: a massive man whose nimble thought danced through his day, entertaining and enlightening millions—including C. S. Lewis, who later testified that Chesterton was his mentor.

JULY

1935 The famous British paperbacks by Penguin Books were first issued.

1945 The USS *Indianapolis,* which had just delivered key components of the Hiroshima atomic bomb to the Pacific island of Tinian, was torpedoed by a Japanese submarine. Only 316 out of 1,196 men survived the sinking in shark-infested waters.

1975 Teamsters Union president Jimmy Hoffa disappeared from his home in suburban Detroit—although he is presumed dead, his remains have never been found.

30

JULY

Born in Scotland, educated at Edinburgh, and a leader among the Presbyterian Jacobites during the great Rising of 1745, John Witherspoon came to America in 1768 to be president of Princeton College. He has been called the most influential professor in American history, not only because of his powerful writing and speaking style but because of the vast number of leaders he trained and sent forth. Nine of the fifty-five participants in the Federal Convention in 1787 were his students—including James Madison. Moreover, his pupils included a president and a vice president, twenty-one senators, twenty-nine representatives, fifty-six state legislators, and thirty-three judges, three of whom were appointed to the Supreme Court.

His sermon, *The Dominion of Providence Over the Passions of Men*, caused a great stir when it was first preached in Princeton and published in Philadelphia on this day in 1776, about two months after he was elected to the Continental Congress.

In the sermon, he made a strong Biblical argument for the Declaration of Independence—and even a war for freedom, if necessary—based on the covenantal violations of king and Parliament as evidence of God's providential dealings in this poor fallen world.

He wrote: "The doctrine of divine providence is very full and complete in the sacred oracles. It extends not only to things which we may think of great moment, and therefore worthy of notice, but to things the most indifferent and inconsiderable; Are not two sparrows sold for a farthing, says our Lord, and one of them falleth not to the ground without your heavenly Father; nay, the very hairs of your head are all numbered. It extends not only to things beneficial and salutary, or to the direction and assistance of those who are the servants of the living God; but to things seemingly most hurtful and destructive, and to persons the most refractory and disobedient. He overrules all his creatures, and all their actions."

He continued asserting, "Thus we are told, that fire, hail, snow, vapor, and stormy wind, fulfill his word, in the course of nature; and even so the most impetuous and disorderly passions of men, that are under no restraint from themselves, are yet perfectly subject to the dominion of Jehovah. They carry his commission, they obey his orders, they are limited and restrained by his authority, and they conspire with every thing else in promoting his glory. There is the greater need to take notice of this, that men are not generally sufficiently aware of the distinction between the law of God and his purpose; they are apt to suppose, that as the temper of the sinner is contrary to the one, so the outrages of the sinner are able to defeat the other; than which nothing can be more false. The truth is plainly asserted, and nobly expressed by the psalmist in the text, Surely the wrath of man shall praise thee; the remainder of wrath shalt thou restrain."

The sermon was instrumental in convincing a large number of very reluctant patriots to see the issues of independence through the lens of covenantal obedience rather than through the lens of revolutionary fervor—a critical distinction. In the end, Witherspoon's argument won the day and independence was declared.

Attachment to the soil is an inescapable aspect of the healthy psyche. Uprootedness is a kind of psychosis—sadly, rampant in our community-less society.

[MARTIN LEMBEC (1909–1990)]

1498 During his third voyage to the Western Hemisphere, Christopher Columbus arrived at the island of Trinidad.

1556 Ignatius Loyola, founder of the Jesuits, died at the age of sixty-five. In his youth, he was a young courtier in Spain who was known for his vanity and pleasure-seeking.

1566 Bartolomé de las Casas, known as the Father to the Indian, was the first Spaniard ordained in the New World. He had come to the American colonies in the footsteps of the conquistadors and like many of the colonists, he settled on a plantation where he enjoyed the forced labor of native conscripts. But following a dramatic conversion in 1509, he labored for the Indians as few men have before or after. His whole life was devoted to that single cause. He wrote books documenting the cruelty of the slave system. He pleaded with those who ruled the colonies. Five times he crossed the ocean to lobby the Hapsburg emperor of the American dominions. On this day, he died. When the news reached the people he had done so much for, they mourned and lamented in their villages and lighted bonfires in honor of his passing. To this day, torchfires are lit throughout the Caribbean world in remembrance of his efforts to overturn the engines of injustice.

1777 The Marquis de Lafayette, a nineteen-year-old French nobleman, was made a major-general in the American Continental army.

1845 Five years after its invention by Belgian instrument maker Adolphe Sax, the saxophone was officially introduced into French military bands.

1874 Georgetown University named Patrick Francis Healy its new president, making Healy the first African American to become president of a predominantly white university.

1875 The seventeenth president of the United States, Andrew Johnson, died in Carter Station, Tennessee, at age sixty-six.

JULY

1919 Germany's post-war Weimar Constitution was adopted.

1953 Senator Robert A. Taft of Ohio, known as Mr. Republican and the father of the modern Conservative movement, died in New York at age sixty-three.

1964 The American space probe *Ranger Seven* transmitted pictures of the moon's surface.

1972 Democratic vice-presidential candidate Thomas Eagleton withdrew from the ticket with George McGovern following disclosures Eagleton had once undergone psychiatric treatment.

449

AUGUST

NATIONAL DAY
   Switzerland
FEAST DAY
   Saints Pistis, Elpis, and Agape
   (Faith, Hope, and Charity); St.
   Peter Julian Eynard; St. Ethelwold
   of Winchester; St. Almedha or Aled;
   St. Alphonse Ligouiri; The Holy
   Macabees

AUGUST

Exhausted from his Herculean labors as a journalist, educator, statesman, theologian, pastor, and social reformer, Abraham Kuyper (1837–1920) came to visit Vienna shortly after his first term in the Dutch Parliament had come to an end. Even as it does today, the city presented him with a jumble of contradictory impressions. The railways, roads, and hotels were all marked by the kind of New World efficiency that was the hallmark of emerging modernity, but the food, drink, and music were all marked by Old World hospitality that was the hallmark of fading antiquity.

Needing rest, Kuyper relaxed in the famous coffeehouses and sidewalk cafés. He feasted on the sagging boards of sausages, strudels, goulashes, and schnitzels at the ornate Biedermeier inns and reveled in the lagers, porters, and stouts at the lively *hofbraus.* He ambled along the Ringstrasse and listened to the street musicians. He took particular pleasure in watching the passing parade of busy Viennese shopkeepers in the early mornings. He visited the great State Opera House, culled the vast library collection of the Hofburg National Bibliothek, and marveled at the shows in the Spanish Riding School at the Hapsburg palace.

But Kuyper quickly discovered that the one place where all the strains of Vienna's wide-ranging heritage were most evident was the gem that dominated the center of the Stephansdomplatz: St. Stephen's Church, the city's beautiful Gothic cathedral. Consecrated in 1147, it was one of the most stunning architectural feats of the Medieval Age. And it changed Kuyper's life.

When he visited the great old church on this day in 1876, it was there that he found the reinvigorating vision he would need for the arduous work that lay ahead of him. He was reminded of the fact that though the imperial House of Hapsburg employed a few master craftsmen at the cathedral, the vast majority of the construction was undertaken by faithful members of the congregation, the ordinary folk of the town. That feat of stupendous architectural beauty was accomplished by the simple men and women at hand.

That, Kuyper realized, was the great lesson of history. Whether building cathedrals like the Stephansdomplatz or toppling the evil empires of revolutionary modernists in his own time, he came to appreciate the fact that all of history's most significant developments had been wrought by babushkas and bourgeoisie, shopkeepers and students, peasants and populists. With that lesson learned, he was ready to return home and launch a revolution of justice, mercy, and Christian charity. And he did.

LAMMAS DAY

In early England, August 1, the first day of harvest for the Celts, was called Lugnasad. Christians observed this day by baking bread from the first corn harvested and dedicating it to God. They called this day the Festival of the First Fruits. With the same concept in mind, Saxons called this day *hlaf-maesse* (loaf-mass), which eventually became Lammas Day.

1252 Friar Giovanni da Piano Carpini died just seven years after the Franciscan had set out on a journey to the heart of Mongol Asia. With him he carried a letter from Pope Innocent IV urging the great Khan to desist from attacking Europe lest he fall under divine wrath. He traveled across the vast expanse of Asia above the Aral and Caspian Seas almost to Karakoram where Güyük Khan was about to be crowned emperor. While waiting for an audience with him, Giovanni created a family tree of the Khans that later proved to be amazingly accurate. He also gathered material for a report on the land and its rulers. When given the opportunity he boldly preached the gospel before the Khan, but in the end the Khan refused baptism. Upon his return Giovanni was made an archbishop—but his greatest achievement was his extraordinary journey halfway around the world.

1768 Merchants of the Boston Colony signed a pact banning the sale of British goods.

1790 The results of the first census in the United States were announced, indicating that the population consisted of some 3,929,214 people with the greatest portion living in Pennsylvania.

1819 American novelist Herman Melville, best known for his stories *Moby Dick* and *Billy Budd,* was born in New York City. He spent several years of his life traveling the world's oceans, which provided the material for his novels of the seas. Although famous at the midpoint of his career, his reclusive death in 1891 garnered no notice or obituaries. His last work, *Billy Budd,* was not published until 1924; however, he has since been recognized as one of America's finest authors.

1873 On Clay Street Hill in San Francisco, the first cable streetcar in the United States was put into operation after inventor Andrew S. Hallidie successfully tested a prototype he had designed for the city.

1876 Colorado was admitted to the Union as the thirty-eighth state.

1893 Henry Perky and William Ford of Watertown, New York, obtained patent number 502,378 for a machine that manufactured shredded-wheat biscuits for breakfast cereal.

1936 The Olympic Games opened in Berlin with a ceremony presided over by Germany's chancellor, Adolf Hitler.

1943 Race riots erupted in New York City, resulting in dozens of deaths.

1944 An uprising broke out in the Jewish ghettos of Warsaw, Poland, against Nazi occupation. The revolt lasted two months before collapsing due to lack of supplies and the overwhelming force of the German military.

1978 Pete Rose of the Cincinnati Reds, who had tied the National League record of hitting in forty-four consecutive games, saw his streak end in a game against the Atlanta Braves.

AUGUST

Merciful service gives itself rich; selfish isolation hoards itself poor.

[THEODORE ROOSEVELT (1858–1919)]

FEAST DAY
*St. Theodota and her Three Sons;
St. Eusebius of Vercelli; St.
Plegmund; St. Stephen I, pope; St.
Syagrius of Autun; St. Sidwell or
Sativola*

A villain to some Southerners and Copperheads, a hero to most others, Abraham Lincoln (1809–1865) has undoubtedly attained greatness—but only in retrospect. In all history there is no more dramatic example of the times making a man rather than a man making the times than the legendary rise of Lincoln from obscurity to the presidency of the shattered Union.

Every conceivable obstacle was there before him: humble birth, ignorance, poverty, and life in the wilderness of the frontier; he was completely without advantages or connections; he was too human ever to be a favorite of the professional politicians; he was too enigmatic, too philosophical, too humorous ever to be a great popular figure. But somehow Lincoln was nominated for the presidency—as the second choice of many. He began his campaign in earnest on this day in 1860—and against all odds, with less than a majority of the popular vote, he managed to be elected just three months later.

Out of those early years of poverty and trial emerged a man uniquely prepared to wage a devastating war against many of his former friends and colleagues—a man of haunting transparency, a man with a probing conscience and a penetrating intellect, a man of deep humanity. After the first ineffectual and indecisive eighteen months in office, Lincoln became a strong, effective leader—firm, unrelenting, and brutal in the prosecution of both war and politics. But, above all, he proved to be a man of vision.

He saw the United States in its largest dimension—as a noble experiment in self-determination that had to be preserved, even if that meant violating the principles of self-determination. In the long history of tyranny and oppression, he believed that the American democracy was man's great hope and that it must be saved even if it was necessary to resort to non-democratic coercion. To him the great ideal of democracy overshadowed the practical realities of democracy. Lincoln's profound conviction of the enduring value of this experiment in a unified government sustained him throughout the long years of war. On the battlefield at Gettysburg it moved him to give the world a glimpse of his vision of the country's true greatness: "a nation conceived in liberty and dedicated to the proposition that all men are created equal." And it moved him to enunciate his ultimate reason for striving to preserve the Union: that "government of the people, by the people, and for the people shall not perish from the earth." One of the truly great political and human statements of all time, the Gettysburg Address, reveals both the ironic complexity and the coarse nobility that mark Lincoln as a legendary figure in American life and culture.

FAST OF AB

On the Hebrew calendar, this date—Ab 9, 5758, or Tisha B'av—is recognized as a day of mourning and memorializing the destructions of the First and Second Temples in Jerusalem (586 B.C. and A.D. 70).

1100 English Norman king William II—known as Rufus—was slain by an arrow during a hunting expedition in the New Forest. He was succeeded by his brother Henry I.

1610 Explorer Henry Hudson entered the bay in northern Canada that now bears his name. He mistakenly thought he had found a passage to the Pacific Ocean.

1643 Isaac Jogues—a French Jesuit who had been lured to Canada by opportunities for evangelism—wept before the Lord in long hours of prayer, asking God to accept his own life if by yielding it the Indians of North America might be won to Christ. One night he heard what he took to be a word from the Lord saying: "Your prayers are granted. It will happen as you have asked. Take heart! Be courageous!" And indeed, his prayer was granted. On this day, the party of Hurons and Frenchmen with whom Jogues was traveling was ambushed by the Iroquois. Jogues, hidden in tall grass, could have escaped. With his own eyes he had witnessed Indian tortures. No one could have blamed him if he stayed hidden. But the idea of flight appalled him. Jogues stepped from the tall grass and was seized with the rest. Terrible tortures followed—but through it all Jogues maintained his Christian witness. Though the Iroquois came to respect him, he was executed. Nevertheless, his testimony caused a rash of conversions among the Indians. Even the executioner eventually came to Christ—taking Isaac Jogues as his baptismal name.

1776 Although it was dated on July 4 and approved four days later, the official signing of the Declaration of Independence by members of the Continental Congress did not take place until this day in the city of Philadelphia.

1876 Frontiersman "Wild Bill" Hickok was shot and killed while playing poker at a saloon in Deadwood, South Dakota.

1909 The Philadelphia Mint issued the first Lincoln penny.

1923 The twenty-ninth president of the United States, Warren G. Harding, suddenly and mysteriously died in office while on a tour of the West Coast.

1934 German President Paul von Hindenburg died, paving the way for Chancellor Adolf Hitler's complete takeover.

1939 Albert Einstein signed a letter to President Roosevelt urging creation of an atomic weapons research program.

1943 A navy patrol torpedo boat, *PT-109*, commanded by Lieutenant John F. Kennedy, sank after being sheared in two by a Japanese destroyer off the Solomon Islands. Though held culpable for the attack, Kennedy was later credited with saving members of the crew.

1945 President Harry Truman, Soviet leader Joseph Stalin, and British Prime Minister Clement Attlee concluded the Potsdam Conference, which consolidated Soviet gains in Eastern Europe and ultimately drew down the Iron Curtain and precipitated the Cold War.

1964 The Pentagon reported the first of two attacks on U.S. destroyers by North Vietnamese torpedo boats in the Gulf of Tonkin.

AUGUST

Ultimately this incident caused a massive escalation of American interests in the war.

1990 Iraq invaded Kuwait, seizing control of the oil-rich emirate. The Iraqis were ultimately driven out by a global alliance led by the United States in Operation Desert Storm.

This is pure and undefiled religion in the sight of our God and Father, to visit the orphans and widows in their distress and to keep oneself unstained by the world.

[JAMES OF JERUSALEM (C. 4–46)]

FEAST DAY
St. Walthen or Waltheof, St.
Germanus of Auxerre, St. Thomas
of Hales or Dover

3

AUGUST

The three little ships in the expedition of Christopher Columbus—the *Niña, Pinta,* and *Santa Maria*—caught a strong sea breeze at the Rio Odiel and put out to sea at the Port of Palos early in the morning on this day in 1492. After a brief stop at the Canary Island of Gomera—in order to make a few last-minute adjustments and repairs—the 119 men in the convoy sailed west into the unknown on September 7.

About ten days later, the ships entered the legendary Sargastso Sea. This vast accumulation of seaweed and rolled fronds in the mid-Atlantic had been known since late antiquity. The testimonies of several famous travelers—including Herodotus, Brendan, and Luriao—had carefully documented and plotted the phenomenon. But it was a frightening and disconcerting sight anyway—and still is to this day. It is one of those things that is invariably misunderstood precisely because it is so often described and explained—like the sciences or the sacraments.

The sailors imagined all manner of sea creatures and sundry monsters of mythic proportions. They fathomed horrors out of the deep recesses of their own souls—where indeed the fiercest horrors do dwell. In spite of their terror though, they somehow mustered the fortitude and determination to stay the course.

And thus, despite modern accounts to the contrary, the expedition sailed through that odd natural obstacle during the next two weeks without incident. In fact, their entire journey passed without much drama to speak of. There were no great storms. There were no real calamities or crises. There was never a serious shortage of provisions. And there were no substantial material or structural failures. Columbus wrote in his logbook that the ships glided lightly on waters "always as calm as the river at Seville."

The only bad news was actually the good news: Strong trade winds continued to push them ever westward. With such an unvarying draught, the men began to worry about the difficulty of an about-face return. Grumbling and murmuring began to sour the onboard atmosphere. More dangerous even than the fears provoked by the Sargasso, such emotions are a kind of diluted and timorous rebellion—just as sentimentality is a kind of diluted and timorous love.

Fortuitously, long before those tensions could ever coalesce into full mutiny, new hope loomed large on the horizon. On the forty-fifth day of the journey—a Sunday—crewmen from two of the ships noticed freshly uprooted vegetation floating on the surface of the water. On Monday a land-living white reed-tailed bird appeared. And over the next three weeks a plethora of other signs gradually convinced them that land was nearby—an unexpected variation in the prevailing winds, the appearance of carved sticks floating in the flotsam and jetsam, and several large flocks of birds flying overhead. Each indicated that they were nearing the end of their storied quest. Indeed they were, because on October 12, the expedition discovered land—they had successfully sailed across the Atlantic to the American continent.

1858 The weekly announcement of death in London from cholera indicated that 1,053 people had died in the previous seven days from the disease.

1872 Ashley Cooper—best known as Lord Shaftesbury—laid the foundation stone for one of the very first housing complexes for the poor at Battersea. Throughout his life he fought for the protection of the neediest of his countrymen. As a member of England's Parliament, he labored long to see that Christian education—what were then called ragged schools—might be provided for London's street urchins. He pressed for improved sewage systems. He backed efforts at evangelization—including the work of Moody, Sankey, and Spurgeon. He struggled to reform the labor laws for women, children, the workday, industrial conditions, and workers' compensation benefits. At his funeral, hundreds of thousands of poor stood hatless in a pouring rain to show their love for the man who had loved them—indeed, he was credited with single-handedly preventing a socialist revolution in England.

1914 Germany declared war on France at the outset of the First World War.

1920 English crime writer Baroness Phyllis Dorothy James, better known as P.D. James, was born in Oxford, England. Known for her strong characterizations and acute sense of atmosphere, she developed an understanding of crime and mysteries while working in the criminal section of the Department of Home Affairs. She first went to work to support her family because her young husband returned from World War II mentally unbalanced and spent the remainder of his life in psychiatric hospitals. James's most famous character is Adam Dalgliesh of Scotland Yard,

who appears in the novels *Unnatural Causes, The Black Tower,* and *Devices and Desires.*

1921 Kennesaw Mountain Landis, the first commissioner of major-league baseball, banned for life the White Sox players charged with throwing the 1919 World Series. Among those banished was "Shoeless" Joe Jackson.

1923 Calvin Coolidge was sworn in as the thirtieth president of the United States, following the sudden death of Warren G. Harding.

1936 The State Department urged Americans in Spain to leave because of that country's bitter civil war.

1943 General George S. Patton slapped a private at an army hospital in Sicily, accusing him of cowardice. Patton was later ordered by General Dwight D. Eisenhower to apologize for this and a second, similar episode.

1948 Whittaker Chambers, a former Communist, publicly accused former State Department official Alger Hiss of having been part of a Communist underground, a charge Hiss denied. It was the beginning of the "Red Scare" in Washington, which led to the McCarthy hearings.

1949 The National Basketball Association was formed.

1958 The nuclear-powered submarine USS *Nautilus* became the first vessel to cross the North Pole underwater.

AUGUST

1981 Unionized air traffic controllers went on strike, despite a warning from President Ronald Reagan that they would be fired. The president made good on his promise and the union was stripped of its power.

How easy is it for one benevolent being to diffuse pleasure around him, and how truly is a kind heart a fountain of gladness, making everything in its vicinity to freshen into smiles.

[WASHINGTON IRVING (1783–1859)]

When the king of Northumbria was killed by enemies in 624, his youngest son, the eleven-year-old Oswald, fled to Scotland. There he took refuge with St. Columba's monks on the isle of Iona where he was ultimately converted. Nine years later, his older brother, Edwin—who had stayed behind in Northumbria to preserve the family's royal prerogative—also perished in battle against Penda and Cadwallon. Oswald was then called to the throne, and the young man reluctantly set aside his monk's cowl to do his duty. Cadwallon ravaged Northumbria, and so Oswald was forced to march against him.

FEAST DAY
St. Molua or Lughaidh, St. Ia, St. Sezni, St. John Baptist Vianney

Oswald's tiny force, like most of the men of Northumbria, were fierce pagans. On the eve of battle Oswald boldly set up a cross, holding it upright while dirt was packed into the hole dug for it. He proclaimed the message of the gospel. He then cried out, "Let us now kneel down and together pray to the almighty and only true God that He will mercifully defend us from our enemy; for He knows that we fight in defense of our lives and country."

That night as Oswald rested, he dreamed that St. Columba of Iona appeared to him, assuring him that he would have victory. The next morning, Oswald went forth boldly into battle despite the fact that the enemy greatly outnumbered his little army. It was on this day in 634 that Oswald won a stunning victory. Amazed, most of his men were immediately converted.

Afterward, Oswald restored order throughout Northumbria and brought missionaries from Scotland to teach his people. Chief among these was Saint Aiden. Oswald himself offered to be Aiden's translator so that his people might hear and understand the gospel. Thousands became Christians. The isle of Lindisfarne was given to Aiden for a bishop's seat, and a famous monastery grew up there. Churches quickly sprang up all across Northumbria.

AUGUST

The king became famous for his prayerful spirit. So often did he praise God and lift petitions to Him that even at meals he kept his hands in an attitude of prayer. In the few short years that he reigned, Oswald's kingdom gained such preeminence that all the other kings of the English domains were subject to him. His charity was particularly renowned—he often journeyed throughout his lands establishing his people in faith and freeing slaves, many of whom he made monks.

Oswald's death, like the deaths of his father and brother, came in battle. The pagan ruler Penda of Mercia, who had defeated Edwin, raised an army in 642 and overwhelmed Oswald. Surrounded by enemies, Oswald prayed one last prayer—for God's mercy on the souls of his soldiers. He was afterward considered a martyr because he died at the hand of a pagan while defending a Christian nation.

1944 Nazi police raided the secret annex of a building in Amsterdam and arrested eight people—including fifteen-year-old Anne Frank, whose diary became a famous account of the Holocaust. Anne later died at the Bergen-Belsen concentration camp.

1756 Fort Oswego in New York was captured by the French under General Montcalm during the French and Indian War.

1790 The Coast Guard was established as the Revenue Cutter Service.

1792 English Romantic poet Percy Bysshe Shelley was born in Field Place near Horsham, Sussex. He was expelled from University College, Oxford, for failing to admit authorship of *The Necessity of Atheism*. His early writing and life centered around illicit relationships and political rhetoric. He eloped with Harriet Westbrook but left her for Mary Wollstonecraft Godwin three years later. After Harriet's suicide, Shelley married Mary. At this point, he was living with Lord Byron, who helped introduce him to art, which greatly influenced his later works, such as *Prometheus Unbound, Ode to the West Wind, To a Skylark,* and *Adonais*—which commemorates the death of John Keats. His work is filled with humanistic idealism. Shelley drowned during a storm off the coast of Italy.

1792 During the French Revolution, the great abbey at Cluny was destroyed. It was just the latest in a series of assaults on the church. From the beginning, the revolution had been hostile to Christianity and to the culture that the faith had built over the centuries. A decree in November 1789 declared that all church property was at the disposal of the nation. A month later a vast amount of church property was ordered sold. Early the next year religious vows were forbidden. On August 26, a decree ordered all nonjuring clergy—those who would not support the political aims of the revolution—out of the nation within two weeks. The sick and aged alone were excused. The penalty was exportation to Guiana. Before it was all said and done, French pastors were hunted, harassed and executed. A deist god was proclaimed by Robespierre, and at last the goddess Reason was made the official deity of a France whose daily, blood-crazed zigzags in policy were anything but reasonable.

1830 Plans for the city of Chicago were laid out.

1875 Children's fairy-tale author Hans Christian Andersen died in Copenhagen, Denmark. Andersen utilized his natural ability to communicate universal elements in his stories with a keen understanding of spoken language. After early success with a fantastic tale, he turned to playwriting, finally achieving recognition for a play depicting the evils of slavery. Several novels followed, but it was not until his first book of children's stories (*Tales, Told for Children*—1835) that he received widespread recognition. Stories such as *The Tinderbox* and *The Princess and the Pea* convey Andersen's empathy with the unfortunate and the outcast.

1914 Because of the German invasion of Belgium, Great Britain declared war on Germany. The Secretary of State for Foreign Affairs, Sir Edward Grey, said, "The lamps are going out all over Europe; we shall not see them lit again in our lifetime."

1916 For $25 million, the United States purchased the Virgin Islands from Denmark.

AUGUST

1987 The Federal Communications Commission voted 4-0 to rescind the Fairness Doctrine, which required radio and television stations to present balanced coverage of controversial issues.

Where there are no good works, there is no faith. If works and love do not blossom forth, it is not genuine faith, the Gospel has not yet gained a foothold, and Christ is not yet rightly known.

[MARTIN LUTHER (1483–1546)]

AUGUST

The famous Cane Ridge Revival began rather inauspiciously through the exhortations of fiery preacher James McGready in Logan County, Kentucky. At a special outdoor Communion service during the summer of 1800, a woman who had for a long time been seeking assurance of salvation suddenly broke into song and shouted with joy. People began to weep and sought a similar assurance. News of their newfound hope spread like wildfire through Kentucky, and people in nearby regions began to attend the services, thirsting to partake of the Lord's salvation.

Throughout the succeeding fall, winter, and spring the flickering flames of revival swept across the entire Western frontier. So charged was the atmosphere in Kentucky that everyone expected great things when the Presbyterian minister Barton W. Stone scheduled a weeklong Communion service the next summer during the first week of August—at the site of the original McGready meeting. Instead of the usual hundreds, people thronged toward Cane Ridge, hungering for a taste of God. Cane Ridge—a small town a day's ride from Lexington—was inundated with thousands of visitors from many miles around. Most came prepared to camp out, hence the name "camp meeting" was given to the services.

Those who came the first night may have been disappointed. Nothing particularly unusual happened—although hundreds of them decided to spend the entire night in prayer. But the next evening a powerful enthusiasm swept through the crowd. Men, women, and children shrieked and fainted. Preachers shouted to the crowd and urged repentance. Some of the penitents became hysterical. Lightheadedness was common. Individuals began to jerk and twitch. Scoffers stood by and mocked them.

On this day in 1801, the services began calmly with Communion. But soon, under the preaching and hymns of a Methodist minister, the crowds grew emotional. Many fell to their knees, crying for forgiveness. People counseled one another on spiritual matters. They sang, shouted, danced, groaned, or wept uncontrollably. Some fell into deep comas. Instead of breaking up on Sunday, services continued through the night and into the following week, lasting until Thursday with as many as twenty-five thousand attending. Thousands professed belief in Christ.

For years afterward preachers and revivalists would pray, "Lord, make it like Cane Ridge." The remarkable occurrences at the Kentucky revival became the model for frontier renewal—and the very name Cane Ridge became practically synonymous with the idea of revivalism.

1861	The Union government levied an income tax for the first time in an effort to finance the prosecution of its invasion of the South during the War Between the States.

1583 The first English colony in North America was founded near St. John's Harbor on the Newfoundland coast. The English navigator and explorer Sir Humphrey Gilbert, arriving on his vessel the *Squirrel*, claimed the area for the queen.

1604 John Eliot, the American "Apostle to the Indians" was born in Hertfordshire, England. He translated the Bible into an Indian tongue, which was the first Bible to be printed in America.

1850 At a literary picnic in New Hampshire, Herman Melville met Nathaniel Hawthorne. The two famed novelists would develop a rich and productive friendship that would fuel both of their considerable imaginations.

1850 The French short-story master Guy de Maupassant was born at Chateau de Miromesnil.

1862 An upright Presbyterian minister, Stephen Soyers epitomized the Christian values and virtues of the Antebellum South. A strong opponent of chattel slavery and the plantation system, he was nonetheless a reluctant supporter of the Confederacy on constitutional grounds. During the War Between the States, the focus of his ministry in central Mississippi was on mercy ministry. He and his wife had an extensive work among the families of war victims—the poor, orphans, widows, the disabled, and the dispossessed. When they discovered on this day in 1862 that a number of midwives and nurse practitioners were performing abortions and dispensing chemical parricides among both the enslaved blacks and free-born whites, they launched a protracted battle against the minions of death. Though he did not survive to see the end of the war, Soyers's work continued long after—laying the foundations for Mississippi's strong pro-life legislation passed at the turn of the century.

1864 Admiral David G. Farragut commanded his fleet to victory at Mobile Bay, Alabama, with such rallying cries as "Damn the torpedoes; full speed ahead!" During the battle, the Union army lost 145 men, but sank all the Confederate army's ships, providing the Union with a stronghold for operations in Mobile.

1884 The cornerstone for the Statue of Liberty was laid on Bedloe's Island in New York Harbor.

1889 Conrad Aiken was born in Savannah, Georgia. Forty years later to the day, he won the Pulitzer Prize for poetry.

1914 The first electric traffic lights were installed, in Cleveland, Ohio.

1924 In the New York *Daily News*, Harold Gray introduced his comic strip "Little Orphan Annie."

1934 American poet and essayist Wendell Berry was born in Port Royal, Kentucky. A literary heir of the Southern agrarians, Berry draws from his experiences as a farmer in his essays and poems on nature, America's rural past, and ecological responsibility.

1957 *American Bandstand*, hosted by Dick Clark, made its network debut on ABC.

AUGUST

1962 Actress Marilyn Monroe, age thirty-six, was found dead in her Los Angeles home. Her death was ruled a "probable suicide" from an overdose of sleeping pills.

1963 The United States, Britain, and the Soviet Union signed a treaty in Moscow banning nuclear tests in the atmosphere, in space, and underwater.

Sowing mercy is life's best investment.

[MALCOLM FORBES (1919–1990)]

NATIONAL DAY
  Bolivia
FEAST OF THE TRANSFIGURATION
FEAST DAY
  *Saints Justus and Pastor; St.
  Hormidsas, pope*

AUGUST

The *National Police Gazette* was undoubtedly the most sensational newspaper in America. Popular, brash, and controversial, the *Gazette* was edited by George Wilkes, a tough veteran of New York City journalism. Popular with the working classes, the paper focused on hard-hitting crime stories drawn from the official interviews, reports, and testimonies of the police themselves.

Often accused of "muckraking" and "yellow journalism," Wilkes maintained that the tabloid paper was actually "a service to both the citizenry and the forces of law and order" because it "portrayed the vices of the criminal element for what they actually are rather than what the bosses of both politics and the underworld would have us to believe."

The *Gazette* was phenomenally successful—able to build both a strong subscriber base and an effective street distribution system. As a result, its advertising space was the most sought-after in New York journalism.

Though the paper regularly filled three of its eight pages with paid commercial advertising—including a strong compliment from patent medicine manufacturers—Wilkes refused to provide any space to abortionists, who advertised freely in all the other papers in the city. In fact, he regularly wrote editorials calling for the criminalization of the industry—calling the practitioners of the procedure "human fiends," "professional murderers," and "child destroyers." He chastised officials for not taking stronger action and predicted a "day of vengeance" for all those who stood idly by.

While other newspapers were silent—largely because they had vested interests in the continued advertising dollars the rich industry afforded them—Wilkes continued to awaken consciences. In fact, the prominent pastor Gardiner Spring and the famed editor Louis Jennings would both later credit Wilkes with having provoked them to action in the fight to protect innocent human life.

The first pro-life bill to go to the floor of the New York Assembly was introduced on this day in 1883 by the young reformer Theodore Roosevelt. The bill was named in honor of George Wilkes.

1945

The United States dropped the first atomic bomb over enemy territory on the Japanese city of Hiroshima from the B-29 bomber, *Enola Gay.* The 8:15 A.M. bombing resulted in the deaths of more than 200,000 civilians, who died either from the explosion or the subsequent radiation fallout. By dropping the bomb known as "Little Boy," President Harry Truman believed he was saving the lives of at least a half-million Americans who would have been at risk in a conventional invasion of Japan.

1637 English poet and dramatist Ben Jonson died. A contemporary of William Shakespeare and Sir Walter Raleigh, he often joined them at the Mermaid Tavern in London, engaging in "wit combats." Second to none in his lifetime—and second only to the Bard in the decades that followed immediately after—his most famous plays were *Volpone* and *The Alchemist*. His simple monument in the Poet's Corner of London's famed Westminster Abbey bears the inscription, "O, rare Ben Jonson."

1786 After doing public penance in church for the sin of fornication, the poet Robert Burns was released from marriage obligations.

1787 The Constitutional Convention in Philadelphia began to debate the articles contained in a draft of the United States Constitution.

1806 The Holy Roman Empire nearly went out of existence when Emperor Francis II abdicated. It was restored almost immediately by Napoleon—who was crowned by the pope—and restored to its Hapsburg heirs when Francis II won the Battle of Leipzig and revived his claims in the Treaty of Vienna in 1815.

1809 English poet Alfred, Lord Tennyson—who succeeded William Wordworth as poet laureate in 1850—was born in Somersby, Lincolnshire. Some of Tennyson's most recognized poems include *The Lady of Shalott, The Charge of the Light Brigade,* and *Idylls of the King.*

1825 Bolivia declared its independence from Peru.

1868 The French poet, essayist, and dramatist Paul Claudel was born in the village of Villeneuve-sur-Fere.

1926 Gertrude Ederle of New York became the first American woman to swim the English Channel, in about fourteen and a half hours.

1926 Warner Brothers premiered its "Vitaphone" sound-on-disk movie system in New York.

1939 Vladimir Saravov served as a deacon in a small parish church on the banks of the Dnieper River near the great city of Kiev. Although his duties were primarily liturgical, he was also responsible to channel his congregation's covert aid to families fleeing Stalin's persecution of Ukrainian kulaks. As he supplied food, clothing, medicines, and shelter to these refugees, he was startled to discover that not only were they victims of socialization, collectivization, and sovietization, many had been coerced to undergo abortion and sterilization procedures. Outraged, Vladimir organized underground resistance to the Red Army doctors in order to rescue both the children and their mothers—by diverting supply lines, hiding refugees, and providing alternative medical care. Though he was martyred for his activities on this day in 1939, several fellow deacons continued his work throughout the tumultuous Stalin years.

1962 Jamaica became an independent dominion within the British Commonwealth.

1965 President Lyndon Johnson signed the Voting Rights Act.

1986 William J. Schroeder died after living nearly two years with the "Jarvik 7" artificial heart.

AUGUST

Be merciful, just as your Father is merciful.

[JESUS CHRIST (C. 3 B.C.–30 A.D.)]

463

AUGUST

James Wilson (1742–1708) called the Constitution, which he helped to draft and later signed, "The best form of government which has ever been offered to the world." Earlier, he also had signed the Declaration of Independence and served as an associate justice of the first Supreme Court.

Although born and educated in Scotland, Wilson became a leader of the patriots after fleeing the English and Hanoverian oppression of his homeland. He studied law under John Dickinson in Philadelphia—and the two served in the Continental Congress together. In 1774, before he was elected to Congress, Wilson wrote a carefully reasoned pamphlet, *Considerations on the Legislative Authority of the British Parliament*, which boldly concluded that Parliament had no authority over the colonies. In Congress he was one of three Pennsylvania members to vote for independence.

In a bizarre incident on this day in 1779, Wilson's home was attacked by a faction of patriots who felt he had betrayed the cause by defending in court merchants charged with treason. However, after the war he continued to represent Pennsylvania—in Congress and at the Constitutional Convention.

At the Constitutional Convention Wilson had a dual role—as a delegate and as spokesman for the elderly and infirm Benjamin Franklin. As a lawyer and political theorist, Wilson was deeply committed to the principle that sovereignty resides with the people, and he advocated popular elections for both the president and Congress. A member of the committee on detail, he wrote a draft of the Constitution that provided the basis for the final document, and throughout the convention he delivered the persuasive words of Franklin that moved the delegates to overlook minor differences and finally approve the Constitution.

Later, in 1787 at the Pennsylvania ratification convention, Wilson delivered a persuasive speech of his own, winning the votes necessary for ratification. Two years later his state called on him to draft a new state constitution. During the first years under the new Constitution, Wilson served on the Supreme Court. In addition, as a lecturer in law at the College of Philadelphia, he undertook to translate the principle of the sovereignty of the people into the realm of law, providing legal justification for the Revolution and the beginnings of a uniquely American system of jurisprudence.

Named among the most influential of all the American Founding Fathers, he brought his Scots zeal, Covenanter steadfastness, and Calvinistic certainty to the civic arena—thus shaping the fledgling experiment in liberty with the distinctive virtues he deemed essential for its ultimate survival.

1782

George Washington established the Order of the Purple Heart as a decoration for "military merit." This was the first honor badge for enlisted and noncommissioned officers. The first recipients (there were only three among Revolutionary War soldiers) were entitled "to wear on facings over the left breast, the figure of a heart in purple cloth or silk, with narrow lace or binding."

1742 Revolutionary War hero Nathanael Greene was born in Potowomut, Rhode Island. He was described as the "ablest military officer of the Revolution under Washington."

1754 To alleviate the ill health that had been plaguing him for more than a decade, novelist Henry Fielding left England for the gentler climate of Lisbon.

1764 James Boswell, age twenty-four, arrived in Holland, having promised himself "to go abroad with manly resolution to improve and correspond with Samuel Johnson" whom he had recently met.

1771 Francis Asbury, then twenty-six years old, attended a Methodist conference held in Bristol, England. For months he had felt a strange call to bring the gospel to the American frontier. It was at the conference on this day that he heard John Wesley issue a plea: "Our brethren in America call aloud for help. Who are willing to go over and help them?" Asbury immediately offered himself. Several other candidates also had stepped forth, but Wesley sensed that Asbury was the man to send. Wesley's choice was ultimately vindicated. No man could have labored harder than Asbury. He visited small, widely scattered congregations. To meet their needs he rode incessantly—5,000 miles a year. He preached 17,000 sermons, ordained 3,000 preachers, founded 5 schools, and distributed thousands of pieces of literature. His organizational skills divided America into circuits. His circuit riders learned the hard life from him. Many, such as Peter Cartwright, became famous in their own right. At Asbury's death the Methodist Episcopal Church was the largest denomination in the United States—his life was ample evidence for what a single dedicated life can accomplish.

1789 The U.S. War Department was established by Congress.

1804 William Blake wrote to biographer and poet William Hayley, "Money flies from me. Profit never ventures upon my threshold."

1903 Anthropologist and author Louis Leakey was born at the British colonial outpost in Kabete, Kenya.

1912 The Progressive Party nominated Theodore Roosevelt for president.

1942 American forces landed at Guadalcanal, marking the start of the first major allied offensive in the Pacific during the Second World War.

1947 The balsawood raft *Kon-Tiki*, which had carried a six-man crew 4,300 miles across the Pacific Ocean, crashed into a reef in a Polynesian archipelago.

1959 The *Explorer VI* satellite took the first photograph of Earth taken from space.

1964 Congress passed the Gulf of Tonkin resolution, giving President Lyndon Johnson broad powers in dealing with reported North Vietnamese attacks on U.S. forces.

1974 French stuntman Philippe Petit walked a tightrope strung between the twin towers of New York's World Trade Center.

1976 Scientists in Pasadena, California, announced that the *Viking 1* spacecraft had found the strongest indications to date of possible life on Mars—indications that have not been verified in the years since.

AUGUST

1987 The presidents of five Central American nations, meeting in Guatemala City, signed an eleven-point agreement designed to bring peace to their region.

1990 President George Bush ordered American troops and warplanes to Saudi Arabia to guard the oil-rich desert kingdom against a possible invasion by Iraq.

You shall love your neighbor more than your own life.

[BARNABAS OF ANTIOCH (C. 180)]

The Augsburg Confession, the most widely accepted confession, or Lutheran statement of faith, was prepared by German Reformer Philip Melanchthon, with Martin Luther's approval. Its twenty-one articles were originally intended to be summary statements for the German nobility, who were called to a diet at Augsburg in June of 1530 by the Holy Roman emperor Charles V to present their Protestant views.

The emperor summarily rejected the confession and Luther, Melanchthon, and the nobles returned to their homes without sanction to continue reforming the church. Undeterred, Melanchthon set about editing, refining, and amending the document.

Born Philipp Schwarzert, Melanchthon was educated by the Brethren of the Common Life and at the universities of Heidelberg and Tübingen. When he entered Heidelberg at the age of twelve, he changed his surname on the advice of his uncle, the German humanist and Hebraist Johann Reuchlin, to Melanchthon—a Greek equivalent, meaning "black earth." Through his uncle's influence he was elected in 1518 to the chair of Greek at the University of Wittenberg. It was during his inaugural address, *Discourse on Reforming the Studies of Youth*, that he first attracted the interest of Martin Luther. He was so profoundly influenced by the great doctor that he turned to the study of theology. In 1521 his *Loci Communes Rerum Theologicarum* (Commonplaces of Theology) contributed substantial rational force to the Reformation, and after Luther's confinement in the castle of Wartburg the same year, he temporarily replaced Luther as leader of the Reformation cause at Wittenberg. In 1526 he became professor of theology.

After amending the Augsburg Confession, he appended several other dogmatic statements—including the Nicene, Apostles', and Athanasian Creeds and Luther's Small and Large Catechisms—and published his greatest work on this day in 1531. It immediately became the standard Lutheran doctrinal statement and formed the creedal basis for Lutheran churches ever afterward.

In its modern form the Augsburg Confession consists of twenty-eight articles. The first twenty-one summarize Lutheran doctrine with special emphasis on justification. The second part of the Confession reviews the "abuses" for which remedy was demanded, such as withholding the cup from the laity in holy Communion and forbidding priests to marry. Because of its conciliatory tone and brevity, the Confession affected the entire Reformation movement, including the Anglican Thirty-nine Articles and the theology of French Reformer John Calvin, who signed a later version in 1540.

The tone of the Confession was so conciliatory that it surprised even Catholics. His Apology, published a year later, vindicated the Confession, and his Variata further reinforced its dogmatic formulations—but as always Melanchthon played the part of peacemaker. Indeed, it was his firm conviction that the reforms it called for were essential for harmony between Protestantism and Roman Catholicism—or for at least a union of Protestant factions. Melanchthon died praying that "the churches might be of one mind in Christ."

1492 In a year best known for the first voyage to America by Christopher Columbus, *St. Jerome's Letters* were published at Bâle, Germany. The title page bore a stunning woodcut portrait of Jerome by a rising young artist named Albrecht Dürer. Though it was his first commission, there would soon be many more. In time he would become the greatest artist of the age and a strong supporter of Martin Luther's Reform movement.

1588 In a speech to her troops at Tilbury, Queen Elizabeth I of England said, "I know I have the body of a weak and feeble woman, but I have the heart and stomach of a king, and a king of England, too; and think foul scorn that Parma or Spain, or any prince of Europe, should dare to invade the borders of my realm."

1672 As part of the war between Holland and England, the Dutch captured New York without firing a shot. They renamed it New Orange.

1815 Napoleon Bonaparte set sail for St. Helena to spend the remainder of his days in exile.

1876 Thomas Alva Edison obtained a patent (No. 180,857) for a mimeograph machine, a "method of preparing autographic stencils for printing." This was the very early forerunner of the copying machine.

1896 Marjorie Kinnan Rawlings was born in Washington, D.C. Her novel *The Yearling* would win the Pulitzer Prize in 1938.

1930 Edmund Wilson advised his friend F. Scott Fitzgerald that "as hard as America can be to live in," it is "a terrible and foolish mistake for American writers to escape abroad."

1942 Six convicted Nazi saboteurs who had landed in the U.S. were executed in Washington, D.C. Two others received life imprisonment.

1945 President Harry Truman signed the United Nations Charter.

1945 The Soviet Union declared war against Japan just as the Second World War was coming to a close.

1953 The United States and South Korea initialed a mutual security pact.

1963 Britain's "Great Train Robbery" took place as thieves made off with 2.6 million pounds in bank notes. A gang ambushed the GPO mail train from Glasgow and were able to make a clean getaway.

1968 Richard M. Nixon was nominated for president at the Republican national convention in Miami Beach.

1973 Vice President Spiro T. Agnew branded as "damned lies" reports that he had taken kickbacks from government contracts in Maryland, and vowed not to yield to the pressure to leave office—but he eventually relented and resigned.

1974 President Richard M. Nixon announced that he would resign following new damaging revelations in the Watergate scandal.

AUGUST

*T*hose who have no concern for their ancestors will, by simple application of the same rule, have none for their descendants.

[RICHARD WEAVER (1910–1963)]

467

AUGUST

1936

Eleanor of Aquitaine was one of the most remarkable women of the Medieval Age—indeed, she was one of the most remarkable of all time. She was the queen consort of both France (1137–1152) and England (1154–1204). In addition, she was the mother of two of the most important kings in the history of England.

Born in Aquitaine in 1122, she inherited the vast duchy along the western coast of France from her father in 1137. Later that same year, she married Louis VII of France. She accompanied her husband on the Second Crusade to the Holy Land, where it was rumored that she committed adultery—a rumor she steadfastly refused to deny in light of her husband's own infidelities.

The scandal, and the fact that she had not given the king a male heir, provoked Louis to seek an annulment of their marriage in 1152 under the pretext of blood kinship between her and the king. The church reluctantly allowed for the dissolution—in an effort to quell any further indignities.

Delighted, Eleanor promptly married and gave her possessions to Henry Plantagenet, count of Anjou, who in 1154 became Henry II, king of England. Their children were largely schooled by her—quite unusual for the time, demonstrating both her great intelligence and her strong will—and were renowned for their strength of character and perceptive discernment.

In 1170, the queen induced her husband to invest their son Richard the Lion-Hearted with her personal dominions of Gascony, Aquitaine, and Poitou. When Richard and his brothers rebelled against their father in 1173, Eleanor, already alienated from the king because of his chronic unfaithfulness, supported her sons. Consequently, she was placed in confinement until 1185.

After her release, she secured the succession of her son Richard, who had become heir apparent at the death in 1183 of his eldest brother. From the death of King Henry II in 1189 until Richard's return from the Third Crusade in 1194, Eleanor ruled the kingdom quite capably as his regent. During Richard's long absence, she foiled the attempt of her son John in 1193 to conspire with sundry French, German, and Austrian lords against the new king. But then, after the return of Richard, she arranged a reconciliation between the two brothers.

Eleanor continued to be prominent in public affairs until she retired to the abbey in Fontevrault, France, where she died on April 1, 1204. There she is buried in a regal tomb next to Richard, as befits the mighty "Warrior Queen."

Jesse Owens won the last of his four medals at the Olympic Games in Germany. He won the 100-meter run on August 3, the broad jump on August 4, the 200-meter run on August 5, and the 400-meter relay on this day. Adolf Hitler, who presided over the Olympics, snubbed Owens because of his African descent.

1387 Henry V, the English king who defeated the French in the Battle of Agincourt, was born in England.

1593 Isaac Walton, author of the *Complete Angler*, was born in Stafford, England.

1631 The poet and critic John Dryden was born at the vicarage of Aldwinkle, All Saints, Northamptonshire.

1787 In Jane Austen's *Persuasion*, Anne Elliot was born in Kellynch Hall, Sommersetshire, to Walter and Elizabeth Elliot.

1790 The *Columbia* returned to Boston Harbor after a three-year voyage, becoming the first ship to carry the American flag around the world.

1842 The United States and Canada resolved a border dispute by signing the Webster-Ashburton Treaty.

1842 Herman Melville escaped from the Typee Valley cannibals with whom he had spent a month in captivity in the Polynesian Marquesas Islands. He had been serving on an American whaling ship—and while he called the experience "more than a little unnerving and fraught with right much unpleasantness," it proved to be the backdrop against which he would build his literary reputation. Indeed, all of his most successful novels were based upon his adventures sailing on the South Seas.

1848 The Free-Soil Party nominated former president Martin Van Buren to be its candidate during a raucous convention in Buffalo, New York.

1854 Henry David Thoreau published his most famous work, *Walden*, a hodgepodge of journal entries, political diatribes, and disjointed philosophical musings. The book dramatically fictionalized his experiences while living near Walden Pond in Massachusetts.

1902 Edward VII was crowned king of England following the death of his mother, Queen Victoria.

1910 A patent for the electric washing machine was awarded to A. J. Fisher of Chicago, Illinois.

1945 Three days after the atomic bombing of Hiroshima, Japan, the American bombers exploded another nuclear device over the city of Nagasaki. At least forty thousand lives were lost.

1965 Singapore proclaimed its independence from the Malaysian Federation.

1969 Actress Sharon Tate and four other people were found brutally murdered in Tate's Los Angeles home. Cult leader Charles Manson and a group of his disciples were later convicted of the crime.

1974 Following the Watergate Affair, President Richard M. Nixon became the first president to resign the office. Gerald Ford, the former Speaker of the House who had only recently gained the role of vice president after the resignation of Vice President Agnew, became president of the United States.

1988 President Ronald Reagan nominated Lauro Cavazos to be secretary of education. Cavazos became the first Hispanic to serve in the cabinet.

AUGUST

To comprehend the history of a thing is to unlock the mysteries of its present, and more, to disclose the profundities of its future.

[HILAIRE BELLOC (1870–1953)]

AUGUST

The "Pinckney Plan" was one of three plans offered to the Constitutional Convention in Philadelphia. No record of it exists, but Charles Pinckney (1757–1824) is generally given credit for many provisions—possibly as many as thirty—of the finished Constitution. In an extremely active career, Pinckney also served four terms as Governor of South Carolina, congressman, senator, and minister to Spain.

Educated in England, Pinckney returned to assist—and then replace—his father (Charles Sr.) and his cousin (Charles Cotesworth Pinckney) in South Carolina's patriotic movement. Before he was twenty he had served on the state's executive council and helped draft its first constitution. In the war he served with the militia, was captured, and spent a year in a British prison.

Elected to the Congress of the Confederation in 1784, Pinckney gradually became convinced of the weakness of the government under the Articles of Confederation. As chairman of a congressional committee considering measures to strengthen the Articles of Confederation, Pinckney gained experience that prepared him for his role at the Constitutional Convention. In 1786, in an address to Congress, he urged that a general convention be called to revise the Articles of Confederation.

When Pinckney arrived at the Constitutional Convention in Philadelphia on this day in May 1787, he had already prepared his "plan." Unfortunately, he presented it to the Convention immediately after Edmund Randolph had completed a three-hour description of his own plan, and Pinckney's was never debated point by point, but simply referred, with other plans, to the committee on detail. And that committee did not identify, in its comprehensive report, the source of each recommended element of the Constitution.

Though the exact extent of Pinckney's contribution to the Constitution remains unknown, Pinckney in later life made such extravagant claims that he became known as "Constitution Charlie." Pinckney also prepared a large part of South Carolina's new constitution, adopted in 1790—a document modeled after the national Constitution. For more than thirty years after the Constitution was ratified, Pinckney served in public office. In the 1790s he left the Federalist Party to support Jefferson. In 1795 he denounced the Jay Treaty, and in the 1800 election, he helped Jefferson carry South Carolina, even though his cousin, Charles Cotesworth Pinckney, was the vice-presidential candidate on the Federalist ticket. President Jefferson's appointment of Pinckney as minister to Spain looked very much like a reward, but Pinckney had little success in dealing with Spain. After his return he continued to be elected to public office, completing his career in the Congress, where one of his final acts was to oppose the Missouri Compromise, believing that it duplicitously dealt with the moral issues inherent in slavery.

1556 German theologian, poet, and composer Philipp Nicolai, who wrote the chorales *How Brightly Shines the Morningstar* and *Wake, Awake for Night Is Flying*, was born in Germany.

1575 Peter Bales, a writing master and miniaturist, presented Queen Elizabeth I with a penny on which he had inscribed the Lord's Prayer, the Creed, the Decalogue, two short prayers in Latin, his own name and motto, the day of the month, the year of the Lord, and the reign of the queen. He later inscribed the entire Bible in a book that fit inside a walnut shell.

1675 At 3:14 P.M., the foundation stone was set for the Royal Observatory at Greenwich. It was commissioned by King Charles II and designed by Sir Christopher Wren, who had himself been a professor of astronomy. Charles II appointed John Flamsteed as the first Astronomer Royal. Flamsteed's task was to "apply himself with the utmost care and diligence to rectifying the tables of the motions of the heavens, and the places of the fixed stars, so as to find out the so much-desired longitude of places for perfecting the art of navigation." Eventually this facility became the fixed spot enabling sailors to determine their longitude.

1787 Wolfgang Mozart wrote perhaps his most famous work, *Eine kleine Nachtmusik*, on this day in Vienna.

1788 Wolfgang Mozart wrote the entirety of his famous Symphony no. 41, *Jupiter*, in Vienna on this day.

1821 Missouri became the twenty-fourth state.

1846 Congress chartered the Smithsonian Institution, named after English scientist James Smithson, whose bequest of half a million dollars had made it possible.

1874 Herbert Clark Hoover, the thirty-first president of the United States, was born in West Branch, Iowa.

1885 Leo Daft opened America's first commercially operated electric streetcar, in Baltimore.

1889 The skeleton of a mammoth was found at St. James, Nebraska. The skeleton's backbone measured thirty-six feet long, and showed that the animal had stood at least fifteen feet tall.

1927 President Calvin Coolidge officially dedicated Mount Rushmore in South Dakota, and Gutzon Borglum began work carving the likenesses of Presidents George Washington, Thomas Jefferson, Abraham Lincoln, and amazingly, the contemporary Theodore Roosevelt.

1949 The National Military Establishment was renamed the Department of Defense.

1969 Leno and Rosemary LaBianca were murdered in their Los Angeles home by members of Charles Manson's cult, one day after actress Sharon Tate and four other people were slain in a similar fashion.

1977 Postal employee David Berkowitz was arrested in Yonkers, New York, accused of being "Son of Sam," the gunman responsible for six slayings and seven other shootings.

10

AUGUST

*H*e spoke with a certain what-is-it in his voice, and *I* could see that, if not actually disgruntled, he was far from being gruntled.

[P. G. WODEHOUSE (1881–1975)]

471

Augustus Montague Toplady, clergyman and writer, was born in 1740 at Farnham, about twenty miles southwest of Windsor, England. He studied at the prestigious Westminster School for a short time but was sent to Ireland in 1755, the same year as his conversion. He had been greatly influenced by the teachings of John Wesley.

Toplady received his degrees of Bachelor of Arts and Master of Arts from Trinity College. During his studies, he gradually came to reject the Arminianism of the Methodists in favor of the doctrines of Sovereign Grace of the Calvinists. Ordained deacon in 1762, he was licensed to the Anglican curacy of Blagdon the same year. He was ordained a priest in 1764, and from then until 1766 he served as curate at Farleigh, Hungerford. For the next two years he held the benefice of Harpford with Venn-Ottery, and for two years after that, of Broad Hembury. During 1775 he took a leave of absence to minister to the French Calvinist Reformed Church in Orange Street, London.

His first published work was a work of verse, *Poems on Sacred Subjects.* But he was best known for his polemical and dogmatic works—including *The Church of England Vindicated from the Charge of Arminianism,* which was published in 1769, and *The Historic Proof of the Doctrinal Calvinism of the Church of England,* which was published five years later in 1774. Those works proved vital in the ongoing theological struggles within the English church and helped to ensure orthodoxy for at least another generation.

Toplady was only thirty-eight when he died, but his short lifespan was enough to produce one of the most beloved of all hymns, "Rock of Ages."

> Rock of Ages cleft for me,
> Let me hide myself in Thee;
> Let the water and the blood
> From Thy riven side which flowed
> Be of sin the double cure;
> Cleanse me from its guilt and power.

AUGUST

The hymn was first published on this day in the *Gospel Magazine* (London, 1776). Today, only a very few nonspecialists read the theological works that established Toplady as one of the most significant men of his day, but nearly all Christians sing his hymn—even the Arminians it was written to confound.

1786

Jean Baptiste Marie Vianney was born near Lyons, France. Though his parents were poor, they were devout. Thus, when the French Revolution unleashed its persecution against the church, the family secreted pastors into the local underground. Though he was too poor to obtain a proper education, he spent the rest of his life serving the church and became renowned for his faith, his merciful service, and his evangelistic zeal.

1860 The nation's first successful silver mine began operation near Virginia City, Nevada.

1877 The first moon orbiting the planet Mars was discovered on this day.

1909 The SOS distress signal was first used by an American ship, the *Arapahoe*, off Cape Hatteras, North Carolina.

1919 Andrew Carnegie, the Scottish-born philanthropist and multimillionaire, died having given more than £70 million and $100 million for such causes as libraries in Great Britain and the United States. He once said, "A man who dies rich dies disgraced."

1921 Author Alex Haley was born in Ithaca, New York. He won the Pulitzer Prize for literature in 1976 with his book *Roots*, which traces the effects of slavery on generations of a black American family.

1934 The first federal prisoners arrived at the island prison of Alcatraz in San Francisco Bay.

1954 A formal peace took hold in Indochina, ending more than seven years of fighting between the French and Communist Vietminh.

1965 The Watts Riots began when looting broke out in the predominantly African-American neighborhoods of Los Angeles. In the week that followed, thirty-four people were killed and more than one thousand injured.

1973 The U.S. Securities and Exchange Commission took Thomas Road Baptist Church to court, accusing the congregation of fraud. The pastor of the church, Jerry Falwell, was born in 1933, the grandson of a backwoods bootlegger. His father died of alcoholism. But Falwell was destined to break that cycle of desperation. Valedictorian of his school, he also excelled in team sports. He entered Lynchburg College, intending to become a mechanical engineer.

About that time, his mother began insisting that the family listen to the *Old Fashioned Revival Hour* radio program. Later, visiting a local church, Falwell gave his life to Christ. He immediately began to study the Bible and transferred to a Bible college. After receiving his theological degree, he returned to Lynchburg and started a church. Within weeks he had a half-hour radio show and six months later a TV show. Meanwhile, his congregation of thirty-five adults grew to more than eight hundred members in a year, largely owing to his aggressive door-to-door evangelization. His *Old-Time Gospel Hour* became one of the most popular religious programs in the nation. On this day, the judge in the SEC case argued that government agents had been overzealous in their actions against the ministry. The good name of the church was untainted, he said. Falwell went on to form the Moral Majority. Many annalists believe that it had much to do with Ronald Reagan's presidential landslide in 1980—but none of it would have been possible if the church had lost its struggle with the government nearly a decade earlier.

1984 President Ronald Reagan joked during a voice test for a paid political radio address that he had "signed legislation that will outlaw Russia forever. We begin bombing in five minutes." The quip caused a furor, but in fact, his policies proved more effective than bombs in defeating the "Evil Empire" of the Soviets.

AUGUST

1997 President Bill Clinton made the first use of the historic line-item veto approved by Congress, rejecting three items in spending and tax bills.

In literature as in love, courage is half the battle. Likewise, in virtue as in fashion, tradition is the surest guide to the future.

[SIR WALTER SCOTT (1771–1832)]

When the esteemed Senate Majority Leader Henry Cabot Lodge addressed his colleagues on this day in 1919, the nation was already in the midst of a "Great Debate" over its future foreign policy. What was then called the Great War—what we call the First World War—had just ended. Should the country now join the new League of Nations that President Woodrow Wilson had hammered into shape at the Versailles Peace Conference, or should the nation retain its traditional commitment to neutrality—as articulated in Washington's hallowed Farewell Address?

Utilizing carefully measured phrases and appealing to the mood of the audience, Lodge's speech somehow bridged the gap between the two positions and unleashed a storm of applause from the packed galleries. A group of marines, just returned from France, pounded their helmets enthusiastically against the gallery railing; men and women cheered, whistled, and waved handkerchiefs and hats. It was minutes before order could be restored, and when a Democratic senator attempted to reply to Lodge's arguments, his remarks were greeted with boos and hisses.

Lodge argued against any possible infringement of America's sovereignty: "I object in the strongest possible way to having the United States agree, directly or indirectly, to be controlled by a league which may at any time, and perfectly lawfully and in accordance with the terms of the covenant, be drawn in to deal with internal conflicts in other countries, no matter what those conflicts may be. We should never permit the United States to be involved in any internal conflict in another country, except by the will of her people expressed through the Congress which represents them."

Likewise, he argued for a strong moral stance regarding the horrors of war while at the same time ringing the bell of patriotism: "In the Great War we were called upon to rescue the civilized world. Did we fail? On the contrary, we succeeded, succeeded largely and nobly, and we did it without any command from any league of nations. When the emergency came, we met it, and we were able to meet it because we had built up on this continent the greatest and most powerful nation in the world, built it up under our own polices, in our own way, and one great element of our strength was the fact that we had held aloof and had not thrust ourselves into European quarrels; that we had no selfish interest to serve. We made great sacrifices. We have done splendid work. I believe that we do not require to be told by foreign nations when we shall do work which freedom and civilization require. I think we can move to victory much better under our own command than under the command of others."

His logic, resounding with the moral fervor of his dear friend Teddy Roosevelt, won the day. In the end, the League of Nations treaty was defeated and the policy Lodge had elaborated became the foundation of all American foreign relations for the rest of the century.

1658 The first police force in America was established in New Amsterdam, later named New York.

1660 Charles II called for the suppression of John Milton's Latin pamphlet, *Defense of the English People.*

1665 During the plague in London, Samuel Pepys wrote in his diary, "The people die so, that now it seems they are fain to carry the dead to be buried by daylight, the nights not sufficing to do it in."

1851 Isaac Singer was granted a patent on his latest invention: the automatic sewing machine.

1852 Isaac Merrit Singer was granted a patent for his improved continuous-stitch sewing machine.

1867 President Andrew Johnson sparked a move to impeach him when he defied Congress by suspending Secretary of War Edwin M. Stanton.

1881 American film producer and director Cecil B. DeMille, renowned for lavish, large-scale films, was born in Ashfield, Massachusetts. Among his credits are the sagas *Cleopatra, King of Kings, The Ten Commandments,* and *The Greatest Show on Earth.*

1898 The peace protocol ending the Spanish-American War was signed.

1898 Hawaii was formally annexed to the United States.

1944 Joseph P. Kennedy Jr., eldest son of Joseph and Rose Fitzgerald Kennedy, was killed with his copilot when their explosives-laden U.S. Navy plane blew up over England.

1953 The Soviet Union conducted a secret test of its first hydrogen bomb.

1961 Communist East Germany further divided the city of Berlin by erecting the Berlin Wall, effectively isolating West Berlin from the rest of Europe.

1972 The last American combat ground troops left Vietnam.

1973 Reading from C. S. Lewis's *Mere Christianity,* Tom Philips—president of Raytheon, a huge electronics firm in Massachusetts—shared the gospel with Chuck Colson—one of the central figures in the Nixon administration's Watergate scandal. Though the words cut into Colson's heart, he said that he was not quite ready to make a commitment. In truth, he did not want to yield to the temptation of foxhole religion. Tom nodded and gave him the book. "Read it," he suggested. "And read the Gospel of John." In his car, Colson found that he couldn't drive. Tears were pouring from his eyes. He started back toward the house, but the lights went out. Sobbing uncontrollably, he started the car and drove a couple hundred feet. There he sobbed aloud. He offered himself to Christ, admitting it wasn't much of an offer. "Take me, take me," he pleaded. For the first time in his life he felt he wasn't alone. It was the beginning of a transformation that would lead him to found Prison Fellowship and make him one of the most respected Christian authors of the day.

AUGUST

1977 The space shuttle *Enterprise* passed its first solo flight test by taking off atop a Boeing 747, separating, then touching down in California's Mojave Desert.

*I*ntent on its ending, they are ignorant of its beginning; and therefore of its very being.

[G. K. CHESTERTON (1874–1936)]

FEAST DAY

St. Simplician of Milan; St. Radegund; St. Wigbert; St. Pontian, pope; St. Benildus; St. Hippolytus of Rome; St. Narses Klaietus; St. Cassian of Imola; St. Maximus the Confessor

AUGUST

A devoted disciple of Jefferson, James Madison (1751–1836) became the active leader of the Democratic-Republican Party when he was elected president. And like his mentor, he was never able to provide the kind of administrative leadership necessary to guide the nation. As had been the case with his friend John Adams, Madison performed his greatest service to the nation before he was elected president.

Increasingly aware of the weaknesses of the confederation that loosely bound the states after the Revolution, he helped frame the Constitution in the Convention of 1787 and eloquently defended it in the Virginia ratifying convention and in the famed *Federalist Papers*. And after the new government was formed, it was Madison who introduced the Bill of Rights to Congress as the first amendments to the Constitution.

The smallest man ever to become president—he stood just over five feet four inches tall and weighed about a hundred pounds—the soft-spoken, retiring Madison was more a scholar than an executive. He developed the habit of serious study at the College of New Jersey—under the tutelage of John Witherspoon—and became a devoted student of history and law.

Besides the Constitution and the *Federalist Papers*, other documents that helped shape the new nation can be traced to his pen: the petition for religious freedom in Virginia, the defense of American navigation rights on the Mississippi, and the Virginia Resolution—a ringing denouncement of the oppressive Alien and Sedition Laws.

Foreign problems dominated Madison's years as president. Conflict with Britain over naval rights finally led to a war that brought little credit to either nation and made Madison the most unpopular president the country had thus far known. The fact that he had to flee Washington on this day in 1814 only made matters that much worse. Federalists demanded that he resign, but he weathered the criticism; with peace he regained a measure of popularity. But nothing that he accomplished as president—or as a member of Congress or secretary of state—won him the high place he had already gained as one of the founders of the nation, a place of enduring fame as the Father of the Constitution.

1521

Spanish conqueror Hernando Cortez captured present-day Mexico City from the Aztec Indians. He had fewer than two dozen men and a few firearms, while the Aztec army numbered more than 100,000 men in arms. So how did Cortez defeat the fierce enemy? Very simply tens of thousands of the oppressed masses rose up against their masters. They saw Cortez as their liberator—and so the shackles of a cruel and bloodthirsty tyranny were thrown off.

1587 The American Indian Manteo converted to Christianity and was baptized into the Church of England. He was the first Native American to embrace Christ.

1624 French King Louis XIII named Cardinal Richelieu his first minister. The wily churchman would dominate European affairs for the next generation.

1704 The Battle of Blenheim was fought during the War of the Spanish Succession, resulting in a victory for English and Austrian forces.

1812 The great Scottish missionary-educator James Stewart landed at Cape Town in the company of David Livingstone's wife, Mary, who was on her way back to Africa to join her husband. At first, Stewart intended to work with Livingstone to establish a new industrial mission, but he eventually decided to focus instead on education. In 1867 he became the principal of Lovedale. He held the post almost forty years and made the school the premier educational establishment for blacks in South Africa. In addition to a general education, Lovedale offered practical arts: blacksmithing, carpentry, masonry, wagon-making. From the start, Lovedale students filled responsible positions throughout Africa. They preached, clerked, taught, and ran businesses. Stewart founded two other mission stations, another school, and a hospital in the later part of his life—and he left a blueprint for a college that was built after his death. He was later lauded as the "educator to a race."

1819 Sir George Grove, an English engineer who became the first director of the Royal College of Music, and the first editor of the *Dictionary of Music and Musicians*, was born on this day.

1846 The American flag was raised for the first time in Los Angeles.

1876 The first complete performance of Richard Wagner's *Der Ring des Nibelungen* (The Ring of the Nibelungs) began on this date and continued for four successive evenings. Wagner based this cycle of operas, *Das Rheingold, Die Walküre, Siegfried*, and *Die Götterdämmerung*, on Scandinavian, German, and Icelandic saga and myths that he developed and altered for his libretto. A special theater, the Festspielhaus, was built in Bayreuth to house the performance, which required various special effects and scene changes.

1899 English master film director Sir Alfred Hitchcock was born in London. He pioneered innovative film techniques while directing the classics *The 39 Steps, Rebecca, Rear Window, North by Northwest, Strangers on a Train, Vertigo, To Catch a Thief,* and *The Birds*, among others.

1932 Adolf Hitler rejected the post of vice chancellor of Germany, saying he was prepared to hold out "for all or nothing."

1934 The satirical comic strip "Li'l Abner," created by Al Capp, made its debut.

1942 Walt Disney's animated feature *Bambi* premiered at Radio City Music Hall in New York.

1960 The first two-way telephone conversation by satellite took place with the help of *Echo 1*.

1961 Berlin was divided as East Germany sealed off the border between the city's eastern and western sectors to halt the flight of refugees and begin building its famous wall.

AUGUST

The family is the only means by which real and substantial change for good might truly be effected.

[JAMES STEWART (1839–1901)]

Every great library begins in the heart of someone with at least three heroic loves: a love for words, a love for truth, and a love for future generations. Libraries begin as a collection of beloved books, but those books generate a love for words, as well—without that, books are mere antiquarian curiosities.

Perhaps the greatest etymologist of all time—and thus, one of the most passionate lovers of word—was James Murray (1837–1915), a self-educated Scots country boy who was the original editor of the monumental *Oxford English Dictionary*.

The dictionary was a mind-bogglingly huge undertaking that practically consumed his life—it documented every single word in the English language, past and present, as well as every possible usage from formal to colloquial. Thus, tens of thousands of entries had to be carefully researched. The etymology of every word was traced. Examples of the use of the word were drawn from the best prose and poetry extant. And it all was arranged and cataloged in as functional and a usable fashion as possible.

Murray was precise with every detail of the Herculean task at hand. His granddaughter later described how he would illumine visitors to his cluttered study as to the vital character of his work—understanding full well the seed truth about language and the precision inherent in the transferal of truth, first foretold in the biblical story of the Tower of Babel.

Thus, Elisabeth Murray wrote, "As he showed the guests round, Dr. Murray would give examples of the unique feature of the dictionary, the application of the historical method. His task was to trace the life history both of every English word now in use and of all those known to have been in use at any time during the last seven hundred years. His starting point was in 1150, and the early history, variations of sense and form of every word current at that date, was to be given in the same detail as the changes which took place in succeeding centuries. In this he was applying the historical principle much more completely than had been attempted in any country. Although James knew that there would be additions and changes in English vocabulary in future ages, he would stress that, every fact faithfully recorded, and every inference correctly drawn from the facts, becomes a permanent accession to human knowledge, part of eternal truth, which will never cease to be true."

It was in 1859, when he was a mere twenty-two years old, that Murray first conceived of the great work—but not until two decades later on this day did he win the confidence of the Philological Society and actually begin the work. Alas, he died before the work was completed. Nevertheless, the organization he put together ensured that the work eventually was published—in 1928.

1934 President Franklin D. Roosevelt signed into law the Social Security Act, designed as a voluntary savings plan creating unemployment insurance and pension plans for the elderly.

1457 A wandering astronomer named Faust published the first known book, *The Book of Psalms*—part of an edition of the Bible that he had begun seven years prior. To sell copies of his book, Faust traveled from Germany to Paris. However, the French threw him into prison because they thought he had conspired with the devil. They believed that only an allegiance with the devil could have produced so many books that agreed exactly with every letter and type. To prove his innocence, Faust had to disclose his process of bookmaking. It is this story upon which the famous theatrical dramas by Marlowe and Goethe found their origin.

1670 Quakers William Penn and William Mead were arrested on this day—apparently for daring to preach in public. The men were jailed and charged—though they were never told just what they were charged with. Twelve jurors were impaneled to determine the guilt of the pair. Penn asked for a written copy of the charges against him. He was refused—not until he had entered his plea would he be given the charges, he was told. Penn pleaded not guilty. The men were summarily returned to lockup. On September 3 they were brought back to court. Their hats were, of course, off. The judge ordered them put on so he could fine them for not removing them. Penn protested. For his defiance Penn was whisked away into an enclosure. He went under protest, saying he would not be silent on a question that affected thousands of other persons. If such proceedings could be taken against him, they could be taken against anyone in England. Mead boldly repeated Penn's arguments—in Latin. In a rage the judge shouted, "You deserve to have your tongue cut out!" Mead stood on his rights as an Englishman.

Thus, Mead, too, was dragged away. The judge demanded that the jury find the two guilty of preaching to the people and drawing a tumultuous crowd after them—and failure to do so would put the members in grave peril. But the jurors would not be cowed. They refused to convict the men. Court officers ranted at the twelve and ordered the verdict changed. When the jurors refused, they were locked up without food, water or a chamber pot. When this still did not bring the jurors to heel, they were sent to prison. Eight of them paid fines to gain immediate release. The remaining four filed a lawsuit. Meanwhile, Penn and Mead were released. Finally, England's highest court ruled in the jurors' favor. Juries could not be coerced. Thus it was that a religious persecution case won for us all one of our most important freedoms.

1848 The Oregon Territory was established.

1900 International forces, including U.S. Marines, entered Beijing to put down the Boxer Rebellion, which was aimed at purging China of all foreigners.

1917 China declared war on Germany and Austria during the First World War.

1941 President Franklin Roosevelt and British Prime Minister Winston Churchill issued the Atlantic Charter, a statement of principles that renounced aggression.

AUGUST

1945 President Harry Truman announced that Japan had surrendered unconditionally, ending the Second World War.

1947 Separated from India, Pakistan became independent of British rule.

There is no other place where the human spirit can be so nurtured as to prosper spiritually, intellectually, and temporally, than in the bosom of the family's rightful relation.

[JOHN CHRYSOSTOM (C. 344–407)]

AUGUST

Sir Walter Scott was born on this day 1771 in Edinburgh, Scotland. He created the genre of historical fiction in a series called the Waverley Novels. In his phenomenally popular works, he managed to arrange the plots and characters so the reader entered into the lives of both great and ordinary people caught up in violent, dramatic changes in history.

To some degree Scott's work shows the influence of the Scottish Enlightenment. For instance, he believed every human was basically decent regardless of class, religion, politics, or ancestry. In fact, tolerance is a major theme in his historical works—he was the first novelist to portray peasant characters sympathetically and realistically, and was equally just to merchants and soldiers. But the novels also expressed his belief in the need for social progress that would not reject the traditions of the past. Thus, he drew on his great Scottish legacy of Calvinism, Covenantalism, and communitarianism. Clearly, his early influences included long evenings of storytelling by his elders, and his prolific reading of poetry, history, and drama, as well as fairy tales and grand romances.

In his introduction to *The Fortunes of Nigel*, Scott remarked, "But no one shall find me rowing against the stream. I care not who knows it; I write for the general amusement." Nevertheless, the works were clearly serious literary and intellectual efforts. In his portraits of Scotland, England, and the Continent from medieval times to the eighteenth century, he showed a keen sense of political and traditional forces and of their influence on the individual. Indeed, Scott wrote frequently about the conflicts between different cultures. *Ivanhoe* (1791) dealt with the struggle between Normans and Saxons. *The Talisman* (1825) described the conflict between Christians and Muslims in the Crusades. But it was for his Scottish novels that he was best known—and most beloved. They have generally garnered the highest praise from critics and common readers alike. They deal with the cataclysmic clashes between the new commercial English culture and the older Scottish clan culture. A number of critics rank *Old Mortality* (1816), *The Heart of Midlothian* (1819), and *St. Ronan's Well* (1824) as Scott's best novels. But several other works in the Waverley series also claim adherents, including *Rob Roy* (1817), *A Legend of Montrose* (1819), and *Quentin Dunward* (1823).

James Fenimore Cooper in America, Honoré de Balzac in France, and Charles Dickens and William Makepeace Thackeray in England were among the many who learned from Scott's panoramic studies of the interplay between social trends and individual character. In Great Britain, he created an enduring interest in Scottish traditions, and throughout the Western world he encouraged the cult of the Middle Ages, which strongly characterized Romanticism.

But besides his books—and the ideas they spawned and the enthusiasms they inculcated—his vast and ornate estate overlooking the Tweed River remains a lasting testimony to the faith, vision, and passion of this remarkable man who almost single-handedly wrenched Scotland out of the dregs of self-immolation. Abbotsford became a combination folly, museum, and worldview proclamation of the great man's quirkiness, amiability, generosity, chivalry, virtue, family pride, and national integrity.

1557 Agnes Prest, one of the famous Exeter martyrs, was martyred during the bitter reign of England's Bloody Mary. Agnes was originally from Cornwall, but lived for a while in Exeter as a servant. Later she returned to Cornwall and married a man who lived in Launceton. They made their living spinning. Agnes was uneducated but learned much of the New Testament by heart from the preaching of Lollards and other itinerant Protestant preachers. She was arrested for her faith and after a long imprisonment during which she refused to return to Catholicism, she was condemned to die. She was led outside the city walls to Southernhay by the sheriff and city officials and burned at the stake. Her last words were, "I am the Resurrection and the Life, saith Christ. He that believeth in Me, though he were dead, yet shall he live, and he that believeth in Me shall never die."

1769 French emperor Napoleon Bonaparte was born on the island of Corsica.

1773 Samuel Johnson, while visiting Edinburgh, met James Boswell's wife, who complained bitterly of his manners and her husband's relationship with him: "I have seen many a bear led by a man, but I never before saw a man led by a bear."

1785 Thomas de Quincey, author of *The Confessions of an English Opium Eater*, was born in Manchester.

1834 Richard Henry Dana left Boston Harbor aboard the brig *Pilgrim*, bound on the journey he would immortalize in *Two Years Before the Mast*. He was just nineteen years old at the time.

1887 Novelist and playwright Edna Ferber was born in Kalamazoo, Michigan. She suggested that, "The ideal view for daily writing, hour on hour, is the blank brick wall of a cold-storage warehouse. Failing this, a stretch of sky will do, cloudless if possible."

1888 T. E. Lawrence, better known as Lawrence of Arabia, was born in Tremadoc, North Wales. Lawrence was a spy for Britain and led the Arab revolt against the Turks during World War I. His book *Seven Pillars of Wisdom* is his account of those events.

1929 The world distance record for a nonstop flight was set by the *Graf Zeppelin*, which flew 6,980 miles from Germany to Tokyo in just under 102 hours.

1935 Humorist Will Rogers and aviator Wiley Post were killed when their airplane crashed near Point Barrow, Alaska.

1945 "VJ Day" was proclaimed by the Allies, a day after Japan agreed to surrender unconditionally.

1947 India became independent after some two hundred years of British rule.

1948 The Republic of Korea was proclaimed.

1969 The infamous Woodstock Music and Art Fair opened at a dairy farm in upstate New York.

1971 President Nixon announced a ninety-day freeze on wages, prices and rents. Afterward, former president Lyndon Johnson commented that the Republican administration of Nixon was "fulfilling all of the campaign promises of the Democratic ticket. You almost don't need the Democrats if the Republicans are willing to do all our dirty work for us."

AUGUST

The lowest subdivision of society, is that by which it is broken into private families; nor do any duties demand more to be explained and enforced, than those which this relation produces; because none are more universally obligatory, and perhaps very few are more frequently neglected.

[SAMUEL JOHNSON (1709–1784)]

FEAST DAY
St. Stephen of Hungary, St. Armel, St. Arascius

For more than forty years Rufus King (1755–1827) served his country as a state legislator, member of Congress, delegate to the Constitutional Convention, senator, minister to Great Britain, and candidate for vice president, and president. He helped draft both the Northwest Ordinance and the Constitution, which he signed and later supported at the Massachusetts ratification convention.

A student during most of the war, King began his public service as a member of the Massachusetts legislature, where he demonstrated his interest in the national cause by championing a bill that provided for regular financial support to the Congress of the Confederation. Later, while serving in Congress, he joined with Jefferson in contributing an antislavery provision to the Northwest Ordinance, the document that prescribed the conditions for the formation of new states from the Northwest Territory. At the Constitutional Convention, where he was recognized as one of the most eloquent speakers, King maintained his position against slavery and supported the idea of a national government with clear authority beyond that of the states.

As a member of the first U.S. Senate, the Federalist King supported the policies and programs of Washington's administration. He backed Hamilton's financial plans and began serving as a director of the Bank of the United States—an institution he helped to establish—on this day in 1794. In 1796 he resigned from the Senate to become minister to Great Britain, a position that taxed his considerable diplomatic ability—helping to keep America neutral while France and Britain were at war.

In the elections of 1804 and 1808, King was a vice presidential candidate, running both times on the unsuccessful Federalist ticket with Charles Cotesworth Pinckney of South Carolina. In 1816 King was himself the Federalist candidate for president, losing to James Monroe.

Back in the Senate, King continued to serve as an eloquent spokesman for Federalist principles. In 1820 he opposed the Missouri Compromise—with the admission of Missouri as a slave state—citing its failure to deal squarely with the problem of slavery. Forcefully but unsuccessfully, he advocated the abolition of slavery. Handsome and sociable, King achieved success as a legislator and diplomat, and he won high praise as a speaker from one of America's most celebrated speakers. Of King, Daniel Webster wrote: "You never heard such a speaker. In strength, and dignity, and fire; in ease, in natural effect, and gesture as well as in matter, he is unequaled."

1861 Despite lacking the authority to impose legal trade sanctions, President Abraham Lincoln prohibited the states of the Union from trading with the seceding states of the Confederacy. The action brought protests and threats of further secession from New York, Delaware, Maryland, Missouri, Iowa, and the president's home state of Illinois.

AUGUST

1762 Samuel Johnson and Joshua Reynolds set out on their famous walking tour of Devonshire.

1772 Like many of his fellow members of the Society of Friends—commonly known as the Quakers—John Woolman resisted use of what he considered "heathen" names for months or days. Thus, throughout his famous journal, the dates are noted in a somewhat cumbersome style: "twelfth of ninth month." This day, the sixteenth of the eighth month of 1772, was a Sunday. Two months earlier Woolman had arrived in England to visit the Quaker community there. He made the arduous six-week trip in steerage from America. As it turned out, the journey had broken his health—thus, the sixteenth day of the eighth month was the last entry in his journal. Two months later he was dead at the age of fifty-two. The journal, which modestly does not describe his own influences, feelings, or struggles, was published shortly afterward, and its unaffected simplicity of style has been recognized ever since as a masterpiece of American literature.

1774 Voltaire wrote to Frederick the Great after hearing of Lord Chesterfield's death, "He was the only Englishman who ever argued for the art of pleasing as the first duty of life."

1777 American forces joined with the independent army of the Republic of Vermont to defeat the British during the Revolutionary War battle of Bennington, Vermont.

1812 Detroit fell to British and Indian forces in the War of 1812.

1858 England's Queen Victoria and U.S. President James Buchanan exchanged introductory messages on the first transatlantic cable. On July 28 of this year, four ships belonging to England and the U.S. met in the mid-Atlantic, spliced wires together, and headed for their respective ports in Valentia, Ireland, and Trinity Bay, Newfoundland, laying the cable as they went. The 1,950 miles of cable proved to be weak, and service was suspended less than a month after it began.

1894 George Meany, pioneering labor union organizer and the first president of the AFL-CIO, was born in New York City.

1898 Edwin Prescott patented the first roller coaster.

1919 Cleveland Indians shortstop Ray Chapman was hit in the head by a pitch from New York's Carl Mays. Chapman's skull was fractured, and he died the next day, becoming the only major-league baseball player ever killed in a game.

1948 Baseball legend Babe Ruth died in New York at age fifty-three.

1949 Margaret Mitchell, author of the blockbuster *Gone with the Wind*, died in Atlanta shortly after being struck by a taxi. She was just forty-eight.

1954 *Sports Illustrated* was first published by the Time-Life magazine group.

1956 Adlai E. Stevenson was nominated for president at the Democratic national convention in Chicago. It would be his second consecutive attempt to defeat the incumbent, Dwight D. Eisenhower.

1960 Britain granted independence to the Crown Colony of Cyprus despite bitter strife between the Greek Christian majority and the Muslim Turkish minority.

1977 Rock-and-roll pioneer Elvis Presley died at his mansion, Graceland, in Memphis, Tennessee, at the age of forty-two.

16

AUGUST

The sin of egotism always takes the form of withdrawal. When personal advantage becomes paramount, the individual passes out of the community.

[RICHARD WEAVER (1910–1963)]

483

NATIONAL DAY
Indonesia
FEAST DAY
St. Joan Delanoue; St. Mamas; St. Liberatus of Capua; St. Rock or Roch; St. Clare of Montefalco; St. Hyacinth; St. Eusebius, pope

AUGUST

Dante Alighieri was born and raised in the vibrant pre-Renaissance environment of medieval Florence. His family was descended from minor nobility, and he was able to maintain a solidly bourgeois status throughout his life. At various times he served as a cavalryman in the Florentine army, an apothecary in the local guild of physicians, an ambassador in the city's diplomatic corps, a political administrator for the municipal government, and an envoy in service to the papacy. But his promising public career came to an end on this day in 1301. He fell out of favor when the political climate in the city changed dramatically, and he was eventually banished.

But what was by all appearances a tragic turn of events for Dante proved to be a propitious and beneficent gift to posterity. It was while he was skulking about Venice in exile that he wrote the bulk of his immortal poetic trilogy, *The Divine Comedy.*

If Venice were not known for its stunning architecture, romantic canals, feats of commercial prowess, naval dominance, glorious art, sumptuous cuisine, or singing gondoliers, it would still have to be remembered for this: Dante was given sanctuary there; and there Dante composed some of the most sublime verses ever set down by mere mortal man.

The masterful work is a kind of spiritual autobiography, mapping the subterranean ecology of his soul. It is an epic allegorical description of a journey through Hell *(Inferno),* Purgatory *(Purgatorio),* and finally Heaven *(Paradisio).* Utilizing soaring images, complex rhyming schemes, brisk plotting, compelling characterizations, and gripping contemporary illustrations, he created both a new vision for vernacular poetry and a new perspective of human psychology. The result is nothing short of stunning.

According to Harold Bloom, besides Shakespeare, "No other literary master, working in any language, so compellingly stretches the boundaries of human creativity, divine passion, and angelic beauty." Arthur Qiller-Couch stated that *Inferno* "broke every literary mold and shattered every artistic expectation." Dante's "eloquence, vitality, and sheer expansive poetic vision," he said, "elegantly reshaped the whole scope of epic literature as only a Homer, a Milton, or a Shakespeare ever has." John Buchan asserted that Dante's *Inferno* was "an essential first component of a well-rounded education, the initial course in a curriculum of wisdom and delight. It is at the core of the Western canon."

How appropriate, then, that it should have been composed to a large degree in Venice, a divine city that earlier had practically invented the ethos of medieval mystery and then later wrenched the Italian city-states toward the Renaissance with its expansive vision and voracious appetites. Theirs was an unplanned and undesired partnership—but one that ultimately shaped the destiny of men and nations in ways that perhaps either alone could never have.

1786 American frontiersman, soldier, and politician Davy Crockett was born in Hawkins County, Tennessee. In his 1834 *Biography*, Crocket wrote, "I leave this rule for others when I'm dead, Be always sure you're right—then go ahead." The hero died during the final defense of the Alamo.

1807 With exclusive rights to operate steamboats in New York granted by the United States Congress, Robert Fulton launched his invention on its first trip. The ship, later named the *Clermont*, made its way from Albany to New York City—150 miles—in 32 hours. Commercial operations began the next year.

1843 In Honolulu, Herman Melville signed aboard the frigate *United States* and began the journey that would form the basis for his novel *White Jacket*.

1858 Lifting off from Lafayette, Indiana, the first air mail in the United States was posted via hot-air balloon.

1863 Federal batteries and ships bombarded Fort Sumter in Charleston Harbor during the War Between the States.

1896 A prospecting party discovered gold in Alaska, a finding that touched off the Klondike gold rush.

1917 John Reed and Louise Bryant set sail for Russia to report on the political upheaval there for Max Eastman's anarchist and socialist tabloid, *The Masses.*

1925 John Hawkes, author of the novel *The Blood Oranges*, was born in Stamford, Connecticut.

1932 Novelist and travel writer V. S. Naipaul was born in Trinidad.

1943 The Allied conquest of Sicily was completed as U.S. and British forces entered Messina.

1945 Indonesian nationalists in the vast Pacific archipelago declared their independence from the Netherlands.

1962 East German border guards shot and mortally wounded eighteen-year-old Peter Fechter, who had attempted to cross the Berlin Wall into the western sector. It was an incident that greatly heightened tensions between East and West and became an emblem of the escalating Cold War.

1969 The Woodstock Music and Art Fair concluded near Bethel, New York after a disastrous week of overcrowding, rain, mud, drugs, nudity, free love, and the near bankruptcy of the promoters.

1978 *The Double Eagle II*, a hot-air balloon, carried three Americans—Ben Abruzzo, Max Anderson, and Larry Newman—across the Atlantic for the first successful crossing in a balloon. They traveled approximately 3,200 miles, from Presque Isle, Maine, to 60 miles west of Paris in 137 hours, 18 minutes.

1987 Rudolf Hess, the last member of Adolf Hitler's inner circle, died at a Berlin hospital near Spandau Prison at age ninety-three, having apparently committed suicide.

17

AUGUST

I try to avoid that species of intensely offensive spiritual pride which takes the form of sniggering conceit in being heterodox.

[THEODORE ROOSEVELT (1858–1919)]

FEAST DAY
*St. Helena, Saints Florus and
Laurus, St. Agapitus, St. Alipius,
St. Beatrice or Brites da Salva*

AUGUST

One of the most influential social critics of the Victorian Age, Thomas Carlyle wrote with a distinctive, energetic voice. The style that fueled his political and historical writings was perhaps best exemplified in his portraits of his contemporaries. On this day in 1840, he met the elderly poet laureate William Wordsworth. The account of the meeting, written sometime afterward by Carlyle, provided readers with a substantial insight into both men.

Carlyle wrote, "On that summer morning I was apprised by Taylor that Wordsworth had come to town, and would meet a small party of us at a certain tavern in St. James's Street, at breakfast, to which I was invited for the given day and hour. We had a pretty little room, quiet though looking streetward (tavern's name is quite lost to me); the morning sun was pleasantly tinting the opposite houses, a balmy, calm and sunlight morning. Wordsworth, I think arrived just along with me; we had still five minutes of sauntering and miscellaneous talking before the whole were assembled. I do not positively remember any of them, except that James Spedding was there, and that the others, not above five or six in whole, were polite intelligent quiet persons, and, except Taylor and Wordsworth, not of any special distinction in the world. Breakfast was pleasant, fairly beyond the common of such things. Wordsworth seemed in good tone, and, much to Taylor's satisfaction, talked a great deal; about poetic correspondents of his own; then about ruralties and miscellanies. Finally, he spoke of literature, literary laws, practices, observances, at considerable length, and turning wholly on the mechanical part, including even a good deal of shallow enough etymology, which was well received. On all this Wordsworth enlarged with evident satisfaction, and was joyfully reverent of the wells of English undefiled; though stone dumb as to the deeper rules and wells of Eternal Truth and Harmony, which you were to try and set forth by said undefiled wells of English or what other speech you had. For the rest, he talked well in his way; with veracity, easy brevity and force, as a wise tradesman would of his tools and workshop—and as no unwise one could."

Carlyle concluded with a remarkably vivid description of the literary lion: "His voice was good, frank and sonorous, though practically clear distinct and forcible rather than melodious; the tone of him businesslike, sedately confident; no discourtesy, yet no anxiety about being courteous. A fine wholesome rusticity, fresh as his mountain breezes, sat well on the stalwart veteran, and on all he said and did. You would have said he was a usually taciturn man; glad to unlock himself to audience sympathetic and intelligent, when such offered itself. His face bore marks of much, not always peaceful, meditation; the look of it not bland or benevolent so much as close impregnable and hard: a man *multa tacere loquive paratus*, in a world where he had experienced no lack of contradictions as he strode along. He had a vivacious strength looking through him which might have suited one of those old steel-grey markgrafs whom Henry the Fowler set up to ward the marches and do battle with the intrusive heathen in a stalwart and judicious manner."

1227 The Mongol conqueror Genghis Khan died. He had united the single largest empire the world had ever known, stretching from the South China Sea to the frontier between Europe and Asia. He left a legacy of organizational efficiency that would enable his heirs to maintain some semblance of the empire for half a millennium.

1587 Virginia Dare was born at Roanoke Island, North Carolina, as the first child born in England's American colonies. She was the daughter of Ananias and Eleanor Dare, who were sent out from England by Sir Walter Raleigh on May 8, 1587.

1773 James Boswell and Samuel Johnson embarked on their seven-week tour of the Hebrides.

1774 Meriwether Lewis, the American explorer of Lewis and Clark fame, was born near Charlottesville, Virginia. Lewis had a special talent for natural history which included botany and zoology. While on the expedition to the Pacific, he made detailed notes about plants and animals that were unfamiliar to Americans and Europeans. Lewis was selected for the trip because of his position as President Thomas Jefferson's personal secretary.

1782 William Blake, age twenty-four, married Sophia Boucher, a beautiful but illiterate peasant whom he would teach to share his love of literature.

1846 American forces led by General Stephen W. Kearney captured Santa Fe, New Mexico, during the Mexican War.

1850 While his wife of five months waited indifferently for the end, Honoré de Balzac died in Paris at age fifty-one, regretting that his own character, Dr. Biachon of *La Comedie Humaine*, was not there to save him.

1894 Congress established the Bureau of Immigration.

1914 President Wilson issued his Proclamation of Neutrality, aimed at keeping the United States out of the First World War.

1920 Tennessee became the thirty-sixth state to ratify the Nineteenth Amendment to the Constitution, which guaranteed the right of all American women to vote.

1958 The lurid novel of obsession and forbidden love *Lolita*, by Vladimir Nabokov, was published in the United States, creating a scandalous uproar.

1963 James Meredith became the first African American to graduate from the University of Mississippi.

1991 Soviet hard-liners launched a military coup aimed at toppling President Mikhail S. Gorbachev, who was vacationing in the Crimea. The coup collapsed three days later when Gorbachev's political rival, Boris Yeltsin, courageously resisted the takeover.

1997 Beth Ann Hogan became the first coed in the Virginia Military Institute's 158-year history.

AUGUST

His honor rooted in dishonor stood,
And faith unfaithful kept him falsely true.

[ALFRED, LORD TENNYSON (1809–1892)]

FEAST DAY

St. Mocha, Saints Agapius and Timothy, St. Sebald, St. Thecla, St. Andrew the Tribune, St. Sixtus III, St. Berulf of Bobbio, St. Louis of Anjou, St. John Eudes, St. Credan of Evesham

AUGUST

The Marquess Archibald Campbell, Earl of Argyll (1598–1661), defied Oliver Cromwell's English Protectorate and invited the exiled Charles II to return to Scotland to receive his crown on this day in 1650. A Scots Presbyterian, Argyll was the leader of the Covenanters, and at the onset of the first phase of the English Revolution, he had forced King Charles I to submit to the demands of the Scottish Parliament—so his role in reestablishing the monarchy was seen as more than a little ironic.

The Covenanters had long been devoted to maintaining Presbyterianism as the faith of Scotland. As a consequence they were largely responsible for establishing the supremacy of Parliament over the monarchy. In reality though, the Covenanters were merely following an old Scottish tradition dating back to the Arbroath Declaration of 1320. Other early covenants—the written documents that bound them to their sacred cause—had been signed as recently as 1557 and 1581 by King James.

When Charles I came to the throne in 1625, he was immediately opposed by the Scottish bourgeoisie because of his policy of oppressive taxation and by the Scottish nobility because of his attempts to impose the Anglican church on Scotland. In 1638 the old covenant of 1581 was revived, and its signatories added a vow to protect the Reformation in their land. Charles, fearing a revolution, convened a General Assembly of Scotland in November 1638. Consisting exclusively of Covenanters, the assembly defied royal authority and abolished the Anglican episcopacy. The resulting First Bishops' War (1639) was settled by referring the dispute to another General Assembly and to a new Scottish Parliament. But the new assembly reaffirmed the decisions of its predecessor, and a Second Bishops' War resulted, during which Charles was defeated at Newburn.

Similar conflicts led the English Parliament to join the Scots in their opposition to Charles, and the Solemn League and Covenant was adopted by the two Parliaments in 1643 launching a united civil war between Royalists and Parliamentarians across the boundaries of the two nations. During the First Civil War (1642–1646) the Covenanters fought side by side with the Parliamentarians. Eventually, Charles surrendered to the Covenanters in 1646. But because he still refused to subscribe to the Solemn League and Covenant, he was turned over to the English.

After the king's execution in 1649, the Scots became increasingly alarmed by the tyrannical ambitions of the English. During what was known as the Second Civil War—the Parliamentarian leader Oliver Cromwell conquered Scotland. As a consequence, Argyll brought Charles II to Scotland and crowned him king of Scotland at Scone. Ironically, Charles II turned on the man most responsible for his restoration. In 1660, Argyll was arrested on a charge of having collaborated with Cromwell in the infamous invasion of Scotland. Though the charges were patently false, Argyll was tried by the Scottish Parliament and was convicted and beheaded.

1646 John Flamsteed, who became the first Astronomer Royal in 1675, was born in England. It was for Flamsteed that Charles II built the Royal Observatory at Greenwich, just outside London.

1812 *Old Ironsides*—officially christened the USS *Constitution*—defeated the British frigate HMS *Guerriere* in a furiously fought naval battle off the coast of Nova Scotia during the War of 1812.

1848 The *New York Herald* reported the discovery of gold in California.

1917 Cameron Townsend said good-bye to his friends and family at the Los Angeles train station and headed for San Francisco to take a ship to South Central Mexico, where he would serve as a missionary distributing the Bible to unreached jungle tribes. Townsend found the work difficult and at times almost despaired of going on. He was revolted by the food, unable to communicate, homesick, heat sick. In addition, he was discouraged to discover that the tribal peoples did not speak or read Spanish. Within a year he determined to translate the Scriptures into the very difficult Cakchiquel language. Overcoming great obstacles, he learned the language, wrote it down, created dictionaries, lexicons, and grammars, and finally translated the Gospel of Mark. His extreme difficulties proved to give birth to a new vision for him. Townsend and several missionary friends founded the Summer Institute of Linguistics—with a course of study specifically designed to teach new missionaries how to break and translate native languages. It became his goal to have someone translate the Bible into each of the languages of Mexico. But as the missionaries began to multiply, Townsend found it necessary to create a whole new mission organization to accommodate the expanding vision. Thus was born the Wycliffe Bible Translators, reportedly the world's largest mission today.

1929 The comedy program *Amos and Andy*, starring Freeman Gosden and Charles Correll, made its network radio debut on NBC.

1934 A plebiscite in Germany approved the vesting of sole executive power in the National Socialist leader Adolf Hitler.

1950 The American Broadcasting Corporation (ABC) began airing Saturday morning television shows for children.

1960 A tribunal in Moscow convicted American U-2 pilot Francis Gary Powers of espionage.

1976 President Ford won the Republican presidential nomination at the party's convention in Kansas City after a fierce challenge by former California governor Ronald Reagan.

1977 Comedian Groucho Marx died in Los Angeles at age eighty-six.

1989 Polish president Wojciech Jaruzelski formally nominated Tadeusz Mazowiecki to become Poland's first non-Communist prime minister in four decades.

1991 Soviet president Mikhail Gorbachev, vacationing in the Crimea, received word that a coup d'état had been staged by a coalition of hard-line Communists in Moscow. Gorbachev had an appointment the next day to sign a treaty that would have given away much of the U.S.S.R.'s centralized government power to its smaller republics. After three days, tremendous public outcry forced the coup leaders to give up their efforts, and they were taken into custody.

AUGUST

Boldness is prudence. Courage is manliness.

[James Longstreet (1821–1904)]

AUGUST

Edward Stratemeyer was arguably among the most prolific and influential American authors. Indeed, he wrote more and sold more than almost any other writer who has ever lived anywhere at any time—some 1,300 novels selling in excess of 500 million copies. He created more than 125 different series—many of them familiar and beloved American cultural icons.

You say you've never heard of him? Well maybe you know him by one of his many pseudonyms: Franklin W. Dixon, Victor Appleton, Carolyn Keene, Roy Rockwood, Laura Lee Hope, or Ralph Bonehill. Still doesn't ring a bell? Surely you're familiar with his famous characters: the Hardy Boys, Nancy Drew, Tom Swift, the Rover Boys, Jack Ranger, Bomba the Jungle Boy, the Dana Girls, the Bobsey Twins, Dave Dashaway, and Don Sturdy. All were invented by this lone writer: Edward Stratemeyer.

At the height of his career in the twenties, he employed an entire syndicate of editors, copywriters, stenographers, coauthors, and secretaries just to keep up with his prodigious creativity. With their assistance he was able to produce an astonishing literary legacy, practically inventing an entirely new genre of juvenile fiction. Alas, since his death in 1930, most of his classic stories for young readers have been ruthlessly modernized and rewritten—with deleterious results—and his familiar characters have been co-opted by the big New York publishing combines. Thus, the recent release of these two volumes is welcome news.

The Minute Boys of Lexington is a vintage Stratemeyer story. It focuses on the daring adventures of a teenager and his pals unexpectedly caught up in breathless action, stirring intrigue, and dark mystery. The hero of this tale, set during the early days of the American War of Independence, is Roger Morse. He is a witness to—indeed, he is a participant in—the remarkable events leading up to the clash of the Lexington and Concord militias with the hated Red Coats of King George's army. Throwing in his lot with the likes of John Hancock, Paul Revere, and Thaddeus Bowman, he left an indelible mark on the unfolding American drama.

The Minute Boys of Bunker Hill finds young Roger and his friends in the thick of the action again, this time just adjacent to Boston at the Battle of Bunker Hill. The awful specter of the battlefield, the hazards of prison, and the deprivations of the home front cannot deter him and his young friends from their patriotic duty. Once again, he stands side by side with some of the greatest men of his day, including Samuel Adams, Joseph Warren, and William Prescott.

Including reproductions of original illustrations, helpful glossaries, crisp typesetting, sturdy bindings, and clean design, these books are part of an impressive enterprise launched by the Lost Classics Book Company to resurrect the ideas and values of an earlier, more enduring American civilization. To have the incomparable work of Edward Stratemeyer at the forefront of such an enterprise bodes well—both for it and for us.

1153   Saint Bernard, one of the greatest influences in medieval monasticism, died in France. He often taught his disciples the great benefits of meditation as opposed to mere ardor and study: "You will find something far greater in the woods than you will find in books. Stones and trees will teach you that which you never will learn from masters."

1591   English poet and cleric Robert Herrick, who also wrote his name as Errick, Heyrick, and Hearick, was born in London. "Whenas in silks my Julia goes,/Then, one thinks how sweetly flows/That liquefaction of her clothes," he wrote in *Upon Julia's Clothes.* Though this work and his other poems tended to be about or for women, he remained a celibate. His most often quoted advice is "Gather ye rosebuds while ye may."

1619   The first slaves brought to the American colonies of England arrived at a Virginia port aboard a Dutch ship.

1866   President Andrew Johnson formally declared the War Between the States was now over—the fighting had actually ended months earlier.

1881   Humorist Edgar Guest was born in Birmingham, England.

1904   The Abbey Theater was founded in Dublin, Ireland.

1914   German forces swept across their northern frontier and occupied Brussels, Belgium, during the First World War.

1940   In a speech extolling the success of the Royal Air Force during the Battle of Britain, Winston Churchill said, "Never in the history of human conflict was so much owed by so many to so few."

1944   During an uprising against the Nazi and Vichy rulers led by the French Resistance in Toulouse, novelist and playwright André Malraux took command of the St. Michel prison.

1964   President Lyndon Johnson launched his War on Poverty. The Department of Health, Education and Welfare was given the monumental task of consolidating and administering each of the initiatives. Eventually, its budget grew to be the third largest in the world, exceeded only by the overall budget of the United States federal government and that of the former Soviet Union. Its strategy involved the creation or expansion of well over one hundred social welfare agencies. Their efforts included major programs such as Social Security, Unemployment Insurance, Medicare, Medicaid, Aid to Families with Dependent Children (AFDC), Supplemental Security Income (SSI), and Food Stamps, as well as a myriad of minor programs, including special supplemental feeding for Women, Infants, and Children (WIC), the Intensive Infant Care Project (ICP), Rent Supplements, Urban Rat Control, and Travelers' Aid.

1968   The Soviet Union and other Warsaw Pact nations began invading Czechoslovakia to crush the Prague Spring liberalization drive of Alexander Dubcek's regime.

1977   The U.S. launched *Voyager 2,* an unmanned spacecraft carrying a twelve-inch copper phonograph record containing greetings in dozens of languages, samples of music, and sounds of nature.

1979   Endurance swimmer Diana Nyad succeeded in her third attempt to swim from the Bahamas to Florida.

AUGUST

*A*wake, awake, put on strength, *A*wake as in the ancient days, in the generations of old.

[ISAIAH OF JERUSALEM (C. 750 B.C.)]

Gerard Groote labored only ten years for Christ, but in that short amount of time he helped to change the face of Europe and pave the way for the Reformation. Born in 1340, he was converted in 1374 after an early life of luxury. Educated in Germany and Poland, as well as at the University of Paris, where he studied theology, medicine, and astronomy, he was solidly entrenched in medievalism's elite.

But immediately after his conversion he gave up almost everything he owned. After two years as a guest in a Carthusian monastery, Groote became a deacon and obtained permission to preach. As a traveling preacher, he worked his way through the Lowlands—Flanders, Guelders, and Holland—teaching the word of God and decrying the abuses prevalent in the church. So severe were Groote's attacks on the errors of the church that his authorization to preach was revoked. Afterward, he gathered a group of men around him who were dedicated to translating the Bible into the vernacular, caring for the poor, and establishing schools for common folk. The band became known as the Brethren of Common Life.

Eventually, the brethren formed dozens of households all over the northern, central, and western regions of Europe. Groote taught them the monastic principles of Augustine of Hippo—though the men did not take monastic vows, nor were they bound to remain celibate. Any could leave the group at any time. Their aim was to live the life of Christ while engaged in service. Their way of life became known as *Devotio Moderna*—the modern way of serving God—which provided a model for reform in the days to come. But the biggest impact of the brethren was in the area of education.

AUGUST

The brethren produced a large number of famous pupils. Nicholas of Cusa, (1401–1464) was a German cardinal, scholar, mathematician, scientist, and philosopher. As a doctor of canon law, he wrote in defense of the conciliar theory that asserted the supremacy of church councils over the pope. The Habsburg archduke Sigismund strongly opposed his elevation to the church hierarchy because of Cusa's proposals for reform.

Another famous student was Thomas à Kempis, who wrote the devotional classic *The Imitation of Christ*. Born in Kempen and educated at a brethren house in Groote's hometown of Deventer, his writings best represented the *Devotio Moderna*.

Yet another pupil, Erasmus Desiderius (1466–1536), was the Dutch writer, scholar, humanist, and the chief interpreter to northern Europe of the intellectual currents of the Italian Renaissance. He became the greatest scholar of his age and an agent of reform.

Likewise, Luther, Melanchthon, and Calvin were all educated in brethren schools. Thus, Groote's efforts proved to be the seedbeds for every significant reform that took place in Europe over the course of the next two centuries, earning him Luther's praise as the "Father of the Reformation."

1560 An eyewitness account of a total eclipse in the Iberian Peninsula stated, "The sun remained obscured for no little time, there was darkness greater than that of night, no one could see where they trod and the stars shone brightly in the sky: the birds, moreover, wonderful to say, fell down to the ground in fright at such startling darkness . . . amid the scream of women who cried that the last day of the world had arrived."

1680 Pueblo Indians took possession of Santa Fe, New Mexico, after driving out the Spanish.

1831 Former slave Nat Turner led a violent insurrection in Virginia. He was later captured, tried, and executed.

1850 At the Pere Lachaise Cemetery in Paris, Victor Hugo delivered a funeral oration for Honoré de Balzac, who had died three days earlier: "Monsieur Balzac was one of the first among the greatest, one of the highest among the best. All his books together make one book—a book of glory and splendor and might."

1858 The famous debates between senatorial contenders Abraham Lincoln and Stephen Douglas began.

1878 The American Bar Association was founded in Saratoga, New York.

1920 Christopher Robin Milne, the son of A. A. Milne and the model for the human hero of the *Winnie the Pooh* books, was born in London. As an adult he would complain bitterly, "The fictional Christopher Robin and his real-life namesake were not always on the best of terms. In pessimistic moments, it seemed to me, almost, that my father had got to where he was by climbing upon my infant shoulders. Quite frankly, I can hardly stand the thought of those books—Pooh and Piglet and Eeyore are but lamentable, even detestable, characters in my sight. I was robbed of my childhood by the very stories that seem to have defined the childhood of myriads of others. Such is the awful irony of celebrity."

1940 Exiled Communist revolutionary Leon Trotsky died in Mexico City from wounds inflicted by an assassin who attacked him in his study with a hatchet.

1945 President Harry Truman ended the Lend-Lease Program that had shipped some $50 billion in aid to America's allies during World War II.

1983 Philippine opposition leader Benigno S. Aquino, ending a self-imposed exile in the United States, was assassinated moments after stepping off a plane at Manila International Airport.

1983 The ribald, raucous, and controversial musical play *La Cage aux Folles* opened on Broadway.

1991 The hard-line military coup against Soviet president Mikhail S. Gorbachev collapsed in the face of a popular uprising led by Russian federation president Boris N. Yeltsin.

1996 Shakespeare's *Two Gentlemen of Verona* was the premiere performance at the new Globe Theatre in London, modeled on the Bard's original venue.

AUGUST

*T*rain your tongue to offer solace, your heart to offer sympathy, and your hand to offer mercy.

[PETER LORIMER (1812–1879)]

When John Witherspoon (1723–1794) was inducted as the new president of Princeton, lamps in every window of the college's Nassau Building were lit and the light shone across the countryside for miles. The fact that he had consented to lead the venerable institution was quite an accomplishment. Witherspoon, a prominent Scottish preacher, had a successful ministry in his homeland and was reluctant to leave it for the New World. His wife was even more reluctant—in fact, it took the fervent persuasion of Benjamin Rush to get her to agree to the move. At last though, Witherspoon relented, sailed for America, and stepped into history as one of the most influential men in the history of America.

Born near Edinburgh and educated at the university there, he joined with many of his Covenanter friends in supporting the great Rising of Bonnie Prince Charlie in 1745 against the English. When the Duke of Cumberland defeated the young Stuart Pretender, Witherspoon was imprisoned for his Jacobite sympathies. Upon his release he held Presbyterian pastorates in and around Fife until 1768, when he came to America.

Besides developing and enlarging the Princeton campus and academic program, Witherspoon furthered the growth of the Presbyterian Church in America. He launched an initiative that helped to plant dozens of new parish churches in the areas affected by the revivals of the Great Awakening.

He was also a strong advocate of freedom in the civic arena. When the colonies began to chafe against the petty tyrannies of Parliament, Witherspoon lent his considerable reputation to the cause of independence. He was a man of presence and of great energy. Indeed, only George Washington commanded more respect than he did. His voice was so influential that Horace Walpole commented, "Cousin America has eloped with the Presbyterian Parson."

A member of the Continental Congress (1776–1779, 1780–1782), he signed the Declaration of Independence and was a delegate to the New Jersey convention of 1787 that ratified the U.S. Constitution. But Witherspoon did not neglect Princeton for politics. He taught a strict Calvinist theology and dramatically upgraded the overall curriculum—he added French, history, international law, philosophy, and speech to course offerings. Of the 478 graduates he trained, many rose to occupy high offices—including one president, several senators and congressmen, dozens of judges, and a multitude of pastors.

It was on this day in 1768 that Witherspoon established his office at the college and launched the remarkable work that would inevitably transform the nation—and through it, the rest of the world.

AUGUST

1485 England's King Richard III was killed in the Battle of Bosworth Field, ending the War of the Roses.

1567 Francis de Boisy—later known as St. Francis of Sales—was born. He was raised in a godly home—for instance, the de Boisy family personally fed five hundred poor a day for several weeks during the terrible famine of 1570. Francis became a Jesuit and preached with great power in the region of Chablais, near Lake Geneva, where by his life and his words he led many Protestants back to Roman Catholicism. His father had resisted this appointment, believing his son would be killed. Indeed, the work at first seemed both fruitless and dangerous. Several times he barely escaped assassins. Once he was treed by wolves and only the kindness of a Calvinist couple saved his life. He wrote and copied little tracts by hand that gradually won over the people of the region. Francis wrote two books, *Introduction to the Devout Life* and *Treatise on the Love of God*, which detail the call of every believer to a holy life—both are widely read to this day. His contemporaries said they had never known another man to demonstrate such a holy life as Francis.

1775 England's King George III declared that his American colonies were in a state of open rebellion.

1787 Inventor John Fitch demonstrated his steamboat on the Delaware River to delegates of the Continental Congress.

1846 The United States annexed New Mexico.

1851 The schooner *America* outraced the *Aurora* off the English coast to win a trophy that became known as the *America's Cup*—named for the ship, not the country.

1862 French innovative composer Claude Debussy was born in St. Germain-en-Laye. Debussy frustrated his music instructors because his intuitive style of composition broke all the established rules of harmony and counterpoint. His instinct for orchestral color and sound enhanced the ability of his music to convey the essence or impression of a poem or nature. His music is the aural equivalent to a painting by Monet.

1893 Author, poet, critic, and wit Dorothy Parker was born in West Bend, New Jersey.

1902 President Theodore Roosevelt became the first U.S. chief executive to ride in an automobile, in Hartford, Connecticut.

1911 It was announced in Paris that Leonardo da Vinci's *Mona Lisa* had been stolen from the Louvre Museum the night before. The painting turned up two years later in Italy.

1956 Incumbent president Dwight Eisenhower and Vice President Richard Nixon were nominated for second terms in office by the Republican national convention in San Francisco.

1968 Pope Paul VI arrived in Bogota, Colombia, for the start of the first papal visit to Latin America.

AUGUST

That religion which God requires, and will accept, does not consist in weak, dull, lifeless wishes, raising us but a little above a state of indifference. God in His Word, greatly insists upon it, that we be in good earnest, fervent in spirit, and our hearts vigorously engaged in mercies.

[JOHN WITHERSPOON (1723–1794)]

NATIONAL DAY
Romania
FEAST DAY
*St. Rose of Lima, Saints Asterius
and Claudius, St. Philip Benizi,
St. Eugene or Eoghan of Ardstraw*

In one of his renowned New York lectures, on this day in 1842, the American transcendentalist poet and essayist Ralph Waldo Emerson called for an authentic American culture to celebrate the common, everyday things in American life. His talk that day, entitled "The Poet," would later act as the basis for one of his most celebrated essays. The topic was familiar. For the past half-century, many American artists and critics like Emerson had sought to establish a truly national culture, not one perceived to be a pale imitation of Europe. The United States had achieved its political independence with the American Revolution, but to many observers, its cultural independence had yet to be achieved.

Emerson's message in "The Poet" was that the search for an authentic American art should be less about formal technique than the ability of the artist to find beauty in the unlikeliest of places. "Readers of poetry see the factory-village and the railway, and fancy that the poetry of the landscape is broken up by these; for these works of art are not yet consecrated in their reading," Emerson explained. He was searching for a poet to celebrate—or even consecrate—the factory and the railroad and all the other things common to workaday American society. Unfortunately, no one had stepped forward to perform such consecrations by creatively exploring topics of everyday life. "I look in vain for the poet I describe," he lamented.

But unknown to Emerson, the young poet Walt Whitman was in the audience that day. He decided that it was his destiny to heed Emerson's call. During the next decade Whitman wrote his renowned *Leaves of Grass*, a book of poems that extolled the people and places of the United States. At the time, Whitman was a twenty-three-year-old editor and occasional reviewer for the New York newspaper *Aurora*. He had already begun to write poems—although he would not publish his first collection for more than a decade—and he admired Emerson's approach. "The lecture was one of the richest and most beautiful compositions, both in manner and style heard anywhere, at any time," Whitman later asserted.

Whitman knew the rhythms of the factory-village and railway far better than Emerson himself. A Long Island farm boy who had come to New York City as a young man, Whitman spent years walking the streets of Manhattan and Brooklyn, talking with—and more important, listening to—its clerks, firemen, prostitutes, and gang members, incorporating their voices into his work. When in 1855 he finally published *Leaves of Grass*, he did so with a strong sense of having answered Emerson's call for an American poet. Indeed, he claimed that he had long been "simmering" until Emerson had brought him "to a boil." Thus were the lives of two of the most important American poets of the nineteenth century intertwined.

1775   King George III of England called upon his loyal subjects in the American colonies—which were now in open rebellion against Crown and Parliament—to act as informants against all disloyal subjects.

1305 The Scottish patriot Sir William Wallace was hanged, drawn, beheaded, and quartered in London. As a message to Scottish freedom fighters, parts of his body were sent to Newcastle, Berwick, Stirling, and Perth. The threat failed to quell the hunger of the Scots for independence, and as a result, the grassroots struggle actually gained a tremendous amount of popular support. Eventually, even the nobility who had delivered Wallace into the hands of the English joined them.

1754 France's ill-fated King Louis XVI was born at Versailles.

1784 The area of modern east Tennessee declared itself to be an independent state named Franklin, after Benjamin Franklin. The Continental Congress rejected this claim and returned control of the territory to the jurisdiction of North Carolina.

1926 Rudolph Valentino, American film actor, died at the age of thirty-three. His funeral in New York City stretched for eleven blocks, and his death resulted in worldwide hysteria and several suicides.

1927 Italian-born anarchists Nicola Sacco and Bartolomeo Vanzetti were executed in Boston for the murders of two men during a 1920 robbery. Despite overwhelming evidence linking them to the crime, Sacco and Vanzetti were absolved of guilt in 1977 by Massachusetts Governor Michael S. Dukakis.

1939 The two great Socialist nations in the world, Nazi Germany and the Soviet Union, signed a nonaggression treaty.

1944 Romanian prime minister Ion Antonescu was dismissed by King Michael, paving the way for Romania to abandon the Axis in favor of the Allies during the Second World War.

1948 The World Council of Churches was established in Amsterdam. Though most Christians regularly professed the truth of the Nicean Creed that there is but "one holy catholic and apostolic church," the reality of a fragmented church professed an entirely different message. Almost from the inception of the Reformation, with its breakup of the Western church, men had tried to restore unity—some by sword, some by reason, and some by goodwill. Martin Bucer worked to iron out divisions within Protantism; Liebnitz tried to gather an international conference to discuss reunification of Lutherans and Catholics; Hugo Grotius cried like a voice in the wilderness not only for international law but also reconciliation; John R. Mott organized the International Missionary Conference held in Edinburgh in 1910; Bishop Charles Brent of the United States returned from Edinburgh and created the World Conference of Faith and Order; following the First World War, Archbishop Nathan Söderblom of Uppsala spearheaded a drive to bring Christian leaders to Stockholm in 1925 for a Life and Work conference at which time he proposed creating a World Council of Churches; in a 1937 meeting at Utrecht, the Life and Faith and the Faith and Order movements united and set up a preliminary headquarters in Geneva; after the Second World War, the hunger for a united ecumenism was greater than ever and the dream of a World Council was at last fulfilled.

1960 Broadway librettist Oscar Hammerstein died in Doylestown, Pennsylvania.

1979 Dancer Alexander Godunov defected from the Soviet Union while the Bolshoi Ballet was on tour in New York.

AUGUST

Custom reconciles us to everything.

[EDMUND BURKE (1729–1797)]

FEAST DAY
St. Bartholomew, The Martyrs of
Utica, St. Audenoeus or Ouen

Catherine de Medici (1519–1589) was the queen of France and mother of the last three Valois kings during one of the most tumultuous eras in European history. She was a major force in French politics during the thirty years of Roman Catholic–Huguenot wars and an instigator of the Massacre of Saint Bartholomew's Day.

Catherine was born on April 13, 1519, in Florence, Italy, the daughter of Lorenzo, Duke of Urbino, and the great-granddaughter of the Florentine ruler Lorenzo de Medici, called Lorenzo the Magnificent. In 1533 she married the duc d'Orléans, who became King Henry II in 1547. On the death of her first son Francis in 1560, the government fell entirely into her hands. She ruled as regent for her second son, Charles IX, until he reached his majority in 1563, and she dominated him for the duration of his reign.

In her determination to preserve royal power at any cost, Catherine devoted her energies to maintaining a balance between the Catholics who were led by the powerful house of Guise and the Protestants—popularly known as the Huguenots—who were ably led by Gaspard de Coligny.

During the religious civil wars that began in 1562, Catherine, a Roman Catholic, usually supported the Catholics; sometimes, however, political expediency led her to switch her support to the Huguenots. Her political manipulations also affected the personal affairs of her family. In 1560 she arranged for her daughter, Elizabeth of Valois, to become the third wife of the powerful Roman Catholic king of Spain, Philip II. But in 1572 Catherine found it propitious to marry another daughter, Margaret of Valois, to the Protestant king Henry of Navarre, who later became Henry IV, king of France.

On this day in 1572 she found the growing Huguenot influence over her son Charles, the French king, frightening, so she instigated the plot to assassinate the Protestant leader Coligny that led to his death and the deaths of an estimated 100,000 other Huguenots in the Massacre of Saint Bartholomew's Day. The massacre spread from Paris to the provinces and sundered the fabric of the entire nation. Despite the horrific consequences of the slaughter, a gleeful Pope Gregory XIII struck a special medallion to commemorate the "holy" act.

The massacre that day was not the end of the matter. When the Protestant Henry of Navarre converted to Catholicism in order to gain the crown of France, he granted his Huguenot compatriots a number of rights under the Edict of Nantes. These rights were gradually eroded. A cycle of Huguenot revolts and persecutions ultimately forced 400,000 to flee the country during the reign of Louis XIV.

79 The city of Pompeii was consumed and buried by hot ash from the sudden eruption of Mount Vesuvius. Years later the site would be unearthed to reveal an amazingly well-preserved Roman culture, providing insight into the halcyon days of the Pax Romana.

1456 The printing of the first Gutenberg Bible was completed in Mainz.

1524 Increasing resentment against the heavy exaction of the feudal system, crop failure in Stühlingen, the writings of Luther, and new biblically derived notions of the equality of man precipitated the tragic Peasant's Revolt of 1524–1525. On this day, Hans Müller gathered a few Stühlingen peasants around him. Calling themselves the "Evangelical Brotherhood," the men swore to emancipate the peasants of Germany. Their twelve-point platform anticipated the liberties that would actually be achieved throughout Christendom after years more of struggle. It was based on Zwingli's teachings. Among its demands was the right of local congregations to choose and dismiss their pastors. Tithes should be collected justly and used for the modest support of pastors, the rest given to alleviate the poor. Serfdom must end. The oppressive rents charged the peasants must be eased. Death taxes must be eliminated, for they robbed widows and orphans. Though the demands seemed reasonable enough, the war-skilled rulers crushed the revolt everywhere with great cruelty. More than 100,000 peasants died, and the misery of those who remained was greatly worsened.

1682 The Duke of York awarded William Penn three counties in the American colonies, which eventually were consolidated into the state of Delaware.

1759 English philanthropist and slave-trade abolitionist William Wilberforce was born on this day. Educated at Cambridge, Wilberforce was elected to Parliament in 1780. He became a Christian in 1784 and worked for social reform from that point on. He was the chief spokesman for the abolition movement in the House of Commons. In 1807, the slave trade was abolished, and in 1833 the Emancipation Bill that abolished slavery went into effect.

1814 The British set fire to the United States Capitol Building and the White House when they took Washington, D.C., during the War of 1812.

1847 Charlotte Brontë dispatched *Jane Eyre* to the publishing house of Smith, Elder & Company under the pseudonym of Currer Bell.

1869 Cornelius Swartwout received a United States patent for the waffle iron.

1892 Two weeks before his death, John Greenleaf Whittier wrote his last poem—an eighty-third-birthday tribute to Oliver Wendell Holmes.

1899 Argentine poet and author Jose Luis Borges was born in Buenos Aires.

1932 Amelia Earhart became the first woman to fly nonstop across the United States, traveling from Los Angeles to Newark, New Jersey, in just over nineteen hours.

1949 The North Atlantic Treaty went into effect.

1954 The Communist Control Act went into effect, virtually outlawing the Communist Party in the United States.

1959 Three days after Hawaiian statehood, Hiram L. Fong was sworn in as the first Chinese-American U.S. senator while Daniel K. Inouye was sworn in as the first Japanese-American U.S. representative.

AUGUST

1968 France became the world's fifth thermonuclear power when it exploded a hydrogen bomb in the South Pacific.

Both the liberals and the conservatives have lost definition. Neither one can make us know what a tradition might.

[ANDREW NELSON LYTLE (1902–1995)]

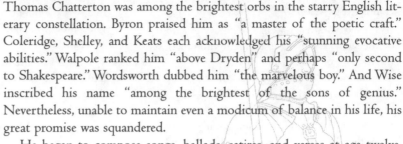

AUGUST

Thomas Chatterton was among the brightest orbs in the starry English literary constellation. Byron praised him as "a master of the poetic craft." Coleridge, Shelley, and Keats each acknowledged his "stunning evocative abilities." Walpole ranked him "above Dryden" and perhaps "only second to Shakespeare." Wordsworth dubbed him "the marvelous boy." And Wise inscribed his name "among the brightest of the sons of genius." Nevertheless, unable to maintain even a modicum of balance in his life, his great promise was squandered.

He began to compose songs, ballads, satires, and verses at age twelve. When his mother, an impoverished widow, secured his apprenticeship with a Bristol scrivener three years later, he turned his hand to political essays, elegies, criticism, and social commentary. In 1768, when he was just sixteen, he startled editors, antiquaries, and critics by publishing a brilliant eyewitness memoir of the dedication of an old bridge by ancient Benedictine friars. The beautiful account—he told the public—was merely translated from a brittle old manuscript found, with others of like character, in a muniment room over the chapel of a local rural parish house.

In short succession he published a whole series of the papers—historical, theological, and poetical—each piquing the interest of experts and common readers alike. Chatterton maintained they were written by a fifteenth-century monk, Thomas Rowley. Though most of the medieval academics of the day questioned the authenticity of the manuscripts, the undeniable beauty and stunning maturity of the pastoral eclogues made them doubt that a neophyte like Chatterton could have manufactured such an elaborate ruse much less have written such magnificent literature.

So despite their persistent misgivings, several publishers began accepting the precocious writer's purported translations for their journals—paying him liberal fees. Chatterton quickly plunged into the rough-and-tumble literary world. He frequented the theaters, dressed fashionably, and drank profligately. He boldly rejected the faith of his childhood and embraced a life of defiant worldliness. As quickly as his star had risen, it suddenly fell. Though his advances and royalties were quickly squandered, he intensified his dissolute lifestyle. Going without food or sleep for days on end, he wrote ceaselessly with a tortured passion unequaled in English letters. Then he would indulge in drinking sprees, carousings, and fierce street brawls.

Such a sad public spectacle made editors reluctant to publish his work—even though its beauty and originality continued to be unimpeachable. Chatterton simply had exhausted his welcome. Tragically, he had exhausted his body as well. Early on this day in 1770, finally weighed down and worn out by circumstances of his own making, the poetic genius took his own life. When the door of his small attic room was broken open the next day, hundreds of small sheets of paper—covered with his florid handwriting—were scattered across the floor. He was just eighteen when the parish sextons buried him in an unmarked pauper's grave.

1531 Thomas Bilney was martyred for his faith. Bilney was a meek man, very scrupulous and tender-minded, who was ordained as a priest in 1519. His reading of both Erasmus and the Bible led him to conclude that salvation came through Christ alone. Rites, rituals, works, he began to believe, were mere emptiness unless done in Christ. His sweetness of character and devotion to Scripture soon won a number of prominent men—including Hugh Latimer, John Lambert, Matthew Parker, and Robert Barnes—to Christ. Freed from the need to work to attain salvation, Bilney worked even harder. He slept seldom, ate little, prayed much, and obtained a license to preach throughout the countryside. Alarmed by Bilney's growing popularity and influence, Cardinal Wolsey had him arrested and condemned. He cheerfully went to his death. After urging a large crowd to godliness, he was burned at the stake. Even as the flames engulfed his body he continued to cry out, "Trust Jesus," and "I believe."

1560 The Protestant faith was formally recognized in Scotland.

1718 The territory of Louisiana welcomed eight hundred French immigrants who eventually founded New Orleans.

1732 The modern missionary movement was launched when several men from Count Zinzindorf's Herrnhut community agreed to serve as missionaries in the far-flung fields of Greenland and the Caribbean. Christian David, a Moravian carpenter, volunteered to go to Greenland, while David Nitschmann and Hans Dober volunteered to serve in St. Thomas.

1814 The United States Library of Congress, along with its three thousand volumes, was destroyed by the British during the War of 1812.

1825 Uruguay declared independence from Brazil.

1875 Captain Matthew Webb became the first person to swim across the English Channel. He swam from Dover, England, to Calais, France, in twenty-two hours.

1916 The National Park Service was established within the Department of the Interior.

1918 American composer, conductor, and educator Leonard Bernstein was born in Lawrence, Massachusetts. Bernstein is known for his contributions to the field of music education as well as his promotion of American music. His most famous compositions include *West Side Story, On the Town, Candide,* three symphonies, and *On the Waterfront.*

1921 The United States signed a peace treaty with Germany, three years after the cessation of hostilities in the First World War.

1944 Paris was liberated by Allied forces after four years of Nazi occupation.

1989 Congressman Barney Frank, a Democrat serving Massachusetts, acknowledged hiring a male prostitute as a personal employee, then firing him after suspecting the aide was selling sex from Frank's apartment.

AUGUST

The great ancients' writings, beside ours,
Look like illuminated manuscripts
Before plain press type.

[PHILIP JAMES BAILEY (1816–1902)]

FEAST DAY
St. Bergwine, Archbishop of Canterbury; St. John Wall; St. Mary Desmaisieres; St. Pandonia; St. Teresa Jornet Ibars

AUGUST

Like the plot in one of his best-selling novels, the life of John Buchan was full of improbable adventures and prodigious achievements. He was one of the most accomplished men of the twentieth century. He was by turns a successful barrister, respected scholar, popular journalist, trusted diplomat, prolific author, efficient colonial administrator, innovative publisher, progressive politician, relentless reformer, and active churchman. Best known for his historical romances and thrilling spy novels—he practically invented the genre—he was also the author of more than a hundred nonfiction works, including an authoritative multivolume history of the First World War and biographies of Oliver Cromwell, Caesar Augustus, Lord Montrose, and Walter Scott.

He was born in Scotland on this day in 1875, the eldest son of a minister in the Presbyterian Free Church. He was of regal Scottish stock—a countess of Buchan had crowned Robert the Bruce, an earl of Buchan had avenged Joan of Arc as constable of France, a Buchan of Auchmacoy had fallen at Flodden beside the king, and another had led the Jacobite remnant after the death of Dundee—but it was his early years in the strict Calvinistic manse that would shape his worldview and stimulate his imagination for the rest of his life. Following a brilliant academic career at the University of Glasgow he transferred to Oxford.

Upon graduation, he joined the foreign service in South Africa. Afterward, he began a successful career in journalism and publishing. But the First World War interrupted his plans. He helped to establish the British spy network during the war and continued his prolific writing. After the war he was elected to Parliament representing the Scottish universities, a position he held until 1935. Meanwhile, between 1922 and 1936 he wrote five books a year. For much of that time he was ranked among the world's best-selling authors alongside his friends and acquaintances Rudyard Kipling, G. K. Chesterton, and Hilaire Belloc. Several of his books were made into full-length motion pictures. Though his work was popular, it often explored serious theological themes and profound human dilemmas.

His great prominence made him an appropriate choice as the king's High Commissioner to the General Assembly of the Church of Scotland for several years. The post enabled him to promote the vital relationship between the dynamics of the Christian life and the preservation of Western civilization—a relationship he believed was threatened by the hubris of modern secularism. It was a theme that resonated throughout all his work. "Our enemies are attacking more than our system of Christian morals on which our civilization is founded" he lamented. "They are attacking Christianity itself, and they are succeeding. Our great achievements in perfecting the scientific apparatus of life have tended to produce a mood of self-confidence and pride. We have too often become gross materialists in our outlook on life." Buchan died suddenly on February 12, 1940, at his official residence in Ottawa residence, where he served as the governor general. The sad news made front-page headlines around the world.

1776 Scottish philosopher and historian David Hume died in Edinburgh.

1826 Felix Mendelssohn completed the "Overture" of *A Midsummer Night's Dream* at the age of seventeen. Mendelssohn's entire mature compositional style was solidified by the age of sixteen or seventeen due to his attentiveness to the masters who had gone before him—including the greatest single influence in his life, Johann Sebastian Bach.

1846 Felix Mendelssohn's oratorio *Elijah* was first performed in Birmingham, England.

1847 The African slave resettlement colony of Liberia was proclaimed an independent republic.

1883 The ever-curious Ralph Waldo Emerson sought out Thomas Carlyle in Cumberland. He was able to wrangle a dinner invitation from the notoriously antisocial Carlyle and thus was begun one of the literary world's most remarkable lifelong friendships.

1893 Jack London returned to San Francisco after spending eight months on a seal-hunting expedition aboard the *Sophia Sutherland.*

1904 Christopher Isherwood was born in Disely, Cheshire. Three years spent in Berlin just before the Second World War would inspire him to write a series of stories about his lover Sally Bowles, providing the source for the play *I Am a Camera,* which in turn became the musical and film *Cabaret.*

1939 The first televised major-league baseball games were shown on experimental station W2XBS. It was a double-header between the Cincinnati Reds and the Brooklyn Dodgers at Ebbets Field.

The Reds won the first game, 5-2, the Dodgers the second, 6-1.

1957 The Soviet Union announced that it had successfully tested an intercontinental ballistic missile.

1958 English composer, teacher, writer, and conductor Ralph Vaughan Williams died on this day. He successfully wove English folk songs into art music forms with such works as *Fantasia on Greensleeves,* the opera *Pilgrim's Progress,* and nine symphonies.

1961 The official International Hockey Hall of Fame opened in Toronto.

1964 President Lyndon Johnson was nominated for a term of office in his own right at the Democratic national convention in Atlantic City, New Jersey.

1972 The summer Olympic Games opened in Munich, West Germany.

1974 Charles Lindbergh, the first man to fly solo, nonstop across the Atlantic, died at his home in Hawaii at age seventy-two.

1978 Cardinal Albino Luciani of Venice was elected the 264th pope of the Roman Catholic Church following the death of Paul VI. The new pontiff took the name Pope John Paul I.

AUGUST

There is the moral of all human tales;
'Tis but the same rehearsal of the past,
First freedom, then glory—when that fails,
Wealth, vice, corruption—barbarism at last,
And history, with all her volumes vast,
Hath but one page.

[LORD BYRON (1788–1824)]

FEAST DAY
St. Caesarius of Arles, St. David Lewis, Little St. Hugh, St. Monica, St. Margaret the Barefooted, St. Marcellus of Tomi, St. Poemen

Though rarely credited as being particularly innovative or farsighted, Harry Truman actually established several important policy precedents during his term in the White House that ultimately helped to define the nation's political tenor for the entire generation that followed. Shortly after taking office upon the death of Franklin Roosevelt, he made the momentous decision to use atomic weapons to end the Second World War. Later he initiated the Truman Doctrine, sending military and economic aid to states threatened by Communism. His Marshall Plan made Europe's postwar recovery possible, and he was instrumental in the establishment of both the United Nations and the North Atlantic Treaty Organization (NATO). His Fair Deal program for domestic reform reduced the centralized power of the lumbering New Deal bureaucracy while achieving improvements in service delivery.

Known for his no-nonsense demeanor and tough-as-nails convictions, he kept two signs on his desk in the Oval Office. One said, "The buck stops here." But the other lesser known sign said, "Always do right. This will gratify some people and astonish the rest." He decided to place the sign on his desk after a particularly difficult day in the Oval Office on this day in 1949.

Both signs spoke volumes about his sense of duty and his moral character. The first bore vivid testimony to the fact that he was willing to accept responsibility for the policies and decisions of his administration. In an age of blame-shifting and finger-pointing, that is admirable in and of itself. But the second sign demonstrated that he accepted a standard of right and wrong that despite its popular neglect remained the barometer of integrity and virtue.

You might be able to argue with his politics—as most conservatives have ever since—but it would be difficult to fault Harry Truman's conviction that in the end there is an absolute of right and wrong that transcends our ever-shifting, ever-changing fashions and fancies.

AUGUST

1770

German philosopher Georg Wilhelm Hegel was born at Stuttgart. Hegel sought to systematize philosophy in a manner that would explain all of life as the Absolute. One of his main thoughts concerned thesis, antithesis, and synthesis. A thesis creates the need for opposition in the antithesis, which eventually leads to a synthesis of the truth present in both the thesis and antithesis. This synthesis is then formed as a thesis, and the process begins again. The cosmic goal of self-consciousness arrives through the rational understanding of the Absolute. At this point, Hegel introduced the idea of God, arguing that "God is God, only in so far as he knows himself." Hegel wrote many influential books that had a profound impact on later thinkers such as Marx, Engels, and Kierkegaard.

55 B.C. At about ten o'clock in the morning, Julius Caesar landed his troops approximately eight miles north of Dover. For his invasion of the lands of the British Celts, he brought some eight thousand Roman marines in eighty ships.

1575 The greatest Venetian painter of the sixteenth century, Titian, died in Venice on this day. His later works provided an alternative to the linear and sculptured look of the Florentine painters. He achieved an equal power and aesthetic by softening the edges of his subjects in a manner that had profound influence on later schools of art.

1660 Because he had written several tracts against the power of the monarchy, John Milton's friends forced him into hiding when Charles II gained the throne of England. They so feared for his life that Milton's friends staged a mock funeral for the author of *Paradise Lost*. When Charles heard of Milton's funeral, he said that he "applauded his policy in escaping the punishment of death by a reasonable show of dying." Unsatisfied with a lack of public spectacle, the king ordered the hangman to burn as many copies of Milton's writing as could be found on this day.

1665 The first play known to be performed in America was *The Bare and Ye Cubb*, presented in Acomac, Virginia.

1667 The first recorded hurricane in North America was reported from Jamestown, Virginia.

1859 Colonel Edwin L. Drake drilled the first successful oil well in the United States near Titusville, Pennsylvania.

1883 Thirty-six thousand people died when the volcano on the island of Krakatoa between Java and Sumatra erupted. The blast was reportedly heard 3,000 miles away, and dozens of ships were sunk by a subsequent tidal wave. A hundred miles away in Batavia, a downpour of thick black mud drenched the area, and ash was scattered over 3,300 miles. The volcano, once spent, collapsed and fell under the sea.

1892 The Metropolitan Opera House in New York City was devastated by fire that destroyed not only the building, but also a million dollars' worth of costumes and scenery.

1894 Congress passed the Wilson-Gorman Tariff Act, which contained a provision for a graduated income tax. The legislation was struck down by the U.S. Supreme Court as unconstitutional.

1908 Lyndon B. Johnson, the thirty-sixth president of the United States, was born near Stonewall, Texas.

1910 Mother Teresa was born in Skopje, Yugoslavia. She spent her life caring for the destitute and discarded in the slums of Calcutta. In 1979, she was awarded the Nobel Peace Prize for her work.

1945 American troops began landing in Japan following the surrender of the Japanese government in the Second World War.

1967 Brian Epstein, manager of the pop music phenomenon the Beatles, was found dead in his London flat from an overdose of sleeping pills. The group never fully recovered from his loss and slowly began to drift apart.

AUGUST

1979 British war hero and mentor to the royal family, Lord Louis Mountbatten, was killed off the coast of Ireland in a boat explosion. Responsibility was claimed by the Irish Republican Army.

As counsel of both times—of the ancient time what is best, and of the latter time what is fittest.

[FRANCIS BACON (1561–1626)]

FEAST DAY

*St. Augustine of Hippo, St.
Alexander of Constantinople, St.
Edmund Arrowsmith, St. Julian of
Brioude, St. Moses of Abyssinia*

The 1963 March on Washington attracted an estimated 250,000 people for a peaceful demonstration to promote civil rights for African Americans. Participants walked down Constitution and Independence Avenues, then—a century after the Emancipation Proclamation—gathered before the Lincoln Monument for speeches, songs, and prayer. Televised live to an audience of millions, the march provided a number of dramatic moments—but the most memorable of all was Dr. Martin Luther King Jr.'s stirring "I Have a Dream" speech. Far larger than any other previous demonstration for any other cause, the march had an obvious and immediate impact, both on the passage of civil rights legislation and on nationwide public opinion. It proved the power of mass appeal and inspired imitators in the antiwar, pro-life, and environmental movements.

As early as 1941 Philip Randolph—international president of the Brotherhood of Sleeping Car Porters, president of the Negro American Labor Council, and vice president of the AFL-CIO—had discussed the possibility of such a march. Thus, he was seen as the chief organizer. But because the march was also sponsored by five of the largest civil rights organizations in the United States, planning was complicated by dissension among the groups. Known in the press as "the big six," the leaders included Randolph and King as well as Whitney Young, president of the National Urban League; Roy Wilkins, president of the NAACP; James Farmer, founder and president of the Congress of Racial Equality; and John Lewis, president of the Student Nonviolent Coordinating Committee. In the end though, they were able to iron out their differences.

On this day the marchers arrived. They came in chartered buses and private cars, on trains and planes—one man even roller-skated to Washington from Chicago. By midday, more than 200,000 had gathered by the Washington Monument, where the march was to begin. It was a diverse crowd: black and white, rich and poor, young and old, Hollywood stars and everyday people. Despite the fears that had prompted extraordinary precautions—including pre-signed executive orders authorizing military intervention in the case of rioting—the marchers walked peacefully to the Lincoln Monument.

Dr. King, the last speaker of the day, was introduced by Randolph as "the moral leader of our nation." His speech, eloquent on the page, was electrifying when spoken. With the passionate, poetic style he had honed in the pulpit, King stirred the audience and built to an extemporaneous crescendo: "I have a dream today. I have a dream that one day every valley shall be exalted, every hill and mountain shall be made low, the rough places will be made plains, and the crooked places will be made straight, and the glory of the Lord shall be revealed and all flesh shall see it together."

As marchers returned home, the organizers met with the president, who encouraged them to continue their work. By all counts, the march was a success. But just three weeks later, the bombing of the Sixteenth St. Baptist Church in Birmingham, Alabama—which killed four young girls—reminded all Americans that the dream had yet to be realized.

AUGUST

430 Theologian, author, apologist, and philosopher St. Augustine, Bishop of Hippo, died on this day. The influential African patriarch was the philosophical founder of Western civilization. His most influential works, essential to the Western Canon of great books, include *Confessions* and *The City of God*.

1609 Henry Hudson discovered Delaware Bay.

1736 While crossing over the Savock River near Preston, Lancashire, a man witnessed a midair collision of two large flocks of birds. The impact was such that more than 180 birds fell to the ground, either unconscious or dead. Not being one to miss opportunity, the man gathered the birds and sold them the same day at the market in Preston.

1748 The first Lutheran synod in the American colonies was established. German Lutherans had begun arriving in Pennsylvania as early as 1683 under the leadership of Frank Pastorius, and many more followed in the succeeding years. In 1741, Pastor Henry Melchior Muhlenberg accepted the call to come to Pennsylvania. He reached Philadelphia on November 15, 1742. He established innumerable congregations in and around the city and helped to launch the first synod. Although very informal, with no constitution in the beginning, the synod gave form and focus to the Lutheran communities throughout the region. From 1754 to 1760 no regular meetings were held, but in 1760, primarily through the influence of Muhlenberg's friend Provost Karl Magnus Wrangel, the synod meetings were revived. The constitution for the mother congregation in Philadelphia, St. Michael's, was written by Muhlenberg and adopted in 1762. It became a model for many Lutheran congregations. By 1781 the constitution of the Evangelical Ministerium of North America was completed.

1749 Johann Wolfgang von Goethe, German poet, dramatist, and scientist, was born in Frankfurt am Main. He was the greatest figure of the German Romantic movement, and his plays and lyrics have influenced generations of authors and composers who came after him. His masterpiece, the drama *Faust*, took fifty-plus years to complete.

1904 Darius Baker, Justice of the First District Court, sentenced a man to five days in the Newport County Jail, Newport, Rhode Island, for speeding in his automobile. This was the man's second offense, as he had been fined $15 on August 21 for driving between 15 and 20 mph.

1930 The Marx Brothers' comedy *Animal Crackers* was released.

1938 The School of Speech of Northwestern University in Evanston, Illinois, conferred an honorary degree on ventriloquist dummy Charlie McCarthy during the NBC broadcast of *The Edgar Bergen-Charlie McCarthy Hour* in Chicago. The degree was "Master of Innuendo and Snappy Comeback."

1947 Legendary bullfighter Manolete was mortally wounded by a bull during a fight in Linares, Spain. He died the following day at age thirty.

1955 Emmett Till, a black teenager from Chicago, was abducted from his uncle's home in Money, Mississippi, by two white men after he had supposedly whistled at a white woman; he was found brutally murdered three days later.

1968 Police and antiwar demonstrators clashed in the streets of Chicago as the Democratic national convention nominated Hubert H. Humphrey for president.

AUGUST

The recollection of the past is only useful by way of provision for the future.

[SAMUEL JOHNSON (1709–1784)]

AUGUST

After the scandals of the previous three administrations the Republican Party was concerned to choose an especially upright candidate in the nation's centennial year, 1876. They found him in Rutherford B. Hayes (1822–1893), a devout, conscientious Midwesterner whose Puritan ancestors had come from New England.

In his third term as governor of Ohio, Hayes was known for an honest administration, constructive reforms, and a strong stand on sound money—one of the leading issues of the day. In addition, he had an outstanding military record—performing gallantly and emerging a major general. He was apparently above reproach. Yet it is one of the quirks of history that such a man should reach the White House through the very questionable settlement of a bitterly disputed election—although most historians believe that Hayes himself was not personally involved.

The settlement was in the hands of a special electoral commission that happened to have a majority of Republicans. But the Republicans had chosen well—better than some of them knew. For President Hayes proved to be too honest and forthright for many of them, who could hardly wait to get him out of office.

Despite political undercurrents, Hayes made good use of his one term to stabilize the government on several fronts. He officially ended Reconstruction on this day in 1877; he withdrew Federal troops from the occupied Southern states; he established reforms in civil service; he took courageous steps to settle the railroad strike of 1877; and he stood firm in enforcing a sound money policy—all in the face of vigorous opposition.

The man chosen to remove the taint of scandal from the government proved to be surprisingly resolute and effective; his dedication to principle and his courageous and forthright actions won him the type of praise earned by very few one-term presidents.

1645

On his deathbed Hugo Grotius lamented the worthlessness of all he had done in his life. He died convinced he was a failure. Born Huig de Groot, by the time he was eleven he was called a second Erasmus. At age fourteen he completely revised Martianus Capella's encyclopedia, having read all the ancient authorities for himself. He followed this with translations of Simon Stevin and Aratus. When he was fifteen he held public disputations and was made attaché to the great John van Barneveld on a crucial peace mission. By age seventeen he had argued his first legal case and at twenty-two had written a book that embodied his best ideas in embryonic form. As a result of the political snarls that engulfed most of Europe during the seventeenth century, he was exiled when he began to propound a new vision of freedom based upon Christian law. His books *Mare Liberum* and *The Law of War and Peace* provided the theoretical basis for the Peace of Westphalia in 1648, which afterward became international law. Alas, he did not live to see his triumph.

1533 Atahualpa, Peru's last Incan king, was killed on orders from Spanish conqueror Francisco Pizarro.

1632 English philosopher John Locke was born in Wrington. He was the first great English philosopher of the Scientific Revolution and his thought greatly influenced the Founding Fathers—especially his manifesto on political freedom, *The Second Treatise on Government.*

1758 The first United States Indian reservation was established by the New Jersey legislature on a tract of 1,600 acres.

1869 Friedrich Ramseyer and his wife, Victoria, departed to become missionaries at Kumassi on the West Coast of Africa. Because the couple's preaching was perceived to be a threat to the Narideggi chieftain Prempeh and his hoard of witch doctors, they were kidnapped and held for four years. Finally rescued in 1874, the Ramseyers left Africa to recover in England. For twenty-two years the Ramseyers prayed that God would provide a way for them to return to Africa. Meanwhile, the denizens of Kumassi groaned under the oppression of the blood-thirsty king. Prempeh killed a slave each night following a lavish feast, solely for his own enter-tainment. Once a year during a "festival of yams," he immolated six hundred of his subjects in a grisly celebration. He had even gone so far as to slaughter four hundred virgins to give the walls of his palace a rich red color by mixing their innocent blood with the mortar. Yielding to the Ramseyers' incessant lobbying and cajol-ing, the British returned to the region in 1895. They immediately deposed the tyrant-king. Soon after, the residents of Kumassi welcomed the missionaries back as long-departed friends, where they worked for another twelve years restructuring the Narideggi society and develop-ing an indigenous law code that would, at long last, fully respect the sanctity of life.

1877 The second president of the Mormon Church, Brigham Young, died in Salt Lake City, Utah.

1896 Chop suey was concocted in New York City by a chef attached to visiting Chinese ambassador Li Hung-Chang, who devised this dish to appeal to both American and Oriental tastes. Chop suey was unknown in China at that time.

1937 Industrialist R. G. LeTourneau and his wife, Evelyn, bought a huge tract of land at Winona Lake outside Chicago to establish Camp Bethel. Using help from students of Wheaton College, the couple, who had long served Christ in innu-merable ways, turned the camp into one of the foremost evangelistic and recreational centers in the nation.

1943 Responding to a clampdown by Nazi occupiers, Denmark scuttled most of its naval fleet.

1944 More than fifteen thousand American troops marched down the Champs Elysees in Paris as the French capital continued to celebrate its lib-eration from the Nazis.

1957 South Carolina Senator Strom Thurmond, then a Democrat, ended a filibuster against a civil rights bill after talking continuously for more than twenty-four hours—at one point he resorted to reading from the Washington phone book.

AUGUST

1965 The *Gemini 5* space cap-sule, carrying astronauts Gordon Cooper and Charles "Pete" Conrad, splashed down in the Atlantic after eight days in space.

1966 The Beatles concluded their fourth American tour with their last public concert at Candlestick Park in San Francisco.

In history's mixture of good and evil, the thing we should note——the thing the historians will note with amazement——is the profundity and the rapidity of change.

[HILAIRE BELLOC (1870–1953)]

FEAST DAY
*Saints Felix and Audauctus, St.
Fantinus, St. Pammachius, St.
Margaret Ward, St. Ruan or
Rumon*

During his term as vice president, Thomas Jefferson traveled to Baltimore on official business. He asked for a room in the city's best hotel. Not recognizing the great man—who always traveled quite modestly without a retinue of servants and dressed comfortably in soiled working clothes—the proprietor turned him away.

Soon after Jefferson's departure, the innkeeper was informed that he had just sent away the author of the Declaration of Independence and a hero of the Revolutionary War. Horrified, he promptly dispatched a number of his employees to find the vice president and offer him as many rooms as he required.

Jefferson, who had already taken a room at another hotel, was not at all flattered or amused. He sent the man who found him back with the message, "Tell the innkeeper that I value his good intentions highly, but if he has no room for a dirty farmer, he shall have none for the vice president."

It was not merely the spirit of democratic solidarity or of judicial propriety that piqued Jefferson's ire in that situation. He had always prided himself as a man of the soil first and foremost. He was America's preeminent agrarian theorist. He was an avid gardener and a skilled botanist. His gardening journals have inspired generations of farmers and planters. And his agricultural innovations helped to make American harvests the envy of the world.

He strongly believed that an attachment to the land was the chief mark of an advanced culture. He believed that the fate of a nation was ultimately decided by the attitude of that nation to its soil. He said, "Widespread distribution and careful stewardship over property is the most tangible attribute of liberty. The faith of a people, the vision of a people, the destiny of a people may be divined by its corporate concern for the soil."

To be sure, Jefferson was often a conflicted intellectual, an inconsistent moralist, and an impractical idealist, but his ideas of land, the dignity of labor, the essential nobleness of common men, and the vitality of the agrarian virtues made Jefferson the undisputed father of American populism.

AUGUST

1686

John Eliot, the first missionary to the American Indians, wrote a final letter to his English sponsors: "I am old, ready to be gone, and desire to leave as many books as I can." He had already left a remarkable legacy. Since his arrival among the Algonquin in 1631 he had learned their language, created its alphabet, and translated all sixty-six books of the Bible, a catechism, a primer, and a number of devotional guides. The Indians so loved their books that they had worn out all their copies of the original printings. Though he did not convert a large number of the Indians—and most of those were caught in the middle of King Philip's War and subsequently massacred—for his tireless labors he is called the "Apostle of the Indians."

Cleopatra, queen of Egypt, lover of Julius Caesar, and wife of Marc Antony, took her own life by allowing an asp to bite her.

1659 John Locke published his defense of Christian orthodoxy, *The Reasonableness of Christianity*. It would be the prototype for the study of apologetics throughout the next century. Indeed, virtually all the apologists who followed Locke argued, like him, that Christianity is rational and that common sense and empirical science provide sufficient reason to believe in the God as He is revealed in the Holy Scriptures.

1797 The creator of *Frankenstein*, Mary Wollstonecraft Shelley, was born in London. She was the daughter of the radical philosopher William Godwin and the feminist activist Mary Wollstonecraft. She would become the wife of poet Percy Bysshe Shelley and write her famous philosophical horror story to amuse him and his friends during a vacation in 1818. In the story, scientist Victor Frankenstein infuses life into a collection of inanimate body parts—but the "birth" of his creation overwhelms Frankenstein with the horror of what he has done.

1829 Felix Mendelssohn visited Holyrood Castle in Edinburgh during an extended visit to Scotland. Inspired by this twilight visit, he jotted down sixteen bars of music that became the opening for his *Scottish Symphony* (completed in 1841–1842).

1862 Union forces were once again defeated by the Confederates at the Second Battle of Bull Run in Manassas, Virginia.

1893 Huey P. Long, the "Kingfish" of Louisiana politics, was born in rural Winn Parish.

1904 After living abroad for two decades, Henry James returned to America for a visit.

1929 The General Electric Company of Schenectady, New York, delivered a combination gas and electric automobile to Colonel E. H. Green. The car had a sixty-horsepower engine and utilized two foot pedals for acceleration instead of a clutch or gearshift.

1945 General Douglas MacArthur arrived in Japan and set up the Allied occupation headquarters.

1963 The "Hot Line" communications link between Washington and Moscow went into operation.

1967 The Senate confirmed Thurgood Marshall's appointment as the first African-American justice of the Supreme Court.

1969 At age seventy-seven and in the last year of her life, Dame Ivy Compton Burnett was asked by the *London Times* to comment on her life. The author of the novels *Mother and Son* and *Dolores* replied, "There's not much to say. I haven't been all that deedy."

1983 Guion S. Bluford Jr. became the first African-American astronaut in space, blasting off aboard the shuttle *Challenger*.

AUGUST

Those who are in rebellion against memory are the ones who wish to live without knowledge.

[RICHARD WEAVER (1910–1963)]

NATIONAL DAY
Malaysia, Trinidad, Tobago
FEAST DAY
St. Paulinus of Trier, St. Aidan of Lindisfarne, St. Raymond Nonnatus, The Servite Martyrs of Prague

Theodore Roosevelt was a voracious learner and an avid reader throughout his extraordinary life. It is hard to imagine though, when he might have found the time—his record of public service and his private interests were astonishingly diverse. How he possibly squeezed reading into the crowded hours of his life was a matter of some substantial speculation among those that observed him flash across the stage of history.

Among his friends he counted the greatest writers, thinkers, scholars, and scientists of his day. And by all accounts he was the best read of them all—being readily conversant on everything from the traditional classics to the most recent philosophical, sociological, or technological musings. He usually read at least five books a week—unless he wasn't too busy, in which case, he read more. And yet his attitude toward the torrid pace of his intellectual pursuit was refreshingly relaxed: "I am old-fashioned, or sentimental, or something about books. Whenever I read one I want, in the first place, to enjoy myself, and, in the next place, to feel that I am a little better and not a little worse for having read it."

His son Quentin claimed that he read every book received at the Library of Congress—which of course, he surely did not. But many of his friends testified that however new the volume they recommended to him, he had always read it already. "His range of reading is amazing," wrote the science fiction writer H. G. Wells. "He seems to be echoing with all the thought of the time, and he has receptivity to the pitch of genius." Guglielmo Marconi, the great Italian physicist and inventor, was amazed by his knowledge in the specialized field of Italian history and literature. "That man actually cited book after book that I've never heard of, much less read. He's going to keep me busy for some time just following his Italian reading." And the English diplomat Lord Charnwood asserted, "No statesman for centuries has had his width of intellectual range."

As a result of his relentless studies and his near-perfect recall, his knowledge was highly integrated, and he was continually crossing boundaries, moving back and forth from one area of human knowledge to another. He was thus able to make connections that mere specialists were unable to make.

According to Viscount Lee, "Whether the subject of the moment was political economy, the Greek drama, tropical fauna or flora, the Irish sagas, protective coloration in nature, metaphysics, the technique of football, or post-futurist painting, he was equally at home with the experts and drew out the best that was in them." Indeed, "In one afternoon," said his son Archie, "I have heard him speak to the foremost Bible student of the world, a prominent ornithologist, an Asian diplomat, and a French general, all of whom agreed that Father knew more about the subjects on which they had specialized than they did."

"If you want to lead, you must read," was a maxim that Roosevelt took seriously. It was merely an extension of his whole philosophy of life: making the most of his mind was a piece with making the most of his body. It was merely an exercise of good stewardship.

AUGUST

651 The Irish priest Saint Aiden, bishop of the island of Lindisfarne, died on this day.

1264 Bonaventure, who besides St. Francis himself was the most eminent of the Franciscan friars, preached a bold sermon before Pope Urban IV and his council calling for fundamental reforms in the church. At the time he was the governor-general of his order. Always zealous for souls, he preached much—to rich and poor alike. And his messages emphasized the sovereign work of grace as the means of salvation. Because of the warmth of his relations, his boldness was excused and the papal delegation did not prosecute Bonaventure. Somehow, he managed to avoid the many pitfalls of medieval corruption—and to this day, it is through his influence that Franciscan thought remains largely Augustinian in orientation.

1290 King Edward I issued a proclamation that demanded the exile of all Jews from England forever, under penalty of death.

1688 English author and minister John Bunyan, best known for his allegory of the Christian life, *Pilgrim's Progress,* died in London. And, just like Pilgrim, "So he passed over, and all the trumpets sounded for him on the other side."

1743 The famed Christian apologist William Paley was baptized. A clumsy youth, he turned to study—and became a masterful thinker. Although Paley was sufficiently good at mathematics to become first wrangler of his school, he was determined to become a clergyman. Once he began his parish ministry, he wrote a number of popular apologetics texts. His *View of the Evidences of Christianity* which argued for the credibility of the biblical miracles, became an immediate best-seller. Its sequel, *Natural Theology,* included his famous "watchmaker" argument: If a savage were to find a watch in the middle of the jungle, he would at once suppose it the work of an intelligent being; nature is far more complex and elaborate than a watch and therefore also requires a designer.

1887 Thomas A. Edison received a patent for his "kinetoscope," a device that produced moving pictures.

1888 Mary Ann Nicholls was found murdered in London's East End. She is generally regarded as the first victim of "Jack the Ripper."

1910 Theodore Roosevelt presented his Square Deal policy, which supported labor protection, a standing army of adequate size, and graduated income tax.

1941 The popular radio program *The Great Gildersleeve* debuted on NBC.

1945 World-renowned violinist virtuoso Itzhak Perlman was born in Tel Aviv, Israel.

1980 Poland's Solidarity labor movement was born with an agreement signed in Gdansk that ended a seventeen-day strike.

AUGUST

All heaven and earth resound with that subtle and delicately balanced truth that the old paths are the best paths after all.

[J. C. RYLE (1816–1900)]

SEPTEMBER

During the nineteenth century Scottish nationalism was reborn after a century during which the once-proud nation had all but surrendered both its distinctiveness and its independence to England. Sir Walter Scott fanned the flames of Scots pride with his swashbuckling historical novels, Robert Burns stirred the embers of Scots romanticism with his affecting bucolic verse, and Thomas Chalmers revived Scots vision with his confident covenantal worldview. There was a reawakening of interest in Scottish culture, Scottish history, and Scottish heroes.

By the middle of the century a group of prominent Scots formed a National Monument Committee. Their idea was to capitalize on the new fascination with all things Scottish to build a lasting testimony to faith, family, and freedom—the essential virtues they saw emerging from Scotland's great legacy. It would be a monument featuring the greatest of all the Scots heroes, William Wallace. Initially, the preferred site for the monument was Glasgow Green; however, on the instigation of the Reverend Dr. Charles Rogers, the chaplain at Stirling Castle, the site at Abbey Craig was selected. The land had much to commend it. A high, craggy mound overlooking the river Forth and the broad field of Bannockburn, it was the site of Cambuskenneth Abbey—which had been founded around 1147 by King David I. But more important, it was also at one time the site of a hill fort where in 1297 William Wallace camped before defeating the English at the Battle of Stirling Bridge.

A public subscription was launched and a design competition was organized. The winner was an Edinburgh architect, J. T. Rochead. His design for the monument was a fanciful baronial construction with a soaring medieval tower arising from a broad Laird's courtyard, with an overlook representing the recently recovered Scottish Crown Royal. It bespoke Victorian excess in the vernacular of Scotland—whimsically combining both secular and ecclesiastical elements.

When the foundation stone was laid in 1863, a crowd of seventy thousand was present. But disputes among the National Monument Committee members and financial problems resulted in construction not being completed for six years. But when it finally was completed on this day in 1869, it almost immediately became an icon of the nation's long-held aspirations and dreams.

The monument soared above the Craig nearly 220 feet. The walls were 18 feet thick at the base, tapering to 5 feet thick at the pinnacle—utilizing more than 30,000 tons of stone. A 15-foot-tall solid bronze statue of Wallace was sculpted by David Watson Stevenson and situated approximately 30 feet above the ground. The total effect was altogether awe-inspiring.

Inside the monument, there were four rooms in the tower, of approximately 25 square feet, with vaulted ceilings 30 feet high. Each of the tower rooms was connected by a spiral staircase—with 246 steps to the top. The rooms were to serve as a national museum—the greatest artifact in the collection being the 700-year-old sword Wallace has used throughout his remarkable career. The sword was a traditional two-handed broad-sword, nearly 6 feet long and weighing nearly 50 pounds. The size of the sword indicated that Sir William must have been at least 6'6" tall.

Amazingly, the monument proved to be a catalyst for an even greater awareness of Scotland's unique identity and heritage. As the designer, Rochead, asserted, "Symbols of things are often more powerful in conveying the essence of those things than the things themselves."

SEPTEMBER

NATIONAL DAY
  Libya
FEAST DAY
  St. Fiacre, St. Giles or Aegidiu, St. Drithelm, St. Lupus or Leu of Sens, St. Sebe, St. Priscus of Capua, St. Verena

256 During the widespread Decian Persecutions, which broke out in the Roman Empire between 250 and 252, many Christians poured out libations to the emperor rather than suffer torture. Others bribed the authorities to obtain certificates saying they had sacrificed even when they had not. Later some of these, who were called the lapsi, felt remorse for their betrayal of Christ, who had suffered and died for them. They asked to be readmitted to the church. But schism developed over the issue. Led by Novatian, a number of Christians broke off from the rest of the church, saying no lapsed person should be readmitted. Others, led by Cyprian, argued that the lapsi should be able to be readmitted if they repented and were rebaptized. On this day the North African synod voted unanimously with Cyprian. Alas, that decision did not end the controversy, and just two years later Cyprian himself died a martyr.

1159 Nicholas Breakspear, the only Englishman to become pope, died as Adrian IV.

1807 Former Vice President Aaron Burr was found innocent of treason in a trial that had transfixed the nation for weeks.

1821 The Santa Fe Trail, an overland route from Independence, Missouri, to Santa Fe (in present-day New Mexico), was first traversed by American trader William Becknell. The trail split into two branches—one through Colorado and one through the Cimarron Desert—but both branches led to Santa Fe. Other trails from Santa Fe continued on to Los Angeles (the Old Spanish Trail) and Mexico City (El Camino Real). The route was used until 1880 when a railroad linked the Midwest to the Southwest.

1878 Miss Emma Nutt of Boston became the first female telephone operator in the United States. She retained this position for thirty-three years.

1897 The first section of Boston's subway system was opened.

1939 Germany started the Second World War when Nazi troops poured into Polish territory and took Danzig.

1969 A military coup in Libya brought a heretofore obscure officer, Colonel Mu'ammar Gadhafi, to power.

1972 In Reykajvik, Iceland, Bobby Fisher defeated Russian master Boris Spassky to become the first American to take the World Chess Championship.

1983 A Soviet interceptor aircraft shot down Korean Airlines flight 007, a commercial flight. The plane, en route from New York to Seoul, Korea, had inadvertently strayed one hundred miles off course, drifting into Soviet airspace and over secret military installations. All 269 people on board—including the prominent conservative congressman Larry MacDonald, who had built his reputation on his denunciations of Communist aggression—perished in the Sea of Japan.

SEPTEMBER

The fear o' hell's a hangman's whip
To haud the wretch in order;
But where ye feel your honor grip,
Let that aye be your border.

[ROBERT BURNS (1759–1796)]

SEPTEMBER

FEAST DAY
St. William of Roskilde, The Martyrs of September 1792, St. Agricolus, St. Antoninus of Pamiers, St. Brocard, St. Castor of Apt

In his masterful novel *The Red Badge of Courage*, Stephen Crane traced the effects of war on a single Union soldier, Henry Fleming, from his dreams of soldiering to his actual enlistment, and through several battles of the War Between the States. Unhappy with his dull, quiet, and boring life at home on the farm, Fleming yearns to somehow earn glory and renown for his heroic achievements in battle. After he enlists, however, he discovers that a soldier's life consists of two parts futility, one part confusion, and one part terror. Set at the Battle of Chancellorsville—though it actually remains unnamed in the story—the young idealistic soldier is forced by the dumb certainties of experience to become a hardened realistic veteran. And in the process, he comes to the difficult realization that boring is actually a virtue, not a vice.

The reality is that boring is what most people are actually yearning for—they just don't know it. Boring is having no people to see, no tasks to accomplish, no expectations to meet, no pressures to deal with—it is the ideal adventure. People go halfway around the world to find a secluded beach or a remote cabin or a mountain chalet, just so they can do nothing. It is dull people who have to be stimulated constantly. Something has always got to be going on.

Most modern men and women are addicted to the razzle-dazzle. We want wow. And we want it now. Our whole culture, from popular entertainment to corporate management, is predicated on the idea that our lives ought to be defined by a frenetic go-go-go sense of busyness. There is no time to reflect. No time to think. No time to do anything at all except be busy.

The more things change, the more they stay the same. Somehow, Stephen Crane realized a century ago what we are still struggling to come to terms with. He realized it too late to wrench his life away from the precipitous decline of debauchery—though his novel remains a morality tale, a steadfast warning for us. He sold an abridged version of *The Red Badge of Courage* to the Bachellor-Johnson Syndicate for ninety dollars on this day in 1894, and it first appeared in the Philadelphia Press about a month later.

Within five years of his greatest achievement, Crane was dead. Suffering from several tuberculosis attacks and a general physical collapse due to his heavy drinking and dissolute lifestyle, Crane was just twenty-eight years old. In his journal he had scratched out a few final words just a day before his death. Though it was destroyed along with all the rest of his effects, an orderly at the sanatorium reported his last desperate cry: "Oh, to find rest, sweet repose. Why must we grind out our lives in search of vain glories when all that is wanted is home?"

1666 The Great Fire of London started in a baker's house in Pudding Lane. In the four days that it raged, the fire destroyed 13,000 houses and more than 80 churches, including St. Paul's Cathedral. Four-fifths of the city lay in ashes. It took the genius of such men as the great English architect Sir Christopher Wren to restore it to its glory.

1729 Sir Richard Steele, age fifty-seven, cofounder with Joseph Addison of the *Tattler* and the *Spectator*, died in Carmarthen, Wales.

1752 Great Britain and her American colonies followed the Julian Calendar for the last time. In accordance with the rest of Europe, who used the Gregorian Calendar, the following day became September 14. Because people thought the government had cheated them of eleven days of their lives, there were riots in the streets.

1789 The U.S. Treasury Department was established.

1857 Edgar Rice Burroughs was born in Chicago. The creator of Tarzan would bemoan, "I am one of those fellows who always seems to get to the fire after it is already out."

1864 During the War Between the States, Union General William T. Sherman's forces occupied Atlanta.

1901 In a speech at the Minnesota State Fair, Vice President Theodore Roosevelt quoted an African proverb, "Speak softly and carry a big stick; you will go far." The phrase became his hallmark.

1903 George Bernard Shaw, in writing to his friend Harley Granville-Barker, denigrated Christopher Marlowe: "He is a barren amateur with a great air."

1917 The popular author and journalist Cleveland Avery was born in Nahant, Massachusetts.

1924 The Rudolf Friml operetta *Rose Marie* opened on Broadway.

1935 Composer George Gershwin finished and signed his name to the completed score of his great American opera, *Porgy and Bess.*

1945 The leader of a grassroots Communist insurgency, Ho Chi Minh, declared Vietnam an independent republic.

1945 Japan formally surrendered in ceremonies aboard the USS *Missouri,* ending the Second World War.

1963 Alabama Governor George C. Wallace prevented the integration of Tuskegee High School by encircling the building with state troopers.

1969 North Vietnamese president Ho Chi Minh died, twenty-four years to the day after he had launched his Communist revolution.

1985 It was announced that a cooperative French-American expedition had located the wreckage of the *Titanic* about 560 miles off Newfoundland.

SEPTEMBER

And I will gladly share with you your pain,

If it turn out I can no comfort bring;

For tis a friend's right, please let me explain,

To share in woeful as in joyful things.

[GEOFFREY CHAUCER (1343–1400)]

Patriot, inventor, scientist, philosopher, musician, editor, printer, and diplomat Benjamin Franklin (1706–1790) brought the prestige of his unparalleled achievements to the public service that consumed over half of his life. He was the living example of the richness of life that man can achieve with the freedom—and the will—to do so. In many senses, he was the first American, and he was a Founding Father of the first rank.

His rise from apprentice to man of affairs was paralleled by an ever-widening circle of interests. His curiosity led him from subject to subject: He mastered printing, learned French, invented a stove, discovered electrical principles, organized a postal service, and helped discover the Gulf Stream. Though a freethinker—an oddity among his overwhelmingly devout Christian peers—he was the close friend and publisher of George Whitefield, the great evangelist.

As his country's representative in England in the 1760s, he defended America's position before hostile, arrogant officials; he helped win repeal of the Stamp Act and pleaded for American representation in Parliament. In the 1770s he continued to try to reason with British officials, but they were inflexible. He returned to America, ready to support the cause of independence. In the Continental Congress, Franklin headed the committee that organized the American postal system, helped draft the Articles of Confederation, and began negotiations with the French for aid. And he helped to draft and then signed the Declaration of Independence.

Franklin was the colonies' best choice as commissioner to France: Well known as a scientist and philosopher, he was warmly welcomed in Paris, and his position as a world figure, coupled with his diplomatic skill, helped him negotiate the alliance with France in 1778, which brought America desperately needed military support. Soon after, he began negotiating with the British for peace. But only after the French fleet had joined with Washington to defeat Cornwallis at Yorktown would the British consider granting independence. Franklin signed the peace treaty on this day in 1783.

After he returned to America, Franklin had one more vital role to play: At the Constitutional Convention his very presence gave weight and authority to the proceedings, and he used his influence to moderate conflicts. Though widely known as a deist and a freethinker, on the final day he appealed to the delegates: "I confess that there are several parts of this Constitution which I do not at present approve, but I am not sure I shall never approve them. For having lived long, I have experienced many instances of being obliged by better information, or fuller consideration, to change opinions even on important subjects, which I once thought right, but found to be otherwise. I cannot help expressing a wish that every member of the Convention who may still have objections to it, would with me, on this occasion, doubt a little of his own infallibility, and to make manifest our unanimity, put his name on this instrument." A few minutes later all but three delegates signed the Constitution.

SEPTEMBER

FEAST DAY
St. Simeon Stylites the Younger, St. Phoebe, St. Remaclus, St. Aigulf or Ayoul of Lerins, St. Gregory the Great, St. Cuthburga, St. Hildelitha, St. Macanisius

1189 Richard the Lion-Hearted, son of Henry II and Eleanor of Aquitaine, was crowned as King Richard I of England at Westminster Abbey. After he was anointed on the head, breast, and shoulders by the Archbishop of Canterbury, the officers of his Royal army invested him with the cap, tunic, swords, spurs, and mantle of a Crusading Knight of Christ—an office he tried to live up to for the rest of his life.

1609 Explorer Henry Hudson, in a search for the Northwest Passage, entered New York Harbor and set sail up the river that was eventually named in his honor.

1658 Oliver Cromwell, the Lord Protector of England, died, creating a power vacuum and throwing the Commonwealth into a panic of uncertainty. Within two years, the monarchy was restored.

1783 The Treaty of Paris between the United States and Great Britain officially ended the Revolutionary War. The treaty was signed by the prominent American patriot leaders John Adams, Benjamin Franklin, and John Jay.

1838 Frederick Douglass escaped from slavery on this day by dressing as a sailor and borrowing identification papers of a retired merchant seaman. He headed for New York City via a train in Maryland, a steamboat in Delaware, and another train, which brought him to the protection of the Underground Railroad network. Douglass used his great oratorical skills as one of the leaders of the antislavery movement.

1849 Sarah Orne Jewett was born in South Berwick, Maine. Her stories of New England life would include *Deephaven* and *The Country of the Pointed Firs*.

1864 Leo Tolstoy was suddenly seized with terror in a country inn and imagined that he was confronting death. The delusion would form the basis for *Notes of a Madman*.

1926 Novelist Alison Lurie—best known for *The War Between the Tates*—was born in Chicago.

1939 Great Britain, New Zealand, Australia, and France all declared war on Germany. On this same day, Winston Churchill was reappointed First Lord of the Admiralty. In a message sent to all Royal Navy ships, the Board of the Admiralty simply stated, "Winston's Back."

1951 The daytime TV soap opera *Search for Tomorrow* debuted on CBS.

1962 The poet e.e. cummings—famed for his odd spelling, grammar, punctuation, and structure—died in North Conway, New Hampshire, at the age of sixty-seven.

1967 Nguyen Van Thieu was elected president of South Vietnam under a new constitution.

1970 Legendary football coach Vince Lombardi died in Washington, D.C.

1976 The unmanned American spacecraft *Viking 2* landed on Mars to take the first close-up, color photographs of the planet's surface.

1978 Pope John Paul II was installed as the 264th pontiff of the Roman Catholic Church.

SEPTEMBER

You can never dictate the future by the past—you may however, ameliorate its illest effects and heighten its greatest delights by its remembrance.

[EDMUND BURKE (1729-1797)]

The renowned avant-garde composer John Cage was born in 1912 in Los Angeles, California. Though trained classically, his rejection of the underlying Christian notions of order, symmetry, and integrity caused him to search for musical forms more able to express his mystical views of chaos and chance.

Thus, he was an early pioneer of experimental music, as well as the use of nontraditional instruments. The use of flowerpots, cow bells, silence, toy pianos, and audience clatter highlighted his philosophy that all sound, no matter what the source or purpose, comprised music. As he often laconically asserted, "Just as beauty is all in the eye of the beholder, so then noise is all in the ear of the hearer."

Influenced by Eastern philosophies, he integrated the use of the Taoist holy book *I Ching* to help govern the supposedly random elements of performances. He called this type of music "indeterminant" because there was no apparently fixed manner in which the composer conveyed to the performer any sort of traditional musical order, structure, or consistency.

One of Cage's most discussed works is a piano piece entitled *4'33"* in which the performer sits on the piano bench for the prescribed length of time without playing a single note. The proposed object lesson is that the music of the piece is created by the ambient sounds of the audience and the performance space during the silence.

In an ironic—and apparently unintentional—analogy to the classic fairy tale "The Emperor's New Clothes," Cage was elected to the American Academy of Arts and Sciences and was also the recipieint of France's highest honor for cultural contributions. His anarchist compositions were lionized—even by those who admitted that they could hardly listen to them. Listening pleasure was not, after all, the point. Not in the least. Rather, they were a philosophical assertion of the absurdity, randomness, and meaninglessness of human existence.

For decades, Cage's life and work have provided a vivid illustration of the fact that when the absolutes of an objective standard—such as the Word of God—are removed from a life or a culture, there are no longer limits that define what is appropriate or artistic. Craftsmanship, artistry, and ability form part of the biblical standard of who and what an artist does. When various artists seek to use their art to shock audiences, they are inevitably driven to greater and greater extremes. The shock value of absurdity, perversity, or inconsistency suffers from the law of diminishing returns.

Similarly, when audiences remain ignorant of objective standards and are swayed by fashion or whimsy, they are increasingly susceptible to treating the ridiculous as serious or sublime. Worldview and philosophy will always permeate the arts in sometimes obvious and other times not so obvious ways—a notion Cage demonstrated throughout his career all too clearly.

SEPTEMBER

FEAST DAY
St. Rosalio; St. Rose of Viterbo; Saints Marcellus and Valerian; St. Marinus of San Marino; St. Boniface I, pope; St. Ultan of Ardbraccan; St. Ida of Herzfeld

688   English Bishop St. Cuthbert died on the island of Lindisfarne. An old Northumbrian legend says that the spirit of Cuthbert rides in the mist when the sea is running high.

1768   Vicomte François-René de Chateaubriand was born at Saint-Malo in Brittany. He would write *Atala* in 1801, re-creating impressions for its background from his trip to America in 1791.

1781   Los Angeles was founded by Spanish missionaries and colonists.

1833   At ten years old, Barney Flaherty became the first newsboy after he answered an advertisement in the *New York Sun*. The ad read, "To the Unemployed—A number of steady men can find employment by vending this paper. A liberal discount is allowed to those who buy to sell again."

1847   The first American missionaries to China, Moses White, Robert Maclay and Henry Hickok, supported by subscription funds of dozens of American Methodist churches, reached Fuchau where they established their ministry.

1886   The last major United States–Indian war came to a close when the Apache Indians under Chief Geronimo surrendered to General Nelson Miles at Skeleton Canyon, Arizona.

1888   George Eastman received a patent for his roll-film camera and registered his trademark, Kodak.

1905   Mary Challans was born in London. She would gain fame and fortune for her Alexandrian-era historical novels such as *The Bull from the Sea*, written under the pseudonym Mary Renault.

1917   The American expeditionary force in France suffered its first fatalities in the First World War.

1935   Simone de Beauvoir—the notorious author and mistress of Jean-Paul Sartre—joined Shakespeare and Company. The unique bookstore and borrowing library in Paris had been set up by American expatriots. When Beauvoir began sharing her interest in Dos Passos and William Faulkner with her high-society friends, having run across them first there at the little bookshop, the American writers began to win great critical acclaim—a success that preceded any such acclaim in their native land.

1948   Queen Wilhelmina of the Netherlands abdicated, citing health reasons.

1951   In the first live, coast-to-coast television broadcast, President Harry Truman addressed the nation from the Japanese peace treaty conference in San Francisco.

1957   The governor of Arkansas, Orval Faubus, called out the National Guard to prevent nine black students from enrolling at Central High School in Little Rock. As access to the school continued to be denied, tensions mounted and some rioting occurred. President Dwight D. Eisenhower sent in federal troops to ensure that the students were able to complete the school year.

1957   Ford Motor Co. began selling its ill-fated Edsel automobile.

1972   American swimmer Mark Spitz won a record seventh Olympic gold medal, in the 400-meter relay at the Munich Summer Olympics.

1984   The Cardinal Prefect of the Congregation for the Doctrine of the Faith in Rome, Joseph Cardinal Ratzinger, denounced aspects of liberation theology—an odd mélange of Marxism and Christianity that had been growing in popularity in Latin American countries. His decree marked the beginning of an all-out war between the Vatican and Communism that would ultimately provoke the collapse of the Soviet Empire.

SEPTEMBER

It is always surprising to the uninitiated, the power that lies in essential and primordial things—discredited though they may be by the concourse of modernity.

[RICHARD WEAVER (1910–1963)]

Who was the first president of the United States? Ask any schoolchild and they will readily tell you "George Washington." And of course, they would be wrong—at least technically. Washington was not inaugurated until April 30, 1789. And yet, the United States continually had functioning governments from as early as September 5, 1774, and operated as a confederated nation from as early as July 4, 1776. During that nearly fifteen-year interval, Congress—first the Continental Congress and then later the Confederation Congress—was moderated by a duly elected president. As the chief executive officer of the government of the United States, the president was recognized as the head of state. Washington was thus the fifteenth—and his administration was the seventeenth—in a long line of distinguished presidents. He just happened to be the first under the current constitution.

When delegates gathered in Philadelphia for the First Continental Congress on this day in 1774, they promptly elected the former king's attorney of Virginia, Peyton Randolph (1723–1775), as the moderator and president of their convocation.

He was a propitious choice. Throughout his life he had been hailed as a genuine prodigy—having mastered multiple languages including Latin, Greek, Hebrew, and French. He had studied law at the Inner Temple in London. And he had served as his native colony's attorney general. All of these accomplishments were achieved before his twentieth birthday.

He went on to have a storied legal and parliamentary career. In addition, he was a renowned professor of rhetoric and oratory. He was a scholar of some renown—having begun a self-guided reading of the classics when he was thirteen. Indeed, he tutored many of the most able men of the South at William and Mary College—including the young Patrick Henry. His home in Williamsburg became the gathering place for Virginia's legal and political gentry—and it remains a popular attraction in the restored colonial capital.

Randolph had served as a delegate in the Virginia House of Burgesses, and had been a commander under William Byrd in the colonial militia. Thus, he was recognized as a mature and tested leader, administrator, and legislator.

There was little doubt among the delegates to the First Continental Congress as to who should bear the double-edged honor and responsibility to lead them into their looming conflict with Crown and Parliament.

Despite suffering poor health, Peyton Randolph served the Continental Congress as president twice, in 1774 from September 5 to October 21, and then again for a few days in 1775 from May 10 to May 23.

He never lived to see independence, yet was numbered among the nation's most revered founders; indeed, he was hailed as the "Father of Our Country," in a congressional eulogy pronounced by one of his presidential successors, John Hancock.

SEPTEMBER

1774 The First Continental Congress assembled in Philadelphia.

1836 Sam Houston, a former congressman, senator, and governor from Tennessee, was elected president of the Republic of Texas.

1870 Novelist Victor Hugo was hailed publicly in Paris upon his return from banishment on Guernsey in the Channel Islands, where he had written *Les Misérables* and *Les Chatiments*, his two greatest works.

1882 The nation's first Labor Day parade was held in New York.

1896 During the Klondike gold rush, some things were worth more than gold. The first beefsteak to reach Circle City, Alaska, sold for $48 per pound, the highest known price ever paid for beef.

1905 The Treaty of Portsmouth, ending the Russo-Japanese War, was signed in New Hampshire under the watchful eye of Theodore Roosevelt who parleyed the peace—and who was later awarded the Nobel Prize for his efforts.

1905 Arthur Koestler, who would indict the police state in *Darkness at Noon*, was born in Budapest, Hungary.

1914 The Battle of the Marne began during the First World War.

1916 Novelist Frank Yerby—whose books included *The Foxes of Harrow* and *A Woman Called Fanny*—was born in Augusta, Georgia.

1921 The Chamber of Commerce in Richmond, Virginia, petitioned the city to consider renaming Main Street in an effort to remove the stigma aroused by Sinclair Lewis's eponymously titled novel.

1939 The United States proclaimed its neutrality in the Second World War.

1945 Iva Toguri D'Aquino, a Japanese American suspected of being wartime broadcaster "Tokyo Rose," was arrested in Yokohama. D'Aquino later served six years in prison. She was finally pardoned in 1977 by President Gerald Ford.

1972 Arab terrorists seized several Israeli athletes and held them hostage during the Olympic Games in Munich. All eleven hostages, the five Palestinian guerrillas and a German policeman lost their lives in a gun battle when negotiations finally collapsed.

1975 President Ford escaped an attempt on his life by Lynette "Squeaky" Fromme, a disciple of Charles Manson, in Sacramento, California.

1997 Mother Teresa died in Calcutta, India, at age eighty-seven.

SEPTEMBER

There is a true glory and a true honor; the glory of duty done—the honor of the integrity of principle.

[ROBERT E. LEE (1807–1870)]

1620

After having failed to sail from England on three earlier occasions and leaving behind her sister ship *Speedwell*, the *Mayflower* sailed from Plymouth for the New World. Aboard were 101 passengers. Just ninety feet long and twenty-six feet wide, it hardly seemed the vessel to alter world history. The sailors cursed the pious passengers, whom they detested. Their food consisted of dried fish, cheese, and beer. The only sanitary accommodation was a single slop bucket. There was nowhere to bathe. Seasickness was rampant during storms. With little air belowdecks, the conditions were nauseating at best. Despite this, only one passenger died at sea. Two months and five days after sailing, the ship landed at Cape Cod. Before going ashore the passengers signed their famous Mayflower Compact. And thus began the saga of the Pilgrims in their new home: America.

Although a kind, gentle man beloved by the American people, William McKinley (1843–1901) did not earn a place in history as a champion of the people. Instead, his administration was closely identified with monopolies, trusts, corporations, and special interests.

At a time when the expanding West and the agrarian South were developing populist movements of growing political significance, the dignified Midwestern lawyer represented the bankers, mercantilists, and industrialists who formed the most powerful bloc in the Republican Party establishment. Both economically and politically, McKinley was a conservative; on the three burning issues of the day—the tariff, currency, and Cuba—he took a conservative position. The McKinley Tariff Bill, passed in 1890, was one of the highest protective tariffs in U.S. history. As president, McKinley supported the gold standard and for a time resisted those who wanted to stampede the U.S. into war with Spain to rescue oppressed Cuba. McKinley had been elected on a platform supporting Cuban independence. American investments in sugar plantations and trade with Cuba were at stake, and the newspapers kept stories of Spanish atrocities in Cuba before the eyes of the public.

The pressure for American intervention—after the sinking of the battle cruiser *Maine* in Havana Harbor—finally moved McKinley to go to war. The remarkable victories of servicemen like Teddy Roosevelt on the field and Dewey on the seas brought Puerto Rico, Guam, and the Philippines into American hands. Ironically, the conservative McKinley launched the nation as a global power.

With McKinley's reelection in 1900, big business seemed secure for four more years. But a series of accidents dramatically altered this serene picture. In the 1900 campaign the progressive governor of New York, Theodore Roosevelt, was put on the ticket as vice president by rival New York Republican leaders who hoped that the post would be his political graveyard. But only six months after the inauguration McKinley was fatally shot by anarchist Leon Czolgosz at the Pan-American Exposition in Buffalo on this day in 1901. And the era of freewheeling big business died with McKinley, the third martyred president.

SEPTEMBER

FEAST DAY
St. Eleutherius of Spoleto; St. Cagnoald or Chainoaldus; Saints Donatian, Laetus, and Others

1837 The Oberlin Collegiate Institute of Ohio became the nation's first genuinely coeducational institution.

1847 Henry David Thoreau, having spent two years in his hut on Walden Pond living solely by the labor of his hands, moved into the Emerson household in Concord, Massachusetts.

1869 Novelist and playwright Felix Salten—author of *Bambi* and *The Emperor's Stallion*—was born in Hungary.

1890 When the captain of the Roi des Belges succumbed to tropical fever on the Congo River, Jospeh Conrad was made master of the ship—an experience he would later draw upon in his novels *Heart of Darkness* and *An Outpost of Progress*.

1909 American explorer Robert Peary sent word that he had reached the North Pole five months earlier.

1941 Jews over the age of six in all German-occupied areas in Europe were ordered to wear yellow Stars of David.

1948 Queen Juliana of the Netherlands was coronated.

1952 Canadian television broadcasting began for the first time in Montreal.

1966 South African Prime Minister Hendrik Verwoerd was stabbed to death by a deranged page during a parliamentary session in Cape Town.

1981 Exactly one month before he was assassinated, Anwar Sadat attempted to appease Islamic fundamentalists in Egypt by sanctioning fierce persecutions against the Christian minority and exiling Shenouda III, the patriarch of the Coptic Church. Christian lands were confiscated. Hundreds of Christians were martyred. And churches were desecrated and destroyed. Officially, the Sadat government attributed all the strife to the besieged Christians. Nevertheless, the ploy failed to satisfy the Islamic hard-liners, and the assassination of Sadat was ordered and carried out.

1989 The National Party, the governing party of South Africa, suffered its worst election setback in four decades in parliamentary elections, losing nearly a quarter of its seats to far-right and anti-apartheid rivals.

1994 Irish Prime Minister Albert Reynolds and Gerry Adams, the head of the IRA's political ally, Sinn Fein, made a joint commitment to peace after their first face-to-face meeting.

1997 Britain bade farewell to Princess Diana with a funeral service at Westminster Abbey.

For God has not given us a spirit of fear, but of power and of love and of a sound mind.

SEPTEMBER

PAUL OF TARSUS (C. 10–65)

The seminal Reformer and theologian John Calvin was born in Noyon, France, in 1509—just eight years before Martin Luther nailed his Ninety-Five Theses on the Wittenberg church door to launch the Reformation. After receiving a classical education at a Brethren of the Common Life school, he received formal instruction for the priesthood at the Collège de la Marche and the Collège de Montaigue, branches of the University of Paris. Encouraged by his father to study law instead of theology, Calvin also attended universities at Orléans and Bourges.

Along with several of his friends he grew to appreciate the humanistic movement of Erasmus as well as the Reformation movement of Luther. As a result, he undertook serious studies in the Greek Bible. In 1532 after he published a commentary on Seneca's _De Clementia_, he was widely regarded as a rising star among a new generation of able humanist scholars.

At about that time, he began to assist Nicholas Cop, the newly elected rector of the University of Paris, as a writer, researcher, and aide. When Cop announced his support in 1535 of Martin Luther, both men were forced to flee the city. Although he seldom spoke of it, Calvin underwent a dramatic conversion about this time.

Over the course of the next two years, Calvin was forced to move frequently to avoid the authorities while he studied, wrote, and formulated from the Bible and Christian tradition the primary tenets of his theology. In 1536 he published the first edition of his _Institutes of the Christian Religion_, a succinct and provocative work that thrust him into the forefront of the Protestant movement as a thinker, systemizer, and spokesman. During the same year, Calvin visited Geneva on his way to Strasbourg and was asked by William Farel to assist in the work of Reform and renewal in that city. Though reluctant at first, Calvin consented to work with Farel in Geneva until 1538, when the town voted to ask both men to leave.

At that point, Calvin completed his interrupted journey to Strasbourg where he pastored a church and participated in that community's dramatic reformation. It was there in Strasbourg that he met and married Idelette de Bure, a widow. Though a very happy marriage, the couple had one child, who died in infancy. At Strasbourg, Calvin also published his _Commentary on Romans_ (1539), the first of his many commentaries on books of the Bible.

On this day in 1541 the Genevans prevailed upon Calvin to return and lead them again in reforming both the church and the city. He remained there for the rest of his life. Although he received a house and stipend from the government, he did not hold office in the government, and he did not even become a citizen of Geneva until 1559. Nevertheless, he was astonishingly productive in giving shape to both the theology and practice of the Reformation, as well as the institutions of freedom and prosperity that would mark the Western world ever after.

Calvin's health was never robust; his illnesses included chronic asthma, indigestion, and catarrh. He became very frail with the onslaught of quartan fever in 1558. Though he was buried in an unmarked grave after his death in 1564, he left his mark on the whole world—which remains as his greatest memorial.

SEPTEMBER

NATIONAL DAY
Brazil
FEAST DAY
St. Anastasius the Fuller, St. Cloud or Clodoald, Saints Alcmund and Tilbert, St. Grimonia, St. Regina or Reine of Alize, St. Sozon, St. John of Nicomedia

1533 Queen Elizabeth I, daughter of King Henry V and his second wife Anne Boleyn, was born on this day.

1716 In Boston, Massachusetts, the first lighthouse in the United States was built.

1776 The American submarine *Turtle* attempted to sink Admiral Howe's flagship, the HMS *Eagle*, in New York Harbor in what was the first use of a submarine in warfare. The mission failed when Sgt. Ezra Lee of the *Turtle* was unable to drill a screw into the ship's copper-clad hull to hang a bomb from it. This first American submarine was later destroyed when another ship sank on top of it.

1825 The Marquis de Lafayette, the French hero of the American Revolution, bade farewell to President John Quincy Adams at the White House.

1829 Felix Mendelssohn's visit to Fingal's cave on Staffa, Scotland, resulted in the sketching of a musical theme that formed the opening of his *Hebrides Overture.*

1892 James J. Corbett knocked out John L. Sullivan to win the world heavyweight crown in New Orleans in the first major prizefight conducted under the Marquis of Queensberry rules.

1901 The Peace of Beijing ended the Boxer Rebellion in China.

1910 The first masterwork by English composer Ralph Vaughan Williams, *Fantasia on a Theme by Thomas Tallis*, was performed at the Three Choirs Festival. Although panned by early critics, this work is regarded as one of Vaughan Williams's most celebrated compositions.

1936 Rock-and-roll legend Buddy Holly was born Charles Hardin Holley in Lubbock, Texas.

1940 Nazi Germany launched its initial "blitz" on London during the Second World War.

1963 The National Professional Football Hall of Fame was dedicated in Canton, Ohio.

1969 Senate Republican leader Everett M. Dirksen died in Washington, D.C. He is best known for his quip about the promiscuity of government spending: "A billion here and a billion there—pretty soon we're talking about real money."

1977 The Panama Canal treaties, calling for the U.S. to eventually turn over control of the waterway to Panama, were signed by President Jimmy Carter in Washington.

1977 Convicted Watergate conspirator G. Gordon Liddy was released from prison after more than four years.

1979 The Entertainment and Sports Programming Network (ESPN) made its cable TV debut.

1986 Desmond Tutu was installed as the first black to lead the Anglican Church in southern Africa.

1998 St. Louis Cardinal Mark McGwire equaled Roger Maris's single-season home run record as he hit number 61 during a game against the Chicago Cubs.

SEPTEMBER

A contempt of the monuments and the wisdom of the past, may be justly reckoned one of the reigning follies of these days, to which pride and idleness have equally contributed.

[SAMUEL JOHNSON (1709–1784)]

1858

In a speech in Clinton, Illinois, Abraham Lincoln uttered the words, "You can fool all of the people some of the time; some of the people all of the time; but not all of the people all of the time."

Samuel Rutherford was born in 1600 near Nisbet, Scotland. Though little is known of his early life, it is clear that he was raised in a pious home that put great emphasis on education. In 1627 he completed his academic work at the University of Edinburgh, where he was appointed Professor of Humanities. On this day that same year he became the pastor of the little parish church in Anwoth.

Anwoth was a rural community, and the people were scattered in farms over the hills. Rutherford apparently had a true pastor's heart, and he was ceaseless in his labors for his flock. Men often said of him, "He was always praying, always preaching, always visiting the sick, always catechising, always writing, and always studying." Even so, his first years in Anwoth were marked by great sadness. His wife was ill for a year and a month before she died in their new home. Two children also died shortly afterward. Nevertheless, his faith never wavered.

Though it was said that he was not a particularly good speaker, his preaching drew great attention. An English merchant said of him, "I came to Irvine, and heard a well-favored, proper old man with a long beard, and that man showed me all my heart. Then I went to St. Andrews, where I heard a sweet, majestic-looking man, and he showed me the majesty of God. After him I heard this little, fair man Rutherford, and he showed me the loveliness of Christ."

In 1636 Rutherford published a book defending the Calvinistic doctrines of grace against Arminanism. This put him in conflict with the church authorities, which were dominated by the English Episcopacy. He was called before the High Court, deprived of his ministerial office, and exiled to Aberdeen. On this day in 1638, the struggles between Parliament and king in England enabled him to slip out of Aberdeen and return to Anwoth—but he was not allowed to stay there as long as he might have wished. The Westminster Assembly began their famous meetings in 1643, and Rutherford was appointed to be one of the five Scottish commissioners invited to attend the proceedings. Although the Scots were not allowed to vote, they had an influence far exceeding their number. Rutherford is thought to have been a major influence on the *Shorter Catechism*.

It was during this period in England that Rutherford wrote his best-known work, *Lex Rex*, which argued for limited government and a refutation of the idea of the divine right of kings. When the monarchy was restored in 1660, it was clear that the author of *Lex Rex* could expect trouble. When the summons came in 1661, charging him with treason, and demanding his appearance on a certain day, Rutherford refused to go. From his deathbed, he answered, "I must answer my first summons; and before your day arrives, I will be where few kings and great folks come." He died a few days later.

SEPTEMBER

FEAST DAY
St. Corbinian; St. Disibod; St. Eusebius; Saints Adrian and Natalia; St. Kingsmark or Cynfarch Oer; St. Sergius I, pope; St. Zeno; St. Nestabus; St. Nestor

1157 Richard the Lion-Hearted was born, the third son of King Henry II and Eleanor of Aquitaine. He ruled England as King Richard I beginning in 1189.

1565 Don Pedro Menendez founded the first American settlement at St. Augustine, Florida.

1636 The General Court of Massachusetts Bay appropriated £400 for the founding of a college with the name of Cambridge. On September 24, 1638, the Reverend John Harvard died, leaving £800 and 300 books to the fledgling college. The name of the college was changed in his honor to Harvard.

1841 Czech composer Antonin Dvořák was born near Prague in Nelahozeves, a small Bohemian village. It was while he served as the director of the National Conservatory of Music in New York City from 1892 to 1895 that Dvořák developed an affinity for spirituals and Native American music. He wrote the Symphony in E minor *(From the New World)* during this time. Although the music does not quote actual themes from spirituals, the melodies have strong characteristic to these influences. Dvořák also utilized Czech and Slavonic influences in his other works in music that reflects strong nationalism and identity.

1892 Former Baptist preacher Francis Bellamy wrote "The Pledge of Allegiance", which first appeared on this day in the *Youth's Companion.*

1900 In a hurricane and resulting twenty-foot tidal surge, between 6,000 and 7,200 people were killed in Galveston, Texas.

1921 Margaret Gorman of Washington, D.C., was crowned the first Miss America in Atlantic City, New Jersey.

1930 Richard Drew developed Scotch tape.

1935 Senator Huey P. Long, the "Kingfish" of Louisiana politics, was shot and mortally wounded. He died two days later.

1949 German composer and conductor Richard Strauss died in Bavaria. Strauss was an innovative master of orchestration and composing for the voice. He utilized Richard Wagner's technique of incorporating a leitmotif system that added dimension to the music through extramusical associations. His contribution of tone poems to the repertoire included *Don Juan* (1888), *Macbeth* (1890), *Tod und Verklärung* (Death and Transfiguration, 1890), *Till Eulenspiegels lustige Streiche* (Till Eulenspiegel's Merry Pranks, 1895), *Also sprach Zarathustra* (Thus Spoke Zarathustra, 1896), *Don Quixote* (1897), and *Ein Heldenleben* (A Hero's Life, 1898). His most famous operas include *Salome* (1905), *Elektra* (1909), and *Der Rosenkavalier* (1911).

1952 The Ernest Hemingway novel *The Old Man and the Sea* was first published.

1974 To former President Richard Nixon, sitting President Gerald Ford granted "a full, free, and absolute" pardon for all federal crimes he may have committed while in office.

1985 Pete Rose of the Cincinnati Reds tied Ty Cobb's career record for hits, singling for hit number 4,191 during a game against the Cubs in Chicago.

1998 Mark McGwire of the St. Louis Cardinals broke major-league baseball's record for home runs in a single season, hitting number 62 off Chicago Cubs pitcher Steve Trachsel and eclipsing the 37-year-old record held by Roger Maris.

SEPTEMBER

People will not look forward to posterity who will not look backward to their ancestors.

[EDMUND BURKE (1729–1797)]

Henryk Sienkiewicz, awarded the Nobel Prize for literature this day in 1905, was an international phenomenon a century ago—at the end of the nineteenth and the beginning of the twentieth centuries. He was trained in both law and medicine. He was a respected historian. He was a successful journalist. He was a widely sought-after critic and editor. He was an erudite lecturer. And in addition to all that, he was an amazingly prolific and wildly popular novelist—selling millions of copies of his almost fifty books in nearly three hundred editions in the United States alone.

He wowed the world with his grace, his learning, his courage, his depth of character, and his evocative storytelling. His writing includes some of the most memorable works of historical fiction ever penned—ranking with the likes of Sir Walter Scott, Robert Louis Stevenson, and Samuel Johnson.

It was an unlikely destiny for a passionately ethnic novelist from the isolated, feudal, and agrarian Podlasie region of Poland to fulfill. Born in 1846, he lived during one of the most tumultuous periods of Central European history. Ideological revolutions, utopian uprisings, base conspiracies, nationalistic movements, and imperialistic expansions wracked the continent in the decades between the fall of Napoleon and the rise of Hitler. Wars and rumors of wars shook the foundations of social order to an extraordinary degree. His own nation was cruelly and bitterly divided between the ambitions of the Prussian kaiser and the Russian czar. The proud cultural and national legacy of Poland was practically snuffed out altogether—all the distinctive aspects of the culture were outlawed and even the language was fiercely suppressed.

Sienkiewicz became a part of the underground movement to recover the Polish arts—music, poetry, journalism, history, and fiction. He used the backdrop of the social, cultural, and political chaos to reflect both the tragedy of his people and the ultimate hope that lay in their glorious tenacity. He was, thus, a true traditionalist at a time when traditionalism had been thoroughly and systematically discredited the world over—the only notable exceptions being in the American South and the Dutch Netherlands. As a result, his distinctive voice rang out in stark contrast to the din of vogue conformity. His novels, therefore, not only introduced the world to Poland, they also offered a stern antirevolutionary rebuke in the face of modernity's smothering political correctness.

His massive *Trilogy*, published between 1884 and 1887, tells the story of an ill-fated attempt to save his homeland from foreign domination during the previous century. When they were first released in the United States, the books became instant bestsellers. They made Sienkiewicz a household name—so much so that Mark Twain could assert that he was the first serious international writer to become an American literary celebrity. Even so, the *Trilogy* did not achieve for him even a fraction of the acclaim that came his way with the publication of *Quo Vadis?* in 1898. It was nothing short of a phenomenon. It was the first book the *New York Times* dubbed a "blockbuster" and became the standard against which all future mega-bestsellers were judged.

SEPTEMBER

FEAST DAY
St. Omer or Audomaurus, St. Peter Claver, St. Ciaran or Kiaran of Clonmacnois, St. Bettelin, St. Joseph of Volokolamsk, St. Gorgonius, St. Isaac or Sahak the Great

1087 William the Conqueror died after falling from his horse.

1776 On this day the Continental Congress decreed that "in all Continental commissions and other instruments, where heretofore the words United Colonies have been used, the style be altered, for the future, to the United States."

1828 Russian novelist and social reformer Count Leo Nikolaevich Tolstoy was born in Yasnaya Polyana. He is best known for his epic works *War and Peace* and *Anna Karenina*.

1850 California became the thirty-first state of the Union.

1926 The National Broadcasting Company (NBC) was created by the Radio Corporation of America (RCA).

1956 Elvis Presley made the first of his three appearances on the nationally televised *Ed Sullivan Show*.

1957 President Dwight Eisenhower signed into law the first civil rights bill to pass Congress since Reconstruction.

1965 Los Angeles pitcher Sandy Koufax pitched a perfect game, beating Chicago 1-0.

1971 Prisoners seized control of the maximum-security Attica Correctional Facility near Buffalo, New York, beginning a siege that ended after claiming forty-three lives.

1976 Communist Chinese leader Mao Tse-tung died in Beijing at age eighty-two.

1982 The three largest Lutheran denominations in the United States, the Association of Evangelical Lutheran Churches, the American Lutheran Church, and the Lutheran Church of America, gathered in simultaneous conventions. Before the meetings were over, their delegates had separately voted by huge majorities to begin the process of a full merger. With tears and joy they connected by phone to pray with one another.

1991 St. Petersburg was officially restored as the name of Russia's second largest city after an act of Russian legislators several days earlier. The city was founded by Peter the Great in 1703, but its name was changed to Petrograd at the beginning of the First World War, and then to Leningrad in 1924 after the death of communist leader Vladimir Lenin.

1993 Palestinian leaders and Israel agreed to recognize each other, clearing the way for a peace accord.

1998 Independent Counsel Kenneth Starr delivered to Congress thirty-six boxes of material concerning his investigation of President Bill Clinton's corruption and perjury charges.

All our debate is voiceless here,
As all our rage, the rage of stone;
If hope is hopeless, then fearless fear,
And history is thus undone.

[ROBERT PENN WARREN (1905–1989)]

SEPTEMBER

533

One of the most remarkable features of the Reformation was the veritable explosion of creativity it produced. Painting, sculpture, music, literature, technology, architecture, oratory, and engineering, the likes of which had not been seen since the halcyon days of High Medievalism, filled cities like Geneva, Frankfurt, London, Zurich, Edinburgh, and Amsterdam. Beauty, goodness, and truth became the natural handmaids of Reformed thought.

Though a good deal of that creativity revolved around the teeming worlds of commerce and industry, not a little focused on reviving the once-moribund services of the church itself. This was particularly evident in the sudden prolificacy of sacred music and hymnody.

In Geneva, the poet Clement Marot and the theologian and Protestant Reformer Theodore Beza collaborated on a magnificent new translation of the book of Psalms into a familiar vernacular French. They also set each psalm to one or another of several standard metrical verse forms, which made them particularly accessible to musicians and composers.

The new translations were introduced by the Reformer John Calvin as a vital part of his liturgical renewal there in Geneva—and from there, they were quickly adopted by the various Reformed churches in France and Switzerland. The French musician Louis Bourgeois either composed new hymn tunes or selected old folk melodies that might be used interchangeably with any number of the psalms—and the result was a lively, refreshing, and dynamic form of worship.

Two other French Reformed musicians, Claude Goudimel and Claude Le Jeune, composed stunning four-voice settings for the Bourgeois melodies that became standard for the churches seeking to conform worship to confessional forms. But visitors—for some reason expecting that the worship of the Reformers might be dour and somber—were often surprised by the vigor and enthusiasm of the new settings. Indeed, these psalms were so lively that they were popularly dubbed Genevan Jigs.

English translations of the Genevan Jigs were published in 1562 by the Puritan writers, printers, and publishers Thomas Sternhold and John Hopkins. And then on this day in 1612 a similar psalter was published in Holland by the English Separatist clergyman Henry Ainsworth—in fact, it was the Ainsworth Psalter that the Pilgrims brought to America on the *Mayflower* in 1620. Thus, quite contrary to the popular caricatures, the music and the worship of the Calvinistic Puritans and Pilgrims—as well as their kith and kin among the Covenanters—was creative, vibrant, and exhilarating.

SEPTEMBER

FEAST DAY

St. Theodard of Maestricht; St. Salvius or Salvy of Albi; St. Ambrose Barlow; St. Aubert of Avranches; Saints Menodora, Metrodora, and Nymphodora; St. Finian of Moville; St. Nemesian; St. Nicholas of Tolentino; St. Pulcheria

534

1608 John Smith assumed the leadership of the Jamestown settlement in the colony of Virginia when he was elected president.

1810 The English romantic poet William Ashbless—a fictional concoction of novelist Tim Powers—wrote the first draft of his most important work, *The Twelve Hours of the Night*, at the Jamaica House Coffee Shop in London.

1813 An American naval force commanded by Oliver H. Perry defeated the British in the Battle of Lake Erie in the War of 1812.

1846 Elias Howe received a patent for his sewing machine.

1890 During a rain shower in Cairo, Illinois, the rain was accompanied by a number of live fish up to four inches in length that fell in various parts of the city.

1912 The multimillionaire William Whiting Borden was ordained. A graduate of both Yale and Princeton, he had always used his wealth for the furtherance of missions and the propagation of the gospel. He had already served as a director of Moody Bible Institute, the National Bible Institute, and the China Inland Mission. After his ordination, Borden offered himself for the China Inland Mission. Upon his acceptance he sailed for Cairo, Egypt, proposing to study Arabic before going on to his work among China's Muslims. In Egypt he contracted cerebrospinal meningitis and died in 1913. He was only twenty-six.

1919 New York City welcomed home General John J. Pershing and twenty-five thousand soldiers who had served in the First Division of the American Expeditionary Force during the First World War.

1922 The release of the short film feature *One Terrible Day* was the debut episode of Hal Roach's long-running comedy series *Our Gang*.

1948 American-born Mildred Gillars, accused of being Nazi wartime radio broadcaster "Axis Sally," was indicted in Washington, D.C., for treason. She was later convicted and served twelve years in prison.

1955 The Western drama *Gunsmoke* premiered on CBS.

1963 Twenty black students entered Alabama public schools following a standoff between federal authorities and Governor George C. Wallace.

1979 Four Puerto Rican nationalists imprisoned for a 1954 attack on the U.S. House of Representatives and a 1950 assassination attempt on President Harry Truman were granted clemency by President Jimmy Carter.

1989 Hungary gave permission for thousands of East German refugees and visitors to emigrate to West Germany. By opening the floodgates, officials realized they were witnessing the beginning of the end of the Communist hold on Europe.

1998 President Clinton met with members of his cabinet to apologize, ask forgiveness, and promise to improve as a person in the wake of the Monica Lewinsky sex, corruption, and perjury scandal.

SEPTEMBER

History must be our deliverer not only from the undue influence of other times, but from the undue influence of our own, from the tyranny of the environment and the pressures of the air we breathe.

[LORD ACTON (1834–1902)]

535

1862

William Sydney Porter—best known as O. Henry—was born in Greensboro, North Carolina. The master of the surprise ending, he was convicted of embezzlement while working as a bank teller early in his career. Following his release from prison he wrote such stories as "The Gift of the Magi" and "The Last Leaf" for syndication in newspapers, literary journals, and magazines. He always worked in what he called a "triple-hinged surprise, to end the scene and make one rub his eyes."

11

SEPTEMBER

Cencio Savelli accepted his election as pope with more than a little reluctance. Already in his sixties, he was said to have sighed with profound reluctance when he was informed of the burden he was called to shoulder. Yet he had many years of able administration behind him, and his pontificate would reveal him to be, by and large, a wise and peaceable man. He took the name Honorius III at his consecration on this day in 1216 at Perugia—though history would call him the Great Pacificator. His eleven-year reign would see some of the church's most significant developments.

To Honorius belongs the honor of approving the rules of three great orders—the governing standards of the Carmelites, the Dominicans and the Franciscans. In addition, he established the guidelines for the first two great universities—a phenomenon heretofore unknown—the universities at Paris and Bologna.

But Honorius is best known as a peacemaker. He appointed worthy legates to oversee the minority of Henry III of England and kept France from warring on the island nation. And he helped to arrange peace for several European nations—including Bohemia, Greece, Burgundy, Hungary, Denmark, Castile, Navarre, and Aragon.

But the two things he longed for most, he never lived to see. The first was the spiritual renewal of the church. The second was the recovery of the Holy Land from the Muslim hoard. He arranged the Fifth Crusade. It quickly captured the Egyptian port of Damietta, but then the crusader armies were soundly trounced when Frederick II failed to appear according to promise. He also authorized the Inquisition against the Albigenses heretics of Acquataine, France, and Provence. The suppression of this Cathar cult turned into a fiasco of greed and brutality.

A man of erudition, Honorius penned biographies of his predecessors Celestine III and Gregory VII and a number of other works of historical interest, including a vast collection of decretals—the papal letters offering authoritative decisions on canon law. When he died in 1227, he was mourned throughout all Christendom.

FEAST DAY
St. Theodora of Alexandria, St. Peter of Chavanon, Saints Protus and Hyacinth, St. Deiniol, St. Patiens of Lyon, St. Paphnutius

1737 George Whitefield is best known for his role in sparking the great Methodist revival in England and the Great Awakening in the American colonies. But the chief concern of his life, and the labor to which all else was subverted, was the erection and maintenance of an orphanage in Georgia. Beginning on this day, Whitefield's unflagging energies focused on the relief of the deplorably destitute children, both fatherless and homeless, scattered in and about Savannah. His lifelong fundraising and zealous perseverance produced schools, hospitals, and homes for boys and girls that endure to this day.

1773 On this day Benjamin Franklin wrote, "There was never a good war or a bad peace."

1777 The Stars and Stripes flag was carried into battle for the first time at the Battle of Brandywine near Wilmington, Delaware, where General George Washington's troops were defeated by the British.

1789 Alexander Hamilton was appointed the first U.S. Secretary of the Treasury.

1814 An American fleet scored a decisive victory over the British in the Battle of Lake Champlain in the War of 1812.

1850 Jenny Lind (1820–1887), Swedish soprano sensation, made her American debut in New York City. Seven thousand music lovers came to see her, and the first ticket sold for $225. Known as the "Swedish Nightingale," Lind was an internationally known coloratura soprano.

1885 Author D. H. Lawrence was born in Eastwood, England.

1936 President Roosevelt dedicated Boulder Dam (later renamed Hoover Dam) by pressing a key in Washington to signal the start-up of the dam's first hydroelectric generator in Nevada.

1944 President Franklin Roosevelt and British Prime Minister Winston Churchill met in Canada at the second Quebec Conference.

1951 *The Rake's Progress*, an opera by Igor Stravinsky, premiered in Venice, Italy. The libretto by W. H. Auden and Chester Kallman was based on a series of lithographs by William Hogarth, the eighteenth-century English artist. This morality tale is summed up in the final words of the opera: "For idle hands and hearts and minds, the devil finds a work to do."

1962 The Beatles made their first recording, "Love Me Do" and "P.S. I Love You," at the EMI studios in London.

1967 The hit variety television program *The Carol Burnett Show* premiered on CBS.

1971 Former Soviet leader Nikita Khrushchev died at age seventy-seven.

1997 Scots voted to create their own Parliament for the first time since their 1707 union with England.

1998 Congress released Kenneth Starr's voluminous report that offered sordid and detailed evidence of President Bill Clinton's sexual misconduct and leveled accusations of perjury and obstruction of justice.

SEPTEMBER

Modernism is in essence a provincialism, since it declines to look beyond the horizon of the moment.

[RICHARD WEAVER (1910–1963)]

1846

Elizabeth Barrett and Robert Browning were secretly married at London's St. Marylebone Church. Afterward, William Wordsworth mused, "Well, I hope they understand one another—nobody else would."

SEPTEMBER

A Yankee cobbler who taught himself law and became a judge and a legislator, Roger Sherman (1721–1793) helped draft four of the major American founding documents—the Declaration of Independence, the Articles of Confederation, the Constitution, and the Bill of Rights.

Sherman had almost twenty years' experience as a colonial legislator behind him when he arrived on this day at the First Continental Congress—a week after it had convened in 1774. He quickly won the respect of his fellow delegates for his wisdom, industry, and sound judgment. John Adams called him "one of the soundest and strongest pillars of the Revolution." In Congress, Sherman was one of the first to deny Parliament's authority to make laws for America, and he strongly supported the boycott of British goods. In the following years he served with Jefferson and Franklin on the committees that drafted the Declaration of Independence and the Articles of Confederation. He also served on the Maritime Committee, the Board of Treasury, and the Board of War—all of first importance to the Revolution.

A Puritan of simple habits who performed all tasks with thoroughness and accuracy, Sherman gained more legislative experience in his years in Congress than any other member; by the time he left he was perhaps the most powerful—and most overworked—of congressmen.

Sherman's greatest and best-known contribution was the "Connecticut Compromise," which he proposed at the Constitutional Convention: By proposing that Congress have two branches, one with proportional, one with equal representation, he satisfied both the small and the large states, providing a solution to one of the most stubborn problems of the Convention. In Connecticut he defended the Constitution, writing articles in the *New Haven Gazette,* and helped win ratification in January 1788. Connecticut was the fifth state to ratify.

Sherman was the oldest man elected to the new national House of Representatives. In the first Congress he served on the committee that prepared and reviewed the Bill of Rights Amendments. By coincidence, the year that the Bill of Rights became part of the Constitution, Sherman was elected senator—so that the man who conceived the "Connecticut Compromise" had the opportunity to represent that state in both of the legislative branches he had helped to create.

FEAST DAY
St. Guy of Anderlecht, St. Aibhe, St. Eanswida

538

1733 Composer, organist, and harpsichordist François Couperin died in Paris, France. He was called Le Grand (the great) because of his status during the French Baroque. His four volumes of harpsichord music influenced J. S. Bach, and his treatise on playing the harpsichord continues to provide understanding of eighteenth-century performance practice. His organ masses are the pinnacle of French Baroque organ compositions.

1740 After having corresponded for years, the French writer Voltaire and the Prussian emperor Frederick the Great finally met.

1832 Hughes Félicité Robert de Lamennais, the father of the French Catholic liberal and Christian socialist movements as well as modern liberation theology, submitted himself entirely to the dictates of the Roman Catholic Church. As a young man Lamennais joined the radicals of the French Revolution in overthrowing the ancien régime. But in 1804 he renounced revolution and became a priest. He was an Ultramontanist, a strong adherent of the pope's prerogatives and infallibility. He believed that since religion in one form or another is the driving principle of society, society cannot ignore what people believe. He published an influential magazine, *L'Avenir*, which forced Catholics to move toward democracy. He was ultimately credited with helping to establish the Second French Republic.

1880 Author and journalist H. L. Mencken was born in Baltimore. The editor, satirist, and author wrote a regular column for the *Baltimore Sun* as well as innumerable important books such as the encyclopedic *The American Language*.

1907 The *Lusitania* arrived in New York Harbor on her maiden voyage. The world's largest ship had set a new transatlantic speed record of 5 days, 54 minutes

1918 During the First World War, American forces led by General John J. Pershing launched an attack on the German-occupied St. Mihiel, north of Verdun, France.

1938 National Socialist leader Adolf Hitler demanded self-determination for the Sudeten Germans in Czechoslovakia.

1943 German paratroopers helped Benito Mussolini escape from the hotel where he was being held by the Italian government.

1974 The Christian emperor Haile Selassie was deposed by a Communist military junta after ruling Ethiopia for fifty-eight years.

1977 South African black student leader Steven Biko died while in police custody, triggering an international outcry.

1986 Joseph Cicippio, acting comptroller at the American University in Beirut, was kidnapped by Islamic hard-liners. He was not released until December 1991.

1989 Manhattan borough president David N. Dinkins won New York City's Democratic mayoral primary, defeating incumbent Mayor Edward Koch and two other candidates on his way to becoming the city's first African-American mayor.

1994 A stolen single-engine Cessna crashed into the South Lawn of the White House, coming to rest against the executive mansion; the pilot, Frank Corder, was killed.

SEPTEMBER

'Tis strange but true; for truth is always strange—stranger than fiction.

[LORD BYRON (1788–1824)]

1788

At an interest rate of 6 percent from the Bank of New York and the Bank of North America, the United States took out its first loan. The money went to pay the salaries of the president and members of Congress.

By all accounts, the very first catechism—a manual of Christian doctrine drawn up in the form of questions and answers for the purpose of instruction in the faith—was compiled by the English scholar Alcuin sometime in the eighth century. It was followed in the next one hundred years by many others, among them those of Notker Labeo, monk of the Abbey of Saint Gall, in Switzerland, and of the German monk Otfried of Weissenburg in Alsace. Nevertheless, catechisms remained relatively rare until the time of the Reformation.

Because of Martin Luther's insistence on the religious instruction of children, the venerable tradition of the catechism was revived—indeed, catechisms became one of the distinctives of Reformation renewal. After Luther published his first little primer of religion, *A Brief Explanation of the Ten Commandments, the Creed, and the Lord's Prayer,* in 1520, several other catechisms were prepared by leading Protestant theologians. Luther's visitation of the Saxon churches in 1528 led him to prepare his *Larger and Smaller Catechisms* the following year.

The Swiss, English, Dutch, and Scottish Reformed also made wide use of catechisms—and a number were published in the sixteenth century. The most noteworthy were the Geneva and Heidelberg catechisms, and those of the German theologian Johannes Oecolampadius of Basel. The Swiss Reformer Heinrich Bullinger produced a catechism in Zürich in 1555. Likewise, John Calvin produced catechisms for the church in Geneva. The Smaller Catechism was published in French in 1536 while the *Larger Catechism* appeared in 1541—both of which were translated into various languages and became acknowledged standards of the Reformed churches.

The Heidelberg, or Palatinate, catechism was compiled in Heidelberg by the German theologians Caspar Olevianus and Zacharias Ursinus, at the request of the Elector Frederick III of the Palatinate. It was published in 1563 and translated into all the languages of Europe. It became the standard of the Dutch and German Reformed churches of America. Soon even the Roman Catholic Church began producing catechisms—the first was prepared by the Council of Trent and published in 1566.

The *Larger* and *Shorter Catechisms,* which, with the Westminster Confession of Faith, became the standard catechisms of the Presbyterian churches throughout the countries of the former British Empire, were compiled by the Assembly of Divines at Westminster between 1645 and 1652. The very familiar *Shorter Catechism* opens with the words "What is the chief end of man? Man's chief end is to glorify God and enjoy him forever."

Amazingly, this little didactic device became the means by which the very foundations of Western culture were reshaped. As Samuel Johnson asserted, "The little questions and answers of the catechisms afford us a glimpse at the inner framework of the Western view of the world."

SEPTEMBER

FEAST DAY
St. John Chrysostum; St. Maurilius of Angers; St. Amatus or Amé, abbot; St. Eulogius of Alexandria

1759 The French and Indian War was brought to an end when the British defeated the French on the Plains of Abraham at Quebec. Killed in the battle were both French General de Montcalm and British General James Wolfe.

1788 The Congress of the Confederation authorized the first national election, and declared New York City as the temporary site for the capital of new United States government.

1792 "Expect great things from God, attempt great things for God" was the famous principle of action first enunciated by the pioneer English missionary, William Carey. Serving as both village pastor and cobbler, on this day in 1792 he wrote *An Inquiry into the Obligations of Christians to Use Means for the Conversion of the Heathens* as a response to the popular pseudo-Calvinism of the day—which held that God would convert the lost when He wished and that nothing men did could possibly alter His timing. That book became the catalyst for a number of new evangelistic endeavors. When the Baptist Missionary Society was formed later that same year, he became its first missionary, leaving almost immediately for India. Carey's remarkable work in literacy training and Bible translation proved to be innovative, efficient, and fruitful—serving as a model for many missions agencies to this day. But he did not limit his efforts to academic work alone. He quickly discovered that India's long-standing legal tradition gave parents the right to kill their children—a right commonly claimed, especially in the case of infant girls. Even the various Hindu sects that forbade the taking of animal life permitted the murder of newborn daughters. Carey went on an all-out campaign to persuade the British government to outlaw the barbaric practice—and ultimately, despite fierce opposition, he succeeded. Shortly before his death, he personally drafted the reform legislation that prohibited child sacrifice at the yearly festival at Gunga Saugor. And, even now, the statute criminalizing infanticide is called the "Carey Edict."

1803 Commodore John Barry, considered by many the father of the American navy, died in Philadelphia.

1943 Chiang Kai-shek became president of China.

1948 Republican Margaret Chase Smith of Maine was elected to the U.S. Senate, becoming the first woman to serve in both houses of Congress.

1949 The Ladies Professional Golf Association of America (LPGA) was formed in New York City, with Patty Berg as its first president.

1971 A four-day inmates' rebellion at the Attica Correctional Facility in Upstate New York ended as police and guards stormed the prison; the ordeal and final assault claimed forty-three lives.

1993 At the White House, Israeli Prime Minister Yitzhak Rabin and Palestinian Liberation Organization chairman Yasser Arafat signed an accord granting limited Palestinian autonomy.

1997 Funeral services were held in Calcutta, India, for Nobel peace laureate Mother Teresa.

1998 Sammy Sosa of the Chicago Cubs hit his 61st and 62nd home runs of the season to pass Roger Maris and pull into a tie with Mark McGwire.

SEPTEMBER

Truth is such a rare thing, it is delightful to tell it.

[EMILY DICKINSON (1830–1886)]

541

Rood is the medieval English word for the "cross of Christ."

The War of 1812 was fiercely raging when Francis Scott Key, a Washington attorney, was sent to the British naval command to secure the release of a prisoner when the fleet began to bombard the placements of American fortifications in Baltimore at Fort McHenry. Key had to watch in agony, wondering if his nation could possibly withstand such a barrage.

Though the battle raged through the night, the American defenses stood firm. The sight of the flag still flying over the fort the next morning inspired the young lawyer to pen the immortal words of "The Star-Spangled Banner"—on this day in 1814.

Later it was set to a popular English hymn tune, "Anacreon in Heaven," and it became a standard in the patriotic repertoire. Congress officially confirmed it as the national anthem more than a hundred years later, just before the First World War.

Though the first verse of the anthem is well known the verses that follow are almost entirely unknown:

> On the shore, dimly seen through the mist of the deep,
> Where the foe's haughty host in dread silence reposes,
> What is that which the breeze, o'er the towering steep,
> As it fitfully blows, half conceals, half discloses?
> Now it catches the gleam of the morning's first beam—
> In full glory reflected, now shines on the stream
> 'Tis the star-spangled banner, O! long may it wave
> O'er the land of the free and the home of the brave.
>
> And where is the band who so vauntingly swore
> That the havoc of war and the battle's confusion
> A home and a country would leave us no more?
> Their blood has washed out their foul footsteps' pollution.
> No refuge could save the hireling and slave
> From the terror of flight or the gloom of the grave!
> And the star-spangled banner in triumph doth wave
> O'er the land of the free and the home of the brave.
>
> O! thus be it ever when freemen shall stand
> Between their loved homes and the foe's desolation;
> Bless'd with victory and peace, may our heaven-rescued land
> Praise the Power that hath made and preserved us a nation.
> Then conquer we must, for our cause it is just—
> And this be our motto—"In God is our trust!"
> And the star-spangled banner in triumph shall wave
> O'er the land of the free and the home of the brave.

SEPTEMBER

335 The empress Helena commissioned the building of a magnificent church in Jerusalem following the discovery of what she thought was the cross of Christ. The church was dedicated on this day with a ceremony of Exaltation of the Holy Cross.

1321 Florentine poet Dante Alighieri, author of the *Divine Comedy*, died in Ravenna, Italy.

1637 John Harvard, a Massachusetts clergyman, bequeathed his library and half of his estate to a local college renamed the following year in his honor.

1716 Guiding sailors into Boston Harbor, the first American lighthouse went into operation on this day.

1741 After working without interruption for twenty-three days, George Frideric Handel completed his greatest oratorio, *Messiah*.

1847 American forces under General Winfield Scott took control of Mexico City during the Mexican War.

1901 Theodore Roosevelt, at age forty-two, became the youngest president when he was sworn in upon the death of President William McKinley.

McKinley died in Buffalo, New York, from gunshot wounds he had received at the Pan-American Exposition on September 6.

1927 Modern dance pioneer Isadora Duncan died in Nice, France, when her scarf became entangled in a wheel of her sports car.

1940 Congress passed the Selective Service Act, providing for the first peacetime draft in American history.

1948 A groundbreaking ceremony took place in New York at the site of the United Nations' world headquarters.

1959 The Soviet space probe *Luna 2* became the first man-made object to reach the moon as it crashed onto the lunar surface.

1975 Pope Paul VI declared Mother Elizabeth Ann Bayley Seton the first American-born saint.

1982 Princess Grace of Monaco, formerly actress Grace Kelly, died at age fifty-two of injuries from a car crash the day before.

1994 On the thirty-fourth day of a strike by players, acting baseball commissioner Bud Selig announced that the 1994 season was over.

Nonsense is nonsense whether it rhymes or not, just as bad half-pennies are good for nothing whether they jingle or lie quiet.

[CHARLES H. SPURGEON (1834–1892)]

SEPTEMBER

His words are among the most recognizable of any of the Founding Fathers: "We the people of the United States, in order to form a more perfect union, establish justice, insure domestic tranquillity, provide for the common defense, promote the general welfare, and secure the blessings of liberty to ourselves and our posterity, do ordain and establish this Constitution for the United States of America."

Gouverneur Morris (1752–1816), who was primarily responsible for the final draft of the Constitution, was also an eloquent, though sometimes windy speaker, and members of the New York legislature, the Constitutional Convention, and the Senate were often swayed by his masterful blend of logic, wit, and imagination. Although he had strong aristocratic tendencies, and as late as 1774 wrote, "It is in the interest of all men to seek for reunion with the parent state," in 1776 Morris spoke in the New York legislature on behalf of the colonies and against the king. He early recognized the need for a united, strong national congress. Of Morris, historian David Muzzey wrote, "He was a nationalist before the birth of the nation."

In the Continental Congress, Morris was chairman of several committees and his gifted pen produced such important documents as the instructions to Franklin as minister to France, and detailed instructions to the peace commissioners, which contained provisions that ultimately appeared in the final treaty. As a member of Congress, he supported and signed the Articles of Confederation.

At the Constitutional Convention, Morris participated in debates more than any other delegate. He argued that the president and the Senate should be elected for life, and that the Senate should represent the rich and propertied, to counterbalance the democratic character of the House of Representatives. This was, of course, rejected, but his proposal for a Council of State led to the idea of the president's cabinet, and he proposed that the President be elected, not by Congress, but by the people. When the Constitution was completed, Morris was given the task of editing and revising it, and he then wrote the famous words of the Preamble.

Once the Constitution was formally accepted, Morris proved one of its most devoted supporters. On September 15, two days before the delegates signed it, Morris made an impassioned speech answering Edmund Randolph, who refused to sign. Many of the delegates later attested that it was his speech that swung the tide of opinion in favor of ratification.

As minister to France in the 1790s, Morris found himself in the wrong country at the wrong time. Although he was recognized by the French revolutionists as one of the leaders of the American Revolution, he was nonetheless a Federalist with clear aristocratic sympathies. In Paris he became involved in attempts to help French nobles escape—including the Marquis de Lafayette and the king, and the revolutionists demanded his removal. After he returned he served in the Senate and, later, as chairman of the group that developed the plan for the Erie Canal, the waterway that opened the path for westward expansion.

But for all of his other accomplishments, he will forever be known as the author of those immortal words in the Preamble to the Constitution.

SEPTEMBER

NATIONAL DAY
Costa Rica
FEAST DAY
St. Nicetus the Goth, St. Nicomedes, St. Aachard or Aichardus, St. Mirin, St. Catherine of Genoa

1782 Congress adopted the Great Seal of the United States with the eagle, arrows, and "E. Pluribus Unum" motto.

1789 American author and historian James Fenimore Cooper was born in Burlington, New Jersey. Best known for the Leatherstocking Tales *(The Deerslayer, The Last of the Mohicans, The Pathfinder, The Pioneers,* and *The Prairie)* and their central character Natty Bumppo, Cooper was instrumental in establishing an independent tradition of American novels.

1821 Independence was proclaimed for Costa Rica, Guatemala, Honduras, Nicaragua, and El Salvador.

1857 William Howard Taft—who would later succeed Theodore Roosevelt as president of the United States and then serve as chief justice of the Supreme Court—was born in Cincinnati, Ohio.

1890 English mystery writer Dame Agatha Christie was born in Torquay, Devon. She wrote numerous books and plays, many featuring detectives Hercule Poirot or Miss Jane Marple, which have sold more than 100 million copies. "Every murderer is probably somebody's old friend."

1917 Russia was proclaimed a republic by Alexander Kerensky, the head of a provisional government after the czar abdicated.

1935 The Nuremberg Laws deprived German Jews of their citizenship and made the swastika the official symbol of Nazi Germany.

1945 American soprano Jessye Norman was born in Augusta, Georgia. Her repertoire consists of works from the baroque period (such as Henry Purcell's *Dido and Aeneas,* 1689) to contemporary works by Stravinsky, Strauss, and Schoenberg. She made her operatic debut in Germany in 1969 and debuted at the Metropolitan Opera House in 1983. Her stage presence, emotional intensity, rich timbre, and expressive range have made her renowned around the world.

1945 Anton Webern, the Austrian composer and follower of the twelve-tone system of music composition, was mistakenly shot and killed by an American soldier.

1949 *The Lone Ranger* premiered on ABC television with Clayton Moore as the masked hero and Jay Silverheels as Tonto.

1963 Unbeknownst to worshippers, approximately fifteen sticks of dynamite had been planted under the back steps of the Sixteenth Street Baptist Church in Birmingham, Alabama. The sermon for the day was, "The Love that Forgives." It was based on Matthew 5:43–44, "You have heard that it was said, 'Love your neighbor and hate your enemy.' But I tell you: Love your enemies and pray for those who persecute you." The lesson was to be grimly appropriate, but before it could be completed, the church exploded, hurling yellow bricks through cars, shattering nearby businesses, collapsing the church rafters, shredding the pews, and shattering the windows. Members of the African-American congregation—wounded, bleeding, and blinded—staggered into the street as rescue crews rushed to the scene. In place of hymns screams and sobs filled the air as they learned that four little girls had died in the racially motivated blast.

1989 Novelist, poet, critic, and multiple Pulitzer Prize winner Robert Penn Warren died on this day. In 1986, he had been named the first poet laureate of the United States.

SEPTEMBER

The mercy of truth is to be truth.

[LAURA RIDING (1901–1991)]

Though he lived only thirty-seven years, Samuel Davies helped to shape American life and culture as few other men had done before or since. Born in Newcastle County, Delaware in 1723, he was descended from sturdy Welsh stock on both sides of his family. His parents were devout, but his mother especially exhibited an ardent piety. Indeed, years later Davies would say, "I am a son of prayer, like my namesake, Samuel the prophet, and my mother called me Samuel, because, she said, I have asked him of the Lord."

When the Reverend Samuel Blair opened his famous school at Fagg's Manor, Pennsylvania, Samuel Davies was put under him and there completed his formal education—both classical and theological. The slender frame of the young man was very weak when he completed his studies; however, he was licensed to preach by Newcastle Presbytery in 1746. The same year he married, and the following year was ordained an evangelist for the purpose of visiting vacant congregations in Virginia. Because of his inexperience, feeble health, and a fear that he would dishonor the ministry, Davies was reluctant to go—but in obedience to the presbytery he set out.

Alas, shortly afterward, on this day in 1747, his wife and son died in a sudden and afflicting manner. The brief notice in his own Bible beside the wife's name says, "September 16, 1747, separated by death, and bereaved of an abortive son." Grief broke his already weakened constitution, and his physical condition gave his friends great concern. In such a condition Davies was unwilling to receive a call to any congregation but traveled from one vacant pulpit to another; his ministrations always being well received so that he received a number of earnest calls for his pastoral services. Among them was one from Hanover County, Virginia, signed by heads of about 150 families and delivered personally by one of their elders.

He accepted the call and sudden blessing was poured out upon the region. At first there were five meetinghouses in which he preached, and then seven in six counties, and later as many as fourteen separate meeting places over which Davies had charge. Some of these were more than thirty miles from one another. Like Whitefield and Wesley, he read while riding on horseback from one charge to another, being all alone in that vast wilderness. The meetinghouse closest to where Davies lived was a plain wooden building in Hanover County capable of holding five hundred people. Amazingly, the building was too small for the multitudes who assembled—including large numbers of black slaves and freedmen. So great and steady was the progress of the church in that region that under the leadership of Davies the first presbytery in Virginia was organized in 1755 with five ministers.

Hanover became the mother presbytery of the Presbyterian Church in the South—and became the seedbed of fervor for independence in the coming conflict with Britain. As Patrick Henry—a congregant in one of the churches established by Davies—later said, "Were it not for him, American freedom would have been still-born. In the gospel he preached, the energy he displayed, and the courage he lived day by day, he modeled the true American temper."

SEPTEMBER

National Day
Mexico
Feast Day
*St. Cornelius, pope; St. Cyprian;
St. Ludmila; St. Ninian; Saints
Abundius and Abundantius; St.
Edith of Wilton; St. Euphemia*

1616 Duke John Maitland Lauderdale, Scottish earl and statesman, was born in Lethington. As a youth he supported the Presbyterians, and from 1643 to 1646 was one of the commissioners to England for the Solemn League and Covenant. In 1647, after King Charles I of England refused to accept Presbyterianism, Maitland was involved in transferring the king, who had been captured by the Scots during the English Revolution, to English custody. Maitland later became a Royalist and gained great influence over Prince Charles, later Charles II of England. In 1651 Maitland, while fighting for Charles, was taken prisoner by troops of the Lord Protector Oliver Cromwell and was not released until 1660. That year, when Charles was restored as king, he appointed Maitland secretary of state for Scotland. Eliminating all his rivals by 1663, Maitland became the virtual ruler of Scotland. He imposed absolute supremacy of the Crown on church and state and persecuted the Covenanters. In 1672 he was created duke of Lauderdale. In spite of the efforts of his enemies to depose him, he held his secretariat until 1680, when Parliament began dismissal proceedings. In 1682, shortly before his death, he was stripped of all his offices.

1638 France's King Louis XIV was born.

1810 Mexico began its revolt against Spanish rule.

1853 Henry Steinway sold his first American-made piano.

1887 Nadia Boulanger, composer, conductor, and teacher, was born in France. She is particularly well known for having been the instructor of Aaron Copland, David Diamond, Elliott Carter, and many other significant American composers.

1893 On this day 100,000 homesteaders rushed onto six million acres of land in what came to be known as the Oklahoma land rush or "Cherokee Strip Day." The land that the United States government had made available for land claims had previously been owned by the Cherokee Nation.

1919 The American Legion was incorporated by an act of Congress.

1940 Samuel T. Rayburn of Texas was elected Speaker of the U.S. House of Representatives.

1949 Warner Brothers introduced the world to Wile E. Coyote (super genius) in the cartoon "Fast & Furry-ous."

1966 The Metropolitan Opera opened its new opera house at New York's Lincoln Center for the Performing Arts.

1974 President Gerald Ford announced a conditional amnesty program for Vietnam War deserters and draft-evaders.

1977 Opera star Maria Callas died in Paris at age fifty-three.

1998 In his first news conference since the release of Kenneth Starr's graphic report, President Clinton said he'd told "the essential truth" about his affair with Monica Lewinsky. As for whether he might resign, Clinton responded that Americans "want me to go on" despite opinion polls showing a very divided citizenry.

SEPTEMBER

A man always has two reasons for doing anything: a good reason and the real reason. Let us be like the man of the frontier and always reveal with utmost honesty our real reasons for all that we do.

[J. P. MORGAN (1837–1913)]

1787 — Though they did not have the authorization of Congress and were, thus, technically in violation of the laws of the land, the delegates attending the Constitutional Convention in Philadelphia completed the Constitution of the United States, and a majority of them signed the great document.

By the time he delivered his Farewell Address to his cabinet in Philadelphia on this day in 1796, George Washington had already served two terms and did not wish to serve a third. His once-immense popularity had dwindled dramatically because of his fierce federalism and his opposition to the formation of political parties—which were emerging nonetheless. In addition, he was tired of being lampooned in the political press.

He asked his most trusted aide, Alexander Hamilton, to draft a kind of manifesto of his greatest concerns and deepest convictions. He considered its message so important that he had the full text published in newspapers around the country two days later so that it would reach a much wider audience. The address warned against foreign involvements, political factions, and sectionalism in the strongest possible terms.

It sounded a distinctly conservative tone: "Toward the preservation of your government and the permanency of your present happy state, it is requisite not only that you steadily discountenance irregular oppositions to its acknowledged authority, but also that you resist with care the spirit of innovation upon its principles, however specious the pretexts."

But perhaps most remarkably, the address promoted the cultural benefits of the Christian faith: "Of all the dispositions and habits which lead to political prosperity, religion and morality are indispensable supports. In vain would that man claim the tribute of patriotism who should labor to subvert these great pillars of human happiness, these firmest props of the duties of men and citizens." Indeed, the address warned, "The mere politician, equally with the pious man, ought to respect and to cherish them. A volume could not trace all their connections with private and public felicity. Let it simply be asked: Where is the security for property, for reputation, for life, if the sense of religious obligation desert the oaths which are the instruments of investigation in courts of justice? And let us with caution indulge the supposition that morality can be maintained without religion. Whatever may be conceded to the influence of refined education on minds of peculiar structure, reason and experience both forbid us to expect that national morality can prevail in exclusion of religious principle."

It was a sober message from the Father of the Nation, all too often quoted yet all too rarely heeded.

SEPTEMBER

FEAST DAY
St. Francis of Camporosso, St. Hildegard, St. Columbia of Cordova, Saints Socrates and Stephen, St. Satyrus of Milan, St. Theodora, St. Lambert of Maastricht, St. Robert Bellarmine, St. Peter Arbues

1630 The name of Trimountain, Massachusetts, was changed to Boston to honor the pastor, John Cotton, formerly of St. Boltoph's Church in Boston, England.

1672 Anne Bradstreet, the first native poet of the American colonies, died in Andover, Massachusetts.

1771 Scottish physician and novelist Tobias Smollett—whose most famous book, *Humphrey Clinker,* set the standard for coming-of-age novels—died at Leghorn at the age of fifty.

1862 Union forces hurled back a Confederate invasion of Maryland in the Battle of Antietam during the War Between the States.

1893 The World's Columbian Exposition, held in Chicago in honor of the four-hundredth anniversary of Columbus' voyage to the New World, was not just a big trade fair. In addition to art exhibitions, technical, engineering, transportation, architectural, and other displays it called together a conference of world religious leaders. This Parliament of World Religions concluded its proceedings on this day. Though many evangelical Christians such as D. L. Moody refused to participate, saying that to do so might imply the essential equality of all religions and might provide a foothold in America for some of the world's most dastardly cults, the Roman Catholic Church sent delegates, as did some liberal Protestant denominations, to meet with a dozen or so Buddhists, eight Hindus, two Shintoists, a Jain, a Taoist, a half dozen Muslims, three or four Confucians, and a couple of Zoroastrians. The Parliament produced a bevy of anti-Christian speeches along with strong denunciations of Christian missions. Following the meetings, Swami Vivekananda of the Hindu tradition and Anagarika Dharmapala of the Buddhists toured the United States in an effort to found Vedanta Societies. D. T. Suzuki, a Buddhist, was dispatched to the United States by another attendee of the conference where he translated works into English and established a Zen presence, including America's first Zen monasteries. Many other Eastern gurus, seeing ripe fields, have also launched new missions in the United States. It seems Moody was right after all.

1908 Thomas Selfridge became the first person to die in an airplane crash. Orville Wright was flying the plane when the propeller was caught in overhead wires. Wright was injured in the crash.

1916 Novelist Mary Stewart was born in Sutherland County, Durham.

1920 In Canton, Ohio, the National Football League was formed.

1939 The Harry James Orchestra—with their lead singer, the young Frank Sinatra—recorded "All or Nothing at All" for Columbia Records.

1947 James V. Forrestal was sworn in as the first U.S. Secretary of Defense as a new National Military Establishment unified America's armed forces.

1948 The United Nations mediator for Palestine, Count Folke Bernadotte, was assassinated in Jerusalem by Jewish extremists.

1964 The situation comedy *Bewitched* premiered on ABC.

1978 After meeting at Camp David, Israeli Prime Minister Menachem Begin and Egyptian President Anwar Sadat signed a framework for a peace treaty.

1980 Former Nicaraguan president Anastasio Somoza was assassinated in Paraguay.

SEPTEMBER

I hope I shall always possess firmness and virtue enough to maintain what I consider the most enviable of all titles, the character of an honest man.

[GEORGE WASHINGTON (1732–1799)]

1729

The Swiss Methodist leader John Fletcher was born. He was educated at Nyon and while visiting England in 1752, fell under the influence of Methodism. He determined immediately to become a pastor. Five years later he was ordained. After assisting John Wesley and preaching to French-speaking Swiss expatriates, he threw himself into his work as the vicar of Madeley. He wrote prolifically—and although born and reared in Switzerland, he adopted the English language so thoroughly that he left fine works in it. He is considered one of the great early Methodist theologians.

18

SEPTEMBER

Born into slavery, Booker T. Washington literally pulled himself up by his own bootstraps to become one of the most articulate and influential educators in the nation. Founder of the Tuskegee Institute, author of a number of books, and a popular speaker, he always emphasized the importance of education, hard work, and self-discipline for the advancement of African Americans. Washington became a celebrity, much in demand as a speaker and lecturer around the country and as a consultant and confidant to powerful politicians and community leaders. Though he was criticized by some because he refused to use his influence for direct political agitation, he had obviously begun the long process toward the reconciliation of long-sundered communities and races.

He was asked to deliver an address at the Cotton States' Exposition on this day in 1895. The invitation was noteworthy in and of itself, since his audience would include both white and black Southerners. As a result, his speech received enormous attention throughout the country—it helped to galvanize public opinion in favor of black self-improvement.

Thus, he argued in that famous speech, "In all things that are purely social we can be as separate as the fingers, yet one as the hand in all things essential to mutual progress. There is no defense or security for any of us except in the highest intelligence and development of all. If anywhere there are efforts tending to curtail the fullest growth of the Negro, let these efforts be turned into stimulating, encouraging, and making him the most useful and intelligent citizen. Effort or means so invested will pay a thousand percent interest. These efforts will be twice blessed—blessing him that gives and him that takes. There is no escape through law of man or God from the inevitable: The laws of changeless justice bind oppressor with oppressed; And close as sin and suffering joined, we march to fate abreast."

Washington had already instilled his philosophy of hard work, competence, and community-mindedness in thousands of students all across the country who were making a substantive difference in the welfare of African-American families, churches, neighborhoods, and businesses. And now, that message was going out to the entire nation, thus ushering in a new era of civil rights for all Americans.

550

1709 Samuel Johnson, the English lexicographer and compiler of the first great dictionary of the English language (1755), was born in Lichfield in Staffordshire. One of the remarkable features of his dictionary was that an example from classical literature was provided for every word. Some of his more famous sayings are: "When a man is tired of London, he is tired of life," "I am willing to love all mankind, except an American," "A cucumber should be well sliced, and dressed with pepper and vinegar, and thrown out as good for nothing," and "When two Englishmen meet, their first talk is of the weather."

1759 The French formally surrendered Quebec to the British.

1793 President George Washington laid the cornerstone of the U.S. Capitol in a secretive Masonic ceremony. This was the last occasion in which the stone was seen despite efforts to find it during renovations in 1958.

1810 Chile declared its independence from Spain.

1830 Essayist and literary critic William Hazlitt died in London at age fifty-two. The last words of his *Memoirs* were, "Well, I have had a happy life."

1850 Congress passed the Fugitive Slave Act, which allowed slaveowners to reclaim slaves who had escaped to other states.

1851 The first edition of the *New York Times* was published. It was originally called the *New York Daily Times* and cost one cent per copy.

1873 The failure of the New York brokerage firm of Jay Cooke and Company set off a panic that resulted in a five-year depression.

1917 Aldous Huxley was hired as a schoolmaster at Eton, where he counted among his unruly pupils Eric Arthur Blair—later best known as George Orwell.

1927 The Columbia Phonograph Broadcasting System (later CBS) made its debut with a network of sixteen radio stations.

1951 The film version of Tennessee Williams's *A Streetcar Named Desire* opened in theaters.

1961 United Nations Secretary-General Dag Hammarskjöld was killed in a plane crash in northern Rhodesia.

1970 Rock guitarist Jimi Hendrix died of a drug overdose in London at age twenty-seven.

1985 Light-night talk show host David Letterman presented his first Top Ten List from the home office.

1997 Voters in Wales narrowly approved a British government offer to set up a Welsh assembly.

How happy is he born or taught
That serveth not another's will;
Whose armor is his honest thought
And simple truth his utmost skill.

[HENRY WOTTON (1568–1639)]

SEPTEMBER

Alfred, Lord Tennyson was one of the greatest idyllic poets ever to write in the English language. He was in many ways, like Dickens and Spurgeon, representative of the whole Victorian Age.

He was born in Somersby, Lincolnshire, in 1809. His initial education was conducted largely by his clergyman father, Dr. George Clayton Tennyson. The boy showed an early interest and talent in poetic composition, working original poems in a variety of meters and also successfully imitating the style of such famous poets as Lord Byron and Sir Walter Scott, both of whom he greatly admired. By the time he was fifteen, he had produced a number of fine blank-verse plays and one long epic.

He gained initial literary recognition from a series of reviews and criticisms he had written while in school. But his first long poem was *The Princess*, a romantic treatment in musical blank verse of the question of women's rights. *In Memoriam*, a tribute to the memory of Arthur Hallam, was one of his greatest poems and was published on this day in 1850. Although the loose organization of this series of lyrics, written over a period of seventeen years, and the intensely personal character of the poem perplexed many of the readers of Tennyson's day, *In Memoriam* has since taken its place as one of the great elegies in English literature.

A short time later, Tennyson married Emily Sarah Sellwood, whom he had been waiting to marry since 1836. Enormously popular, he was appointed poet laureate of Britain the same year, succeeding William Wordsworth in this honor. He settled with his bride at Twickenham near London, three years later moving to his estate, Farringford, near Freshwater on the Isle of Wight. There he resided for at least a part of each year for the remainder of his life. In 1854, *The Charge of the Light Brigade* appeared. It was written as one of the duties of his laureateship to celebrate a memorable action by a British cavalry unit in the Crimean War.

With the composition of *Idylls of the King*, which he began in 1859 and completed in 1885, Tennyson returned to the subject of the Arthurian cycle. He dealt with the ancient legends in an episodic rather than a continuous narrative structure, the result being a loosely strung series of metrical romances. Rich in medieval pageantry and vivid, noble characterization, the poems contain some of Tennyson's best writing.

Tennyson was made a peer in 1884, taking his seat in the House of Lords as Baron Tennyson of Freshwater and Aldworth. He died at Aldworth House, Hazlemere, Surrey, on October 6, 1892, his reputation secure for the ages.

SEPTEMBER

FEAST DAY

St. Januarius of Benevento, St. Peleus and his Companions, St. Emily de Rodat, St. Mary of Cerevellon, St. Goericus or Abbo, St. Theodore of Canterbury, St. Susanna of Eleutheropolis, St. Sequanus or Seine

1777 During the Revolutionary War, American soldiers won the first Battle of Saratoga.

1783 Jacques-Etienne Montgolfier launched a duck, a sheep, and a rooster aboard a hot-air balloon at Versailles in France.

1819 John Keats, English poet, wrote "To Autumn," a three-stanza ode inspired by the beauty of the changing season.

1846 English poet Elizabeth Barrett, in the company of her dog Flush and her devoted maid Wilson, escaped her tyrannical father when she eloped with Robert Browning, to whom she had been secretly married a week earlier.

1881 The twentieth president of the United States, James A. Garfield, died of wounds inflicted by an assassin.

1888 The renowned missionary to China, Jonathan Goforth, began a tour of the North Honan region of China where he would spend the rest of his life proclaiming the gospel, establishing churches, and ministering to the needy. He was convicted of the need to go to the foreign mission field while reading the memoirs of the famed preacher Robert Murray McCheyne. A student at Knox College, Toronto, he immediately offered himself for missionary service—first with Hudson Taylor's China Inland Mission and later with the Presbyterian Foreign Mission Society. His service proved to be one of the most effective in the entire world.

1911 English novelist and Nobel Prize winner for literature in 1983, Sir William Golding was born in Colomb Minor in Cornwall. His first and most famous novel was *Lord of the Flies.*

1928 The first animated talking cartoon, Walt Disney's "Steamboat Willie" featuring Mickey Mouse, was shown at the Colony Theatre in New York City.

1934 Bruno Hauptmann was arrested in New York and charged with the kidnap-murder of the Lindbergh infant.

1955 President Juan Peron of Argentina was ousted after a revolt by the army and navy.

1957 In the Nevada desert, the United States conducted its first underground nuclear test.

1959 Soviet leader Nikita Khrushchev reacted angrily during a visit to Los Angeles upon being told that, for security reasons, he wouldn't be allowed to visit Disneyland.

1960 Cuban leader Fidel Castro, in New York to visit the United Nations, angrily checked out of the Shelburne Hotel after a dispute with the management.

1973 Novelist and journalist Paul Theroux set out from London's Victoria Station for Folkstone and Paris on the journey he would chronicle in his classic travel book *The Great Railway Bazaar.*

1984 Britain and China completed a draft agreement on transferring Hong Kong from British to Chinese rule by 1997.

SEPTEMBER

There is no well-defined boundary line between honesty and dishonesty. The frontiers of one blend with the outside limits of the other, and he who attempts to tread this dangerous ground may be sometimes in the one domain and sometimes in the other.

[O. Henry (1862–1910)]

1224

On this day of the Feast of the Holy Cross, Francis of Assisi had a vision while communing with the Lord at a retreat on Mt. Alvernia. An angel appeared to him and commanded him to give three gifts back to the Lord, to his Franciscan brothers, and to the world—the three gifts were, he later attested, as golden balls in his bosom: poverty, chastity, and obedience. When the angel left, in what is regarded as one of the classic experiences of all Christian history, Francis's hands, feet, and sides bore the wounds of Christ, the marks of the stigmata. Within two years the saint was dead.

SEPTEMBER

Although the nomination and election of the dark-horse candidate James Garfield surprised many Americans, the nomination of Chester A. Arthur (1830–1886) as vice president was even more of a shock. Many a citizen feared the worst when Garfield died with three and a half years of his term remaining. And for good reason.

Arthur, who loved fine clothes and elegant living, had been associated with the corrupt New York political machine for almost twenty years. In 1878 he had even been removed from his post as collector of the Port of New York by President Hayes, who had become alarmed at his misuse of patronage.

But in spite of his questionable record, Arthur was nominated vice president—largely to appease the powerful party establishment. Thus, when Arthur became president on this day in 1881 following the assassination of President Garfield, there was every expectation that the freewheeling spoils system that had reigned in New York would be firmly established in Washington. But Chester Arthur fooled everyone—friends and enemies alike. Somehow the responsibilities of that high office seemed to transform this corrupt, petty politician into a man sincerely dedicated to the good of the country. Courageously he established his independence by vetoing a graft-laden rivers-and-harbors bill, by breaking with his former machine cronies, and by vigorously prosecuting members of his own party accused of defrauding the government. And, most important, instead of a spoils system, he supported a Federal Civil Service based on competitive examinations and a nonpolitical merit system.

By his courageous acts Arthur won over many who had first feared his coming to power, but he lost the support of the political bosses. Although he was not an inspiring leader of men, he earned the nation's gratitude as the champion of the Civil Service system.

FEAST DAY
Saints Fausta and Evilasius; St. Candida of Carthage; St. Vincent Madelgarius; Saints Theodore, Philippa, and their Companions

331 B.C.	Alexander the Great crossed the Tigris River and began his assault on the ancient empire of Persia.

451	Attila the Hun was defeated by the Romans in France
1258	The great cathedral at Salisbury, England, was consecrated on this day.
1440	King Henry VI founded the school at Eton.
1519	Portuguese navigator Ferdinand Magellan set out from Spain on a voyage to find a western passage to the Spice Islands in Indonesia. Magellan was killed en route, but one of his ships eventually was able to circle the world.
1865	In Poughkeepsie, New York, Vassar College for women was opened.
1870	Italian troops took control of the Papal States, leading to the unification of Italy for the first time since the fall of the Roman Empire in the fifth century.
1873	On the floor of the New York Stock Exchange, panic followed news of railroad bond defaults and bank failures. In New York, all banks were closed for ten days.
1881	Chester A. Arthur was sworn in as the twenty-first president of the United States, succeeding James A. Garfield, who had been assassinated.
1884	The Equal Rights Party was formed during a convention of suffragists in San Francisco. The convention nominated Belva Ann Bennett Lockwood for president.

1947	Former New York City Mayor Fiorello La Guardia died.
1958	At a public appearance in a Harlem department store, Martin Luther King Jr. was seriously wounded by an apparently deranged African-American woman who stabbed him in the chest.
1962	James Meredith was blocked from enrolling at the University of Mississippi by Governor Ross R. Barnett. Meredith was later admitted and became the first African-American graduate of the school.
1973	Singer-songwriter Jim Croce died in a plane crash near Natchitoches, Louisiana; he was thirty.
1973	In their so-called "Battle of the Sexes," tennis star Billie Jean King defeated Bobby Riggs in straight sets, 6-4, 6-3, 6-3, at the Houston Astrodome.
1979	Jean-Bedel Bokassa, self-styled head of the Central African Empire, was overthrown in a French-supported coup while on a visit to Libya.
1984	A suicide car bomber attacked the U.S. Embassy annex in north Beirut, killing a dozen people.
1989	Soviet leader Mikhail S. Gorbachev succeeded in completely realigning the Soviet Communist Party, dropping three Politburo members.
1998	After 2,632 consecutive games, Cal Ripken of the Baltimore Orioles sat out a game against the New York Yankees, ending a sixteen-year run.

SEPTEMBER

The greatest homage we can pay to truth is to use it.

[RALPH WALDO EMERSON (1803–1882)]

Charles V was one of the most remarkable men in history, serving as king of Spain and as holy Roman emperor for forty years. He very nearly succeeded in uniting the world into a vast Roman Catholic fiefdom—stretching from the Americas to the frontiers of Asia.

He was born with the most royal pedigree of any man since the time of the Caesars: He was the son of Philip I, king of Castile; maternal grandson of Ferdinand V of Castile and Isabella I; paternal grandson of the Hapsburg Holy Roman emperor Maximilian I; and great-grandson of Charles the Bold, duke of Burgundy. On the death of his father in 1506, he inherited the Burgundian realm; following the death of Ferdinand in 1516, he became ruler of the vast interconnected Spanish kingdoms; and when Maximilian died in 1519, he gained the Hapsburg lands in central Europe, where his younger brother, Ferdinand, later Emperor Ferdinand I, was governor. Also in 1519, Charles, having bribed the electors, was designated Holy Roman emperor.

Thus, before his twentieth birthday, Charles was by far the most powerful sovereign in Christendom. His inherited lands far exceeded those of the Frankish emperor Charlemagne. His territory included the Spanish realms of Aragdoms; and when Maximilian died ; the Italian states of Naples, Sicily, and Sardinia; Spanish conquests in America and Africa; and all the Habsburg lands of Germany and Central Europe.

Yet, his hegemony was not without challenges. He ascended the Imperial throne at a time when Germany was agitated by Martin Luther and his Protestant movement. In an unsuccessful attempt to restore order and tranquillity, a great diet was held in Worms in 1521, before which Luther made a memorable defense of his doctrines. The diet rejected his position, and Charles subsequently issued an edict condemning Luther—but the Reformer enjoyed the protection of several German electors.

Meanwhile, Charles was distracted by the rivalry between England, France, and Spain over various Italian lands. War resulted, so Charles was unable to prosecute his assault on the Lutherans. And as if that were not bad enough, the Ottoman Turks under the able leadership of Sultan Suleiman were threatening to overrun Europe. The Turks already controlled the Balkan Peninsula, and in 1526, the Moslem hoard swept over the Hapsburg lands of Hungary. Then just three years later, the Turks laid siege to Vienna.

Though Charles was finally able to quell the rivalries in Europe and hold Suleiman at bay, the spread of disorder during the Reformation emboldened the German princes to seek autonomy for their states. The peasants took advantage of the turmoil in 1524 and revolted.

In the end, it seemed that one thing or another would always conspire against his attempt to unite all of Christendom once again. Weary of the constant struggles and heavy responsibilities of his scattered realms, Charles in 1555 resigned the Netherlands and, in 1556, Spain, to his son Philip II. In 1556 Charles announced his intention to abdicate the Imperial crown in favor of his brother, Ferdinand I, who officially became emperor in 1558. Charles retired that year to the monastery of San Jerónimo de Yuste in Extremadura, Spain, where he died on this day in 1558.

SEPTEMBER

NATIONAL DAY
Malta
FEAST DAY
St. Theodore of Chernigov, The Martyrs of Korea, St. Michael of Chernigov, St. Matthew, St. Maures of Troyes

19 B.C. The author of the epic poem the *Aeneid*, Publius Vergilius Maro, known simply as Virgil, died on this day.

1792 The French National Convention voted to abolish the monarchy.

1866 Herbert George Wells, English novelist and science-fiction pioneer, was born on this day. His most famous works include *The Time Machine*, *War of the Worlds*, and *The Invisible Man*.

1874 English composer Gustav Holst was born in Cheltenham. Primarily known for his orchestral suite *The Planets* (1916), Holst also wrote several choral and orchestral works that utilized elements of English folk songs.

1893 Frank Duryea and his brother Charles took the gasoline-powered automobile they had developed for a test drive in Springfield, Massachusetts. This is believed to have been the first such automobile in the United States.

1897 In response to a letter by eight-year-old Virginia O'Hanlon, the *New York Sun* printed an editorial titled "Yes, Virginia, There Is a Santa Claus."

1915 On England's Salisbury Plain, Stonehenge was auctioned to C. H. E. Chubb of Salisbury for £6,600.

1931 Britain went off the gold standard.

1938 New York and New England ware battered by 180-mile-per-hour winds in a hurricane that killed more than six hundred people, caused widespread damage, and literally split Long Island in two.

1944 The growth of religious programming on radio led to the formation of the National Religious Broadcasters at a convention in Chicago's Moody Memorial Church.

1945 On Secretary of War Henry Stimson's recommendation, President Truman approved the use of the "Second World War" as the official designation of the war.

1948 Vaudeville star Milton Berle made his debut as permanent host of *The Texaco Star Theater* on NBC television.

1949 The People's Republic of China was proclaimed by its Communist leaders.

1998 President Clinton's videotaped grand jury testimony was publicly broadcast; in it, Clinton quibbled with prosecutors over "the truth of my relationship" with Monica Lewinsky—at one point asking the grand jury to clarify the meaning of the word *is*.

21

No legacy is so rich as honesty.

[WILLIAM SHAKESPEARE (C. 1564–1616)]

SEPTEMBER

Few provincial cities anywhere are more crowded with incident and achievement than the English University city of Oxford. In a short stroll visitors may pass the house where Edmund Halley discovered his comet; the site of Britain's oldest public museum, the Ashmolean; the hall where architect Christopher Wren drew his first plans; the pub where Thomas Hardy scribbled his notes for *Jude the Obscure*; the track where Roger Bannister ran the first sub-four-minute mile; the meadow where a promising young mathematician named Charles Lutwidge Dodgson refined *The Formulae of Plane Trigonometry, An Elementary Treatise on Determinants* and, of course, his famous children's trifle called *Alice's Adventures in Wonderland*.

As they walk down the broad and curving High Street, thought by many to be the most beautiful in England, or through the maze of back lanes that wander among the golden, age-worn college buildings, visitors may follow in the footsteps of Samuel Johnson, Adam Smith, Edward Gibbon, Jonathan Swift, John Donne, Roger Bacon, Cardinal Wolsey, Oscar Wilde, Graham Greene, Evelyn Waugh, T. S. Eliot, C. S. Lewis, Percy Bysshe Shelley, Indira Gandhi, and Margaret Thatcher, to name just a few who have worked and studied here.

The heart of the city is Carfax—from the Latin *quadrifurcua*, "four-forked"—from which the main streets run to the four points of the compass. This was the center of the walled medieval city—built on the foundations of an early Saxon trading settlement located near the ford in the river there.

It was in this remarkable environment on this day in 1921 that the esteemed professor of etymology, J. R. R. Tolkien, began to recount the stories of Bilbo and Frodo Baggins, hobbits of Middle Earth—one of the most remarkable achievements in English literature.

John Ronald Reuel Tolkien was born in South Africa in 1892. After a brilliant undergraduate career, he became a medieval scholar, philologist, and professor at the university. His scholarly work concerned Anglo-Saxon and medieval literature.

His depth and breadth of scholarship are most evident in the epic works he created about the fantasy world he called Middle Earth. He wrote *The Hobbit* in 1937 as a children's book. Its sequel, the trilogy entitled *The Lord of the Rings*—finally published after much anticipation in 1954 and 1955—included *The Fellowship of the Ring, The Two Towers,* and *The Return of the King*. The work is an imaginative masterpiece that has captured the imagination of generations ever since. It is a profound tale of the conflict between good and evil told against a backdrop of rich cultures, vibrant characters, and stunning prose and poetry.

Tolkien's close friend and fellow professor, C. S. Lewis, commented that "such a tale, told by such an imaginative mind, could only have been spawned in such a place as Oxford."

SEPTEMBER

FEAST DAY
St. Felix II, pope; St. Landus or Lô; St. Bodo; St. Emmeramus; St. Maurice of Agaunum; St. Thomas of Villanova; The Theban Legion; St. Phocas the Gardener; St. Salaberga

1598 The playwright Ben Jonson—the man most responsible for identifying William Shakespeare—was indicted for manslaughter after killing another actor in a duel.

1692 In Salem, Massachusetts, seven women and two men were convicted of witchcraft and executed.

1776 Nathan Hale, the American soldier and patriot, was hanged for spying on British troops. He was not given the opportunity to have a clergyman attend him, and letters to his mother and friends were destroyed. As he was about to die, his last words were, "I regret that I have but one life to give for my country."

1784 The Russians established their first settlement in Alaska, on Kodiak Island.

1789 Congress authorized the office of postmaster general.

1792 The French Republic was proclaimed.

1862 President Abraham Lincoln issued a preliminary Emancipation Proclamation, declaring all slaves in rebel states should be free—though he said nothing about any of the slaves in the Union states of Missouri, Maryland, Delaware, Kentucky, West Virginia, or even the District of Columbia.

1914 T. S. Eliot and Ezra Pound met at Pound's flat in Kensington, beginning a long standing friend-ship.

1926 Though they were on the same tour bus visiting the site of the Battle of Waterloo, James Joyce and Thomas Wolfe did not meet.

1949 The Soviet Union exploded its first atomic bomb.

1964 Starring Zero Mostel, the musical *Fiddler on the Roof* made its Broadway debut at the Imperial Theater. It was the beginning of a run of 3,242 performances.

1969 Willie Mays of the San Francisco Giants hit his 600th career home run, during a game against San Diego.

1975 Sara Jane Moore attempted to shoot President Gerald Ford outside a San Francisco hotel, but missed.

1980 The Persian Gulf conflict between Iran and Iraq erupted into full-scale war.

1989 Irving Berlin, one of America's most prolific songwriters, died in New York City at age 101.

1993 Nearly fifty people were killed when an Amtrak passenger train derailed and crashed into Bayou Canot near Mobile, Alabama. Among the sur-vivors was renowned theologian R. C. Sproul, who took the train for fear of flying.

SEPTEMBER

Never laugh at live dragons.

[J. R. R. Tolkien (1892–1973)]

559

Ever since the advent of the nineteenth century, fictional portrayals of the persecuted church in Nero's Rome have been a favored form of the Christian novel. Most have hardly been particularly noteworthy—indeed, a rather predictable formula made them all too facile. The plots were constructed to contrast the corrupt brilliance of pagan Rome with the austere and pious life of the early church. Most readers can recount such business by heart: the orgies, the arena, the glimpse of the bloated and sensual figure of the emperor and his perversely corrupted court, the delicate and beautiful Christian maiden with her hair let down her back, the ill-fated love affair between her and some swashbuckling, worldly wise, well-placed Roman soldier, the soldier's reluctant conversion just in the nick of time, the dim passageways and fleeting sanctuaries of the catacombs, the horrific conflagration of Nero's fire, and the sad but heroic martyrdom of each of the protagonists in turn. Such pulp protocols seem to lie altogether outside the pale of literature, reserved entirely for the dogmatic propagandist. But there have been more than a few remarkable exceptions.

There were such early marvels as Zygmunt Krasinski's tragedy, *Iridion*. It portrays a Greek rebel who tried to turn the Christian dissenters into revolutionaries. John Henry Newman's *Callista* captures the universality of the Christian message in a time of heaving uncertainty, Paul Bereille's *Emilie,* Hermann Geiger's *Lydia*, George Whyte-Melville's *The Gladiators*, Ren du Mesnil Marincourt's *Viva,* Josef Kraszewski's *Caprea and Roma*, and F. N. Farrar's *Darkness and Dawn* all revolve around the lives, loves, and sacrifices of the early martyrs—each considered a classic in its own right. *Act* by Alexandre Dumas and *Salammbo* by Gustave Flaubert, though hardly counted among their best-known works, are undoubtedly among their best-written ones—in large part because they were the passionate vehicles for their authors' own struggles regarding the gospel.

In the United States, amid a torrent of maudlin and sentimental tomes, a few works were able to emerge as genuinely edifying fictional narratives. Lew Wallace, a bitter Union general during the War Between the States, began writing *Ben Hur* to disprove the claims of Christianity. But, much to his surprise, he himself was converted as he researched the period and developed the characters. The result was an invigorating paean to the faith. Lloyd Douglas likewise turned his experienced fictional hand to the days of the early church. As a result, he not only produced two classics of the genre, *The Big Fisherman* and *The Robe*, he also reinvigorated his own flagging faith.

But as fine as each of these books is, all of them pale in comparison with *Quo Vadis*. The triumph of Sienkiewicz sets his work altogether apart. As late as 1937, the French *Larousse Encyclopedia* asserted that the book was "one of the most extraordinary successes registered in the history of the book—both in terms of sales and in terms of literary merit." The American literary critic Nathan Haskell Dole was hardly exaggerating when he commented, "It is said that if a person standing at the foot of Niagara merely touches the awful sheet of water with a finger, he is drawn irresistibly in; and so if a person begins this book, the torrential sweep of its immensity becomes instantly absorbing. It is one of the great books of our day."

SEPTEMBER

NATIONAL DAY
  Saudi Arabia
FEAST DAY
  Saints Andrew, John, Peter, and Antony; St. Adamnan or Euanan of Iona

63 B.C. The founder of the Roman Empire, Caius Octavias—later known as Caesar Augustus—was born in Rome.

1642 Harvard College in Cambridge, Massachusetts, held its first commencement.

1758 Robert Adam and his three brothers, John, James, and William, all followed in their architect father's footsteps. Robert and James set up a practice in London on this day, developing there an integrated style, an elegant sense of proportion, and unified façades such as in Portland Place and the Adelphi. In 1762 Robert Adam was appointed as a royal architect and became the most fashionable architect in England. He had a great impact on interior design with elaborate plaster work and neoclassical figures. Adam spent the last ten years of his life in Scotland where he influenced the design of the New Town, Edinburgh, particularly in the wonderful Charlotte Square and also Register House and the Old College of Edinburgh University. A high point in Robert's work was Culzean Castle for the Earl of Cassilis. In addition though, he was a preservationist—a strong advocate of protecting the ancient ruins of the architectural legacy of the nation. Adam was far and away the most influential architect of the time and at his death was buried in Westminster Abbey.

1779 During the Revolutionary War, the American warship *Bon Homme Richard* defeated the HMS *Serapis* after the American commander, John Paul Jones, is said to have declared: "I have not yet begun to fight!"

1780 British spy John Andre was captured along with papers revealing Benedict Arnold's plot to surrender West Point to the British.

1800 Today in Washington County, Pennsylvania, William Holmes McGuffey, educator and author of the *McGuffey Readers*, was born.

1806 After two years and four months, Meriwether Lewis and William Clark returned from the first successful expedition to the United States Pacific Coast.

1846 The planet Neptune was discovered by German astronomer Johann Gottfried Galle.

1911 The first airmail service offered by the United States Post Office began operations when "airmail pilot number one," Earl Ovington, delivered mail from Long Island to Mineola, New York, a mere six miles away. Ovington's plane, the *Dragon Fly*, was a Biériot monoplane.

1939 Sigmund Freud, the founder of the dubious practice of psychoanalysis, died in London.

1952 Republican vice-presidential candidate Richard M. Nixon went on television to deliver what came to be known as the "Checkers" speech as he refuted allegations of improper campaign financing.

1957 Nine African-American students who had entered Little Rock Central High School in Arkansas were forced to withdraw because of a white mob outside.

1980 For a price of $50,000, Microsoft Corporation purchased QDOS (Quick and Dirty Operating System) from a company called Seattle Computer. Licensing revenues from the system, later known as DOS, and from its subsequent Windows programs, turned Bill Gates, president of the company, into the world's richest man.

SEPTEMBER

23

A ruin should always be protected but never repaired— thus may we witness full the lingering legacies of the past.

[SIR WALTER SCOTT (1771–1832)]

HARVEST DAY

Traditionally, the people of medieval England began the fall harvesting on or near this day, at the Feast of Ungathering or Harvest Home. To celebrate, wagons were decorated with fruits of the harvest, amid celebration and song.

Harvest-home, harvest-home
We have ploughed, we have sowed,
We have reaped, we have mowed,
We have brought home every load,
Hip, hip, hip, harvest-home, hurrah!

On this day in 1904, after several years of experience publishing quality books at popular prices, Joseph Malaby Dent (1849–1926) began to flesh out an ambitious vision for a series of reprints he would call the Everyman's Library. It was to be a massive and diverse selection of one thousand classics—practically the whole canon of Western civilization's great books—sold at affordable prices.

Though the experts had decreed that the classics were dry, uninspiring, and hardly suited for the fast-paced industrial world of the twentieth century, Dent believed that properly presented, the great books would prove to be as appealing as ever. He also believed that the classics had an inevitable transforming effect on the reader's self-understanding—stretching, shaping, and confronting him. He thought they invited and rewarded frequent rereadings—they were ever new. They had the uncanny ability to adapt themselves to various times and places and thus provided a sense of the shared life of humanity over the course of space and time. And finally, he held that their mere endurance across all the varied times and seasons of human experience demonstrated an interminable permanence amid modern temporality that was simultaneously comforting and challenging.

Though the venture was obviously a commercial risk, Dent was confident that the very thing that made the classics classic would ensure success for the series. He was right. Public demand for books in Everyman's Library exceeded every expectation. Production began in 1906 and more than 150 titles were issued by the end of that first year.

Wartime inflation and shortages of supplies more than doubled the price of each volume during the First World War. After the conflict, inflation and shortages actually worsened. Dent responded to the setbacks by expanding book sales to international markets. He expanded distribution to North America by setting up a Canadian subsidiary and by allowing E. P. Dutton to distribute Everyman titles throughout the United States. In addition, Dent hired agents to sell Everyman titles in Australia, New Zealand, South Africa, and most of continental Europe.

In just fifty years total sales of the Everyman's series exceeded sixty million copies of the classics. Though his company was finally sold by his heirs in 1988, almost exactly a century after he founded it, the impact of the little publisher who dared stand against the tide of the modern conventions of uniformity, conformity, and efficiency is still felt.

SEPTEMBER

FEAST DAY
St. Pacifico of San Severino, St. Robert Flower of Knaresborough, St. Geremarus or Germer, St. Gerard of Csanad

1789   Congress passed the First Judiciary Act, which provided for an attorney general and a Supreme Court.

1869   Thousands of businessmen were ruined in a Wall Street panic after financiers Jay Gould and James Fisk attempted to corner the gold market.

1896   Jazz Age novelist and short-story author F. Scott Fitzgerald was born in St. Paul, Minnesota. He was named for the great Christian patriot—his full name was actually Francis Scott Key Fitzgerald. He was best known for the novels *This Side of Paradise, The Great Gatsby*, and *Tender Is the Night*.

1929   Lieutenant James H. Doolittle guided a Consolidated NY-2 biplane over Mitchell Field in New York in the first all-instrument flight.

1936   Jim Henson, creator of the Muppets and such characters as Kermit the Frog, Miss Piggy, Fozzie Bear, and Rowlf, was born in Greenville, Mississippi.

1955   President Dwight Eisenhower suffered a heart attack while on vacation in Denver.

1957   The Brooklyn Dodgers played their last game at Ebbets Field, before moving to Los Angeles. The team defeated the Pittsburgh Pirates 2-0.

1960   The USS *Enterprise*, the first nuclear-powered aircraft carrier, was launched at Newport News, Virginia.

1969   The trial of the "Chicago Seven" began—originally there were eight defendants, but one successfully appealed for a separate trial. Five of the defendants were convicted of crossing state lines to incite riots at the 1968 Democratic national convention, but the convictions were ultimately overturned.

1976   Newspaper heiress Patricia Hearst was sentenced to seven years in prison for her part in a 1974 bank robbery. Though she had been kidnapped by the Symbionese Liberation Army, she had apparently become sympathetic with the underground group's aims. She was released after twenty-two months upon receiving clemency from President Jimmy Carter.

Just as a loss of memory in an individual is a psychiatric defect calling for medical treatment, so too any community which has no social memory is suffering from an illness.

[JOHN H. Y. BRIGGS (1922–)]

SEPTEMBER

Samuel Doak crossed over the Appalachian Mountains to the Tennessee wilderness in 1777 and became one of the most renowned men in the history of the western frontier. He had studied at Princeton and then served on the faculty of the college, and had been ordained by the energetic Hanover Presbytery of Virginia. Loving an educated ministry, the settlers of the Watauga region welcomed Doak with open arms.

Shortly after he arrived he happened upon some men who were felling trees. "Learning that he was a minister, they requested him to preach to so many of them as could be assembled immediately. He complied, using his horse for a pulpit and the shady grove for a sanctuary. They entreated the preacher to tarry long with them. He yielded to their entreaty, and this led to his permanent settlement among them." It would be the first of seven churches he would plant in the region. Doak built schools as well. In 1783 he secured a charter for a classical school—the first literary institution of the West, which would eventually become the mighty University of Tennessee.

On this day in 1780, a few days before the famous Revolutionary War battle at Kings Mountain, the local militia had gathered at Sycamore Shoals to prepare for the engagement. Doak was asked to speak to the men and say a prayer over them. He spoke beyond the immediate occasion and captured what some have called the "American spirit," that broader sense of the divine destiny of the nation:

"My countrymen, you are about to set out on an expedition which is full of hardships and dangers, but one in which the Almighty will attend you. The Mother country has her hands upon you, these American colonies, and takes that for which our fathers planted their homes in the wilderness—our liberty. Taxation without representation and the quartering of soldiers in the homes of our people without their consent are evidence that the Crown of England would take from its American subjects the last vestige of freedom. Your brethren across the mountains are crying the Macedonia unto your help. God forbid that you shall refuse to hear and answer their call—but the call of your brethren is not all. The enemy is marching hither to destroy your homes. Brave men, you are not unacquainted with battle. Your hands have already been taught to war and your fingers to fight. You have wrested these beautiful valleys of the Holston and Watauga from the savage hand. Will you tarry now until the other enemy carries fire and sword to your very doors? No, it shall not be. Go forth then in the strength of your manhood to the aid of your brethren, the defense of your liberty and the protection of your homes. And may the God of justice be with you and give you victory."

And then, each family huddled tightly together, the men heard Doak pray a prayer that men destined for battle would quote for generations to come. He then led them in lustily singing an old Celtic battle Psalm. When they set off to the battle, the "Tennessee Volunteers" decisively defeated the British forces in sixty-five minutes.

FEAST DAY
St. Sergius of Radonezh, St. Vincent Strambi, St. Aunacharius or Aunaire, St. Albert of Jerusalem, St. Firminus of Amiens, St. Ceolfirth, St. Fibar or Bairre

564

1066 At the Battle of Stamford Bridge in Yorkshire, King Harold II of England defeated the forces of the king of Norway, Harald Hardrada. King Hardrada and Harold's treacherous brother Tostig were both killed in the conflict.

1492 Crew members aboard one of Christopher Columbus's ships, the *Pinta*, shouted that they could see land; it turned out to be a false sighting.

1493 Christopher Columbus set sail from Cadiz, Spain, with a flotilla of seventeen ships—as well as 1,500 crewmen intent on beginning a new colony in the New World—for his second voyage to the Western Hemisphere.

1513 Vasco Núñez de Balboa, after having traversed the Isthmus of Panama, first discovered the Pacific Ocean.

1775 Revolutionary War hero Ethan Allen—who fought for the independent Republic of Vermont, not the United States—was captured by the British as he led an attack on Montreal.

1789 The first United States Congress adopted twelve amendments to the Constitution and sent them to the states for ratification. Ten of the amendments eventually passed and became the Bill of Rights.

1890 President Benjamin Harrison signed a measure establishing Sequoia National Park.

1898 Southern author William Faulkner was born in New Albany, Mississippi. His unique style of writing is evident in such works as *Light in August*, *The Sound and the Fury*, *As I Lay Dying*, and *The Reivers*. He received the 1949 Nobel Prize for literature.

1906 Russian composer Dmitri Shostakovich was born in St. Petersburg. His tenuous and strained relation with the Soviet government often hindered his creativity; however, his fifteen symphonies and fifteen string quartets are among the finest in the contemporary repertoire. His music has a rhythmic vitality, melodic richness, and mastery of orchestral technique.

1957 With three hundred U.S. Army troops standing guard, nine black children who had earlier been forced to withdraw from Central High School in Little Rock, Arkansas, because of unruly white crowds were escorted back to class.

1973 The three-man crew of the U.S. space laboratory *Skylab 2* splashed down safely in the Pacific Ocean after spending fifty-nine days in orbit.

1979 The musical *Evita* opened on Broadway.

1981 Sandra Day O'Connor was sworn in as the first female justice on the Supreme Court.

*T*he antiquary of tradition is the preserver of all that is right and good and true. It is the wisest and most progressive of all the human impulses–for it guarantees continuity for the uncertain days of the future. Let every man and woman warmly embrace the lessons of the past.

[CALVIN COOLIDGE (1872–1933)]

SEPTEMBER

At the beginning of the twentieth century, eugenics was perhaps the most revolutionary of the pseudo-sciences spawned by the wild-eyed vision of scientism—the almost religious belief that somehow science could solve all the problems of humanity. Having convinced an entire generation of scientists, intellectuals, and social reformers that the world was facing an imminent economic crisis caused by unchecked human fertility, the followers of Malthusianism quickly turned their attentions to practical programs and social policies.

Some of these managerial Malthusians believed that the solution to the imminent crisis was political: restrict immigration, reform social welfare, and tighten citizenship requirements. Others thought the solution was technological: increase agricultural production, improve medical proficiency, and promote industrial efficiency. But many others felt that the solution was genetic: restrict or eliminate "bad racial stocks," and gradually "help to engineer the evolutionary ascent of man."

This last group became the adherents of a malevolent new voodoo-science called eugenics. They quickly became the most influential and powerful of all the insurgent ideologists striving to rule the affairs of men and nations. In fact, for the rest of the twentieth century they would unleash one plague after another—a whole plethora of designer disasters—upon the unsuspecting human race.

The eugenicists unashamedly espoused an elitist white supremacy. Or to be more precise, they espoused an elitist Northern and Western European white supremacy. It was not a supremacy based on the crass ethnic racism of the past but upon a new kind of "scientific" elitism deemed necessary to preserve "the best of the human race" in the face of impending doom. It was a very refined sort of supremacy that prided itself on rationalism, intellectualism, and progressivism.

This racial supremacy, they believed, had to be promoted both positively and negatively. Through selective breeding, the Eugenicists hoped to purify the bloodlines and improve the stock of the "superior" Aryan race. The "fit" would be encouraged to reproduce prolifically. This was the positive side of Malthusian eugenics.

Negative Malthusian eugenics, on the other hand, sought to contain the "inferior" races through segregation, sterilization, birth control, and abortion. The "unfit" would thus be slowly winnowed out of the population as chaff is from wheat. By the first two decades of this century, according to feminist author Germaine Greer, "the relevance of Eugenic considerations was accepted by all shades of liberal and radical opinion, as well as by many conservatives."

Some forty states had enacted restrictive containment measures and established eugenic asylums. Eugenics departments were endowed at many of the most prestigious universities in the world including Harvard, Princeton, Columbia, and Stanford. Funding for eugenics research was provided by the Rockefeller, Ford, and Carnegie Foundations. And eugenic ideas were given free rein in the literature, theater, music, and press of the day. Ideas have consequences. When the ideas of Christianity were replaced in our society by the ideas of scientism, it was inevitable that calamities would result—thus, the horrors of the Holocaust, the abortion pandemic, and ethnic genocide.

SEPTEMBER

FEAST DAY
Saints Cosmas and Damian, St. Nilus of Rossano, St. Colman of Lann Elo, St. Teresa Couderc, St. John of Meda

566

1580 After a voyage of more than thirty-three months, Sir Francis Drake and the fifty sailors that comprised the crew of the *Golden Hind* returned to Plymouth as the first Englishmen to circumnavigate the globe.

1607 Citizens of Ursa Major and Serpentis reported seeing a comet that looked like "a flaming lance."

1772 For the first time, doctors in New Jersey were required by law to hold a medical license. The New Jersey legislature gave exceptions to anyone who pulled teeth, drew blood, or gave free medical advice.

1777 British troops occupied Philadelphia during the American Revolution.

1789 All in one day, Thomas Jefferson was appointed as the United States' first secretary of state, John Jay was named the first chief justice, Samuel Osgood became the first postmaster general, and Edmund Jennings Randolph became the first attorney general.

1888 Poet and playwright Thomas Stearns Eliot was born in St. Louis, Missouri. He once wrote, "There never was a time when those that read at all, read so many more books by living authors than books by dead authors; there never was a time so completely parochial, so shut off from the past."

1892 American bandleader John Philip Sousa had his band play his "Liberty Bell March" at their first American concert.

1898 American composer and songwriter George Gershwin was born in Brooklyn, New York. His best-known songs include "I Got Rhythm," "Fascinating Rhythm," "The Man I Love," "Swanee," and "Strike Up the Band."

1913 A tugboat made the first voyage through the Panama Canal.

1914 The Federal Trade Commission was established.

1957 Leonard Bernstein's *West Side Story* opened in New York City. With contributions by Stephen Sondheim and Jerome Robbins, this musical made a profound impact on theater.

1960 The first televised debate between presidential candidates Richard M. Nixon and John F. Kennedy took place in Chicago.

1964 Hey, little buddy! *Gilligan's Island* premiered on CBS, and it has reportedly not gone off the air since.

1969 The family comedy series *The Brady Bunch* premiered on ABC.

1991 Four men and four women began an ill-fated two-year stay inside a sealed-off structure in Oracle, Arizona, called *Biosphere II.*

SEPTEMBER

Error lives but a day. Truth is eternal.

[JAMES LONGSTREET (1821–1904)]

Though quite obviously anointed with divine favor, Jonathan Edwards (1703–1758)—best known today for his sermon "Sinners in the Hands of an Angry God"—was not without controversy. Many said that Edwards illegitimately played upon people's emotions. Others said that he shamelessly exploited the popular fears and phobias of the day. Still others said that he appealed to the innate intolerance, bigotry, and mob instincts of unsuspecting simple-minded people.

For the record, Edwards claimed that all of his sermons and books were modeled on the admonition of the apostle Paul: "Knowing therefore the terror of the Lord, we persuade men" (2 Corinthians 5:11). He told his own parish, "I don't desire to go about to terrify you needlessly or represent your case worse than it is, but I do verily think that there are a number of people belonging to this congregation in imminent danger of being damned to all eternity."

It was that kind of pastoral concern and evangelistic passion that enabled Edwards to wisely lend leadership and direction to the Great Awakening—perhaps the most sweeping revival in modern history. It enabled him to become the "acknowledged dean" of American evangelicalism. And it thrust him into the international limelight alongside Whitefield and Wesley as a spokesman for Christian unity and cooperation.

Even so, the controversy stirred by his unbending commitment to an unadulterated substantiveness never entirely went away. After nearly a quarter century of service to his Northampton congregation, a small disgruntled faction—advocates of what historian Perry Miller called a kind of "early pluralism" who desired less stringent moral standards for church membership than Edwards would allow—secured his ouster. They were apparently offended by his insistence that the message of justice—temporal and eternal—was inseparable from the message of faith. On this day in 1750 he was exiled to the frontier where he lived out his days as a missionary to the Indians.

But he had no regrets. He knew that the substantiveness of the faith was not a matter to be trifled with. He knew that both the imminence and the finality of eternal judgment mitigated lowering the standards, diluting the ethics, or compromising the integrity of his proclamations. He knew that hell was the best argument against muddled and mitigated morals. His position was simple: "The Good News is that the bad news is bad—and yet hope remains." Knowing this, Jonathan Edwards threw caution to the wind and pleaded for his congregation to hear and heed a message of substantive wisdom: "You hang by a slender thread, with the flames of divine wrath flashing about it, and ready every moment to singe it and burn it asunder. God hath had it on His heart to show angels and men, both how excellent His love is, and also how terrible His wrath is."

He was unwilling—regardless of the cost—to dumb down his message, to make it more user friendly, to reduce it to the lowest common denominator. He was convinced that to do so would be a betrayal of wisdom. As G. K. Chesterton later remarked, "If the world grows too worldly, it can be rebuked by the church; but if the church grows too worldly, it cannot be adequately rebuked for worldliness by the world." So Edwards stuck by his guns. Cost him it did. His struggle for substantiveness appeared to be a lost cause toward the end of his life. But in the end his weighty refusal to compromise ensured his reputation.

SEPTEMBER

FEAST DAY
St. Elzear of Sabran, St. Barrog or Barnoch, St. Vincent de Paul

1498 One of the cruelest men who ever lived, the inquisitor Tomás de Torquemada died. Of Jewish blood himself, born into a family of converts, he turned most of his fury against his own people. After studying theology at the Dominican convent of San Pablo in Valladolid, he became prior of the Santa Cruz convent in Segovia. He also became confessor to the royal court. There he whispered in the ears of King Ferdinand of Aragon and Queen Isabella of Castile that many Jewish converts were secretly practicing Judaic rites while outwardly pretending the Christian faith. He helped the royal couple draft a request for an inquisition into this matter. The request was granted. In 1483, Torquemada was made grand inquisitor. Thousands of individuals were brought before his courts. Most of them were completely at a loss as to what they were supposed to have done. One-third were tortured. The three most common tortures were to be hung by the arms so that the arms were pulled from their joints, to be forced to swallow gallons of water; and to be racked. Worse than the tortures was the fear of immolation. Torquemada burned more than two thousand "guilty" victims. He was so loathed that he found it necessary to go about with bodyguards. But even the pope could not stop his cruel work. Finally, in 1492, he had all unconverted Jews expelled from all the Spanish kingdoms.

1710 The author of *Gulliver's Travels*, Jonathan Swift, wrote to a friend in London, "I lodge in Bury Street, where I removed a week ago. I have the first floor, a dining-room, and a bed chamber, at eight shillings per week; plaguey deep, but I spend nothing for eating, never to a tavern, and very seldom in a coach; yet, after all, it will be expensive."

1854 The first great disaster involving an Atlantic oceanliner occurred when the steamship *Arctic* sank with three hundred people aboard.

1911 "Memphis Blues" by W. C. Handy was the first blues song ever published.

1935 Charles Willis Howard instructed six students for a week in the finer points of playing the role of St. Nick at the first Santa Claus School opened in Albion, New York.

1942 Glenn Miller and his Orchestra performed together for the last time, at the Central Theater in Passaic, New Jersey, prior to Miller's entry into the army.

1943 Bing Crosby, the Andrews Sisters, and the Vic Schoen Orchestra recorded "Pistol Packin' Mama" and "Jingle Bells" for Decca Records.

1954 *The Tonight Show*, hosted by Steve Allen, made its debut on NBC.

1964 The Warren Commission issued a report concluding that Lee Harvey Oswald had acted alone in assassinating President Kennedy.

1979 Congress gave final approval to Jimmy Carter's plan to form the Department of Education, the thirteenth cabinet agency in U.S. history.

1994 More than 350 Republican congressional candidates gathered on the steps of the U.S. Capitol to sign the Contract with America, a ten-point platform they pledged to enact if voters sent a GOP majority to the House.

1998 Gerhard Schroeder and his Social Democrats won national elections in Germany, following sixteen years of conservative rule under Chancellor Helmut Kohl's Christian Democrats.

SEPTEMBER

1998 St. Louis Cardinal Mark McGwire's record-breaking season ended with his 69th and 70th home runs.

An honest man's the noblest work of God.

[Alexander Pope (1688–1744)]

1943

William Franklin Graham—best known as Billy—became the pastor of the First Baptist Church of Western Springs, Illinois. He was born in Charlotte, North Carolina, in 1918. Educated at Bob Jones University, the Florida Bible Institute, and Wheaton College, he was ordained in the Southern Baptist Convention in 1939 before briefly entering the pastorate. Graham turned to large-scale evangelism in 1949 and embarked on a series of tours of the United States and Europe. A forceful, eloquent, and charismatic preacher, he attracts audiences that total in the millions to his meetings. Graham also became known through televised films of his rallies; through his own motion pictures; through *Decision,* the magazine of his eponymous evangelistic association; through the radio program *The Hour of Decision;* and through a syndicated newspaper column. Graham's numerous best-selling books include *Peace with God* (1953), *The Secret of Happiness* (1955), *World Aflame* (1965), *How to Be Born Again* (1977), *A Biblical Standard for Evangelists* (1984), and *Hope for the Troubled Heart* (1991). His autobiography, *Just As I Am,* was published in 1997.

SEPTEMBER

An industrious youth who mastered his studies of the law without the advantage of a school, a tutor, or a master—borrowing books and snatching opportunities to read and research between odd jobs—Samuel Huntington (1732–1796) was one of the greatest self-made men among the American Founders.

He was also one of the greatest legal minds of the age. His poverty-stricken youth was set behind him forever when in 1764, in recognition of his obvious abilities and initiative, he was elected to the General Assembly of Connecticut. The next year he was chosen to serve on the Executive Council. In 1774 he was appointed associate judge of the Superior Court and, as a delegate to the Continental Congress, was acknowledged to be a legal scholar of some respect.

He served in Congress for five consecutive terms, during the last of which he was elected president. He was chosen to follow John Jay in that office on this day in 1779—at a time when the demands of war, the pressures of diminishing resources, and internal dissentions made the presidency one of the least desirable offices imaginable. Nevertheless, he faithfully served his nation and the cause of freedom until ill health forced him to resign on July 9, 1781. He returned to his home in Connecticut—and as he recuperated, he accepted more council and bench duties.

He again took his seat in Congress in 1783, but left it to become chief justice of his state's Superior Court. He was elected lieutenant governor in 1785 and governor in 1786. Regardless of the office he held, he always served with purposeful zeal, discerning wisdom, and forthright courage. In addition, he was a careful legal scholar and greatly refined the fledgling nation's legal foundation. Indeed, according to John Jay, he was "the most precisely trained Christian jurist ever to serve his country."

1066 William the Conqueror (1027–1087), a Norman prince and a cousin to the royal family of Saxon England, launched an invasion by crossing the English Channel in an effort to claim the crown from his cousin, King Harold. Born in Falaise, France, William was the illegitimate son of Robert I, duke of Normandy. Upon the death of his father, the Norman nobles, honoring their promise to Robert, accepted William as his successor. Rebellion against the young duke broke out almost immediately, however, and his position did not become secure until 1047 when, with the aid of Henry I, king of France, he won a decisive victory over a rebel force near Caen. During a visit in 1051 to his childless cousin, Edward the Confessor, king of England, William is said to have obtained Edward's agreement that he should succeed to the English throne. In 1053, defying a papal ban, William married Matilda of Flanders, daughter of Baldwin V, count of Flanders and a descendant of King Alfred the Great, thereby strengthening his claim to the crown of England. When Edward died, however, the powerful English noble Harold, Earl of Wessex, was elected king. Determined to make good his claim, William invaded. Just two weeks later, on October 14, the Normans defeated the English forces at the celebrated Battle of Hastings, in which Harold was slain. On Christmas Day he was crowned king of England in Westminster Abbey.

1542 Portuguese navigator Juan Rodriguez Cabrillo arrived at present-day San Diego.

1745 Following Bonnie Prince Charlie's defeat of the English forces under Sir John Cope, English theater patrons sang "God Save the King" for the first time.

1781 American forces in the Revolutionary War, backed by a French fleet, began their siege of Yorktown Heights, Virginia.

1787 Congress voted to send the just-completed Constitution of the United States to state legislatures for their approval.

1850 Flogging was abolished as a form of punishment in the U.S. Navy.

1913 Edith Pargeter, renowned author of the more than twenty Brother Caedfael mysteries, and writer of haunting historical fiction, was born in Horsehay, Shropshire.

1920 Eight baseball players with the Chicago White Sox were indicted for "throwing" the previous year's World Series against the Cincinnati Reds.

1924 Two U.S. Army planes landed in Seattle, Washington, having completed the first round-the-world flight in 175 days.

1931 C. S. Lewis was converted while riding to a zoo in his brother's motorcycle sidecar. "When we set out I did not believe that Jesus is the Son of God and when we reached the zoo I did." Lewis had already become a theist, but his conversion followed a long talk he'd had the week before with two Christian friends: J. R. R. Tolkien and Hugo Dyson.

1967 Walter Washington took office as the first mayor of the District of Columbia.

1995 Israeli Prime Minister Yitzhak Rabin and PLO chairman Yasser Arafat signed an accord to transfer much of the West Bank to the control of its Arab residents.

SEPTEMBER 28

Truth may be stretched but cannot be broken, and always gets above falsehood, as oil does above water.

[MIGUEL CERVANTES (1547–1616)]

571

MICHELMAS DAY

The Feast of Saint Michael recognizes the archangel and all the heavenly hosts. Michael is often thought of in battle gear, standing victorious over the defeated fallen angel Satan.

When Rudyard Kipling interviewed Mark Twain on this day in 1889, Kipling was still making his reputation while Twain was at the height of his fame. Kipling's entertaining account of the meeting began in a flourish of braggadocio: "You are a contemptible lot, over yonder. Some of you are Commissioners, and some Lieutenant-Governors, and some have the Victoria Cross, and a few are privileged to walk about the Mall arm in arm with the Viceroy; but I have seen Mark Twain this golden morning, have shaken his hand, and smoked a cigar—no, two cigars—with him, and talked with him for more than two hours! Understand clearly that I do not despise you; indeed, I don't. I am only very sorry for you, from the Viceroy downward. To soothe your envy and to prove that I still regard you as my equals, I will tell you all about it."

Kipling described all the trials and tribulations of tracking down Twain at his gothic mansion there in central New York—the hassles, the runarounds, the delays, and the off-putting diversions that almost deterred him from his task: "They said in Buffalo that he was in Hartford, and again they said, perchance he is gone upon a journey to Europe—which information so upset me that I embarked upon the wrong train, and was incontinently turned out by the conductor three-quarters of a mile from the station, amid the wilderness of railway tracks. Have you ever, encumbered with great-coat and valise, tried to dodge diversely-minded locomotives when the sun was shining in your eyes? But I forgot that you have not seen Mark Twain, you people of no account!"

But at last the men met and Kipling was awestruck: "The thing that struck me first was that he was an elderly man; yet, after a minute's thought, I perceived that it was otherwise, and in five minutes, the eyes looking at me, I saw that the grey hair was an accident of the most trivial. He was quite young. I was shaking his hand. I was smoking his cigar, and I was hearing him talk—this man I had learned to love and admire fourteen thousand miles away. Reading his books, I had striven to get an idea of his personality, and all my preconceived notions were wrong and beneath the reality. Blessed is the man who finds no disillusion when he is brought face to face with a revered writer. That was a moment to be remembered; the landing of a twelve-pound salmon was nothing to it. I had hooked Mark Twain, and he was treating me as though under certain circumstances I might be an equal."

The two men talked of publishing and writing and gardening. They discussed the novels of Scott, the stories of Hart, and the verse of Burns. Then Kipling got to the heart of the matter: "Growing bold, and feeling that I had a few hundred thousand folk at my back, I demanded whether Tom Sawyer married Judge Thatcher's daughter and whether we were ever going to hear of Tom Sawyer as a man." Twain replied that he hadn't decided yet. And then the two men dreamed and conspired and imagined what might be, what ought not be, and what should be until the waning hours of the night.

The interview was, as Kipling asserted, "a holy moment when the sub-creative genius of the Almighty is suddenly made manifest."

SEPTEMBER

FEAST DAY
Saints Rhipsime, Gaiana, and Companions; St. Theodota of Philippolis; St. Michael, St. Raphael, St. Gabriel, archangels

1399 Henry IV deposed his cousin Richard II and ascended the English throne.

1413 Sir John Oldcastle, a follower of John Wycliffe and supporter of the Lollards, was condemned of heresy by the archbishop Arundel. Because of Oldcastle's friendship with King Henry V and his high social standing—many scholars believe that Oldcastle was the model for Shakespeare's Flagstaff—he was given forty days to recant. During that time, he escaped and hid in Wales. An immense reward was offered for him dead or alive. Nonetheless, he remained hidden for four years. At last someone betrayed his whereabouts. Oldcastle was captured and hung in iron chains over a fire until he died.

1565 Nearly five hundred Huguenot settlers in Florida—having fled persecution in their native France—were slaughtered by Spanish soldiers in the worst single case of religious persecution on the North American continent.

1758 English Admiral Horatio Nelson was born.

1789 A 1,000-man standing army was established by authorization from Congress.

1829 Regular police patrols began on the streets of London. They came to be known as "bobbies" after Sir Robert Peel who, as the Home Secretary, had helped to reorganize London's police force.

1902 Impresario David Belasco opened his first Broadway theater.

1918 The first performance of Gustav Holst's *The Planets* by the Queen's Hall Orchestra under Adrian Boult was held on this day. This performance during a time of severe wartime restrictions was arranged privately for Holst as gift from his friend Balfour Gardiner. The first public performance took place five months later.

1943 General Dwight D. Eisenhower and Italian Marshal Pietro Badoglio signed an armistice aboard the British ship *Nelson* off the coast of Malta.

1963 The second session of the Second Vatican Council opened in Rome.

1973 Anglo-American poet and man of letters W. H. Auden died in Vienna, Austria. Possessed with lyricism, psychological insight, ironic wit, and deep religious and social convictions, his master craftsmanship placed him in the limelight of contemporary poets.

1978 Pope John Paul I was found dead in his Vatican apartment just over a month after ascending the papal throne of the Roman Catholic Church.

1979 Pope John Paul II became the first pope to visit Ireland as he arrived for a three-day tour.

SEPTEMBER

A little integrity is better than any career.

[RALPH WALDO EMERSON (1803–1882)]

Though he was best known as a world-renowned author, preacher, and philanthropist, the bookshops of London knew Charles Spurgeon as a voracious reader and an avid collector. He was the most famous preacher in the world for most of the nineteenth century. In 1854, just four years after his conversion, Charles Spurgeon, then just barely twenty years old, became pastor of London's famed New Park Street Church—formerly pastored by the famous Puritans John Gill and John Rippon. The young preacher was an immediate success. The congregation quickly outgrew the building, moved to Exeter Hall, then to Surrey Music Hall. In these venues Spurgeon frequently preached to audiences numbering in the tens of thousands—all in the days before electronic amplification. In 1861 the congregation moved permanently to the newly constructed Metropolitan Tabernacle. It quickly became the largest congregation in the world.

In addition to pastoring that remarkable church, he was also the founder of more than sixty philanthropic institutions including orphanages, colportage societies, schools, colleges, clinics, and hospitals. He also established more than twenty mission churches and dozens of Sunday and Ragged Schools throughout England.

But in the midst of the busyness of his life and ministry, he always found time to read. Books were his most constant companions and bookstores were his most regular haunts. He was born in the little Essex village of Kelvedon in 1834. Both his father and grandfather were pastors, and so he was raised around books, reading, and piety. As a youngster, he began a lifelong habit of diligent and unending reading—typically he read six books per week, and was able to remember what he had read and where he had read it many years later. He particularly loved old books. He claimed in his autobiography that even before the age of ten, he preferred to go into his grandfather's study and pull down an old Puritan classic and read rather than go outside and play with friends.

As he grew older, his passion for books, and the little shops that sold them, remained unabated. Each day Spurgeon would scour the newspapers to find when an antiquarian bookshop might be selling certain books. He would then beat a hasty path to the shop to purchase the treasure—or if he was too busy that day with appointments, he would send his secretary to buy the book. In time, his personal library numbered more than twelve thousand volumes.

The books were all shelved in Spurgeon's study at Westwood, his family home. Of course, Spurgeon was not merely a collector. He was utilitarian if anything. He viewed his books as the tools of his trade. And the shops where he found them were essentially his hardware stores. As a result, the books were used. They were hardly museum pieces, despite their scarcity or value. They were the natural extensions of his work and ministry. He once wrote, "My books are my tools. They also serve as my counsel, my consolation, and my comfort. They are my source of wisdom and the font of my education. They are my friends and my delights. They are my surety, when all else is awry, that I have set my confidence in the substantial things of truth and right."

SEPTEMBER

NATIONAL DAY
Botswana
FEAST DAY
St. Jerome, St. Simon of Crépy, St. Gregory the Enlightener, St. Honorius of Canterbury

1791 Wolfgang Mozart's opera *The Magic Flute* premiered at the Theatre auf der Wieden in Vienna. This was the first great work of music composed with the mass populace in mind. The fairy-tale-like aspects of the story as well as the music are said to be of Masonic significance. Although Mozart wrote this opera for the sake of money, when he fell ill and was confined to his deathbed less than three months later each night he held a watch in his hand and followed the progress of each performance in his mind.

1846 Dentist William Morton used ether as an anesthetic for the first time on a patient in his Boston office.

1927 Babe Ruth hit his 60th homer of the season to break his own major-league record.

1935 George Gershwin's folk opera *Porgy and Bess* was first performed by the Theater Guild in Boston. The story was adapted from a successful play, *Porgy*, written by Du Bose and Dorothy Heyward in collaboration with Ira Gershwin. Set in Catfish Row in Charleston, North Carolina, the opera tells the story of the lives and loves in the black tenement community with such familiar songs as "Summertime," "I Got Plenty of Nuthin'," "Bess, You Is My Woman Now," and "It Ain't Necessarily So."

1938 The leaders of Great Britain, France, Germany, and Italy (Chamberlain, Daladier, Hitler, and Mussolini) signed the Munich agreement. British Prime Minister Neville Chamberlain said, "This is the second time in our history that there has come back from Germany to Downing Street Peace with Honour: I believe it is peace for our time." The policy of appeasement failed miserably as Germany became increasingly aggressive.

1939 The first college football game to be televised was shown on experimental station W2XBS in New York as Fordham University defeated Waynesburg College, 34-7.

1946 An international military tribunal in Nuremberg, Germany, found twenty-two top Nazi leaders guilty of war crimes.

1954 The first atomic-powered vessel, the submarine *Nautilus*, was commissioned by the navy.

1955 Actor James Dean was killed in a two-car collision near Cholame, California.

1962 African-American student James Meredith succeeded on his fourth try in registering for classes at the University of Mississippi.

1989 Thousands of East Germans who had sought refuge in West German embassies in Czechoslovakia and Poland began emigrating under an accord between Soviet bloc and "NATO" nations.

SEPTEMBER

He that is warm for truth, and fearless in its defense, performs one of the duties of a good man; he strengthens his own conviction, and guards others from delusion; but steadiness of belief, and boldness of profession, are yet only part of the form of godliness.

[SAMUEL JOHNSON (1709–1784)]

OCTOBER

<table>
<tr><td>1861</td><td>The U.S. Army Balloon Corps, comprised of fifty men and five balloons, was formed under the command of Thaddeus Sobieski Coulincourt Lowe. Four of the balloons were ready for service by November 10, 1861.</td></tr>
</table>

English novelists were among the first to write spy thrillers. The most prominent included Erskine Childers with *The Riddle of the Sands*, W. Somerset Maugham with *Ashenden*, and Graham Greene with *A Gun for Sale*. In the United States, *Sanctuary* by William Faulkner, *The Postman Always Rings Twice* by James M. Cain, and *No Pockets in a Shroud* by Horace McCoy were novels with strong thriller elements.

The real development of the spy thriller, however, came with the Richard Hannay thrillers of John Buchan (1875–1940). They included *The Thirty-Nine Steps*, *Greenmantle*, *Mr. Standfast*, *The Three Hostages*, *The Courts of Morning*, and *The Island of Sheep*. Buchan—who later became Baron Tweedsmuir—was a Scottish writer and statesman, born in Perth. An active politician, he wrote in his spare time, producing more than four dozen other fine books besides his thrillers. A history of the First World War was published as *History of the Great War* in twenty-four volumes. His biography of Sir Walter Scott was hailed as a masterpiece by readers and critics alike.

Nevertheless, his worldwide reputation rested on his exciting adventure-mystery novels. Readers found Buchan's work to be a rich and pleasurable journey into the best of Edwardian England and Georgian Scotland. His harum-scarum spy novels were full of action, thrills and spills, twists and turns, and betrayals and salvations. They were also richly literary and full of subtle references to both theological traditions and great literary classics. *The Thirty-Nine Steps*, for instance, was filled with references to the Thirty-Nine Articles of Anglicanism. *Midwinter* was a literary unfolding of the concepts of the Covenanters. And *Mr. Standfast* was overflowing with allusions to *Pilgrim's Progress*. Every one of his books seemed to operate on several levels simultaneously.

It was upon Buchan's considerable shoulders that English writer Ian Fleming built the concept for his James Bond novels. Likewise, John Le Carré and Len Deighton and the other masters of the genre—right up to Tom Clancy and Robert Ludlum—followed along the path that Buchan had forged a full generation earlier.

OCTOBER

NATIONAL DAY
China, Nigeria, Cyprus
FEAST DAY
St. Romanus the Melodist, St. Melorus or Mylor, St. Bavo or Allowin, St. Thérèse of Lisieux

1529 The Colloquy of Marburg—the first council of Protestant Christians—was held in an attempt to resolve the controversies that had arisen between the two Reformers Ulrich Zwingli and Martin Luther. Strong disagreement had arisen over the meaning of Holy Communion. The Roman Catholic Church taught that in the ceremony of the Mass, the bread and wine were transformed into the literal body and blood of Christ. Neither Zwingli nor Luther found that view scripturally supportable or acceptable. Luther believed that Christ was spiritually present in the bread and wine. Zwingli believed the whole ceremony of Communion was a memorial of Christ's death for us, but Christ was not present in the elements, either physically or spiritually. Neither Zwingli nor Luther could accept the other's viewpoint, and the debate often became harsh and unpleasant. Philip of Hesse, one of the German rulers, invited the Reformers to come to his territory to resolve their differences. Behind Philip's desire for peace between Zwingli and Luther was the hope that a political alliance of the Protestant states might eventually be made, thus weakening the Catholic Hapsburgs and the Holy Roman Empire. Peace was not to be had, however. Though the Reformers could agree on the doctrines of the Trinity, the person of Christ, His death and resurrection, original sin, justification by faith, the Holy Spirit, and the sacraments, they could not agree on the nature of Communion.

1800 Spain ceded Louisiana to France in a secret treaty.

1880 Edison Lamp Works in Menlo Park, New Jersey, started production of light bulbs.

1885 Special-delivery mail service began in the United States.

1885 Poet and anthologist Louis Untermeyer was born in New York City. On his ninetieth birthday he would comment that he was writing his third autobiography: "The other two were obviously premature."

1896 The U.S. Post Office established Rural Free Delivery, with the first routes in West Virginia.

1903 The first modern World Series was played between the Boston Americans of the American League and the Pittsburgh Pirates of the National League

1909 With a price tag of $850, the Model T, was introduced to consumers by the Ford Motor Company.

1936 General Francisco Franco was proclaimed the regent of a Spanish commonwealth.

1949 Communist Party Chairman Mao Tse-tung raised the first flag of the People's Republic of China during a ceremony in Beijing.

1961 Roger Maris of the New York Yankees hit his 61st home run during a 162-game season, compared to Babe Ruth's 60 home runs during a 154-game season.

1964 The Free Speech Movement was launched at the University of California at Berkeley.

1971 Walt Disney World opened in Orlando, Florida.

1979 Pope John Paul II arrived in Boston for the start of a tour of the United States.

1989 Thousands of East Germans received a triumphal welcome in West Germany after the Communist government agreed to let them flee to freedom in the West.

OCTOBER

Let liars fear, let cowards shrink,
Let traitors turn away,
Whatever we have dared to think
That we dare to say.

[James Russell Lowell (1819–1891)]

1836	Charles Darwin returned from his four-year voyage on the HMS *Beagle* during which he had begun to formulate his controversial *Theory of Natural Selection*. His new evolutionary views would ultimately cause him to deny his lifelong faith in the truth of Christianity.

OCTOBER

Although Woodrow Wilson (1856–1924) held only one political office before he became president, his years as a professor of history provided him with a detailed knowledge of political processes; as president of Princeton University and governor of New Jersey he proved himself an able, dedicated administrator, unafraid to institute reforms. Thus Wilson's philosophy, knowledge, and ability uniquely equipped him for the nation's highest office. It was ironic, then, that he came to office having won only a tiny plurality of the votes in a fractious election and afterward that his policies were, for the most part, dictated by a secretive band of political cronies led by a mysterious wheeling-and-dealing conspiratorialist named Colonel House.

The administration's misguided conspiratorial energies were first directed toward domestic issues: a lower tariff, stronger antitrust measures, a child labor law, the first income tax law, and the Federal Reserve Act—the last greatly centralizing the economy and the control of money through the establishment of a semiprivate national bank.

But the country that had emerged as a world power under William McKinley and Teddy Roosevelt could not long ignore the growing conflict in Europe. Wilson kept the country out of war during his first term, but America's sympathy with the Allies made his ostensible neutrality difficult to maintain. "To make the world safe for democracy," Wilson finally led the nation into the First World War in 1917.

In directing the war effort Wilson cooperated with a Congress that gave him vast emergency powers. While mobilizing the industrial as well as the military forces of the nation, he labored over plans for peace—his great hope was for a kind of multinational government called the League of Nations. But his dedication to the noble ideal of the League's covenant led to a bitter conflict with Congress when the covenant, already signed by the European powers, was before them for approval. When Congress rejected it, Wilson suffered his greatest defeat. During the last several months of his administration, he was deathly ill, having suffered a stroke on this day in 1919. His cronies practically ran what they could of the government as their personal fiefdom. He died three years later, a broken man.

FEAST DAY
The Guardian Angels, St. Leger or Leodegarius, St. Eleutherius of Nicomedia

322 B.C. Greek philosopher Aristotle is believed to have died on this day. A student of Plato and a teacher of Alexander the Great, Aristotle influenced generations of scholars through his works such as *Poetics, Politics,* and *The Art of Rhetoric.*

1780 British spy John Andre was hanged in Tappan, New York.

1792 The twelve ministers from small churches in the district of Kettering, England, formed the Baptist Missionary Society for Spreading the Gospel Among the Heathen. The group included the young William Carey, who had written a small book the previous May entitled *An Enquiry into the Obligation of Christians to Use Means for the Conversion of the Heathens.* Carey encouraged his readers to "expect great things from God; attempt great things for God." Carey's pamphlet and impassioned address on missions at the semiannual Kettering ministers' meeting stirred the other men to action. Thus was born the fledgling missionary society. The next year the men sent Carey to India where he translated the New Testament into Bengali and launched the modern missions movement.

1835 The first battle of the Texas Revolution took place as American settlers defeated a Mexican cavalry near the Guadalupe River.

1890 Julius Henry "Groucho" Marx, the American comedian and foremost member of the Marx Brothers, was born on this day. He was known as the irreverent, wisecracking, cigar-smoking, mustached member of the group.

1904 British novelist and playwright Graham Greene was born in Berkhamstead, Hertfordshire. Writing from his Catholic background, much of his work centers around characters facing salvation or damnation in their world of chaos.

1926 Writer James Morris was born in Wales. He would change his name to Jan Morris following a sex-change operation—it was as Jan that he gained international fame as a travel writer.

1939 The Benny Goodman Sextet recorded "Flying Home."

1950 Good Grief! Charlie Brown, Snoopy, Woodstock, Linus, Lucy, Sally, and all the gang debuted in the "Peanuts" comic strip by Charles M. Schulz. The strip appeared in nine newspapers.

1958 The former French colony of Guinea in West Africa proclaimed its independence.

1959 Rod Serling's *The Twilight Zone* made its debut on CBS television.

1967 Thurgood Marshall was sworn in as an associate justice of the Supreme Court; he was the first African American appointed to the nation's highest court.

1989 Nearly ten thousand people marched through Leipzig, East Germany, demanding legalization of opposition groups and adoption of democratic reforms in the country's largest protest since 1953.

Since the time of Bacon the world has been running away from, rather than toward, first principles, so that, on the verbal level, we see fact substituted for truth.

[RICHARD WEAVER (1910–1963)]

OCTOBER

Much has changed in New York since the two-week visit of Alexis de Tocqueville and Gustav de Beaumont in 1831. They described the city then as a rather disagreeable provincial town with badly paved roads, garish arts, teeming confusion, pretentious architecture, and bizarrely rude manners. While some critics might well still make such charges against the city, clearly New York has come of age in the interval between then and now.

The two aristocratic travelers were at the beginning of what would be a nine-month tour of the fledgling United States. They had an official mandate from the French government to study the land's criminal justice system—but they were actually interested in seeing far more than America's courts and jails. They wanted to explore the essence of the American spirit, discover the secret to American ingenuity, and plumb the depths of the American soul. Eventually they would visit nineteen of the country's then twenty-four states, stopping in more than fifty towns and villages from the thronging urban centers of the East to the rough and tumble frontier settlements of the West. They covered more than eight thousand miles, mostly on foot, on horseback, in steamboats, and on stage coaches. As de Tocqueville later wrote, "I confess that in America, I saw more than America; I sought there the image of democracy itself, with its inclinations, its character, its prejudices, and its passions, in order to learn what we have to fear or to hope from its progress."

New York was the young republic's thriving banking and trading center. Though it had spread across only about half of Manhattan Island—the rest was still divided between country estates, a few farms, and even a bit of wild forestland—the city had already become densely populated and was growing rapidly. It was shot through with the great American optimism of the Jacksonian Age. It was already the nation's largest city, and it hummed with commerce. Of course, there was no Empire State Building, no Statue of Liberty, no Times Square, no Central Park, no Radio City Music Hall, and no Rockefeller Center—each of these New York landmarks would come in the succeeding years. Nevertheless, much of what would ultimately give the city its unique character and culture was already in evidence.

He attributed the city's remarkable dynamism to the freedom Americans seemed to enjoy—indeed, and thrive upon. He wrote, "Here freedom is unrestrained, and subsists by being useful to everyone without injuring anybody. There is something undeniably feverish in the activity it imparts to industry and to the human spirit." It was an observation that he would recall again and again as he traveled throughout the land—but it was especially evident in his visit to New York.

Though the city was then under the control of a handful of politicians led by Martin van Buren—its seems the city has always had its machines from Aaron Burr's Chase Manhattan clique to Boss Tweed's Tammany Ring—it was marked by a persistent independence of heart, soul, mind, and spirit. This was, to de Tocqueville, the greatest landmark of the already amazing New York City profile. And so it was in New York that the visitors first observed all that was right and all that was wrong with America. It was there that he first caught a glimpse of liberty's great power, great promise, and great purpose. It was also there that he first felt the gnawing certainty that something so great could greatly disappoint.

OCTOBER

Feast Day
St. Hesychius, St. Thomas
Cantelupe of Hereford, St.
Attilanus, St. Gerard of Brogne,
St. Froilan, St. Ewald the Fair, St.
Ewald the Dark

582

1226 Francis of Assisi, the founder of the Order of the Franciscan Friars Minor, died on this day. Francis, who was born Giovani Francesco Bernardone, led a wild and decadent early life. When he recovered from a violent illness at the age of twenty-five, he vowed to dedicate his life to the church and never to refuse alms to a poor person. He lived the rest of his life in piety and poverty. He was canonized just two years after his death on this day in 1228.

1789 By presidential proclamation, George Washington declared that the first national Thanksgiving Day would be observed on the twenty-sixth of November.

1862 President Abraham Lincoln set aside the last Thursday in November as a national day of Thanksgiving. Earlier, he had designated other days of thanksgiving in order "to subdue the anger which has produced and so long sustained a needless and cruel rebellion."

1900 *The Dream of Gerontius,* an oratorio by English composer Sir Edward Elgar based on a poem by Cardinal Newman, was first performed at the Birmingham Festival. Although critics appreciated its premiere (including Bernard Shaw), it was not until subsequent performances that the English public regarded it with great acclaim as a masterpiece only rivaled by Handel's *Messiah* and Mendelssohn's *Elijah.*

1916 Beloved author and veterinarian James Herriott was born in Glasgow, Scotland. *All Creatures Great and Small* (1974) is one of his twelve books that relate his life in the Yorkshire countryside.

1929 The Kingdom of Serbs, Croats, and Slovenes formally changed its name to the Kingdom of Yugoslavia.

1960 The first episode of *The Andy Griffith Show*—"The New Housekeeper"—was aired by CBS on Monday night at 9:30. Aunt Bee won the heart of Opie after she came to live with her widowed nephew and his son.

1974 Frank Robinson was named major-league baseball's first African-American manager as he was placed in charge of the Cleveland Indians.

1990 East and West Germany reunited after forty-five years of division. Adopting the constitution of the former West Germany, the new country took the name the Federal Republic of Germany.

Truth: that long, clean, clear, simple, undeniable, unchallengable, straight, and shining line, on one side of which is black and on the other of which is white.

[WILLIAM FAULKNER (1897–1962)]

OCTOBER

1957

The Space Race began when the Soviet Union successfully launched the first man-made Earth satellite. *Sputnik*—a Russian word meaning "fellow traveler of Earth"—transmitted a radio signal for twenty-one days.

In 1828, the world's greatest storyteller sat down to weave yet another yarn. Over the past dozen years or so he had almost single-handedly revived Scottish pride—he had recovered the Royal Honors of Crown in Edinburgh Castle in 1818, more than a century after they had been locked away after the Union of Parliaments in 1707. And of course, his novels had fanned the flames of passion for the kilts, bagpipes, and the highland burr of the Scots. He had become the world's spokesman for all things Celtic.

But now he had something entirely different in mind. His *Tales of a Scottish Grandfather* proved to be his most intimate, most accessible, and most dramatic stories of all. The reason was simple: He was no longer telling his stories to the world. He was telling them to his own grandson.

Sir Walter Scott was far and away the most popular writer of the nineteenth century. Often mentioned in the same breath with Chaucer, Shakespeare and Milton, his output was prodigious: twenty-seven novels, five major works of epic poetry, three biographies, fourteen histories, and a half dozen collections of tales, legends, and ballads. All remain classics to this day. But it was for his popularization of his native Scotland that he is best remembered. Scott created and popularized historical fiction in a series called the Waverley Novels—which included such works as *Old Mortality* (1816), *Rob Roy* (1817), *The Heart of Midlothian* (1819), *Quentin Dunward* (1823), and *St. Ronan's Well* (1824). In these stories Scott arranged the plots and characters so the readers entered into the lives of both great and ordinary people caught up in violent, dramatic changes in history. They included romance, adventure, action, and an incredibly vivid eye and ear for detail.

Scott was proud of his work, and rightly so. Works such as *Ivanhoe* (1819) and *The Chronicles of Canongate* are marvels of the literary craft. But he was especially proud of these volumes. In *Tales of a Scottish Grandfather* he had recovered the whole story of his beloved Scotland—its actual history, not some fictionalized approximation. From William Wallace and Robert the Bruce to John Knox and Mary Queen of Scots, from the subjugation of Rob Roy and the rising of the Jacobites to the crusade of Bonnie Prince Charlie and the quest of the Duke of Cumberland, the entire romantic story is told—not as a historian would tell it, but as a grandfather would.

OCTOBER

NATIONAL DAY
Lesotho
FEAST DAY
St. Petronius of Bologna, St. Francis of Assisi, St. Ammon

1636 The first legal code composed in North America was instituted in the Plymouth Colony.

1777 George Washington's troops launched an assault on the British at Germantown, Pennsylvania, resulting in heavy American casualties.

1822 The nineteenth president of the United States, Rutherford B. Hayes, was born in Delaware, Ohio.

1862 Edward L. Stratemeyer was born in Elizabeth, New Jersey. He—and his syndicate of secretaries and writers—created a number of the world's most beloved series of children's books, including The Bobbsey Twins, The Hardy Boys, Nancy Drew, Bomba the Jungle Boy, and Tom Swift. Utilizing at least fifty pen names, he produced more than eight hundred books.

1887 The first issue of the *International Herald Tribune*—an English language daily newspaper for Europeans and expatriate Americans—was published as the *Paris Herald Tribune.*

1895 The first U.S. Open golf tournament was held, at the Newport Country Club in Rhode Island.

1895 Alfred Nobel drew up the plans for his famous philanthropic prizes in his final will and testament. The Swedish chemist, inventor, and philanthropist was born in Stockholm in 1833. After receiving an education in Saint Petersburg, Russia, and in the United States, where he studied mechanical engineering, he returned to St.

Petersburg to work under his father, developing mines, torpedoes, and other explosives. In a family-owned factory in Heleneborg, Sweden, he sought to develop a safe way to handle nitroglycerin after a factory explosion in 1864 killed his younger brother and four other people. In 1867 Nobel achieved his goal; by using an organic packing material to reduce the volatility of the nitroglycerin, he produced what he called dynamite. He later produced ballistite, one of the first smokeless powders. At the time of his death he controlled factories for the manufacture of explosives in many parts of the world. His will provided that the major portion of his $9 million estate be set up as a fund to establish yearly prizes for merit in physics, chemistry, medicine and physiology, literature, and world peace.

1931 The comic strip "Dick Tracy," created by Chester Gould, made its debut.

1940 Adolf Hitler and Benito Mussolini conferred at Brenner Pass in the Alps, where the Nazi leader sought the Italian Fascist's help in fighting the British.

1958 The first transatlantic passenger jetliner service was begun by British Overseas Airways Corporation (BOAC) with flights between London and New York.

1978 Funeral services were held at the Vatican for Pope John Paul I.

Commend me to sterling honesty, though clad in rags.

[SIR WALTER SCOTT (1771–1832)]

OCTOBER

While incarcerated in a grim Hapsburg gaol for embezzlement, Miguel de Cervantes Saavedra—a weathered old soldier then in service to the Spanish Crown as a tax collector—conceived the story of a lunatic knight errant and his peasant squire. Enduring all manner of hardships and setbacks, he set the semiautobiographical story to paper—and thus was born not only a masterpiece of comic writing but the prototype of the modern novel as well.

That first edition of *Don Quixote*—published on this day in 1605—was a huge success. There was little about the life and career of Cervantes that would have indicated a predilection to a successful literary career—his family had once been proud and influential but had fallen on hard times. Though his childhood was apparently fraught with difficulty, he was able to obtain an excellent education that filled him with aspirations to restore his family's fortunes. The young Cervantes chose the life of a professional soldier—the surest and quickest path to fame, glory, riches, and royal favor.

Service to the king of Castile led him into the fierce conflict between Christendom and Islam, still raging after nearly a millennium. His participation in the great Battle of Lepanto—in which the allied forces of Austria, Castile, Aragon, Navarre, Portugal, Venice, Lombardy, Genoa, Naples, and Rome surprisingly crushed the naval superiority of the Ottomans—marked him as a skilled and courageous warrior. During the fierce fighting he was severely wounded—permanently losing the use of his left arm. He was rewarded for his heroism and sent to Naples to recover.

It was there in the climes of the Italian Renaissance—surrounded by vibrant academies, passionate salons, and literary cenacles—that the young soldier steeped himself in the writings of Dante, Petrarch, Boccaccio, Bembo, and Aretino. He also became familiar with the innovative chivalric chapbooks written by Boiardo and Ariosto—whose style would greatly influence him later in life. Once he had regained his full strength, Cervantes was assigned minor administrative duties that allowed him to continue to drink deeply from those cultural wells.

Sadly, this refreshing period of his life was cut short when he was captured by the Turks while on a short journey and then sold into slavery in Algiers. For the next five years he was to suffer unmentionable tortures and atrocities in the Saracen prisons. Once again, he displayed exemplary courage throughout the ordeal—he escaped four times and became the tacit leader of the Christian detainees.

Back in Castile, he accepted the noxious task of a roving commissary—or auxiliary tax collector. But apparently, Cervantes was entirely unsuited for the task. His accounting was indecipherable, his work habits were inconsistent, and his diligence was suspect—in other words, he was a frustrated writer caught in a dead-end job. When his ledgers failed to add up, he was arrested and charged with fraud. But what was obviously a personal calamity for him turned out to be a cultural accretion for the world.

The achievement of Cervantes is stunning. With *Don Quixote*, he changed the shape of literature the world over. When he died in 1616—presumably the same year that William Shakespeare passed away—he left a huge void in Spanish letters that has never been entirely filled.

OCTOBER

Feast Day
St. Flora of Beaulieu, St. Maurus,
St. Magenulf or Meinulf, St.
Apollinaris of Valence, St. Galla

1703 Jonathan Edwards, theologian and leader of the Great Awakening, was born at East Windsor, Connecticut. He is best known for his writings in *Religious Affections* and his powerful sermon "Sinners in the Hands of an Angry God."

1735 The famed English clergyman and hymnist Charles Wesley (1707–1788) was ordained in the Church of England. Later that year he went to Georgia with his brother John as secretary to the colonial governor James Edward Oglethorpe. Ill health forced him to relinquish that post, however, and he returned to England the following year. Born in the rectory at Epworth, Lincolnshire, he was educated at Westminster School and Christ Church, University of Oxford. While at Oxford, he was a member, with his older brother John, of the Holy Club. On May 21, 1738, Charles Wesley experienced a religious awakening similar to that which his brother John was to undergo three days later. Charles subsequently was closely associated with the Wesleyan movement and traveled extensively as an evangelical preacher. After 1756 he carried on his work chiefly in Bristol and in London, where he lived from 1771 on. The two Wesleys differed on certain doctrinal matters—with Charles staying much more in line with Protestant and Reformed orthodoxy. In addition, Charles strongly opposed steps that might lead to separation from the Church of England and thus disapproved of John's ordinations. Charles Wesley is often called the "poet of the Methodist movement." He composed almost seven thousand hymns, many of which are still sung in Protestant churches. Among the most widely known are "Jesus, Lover of My Soul," "Hark! The Herald Angels Sing," and "Love Divine, All Love Excelling."

1830 The twenty-first president of the United States, Chester Arthur, was born in Fairfield, Vermont.

1892 The Dalton Gang, notorious for its train robberies, was practically wiped out while attempting to rob a pair of banks in Coffeyville, Kansas.

1921 The World Series was broadcast on radio for the first time.

1930 The Columbia Broadcasting System (CBS) aired the first of its live Sunday night radio broadcasts of the New York Philharmonic.

1941 Former Supreme Court Justice Louis D. Brandeis—the first Jewish member of the nation's highest court—died in Washington, D.C., at age eighty-four.

1947 President Harry Truman delivered the first televised White House address.

1962 The Beatles released their first hit, "Love Me Do," to mixed reviews in the United Kingdom.

1969 The surreal comedy *Monty Python's Flying Circus* made its debut on BBC television.

1989 A jury in Charlotte, North Carolina, convicted former PTL evangelist Jim Bakker of using his television show to defraud followers.

1998 The House Judiciary Committee voted to investigate whether President Bill Clinton should be removed from office on charges of corruption and perjury.

OCTOBER

Aye, sir; to be honest, as this world goes, is to be one man picked out of ten thousand.

[WILLIAM SHAKESPEARE (c. 1564–1616)]

James Whistler was one of the most remarkable and innovative artists in American history—renowned as a fine portrait painter and an unparalleled etcher, who incongruously assimilated the distinctive features of East and West, made innumerable technical innovations, and championed the cause of modern art.

He was born on July 10, 1834, in Lowell, Massachusetts, and entered the United States Military Academy at West Point in 1851. He did not do well in his studies, however, and was forced to leave the academy in 1854 to take a job as a draftsman with the government's Coastal Survey Corps. One year later, on this day, he went to Paris, where he became a pupil of the Swiss classicist painter Charles Gabriel Gleyre. Formal instruction influenced him less, however, than his acquaintance with the French realist painter Gustave Courbet and his own study of the great masters. It was also in Paris that he became fascinated with traditional Chinese and Japanese styles.

Whistler won recognition as an etcher when his first series of etchings, *Twelve Etchings from Nature*—commonly called *The French Set*—appeared in 1858. Soon after he moved to London where his paintings, which had been repeatedly rejected by the galleries of Paris, found ready acceptance and acclaim. *At the Piano* was shown by the Royal Academy of London in 1860. Thereafter, exhibitions of his work aroused increasing international interest, as did his flamboyantly eccentric personality.

Three of Whistler's best-known portraits, *Arrangement in Black and Grey No. 1: The Artist's Mother*—the official title of that famous painting best known simply as *Whistler's Mother*—*Arrangement in Grey and Black No. 1: Thomas Carlyle*, and *Harmony in Grey and Green: Miss Cicely Alexander*, were all painted during a very productive period of his life around 1872. In 1877 he exhibited a number of landscapes done in the Japanese manner; these paintings, which he called nocturnes, outraged conservative art opinion, which did not understand his deliberated avoidance of what he called "narrative detail." The famous traditionalist art critic John Ruskin wrote a caustic article, and Whistler, charging slander, sued Ruskin for damages. He won the case, one of the most celebrated of its kind, but the expense of the trial forced him into bankruptcy. Selling the contents of his studio, Whistler left England, worked intensively from 1879 to 1880 in Venice, then returned to England and resumed his attack on the academic art tradition.

In his later years Whistler devoted himself increasingly to etching, drypoint, lithography, and interior decoration—he was one of the first serious artists to turn to what he called "decorative architecture" to express his Christian worldview in "tangible, livable forms." *The Peacock Room* which he painted for a private London residence, was the most noteworthy example of his interior decoration, but he actually worked extensively in the field, arguing that "to live in art is a far more biblical notion than to merely pander to the critics and collecting classes." And so, until his death in 1903, that was his preferred medium.

OCTOBER

FEAST DAY
St. Mary Frances of Naples, St. Faith of Agen, St. Nicetas of Constantinople, St. Bruno

1536 The English translator of the New Testament, William Tyndale, was martyred at Vilvorde, in Flanders. He was strangled and burned at the stake for heresy.

1870 Louis Jennings was a pioneer in American journalism. The editor of the *New York Times* during the last decades of the nineteenth century, he helped to build the reputation of that paper—ultimately making it the premier daily in the entire nation. He was also a committed Christian and a stalwart in the struggle for life. On this day Jennings began a crusade against abortion on the editorial pages of his paper that ultimately lead to the criminalization of the procedure in every state in the Union. He understood the power of the printed page and utilized it expertly. He knew only too well that it would be necessary to provoke a public outrage over the issue, not simply a stiffening of legislation that might go unenforced. It was his leadership, and the national visibility of his paper, that ultimately swayed both the legal and the medical establishments to publicly denounce abortion as murder.

1884 The Naval War College was established in Newport, Rhode Island.

1889 The Moulin Rouge in Paris first opened its doors to the public.

1891 Charles Stewart Parnell, the "Uncrowned King of Ireland," died in Brighton, England.

1927 The era of talking pictures arrived with the opening of *The Jazz Singer*, a film starring Al Jolson and released by Warner Brothers Studio.

The movie premiered in New York City and featured both silent and sound-synchronized scenes.

1939 In an address to the Reichstag, Adolf Hitler denied having any intention of war against France and Britain.

1949 American-born Iva Toguri D'Aquino, convicted of being Japanese wartime broadcaster "Tokyo Rose," was sentenced in San Francisco to ten years in prison and fined ten thousand dollars.

1965 Georgi Vins, a courageous Russian Baptist pastor, helped to pioneer a new organization entirely independent of the Communist government-sanctioned religious union. The creation of the CCECB—the Council of Churches of Evangelical Believers—would unleash a vicious cycle of persecution against the confessing church—but it would also pave the way to more substantive resistance to the Soviet regime.

1973 War erupted in the Middle East as Egypt and Syria attacked Israel during the Yom Kippur holiday.

1979 Pope John Paul II, on a weeklong American tour, became the first pontiff to visit the White House, where he was received by President Jimmy Carter.

1981 Egyptian President Anwar Sadat was shot to death by Islamic extremists while reviewing a military parade.

1983 Cardinal Terence Cooke, the spiritual head of the archdiocese of New York, died at age sixty-two.

Genuine simplicity of heart is a healing and cementing principle.

[Edmund Burke (1729–1797)]

OCTOBER

The life of Edgar Allan Poe—who died on this day in 1849 in Baltimore, Maryland—was as haunting, as mysterious, and as provocative as his stories and verse. The master of the psychological thriller, the procedural mystery, and the horror tale was a man who lived a conflicted life and left a controversial legacy. As a result, there have been very few literary figures who have elicited more interest than Poe.

A common, almost automatic assumption about Poe is that he was an irredeemable atheist. As with so many other aspects of Poe's life, however, the truth is far less simplistic. Unfortunately, nowhere in Poe's writings do we find a straightforward and definitive statement of his position on this topic—nor, perhaps, should we expect one. Those who knew Poe and were quick to recall him as having no religion were often themselves quite zealous in their views. Effusive enthusiasm was likely to raise Poe's sense of the contrary. Poe loved to startle or surprise, and was likely to say things just for effect. Others made assumptions based on the negative evidence—that there is no overtly moral preaching and relatively little mention of religion in his writings. Some have suggested, rather dramatically, that Poe's only god was art.

But there is much to contradict this standard view. Poe's upbringing appears to have been quite typical for his era. He was, for instance, baptized and confirmed at Monumental Episcopal Church. Indeed, the dominant role of Christianity in the United States in the nineteenth century, especially before promulgation of Darwin's theory of evolution and the unutterable horrors of the War Between the States would have made it nearly impossible for him to have avoided being bathed in a general consensus of the truth and importance of the gospel. In addition though, Poe was carefully instructed in the catechism of the Church of England when he was in school in London.

Poe's small Bible, given to him by a lady friend in 1846, was one of the books in his trunk when he died. Another book Poe owned at the time was the 1833 edition of *On the Power, Wisdom, and Goodness of God* by Thomas Chalmers. It is clear from the notes written in his own hand in the margins of the book that he read it for personal rather than merely professional reasons.

In Poe's writings there are other clues to his spiritual estate. There are brief references to Christ and Christian behavior in letters and in marginalia, but while hardly typical of an atheist, such phrases may be little more than clichés or figures of speech. At best, they are rather vague and lend themselves to multiple interpretations. Nevertheless, at least a few seem to be rather enlightening. In one letter he wrote, "After reading all that has been written, and after thinking all that can be thought, on the topics of God and the soul, the man who has a right to say that he thinks at all, will find himself face to face with the conclusion that, on these topics, the most profound thought is that which can be the least easily distinguished from the most superficial sentiment." In another letter he wrote, "A strong argument for the religion of Christ is this—that offenses against Charity are about the only ones which men on their death-beds can be made not to understand, but to feel—as crime." Clearly, Poe also knew his Bible well, at least as literature—adding depth and breadth to his already rich legacy as a writer.

OCTOBER

1555 Charles V, the Holy Roman emperor, held the Diet of Augsburg during which Lutherans were given legal standing. Not until the Peace of Westphalia in 1648 however, were Calvinists added to the list of tolerated religions.

1644 John Evelyn wrote in his diary about his visit aboard the *Gally Royal,* a slave ship. He wrote, "the spectacle was to me new and strange, to see so many hundreds of miserably naked persons, their heads being shaved close, and having only high red bonnets, a pair of coarse canvas drawers, their whole backs and legs naked, double-chained about their waist and legs, in couples and made fast to their sheets, and all commanded in a trice by a cruel and imperious seaman."

1765 The Stamp Act Congress convened in New York to draw up colonial grievances against England.

1777 The second Battle of Saratoga began during the American Revolution. British forces under General John Burgoyne surrendered ten days later.

1826 The first railroad in the United States was completed. It spanned the three miles between Quincy, Massachusetts, and the Neponset River.

1916 The most lopsided game of intercollegiate football occurred on this day in Atlanta, Georgia, when Georgia Tech humiliated Cumberland University with a score of 222-0.

1949 The Communist junta of East Germany was formed.

1954 Marian Anderson became the first African-American singer hired by the Metropolitan Opera Company in New York.

1968 The Motion Picture Association of America adopted its film rating system.

1979 Pope John Paul II concluded his weeklong tour of the United States with a Mass on the Washington Mall.

1981 Egypt's parliament named Vice President Hosni Mubarak to succeed the assassinated Anwar Sadat.

1982 The Andrew Lloyd Webber–Tim Rice musical *Cats,* featuring the popular song "Memory," opened on Broadway.

1985 Palestinian gunmen hijacked the Italian cruise ship *Achille Lauro* in the Mediterranean with more than four hundred people aboard.

1989 Hungary's Communist Party renounced Marxism in favor of democratic socialism during a party congress in Budapest.

Behold all the leaders who have been handed down to posterity as instances of an evil fate—yet among them the good, the true, and the great.

[SENECA (C. 5–65)]

OCTOBER

At a campaign stop in Milwaukee on this day in 1912, a deranged, out-of-work bartender emerged from a crowd and shot Theodore Roosevelt in the chest at point-blank range. Staggered by the impact of the bullet and the shock of the injury, the great man nevertheless righted himself. As the crowd converged on the man, the wounded former president cried, "Stand back! Don't hurt the man! Bring him to me!" After examining his would-be assassin with a dismissive glare, he told his aides to get him to the rally. "This may be the last speech I deliver," he admitted. Seeing that he was bleeding heavily, several doctors in Roosevelt's party wanted to rush him to the hospital at once, but he waved them aside. "You just stay where you are," he ordered. "I am going to make this speech and you might as well compose yourselves." When they persisted, he said, "Get an ambulance or a carriage or anything you like at ten o'clock and I'll go to the hospital, but I won't go until I've finished my speech." He then demanded that his driver proceed to the auditorium.

The crowd was told what had happened. But as Roosevelt appeared on the platform, the familiar figure smiled and waved weakly to the awestruck crowd. "It is true," he whispered in a hoarse voice, "I have just been shot. But it takes more than that to kill a Bull Moose." Now beginning to gain his composure, he said, "Friends, I should ask you to be as quiet as possible. And please excuse me from making a long speech. I'll do the best I can." He then took his manuscript from his jacket; it had been pierced through by the bullet and was soaked with blood. "It is nothing," he said as the people gasped. "I am not hurt badly. I have a message to deliver and will deliver it as long as there is life in my body." The audience became deathly still as he went on to say, "I have had an A-1 time in life and I am having it now."

He always had the ability to cast an intoxicating spell over crowds. Even now, his physical presence was dominating. Though he was bleeding profusely, he went on to speak for an hour and a half. By the end he had almost completely regained his typical stump fervor—rousing the crowd to several extended ovations. When at last he allowed his concerned party to take him to the hospital, the audience reached a near frenzy, chanting, "Teddy! Teddy! Teddy!"

At the hospital he joked and talked politics with his attendants. But his condition was hardly a joking matter. The surgeons found that the bullet had fractured his fourth rib and lodged close to his right lung. "It is largely due to the fact that he is a physical marvel that he was not mortally wounded," observed one of them later. "He is one of the most powerful men I have ever seen on an operating table."

Nevertheless, he was no longer a young buck at the age of fifty-four. He was required—against his quite considerable will—to sit out the remainder of the campaign. Later, his biographers would view the incident as quintessential Roosevelt: imposing the sheer force of his will upon a seemingly impossible circumstance, and yet prevailing.

OCTOBER

FEAST DAY
St. Simeon Senex, St. Pelagia (or Margaret) the Penitent, St. Demetrius, St. Keyne, St. Thaïs, St. Marcellus, St. Reparta of Caesarea

1179 Medieval abbess, musician, and author Hildegarde of Birgen—known as Sybil of the Rhine—died after a long life of extraordinary impact. Her output was prodigious and varied. She compiled an encyclopedia of natural science and clinical medicine. She wrote the first known morality play and a song cycle. Hundreds of her letters of advice and rebuke went out to kings and commoners alike. She wrote highly regarded biographies of two saints. Her book of visions, *Scivias,* took her ten years to complete and was a devotional masterpiece. And she pioneered a remarkable new approach to liturgical music that remains vibrant and dynamic to this day. This output, coming from the pen of a woman, was extraordinary in an age when women seldom learned to read. She was considered a prophetess. St. Bernard of Clairvaux and popes endorsed her visions. All listened to her.

1869 The fourteenth president of the United States, Franklin Pierce, died in Concord, New Hampshire.

1871 The Great Fire of Chicago started on this day when, as legend tells it, Mrs. O'Leary's cow kicked over a lantern. The city, whose buildings were constructed mostly of wood, was almost entirely destroyed, several hundred people died, and around $200 million in property was consumed by the flames. In excess of 17,000 buildings were leveled and almost 100,000 people were left homeless.

1886 The statue *Liberty Enlightening the World,* commonly known as the *Statue of Liberty,* was unveiled in New York Harbor. This gift from the people of France was a given for the commemoration of the one-hundredth anniversary of American independence. The right hand and torch of the statue designed by Frédéric Auguste Bartholdi were exhibited in 1876 in Philadelphia at the Centennial Exhibition. The statue is 151 feet high and stands on a 155-foot granite pedestal, which was provided through subscription in America.

1890 American aviation hero Eddie Rickenbacker was born in Columbus, Ohio.

1918 Stationed in the Argonne Forest in France during the First World War, Sergeant Alvin C. York single-handedly killed 25 German soldiers, captured 132 more, and confiscated 35 machine guns while separated from his patrol.

1929 The first in-flight movie, consisting of two cartoons and a newsreel, was shown by Transcontinental Air Transport of America at some five thousand feet in the air.

1944 The situation comedy *The Adventures of Ozzie and Harriet* made its debut on CBS Radio.

1945 President Harry Truman announced that the secret of the atomic bomb would be shared with only Britain and Canada.

1956 Don Larsen pitched the first perfect game in a World Series as the New York Yankees defeated the Brooklyn Dodgers.

1982 All labor organizations in Poland, including Solidarity, were banned.

1998 The House triggered an open-ended impeachment inquiry against President Clinton in a momentous bipartisan vote.

OCTOBER

*T*o know that which before us lies in daily life is the prime wisdom.

[JOHN MILTON (1608–1674)]

1707

English theologian and hymn writer Isaac Watts (1674–1748) published his first collection of groundbreaking Puritan and Reformed hymns. Born in Southampton, he was educated at an academy for dissenters at Stoke Newington—now part of London. After some years as a tutor, preacher, and assistant pastor, he became minister of a dissenting church in London in 1702. Watts's books on theological subjects were well known, including his *Scripture History,* which was first published in 1732. Even better known, however, were his *Horae Lyricae,* a collection of Puritan poems, and his beloved hymn texts. He published two hymn collections, *Hymns* and *The Psalms of David.* Among his hymns still sung are "When I Survey the Wondrous Cross" and "O God, Our Help in Ages Past."

OCTOBER

NATIONAL DAY
Uganda
FEAST DAY
St. Demetrius of Alexandria,
Saints Andronicus and Athanasia,
St. Denis or Dionysius of Paris,
St. Dionysius the Aeropagite, St.
Savin, St. Publia, St. Louis
Bertrán, St. Ghislain or Gislenus

Grandson of a president and great-grandson of a signer of the Declaration of Independence, Benjamin Harrison (1833–1901) carried a distinguished American name into the White House, but most historians generally agree that he added very little distinction to it during his stay there.

Harrison's early years were filled with promise and success—admitted to the Indiana bar at the age of twenty, he became one of the state's ablest lawyers, and he interrupted his law career only to become a brigadier general for the Union army in the War Between the States at the age of thirty-two.

But the success that marked his early years was rather spotty when he entered politics after the war. Shortly after returning to Indiana he was defeated running for governor. After one term in the U.S. Senate he failed to be reelected in 1887. And his victory over Cleveland in the presidential election of 1888 was matched by a defeat at his hands when the two ran against each other in 1892.

Although he performed bravely on the battlefield, Harrison was not a bold president. Strongly supported and influenced by the mammoth trusts and other business interests, he signed into law one of the highest protective tariffs the country has ever known; and even when bills to curb the trusts managed to be passed, his administration did virtually nothing to enforce them. Ironically, he signed the Sherman Anti-Trust Act into law on this day in 1890—and though its provisions were enforced by his administration, it became the means by which the consuming monopolies were temporarily reined in a decade later.

In spite of such concessions to big business, the economy grew worse. Harrison permitted the country's gold reserves to be severely depleted by a questionable pension plan for war veterans. By the close of his administration the signs of depression had multiplied. As is almost always the case, what was good for the huge corporate trusts had not proved to be good for the nation. The cautious man who was afraid of the new electric lights in the White House had failed to convince the country that he could lead on to better times, and he was succeeded by his predecessor.

1000 People in Norway celebrate Leif Ericson Day as the day when the explorer landed at Vinland, which is thought to have been New England.

1635 Political and religious dissident Roger Williams was banished from the Massachusetts Bay Colony for disturbing the peace, refusing to submit to the governance of the state, and advocating heretical views.

1701 The Collegiate School of Connecticut—later renamed Yale University—was chartered in New Haven by the colonial legislature of Connecticut.

1776 A group of Spanish missionaries settled in present-day San Francisco.

1835 French composer Camille Saint-Saëns was born in Paris. His precise, lyrical compositions were in keeping with French classicism. His best-known works are the opera *Samson et Dalila* (1877), *Danse Macabre* (1874), the *Third Symphony in E-flat Minor* (1886), and *Le Carnaval des Animaux* (Carnival of the Animals, 1886). One of his pupils was Gabriel Fauré.

1888 The public was first admitted to the Washington Monument.

1917 Mr. Clarence Saunders of Memphis, Tennessee, was awarded a patent for his self-service method of running a food store. Thus, the first supermarket.

1919 Under questionable circumstances, the Cincinnati Reds defeated the Chicago White Sox in the World Series. Known as the Black Sox Scandal, eight players were banned from baseball because they intentionally lost the game or knew of the plan to do so.

1936 The first generator at Boulder Dam—later renamed Hoover Dam—began transmitting electricity to Los Angeles.

1946 The Eugene O'Neill drama *The Iceman Cometh* opened at the Martin Beck Theater in New York.

1958 Pope Pius XII died, nineteen years after he was elevated to the papacy. He was succeeded by Pope John XXIII.

1967 Latin American guerrilla leader Che Guevara was executed while attempting to incite revolution in Bolivia.

1974 Czech-born German businessman Oskar Schindler, credited with saving about 1,200 lives during the Holocaust, died in Frankfurt, West Germany. At his request, he was buried in Jerusalem.

1975 Dissident Soviet scientist Andrei Sakharov was awarded the Nobel Peace Prize.

1989 The official Soviet news agency *Tass* reported that a spaceship of some kind, complete with a trio of tall aliens, had visited a park in the city of Voronezh.

The future is purchased at the price of vision in the present.

[SAMUEL JOHNSON (1709–1784)]

OCTOBER

Abraham Kuyper was one of the most remarkable men of the twentieth century. A true polymath, the Dutch statesman made his mark as a pastor, theologian, journalist, educator, orator, publisher, politician, and reformer.

He was born in 1837, just seven years after Belgium and the Netherlands separated. Though his pious family background, quiet rural community, and meager local schooling combined to afford him only very humble resources, he was a bright student and was early on marked for great things. He attended the university at Leiden and quickly demonstrated an aptitude for serious scholastic work. Following his postgraduate work, he pastored a succession of churches—first in Beesd, then in Utrect, and finally in Amsterdam. He became the leader of the theological conservatives who were working hard to hold at bay the encroachments of modernists and liberals.

By 1872, he had begun publishing a daily newspaper, *De Standaard.* He was already the editor of the inspirational monthly magazine *De Heraut.* In addition, he had founded a new legal organization to protect the concerns of private Christian schools and had spearheaded the reorganization of the political conservatives into the Anti-Revolutionary Party. He was elected to the lower assembly and quickly became the leading exponent and spokesman for spiritual orthodoxy, fiscal restraint, and judicial tradition. As if all these activities were not enough, he continued the serious academic research he had begun at the university. He wrote a flurry of books, pamphlets, and broadsides, and he managed a heavy speaking schedule at home and abroad. In later years he would also establish the Free University of Amsterdam, give vision and direction to the new Dutch Reformed Church, and lead a coalition government as the prime minister. He was a genuine renaissance man in every respect.

He first entered politics as a member of the lower chamber of the Dutch legislature, at the head of a new Conservative and Christian coalition party. After breaking with the national church and forming the Free Reformed Church in 1886, he united the Calvinist and Catholic parties and in 1901 formed a reformed Christian Conservative ministry, serving as minister of the interior until 1905 and prime minister until 1907. He served in the upper house of the legislature from 1913 to 1920.

Beginning on this day in 1898, he gave an influential series of lectures at Princeton University in New Jersey in which he developed the idea of a comprehensive and universal Christian woldview—rooted in the Reformation doctrines of Calvinism. Before his death in 1920, he was able to successfully mobilize the ordinary citizens of the great Dutch nation to do the difficult work of social transformation—through the consistent application of the Christian worldview he so articulately espoused.

OCTOBER

FEAST DAY
St. Francis Borgia, St. Daniel, St. Cerbonius, Saints Eulampius and Eulampia, St. Paulinus of York, St. Maharsapor, St. Gereon

1582 The pious and learned Carmelite nun Teresa of Avila died in Alba de Tormes. The Carmelite order was founded by St. Berthold in Palestine around 1154, claiming descent from hermits who had lived on the holy mountain of Carmel in biblical times. The order achieved great success under St. Simon Stock, a thirteenth-century Englishman who was general from about 1247. The brown robe and scapular and white cape were the same for men and women, although the women added the white wimple and black veil. Teresa was born in 1515, just twenty-three years after Columbus claimed America for Spain. After much soul-searching during her teen years, in 1536 she entered the Carmelite Convent of the Incarnation at Avila. Between 1567 and 1582, she founded sixteen other convents of Discalced Carmelites. She was canonized in 1622, only forty years after her death.

1746 The great Puritan composer and hymn writer William Billings was born in Boston, Massachusetts. Though he had no musical training and was never able to earn his living as a musician, he was an enthusiastic singing master and a popular composer. In 1770 he published a collection of songs entitled *The New England Psalm Singer*. Its first written edition was engraved by Paul Revere. Billings later published six other collections of music, often including his original compositions. He especially favored fugue tunes but also included plain songs and anthems in his collections. One of the musical schools organized by William Billings in 1774 was at Stoughton, Massachusetts. In 1786 this was more formally organized into the Stoughton Musical Society, which is today the oldest musical society in the United States.

1845 The U.S. Naval Academy opened in Annapolis, Maryland.

1911 Revolutionaries under Sun Yat-sen overthrew China's venerable Manchu dynasty.

1914 By detonating one last explosion, President Woodrow Wilson ceremoniously completed the construction of the Panama Canal.

1931 *Belshazzar's Feast*, the dramatic and colossal oratorio by English composer Sir William Walton, received its premiere at the Leeds Festival. Because Walton knew the vast resources that would be available to him at the festival, he wrote the piece for a six-part choir, large orchestra, and brass bands. The biblical text compiled by Osbert Sitwell faithfully recounts the story from the book of Daniel with interpolations from the Psalms.

1935 After several private showings over the course of the previous month, George Gershwin's opera *Porgy and Bess* opened to the public on Broadway.

1938 Germany completed its annexation of the Czech Sudetenland.

1943 Chiang Kai-shek took the oath of office as president of China.

1959 The first global airline service was announced by Pan American Airlines.

1970 Fiji became independent after nearly a century of British rule.

1973 Vice President Spiro T. Agnew, accused of accepting bribes, pleaded no contest to one count of federal income tax evasion, and resigned his office.

1978 President Jimmy Carter signed a bill authorizing the ill-fated Susan B. Anthony dollar coin.

1990 The United States government began paying reparation to Japanese Americans placed in internment camps during the Second World War.

OCTOBER

Understanding is knowing what to do; wisdom is knowing what to do next; virtue is actually doing it.

[TRISTAN GYLBERD (1954–)]

597

Calvin Coolidge was the only son of a stern Puritan storekeeper, John Calvin Coolidge. The boy was born in 1872 in the dwelling at the rear of his father's combined general store and post office in Plymouth Notch and was schooled on hard work, pious manners, and the *Shorter Catechism*. It was a combination that would make him one of America's most uncompromisingly principled political figures and as a consequence, one of its greatest presidents. His straightforward homespun personality captivated the nation, and to this day he remains a symbol of his era.

His philosophy was direct: Success came to those, like himself, who worked hard and were honest. Provincial in background and outlook, he nevertheless had a remarkable grasp of the difficulties the nation faced as it advanced through the tumultuous decades at the beginning of the twentieth century. Coolidge was opposed to the ideological notions of liberal government interventionism, and he was equally against any measures that would interfere with the marketplace. "The chief business of America is business" expressed his concept of the nation's destiny.

Following his graduation from Amherst College in 1895, Coolidge studied law in Northampton, Massachusetts, and was admitted to the practice of law in 1897. The following year he opened his own law office in Northampton, and maintained a practice there until 1919. Coolidge devoted as much time as his law practice would permit to Republican Party politics. In 1898 he was elected city councilman of Northampton. Although he lacked the public friendliness of a professional politician, he won elections based on his forthrightness and integrity. He formed the habit of visiting his constituents and simply saying, "I want your vote. I need it. I shall appreciate it." Between 1900 and 1911 he served as city solicitor, clerk of courts, representative in the Massachusetts legislature, and mayor of Northampton. He then served as senator in the state legislature, as lieutenant governor, and as governor. It was then that he gained national renown when he broke the Boston police strike.

In 1920 the Republican National Convention chose him to be the running mate of Senator Warren G. Harding, an Ohio conservative. The men easily defeated the Democratic ticket of James M. Cox and future president Franklin D. Roosevelt—largely due to the unpopularity of the previous Wilson administration.

When Harding died suddenly and mysteriously on August 2, 1923, Coolidge took the presidential oath in his father's farmhouse parlor by the light of kerosene lamps. It fell to the new president to clean up the scandals and economic chaos of his predecessor's administration. He performed the task competently, bringing America unprecedented prosperity while slashing federal spending and taxation.

In 1924, Coolidge was reelected in his own right, riding a wave of popularity. Known as Silent Cal for his taciturn persona, he lived and governed by a set of unchanging principles drawn from his Puritan heritage and strong personal faith. Though his policies were quickly abandoned by his successor, Herbert Hoover—to disastrous results—his example provided the basis for a growing Conservative movement in America that would gain cultural dominance within half a century.

OCTOBER

FEAST DAY
St. Mary Soledad; Saints Andronicus, Tarachus, and Probus; St. Agilbert; St. Alexander Sauli; St. Nectarius of Constantinople; St. Bruno the Great of Cologne; St. Gummarus or Gomaire; St. Canice or Kenneth

1492 About an hour before moonrise on this day, Christopher Columbus was standing on the sterncastle of the *Santa Maria*, slightly higher than the prow. From there, he saw—or thought he saw—a light in the darkness along the western horizon. Later he wrote that it appeared to be "like a little wax candle rising and falling." Columbus excitedly summoned Pedro Gutierrez—one of the ship's several experienced and ably trained *marineros*—who confirmed the sighting. But the lights quickly faded from view. Sometime after midnight, with the moon in its last quarter illuminating the waves, Rodrigo de Triana—a lookout on the *Pinta*'s forecastle—caught sight of what appeared to be a whitish sand dune gleaming in the half-light. Then he saw another. Finally he glimpsed a dark mass of rocks connecting the two. *"Tierra! Tierra!"* he cried out. And indeed it was. It was not Asia as they all had hoped. But it was land—lying just six miles ahead. It had been nearly three months since they had left the familiar realms of Christendom. It had been more than eight years since Columbus had first proposed the expedition—and more than a decade since he had first conceived it. He had had to overcome the objections of the greatest minds of the day. He had had to convince reluctant merchants, courtiers, mariners, and churchmen. He had had to outwit men made ignorant by their experience. Again and again, he had persevered in the midst of disappointment, humiliation, poverty, frustration, and betrayal. There was, thus, glory in this moment of discovery.

1531 Ulrich Zwingli, the Swiss Reformer, died at the Battle of Kappel, which brought to a swift close the Swiss religious wars.

1776 The first naval battle of Lake Champlain was fought during the American Revolution. American forces led by General Benedict Arnold suffered heavy losses, but managed to stall the British.

1779 Polish nobleman Casimir Pulaski was killed while fighting for American independence during the Revolutionary War Battle of Savannah, Georgia.

1811 The first steam-powered ferryboat, the *Juliana*, was put into operation between New York City and Hoboken, New Jersey.

1889 *London Morning Post* chief correspondent Winston Churchill sailed to South Africa to cover the Boer War.

1890 The Daughters of the American Revolution was founded in Washington, D.C.

1896 Austrian composer Anton Bruckner died in Vienna. His sincere religious beliefs greatly influenced his works, which included chorale-like elements in his symphonies.

1948 The musical comedy *Where's Charley?*, starring Ray Bolger and featuring songs by Frank Loesser, opened on Broadway.

1975 NBC's *Saturday Night* made its debut with guest host George Carlin.

1984 Space shuttle *Challenger* astronaut Kathy Sullivan became the first American woman to walk in space.

1998 Pope John Paul II decreed the first Jewish-born saint of the modern era: Edith Stein, a nun killed in the gas chambers of Auschwitz.

OCTOBER

The art of being wise is the art of knowing what to overlook.

[WILLIAM JAMES (1842–1910)]

732

Charles Martel, Mayor of the Palace of the Franks and his stalwart Merovingian knights fought Islamic invaders between Poitiers and Tours in a battle that lasted several days. The Franks were on foot while the Muslims had a mighty cavalry. Even so, the Franks routed the invaders—and as a consequence Europe was spared the terrible fate of the Christian lands of the Middle East and North African Muslims. Europe would remain Christian territory. After beating back the Islamic hoard, Charles Martel gained great prominence—and his descendants had great influence on European history. Indeed, his grandson became the famous emperor Charlemagne.

His thick woolen doublet was sticky against his breast as he labored forward in the sweltering humidity. Briny water sloshed about in his boots. A gritty, sugary sand, whisked by the wind, clung to his skin and found its way between the folds of his clothing. For seventy-one days he had endured the close quarters and meager rations of a tiny caravel out on the open seas. During the last three weeks of that long journey, he had to calm the fears and control the anxieties of ninety restless sailors. Over the past thirty-six hours he had not slept at all. He was hot, dirty, and exhausted.

But in this moment of victory, he felt no discomfort—only exhilaration. At last he had made land-fall in what he believed to be the fabled Indies. In fact, Christopher Columbus had just discovered America—though it would be some time before he fully comprehended the real significance of that feat.

It was early in the morning on this day in 1492. Columbus left his command of the *Santa Maria* in a tiny skiff. A few yards from the shore, he plunged into the shallows and collapsed on the beach. And prostrate there on the tiny Guanahani island of the Bahamian archipelago, he wept tears of joy.

After a few moments, he lifted his head toward heaven and cried out with the words of the traditional dawn-watch canticle—the *Bendita Sea la Luz*—in exultant thanksgiving: "Blessed be the light of day, and the Holy Cross we say; and the Lord of Verity, and the Holy Trinity. Blessed be the immortal soul, and the Lord who keeps it whole, blessed be the light of day, and He who sends the dark away."

With several of his crewmen giddily gathered around him—including many of the experience-hardened *marineros, grumetes,* and *oficiales* of the expedition—he rose to his feet and unfurled the royal standard of Castile's beloved Queen Isabella. The two Pinzon brothers—Martin, who captained the *Pinta,* and Vicente, who captained the *Niña*—likewise solemnly displayed the banners of Aragon's revered King Ferdinand.

Afterward, Columbus summoned the secretary of his little armada and formalized his perpetration. With whatever pomp and ceremony he could muster in such circumstances, he intoned gravely the holy decrees and contentions. He claimed the island for his liege lord. And he named it for his divine Lord. Thus was the thirteen-mile stretch of coral and sand rechristened San Salvador. The men began to celebrate. They danced and shouted and clapped one another on the back. They sang and wept and made gracious amends. Besides grief, there is no emotion that elicits such free expression as relief.

OCTOBER

FEAST DAY
St. Maximilian of Lorch, Saints Felix and Cyprian, St. Edwin, St. Wilfrid of York, St. Ethelburga of Barking

600

451 The Second Ecumenical Council began in earnest after several days of ceremonial preliminaries. In 325 the First Ecumenical Council had taken place at Nicea to settle disputes over the nature of Christ. The council issued the Nicene Creed, agreeing that Christ was both man and God, and that as the Son of God He had the same divine nature as the Father. At this second synodical meeting, nearly six hundred bishops once again debated the nature of the incarnation of Christ. After several days of debate, the Chalcedonian creed was adopted, which reaffirmed the divine and human natures of Christ recognized at Nicea, and further stated that the two natures of Christ were "without confusion, without conversion, without severance, and without division." Jesus was affirmed as being both fully divine and human.

1654 Dutch painter Carel Fabritius was one of many killed by a great explosion in Delft while he was working on a portrait. Fabritius was one of Rembrandt's best-known students, and also a teacher of Vermeer.

1870 The scion of one of America's most prominent founding families, Robert E. Lee died in Lexington, Virginia, at age sixty-three.

1872 English composer, teacher, writer, and conductor Ralph Vaughan Williams was born in Down Ampney, Gloucestershire. Considered the greatest of England's nationalistic composers, Vaughan Williams fused traditional English folk music with art music composition techniques.

1901 The Executive Mansion was renamed the "White House" by President Theodore Roosevelt.

1915 English nurse Edith Cavell was executed by the Germans in occupied Belgium during the First World War.

1920 Construction began on the Holland Tunnel, connecting Twelfth Street in Jersey City, New Jersey, and Canal Street in New York City.

1933 Bank robber John Dillinger escaped from a jail in Allen County, Ohio, with the help of his gang, who killed the sheriff.

1935 Italian tenor Luciano Pavarotti was born in Modena and raised in poverty. He debuted as Rodolfo in *La Bohème* in Italy after years of vocal lessons. His debut at Covent Garden in 1965 launched his international career. He has performed around the world in major opera houses and successfully brought art music and specifically opera to nontraditional listeners. He is best known for his clear and full vocal quality throughout his range including a penetrating high register.

1960 Soviet Premier Nikita Khrushchev, angered by delegates refusing to vote on the Soviet draft declaration against colonialism, pounded one of his shoes on his desk at the United Nations General Assembly.

1973 President Richard Nixon nominated House Minority Leader Gerald R. Ford of Michigan to succeed Spiro T. Agnew as vice president.

1997 Folk singer John Denver was killed in the crash of his privately built aircraft in Monterey Bay, California.

OCTOBER

What you do when you don't have to, determines what you will be when you can no longer help it.

[RUDYARD KIPLING (1865–1936)]

1925 | Baroness Margaret Thatcher of Kesteven was born in the county of Lincolnshire, England. She served as Britain's first female prime minister, taking up her office in 1979. She was also the longest-serving prime minister of the twentieth century.

Stephen Crane sold an abridged version of his famous novel, *The Red Badge of Courage*, to the Bachellor-Johnson Syndicate for ninety dollars. A month later it first appeared in the *Philadelphia Press*—on this day in 1894.

The novel is full of spectacular descriptions—vivid scenes to satisfy a growing consumer society's desire for thrilling spectacle. Written in a post-photographic age, the novel discards contemporaneous conventions of battlefield prose for a discontinuous succession of flashing images that yield photographic revelations. Crane limited the novel's point of view and fragmented its narrative to focus the impact of each of his battle pictures. He wanted to somehow make his readers see the truth of his descriptions.

He focused the narrative on the physical, emotional, and intellectual responses of people under extreme pressure, nature's indifference to humanity's fate, and the consequent need for compassionate collective action. He explored the effect of colors on the human mind, the harsh realities of war and fighting on the social fabric, the lasting impact of father-son relationships on community life, the interlacing themes of sin and virtue on the cultural consensus. The result was nothing short of riveting.

The English critic Sydney Brooks, totally convinced by Crane's depictions of combat in *Red Badge*, assumed that Crane had fought in the Civil War. If *Red Badge* were "altogether a work of the imagination, unbased on personal experience," Brooks asserted, "its realism would be nothing short of a miracle."

In fact though, Crane was not born until nearly a decade after the conflicts depicted in the novel took place. When he wrote those scenes, he had not seen any form of warfare at all. Indeed, though informed by a certain amount of research, the book was entirely the work of a fantastic imagination. His realism was completely made up. In that sense, he was a romantic of the basest sort.

In writing about the life and legacy of King Alfred the Great, G. K. Chesterton quipped, "King Alfred is not a legend in the sense that King Arthur may be a legend; that is, in the sense that he may possibly be a lie. But King Alfred is a legend in this broader and more human sense, that the legends are the most important things about him." Chesterton recognized that sometimes that which appears to be most realistic is actually most fantastic and that which appears to be most fantastic is actually most realistic. In the case of Stephen Crane, we have a remarkable writer known for his authenticity, but whose realism was in fact just a romance.

Modern critics have assumed that Crane produced a new thing—a kind of fictionalized journalism. In fact, what he produced in *Red Badge* was a fairy tale with a moral.

OCTOBER

FEAST DAY
Saints Januarius and Martial, St. Gerald of Aurillac, St. Edward the Confessor, St. Coloman, St. Comgan, St. Faustus of Cordova, St. Maurice of Carnoët

54   Tiberius Claudius Caesar Augustus Germanicus, the Roman emperor who extended Roman rule in North Africa and added Britain as a Roman province, died on this day. After thirteen years as Caesar, he was poisoned by his wife, Agrippina.

1775 The Continental Congress ordered the construction of two warships, thus launching the United States Navy.

1792 The cornerstone was laid for the executive mansion, the first building erected by the government in Washington, D.C. Modeled after the palace of the Duke of Leinster in Ireland, the mansion was first occupied by President John Adams in 1800. Only the four walls were left standing after it was burned by the British in 1814. During the restoration in 1818, the stones were painted white to obliterate the marks of the fire.

1843 The Jewish organization B'nai B'rith was founded in New York City.

1845 Texas ratified a state constitution after joining the United States a decade after gaining independence from Mexico.

1943 Italy declared war on Germany, its one-time Axis partner.

1952 Flannery O'Connor published her first novel, *Wise Blood*. Born in Savannah, Georgia, O'Connor was educated at the Georgia State College for Women and the State University of Iowa. Most of her life was spent in Milledgeville, Georgia, where she raised peacocks and wrote. Her novels and short stories, which focused on humanity's spiritual deformity and flight from redemption, offered readers an unlikely mixture of Southern Gothic, prophecy, and evangelistic Christianity. O'Connor was frequently compared to the American novelist William Faulkner for her portrayal of Southern character and milieu, and to the Austrian writer Franz Kafka for her preoccupation with the grotesque. A basic theme of her work is the individual's vain attempt to escape the irresistible grace of God. She died of lupus, a disease that crippled her during the lone decade of her career.

1960 Richard M. Nixon and John F. Kennedy participated in the third televised debate of their presidential campaign.

1962 *Who's Afraid of Virginia Woolf?*, by Edward Albee, opened on Broadway.

1974 Longtime television host Ed Sullivan died in New York City at age seventy-two.

1975 Lars Tanner was raised in a large working-class Norwegian Lutheran home in Oslo. When he was a teenager, his family moved to Stockholm where he lived and worked as a cobbler for the rest of his life. A series of devastating miscarriages suffered by his wife provoked him to delve into the Bible's teaching about children. Startled by what he discovered, he began to wonder why the church had not taken a stronger stand the previous year when many restrictions on abortion were lifted. Beginning with a small newsletter printed on a crude press in his cellar, he dedicated himself to an educational campaign that would eventually span nearly four decades—testifying before hospital committees and government hearings, lecturing to secondary and university students, lobbying candidates for political office, and organizing protests at abortuary sites. By the time of his death in 1975, he had laid the groundwork for a resurgent pro-life movement in Sweden and had set an example of faithfulness for thousands of Christians throughout Scandinavia.

OCTOBER

*I*nstruct a wise man and he will be wiser still; teach a righteous man and he will add to his learning.

[KING SOLOMON (C. 1000 B.C.)]

Following the death of Edward the Confessor, Harold Godwin, a member of the most powerful noble family in England and Earl of Wessex, was crowned King Harold II. Although the late king had apparently approved Harold's succession, Harold's brother, Tostig, also declared his right to the throne, and along with King Harold III of Norway launched an invasion of England from Scotland. In September, Harold defeated the combined forces of Tostig and the Norwegian king at Stamford Bridge, and both leaders were killed.

Five years earlier, Harold had been shipwrecked on the Norman coast and taken prisoner by William the Conqueror (1027–1087), a Norman prince and a cousin to the royal family of Saxon England. He secured his release by swearing to support William's succession claims to the English throne.

Now, with his troops exhausted from their bitter struggle with Tostig, Harold had to face the wrath of his slighted cousin. Even though the witenagemot—the royal council—had deliberately bypassed William in favor of Harold, William was determined to make good his claim. He secured the sanction of Pope Alexander II for a Norman invasion of England and the duke, with his powerful army, crossed the English Channel and landed at Pevensey on September 28, 1066.

On October 14, the Normans defeated the English forces at the celebrated Battle of Hastings, in which Harold was slain—shot through the eye with an arrow. William then proceeded to London, crushing the resistance he encountered on the way. On Christmas Day he was crowned king of England in Westminster Abbey.

The English did not accept foreign rule without a struggle. William met the opposition, which was particularly violent in the north and west, with strong measures; he was responsible for the devastation of great areas of the country, particularly in Yorkshire, where Danish forces had arrived to aid the Saxon rebels. By 1070 the Norman conquest of England was complete.

William invaded Scotland in 1072 and forced the Scottish king Malcolm III MacDuncan to pay him homage. During the succeeding years the Conqueror crushed insurrections among his Norman followers, including that incited in 1075 by Ralph de Guader, 1st Earl of Norfolk, and Roger Fitzwilliam, Earl of Hereford, and a series of uprisings in Normandy led by his eldest son Robert, who later became Robert II, duke of Normandy.

One feature of William's reign as king was his reorganization of the English feudal and administrative systems. He dissolved the great earldoms, which had enjoyed virtual independence under his Anglo-Saxon predecessors, and distributed the lands confiscated from the English to his trusted Norman followers. He introduced the Continental system of feudalism; by the Oath of Salisbury of 1086 all landlords swore allegiance to William, thus establishing the precedent that a vassal's loyalty to the king overrode his fealty to his immediate lord. The feudal lords were compelled to acknowledge the jurisdiction of the local courts, which William retained along with many other Anglo-Saxon institutions. The ecclesiastical and secular courts were separated, and the power of the papacy in English affairs was greatly curtailed. He was, in a very real sense, the founder of an altogether new England.

OCTOBER

NATIONAL DAY
Madagascar
FEAST DAY
St. Callixtus I, St. Angadiama, St. Justus of Lyons, St. Burchard of Würzburg, St. Manaccus, St. Manechildis, St. Dominic Lauricatus

1531 Ulrich Zwingli, pastor of the church in Zurich and a prominent leader of the Reformation, was killed at the Battle of Kappel as Catholic forces laid siege on the city's defenses. Born the first of January 1481, as a boy Zwingli handcopied and memorized Paul's letters in the original Greek. Impressed by the Reform writings of the great humanist scholar Erasmus, he espoused a Protestant theology even before Martin Luther did. He was the pastor of the influential church at Zurich beginning in 1519. He joined the troops on the day of his death to encourage them to continue to stand for their faith and their families.

1644 English Reformer and founder of Pennsylvania, William Penn was born in London, England. Educated at Christ Church, Oxford, he converted to Quakerism. In and out of jail for his religious beliefs, Penn wrote tracts and books including *No Cross, No Crown* in 1669. He was granted territory in North America in exchange for a debt owed to his father. Along with several friends, he sailed to what became Pennsylvania. He planned the city of Philadelphia, and governed the colony well.

1822 When Victor Hugo married the beautiful Adel Foucher, his older brother suddenly went mad at the wedding breakfast—apparently insane with jealousy. The scene would haunt the writer for the rest of his life and would recur in all of his most famous plots and characters.

1843 Felix Mendelssohn conducted the premiere of his incidental music for *A Midsummer Night's Dream*, which was commissioned by Friedrich Wilhelm IV of Prussia and performed in the New Palace at Potsdam.

1890 Dwight D. Eisenhower, thirty-fourth president of the United States, was born in Denison, Texas.

1933 Nazi Germany announced it was withdrawing from the League of Nations.

1944 German Field Marshal Erwin Rommel committed suicide rather than face execution for allegedly conspiring against Adolf Hitler.

1947 Captain Charles E. Yeager broke the sound barrier with the *XS-1*, a United States Army rocket airplane at Muroc, California.

1960 The idea of a Peace Corps was first suggested by Democratic presidential candidate John F. Kennedy to an audience of students at the University of Michigan.

1964 Dr. Martin Luther King Jr. became the youngest recipient of the Nobel Peace Prize. The civil rights leader donated the entirety of the prize money, $54,000, to further the cause for which he eventually gave his life.

1977 Singer Bing Crosby died outside Madrid, Spain, at age seventy-three.

1990 Composer-conductor Leonard Bernstein died in New York at age seventy-two.

To be wise, one must take time to deliberate. But when the time for action has arrived, one must stop deliberating and boldly act.

[NAPOLEON BONAPARTE (1769–1821)]

OCTOBER

The Roman epic poet Publius Virgilius Maro was born on this day in 70 B.C. at Andes, near Mantua, in Cisalpine Gaul. He died fifty-one years later in 19 B.C. at Brundisium. He was thought to have been sickly, slow of speech, and of a countrified appearance. His writing was sometimes criticized for its rusticity, too. Nevertheless, he was able to create one of literature's greatest enduring masterpieces.

Though wealth, privilege, and power were not part of his inheritance, he had the good fortune to win the friendship and patronage of a number of very influential men. Eventually, he became a favorite of the emperor—and in fact, his greatest works were actually commissioned by Caesar for the purpose of lauding the new Imperial social and political structure.

Augustus commissioned the *Aeneid* to glorify Rome and the Roman people by means of a Homeric epic about the adventures of Aeneas, ancestor of Romulus and the Julian line. Thus, the real subject of the *Aeneid* was not Aeneas, but rather Rome and the glories of her empire, seen as the Romanticist sees the great past. Indeed, the first title of the *Aeneid* was *The Deeds of the Roman People.* Aeneas was important only because he carried Rome's destiny—he was to be her founder by the high decrees of fate.

The great poem was an arduous undertaking—after eleven years, it was still incomplete at the poet's death. Virgil had asked that it be burned, not published, should he die before it was finished, but Augustus countermanded these instructions—and as a result the world was given one of the most remarkable epics ever penned by the hand of man.

Long after the poet's death, his poem attained a kind of immortality. Augustine believed Virgil had foretold the birth of Jesus—and so Christians thoughout the Patristic and Medieval Ages looked to the *Aeneid* as a model of proto-Christian verse. Later, a fictional Virgil would act as the guide to Dante Alighieri, in the *Divine Comedy.* Francesco Petrarch modeled his *Africa* on *Aeneid.* Giovanni Boccaccio wrote the *Theseid* in the classical form of twelve books and in precisely the same number of lines as *Aeneid.* He is said to have started its composition sitting in Virgil's tomb. Geoffrey Chaucer summarized the *Aeneid* in *The House of Fame* and *The Legend of Dido.*

During the Renaissance, Virgil's *Aeneid* appeared translated into prose or paraphrased into French, Gaelic, Italian, and Catalonian, Castilian, and Aragonese by the fifteenth century. Shortly thereafter there were German, English, and Russian versions. Matthew Arnold, Alfred, Lord Tennyson, and John Keats all created prose translations of the entire *Aeneid* as teenagers, as well as Victor Hugo, who translated Virgil at sight at age nine in the entrance exam for his school. Thus, the Augustan poet was, as John Buchan asserted, the literature instructor to all the world of Christendom.

OCTOBER

FEAST DAY
  St. Teresa of Avila, St. Leonard of Vandoeuvre, St. Thecla of Kitzingen, St. Euthymius the Younger

1582 Italy, France, Spain, and Portugal adopted the Gregorian, or New Style, Calendar. As a result, the date before this day was October 4. The intervening ten days were subsequently lost to history to reconcile the two calendars.

1844 German philosopher Friedrich Wilhelm Nietzsche was born in Rocken. His influential ideas included the Will to Power and contempt for the weak. His concept of the superman was adopted by Hitler and his designs for the master race. Nietzsche went insane ten years before his death in 1900.

1878 The first electric company, Edison Electric Light, was incorporated in New York City , and issued 3,000 stock shares of a value of $100 each for the purpose of financing Mr. Edison in his efforts to invent the incandescent lamp.

1880 After six hundred years of construction, the Grand Cathedral in Cologne, Germany, was finally completed, to the glory of God, and with great rejoicing of the people.

1881 P. G. Wodehouse (Sir Pelham Grenville Wodehouse) was born in Guilford, Surrey, England. Plum, as he was known to his friends, was best known as the creator of Jeeves, the quintessential gentleman's gentleman, and Bertie Wooster, his flighty but good-hearted employer. Wodehouse wrote more than ninety novels, collaborated on more than thirty plays and musical comedies (including those of George Gershwin, Jerome Kern, and Victor Herbert), and wrote over twenty film scripts. His incredible comic timing, pointed wit, and skillful dialogue are surpassed only by his masterful use of the English language.

1902 The first jazz music to be written down, the "New Orleans Blues," was performed and recorded by Jelly Roll Morton.

1928 The German dirigible *Graf Zeppelin* landed in Lakehurst, New Jersey, on its first commercial flight across the Atlantic.

1939 New York Municipal Airport, later renamed LaGuardia Airport, was dedicated.

1945 The former premier of Vichy France, Pierre Laval, was executed.

1946 Nazi war criminal Hermann Goering poisoned himself hours before he was to have been executed.

1962 President John Kennedy was informed that reconnaissance photographs indicated the presence of missile bases in Cuba, thus launching the Cuban Missile Crisis.

1966 President Lyndon Johnson signed a bill creating the Department of Transportation.

1976 In the first debate of its kind between vice-presidential nominees, Democrat Walter F. Mondale and Republican Bob Dole faced off in Houston.

1989 Wayne Gretzky of the Los Angeles Kings surpassed Gordie Howe's scoring record of 1,850 points, during a game against the Edmonton Oilers.

1990 Soviet President Mikhail S. Gorbachev was named the winner of the Nobel Peace Prize.

1991 Despite sexual harassment allegations by Anita Hill, the Senate narrowly confirmed the nomination of Clarence Thomas to the Supreme Court, 52-48.

OCTOBER

That which seems to be the height of absurdity in one generation often becomes the height of wisdom in the next.

[JOHN STUART MILL (1806–1873)]

In 1900, most Americans greeted the twentieth century with the proud and certain belief that the next hundred years would be the greatest, the most glorious, and the most glamorous in human history. They were infected with a sanguine spirit. Optimism was rampant. A brazen confidence colored their every activity.

Certainly there was nothing in their experience to make them think otherwise. The twentieth century has moved so fast and furiously that those of us who have lived in it feel sometimes giddy, watching it spin; but the nineteenth moved faster and more furiously still. Railroads, telephones, the telegraph, electricity, mass production, forged steel, automobiles, and countless other modern discoveries had appeared at a dizzying pace, expanding visions and expectations far beyond anyone's wildest dreams. It was more than unfounded imagination, then, that lay behind the *New York World*'s New Year's prediction that the twentieth century would "meet and overcome all perils and prove to be the best that this steadily improving planet has ever seen."

What they did not know was that dark and malignant seeds were already germinating just beneath the surface of the new century's soil. Joseph Stalin was a twenty-one-year-old seminary student in Tiflis, a pious and serene community at the crossroads of Georgia and Ukraine. Benito Mussolini was a seventeen-year-old student teacher in the quiet suburbs of Milan. Adolf Hitler was an eleven-year-old aspiring art student in the quaint upper Austrian village of Brannan. And Margaret Sanger was a twenty-year-old out-of-sorts nursing school dropout in White Plains, New York. Who could have ever guessed on that ebulliently auspicious New Year's Day that those four youngsters would, over the span of the next century, spill more innocent blood than all the murderers, warlords, and tyrants of past history combined? Who could have ever guessed that those four youngsters would together ensure that the hopes and dreams and aspirations of the twentieth century would be smothered under the weight of holocaust, genocide, and triage?

No one in his right mind would want to rehabilitate the reputations of Stalin, Mussolini, or Hitler. Their barbarism, treachery, and debauchery will make their names live on in infamy forever. Amazingly though, Sanger has somehow escaped their wretched fate. In spite of the fact that her crimes against humanity were no less heinous than theirs, her place in history has effectively been sanitized and sanctified. In spite of the fact that she openly identified herself in one way or another with their aims, intentions, ideologies, and movements, her faithful minions have managed to manufacture an independent reputation for the perpetuation of her memory.

In life and death, the progenitor of the grisly abortion industry and the patron of the devastating sexual revolution has been lauded as a courageous reformer. Yet it was on this day in 1916 that she began her deleterious work. Sanger, as a part of her eugenic effort to limit the offspring of minorities, opened the first birth control clinic in Brooklyn, New York—the progenitor of the Planned Parenthood movement.

16

OCTOBER

FEAST DAY
Saints Martinian and Maxima, St. Margaret-Mary, St. Anastasius of Cluny, St. Hedwig, St. Bertrand of Comminges, St. Becharius, St. Mommolinus, St. Lull, St. Gerard Majella, St. Gall

1555 Across from Balliol College in Oxford, Bishop Hugh Latimer and Bishop Nicholas Ridley were burned at the stake for heresy. Protestant martyr Latimer turned to Ridley and said, "Be of good comfort, Master Ridley, and play the man. We shall this day light such a candle by God's grace in England, as I trust never shall be put out."

1621 Netherlands composer, teacher, and organist Jan Pieterszoon Sweelinck, who wrote one of the finest collections of polyphonic psalm settings, died on this day.

1758 American teacher and journalist Noah Webster was born in West Hartford, Connecticut. His dictionary of American English helped to codify uniquely American spelling practices.

1793 During the French Revolution, Queen Marie Antoinette was beheaded.

1829 The Tremont House Hotel in Boston celebrated its grand opening as the first modern first-class hotel. The hotel contained 170 rooms at a rate of $2 a day, which included four meals. Some of the innovations of this hotel included the opportunity to rent a single room (as opposed to doubling up with strangers three or four to a bed—some of whom may have arrived in the middle of the night), a key for each room, a wash bowl, a free cake of soap, gas lights, and eight "bathing rooms" with running water in the basement.

1859 Abolitionist John Brown led a group of about twenty men in a raid on Harper's Ferry.

1900 British author, lecturer, statesman, and anthologist Sir Arthur Thomas Quiller-Couch (1863–1944), published the first edition of his immortal *Oxford Book of English Verse*. Born in Fowey in Cornwall, Q—as he was best known to his friends, students, and readers—was to call the beloved little fishing village his home throughout his life. He memorialized it in his novels as Troy Town—and indeed, in 1937, he was elected the town's mayor. After editing *The Speaker* from 1887 to 1892, he became professor of English literature at Cambridge University and was knighted in 1910. In his later years he was best known as a scholar and as the editor of anthologies of verse, prose, ballads, lectures, and essays. A close friend of G. K. Chesterton and Hilaire Belloc, he was nevertheless a lifelong Anglican and held to an orthodox Reformed and Protestant worldview.

1901 President Theodore Roosevelt received harsh criticism when he invited his friend Booker T. Washington to the White House. Surprised at the uproar over race, Washington told the president that the nation would be unable to accept racial reconciliation because the church did not yet accept it.

1946 Ten convicted Nazis were hanged at Nuremberg for war crimes. An eleventh criminal, Hermann Goering, committed suicide the day before within hours of his scheduled execution.

1969 The New York Mets capped a miraculous season as they won the World Series, defeating the Baltimore Orioles.

1978 The College of Cardinals of the Roman Catholic Church chose Cardinal Karol Wojtyla to be the new pope. He took the name John Paul II.

OCTOBER

To establish the fact of decadence is the most pressing duty of wisdom in our time.

[RICHARD WEAVER (1910–1963)]

Known for his witty style, the amazingly prolific author G. K. Chesterton wrote in many genres, including fiction, biography, poetry, theology, history, as well as a myriad of essays. He was one of the most beloved writers in England during the first part of the twentieth century.

On this day in 1912, biographer Hugh Lunn interviewed Chesterton for the *Hearth and Home* magazine. He began with a description of the great man: "Everyone knows Mr Chesterton's appearance, a good portly man, i' faith, and a corpulence, like Falstaff. His writings, too, have become familiar, winning many disciples, especially among the young. At Oxford the Chestertonian and the Shavian are well-known types: the Shavian enthroned above human emotion is clever, but a prig; the Chestertonian, less brilliant, is more likeable. He doesn't care for advanced ideas, but he would like to combine wit and probity. So he welcomes a writer who defends old modes of thought with humor, and attacks modern thinkers on the ground that they are antiquated bores in disguise."

Lunn was soon to discover that with Chesterton, there was much more than met the eye—despite the fact that his rotund figure was sufficient to fill the eye. With a glint of good humor, Chesterton began with characteristic words: "I am always ready to be interviewed, for I hold the theory, nowadays completely forgotten—as forgotten as this matchbox was still this moment (fishing a box out of a bowl on the mantelpiece)—the theory that the Press is a public agora. I should not refuse an interview even to a paper owned by one of those capitalist millionaires, whom I hate. Nowadays the Press merely echoes the powerful; its real aim should be to give the public a chance to state its views."

Lunn could hardly get a word in edgewise, so the interview turned into something of a monologue—a forum for the great man to hold forth on all manner of ideas, much like his writing: "And now what do you want me to talk about? I am ready to give my opinion on any question, whether I know something about it or not. No, I'm not an Imperialist in the modern sense; the only theory of Imperialism that seems to me sound is Dante's. He defended the Roman Empire as the best human government, on the definite ground that the best human government would probably crucify God. Caesar had to be lawful; because Christ had to be killed by law."

With that, he paused with a smile to ask Lunn what questions he really wanted to put upon the table. He should not have bothered. Before he could reply, Chesterton was off again: "I do not believe in Cosmopolitanism, you know: nowadays it's either run by financiers for their own profit, or it's the product of Atheistic Socialism, as in Germany. Christ didn't come to bring peace among the nations. When He said that a man should turn the other cheek, I fancy He meant that a man, when attacked, should humiliate his enemy by treating him with sudden and unexpected contempt."

And so it went for nigh on an hour. Lunn had to admit afterward, "I had altogether underestimated the tornado of thought and creativity and imagination that the jolly figure of Chesterton contained." To which Chesterton later retorted, "It is always better to be underestimated than overestimated—that way, all good things are taken as if by surprise and are therefore all the more appreciated." Appreciated, Chesterton surely is.

OCTOBER

FEAST DAY
The Ursuline Martyrs of Valenciennes, Saints Ethelbert and Ethelred, St. John the Dwarf, St. Anstrudis or Austrude, St. Seraphino, St. Nothelm, St. Ignatius of Antioch, St. Rule

1711 With the publication of his eighty-eight-line poem "An Evening Thought," Jupiter Hammon became the first published African-American poet. He was born as a slave on this day on Long Island, New York.

1777 British forces under General John Burgoyne surrendered to American troops in Saratoga, New York, in a turning point of the Revolutionary War.

1845 The *Boston Transcript* newspaper reported that Edgar Allan Poe's reading of his poem *The Raven* the night before had been such that the audience at the Lyceum had walked out on him. Poe responded that he was ashamed of having been born in such a city.

1892 English composer Herbert Howells, organist and master of the English anthem, was born on this day. His mastery of vocal and organ writing have established him as a seminal figure in the development of the English choral anthem. His music was played at both the 1937 and 1953 coronations.

1915 American playwright Arthur Miller was born in New York City. His greatest work was *Death of a Salesman* (1949), which won the Pulitzer Prize for Drama and the New York Drama Critics' Circle Award. Miller often wrote in a realistic manner, but relied on techniques such as memory and internal struggles to convey the action of the drama.

1919 The Radio Corporation of America (RCA) was created.

1931 Mobster Al Capone was convicted of income tax evasion and sentenced to eleven years in prison. He was released eight years later.

1933 Fleeing from Nazi Germany, Albert Einstein arrived in the United States as a refugee.

1939 Frank Capra's film classic *Mr. Smith Goes to Washington*, starring Jimmy Stewart, premiered in Washington, D.C.

1945 Colonel Juan Peron staged a coup, becoming absolute ruler of Argentina.

1957 French author Albert Camus was awarded the Nobel Prize in literature.

1960 Charles van Doren was arrested for perjury after lying to a grand jury concerning whether he had received answers prior to being a contestant on a television quiz show.

1978 President Jimmy Carter signed a bill restoring U.S. citizenship to former Mississippi Senator and Confederate President Jefferson Davis.

1989 Just as the 1989 World Series was about to begin, an earthquake measuring 7.1 on the Richter scale shook the San Francisco Bay area. Sixty-seven people were killed, and the quake caused $10 billion in physical damage.

1997 The remains of revolutionary Ernesto "Che" Guevara were laid to rest in his adopted Cuba, thirty years after his execution in Bolivia.

OCTOBER

Learn from the mistakes of others—you don't have nearly enough time to make them all yourself.

[TRISTAN GYLBERD (1954–)]

Washington's most valued assistant in war and peace, Alexander Hamilton (1755–1804) was probably the most brilliant writer, organizer, and political theorist among the Founding Fathers. Time after time from 1776 to 1795 he brought his great powers of intellect to bear on the most critical problems facing the new nation—from obtaining a truly national constitution to establishing a sound national financial system.

Born in the British West Indies, he came to America as a teenager. William Livingston of New Jersey, who later joined Hamilton in signing the Constitution, gave the talented young man a home and sent him to King's College—later Columbia University—in New York on this day in 1772. By 1775 Hamilton had written two pamphlets defending the American cause that displayed an exceptional grasp of the principles of government. During the war Hamilton distinguished himself in battle and served as Washington's aide. He organized Washington's headquarters and wrote many of Washington's statements and a complete set of military regulations.

An advocate of a strong central government, Hamilton led the delegates at the inconclusive Annapolis Convention to agree to meet in Philadelphia the next year "to take into consideration the situation of the United States, to render the Constitution of the Federal Government adequate to the exigencies of the Union." His carefully worded proposal permitted more than it seemed to say: He opened the way for the Constitutional Convention.

His influence was not so great at the Convention as after it, when he wrote fifty of the eighty-five *Federalist Papers*, which won necessary public support. As first secretary of the Treasury, Hamilton devised a comprehensive financial system that proved almost immediately successful: He proposed that the federal government assume the states' war debts, and, to settle these and foreign debts, that there be an excise tax, a national bank, and a protective tariff, which would also encourage American industry. The businessmen favored by these measures gradually grew into a political party under Hamilton. As first leader of the Federalist Party, Hamilton was, with Jefferson—who founded the Democratic-Republican Party—a founder of the two-party system.

Hamilton, who had little faith in mass democracy, stood for a more representative and republican form of government, an industrial society, and an aristocracy of power. Jefferson, on the other hand, who was convinced by the egalitarian rhetoric of the French Revolution, stood for a more agricultural society, strong states' rights, and mass democracy. Jefferson was more concerned with individualism as the pathway to freedom, while Hamilton was convinced that societies and communities needed to be the first hedge against tyranny.

Rivalry between the factions came to a head when Hamilton was killed in a duel with his New York rival, Aaron Burr. The Constitution and the *Federalist Papers*, the national financial system and the American two-party system—in a very real sense these are the legacy of the brilliant man who came to America a penniless immigrant.

OCTOBER

FEAST DAY
*St. Luke, St. Gwen of Cornwall,
St. Justus of Beauvais*

1534 Alessandro Farnese was elected pope. He took the name of Paul III and soon took steps to try to put the affairs of the Roman Church in order. He appointed Reform-minded men to the College of Cardinals and set up a papal reform commission to recommend reforms to the church. In its report the commission emphasized that the papal office had become too worldly. He began a reform of the papal bureaucracy and ordered an end to the taking of money for spiritual favors. He also forbade the previous widespread practice of begging and selling church appointments. To deal with the split in the church caused by the Reformation, Pope Paul called a council to meet at Trent. The Council of Trent met in three sessions from 1545 to 1563. It was said by some to be perhaps the most important ecumenical council between Nicea in the fourth century and Vatican II in the twentieth. The council strongly supported many of the Roman Catholic doctrines the Reformers had opposed—transubstantiation, justification by faith and works, the Mass, the seven sacraments, celibacy of the priesthood, purgatory, indulgences, and papal authority. To further strengthen the church's authority, Pope Paul III revived the Inquisition in Italy in 1542, established censorship in 1543, and in 1540 approved the new monastic order of the Jesuits to combat heresy. Needless to say, though he accomplished much, his aim of healing the rift of the Reformation was not accomplished—indeed, the findings of Trent only exacerbated it.

1685 King Louis XIV of France revoked the Edict of Nantes, which had established legal toleration of France's Protestant population, the Huguenots.

1767 The eighty-six-year-old border dispute between Maryland and Pennsylvania was brought to an end with the drawing of the Mason-Dixon Line, later the recognized boundary between North and South.

1867 For a price of $7.2 million, the United States purchased Alaska from Russia.

1875 England's Cambridge University opened Newnham College for women.

1892 The first long-distance telephone line between Chicago and New York was formally opened.

1898 The American flag was raised in Puerto Rico shortly before Spain formally relinquished control of the island to the U.S.

1931 Inventor Thomas Alva Edison died in West Orange, New Jersey, at age eighty-four.

1946 The Boston Symphony under the direction of Koussevitzy premiered Aaron Copland's masterwork *Third Symphony*. Koussevitzy said that "this is the greatest American symphony—it goes from the heart to the heart."

1961 The film version of Leonard Bernstein's American classic *West Side Story* premiered at the Rivoli Theater in New York. The film went on to receive ten Academy Awards.

1967 A Soviet spacecraft made the first soft landing on the planet Venus.

1968 The U.S. Olympic Committee suspended Tommie Smith and John Carlos for giving a Black Power salute as a protest during a victory ceremony in Mexico City.

1982 Former first lady Bess Truman died at her home in Independence, Missouri, at age ninety-seven.

1989 After nearly two decades in power, Erich Honecker was ousted as leader of Communist East Germany in the face of growing pro-democracy protests.

OCTOBER

The idle man does not know what it is to enjoy rest.

[ALBERT EINSTEIN (1879–1955)]

1860

In response to Grace Beddell, an eleven-year-old girl, Abraham Lincoln wrote a letter saying, "My dear little Miss . . . as to whiskers, having never worn any, do you not think people would call it a piece of silly affectation if I were to begin it now?" The girl had written to the presidential candidate that she would try to persuade her four brothers to vote for him if he would grow whiskers. By November, he was sporting an early beard.

A wealthy Virginia planter and political leader, Benjamin Harrison (1726–1791) risked his vast holdings along the James River by embracing the cause of independence from the time of the Stamp Act through the Revolution—and suffered severe losses during the war when British troops plundered his property. He was the scion of one of America's greatest political families.

While serving in the Virginia legislature, Harrison helped draft an official protest against the Stamp Act, and his activities as a member of the committee of correspondence and of the First Provincial Congress led to his selection as a delegate to the Continental Congress. There he served on three important committees, dealing with foreign affairs, the army, and the navy—the working committees that formed the nucleus of what later became major departments of the federal government. Harrison also served in Congress as chairman of the Committee of the Whole, and, on July 2, 1776, he presided over the discussions that led to the vote in favor of Richard Lee's resolution for independence. Harrison's signature on the Declaration of Independence is next to that of his fellow Virginian, Thomas Jefferson. In the Congress Harrison also presided over the debates that led to the adoption of the Articles of Confederation.

During the war Harrison served as speaker of the Virginia legislature and as governor, the position he held when the British surrendered at Yorktown on this day in 1781. During his tenure in that latter office, Virginia ceded to the federal government its claim to the lands north and west of the Ohio River, an action in which Jefferson played a major role, and one that helped strengthen the new Union.

As a member of the Virginia convention that met to consider ratifying the Constitution, Harrison was chairman of the committee on elections, but he did not participate in many debates. He did, however, join Patrick Henry in refusing to support the Constitution without a Bill of Rights.

Of all the Founding Fathers, Harrison left perhaps the greatest personal legacy: He was the only one who had the distinction of having two direct descendants—a son and a great-grandson—serve as president of the United States. His son, William Henry Harrison, was the ninth president under the current constitution and his great-grandson, Benjamin Harrison, was the twenty-third.

OCTOBER

FEAST DAY
St. Paul of the Cross, St. Philip Howard, St. Ethbin, St. Aquilinus of Evreux, St. Cleopatra, St. Frideswide, St. Peter of Alcántara, St. John de Brébeuf, St. René Goupil, St. Varus, Saints Ptolemy and Lucius

1656 Massachusetts passed a law prohibiting the further immigration of Quakers into the Puritan colony—this ultimately led to the establishment of Pennsylvania.

1765 The Stamp Act Congress, meeting in New York, drew up a declaration of rights and liberties.

1779 William Cowper, the pastoral English poet, collaborated with the curate John Newton in publishing the *Olney Hymns*—a classic collection of Evangelical and Reformed hymns. Cowper, who generally wrote about simple pleasures of country life and expressed a deep concern with human cruelty and suffering, was born in Great Berkhampstead, Hertfordshire. Though he suffered periods of acute depression, he lived with the evangelical cleric Morley Unwin and his wife, Mary. In 1773 Cowper was seized by a severe despondency, rooted in religious doubts and fears that plagued him all his life. It was apparently the care of Mrs. Unwin, who encouraged him to compose poetry, that enabled him to recover. And thus, out of the depths of despair was the church given the great gift of his verse.

1781 General Charles Cornwallis surrendered his eight thousand British troops at Yorktown, effectively ending the Revolutionary War.

1812 French forces under Napoleon Bonaparte began their retreat from Moscow.

1864 A small band of Confederate soldiers slipped across the Canadian border into Vermont, robbed three banks in the town of St. Albans, and stole $250,000. Plans to burn the town were thwarted by locals, but eleven of the raiders were able to cross back into Canada. They were apprehended, but later released by Canadian officials because of lack of jurisdiction.

1864 Confederate General Jubal A. Early attacked Union forces at Cedar Creek, Virginia. The Union troops were able to rally and defeat the Confederates.

1872 One of the most hated, and at the same time most admired, men in nineteenth century America was Anthony Comstock. As a special prosecutor for the U.S. Post Office and director of the New York Society for the Suppression of Vice, he led a lifelong massive anti-obscenity campaign. He was responsible for innumerable legislative initiatives that banned pornography and other sexually explicit materials from the mails. In addition, between 1872 and 1880 he oversaw the arrest and conviction of fifty-five abortionists operating up and down the East Coast, including the notorious Anna Lohman. Even after he had relinquished his post, the legislation he had drafted was used to prosecute a number of the abortion industry's stellar personalities—from Margaret Sanger, the infamous founder of Planned Parenthood, to Julius Hammer, father of Armand and co-founder of the American Communist Party.

1879 Thomas A. Edison publicly exhibited his incandescent electric light bulb.

1960 The United States imposed an embargo on exports to Cuba covering all commodities except medical supplies and certain food products.

1977 The supersonic *Concorde* made its first landing in New York City.

OCTOBER

*K*nowledge is proud that he has learned so much; wisdom is humble that he knows no more.

[WILLIAM COWPER (1731–1800)]

The pioneering African-American scientist George Washington Carver developed a keen interest in plants at an early age. Growing up in post-emancipation Missouri under the care of his parents' former owners, Carver collected a variety of wild plants and flowers, which he planted in a garden. At the age of ten, he left home of his own volition to attend a school for freed slaves in the nearby community of Neosho, where he did chores for an African-American family in exchange for food and a place to sleep. He maintained his interest in plants while putting himself through high school in Minneapolis, Kansas, and during his first and only year at Simpson College in Iowa. During this period, he made many sketches of plants and flowers. He made the study of plants his focus in 1891, the year he enrolled at Iowa State College. After graduating in 1894 with degrees in botany and agriculture, he spent two additional years at Iowa State to complete a master's degree in the same fields. During this time, he taught botany to undergraduate students and conducted extensive experiments on plants while managing the university's greenhouse. These experiences served him well during the first few years after he joined the faculty of Booker T. Washington's Tuskegee Institute.

Carver used scientific means to tackle the widespread poverty and malnutrition among the local African-American farmers in south Alabama. Year after year, farmers had planted cotton on the same plots of land and thereby exhausted the topsoil's nutrients. By testing the soil, he discovered that a lack of nitrogen in particular accounted for consistently low harvests. While at Iowa State, Carver had learned that certain plants in the pea family extracted nitrogen from the air and deposited it in the soil. To maintain the topsoil's balance of nutrients, Carver advised farmers to alternate planting cotton and peanuts. This farming method proved effective, and within a few years, farmers saw a dramatic increase in their crop production. Carver then created an outreach program in which he would travel once a month to rural parts of Alabama to give hands-on instruction to farmers in this and other innovative farming techniques.

Because of Carver's emphasis on the cultivation of the peanut, peanuts flooded the market and their prices dropped. This predicament presented Carver with yet another challenge—how to prevent farmers from resorting to the exclusive cultivation of cotton, which had a higher market value. Carver began to explore alternative uses for the peanut that would increase its market value. He developed more than three hundred peanut products that included peanut butter, cheeses, flours, ice creams, and stains. Then, on this day in 1921, he helped the United Peanut Growers Association persuade Congress to pass a bill calling for a protective tariff on imported peanuts.

The development of the peanut also helped Carver resolve the problem of malnutrition in the rural South. He stressed that the peanut was a valuable source of protein that could enrich farmers' diets and improve their health. As part of his extension program, Carver taught farmers' wives how to preserve food and prepare tasty, well-balanced meals. For many African-American Southerners who had never given thought to eating a tomato, which was once widely believed to be poisonous, Carver explained its nutritional value and demonstrated several recipes in which it could be used. Carver was also innovative with the sweet potato and the pecan, introducing approximately one hundred uses for each of those two foods.

OCTOBER

FEAST DAY
St. Artemius, St. Andrew the Calybite of Crete, St. Caprasius of Agen, St. Bertilla Boscardin, St. Acca

751 Pepin the Short (714–768) deposed the last of the Merovingian kings, Childeric III, to become the first king of the Carolingian dynasty. He was the son of the Frankish hero Charles Martel and had served the Merovingians as mayor of the palace of Austrasia. Following his violent coup, he was crowned by Pope Stephen II in 754. In turn, when the pope was threatened by the Lombards of northern Italy, Pepin led an army that defeated them (754–755). He then ceded to the pope all the territory he captured—which included Ravenna and several other major cities. This grant, called the Donation of Pepin, laid the foundation for the Papal States. Afterward Pepin enlarged his own kingdom by capturing Aquitaine in southwestern France. He was succeeded by his sons Carloman and Charlemagne as joint kings.

1803 The United States Senate ratified the Louisiana Purchase Treaty by a vote of 24-7. The vast region encompassed more than 800,000 square miles of territory and comprised present-day Arkansas, Missouri, Iowa, Minnesota west of the Mississippi River, North Dakota, South Dakota, Nebraska, Oklahoma, nearly all of Kansas, the portions of Montana, Wyoming, and Colorado east of the Rocky Mountains, and Louisiana west of the Mississippi River as well as the city of New Orleans. At the time of purchase, Thomas Jefferson was concerned about the constitutionality of making a land acquisition without adding a covering amendment to the U.S. Constitution. The law of the land, however, did give the president treaty-making power, and the Louisiana Purchase was ratified into law as a treaty by the U.S. Senate. The Louisiana Purchase stands as the largest area of territory ever added to the U.S. at one time.

1820 For a price tag of $5 million, the United States purchased the eastern part of Florida from Spain.

1822 The British weekly newspaper the *Sunday Times* made its debut.

1879 The Reading Room of the British Museum in London was illuminated by electric lights for the first time.

1903 A joint commission ruled in favor of the United States in a boundary dispute between the Alaskan Territory and Canada.

1944 During the Second World War, General Douglas MacArthur stepped ashore at Leyte in the Philippines, two and a half years after he had said, "I shall return."

1947 The House Un-American Activities Committee opened hearings into alleged Communist influence and infiltration within the American motion picture industry.

1964 The thirty-first president of the United States, Herbert Hoover, died in New York at age ninety.

1967 Seven men were convicted in Meridian, Mississippi, of violating the civil rights of three murdered civil rights workers.

1973 In the so-called "Saturday Night Massacre," special Watergate prosecutor Archibald Cox was dismissed and Attorney General Elliot L. Richardson and Deputy Attorney General William B. Ruckelshaus resigned.

OCTOBER

Every honest man will suppose honest acts to flow from honest principles.

[THOMAS JEFFERSON (1743–1826)]

Dante Alighieri (1265–1321), one of the supreme figures of world literature, was admired for the depth of his spiritual vision and for the range of his intellectual accomplishment. Indeed, the brilliance of his vision was almost immediately recognized throughout the Western world. Samuel Johnson claimed that Dante's poetic vision "was the seminal creative impulse which spawned the great literary flowering of High Medievalism and was the enlightening portent of all which would follow in the Renaissance." Geoffrey Chaucer, Thomas Malory, Giovanni Boccaccio, and Francesco Petrarch all counted him as a vital primary influence and stirring inspiration for their own pioneering work. He was among the first thinkers and poets to attempt a thoroughgoing integration of Christian ideals with the culture of pagan antiquity—a conception that would ultimately become a cornerstone of Renaissance thought, life, and culture.

Though brimming over with historical and political ideas, issues, and personalities, his greatest work, *The Divine Comedy*, was not essentially a covert work of social commentary—an attempt to lampoon political enemies or spiritualize ideological agendas. Neither was it an attempt to paint an accurate portrait of an actual hell or heaven—though it certainly drew upon traditional Catholic teachings for its prevailing images. It was instead an allegory aimed at an exploration of the human psyche. It was an expansive humanistic discourse on the nature of virtue and vice, achievement and despair, redemption and damnation, glorification and vilification. Mingling the Christian wisdom of Augustine, Aquinas, Boethius, and Cassiodorus with the Heathen aesthetic of Virgil, Ovid, Thucidides, and Plutarch, it was a symbolic investigation into the essence of grace and disgrace, orthodoxy and heresy, eternal and temporal, spiritual and carnal.

Dante presaged the radical shift in Christendom from the prevailing orthodoxy of High Medievalism to the corrosive humanism of the Renaissance. Indeed, it was pioneered by him. Thus, it might be stated with fairness that he was the first prophet of modernity. Though neither primarily political nor theological, his work essentially marked the beginning of the end of the Old World Order—thus, its impact may well have been far more profound than any of the political tracts or theological tomes of his day.

Dante, believing that he had somehow strayed from the "true way" into worldly woe, told of a terrifyingly detailed vision he had—a vision in which he traveled through all the levels of Hell, up the mount of Purgatory, and finally through the realms of Paradise, where he was at last allowed a brief glimpse of God.

Dante entitled his three-volume work *The Comedy*. The term "comedy" was used in its classical sense to denote a story that begins in great suspense but ends well. By combining innumerable devices, symbols, historical references, and contemporary themes—all utilizing his native Tuscan dialect—Dante created a revolutionary work. It presciently laid the foundations of Renaissance literature and philosophy—and was quickly recognized as a masterpiece. Indeed, it was so highly regarded that shortly after his death, the title was changed from *The Comedy* to *The Divine Comedy*.

OCTOBER

FEAST DAY
St. Hilarion, St. Fintan or Munnu of Taghmon, St. Condedus, St. Tuda, St. John of Bridlington, St. Malchus

1555 Five days after Nicholas Ridley and Hugh Latimer were burned at the stake, Bloody Mary, the daughter of King Henry VIII, launched a series of fierce persecutions against Protestants in which more than two hundred men, women, and children were put to death for their faith. Ridley had been a chaplain to King Henry VIII and was the Bishop of London under his son Edward. Latimer was the Bishop of Worcester. Both men were renowned for their piety and compassion. When Mary became Queen of England, one of her first acts was to arrest Bishop Ridley, Bishop Latimer, and Archbishop Thomas Cranmer. After serving time in the Tower of London, the three were taken to Oxford in September 1555 to be examined by the Lord's Commissioner in Oxford's Divinity School. Sensing the groundswell of support the men had throughout England, it was determined to make a public spectacle of their executions. Mary and her minions were startled to discover that the martyrdoms only intensified Protestant zeal. Thus, the horrors of the bloody persecution were unleashed to quash the confessing church—in the end though, it had quite the opposite effect.

1797 The U.S. Navy frigate *Constitution*, also known as *Old Ironsides*, was launched in Boston's harbor.

1805 A painting placed in the Royal Post Office near Charring Cross in London commemorated the Battle of Trafalgar: "This famous naval action on October 21, 1805, between the British Royal Navy and the combined French and Spanish fleets, removed forever the threat of Napoleon's invasion of England. The British victory, off Trafalgar, set the seal of eternal fame on Viscount Horatio Nelson, who died in the moment of victory."

1879 Thomas A. Edison invented a practical incandescent lamp in his laboratory at Menlo Park, New Jersey. "The longer it burned," he said, "the more fascinated we were . . . there was no sleep for any of us for forty hours."

1959 The striking Solomon R. Guggenheim Museum of Contemporary Art, designed by Frank Lloyd Wright, opened in New York City.

1960 Democrat John F. Kennedy and Republican Richard M. Nixon clashed in their fourth and final presidential debate.

1967 Tens of thousands of Vietnam War protesters marched in Washington D.C.

1987 The United States Senate failed to ratify the appointment of Judge Robert Bork to the Supreme Court by a margin of 58-42.

1998 The Earth Liberation Front—a radical environmentalist group—claimed responsibility for fires that caused $12 million in damage at the nation's busiest ski resort in Vail, Colorado.

The enemies of the truth are always awfully nice.

OCTOBER

[CHRISTOPHER MORLEY (1890–1957)]

| 1836 | Former Tennessee congressman, senator, and governor Sam Houston was inaugurated as the first constitutionally elected president of the Republic of Texas. |

America's second elected president—fourteen administrations prior to that of George Washington—was one of the wealthiest planters in the South, the patriarch of the most powerful families anywhere in the nation. Henry Middleton (1717–1784) evidenced a strong public spirit from an early age.

He was a member of South Carolina's Common House from 1744 to 1747. During the last two years he served as the speaker. During 1755 he was the King's Commissioner of Indian Affairs. He was a member of the South Carolina Council from 1755 to 1770. His valor in the War with the Cherokees during 1760–1761 earned him wide recognition throughout the colonies—and demonstrated his cool leadership abilities while under pressure.

His wealth and prestige were never an obstacle to Middleton, who apparently had never met a stranger, was practical and down to earth, and never bore ostentatious airs about himself or his family. He was an amiable man who demonstrated great ability in everything to which he set his mind.

Enjoying wide local popularity, he was elected as a delegate to the first session of the Continental Congress, and when Peyton Randolph was forced to resign the presidency, his peers immediately turned to Middleton to complete the term on this day in 1774. He served as the fledgling coalition's president until Randolph was able to resume his duties briefly beginning on May 10, 1775.

After his term as chief executive officer, he continued to serve in Congress—first as a member of the Congressional Council of Safety and later as a special commissioner charged with the task of establishing the young nation's policy toward the encouragement and support of education.

In February 1776 he was forced to resign from all his political involvements to prepare his family and lands for what he believed was inevitable war with Crown and Parliament—but he was replaced by his son Arthur. Thus, he ensured that a Middleton would eventually have the opportunity to sign both the Declaration of Independence and the Articles of Confederation. In addition to filling his father's seat admirably, the younger Middleton served time as an English prisoner of war, and was twice elected governor of his state. Thus, the family constituted the first political dynasty of the South—and one of the first in the entire nation.

OCTOBER

FEAST DAY
St. Philip of Heraclea and his Companions, St. Mellon or Mallonus, St. Abercius, Saints Nulino and Alodia, St. Donatus of Fiesole

1797   French balloonist Andre-Jacques Garnerin made the first parachute descent, landing safely from a height of about three thousand feet.

1856   Just three days after the great disaster at Surrey Gardens, Charles Haddon Spurgeon met with members of the press to announce he was taking a sabbatical from the pulpit for an indeterminate amount of time. The elders had leased the Surrey Music Hall in the Royal Surrey Gardens for services because all the available spaces had proven too small to house the large numbers of worshippers who wanted to see Spurgeon. This was London's largest and most beautiful building and held ten to twelve thousand people. It was packed to overflowing on October 19 with nearly as many outside the building as were able to get in. Sadly, the service had only just begun when hooligans began shouting, "Fire! The galleries are giving way, the place is falling!" In the ensuing panic, a number of people were trampled. Seven died and many others were seriously injured. Spurgeon was tremendously depressed over the event, and his grief was so deep some feared his reason had left him. He spent hours "in tears by day, and dreams of terror by night." Within two weeks, however, Spurgeon had recovered sufficiently to preach again. The crowds were even bigger than before. Then, in the spring of 1861, the congregation's new home, the Metropolitan Tabernacle, was completed. This was to be Spurgeon's pulpit for the next thirty-one years. Throughout those years an average of five thousand people attended each morning and evening Sunday service. Though he constantly preached to a sea of faces, Spurgeon trembled at the multitudes who came to hear him—always mindful of the horror of the Surrey Garden disaster.

1928   Republican presidential nominee Herbert Hoover spoke of the "American system of rugged individualism" in a speech at New York's Madison Square Garden.

1938   Chester F. Carlson demonstrated his machine for "xerography", meaning dry writing, or copying.

1944   David Diamond's Symphony no. 2 was premiered by the Boston Symphony Orchestra, under the direction of Natalie Koussevitzky.

1962   President John Kennedy announced an air and naval blockade of Cuba, following the discovery of Soviet missile bases on the island.

1978   Negotiators for Egypt and Israel announced in Washington that they had reached tentative agreement on the main points of a peace treaty.

1979   The U.S. government allowed the deposed Shah of Iran to travel to New York for medical treatment—a decision that precipitated the Iran hostage crisis.

My books are my tools. They also serve as my counsel, my consolation, and my comfort. They are my source of wisdom and the font of my education. They are my friends and my delights. They are my surety, when all else is awry, that I have set my confidence in the substantial things of truth and right.

[CHARLES SPURGEON (1834–1892)]

OCTOBER

Considered one of the finest authors of short stories and fiction, Rudyard Kipling in 1907 became the first English author to win the Nobel Prize in literature. Kipling lived briefly in the United States after marrying an American woman in 1892. When a reporter from the *Boston Sunday Herald* approached Kipling on a Vermont roadway for an interview, the author refused and fled. But the persistent reporter pursued the unwilling Kipling to his house and on this day in 1892, the newspaper published an antagonistic interview.

Kipling opened with a grand caveat, "Yes, I am a boor. I am glad of it. I don't care. I want people to know it." The reporter agreed, "That's what Mr Rudyard Kipling is. It's so, for 'he himself hath said it', and those were his last words to the writer as he left him the other day, after having had an interview with a man who is probably one of the most peculiar persons in the world."

The persistent scribe went on to describe his subject, "A little, short, stocky body stopped at a barbed wire fence. The legs that supported the body were not very stout. They were covered with a pair of old, skin-tight, brownish, trousers. He wore a very faded greenish Norfolk jacket. An informal neglige shirt collar and black silk four-in-hand necktie, showed at the neck. His face is dark, he has a crisp, dark brown mustache, determined mouth, sharp, rather retreating eyes, covered by double lens gold bowed spectacles, topped by heavy eyebrows, and his full, broad forehead is covered by not very thick brown hair. He wore a huge, light gray slouch hat, which is his invariable headgear, and by which he is known for miles as a landmark, as it were. This hat makes him look too heavy. In his right hand was a tall staff, that he always carries. His strange looks would betoken a strange man. His appearance was consistent with what was expected. He halted at the fence at my inquiry."

But the moment the reporter identified himself as a reporter, Kipling retorted with a muttered exclamation in violation of the third commandment, and he pushed between the barbed-wire strands regardless of clothes or limb. Not to be outdone, the reporter got out of his buggy and followed after the doughty Kipling. But the great man was resolute: "I refuse to be interviewed. It is a crime. You have no more right to stop me for this than to hold me up like a highwayman. It is an outrage to assault a man on the public way. If you have anything to ask, submit it in writing to me at my house." With this he darted away.

The ambitious journalist refused to take a hint. It was then that Kipling let him know in no uncertain terms why it was that he abhorred the notion of interviews: "Why do I refuse to be interviewed? Because it is immoral! It is cowardly and vile. No respectable man would ask it, much less give it. What good are reporters, anyway? What do you expect to become or get out of it? The American press is dirty and rotten. The American reporter is a blot on the journalistic escutcheon, and when one perpetrates a crime, as you have done, he ought to be locked up where he couldn't do any harm. There is nothing in American journalism to admire and less to respect. All I have to say, I put in my books."

With that the interview was ended—and a far more enlightening exchange had taken place than perhaps either of the participants might have ever known.

OCTOBER

Feast Day
  St. Severino Boethius, St. Severinus or Seurin of Bordeaux, St. Elfleda or Ethelfled, St. Allucio, St. Ignatius of Constantinople, St. Theodoret, St. Romanus of Rouen, St. John of Capistrano

525 Philosopher Anincius Manlius Severinus Boethius lost his head per the command of Theodoric, king of the Ostrogoths, for false accusations of treason. It was during his imprisonment before his execution that he wrote *De Consolatione Philosophiae* or *The Consolation of Philosophy*. This work was later translated by King Alfred the Great and Geoffrey Chaucer, among others, and was influential in the Medieval Period. His other treatises included works on logic, which shaped the terminology of medieval studies, and translations of Aristotle, and other works on music, arithmetic, and theology.

1366 Much of Europe experienced a great meteor shower, which actually left parts of meteors on the ground.

1781 Three days after French troops under the command of Jean Baptiste de Vimeur, comte de Rochambeau, and the Marquis de Lafayette helped George Washington's ragged forces defeat the British army, the men celebrated the formal surrender of Lord Cornwallis. The British band played the popular song "The World Turned Upside Down" as they stacked up their arms. The last major fighting of the American War for Independence had somehow ended in a resounding American victory. Washington and the others could not help but recognize God's hand in the victory. Indeed, it was when the American forces were at their weakest that victory had finally

come. Accordingly, Washington issued orders to the army that "Divine service is to be performed in the several brigades and divisions. The commander-in-chief recommends that the troops not on duty should universally attend with that seriousness of deportment and gratitude of heart which the recognition of such reiterated and astonishing interpositions of Providence demand of us."

1915 Twenty-five thousand women, popularly known as suffragettes, marched in New York City, demanding the right to vote.

1946 The United Nations General Assembly convened in New York for the first time, at an auditorium in Flushing Meadow.

1956 An anti-Stalinist revolt that was subsequently crushed by Soviet troops began in Hungary.

1958 Boris Pasternak was named winner of the Nobel Prize in literature—however, Soviet authorities pressured Pasternak into relinquishing the award.

1973 President Nixon agreed to turn White House tape recordings requested by the Watergate special prosecutor over to Judge John J. Sirica.

1983 In Beirut, Lebanon, a suicide truck-bomber crashed his vehicle into the U.S. compound at the Beirut International Airport, killing 241 marines and sailors. A near-simultaneous attack on French forces killed 58 paratroopers.

To live for a time close to great minds is the best kind of education.

[JOHN BUCHAN (1875–1940)]

OCTOBER

Henryk Sienkiewicz was an international phenomenon a century ago—at the end of the nineteenth and the beginning of the twentieth centuries. He was trained in both law and medicine. He was a respected historian. He was a successful journalist. He was a widely sought-after critic and editor. He was an erudite lecturer. And in addition to all that, he was an amazingly prolific and wildly popular novelist—selling millions of copies of his almost fifty books in nearly three hundred editions in the United States alone.

Quo Vadis?, published in 1898, was his most successful book and became a publishing phenomenon—it was the standard against which all future mega-bestsellers were judged. The book was intended to be an epic retelling of the Great Fire of Rome in A.D. 64. Its broad, biblical sweep of events includes the machinations of Nero's court, the rising tide of persecutions against the fledgling Christian community, the movements of the Germanic tribes along the Roman frontier—not surprisingly featuring the Polish Ligians—and the ministries of the apostles Paul and Peter. According to an old Christian legend, Peter was fleeing the emperor's persecutions when he had a vision of Christ along the Appian Way. Awestruck, the apostle addressed the Lord, asking, *"Quo vadis?"* or "Whither do You go?" Jesus answered him, "To Rome, to be crucified anew, inasmuch as you have abandoned My sheep." Fully comprehending the rebuke, Peter returned to the city to face his inevitable martyrdom.

In the hands of Sienkiewicz, the legend comes alive with bristling dialogue, fully dimensional characters, abiding faith, and informed political rage. His ability to relate the struggle of the first generation of believers against the juggernaut of messianic Caesarism to the struggle of modern believers against the juggernaut of messianic Statism is nothing less than brilliant. The story is never compromised by a propagandistic message; nevertheless, Sienkiewicz's message of anti-revolutionary, anti-ideological, and anti-modernist traditionalism sounds out, loud and clear. Indeed, the way Sienkiewicz weaves the historical narrative, the plot line, the character development, and the message of the gospel, it is evident that he was working out of the same worldview context as his Dutch contemporaries, Groen van Prinsterer and Abraham Kuyper, as well as the later English Distributists and Southern Agrarians. For many readers, the transformation of that kind of confessional faith into vibrant art is a kind of revelation in itself—akin to discovering G. K. Chesterton, Hilaire Belloc, Thomas Chalmers, Caroline Gordon, or Walter Scott for the first time.

OCTOBER

NATIONAL DAY
Zambia
UNITED NATIONS DAY
FEAST DAY
St. Martin or Mark, St. Martin of Vertou, St. Elesbaan, St. Felix of Thibiuca, St. Antony Claret, St. Evergislus, St. Aretas, St. Senoch, St. Maglorius or Maelor, St. Proclus of Constantinople, The Martyrs of Najran

1537 Jane Seymour, the third wife of England's King Henry VIII, died twelve days after giving birth to Prince Edward, later King Edward VI.

1648 The Peace of Westphalia ended the Thirty Years' War and effectively stripped the Holy Roman Empire of any real power.

1725 Composer Alessandro Scarlatti, the first great master of the Neapolitan opera, died in Naples, Italy.

1861 Marked by a message sent from San Francisco to Washington, D.C., the first transcontinental telegraph system was completed, making the Pony Express obsolete. The telegram was sent by Justice Stephen J. Field of California to President Abraham Lincoln.

1901 Anna Edson Taylor became the first person to go over Niagara Falls in a barrel for the purpose of raising money due on a loan on her Texas ranch. The barrel was 4½ feet tall and 3 feet in diameter. A leather harness and cushions inside the barrel protected the 43-year-old widow.

1931 New York and New Jersey were linked by the opening of the George Washington Bridge.

1939 Nylon stockings were sold publicly for the first time, in Wilmington, Delaware.

1939 Benny Goodman and his orchestra recorded their signature theme, "Let's Dance," for Columbia Records in New York.

1940 The forty-hour work week went into effect under the Fair Labor Standards Act of 1938.

1945 The United Nations officially came into existence as its charter took effect.

1952 Republican presidential candidate Dwight D. Eisenhower declared, "I shall go to Korea," as he promised to end the conflict.

1962 The U.S. blockade of Cuba during the missile crisis officially began under a proclamation signed by President John Kennedy.

1989 Former television evangelist Jim Bakker was sentenced by a judge in Charlotte, North Carolina, to forty-five years in prison for fraud and conspiracy. The sentence was later reduced to eight years and then further reduced to four for good behavior.

When you sell a man a book you don't sell him just twelve ounces of paper and ink and glue—you sell him a whole new life. Love and friendship and humor and ships at sea by night—there's all heaven and earth in a book, a real book I mean.

[CHRISTOPHER MORLEY (1890–1957)]

OCTOBER

SAINT CRISPIN'S DAY

Saint Crispin and his brother Crispinian were Christians who were martyred during the persecution by the emperor Maximian in Rome. They preached to people during the day and made shoes at night to earn their living.

OCTOBER

The number of truly masterful American writers can probably be numbered on two hands—Cotton Mather, James Fenimore Cooper, Nathaniel Hawthorne, Washington Irving, Mark Twain, Edgar Allan Poe, Henry Wadsworth Longfellow, Henry Adams, William Faulkner, and of course Herman Melville. Each of these authors achieved great success during their lifetimes and were mourned at their deaths—all except Melville. In fact, he died in his New York City home in 1891 at the age of seventy-two in utter obscurity—his brilliant career and voluminous writings by then long-forgotten.

A short obituary appearing the day afterward in the *New York Press* recalled, "Melville had once been one of the most popular writers in the United States," but added, "The later years of his life had been so quiet that probably even his own generation has long thought him dead." Another paper in the city, the *Daily Tribune*, noted, "The deceased had won considerable fame as an author by the publication of a book entitled *Typee*, which was the account of his experience while a captive in the hands of the savages of the Marquesas Islands. This was his first and best work although he later wrote a number of other stories, which were published more for private than public circulation."

The obituaries demonstrate one of the most remarkable ironies in the history of American letters—aside from some early renown as an adventure writer, Melville was a publishing failure. During the eleven short years of his literary activity, he was either misunderstood and miscast or castigated and ignored. Even so, some of the best fiction ever produced in the English language flowed from his pen—*Moby Dick, Billy Budd, Redburn, The Piazza Tales, The Confidence Man, White-Jacket,* and *Omoo.* By the time he had reached forty though, he had abandoned his writing to provide for his family.

It was not until some thirty years after his demise that academics rediscovered his genius. They marveled at the richness of his prose, the depth of his characterizations, the complexity of his symbiology, and the passion of his theology. *Moby Dick*, in particular, was widely heralded as a genuine masterpiece, while several of his other works were made the subjects of serious critical acclaim. Soon Melville was deservedly enshrined in the pantheon of literary greatness.

FEAST DAY
Saints Crispin and Crispinian, Saints Fronto and George, The Forty Martyrs of England and Wales, Saints Crysanthus and Daria, St. Richard Gwyn, St. Gaudentius of Brescia

1400 Middle English poet Geoffrey Chaucer died in London, and was buried in Westminster Abby. His *The Canterbury Tales* was written in more than seventeen thousand lines of poetry.

1415 England's King Henry V defeated the overwhelming force of the French army in the fields of Agincourt inspiring Shakespeare's famous monologue: "If we are marked to die, we are enough to do our country loss; and if to live, the fewer the men, the greater share of honor. God's will, I pray thee, wish not one man more. This story shall the good man teach his son, and Crispin Crispian shall ne'er go by from this day to the ending of the world but we in it shall be remembered. We few, we happy few, we band of brothers. For he today that sheds his blood with me shall be my brother; be he ne'er so vile, this day shall gentle his condition. And gentlemen in England now abed shall think themselves accursed they were not here, and hold their manhoods cheap whiles any speaks that fought with us on St. Crispin's Day."

1760 Britain's ill-fated Hanoverian king, George III, succeeded his late grandfather, George II.

1854 The Charge of the Light Brigade took place during the Crimean War. It was the climax of the Battle of Balaklava during the Crimean War. The battle, which has been long regarded as one of the most famous military blunders in history, took place in the Crimea, Ukraine, between an allied Anglo-French army and a Russian force commanded by General Liprandi. The Light Brigade consisted of five regiments totaling 661 men. The men were ordered to attack a well-entrenched Russian force—it was a certain slaughter but due to confused communications and conflict within the officer corps, the men advanced into a withering line of fire. Amazingly, despite heavy casualties, the men achieved their objective. The charge lasted no more than twenty minutes. When the brigade was mustered afterward, there were only 195 mounted men left. Though the maneuver was a complete disaster, General Liprandi was deeply impressed by the stature and composure of the prisoners. The moral effect on the Russians of the discipline, courage, and resolve of the Light Brigade was immense. For the rest of the war, the Russian cavalry refused combat with the British, even when vastly superior in numbers. Long afterward, the fact that a single, understrength brigade of light cavalry had captured a battery of guns and driven off a far larger body of Russian horses was the admiration of Europe.

1881 Spanish artist Pablo Picasso was born in Malaga. Considered as possibly the greatest artist of the twentieth century, Picasso excelled as a painter, sculptor and engraver. He once said, "I am only a public entertainer who has understood his time."

1885 The last symphony by Johannes Brahms, the Symphony no. 4 in E Minor, was first performed in Meiningen.

1939 The drama *The Time of Your Life*, by William Saroyan, opened in New York.

1962 U.S. Ambassador Adlai E. Stevenson presented photographic evidence of Soviet missile bases in Cuba to the United Nations Security Council.

1971 The United Nations General Assembly voted to admit mainland China and expel Taiwan.

1983 An American-led force invaded Grenada at the order of President Ronald Reagan, who said the action was needed to protect U.S. citizens there.

OCTOBER

I love the smell of book ink in the morning.

[UMBERTO ECO (1929–)]

On this day in 1633, the little Puritan and Pilgrim congregation at Newton, in the fledgling Massachusetts Bay Colony—since renamed Cambridge—held a day of fasting and prayer at the end of which they chose Thomas Hooker as their pastor. Hooker had arrived in the colony only the previous month, but his zeal for the doctrines of grace and his pastoral qualifications had been amply demonstrated in years of difficult service in England.

Born in 1586 in Leicestershire, Hooker studied theology at Cambridge University and became a popular lecturer and an able assistant to the rector of the parish church in Chalmsford. Though Hooker accepted most of the doctrines of the Church of England, he did not believe its liturgy or ecclesiology was biblical—in other words, he was a dissenter when it came to worship and church government. Accordingly, in 1630 he came under the discipline of Archbishop Laud—a fierce persecutor of nonconformity. When he was summoned to appear before the dreaded High Commission, Hooker fled to Holland where he preached to exiled Puritans in both Delft and Rotterdam. He became an assistant to the renowned theologian William Ames and wrote a pamphlet entitled *A Fresh Suit Against Human Ceremonies in God's Worship.*

In 1633, Hooker, along with the Puritan preachers John Cotton and Samuel Stone, fled to America aboard the *Griffen.* When the three prominent men arrived in Boston in September, several Puritans quipped that they now had "Cotton for their clothing, Hooker for their fishing, and Stone for their building." It was not surprising that the Newton congregation so quickly chose Hooker as their pastor.

In Massachusetts, however, Hooker began to question the form of government established by the Massachusetts Bay Colony. He questioned the validity of a church covenant forming the basis for a civil government. Hooker did not believe that participation in the government should be limited to church members. Rather, he asserted that all civil government should be based on voluntary submission to some kind of civil covenant, just as the churches were established on a covenant of spiritual things. The foundation of government, he thought, lay in the free choice of the people, who were to choose public officials according to God's will and law. Hooker's views on government were much more democratic than those espoused by the leaders of the Massachusetts Colony.

Because of these differences, Hooker peacefully left Massachusetts with a number of members from his Newton congregation and established the town of Hartford in Connecticut. In 1638, three of the Connecticut towns met to form a government. In a sermon preached to the General Court at that time, Hooker maintained that the foundation of government authority is "laid in the free consent of the people, that the choice of public magistrates belongs unto the people by God's own allowance." The text from which Mr. Hooker derived his sermon was Deuteronomy 1:13, "Take you wise men, and understanding, and known among your tribes, and I will make them rulers over you."

The resulting government, The Fundamental Orders of Connecticut, was the first written Constitution in America.

OCTOBER

NATIONAL DAY
Iran, Austria
FEAST DAY
Saints Lucian and Marcian, St. Bean, St. Rusticus of Narbonne, St. Eata, St. Cedd

1277 Merton College of Oxford was founded by Walter de Merton.

1685 Composer and renown harpsichordist Domenico Scarlatti was born in Naples, Italy.

1774 The First Continental Congress adjourned in Philadelphia.

1825 The Erie Canal opened, providing a water route between Lake Erie and the Hudson River. Construction of the waterway took eight years and cost $7.6 million. It had been the super-highway of antebellum America. When it opened it was a marvel of engineering and human labor. From Albany to Buffalo, it opened up the American frontier and made westward expansion inevitable. It turned New York Harbor into the nation's number one port. It shaped social and economic development. With branches crisscrossing the entire state, cities and industries developed along the canal and flourished—chief among them were Rochester, Syracuse, and Binghamton. Until the American colonies declared independence in 1776, European settlement of the New World was largely confined to the eastern seaboard. The Appalachian Mountains were a formidable obstacle to westward movement. Only the Mohawk River Valley in New York offered both a land and a water passage through the mountains. By 1817, plans for a man-made waterway fed by the Mohawk River and bypassing its waterfalls and rapids had been made. The plan was to traverse the entire state of New York, connecting the Hudson River in the east with the Great Lakes in the west. When it was opened, vast parcels of land became accessible for the first time. Shipping costs dropped dramatically. Immigrants to America, in search of new lands and new opportunities in the West, crowded canal boats. The westward movement of the nation was begun.

1854 In South Africa, nine hundred tribesmen were killed by the Boers.

1870 Anthony Claret, a famed Spanish Claretian friar, died. He was the founder of an evangelistic religious order, the Missionary Sons of the Immaculate Heart of Mary. In 1850 he was appointed an archbishop to Cuba. He served the poor there—and most notably, he smashed racial barriers by uniting thousands of interracial couples in marriage who would otherwise have lived only in concubinage. In his later years he became confessor to Isabelle II and bishop of Santiago.

1967 The Shah of Iran crowned himself and his queen after having already reigned twenty-six years on the great Peacock Throne of Persia.

1972 National security adviser Henry Kissinger declared, "Peace is at hand" in Vietnam following negotiations in Paris with the Communist government of the north.

1977 The experimental space shuttle *Enterprise* glided to a bumpy but successful landing following its maiden flight at Edwards Air Force Base in California.

1979 President Park Chung-hee of Korea was assassinated by his own national security chief—the head of the Korean Central Intelligence Agency, Kim Jae-kyu.

1984 Baby Fae, a newborn with a severe heart defect, was given the heart of a baboon in an experimental transplant in Loma Linda, California. The child lived twenty-one days following the transplant.

26

OCTOBER

A lie stands on one leg, truth on two.

[BENJAMIN FRANKLIN (1706–1790)]

Before his fiftieth birthday he had served as a New York State legislator, the Undersecretary of the U.S. Navy, Police Commissioner for the city of New York, U.S. Civil Service Commissioner, the governor of the state of New York, the vice president under William McKinley, a colonel in the U.S. Army, and two terms as the president of the United States. In addition, he had run a cattle ranch in the Dakota Territories, served as a reporter and editor for several journals, newspapers, and magazines, and conducted scientific expeditions on four continents. He read at least five books every week of his life and wrote nearly fifty on an astonishing array of subjects—from history and biography to natural science and social criticism. He enjoyed hunting, boxing, and wrestling. He was an amateur taxidermist, botanist, ornithologist, and astronomer. He was a devoted family man who lovingly raised six children. And he enjoyed a lifelong romance with his wife.

During his long and varied career Theodore Roosevelt (1858–1919) was hailed by supporters and rivals alike as the greatest man of the age—perhaps one of the greatest of all ages. A Reformer and fighter, he was the most colorful and the most controversial president since Lincoln, the most versatile since Jefferson.

Born to wealth on this day in 1858, Roosevelt was imbued with a strong sense of public service; in every position he held, he fought for improvement and reform. His was largely a moral crusade: He saw his chief enemy as non-Christian corruption and weakness, and he vigorously fought it wherever he found it—in business or in government.

In the White House the many-sided personality of Roosevelt captured the American imagination. The youngest man to become president, this dynamic reformer who combined a Harvard accent with the toughness of a Dakota cowboy was a totally new kind of president. Fighting the "malefactors of great wealth," Roosevelt struck out against the mammoth trusts that appeared to be outside of government regulation. The railroads, the food and drug industries, and enterprises using the natural wealth of the public lands all were subjected to some form of regulation, for the protection of the public interest. Many conservation practices began with Roosevelt. In the seven and a half years he led the nation, he was the first president to ride in a car, to submerge in a submarine, or to fly in an airplane.

A reformer at home, he was an avowed expansionist abroad. He supported the Spanish War and led his "Rough Riders" to fame; when president, he acquired the Canal Zone from Panama and sent U.S. battleships on a world cruise—to show off America's growing strength. Perhaps most notable were Roosevelt's efforts to end the Russo-Japanese War, an achievement that won him the Nobel Peace Prize. But this peacemaker, soldier, explorer, hunter, scientist, writer and progressive statesman left many a mark upon history: To government he brought the fresh winds of reform, and the courage, vigor, and tenacity to make his reforms an enduring part of the American scene.

OCTOBER

FEAST DAY
St. Otteran or Odhran of Iona, St. Frumentius of Ethiopia

1746 The Scottish Presbyterian pastor and theologian William Tennent obtained a charter for the College of New Jersey—later to be called Princeton University. He founded the school in 1726 as a seminary at Neshaminy to train his sons and others for the gospel ministry. Critics derisively called the school the Log College because of its frontierlike facilities, but the young men trained under Tennent became pastors who clearly taught the gospel and spread revival throughout the middle section of America's thirteen colonies. The first president of the school was Jonathan Dickenson of Massachusetts. His successor, Aaron Burr, moved the college to Princeton. Jonathan Edwards succeeded him but died within a few months from a smallpox inoculation. The next president, Samuel Davies, died within two years. Finally, in 1768, the Reverend John Witherspoon of Scotland was chosen as president. Recognized for scholarship in both Britain and America, Witherspoon led Princeton, as the college became known, to a place of great prominence in the new American nation.

1787 A New York City newspaper printed the first of the eighty-five *Federalist Papers.* Alexander Hamilton, James Madison, and John Jay wrote these essays, which argued for the adoption of the new Constitution.

1880 Theodore Roosevelt married Alice Lee, his first wife, who died just over three years later during childbirth.

1904 The first leg of the famed New York City subway system—the IRT—was opened by Mayor George M. McClellan. It ran from City Hall to West 145th Street.

1914 Welsh poet Dylan Thomas was born in Swansea, Glamorgan, Wales. He is best known for his many poems including "Do Not Go Gentle into That Good Night," and his short story "A Child's Christmas in Wales," a nostalgic remembrance of his boyhood, which has become a Christmas classic. His writing is characterized by a mix of humor and pathos.

1938 Du Pont announced the development of a new synthetic yarn, calling the remarkable fiber Nylon.

1941 The *Chicago Daily Tribune* dismissed the possibility of war with Japan, editorializing, "She cannot attack us. That is a military impossibility. Even our base at Hawaii is beyond the effective striking power of her fleet." Less than two months later the editors discovered how wrong they were.

1947 *You Bet Your Life*, starring Groucho Marx, premiered on ABC Radio. It later became a television show for NBC.

1954 Walt Disney's first television program, called *Disneyland* after his yet-to-be completed theme park, premiered on ABC.

1967 The Canadian world's fair, Expo '67 closed in Montreal.

1978 President Anwar Sadat of Egypt and Prime Minister Menachem Begin of Israel were named winners of the Nobel Peace Prize for their progress toward achieving a Middle East accord.

*F*ar better it is to dare mighty things, to win glorious triumphs, even though checkered by failure, than to take rank with those poor spirits who neither enjoy much nor suffer much because they live in the gray twilight that knows neither victory nor defeat.

[THEODORE ROOSEVELT (1858–1919)]

OCTOBER

1903   English satirical novelist Evelyn Waugh was born in London. Educated at Oxford, he published five novels between 1928 and 1938 that satirized aspects of upper-class British life such as colonialism, public schools, and manners and morals—*Decline and Fall* (1928), *Vile Bodies* (1930), *Black Mischief* (1932), *A Handful of Dust* (1934), and *Scoop* (1938). His greatest novel was *Brideshead Revisited* (1945), which was profoundly influenced by his conversion to Roman Catholicism in 1930.

John of Salisbury was an English philosopher and humanist, a leader of the twelfth-century literary renaissance. He was an intimate friend of Pope Hadrian IV and Bernard of Clairvaux. He was trained by the infamous scholar Peter Abelard. He served as secretary to two archbishops of Canterbury and was wounded when Archbishop Thomas à Becket was hacked to death by four ruthless knights. John wrote extensively, and many of his writings cast light upon the lives, events, and schools of his day. It is little wonder, then, that his era is sometimes called the Age of John of Salisbury.

John's close association with Becket cost him dearly. He was forced into exile on the Continent—even before his master was forced to flee from the wrath of Henry II. When the archbishop was killed, John wrote his biography in such terms as would ensure his canonization—but it also ensured permanent enmity with the English Crown.

Despite all his dealings with the famous men of his day, it was as a scholar that John actually won his greatest renown. He was a passionate champion of the ideas of Aristotelian logic and wrote a number of influential books on the subject. He also developed a political theory that prefigured later works such as *Lex Rex* by Samuel Rutherford—he argued that a monarch is subject to God's laws, just as any other man would be, and therefore could be disciplined and perhaps even executed if he violated those laws.

He was widely respected in his own time as a scholar, literary master, theoretician, rhetoretician, and Latinist. The two principal works of his later years were the *Policraticus*, a treatise on the principles of free government; and the *Metalogicon*, a discussion of the plaguing philosophical and theological dilemmas of the day and an argument for the foundational character of Augustine's grammar, rhetoric, and logic—the so-called classical trivium—for the general course of education.

His greatest historical work, *Historia Pontificalis*, and his letters, some of which were written in the name of the archbishops whom he served, became some of the most important documentary sources of the time. He also wrote a number of practical commonsense works for distribution among the common people and the emerging middle class on the foolishness of superstitions, premonitions, astrology, occultism, and any number of other medieval wives' tales.

He became bishop of Chartres in 1176 and remained there for the rest of his life. Most of his works were completed, copied, and published there and sent around the Christian world, affording him great influence. It was there that he died just four years later, on this day in 1180.

OCTOBER

FEAST DAY
Saints Anastasia and Cyril, St. Faro, St. Abraham of Ephesus, St. Salvius or Saire, St. Simon, St. Jude or Thaddeus, St. Fidelis of Como

901 Alfred the Great, king of England, died on this day. The Saxon king proved to be an effective leader against the invasion of the Danes, as well as an equitable ruler and scholar.

1553 Michael Servetus was condemned to death for the crimes of subversion of the public morality, blasphemy, and heresy in the city of Geneva. Born in Spain in 1509, he had a gifted mind, was trained by the Dominicans, and then went to the University of Saragossa. There he began studying the Bible, whose authority he thoroughly recognized, but his own fanciful interpretations brought him into conflict with the Orthodox Church. In 1531 Servetus published a work called the *Errors of the Trinity*, in which he argued that Trinitarians were actually tritheists or atheists. He said the gods of the Trinitarians were a three-headed monster and a deception of the devil. Both Protestants and Catholics found the work blasphemous, and the emperor had it banned. Servetus fled to France where he assumed the identity of Michel de Villeneuve. He studied mathematics, geography, astrology, and medicine. He gained great fame as a physician, having discovered pulmonary circulation of the blood and published a frequently studied book on the use of syrups in medicine. Nevertheless, in 1553 he once again published a book denying the Trinity, *The Restitution of Christianity*. Shortly afterward, he was brought to trial for heresy by the Roman Catholic authorities. Though he was convicted and condemned, he somehow managed to escape. He fled to Geneva where he quickly ran afoul of the law there too. Though the pastor of the church there, John Calvin, pleaded with the magistrates for mercy in his case, Servetus refused his aid. Thus, he was executed.

1636 The General Court of Massachusetts founded Harvard College.

1793 Eli Whitney applied for a patent for his cotton gin. The patent was granted the following March.

1886 The Statue of Liberty, a gift from the people of France, was dedicated in New York Harbor by President Grover Cleveland.

1893 Peter Ilyich Tchaikovsky conducted the first public performance of his Symphony no. 6 in B Minor (*Pathetique*) in St. Petersburg, Russia, just nine days before his death.

1922 Fascism became the dominant ideology of Italy when Benito Mussolini took control of the government.

1936 President Franklin Roosevelt rededicated the Statue of Liberty on its fiftieth anniversary.

1958 The Roman Catholic patriarch of Venice, Angelo Giuseppe Roncalli, was elected pope. He took the name John XXIII.

1960 The immediate threat of nuclear war due to the Cuban Missile Crisis came to an end when Premier Nikita Khrushchev of the Soviet Union agreed to dismantle and withdraw all missile bases from Cuba.

1965 The world's tallest monument, the St. Louis Arch, called "The Gateway to the West," was completed. It stands 630 feet tall and 630 feet wide at its base.

28

OCTOBER

The prevailing spirit of the present age seems to be the spirit of skepticism and captiousness, of suspicion and distrust in private judgment; a dislike of all established forms, merely because they are established, and of old paths, because they are old.

[SAMUEL JOHNSON (1709–1784)]

On this day in 1907, the entire nation of the Netherlands celebrated the seventieth birthday of Abraham Kuyper. A national proclamation recognized that "the history of the Netherlands, in Church, in State, in Society, in Press, in School, and in the Sciences the last forty years, cannot be written without the mention of his name on almost every page, for during this period the biography of Dr. Kuyper is to a considerable extent the history of the Netherlands."

The boy who was born in 1837 was at first thought to be dull, but by the time he was twelve he had entered the Gymnasium. Years later he would graduate with the highest possible honors from Leyden University. In short order he earned his master's and doctoral degrees in theology before serving as minister at Breesd and Utrecht.

The brilliant and articulate champion of biblical faithfulness was called to serve in the city of Amsterdam in 1870. At the time, the religious life of the nation had dramatically declined. The church was cold and formal. There was no Bible curriculum in the schools, and the Bible had no real influence in the life of the nation. Kuyper set out to change all this in a flurry of activity.

In 1872, Kuyper founded the daily newspaper, *De Standaard.* Shortly afterward he also founded *De Heraut,* a weekly devotional magazine. He continued as editor of both newspapers for more than forty-five years—and both became very influential in spreading the winsome message of a consistent Christian worldview.

Two years later, in 1874, Kuyper was elected to the lower house of Parliament as the leader of the Anti-Revolutionary Party-and he served there until 1877. Three years later he founded the Free University of Amsterdam, which asserted that the Bible was the foundation of every area of knowledge.

Following a stunning victory at the polls, Kuyper was summoned in 1902 by Queen Wilhelmena to form a cabinet and become prime minister of the nation—a position he held for three years. A number of politicians were dissatisfied with Kuyper's leadership because he refused to separate his theological and political views. To him, they were identical interests since Christ was King in every arena of human life. He believed that Christ rules not merely by the tradition of what He once was, spoke, did, and endured, but by a living power which even now, seated as He is at the right hand of God, He exercises over lands, nations, generations, families, and individuals.

Kuyper was undoubtedly a man of tremendous versatility—he was a noted linguist, theologian, university professor, politician, statesman, philosopher, scientist, publisher, author, journalist, and philanthropist. But amazingly, in spite of his many accomplishments and his tremendous urgency to redeem the times, Kuyper was also a man of the people.

In 1897, at the twenty-fifth anniversary of his establishment of *De Standaard*, Kuyper described the ruling passion of his life: "In spite of all worldly opposition, God's holy ordinances shall be established again in the home, in the school, and in the State for the good of the people; to carve as it were into the conscience of the nation the ordinances of the Lord, to which Bible and Creation bear witness, until the nation pays homage again to God."

OCTOBER

NATIONAL DAY
Turkey
FEAST DAY
The Martyrs of Douay, St. Theuderius or Chef, St. Colman or Kilmacduagh, St. Narcissus of Jerusalem

1618 Under a fifteen-year-old conviction of conspiracy against James I, Sir Walter Raleigh was beheaded at Whitehall. When asked which way he wished to lay his head on the block, he responded, "So the heart be right, it is no matter which way the head lies."

1652 The Massachusetts Bay Colony declared itself an independent commonwealth.

1682 The founder of Pennsylvania, William Penn, landed at what is now Chester, Pennsylvania.

1740 James Boswell, friend and biographer of Samuel Johnson, was born in Edinburgh, Scotland.

1901 President William McKinley's assassin, Leon Czolgosz, was executed by electrocution.

1911 American newspaperman Joseph Pulitzer died in Charleston, South Carolina.

1923 The Republic of Turkey was proclaimed following the collapse of the old Ottoman Empire.

1929 Black Tuesday descended upon the New York Stock Exchange. Prices collapsed amid panic selling and thousands of investors were wiped out as America's Great Depression began.

1945 Gimbel's of New York City sold the first ballpoint pen for $12.50.

1947 Former first lady Frances Cleveland Preston died in Baltimore at age eighty-three.

1956 During the Suez Canal crisis, Israel launched an invasion of Egypt's Sinai Peninsula.

1956 *The Huntley-Brinkley Report* premiered as NBC's nightly television newscast, replacing *The Camel News Caravan.*

1966 The feminist political organization, the National Organization for Women, was founded.

1989 At least twenty thousand East Berliners observed a minute of silence for those killed while attempting to flee over the Berlin Wall, the first such public mourning since Communist Party authorities built the wall in 1961.

1998 Senator John Glenn, at age seventy-seven, roared back into space aboard the shuttle *Discovery,* retracing the trail he'd blazed for America's astronauts thirty-six years earlier.

Opinion is a flitting thing
But truth, outlasts the sun;
If we cannot own them both,
Possess the oldest one.

[EMILY DICKINSON (1830–1886)]

OCTOBER

1944

Aaron Copland's ballet *Appalachian Spring* was first performed in the Coolidge Auditorium of the Library of Congress in Washington, D.C., with Martha Graham as choreographer and in the lead role. Copland utilized excerpts from the Shaker tunes of the Pennsylvania mountain people. Copland won the Pulitzer Prize for the symphonic suite that was adapted from the ballet score.

On this day in 1517, German theologian Martin Luther recopied the scroll of his soon to be revealed *Disputation on the Power and Efficacy of Indulgences*—a document that would be popularly called the *Ninety-Five Theses.* The next day he would post the scroll, consisting of ninety-five propositions that established a theological basis for opposing the sale of indulgences. Though written in Latin and designed to provoke only a limited academic discussion, Luther's manifesto would almost immediately be translated into the vernacular and then widely distributed, causing a great public controversy leading to the Reformation. Who would have ever dreamed that in the little town of Wittenberg, Germany, all of Europe would be shaken by the simple act of provoking a series of questions? Certainly not Luther. But in fact, his little academic exercise would lead to a dramatic realignment of men and nations—indeed, he would eventually be excommunicated by the Roman Catholic Church and become the founder of Protestantism.

But as he prepared the scroll, he certainly had none of that in mind. Indeed, the tone of the document was clearly a moderate call for little more than a bit of dialogue and some serious theological investigation. He wrote, "A disputation on the power and efficacy of indulgences: out of love for the truth and the desire to bring it to light, the following propositions will be discussed at Wittenberg, under the presidency of the Reverend Father Martin Luther, Master of Arts and of Sacred Theology, and Lecturer in Ordinary on the same at that place. Wherefore he requests that those who are unable to be present and debate orally with us, may do so by letter."

The theses themselves were not any more incendiary. Instead, they discussed the character and nature of true repentance, the core values of the gospel, and the essence of the justice and mercy of God. Hardly the sort of material one might expect to cause a furor.

Nevertheless, the faithful Augustinian monk's attempt to open a dialogue was, in the good providence of God, the catalyst for a movement that would ultimately reshape the whole of Western civilization.

OCTOBER

FEAST DAY
St. Marcellus the Centurion, St. Alphonsus Rodriguez, St. Germanus of Capua, St. Serapion of Antioch, St. Asterius of Amasea, St. Ethelnoth

1485 One of the first commands issued by King Henry VII as a newly crowned monarch was the institution of the Yeomen of the Guard to act as Royal attendants. This guard body eventually became known as the Beefeaters.

1735 The second president of the United States, John Adams, was born in Braintree, Massachusetts.

1795 John Keats was born in his father's livery stable in Finsbury Pavement.

1811 Jane Austen's *Sense and Sensibility* was published anonymously in three volumes by Thomas Egerton. Embarrassed, the author took special pains to hide the fact that her first novel—which caused a literary sensation—was published at all.

1830 George Mueller—a Prussian-born English pastor and philanthropist—explained to his congregation that he would no longer accept a salary from them. A box would be put up in the chapel, and people would be able to contribute as they desired before the Lord, without any man having to know the giver or the amount. Mueller made it a point never to ask for money or even let his needs be known lest it appear he was appealing for funds. His appeals were always to his heavenly Father, who in turn would direct His people to care for His own. The gifts Mr. Mueller received were many and varied—a bride and bridegroom gave money to the Lord's work rather than buy an engagement ring; a lady sold all of her jewelry and gave the proceeds to the Lord; one man sent in a gold watch and chain with a note, "A pilgrim does not want such a watch as this to make him happy; one of an inferior kind will do to show him how swiftly time flies and how fast he is hastening on to that Canaan where time will be no more." George Mueller's ministry was worldwide and included ten churches in the Bristol area, orphanages that cared for and educated eight thousand orphans in his lifetime, and a vast ministry of printing and distributing biblical literature. In all of his ministry, Mueller looked to the Lord alone for his supply. As Mueller himself said, "I have joyfully dedicated my whole life to the object of exemplifying how much may be accomplished by prayer and faith."

1871 French philosopher Paul Valery was born in Sete.

1913 Historian Will Durant, age twenty-seven—a member of the radical Greenwich Village coterie that included Mable Dodge, Edna St. Vincent Millay, and Margaret Sanger—married his fifteen-year-old live-in girl friend, Ariel, at New York City Hall.

1938 The radio dramatization of H. G. Wells's *The War of the Worlds* by Orson Welles created national panic when listeners mistook the simulated news bulletins of Martian invasion to be real.

1961 The Soviet Union tested a hydrogen bomb with a force estimated at fifty-eight megatons.

1961 The Soviet Party Congress unanimously approved a resolution ordering the removal of Joseph Stalin's body from the Red Square Mausoleum—leaving only Nicolai Lenin's body enshrined there.

1974 Muhammad Ali knocked out George Foreman in the eighth round of a fifteen-round bout in Kinshasa, Zaire, to regain his world heavyweight title.

1989 Mitsubishi Estate Company, a major Japanese real estate concern, announced it was buying 51 percent of Rockefeller Group Incorporated of New York.

OCTOBER

The brilliant passes, like the dew at morn;

The true endures, for ages yet unborn.

[JOHANN GOETHE (1749–1832)]

Martin Luther was born in Eisleben on November 10, 1483. He was descended from the peasantry, a fact in which he took great pride. His father was a copper miner in the mining area of Mansfeld—but humble as he was, he determined to procure a sound education for his children. Thus, Luther received a Brethren of the Common Life education at Mansfeld, Magdeburg, and Eisenach. In 1501, he enrolled at the University of Erfurt, receiving his undergraduate degree in 1502 and his master's degree in 1505. He then intended to study law, as his father wished. But in the summer of 1505, he suddenly abandoned his studies, sold his books, and entered the Augustinian monastery in Erfurt. The decision surprised his friends and appalled his father. Later in life, Luther explained it by recalling several brushes with death that made him astutely aware of the fleeting character of life. Luther made his profession as a monk the following year and was ordained as a priest the year after that.

After his ordination, Luther was asked to study theology to become a professor at one of the many new German universities. The following year he was assigned by Johann von Staupitz, vicar-general of the Augustinians and a friend and counselor, to the University of Wittenberg, which had been founded just six years earlier. He was to give introductory lectures in moral philosophy. Two years later, he had the opportunity to visit Rome and was shocked by the worldliness of the Roman clergy.

Increasingly concerned about corruption within the church—both material and spiritual—Luther suddenly became a public and controversial figure when he published his Ninety-Five Theses on this day in 1517. They were supremely academic in character—Latin propositions opposing the manner in which indulgences were being sold to raise money for the construction of Saint Peter's in Rome. The Theses caused great excitement and were immediately translated into German and widely distributed. Luther's spirited defense and further development of his position through public university debates in Wittenberg and other cities resulted in an investigation by the Roman Curia that led to his condemnation three years later and his excommunication a year after that in 1521.

Summoned to appear before Emperor Charles V at the Diet of Worms in April 1521, he was asked before the assembled secular and ecclesiastical rulers to recant. He refused firmly, asserting that he would have to be convinced by Scripture and clear reason in order to do so: "Here I stand, I can do no other."

Condemned by the emperor, Luther was spirited away by his prince, the elector Frederick the Wise of Saxony, and kept in hiding at Wartburg Castle. There he began his translation of the New Testament from the original Greek into German, a seminal contribution to the development of a standard German language. Disorders in Wittenberg caused by some of his more extreme followers forced his return to the city in March 1521, and he restored peace through a series of sermons.

By that time, it was clear that the protesting churches—or Protestants—would not succeed in reforming the whole church as Luther had wished, and so they established a new ecclesiastical structure rooted in the idea of *Sola Scriptura* (Scripture Alone). Thus was born the Reformation.

OCTOBER

ALL HALLOWS' EVE *(Halloween)*
FEAST DAY
 *St. Quentin or Quintinus, St. Bee
 or Bega, St. Wolfgang, St. Foillan
 of Fosses*

1864 Nevada became the thirty-sixth state.

1926 Magician Harry Houdini died in Detroit of gangrene and peritonitis resulting from a ruptured appendix.

1941 The U.S. Navy destroyer *Reuben James* was torpedoed by a German U-boat off Iceland with the loss of 115 lives, even though America had not yet entered the Second World War.

1956 Rear Admiral G. J. Dufek became the first person to land an airplane at the South Pole.

1959 Lee Harvey Oswald, a former U.S. Marine from Fort Worth, Texas, announced in Moscow that he would never return to the United States.

1968 President Lyndon Johnson ordered a halt to all U.S. bombing of North Vietnam, saying he hoped for fruitful peace negotiations.

1980 Reza Pahlavi, eldest son of the late shah, proclaimed himself the rightful successor to the Peacock Throne of Iran.

1984 Indian Prime Minister Indira Gandhi was assassinated by two Sikh security guards.

1998 A genetic study was released suggesting that someone from the family of Thomas Jefferson was the father of the children of his slave Sally Hemings—though there was no evidence that this male line ran through Jefferson himself.

ALL HALLOW'S EVE

Samhain, a holiday observed by the ancient Celts, was the most important of the ancient late autumn holidays celebrated in Europe. It marked the end of one year and the beginning of the next. According to tradition, the spirits of those who had died in the preceding year roamed the earth on Samhain evening. The Celts sought to ward off these spirits with offerings of food and drink. They also built bonfires at sacred hilltop sites and performed rituals, often involving human and animal sacrifices. When the Celts were absorbed into the Roman Empire, many of their traditions were adapted by the conquerors as part of their own celebrations. In Britain, Romans blended Samhain customs with their own pagan harvest festival honoring Pomona, goddess of fruit trees—from which the game of bobbing for apples was derived. Even after Samhain was abandoned during the early Middle Ages, pagan folk observances were often linked to some Christian holidays. Thus, many of the old Samhain traditions thought to be incompatible with Christianity often became linked with Christian folk beliefs about evil spirits in the celebration of Halloween. Although such superstitions varied from place to place, many of the supernatural beings now associated with the holiday became fixed in the popular imagination during the Renaissance. In British folklore, small magical beings known as fairies became associated with Halloween mischief. The jack-o'-lantern, originally carved from a large turnip rather than a pumpkin, originated in medieval Scotland. As belief in many of the old superstitions waned during the late nineteenth century, Halloween was increasingly regarded as a children's holiday. Beginning in the twentieth century, Halloween mischief gradually transformed into the modern ritual of trick-or-treating. Eventually, Halloween treats were plentiful while tricks became rare.

OCTOBER

Keep steadily in the view of the great principles for which you contend: the safety of your homes and the lives of all you hold dear depend upon your courage and exertions. Let each man resolve to be victorious, and that the right of self-government, liberty, and peace shall find him a defender.

[ROBERT E. LEE (1807–1870)]

November

ALL SAINT'S DAY

In the earliest years of the church, so many martyrs died for their faith, Christians set aside special days to honor them. For example, in 607 Emperor Phocas presented the beautiful Roman Pantheon to the church. Pope Boniface IV quickly removed the statues of Jupiter and the pagan gods and consecrated the Pantheon to all the martyrs who had suffered during the Roman persecution in the first three hundred years after Christ—that great cloud of witnesses to the Christian faith. Originally celebrated on May 1, the festival in commemoration of all the saints was eventually moved to November by Pope Gregory IV as a time of remembrance of all those who had suffered persecution for their faith.

NATIONAL DAY
Algeria
FEAST DAY
All Saints; St. Benignus of Dijon;
Saints Caesarius and Julian;
St. Austremonius or Stremoine;
St. Cadfan; St. Mary, martyr;
St. Vigor; St. Marcellus of Paris;
Saint Mathurin or Maturinus

The only American president ever to be held as a prisoner of war by a foreign power, Henry Laurens (1724–1792) was heralded after he was released as "the father of our country," by no less a personage than George Washington. He was of Huguenot extraction, his ancestors having come to America from France after the revocation of the Edict of Nantes made the Reformed faith illegal.

Raised and educated for a life of mercantilism at his home in Charleston, he also had the opportunity to spend more than a year in continental travel. It was while in Europe that he began to write revolutionary pamphlets—gaining him renown as a patriot. He served as vice president of South Carolina in 1776. He was then elected to the Continental Congress. He succeeded John Hancock as President of the newly independent but war-beleaguered United States on this day in 1777.

He served as the nation's chief executive until December 9, 1778, at which time he was appointed ambassador to the Netherlands. Unfortunately for the cause of the young nation, he was captured by an English warship during his transatlantic voyage and was confined to the Tower of London until the end of the war.

After the Battle of Yorktown, the American government regained his freedom in a dramatic prisoner exchange—President Laurens for Lord Cornwallis. Ever the patriot, Laurens continued to serve his nation as one of the three representatives selected to negotiate terms at the Paris Peace Conference in 1782.

NOVEMBER

1604 William Shakespeare's tragedy *Othello* was first presented at Whitehall Palace in London.

1611 The Shakespearean romantic comedy *The Tempest* was first presented at Whitehall Palace.

1755 Lisbon, Portugal, was destroyed by an earthquake in the Atlantic that came in the form of twenty-two rapid shocks. The entire Iberian Peninsula coast was shaken by the tremors as well as washed away by huge tidal waves. An entire town in Morocco of eight thousand people disappeared into a crack that formed in the earth's crust. In all, some sixty thousand people were killed.

1765 The Stamp Act went into effect in the colonies with much resistance. The purpose of the Stamp Act was for Great Britain to raise revenue with which to maintain the military defenses of the colonies by requiring all legal documents, licenses, commercial contracts, newspapers, pamphlets, and playing cards to carry a stamp tax. The colonists balked at being taxed when they had no representation in Parliament.

1800 John Adams moved into the White House, becoming the first president to reside there.

1861 General George B. McClellan was made general-in-chief of the Union armies. He would later be removed by Abraham Lincoln only to emerge as Lincoln's fiercest political critic and rival in the Northern Union during the War Between the States.

1870 Using telegraph reports from twenty-four locations, the United States Weather Bureau made its first meteorological observations.

1873 Joseph F. Glidden invented barbed wire.

1897 The Library of Congress opened to the public.

1913 Knute Rockne helped the Notre Dame Fighting Irish football team to beat Army with a score of 35-7 with the innovation of the forward pass.

1940 Bud Abbott and Lou Costello's first film was released with the title *One Night at the Tropics.*

1944 *Harvey,* a comedy by Mary Chase about a man and his friend, an invisible six-foot rabbit, opened on Broadway.

1950 Two Puerto Rican nationalists tried to force their way into Blair House in Washington to assassinate President Harry Truman. The attempt failed, and one of the pair was killed.

1952 The United States exploded the first hydrogen bomb at Eniwetok in the Marshall Islands.

1954 The western African nation of Algeria began a rebellion against French rule that would ultimately sunder the deteriorating fabric of European colonialism throughout Africa and Asia.

1973 Following the so-called "Saturday Night Massacre," acting Attorney General Robert H. Bork appointed Leon Jaworski to be the new Watergate special prosecutor, succeeding Archibald Cox.

1979 Former first lady Mamie Eisenhower died in Washington, D.C. at age eighty-two.

1989 East Germany reopened its border with Czechoslovakia, prompting tens of thousands of refugees to flee to the West.

If you tell the truth you don't have to remember anything.

[MARK TWAIN (1835–1910)]

NOVEMBER

ALL SOULS' DAY

In the tenth century, Abbot Odela of the Cluny monastery decided to add to the celebration of All Saints' Day—a feast set aside to remember the martyrs of the faith through the ages—by declaring the following day as the Feast of All Souls' Day. His purpose was to honor not just the martyrs, but all Christians who had died and gone on to their eternal reward in heaven.

Though he thought of himself as merely a farmer, it is not as a humble agrarian that Thomas Jefferson is best remembered today. Jefferson placed as much emphasis on books and libraries as he did on farms and agriculture. He was constantly recommending books. He was as renowned for his reading lists and catalogs as he was for his hybrid tomatoes and broad leaf tobacco.

The Library of Congress was founded in 1800, making it the oldest federal cultural institution in the nation. Jefferson, who became president the following year, gleefully appointed the first two librarians of Congress, taking a keen interest in the library and its collection. Jefferson passionately held that the power of the intellect could and should shape a free and democratic society. Even after he returned to civilian life, he continued to offer his advice and counsel to the librarians in Washington.

In 1814, the invading British army swept into the city of Washington and burned the Capitol, including the entire Library of Congress. The following year, on this day, Jefferson offered to sell his vast personal library, the largest and finest in the country, to the Congress to recommence its library. Congress gladly accepted his generous offer.

FEAST DAY
All Souls, St. Victorinus of Pettau, Saint Marcian of Cyrrhus

NOVEMBER

The catalog of books that Jefferson sold to Congress not only included more than twice the number of volumes that had been in the destroyed Library of Congress, it also expanded the scope of the Library far beyond the bounds of a legislative library devoted primarily to legal, economic, and historical works. Jefferson was a man of encyclopedic interests, and his library included works on architecture, the arts, science, literature, and geography. It contained books in French, Spanish, German, Latin, Greek, and one three-volume statistical work in Russian. Anticipating the argument that his collection might be too comprehensive, he argued that there was "no subject to which a Member of Congress may not have occasion to refer."

The Jeffersonian concept of universality is the rational for the comprehensive collecting policies of today's Library of Congress. Jefferson's belief in the power of knowledge and the direct link between knowledge and democracy shaped the library's philosophy of sharing its collections and services as widely as possible. Today, the Library of Congress is the largest library in the world, with more than 115 million items on approximately 530 miles of bookshelves. The collections include some 17 million books, 2 million recordings, 12 million photographs, 4 million maps, and 50 million manuscripts. Jefferson's vision has been realized in magnificent fashion.

1533 When the apostle Paul escaped from the city of Damascus by being lowered over the wall in a basket it would not be the last time that a Christian evangelist would be forced to dramatically flee from persecution. On this day in 1533, John Calvin made a similarly thrilling escape from the city of Paris. To be sure, Calvin was hardly a prime candidate for such adventures. Always of frail health as well as retiring, serious, and scholarly, his greatest aspiration was simply to be left alone so that he might quietly pursue his studies. Nevertheless, his stalwart theology forced him to live a stalwart existence. After having written a series of Reformation pamphlets and sermons, Calvin had to flee for his life with the police hot on his heels. Calvin lowered himself from a window on tied-together bedsheets, and escaped Paris dressed as a farmer with a hoe on his shoulder. For three years he wandered as a fugitive evangelist under assumed names. He finally settled in Geneva, where he became perhaps the greatest theologian of the Reformation.

1734 Frontiersman, explorer, and militia officer Daniel Boone was born in Berks County near Reading, Pennsylvania. His many adventures included his abduction by Shawnee Indians (who adopted him and named him "Big Turtle") and his capture by the British in 1781. An avid sportsman, Boone continued hunting into his eighties. In his famous poem *Don Juan*, Lord Byron immortalized the woodsman by saying:

> Of all the men, saving Sylla, the man-slayer,
> Who passes for in life and death most lucky,
> Of the great names which in our faces stare,
> The General Boone, back-woodsman of Kentucky,
> Was happiest among mortals anywhere;
> For killing nothing but a bear or buck, he
> Enjoy'd the lonely, vigorous, harmless days
> Of his old age in wilds of deepest maze.

1873 The enthusiastic reception by critics to the premiere of Johannes Brahms's *Variations on a Theme by Haydn* in Vienna encouraged the forty-year-old composer to undertake the writing of his first symphony, which was completed in 1876.

1889 North Dakota and South Dakota became the thirty-ninth and fortieth states.

1930 Haile Selassie was crowned the Christian emperor of Ethiopia.

1948 President Harry Truman surprised the experts by being narrowly reelected in an upset over Republican challenger Thomas E. Dewey.

1954 Strom Thurmond became the first senator elected by write-in vote during elections in South Carolina.

1963 The Christian South Vietnamese president Ngo Dihn Diem was assassinated in a military coup provoked and financed by the American government.

Truth crushed to earth shall rise again,
The eternal years of God are hers.

[WILLIAM CULLEN BRYANT (1794–1878)]

NOVEMBER

1871

American journalist Henry Morton Stanley sought out and finally found the missionary Dr. David Livingstone at Ujiji in Africa. Upon their meeting, Mr. Stanley is said to have declared, "Dr. Livingstone, I presume." Stanley found the pale, careworn, gray-headed old man "dressed in a red shirt and crimson jo-ho, with a gold band around his cap, an old pair of tweed pants, and his shoes looking worse for wear."

The story that Herman Melville (1819–1891) conceived as his magnum opus was published after he had attained his minor popularity as a writer of pulp thrillers. But he aspired to something far greater than merely an intrepid tale of sea adventure. He wanted to write great and enduring literature. Alas, that was hardly the kind of pap that publishers in the middle of the nineteenth century were looking for. The more things change, the more they stay the same.

NATIONAL DAY
Panama
FEAST DAY
St. Rumwald, St. Malachy of Armagh, St. Amicus, St. Winifred or Gwenfrewi, St. Martin de Porres, St. Pirminus

Undeterred, the big, brash, and boisterous book he wrote, *Moby Dick*, proved to be a multilayered novel of expansive scope, subtle intrigue, and stunning exploits. Like much of his writing, the story was constructed as a kind of literary and theological puzzle. But this surprising and scintillating double-coded labyrinth—which apparently was intended to follow the thematic structure of a great Puritan sermon—never obstructed the pace or the sense of the story. Powerful scenic images and a rip-roaring series of illusions, cons, ploys, and deceptions gave the book an immediacy and a page-turning quality generally unknown in serious literary works. It was, in short, brilliantly conceived and passionately executed.

Born in 1819 the son of a struggling merchant, Melville had an adventurous youth serving on whaling vessels and trading ships throughout the Pacific and across the Atlantic. His literary career, such as it was, grew out of a desire to tell of those experiences. His maturity as a writer blossomed quickly, and he was drawn into the highbrow literary circle that included Longfellow and Hawthorne. But his unwillingness to compromise either his style or his content to suit popular tastes doomed his commercial appeal. When he quit writing altogether in 1857, he asserted that he'd rather lay down his pen than lower his standards: "What I feel most moved to write will not pay. Yet write the other way, I cannot."

NOVEMBER

Thus, with the force of an unerring moral compunction, he put away his parchments and went to work as an inspector at the busy New York Harbor. That kind of uncompromising ethical conviction is readily apparent in *Moby Dick*. The book is an unrestrained expression of originality and verve. But it is also a forceful exertion of will against all odds erupting upon the intellectual stage with a lusty obsession for truth and resolution: "Unconsciously my chirography expands into placard capitals. Give me a condor's quill. Give me Vesuvius's crater for an inkstand."

He wrote of leviathans. Indeed, he was himself a leviathan.

1723 Samuel Davies was born this day. His mother wanted her son to be dedicated to the Lord's work. In later life, Samuel wrote a friend that God's prompt answers to the prayers of a Christian mother accounted for the most important blessings in his life. In 1740, although Virginia's colonial government took a dim view of any kind of ministry outside the official Church of England, it gave Davies a license to preach as a Presbyterian minister in four counties, and he used it to promote tolerance for all denominations. The persuasive reasoning of Davies's eloquent sermons electrified his audiences by combining Scripture with practical teaching. The patriot orator Patrick Henry frequently attended Davies's services, and gained some of his eloquent style from him. Davies also regularly invited three hundred slaves to his home on Saturday evenings—their only free time. He taught them to read and to sing hymns, many of which he wrote himself. His "Great God of Wonders" and other gospel songs are still found in many hymnbooks. Realizing the importance of education, Davies helped found Princeton University, and was chosen its president after Jonathan Edwards's sudden death. Yet Davies, too, died early, at age thirty-eight.

1794 The American poet William Cullen Bryant was born in Cummington, Massachusetts. His greatest works, *Thanatopis* and *To a Waterfowl*, would both be published in 1817 to great acclaim from readers and critics alike.

1901 The French novelist, archaeologist, art theorist, political activist, and statesman Andre Malraux was born into a prosperous Parisian family and educated at the School of Oriental Languages. In 1923 he went to Indochina to do archaeological research. He became active in the struggle of Vietnamese revolutionists to win self-rule from France. Malraux used his Asian experiences as background for three novels, *The Conquerors*, *The Royal Way*, and *Man's Fate*. His next novel, *Days of Wrath*, was inspired by a visit to Germany, then under the dictatorship of Adolf Hitler. His experiences as a pilot with a Loyalist air squadron during the Spanish Civil War were the basis for the novel *Man's Hope*. In the Second World War, Malraux volunteered as a private, was captured by the Germans, escaped, and served as a colonel in the French Resistance but was recaptured. In 1945–1946 he joined the provisional government of Charles de Gaulle. After the war he served as minister for cultural affairs. He retired to a suburb of Paris, where he continued to write until his death in 1976.

1941 The United States ambassador to Japan sent a cable to Washington, D.C., stating that a surprise attack on the United States had been planned. His warning went unheeded.

1948 Readers awoke this morning to a large banner headline in the *Chicago Tribune* announcing the results of the presidential election as "Dewey Defeats Truman." In actuality, Harry S Truman defeated the Republican candidate.

1989 East German leader Egon Krenz delivered a nationally broadcast speech in which he promised sweeping economic and political reforms, and called on East Germans to stay. His pleas fell on deaf ears as a flood of refugees poured out of the country to freedom in the West.

Truth is the trial of itself,
And needs no other touch;
And purer than the purest gold,
Refine it ne'er so much.

[Ben Jonson (1572–1637)]

NOVEMBER

Alexis de Tocqueville was born into the aristocracy in 1805, during the halcyon days of the Napoleonic Empire. His family had suffered much during the French Revolution—as had so many of noble birth. But Napoleon restored their fortunes. As a result, de Tocqueville was able to enjoy a privileged upbringing despite all the vicissitudes of the time. As a young adult, he served the ever-changing French governing institutions—thus preserving his family's fortunes. It was in that capacity that he made his famous trip to America to discover the secret of that fledgling nation's vitality.

When he returned to France, de Tocqueville sat down to document his experiences and to sort through his conclusions. Eventually, he published his observations in a massive two-volume work entitled *The Republic of the United States of America*—later retitled *Democracy in America*. The book became an instant classic. It helped to explain the American phenomenon to Europeans. But it also provided a rare objective look at the culture of America for Americans. And his discoveries were thus woven into the mythos and the consciousness of thoughtful men and women the world over. Many historians believe that it was the way de Tocqueville articulated those discoveries that provided the philosophical paradigm shift necessary for the ultimate American triumph and the advent of the American century.

Essentially what he discovered was that America was the only modern nation in the world that was founded on a creed. Other nations found their identity and cohesion in ethnicity, or geography, or partisan ideology, or cultural tradition. But America was founded on certain ideas—ideas about freedom, human dignity, and social responsibility. It was this profound peculiarity that most struck him. He called it "American exceptionalism."

He simultaneously concluded that if their great experiment in liberty, their extraordinary American exceptionalism, were to be maintained over the course of succeeding generations, then an informed patriotism would have to be instilled in the hearts and minds of the young. Not surprisingly, then de Tocqueville has oft been quoted—perhaps apocryphally, but nevertheless true to the basic tenets of his evident opinion—as saying: "I sought for the greatness and genius of America in her commodious harbors and her ample rivers, and it was not there; in her fertile fields and boundless prairies, and it was not there; in her rich mines and her vast world commerce, and it was not there. Not until I went to the churches of America and heard her pulpits aflame with righteousness did I understand the secret of her genius and power. America is great because she is good and if America ever ceases to be good, America will cease to be great."

His remarkable chronicle was offered in the hope that the ideas that made America both great and good might remain the common currency of the national life. He felt that the world needed to know those things—because the world needed to share those things.

NOVEMBER

1740 English clergyman Augustus Montague Toplady, author of "Rock of Ages," was born on this day.

1842 Abraham Lincoln married Mary Todd in Springfield, Illinois. It was to prove to be a melancholy match for both.

1847 German composer Felix Mendelssohn died in Leipzig. He helped to spark an interest in the works of J. S. Bach through an 1829 revival of the *St. Matthew Passion*. He also contributed several works to the repertoire that are imbued with splashes of orchestral color and clear, lyrical melodies.

1876 The Symphony no. 1 by Johannes Brahms was premiered in Karslruhe after nearly twenty-one years of work and refining. It was met with resounding praise that encouraged Brahms to continue writing in the symphonic form. Brahms had already had a remarkable career. After studying the violin and cello with his father, a double bass player in the city theater, Brahms mastered the piano and began to compose under the guidance of the German music teacher Eduard Marxsen, whose conservative tastes left a lasting imprint on him. In 1853 Brahms went on a concert tour as accompanist to the Hungarian violinist Eduard Reményi. In the course of the tour he met the Hungarian violinist Joseph Joachim, who introduced him in turn to the German composer Robert Schumann. Schumann was so impressed by Brahms's unpublished compositions that he wrote a wildly enthusiastic magazine article about him. Brahms cherished a deep affection for both Schumann and his wife, Clara,

a famous pianist. The friendship and encouragement he received from them gave impetus to his work. In 1857 Brahms secured an appointment as conductor at the court theater in Detmold, where he remained until 1859; for several years thereafter he traveled in Germany and Switzerland. His first major work to be publicly presented was the Piano Concerto no. 1 in D minor, which he performed in Leipzig in 1859. In 1868 Brahms won fame throughout Europe following the performance of his *German Requiem*, in which he departed from Catholic tradition by using a German rather than a Latin text. Eventually, he wrote in every medium except opera. He died in 1897 in Vienna.

1897 Humorist Will Rogers was born near Oolagah in the Oklahoma Indian Territory. His epitaph would one day read, "I joked about every prominent man in my lifetime, but I never met one I didn't like."

1922 The entrance to King Tutankhamen's tomb was discovered in Egypt.

1939 The United States modified its neutrality stance in World War II, allowing cash-and-carry purchases of arms by belligerents, a policy favoring Britain and France.

1956 Soviet troops moved in to crush the popular Hungarian pro-democracy movement.

1979 Sixty-five Americans were seized as hostages by Iranian militants at the American embassy in Teheran—it was the start of 444 days of captivity.

The community is the true sphere of human virtue. In social, active life, difficulties will perpetually be met with; restraints of many kinds will be necessary; and studying to behave right in respect of these, is a discipline of the human heart, useful to others, and improving to itself.

[SAMUEL JOHNSON (1709–1784)]

NOVEMBER

<table>
<tr><td>1605</td><td>Englishman Guy Fawkes and at least ten other conspirators sought to blow up Parliament, kill King James I, and establish a Catholic monarchy. A Protestant by birth, he became a Roman Catholic after the marriage of his widowed mother to a man of Catholic background and sympathies. In 1593 he enlisted in the Spanish army in Flanders and in 1596 participated in the capture of the city of Calais by the Spanish in their war with Henry IV of France. He became implicated with Thomas Winter and others in the Gunpowder Plot to blow up Parliament as a protest against the anti–Roman Catholic laws. On this night, Fawkes was apprehended in a vault under the Old House of Lords with incendiary devices and a cache of more than twenty barrels of gunpowder. After severe torture he disclosed the names of his accomplices, and with them he was hanged. Guy Fawkes Day is celebrated on November 5 in the United Kingdom and some other parts of the British Commonwealth with bonfires and fireworks.</td></tr>
</table>

FEAST DAY
Saints Elizabeth and Zachary, St. Galation, St. Bertilla of Chelles, St. Episteme

He was the heir of one of the greatest family traditions in the colonies and became the patriarch of a long line of American patriots—his great-grandfather died at Lutzen beside the great King Gustavus Adolphus of Sweden; his grandfather was one of the founders of New Sweden along the Delaware River in Maryland; one of his nephews was the military secretary to George Washington; another was a signer of the Declaration; still another was a signer of the Constitution; yet another was governor of Maryland during the Revolution; and still another was a member of the First Congress; two sons were killed in action with the Continental army; a grandson served as a member of Congress under the new Constitution; and another grandson was a Maryland senator.

Thus, even if John Hanson (1715–1783) had not served as president himself, he would have greatly contributed to the life of the nation through his ancestry and progeny. As a youngster he began a self-guided reading of classics and rather quickly became an acknowledged expert in the juridicalism of Anselm and the practical philosophy of Seneca—both of which were influential in the development of the political philosophy of the great leaders of the Reformation. It was based upon these legal and theological studies that the young planter whose farm, Mulberry Grove, was just across the Potomac from Mount Vernon, began to espouse the cause of the patriots.

In 1775 he was elected to the Provincial Legislature of Maryland. Then in 1777, he became a member of Congress where he distinguished himself as a brilliant administrator. He was thus elected president in 1781. He served in that office from November 5, 1781, until November 3, 1782. He was the first president to serve a full term after the full ratification of the Articles of Confederation—and like so many of the Southern and New England Founders, he was strongly opposed to the Constitution when it was first discussed. He remained a confirmed anti-Federalist until his untimely death.

NOVEMBER

1639 The first colonial post office was established in Massachusetts.

1664 Samuel Pepys wrote in his diary that he had been to see *Macbeth*, "a pretty good play."

1768 The League of Iroquois sold land to the United States that became parts of western Pennsylvania, southwestern New York, West Virginia, Tennessee, and Kentucky.

1782 The Continental Congress elected John Hanson of Maryland its chairman, giving him the title of "President of the United States in Congress Assembled."

1872 Suffragist Susan B. Anthony was fined $100 for attempting to vote for President Ulysses Grant. She never paid the fine.

1885 Historian and socialist reformer Will Durant was born in North Adams, Massachusetts.

1893 American writer and journalist Willa Cather began contributing to the *Nebraska State Journal* for which she was paid $1 per column. She would later become one of the country's foremost novelists, whose carefully crafted prose conveys vivid pictures of the American landscape and the people it molded. Influenced by the prose of the American regional writer Sarah Orne Jewett, Cather set many of her works in Nebraska and the American Southwest, areas with which she was familiar from her childhood.

1911 Calbraith P. Rodgers arrived in Pasadena, California, completing the first transcontinental airplane trip in forty-nine days.

1930 When Sinclair Lewis received a phone call from a Swedish newspaper correspondent telling him he was the first American to win the Nobel Prize for literature, Lewis thought it was a prank and began imitating the man's accent.

1938 Arturo Toscanini conducted the premiere performances of Samuel Barber's *Adagio for Strings and Essay for Orchestra no. 1* with the NBC Symphony in New York City. This was the first time that Toscanini and the NBC Orchestra performed works by an American composer.

1940 President Franklin Roosevelt won an unprecedented third term in office as he defeated Republican challenger Wendell L. Willkie.

1946 Republicans captured control of both the Senate and the House in midterm elections after more than a decade and a half of New Deal Democratic rule.

1956 Britain and France started landing forces in Egypt during fighting between Egyptian and Israeli forces around the Suez Canal. A cease-fire was declared two days later.

1974 Ella T. Grasso was elected governor of Connecticut, the first woman to win a gubernatorial office without succeeding her husband.

Such is the irresistible nature of truth that all it asks, and all it wants, is the liberty of appearing.
[THOMAS PAINE (1737–1809)]

NOVEMBER

<table>
<tr><td>1646</td><td>The fledgling Massachusetts Bay Colony passed a law prohibiting its people from denying that the Bible is the Word of God. For the Puritans who founded the colony, and for John Cotton, their leader, it made sense for them to have a theocratic government in which the laws ruling society are also the laws of God as found in the Bible. Though they did not strictly combine church and state, they believed that both institutions had their source in God, and both should look to the Bible as the source for standards, direction, and guidance.</td></tr>
</table>

FEAST DAY

St. Demetrian of Khytri, St. Melaine, St. Barlaam of Khutyn, St. Leonard of Noblac, St. Winnoc, St. Illtud

6

The distinctively American bandmaster John Philip Sousa was born on this day in 1854 in the nation's capital. It was an appropriate place for him to make his entry into the world because he would ultimately be known for his patriotic marches.

From his earliest childhood, he was musically inclined. He took up instruments like other children took up hobbies. By the age of thirteen he was apprenticed to the Marine Band, the official band of the president of the United States, and by the time he was eighteen he had begun to play the violin in theater orchestras. Appointed leader of the Marine Band in 1880, he resigned twelve years later to form his own band—through which he was able to achieve great popularity during many tours of America and Europe.

Sousa was an uncompromising perfectionist. As a result he was able to raise the performance and instrumentation of his concert band to a whole new level. He wed popular music with art music in a way that had not been attempted since the early days of the baroque period.

Though he was actually quite diverse in his sundry compositions, he wrote so many marches that he eventually became known as the "March King." Indeed, his marches were immediately recognizable as both distinctively American and musically innovative. His most stirring works included "Semper Fidelis" (1888), "The Washington Post March" (1889), "King Cotton" (1897), and the most popular of all, his classic "Stars and Stripes Forever" (1897).

In addition to his marches, Sousa composed eleven comic operas and two symphonic poems. He also invented the sousaphone, a large bass tuba with circular coiling chamber and an upright bell, which was particularly useful for marching bands.

He wrote an autobiography, *Marching Along* (1928), which documented his remarkable career in music as well as profiled the tumultuous world of the fine arts at the turn of the century.

NOVEMBER

1315 Dante Alighieri was sentenced to death, in abstentia, by the city magistrates in Florence after he ignored their efforts to force his return from exile in Venice where he was working on his literary masterpiece *The Divine Comedy*.

1558 The English dramatist Thomas Kyd was born in London.

1671 Colley Cibber—the English actor, dramatist, poet, and hero of Alexander Pope's famous epic *Dunciad*—was born in London.

1860 Polish patriot, composer, and pianist Ignace Jan Paderewski was born at Kurylowka, Powdolia. When he died in 1941 during the Second World War, he was interred at Arlington National Cemetery until the end of the war, but his family decided to leave his remains there when Poland fell into the hands of the Soviets. In May of 1963, President John F. Kennedy dedicated a plaque to Paderewski and pledged that he could be returned to his native land when it was freed. Paderewski's remains were moved to Poland in 1992, following the fall of Communism and Poland's first free national elections.

1861 Jefferson Davis, a former United States senator from Mississippi, was elected to a six-year term as president of the Confederacy.

1880 Novelist Robert Musil was born in Klagenfurt, Austria.

1888 Benjamin Harrison of Indiana won the presidential election, defeating incumbent Grover Cleveland by gaining the required number of electoral votes, even though Cleveland led in the popular vote.

1893 Composer Peter Ilyich Tchaikovsky died in St. Petersburg, Russia, at age fifty-three.

1913 Mohandas K. Gandhi was arrested as he led a march of Indian miners in South Africa. He was born in Porbandar in 1869, and educated in law at University College, London. Gandhi was hired by an Indian law firm to represent their interests in South Africa. Arriving there, Gandhi was appalled at the widespread denial of civil liberties and political rights to Indian immigrants. It was during his time there that he began to teach a policy of passive resistance to and noncooperation with the authorities. Part of the inspiration for this policy came from the Russian writer Leo Tolstoy, whose influence on Gandhi was profound. Following the First World War, he began advocating home rule for his homeland. Indeed, he soon became the international symbol of a free India. He lived a spiritual and ascetic life of prayer, fasting, and meditation. Many began to call him *Mahatma* or "Great Soul," and he was revered as a saint. Eventually his long and arduous campaign won Indian independence. But just four years later, as he was on his way to his evening prayer meeting, he was assassinated by a Hindu fanatic. Nevertheless, the teachings of Gandhi came to inspire nonviolent movements elsewhere, notably in the U.S. under the civil rights leader Martin Luther King Jr.

1928 In a first, the results of Herbert Hoover's election victory over Alfred E. Smith were flashed on an electric sign outside the *New York Times* Building.

*M*ake yourself an honest man, and then you will be sure there is one rascal less in the world.

[THOMAS CARLYLE (1795–1881)]

NOVEMBER

Ralph Abernathy, a civil rights pioneer, was confirmed as the president of the Southern Christian Leadership Council—an organization he had founded with Martin Luther King Jr. eleven years earlier—on this day in 1968. Both the movement and the organization were still wracked by grief following the assassination of King the previous April. Nevertheless, Abernathy soldiered on in the cause of justice for the poor and dispossessed.

He was born in rural Alabama in 1926. His parents determined that he would have the educational advantages they never had—just three generations removed from slavery. He studied at Alabama State College and was ordained a Baptist minister in 1948. In 1951, he moved to Montgomery where he received a master's in sociology and became pastor of the prestigious First Baptist Church. He befriended a fellow pastor in the community, Martin Luther King Jr., and together the men led the successful boycott of the Montgomery bus system in 1955, protesting segregated public transportation.

In 1957, convinced that their efforts should be replicated all across the country, the men joined with several other prominent African-American clergymen in establishing the SCLC to coordinate nonviolent resistance to segregation. The organization quickly became the dynamic center of the cluster of organizations that made up the civil rights movement. It differed from such broad-based national organizations as the Student Nonviolent Coordinating Committee and the National Association for the Advancement of Colored People, because it concentrated all its energies on justice for the poor—regardless of race. Some observers criticized the SCLC for being too dependent on white liberal support and, at a time of the rising Black Power movement, too moderate.

NOVEMBER

Abernathy demonstrated the brilliant strategic power of moderated nonviolence when in 1963 he organized a demonstration for seven hundred African-American children who marched from the 16th Street Baptist Church through town. After police wagons were filled, the children were carted to jail in school buses. When 2,500 more young protesters marched the next day, the police turned fire hoses on them, and the international press turned their lenses on Birmingham's police. The world saw pictures of black children being knocked down by a force of water so powerful that it tore the bark off nearby trees. Now under international pressure and the growing threat of a riot, Birmingham's officials returned to the bargaining table more willing to deal with SCLC. As a result of the Birmingham protest, SCLC won a desegregation settlement. More important, the protest laid the groundwork for the nation's 1964 Civil Rights Act.

After the assassination of Dr. King, criticism of Abernathy increased, and in 1977 he resigned from the organization he had founded to focus on his work as a pastor. He became increasingly alienated from the new liberal leadership and became one of the founders of the new black conservative movement—a movement he claimed his friend Dr. King would have heartily endorsed.

1811 William Henry Harrison and his soldiers defeated the Indians at the Tippecanoe River in Indiana. Harrison's acquired nickname of Tippecanoe served him well in successful political campaigns for governor of Indiana and president of the United States.

1874 The elephant was first associated with the Republican Party in a satirical cartoon by Thomas Nast published in *Harper's Weekly*.

1917 Russia's Bolshevik Revolution took place as forces led by Vladimir Ilyich Lenin overthrew the democratic government of Alexander Kerensky in the city of St. Petersburg. A bitter civil war would take place over the course of the next six years in an effort to consolidate Communist rule over all of Russia and its neighboring states.

1918 Christian evangelist Billy Graham was born in Charlotte, North Carolina. His evangelistic crusades would ultimately reach nearly a quarter billion people in person, and millions more were able to see or hear him on radio, television, and film. He was welcomed behind the Iron Curtain, into China and North Korea, and on every continent. His life story is one of the most remarkable of any other man during the last half of the twentieth century. The son of a North Carolina farmer, Graham was educated at Bob Jones University, the Florida Bible Institute, and Wheaton College. He was ordained in 1939 and became pastor of a local church in Western Springs, Illinois, a few years later. But in 1949 Graham turned to large-scale evangelism and embarked on a series of tours of the United States and Europe. A forceful, eloquent, and charismatic preacher, he attracted vast and enthusiastic audiences to his meetings. Graham also became known through televised films of

his rallies; through his own motion pictures; through *Decision* magazine; through the radio program *The Hour of Decision;* and through a syndicated column. He also wrote a host of bestselling books including *Peace with God, The Secret of Happiness, World Aflame, How to Be Born Again,* and *Hope for the Troubled Heart*. In his autobiography, *Just As I Am,* he discussed his relationship with heads of state as diverse as Queen Elizabeth II, the Shah of Iran, Kim Il Sung, every president from Truman to Clinton, and every Soviet premier from Khrushchev to Gorbachev. Graham also shares such memorable encounters as his plane trip with civil rights leader Martin Luther King, during which an engine caught fire, and his tragic unsuccessful attempt to warn President Kennedy about the danger of his trip to Dallas. He became, without question, the single greatest evangelist of the modern era.

1929 The Museum of Modern Art in New York City opened to the public.

1933 The Marx Brothers' *Duck Soup* was released in theaters. This movie contains some of the most memorable scenes of the wacky brothers.

1962 Richard M. Nixon, having lost California's gubernatorial race, held what he called his "last press conference," telling reporters, "You won't have Dick Nixon to kick around anymore."

1962 Former first lady Eleanor Roosevelt died in New York City.

1973 Congress overrode President Richard Nixon's veto of the War Powers Act, which would have expanded a chief executive's power to wage war without congressional approval.

1998 John Glenn returned to Earth aboard the space shuttle *Discovery*, visibly weak but elated after a nine-day mission.

*T*he honest man takes pains, and then enjoys pleasures; the knave takes pleasure, and then suffers pains.

[BENJAMIN FRANKLIN (1706–1790)]

NOVEMBER

On this day in 1787, Richard Allen and a number of other African-American Methodists arrived at St. George's Methodist Episcopal Church in Philadelphia, Pennsylvania, to attend Sunday services. They were directed toward a newly built seating gallery, and mistakenly sat in its "white" section. During a prayer, white ushers pulled the black worshippers to their feet and demanded that they sit in the "proper" section. Humiliated, Allen—a former slave from Delaware who had joined the Wesleyan movement because of its work against slavery and who eventually became a licensed Methodist preacher—and several others left the church at the prayer's end. "They were no more plagued with us in the church," he later said dryly.

Similar indignities were suffered by African-American Christians all across both the North and the South. There were incidents where children were refused baptism because white pastors refused to take the infants into their arms. Likewise free black parishioners were often forced to wait until all the whites had been served the Lord's Supper before they were admitted to the table. There were even conflicts over access to cemeteries.

In response to such discrimination, African-American Methodists in Baltimore and Philadelphia began holding separate prayer meetings as early as 1786, two years after Methodism had made its way to American shores. Allen tried to buy a separate building for such meetings, but abandoned his plan in the face of white hostility. Recognizing the importance of black self-reliance, Allen, Absalom Jones, and others formed the Free African Society—a benevolent organization whose commitment to abolition and the aiding of blacks in times of need became a model for other societies nationwide. But they were still dependent on dominant Methodist institutions.

By 1794 Philadelphia's black Methodists had raised enough money to build their own church, which a majority of the congregation voted to align with the Episcopalians rather than with the Methodists. They named it the St. Thomas African Episcopal Church. Allen, however, believed that "no religious sect or denomination would suit the capacity of the colored people as well as the Methodists, for the plain and simple gospel suits best for any people." Thus, he purchased a blacksmith shop with his own money and converted it into a storefront church. Methodist Bishop Frances Asbury named it the Bethel African Methodist Episcopal Church.

By 1816 black Methodists, still facing persistent discrimination, had come to believe that separate churches were not enough. Allen and a number of other prominent African-American pastors decided to organize under the name the African Methodist Episcopal Church. Afterward, they successfully sued for independence before the Supreme Court of Pennsylvania. Not surprisingly, Richard Allen became the first AME bishop.

FEAST DAY
The Four Crowned Martyrs, St. Cuby or Cybi, St. Godfrey of Amiens, St. Deusdedit, St. Willehad, St. Tysilio or Suliau

NOVEMBER

1414 In the Swiss town of Constance in excess of fifty thousand people from all of Europe convened at the Council of Constance. The throng included 33 cardinals, 238 bishops, a thousand university scholars, representatives of 83 kings, and 2,000 musicians. It was reported that 700 prostitutes also converged on the city. The atmosphere was more like a fair with tournaments, dances, acrobatic shows, and music. It was hardly the scene of sober piety one might have expected at a church gathering. The council met from 1414 to 1417 to resolve the Great Schism between Gregory, Benedict, and John XXIII, each of whom claimed to be pope. Ridding the church of all three, the council persuaded Gregory and Benedict to resign, and deposed John by convicting him on charges of simony, sodomy, lying, and unchastity. The council then elected Martin V as the new pope. John Wycliffe's translation of the Bible into English was branded as heresy, and the Bohemian Jan Hus was likewise condemned.

1731 The first circulating library in the United States was organized by Benjamin Franklin in Philadelphia.

1793 William Carey, the father of modern missions, landed in India to begin his ministry there. At Calcutta, Carey and his family had to sneak ashore in a rowboat because East India Company laws forbade missionaries to land there. Over the next few years, suffering from poverty, malaria, and the deaths of his son and invalid wife, Carey struggled forward. He supervised the translation of the Bible into thirty-four Asian languages, wrote dictionaries in four Indian languages, started the Horticultural Society of India, and founded the still-influential Serampore College. Carey also founded nineteen mission stations, more than one hundred schools, the first newspaper in India, and led the successful fight to outlaw sati, the practice of burning widows. A motto from one of Carey's sermons tells the story of his life: "Expect great things from God; attempt great things for God."

1802 British politician Sir Benjamin Hall was born in England. As the Minister of Works, his name became attached to the famous clock tower above the Houses of Parliament—Big Ben.

1889 Montana became the forty-first state.

1923 Adolf Hitler launched his first attempt at seizing power with a failed coup in Munich, Germany, that came to be known as the Beer-Hall Putsch.

1933 President Franklin Roosevelt created the Civil Works Administration, designed to create jobs for more than four million unemployed during the Great Depression.

1939 The play *Life with Father,* based on the book by Clarence Day, opened on Broadway.

1950 During the Korean conflict, the first jet-plane battle took place as American Air Force Lieutenant Russell J. Brown shot down a North Korean MiG-15.

1966 Former actor and conservative commentator Ronald Reagan was elected governor of California.

1994 Midterm elections resulted in Republicans winning a majority in the Senate while at the same time gaining control of the House for the first time in forty years.

I had rather starve and rot and keep the privilege of speaking the truth than of holding all the offices that capital has to give, from the presidency downward.

[Henry Adams (1838–1918)]

NOVEMBER

On this day, the Berlin Wall, the most visible physical manifestation of the Iron Curtain, was breached and subsequently dismantled, and citizens from both West and East Berlin moved freely back and forth for the first time in twenty-eight years. The scene was veritable pandemonium as men and women, young and old, celebrated the symbolic collapse of Communism.

Built in 1961 at the insistence of their Communist masters in the Soviet Union, the wall was maintained by the German Democratic Republic, commonly known as East Germany. It quickly became a symbol of the Cold War, the struggle between the Communist East and the Democratic West.

At the end of the Second World War in 1945, while the Western Allies helped to rebuild a free Germany in the areas they controlled, the Soviets imposed a fierce Communist regime in areas they continued to control. Thus, the nation was divided into a free West Germany and an enslaved East. The city of Berlin, though entirely surrounded by the Soviet sphere, was similarly partitioned into East Berlin and West Berlin. Between 1949 when East Germany was established and the middle of 1961, nearly three million people fled the tyranny of the East German regime—more than half of them through West Berlin.

In 1961 the East German government decided to stop this flight to the West. Its standing military and members of its militia surrounded West Berlin with temporary fortifications that were rapidly replaced by a concrete wall, 12 feet high and 103 miles long, of which 28 miles lay between two sides of the city. Where a wall was not possible, buildings were bricked-up. The only openings in the wall were two closely guarded crossing points. Although the Communist government announced that the wall was needed to prevent military aggression and political interference from West Germany, the East Germans built tank traps and ditches along the eastern side of the wall, demonstrating that it was actually constructed to keep its own citizens within the prison state. Between 1961 and 1989, a few desperate East Germans managed to escape to West Berlin, but at least a hundred people died trying to cross the border.

In the summer of 1989, the Berlin Wall became practically irrelevant when Hungary allowed East Germans to pass through Hungary on their way to Austria and West Germany. Following a dramatic revival of the Lutheran churches in the city and the near collapse of the East German regime, enthusiastic citizens began to demolish whole sections of the wall without interference from government officials. East Germany eventually reunited with West Germany as one nation.

The Berlin Wall is now commemorated by a few remaining sections and by a museum and shop near the site of the most famous crossing point, Checkpoint Charlie.

NATIONAL DAY
Cambodia
FEAST DAY
St. Theodore the Recruit, St. Vitronus or Vanne, St. Benignus or Benen

NOVEMBER

1674 The great English poet John Milton died at the age of sixty-five in London. He was buried next to his father in the chancel of St. Giles in Cripplegate.

1900 Theodore Dresser's first novel, *Sister Carrie,* was published by Doubleday and Page. The book sold only 456 copies before it was pulled from bookstore shelves. Nevertheless, Dresser went on to attain literary fame and is counted among the most influential writers of the century.

1906 Theodore Roosevelt became the first president to visit countries outside of the United States in an official capacity when he took a seventeen-day trip to Puerto Rico and Panama.

1918 Germany's Kaiser Wilhelm II announced he would abdicate. He then fled to the Netherlands where he lived out his days.

1938 Known as *Kristallnacht* (Night of Broken Glass) for the smashing of storefront windows, on this night more than thirty thousand Jews were arrested while synagogues and Jewish businesses were destroyed throughout Germany.

1953 Author-poet Dylan Thomas died in St. Vincent's Hospital at age thirty-nine. His death was the result of drinking eighteen straight whiskeys in a New York tavern.

1965 The Great Northeast Blackout, in which 80,000 square miles were affected, began at 5:16 P.M. The power failure hit 30 million people in New York, Connecticut, Rhode Island, Massachusetts, Vermont, New Hampshire, and Ontario, Canada, for up to thirteen and a half hours. Since the blackout occurred during rush hour, 800,000 people were trapped in New York subways, elevators, and skyscrapers until power was restored.

1970 Former French president and hero of the Second World War, French general and statesman, the architect of the Fifth French Republic and its first president, Charles de Gaulle, died at age seventy-nine. During the First World War he served with distinction at the Battle of Verdun, was wounded three times, and was finally taken prisoner by the Germans. After the war he was aide-de-camp to Marshal Henri Pétain. De Gaulle won prominence for his advocacy of a highly mechanized French army that he described in his books on military tactics. After the fall of France at the beginning of the Second World War he escaped to London, where he announced the formation of a French national committee in exile. As president of the Free French, de Gaulle commanded French troops fighting with the Allied armies as well as those participating in the Resistance in German-occupied France. After the Allies liberated France, De Gaulle became provisional premier. Two months later though, he resigned due to political wrangling. In 1947 he organized a new political movement, the Rassemblement du Peuple Français. In the 1951 elections, the RPF won the largest number of seats in the French Assembly. The RPF worked to strengthen the central government, balance the budget, promote private enterprise, and remove state controls on the economic life of France. Once again De Gaulle felt he could retire. But conflicts tore at the fabric of France again and he was recalled to serve as premier. The National Assembly granted him power to rule by decree for six months and to supervise the drafting of a new constitution. The new charter was overwhelmingly approved by the French voters. The following December De Gaulle was elected president of the newly created Fifth Republic. In 1969 he retired once again to his private estate in Colombey-les-deux-Églises, and there he continued to work on his memoirs until his death.

NOVEMBER

The graveyards of Paris are filled with indispensable men.

[CHARLES DE GAULLE (1890–1970)]

1919

The American Legion held its first national convention, in Minneapolis. Its mission was to offer support for American veterans and their families. The forerunner of the Veterans Administration was created in 1921 as a result of efforts by the Legion. The organization also authored the first draft of the Serviceman's Readjustment Act, and became a major sponsor of the Boy Scouts.

According to tradition, on this day in the year 432, a young British monk—formerly held captive as a slave by the very people he now sought to serve—arrived in Ireland to begin his ministry.

Patrick was said to have been born at one of the little Christian towns near present-day Glasglow—either Bonavern or Belhaven. Although his mother taught him the Christian faith, he preferred the passing pleasures of sin. One day while playing by the sea, Irish pirates captured Patrick and sold him into slavery on a farm in Ireland. Alone in the fields, caring for sheep, Patrick began to remember the Word of God his mother had taught him. Regretting his past life of selfish pleasure-seeking, he turned to Christ as his Savior.

Writing of his conversion, Patrick later wrote, "I was sixteen years old and knew not the true God and was carried away captive; but in that strange land the Lord opened my unbelieving eyes, and although late I called my sins to mind, and was converted with my whole heart to the Lord my God, who regarded my low estate, had pity on my youth and ignorance, and consoled me as a father consoles his children. Every day I used to look after sheep and I used to pray often during the day, the love of God and fear of him increased more and more in me and my faith began to grow and my spirit stirred up, so that in one day I would pray as many as a hundred times and nearly as many at night. Even when I was staying out in the woods or on the mountain, I used to rise before dawn for prayer, in snow and frost and rain, and I felt no ill effect and there was no slackness in me. As I now realize, it was because the Spirit was glowing in me."

Eventually rescued through a remarkable turn of events, Patrick returned to his family in Britain. But his heart increasingly longed to return to his Irish captors and share the gospel of Jesus Christ with them. He sought theological training on the Continent and gained a warrant to evangelize his former captors in Ireland.

When he finally did return, Patrick preached to the pagan tribes in the Irish language he had learned as a slave. Many accepted Christ, and soon heathen songs were replaced with hymns praising Jesus Christ as Lord. Patrick once wrote that God's grace had so blessed his efforts that thousands were "born again to God" through his ministry. Killen, a prominent historian of Ireland, wrote, "There can be no reasonable doubt that Patrick preached the gospel, that he was a most zealous and efficient evangelist, and that he is entitled to be called the Apostle of Ireland."

Patrick ministered to the Irish for more than fifty years until he died in 493. Tradition asserts that he reached and baptized in excess of a hundred thousand people.

FEAST DAY
St. Leo the Great, St. Justus of Canterbury, St. Aedh MacBrice, St. Theoctista, St. Andrew Avellino

10

NOVEMBER

1483 Martin Luther, the Augustinian monk who became the founder and leader of the German Reformation, was born in Eisleben, Saxony.

1697 William Hogarth, the famed English painter and engraver, was born in London.

1759 German poet, historian, and dramatist Friedrich von Schiller was born in Marbach. The son of an army officer and estate manager for the duke of Württemberg, he was educated at the duke's military school and then studied law and medicine. In 1780 he was appointed physician to a military regiment stationed in Stuttgart. As a student, Schiller wrote poetry and finished his first play, *The Robbers*, which was successfully presented in 1782 at the National Theater in Mannheim. Arrested by the duke for leaving Württemberg without permission in order to witness the production, Schiller was forbidden to publish further dramatic works, but in September 1782 he escaped from prison. During the next ten years, Schiller lived and wrote, often under assumed names to avoid discovery and possible extradition to Württemberg, in various parts of Germany, including Mannheim, Leipzig, Dresden, and Weimar. On the strength of his *Defection of the Netherlands* and through the recommendation of the poet Johann Wolfgang von Goethe, he was appointed professor of history at the University of Jena in 1790. Through Goethe's influence Schiller turned from philosophical writing back to the writing of poetry and plays, and his last years proved to be the most productive of his life. In 1799 he completed his masterpiece, *Wallenstein*, a three-part work in verse that includes a narrative prologue and two full-length dramas. Among his other remarkable works were the *History of the Thirty Years' War, Letters on the Aesthetic Education of Man, The Song of the Bell*, and the famed *Ode to Joy*—which was set to music by the composer Ludwig van Beethoven in the Ninth Symphony. If Goethe was Germany's Shakespeare then Schiller was her Milton.

1885 Paul Daimler, son of the German engineer Gottlieb Daimler, test-drove his father's new invention—the motorcycle.

1888 At the age of thirteen, Austrian violinist Fritz Kreisler made his American debut at Steinway Hall in New York, beginning a long and distinguished career.

1928 Hirohito was enthroned as emperor of Japan.

1951 Direct-dial coast-to-coast telephone service began as the mayor of Englewood, New Jersey, called his counterpart in Alameda, California.

1954 The Iwo Jima Memorial—the only memorial to the veterans of the Second World War in or around the nation's capital—was dedicated.

1969 The Children's Television Workshop presented the debut of *Sesame Street* on 170 Public Broadcasting Stations and 20 commercial outlets. Since that time, whole generations of children have learned that education must be passive and entertaining, that information does not build on itself from yesterday's program, and that daycare, alternative lifestyles, and other such elements of liberal politics are normal.

1982 The newly completed Vietnam Veterans Memorial was opened to its first visitors in Washington, D.C.

We should remember that it is no honor or profit merely to appear in the arena, but the wreath is for those who contend aright.

[JAMES A. GARFIELD (1831–1881)]

NOVEMBER

Martin of Tours was a bishop who was martyred on this day in 397. Also on this day in 655, Martin of Umbria was martyred during the great Monothelite controversy. Both men demonstrated perseverance in the face of political persecution, personal humiliation, torture, starvation, and eventually, death, which made them models of faith during the early medieval period. According to legend, Martin of Tours once cut his own coat in half to share it with a beggar. Part of the cloak was saved and considered a holy relic in France, with monarchs going so far as to carry it into battle. The cloak was kept in a "chapelle," from the French word *chape,* meaning "cape," and its overseer was the "chapelain," from which, of course, we get our words *chapel* and *chaplain.* During his final imprisonment, Martin of Umbria diligently kept the fasts of the Little Pascha, as Advent was then called, though he was already dying of hunger.

FEAST DAY
St. Martin of Tours, St. Bartholomew of Grottaferata, St. Mannas of Egypt, St. Theodore the Studite

Drafted and signed on board the *Mayflower* as that ship approached Cape Cod on this day in 1620, the Mayflower Compact is regarded as one of the most important documents in American history. It proves the determination of the small group of English separatist Christians to live under a rule of law, based on the consent of the people, and to set up their own civil government. The parchment has long since disappeared—the current text was first printed in London in 1622 in a pamphlet generally known as *Mourt's Relation,* which contained extracts from the fledgling colony's journals and histories.

In an oration delivered at Plymouth in 1802, John Quincy Adams declared that it was "perhaps the only instance, in human history, of that positive, original social compact, which speculative philosophers have imagined as the only legitimate source of government." Thus, the Pilgrim Fathers had anticipated the social contract 70 years before John Locke and 140 years before Jean Jacques Rousseau.

The document was concise and to the point, beginning with the commitment of the signers to providence, "In the name of God Amen." With that invocation, the document declared the intention of their compact: "We whose names are underwritten, the loyal subjects of our dread sovereign Lord King James by the grace of God, of Great Britain, France, and Ireland king, defender of the faith, having undertaken, for the glory of God, and advancements of the Christian faith and honor of our king and country, a voyage to plant the first colony in the Northern parts of Virginia, do by these presents solemnly and mutually in the presence of God, and one of another, covenant and combine our selves together into a civil body politic; for our better ordering, and preservation and furtherance of the ends aforesaid; and by virtue hearof to enact, constitute, and frame such just and equal laws, ordinances, acts, constitutions, and offices, from time to time, as shall be thought most meet and convenient for the general good of the Colony: unto which we promise all due submission and obedience."

NOVEMBER

Following those declarations the new experiment in American liberty was sealed by the signatures of forty-one of the Pilgrims. One of the greatest chapters in human history had just begun.

1647 Massachusetts passed the first compulsory school law in the colonies.

1821 Russian novelist Fyodor Mikhaylovich Dostoyevsky was born in Moscow. Author of *The Brothers Karamazov, Crime and Punishment,* and *The Idiot,* Dostoyevsky was convicted of being a political revolutionist and, rather than having his death sentence carried out, was sent to a prison in Siberia, where he eventually served in the army.

1831 Former slave Nat Turner, who had led a violent insurrection, was executed in Jerusalem, Virginia.

1851 Alvan Clark of Cambridge, Massachusetts, patented the telescope.

1889 Richard Strauss's tone poem "Don Juan" was premiered and conducted by the composer in Weimar. He wrote that "the sound was wonderful, with an immense glow and sumptuousness." The audience received it most enthusiastically.

1889 Washington became the forty-second state.

1909 The construction of the naval base at Pearl Harbor began in a location chosen because "it is defensible against any potential threat from Japan."

1918 At 5:00 A.M., in a railway car in the Forest of Compiegne, France, Allied and Central Powers signed the armistice that ended the First World War. The cease-fire was to commence six hours later—thus Winston Churchill's immortal phrase, "At the eleventh hour on the eleventh day of the eleventh month silence fell across the battlefields of Europe."

1921 President Warren Harding dedicated the Tomb of the Unknown Soldier in Arlington National Cemetery.

1922 American novelist Kurt Vonnegut Jr. was born in Indianapolis, Indiana. Known for his pessimistic and satirical novels, he is most famous for his blending of fantasy and science fiction with historical fact to heighten the horror of twentieth-century life. His novel *Slaughterhouse-Five* blends his experiences as a prisoner of war during World War II with aliens who are resigned to a fatalistic philosophy.

1939 Kate Smith first sang Irving Berlin's "God Bless America" on network radio.

1940 The jeep was introduced as a vehicle for the American armed forces. It was designed to combine the sturdiness and capacity of a truck with the speed and mobility of a car. It was called a peep at first, but during the Second World War, the name jeep was attached to it from the contraction of General-Purpose or "GP" vehicle.

1972 The U.S. Army turned over its base at Long Bihn to the South Vietnamese army, symbolizing the end of direct American military involvement in the Vietnam War.

1992 Despite twenty centuries of consensus on the biblical imperatives, the Church of England voted to ordain women as priests.

All the evils in our now extensive catalogue flow from a falsified picture of the world which, for our immediate concern, results in an inability to interpret current happenings.

[RICHARD WEAVER (1910–1963)]

NOVEMBER

663

A patriot who signed the Declaration of Independence and the Articles of Confederation but refused to sign the Constitution, Elbridge Gerry (1744–1814) worked vigorously for independence from the "prostituted government of Great Britain," yet feared the dangers of "too much democracy." At the Constitutional Convention, Gerry refused to sign the Constitution because he could not accept the proposed division of powers or the absence of a Bill of Rights. Although he championed the people and their rights, he believed that the common man could be too easily swayed by unprincipled politicians for democracy to work. But he was not altogether consistent, for he was also jealous of power, fearful of possible tyranny.

Devoted to the patriots' cause in the early 1770s, Gerry was active as a member of the Massachusetts committee of correspondence and the first Provincial Congress. As one of the Congress's committee of safety, he was almost captured by British troops the night before the Battles of Lexington and Concord. In the Continental Congress he supported the Articles of Confederation—with equal representation for all states, large and small.

Gerry represented his district in the first session of the Congress, but he refused to run after two terms. However, he was called to further service when, in 1797, President Adams selected him as a commissioner to France, along with John Marshall and Charles Pinckney, to attempt to improve American relations with the revolutionary French government. French agents—identified as X, Y, and Z—insulted the commissioners by seeking bribes, and Marshall and Pinckney left. Gerry stayed and tried to negotiate with Talleyrand—albeit unsuccessfully. Even so, upon his return on this day a year later, Gerry was able to claim credit for reducing the tensions between France and America.

As governor of Massachusetts, in 1812 Gerry approved an unusual redistricting that favored his Democratic-Republican Party; one of the more extreme districts, shaped something like a salamander, was depicted by a cartoonist as a beast labeled "Gerrymander"—a term that has become a part of America's political language. Gerry was elected vice president when Madison was elected to a second term in 1812, and was serving in his official capacity when he died suddenly. Ironically, he was riding to the Capitol to perform the duties of president of the Senate, a constitutional function of the vice president that he had objected to in 1787, and one of the reasons he had refused to sign the U.S. Constitution.

NOVEMBER

1840 French sculptor Auguste Rodin was born in Paris. He studied art on his own and in a free school for artisans. A trip to Italy in 1875 brought him in contact with the works of Donatello and Michelangelo from which he learned aspects of movement. His goal was to portray a truthful representation of the psychological inner state of the subject through texture and modeling. For Rodin, beauty in art consisted in the truthful representation of inner states, and to this end he often subtly distorted anatomy. His sculpture, in bronze and marble, falls generally into two styles. The more characteristic style reveals a deliberate roughness of form and a painstaking surface modeling; the other is marked by a polished surface and delicacy of form.

1912 Frederick Rodman Law, the first stunt actor, jumped from a dynamited balloon into the Hudson River. Previously that year, he had parachuted from the Statue of Liberty in January and jumped from the Brooklyn Bridge on April 14.

1920 Baseball got its first czar as Judge Kenesaw Mountain Landis was elected commissioner of the American and National Leagues. He was born in Millville, Ohio, and practiced law in Chicago from 1891 until 1905, when he was appointed United States district judge for the northern district of Illinois by President Theodore Roosevelt. In 1907 he found the Standard Oil Company of Indiana guilty of illegal rebating and imposed a fine of more than $29 million. The judgment was later reversed by a higher court, but the trial attracted national attention. In 1920, when it was discovered that several players of the Chicago White Sox, an American League baseball team, had apparently accepted bribes from gamblers and deliberately lost the 1919 World Series, baseball club owners appointed Landis commissioner for the major and minor leagues. As baseball's first commissioner, Landis was granted absolute powers to govern every phase of the game and eliminate all dishonest and unfair practices. He served in this office until his death, and his rigid supervision and impartial judgments renewed public esteem for baseball. Landis was elected to the Baseball Hall of Fame in 1944, the year of his death.

1921 Representatives of nine nations gathered for the start of the Washington Conference for Limitation of Armaments.

1927 Joseph Stalin became the undisputed ruler of the Soviet Union as Leon Trotsky was expelled from the Communist Party.

1929 Grace Kelly—the future movie star and Princess of Monaco—was born in Philadelphia.

1948 Former Japanese premier Hideki Tojo and several other World War Two Japanese leaders were sentenced to death by a war crimes tribunal.

1980 Scientists learned much more about Saturn, including the discovery of many more rings, when *Voyager 1* flew within seventy-seven thousand miles of the planet.

1981 The space shuttle *Columbia STS-2* was launched from Kennedy Space Center, Florida, as the first spacecraft to be launched for a second orbiting mission. Aboard were astronauts Joe Engle and Richard Truly.

1982 Former KGB chief Yuri V. Andropov was elected to succeed the late Leonid I. Brezhnev as general secretary of the Soviet Communist Party's Central Committee.

1990 Emperor Akihito of Japan formally assumed the Chrysanthemum Throne.

The streets of hell are paved with good intentions.

[MARK TWAIN (1835–1910)]

NOVEMBER

Robert Louis Balfour Stevenson was born on this day in 1850. His father was a remarkably gifted and driven engineer responsible for the building of more than forty lighthouses around Britain. Stevenson was an only child who suffered from ill health, but under the weight of paternal expectations he started an engineering course at Edinburgh University.

But his heart's desire—from the time he was a small boy—was to become a professional writer and eventually, as a compromise with his father, he determined to study instead for a law degree, becoming an advocate in 1875. He thought that he might follow in the footsteps of his hero Sir Walter Scott—practicing law by day and writing by night. Alas, he was never patient enough or strong enough for that.

He began to write far more than he practiced law. His earliest works were actually descriptions of his journeys taken while on holiday—for example, *An Inland Voyage*, about a canoe trip through Belgium and France in 1876, and *Travels with a Donkey in the Cévennes*, an account of a journey on foot through mountains in southern France in 1878. On yet another holiday in France he met Fanny Vandegrift Osbourne, an American who was ten years his senior. Despite disapproval from his father, he followed her across America and married her in San Francisco. However, he had contracted tuberculosis and spent the following years trying to find places conducive to allaying his symptoms. Stevenson and his wife moved to Saranac Lake, New York, in 1887. In 1888 they sailed from San Francisco on a cruise across the South Pacific. In 1889 they settled in Samoa on the island of Upolu in a final effort to restore Stevenson's health.

Despite such restlessness and his chronic ill health, Stevenson was amazingly productive. He published the classic pirate story *Treasure Island* in 1882 and the thriller *Dr. Jekyll and Mr. Hyde* and *Kidnapped* in 1886. While in America he started *The Master of Ballantrae*, set in Scotland and America, and he completed his classic tale of adventure *The Black Arrow*.

Stevenson wrote skillfully in a variety of genres. He employed the forms of essay and literary criticism in *Virginibus Puerisque*, *Familiar Studies of Men and Books*, and *Memories and Portraits*. Also critically well received were such travel and autobiographical pieces as *The Silverado Squatters*, which records Stevenson's impressions of his stay at a California mining camp, as well as *In the South Seas*, which describes his life in Polynesia. *A Child's Garden of Verses*, containing some of Stevenson's best-known poems, is regarded by many as one of the finest collections of poetry for children. His other verse collections include *Underwoods* and *Ballads*. Stevenson's short stories were published in *The New Arabian Nights* and *Island Nights' Entertainments*. He also collaborated with his stepson, American writer Lloyd Osbourne, in writing the novels *The Wrong Box* and *The Wrecker*.

NOVEMBER

He continued his flurry of literary activity throughout the sickly days he spent in Polynesia but unexpectedly died of a stroke in 1894. During his short life, he left a remarkable legacy—including some of the most beloved stories in the English literary tradtion.

354 The great African theologian Augustine of Hippo was born in Tagaste, Numidia, in present-day Algeria. His father, Patricius, was a pagan, but his mother, Monica, was a devout Christian who labored untiringly for her son's conversion and who was canonized by the church. Augustine was educated as a rhetorician in the North African cities of Madaura and Carthage. As a young man, he lived a dissolute life—indeed, between the ages of fifteen and thirty, he lived with a Carthaginian concubine who bore him a son, whom he named Adeodatus. Nevertheless, he was an inspired intellectual and thus, Augustine became an earnest seeker after truth. He considered becoming a Christian, but experimented with several philosophical systems before finally entering the church while teaching rhetoric in the city of Milan. Shortly afterward, he returned to North Africa and was ordained in 391. He became bishop of Hippo in 395, an office he held until his death. It was a period of political and theological unrest, for while the barbarians pressed in upon the empire, even sacking Rome itself in 410, schism and heresy also threatened the church. Augustine threw himself wholeheartedly into the theological battle, writing innumerable works of lasting significance—chief of which are his *Confessions* and *City of God*. Many scholars believe that in a very real sense these works established the principles upon which Western civilization would be established.

1789 Benjamin Franklin wrote a letter to a friend in which he said, "In this world nothing can be said to be certain, except death and taxes."

1797 The epic poem *The Rhyme of the Ancient Mariner* was begun as a collaborative effort of Samuel Taylor Coleridge and William Wordsworth while walking through the Valley of Stones near Lynmouth.

1868 Italian opera composer Giacchino Rossini died in Paris, France. He is best known for his operas *The Barber of Seville* and *William Tell*.

1895 The first canned pineapple from Hawaii arrived in the United States.

1927 The Holland Tunnel, the first underwater tunnel in the United States, opened to move traffic under the Hudson River from New York City to Jersey City, New Jersey. The tunnel consists of two tubes large enough for two lanes of traffic each.

1940 The Broadway theater in New York was the site of the premier of the Walt Disney animated film *Fantasia*—the first film to feature stereo sound. It was a box office failure until its 1967 rerelease.

1942 The minimum draft age was lowered from twenty-one to eighteen.

1956 The Supreme Court struck down laws calling for racial segregation on public buses.

1977 The comic strip "Li'l Abner" by Al Capp appeared in newspapers for the last time.

1979 Former California governor Ronald Reagan announced in New York his candidacy for the Republican presidential nomination.

1982 The Vietnam Veterans Memorial was officially dedicated in Washington.

1989 Polish labor-union leader Lech Walesa received the Medal of Freedom from President Bush during a White House ceremony.

We should learn to see things in a higher light.

[BOOKER T. WASHINGTON (1856-1915)]

NOVEMBER

1900

American composer Aaron Copland—best known for *Fanfare for the Common Man,* the ballets *Appalachian Spring, Rodeo,* and *Billy the Kid,* and his expansive American sound—was born in Brooklyn. He studied in New York City with the American composer Rubin Goldmark and in Paris with the influential French teacher Nadia Boulanger. Although his earliest work was heavily influenced by the French impressionists, he soon began to develop a personalized style. After experimenting with jazz rhythms in *Music for the Theater,* Copland turned to more austere and dissonant compositions. Concert pieces such as *Piano Variations* and *Statements* rely on nervous, irregular rhythms, angular melodies, and highly dissonant harmonies. But within a decade Copland turned to a simpler style, more melodic and lyrical, frequently drawing on elements of American folk music. His best works expressed distinctly American themes; in *Lincoln Portrait,* for orchestra and narrator, and in the ballets *Billy the Kid, Rodeo,* and *Appalachian Spring,* he utilized native themes and rhythms to capture the flavor of early American life. His music for films included *Of Mice and Men, Our Town,* and *The Heiress,* which won the Academy Award for best film score. Teaching at the Berkshire Music Center, Copland was a champion of the music of contemporary composers. His books include *What to Listen for in Music, Our New Music, Music and Imagination,* and *Copland on Music.*

FEAST DAY
St. Laurence O'Toole, St. Adeotus Aribert, St. Nicholas Tavelic, St. Dubricius or Dyfrig, St. Stephen of Como, St. Peter of Narbonne

NOVEMBER

Leonard Bernstein's rise to fame was the result of both diligent preparation and a stroke of providence. Bernstein studied composition at Harvard University and continued his studies in conducting, orchestration, and piano after he graduated. He further honed his conducting skills with Serge Koussevitsky at the Tanglewood Festival during the summers of 1940 and 1941. Due to his proficiency in conducting, he was appointed assistant conductor of the New York Philharmonic in 1943 at the age of twenty-five.

Bernstein's first recognition came on November 14, 1943, when he replaced an ailing conductor at the last moment in a nationally broadcast concert of the Philharmonic. His performance and skill earned him immediate attention and led to a series of conducting and teaching positions.

Bernstein eventually became the music director of the New York Philharmonic in 1958 as the first American-born and American-trained musician to attain such a prominent post. Bernstein helped to educate Americans in the area of music with his television broadcasts and series of best-selling books (*The Joy of Music, Leonard Bernstein's Young People's Concerts,* and *The Infinite Variety of Music*).

Although he was not a paragon of virtue and his own music openly displays his search for truth and meaning, Bernstein remains a good example of one who was faithful in the little things.

1615   The Puritan minister and writer Richard Baxter was born. In 1641 he became pastor in the church at Kidderminster, and his powerful preaching soon transformed the town. Visiting travelers reported that instead of widespread immorality, they began to hear praise and prayer coming from every house. With the outbreak of England's Civil War between king and Parliament, Baxter served for a time as chaplain to the parliamentary forces. Suffering from failing health and seemingly at the point of death, Baxter wrote the classic devotional works *The Saints' Everlasting Rest* and *Call to the Unconverted.*

1840   French impressionist painter Claude Monet was born in Paris. By the age of nineteen, he had committed himself to a career in art and he associated with Édouard Manet as well as rising artists Camille Pissarro, Pierre Auguste Renoir, and Alfred Sisley. Monet's desire was to capture the transient effects of light on canvas, and he sought to paint outside instead of in the studio. In 1874, he and other artists organized the first exhibition of this new style, which the press labeled Impressionism after Monet's painting *Impression: Sunrise* and the unfinished look of the works. He often painted the same subject numerous times at different points in the day, in different light, and in changing seasons.

1881   Charles J. Guiteau went on trial for assassinating President James Garfield. Guiteau was convicted and hanged the following year.

1889   Inspired by the fiction of Jules Verne, *New York World* reporter Nellie Bly set out to travel around the world in less than eighty days. She made the trip in seventy-two days.

1910   For the first time, an airplane took off from the deck of a ship—the USS *Birmingham*—off the coast of Norfolk, Virginia.

1922   The British Broadcasting Corporation began its domestic radio service.

1935   President Franklin Roosevelt proclaimed the Philippine Islands a free commonwealth.

1940   During the Second World War, German planes destroyed most of the English town of Coventry in a bombing raid.

1944   Tommy Dorsey and Orchestra recorded "Opus One" for RCA Victor.

1963   Off the coast of Iceland, a volcanic island lifted itself out of the ocean, rising to 567 feet in height and a mile in length in a matter of weeks. It was named Surtsey in honor of the legendary Norse giant.

1969   *Apollo 12* blasted off for the moon.

1972   The Dow-Jones industrial average closed above the 1,000 level for the first time, ending the day at 1000.16.

Things just don't turn up in this world until someone turns them up.

[JAMES A GARFIELD (1831–1881)]

NOVEMBER

669

The first constitution of the newly independent American nation was sent to the states for ratification on this day in 1777—though it would not be adopted until March 1, 1781. Throughout the Revolutionary War the Federal Union had been held together by a provisional government and both the nascent presidency and the assembled Congress had only such powers as the states afforded them by proxy. The new constitution—called the Articles of Confederation—enumerated the powers of both the federation and the individual states and was heralded as a great leap forward in republicanism.

The document began with a clear delineation of powers and authorities: "To all to whom these presents shall come, we the undersigned delegates of the states affixed to our names send greeting. Whereas, The delegates of the United States of America in Congress assembled did on the fifteenth day of November in the year of Our Lord one thousand seven hundred and seventy-seven, and in the second year of the independence of America, agree to certain articles of confederation and perpetual union between the states of New Hampshire, Massachusetts Bay, Rhode Island and Providence Plantations, Connecticut, New York, New Jersey, Pennsylvania, Delaware, Maryland, Virginia, North Carolina, South Carolina, and Georgia in the words following, viz: Articles of Confederation and perpetual union between the states of New Hampshire, Massachusetts Bay, Rhode Island and Providence Plantations, Connecticut, New York, New Jersey, Pennsylvania, Delaware, Maryland, Virginia, North Carolina, South Carolina, and Georgia. Done at Philadelphia in the state of Pennsylvania the ninth day of July in the year of Our Lord one thousand seven hundred and seventy-eight, and in the third year of the independence of America."

The Articles were actually written in 1776 and 1777 during the early part of the American Revolution by a committee of the Second Continental Congress. The head of the committee, John Dickinson, presented a report on the proposed articles to the Congress on July 12, 1776, eight days after the signing of the Declaration of Independence. Dickinson initially proposed a strong central government, with control over the western lands, equal representation for the states, and the power to levy taxes.

Because of their bitter experience with Great Britain, the thirteen states feared a powerful central government; consequently, they changed Dickinson's proposed articles drastically before they sent them to all the states for ratification. The Continental Congress had been careful to give the states as much independence as possible and to specify the limited functions of the federal government. Despite these precautions, several years passed before all the states ratified the Articles. The delay resulted from preoccupation with the Revolution and from disagreements among the states.

The final document laid out a kind of decentralized authority and a mixed government of checks and balances. Though it was eventually superceded by the new Constitution of 1789, the Articles of Confederation set the pattern for virtually all the guaranteed liberties that would become the hallmark of the American experiment in freedom.

FEAST DAY
St. Leopold of Austria; Saints Abibus, Gurias, and Samonas; St. Fintan of Rheinau; St. Malo or Machutus; St. Albert the Great; St. Desiderius or Didier of Cahors

NOVEMBER

1280 German theologian and music theorist Albertus Magnus—or Albertus de Bollstadt—who taught Thomas Aquinas, died on this day. Albertus wrote that a balance of proportions in music is delightful and a lack of it distasteful. He further wrote that just as beauty in the universe consists in antithesis, so in music "when rests are interposed in choral singing, it becomes sweeter than continuous sound." He brought together Scripture, the church fathers, earlier medieval exegesis, and scholarly writings including Aristotle.

1492 In his journal, Christopher Columbus noted the use of tobacco among the Indians. This was the first recorded reference to smoking.

1731 English poet and hymn writer William Cowper was born on this day in Great Berkhampstead, Hertfordshire. Despite bouts of depression, he wrote such hymns as "God Moves in a Mysterious Way" and "There Is a Fountain Filled with Blood."

1806 Explorer Zebulon Pike sighted the mountaintop now known as Pikes Peak.

1862 Nobel Prize–winning dramatist, poet, and novelist Gerhart Hauptmann was born in Ober-Salzbrunn in the German Silesia.

1886 In a production of Charles A. Gardiner's play *Karl the Peddler*, the fictitious theater name George Spelvin appeared for the first time. George Spelvin (or its female equivalent Georgina or Georgetta) is used in a program to conceal the fact that an actor is playing more than one role. The name of Spelvin has been seen in more than ten thousand Broadway performances. The British equivalent name is Walter Plinge.

1887 One of America's greatest modern artists, Georgia O'Keeffe, was born in Sun Prairie, Wisconsin. Her work is considered abstract, although the subject matter of flowers or southwestern motifs are painted in a representational manner. The close-up view of the subjects makes the familiar unfamiliar while emphasizing the linear and pure quality of their designs.

1887 Poet Marianne Moore was born in St. Louis. She would write, "Any writer overwhelmingly honest about pleasing himself is almost sure to please others."

1889 Brazil's monarchy was overthrown.

1926 The National Broadcasting Company debuted with a radio network of twenty-four stations.

1939 President Franklin Roosevelt laid the cornerstone of the Jefferson Memorial in Washington, D.C.

1940 The first seventy-five thousand men were called to armed forces duty under peacetime conscription.

1969 A quarter of a million protesters staged a peaceful demonstration in Washington against the Vietnam War.

Example is the school of mankind, and they will learn at no other.

[EDMUND BURKE (1729–1797)]

NOVEMBER

Michael Higgins was an Irish Catholic immigrant who fancied himself a radical freethinker and a freewheeling skeptic. As a youngster he had enlisted in General William Sherman's notorious Twelfth New York Cavalry and proudly participated in the nefarious campaign that ravaged the South across Tennessee, through Atlanta, and to the sea—a campaign that began on this day in 1864. He achieved notable infamy among his peers when he was honored by his commander for special treachery in fiercely subduing the captive population. Not surprisingly, that cruel and inhuman experience apparently hardened and embittered him. Genocide is not easily forgotten by either victims or perpetrators. His criminal inhumanity constituted a kind of spiritual calamity from which he, like so many others of his region, never fully recovered. Afterward he was pathetically stunted, unable to maintain a modicum of normalcy in his life or relations.

He worked sporadically as a stonemason and a tombstone carver but was either unwilling or unable to provide adequately for his large family. His wife, Anne Purcell, was a second-generation American from a strict Irish Catholic family. She was frail and sickly but utterly devoted to her unstable and unpredictable husband, as well as their ever-growing brood of children. The family suffered from cold, privation, and hunger. That was the common lot of thousands of other families in nineteenth-century America. But the Higginses also suffered grievously from scorn, shame, and isolation—because of Michael's sullen improvidence. And like many a man who is proudly progressive in public, he was repressively remonstrant at home. He regularly thrashed his sons "to make men of them." And he treated his wife and daughters as "virtual slaves." And when he drank—which was whenever he could afford it—his volatile presence was even more oppressive than normal.

The Higginses not only had to endure grave social and material lack, they were spiritually deprived as well. As a confirmed skeptic, Michael mocked the sincere religious devotion of most of his neighbors. He openly embraced radicalism, socialism, and atheism. And he had little toleration for the modicum of morality that his poor wife tried to instill in the lives of their hapless children. One day for example, when his youngest daughter was on her knees saying the Lord's Prayer, she came to the phrase "Give us this day our daily bread," and her father snidely cut her off. "Who were you talking to?" he demanded. "To God," she replied innocently. "Well, tell me, is God a baker?" With no little consternation, she said, "No, of course not. But He makes the rain, the sunshine, and all the things that make the wheat, which makes the bread." After a thoughtful pause her father rejoined, "Well, well, so that's the idea. Then why didn't you just say so? Always say what you mean, my daughter, it is much better."

The little girl would grow up to be the infamous Margaret Sanger, the founder of Planned Parenthood and patron of the global abortion holocaust. If it is true that "The hand that rocks the cradle, rules the world," it is equally true that "The hand that wrecks the cradle ruins the world."

NOVEMBER

1776 British troops captured Fort Washington during the American Revolution.

1824 Fifth Avenue in New York City was opened for real estate development and commercial enterprise.

1838 A Gothic cross was erected in Oxford, England, commemorating the memory of three notable figures in the English Reformation: Bishop Nicholas Ridley (1500–1555), Bishop Hugh Latimer (1485–1555) and Archbishop Thomas Cranmer (1489–1556). The men were executed for their faith across from the main entrance of Balliol College on Broad Street during the persecutions of Bloody Mary.

1864 General William T. Sherman and his Union troops began their infamous March to the Sea during the bitter War Between the States.

1889 American comic playwright, director, and producer George S. Kaufman, most known for *The Man Who Came to Dinner*, was born in Pittsburgh, Pennsylvania. He was a master of hilarious dialogue, and most successful works were written with others including: Morrie Ryskind—*Animal Crackers* (1928) and *Of Thee I Sing* (1931), for which he won the Pulitzer Prize; Moss Hart—*You Can't Take It With You* (1936; Pulitzer Prize) and *The Man Who Came to Dinner* (1939); Edna Ferber—*Dinner at Eight* (1932) and *Stage Door* (1936). He was the sole author of the 1927 George Gershwin musical *Strike Up the Band*.

1895 German composer, theorist, teacher, violist, and conductor Paul Hindemith was born in Hanau. He gained recognition as a composer in the 1920s, but his compositions were banned by Hitler's regime because of their modernism. He emigrated to the United States where he taught at Yale. He based his compositions on a hierarchy of tension and relaxation, and his books include *The Craft of Musical Composition* (1941), which discusses this technique. He died in Frankfurt on December 28, 1963.

1907 Oklahoma became the forty-sixth state of the Union.

1933 The United States and the Soviet Union established diplomatic relations for the first time since the Communist Revolution of 1917.

1959 The Rodgers and Hammerstein musical *The Sound of Music* opened on Broadway.

1961 House Speaker Samuel T. Rayburn died in Bonham, Texas, having served as Speaker almost continually since 1940.

1966 Dr. Samuel H. Sheppard—the man who inspired the television programs and the Hollywood film *The Fugitive*—was acquitted in his second trial on charges he had murdered his pregnant wife, Marilyn, in 1954.

1973 *Skylab 3*, carrying a crew of three astronauts, was launched from Cape Canaveral, Florida, on an eighty-four-day mission.

What great men do, the less will prattle of.

[WILLIAM SHAKESPEARE (c. 1564–1616)]

NOVEMBER

Elizabeth I ascended the English throne upon the death of Bloody Mary on this day in 1558. She was the daughter of Henry VIII and his second wife, Anne Boleyn. Elizabeth ultimately became the longest-reigning English monarch in nearly two centuries and the first woman to successfully occupy the English throne. Called Glorianna, the Virgin Queen, Virginia, and Good Queen Bess, Elizabeth enjoyed enormous popularity during her life and became an even greater legend after her death.

When she was born at Greenwich Palace in 1533, her parents were deeply disappointed—they had wanted a son as heir. When she was two her mother was beheaded for adultery, and Elizabeth was exiled from court. She was later placed under the protection of Catherine Parr, Henry's sixth wife, and educated in the same household as her half brother, Edward. Both were raised as Protestants. The noted scholar Roger Ascham later served as her tutor, and he educated her as a potential heir to the throne rather than as an insignificant daughter of the monarch. Elizabeth underwent rigorous training in Greek, Latin, rhetoric, and philosophy and was an intellectually gifted pupil.

Edward succeeded his father in 1547 at the age of nine—but he was sickly and reigned only six years. When her Roman Catholic half sister, Bloody Mary inherited the crown in 1553, Elizabeth was imprisoned in the Tower of London, briefly threatened with execution, and then placed under house arrest. Elizabeth lived quietly at her family's country retreat north of London during the terrible persecutions of Mary's reign.

When Elizabeth succeeded to the throne, she ended the horror of the English Counter-Reformation. Under Mary, prominent Protestant clergymen were either executed or forced to flee the country. Elizabeth firmly established Protestantism and ended the persecutions—but she did so with an even and judicious hand, never allowing retribution or vigilantism.

Elizabeth also encouraged English enterprise and commerce, established a consistent legal code, and defended the nation against the powerful Spanish naval force known as the Spanish Armada. Her reign was noted for the English Renaissance, an outpouring of poetry and drama led by William Shakespeare, Edmund Spenser, and Christopher Marlowe that remains unsurpassed in English literary history. She was the last of the Tudor monarchs, never marrying or producing an heir, and was succeeded by her cousin, James VI of Scotland.

It was during Elizabeth's reign that England began to expand trade overseas and the merchant community grew dramatically. Private shipbuilding boomed and navigational advances made long sea voyages safer. England's chief commodity was woolen cloth, traded mostly at the Dutch port of Antwerp for finished goods and such luxuries as French wines. At the same time, new enterprises like the Muscovy Company were chartered to find outlets for English products. In 1600 the government granted the English East India Company a monopoly to trade in Asia, Africa, and America. The desire to expand overseas trade was also a motive in the ventures of English explorers such as Sir Francis Drake, Sir Humphrey Gilbert, and Sir Walter Raleigh. Such adventurers established the first English outposts in North America.

FEAST DAY

St. Hilda, Saints Acisclus and Victoria, St. Anianus or Aignan of Orléans, Saints Alphaeus and Zachaeus, St. Elizabeth of Hungary, St. Gregory of Tours, St. Gregory the Wonderworker, St. Dionysius of Alexandria, The Martyrs of Paraguay, St. Hugh of Lincoln

NOVEMBER

1800 After meeting at various times in Philadelphia; York and Lancaster, Pennsylvania; Princeton, New Jersey; Baltimore and Annapolis in Maryland; New York City; and again in Philadelphia, the Congress of the United States held its first session in Washington, D.C.

1839 Italy's Giuseppe Verdi, composer of such classic operas as *Aida*, *Rigoletto*, *Il Trovatore*, *Falstaff*, and *La Traviata*, debuted his first opera, *Oberto*. Born in 1813, in Roncole in the former duchy of Parma, he first studied music in the neighboring town of Busseto. Then, upon being rejected in 1832 because of his age by the Milan Conservatory, he became a pupil of the Milanese composer Vincenzo Lavigna. He returned to Busseto in 1833 as conductor of the Philharmonic Society. At the age of twenty-five Verdi again went to Milan. His first opera was produced at La Scala with some success. His next work though, the comic opera *Un giorno di regno*, was a failure, and Verdi, lamenting also the recent deaths of his wife and two children, decided to give up composing. After more than a year, however, the director of La Scala succeeded in inducing him to write *Nabucco*. This time his composition created a sensation; its subject matter dealt with the Babylonian captivity of the Jews, and the Italian public regarded it as a symbol of the struggle against Austrian rule in northern Italy. *I Lombardi* and *Ernani*, both great successes, followed, but of the next ten only *Macbeth* and *Luisa Miller* have survived in the permanent operatic repertory. Verdi's three following works, *Rigoletto*, *Il Trovatore*, and *La Traviata*, brought him international fame and remain among the most popular of all operas. Verdi's works are most noted for their emotional intensity, tuneful melodies, and dramatic characterizations. He transformed the Italian opera, with its traditional set pieces, old-fashioned librettos, and emphasis on vocal displays, into a unified musical and dramatic entity.

1869 The Suez Canal was officially opened in Egypt, in the presence of more than six thousand foreign guests and dignitaries. The first yacht to pass through the locks carried Emperor Franz-Josef of Austria-Hungary, Empress Eugénie of France, and the khedive of Egypt.

1888 Breaking several years of musical silence, Symphony no. 5 by Peter Ilyich Tchaikovsky was premiered in St. Petersburg. His fear of having nothing more to write was expressed in a letter when he wrote, "Not the slightest musical idea in my head! . . . I am beginning to fear that my muse has flown far, far away." Although not widely received at the time, Symphony no. 5 was soon regarded as one of Tchaikovsky's masterpieces that served to increase his fame and financial security.

1917 Sculptor August Rodin died in Meudon, France.

1934 Lyndon Baines Johnson married Claudia Alta Taylor, better known as Lady Bird.

1962 Washington's Dulles International Airport was dedicated by President John Kennedy.

1966 In less than twenty minutes, more than forty-six thousand meteoroids fell over Arizona.

1973 President Richard Nixon told Associated Press managing editors meeting in Orlando, Florida, "People have got to know whether or not their president is a crook. Well, I'm not a crook."

The true discoverer is not he who stumbles across that which none else has stumbled but he who beholds its wonder and tells of its glory and makes use of its stewardship.

[SENECA (C. 5–65)]

NOVEMBER

1985

Bill Waterson's comic strip "Calvin and Hobbes" debuted in newspapers. The strip would gain astonishing popularity through its ability to work on several levels at once: It was executed with the gleeful impishness of a child, its artistry was head and shoulders above the standard comic fare, and its ribald humor was remarkably consistent, yet it was based upon a rather heady concept—John Calvin was the preeminent Protestant Reformer while Thomas Hobbes was the preeminent Humanistic Secularist. Still, Waterson's piquant social commentary was nonideological and nonpartisan.

FEAST DAY
St. Odo of Cluny, St. Romanus of Antioch, St. Mawes or Maudez

When vice president Millard Fillmore (1800–1874) succeeded to the presidency upon the death of Zachary Taylor, he became one of the select group of presidents who have made the American myth "from a log cabin to the White House" a reality. But Fillmore's rise from humble apprentice to the highest office in the land was more inspiring than his performance in that office.

When the short, stocky Taylor was still in the White House, Washingtonians observed that the tall, dignified Fillmore looked more like a president than the president himself. Born in a log cabin in Cayuga County, New York, Fillmore overcame extreme handicaps—he had little formal education, worked on his father's farm, and at fifteen was apprenticed to a wool carder. While serving his apprenticeship he belatedly began his studies and gradually learned enough to teach school himself, so that he could afford to study law. At twenty-three he was admitted to the bar; by the time he was thirty he had established himself in Buffalo and won a seat in the New York State Assembly.

In politics Fillmore generally followed a moderate course, although in Congress he did espouse an unpopular cause by supporting John Quincy Adams in his fight against the "gag rule" denouncing antislavery bills. But as president he accepted Henry Clay's compromise measures on slavery and signed his political life away when he enacted the Fugitive Slave enforcement standards on this day in 1850.

Part of the Compromise of 1850, the notorious Fugitive Slave Act, permitted slaveowners to seize any suspected runaways in the North as fugitives without process of law. The act aroused extreme bitterness in the North; instead of improving conditions, it drove North and South ever farther apart. Although Fillmore could not then have realized it, his political career was practically over.

The man who looked the part of a president was not even nominated by his own party to play the role again—though he continued to be a third-party threat for nearly another quarter century.

NOVEMBER

1095 Pope Urban II called six hundred clergymen and laymen to the Council of Clermont. He addressed the council with a sermon that tugged at the heartstrings of Christians everywhere. He asked Europe to recapture the Holy Land from the Turks and to free Antioch, where men had first been called Christians. Nine days later he would issue the dramatic call that resulted in the successful mobilization and deployment of a vast crusading army.

1307 In Switzerland, William Tell was made to shoot an apple off his son's head with a bow and arrow for his failure to salute the despotic Austrian ruler. Tell succeeded in the task but was imprisoned when he threatened the life of the governor. He later ambushed the governor and killed him in an act that sparked the uniting of the Swiss against their Austrian rulers. This resulted in the independence of the Swiss nation. The legend of William Tell first appeared in a fifteenth-century ballad and formed the basis of the drama *Wilhelm Tell* (1804) by Friedrich von Schiller and the opera *Guillaume Tell* (1829) by Gioacchino Rossini.

1626 In Vatican City, Rome, the newly rebuilt Basilica of Saint Peter was consecrated.

1789 French painter and inventor Louis Daguerre was born on this day. He invented the first practical process of photography, the daguerrotype, some examples of which still survive.

1820 Captain Nathaniel Brown Palmer and a crew of five discovered Antarctica at a point near latitude 64 degrees south and longitude 60 degrees west.

1902 Morris Michton, a toymaker in Brooklyn, New York, named the teddy bear after Theodore Roosevelt because of an incident that occurred while Roosevelt was hunting.

1903 In a treaty signed on this day, the United States promised the country of Panama $10 million and $250,000 annually for the right to build a canal across the isthmus connecting the Atlantic and Pacific Oceans.

1928 The first successful sound-synchronized animated cartoon, Walt Disney's "Steamboat Willie," starring Mickey Mouse, premiered in New York.

1949 Jackie Robinson of the Brooklyn Dodgers was named the National League's Most Valuable Player. He began his professional baseball career in 1945 with the Kansas City Monarchs, one of the leading teams of the Negro Leagues. Later that year, Robinson signed with Branch Rickey, the general manager of the Dodgers. After one season in the minor leagues, Robinson was called up to the majors in 1947, becoming the first African American to play major-league baseball. Starting at first base, he made his debut in a Brooklyn uniform on April 15, 1947. Breaking baseball's color barrier was a serious challenge, and Robinson met fierce resistance from many players and fans. The determined Robinson survived the abuse and helped the Dodgers win the National League pennant. Sportswriters named the courageous and talented Robinson rookie of the year. Over ten seasons Robinson executed one of baseball's rarest and most exciting plays—stealing home—not once but nineteen times. His success with the Dodgers also opened the way for other black players to sign major-league contracts. But not until 1959 did all sixteen major-league clubs field at least one black ballplayer.

We are perpetually being told that what is wanted is a strong man who will do things. What is really wanted is a strong man who will undo things; and that will be the real test of strength.

[G. K. CHESTERTON (1874–1936)]

NOVEMBER

Though he was not even the main speaker at the dedication of a cemetery on the site of the bloody Gettysburg battlefield, the tantalizingly short speech Abraham Lincoln gave on this day in 1863 is a masterpiece of both penetrating rhetoric and moral politics. These words, though few, have proven to be immortal.

Carl Sandburg in 1946 hailed the address as one of the great American poems. "One may delve deeply into its unfolded meanings," he wrote, "but its poetic significance carries it far beyond the limits of a state paper. It curiously incarnates the claims, assurances, and pretenses of republican institutions, of democratic procedure, of the rule of the people. It is a timeless psalm in the name of those who fight and do in behalf of great human causes rather than talk, in a belief that men can 'highly resolve' themselves, and can mutually 'dedicate' their lives to a cause."

The words Lincoln had scribbled on the back of an envelope during the train journey from Washington to the Pennsylvania town were astonishingly potent: "Fourscore and seven years ago our fathers brought forth, on this continent, a new nation, conceived in liberty, and dedicated to the proposition that all men are created equal. Now we are engaged in a great civil war, testing whether that nation, or any nation so conceived, and so dedicated, can long endure. We are met on a great battlefield of that war. We have come to dedicate a portion of that field, as a final resting-place for those who here gave their lives, that that nation might live. It is altogether fitting and proper that we should do this."

He concluded his oratory with a poignant plea—as if he yearned for some sacred meaning to be forged from the horrors of the war he had wrought: "But, in a larger sense, we cannot dedicate—we cannot consecrate—we cannot hallow—this ground. The brave men, living and dead, who struggled here, have consecrated it far above our poor power to add or detract. The world will little note, nor long remember what we say here, but it can never forget what they did here. It is for us the living, rather, to be dedicated here to the unfinished work which they who fought here have thus far so nobly advanced. It is rather for us to be here dedicated to the great task remaining before us—that from these honored dead we take increased devotion to that cause for which they here gave the last full measure of devotion—that we here highly resolve that these dead shall not have died in vain—that this nation, under God, shall have a new birth of freedom—and that government of the people, by the people, for the people, shall not perish from the earth."

FEAST DAY
St. Ermenburga, St. Barlaam of Antioch, St. Nerses I

NOVEMBER

1632 During the aftermath of the Battle of Lutzen— one of the most crucial engagements in the bloody Thirty Years' War—it was announced to the world that King Gustavus Adolphus of Sweden had died. During the course of the battle, the king had been surrounded by enemy soldiers. Before taking his life, they demanded his name. Gustavus replied, "I am the King of Sweden! And this day I seal with my blood the liberties and religion of the German nation." During the horrific conflict, during which Gustavus defended the cause of the Protestants against Emperor Ferdinand II, a staunch Roman Catholic, the people of Europe suffered terribly. Out of a German population of sixteen million people, only four million survived. The town of Augsburg had a population of 80,000 people at the beginning of the conflict but only 18,000 survived to the end. Indeed, before the awful war had concluded an estimated 30,000 villages were destroyed. It was one of the saddest chapters in the long history of man—and the loss of Gustavus was a bitter loss for all the advocates of freedom.

1794 The United States and Britain signed the Jay Treaty, which resolved some issues left over from the Revolutionary War.

1828 Art song composer Franz Peter Schubert died in Vienna, Austria, at the age of thirty-one. The son of a parish schoolmaster, he became a choirboy in the Imperial Chapel in 1808 and began studies at the Konvict, the school for court singers. He also played violin in the school orchestra and began to compose seriously. When his voice changed in 1813, Schubert left the Konvict and began teaching in his father's school—and he produced a steady stream of new compositions. His earliest instrumental works which were clearly influenced by Mozart, Haydn, and Beethoven, but he eventually broke free to pioneer a romantic style notable for its sonority and distinctive harmonic and melodic richness. Although he wrote a large number of these chamber and symphonic works, he excelled most in the small-form structure of the German lieder—or art song—of which he wrote more than six hundred. His tombstone is inscribed with the words "Music has buried here a rich treasure, but fairer hopes."

1831 The twentieth president of the United States, James Garfield, was born in Orange, Ohio.

1899 Poet, critic, and biographer Allen Tate was born in Clarke County, Kentucky. He would be one of the leading lights of the Southern Agrarians—a remarkable literary coterie at Vanderbilt University during the first half of the twentieth century.

1919 Following a brilliant oratory by Henry Cabot Lodge, the Senate rejected the Treaty of Versailles by a vote of fifty-five in favor to thirty-nine against—well short of the two-thirds majority needed for ratification.

1949 Monaco held a coronation for its new ruler, Prince Rainier III, six months after he succeeded his grandfather Prince Louis II.

1969 *Apollo 12* astronauts Charles Conrad and Alan Bean made man's second landing on the moon.

1979 President Anwar Sadat of Egypt became the first Arab leader to visit Israel following the historic signing of the Camp David Accords with Israel's prime minister, Menachem Begin, and President Jimmy Carter.

Speak softly and carry a big stick; you will go far. It sounds rather as if that were but a homely old adage, yet as is often the case with matters of tradition, this truism is actually true.

[THEODORE ROOSEVELT (1858–1919)]

NOVEMBER

This is a season of preparation. For centuries Christians have used the month prior to the celebration of Christ's incarnation to ready their hearts and their homes for the great festival. While we moderns tend to do a good bit of bustling about in the crowded hours between Thanksgiving and Christmas, it often doesn't constitute the kind of preparation Advent calls for. Indeed, traditionally Advent has been a time of quiet introspection, personal examination, and repentance. It is a time to slow down, to take stock of the things that matter the most, and to do a thorough inner housecleaning. Advent is, as the ancient dogma of the church asserts, a *Little Pascha*—a time of fasting, prayer, confession, and reconciliation.

FEAST DAY
St. Edmund the Martyr, St. Maxentia of Beauvais, St. Nerses of Sahgerd, St. Bernward, St. Felix of Valois, St. Dasius

NOVEMBER

When was Jesus born in Bethlehem? The Bible describes with great certainty the fact of Christ's birth as well as the place. But not the exact date. One of the greatest of the Patristic writers, Basil of Caesarea, believed Christ was born on this day in the year 4 B.C. Another, Clement of Alexandria, speculated that Christ was born on November 17 in the year 3 B.C. Still others, such as John Chrysostom, speculated that since shepherds were in the field the night Christ was born, it must have been in spring or summer. Similarly, Athanasius argued for a date of May 20. Cyril of Jerusalem reasoned for the date to be on either April 19 or 20. And Ambrose of Milan made a strong traditional case for March 25. Quite obviously though, no one really knew with any degree of certainty.

In 354, the bishop of Rome started to observe December 25 as the date of Christ's birth. Four major Roman festivals were held in December, including Saturnalia, which celebrated the returning sun god. It was easy to adapt this to the Christian celebration of the coming of the Son of God.

In fact, Christians had already been celebrating the incarnation and nativity of the Lord Jesus on that day since at least the early part of the third century—just a few generations removed from the days of the Apostles. Thus, by 336, when the Philocalian Calendar—one of the earliest documents of the Patriarchal Church—was first utilized, Christmas Day was already a venerable and tenured tradition. Though there is no historical evidence that Christ was actually born on that day—indeed, whatever evidence there is points to altogether different occasions—the conversion of the old pagan tribes of Europe left a gaping void where the ancient winter cult festivals were once held. It was both culturally convenient and evangelically expedient to exchange the one for the other. And so joy replaced desperation. Celebration replaced propitiation. Christmas feasts replaced new moon sacrifices. Christ replaced Baal, Molech, Apollo, and Thor.

Like so many calendar dates, the many different customs of Christmas ultimately melded together. And thus emerged the traditional Advent season—a four-week anticipation of Christmas beginning in late November and marked by a series of important feasts, fasts, rituals, and rites all the way through the designated date of the Incarnation itself.

967 Arab scholar Abu al-Faraj al-Isbahani died in Baghdad. His major work, *Kitab al-aghan* (The Book of Songs), contains much information on the life and customs of the early Arabs as well as songs and information on composers, poets, and musicians.

1497 Portuguese explorer Vasco da Gama was the first European to round the Cape of Good Hope on the southern tip of Africa. Three vessels and 160 men accompanied the explorer on his successful trip to India.

1620 Peregrine White, the son of William and Susanna White, was the first child to be born on the *Mayflower*.

1789 The first state to ratify the Bill of Rights was New Jersey.

1805 *Fidelio*, Ludwig van Beethoven's only opera, was first performed at the Theater an der Wien in Vienna. Set in Seville, the story tells of Leonore, who disguises herself as a boy (Fidelio), to save her husband from death in a Spanish prison.

1910 Revolution broke out in Mexico, led by Francisco I. Madero.

1945 Two dozen Nazi leaders went on trial before an international war crimes tribunal in Nuremberg, Germany.

1975 After nearly four decades of near-absolute rule, Spain's General Francisco Franco died two weeks before his eighty-third birthday. He rose to power during the Spanish Civil War and afterward steered the country toward peace and prosperity. Following a brilliant military career,

Franco and a number of other conservatives were disturbed by the anti-Christian character of the Second Republic—which abolished the monarch, persecuted the church, promoted Communist ideals, and ushered in a host of liberal reforms. The country suffered from economic depression, revolutionary insurrections, and government scandals. In 1936, Franco joined a group of conspirators in an attempt to overthrow the Leftist government—and thus began the Civil War. By the end of the war, the provisional ruling military junta had chosen Franco as both the *Generalísimo* (commander in chief) and *el Caudillo* (leader of the Spanish state). He ruled absolutely and with an iron fist. During the Second World War, though friendly with both Italy and Germany, he was able to maintain Spanish neutrality. By avoiding direct involvement in the war, he spared Spain the wide-scale death and destruction suffered by most of Europe. In 1969, Franco named Don Juan Carlos de Borbón, grandson of former king Alfonso XIII, as heir to the Spanish throne and his successor. Although he had been carefully groomed as Franco's successor, Juan Carlos began working with politicians and labor groups to bring about Spain's relatively smooth transition to democracy. Whether Franco should be remembered as a hero or villain will no doubt continue to stir debate—but what few will dispute is that he was one of the most intriguing figures of his day.

How proper it is that Christmas should follow Advent. For him who looks toward the future, the manger is situated on Golgotha, and the cross has already been raised in Bethlehem.

[DAG HAMMARSKJÖLD (1905–1961)]

NOVEMBER

The English Puritan Philip Doddridge was born in 1702, the youngest of twenty children. His parents died when he was a boy, and he was raised by friends in their nonconformist parish church. By all accounts, he was a diligent and disciplined child—demonstrating a profound piety from an early age.

Because he could not accept the tenets of the Anglican Church, he refused a generous scholarship offer to attend Cambridge and instead, decided to attend a nonconforming seminary where he excelled. He was a particularly gifted orator in addition to being a fine poet and musician.

For several years he served in small Puritan congregations, assisting ministers with their pastoral work, evangelizing the community, visiting in the prisons, and providing informed research for sermons and Bible lessons. He was widely considered to be one of the finest young scholars among the swelling ranks of dissenting nonconformist ministers.

At the age of twenty-seven, Doddridge was called to pastor the Castle Hill congregational chapel in Northampton, England, where he remained for twenty-two years. In addition to his regular parish responsibilities, he spent much of his time in Northampton training other young men for the ministry in independent churches. He taught nearly two hundred men Hebrew, Greek, math, philosophy, the Bible, and theology. In addition, he wrote several books on theology and over four hundred hymns. Many of those hymns were written as summaries of his sermons so that the congregation was able to express their response to the truths taught. One of the most beloved of his hymns was written for his parish's Advent services on this day in 1748. "Hark the Glad Sound!" captures the Puritan emphasis on anticipating the Incarnation with great joy:

FEAST DAY
St. Geasius, pope; St. Albert of Louvain

> Hark the glad sound! The Saviour comes,
> The Saviour promised long:
> Let every heart prepare a throne, and every voice a song.
> He comes, the prisoners to release
> In Satan's bondage held;
> The gates of brass before Him burst, the iron fetters yield.
> He comes, the broken heart to bind,
> The bleeding soul to cure,
> And with the treasures of His grace, to bless the humble poor.
> Our glad hosannas, Prince of peace,
> Thy welcome shall proclaim,
> And heaven's eternal arches ring, with Thy beloved Name.

NOVEMBER

Always plagued by ill health, Doddridge contracted tuberculosis and died in Lisbon, Portugal, while seeking a respite from the disease. He was not yet fifty—even so, the catalog of his works is astonishingly rich and continues to supply the church with a substantive expression of the gospel.

1695 Regarded as the greatest English composer, Henry Purcell died in London at the young age of thirty-six. He is best known for his operas *Dido and Aeneas,* which is considered to be a landmark in English music, and *The Fairy Queen.* He is buried in Westminster Abbey.

1789 North Carolina became the twelfth state to ratify the U.S. Constitution.

1800 In a letter to her sister, Abigail Adams, having arrived in Washington less than a week before, wrote, "Not one room is finished of the whole . . . it is habitable by fires . . . thirteen of which we are obliged to keep daily, or sleep in wet or damp places . . . we have not the least fenceyard . . . and the great unfinished audience room I make a drying room of, to hang the clothes in."

1806 Isaac Backus, one of New England's great preachers and the father of American religious liberty, died on this day. Born into a staunch Puritan home in 1724 in Norwich, Connecticut, he was profoundly influenced by the Great Awakening and the preaching of George Whitefield. Shortly after the revivals broke out, Backus was ordained as a Reformed Baptist preacher. For the next sixty years, he traveled more than seventy thousand miles all across the American frontier preaching the gospel. In 1774, at the First Continental Congress in Philadelphia, Backus represented the independent churches and the Baptists—urging religious liberty for the fledgling republic. Later, as a delegate for Massachusetts, he voted for the U.S. Constitution's protection of free worship.

1863 Sir Arthur Quiller-Couch, fondly known simply as "Q," was born in Bodmin, Cornwall. One of his greatest accomplishments was the compilation of *The Oxford Book of English Verse 1250–1900.* He was a lecturer in classics at Oxford and a professor at Cambridge. In addition to publishing several volumes of poetry, he wrote books on literature such as *On the Art of Reading, On the Art of Writing, Studies in Literature,* and *Shakespeare's Workmanship.*

1877 Inventor Thomas A. Edison announced the invention of his phonograph.

1899 Vice President Garret A. Hobart, serving under President McKinley, died in Paterson, New Jersey, at age fifty-five.

1922 Rebecca L. Felton of Georgia was sworn in as the first woman to serve in the United States Senate.

1937 Dmitri Shostakovich premiered his Symphony no. 5 in D Minor. This symphony marked his return to favor with the Soviet government, a continual love-hate relationship. The *Moscow Daily News* called it a "work of great depth, with emotional wealth and content, and is of great importance as a milestone in the composer's development."

1942 The Alaska highway across Canada was formally opened.

1964 New York's Verrazano Narrows Bridge opened.

1973 President Richard Nixon's attorney, J. Fred Buzhardt, revealed the existence of an 18½ minute gap in one of the White House tape recordings related to Watergate.

When I get a little money, I buy books; and if there is any left, I buy food and clothes.

[DESIDERIUS ERASMUS (1466–1536)]

NOVEMBER

Long before the bane of television invaded our every waking moment, C. S. Lewis commented that while most people in modern industrial cultures are at least marginally able to read, they just don't. In his wise and wonderful book *An Experiment in Criticism* he said, "The majority, though they are sometimes frequent readers, do not set much store by reading. They turn to it as a last resource. They abandon it with alacrity as soon as any alternative pastime turns up. It is kept for railway journeys, illnesses, odd moments of enforced solitude, or for the process called reading oneself to sleep. They sometimes combine it with desultory conversation; often, with listening to the radio. But literary people are always looking for leisure and silence in which to read and do so with their whole attention. When they are denied such attentive and undisturbed reading even for a few days they feel impoverished."

Lewis went further, admitting that there is a profound puzzlement on the part of the mass of the citizenry over the tastes and habits of the literate. "It is pretty clear that the majority," he wrote, "if they spoke without passion and were fully articulate, would not accuse us of liking the wrong books, but of making such a fuss about any books at all. We treat as a main ingredient in our well-being something which to them is marginal. Hence to say simply that they like one thing and we another is to leave out nearly the whole of the facts."

C. S. Lewis was the happy heir of a great tradition of books and the literary life. His brilliant writing—in his novels like *The Lion, the Witch, and the Wardrobe; The Screwtape Letters;* and *Perelandra,* as well as in his nonfiction like *The Four Loves, Surprised by Joy, The Abolition of Man,* and *A Grief Observed*—evidence voracious reading. He was born in 1898 and died on this day in 1963, just seven days shy of his sixty-fifth birthday. During his life he became renowned as a popular best-selling author, a brilliant English literary scholar and stylist, and one of the foremost apologists for the Christian faith. Recalling his formative childhood years, he wrote, "I am the product of long corridors, empty sunlit rooms, upstairs indoor silences, attics explored in solitude, distant noises of gurgling cisterns and pipes, and the noise of wind under the tiles. Also, of endless books."

Throughout his life, Lewis celebrated everything that is good and right and true about the literary life. The result was that he was larger than life in virtually every respect. Though he knew that this was little more than a peculiarity in the eyes of most, he did not chafe against it. Instead, he fully embraced it. He explained, "Those of us who have been true readers all our life seldom fully realize the enormous extension of our being which we owe to authors. We realize it best when we talk with an unliterary friend. He may be full of goodness and good sense but he inhabits a tiny world. In it, we should be suffocated. The man who is contented to be only himself, is in a prison. My own eyes are not enough for me. I will see through those of others." This is because, he argued, "Literary experience heals the wound, without undermining the privilege, of individuality. Here, as in worship, in love, in moral action, and in knowing, I transcend myself; and am never more myself than when I do."

NOVEMBER

1247 Robin of Locksley, known as Robin Hood, died in a convent in Kirklees, Yorkshire. *A Lytell Geste of Robyn Hood*, the fourteenth-century manuscript on the life of Sherwood Forest crusader, recounts his last instructions to his deputy Little John: "Give me my bent bow in my hand/And an arrow I'll let free,/And where the arrow is taken up,/there let my grave digged be." A monument to Robin Hood stands on the edge of Kirklees Park, where the arrow fell.

1698 John Dryden wrote a poem of praise to Saint Cecilia, the patron saint of music, in *Alexander's Feast*:

> At last divine Cecilia came,
> Inventress of the vocal frame;
> The sweet enthusiast from her sacred store
> Enlarged the former narrow bounds,
> To harmonious, melodious sounds,
> With nature's mother's wit, and arts unknown before.

1718 English pirate Edward Teach—better known as Blackbeard—was killed during a battle off the Virginia coast.

1819 English novelist Mary Ann Evans, who wrote under the pseudonym George Eliot, was born in Chilvers, Coton, Warwickshire. She was the author of such beloved works as *Silas Marner, The Mill on the Floss, Adam Bede,* and *Middlemarch.*

1913 English composer Benjamin Britten, Baron Britten of Aldeburgh, was born in Lowestoft, Suffolk. Educated at the Royal College of Music, he is best remembered for his operas—among the finest English language operas of the twentieth century. These works include *Peter Grimes* (1945), *Billy Budd* (1951), and *Gloriana* (1953)—about Queen Elizabeth I and written in honor of the coronation of Elizabeth II. His music ranges from the simple and lyrical to complex yet effective atonality.

1940 Actor, writer, and director Terry Gilliam was born in Minneapolis, Minnesota. His most fascinating films include *Brazil, The Fisher King,* and *12 Monkeys.*

1943 Lyricist Lorenz Hart died in New York at age forty-eight.

1963 President John F. Kennedy was assassinated in Dallas, Texas, as he rode in a motorcade. Largely overshadowed on the same day were the deaths of English authors C. S. Lewis and Aldous Huxley.

1965 The musical *Man of La Mancha* opened in New York.

STIRRING DAY

Stirring Day, or Stir-Up Sunday as it is sometimes called, is the first Sunday before Advent—usually falling on the Sunday after our American Thanksgiving. A holiday borrowed from the Victorians, it provides a wonderful way to make the transition into the Advent season. On this day mothers and grandmothers gather their whole family into the kitchen, assign various chopping, stirring, measuring, and cleanup tasks and bake the Christmas Plum Pudding together. Then, pudding baked and aging nicely in a cool, dark spot, they relax with the feeling of satisfaction that although the busy Yuletide season is soon to be upon them, at least some of the preparation for Christmas Dinner was completed.

If a book is worth reading, it is worth buying.

[JOHN RUSKIN (1819–1900)]

NOVEMBER

Blaise Pascal was a genuine Renaissance man. He was a prominent mathematician, physicist, inventor, and philosopher. He made important contributions to geometry, calculus, and developed the theory of probability. In physics, Pascal's law is the basis for all modern hydraulic operations. When he was still a teenager he invented the first mechanical calculator. He even created the theoretical basis for a computer language—known as Pascal—long before the technology was available to use it.

Pascal was born in Clermont-Ferrand in 1623, and his family settled in Paris in 1629. Under the tutelage of his father, Pascal soon proved himself a mathematical prodigy, and at the age of sixteen he formulated one of the basic theorems of projective geometry, known as Pascal's theorem and described in his *Essay on Conics.* He proved by experimentation in 1648 that the level of the mercury column in a barometer is determined by an increase or decrease in the surrounding atmospheric pressure rather than by a vacuum, as previously believed. This discovery verified the hypothesis of the Italian physicist Evangelista Torricelli concerning the effect of atmospheric pressure on the equilibrium of liquids. Six years later, in conjunction with the French mathematician Pierre de Fermat, Pascal formulated the mathematical theory of probability, which has become important in such fields as actuarial, mathematical, and social statistics and as a fundamental element in the calculations of modern theoretical physics. Pascal's other important scientific contributions include the derivation of Pascal's law or principle, which states that fluids transmit pressures equally in all directions, and his investigations in the geometry of infinitesimals. His methodology reflected his emphasis on empirical experimentation as opposed to analytical, a priori methods, and he believed that human progress is perpetuated by the accumulation of scientific discoveries resulting from such experimentation.

FEAST DAY
St. Clement I, pope; St. Alexander, prince; St. Columbanus; St. Amphilochius; St. Trudo or Trond; St. Gregory of Girgenti; St. Felicitas

On this day in 1654 Pascal underwent a dramatic conversion experience. Afterward, he became a part of the Jansenist community at Port Royal, where he led a rigorously ascetic life until his death eight years later. The Jansenists were reformers within the Catholic Church who sought to bring a kind of Protestant theological emphasis to the church without disrupting its liturgy or hierarchy. The movement was founded by the Flemish theologian and bishop of Ieper, Cornelis Jansen, whose ideas were summarized in the treatise *Augustinus*—a profoundly orthodox interpretation of Augustine's biblical worldview. Under the sway of this teaching, Pascal wrote his famous *Lettres provinciales,* in which he attacked the anti-Reform Catholics—and especially the Jesuits—for their attempts to reconcile humanistic naturalism with Christianity. He also wrote a defense of the faith, *Apologie de la Religion Chrétienne,* in preparation for his magnum opus, *Pensées sur la Religion.* In the *Pensées* Pascal attempted to explain and justify the difficulties of human life by the doctrine of original sin, and he contended that revelation can be comprehended only by faith, which in turn is justified by revelation. A genius, yielded to the purposes of Christ, Pascal was one of the most remarkable men ever to grace the church.

NOVEMBER

c. 100 Serving as the bishop of Rome after Peter, Linus, and Cletus at the end of the first century, Clement was one of the greatest stalwarts of the early church. His letters, sermons, and commentaries remain some of the best testimonies of the dynamism of the fledgling Christian witness. A constant encouragement to others, he was responsible for the establishment of at least seventy-five churches. His martyrdom apparently occurred on November 23 and, as a result, believers have long remembered him on that day. Celebrated as the first day of winter, it has been marked by community or guild suppers—where coworkers gather to sing, to roast apples, and to offer mutual encouragement in the faith.

1585 Thomas Tallis, the Father of English Cathedral Music, died on this day. He served as gentleman of the chapel royal during the reigns of Henry VIII, Edward VI, Mary I, and Elizabeth I. Along with his pupil and fellow organist William Byrd, he published the *Cantiones Sacrae*, which consisted of sixteen motetes by Tallis and eighteen by Byrd. One of his most famous works is the motet *Spem in Alium* which is written in forty parts for eight five-part choirs.

1621 John Donne was elected Dean of St. Paul's Cathedral in London.

1765 Frederick County, Maryland, repudiated the British Stamp Act—it was the first act of open rebellion through the agency of magistratal interposition, and it established a pattern for the fledgling American patriot movement.

1804 The fourteenth president of the United States, Franklin Pierce, was born in Hillsboro, New Hampshire.

1874 *Far from the Madding Crowd* by Thomas Hardy was first published.

1889 The first jukebox made its debut in San Francisco, at the Palais Royale Saloon.

1896 Discussing Southern cuisine, the *Homemaker's Magazine* declared, "The barbecue is to Georgia what the clambake is to Rhode Island, what a roast beef dinner is to our English cousins, what canvasback duck is to the Marylander, and a pork and bean supper is to the Bostonian."

1903 Singing the role of the duke in *Rigoletto*, famed Italian tenor Enrico Caruso made his American debut at the Metropolitan Opera House in New York City.

1913 Jean Cocteau reviewed Marcel Proust's *Swan's Way:* "It resembles nothing that I know of, and reminds me of everything I admire."

1936 *Life*, the pioneering photojournalism magazine created by Henry R. Luce, was first published.

1945 Most American wartime rationing, including limits on the purchase and consumption of meat and butter, ended.

1959 The musical *Fiorello!*, with music by Jerry Bock and lyrics by Sheldon Harnick, opened on Broadway.

Bookselling is the most ticklish and unsafe and hazardous of all professions scarcely with the exception of horse jockeyship.

[WALTER SCOTT (1771–1832)]

NOVEMBER

According to tradition, John Knox was born at Haddington in East Lothian on this day in 1505. His father, William, ensured that he obtained a liberal education in grammar school, and at the age of sixteen sent him to the University of Glasgow, where John Majors was professor of moral philosophy and theology. Majors was one of the leading intellectuals of Europe and he not only lectured on Peter Lombard's *Books of the Sentences*—the standard classical text of the day—he also introduced his students to the text of the Latin Bible. Despite his proficient studying, Knox left the university without obtaining a master's degree, and afterward taught in some capacity at the University of St. Andrews. It appears that he also took the orders of the Catholic priesthood—sometime around 1530—and served the parish of Haddington over the course of the next decade, functioning as a notary and as a private tutor.

The Protestant faith first appeared in Scotland at the beginning of the fifteenth century, when the Lollard followers of Wycliffe fled persecution in England and found their way across the border. Shortly thereafter, the ideas and books of Martin Luther began filtering into the university towns. At about the time Knox began teaching at St. Andrews University, George Wishart, a zealous Protestant, also began his preaching and teaching ministry there. Knox, still a Catholic priest, was attracted to the beauty, goodness, and truth he saw in Wishart's message. Knox offered to serve as a bodyguard for the evangelist—but soon afterward, Wishart was arrested, condemned as a heretic, and burned at the stake. His martyrdom provoked Knox's dramatic conversion—he would never be the same again and neither would Scotland.

In 1546 a group of ardent Protestants took over the city of St. Andrews and garrisoned themselves there—it was their attempt to usher in the Reformation by force. Though Knox was not party to the conspiracy, he decided to join the men in the garrison for the purspose of ministering to them. The castle was stormed by the French and Scots, and the Protestants were consigned to the French as galley slaves.

Knox was undeterred. After securing his release after several months of hard labor, he spent the rest of his life working for the Reformation—sometimes in exile in England or Geneva, sometimes in his native Scotland. He was clearly, as Calvin called him, "God's firebrand." He wrote incendiary books like *The First Blast of the Trumpet Against the Monstrous Regiment of Women* during the horrific persecutions of Bloody Mary, Mary Queen of Scots, and Mary Guise. He helped to create the Genevan Bible. He served in the court of Edward VI. But all the while, his heart cry was for his homeland, "Give me Scotland or I die."

In 1559, he came home to Scotland to stay. The Reformation he unleashed swept across the land in a torrent. His *Confession of Faith Professed and Believed by the Protestants within the Realm of Scotland* was approved by the Scottish Parliament in1560. He became the pastor of Gileskirk, the great cathedral on High Street in Edinburgh. He made great plans for the comprehensive application of the gospel to all of Scottish life—he wanted a school in every parish, a college in every town, and a university in every city. And he wanted regular, organized provision for the nation's poor. When he died in 1572, his heart cry had been answered.

NOVEMBER

1632 Dutch philosopher Barouch Spinoza was born in Amsterdam to Spanish-Portuguese Jewish parents. He stated, "Peace is not an absence of war. It is a virtue, a state of mind, a disposition for benevolence, confidence, justice." His philosophy of essences and causation made him one of the most influential thinkers, especially in the realm of pantheism.

1784 Zachary Taylor, the twelfth president of the United States, was born in Orange County, Virginia.

1849 Frances Hodgson Burnett, author of the beloved children's stories *The Secret Garden* (1911) and *Little Lord Fauntleroy* (1886), was born Manchester, England. She immigrated to the United States at the close of the Civil War. Her forty-plus novels and plays stress themes of romantic sentimentalism.

1859 British naturalist Charles Darwin published *On the Origin of Species*, which attempted to provide a basis for his theory of evolution.

1868 American ragtime composer and pianist Scott Joplin—best known for "The Entertainer" and "Maple Leaf Rag"—was born in Texarkana, Texas.

1925 William F. Buckley, editor of *The National Review* and author of *God and Man at Yale*, was born in New York City.

1947 A group of writers, producers, and directors that became known as the Hollywood Ten was cited for contempt of Congress after refusing to answer questions about alleged Communist influence in the movie industry.

1947 John Steinbeck's novel *The Pearl* was first published.

1963 Jack Ruby shot and mortally wounded Lee Harvey Oswald, the accused assassin of President Kennedy, in a scene captured live on television.

1971 Hijacker D. B. Cooper parachuted from a Northwest Airlines 727 over Washington State with $200,000 in ransom money—his fate remains unknown to this day.

1992 After almost one hundred years of military presence on the island, the United States military left the Philippines after the Philippine Senate rejected a new lease for bases.

1998 The first Palestine Airlines flight touched down at Gaza International Airport.

The age is weary with work and gold;

And high hopes wither, and memories wane,

On hearths and altars the fires are dead;

But that brave faith hath not lived in vain.

[FRANCES BROWN (1816–1864)]

NOVEMBER

689

The first few winters in the New World were treacherous for the new American colonists. Nevertheless, from the beginning the settlers expressed their thanksgiving for the evidence of God's good providence in their lives—despite all the hardships they faced, they recognized the peculiar opportunity they had been afforded. Many years later, the patriotic poet and balladeer Hezekiah Butterworth attempted to capture that remarkable paradox of faith in his lyrical verse, "Five Kernels of Corn."

'Twas the year of the famine in Plymouth of old,
The ice and the snow from the thatched roofs had rolled;
Through the warm purple skies steered the geese o'er the seas,
And the woodpeckers tapped in the clocks of the trees;
And the boughs on the slopes to the south winds lay bare,
And dreaming of summer, the buds swelled in the air.
The pale Pilgrims welcomed each reddening morn;
There were left but for rations Five Kernels of Corn.
Five Kernels of Corn! Five Kernels of Corn!
But to Bradford a feast were Five Kernels of Corn!

Five Kernels of Corn! Five Kernels of Corn!
Ye people, be glad for Five Kernels of Corn!
So Bradford cried out on bleak Burial Hill,
And the thin women stood in their doors, white and still.
Lo, the harbor of Plymouth rolls bright in the Spring,
The maples grow red, and the wood robins sing,
The west wind is blowing, and fading the snow
And the pleasant pines sing, and arbutuses blow.
Five Kernels of Corn! Five Kernels of Corn!
To each one be given Five Kernels of Corn!

O Bradford of Austerfield haste on thy way.
The west winds are blowing o'er Provincetown Bay,
The white avens bloom, but the pine domes are chill,
And new graves have furrowed Precisioners' Hill!
Give thanks, all ye people, the warm skies have come,
The hilltops are sunny, and green grows the holm,
And the trumpets of winds, and the white March is gone,
And ye still have left you Five Kernels of Corn.
Five Kernels of Corn! Five Kernels of Corn!
Ye have for Thanksgiving Five Kernels of Corn!

The raven's gift eat and be humble and pray,
A new light is breaking, and Truth leads your way;
One taper a thousand shall kindle: rejoice
That to you has been given the wilderness voice!
O Bradford of Austerfield, daring the wave,
And safe though the sounding blasts leading the brave,
Of deeds such as thine was the free nation born,
And the festal world sings the Five Kernels of Corn.
Five Kernels of Corn! Five Kernels of Corn!
The nation gives thanks for Five Kernels of Corn!
To the Thanksgiving Feast bring Five Kernels of Corn!

FEAST DAY
St. Moses the Martyr, St. Mercurius of Caesarea

NOVEMBER

Long a part of the traditional New England holiday tradition—before the turkey is carved, each member of the family is served a mere five kernels of corn after which this inspiring poem is recited—the remembrance of Plymouth has become a symbol of the incredible blessing of this land.

1748 English cleric and hymn writer Isaac Watts died on this day. He published two hymn collections including a versification of the *Psalms of David* in 1719. His many hymns include "O God, Our Help in Ages Past," "When I Survey the Wondrous Cross," "Joy to the World," and "How Sweet and Awesome Is This Place."

1758 In the French and Indian War, the British captured Fort Duquesne in present-day Pittsburgh.

1783 The British evacuated New York, their last military position in the United States during the Revolutionary War.

1792 *The Farmer's Almanac* was first published by Robert Bailey Thomas in West Boylston, Massachusetts. He compiled the almanac for fifty-four years. It is still the oldest continuously published periodical in the United States.

1835 American industrialist Andrew Carnegie was born in Dunfermline, Scotland.

1947 Movie studio executives meeting in New York agreed to blacklist the Hollywood Ten who were cited for contempt of Congress the day before.

1952 The Ambassadors Theatre in London presented the first performance of Agatha Christie's murder mystery *The Mousetrap*, beginning the longest continuous run of any show in the world. It can be enjoyed in London to this day, where audiences are sworn not to reveal whodunit.

1963 The body of President Kennedy was laid to rest at Arlington National Cemetery.

1974 The Burmese diplomat and former United Nations Secretary-General U Thant died in New York at age sixty-five.

Well, if we are to die, let us die like men.

[PATRICK CLEBURNE (1831–1864)]

NOVEMBER

In 1950, when William Faulkner was awarded the Nobel Prize for literature, he had published twenty books—including the classics *As I Lay Dying, Light in August, Absalom, Absalom!* and *Co Down, Moses.* Southerners noted that he was the first writer from that region to win the prize and praised his brilliant and articulate colloquialism. All his life he had avoided speeches and insisted that he not be taken as serious poet, "I'm just a farmer who likes to tell stories." Because of his known aversion to making formal pronouncements, there was much interest in what he would say in the speech that the Nobel custom obliged him to deliver. He evidently wanted to set the record straight concerning the place of the regionalist poet in the discourse of a wider culture—and that he did in a speech he wrote on this day as he traveled to Stockholm to receive the prize.

He began with typical humility, "I feel that this award was not made to me as a man but to my work—a life's work in the agony and sweat of the human spirit, not for glory and least of all for profit, but to make out of the material of the human spirit something which was not there before; so this award is only mine in trust."

The inventive novelist, known for his epic portrayal of the tragic conflict between the old and the new South as well as for his complex plots and narrative style, asserted that the literary arts were an essential part of the redemption of the modern world: "Our tragedy today is a general and universal physical fear so long sustained by now that we can even bear it. There are no longer problems of the spirit. There is only the question: When will I be blown up? Because of this, the young man or woman writing today has forgotten the problems of the human heart in conflict with itself which alone can make good writing because only that is worth writing about; worth the agony and the sweat. He must learn them again, he must teach himself that the basest of all things is to be afraid, and teaching himself that, forget it forever leaving no room in his workshop for anything but the old verities and truths of the heart, the old universal truths lacking which any story is ephemeral and doomed—love and honor and pity and pride and compassion and sacrifice. Until he does so, he labors under a curse. He writes not of love but of lust, of defeats in which nobody loses anything of value, of victories without hope and, worst of all, without pity or compassion. His griefs grieve on no universal bones, leaving no scars. He writes not of the heart but of the gland. Until he relearns these things, he will write as though he stood among and watched the end of man. I do not believe in the end of man."

He concluded his remarks by saying, "I believe man will not merely endure, he will prevail. He is immortal, not because he, alone among creatures, has an inexhaustible voice but because he has a soul, a spirit, capable of compassion and sacrifice and endurance. The poet's—the writer's—duty is to write about these things. It is his privilege to help man endure by lifting his heart, by reminding him of courage and honor and hope and pride and compassion and pity and sacrifice which have been the glory of his past. The poet's voice need not merely be the record of man, it can be one of the props to help him endure and prevail."

FEAST DAYS
St. Conrad of Constance, St. Peter of Alexandria, St. John Berchmans, St. Basolus or Basle, St. Siricius, St. Leonard of Porto Maurizio, St. Silvester Gozzolini

NOVEMBER

1789 George Washington designated this day as a day of general thanksgiving for the adoption of the new American Constitution. This was the first national Thanksgiving Day declared by presidential proclamation.

1825 The first college social fraternity, Kappa Alpha, was formed at Union College in Schenectady, New York.

1832 Public streetcar service began in New York City. The fare was 12½ cents.

1862 On meeting Harriet Beecher Stowe, author of the novel *Uncle Tom's Cabin*, Abraham Lincoln commented, "So this is the little lady who made the big war."

1864 Alice Liddel, the twelve-year-old daughter of a country clergyman, received an early Christmas gift from Charles L. Dodgson, a young mathematics professor at Oxford University. The gift was a handwritten manuscript describing *Alice's Adventures Underground* signed with the pen name of Lewis Carroll.

1940 The half million Jews of Warsaw, Poland, were forced by the Nazis to live within a walled ghetto.

1942 The movie *Casablanca*—remembered for outstanding performances by Humphrey Bogart and Ingrid Bergman and the song "As Time Goes By"—premiered at the Hollywood Theater in New York. The original release date of June 1943 was moved up because of the landing of Allied troops in North Africa. The nationwide release occurred on January 23, 1943, to coincide with the Churchill-Roosevelt conferences in Casablanca.

1942 President Franklin Roosevelt ordered nationwide gasoline rationing in light of the provisioning needs of American war efforts.

1949 India adopted a constitution as a republic within the British Commonwealth.

1950 China entered the Korean conflict, launching a counteroffensive against soldiers from the United Nations, the U.S., and South Korea.

1983 Britain's most costly theft took place at the Brinks-Mat warehouse in Middlesex when thieves absconded with gold bars, platinum, and diamonds worth some £26 million.

1992 Prime Minister John Major of Great Britain announced that Queen Elizabeth had decided to begin paying income taxes on her personal income.

Learn all you can, but learn to do something, or your learning will be useless and your vision will depart.

[BOOKER T. WASHINGTON (1856–1915)]

NOVEMBER

KLOPFELNACHTE

Literally "Knocking Night," each Thursday in Advent is celebrated throughout German communities by youngsters walking from house to house, beckoning upon the door stoops, singing carols, and offering gifts of fruit and candies. A reversal of the "Trick or Treat" ritual, the Klopfelnachte tradition is a joyous and selfless expression of commitment in a covenantal community.

FEAST DAY
St. James Intercisus, St. Cungar of Somerset, Saints Barlaam and Josaphat, St. Maximus of Riez, St. Fergus of Strathern, St. Virgin of Salzburg, St. Secundinus or Sechnall

The idea of some kind of a holy war to avenge the subjugation of Christian lands first occurred to Pope Gregory VII, and then to his successor, Victor III, but affairs closer to home kept them both more than a little preoccupied. Soon though, stories of gross atrocities against captive churches began to reach the West. The brutal conquest of Egypt, Syria, and Iraq sent shudders of fear throughout the kingdoms of the West. The penetration of Muslim armies into Spain, France, and Italy, and the slaughter of whole communities of believers shook their confidence even more. The vulnerability of the once-invulnerable Byzantine Empire was utterly terrifying to them. And horrific stories of the occupation of the Holy Land—Jerusalem and Palestine—and the desecration of the sacred sites of the Christian faith there distressed them no end. Soon, they could no longer ignore such abscesses of despotism.

At the Council of Clermont on this day in 1095, Pope Urban II issued a call for concerted and forthright action that was heard throughout Europe: "From the confines of Jerusalem and from the city of Constantinople a horrible tale has gone forth. An accursed people, a people utterly alienated from God, has invaded the lands of those Christians and depopulated them by the sword, plundering, and fire."

He went on to list in detail the outrages of Ji'had and Dhimma: the plunder of churches, the rape of Christian women, the torture of priests and monks, the pilfering of villages and towns, and the occupation of the territories. He appealed to both their sense of Christian mercy and their sense of European honor: "Recall the greatness of Charlemagne. O most valiant soldiers, descendants of invincible ancestors, be not degenerate. Let all hatred between you depart, all quarrels end, all wars cease. Start upon the road to the Holy Sepulcher, to tear that land from a wicked race and subject it to yourselves thereby restoring it to Christ. I call you to take the cross and redeem defiled Jerusalem."

Immediately a stirring chant arose from the crowd there at Clermont: *"Deus Vult"*—God wills it. It was a chant that would quickly spread throughout Europe. The following year, their campaign of liberation the historians now call the Crusades began in earnest resulting in the emancipation of all the lands from Edessa to the Gaza—including the Holy City of Jerusalem—less than four years later.

NOVEMBER

8 B.C. Roman lyric poet and satirist Horace died in Rome. Born Quintus Horatius Flaccus in 65 B.C., Horace was educated in Rome and then in Athens where he studied Greek philosophy and poetry. He was recruited into the Republican army by Brutus after the assassination of Julius Caesar in 44 B.C. His poetry attracted the attention of then poet laureate Virgil who helped to get him situated in literary and political circles. Horace produced several extant books of poetry in the form of satires, epodes, odes, and epistles. His odes praised peace, patriotism, love, friendship, wine, and simplicity and were the inspiration for many eighteenth- and nineteenth-century English poets. He became poet laureate in 19 B.C.

1746 Robert R. Livingston, farmer, diplomat, and member of the Continental Congress, was born in New York City. In 1789 he administered the oath of office to President George Washington.

1759 Reverend Francis Gastrell was ejected from his home in Stratford-upon-Avon. It seems that Gastrell was living in the former home of William Shakespeare, and he cut down the 150-year-old mulberry tree that Shakespeare had planted. He had grown tired of the many visitors and Bard enthusiasts who would trespass in order to view the tree. Although he sold the tree for firewood, Thomas Sharp, a jeweler and woodcarver, recovered the wood and carved hundreds of relics. Gastrell and his wife, Jane, were removed from Stratford "amid the ragings and cursings of its people" for one of "the meanest and petty infamies in our annals."

1843 The Irish composer Michael Balfe premiered his opera *The Bohemian Girl* at the Drury Lane Theatre in London. This opera about gypsies and an Austrian royal family is most remembered for its aria "I Dreamt That I Dwelt in Marble Halls" and the ballad "Then You'll Remember Me."

1901 The Army War College was established in Washington, D.C.

1910 New York's Penn Station opened.

1939 The play *Key Largo*, by Maxwell Anderson, opened at the Ethel Barrymore Theater in New York.

1942 During the Second World War, the French navy at Toulon, disobeying orders from Paris, scuttled its ships and submarines to keep them out of the hands of the Nazis.

1945 General George C. Marshall was named special American envoy to China to try to end hostilities between the Nationalists and the Communists. Negotiations broke down within a week.

1953 Playwright Eugene O'Neill died in Boston at age sixty-five.

1970 Pope Paul VI, visiting the Philippines, was slightly wounded at the Manila airport by a dagger-wielding Bolivian painter disguised as a priest.

1973 The Senate voted 92-3 to confirm Gerald R. Ford as vice president, succeeding Spiro T. Agnew, who had resigned in disgrace.

1985 The British House of Commons approved the Anglo-Irish accord, giving Dublin a consultative role in the governing of British-ruled Northern Ireland.

1991 Both houses of the United States Congress approved the $70 billion bailout of banks and savings and loan institutions.

*I*nnocence prolonged ignores experience; knowledge denied becomes a stone in the head.

[ANDREW NELSON LYTLE (1902–1995)]

NOVEMBER

27

1582

Guillame Shakspar—who most scholars believe was the author of the remarkable works of William Shakspeare despite the fact that there is no evidence that he was even literate—posted a bond to secure his marriage with Anne Hathaway at Stratford upon Avon.

NOVEMBER

William Blake was an English poet, painter, and engraver who created a unique form of illustrated verse and who was among the most original, lyrical, and prophetic writers ever to work in the English language. Best known for his poems *The Lamb* and *The Tyger*, he was born in London on this day in 1757.

Largely self-taught, he was, however, widely read, and his poetry shows such varied influences as the German mystic Jakob Boehme and the religious reformer Emanuel Swedenborg. As a child, Blake wanted to become a painter, so he was sent to drawing school and at the age of fourteen was apprenticed to James Basire, an engraver. After his seven-year term was over, he studied briefly at the Royal Academy, but he rebelled against the Christian aesthetic of its president, Sir Joshua Reynolds. Blake did, however, later establish friendships with such academicians as John Flaxman and Henry Fuseli, whose work may have influenced him.

In 1784 he set up a printshop, but it failed after only a few years. So, for the rest of his life Blake attempted to eek out a living as an engraver and illustrator. It was not an easy task—despite his obvious talent—due to the fact that he constantly defied eighteenth-century artistic and social conventions. Always stressing imagination over reason, he felt that ideal forms should be constructed from inner visions rather than from observations of nature. His rhythmically patterned style was also a repudiation of the painterly approach popular in his day. Blake's attenuated, fantastic figures go back, instead, to the medieval tomb statuary he copied as an apprentice.

In 1800 Blake moved to the seacoast town of Felpham, where he lived and worked until 1803 under the patronage of William Hayley. There he had a series of profound spiritual experiences that prepared him for his mature work, the great visionary epics written and etched between about 1804 and 1820. Not surprisingly, most of those works were focused on Christian subjects—including a bevy of illustrations for the work of the great Puritan John Milton, who was his favorite poet. He also did a series of illustrations for John Bunyan's *Pilgrim's Progress*, and for the Bible, including two dozen illustrations for the book of Job.

Blake's final years were cheered by the admiring friendship of a group of younger artists who believed he had pioneered a remarkable fusion of the arts and faith. He died in London in 1827, leaving uncompleted a cycle of drawings inspired by Dante's *The Divine Comedy*.

1520 Portuguese navigator Ferdinand Magellan reached the Pacific Ocean after passing through the South American strait that now bears his name.

1628 English author John Bunyan, best known for his Christian allegory *Pilgrim's Progress*, was born in Elstow, Bedfordshire, England. His home was a small thatched cottage, and his father was a tinker, who spent his days pushing a cart along the roads, stopping at homes to fix metal pots. Young John received a grammar school education, but like most sons of his day, he learned his father's trade. His adventurous life—including service in the Puritan Parliamentary Army during the Civil War, imprisonment for his nonconformist beliefs, and his travels as a tinker—provided all the images for his remarkable allegorical works, which ultimately made him the best-selling author of all time. Indeed, his magnum opus *Pilgrim's Progress* has in the years since it was written outsold every other book ever written—except, of course, the Bible.

1826 Jedidiah Strong Smith entered California's San Bernardino Valley to become the first American to cross the southwestern part of the American continent. Smith was not a typical mountain man. He was tall, silent, and never used tobacco or profanity. Reared a devout Methodist, Smith was a passionate evangelical Christian who always remained a gentleman even in the wildest frontier company. As he explored the areas of the West, Smith filled his journal describing the wonders of God's creation. When he faced hardship or peril, he looked to Scripture for strength.

1859 Washington Irving died in Tarrytown, New York, shortly after publishing the fifth and final volume of his biography of George Washington—in which he immortalized the apocryphal tale of the cherry tree.

1919 American-born Lady Astor was elected the first female member of the British Parliament.

1925 *The Grand Ole Opry*, Nashville's famed home of country music, made its radio debut on station WSM.

1942 The rationing of coffee in the United States began on this day and lasted throughout the Second World War.

1942 Almost five hundred people died during a fire at the popular Cocoanut Grove nightclub in Boston.

1943 President Franklin Roosevelt, Prime Minister Winston Churchill and Soviet leader Joseph Stalin met in Tehran during the Second World War.

1958 The African nation of Chad became an autonomous republic within the French community.

1964 The United States launched the space probe *Mariner 4* on a course to Mars.

1975 President Gerald Ford nominated Federal Judge John Paul Stevens to the U.S. Supreme Court seat vacated by William O. Douglas.

1990 Margaret Thatcher resigned as prime minister of Britain during an audience with Queen Elizabeth II, who conferred the premiership on John Major.

A pound of pluck is worth a ton of luck.

[JAMES A. GARFIELD (1831–1881)]

NOVEMBER

Theodore Roosevelt was never afraid to fail. In fact, he often wore his failures as badges of honor. To him, the attempt, the effort, and the sheer pluck of involvement were what really mattered in the end: "Far better it is to dare mighty things, to win glorious triumphs, even though checkered by failure, than to take rank with those poor spirits who neither enjoy much nor suffer much because they live in the gray twilight that knows neither victory nor defeat."

Though he enjoyed many successes throughout his career, he had his share of failures. He never allowed them to stymie his sense of responsibility and calling. He was often knocked down, but never out.

In addition, he was eager to learn from his mistakes. On this day in 1905, when his administration had lost a strategic legislative battle on the floor of the Senate, he called each of the men who had led the opposition to the White House. Expecting an angry tirade or a hysterical harangue, the senators were surprised when Roosevelt anxiously gathered them around his desk and asked for their advice. "How could I have handled this bill better? What did I say or not say to cause you to oppose it? What should I do in the future to better advance my principles?" The men were stunned. There was no recrimination. There were no lectures. There were no threats. Instead, they found in the president an eager learner—ready to accept the blame for his own shortcomings and then to try to move on and do better on another day. One of them later confessed, "I learned more about leadership and greatness in that one incident than in all my previous years in politics."

FEAST DAY
St. Radbod; St. Brendan of the Birr; St. Saturnius, martyr; St. Saturnius or Sernin or Toulouse

Elihu Root, who served as Roosevelt's secretary of state, called him "the most advisable man I ever knew." "If he was convinced of your sincerity," said the Progressive leader Albert Beveridge, "you could say anything to him you liked. You could even criticize him personally." And the author and social reformer Herbert Croly remarked that he had "never met a man so eager to learn from his mistakes—or even so ready to admit them. It was as if he had no ego."

Roosevelt was not simply a hopeless romantic or an unrealistic optimist in this regard. Rather, he was a man who was secure enough in his calling and purpose in life to remain undeterred by obstacles along the way—be they great or small. His son, Kermit, explained, "Some men have a strong sense of destiny. I cannot say that Father could ever fully identify such sentiments in his own experience. But I am quite certain that he knew what to work toward. Whether he ever actually attained to it was another matter altogether—and one of little concern to him."

For Roosevelt, true leadership not only involved a strength of character that was unafraid to admit failure, was willing to learn from error, and was quick to accept wise counsel, it also involved a sense of calling that was able to integrate such virtues into life with real confidence. For him, failure was merely the back door to success.

NOVEMBER

1530 Cardinal Thomas Wolsey, onetime adviser to England's King Henry VIII, died in disfavor, having failed to secure an annulment for the king's marriage to Catherine of Aragon.

1643 Composer Claudio Monteverdi died in Venice, Italy. He was the most important figure in the transition from the Renaissance to the baroque period through his deemphasis of polyphonic independent lines and his emphasis on the bass line and melody with harmonic support. His 1607 work *Orfeo* presented opera as a serious art form that expressed great emotional content. Monteverdi's impact on subsequent generations of composers and the development of the baroque period was profound.

1799 American novelist Louisa May Alcott was born in Philadelphia, Pennsylvania. Her story of sisters Meg, Jo, Beth, and Amy form her classic tale *Little Women.*

1890 The Imperial Diet, forerunner of Japan's current national legislature, opened its first session, four days after its members were summoned by Emperor Meiji.

1898 Christian novelist, essayist, scholar, and apologist C. S. Lewis (Clive Staples Lewis) was born in Belfast, Ireland. Best known for his novels of The Narnia Chronicles and The Space Trilogy (*Out of the Silent Planet, Perelandra,* and *That Hideous Strength*), Lewis's other fiction included *The Screwtape Letters* and *Till We Have Faces,* the retelling of the Cupid and Psyche myth. In addition, his scholarly works, *The Discarded Image, Allegory of Love,* and *An Experiment in Criticism,* were regarded as landmarks in medieval and Renaissance learning. *Mere Christianity* expressed Lewis's apologetics of the faith.

1924 Italian composer Giacomo Puccini died in Brussels before he could complete his opera *Turandot.* It was later finished by his friend Franco Alfano.

1929 Navy Lieutenant Commander Richard E. Byrd radioed that he'd made the first airplane flight over the South Pole.

1947 The United Nations General Assembly passed a resolution calling for the partitioning of Palestine between Arabs and Jews.

1952 Despite the cautions of the Secret Service and the military high command, President-elect Dwight D. Eisenhower kept his campaign promise to visit Korea to assess the ongoing conflict.

1961 Enos the chimp was launched from Cape Canaveral aboard the *Mercury-Atlas 5* spacecraft, which orbited earth twice before returning. Afterward, Enos was reportedly quite happy to disembark the craft.

1963 President Lyndon Johnson named a commission headed by Earl Warren to investigate the assassination of President Kennedy.

1989 In response to a growing pro-democracy movement in Czechoslovakia, the Communist-run Parliament ended the party's forty-year monopoly on power.

The invulnerable thing is not that which is not struck, but that which is not hurt—that which endures if only in aspiration.

[SENECA (c. 5–65)]

NOVEMBER

Chartwell was a refuge and sanctuary for Winston Churchill. The odd conglomeration of structures and additions on the Kentish weald southeast of London was, for him, an earthly paradise. In fact, he often asserted that "A day away from Chartwell is a day wasted." It was home.

And if ever a man needed a home, an earthly elysium to recharge, recoup, and reinvigorate, it was Churchill. He was born into privilege on this day in 1874—the son of the parliamentary master, Lord Randolph Churchill, and thus one of the heirs of the Marlborough legacy. Educated at Harrow and Sandhurst, he entered the Imperial service as a hussars officer. After notable tours of duty in India, Sudan, and South Africa, he entered Parliament himself.

Having already acquired notoriety, he rose quickly through the political ranks. By 1908 he moved from the back benches to become president of the Board of Trade. Two years later he became Home Secretary. The next year he was appointed First Lord of the Admiralty, presiding over the naval expansion that preceded the First World War. He was evidently a man of extraordinary gifts and abilities.

A series of disastrous defeats—including the failure of the Dardanelles expedition, which he had championed—Churchill lost his Admiralty post and served out the remainder of the war on the front lines in France. He undertook a painstakingly slow and difficult political rehabilitation in the years that followed. Most analysts believed his career was essentially over—he was now relegated to the outer fringe of political influence. His dire warnings of the threat from Hitler's Nazi regime in Germany went unheeded. During those difficult years, Churchill bought and renovated the old estate of Chartwell. It was a place where he could rest and reflect, read and write, paint and build, garden and walk. He once asserted, "We shape our dwellings and afterwards, our dwellings shape us." There can be little doubt that he shaped Chartwell to suit his peculiar interests and concerns. There his soul was braced for the great trials ahead.

When the Second World War broke out, the hapless prime minister, Neville Chamberlain, was forced to bring Churchill into the government—even though he was now sixty-five years old. He was appointed First Lord of the Admiralty. The following May, when Chamberlain was forced to resign, Churchill was asked by the king to form a new government and accept the office of Prime Minister.

Over the next five years, he stood practically alone against the Nazi menace. Almost single-handedly he saved Western civilization, stirring the British people to unimaginable feats of valor with his bold oratory and even bolder leadership. His unflagging energy and his stubborn refusal to make peace until Adolf Hitler was crushed were crucial in turning the tide of the war and ultimately leading the Western Allies to victory. After the war, he returned to Chartwell. Extraordinary vitality, imagination, and boldness characterized his whole career. But, he was the first to admit, if he had not had Chartwell—its libraries and gardens, its hearthsides and hedgerows, its peace and quiet—he would never have been able to do what he was called to do.

NOVEMBER

1667 This date marks the birth of Irish novelist and satirist Jonathan Swift, best known for *Gulliver's Travels*, for which he received £200, the only money he ever received for any of his writing.

1782 The United States and Britain signed preliminary peace articles in Paris, ending the Revolutionary War.

1804 Supreme Court Justice Samuel Chase went on trial, accused of political bias. He was ultimately acquitted by the Senate.

1835 Mark Twain—best known as a great American humorist and the creator of Tom Sawyer and Huckleberry Finn—was christened as Samuel Langhorne Clemens, in the little Missouri village of Florida, astride the Mississippi River.

1864 The decisive Battle of Franklin was fought just south of Nashville. Though the forces of the Confederate Army of Tennessee under the command of General Hill technically won the engagement, their losses were so great that they never were able to muster a full fighting force again, thus heralding the end of the bitter War Between the States.

1900 Irish author Oscar Wilde died in Paris.

1935 Author and theologian Dietrich Bonhoeffer returned to Germany from pastoring the exile community in London in order to lead the church's opposition to Adolf Hitler's Nazi regime—it was a decision that would cost him his freedom and ultimately his life. In 1944, he was implicated in a conspiracy that had been linked to the German resistance and was imprisoned at Flossenburg. Convicted of treason, he was sent to the gallows the following year—just days before the Allied liberation.

1936 London's famed Crystal Palace, constructed for the International Exhibition of 1851, was destroyed in a fire.

1939 The Russo-Finnish War began as Soviet troops invaded Finland.

1943 Nat King Cole and his trio made their first recording, "Straighten Up and Fly Right," for Capitol Records.

1962 U Thant of Burma was elected secretary-general of the United Nations, succeeding the late Dag Hammarskjöld.

If you cannot read all your books, at any rate handle, or as it were, fondle them—peer into them, let them fall open where they will, read from the first sentence that arrests the eye, set them back on the shelves with your own hands, arrange them on your own plan so that you at least know where they are. Let them be your friends; let them be your acquaintances.

[WINSTON CHURCHILL (1874–1965)]

NOVEMBER

701

DECEMBER

The civil rights movement was suddenly launched in 1955 when Rosa Parks, exhausted after a hard day's work, refused to surrender her bus seat to a white passenger. She was ultimately arrested, and the humiliating incident galvanized a growing movement to desegregate public transportation, and marked a historic turning point in the African-American struggle for freedom and equality.

Rosa Louise McCauley Parks was born in 1913 in Tuskegee, Alabama, where she grew up in the shadows of Booker T. Washington and George Washington Carver. The granddaughter of former slaves, the future civil rights leader attended the all-black Alabama State College in Montgomery, Alabama. In 1932 she married Raymond Parks, a barber, with whom she became active in Montgomery's chapter of the National Association for the Advancement of Colored People.

In 1943, when Rosa Parks joined the NAACP herself, she helped to mobilize a voter registration drive in Montgomery. That same year Parks also was elected secretary of the Montgomery branch. Six months before her famous protest, Rosa Parks received a scholarship to attend a workshop on school integration for community leaders.

The segregated seating policies on public buses had long been a source of resentment within the black community in Montgomery and in other cities throughout the Deep South. African Americans were required to pay their fares at the front of the bus, and then reboard through the back door. The white bus drivers, who were invested with police powers, frequently harassed blacks, sometimes driving away before African-American passengers were able to get back on the bus. At peak hours, the drivers pushed back boundary markers segregating the bus, crowding those in the "colored section" so that whites could be provided with seats. On the day of her protest, Parks took her seat in the front of the "colored section" of a Montgomery bus. When the driver asked Parks and three other black riders to relinquish their seats to whites, Parks simply refused. The driver called the police, and Parks was arrested.

The Montgomery chapter of the NAACP had been looking for a test case to challenge the legality of segregated bus seating and to woo public opinion with a series of protests. Within twenty-four hours of her arrest, the community had mobilized a massive boycott of the bus system. By December 5, the city buses went through their routes virtually empty. Martin Luther King Jr., who had just moved to Montgomery as the new pastor at the Dexter Avenue Baptist Church, helped to mobilize and inspire the entire African-American community to stand by their principles. The boycott lasted 381 days, during which time 42,000 protesters walked, carpooled, or took taxis, rather than ride the segregated city buses of Montgomery. It was the beginning of the end of segregation.

Of course, the protest proved to be costly for Parks. She lost her job and was unable to find other work in Montgomery. Parks and her husband finally were forced to relocate to Detroit, Michigan, in 1957, where they continued to struggle financially for years. Even so, she remained unwavering in her conviction that she had done what was right. And so was the freedom of millions of Americans secured by her solitary courage.

FEAST DAY
St. Edmund Campion, St. Agericus or Airy, St. Eligius or Elroy, St. Alexander Briant, St. Anasanus, St. Tudwal, St. Ralph Sherwin

DECEMBER

1581   After being tortured, Edmund Campion and other Jesuit martyrs were hanged for sedition at Tyburn.

1789   General George Washington, in a diplomatic letter to his friend Sidi Mohammad, emperor of Morocco, enclosed a copy of the new American Constitution.

1878   The first telephone was installed on this day in the White House.

1879   Gilbert and Sullivan presented *HMS Pinafore* to a New York audience at the Fifth Avenue Theatre. Arthur Sullivan conducted the pit orchestra, while William S. Gilbert played the role of a sailor in the chorus.

1891   James Naismith instructed his students to toss soccer balls into one of two peach buckets that he had nailed to opposite ends of a gym. Basketball was born from the desire to create an indoor sport for exercise in the winter.

1913   Henry Ford introduced the continuous moving assembly line in Dearborn, Michigan, and the first drive-in gas station opened for business in Pittsburgh, Pennsylvania.

1917   Father Ed Flanagan founded Boys Town—a home for poor, orphaned, or problem children—in an old house in Omaha, Nebraska. He borrowed $90 from a friend to pay the first month's rent. For dinner the first Christmas, the boys had a barrel of sauerkraut donated by another friend of the priest. Father Flanagan believed there is no such thing as a boy beyond hope, and he strove to provide a home for the wayward youths where they could grow into the best men possible. He soon moved from the old house in Omaha to a large site outside town called Overlook Farm. The site expanded to hundreds of acres. Before his death in 1948, Father Flanagan traveled around the world spreading his ideas of how to deal with delinquent boys.

1924   George Gershwin's first smash-hit musical, *Lady, Be Good!*, premiered on Broadway, starring Fred and Adele Astaire as Richard and Susie Trevor. This first successful collaborative effort with his brother Ira Gershwin included the songs "Fascinating Rhythm" and "Hang On to Me."

1944   The stunning and scintillating *Concerto for Orchestra* by Hungarian composer Béla Bartók was premiered by the Boston Symphony Orchestra. Bartéok wrote this piece as a commissioned work while dying of leukemia. He was living in American, not respected as a composer, and virtually penniless; he received medical care only from the generosity of others. The *Concerto* was one of the few pieces he had written that was enthusiastically received by audiences. He died in New York on September 26, 1945. One of his final statements was, "The trouble is that I have to go with so much left to say." Within a few months of his death, his works received unprecedented acceptance and notoriety.

1956   Based on Voltaire's allegory, Leonard Bernstein's Broadway musical *Candide* opened.

The oppression of the people is a terrible sin; but the depression of the people is far worse.

[G. K. CHESTERTON (1874–1936)]

DECEMBER

The Monroe Doctrine, excerpted from the president's message to Congress on this day in 1823, was actually formulated by Secretary of State John Quincy Adams. Its design was to head off the colonial intentions of both the Russians—who claimed the coastal lands from the Bering Straits south to an undetermined line in the American Northwest—and the Spanish—who were determined to put down a rash of rebellions in their American colonies.

The foreign policy manifesto began with an explanation:

At the proposal of the Russian imperial government, made through the minister of the Emperor residing here, a full power and instructions have been transmitted to the Minister of the United States at St. Petersburg, to arrange, by amicable negotiation, the respective rights and interests of the two nations on the northwest coast of this continent. A similar proposal has been made by his Imperial Majesty to the government of Great Britain, which has likewise been acceded to. The government of the United States has been desirous, by this friendly proceeding, of manifesting the great value which they have invariably attached to the friendship of the emperor, and their solicitude to cultivate the best understanding with his government. In the discussions to which this interest has given rise, and in the arrangements by which they may terminate, the occasion has been judged proper for asserting, as a principle in which the rights and interests of the United States are involved, that the American continents, by the free and independent condition which they have assumed and maintain, are henceforth not to be considered as subjects for future colonization by any European powers.

After discussing the turmoil among the colonial powers of Europe, the document concluded,

The late events in Spain and Portugal, shew that Europe is still unsettled. Of this important fact, no stronger proof can be adduced than that the allied powers should have thought it proper, on any principle satisfactory to themselves, to have interposed, by force, in the internal concerns of Spain. To what extent such interposition may be carried, on the same principle, is a question, in which all independent powers, whose governments differ from theirs, are interested; even those most remote, and surely none more so than the United States. Our policy, in regard to Europe, which was adopted at an early stage of the wars which have so long agitated that quarter of the globe, nevertheless remains the same, which is, not to interfere in the internal concerns of any of its powers; to consider the government de facto as the legitimate government for us; to cultivate friendly relations with it, and to preserve those relations by a frank, firm, and manly policy, meeting, in all instances, the just claims of every power; submitting to injuries from none. But, in regard to those continents, circumstances are eminently and conspicuously different.

It is impossible that the allied powers should extend their political system to any portion of either continent, without endangering our peace and happiness; nor can any one believe that our Southern Brethren, if left to themselves, would adopt it of their own accord. It is equally impossible, therefore, that we should behold such interposition, in any form, with indifference. If we look to the comparative strength and resources of Spain and those new governments, and their distance from each other, it must be obvious that she can never subdue them. It is still the true policy of the United States, to leave the parties to themselves, in the hope that other powers will pursue the same course.

Though rarely enforced until the administration of Theodore Roosevelt, the statement quickly was recognized as the clearest enunciation of American foreign policy—and has remained so to this day.

DECEMBER

1552   Founder of the Jesuits, St. Francis Xavier, died on this day while attempting a missionary journey to China. He had previously done missionary work in India and Ceylon (Sri Lanka) before traveling to Japan where he learned the language and preached which great success.

1697   The dedication ceremony for the newly rebuilt St. Paul's Cathedral was held in London. A church had stood on Ludgate Hill since the seventh century and a magnificent medieval cathedral was built there in 1087, twenty years after the Norman conquest. But this medieval cathedral was destroyed by the Great Fire that swept through London in September 1666. The royal architect Christopher Wren was chosen to design the new cathedral—and his baroque and classical design was stunning, with a main aisle of more than 150 yards and a dome soaring 366 feet above it. Construction began on June 21, 1675. Dedication ceremonies were held over twenty years later on this day. The church quickly became a London landmark. Many famous Britons were buried there in the years that followed, including the Duke of Wellington, Lord Nelson, and Sir Christopher Wren himself. During the Nazi Blitz of the Second World War, the dome of St. Paul's towering through the haze was a beacon of hope and a comfort to the embattled population of London.

1804   Napoleon Bonaparte, with Josephine by his side, was inaugurated by Pope Pius VII, and crowned himself Emperor Napoleon I at the Cathedral of Notre Dame in Paris.

1859   The French painter who developed the pointillism technique, Georges Seurat, was born in Paris. His greatest work was *A Sunday Afternoon on the Island of La Grande Jatte* (1884–1886).

1859   Militant abolitionist John Brown was hanged for his raid on Harper's Ferry the previous October.

1863   A groundbreaking ceremony in Omaha, Nebraska, marked the beginning of construction on the Union Pacific Railroad.

1867   Charles Dickens gave his first reading in New York City. Before the box office opened people stood in two lines almost a mile long waiting for tickets.

1883   Johannes Brahms continued his mastery of the symphonic form with the premier of his Symphony no. 3 in F in Vienna.

1923   Greek-American opera singer Maria Callas was born in New York City. She moved to Greece at the age of thirteen, where she made her debut five years later in *Tosca*. She helped to revive several forgotten operas with her distinctive voice and dramatic gift.

1927   Automobile maker Henry Ford unveiled his Model A Ford. This successor to the Model T generated so much interest that an estimated one million people made their way to Ford Headquarters in New York City just to look at it. The roadster sold for $385.

1942   Beneath the stands of the University of Chicago's football stadium, physicist Enrico Fermi and a team of scientists built the first simple nuclear reactor. On this day, they achieved a self-sustaining, controlled nuclear chain reaction.

Clear and round dealing is the honor of a man's nature, and that mixture of falsehood is like alloy in coin of gold and silver, which makes the metal work the better, but debases it.

[Francis Bacon (1561–1626)]

DECEMBER

1833

Oberlin College in Oberlin, Ohio, became the first fully coeducational institution of higher learning in the United States, with twenty-nine males and fifteen females enrolling for classes. Oberlin was also the first college to champion the abolition of slavery and to welcome blacks as a fully integrated part of the student body. The college was an outgrowth of the revival movement led by Charles G. Finney, who later became president of the college.

FEAST DAY
Saints Claudius, Hilaria, and their Companions; St. Birnius; St. Lucius of Britain; St. Cassian of Tanger, St. Francis Xavier

3

DECEMBER

When Herman Melville first visited Washington on this day in 1862, the nation was in the midst of its terribly uncivil War Between the States. The city itself was in a awful state. Even in the best of circumstances, it would have looked dramatically different than it does today—the Washington Monument was not yet built, the Smithsonian Institution was contained in a single small building, the new cast-iron dome for the Capitol had only been partially constructed, and the great parks were rough, unkempt, and untended. The streets were muddy, ill-managed, and clogged with commercial wagons. The government offices were crowded, poorly administered, and badly maintained. And worse, these were hardly the best of circumstances.

Wartime Washington was a awash in the detritus of strife. Melville was shocked by the numbers of wounded soldiers that walked the streets near the Federal hospitals. He was outraged by the sight of the continuing slave trade just blocks from President Lincoln's residence in the White House. And he was baffled by the sense of doom that seemed to pervade every conversation. A goodly number of the citizens—and many of the most prominent leaders—seemed gripped by an almost irrational frenzy of fear and trepidation. Indeed, it seemed that the Confederate forces under the able leadership of General Lee and Jackson might sweep across the Virginia border any day—as they had been threatening to do since the beginning of the armed hostilities—sending the government fleeing into an ignominious exile.

Melville was an eminent man of letters—but he was not visiting Washington as a writer. Rather, he had come as a government official. He worked in New York at the Port Authority as a customs inspector, having given up writing some five years earlier.

Thus, in 1862, both the man and the city were rather out of sorts.

When he visited Washington in 1862, he could not help but see the sad parallels between the squandered promise of his own life and the squandered promise of the national life. Everything that was necessary for greatness in both was everywhere evident, yet the expediencies of the moment and the exigencies of circumstances demanded otherwise.

After his short visit, during which he tended to what he called "the banal administrative chores typical of Washington politics," he returned to his home, saddened by the irony of it all.

1818 Illinois was admitted as the twenty-first state.

1828 Andrew Jackson was elected president of the United States.

1846 Leslie Printice was a young widow in New York City when she first became active in the pro-life movement. A member of Gardiner Spring's congregation at the prominent Brick Presbyterian Church, she was encouraged by his sermons on child-killing to take a bold and active stand. She organized several meetings in her midtown Manhattan brownstone of doctors, lawyers, politicians, judges, and community leaders to hear the facts about the abortion trade. Under the auspices of the church she set up the New York Parent and Child Committee. The committee established prayer networks, sidewalk counseling shifts, and even alternative care programs with Christian doctors. It also organized regular protests in front of Anna Lohman's five area abortion franchises—known professionally as Madame Restell, Lohman was the boldest, richest, and most visible child-killer. Tenacious and unrelenting, Leslie led a rally outside Lohman's lavish home on this day that was by turns emotional, physical, and fierce. When Lohman went to trial for the first time the next year, Leslie was there—despite innumerable threats on her life from a number of the gangsters on Lohman's payroll—to testify with several children "saved from the butcher's knife." Nearly half a century later, her efforts were recognized in Albany by Theodore Roosevelt as the primary catalyst for the state's tougher legislation and stiffer enforcement.

1857 Novelist Joseph Conrad, best known for *Heart of Darkness* and *Lord Jim*, was born in the Ukraine to Polish parents who were in exile. His adventurous life on the seas—including stints in the French Merchant Marine, the British Merchant Navy, and as captain of his own ship—led him to such exotic locales as the West Indies, Constantinople, the Far East, India, Java, and Bangkok. His four months of command on a Congo River steamboat provided much of the inspiration for *Heart of Darkness*.

1925 Concerto in F, the first jazz concerto for piano and orchestra, was premiered by its composer George Gershwin at a concert in Carnegie Hall in New York City.

1947 Tennessee Williams debuted his play *A Streetcar Named Desire* starring Marlon Brando and Jessica Tandy. Williams won his first Pulitzer Prize for the play.

1954 William Walton's opera *Troilus and Cressida* premiered in London. The sources for the opera were the stories by Boccaccio (1340) and Chaucer (1380) rather than the treatments of the same story in the plays of Shakespeare (1600) and Dryden (1678). The setting for the opera is Troy during the twelfth century B.C.

1960 The musical *Camelot* opened on Broadway.

1962 A dense fog blanketed the city of London for a period of four days and virtually shut down all transportation. When the fog finally lifted, 106 people had died in the city—most of them from breathing the high content of sulfur dioxide that was in the air.

1967 Dr. Christian Barnard led a team of surgeons in performing the first heart transplant in humans in Cape Town, South Africa. Louis Washkansky lived eighteen days with the new heart.

1984 The worst industrial accident in history occurred on this night at the Union Carbide Plant in Bhopal, India, when a leak of the deadly gas methyl isocyanate took the lives of more than 2,000 people and injured an additional 200,000.

This is a practice as full of labor as a wise man's art, for folly that he wisely shows is fit, but wise men, folly-fall'n, quite taint their wit.

[WILLIAM SHAKESPEARE (C. 1564–1616)]

DECEMBER

A prophet is not without honor except in his own town, or perhaps in his own time. Thomas Carlyle was widely acknowledged along with William Cobbett, John Ruskin, and William Morris as one of the great Jeremiahs of the Victorian Age. Like them, he railed against the bold materialism, the bare rationalism, and the brazen skepticism of his time with an untempered fervor rivaling the seers of yore. And consequently, he was less than esteemed by his peers. But he has proved more relevant than almost all of them—to our time and to all time.

Chided as a contentious crank and pilloried as a bombastic buffoon, Carlyle nonetheless set the standard for philosophical commentary and almost single-handedly changed the shape of historical research for several generations to come. By turns scholarly and theatrical, sober and whimsical, furtive and satirical, he challenged the staid notions of the dispassionate academic literary establishment and championed the popularization of revisionist and partisan chronicling.

He was born on this day in 1795, the first of nine children, in the small market town of Ecclefechan in the Scottish county of Dumfriesshire, not far from the north shore of the Solway Firth. The roots of his family in that Annandale soil were deep and tenacious. His father was a stonemason and a farmer who raised his progeny in the proud but stern providence of the Burgher Secession Church—one of the numerous splinter groups that had rebelled against the laxity of the established national church. Though young Carlyle fled to the intellectual environs of literary London at the earliest opportunity, he was never to escape the tug of those strong childhood influences: He was a resolute Scot, a hardworking commoner, and a convinced Calvinist. Furious episodes of rebellion from these standards would punctuate his life and career, but he always returned—thus demonstrating his contention that what a man is ultimately determines what he does, not the other way around.

Carlyle abandoned his first ambition to be a clergyman for a career as an economist and mathematician—but before long his wide-ranging intellect felt too constrained even by that. He read voraciously and omnivorously of the medieval classics and the *chansons de chivalry,* realizing before long that his emerging worldview—rooted in that profound heritage of near-forgotten Christendom—was utterly at odds with the prevailing Enlightenment view of his time. So he began to write—or rather to prophesy.

In 1834 Carlyle moved to the Chelsea section of London, where he soon became known as the Sage of Chelsea and was a member of a literary circle that included the essayists Leigh Hunt and John Stuart Mill. It was there that Carlyle wrote his magisterial two-volume history, *The French Revolution.* This was followed by a series of lectures, including *On Heroes and Hero-Worship, Chartism,* and *Past and Present.* Profoundly influenced by the theologian and reformer Thomas Chalmers, his work inevitably betrayed his Scottish Presbyterian roots.

DECEMBER

1783 General George Washington bade farewell to his officers at Fraunces Tavern in New York City.

1816 James Monroe of Virginia was elected the fifth president of the United States, ushering in the "Era of Good Feeling."

1839 The Whig Party opened a national convention in Harrisburg, Pennsylvania, during which delegates nominated William Henry Harrison for president.

1856 Samuel Taylor was a prototypical mild-mannered small-town pharmacist. A family man, community leader, and life-long Methodist, he had a natural Midwestern aversion to controversy. But when the daughter of one of his customers was nearly poisoned by a dose of mail-order abortifacient pills, he sprang into action. He discovered that the abortifacient business was booming all over the United States—and that it was an entirely unrestricted, unregulated, and unmonitored industry. Without the benefits of a government agency, an institutional largess, or a corporate sponsor, he began a one-man educational campaign—first with his fellow pharmacists, later expanding to physicians, and finally with state legislators—to alert the public to the physical dangers and the moral liabilities of the child-killing trade. Taylor testified before the Ohio, Illinois, and Indiana legislatures—winning their support for a ban on the sale of all chemical parricides and abortifacients—and he drafted model legislation that was approved by fourteen other states.

1866 Russian painter Wassily Kandinsky, who cofounded the *Der Blaue Reiter* (The Blue Rider) group of artists was born on this day. He was instrumental in the development of abstract art.

1915 Henry Ford led a private peace expedition to Europe to "get the boys out of the trenches by Christmas." The group was unable to agree among themselves and broke up soon after arriving in Europe.

1918 President Wilson set sail for France to attend the Versailles Peace Conference where he would present his famous Fourteen Points.

1942 President Franklin Roosevelt ordered the dismantling of the Works Progress Administration, which had been created to provide jobs during the Great Depression.

1945 The Senate approved American participation in the United Nations.

1965 The United States launched *Gemini 7* with Air Force Lieutenant Colonel Frank Borman and Navy Commander James A. Lovell aboard.

1978 San Francisco got its first female mayor as City Supervisor Dianne Feinstein was named to replace the assassinated George Moscone.

1996 The *Mars Pathfinder* lifted off from Cape Canaveral and began speeding toward Mars on a 310-million-mile odyssey to explore the Red Planet's surface.

Only for a little of the first fruits of wisdom— only a few fragments of the boundless heights, breadths, and depths of truth—does the world yearn for from our table of grace.

[MARTIN LUTHER (1483–1546)]

DECEMBER

1815

On a Tuesday, the Earl of Home led the men of Ettrick against Sir Walter Scott and his team from Yarrow in a game of football. In honor of the match, which took place at Carterhaugh in Ettrick Forest, Scotland, the poet penned two songs to inspire his team, including the words:

Then strip lads, and to it, though sharp be the weather,
And if by mischance, you should happen to fall,
There are worse things in life than a tumble in the heather,
And life is itself but a game of foot-ball!

On this day in 1955, Martin Luther King Jr. launched the Montgomery bus boycott in Montgomery, Alabama. Though he would one day gain recognition as the undisputed leader of the American civil rights movement and the consensus winner of the Nobel Peace Prize, at the time he was still just a young and untested pastor of a local congregation, the Dexter Avenue Baptist Church.

He was born in Atlanta, Georgia, the eldest son of Martin Luther King Sr., a Baptist minister at the historic Ebenezer Baptist Church. King attended local segregated public schools, where he excelled. He entered nearby Morehouse College at age fifteen and graduated with a bachelor's degree in sociology in 1948. After graduating with honors from Crozer Theological Seminary in Pennsylvania in 1951, he went to Boston University where he earned a doctoral degree in systematic theology in 1955.

NATIONAL DAY
Thailand
FEAST DAY
St. Christian, St. Sabas, St. Justinian or Iestin, St. Crispina, St. Nicetius of Trier, St. Sigiramnus or Cyran, St. John Almond

King's public-speaking ability—which would become renowned as his stature grew in the civil rights movement—was already well-developed when he came to Montgomery in 1954, and he quickly emerged as a community leader.

Montgomery's African-American community had long-standing grievances about the mistreatment of blacks on city buses. Many white bus drivers treated blacks rudely, often cursing them and humiliating them by enforcing the city's segregation laws, which forced them to sit in the back of buses and give up their seats to white passengers on crowded buses. On December 1, 1955, Rosa Parks, an active member of the NAACP, was ordered by a bus driver to give up her seat to a white passenger. When she refused, she was arrested and taken to jail. Local leaders of the NAACP recognized that the arrest of the popular and highly respected Parks was the event that could rally local blacks to a bus protest.

The Montgomery bus boycott lasted for more than a year, demonstrating a new spirit of unity among African Americans. King's serious demeanor and consistent appeal to Christian brotherhood and American idealism made a positive impression on whites outside the South. Incidents of violence against black protesters, including the bombing of King's home, focused media attention on Montgomery. By the time the Supreme Court ruled in favor of desegregation, King had become a national figure. Neither Montgomery nor the nation would ever be the same again.

DECEMBER

1057 Macbeth, the Scottish king, died on this day. He served as a commander for King Duncan I and a chieftain for the Moray District. Macbeth claimed the throne after murdering Duncan in 1040. He ruled for seventeen years before being killed in battle by Malcolm Canmore, one of the sons of Duncan I, who eventually became Malcolm III, king of Scotland.

1776 The first scholastic fraternity in America, Phi Beta Kappa, was organized at the College of William and Mary in Williamsburg, Virginia.

1784 African-American poet Phyllis Wheatley died in Boston. Born in Africa, she was brought to the American colonies in 1761 and purchased by John Wheatley, a tailor of Boston. She was granted the unusual privilege of an education, and she began writing poetry at the age of fourteen. With the publication of *Poems on Various Subjects, Religious and Moral* in 1773, her fame spread throughout Europe. In 1776, George Washington invited her to visit his army headquarters after reading a poem she had written about him.

1791 Austrian composer Wolfgang Amadeus Mozart died in Vienna, Austria, at the age of thirty-six while working on the *Requiem* for choir and orchestra. He was buried in an unmarked pauper's grave.

1830 English poet Christina Georgina Rossetti, sister of poet Dante Gabriel Rossetti, was born in London. She was the most important female poet in her era, due to the breadth of her range and the quality of her works. She was best known for her works of fantasy, children's poems, and especially religious works such as *None Other Lamb* and *Love Came Down at Christmas*.

1901 Movie producer Walt Disney was born in Chicago.

1906 Just after receiving the Nobel Peace Prize, President Theodore Roosevelt wrote to his son, Kermit, and explained why he could not accept the award money that went along with the prize. "It appears that there is a large sum of money— they say about $40,000—that goes with it. Now, I hate to do anything foolish. . . . But Mother and I talked it over and came to the conclusion that . . . I could not accept any money given to me for making peace between two nations, especially when I was able to make peace simply because I was President." Roosevelt had masterminded the peace ending the Russian-Japanese War.

1932 German physicist Albert Einstein was granted a visa, making it possible for him to travel to the United States.

1933 National Prohibition came to an end as Utah became the thirty-sixth state to ratify the Twenty-first Amendment to the Constitution, repealing the Eighteenth Amendment.

1946 World-renowned operatic tenor José Carreras was born in Barcelona, Spain. He is known for his pure tone and lyricism.

1955 The American Federation of Labor and the Congress of Industrial Organizations merged to form the AFL-CIO under its first president, George Meany.

Education is not the filling of a pail but the lighting of a fire. Of such is wisdom.

[WILLIAM BUTLER YEATS (1865–1939)]

DECEMBER

The fourth-century pastor who inspired the tradition of Santa Claus may not have lived at the North Pole or traveled by reindeer and sleigh, but he certainly was a paradigm of graciousness, generosity, and Christian charity. Nicholas of Myra's great love and concern for children drew him into a crusade that ultimately resulted in protective Imperial statutes that remained in place in Byzantium for more than a thousand years.

Though little is known of his childhood, he was probably born to wealthy parents at Patara in Lycia, a Roman province of Asia Minor. As a young man noted for his piety, judiciousness, and charity, he was chosen bishop of the then rundown diocese of Myra. There he gained renown for his personal holiness, evangelistic zeal, and pastoral compassion.

Early Byzantine histories reported that he suffered imprisonment and made a famous profession of faith during the persecution of Diocletian. He was also reputedly present at the Council of Nicaea, where he forthrightly condemned the heresy of Arianism—one story holds that he actually slapped the heretic Arius. But it was his love for and care of children that gained him his greatest renown. Though much of what we know about his charitable work on behalf of the poor, the despised, and the rejected has been distorted by legend and lore over the centuries, it is evident that he was a particular champion of the downtrodden, bestowing upon them gifts as tokens of the grace and mercy of the gospel.

One legend tells of how a citizen of Patara lost his fortune, and because he could not raise dowries for his three young daughters, he was going to give them over to prostitution. After hearing this, Nicholas took a small bag of gold and threw it through the window of the man's house on the eve of the Feast of Christ's Nativity. The eldest girl was married with it as her dowry. He performed the same gracious service for each of the other girls on each of the succeeding nights. The three purses, portrayed in art with the saint, were thought to be the origin of the pawnbroker's symbol of three gold balls. But they were also the inspiration for Christians to begin the habit of gift giving during each of the twelve days of Christmas—from December 25 until Epiphany on January 6.

In yet another legend, Nicholas saved several youngsters from certain death when he pulled them from a deep vat of vinegar brine—again, on the Feast of the Nativity. Ever afterward, Christians remembered the day by giving one another large crisp pickles.

The popular cultural representation of St. Nicholas as Father Christmas or Santa Claus, though drawing on a number of such legends, was based primarily on a the Dutch custom of giving children presents—slipping fruits, nuts, and little toys into shoes or stockings drying along the warm hearthside—on his feast day, December 6. Throughout the rest of Europe during the Middle Ages, that day was marked by festively decorating homes and by a sumptuous feast that interrupted the general fasting of Advent. And in Scandanavia it was celebrated as a day of visitation, when the elders of all the remote country churches would bundle themselves in their thick furs and drive their sleighs laden with gift pastries, through the snowy landscape to every home within the parish.

6

DECEMBER

714

1790 Congress moved from New York to Philadelphia.

1849 Harriet Tubman, who later founded the Underground Railroad, escaped from slavery in Maryland.

1877 American inventor Thomas Alva Edison created the first known recording of sound when he recited "Mary Had a Little Lamb" into his newly invented phonograph.

1884 The Washington Monument was completed when the 3,300-pound marble capstone was placed on top of the 555-foot-tall obelisk after thirty-six years of work.

1889 Jefferson Davis, the first and only president of the Confederate States of America, died in New Orleans.

1896 Pulitzer Prize–winning lyricist Ira Gershwin was born in New York City. Perhaps his best-known works were through his collaboration with brother George, which resulted in such memorable songs as "The Man I Love," "Someone to Watch Over Me," "I Got Rhythm," and "Lady, Be Good!"

1923 A presidential address was broadcast on radio for the first time as President Calvin Coolidge spoke to a joint session of Congress.

1935 The Marx brothers' *A Night at the Opera*, which contains the hilarious boat cabin scene as well as the contract scene, opened at the Capitol.

1945 The patent for the microwave was issued.

1947 Everglades National Park in Florida was dedicated by President Harry Truman.

1969 A concert by The Rolling Stones at the Altamont Speedway in Livermore, California, was marred by the deaths of four people, including one who was stabbed by a Hell's Angel.

1973 Gerald R. Ford, the House minority leader, was sworn in as the first un-elected vice president. He replaced Spiro T. Agnew who had resigned in October over a series of personal, financial, and political scandals.

SANTA

The transformation of St. Nicholas into Santa Claus is rooted in a number of intertwined traditions, legends, and archetypes. But perhaps more than any other source, the advertising of soft drink manufacturer Coca Cola and the holiday cartoons of New York newspaperman Thomas Nash have profoundly shaped our perception. Coca Cola's serving trays, signage, and print ads popularized the Nash caricature of a rotund, jolly, fur-draped, gift-laden, and unbidden visitor who pops down chimneys and distributes gifts to children all over the world. Alas, thus stripped of his pastoral function and parish proximity, Santa has become almost fairylike in his mythic proportions.

The giver of every good and perfect gift has called upon us to mimic His giving, by grace, though faith, and this not of ourselves.

[NICHOLAS OF MYRA (c. 288–354)]

DECEMBER

Ambrose of Milan was one of the most celebrated pastors, theologians, and statesmen during the Patristic Age of the church. His life and work was one of the most remarkable in the late Roman Empire.

He was born in Trier—now in Germany—and educated in Rome. His father was the Roman Imperial Prefect of Gaul. With his patronage, Ambrose was able to study law, enter the civil service, and rise quickly through the ranks of the bureaucracy and diplomatic corps. In about the year 370 he was appointed governor of Aemilia and Liguria, with his headquarters at Milan. In this office his kindness and wisdom won the esteem and love of the public, who called him to be bishop of Milan on this day in 374.

Although he had converted some years before, he had not yet been baptized—so, he was actually consecrated as a bishop before he had even formally entered into the covenant of church membership, much less been ordained. Nevertheless, he took his responsibilities very seriously. He devoted himself to the study of Scripture and the writings of Origen and Basil, becoming an influential protagonist of their thought in the West.

Because Milan was the administrative capital of the Western Empire, Ambrose came to play an important role in the politics of his day—indeed, he was bold in his counsel, reproof, and discipline of the civil magistrates. To the young emperor Gratian, for instance, he wrote a work entitled *On the Faith,* warning of the dangers of Arianism. He also refused to give over a church in Milan for use by Arians at the Imperial court despite pleas from the emperor himself. He went so far as to excommunicate Emperor Maximus for the unjust execution of the heretic Priscillian, and he imposed a public penance on Emperor Theodosius I for ordering a massacre in Thessalonica. In addition, he intervened with Emperor Valentinian II to prevent the restoration of a statue of the goddess Nike to the Senate house in Rome.

In addition, he was active in the reform of the church, its liturgy, and its music. He developed the Ambrosian chant and introduced the singing of hymns in the Latin church. Tradition says that he and Augustine spontaneously composed the *Te Deum* in alternating verses on the occasion of Augustine's baptism.

And in fact, it was for that remarkable event that Ambrose is best known—he was the man God used to draw the brilliant Augustine of Hippo to faith in Christ. It was his clear proclamation of the gospel that finally knocked down the walls of Augustine's doubt, and it was his gracious encouragement that welcomed Augustine into the covenant community.

After his death in 397, Ambrose was quickly adopted as the patron saint of Milan, and the Ambrosian Library in that city was named in his honor.

FEAST DAY
St. Martin of Saujon, St. Ambrose of Milan, St. Eutychianus, St. Servus, St. Buithe or Boethius

DECEMBER

43
B.C. Roman statesman, scholar, and author Marcus Tullius Cicero was murdered on this day. His writings preserve much of Greek thought as well as provide a glimpse into the political machinations of first-century B.C. Roman politics.

1598 Giovanni Lorenzo Bernini, the Italian sculptor and architect, was born in Naples. He is considered to be the single most important artistic talent of the Italian baroque. He worked as a painter, draftsman, stage designer, playwright, and designer of fireworks displays. He was able to capture emotion and movement in his sculptures with great energy. Perhaps his greatest work is *The Ecstasy of Saint Teresa*.

1787 By a unanimous vote, Delaware became the first state to ratify the U.S. Constitution.

1796 Electors chose John Adams to be the second president of the United States.

1836 Martin Van Buren was elected the eighth president of the United States.

1842 The New York Philharmonic performed works by Ludwig van Beethoven and Karl Maria von Weber during its premier concert.

1873 American frontier novelist Willa Cather—best known for her novels *O Pioneers!* (1913), *My Antonia* (1918), *Death Comes for the Archbishop* (1927), and *Song of the Lark* (1915)—was born in Winchester, Virginia. She was awarded the Pulitzer Prize in 1922 for her novel *One of Ours*.

1941 On this "date which will live in infamy," a surprise attack by the Japanese at Pearl Harbor, Hawaii, thrust the United States into the Second World War. At anchor in the harbor was nearly the entire United States Pacific fleet. In the attack that lasted for just over one hour, several ships were sunk, two hundred airplanes were destroyed on the ground, and almost three thousand people lost their lives.

1972 America's last moon mission to date was launched as *Apollo 17* blasted off from Cape Canaveral.

1987 The Communist dictator of the Soviet Union, Mikhail S. Gorbachev, set foot on American soil for the first time, arriving for a Washington summit with President Ronald Reagan.

1989 East Germany's Communist Party agreed to cooperate with the opposition in paving the way for free elections and a revised constitution.

To be genuinely wise, one must make haste slowly.

[BENJAMIN FRANKLIN (1706–1790)]

DECEMBER

717

The day after the Japanese military conducted a surprise attack on the American naval base at Pearl Harbor, Hawaii, President Franklin Delano Roosevelt addressed Congress and the nation in a broadcast heard worldwide.

In somber tones, the president began his speech, "Yesterday, December 7, 1941—a date which will live in infamy—the United States of America was suddenly and deliberately attacked by naval and air forces of the Empire of Japan."

With evident emotion, even anger, he continued, "The United States was at peace with that nation and, at the solicitation of Japan, was still in conversation with its government and its emperor looking toward the maintenance of peace in the Pacific.

His reasoned argument was an clear indictment of Japanese intentions: "It will be recorded that the distance of Hawaii from Japan makes it obvious that the attack was deliberately planned many days or even weeks ago. During the intervening time the Japanese government had deliberately sought to deceive the United States by false statements and expressions of hope for continued peace. The attack yesterday on the Hawaiian Islands has caused severe damage to American naval and military forces. Very many American lives have been lost. In addition American ships have been reported torpedoed on the high seas between San Francisco and Honolulu."

He then listed a whole litany of transgressions: "Yesterday the Japanese government also launched an attack against Malaya. Last night Japanese forces attacked Hong Kong. Last night Japanese forces attacked Guam. Last night Japanese forces attacked the Philippine Islands. Last night the Japanese attacked Wake Island. This morning the Japanese attacked Midway Island. Japan has, therefore, undertaken a surprise offensive extending throughout the Pacific area. The facts of yesterday speak for themselves. The people of the United States have already formed their opinions and well understand the implications to the very life and safety of our nation."

He then concluded: "As commander in chief of the army and navy I have directed that all measures be taken for our defense. Always will we remember the character of the onslaught against us. No matter how long it may take us to overcome this premeditated invasion, the American people in their righteous might will win through to absolute victory. I believe I interpret the will of the Congress and of the people when I assert that we will not only defend ourselves to the uttermost but will make very certain that this form of treachery shall never endanger us again. Hostilities exist. There is no blinking at the fact that our people, our territory, and our interests are in grave danger. With confidence in our armed forces—with the unbounded determination of our people—we will gain the inevitable triumph—so help us God."

Later that afternoon, Congress overwhelmingly passed a resolution declaring war on Japan and the Axis powers. America had entered the Second World War.

FEAST DAY

The Immaculate Conception, St. Romaric, St. Eucharius, St. Sophronius of Cyprus, St. Patapius

DECEMBER

65 B.C. The Latin poet Quintus Horatius Flactus, better known as Horace, was born on this day. His best-known writings include *Satires, Odes, Epodes, Epistles,* and *Ars Poetica.*

1660 For the first time, an English actress—thought to have been one Mrs. Norris—played a female lead in a Shakespearean play as Desdemona in *Othello.*

1776 George Washington's retreating army in the American Revolution crossed the Delaware River from New Jersey to Pennsylvania.

1854 Pope Pius IX proclaimed the dogma of the Immaculate Conception.

1863 President Abraham Lincoln announced his plans for the reconstruction of the South including amnesty for Confederate deserters.

1865 Finnish late-Romantic composer Jean Sibelius was born in Hämeenlinna. He was educated at the Helsinki Conservatory, taught there, and spent the rest of his life in the Helsinki area. His intensely nationalistic music was inspired by Finnish legends and the melodic and rhythmic patterns of Finnish poetry and music. One of his characteristics was to use short motifs that continue to be transformed and evolved until they finally are metamorphosed into a complete melody. He stopped composing in 1929 and died at the age of ninety-one on September 20, 1957.

1886 The American Federation of Labor was founded in Columbus, Ohio.

1914 *Watch Your Step,* Irving Berlin's first musical revue, opened in New York.

1949 The Chinese nationalists, consisting of the government of Chiang Kai-shek, moved to Formosa—the island of Taiwan—after the Communists drove them out of mainland China.

1978 Former American schoolteacher and prime minister of Israel Golda Meir died in Jerusalem at age eighty.

1980 Former Beatle star John Lennon was shot to death outside his New York City apartment building by an apparently deranged fan.

1987 President Ronald Reagan and Soviet dictator Mikhail S. Gorbachev signed a treaty calling for destruction of intermediate-range nuclear missiles.

1991 In a signed agreement in Minsk, the Union of Soviet Socialist Republics dissolved into the Commonwealth of Independent States, led by Russia, Belorussia, and the Ukraine.

1993 President Bill Clinton signed into law the North American Free Trade Agreement—a measure designed to remove trade barriers between Canada, the U.S., and Mexico.

1996 Homegoing of Andy Tant—friend, student, and servant.

Be courteous to all, but intimate with few, and let those few be well tried before you give them your confidence. True friendship is a plant of slow growth, and must undergo and withstand the shocks of adversity before it is entitled to the appellation.

[GEORGE WASHINGTON (1732–1799)]

DECEMBER

1640 — Because he declared himself free of original sin, Hugh Bewitt was banished from the Massachusetts Colony.

Three hundred years ago the American Puritan pastor Cotton Mather completed a book of historical reflection he had worked on "in snatches" for a little more than four years. Toward the end of 1693 he became convinced that in order to facilitate a spiritual reformation in the life of the American church—and those abroad—a survey of the heretofore untold "mighty works of grace" needed to be made public. Though it would not be published until 1702, *Magnalia Christi Americana* is clearly marked by the concerns of the *fin de siècle*—or end of the century—in which it was written.

The more things change, the more they stay the same. Then, as now, the speculations of men ran to the frantic and the frenetic. Ecstatic eschatalogical significance was read into every change of any consequence—be it of the weather or of the government. Apocalyptic reticence was chided as faithlessness, while practical intransigence was enshrined as faithfulness. Fantastic common wisdom replaced ordinary common sense, and plain selfish serenity replaced plain selfless civility.

Mather wrote three hundred years ago, but he wrote in a time very much like our own. What he wrote was a jeremiad—a stern warning. It is a mode of address that we would do well to hear and heed. Though his subject was a survey of the ecclesiastical history of New England—from the founding at Plymouth, the establishment of culture at Boston, and the erection of institutions like Harvard to the desperate struggles of the frontier, the disputations of heretics like Roger Williams and Anne Hutchinson, and the wars against the Indians—his purpose was the restoration of the original vision of the pioneers who had come to America to "set a city on a hill." He desired, first and foremost, to revive the traditions of the "New England way" and the fervor of the old "errand into the wilderness." His fear was that the growing prosperity of the land had "softened the resolve and hardened the hearts" of the "heirs of the Pilgrims and Puritans."

Reading *Magnalia Christi Americana* is thus satisfying on several levels. First, it affords readers insight into the colonial era unclouded by the palimpsests of modern skeptics and cynics—instead, the remarkable achievements of our Pilgrim and Puritan fathers are confirmed through the lens of faith. Second, it reveals the breadth and depth of the spiritual foundations upon which American liberty was based—freedom was clearly not conceived in a worldview vacuum. Third, it recasts the image of American education—its character and its purpose—by recalling the remarkable early days of classical and covenantal learning at Harvard and Yale. Fourth, it presents a lucid literary approach to the task of writing history—one that became a model of moral philosophy for many of America's finest historians and writers in the years to come.

NATIONAL DAY
Tanzania
FEAST DAY
*The Seven Martyrs of Samosata,
St. Peter Fourier, St. Budoc or
Beuzec, St. Gorgonia, St. Leocadia*

DECEMBER

1608 One of the greatest poets of the English language, John Milton, author of *Paradise Lost*, was born in Bread Street, Cheapside, London. Writing in a grand style, he portrayed the fall of Lucifer and the subsequent fall of man with great power and majesty of language. *Paradise Lost* and Milton's other epics, *Paradise Regained* and *Sampson Agonistes*, were all written fifteen to twenty years after the poet went blind. A defender of the Puritan cause, Milton was arrested after the restoration of Charles II. However, his reputation helped shorten the length of his imprisonment. He died on November 8, 1674.

1848 American author and creator of the Uncle Remus stories, Joel Chandler Harris, was born in Eatonton, Georgia. The shenanigans of Brer Rabbit, Brer Fox, and Brer Bear owe much to Harris's familiarity with folklore and the creation of a distinctive type of dialect literature.

1854 Alfred, Lord Tennyson's famous poem, "The Charge of the Light Brigade," was published in England.

1886 Clarence Birdseye, the American industrialist who developed the method of deep-freezing foods, was born in Brooklyn, New York. As one of the founders of General Foods Corporation, he revolutionized the way Americans ate.

1907 Christmas seals went on sale for the first time, at the Wilmington, Delaware, post office; proceeds went to fight tuberculosis.

1917 The Ottoman Turks surrendered Jerusalem to the British as the conflict of the First World War drew to a close. A month earlier, the British foreign office had issued the Balfour Declaration, which promised British help in establishing a Jewish nation in their ancestral homeland of Palestine. By that time the British had already routed the Turks in the southern portion of the land. British General Allenby took the port city of Jaffa and marched on Jerusalem. After Allenby took the Nablus highway north of Jerusalem, he was able to march directly to the city. Seven hundred years of rule by the Muslim Turks came to an end; for the first time since the Crusades the country was governed by a Christian nation. Palestine remained a protectorate of Great Britain until Israel became independent in 1948.

1939 Cardinal Pacelli succeeded Pius XI as Pope Pius XII and continued Catholic opposition to "the neo-pagan doctrines" of the Nazis. In his first encyclical, *Summi Pontificatus*, he condemned "exacerbated nationalism, the idolatry of the state, totalitarianism, racism, the cult of brutal force, contempt of international agreements," and, in short, "all the characteristics of Hitler's political system." When Jews were rounded up in France and deported to Germany in 1942, the collaborating governments tried to get at least partial support from the Vatican but were severely rebuffed. Pius XII twice agreed to directly contact the highest level of the German civil and military Resistance in order to represent it before the London War Cabinet. Though events led to the cancellation of the plan, the pope led many in the church, both Catholic and Protestant, to reject Nazi ideology as anti-Christian paganism and actively resist and rescue. More than once he publicly brought attention to "the anxious supplications of all those who, because of their nationality or their race, are overwhelmed by the greatest trials and most acute distress, and at times even destined, without any personal fault, to measures of extermination."

1958 The anti-Communist John Birch Society was formed in Indianapolis.

1965 *A Charlie Brown Christmas* first aired on CBS featuring the jazz music of the Vince Guaraldi Trio. The highlight of the show is the acceptance of Charlie Brown's Christmas tree, the reciting of the Christmas story, and the singing of all the verses of "Hark! The Herald Angels Sing."

*W*here is human nature so weak as in the bookstore?

[HENRY WARD BEECHER (1813–1887)]

DECEMBER

YULETIDE

The holiday season—what we generically call Christmastime—is actually a long sequence of holy days, festal revelries, and liturgical rites stretching from the end of November through the beginning of January that are collectively known as Yuletide. Beginning with Advent, a time of preparation and repentance, proceeding to Christmas, a time of celebration and generosity, and concluding with Epiphany, a time of remembrance and thanksgiving, Yuletide traditions enable us to see out the old year with faith and love while ushering in the new year with hope and joy. It is a season fraught with meaning and significance. Unfortunately, it is also such a busy season that its meaning and significance can all too easily be obscured, either by well-intended materialistic pursuits—frenzied shopping trips to the mall to find just the right Christmas gift—or by the less benign demands, desires, wants, and needs, which are little more than grist for human greed. The traditions of Yuletide were intended to guard us against such things—and thus, are actually more relevant today than ever before.

FEAST DAY

St. Gregory, pope; St. Edmund Gerhings; St. Eustace White; St. John Roberts; St. Eulalia of Merida; St. Swithin Wells; Saints Mannas, Hermogenes, and Eugrphus; St. Polydore Plaaden; St. Melchiades or Miltiades

Though rarely credited as being particularly innovative or farsighted, Harry Truman actually established several important policy precedents during his term in the White House that ultimately helped to define the nation's political tenor for the entire generation that followed.

He was a man who had literally pulled himself up by his own bootstraps. In 1901, when he graduated from high school, his future was uncertain. College had been ruled out by his family's financial situation, and appointment to the U.S. Military Academy at West Point was eliminated by his poor eyesight. He began work as a timekeeper for the Santa Fe Railroad at $35 per month, and in his spare time he read histories and encyclopedias. He later moved to Kansas City, where he worked as a mail clerk for the *Kansas City Star,* then as a clerk for the National Bank of Commerce, and finally as a bookkeeper for the Union National Bank. In 1906 he was called home to help his parents run the large farm of Mrs. Truman's widowed mother in Grandview, Missouri. For the next ten years, Truman was a successful farmer. It was not until 1916 that he got involved in politics when he joined Mike Pendergast's Kansas City Tenth Ward Democratic Club, the local Democratic Party organization. His slow ascent to prominence was marked by pluck, integrity, and humility—a rare set of attributes for an American politician.

You might be able to argue with his politics—as most conservatives have ever since—but it would be difficult to fault Harry Truman's conviction that in the end there is an absolute of right and wrong that transcends our ever-shifting, ever-changing fashions and fancies.

DECEMBER

1282   The forces of King Edward I of England ambushed and beheaded Llewellyn, the last native Welshman to be the Prince of Wales. The head was presented to King Edward in London where he had it placed upon one of the highest turrets of the Tower of London. Known as Longshanks, Edward was the proud heir of the house of Plantagenet. He was the eldest son of King Henry III and was renowned for his ferocity in battle. In 1270 he left England to join the Seventh Crusade; his father died two years later while he was still abroad. Edward was recognized as king by the English barons and in 1273, on his return to England, he was crowned. The first few years of Edward's reign were devoted to consolidating his power. Afterward, he was brutal in extending it—annexing Wales and Scotland, expelling the Jews, and tyrannizing Gascony. Until his death in 1307, he was known as the "Scourge of the North."

1520   Martin Luther publicly burned the papal edict demanding that he recant or face excommunication. Afterward he exulted, "I stand fast on the truth and no other. Fear of power shall never sway me, for God is God and man is naught."

1817   Mississippi became the twentieth state to join the Union.

1830   American poet Emily Dickinson was born in Amherst, Massachusetts. Because of her frail health and reclusive tendencies, neither she nor her poems were known to many people. After her death, her original and influential works—almost two thousand poems written on scraps of paper and the backs of envelopes—were discovered by her sister, Lavinia. The poems were gradually published over a span of fifty years, beginning in 1890.

1869   Women were granted the right to vote in the Wyoming Territory.

1879   Illustrator E. H. Shepard (Ernest Howard Shepard), best known for his drawings of Pooh, Piglet, Eeyore, and Tigger in the works of A. A. Milne and of Mr. Toad and the gang for Kenneth Grahame's *Wind in the Willows*, was born in England.

1896   Nobel Prizes in the fields of physics, chemistry, medicine, literature, economics, and service to the cause of peace are traditionally awarded on this day, the anniversary of the death of Alfred Bernhard Nobel. The Swedish chemist and engineer, inventor of dynamite and other explosives, provided for the annual awards in his will. The Nobel Peace Prize is presented at the Oslo City Hall in Norway and is awarded by a committee of the Norwegian Parliament. The other prizes are presented in a ceremony in Stockholm, Sweden.

1906   President Theodore Roosevelt became the first American to be awarded the Nobel Peace Prize, for helping to mediate an end to the Russo-Japanese War.

1915   The Ford Motor Company built its one millionth Model T automobile.

1930   Duke Ellington and his Orchestra recorded "Mood Indigo" for Victor Records.

1931   Jane Addams became a co-recipient of the Nobel Peace Prize, the first American woman so honored.

1964   Dr. Martin Luther King Jr. received the Nobel Peace Prize during ceremonies in Oslo, Norway.

1984   Bishop Desmond Tutu of South Africa received the Nobel Peace Prize.

Never get into a rut. You cannot afford to do a thing poorly. You are more injured in shirking your work or half-doing a job than the person for whom you are working.

[BOOKER T. WASHINGTON (1856–1915)]

DECEMBER

America's first secretary of state, first chief justice of the Supreme Court, one of its first ambassadors, and author of some of the celebrated *Federalist Papers*, John Jay (1745–1829), was a Founding Father who, by a quirk of fate, missed signing the Declaration of Independence. At the time of the vote for independence and the signing, he had temporarily left the Continental Congress to serve in New York's revolutionary legislature. Nevertheless, he was chosen by his peers to succeed Henry Laurens as president of the United States—serving a term from December 10, 1778 to September 27, 1779.

A conservative New York lawyer who was at first against the idea of independence for the colonies, the aristocratic Jay in 1776 turned into a patriot who was willing to give the next twenty-five years of his life to help establish the new nation. During those years, he won the regard of his peers as a dedicated and accomplished statesman and a man of unwavering principle. In the Continental Congress Jay prepared addresses to the people of Canada and Great Britain. In New York he drafted the state constitution and served as chief justice during the war. He was president of the Continental Congress before he undertook the difficult assignment as ambassador of trying to gain support and funds from Spain.

After helping Franklin, Jefferson, Adams, and Laurens complete peace negotiations in Paris in 1783, Jay returned to become the first secretary of state, called "Secretary of Foreign Affairs," under the Articles of Confederation. He negotiated valuable commercial treaties with Russia and Morocco and dealt with the continuing controversy with Britain and Spain over the southern and western boundaries of the United States. He proposed that America and Britain establish a joint commission to arbitrate disputes that remained after the war—a proposal that, though not adopted, influenced the government's use of arbitration and diplomacy in settling later international problems. In this post Jay felt keenly the weakness of the Articles of Confederation and was one of the first to advocate a new governmental compact. He wrote five *Federalist Papers* supporting the Constitution, and he was a leader in the New York ratification convention.

As first chief justice of the Supreme Court, Jay made the historic decision that a state could be sued by a citizen from another state, which led to the Eleventh Amendment to the Constitution. On a special mission to London he concluded the "Jay Treaty," which helped avert a renewal of hostilities with Britain but won little popular favor at home—and it is probably for this treaty that this Founding Father is best remembered.

DECEMBER

1640 A petition with fifteen thousand signatures of the citizens of London was presented to the English Parliament. Known as the Root and Branch Petition, it sought to sweep away the whole church hierarchy from its "roots to its branches." The House of Commons accepted the petition and soon passed a corresponding bill. The House of Lords, however, opposed the notion entirely. Many of its members were bishops, and they resented any pressure from the people to reorganize their House. The bill was ultimately rejected by a narrow vote, and the Episcopal organization of the Church of England was able to survive.

1719 The first reported display of the aurora borealis was recorded in New England: "This evening, about eight o'clock, there arose a bright and red light in the east-northeast like the light which arises from an house when on fire . . . which soon spread itself through the heavens from east to west."

1792 King Louis XVI of France went before the Revolutionary Convention to face charges of treason. Louis was convicted, and executed the following month.

1816 Indiana became the nineteenth state.

1872 America's first African-American governor took office as Pinckney Benton Stewart Pinchback became acting governor of Louisiana.

1918 Russian author and former exile Aleksandr Solzhenitsyn, winner of the 1970 Nobel Prize for literature, was born in Kislovodsk, U.S.S.R. His exposé of Soviet life in such works as *Cancer Ward, One Day in the Life of Ivan Denisovich,* and his magnum opus *The Gulag Archipelago* brought him great acclaim in the West and condemnation from the Soviet government. He spent years in exile before returning to his homeland after the fall of the Communist regime.

1928 Police in Buenos Aires thwarted an attempt on the life of President-elect Herbert Hoover.

1931 Actress, singer, and dancer Rosita Dolores Alverio (Rita Moreno) was born. To date she is the only person to have won an Oscar, Tony, Grammy, and Emmy.

1936 Britain's King Edward VIII abdicated the throne in order to marry American divorcée Wallis Warfield Simpson.

1961 An American aircraft carrier carrying army helicopters arrived in Saigon—the first direct American military support for South Vietnam's battle against Communist guerrillas.

1981 The United Nations Security Council chose Javier Perez de Cuellar of Peru to be the fifth secretary-general of the world body.

1998 The House Judiciary Committee handed down three articles of impeachment against President Bill Clinton for high crimes and misdemeanors following a shameful public scandal and cover-up—the first American president to be so indicted since Andrew Johnson.

He that is warm for truth, and fearless in its defense, performs one of the duties of a good man; he strengthens his own conviction, and guards others from delusion; but steadiness of belief, and boldness of profession, are yet only part of the form of godly vision.

[SAMUEL JOHNSON (1709–1784)]

DECEMBER

1863

Norwegian artist Edvard Munch was born in Løten. His early angst-filled works are filled with grief, pain, and unfulfilled obsessions. His best known work is *The Scream* (1893), which portrays a person in anguish under blood-red clouds. He was hospitalized for anxiety in 1908, and the treatment he received was reflected in the rest of his work. For the next thirty years, Munch painted tranquil, brightly colored pieces such as landscapes.

NATIONAL DAY
Kenya
FEAST DAY
St. Jane Frances de Chantel, St. Corentin or Cury, Saints Epimachus and Alexander, St. Edburga of Minister, St. Vicelin, St. Finnian of Clonard

The heir of a substantial Philadelphia business and banking fortune, George Clymer (1739–1813) risked everything to become a leader of the patriots in the early days of the conflict with the king, served in public office for more than twenty years, and signed both the Declaration of Independence and the Constitution. A man of unusual intellectual curiosity, he also served as an officer of the Philadelphia Academy of Fine Arts and the Philadelphia Agricultural Society.

One of the first members of Pennsylvania's committee of safety, and one of the first to advocate complete independence from Britain, Clymer was called upon by the Continental Congress to serve as the first treasurer for the United States, and he undertook the almost impossible assignment of raising money to support the government's operations, chief of which was the new Continental army. And Clymer devoted not only his great energy, but also his own fortune to the cause, exchanging all his money, which was in hard coin, for the shaky Continental currency.

On this day in 1776, when Congress fled a threatened Philadelphia, Clymer was one of the committee of three left behind to maintain essential government activities. During this crisis Clymer drove himself almost to a state of exhaustion. Shortly after this ordeal, the British captured Philadelphia and plundered and destroyed his home.

In Congress, Clymer performed valuable services as a member of committees dealing with financial matters. During the final years of the war, he was again responsible for obtaining funds for the army. At the Constitutional Convention Clymer, who was not an exceptional speaker, distinguished himself by his work in committees dealing with his specialty—finance. In 1791, after a term in the First Congress, Clymer served as Federal collector of the controversial tax on liquor, which led to the Whiskey Rebellion.

He concluded his career by negotiating an equitable peace treaty between the United States and the Creek tribe in Georgia. Clymer served the cause from the beginnings of the movement for independence and established his place among the Founding Fathers, although he never sought a public office.

DECEMBER

1787 Pennsylvania became the second state to ratify the U.S. Constitution.

1792 Twenty-two-year-old Austrian composer Ludwig van Beethoven received his first music lesson from Franz Joseph Haydn for which he paid the equivalent of nineteen cents.

1821 French literary master Gustave Flaubert was born in Rouen.

1870 Joseph H. Rainey of South Carolina became the first African-American lawmaker sworn in to the U.S. House of Representatives.

1882 The Bijou Theater in Boston became the first American stage lit by electric lamps. More than three hundred lights were used.

1889 The English poet Robert Browning died in Venice twenty-eight years after the death of his beloved wife, Elizabeth. Because the little grave-yard where she was buried was closed to further interments, he was buried in the Poet's Corner of Westminster Abbey.

1913 Authorities in Florence, Italy, announced that Leonardo da Vinci's masterpiece, *Mona Lisa*—which had been stolen from the Louvre Museum in Paris in 1911—had been recovered.

1925 The first motel—the Motel Inn—designed for motorists to drive right to the door of their room, opened in San Luis Obispo, California.

1936 Bishop Clemens Count von Galen of Munster delivered a devastating sermon condemning the Nazi extermination of handicapped adults deemed "unfit" by Hitler's "race hygiene" program. He articulated the historic orthodox position that the Christians must protect the inno-cent even at the risk of their own lives: "It is said of these patients: They are like an old machine which no longer runs, like an old horse which is hopelessly paralyzed, like a cow which no longer gives milk. But these are horridly false metaphors. We are not talking here about a machine, a horse, nor a cow. No, we are talking about men and women, our compatriots, our brothers and sisters. Poor unproductive people if you wish, but does this mean that they have lost their right to live?" He prophesied God's wrath on those "sending innocent people to their death," and he spoke for the Christian community, asserting, "We wish to withdraw ourselves and our faithful from their influence, so that we may not be contaminated by their thinking and their ungodly behavior, so that we may not participate and share with them in the punishment which a just God should and will pronounce upon all those who—like ungrateful Jerusalem—do not wish what God wishes." Galen's sermon was widely distributed throughout Germany and proved to be one of the primary catalysts for the underground resistance in both the occupied regions and in Germany itself.

1946 Tide detergent was introduced.

1947 The United Mine Workers union withdrew from the American Federation of Labor.

1963 Kenya gained its independence from Britain.

1998 The House Judiciary Committee approved a fourth and final article of impeachment, this one accusing President Clinton of abuse of power.

*K*nowledge comes, but wisdom lingers.

[ALFRED, LORD TENNYSON (1809–1892)]

DECEMBER

SANTA LUCIA'S DAY

A beautiful and wealthy Sicilian who was martyred during the persecutions of Diocletian, Lucia of Syracuse (c. 304) was known as the patron of light. For her, Advent was always a celebration of the approach of Light and Life. Interestingly, her feast day, held on December 13, is one of the shortest and darkest days of the year. Thus, a great festival of lights is traditionally held in her memory—particularly in Scandinavian cultures. Candles are set into evergreens. Garlands are spread, full of twinkling lights. Torchlight parades are held. And fireworks brighten the evening sky.

FEAST DAY
St. Lucy, St. Aubert of Cambrai, St. Othilia or Odilia, St. Eustratius of Sebastea, St. Judocus or Josse

Two centuries after Patrick had carried the gospel of Christ to Ireland, Columba was born in the Irish town of Donegal on this day in 521. He was a member of the royal family—though his parents were devout Christians, and as a boy Columba attended the first church established by Patrick.

Columba was ordained and established several churches and monasteries in Ireland, but in 563 he left his native land and went on a pilgrimage for Christ. With twelve companions he sailed to Iona, a rugged island just off the west coast of Scotland. There he established a monastery that would serve as a base of evangelism among the barbarian Scots and the Picts.

He and his pioneer evangelists courageously preached to these fierce people who were still under the strong influence of the Druid religion. Brude, king of the Picts, was converted under Columba's influence, and Christianity began to spread quickly and have a strong influence on the region.

The monastery Columba founded at Iona became a center of learning and piety. In a day when the Roman Church was becoming more ceremonial and priestly, the school at Iona emphasized the Bible as the sole rule of faith. For these Celtic Christians, Christ alone was Head of the church—they did not follow the hierarchical authority or the liturgical ceremonies of the Roman Church.

From Iona, a vast number of missionaries went out to the lands of Holland, France, Switzerland, Germany, and Italy. As a result, the island became a favorite burying place for kings—more than seventy Irish, Scots, Norse, and Fleming kings sought to be interred within its holy confines.

By the end of the sixth century, Pope Gregory tried to bring the movement Columba had begun under the authority of the Roman Church. He sent the missionary Augustine to Britain in 592 and established him as bishop at Canterbury. For a century there was a struggle between the British Church and the Roman Church for authority in the region. At last though, in the seventh century, at the synod of Whitby in 664, the authority of the Roman Church was affirmed and accepted by all but a few of the churches. Even those few recalcitrant parishes in the Highlands of Scotland eventually acceded to Rome's control by the end of the eighth century, and Columba's vision was all but lost—until its revival under John Knox and George Buchanan during the Scottish Reformation during the sixteenth century.

DECEMBER

1577 Sir Francis Drake of England set out with five ships on a nearly three-year journey that would take him around the world.

1642 Dutch navigator Abel Tasman arrived in present-day New Zealand.

1759 The first music store in the colonies opened in Philadelphia.

1769 Dartmouth College, in New Hampshire, received its charter.

1835 Phillips Brooks, the American Episcopal bishop who wrote the words to "O Little Town of Bethlehem," was born in Boston.

1862 Union forces suffered a major defeat to the Confederates at the Battle of Fredericksburg during the War Between the States.

1887 Sergeant Alvin C. York, the "greatest civilian soldier" of World War I, was born in Pall Mall, Tennessee. He was awarded the Congressional Medal of Honor and the French Croix de Guerre for his acts of bravery in World War I. He later established a foundation to help educate the children living in the poor sections of the mountains of Tennessee.

1918 President Wilson arrived in France, becoming the first chief executive to visit Europe while in office.

1927 Violinist Yehudi Menuhin made his New York debut at Carnegie Hall at the age of ten. The audience forced their way backstage to congratulate the little boy, but Menuhin wanted nothing more than some ice cream.

1928 Carnegie Hall was the site for the world premiere of George Gershwin's composition for piano and orchestra, *An American in Paris.*

1930 *Symphony of Psalms*—a work for chorus and orchestra by Igor Stravinsky—was premiered in Brussels. Divided into three sections, the piece is a setting of the Vulgate of Psalms 39, 40, and 150. The text moves from a prayer for divine pity ("Hear my prayer, O Lord, and give ear unto my cry, Hold not Thy peace at my tears") to an expression of gratitude for God's grace ("I waited patiently for the Lord, and he inclined unto me, and heard my cry.") and finally a hymn of praise and glory ("Praise ye the Lord, Praise God in his sanctuary."). Stravinsky, who began each day with prayer, believed that "the principal virtue of music is a means of communication with God."

1978 The Philadelphia Mint began stamping the Susan B. Anthony dollar, which went into circulation the following July.

1989 President F. W. de Klerk of South Africa met for the first time with imprisoned African National Congress leader Nelson Mandela—who had been convicted of treason, terrorism, and conspiracy to overthrow the government in 1962—at de Klerk's office in Cape Town.

1998 Voters in Puerto Rico rejected U.S. statehood.

Our Savior, Christ Jesus, was a carpenter and got His living with great labor. Therefore, let no man disdain to follow Him in a common calling and occupation.

[HUGH LATIMER (1485–1555)]

DECEMBER

The colors of the church have special symbolism throughout the year, and this fact is readily apparent during the time of Advent, Christmas, and Epiphany. Paraments are the altar cloths, pulpit cloths, and sometimes banners that proclaim the color of the church or liturgical year. The first color of the season is the Advent color of purple. Purple is the color of royalty because of its scarcity in the Ancient world. Purple is used during the penitential seasons of Advent and Lent as a reminder of the sacrifice of Christ and the scorn that He endured for our salvation. Ecclesiastical purple should invoke a daily reminder of the need for all Christians to humbly give attention to a life of repentance. White is the color of purity and completeness, and is, therefore, the color appointed for such festive Sundays as Christmas and its twelve days; Epiphany (January 6) and the first Sunday following it, which is usually observed as the baptism of our Lord. The incarnation of Christ as Emmanuel, God-with-us, as well as the culmination of God's plan for redemption are symbolized in the color white. The color red symbolizes passion and blood. As a parament, red is used during the week leading to Easter, Pentecost, and for the days set aside in honor of martyrs. The red blood of the martyrs shed in defense of the gospel offers perpetual encouragement for God's people to be resolute in living the faith. Green is the color utilized through the season of Epiphany. The coming of the Magi is a reminder of the gift of salvation that is offered not just to Jews but to Gentiles as well. Green represents growth and vitality as in the spreading of the gospel to all the ends of the earth.

LITURGICAL COLORS

FEAST DAY
St. John of the Cross, Saints Fingar or Gwinnear and Phiala, St. Spiridion, St. Venantius Fortunatus, St. Nicasius of Reims

On this day in 1877, Anton Bruckner conducted the premiere performance of his Symphony no. 3 in D Minor because no other conductor would do it. The score had earlier been discarded by the Vienna Philharmonic after one rehearsal because all of the musicians but one refused to play it. During the performance, the audience laughed and jeered. After the concluding chord, Bruckner turned to face the crowd, which had dwindled to only twenty-five people in the large auditorium. Dazed, he stood rooted to the platform while tears streamed down his cheeks. He continued to remain frozen in place, and finally said to the few admirers, "Let me go. The people don't want to know anything of me."

His earlier works had not fared much better, and he had paid almost a year's salary to have his Symphony no. 2 in C Minor performed in 1873. His works were rejected again and again, but he held an unswerving confidence in his God-given creative power. He once said, "When God calls me to Him and asks me: 'Where is the talent which I have given you?' Then I shall hold out the rolled-up manuscript of my *Te Deum* and I know He will be a compassionate judge."

Bruckner continued to patiently wait and write. Finally on February 20, 1881, his Fourth Symphony in E-flat major received an enthusiastic response, and his Seventh Symphony in E major in 1884 was met with even greater acclaim. Critics responded by asking, "How is it possible that he could remain so long unknown to us?"

Triumph followed triumph for the rest of the life of this former church organist. Although he did not write a great work until he was forty-one and was not widely known until he was sixty, God used his piety and faithfulness and blessed him late in life with the full utilization of his gifts.

DECEMBER

1417 Sir John Oldcastle was executed by hanging and was burned on the scaffold. Oldcastle was the prototype of Shakespeare's Falstaff. He served under King Henry IV in the effort to put down the Welsh rebel Owen Glendower. It was during this time that he became a close friend of Prince Hal, who later became Henry V of England. He served in the House of Commons and the House of Lords, but he was condemned for joining the Lollards, a dissident Christian sect. Henry V granted him a forty-day reprieve in the hopes that his old friend would recant; however, Oldcastle escaped from the Tower of London and led a Lollard revolt against the throne. After four years in hiding, he was captured on this day.

1713 Alexander Pope wrote on this day, "What a bustle we make about passing our time, when all our space is, but a point! What aims and ambitions are crowded into this little instant of life! Our whole extent of being is no more in the eye of Him who gave it than a scarce perceptible moment of duration."

1788 Composer Carl Philipp Emanuel Bach, son of J. S. Bach, died in Weimar. His innovations, technique, and compositions for the keyboard paved the way for the compositions of Haydn, Beethoven, and Schubert.

1799 George Washington died at his Mount Vernon home at age sixty-seven.

1819 Alabama joined the Union as the twenty-second state.

1836 The first railway from London was opened today to Greenwich.

1861 Prince Albert, husband of Queen Victoria, died in London.

1911 Norwegian explorer Roald Amundsen became the first man to reach the South Pole, just beating out an expedition led by Robert F. Scott.

1939 The Soviet Union was expelled from the League of Nations.

1946 The United Nations General Assembly voted to establish its headquarters in New York City.

1962 The American space probe *Mariner 2* approached Venus, transmitting information about the planet.

1980 Fans around the world paid tribute to John Lennon, six days after he was shot to death in New York City.

1981 Israel annexed the Golan Heights, which it had seized from Syria in 1967.

The antiquary of tradition is the preserver of all that is right and good and true. It is the wisest and most progressive of all the human impulses—for it guarantees continuity for the uncertain days of the future. Let every man and woman warmly embrace the lessons of the past.

[CALVIN COOLIDGE (1872–1933)]

DECEMBER

1979 The deposed shah of Iran left the United States for Panama, the same day the International Court of Justice in the Hague ruled that Iran should release all its American hostages.

Because of the opposition to the adoption of the Constitution by the anti-Federalists, several states proposed amending the document to better protect the states as well as individuals from the incursions of the centralized federal government. Thus these ten new planks were drafted, debated, and eventually adopted. They became the first ten amendments to the Constitution—finally ratified on this day in 1791. Ultimately, this Bill of Rights proved to be the cornerstone of American liberty.

The preamble—often edited out of schoolbook copies of the Bill of Rights—laid out the purposes of the amendments as well as the character of the fledgling Federal Union: "The conventions of a number of states having at the time of their adopting the Constitution, expressed a desire, in order to prevent misconstruction or abuse of its powers, that further declaratory and restrictive clauses should be added; and as extending the ground of public confidence in the government, will best insure the beneficent ends of its institution."

The first of the amendments, quite contrary to modern interpretation, clearly prohibited the new federal government from restricting religion in any way, shape, or form, as well as providing for free speech and expression: "Congress shall make no law respecting an establishment of religion, or prohibiting the free exercise thereof; or abridging the freedom of speech, or of the press; or the right of the people peaceably to assemble, and to petition the government for a redress of grievances."

The second of the amendments clearly expresses the need for citizens to be able to defend themselves against the incursions of oppressors—including those that might come from the government itself: "A well-regulated militia, being necessary to the security of a free state, the right of the people to keep and bear arms, shall not be infringed."

The third, fourth, fifth, sixth, seventh, and eighth amendments secured legal rights for the citizens against possible incursions by the government, while the ninth asserted the extremely limited nature of government allowable by the new constitution—only those prerogatives specifically enumerated by the covenant could be exercised, and no more: "The enumeration in the Constitution, of certain rights, shall not be construed to deny or disparage others retained by the people."

Finally, the tenth amendment asserted that any governmental powers not specifically assigned to the new Federal Union automatically remained in the hands of either the states or the people: "The powers not delegated to the United States by the Constitution, nor prohibited by it to the states, are reserved to the states respectively, or to the people."

It was a remarkable hedge of protection that served for many years to preserve the unprecedented freedoms of the American people.

FEAST DAY
St. Nino, St. Valerian, St. Mary di Rosa, St. Paul of Latros

DECEMBER

1675 Dutch painter Jan Vermeer died in Delft, leaving a widow, eleven children, and many debts. Only thirty-five of Vermeer's works survived. Many of his canvases depict interior settings of everyday life painted in warm, rich hues. In his lifetime he was known as an art dealer rather than an artist, but subsequent generations have recognized his ability to convey pure color with great subtlety and delicacy.

1877 Thomas Edison filed a patent for the phonograph.

1890 Sioux Indian Chief Sitting Bull and eleven other tribe members were killed in Grand River, South Dakota, during a fracas with Indian police.

1939 The motion picture *Gone with the Wind* had its world premiere at the Loew's Grand Theater in Atlanta.

1944 A single-engine plane carrying bandleader Glenn Miller disappeared into a thick fog over the English Channel while en route to Paris.

1944 Henry Harley Arnold, Dwight David Eisenhower, Douglas MacArthur, and George Catlett Marshall received appointments as the first five-star generals of the U.S. Army after that particular rank of general was established by an act of Congress the day before.

1948 Former State Department official Alger Hiss was indicted by a federal grand jury in New York on charges of perjury. He was convicted in 1950.

1961 Former Nazi official Adolf Eichmann was sentenced to death by an Israeli court.

1973 The American Psychiatric Association reversed its position and declared that homosexuality was not a mental illness. They have recently made similar steps regarding pedophilia.

1989 A popular uprising that eventually resulted in the downfall of Romania's brutal dictator Nicolae Ceausescu began as demonstrators gathered in Timisoara to prevent the arrest of Laszlo Tokes, a prominent evangelical pastor. In post-war Communist Romania Ceausescu held several party posts, becoming a member of the ruling Politburo in 1955. He succeeded Gheorghe Gheorghiu-Dej, the Romanian Communist leader, as first secretary of the party and the effective ruler of Romania. Then in 1967 he also became the country's president. He imposed a bitter austerity program to liquidate Romania's foreign debt, a program of forced relocation of rural population, and an extreme cult of personality, while rejecting political and economic reforms introduced in the Soviet Union and other East European countries. His brutal suppression of the church ultimately sparked widespread demonstrations against his dictatorship and the Communist Party rule and turned the army against him. His attempt to flee Bucharest on December 22 with his wife Elena, herself a member of the Politburo, was unsuccessful. Captured and tried secretly, they were executed on December 25.

It was the best of times, it was the worst of times, it was the age of wisdom, it was the age of foolishness, it was the epoch of incredulity, it was the season of Light, it was the season of Darkness, it was the spring of hope, it was the winter of despair, we had everything before us, we had nothing before us.

[CHARLES DICKENS (1812–1870)]

DECEMBER

HOLLY AND IVY

Throughout the Celtic lands, holly and ivy were symbols of victory won. Holly, representing masculine triumph, and ivy, representing feminine triumph, were often woven together as a sign that men and women need one another. Homes were decorated during Advent with both—often woven together—as a picture of the healthy family under God's gracious providential hand.

On this day in 1773, colonial leaders grown weary with England's increasingly intrusive government, carried out a remarkable protest in Boston Harbor. Disguised as Indians, they boarded a British ship and threw its cargo of more than three hundred chests of imported tea overboard. This action, more than almost any other, demonstrated the resolve of the colonists to maintain the standard of liberty guaranteed by English common law. The well-known tale of the Boston Tea Party was set to verse by a master of nineteenth-century American poetry, Oliver Wendell Holmes.

FEAST DAY
St. Irenion; Saints Ananiah,
Azariah, and Michael; St. Adelaide

No! never such a draught was poured
    Since Hebe served with nectar
The bright Olympians and their Lord,
    Her over-kind protector,
Since Father Noah squeezed the grape
    And took to such behaving
As would have shamed our grand-sire ape
    Before the days of shaving,
No! ne'er was mingled such a draught
    In palace, hall, or arbor,
As freemen brewed and tyrants quaffed
    That night in Boston Harbor!
It kept King George so long awake
    His brain at last got addled,
It made the nerves of Britain shake,
    With seven score millions saddled;
Before that bitter cup was drained,
    Amid the roar of cannon,
The Western war-cloud's crimson stained
    The Thames, Clyde, and Shannon;
Full many a six-foot grenadier
    The flattened grass had measured,
And, many a mother many a year
    Her tearful memories treasured;
Fast spread the tempest's darkening pall,
    The mighty realms were troubled,
The storm broke loose, but first of all
    The Boston teapot bubbled!
An evening party—only that,
    No formal invitation,
No gold-laced coat, no stiff cravat,
    No feast in contemplation,
No silk-robed dames, no fiddling band,
    No flowers, no songs, no dancing,
A tribe of red men, axe in hand,
    Behold the guests advancing!

O woman, at the evening board
    So gracious, sweet, and purring,
So happy while the tea is poured,
    So blest while spoons are stirring,
What martyr can compare with thee,
    The mother, wife, or daughter,
That night, instead of best Bohea,
    Condemned to milk and water!
Ah, little dreams the quiet dame
    Who plies with rock and spindle
The patient flax, how great a flame
    Yon little spark shall kindle!
The lurid morning shall reveal
    A fire no king can smother
Where British flint and Boston steel
    Have clashed against each other!
Old charters shrivel in its track,
    His Worship's bench has crumbled,
It climbs and clasps the Union Jack,
    Its blazoned pomp is humbled,
The flags go down on land and sea
    Like corn before the reapers;
So burned the fire that brewed the tea
    That Boston served her keepers!
The waves that wrought a century's wreck
    Have rolled o'er Whig and Tory;
The Mohawks on the Dartmouth's deck
    Still live in song and story;
The waters in the rebel bay
    Have kept the tea-leaf savor;
Our old North-Enders in their spray
    Still taste a Hyson flavor;
And Freedom's teacup still o'erflows
    With ever fresh libations,
To cheat of slumber all her foes
    And *cheer* the wakening nations!

DECEMBER

1653 Oliver Cromwell became lord protector of England, Scotland, and Ireland.

1770 Composer Ludwig van Beethoven, who was the transition figure between the Classical and Romantic periods, was born in Bonn, Germany. He began losing his hearing before the age of thirty and later became completely deaf. His temperament was stormy, as seen in a letter he wrote while revising some music: "I have spent no less than the whole morning and the whole of yesterday afternoon over the correction of the two pieces, and am quite hoarse with swearing and stamping."

1775 English novelist Jane Austen, best known for her novels *Pride and Prejudice, Sense and Sensibility,* and *Emma,* was born in Steventon, Hampshire, England.

1809 Napoleon Bonaparte was divorced from Empress Josephine by an act of the French Senate.

1893 *The New World Symphony* (Symphony no. 9 in E Minor) by Antonín Dvořák was premiered at Carnegie Hall by the New York Philharmonic. The Czech composer had only been in the United States for a year before writing this work, which contains melodic elements derived from spirituals.

1899 Sir Noel Coward, the English actor, playwright, and composer, was born in London.

1916 Grigori Rasputin, the monk who had wielded powerful influence over the Russian royal family, was murdered by a group of noblemen.

1944 The Second World War Battle of the Bulge began as German forces launched a surprise counterattack against Allied forces in Belgium.

1950 President Harry Truman proclaimed a national state of emergency to fight Communist Imperialism.

1991 The United Nations General Assembly rescinded its 1975 resolution equating Zionism with racism by a vote of 111-25.

Intelligent children, whether they believed or not in the sacred and benevolent burglary every Christmas Eve, would feel that the magi, the saint, and the heathen god did not really make up the image of the old man with the furred coat and the reindeers: or if they did not feel so, they would have developed their intelligence at the ruinous expense of their childhood. But indeed, in such cases, childhood and intelligence fail together.

[G. K. CHESTERTON (1874–1936)]

DECEMBER

REINDEER	Scandanavian images have greatly influenced our modern vision of the traditional Christmas—from the thick fur garb of Santa to the manner of his transport. The romantic image of reindeer pulling his sleigh was grafted into our cultural vocabulary by Danish, Swedish, and Norwegian immigrants to America during the nineteenth century.

SLEIGH RIDES	Mimicking the supposed pattern of pastoral care practiced by Nicholas of Myra, the sleigh ride—particularly on Christmas Eve—was gradually woven into the joyous celebration of Christmas. Beginning in Scandanavia, spreading to Germany, England, Scotland, and finally New England, the sounds of the jingling bells, the tramping of horses through the snow, and the brisk wind through the trees became essential elements in provoking the Yuletide spirit.

Henry Wadsworth Longfellow was one of the most popular and celebrated poets of his time. Born in Portland, Maine, Longfellow was educated at Bowdoin College, intending to spend the rest of his life as an academic. After graduating in 1825 he traveled in Europe in preparation for a teaching career. He taught modern languages at Bowdoin from 1829 to 1835. In late 1835, during a second trip to Europe, Longfellow's wife, Mary Storer Potter, died in Rotterdam, the Netherlands.

Grief turned him toward serious writing. Though he returned to the United States in 1836 and began teaching at Harvard University, he had lost all desire to labor in the classroom—only writing gave him solace.

FEAST DAY
St. Lazarus, St. Sturmi, St. Begga, St. Wivina, St. Olympias

Longfellow began to receive wide public recognition with his initial volume of verse, *Voices of the Night,* which contained the poem "A Psalm of Life." His subsequent poetic work, *Ballads,* introduced some of his most famous poetry, such as "The Wreck of the Hesperus," "The Village Blacksmith," "The Skeleton in Armor," and "Excelsior." He also wrote three notable long narrative poems on American themes—*Evangeline* was about lovers separated during the French and Indian War, *The Song of Hiawatha* addressed the romance of Native American Indian cultures, and *The Courtship of Miles Standish* was about a love triangle in colonial New England. About this time he also made a verse translation of *The Divine Comedy* by Italian poet Dante Alighieri.

In 1843 he remarried and a few years later retired from Harvard to devote himself exclusively to writing. He was utterly devastated when on this day in 1861 his second wife was burned to death in a household accident.

Though never particularly appreciated by professional literary critics, Longfellow remains one of the most popular of American poets, primarily for his simplicity of style and theme and for his technical expertise, but also for his role in the creation of an American mythology. His verse was also instrumental in reestablishing a public audience for poetry in the United States.

In 1884 a bust of Longfellow was placed in the Poet's Corner of Westminster Abbey in London—the first American to be thus honored.

DECEMBER

736

1777 France recognized American independence.

1777 The army under George Washington established winter headquarters at Valley Forge, Pennsylvania.

1790 While repairing the Central Plaza in Mexico City, workmen uncovered the Aztec Calendar, or Solar Stone. Believed to have been carved in 1479, the stone is 11'8" in diameter and weighs almost twenty-five tons. The fifty-two-year cycle depicted on the stone regulated the ceremonies and festivals of the Aztecs and stood in their Great Temple.

1791 New York City established the first one-way street.

1830 South American revolutionary Simon Bolivar died in Colombia.

1889 Dwight L. Moody founded the Bible Institute—now known as the Moody Bible Institute—in Chicago to train Christian workers. Moody was an American evangelist, born in Northfield, Massachusetts. A Unitarian, he was converted to evangelical Christianity and in 1856 left his work as a shoe salesman in Boston to engage in missionary work in Chicago. His Sunday school in North Market Hall grew into the Illinois Street Church and afterward became the Chicago Avenue Church, of which he was lay pastor—it was later rechristened the Moody Memorial Church. In 1870 he was joined by the American singer and hymn composer Ira Sankey. The two began a series of revival meetings in America and also visited Britain. In 1879 Moody opened the Northfield Seminary for Young Women and in 1881 the Mount Hermon School for Boys, both in his hometown. He was the preeminent evangelist of his day—setting precedents that would be followed by every great revivalist afterward from Billy Sunday to Billy Graham.

1894 Arthur Fiedler, the American conductor of the Boston Pops Orchestra for almost fifty years, was born on this day.

1903 In Kill Devil Hills, North Carolina, Wilbur and Orville Wright, bicycle shop owners, successfully completed the first flight of their flying machine. The flight lasted about twelve seconds at a height of eight to twelve feet.

1957 The United States successfully test-fired the Atlas intercontinental ballistic missile for the first time.

1969 The U.S. Air Force closed its Project Blue Book by concluding there was no evidence of extraterrestrial spaceships behind thousands of UFO sightings.

1969 An estimated fifty million TV viewers watched singer Tiny Tim marry his fiancée, Miss Vicky, on NBC's *Tonight Show*.

Hail to the King of Bethlehem
Who weareth in His diadem
The yellow crocus for the gem
Of His authority.

[HENRY W. LONGFELLOW (1807–1882)]

DECEMBER

On this day in 1979, Francis Schaeffer gave a historic speech that would form the basis of his landmark book *A Christian Manifesto*. He asserted that "the basic problem with Christians in this country" over the last two generations or more has been that "they have seen things in bits and pieces instead of totals." The result has been a kind of hesitant hit-or-miss approach to the dire dilemmas of our day: "They have very gradually become disturbed over permissiveness, pornography, the public schools, the breakdown of the family, and finally abortion. But they have not seen this as a totality—each thing being a part, a symptom, of a much larger problem."

He said that part of the reason for this was: "They failed to see that all of this has come about due to a shift in worldview—that is, through a fundamental change in the overall way people think and view the world and life as a whole."

When the subject of worldview comes up, we generally think of philosophy. We think of intellectual niggling. We think of the brief and blinding oblivion of ivory tower speculation, of thickly obscure tomes, and of inscrutable logical complexities.

In fact, a worldview is as practical as potatoes. It is less metaphysical than understanding marginal market buying at the stock exchange or legislative initiatives in Congress. It is less esoteric than typing a book into a laptop computer or sending a fax across the continent. It is instead as down to earth as tilling the soil for a bed of zinnias.

The word itself is a poor English attempt at translating the German *weltanshauung*. It literally means "a life perspective or a way of seeing." It is simply the way we look at the world.

You have a worldview. I have a worldview. Everyone does. It is our perspective. It is our frame of reference. It is the means by which we interpret the situations and circumstances around us. It is what enables us to integrate all the different aspects of our faith, life, and experience.

Alvin Toffler, in his book *Future Shock*, said: "Every person carries in his head a mental model of the world, a subjective representation of external reality."

This mental model is, he says, like a giant filing cabinet. It contains a slot for every item of information coming to us. It organizes our knowledge and gives us a grid from which to think. Our mind is not as Pelagius, Locke, Voltaire, or Rousseau would have had us suppose—a *tabla rasa*, a blank and impartial slate. None of us are completely open-minded or genuinely objective. "When we think," said economic philosopher E. F. Schumacher, "we can only do so because our mind is already filled with all sorts of ideas with which to think." These more or less fixed notions make up our mental model of the world, our frame of reference, our presuppositions—in other words, our worldview.

Thus, a worldview is simply a way of viewing the world. Nothing could be simpler. But by raising the issue when he did and in the way he did, Francis Schaeffer altogether altered the terms of the theological debate in America and ushered in a new wave of reform.

DECEMBER

1707 English hymn writer Charles Wesley, the younger brother of John Wesley, was born in the rectory in Epworth, Lincolnshire. He wrote more than 6,500 hymns including "Jesus, Lover of My Soul," "Hark! The Herald Angels Sing," "Love Divine, All Loves Excelling," and "And Can It Be That I Should Gain."

1737 Antonio Stradivari, the incomparable Italian violin maker, died in Cremona. Stradivari improved the instruments by making certain changes to the proportions. However, the secret of his instruments is still unknown. Several hundred of his violins survive, but his cellos and violas are more rare. He continued making instruments into his nineties.

1777 The first nationwide Thanksgiving Day celebration was held in commemoration of the surrender of Lieutenant General John Burgoyne on October 17, 1777, in New York. The Continental Congress appointed Samuel Adams and others to draft a recommendation "to set apart a day of thanksgiving for the signal success lately obtained over the enemies of the United States." The resolution was passed on November 1, 1777.

1786 Composer Carl Maria von Weber, the Hero of German Romantic opera, was born in Eutin, Germany. His major contributions to opera include *Der Freischütz* (The Free-Shooter, 1821), *Euryanthe* (1823), and *Oberon* (1826). His use of leitmotifs and orchestral coloring provided inspiration for Richard Wagner.

1787 New Jersey became the third state to ratify the U.S. Constitution.

1861 American composer Edward MacDowell was born in New York City. Known primarily for his compositions for piano and voice, he also wrote orchestral music. He studied in the United States, France, and Germany, where he taught for several years. An association named for him maintains his former home in Peterborough, New Hampshire, as an artists' colony.

1865 The Thirteenth Amendment to the Constitution, abolishing slavery, was declared in effect.

1892 Peter Ilyich Tchaikovsky's *The Nutcracker Suite* premiered in St. Petersburg, Russia.

1914 Great Britain claimed Egypt as a protectorate.

1915 President Woodrow Wilson, widowed the year before, married Edith Bolling Galt at her Washington home.

1940 Adolf Hitler signed a secret directive ordering preparations for a Nazi invasion of the Soviet Union. Operation Barbarossa was launched in June 1941.

1971 The Reverend Jesse Jackson announced the founding of a new civil rights organization in Chicago—Operation PUSH.

The true Christian religion is incarnational and thus does not begin at the top, as all other religions do; it begins at the bottom. You must run directly to the manger and the mother's womb, embrace the Infant and Virgin's Child in your arms and look at Him—born, being nursed, growing up, going about in human society, teaching, dying, rising again, ascending above all the heavens, and having authority over all things.

[MARTIN LUTHER (1483–1546)]

DECEMBER

CAROLING

Carols are songs that are usually narrative and celebratory in nature with a simple spirit and often in verse form. The term "carol" has a varied and interesting past and is derived from several foreign words that include the idea of dancing as well as singing. It has been often mentioned that the first carol was sung by the angels to the shepherds on the night of Christ's birth. Mary's song, the Magnificat, could also fit in the category of early Christmas music. The idea of caroling from one home to another seems to have started sometime during the eighteenth century or earlier. Carolers would visit each house of a parish on Christmas night to sing songs of the Nativity and to call forth blessings on every home. The term "wassail" means "Good health!" Carolers would often receive food, money, and drink for the spreading of good cheer.

FEAST DAY
St. Timothy, St. Gregory of Auxerre, St. Anastasius I of Antioch, St. Nemesius of Alexandria

Charles Haddon Spurgeon is commonly heralded as the greatest preacher to grace the Christian pulpit since the apostle Paul. His Metropolitan Tabernacle was undoubtedly a dynamic force for righteousness in Victorian England. But his many years of ministry were marked not only by his masterful pulpiteering, but by his many labors on behalf of the poor and needy as well.

On this day in 1861, he erected an almshouse for the elderly. In 1864, he established a school for the needy children of London. In 1866, he founded the Stockwell Orphanages. And, in 1867, to these many enterprises was added still another, a private hospital.

Explaining this furious activity on behalf of the poor, Spurgeon said, "God's intent in endowing any person with more substance than he needs is that he may have the pleasurable office, or rather the delightful privilege, of relieving want and woe. Alas, how many there are who consider that store which God has put into their hands on purpose for the poor and needy, to be only so much provision for their excessive luxury, a luxury which pampers them but yields them neither benefit nor pleasure. Others dream that wealth is given them that they may keep it under lock and key, cankering and corroding, breeding covetousness and care. Who dares roll a stone over the well's mouth when thirst is raging all around? Who dares keep the bread from the women and children who are ready to gnaw their own arms for hunger? Above all, who dares allow the sufferer to writhe in agony uncared for, and the sick to pine into their graves unnursed? This is not small sin: it is a crime to be answered for, to the Judge, when He shall come to judge the quick and the dead."

DECEMBER

960 After it was destroyed by fire, the Japanese Imperial Palace in Kyoto was reconstructed.

1155 Henry II and his wife, Eleanor of Aquitaine, were crowned king and queen of England.

1562 With the Battle of Dreux, the French religious wars between the Huguenots and the Catholics began in earnest.

1732 Under the name of Richard Saunders, Benjamin Franklin began publishing *Poor Richard's Almanac* in Philadelphia.

1776 In his first American crisis essay in the *Pennsylvania Journal*, Thomas Paine wrote, "These are the times that try men's souls."

1843 *A Christmas Carol*, by Charles Dickens, was first published in England.

1932 The British Broadcasting Corporation began transmitting overseas with its Empire Service to Australia.

1946 French and Communist forces began skirmishes in Vietnam.

1957 The musical play *The Music Man* opened on Broadway.

1959 The last surviving veteran of the American War Between the States, Walter Williams, died in Houston, Texas, at the age of 117.

1972 *Apollo 17* splashed down in the Pacific, winding up the Apollo program of manned lunar landings.

1974 Nelson A. Rockefeller was sworn in as the forty-first vice president of the United States.

1984 Britain and China signed an accord that would return Hong Kong to Chinese sovereignty on July 1, 1997.

1998 President Bill Clinton was impeached by the United States House of Representatives for perjury and obstruction of justice. The forty-second chief executive became only the second in history to be ordered to stand trial in the Senate, where, like Andrew Johnson before him, he was eventually acquitted. Full impeachment trials have been held in the Senate fourteen other times in American history. Twelve federal judges have been tried, and seven were convicted. The Senate acquitted four judges, and one resigned before the trial was complete. The Senate also tried and acquitted William W. Belknap, secretary of war during the administration of President Ulysses S. Grant. In cases of presidential impeachment, the Constitution stipulates that the chief justice of the Supreme Court of the United States preside over the trial. In cases involving officials other than the president, the vice president presides. In all impeachment trials, a two-thirds majority of the Senate is required to convict. Officials who are convicted by the Senate are disqualified from holding other federal offices.

In the holiday season, the corruptions of men in places of high authority are highlighted all the more by the absolute perfection of Christ who came among the rich and mighty and powerful to save just as surely as among the poor and despised and rejected.

[C. S. Lewis (1898–1963)]

DECEMBER

| 1820 | The Bachelor Tax went into effect today in Missouri. All unmarried men between the ages of twenty-one and fifty were required to pay a tax of $1 a year. |

Winslow Homer was undoubtedly one of the greatest artists America has ever produced. Amazingly, he was almost entirely self-taught. Born in 1836 in Boston, he began sketching and painting as a boy—but he never had any encouragement or support from his family, much less any formal training. Nevertheless, his extraordinary talents were so obvious that by 1857 he had already become a regular contributor to the popular *Harper's Weekly*. His illustrations—primarily engravings at that time—were characterized by clean outlines, simplified forms, dramatic contrasts of light and dark, and lively groupings of figures.

During the American War Between the States, Homer made several trips to the Virginia front for *Harper's*. It was then that he experimented with his first oil painting, *Prisoners from the Front*. It was a breathtaking work—notable for its cool objectivity and vigorous realism. After the war, he also began experimenting with watercolor—it seemed that there was no artistic medium that his raw talent and sheer pluck would not enable him to master. His favorite subjects in those days were primarily rural or idyllic—scenes of farm life, children at play, or resort scenes.

But a stay in England beginning in 1881, during which Homer lived in a tiny fishing village that reminded him of his childhood by the sea in New England, led to a permanent change in his interests. Thereafter he concentrated on large-scale scenes of nature, particularly scenes of the sea, of its fishermen, and of their families. Taking up solitary residence on the Maine coast at Prout's Neck, he produced such masterpieces of realism as *Eight Bells*, where the drama of the sea is imbued with an epic, heroic quality.

In addition, he spent a great deal of time in the Florida Keys, the Bahamas, and Cuba. His many scenes of the Tropics were painted mostly in watercolor, and his technique was the most advanced of its day—loose, fresh, spontaneous, almost impressionistic, although it never lost its basic grounding in naturalism.

As was the case with the practitioners of the earlier Hudson River School, it was Homer's Christian faith that enabled him to embody such distinctive ideals as the heroism of ordinary people and their rugged sort of covenantalism—after all, his own life was an extraordinary example of the power of the Protestant work ethic. The grandeur of his themes and the strength of his designs—and all that rooted in an uncommon commonness—enabled Homer to become a dominant influence on the American realist and expressionist styles of painting.

FEAST DAY
St. Dominic of Silos, St. Ammon and his Companions, St. Ursicinus, St. Philogonius

DECEMBER

1606 The *Susan Constant,* the *Godspeed,* and the *Discovery* departed from London carrying the 120 or so colonists to the New World to establish the royally chartered Virginia Company's first settlement at Jamestown.

1790 The first successful cotton mill in the United States began operating at Pawtucket, Rhode Island.

1860 South Carolina became the first state to secede from the Union.

1864 Confederate forces evacuated Savannah, Georgia, as Union General William T. Sherman continued his March to the Sea.

1879 Thomas A. Edison privately demonstrated his incandescent light at Menlo Park, New Jersey.

1946 *It's a Wonderful Life* was shown in a charity preview at New York's Globe Theatre the day before its official premiere. The film, directed by Frank Capra and starring Jimmy Stewart, became an instant holiday classic. Based on the story *The Greatest Gift* by Philip Van Doren Stern, it focuses on a man who believes he is a failure because he never left the small town where he grew up. George Bailey has run the town savings and loan since his father retired, something he swore as a child he'd never do. Bailey, a decent and good man who serves his town well, struggles to make ends meet at the job he has never really loved. When disaster strikes and the savings and loan funds are lost, Bailey decides to commit suicide. In a *Christmas Carol*–like twist of fate, an angel helps George see what life would have been like in the town if he had never been born. *It's a Wonderful Life* was reportedly the favorite work of both actor Stewart and director Capra from their long and illustrious careers.

1963 The Berlin Wall was opened for the first time to West Berliners, who were allowed one-day visits to relatives in the Eastern sector for the holidays.

1968 John Steinbeck died in New York at age sixty-six. The Pulitzer Prize–winning American writer and Nobel laureate described in his work the unremitting struggle of people who depend on the soil for their livelihood. His books included such classics as *Tortilla Flat, The Pearl, Travels with Charley, The Moon Is Down, Cannery Row, East of Eden* and *Of Mice and Men.* His greatest work was *The Grapes of Wrath,* the stark account of the Joad family from the impoverished Oklahoma Dust Bowl and their migration to California during the Great Depression. The controversial novel, received not only as realistic fiction but also as a moving document of social protest, is an American classic. Steinbeck took as his central theme the quiet dignity he saw in the poor and the oppressed. Although his characters are often trapped in an unfair world, they remain sympathetic and heroic—even if defeated—human beings.

1989 After General Manuel Noriega declared war on the United States, twelve thousand American troops arrived in Panama—launching Operation Just Cause—to overthrow the Noriega government and restore democracy.

There is something about saying, "We always do this," which helps keep the years together. Time is such an elusive thing that if we keep on meaning to do something interesting, but never do it, year would follow year with no special thoughtfulness being expressed in making gifts, surprises, charming table settings, and familiar, favorite food. Tradition is a good gift intended to guard the best gifts.

[EDITH SCHAEFFER (1916–)]

DECEMBER

Charles Dickens burst onto the literary scene in England with a series of prose sketches published in a monthly magazine and later in a daily newspaper. The young journalist—who had endured dire poverty and deep shame as a child—was suddenly thrust to the forefront of celebrity and fame. The stunning success of those first sketches—later published in book form as *Sketches by Boz* and *The Pickwick Papers*—was followed in quick succession by *Oliver Twist, Nicholas Nickleby, David Copperfield, Bleak House, Hard Times, A Tale of Two Cities,* and *Great Expectations.* There was little doubt that Dickens had become the most influential novelist in the English language. His plots, his characters, and his images defined for many the Victorian dystopic standard. But more than that, his prolificacy, his versatility, and his creativity defined the modern literary standard. As G. K. Chesterton later said, "The boors in his books are brighter than the wits in other books."

He became the Victorian equivalent of a pop star—rich, famous, pampered, and lionized. His was a rags-to-riches dream come true. Never entirely comfortable with his exalted role though, Dickens began a deep and impassioned search for professions. He tried his hand at lecturing. He dabbled in acting and theater production. He launched innumerable journals, tabloids, magazines, and newspapers. Finding little satisfaction even in these professional successes, he turned to arcane philosophies and sundry esoterica. He explored the occult. And he sated himself in the pleasures of the flesh.

But the great fascination of his life was the Christian faith. At the heart of most of his novels is evidence of an impassioned quest for significance—in and through the spiritual system that ultimately gave flower to the wonder of Western civilization. He wrote innumerable essays on the disparity between Christian teaching and Christian practice. He lectured widely on the nature of Christian ethics and society. And he penned a groping, probing, yearning sketch of the life of Christ.

But the forum for his most sophisticated musings on the faith came in his annual Christmas stories. There, he not only rehearsed his own tragedies and commemorated his own injuries, but he also cast about for some metaphysical meaning or comfort for them.

The stories were written beginning in 1843, when Dickens was at the pinnacle of his writing prowess. The first—and probably the best—was *A Christmas Carol.* It is the familiar story of Scrooge, Marley, Cratchit, Tiny Tim, and ghosts from the past, present, and future. It is also the recollection of that strange mixture of joys and sorrows, victories and defeats, sanctities and perversities, approbations and imprecations inherent in this poor fallen world.

With unsurpassed artistry Dickens painted a picture of depravity, dispossession, and depression with an impressionistic palate—while vividly portraying the power of repentance, redemption, and resurrection with the clarity of a photo. This was undoubtedly the master at his best. Not only did Dickens do something special for Christmas, but Christmas did something special for Dickens.

DECEMBER

1375 Italian scholar, poet, and author of *The Decameron*, Giovanni Boccaccio died in Tuscany on this day. *Il Decamerone* (Ten Days' Work) is a collection of one hundred tales that seven women and three men tell to one another to pass the time while escaping from an outbreak of the plague. The ten friends spend their ten days of retreat in a country villa outside of Florence telling stories of tragedy interspersed with earthy humor. This is considered to be the best prose masterpiece of the Italian Renaissance due to its craftsmanship, classical allusion, character analysis, and pointed observations.

1620 Forefathers Day is celebrated as the day on which an exploratory party from the *Mayflower* first landed at Plymouth Rock.

1872 Phileas Fogg, from Jules Verne's *Around the World in Eighty Days*, walked into the Reform club to claim his £20,000 wager. He announced, "Here I am, gentlemen!" seventy-nine days, twenty-three hours, fifty-nine minutes, and fifty-nine seconds after the start of his trip.

1898 Scientists Pierre and Marie Curie discovered the radioactive element radium.

1913 The first crossword puzzle was published in the supplement of the *New York World* and prepared by Arthur Winn.

1937 *Snow White and the Seven Dwarfs* premiered in Hollywood, California, as the first full-length cartoon with color and sound.

1945 General George S. Patton died in Heidelberg, Germany, of injuries from a car accident.

1948 The state of Eire—formerly the Irish Free State—declared its independence from Great Britain.

1958 Charles de Gaulle was elected to a seven-year term as the first president of the Fifth Republic of France.

1991 Eleven of the twelve former Soviet republics proclaimed the birth of the Commonwealth of Independent States.

1995 The city of Bethlehem passed from Israeli to Palestinian control.

ST. THOMAS DAY	Though he was doubter at first, the apostle Thomas (c. 10–60) came to believe that Christ was not only risen from the dead, but proclaimed Him "My Lord and my God." His anticipation of the full revelation of the kingdom is celebrated on December 21. Traditionally this has been a day for well-wishing—friends, neighbors, and loved ones going out of their way to remember others and to bless one another. Though Christmas cards are a Victorian innovation, they were conceived as a kind of St. Thomas Day gesture of kindness, encouragement, and graciousness.

Christmas time changes our hearts, its seems, whether we wish it so or not. There is a power the coming of Christ has over even the most obdurate unbeliever that simply cannot be escaped.

[CHARLES DICKENS (1812–1870)]

DECEMBER

Gilbert Keith Chesterton was surely among the brightest minds of the twentieth century—a prolific journalist, best-selling novelist, insightful and popular debater, astute literary critic, grassroots reformer, and profound humorist. Recognized by friend and foe alike as one of the most perspicacious, epigrammatic, and jocose prose stylists in the entire literary canon, he is today the most quoted writer in the English language besides William Shakespeare.

His remarkable output of books—more than a hundred published in his lifetime and half again that many afterward—covered an astonishing array of subjects from economics, art, history, biography, and social criticism to poetry, detective stories, philosophy, travel, and religion. His most amazing feat was not merely his vast output or wide range but the consistency and clarity of his thought, his uncanny ability to tie everything together. In the heart of nearly every paragraph he wrote was a jaw-dropping aphorism or a mind-boggling paradox that left readers shaking their heads in bemusement and wonder.

But Chesterton was not only a prodigious creator of characters, he was also a prodigious character in his own right. At over six feet and three hundred pounds his romantically rumpled appearance—often enhanced with the flourish of a cape and a swordstick—made him appear nearly as enigmatic, anachronistic, and convivial as he actually was. Perhaps that was a part of the reason why he was one of the most beloved men of his time—even his ideological opponents regarded him with great affection. His humility, his wonder at existence, his graciousness, and his sheer sense of joy set him apart not only from most of the artists and celebrities during the first half of the twentieth century, but from most anyone and everyone.

He was amazingly prescient—predicting such things as the mindless faddism of pop culture, the rampant materialism permeating society, the moral relativism subsuming age-old ethical standards, disdain of religion, the unfettered censorship by the press (as opposed to censorship of the press), the grotesque uglification of the arts, and the rise of the twin evils of monolithic business and messianic government. It seems that his words ring truer today than when they were first written nearly a century ago.

But perhaps the most remarkable thing about Chesterton was not his prodigious literary output, his enormous popularity, or his cultural sagacity. Instead, it was his enormous capacity to love—to love people, to love the world around him, and to love life. His all-encompassing love was especially evident at Christmastime.

Maisie Ward, Chesterton's authoritative biographer and friend, asserted, "Some men, it may be, are best moved to reform by hate, but Chesterton was best moved by love and nowhere does that love shine more clearly than in all he wrote about Christmas." Indeed, he wrote a great deal about Christmas throughout his life—and as a result his love shines abroad even now, nearly three-quarters of a century after his death. He wrote scintillating Christmas essays, poignant Christmas verse, and adventurous Christmas stories. He wrote Christmas reviews, editorials, satires, and expositions. He wrote of Christmas recipes and Christmas presents and Christmas sermons. They all bespeak the stalwart faith, the abiding hope, and the infectious joy he drew from the celebration of Christ's incarnation.

DECEMBER

1808 Ludwig van Beethoven's Symphony no. 5 in C Minor was first performed. He utilized a four-note motif to unify the work melodically and rhythmically in the contrasting sections of the entire piece.

1858 Italian opera composer Giocomo Puccini was born in Lucca to a family of church musicians. His operas contain intense emotion expressed through lyrical vocal lines and rich orchestration. His most famous works include *Manon Lescaut* (1893), *La Bohéme* (1896), *Tosca* (1900), *Madama Butterfly* (1904), and *Turandot* (1924).

1880 English novelist Mary Ann Evans—best known by her nom de plume, George Eliot—died suddenly this evening at her home in Cheyne Walk, London. She was known for her penetrating feeling and accurate portrayal of common lives in such works as *Adam Bede* (1859), *The Mill on the Floss* (1860), and what is considered by some to be one of the most perfect short stories in the English language, *Silas Marner* (1861). All three of these novels deal with life in the Warwickshire countryside where Eliot grew up. She rejected dogmatic religion early in life and lived as a rationalist.

1894 Claude Debussy wrote *L'Après-midi d'un Faune* (The Afternoon of a Faun), an orchestral prelude that marked the development of the highly individual and exquisite style of composition that came to be known as Impressionism.

1894 French army officer Alfred Dreyfus was convicted of treason in a court-martial that triggered worldwide charges of anti-Semitism. Dreyfus was eventually vindicated, but not before inspiring the formation of the Zionist movement.

1938 Off the coast of South Africa in the Bay of Chalumna, the first example of a coelacanth fish was caught and identified. Evolutionary scientists had believed that this species had been extinct for more than fifty million years.

1942 Beatrix Potter died at the age of seventy-seven, after a multifaceted life as a best-selling children's author and painter and a respected Herdwick sheep breeder. She left her fourteen farms totalling more than four thousand acres to the British National Trust.

1963 An official thirty-day mourning period following the assassination of President Kennedy came to an end.

1989 President Nicolae Ceausescu of Romania, the last of Eastern Europe's hard-line Communist rulers, was toppled from power in a popular uprising.

1990 Lech Walesa, a former electrician and leader of the Solidarity Union movement, took the oath of office as Poland's first popularly elected president.

Weak things must boast of being new, like so many new German philosophies. But strong things can boast of being old. Strong things can boast of being moribund.

[G. K. CHESTERTON (1874–1936)]

DECEMBER

BELLS

Some early bell-ringers believed that the sound of bells would frighten away evil spirits. The church has used bells throughout the centuries to spread news of victory, death, and celebration. Whatever the form, the pealing of bells are distinctive heralds to the good news of Christmas. On the island of Guernsey, the church bells tolled all through the day of December 23—which was known as *La Longue Vielle*. It was a pre-Christmas celebration—worshippers stayed up late eating biscuits and cheese while drinking mulled wine. It was also a collective time for preparing Christmas goods for the market.

Following his successful campaign to ensure the independence of his new nation, General George Washington surrendered his commission to President Thomas Mifflin and the assembled Congress of the United States on December 23, 1783. Though his troops were ready to declare him king, he desired to honor the federal government as it was then constituted. He then retired to private life at his home on the Potomac River, Mount Vernon. It would only be a short retirement, however; the controversy over a new form of Federalism ultimately brought him back into public life and ultimately to the presidency itself. John Greenleaf Whittier wrote a ballad to celebrate his extraordinary commitment and submission to authority.

FEAST DAY
The Ten Martyrs of Crete, St. Dagobert II of Austria, St. John of Kanti, Saints Victoria and Anatolia, St. Frithebert, St. Servulus, St. Thorlac

The sword was sheathed: In April's sun
Lay green the fields by Freedom won;
And severed sections, weary of debates,
Joined hands at last and were United States.

O City sitting by the Sea!
How proud the day that dawned on thee,
When the new era, long desired, began,
And, in its need, the hour had found the man!

One thought the cannon salvos spoke,
The resonant bell-tower's vibrant stroke,
The voiceful streets, the plaudit-echoing halls,
And prayer and hymn borne from Saint Paul's!

How felt the land in every part
The strong throb of a nation's heart,
As its great leader gave, with reverent awe,
His pledge to Union, Liberty, and Law!

That pledge the heavens above him heard,
That vow the sleep of centuries stirred;
In world-wide wonder listening peoples bent
Their gaze on Freedom's great experiment.

Could it succeed? Of honor sold
And hopes deceived all history told.
Above the wrecks that strewed the mournful past,
Was the long dream true at last?

Thank God! The people's choice was just,
The one man equal to his trust,
Wise beyond lore, and without weakness good,
Calm in the strength of flawless rectitude!

His rule of justice, order, peace,
Made possible the world's release;
Taught prince and serf that power is but a trust,
And rule alone, which serves the ruled, is just.

That Freedom generous is, but strong
In hate of fraud and selfish wrong,
Pretence that turns her holy truth to lies,
And lawless license masking in her guise.

Land of his love! With one glad voice
Let thy great sisterhood rejoice;
A century's suns o'er thee have risen and set,
And, God be praised, we are one nation yet.

And still we trust the years to be
Shall prove his hope was destiny,
Leaving our flag, with all its added stars,
Unrent by faction and unstained by wars.

Lo! Where with patient toil he nursed
And trained the new-set plant at first,
The widening ranches of a stately tree
Stretch from the sunrise to the sunset sea.

And in its broad and sheltering shade,
Sitting with none to make afraid,
Were we now silent, through mighty limb,
The winds of heaven would sing the praise of him.

DECEMBER

37 Nero, the notorious Roman despot, was most likely born on this day—though some historians place the date several days earlier, others a few days later. Nero was the last of the family of Julius Caesar to be emperor of Rome. He came to the throne at the age of sixteen, after his mother, Agrippina, poisoned her husband, the emperor Claudius. During his early reign he was guided by the philosopher Seneca and Burius, the commander of his guard. Roman rule spread from Britain to Armenia, but Nero was more concerned with promoting his own power than the might of Rome. The last years of his rule were years of terror and self- indulgence. When a conspiracy against him failed, Nero became even more repressive. When Rome burned in 64, Nero was so fascinated with the fire and the opportunity it provided to rebuild the city that many suspected him of setting the blaze. To direct blame away from himself, Nero blamed the fire on the Christians—beginning the first wave of cruel persecutions against the church, which resulted in thousands of martyrdoms including those of the apostles Peter and Paul.

1788 Maryland ceded one hundred square acres for the District of Columbia.

1823 *A Visit from St. Nicholas*—best known as *'Twas the Night Before Christmas*—was published anonymously in the *Troy Sentinel* in New York. The poem was by Clement C. Moore.

1893 The Engelbert Humperdinck opera *Haensel und Gretel* was first performed, in Weimar, Germany.

1928 The National Broadcasting Company set up a permanent, coast-to-coast network.

1948 Former Japanese premier Hideki Tojo and six other Japanese war leaders were executed in Tokyo.

1968 Eighty-two crew members of the U.S. intelligence ship *Pueblo* were released by North Korea, eleven months after they had been captured.

1975 Congress adopted the Metric Conversion Act, inteded to make the metric system the basic system of measurement in the United States.

Neither in halls nor yet in bowers
Born would he not be,
Neither in castles nor yet in towers
That seemly were to see;
But at his Father's will
The prophecy to fulfill,
Betwixt an ox and an ass
Jesus, this king, born he was.
Heavén he bring us till!

[COVENTRY MYSTERY PLAY (C. 1200)]

DECEMBER

CHRISTMAS EVE	The night before the Feast of Christ's Nativity has always been a time of special anticipation for Christian families. The end of the Advent preparation marks a time of special feasting. There is always good food to look forward to—and the aromas of the last round of baking fills homes with delight. In addition, the special tradition of gift giving, almost universally practiced by the end of the fourth century or so, particularly excites the imaginations of children. As a result, the evening has become a kind of vigil for everyone, young and old alike.
ANGELS	They were the first heralds of the miracle of the Incarnation in Bethlehem two millennia ago. Not surprisingly then, representations of angels have accompanied Christmas celebrations ever since. They appear atop Christmas trees, in tabletop arrangements, adorning evergreen wreaths, outlined in lights along the hearthside, and astride candles and candelabras. They play a prominent role in Christmas carols, Christmas tales, and Christmas decorations. They are featured in Christmas arts, crafts, and designs. Indeed, they lend solemnity and credulity to the Yuletide season.

FEAST DAY

St. Gregory of Spoleto, Saints Tharsilla and Emiliana, St. Adela, St. Irmina, St. Delphinus, St. Sharbel Makhlouf

DECEMBER

The traditional holiday Service of Lessons and Carols is most closely associated with the King's College Chapel, Cambridge. The service consists of nine Scripture lessons that alternate with carols of a similar theme. The lessons and carols tell of the fall of man, the promise of a Savior by the prophets, the annunciation to Mary, the shepherds and angels, and ends with the reading of John chapter one.

This Christmas Eve service follows the form laid down in 1918 by the King's College Dean, Eric Milner-White. As he saw it, the strength of the service lay in the Scripture readings, which outline the need for redemption, the promise of a Savior, and the Nativity itself. Milner-White patterned his 10:00 P.M. Christmas Eve service on an order of worship that had been drawn up by E. W. Benson, later Archbishop of Canterbury, for use in the wooden shed that served as his cathedral in Truro in 1880. A. C. Benson recalled: "My father arranged from ancient sources a little service for Christmas Eve—nine carols and nine tiny lessons, which were read by various officers of the Church, beginning with a chorister, and ending, through the different grades, with the Bishop." The suggestion for the service had come from G. H. S. Walpole, who later became the bishop of Edinburgh. The service in Cambridge has been adapted and emulated throughout the world. With the exception of the year 1930, the BBC has broadcast the concert annually since 1928. This includes the period of the Second World War, when the ancient glass (and also all heat) had been removed from the chapel and the name of King's College could not be broadcast for security reasons. The combination of prayers, liturgy, carols, Scripture, and congregational worship creates a solemnity that recognizes the historic nature of the Christian faith as well as a celebration of the fulfilled promise of redemption.

1524 Portuguese navigator Vasco da Gama—who had discovered a sea route around Africa to India—died in Cochin, India.

1818 Franz Gruber and Joseph Mohr composed *"Stille Nacht, Heilige Nacht"*—"Silent Night, Holy Night"—to be sung at the village church in Oberndorff, Austria, the following day. Since then the carol has been translated into more than ninety languages and dialects. However, there has been much lore and legend surrounding the composition of this quintessential Christmas carol. Franz Gruber (1787–1863), the composer of the tune, gives the definitive version of the story in a signed statement issued by him: "It was on December 24 of the year 1818 when Joseph Mohr, then assistant pastor of the newly established St. Nicholas parish church in Oberndorf, handed to Franz Gruber, who was attending to the duties of organist (and was at the same time a schoolmaster in Arnsdorf) a poem, with the request that he write for it a suitable melody arranged for two solo voices, chorus, and a guitar accompaniment. On that very same evening the latter, in fulfillment of this request made to him as a music expert, handed to the pastor his simple composition, which was thereupon immediately performed on that holy night of Christmas Eve and received with all acclaim."

1822 English poet Matthew Arnold was born in Laleham, Middlesex, England. Perhaps his most famous poem is "Dover Beach."

1851 Fire destroyed more than two-thirds of the books in the Library of Congress.

1871 The first performance of Giuseppe Verdi's opera *Aïda* was held at the opening of a new opera house in Cairo. This tragic story of an Ethiopian slave girl in Egypt was written by Verdi at the request of the khedive of Egypt in celebration of the opening of the Suez Canal. The Italian text was based on prose by an Egyptologist through a French verse translation.

1906 Canadian physicist Reginald A. Fessenden became the first person to broadcast a music program over radio, from Brant Rock, Massachusetts.

1920 Enrico Caruso gave his last public performance, singing in Jacques Halevy's *La Juive* at the Metropolitan Opera in New York.

1928 The Service of Lessons and Carols was first broadcast from King's College Chapel, Cambridge, by the BBC.

1951 Gian Carlo Menotti's *Amahl and the Night Visitors,* the first opera written specifically for television, premiered on NBC-TV.

1968 The *Apollo 8* astronauts, orbiting the moon, read passages from the Old Testament book of Genesis during a Christmas Eve television broadcast.

1989 Ousted Panamanian ruler Manuel Noriega, who had succeeded in eluding American forces, took refuge at the Vatican's diplomatic mission in Panama City.

When I think of Christmas Eves, Christmas feasts, Christmas songs, and Christmas stories, I know that they do not represent a short and transient gladness. Instead, they speak of a joy unspeakable and full of glory. God loved the world and sent His Son. Whosoever believes in Him will not perish, but have everlasting life. That is Christmas joy. That is the Christmas spirit.

[CORRIE TEN BOOM (1892–1983)]

DECEMBER

751

Boniface of Crediton spent the first forty years of his life in quiet service to the church near his home in Exeter. But in 718, Boniface became a missionary to the savage Teutonic tribes of Germany. Stories of his courageous intervention on behalf of the innocent abound. He was constantly jeopardizing his own life for the sake of the young, the vulnerable, the weak, the sick, and the poor—often imposing his body between the victims and their oppressors. Indeed, it was during one of his famed rescues that his name was forever linked to the celebration of Advent during Yuletide.

Wherever he went among the fierce Norsemen who had settled along the Danish and German coast, he was forced to face the awful specter of their brutal pagan practices—which included human mutilations and vestal sacrifices. Boniface decided to strike at the root of such superstitions. He publicly announced that he would destroy their gods. He then marched toward their great sacred grove. The awestruck crowd at Geismar followed along and then watched as he cut down the sacred Oak of Thor, an ancient object of pagan worship standing atop the summit of Mount Gudenberg near Fritzlar. The pagans, who had expected immediate judgment against such sacrilege, were forced to acknowledge that their gods were powerless to protect their own sanctuaries.

A young boy from a neighboring village, hearing of such boldness, rushed into the missionary camp of Boniface three evenings later. It was just about twilight on the first Sunday in Advent. He breathlessly told of a sacrifice that was to be offered that very evening—his sister was to serve as the vestal virgin. Hurrying through the snowy woods and across the rough terrain, Boniface and the boy arrived at the dense sacred grove just in time to see the Druid priest raise his knife into the darkened air. But as the blade plunged downward Boniface hurtled toward the horrid scene. He had nothing in his hands save a small wooden cross. Lunging forward, he reached the girl just in time to see the blade of the knife pierce the cross—thus, saving her life. The priest toppled back. The huddle of worshippers were astonished. Their was a brief moment of complete silence. Boniface seized upon it. He proclaimed the gospel to them then and there, declaring that the ultimate sacrifice had already been made by Christ on the cross at Golgotha—there was no need for others.

Captivated, the small crowd listened intently to his words. After explaining to them the once and for all provision of the gospel, he turned toward the sacred grove. With the sacrificial knife in hand, he began hacking off low-hanging branches. Passing them around the circle, he told each family to take the small fir boughs home as a reminder of the completeness of Christ's work on the tree of Calvary. They were to adorn their hearths with the tokens of His grace. They could even chop great logs from the grove as fuel for their home fires—not so much to herald the destruction of their pagan ways but rather to memorialize the provision of Christ's coming.

Such exploits inspired a number of Advent traditions. The Advent wreath was quickly established as a means of reenacting the gospel lesson of Boniface. In addition, the Christmas tree, decorated with candles and tinsel, strings of lights and garlands under the eaves and across the mantels, and the Yule log burning in the fireplace were favorite reminders of the season's essential message.

CHRISTMAS DAY
FEAST DAY
The Martyrs of Nicomedia, St. Eugenia, St. Alburga, St. Anastasia of Sirmium

DECEMBER

1541 The Unlawful Game Act in England proclaimed that only archery could be played on Christmas Day.

1642 English scientist, mathematician, and author Sir Isaac Newton was born in Woolsthorpe, Lincolnshire. He enunciated his famous three laws of motion in *Philosophiae Naturalis Principia Mathematica* (1687). He is buried in Westminster Abbey.

1821 Clara Barton, nurse and founder of the American Red Cross, was born in Oxford, Massachusetts.

1831 Arkansas and Louisiana became the first two states to celebrate Christmas as a legal holiday.

1896 John Philip Sousa wrote the "Stars and Stripes Forever" march.

1909 On the first Christmas during World War I, British and German troops along the Western Front observed an unofficial truce that included the exchange of gifts and the playing of soccer in "no man's land."

1939 Rudolph was introduced as the ninth reindeer by Montgomery Ward.

1943 In his Christmas Fireside Chat via radio, President Franklin Roosevelt spoke soberly: "The war is now reaching the stage when we shall have to look forward to large casualty lists—dead, wounded, and missing. War entails just that. There is no easy road to victory. And the end is not yet in sight."

1991 The dictator of the Soviet Union for almost seven years, Mikhail Gorbachev announced his resignation. As a result, the Communist nation and its Eastern Bloc allies dissolved the Iron Curtain and started a massive reform of government.

CHRISTMAS

Christians have celebrated the incarnation and nativity of the Lord Jesus on December 25 since at least the early part of the third century—just a few generations removed from the days of the apostles. By 336, when the Philocalian Calendar—one of the earliest documents of the Patriarchal Church—was first utilized, Christmas Day was already a venerable and tenured tradition. Though there is no historical evidence that Christ was actually born on that day—indeed, whatever evidence there is points to altogether different occasions—the conversion of the old Pagan tribes of Europe left a gaping void where the ancient winter cult festivals were once held. It was both culturally convenient and evangelically expedient to exchange the one for the other. And so joy replaced desperation. Celebration replaced propitiation. Christmas feasts replaced new moon sacrifices. Christ replaced Baal, Molech, Apollo, and Thor. Glad tidings of great joy, indeed.

Let us stand fast in what is right and prepare our souls for trial. Let us be neither dogs that do not bark nor silent onlookers nor paid servants who run away before the wolf.

[BONIFACE OF CREDITON (680–755)]

DECEMBER

On this day in 1223, Francis of Assisi assembled one of the first Nativity scenes, in Greccio, Italy. The tradition caught on and by the sixteenth century, the tradition of Francis was made an integral part of the Coventry Pagent in England. The Shearmen and Tailors guilds put on the pageant as a didactic tool to teach the people about the Bible and theology. It included a series of plays, hymns, and carols performed on carts drawn through the streets.

In one of the plays, just before the introduction of the Bethlehem shepherds, Mary sends Joseph in search of a midwife because the birth of Christ is imminent. As three shepherds gather together for food and shelter, the star is revealed, and the third shepherd exclaims:

> A ha! Now ys cum the tyme that old fathurs [prophets] hath told,
> Thatt in the wynturs nyght soo cold
> A chyld of meydyn borne be he wold
> In whom all profeciys schalbe fullfyld.

The angels sing "'Glorea in excelsis Deo' above in the clowdis." The first shepherd suggests:

> Mow goo we hence
> To worschippe thatt chyld of hy manyffecence,
> And that we ma syng in his prescence
> "Et in tarra pax omynibus."

The shepherds sing the first verse of "Ase I owt Rodde" followed by dialogue from Joseph, the singing of the angels, and a blessing from Mary. "There the Scheppardis syngith ageyne and goth forthe of the place."

It is because of the immense popularity of this great drama that ever since, representative reminders of the crèche in Bethlehem have been central to the Christmas celebrations of Christians around the world. Eventually, most of the great European cathedrals, town squares, castles, and palaces were thereafter adorned with scenes of the wise men, shepherds, and stable animals gathered around the holy family of Mary, Joseph, and the baby Jesus. Along the Mediterranean, scenes carved from olive wood were especially prized beginning in the sixth century—and so remain to this day.

DECEMBER

c. 35 Like Good King Wenceslaus, Stephen was killed because of his convictions about the revelation of Christ in the world. Indeed, according to the book of Acts, he was the very first martyr of the Christian faith—bearing testimony to his accusers of the historicity and transforming power of the gospel. For centuries, Christians have remembered his boldness, courage, and faithfulness on the day after Christmas, December 26. Because Stephen was a deacon in the early church—charged with caring for the orphans and widows in their distress—his day has generally been set aside as a day for selfless care of the poorest of the poor, the despised, the rejected, and the unloved.

800 The day after he was crowned emperor of the Holy Roman Empire, Charlemagne was presented to his subjects by the pope.

1066 The day after he was crowned the king of England, William the Conqueror began to consolidate his reign by pardoning the most powerful and influential Saxon lords who had previously opposed him.

1716 English poet Thomas Gray was born in Cornhill, London. He was best known for his "Elegy Written in a Country Churchyard," which contains the following lines:

Far from the madding crowd's ignoble strife,
Their sober wishes never learned to stray;
Along the cool sequestered vale of life
They kept the noiseless tenor of their way.

The curfew tolls the knell of the parting day,
The lowing herd winds slowly o're the lea,
The ploughman homeward plods his weary way,
And leaves the world to darkness and to me.

1799 In a eulogy of George Washington delivered to both houses of Congress, Henry Lee of Virginia described him as "first in war, first in peace and first in the hearts of his country-men."

1931 George Gershwin's musical *Of Thee I Sing* opened at the Music Box Theatre in New York City. It was the first musical to be awarded a Pulitzer Prize.

1947 The children's television program *Howdy Doody* made its debut on NBC.

1949 Queen Juliana of the Netherlands signed an act granting sovereignty to Indonesia after more than three centuries of Dutch rule.

1970 *Hello, Dolly!* closed on Broadway after a run of 2,844 performances.

1979 Soviet forces seized control of Afghanistan. President Hafizullah Amin, who was overthrown and executed, was replaced by the Communist puppet Babrak Karmal.

The Son of God became a man to enable men to become the sons of God.

[C. S. Lewis (1898–1963)]

DECEMBER

The brilliant Scottish critic and historian Thomas Carlyle published his greatest work, *Sartor Resartus*, on this day in 1828 after having lived and worked for a time in London. At the time, the city was in the process of becoming the first truly great industrial center in the world. The venerable old city was rapidly disappearing. In its place was emerging the remarkable innovation of modern machinery and the urban center—the inhuman humanism of commercial progress.

Carlyle was attracted and repulsed simultaneously. His writing ably demonstrated that wrenching paradox as did the similarly conflicted novels of his friend Charles Dickens. Part novel, part autobiography, part history, and part social commentary, *Sartor Resartus* was one of the most original works of prose ever written in the English language. The conservative publishers along Charing Cross Road and Paternoster Row in London were frightened away at first by its ostentatiously fantastic vision, and so it was serialized in the newly established *Fraser's Magazine*. Only later—because of intense public demand—was it published independently for the trade.

At first sight the book appeared to be the bizarre account—recorded by an admiring but dubious editor—of a work by an outlandish German philosopher named Diogenes Teufelsdrockh (literally, Devil's Dung), who was Professor of Things in General at the University of Weissnichtwo (literally, Don't Know Where), on the Philosophy of Clothes (or more specifically, on the philosophy of hidden and revealed covenants). The whole story turns out to be an ingenious and amusing metaphor comparing and contrasting Lutheran Pietism with Calvinistic Covenantalism—the eccentricity of Teufelsdrockh is somehow symbolic of God's providential working in the lives of the mundane and ordinary men to accomplish marvelous and extraordinary deeds, while his strange fixation on clothes is symbolic of this poor fallen world, which at once disguises and conceals, but also reveals and expresses the gracious workings of the Spirit of God behind the spirit of men.

Most students of the work of Carlyle contend that his thought did not reach full maturity until the appearance of his great historical and biographical works—*The French Revolution, Heroes and Hero Worship, Life and Letters of Cromwell, Life of Sterling,* the multivolume *History of Frederick the Great,* and *The Portraits of John Knox.* But the philosophical grid for those later works was first established in *Sartor Resartus.*

It was in the novel that he argues that history is itself a kind of dim gospel—the veiled revelation of a just providence working in the affairs of men. It was not a gospel that could be read simplistically, of course; rather it was one that bids us all to "pause over the mysterious vestiges of Him, whose path is in the great deep of Time, whom history indeed reveals, but only in all of history, and in Eternity—not merely in swatches—will He clearly be revealed."

It was in the novel that he best enunciated his belief that we can see the ultimate reality of God's glory in the brute obscurity of recorded events knowing that "Man's history is a perpetual Evangel—an inarticulate Bible—a loud-roaring loom of time, with all its French Revolutions and Jewish Revelations weaving the vesture thou seest Him by."

DECEMBER

1571 German astronomer Johannes Kepler, who named three important laws of planetary motion, was born in Wurttemberg. He was known as the father of modern astronomy.

1742 David Brainerd was a legendary pioneer missionary to the American Indians. He died in 1747 when he was only twenty-nine years old. But his journal—edited and published by his friend and intended father-in-law, Jonathan Edwards—has served as an inspiration to generations of Christians ever since. On this day he wrote of his experience as a believer who has diligently pursued the presence of God. He asserted that he "had a sweet melting sense of divine things, of the pure spirituality of the religion of Christ Jesus. Oh, the sweetness, the tenderness I felt in my soul! If ever I felt the temper of Christ, I had some sense of it now. Blessed be my God, I have seldom enjoyed a more comfortable and profitable day than this. Oh, that I could spend all my time for God."

1814 The gospel was preached to Maori people of New Zealand for the first time by Samuel Marsden, an Anglican missionary from Sydney, Australia. Marsden was born at Horsforth near Leeds, England, in 1764. He attended grammar school at Hull, and after school helped his father in his shop at Leeds. Following his conversion he joined the Methodist Church, but later embraced the Church of England and entered St. John's College, Cambridge. He was ordained in 1793, and the very next year he was sent to be the chaplain of the penal colony at Parmatta, near Sydney, Australia. Reverend Marsden was responsible for starting a farm there, considered one of the finest in Australia, for the benefit of training the convicts. At his own expense Marsden outfitted a ship and sailed with his two new associates from Australia to New Zealand, landing at the Bay of the Islands. The Maoris welcomed the missionaries warmly and graciously, and Marsden returned to New Zealand six times over the next twenty-five years.

1927 The Hammerstein-Kern musical *Showboat* was opened in New York by Florenz Ziegfeld. Based on Edna Ferber's novel, the use of idioms and authenticity to portray the lives of the people on the *Cotton Blossom* was unique in American theater.

1932 Radio City Music Hall at the Rockefeller Center in New York City was opened to the public.

1940 Germany released a propaganda statement declaring that P. G. Wodehouse, the British novelist and humorist, was writing a novel about American swindlers. At the time Wodehouse was being held in a German internment camp.

ST. JOHN'S DAY

John, the beloved apostle, was one of the founders of the church in Ephesus. He carried out his pastoral charge with particular compassion to the hurting and forlorn. As a result, his testimony has long been commemorated during this season of practical charity. It is on December 27 that the winter beers are uncasked, distributed to the poor, and that the dark is drawn for the blessing and benefit of all the townspeople and those who live beyond in field and forest.

Writing for a living ought to be a crime—a bit like taking candy from children. Though I must say, it is pretty nice work if you can get it.

[PELHAM GRENVILLE WODEHOUSE (1881–1975)]

DECEMBER

Often called Childermas, this day on the Christian calendar has traditionally been celebrated as the Feast of the Holy Innocents. It is a day that solemnizes the slaughter of the children of Judea by Herod the Great following the birth of Christ.

It has always been the focus of the Christian's commitment to protect and preserve the sanctity of human life—thus serving as a prophetic warning against the practicioners of abandonment and infanticide in the age of antiquity, oblacy, and pessiary in the medieval epoch, and abortion and euthanasia in these modern times. Generally set aside as a day of prayer, it culminates with a declaration of the covenant community's unflinching commitment to the innocents who are unable to protect themselves.

Virtually every culture in antiquity was stained with the blood of innocent children. Unwanted infants in ancient Rome were abandoned outside the city walls to die from exposure to the elements or from the attacks of wild foraging beasts. Greeks often gave their pregnant women harsh doses of herbal or medicinal abortifacients. Persians developed highly sophisticated surgical curette procedures. Chinese women tied heavy ropes around their waists so excruciatingly tight that they either aborted or passed into unconsciousness. Ancient Hindus and Arabs concocted chemical pessaries— abortifacients that were pushed or pumped directly into the womb through the birth canal. Primitive Canaanites threw their children onto great flaming pyres as a sacrifice to their god Molech. Polynesians subjected their pregnant women to onerous tortures—their abdomens beaten with large stones or hot coals heaped upon their bodies. Egyptians disposed of their unwanted children by disemboweling and dismembering them shortly after birth—their collagen was then harvested for the manufacture of cosmetic creams.

FEAST DAY
The Holy Innocents, St. Antony of Lérins, St. Theodore the Sanctified

Abortion, infanticide, exposure, and abandonment were so much a part of human societies that they provided the primary literary leitmotif in popular traditions, stories, myths, fables, and legends. The founding of Rome was, for instance, presumed to be the happy result of the abandonment of Romulus and Remus. Likewise, Oedipus, Jupiter, Poseidon, and Hephaistos were all victims of failed infanticides.

Because they had been mired by the minions of sin and death, it was as instinctive as the autumn harvest for them to summarily sabotage their own heritage. They saw nothing particularly cruel about despoiling the fruit of their wombs. It was woven into the very fabric of their culture. They believed that it was completely justifiable. They believed that it was just and good and right.

The gospel therefore came into the world as a stern rebuke. God, who is the giver of life (Acts 17:25), the fountain of life (Psalm 36:9), and the defender of life (Psalm 27:1), not only sent us the message of life (Acts 5:20) and the words of life (John 6:68), He sent us the light of life as well (John 8:12). He sent us His only begotten Son—the life of the world (John 6:51)—to break the bonds of sin and death (I Corinthians 15:54–56). For God so loved the world, that He sent His only begotten Son, that whosoever believeth in Him should not perish, but have everlasting life (John 3:16).

DECEMBER

1832 John C. Calhoun became the first vice president of the United States to resign, stepping down over differences with President Andrew Jackson.

1846 Iowa became the twenty-ninth state to be admitted to the Union.

1856 The twenty-eighth president of the United States, Thomas Woodrow Wilson, was born in Staunton, Virginia.

1869 William F. Semple of Mt. Vernon, Ohio, received a patent for chewing gum. He claimed that the "combination of rubber with other articles, in any proportions, adapted to the formation of an acceptable chewing gum."

1897 The play *Cyrano de Bergerac*, by Edmond Rostand, premiered in Paris.

1917 The *New York Evening Mail* published a facetious essay by H. L. Mencken on the history of bathtubs in America. The essay claimed, for example, that Millard Fillmore was the first president to have a bathtub installed in the White House.

1917 The insurgent Communist government of the Bolshevik Revolution confiscated all Russian church lands, canceled state subsidies for church schools, decreed marriage a civil ordinance, and nationalized all charitable institutions, thus effectively abolishing all religious influence in the culture—imposing what Chairman Lenin called "a separation of church and state." The leader of the Russian Orthodox Church, Patriarch Tikhon, was outraged. He angrily charged the men with all the insanity of modern-day Herods—a notion history would ultimately justify: "Think what you are doing, you madmen! Stop your bloody outrages! Your acts are not merely cruel, they are the works of Satan, for which you will burn in hell fire in the life hereafter and will be cursed by future generations in this life." Not surprisingly, a week later the patriarch was arrested by the Communists and martyred.

1945 Congress officially recognized the Pledge of Allegiance.

1963 German composer, theorist, teacher, violist, and conductor Paul Hindemith died in Frankfurt. His great operatic masterpiece, *Mathis der Maler* (1938), was based on the life of German painter Matthias Grünewald.

1973 Aleksandr Solzhenitsyn published *Gulag Archipelago*, an exposé of the Soviet prison system.

1981 Elizabeth Jordan Carr, the first American "test-tube" baby, was born in Norfolk, Virginia.

1989 Alexander Dubcek, the former Czechoslovak Communist leader who was deposed in a Soviet-led Warsaw Pact invasion in 1968, was named chairman of the country's Parliament.

There is no fortress of man's flesh so made, but subtle, treacherous time comes creeping in. Oh, long before his last assaults begin, the enemy's on; the stronghold is betrayed; and the one lonely watchman, half-dismayed, beyond the covering of dark, he hears them come: the distant hosts of death that march with muffled drum.

[Hilaire Belloc (1871–1953)]

DECEMBER

When he was a teenager, the Russian mystic Grigori Efimovich Rasputin had a vision of the Virgin of Kazan and became convinced that he was chosen for some special purpose. He was filled with a holy zeal that many believed bordered on madness. Ostracized from his own family and village, he took to the roads, becoming one of thousands of "holy wanderers" who roamed Russia traveling from one religious shrine to another at the beginning of the twentieth century.

He was born into humble peasant stock and was raised in an isolated Siberian village where memories of the pagan past still survived. It seems that many of his mystical beliefs were adapted from the old superstitions and folk tales he had heard as a child. Ultimately, he accepted the belief of a strange sect that taught that communion with God came only after committing sin. He spent his life on a pendulum swinging from days of wanton orgy to days of abject penance. Indeed, his very name, Rasputin, was derived from his scandalous sexual exploits—it literally meant "debauchee."

In 1903 he arrived in Saint Petersburg, where he owed his entry into high society to the fad for spiritualism, exoticism, and popular religion fashionable in some circles at that time. Although he was unordained, Rasputin enjoyed the favor of some prominent leaders in the Russian Orthodox Church. He first met the Russian emperor Nicholas II and the Empress Alexandra in the autumn of 1905, when Russia was in the midst of an uprising against the monarchy. The Imperial family was also shaken by the discovery that Alexis, the heir to the throne, had hemophilia. Rasputin seemed to embody the simple peasant faith in the monarchy that Nicholas saw as the chief support for his dynasty and the main justification of his role as autocrat and protector of his people. Above all, Rasputin appeared to be uniquely able to alleviate the incurable illness of Alexis, on occasion intervening successfully to end dangerous attacks of bleeding. This won him the passionate support of the worried empress.

Between 1906 and 1914, Rasputin's association with the Imperial family was used against the regime by politicians and journalists who wished to undermine the dynasty's credibility, force the emperor to renounce any political role, and assert the independence of the Russian Orthodox Church from the state. Rasputin helped the propaganda by boasting about his influence on the imperial couple, by his debauched lifestyle, and by a number of public disputes with church figures.

Fearing the evil tongues of the tsar's enemies, and wishing to be rid of Rasputin, a few men decided to murder him. He was brought to the palace of Prince Yusupov in St. Petersburg, where he was poisoned. The poison had little effect, so both the prince and another assassin shot him several times. His body was dumped into the Neva River and was not found until January 2. An autopsy indicated that he was still alive when he was put in the water and may have even survived for several days. It was clear though that he had done such damage to the royal family that the monarchy would not survive much longer than that—and thus heresy paved the way for revolution.

DECEMBER

29

1170 St. Thomas à Becket, the thirty-ninth archbishop of Canterbury, was murdered in Canterbury Cathedral on the order of King Henry II by four of his knights. T. S. Eliot's play *Murder in the Cathedral* (1935) is based on these events: "What a parcel of fools and dastards have I nourished in my house, that not one of them will avenge me of this one upstart clerk."

1777 Faced with starvation and mutiny, George Washington urged the camp chef to prepare a warming dish to raise moral against the bitter cold. The chef secured a large quantity of tripe, some peppercorns, and some vegetables, which he concocted into the "Philadelphia Pepper Pot."

1808 The seventeenth president of the United States, Andrew Johnson, was born in Raleigh, North Carolina.

1845 Texas was admitted as the twenty-eighth state.

1851 The first American Young Men's Christian Association was organized, in Boston.

1852 Emma Snodgrass was arrested in Boston for wearing pants.

1890 The Wounded Knee Massacre took place in South Dakota as some three hundred Sioux Indians were killed by U.S. troops sent to disarm them.

1916 After having been serialized by Ezra Pound in the *Egoist* during 1914 and 1915, James Joyce's *Portrait of the Artist as a Young Man* was published in New York.

1940 During the Second World War, Germany began dropping incendiary bombs on London.

1957 Singers Steve Lawrence and Eydie Gorme were married in Las Vegas, Nevada.

1989 Playwright Vaclav Havel was elected president of Czechoslovakia by the country's Federal Assembly, becoming the first non-Communist to attain the post in more than four decades.

THE TWELVE DAYS OF CHRISTMAS

Every day, from December 25 to January 6, is traditionally a part of the Yuletide celebration. Dedicated to mercy and compassion—in light of the incarnation of heaven's own mercy and compassion—each of those twelve days between Christmas and Epiphany is to be noted by selfless giving and tender charity. In many cultures, gift giving is not concentrated on a single day, but rather, as in the famous folk song, spread out through the entire season. All of the gifts in the folk song "Twelve Days of Christmas" represent some aspect of the blessing of Christ's appearing. They portray the abundant life, the riches of the Christian inheritance, and the ultimate promise of heaven. They also depict the essential covenantal nature of life lived in community and accountability.

A friend loves at all times and a brother is born for adversity.

[KING SOLOMON (PROVERBS 17:17)]

DECEMBER

By the end of the nineteenth century most Americans looked forward to the future with the proud and certain belief that the next hundred years would be the greatest, the most glorious, and the most glamorous in human history. They were infected with a sanguine spirit. Optimism was rampant. A brazen confidence colored their every activity.

There was nothing in their experience to make them think otherwise. Never had a century changed people's lives as dramatically as the one just past. Railroads, telephones, the telegraph, electricity, mass production, forged steel, automobiles, and countless other modern discoveries had all come upon them at a dizzying pace, expanding their horizons far beyond their grandfathers' wildest dreams.

The wrenching disruption of the War Between the States was now past. The moral blight of slavery had been wiped out of existence. Prosperity had returned. Brash vitality and assurance were now the common currencies of the day. Things couldn't have been better—or at least, so it seemed.

It was more than unfounded imagination, then, that lay behind the *New York World*'s prediction that the twentieth century would "meet and overcome all perils and prove to be the best that this steadily improving planet has ever seen."

Most Americans were cheerfully assured that control of man and nature would soon lie entirely within their grasp and would bestow upon them the unfathomable millennial power to alter the destinies of societies, nations, and epochs. They were a people of manifold purpose. They were a people of manifest destiny.

What they did not know was that dark and malignant seeds were already germinating just beneath the surface of the new century's soil. Even as the new epoch dawned, ideological revolutions, nationalistic passions, and unbridled new technological powers drew the entire world toward a century of the unimagined and unimaginable horrors of war, despotism, injustice, prejudice, discrimination, and totalitarianism.

Who could have ever guessed during those ebulliently auspicious days of anticipation and celebration that a mere handful of ideologues would, over the span of the next century, spill more innocent blood than all the murderers, warlords, and tyrants of past history combined? Who could have ever guessed that they would together ensure that the hopes and dreams and aspirations of the twentieth century would be smothered under the weight of holocaust, genocide, and triage?

While the church had been forced to face grave and difficult challenges in the past, its challenges in this new century would be unprecedented. From both within and without the community of faith would be buffeted by forces of fierce virulence. And its response would ultimately determine the destiny of both men and nations.

The founders of the great American experiment in liberty—from the Pilgrim and Puritan pioneers to the constitutional framers—imagined that this land might be a "city on a hill," a "light to the nations," and a "great and final hope for mankind." The difficult days of the twentieth century would test that proposition as it had never before been tested. And as always, judgment would begin at the house of God.

30

DECEMBER

1384 John Wycliffe died after suffering a stroke—but there would be no rest for his bones. Almost thirty years later the Church Council of Constance condemned Wycliffe's teachings and ordered his bones dug up and burned. But of course, the burning of his bones would not end John Wycliffe's influence. Wycliffe had been a leading scholar at Oxford and a chaplain to the King of England. He boldly spoke out against the pope, the organizational hierarchy of the Roman Church, and the corruption of the clergy. He criticized not only the organization of the medieval church but its theology as well. He believed the church should return to the Scriptures. Pastors should live lives of simplicity and holiness, shepherding the flock the Lord had given them. Under Wycliffe's direction, the entire Bible was translated into English for the first time. The translation was completed by Wycliffe's associates in 1395, eleven years after his death. Though repeatedly condemned and burned by the authorities, copies of Wycliffe's Bible continued to bring the truth to England for more than a century. It greatly influenced William Tyndale and the translators of the King James Version. John Foxe in his book of martyrs well described Wycliffe's influence when he said, "Though they digged up his body, burnt his bones, and drowned his ashes, yet the Word of God and the truth of his doctrine, with the fruit and success thereof, they could not burn; which yet to this day doth remain."

1731 Peter Pelham's great room in Boston, Massachusetts, was the site of the first music concert in the colonies.

1853 The United States bought some forty-five thousand square miles of land from Mexico in a deal known as the Gadsden Purchase.

1865 Rudyard Kipling, the first Englishman to be awarded the Nobel Prize for literature in 1907, was born in Bombay, India. Kipling was a poet, novelist, and short-story author whose best-known works include the *Jungle Book* and *Just So Stories*. He traveled around the world as a journalist, married an American, and lived in Vermont for several years. He died in London on January 18, 1936.

1877 Symphony no. 2 in D by Johannes Brahms was premiered in Vienna just a little over a year after the premiere of his first symphony.

1911 Sun Yat-sen was elected the first president of the Republic of China.

1922 Vladimir I. Lenin proclaimed the establishment of the Union of Soviet Socialist Republics.

1944 King George II of Greece proclaimed a regency to rule his country, virtually renouncing the throne.

1947 King Michael of Romania agreed to abdicate, but charged he was being forced off the throne by Communists.

1948 The Cole Porter musical *Kiss Me, Kate* opened on Broadway.

1993 Israel and the Vatican agreed to recognize each other diplomatically.

The world does not need more Christian writers— it needs more good writers, and composers, who are Christians.

[C. S. LEWIS (1898–1963)]

DECEMBER

763

The old Church of St. Peter in Rome was thronged with the faithful. Originally erected by Constantine the Great some six and a half centuries previous, the vast decrepit basilica would not be revitalized by Michaelangelo's artistry until some five centuries hence. Those who crowded into the transepts, around the apse, throughout the nave, and into the narthex that day would not have expected that the creaking timbers and worn stones around them would have any need to endure the long span of all those years. Weeping and wailing, they had gathered there to await the end of the world.

Just before midnight, a great liturgical procession began to slowly make its way along the shadowy aisles toward the iconostasis and the choir, altar, and focault beyond. The tormented cries of the people hung in the air, thick like incense. The great bells in the towers above the adjacent courtyard began to toll ominously. Every sight, sound, texture, and aroma bore the manifest taint of judgment. Grievous, they were observing a wake for the world.

The holy seers had all foretold this dreadful day—indeed, most had expected it for quite some time. Centuries before, when Rome was sacked by the Vandals, the apocalypticists were certain that the end was nigh. Later, when successive waves of Persians and Muslims swept through Byzantium, making the great Christian centers of Jerusalem, Alexandria, Damascus, and Antioch captive to fierce pagan warlords, they became convinced that the last days had finally come. It seemed that the end of each successive century was always marked by a new interest in the harbingers of doom. Up until now, the prophets had been inaccurate, erroneous, and premature, even in their most painstaking calculations.

NEW YEAR'S EVE
FEAST DAY
  *St. Silvester I, pope; St. Melania
  the Younger; St. Columba of Sens*

But here at the end of the millennium, the signs were practically unmistakable. The beloved Pope Gregory, just before his untimely demise earlier that year, had assured good men and women of faith that the wars and rumors of wars, that the nations rising against nations and the kingdoms rising against kingdoms, the famines, the pestilences, and the earthquakes in diverse places— all seen in abundance in recent days—were clear portents of the consummation of the ages. His successor in the office of the Holy See, with the concurrence of each of the venerable Patriarchs of the East, confirmed that time had run out for this, the terminal generation.

Some of those who were gathered at the Vatican that evening had rid themselves of all their earthly possessions as a final act of contrition. Some gave their lands, homes, money, foodstuffs, and household goods to the poor. Others simply left their fields, shops, and villages vacant. Still others resigned themselves to an "eat, drink, and be merry, for tomorrow we die" debauchery. In most cases, little or no preparation was made for the future—because of course, there was no future. Now, it was New Year's Eve in the year 999.

At long last, the hour arrived. A hush fell over the congregation as the bells slowly tolled the end of the year, the end of the century, the end of the millennium, the end of the world. And then . . . nothing happened. Nothing at all. The silence was deafening. Everyone looked around at one another in astonished relief. The terror was past. And that was when the real trouble began. Preparing for the end, though perhaps dispiriting, is not nearly so difficult as preparing for what comes after the end.

DECEMBER

1640 The father of modern chemistry, Robert Boyle, was converted to the Christian faith. He is remembered as a founder of the Royal Society and for his scientific studies, especially his discovery of the law relating gas pressures to temperature and volume. But Boyle himself considered his scientific studies simply one aspect of his Christian life and walk. In his account of his boyhood, he gave himself the Greek name Philaretus, meaning "fond of virtue." On this day in 1640, when he was thirteen, Boyle had a conversion experience that he later marked as the turning point of his life. He recounted that at night he "suddenly awoke in a fright by loud claps of thunder and every clap was both preceded and attended with flashes of lightning so frequent and so dazzling, that Philaretus began to imagine them the sallies of that fire that must consume the world. The long continuance of that dismal tempest, when the winds were so loud, as almost drowned the noise of the very thunder, and the showers so hideous, as almost quenched the lightning, ere it could reach his eyes confirmed Philaretus in his apprehensions of the day of judgment's being at hand. Whereupon the consideration of his unpreparedness to welcome it, and the hideousness of being surprised by it in an unfit condition, made him resolve and vow, that if his fears were that night disappointed, all his future additions to his life should be more religiously and watchfully employed. The morning came, and a serene cloudless sky returned, when he ratified his determination so solemnly, that from that day he dated his conversion."

1775 The British repulsed an attack by Continental army generals Richard Montgomery and Benedict Arnold at Quebec; Montgomery was killed.

1805 The French Revolutionary Calendar which centered dates around the Revolution since 1793, was last officially used.

1862 President Abraham Lincoln signed an act admitting West Virginia to the Union, despite direct constitutional prohibitions.

1879 Thomas Edison first publicly demonstrated his electric incandescent light in Menlo Park, New Jersey.

1897 Brooklyn, New York, spent its last day as a separate entity before becoming part of New York City.

1946 President Harry Truman officially proclaimed the end of hostilities in the Second World War.

1960 In Great Britain, the farthing, which had been legal tender since the thirteenth century, was removed from circulation.

1961 The Marshall Plan expired after distributing more than $12 billion in foreign aid.

1974 Private American citizens were allowed to buy and own gold for the first time in more than forty years.

1978 Taiwanese diplomats struck their colors for the final time from the embassy flagpole in Washington, marking the end of diplomatic relations with the U.S.

1998 Europe's leaders proclaimed a new era as eleven nations merged currencies to create the euro, a shared money they said would boost business, underpin unity, and strengthen their role in world affairs.

Christianity is the basis of all science—if there is any science not so rooted in the truth, it is no science at all.

[ROBERT BOYLE (1627–1691)]

DECEMBER

INDEX

A

Aaron, Hank, 85, 133, 207, 215, 245
Abbey Theater, 491
Abbotsford, 480
Abbott, Bud, 643
Abdul Illah, 415
Abdulla Ibn Ul-Hussein, 311, 427
Abel, Rudolph Ivanovich, 95
Abelard, Peter, 241, 632
Abernathy, Ralph, 654
Abruzzo, Ben, 485
Abu al-Faraj al-Isbahani, 681
Academie Française, 15
Academy Awards, 173, 269, 293
Academy of Motion Picture Arts and Sciences, 269
Account of the Growth of Popery, An, 177
Achille Lauro, 591
ACLU, 161, 271
Acquinas, Thomas, 671
Acton, Lord, 535
Adalbert of Prague, 245
Adam, Robert, John, James, and William, 561
Adams, Abigail, 409, 683
Adams, Ansel, 115
Adams, Gerry, 527
Adams, Henry, 107, 237, 657
Adams, John, 92, 142, 241, 247, 308, 347, 394, 395, 409, 476, 521, 538, 603, 637, 643, 717
Adams, John Quincy, 44, 92, 116, 121, 170, 409, 529, 662, 676, 706
Adams, Samuel, 234, 308, 490, 739
Addai of Edessa, 92
Addams, Jane, 723
Addison, Joseph, 263, 341, 519
Adler, Max, 281

Adrian IV, 517
Advent, 9, 680
Adventures of Huckleberry Finn, The, 111
Adventures of Ozzie and Harriet, The, 593
Adventures of Superman, The, 99
Aeneid, 557
Aeronautical Society of Great Britain, 35
Afghanistan, 291, 755
AFL-CIO, 713
Afra of Augsburg, 183
African Methodist Episcopal Church, 217, 656
Agca, Mehmet Ali, 287
Agincourt, 627
Agnew, Spiro T., 467, 469, 597, 601, 695, 715
Agrarians, The, 34, 127, 418
Aid to Families with Dependent Children (AFDC), 491
Aida, 751
Aiden, Saint, 458, 513
Aiken, Conrad, 461
Ainsworth, Henry, 534
Air Force Academy, 409
Akihito, 219
Alabama, 731
Alabama, University of, 347
Alamo, 121, 147, 485
Alaska, 195, 401
Alaska highway, 683
Alban of Verlamium, 94
Alban, Saint, 371
Albert, Prince (of Saxe-Coburg-Gotha), 95
Alcatraz, 177, 473
Alcoholics Anonymous, 345
Alcott, Louisa May, 699
Alcuin, 540
Alcuin of York, 299
Aldrin, Edwin "Buzz," 427

Alexander II, 604
Alexander VI, 162
Alexander of Alexandria, Bishop, 300
Alexander the Great, 555
Alexander's Feast, 685
Alfano, Franco, 249, 699
Alfonso XIII of Spain, 227, 681
Alfred the Great, 23, 273, 356, 571, 602, 623, 633
Alfred P. Murrah Federal Building, 237
Alger, Horatio, 37
Algeria, 393, 643
Ali, Muhammad, 255, 365, 377, 637
Alice's Adventures Underground, 693
Alien and Sedition Laws, 476
Aliened-American, 236
Alighieri, Dante, 65, 155, 316, 484, 543, 618, 653, 736
Alka-Seltzer, 117
All Creatures Great and Small, 583
All in the Family, 47
All Hallow's Eve, 639
"All or Nothing at All," 549
All Saint's Day, 642
All Souls' Day, 644
Allen, Bryan, 349
Allen, Ethan, 31, 182, 281, 565
Allen, Richard, 217, 656
Allen, Steve, 569
Almayer's Folly, 38
Alonso, Mateo, 160
Alphege, Saint, 237
Altamont Speedway, 715
Ambassadors Theatre in London, 691
Ambrose, 26
Ambrose of Milan, 680, 716
Ambrose, Saint, 207